MACMILLAN LITERATURE SERIES

Introducing
Literature

Enjoying
Literature

Understanding
Literature

Appreciating
Literature

American
Literature

English and Western
Literature

General Adviser and Writer

George Kearns
Director, Expository Writing Program
English Department
Rutgers University
New Brunswick, New Jersey

Advisers

Elizabeth Ackley
Teacher
Indian Hill High School
Cincinnati, Ohio

Paula A. Calabrese
Assistant Principal, Ingomar Middle School
North Allegheny School District
Pittsburgh, Pennsylvania

Sandra A. Cavender
Teacher
Nathan Hale High School
West Allis, Wisconsin

Bernarr Paul Folta
Teacher
West Lafayette High School
West Lafayette, Indiana

Carolyn Dennis Jones
Assistant to Superintendent
Office of Manhattan High Schools
New York, New York

Judi Purvis
Department Head
Irving High School
Irving, Texas

Robert Ranta
Department Head
Lacey Township High School
Lanoka Harbor, New Jersey

Pearl Thomas
Assistant Principal, English Department
Norman Thomas High School
New York, New York

Donna Townsend
Educational Consultant
Austin, Texas

Marjory Carter Willis
Teacher
Midlothian High School
Midlothian, Virginia

Contributing Writers

Cosmo F. Ferrara
Consultant and Writer
Former English Department Head

Philip McFarland
English Teacher

Gail Mack
Educational Writer

Catherine Sagan
English Department Head

MACMILLAN LITERATURE SERIES

American Literature

SCRIBNER EDUCATIONAL PUBLISHERS

NEW YORK

MACMILLAN PUBLISHING COMPANY

NEW YORK

COLLIER MACMILLAN PUBLISHERS

LONDON

SPECIAL ACKNOWLEDGMENTS

The Publisher is grateful for assistance and comments from the following people:

Jack V. Booch, Theatre Guild, New York, New York

Mrs. Rosalie Clark, Austin High School, Decatur, Alabama

Mr. Albert G. Craz, Northport–East Northport High School, Northport, New York

Mrs. Doris E. R. Gilbert, Syracuse City Schools, Syracuse, New York

William Ince, Stuyvesant High School, New York, New York

Iris Gates McAnear, Austin High School, Decatur, Alabama

Scribner Educational Publishers
Macmillan Publishing Company
866 Third Avenue
New York, New York 10022
Collier Macmillan Canada, Inc.

Printed in the United States of America

ISBN 0-02-192680-8
9

ACKNOWLEDGMENTS

Grateful acknowledgment is given authors, publishers, and agents for permission to reprint the following copyrighted material. Every effort has been made to determine copyright owners. In the case of any omissions, the Publisher will be pleased to make suitable acknowledgments in future editions.

Margaret Walker Alexander
MARGARET WALKER ALEXANDER: "Lineage" from *For My People.* Reprinted by permission of Margaret Walker Alexander.

Robert Bly
ROBERT BLY: "Driving to Town Late to Mail a Letter" from *Silence in the Snowy Fields.* Published by Wesleyan University Press, 1962. Copyright © 1962 by Robert Bly. Reprinted by permission of Robert Bly.

The Bodley Head
F. SCOTT FITZGERALD: "Basil: He Thinks He's Wonderful" from *The Bodley Head Scott Fitzgerald.* Reprinted by permission of The Bodley Head.

Brandt & Brandt Literary Agents, Inc.
JEROME WEIDMAN: "My Father Sits in the Dark" from *My Father Sits in the Dark & Other Stories.* Copyright 1934 and renewed 1962 by Jerome Weidman. Reprinted by permission of Brandt & Brandt Literary Agents, Inc.

Olga Cabral
OLGA CABRAL: "(HELP!)" from *The Darkness in My Pocket.* Copyright © 1976 by Olga Cabral. Reprinted by permission of Olga Cabral.

Jonathan Cape Ltd.
SHERWOOD ANDERSON: "Sophistication" from *Winesburg, Ohio.* Reprinted by permission of the Estate of Sherwood Anderson and Jonathan Cape Ltd.
ROBERT FROST: "Acquainted With the Night," "Birches," "Desert Places," "Fire and Ice," "Mending Wall," "Nothing Gold Can Stay," "The Road Not Taken," and "Stopping by Woods on a Snowy Evening" from *The Poetry of Robert Frost* edited by Edward Connery Lathem. Reprinted by permission of the Estate of Robert Frost, Robert Connery Lathem, and Jonathan Cape Ltd.
ERNEST HEMINGWAY: "In Another Country" from *The First Forty-Nine Stories.* Reprinted by permission of the Executors of the Ernest Hemingway Estate and Jonathan Cape Ltd.

CREDITS

CANADA

Kerouac's
Desolation Peak

• Roethke teaches

WASHINGTON

MONTANA

Chief Joseph
surrenders

NORTH DAKOTA

Chief Joseph born

• Malamud teaches

IDAHO

Garland's
stories

OREGON

• Pound born

WYOMING

SOUTH DAKOTA

Momaday's
Devil's Tower

CALIFORNIA

NEVADA

UTAH

• Twain writes

COLORADO

NEBRASKA

Cather's stories •

• Van Tilburg Clark's home
• Twain meets Artemus Ward

KANSAS

Katherine Anne
• Porter
lives

Gwendol
Broo
bc

Twain's Calaveras County
Harte's Poker Flat •

William Stafford
born •

• Frost born

Saroyan's
• hometown

ARIZONA

NEW MEXICO

OKLAHOMA

• Steinbeck's stories

Ellison
born

•

• Ortiz writes

Navaho
rain
chant

Momaday's
Rainy Mountain

Katherine Anne Porter born

PACIFIC
OCEAN

Wilder
writes
•

TEXAS

ALASKA

London's
Klondike

HAWAII

London, Melville,
Twain write

MEXICO

x

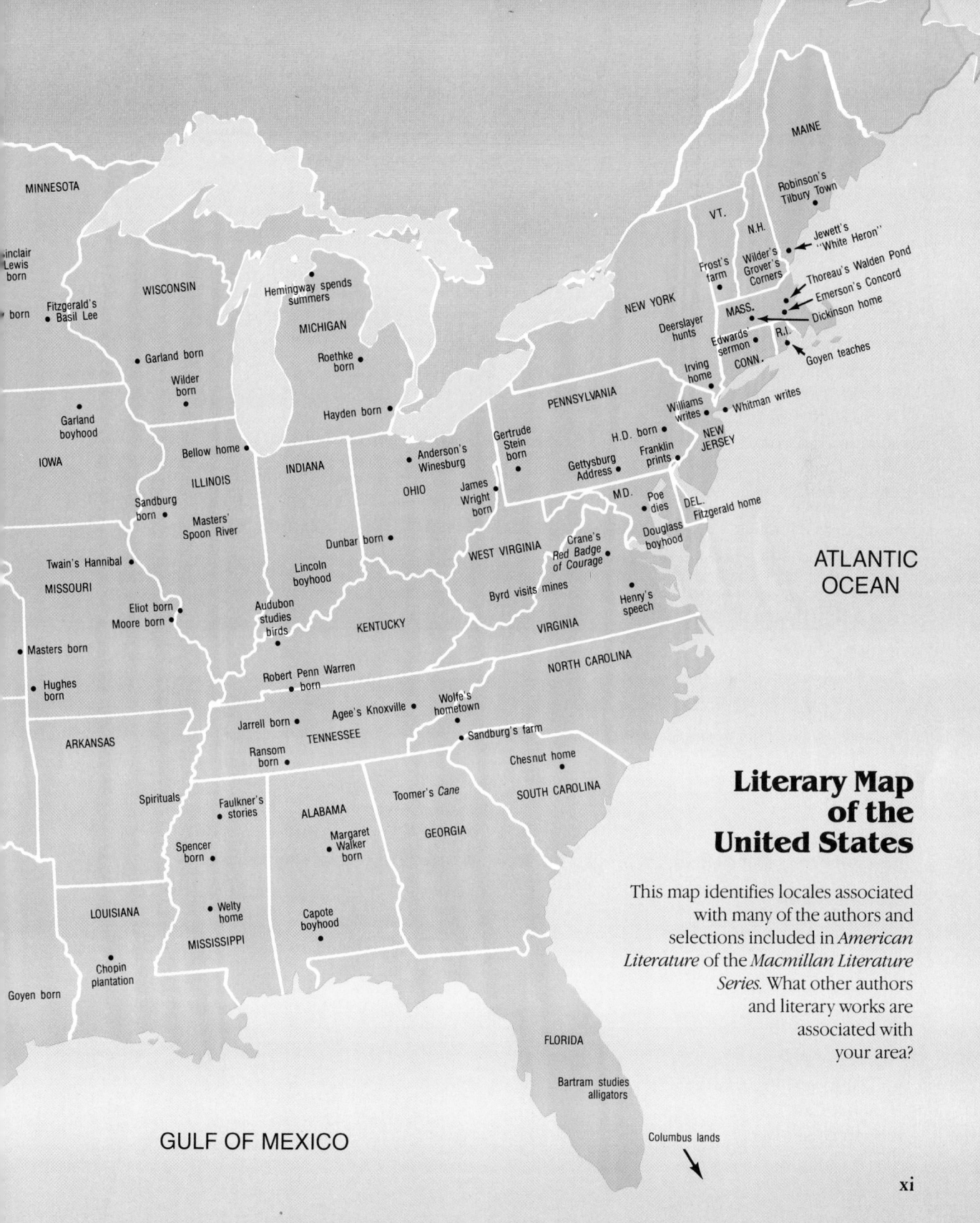

Literary Map of the United States

This map identifies locales associated with many of the authors and selections included in *American Literature* of the *Macmillan Literature Series*. What other authors and literary works are associated with your area?

MINNESOTA

Sinclair Lewis born

born

Fitzgerald's Basil Lee

WISCONSIN

Garland born

Wilder born

Garland boyhood

IOWA

Hemingway spends summers

MICHIGAN

Roethke born

Hayden born

Bellow home

ILLINOIS

INDIANA

Anderson's Winesburg

Gertrude Stein born

MAINE

Robinson's Tilbury Town

VT.

N.H.

Jewett's "White Heron"

Frost's farm

Wilder's Grover's Corners

Thoreau's Walden Pond

Emerson's Concord

MASS.

Dickinson home

R.I.

Goyen teaches

NEW YORK

Deerslayer hunts

Edwards' sermon

CONN.

Irving home

Williams writes

Whitman writes

NEW JERSEY

PENNSYLVANIA

H.D. born

Franklin prints

Sandburg born

Masters' Spoon River

Dunbar born

OHIO

James Wright born

Gettysburg Address

MD.

Poe dies

DEL.
Fitzgerald home

Twain's Hannibal

MISSOURI

Eliot born
Moore born

Lincoln boyhood

Audubon studies birds

KENTUCKY

WEST VIRGINIA

Crane's Red Badge of Courage

Byrd visits mines

VIRGINIA

Douglass boyhood

Henry's speech

ATLANTIC OCEAN

Masters born

Hughes born

Robert Penn Warren born

NORTH CAROLINA

ARKANSAS

Jarrell born

Ransom born

TENNESSEE

Agee's Knoxville

Wolfe's hometown

Sandburg's farm

Chesnut home

SOUTH CAROLINA

Spirituals

Faulkner's stories

ALABAMA

Margaret Walker born

Toomer's *Cane*

GEORGIA

LOUISIANA

Spencer born

Welty home

MISSISSIPPI

Capote boyhood

Goyen born

Chopin plantation

FLORIDA

Bartram studies alligators

GULF OF MEXICO

Columbus lands

xi

CONTENTS

American Literature

Key to Illustrations appears on page 47.

EARLY AMERICA

To 1750

American Beginnings

America has always been a land of beginnings. After Europeans "discovered" America in the fifteenth century, the mysterious New World became for many people a genuine hope of a new life, an escape from poverty and persecution, a chance to start again. We can say that, as a nation, America begins with that hope. When, however, does American *literature* begin?

American literature begins with American experiences. Long before the first colonists arrived, before Christopher Columbus, before the Northmen who "found" America about the year 1000, Native Americans lived here. Each tribe's literature was tightly woven into the fabric of daily life and reflected the unmistakably American experience of living with the land. Another kind of experience, one filled with fear and excitement, found its expression in the reports that Columbus and other explorers sent home in Spanish, French, and English. In addition, the journals of the people who lived and died in the New England wilderness tell unforgettable tales of hard and sometimes heartbreaking experiences of those early years.

Experience, then, is the key to early American literature. The New World provided a great variety of experiences, and these experiences demanded a wide variety of expressions by an even wider variety of early American writers. These

Title page of *The General History of Virginia, New England, and the Summer Isles,* John Smith, 1624.

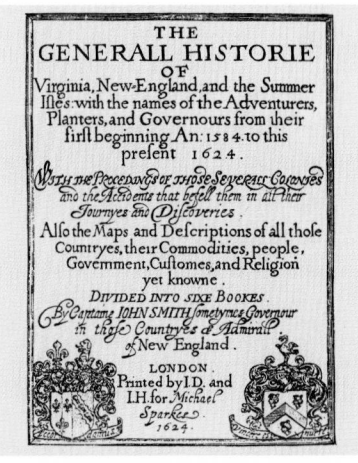

writers included John Smith (page 19), who spent only about two-and-one-half years on the American continent. They included Jonathan Edwards (page 40) and William Byrd (page 35), who thought of themselves as British subjects, never suspecting a revolution that would create a United States of America with a literature of its own. American Indians, explorers, Pilgrims, Puritan ministers, frontier wives, plantation owners—they are all the creators of the first American literature.

The Puritans

The ship *Mayflower* carried about one hundred passengers (their leader called them Pilgrims, or travelers) and took sixty-six days to beat its way across the Atlantic. In December of 1620, the *Mayflower* put the Pilgrims ashore at Plymouth, Massachusetts. Before the unrelenting winter was over, half of them were dead. Within the next few years, however, those who survived were joined by more settlers from England. Only some of these first colonists were *Puritans,* but it was the Puritans, led by their clergymen, who dominated the government, the religious outlook, and the literature of the communities they established.

Who were these extraordinary people? The Puritans were devout Christians who wanted to *purify* their lives and their church of what they saw as the

corruptions of English society and its state religion, the Church of England. They called themselves Saints or Separatists, but they are now generally called Puritans—a name that became a sign of their separateness.

The Puritans believed in an all-powerful God who freely granted to his "Saints" the gift of *grace.* Grace was a complicated matter for the Puritans, but it can be described as the spirit that would guarantee salvation—eternal happiness with God. In their daily lives the Puritans wanted to demonstrate at every moment that they possessed grace or that they were worthy of it.

For the Puritans everything was, ideally, aimed at personal salvation and the building of a new, God-centered society. They were willing to risk their lives for such a world. It would be a place where they would practice their religion freely and raise their children free from the frivolities and temptations of the Old World. As we listen to their language, which refers to the Bible easily and frequently,

their passionate desire to establish a New Jerusalem becomes clear. In their dreams they would build the City of God on earth.

Life for the average Puritan in the New World was essentially a life of work and prayer, but it was not a fanatically austere life. The Puritans worked long and hard under extremely difficult conditions so that their farms and trading enterprises would prosper. In fact, they believed prosperity was a sign of *election,* or God's special favor. Nevertheless, they did not turn away from eating and drinking, the pleasure of social gatherings, and the joys of a close family life. They simply kept reminding themselves that their souls were the constant battlegrounds of God and Satan and that every act and thought had to be judged according to whether or not it truly glorified God.

In the pursuit of virtue, the Puritans passed laws against many activities that would distract good souls from their real task. Certain "delights" were forbidden, such as bowling, Maypole dancing, gambling, attending plays, and "unprofitable" hunting (for someone who was a bad shot, it was a sin to waste time and ammunition). Virtue was learned primarily at home, where the father had complete authority. The family was the center of activity; the aged were always cared for; young people were apprenticed to learn trades the community needed.

Writing was an important part of Puritan life; it was often

A page of the rhymed alphabet from the earliest extant edition of *The New England Primer,* Boston, 1727.

G As runs the Glafs
Mans life doth pafs.

H My Book and Heart
Shall never part.

J Job feels the Rod
Yet bleffes GOD.

K Our KING the good
No man of blood.

L The Lion bold
The Lamb doth hold.

M The Moon gives light
In time of night.

an extension of religion. In fact, the first book published in America was the *Bay Psalm Book* (1640), a translation of the biblical Psalms. Many Puritans kept journals to help them carefully examine their spiritual lives. These journals and diaries, detailed and intense, were usually meant to be purely private writings. Even when they did write for a public, however, the Puritans wrote to instruct others or to testify to their experience of divine grace; they wrote spiritual autobiographies.

Puritan writing, in other words, was *practical.* The writers were not merely providing entertainment; they were deeply involved with their spiritual selves and attempts to improve them. They wrote no fiction, nor did they even approve of reading fiction, and they wrote no plays because they disapproved violently of the theater. Their writings consisted largely of journals, sermons, hymns, histories, and poems.

Just as the Puritans sought to purify their lives, so too they sought to purify their language. Everything they wrote avoided **Ornate Style,** the complicated and decorative style of their European contemporaries. They preferred to write in what they called **Plain Style,** even as they strove for plainness in their architecture, clothing, food, and household furnishings. Plain Style was meant simply to communicate ideas as clearly as possible. Writing was not a way of showing off cleverness or learning

but a way of serving God and the community. The whole Puritan way of life is summed up in William Bradford's desire to tell the story of Plymouth Plantation (page 24) in "a plain style, with singular regard unto the simple truth in all things."

The Southern Colonies

Life in the southern colonies, begun in 1607 with Jamestown, Virginia, developed quite differently from life in New England. Unlike the Puritans, who lived fairly closely together, much of the southern population lived on farms or plantations that were distant from one another. Often like little colonies of their own, these plantations were largely self-sufficient.

The larger estates were owned and operated by wealthy and well-educated colonists who developed a more social and outgoing way of life than the Puritans. Different things became important to them: cultivation of nature and of society, sophistication, and public service.

Southern colonial literature reflects that experience. For the most part, southern gentlemen and ladies carried on correspondence with friends who often lived at great distances from them, as well as with family and friends back in England. Many of the southern colonists belonged to the Church of England, the church that the Puritans had attempted to reform, and their ties with the Old World were stronger. As a result, they did not have the reasons the Puritans had to create a literature of their own.

Still, in their letters, journals, and public reports, southern writers recorded the details of their way of life. The realities of science and politics blend, in their writings, with a New World sense of excitement and discovery. After all, the southern wilderness too had to be explored, mapped, and described.

Of course, not all the residents of the southern colonies were the prosperous owners of plantations. Most were hard-working tradespeople, artisans, small farmers, indentured servants, and slaves. Yet the sophisticated gentleman and lady dominate our sense of the early southern colonies as we meet them in literature. We can hear at once, in the voice of a man like William Byrd (page 35), a strong contrast between the more worldly and witty southerners and the intense, self-examining Puritans. This contrast, too, is an important part of the American experience.

TIME LINE

pre-1400   Hundreds of American Indian tribes inhabit the Americas before European explorers arrive

1492   Columbus lands in New World

1509   New World named America after Amerigo Vespucci

1519–1522   Magellan sails around the world

Columbus XMY VIREY

1540   Coronado explores Southwest

1541   De Soto explores the Mississippi

1565   Spanish found St. Augustine, Florida, oldest permanent settlement in what is now the United States

1600–1649   1600–1649

1603   England: Bubonic plague kills 30,000 people

1605   England: Shakespeare completes *Macbeth*

1607   Jamestown, Va., founded

1608   John Smith, *A True Relation of Virginia*

1609   Henry Hudson explores Hudson River

1609   Italy: Galileo builds first telescope

1610   Colonial population estimate: 210

1611   England: King James translation of Bible

1616   John Smith, *A Description of New England*

1616   England and Spain: Deaths of Shakespeare and Cervantes

1620   Pilgrims land at Plymouth, Mass.

1624   Dutch establish New Amsterdam

1630 William Bradford begins *History of Plymouth Plantation*

John Winthrop settles Boston

1635 First public school in America

1636 Harvard, first college in America

1638 First printing press in America at Cambridge, Mass.

1640 *Bay Psalm Book,* first book published in America

Colonial population estimate: 27,950

1643 Roger Williams, *A Key to the Language of America*

First American restaurant opens in Boston

1628 England: William Harvey describes circulation of blood

1630 France: Beginning of public advertising

1644 China: Ming Dynasty falls

France: Blaise Pascal completes calculating device, forerunner of modern digital calculator

1650–1699   **1650–1699**

1650 Anne Bradstreet, *The Tenth Muse Lately Sprung Up in America*

1653 John Eliot, *Catechism in the Indian Language*

1664 English capture New Amsterdam, rename it New York

1669 La Salle explores Great Lakes

1670 Colonial population estimate: 114,500

1671 Edward Taylor becomes minister of Westfield, Mass.

1663 Germany: First electric generator invented

1667 England: John Milton completes *Paradise Lost*

1673 Regular New York–Boston mail service

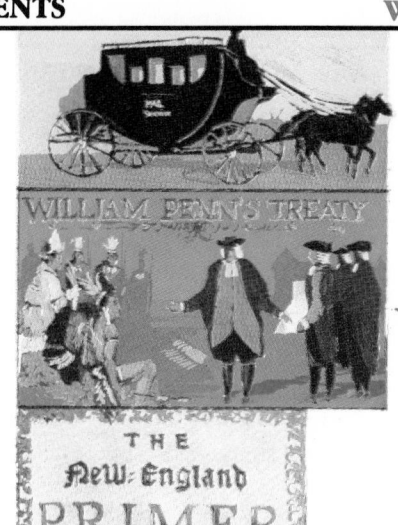

1674 Holland: Leeuwenhoek observes bacteria

1680 France: King Louis XIV at height of power

1682 William Penn founds Pennsylvania

La Salle explores Mississippi

1690 *New England Primer*

Paper money issued for first time in America

1692 Witchcraft trials in Salem, Mass.

1700–1750   1700–1750

1701 Detroit founded

1704 First American newspaper, *Boston News Letter*

1709 Germany: Gabriel Fahrenheit invents thermometer

1714 Tea introduced in colonies

1718 New Orleans founded

1719 England: Daniel Defoe, *Robinson Crusoe*

1726 England: Jonathan Swift, *Gulliver's Travels*

1729 Baltimore founded

First arithmetic textbook in America published in Boston

1731 First public library in America founded in Philadelphia

1732 William Byrd, *Progress to the Mines*

1737 William Byrd founds Richmond, Va.

1741 Jonathan Edwards, *Sinners in the Hands of an Angry God*

1749 Franklin invents lightning rod

1750 Colonial population estimate: 1,207,000

American Indians

When European explorers first set foot in the New World, they encountered people who had been native to the Americas for thousands of years. Because the Europeans thought they had landed in the "Indies," or the Far East, they called the natives Indians. No one name, however, would adequately describe the variety of cultures that flourished from one end of America to the other.

Generation after generation these Native Americans had told stories, sung songs, and recited groups of tales that embodied their past and told of their close relationship with the natural world. Their mythologies, songs, and ritual chants were rarely written down, though some tribes, such as the Delaware, did develop forms of writing. Most of these works of literature survived through oral tradition, each generation transmitting its literature to its young people by word of mouth. The result is a literature that is timeless, a literature created by no one author. It is a literature made by its people.

Some American Indian tribes of the New World.

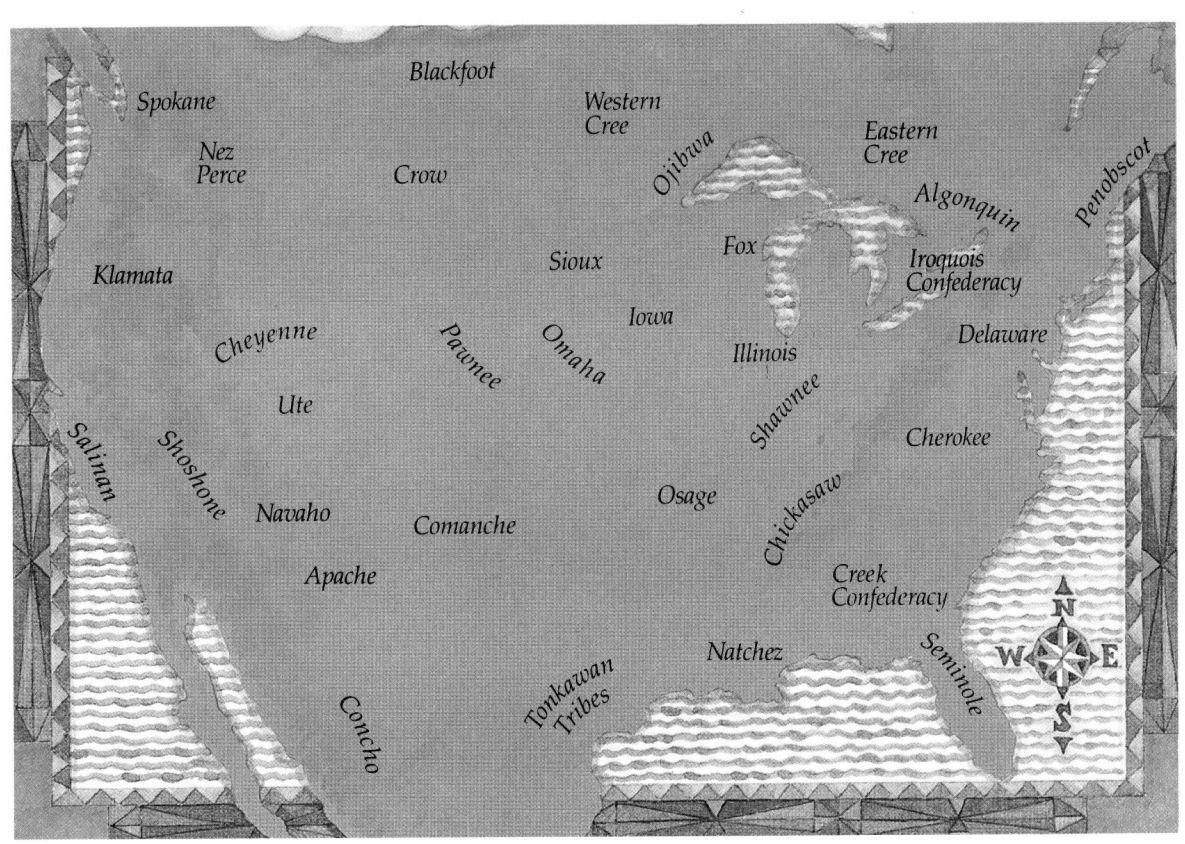

The *Walum Olum* is a creation myth of the Delaware, a people who lived in the areas we now call New Jersey, Delaware, and parts of New York and Pennsylvania. The *Walum Olum* ("Painted Record") is a chronicle of the beginning of the world and the origins of the Delaware people in the far Northwest.

Through this myth the Delaware kept in touch with their own past and placed themselves within a framework of history as they remembered it. The ancient words also celebrated the Manito, the supernatural force, or spirit, believed by the Delaware to be the source of both good and evil.

The form of writing developed by the Delaware was not based on a phonetic representation of sounds, as English is, but upon a kind of picture writing. In the following passage each of the original drawings, or pictographs, is accompanied by an English translation of its meaning. In some of these pictographs, we can clearly see the meaning. We can easily find the sun, men, women, fish, and birds. However, other pictographs demand a detailed knowledge of the Delaware language—or an act of imagination.

Delaware Traditional

from **The Walum Olum**

At first, in that place, at all times, above the earth,

On the earth, an extended fog, and there the great Manito was.

At first, forever, lost in space, everywhere, the great Manito was.

He made the extended land and the sky.

He made the sun, the moon, the stars.

He made them all to move evenly.

Then the wind blew violently, and it cleared, and the water flowed off far and strong.

And groups of islands grew newly, and there remained.

Anew spoke the great Manito, a manito to manitos,

To beings, mortals, souls and all,

And ever after he was a manito to men, and their grandfather.

He gave the first mother, the mother of beings.

He gave the fish, he gave the turtles, he gave the beasts, he gave the birds.

But an evil Manito made evil beings only, monsters.

He made the flies, he made the gnats.

All beings were then friendly.

Truly the manitos were active and kindly

To those very first men, and to those first mothers; fetched them wives,

And fetched them food, when first they desired it.

All had cheerful knowledge, all had leisure, all thought in gladness.

But very secretly an evil being, a mighty magician, came on earth,

And with him brought badness, quarreling, unhappiness,

Brought bad weather, brought sickness, brought death.

All this took place of old on the earth, beyond the great tide water, at the first.

STUDY QUESTIONS

Recalling

1. According to the *Walum Olum,* how were good things and evil things created?
2. List three good things and three evil things that the manitos did for mortals.

Interpreting

3. What kind of relationship is depicted between the manitos, or spiritual forces, and mortals?
4. Identify two pictographs in which there is a clear relationship between the picture and the translated meaning. Then find two abstract pictographs in which the relationship between picture and meaning is not obvious. For one of the abstract pictographs, tell how it nevertheless suggests the meaning given in the translation.

The Navaho are a large and varied group who settled in the American Southwest, where their culture still flourishes. An agricultural people, the Navaho composed ritual songs like "Listen! Rain Approaches!" to celebrate the growth of crops and to control the coming of the vitally important rains. The repetition of words and lines (sometimes with variations) is characteristic of Native American ritual chants and songs. Imagine this song as part of a ceremony including dancing, music, and elaborate costumes.

Navaho Traditional

Listen! Rain Approaches!

Truly in the East
The white bean
And the great corn plant
Are tied with the white lightning.
5 Listen! It approaches!
The voice of the bluebird is heard.

Truly in the East
The white bean
And the great squash
10 Are tied with the rainbow.
Listen! It approaches!
The voice of the bluebird is heard.

Whirling Rainbow People, 1948. This sand painting shows eight rainbow goddesses swirling clockwise around a dark, cloud-covered lake.

"Calling One's Own" is a song of the Ojibwa, also known as the Chippewa, a group of people who lived around the Great Lakes and throughout the Great Plains. It is a song that sounds much like the love songs of English-language poetry. The imagery of the song is drawn from the natural world, showing the close relationship between the Ojibwa and the landscape of waters, flowers, trees, and skies that surrounded them.

Ojibwa Traditional

Calling One's Own

Awake! Flower of the forest, sky treading bird of the prairie.

Awake! Awake! Wonderful fawn-eyed One.
When you look upon me I am satisfied, as flowers that
    drink dew.
The breath of your mouth is the fragrance of flowers in
    the morning,
5 Your breath is their fragrance at evening in the moon of
    fading-leaf.

Do not the red streams of my veins run toward you
As forest streams to the sun in the moon of bright nights?
When you are beside me my heart sings; a branch it is, dancing,
Dancing before the Wind spirit in the moon of strawberries.

10 When you frown upon me, beloved, my heart grows dark—
A shining river the shadows of clouds darken;
Then with your smiles comes the sun and makes to look
    like gold
Furrows the cold wind drew in the water's face.

Myself! Behold me! Blood of my beating heart.
15 Earth smiles—the waters smile—even the sky of clouds smiles—
    but I,
I lose the way of smiling when you are not near.
Awake! Awake! My beloved.

Wheelright Museum of the American Indian

STUDY QUESTIONS

Listen! Rain Approaches!

Recalling

1. Which lines in the first stanza are repeated in the second stanza? Which lines are varied?
2. What two specific elements of a rainstorm does the song mention in lines 4 and 10?

Interpreting

3. What does the verb repeated in lines 4 and 10 imply about the relationship of things in nature? In what way does the other repetition in the poem contribute to this idea?
4. What stages of a storm does the variation in lines 4 and 10 represent? What broader characteristic of nature do these lines suggest?

Extending

5. What purposes, besides bringing rain, do you think someone might have for singing a ritual song?

Calling One's Own

Recalling

1. With what phrases is the beloved described in the first two lines? To what does the speaker compare his singing heart in stanza 2?
2. According to stanza 3, what happens in nature when the beloved frowns? When the beloved smiles?

Interpreting

3. What is the one general thing that the speaker and the beloved are compared to throughout the poem? What seems to be its importance in the life of the Ojibwa?
4. Which images of the beloved do you find most moving or expressive, and why?

Extending

5. Remember that this song is a translation from an Indian language. How is it like English-language love poems that you have read? In what ways, if any, is it different?

LITERARY FOCUS

Techniques of Oral Literature

Imagine yourself in a time and a place where there are no books to read. Anything you want to record, any event or story or song, must live in your memory and the memories of the people around you. You depend upon oral tradition.

Oral tradition is the name we give to the process of passing on literature by word of mouth. If a prayer or a history or a myth is important to a group, someone in the group must remember it. Otherwise, it will fade into oblivion. Its power and its pleasure will be lost.

Traditionally, it was the tribal poet whose job it was to remember the tribe's history, its line of leaders, its victories, its gods and rituals. In a sense the first poets were memory banks, able to call up the treasure of the tribe's past whenever asked to do so. To make recitation surer, the poets used certain formulas and memory tricks.

One technique was to repeat certain lines, sometimes varying one word or part of a word. Another technique was to make sure that each line had a certain number of syllables or a certain number of rhythmic beats. Sometimes a poet used standard words to represent things commonly referred to, and these stock words became so common that the listeners came to expect to hear them. In fact, the poet was eventually not allowed to leave out a certain word or deviate from the expected pattern.

Thinking About Oral Literature

■ Find examples of words and parts of lines that are repeated throughout "Listen! Rain Approaches!" and "Calling One's Own." Why do you think these particular words are repeated?

VOCABULARY

Native American Words

Native American languages have contributed a large number of words to the American vocabulary. The map of North America, for example, is dotted with Indian place names. *Mississippi* means "great river" in Ojibwa, *Oklahoma* means "red people" in Choctaw, and *Ohio* means "beautiful river" in Iroquois.

We have also incorporated many American Indian common nouns into our everyday speech. The Algonquian language family contributed *chipmunk* and *toboggan*. The Aztec language, known as Nahuatl, gave us *tomato* and *avocado*.

Look up the following words in a dictionary or a book of word origins, and tell what they mean and which Indian language they come from.

totem	Chicago	skunk
powwow	Miami	hammock
squash	hominy	savannah

Christopher Columbus   1451–1506

The dramatic story of the Italian explorer Christopher Columbus has become a familiar part of our culture. For years Columbus tried to convince his patrons that he could reach the riches of the East by sailing west, that he would not sail off the edge of the earth. Finally, with the support of Spain's Queen Isabella, he was able to pursue his dream with his three ships, the *Niña,* the *Pinta,* and the *Santa Maria.*

The discovery of the New World brought Columbus fame and an appointment as Admiral of the Ocean Sea. His later attempts to establish colonies in America were not successful, however, and his last years were filled with disappointments and a sense of failure.

Here is Columbus' own account, from his journal, of the final days of his first and most extraordinary voyage and the landing on the island of San Salvador in 1492. Columbus' nonfiction, real-life adventure might be considered the first American story—both a quest for a dream and a record of hard fact.

This version from the Spanish was made by the twentieth-century American poet William Carlos Williams.

Christopher Columbus

from **The Journal**

A Modern Version by William Carlos Williams

The seventeenth of September, Monday, I proceeded on the west course and made over fifty leagues[1] in the day and night, counting only forty-seven. A favorable current aided us on our way. . . .

At dawn we observed much more weed appearing, like herbs from a river, in which one of the men discovered a live crab. This I kept that all might see it and believe on the land. The sea water was found to be less salt than it had been since leaving the Canaries.[2] This I caused many to taste. The breezes were always soft. Everyone was pleased and the best sailors went ahead to sight the first land. Many tunnyfish passed on all sides of us and the crew of the *Niña* killed one. All these signs came from the west, in which direction I trust in that high God in whose hands are all victories that very soon we shall see land. On that morning there appeared a white bird, called boatswainbird, which is not in the habit of sleeping on the sea. . . .

Saturday, September twenty-second, I shaped my course W.N.W. more or less, her head turning from one to the other point, and made thirty leagues. This contrary wind was very necessary to me because my people had become much excited at the thought that in

---

1. **leagues:** One league is about three miles. Columbus deliberately underestimates the distance for his crew.
2. **the Canaries:** the Canary Islands, off the coast of northwestern Africa.

these seas no wind ever blew in the direction of Spain. In the morning there was no weed but in the afternoon it was very thick. . . .

Tuesday, calm and afterwards wind. . . . At sunset Martin Alonzo went up on the poop of his ship and with joy called out that he had sighted land. I fell on my knees and gave thanks to the Lord, so heavy had been my burdens these latter days at the despair among the men and the murmurs going among them that I should have to turn back. And Martin Alonzo said the *Gloria in Excelsis*[3] with his people. My own crew did the same. Those of the *Niña* all went up on the mast and into the rigging and declared that it was land. It seemed distant twenty-five leagues. So it appeared until night. I ordered the course to be altered from west to S.W. in which direction the land had appeared. Four leagues that day on a west course and seventeen S.W. during the night,

in all twenty-one, but I told the men that thirteen was the distance made good. The sea was very smooth so that many sailors bathed alongside. We saw many giltheads and other fish.

Wednesday, what had been said to be land was only clouds and I continued on the west course till afternoon, then altered to S.W. Day and night thirty-one leagues, counting twenty-four for the people. The sea was like a river, the air pleasant and mild. The despair of the crew redoubled at this disappointment but I comforted them as best I could, begging them to endure a while longer for all that would be theirs in the end. . . .

Tuesday, west, day and night thirty-nine leagues, counted for the crew thirty. The weed, many thanks to God, coming from east to west, contrary to the usual course. Many fish seen and one killed. A white bird like a gull.

Wednesday, still the west course, and made good forty-seven leagues, counted forty. Sandpipers appeared, and much weed, some old and

---

3. *Gloria in Excelsis* [glôr′ē ə in ek sel′ sis]: *Glory in the Highest,* a Latin prayer of praise to God.

some quite fresh and having fruit. No birds. So I gave it out that we had left the islands behind that were depicted on the chart. Here many called upon me to turn about and search for the land but I did not wish to keep the ships beating about, although I had certain information of islands in this region. It would not have been good sense to do this since the weather was favorable and the chief intention was to go in search of the Indies by way of the west. This was what I had promised to the King and Queen, and they had sent me for this purpose.

Thursday, west sixty-three leagues, counted forty-six. . . . The crew here became even louder in their complaints but I gave as little heed as I was able though many were now openly mutinous and would have done me harm if they dared. . . .

Thursday, eleventh of October. The course was W.S.W. More sea than there had been during the whole of the voyage. Sandpipers and a green reed near the ship. And for this I gave thanks to God as it was a sure sign of land. Those of the *Pinta* saw a cane and a pole, and they took up another small pole which appeared to be worked[4] with iron; also another bit of cane, a land plant and a small board. The crew of the caravel *Niña* also saw signs of land, and a small plant covered with berries.

After sunset I returned to the west course. Up to two hours past midnight we had gone ninety miles, when the *Pinta,* which was the fastest sailer and had gone ahead, found the land and gave the signals. The land was first seen by Rodrigo de Triana. . . .

On Friday, the twelfth of October, we anchored before the land and made ready to go on shore. Presently we saw naked people on the beach. I went ashore in the armed boat and took the royal standard and Martin Alonzo and Vincent Yañez, his brother, who was captain of the *Niña.* And we saw the trees very

---

4. **worked:** carved or shaped.

green, and much water and fruits of divers[5] kinds. Presently many of the inhabitants assembled. I gave to some red caps and glass beads to put round their necks, and many other things of little value. They came to the ships' boats afterward, where we were, swimming and bringing us parrots, cotton threads in skeins, darts—what they had, with good will. . . .

On Saturday, as dawn broke, many of these people came to the beach, all youths. Their legs are very straight, all in one line and no belly. They came to the ship in canoes, made out of the trunk of a tree, all in one piece, and wonderfully worked, propelled with a paddle like a baker's shovel, and go at a marvelous speed.

Bright green trees, the whole land so green that it is a pleasure to look on it. Gardens of the most beautiful trees I ever saw. . . . I

_____
5. **divers** [dī′vərz]: diverse or various.

saw many trees very unlike those of our country. Branches growing in different ways and all from one trunk; one twig is one form and another is a different shape and so unlike that it is the greatest wonder in the world to see the diversity; thus one branch has leaves like those of a cane, and others like those of a mastic tree; and on a single tree there are five different kinds. The fish so unlike ours that it is wonderful. Some are the shape of dories and of the finest colors, so bright that there is not a man who would not be astounded, and would not take great delight in seeing them. There are also whales. I saw no beasts on land save parrots and lizards.

On shore I sent the people for water, some with arms, and others with casks; and as it was some little distance, I waited two hours for them.

During that time I walked among the trees which was the most beautiful thing which I had ever seen.

STUDY QUESTIONS

Recalling

1. According to the entry for September 22, why was the "contrary wind" necessary for Columbus?
2. What event took place on Tuesday, September 25? What happened the following day?
3. Summarize the important events described in the entry for October 11.
4. From the entry for Saturday, October 13, list several adjectives that Columbus uses to describe the land, trees, and fish that he encountered.

Interpreting

5. In what way did Columbus report the distance traveled each day to his crew? What reason would he have for reporting the distance in this manner?
6. Based on the entry for October 13, how would you characterize Columbus' general impression of the New World?

Extending

7. Why do you think so many early explorers and settlers described the New World as Columbus did? What hopes might they have had for this land?

John Smith   *1580–1631*

John Smith lived a life crammed with adventure and achievement during a great age of exploration. It had not taken long for adventurers and merchants to begin to explore the New World Columbus had discovered. The Spanish to the south, the French to the north, the English along the mid-Atlantic coast, the Dutch, the Swedes, the Portuguese—all of Europe seemed to be moving west. By Smith's time, about 1600, exploration and the search for gold were still important, but the desire to establish permanent settlements was growing. Smith—strong-willed, imaginative, a born leader—was in the right place at the right time.

In 1585 Sir Walter Raleigh had commissioned an English settlement on Roanoke Island, off the coast of what is now North Carolina, but it lasted only a year. In 1587 another colony was established on Roanoke, but when the English ships returned in 1590, the colony had mysteriously disappeared. Success finally came in 1607 when the first permanent English settlement, Jamestown, Virginia, was founded. It was made up of one hundred men and four boys, and the man in charge was the twenty-seven-year-old Captain John Smith.

It was at Jamestown that Smith may or may not have had the most famous of his adventures. Scholars are still not sure to what extent he was embroidering the truth when he claimed to have been captured by Chief Powhatan and rescued from death by the chief's beautiful daughter, Pocahontas. The story seemed to grow more romantic and exciting each time Smith related it. There is no doubt, however, of the quality of Smith's leadership; the colony would not have survived without him. As it was, over half the colonists died during the first winter. After two years in Jamestown, Smith returned to England.

In 1614 a group of English merchants, who hoped to get rich from gold, whale oil, and furs, financed a six-month expedition to New England for Smith. He explored the coast from Maine to Cape Cod, made maps, traded with Indians, and went back to England, never to return to America.

Yet Smith wanted to return, as we can see from his *Description of New England,* published in 1616. Although he calls this work a description, Smith's main purpose is not to describe but to persuade. This pamphlet is essentially an advertisement, a kind of seventeenth-century "commercial." It is an effort to raise money for another new expedition and to convince Englishmen to join Smith in establishing a new colony of which he hoped to be governor.

The Peaceable Kingdom, Edward Hicks, c. 1839.

John Smith

from **A Description of New England**

Who can desire more content, that has small means or but only his merit to advance his fortune, than to tread and plant that ground he has purchased by the hazard[1] of his life? If he have but the taste of virtue and magnanimity, what to such a mind can be more pleasant than planting and building a foundation for his posterity, got from the rude earth by God's blessing and his own industry, without prejudice to any? If he have any grain of faith or zeal in religion, what can he do less hurtful to any or more agreeable to God than to seek to convert those poor savages[2] to know Christ and humanity? . . . What so truly suits with honor and honesty as the discovering things unknown, erecting towns, peopling countries, informing the ignorant, reforming things unjust, teaching virtue, and gain to our native mother-country a kingdom to attend her, find employment for those that are idle because they know not what to do? [This is] so far from wronging any as to cause posterity to remember thee, and remembering thee, ever honor that remembrance with praise. . . .

Here nature and liberty afford us that freely which in England we want,[3] or it costs us dearly. What pleasure can be more than (being tired with any occasion ashore, in planting

---

1. **hazard:** risk.
2. **savages:** The earliest European settlers considered the Native Americans savages because they lacked what seemed to Europeans the advantages of "civilization."

3. **want:** lack.

vines, fruits, or herbs, in contriving their own grounds, to the pleasure of their own minds, their fields, gardens, orchards, buildings, ships, and other works, etc.) to recreate themselves before their own doors, in their own boats upon the sea, where man, woman, and child, with a small hook and line, by angling may take divers sorts of excellent fish at their pleasures? And is it not pretty sport to pull up two pence, six pence, and twelve pence as fast as you can haul and veer[4] a line? He is a very bad fisher [who] cannot kill in one day with his hook and line, one, two, or three hundred cods, which dressed and dried, if they be sold there for ten shillings the hundred [pounds], though in England they will give more than twenty, may not both the servant, the master, and merchant be well content with this gain? If a man work but three days in seven he may get more than he can spend, unless he will be excessive. . . .

For hunting also, the woods, lakes, and rivers afford not only chase sufficient for any that delight in that kind of toil or pleasure, but such beasts to hunt that besides the delicacy of their bodies for food, their skins are so rich as may well recompense thy daily labor with a captain's pay.

For laborers, if those [in England] that sow hemp, turnips, parsnips, carrots, cabbage, and such like, give 20, 30, 40, 50 shillings yearly

---

4. **haul and veer:** pull in and let out.

[rent] for an acre of ground, and meat, drink, and wages to use it and yet grow rich, [then] when better or at least as good ground may be had [in New England] and cost nothing but labor, it seems strange to me any such should there grow poor.

My purpose is not to persuade children from their parents, men from their wives, nor servants from their masters, only such as with free consent may be spared. But [if] each parish or village, in city or country, that will but apparel their fatherless children of thirteen or fourteen years of age, or young married people that have small wealth to live on, here by their labor [they] may live exceeding well, provided always that first there be a sufficient power to command them, houses to receive them, means to defend them, and meet[5] provisions for them, for any place may be overlain[6] and it is most necessary to have a fortress and sufficient masters (as, carpenters, masons, fishers, fowlers, gardeners, husbandmen,[7] sawyers, smiths, spinners, tailors, weavers, and such like) to take ten, twelve, or twenty, or as there is occasion, for apprentices. The masters by this may quickly grow rich; these [apprentices] may learn [by] their trades themselves to do the like, to a general and an incredible benefit for king and country, master and servant.

---

5. **meet:** sufficient.
6. **overlain:** overwhelmed by an enemy.
7. **husbandmen:** farmers.

STUDY QUESTIONS

Recalling

1. According to the first sentence, to people of what economic "means" and "fortune" is Smith addressing his words?
2. From the first paragraph name at least one attraction of life in New England that appeals to the following qualities: virtue, faith, honor.
3. Name three means of earning a living in New England that Smith discusses at length in paragraphs 2–4. Name five other trades that will be needed in New England, according to paragraph 5.
4. According to the last paragraph, whom is Smith not trying to persuade to move to New England? Who does he think should journey to America?

5. According to the final sentence, who will benefit from the establishment of New England settlements?

Interpreting

6. What general impression does Smith give of life in New England?
7. Does Smith describe the drawbacks of settling in New England? Why or why not?
8. For what reason other than describing New England did Smith write this piece? In what paragraph and through what specific recommendations does that additional reason become most apparent?

LITERARY FOCUS

Persuasion

Persuasion attempts to sway the reader to think or act in a particular way. Although Smith says he is writing a "description," he is actually trying to persuade English men and women of the advantages of settling in the New World.

Four elements must be considered when writing or evaluating persuasion:

The writer. The persuasive writer calls upon personal experience for support. As one of the few Europeans who had been to America, Smith speaks about the New World with first-hand knowledge. His reputation as a leader and his fact-filled descriptions help convince his audience of the truth of what he says.

The audience. The persuasive writer pinpoints the people whose minds are to be changed and considers what they already believe and feel. Smith recognizes that only people without wealth and position are likely colonists, but he also addresses people who might help to finance the expedition. He stresses economic opportunities but does not neglect patriotic and religious motives.

The occasion. The persuasive writer takes advantage of current events in the mind of the reader. Smith makes the most of the curiosity of Europeans about America in the early seventeenth century. He plays upon their eagerness to know and their desire to better their own lives.

The purpose. Effective persuasion has a clear purpose: to move the reader to take a particular action. Smith's purpose is clear: He wants to persuade people "with free consent" to settle in New England.

Thinking About Persuasion

Which of the benefits that Smith describes seem directed at persuading people to join his expedition? Which benefits seem directed at people who might help finance a new colony?

VOCABULARY

Synonyms

Synonyms are words that have the same or nearly the same meaning. *Change* and *alter* are synonyms.

The words in capital letters are from *A Description of New England.* Choose the word that is *nearest* to the meaning of each word in capitals, *as the word is used in this selection.* Write the number of each item and the letter of your choice on a separate sheet.

1. HAZARD: (a) risk (b) choice (c) opportunity (d) desire
2. MAGNANIMITY: (a) daring (b) size (c) generosity (d) prudence
3. POSTERITY: (a) fortune (b) honor (c) ancestors (d) descendants
4. ANGLING: (a) fishing (b) carving (c) dangling (d) hunting
5. RECOMPENSE: (a) thought (b) treat (c) reward (d) correction

COMPOSITION

Developing a Thesis Statement

Write a brief essay about Smith's technique of piling up details. First create a thesis statement about this technique. Then demonstrate with examples how Smith adds detail after detail, not stopping with one noun or one adjective. Finally describe the effect you think Smith's technique would have had on a reader's view of the New World. *For help with this assignment, refer to Lesson 1 in the Writing About Literature Handbook at the back of this book.*

Writing a Letter

Assume the role of an English person in 1616. A copy of Smith's *Description* has fallen into your hands. Write a letter to a friend in which you react to Smith's appeals, discussing the positive and the negative aspects of joining Smith's proposed expedition.

William Bradford   *1590–1657*

While Jamestown was continuing its struggle for survival, another group of colonists, known as the Pilgrims, landed farther north. They were led by William Bradford, a Yorkshire farmer who had been converted as a teen-ager to an extreme form of Puritanism. Many Puritans hoped to remain members of the Church of England and to reform it from within. Bradford's Separatist group, however, saw no compromise and suffered heavy persecution for their beliefs. They fled to Holland and later decided to establish their own colony in Virginia.

Bradford and the Pilgrims sailed from Leyden in Holland in 1620, but because of storms they never reached Virginia. Instead, they landed their ship *Mayflower* at Plymouth on the coast of Massachusetts. In the Mayflower Compact, an agreement they signed before they left the ship, they decided to form a government and follow an elected leader. When their first governor, John Carver, died in April 1621, the people chose Bradford to take his place. He was so successful that he was reelected thirty times. In 1630 he began writing *Of Plymouth Plantation,* his history of these early Americans and their long geographical and spiritual pilgrimage.

Bradford is a gifted writer. His chronicle conveys not only facts but also feelings because he imaginatively projects himself and his readers into the experience of each moment. He makes a personal story out of the voyage, the settlement, and the grim realities of "the starving time." Through him, we share the struggle, the fears, and the victories over the elements, as well as the gradual changes that overtake the colony as people move away, as children grow up, as the original vision fades.

Year after year Bradford always keeps sight of the signs of God's judgment and providence. He sees the signs everywhere, so that, for example, the Indian interpreter Squanto becomes "an instrument sent of God for their good." For Bradford the Puritans' flight from Europe is guided by God in the same way as the Israelites' exodus from Egypt.

Bradford writes in the Puritan Plain Style, seldom using any metaphors or decorative language. Certainly he found no need to decorate a chronicle of events so charged with excitement, danger, and emotion. Bradford's plain language reflects his belief that everything in the Puritan way of life should have the power of simplicity. As one of the great Puritan ministers, John Cotton, said, "God's altar needs no polishing."

The Pilgrims' First Winter in Massachusetts, 1620. Nineteenth-century engraving.

William Bradford

from **Of Plymouth Plantation**

Arrival

After long beating at sea they fell with[1] that land which is called Cape Cod; the which being made and certainly known to be it, they were not a little joyful. . . .

Being thus arrived in a good harbor, and brought safe to land, they fell upon their knees and blessed the God of Heaven who had brought them over the vast and furious ocean, and delivered them from all the perils and miseries thereof, again to set their feet on the firm and stable earth, their proper element. . . .

But here I cannot but stay and make a pause, and stand half amazed at this poor people's present condition; and so I think will the reader, too, when he well considers the same. Being thus passed the vast ocean, and a sea of troubles before in their preparation (as may be remembered by that which went before), they had now no friends to welcome them nor inns to entertain or refresh their weatherbeaten bodies; no houses or much less towns to repair to, to seek for succor. It is recorded in Scripture[2] as a mercy to the Apostle and his shipwrecked company, that the barbarians showed them no small kindness in refreshing them, but these savage barbarians, when they

---

1. **fell with:** arrived at.

2. **Scripture:** Acts of the Apostles, Chapter 28, Verse 2, tells how strangers helped Saint Paul after he was shipwrecked.

met with them (as after will appear) were readier to fill their sides full of arrows than otherwise. And for the season it was winter, and they that know the winters of that country know them to be sharp and violent, and subject to cruel and fierce storms, dangerous to travel to known places, much more to search an unknown coast. Besides, what could they see but a hideous and desolate wilderness, full of wild beasts and wild men—and what multitudes there might be of them they knew not. Neither could they, as it were, go up to the top of Pisgah[3] to view from this wilderness a more goodly country to feed their hopes; for which way soever they turned their eyes (save upward to the heavens) they could have little solace or content in respect of any outward objects. For summer being done, all things stand upon them with a weather-beaten face, and the whole country, full of woods and thickets, represented a wild and savage hue. If they looked behind them, there was the mighty ocean which they had passed and was now as a main bar and gulf to separate them from all the civil parts of the world. If it be said they had a ship to succor them, it is true; but what heard they daily from the Master[4] and company? But that with speed they should look out a place (with their shallop[5]) where they would be, at some near distance; for the season was such as he would not stir from thence till a safe harbor was discovered by them, where they would be and he might go without danger; and that victuals consumed apace but he must and would keep sufficient for themselves and their return. Yea, it was muttered by some[6] that if they got not a place in time, they would turn them and their goods ashore and leave them. Let it also be considered what weak hopes of supply and succor they left behind them that might bear up their minds in

this sad condition and trials they were under; and they could not but be very small. It is true, indeed, the affections and love of their brethren at Leyden[7] was cordial and entire towards them, but they had little power to help them or themselves.

What could now sustain them but the Spirit of God and His grace? May not and ought not the children of these fathers rightly say: "Our fathers were Englishmen which came over this great ocean, and were ready to perish in this wilderness; but they cried unto the Lord, and He heard their voice and looked on their adversity,"[8] etc. "Let them therefore praise the Lord, because He is good: and His mercies endure forever." "Yea, let them which have been redeemed of the Lord, show how He hath delivered them from the hand of the oppressor. When they wandered in the desert wilderness out of the way, and found no city to dwell in, both hungry and thirsty, their soul was overwhelmed in them. Let them confess before the Lord His lovingkindness and His wonderful works before the sons of men."[9]

The Starving Time

But that which was most sad and lamentable was that in two or three months' time half of their company died, especially in January and February, being the depth of winter, and wanting houses and other comforts; being infected with the scurvy[10] and other diseases which this long voyage and their inaccommodate condition had brought upon them. So as there died some times two or three of a day in the foresaid time, that of 100 and odd persons, scarce fifty remained. And of these, in the time of most distress, there was but six or

---

3. **Pisgah** [piz′gə]: Moses viewed the Promised Land from Mount Pisgah (Deuteronomy 34: 1–4).
4. **Master:** Christopher Jones, the captain of the *Mayflower.*
5. **shallop** [shal′əp]: small open boat with oars or sail.
6. **some:** some of the sailors.

7. **Leyden** [līd′ən]: city in Netherlands where the Pilgrims lived before coming to America.
8. **"Our fathers . . . their adversity":** Bradford recalls Deuteronomy 26 : 5–7, the outcry of the Israelites to be delivered from Egyptian bondage.
9. **"Yea, let . . . sons of men":** Bradford paraphrases Psalm 107, comparing Puritan "captivity " and "wandering" with the captivity of the Israelites in Egypt and their wandering in the desert as they searched for the Promised Land.
10. **scurvy:** disease caused by vitamin C deficiency.

seven sound persons who to their great commendations, be it spoken, spared no pains night nor day, but with abundance of toil and hazard of their own health, fetched them wood, made them fires, dressed[11] them meat, made their beds, washed their loathsome clothes, clothed and unclothed them. In a word, did all the homely[12] and necessary offices for them which dainty and queasy stomachs cannot endure to hear named; and all this willingly and cheerfully, without any grudging in the least, showing herein their true love unto their friends and brethren; a rare example and worthy to be remembered. Two of these seven were Mr. William Brewster, their reverend Elder, and Myles Standish, their Captain and military commander, unto whom myself and many others were much beholden in our low and sick condition. And yet the Lord so upheld these persons as in this general calamity they were not at all infected either with sickness or lameness. And what I have said of these I may say of many others who died in this general visitation,[13] and others yet living; that whilst they had health, yea, or any strength continuing, they were not wanting to any that had need of them. And I doubt not but their recompense is with the Lord.

But I may not here pass by another remarkable passage not to be forgotten. As this calamity fell among the passengers that were to be left here to plant, and were hasted ashore and made to drink water that the seamen might have the more beer, and one[14] in his sickness desiring but a small can of beer, it was answered that if he were their own father he should have none. The disease began to fall amongst them[15] also, so as almost half of their company died before they went away, and many of their officers and lustiest[16] men, as the boatswain, gunner, three quartermasters, the cook and others. At which the Master was something stricken and sent to the sick ashore and told the Governor he should send for beer for them that had need of it, though he drunk water homeward bound.

But now amongst his company there was far another kind of carriage[17] in this misery than amongst the passengers. For they that before had been boon[18] companions in drinking and jollity in the time of their health and welfare began now to desert one another in this calamity, saying they would not hazard their lives for them: they should be infected by coming to help them in their cabins, and so, after they came to lie by it, would do little or nothing for them but, "if they died, let them die." But such of the passengers as were yet aboard showed them what mercy they could, which made some of their hearts relent, as the boatswain (and some others) who was a proud young man and would often curse and scoff at the passengers. But when he grew weak, they had compassion on him and helped him; then he confessed he did not deserve it at their hands, he had abused them in word and deed. "Oh!" (saith he) "you, I now see, show your love like Christians indeed one to another, but we let one another lie and die like dogs." Another lay cursing his wife, saying if it had not been for her he had never come this unlucky voyage, and anon cursing his fellows, saying he had done this and that for some of them; he had spent so much and so much amongst them, and they were now weary of him and did not help him, having need. Another gave his companion all he had, if he died, to help him in his weakness; he went and got a little spice and made him a mess[19] of meat once or twice. And because he died not so soon as he expected, he went amongst his fellows and swore the rogue would cozen[20] him, he would see him choked before he made him any more meat; and yet the poor fellow died before morning.

11. **dressed:** prepared.
12. **homely:** domestic and everyday.
13. **visitation:** affliction or disaster.
14. **one:** Bradford notes that this "one" was himself.
15. **them:** the sailors.
16. **lustiest:** healthiest and strongest.

17. **carriage:** behavior.
18. **boon:** merry.
19. **mess:** a meal.
20. **cozen** [kuz′ən]: cheat.

Squanto Teaching the Pilgrims How to Plant Corn, C. W. Jefferys.

Compact with the Indians

All this while the Indians came skulking about them, and would sometimes show themselves aloof off, but when any approached near them, they would run away; and once they stole away their tools where they had been at work and were gone to dinner. But about the 16th of March, a certain Indian came boldly amongst them and spoke to them in broken English, which they could well understand but marveled at it. At length they understood by discourse with him that he was not of these parts, but belonged to the eastern parts where some English ships came to fish, with whom he was acquainted and could name sundry of them by their names, amongst whom he had got his language. He became profitable to them in acquainting them with many things concerning the state of the country in the east parts where he lived, which was afterwards profitable unto them; as also of the people here, of their names, number and strength, of their situation and distance from this place, and who was chief amongst them. His name was Samoset. He told them also of another Indian whose name was Squanto, a native of this place, who had been in England and could speak better English than himself.

Being, after some time of entertainment and gifts, dismissed, a while after he came again, and five more with him, and they brought again all the tools that were stolen away before, and made way for the coming of their great Sachem,[21] called Massasoit. Who, about four or five days after, came with the chief of his friends and other attendance, with the aforesaid Squanto. With whom, after friendly entertainment and some gifts given him, they made a peace with him (which hath now continued this twenty-four years) in these terms:

1. That neither he nor any of his should injure or do hurt to any of their people.
2. That if any of his did hurt to any of theirs, he should send the offender, that they might punish him.
3. That if anything were taken away from any of theirs, he should cause it to be restored; and they should do the like to his.

---

21. **Sachem** [sā′chəm]: chief.

4. If any did unjustly war against him, they would aid him; if any did war against them, he should aid them.
5. He should send to his neighbors confederates to certify them of this, that they might not wrong them, but might be likewise comprised in the conditions of peace.
6. That when their men came to them, they should leave their bows and arrows behind them.

After these things he returned to his place called Sowams, some forty miles from this place, but Squanto continued with them and was their interpreter and was a special instrument sent of God for their good beyond their expectation. He directed them how to set their corn, where to take fish, and to procure other commodities, and was also their pilot to bring them to unknown places for their profit, and never left them till he died.

STUDY QUESTIONS

Recalling
1. What was the Pilgrims' first action upon landing in the New World?
2. Identify four specific hardships that the Pilgrims faced in the New World, according to the third paragraph. What sustained them, according to the fourth paragraph?
3. As "calamity fell among the passengers," what did the sailors do? When calamity struck the sailors, what did the Pilgrims still on board do?
4. How did the Indians act at first, according to Bradford? What did they do after "friendly entertainment and some gifts"? What information did Samoset and Squanto provide for the Pilgrims?

Interpreting
5. State two dominant characteristics of the *Mayflower* Pilgrims as they are pictured by Bradford during their first months of hardship in America.

6. Which words and statements by Bradford create a picture of the Pilgrims as God's "chosen people"?
7. Describe Bradford's initial attitude toward the Indians and his attitude in the section "Compact with the Indians." How has Bradford changed? What seems to have caused the change?

Extending
8. Judging from Bradford's account, what qualities do you think would be necessary for a man or woman to survive for any length of time in the American wilderness? What attitudes brought from Europe had to be abandoned?

VIEWPOINT

Throughout this book "Viewpoint" will present a quotation about an author or a selection you have read. Most of these quotations come from literary critics; some come from the authors themselves. Each quotation is followed by one or two questions to help you consider the quoted opinion in light of your own reading of the selection.

Perry Miller, an expert on early American literature, writes:

No other writer will lead us so directly to the core of Puritanism as Bradford; none with such charm, generosity, largeness of spirit, with such calm assurance and massive strength will so completely reveal the essential frame of mind, the type of character, the quality of life that underlay the theology.
—*The New England Mind*

■ Find three passages in *Of Plymouth Plantation* supporting Miller's statement that Bradford reveals the essence of Puritanism. What conclusions about Puritanism can you draw from the details of Bradford's story?

LITERARY FOCUS

Allusions: The Use of the Bible

For centuries English-speaking writers and their readers knew the Bible very well. After 1611 the version they knew best was the King James translation, which has had a powerful influence on English and American literature. Poets, storytellers, and orators referred to the Bible frequently, and phrases from the King James version became part of everyone's vocabulary. The Puritans, especially, based their religion directly on a reading of the Bible, and their writers naturally made allusions to it.

An **allusion** is a short reference to a person, a place, an event, or another work of literature. When Bradford alludes to the "top of Pisgah," he knows his audience will understand that he is referring to the mountain from which Moses saw the Promised Land.

Writers use allusions to extend the meanings of their works. Sometimes they want to show that a particular experience is also a universal experience. Sometimes they want to remind us of connections we might not have thought of ourselves.

Thinking About Allusions

■ Find the two biblical allusions in Bradford's third paragraph. Why were these specific references appropriate to the experience of the Pilgrims?

VOCABULARY

Sentence Completions

Each of the following sentences contains a blank with four possible words for completing the sentence. The words are from *Of Plymouth Plantation*. Choose the word that completes each sentence correctly, using the word *as it is used in this selection*. Write the number of each item and the letter of your choice on a separate sheet.

1. The colonists could not hope for supply and _____ in the desolate wilderness.
   (a) succor   (c) shallop
   (b) scurvy   (d) carriage

2. The Pilgrims faced much _____ during their hard sea voyage.
   (a) abundance   (c) solace
   (b) boon   (d) adversity

3. One of the many _____ that befell the settlers was death from scurvy.
   (a) recompenses   (c) calamities
   (b) commendations   (d) commodities

4. Many sailors did not want to risk infection or to _____ their lives.
   (a) scoff   (c) relent
   (b) hazard   (d) cozen

5. The Pilgrims had lengthy _____ with Samoset.
   (a) commendation   (c) hue
   (b) solace   (d) discourse

COMPOSITION

Writing a Comparison/Contrast

■ Compare and contrast the promises that John Smith makes in his *Description of New England* (page 20) and the reality of the settlers' lives as Bradford describes it. You may want to write first about Smith's ideal vision and then about Bradford's genuine history. *For help with this assignment, refer to Lesson 2 in the Writing About Literature Handbook at the back of this book.*

Writing a Diary

■ Imagine yourself one of the Plymouth settlers, and write a diary chronicling several days of your adventures. Consider including details of your problems with weather, animals, food, clothes, the native inhabitants, and the organization of your first government.

Anne Bradstreet *1612–1672*

Anne Bradstreet came to the Massachusetts Bay Colony with her husband and her parents in 1630. The Bradstreets settled in the frontier village of Andover, where Anne, under difficult conditions that tried her faith, maintained a household and raised eight children. She had to defend her right to compose verses, for many Puritans, who did not disapprove of poetry itself, wondered if a woman should write it. Yet her first book, *The Tenth Muse Lately Sprung Up in America,* was published in England in 1650 and was a great success.

Bradstreet's finest poems are those closest to her personal experience as a Puritan wife and mother living on the edge of the wilderness. Like other Puritans, she found similarities between the domestic details of daily life and the spiritual details of her religious life. For Bradstreet the everyday and the everlasting were simply two sides of the same experience.

In a poem called "Upon the Burning of Our House" Bradstreet records both her earthly sorrow and the faith that sustains her:

> Thou hast a house on high erect,
> Framed by that mighty Architect,
> With glory richly furnished,
> Stands permanent though this be fled.
>   *   *   *
> The world no longer let me love,
> My hope and treasure lies above.

Similarly, in her tender poem "To My Dear and Loving Husband" Bradstreet places her earthly married life within the framework of eternity. Anne Bradstreet was not an innovative poet, but her directness and her sincerity are moving.

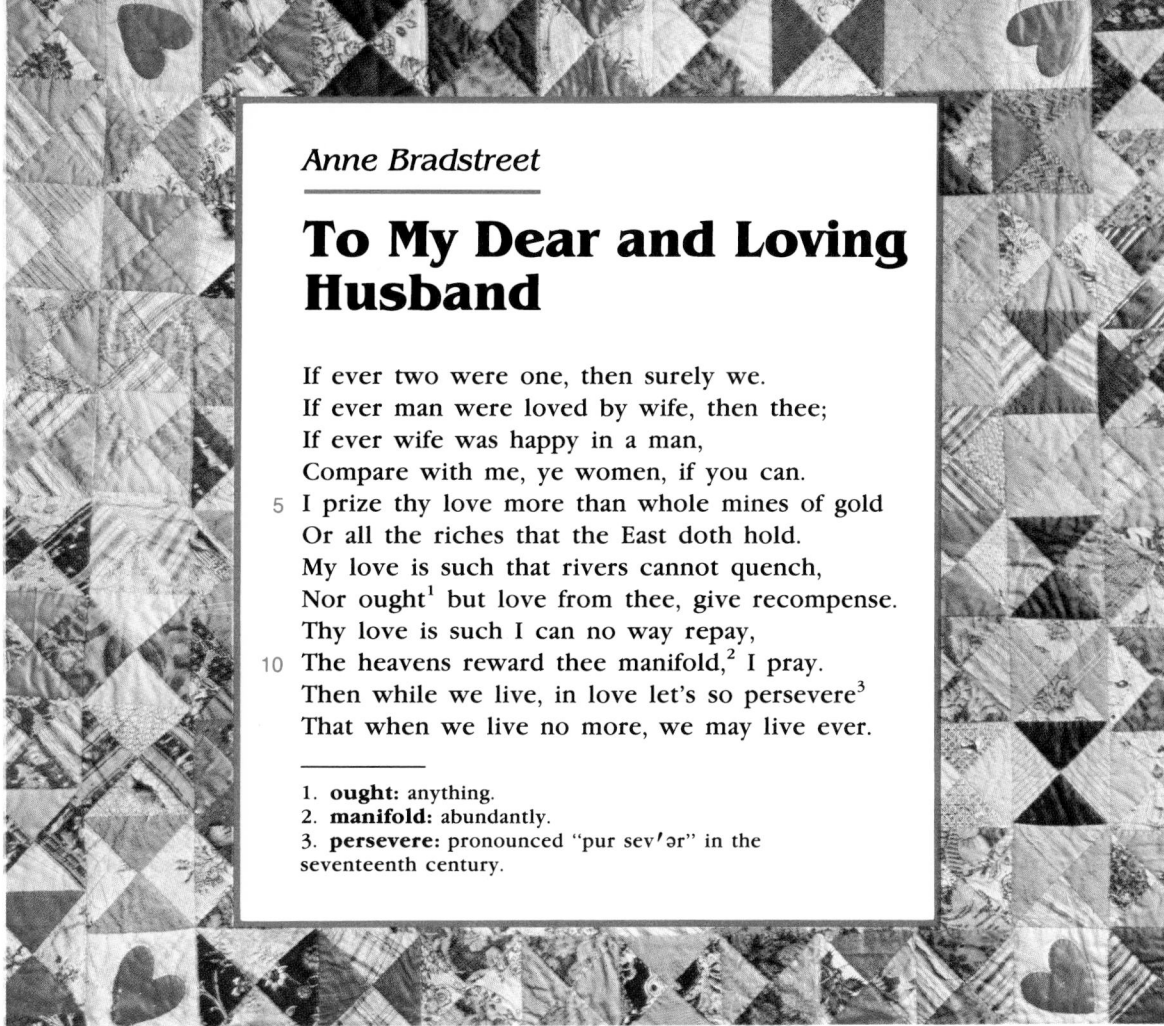

Anne Bradstreet

To My Dear and Loving Husband

If ever two were one, then surely we.
If ever man were loved by wife, then thee;
If ever wife was happy in a man,
Compare with me, ye women, if you can.
5 I prize thy love more than whole mines of gold
Or all the riches that the East doth hold.
My love is such that rivers cannot quench,
Nor ought[1] but love from thee, give recompense.
Thy love is such I can no way repay,
10 The heavens reward thee manifold,[2] I pray.
Then while we live, in love let's so persevere[3]
That when we live no more, we may live ever.

---

1. **ought:** anything.
2. **manifold:** abundantly.
3. **persevere:** pronounced "pur sev′ər" in the seventeenth century.

STUDY QUESTIONS

Recalling
1. What does the poet prize "more than whole mines of gold"? What is it that "rivers cannot quench"?
2. Which words tell us what will happen when she and her husband die if they persevere in love while they live?

Interpreting
3. What does Bradstreet actually mean by the seeming paradox in the last line about living "no more" yet living "ever"?
4. Besides declaring her human love for her husband during her earthly marriage, what other typical Puritan concern does this poem celebrate in lines 9–10?

VIEWPOINT

The contemporary American poet Adrienne Rich writes of Bradstreet:

It is worth observing that Anne Bradstreet happened to be one of the first American women, inhabiting a time and place in which heroism was a necessity of life, and men and women were fighting for survival both as individuals and as a community.

—Introduction to
The Works of Anne Bradstreet

■ What personal qualities and beliefs does Bradstreet reveal in "To My Dear and Loving Husband" that made such heroism possible for her?

Edward Taylor   *1642–1729*

For fifty-eight years Edward Taylor was both minister and physician to the people of Westfield, Massachusetts, bordering what he called the "howling wilderness." Because Taylor considered his poems a private record of his religious experience, he asked his heirs never to publish them. As a result, the work of this major New England poet was unknown for 210 years after his death.

Perhaps another reason Taylor did not wish to publish his work was that his poetry was not written in the Plain Style of the Puritans. At first reading we can see that Taylor uses elaborate imagery. In one poem, *God's Determinations,* the poet meditates on the wonders of the created world and compares God to a builder, an ironmonger, a weaver, and a bowler rolling forth the great bowling ball of the sun. He focuses on images of God as an artisan, a maker:

> His hand hath made this noble work which stands
> His Glorious Handiwork not made by hands.

"Huswifery" [hoōs'wif rē] is also a complicated poem, a prayer in which the poet compares God's granting of grace to the work of a housewife who spins, weaves, and dyes a piece of cloth. By *huswifery,* Taylor meant not only "housekeeping," but "managing well."

Taylor's poems use an extravagant imagery. Their emotion, however, is still the typically Puritan one of submissiveness and wonder in the face of God's grace and power.

Edward Taylor

Huswifery

Make me, O Lord, Thy spinning[1] wheel complete.
    Thy holy word my distaff make for me.
Make mine affections[2] Thy swift flyers neat,
    And make my soul Thy holy spool to be.
5   My conversation make to be Thy reel,
    And reel the yarn thereon spun of Thy wheel.

Make me Thy loom then, knit therein this twine;
    And make Thy holy spirit, Lord, wind quills;[3]
Then weave the web Thyself. The yarn is fine.
10   Thine ordinances[4] make my fulling mills.[5]
    Then dye the same in heavenly colors choice,
    All pinked[6] with varnished flowers of paradise.

Then clothe therewith mine understanding, will,
    Affections, judgment, conscience, memory,
15 My words and actions, that their shine may fill
    My ways with glory and Thee glorify.
    Then mine apparel shall display before Ye
    That I am clothed in holy robes for glory.

---

1. **spinning:** making yarn by twisting woolen fibers. On a spinning wheel, the *distaff* holds the fibers to be spun; the *flyers* twist them into yarn, which is then wound on a *spool* or *reel.*
2. **affections:** emotions.
3. **quills:** weaver's spindles.
4. **ordinances:** religious rites.
5. **fulling mills:** mills in which cloth is cleaned and thickened.
6. **pinked:** decorated.

STUDY QUESTIONS

Recalling

1. What devices are mentioned in lines 1 and 7?
2. With what verb does the poem begin? What are the subject and object of this verb? In what lines of the poem is the verb repeated?
3. According to lines 17–18, what does the poet want his "apparel" to "display" and to whom?

Interpreting

4. What process and what stages in that process are described in the poem? What role does the poet play in this process? What role does God play?
5. What does the verb repeated throughout the poem suggest about how the poet views God's role in his life?
6. In the third stanza, particularly in line 16, what does Taylor suggest is his ultimate goal?
7. Does Taylor believe one can achieve grace through one's own efforts, or must grace come as a gift from God? Supply evidence from the poem for your answer.

VIEWPOINT

One writer who has studied the Puritans says that Edward Taylor

> brings religious vision and the actualities of earth together in his verses, striking poetic sparks from the contrast. Again and again he makes articulate the drama inherent in man's quest for a beauty which is beyond earth. . . .
> —*Literary History of the United States*

■ The writer, Kenneth Murdock, points to a dramatic contrast in Taylor's poetry. How does "Huswifery" contrast a heavenly vision with the everyday things of earth?

LITERARY FOCUS

Controlling Imagery

When we speak of an **image** in literature, we usually mean that the words create a "picture" in our minds. Images can be visual, of course, but they can also describe other sensory experiences, such as tasting, smelling, feeling, or hearing. Sometimes poets use a variety of images in a single poem. Sometimes they use only one, allowing it to *control*, or dominate, the poem.

In "Huswifery" Taylor controls the many separate images of the poem with the single larger image of clothmaking. An extended image like this, especially one that sets up a rather surprising or unusual comparison (God as a clothmaker), is sometimes called a **conceit.**

Taylor sets up the controlling image in the first line as he asks to be God's instrument, a spinning wheel. Then he compares the Bible ("Thy holy word") to part of the spinning wheel—the distaff, the strong stick that holds the raw wool.

Thinking About Controlling Imagery

■ To what does Taylor compare his emotions and his soul? How does the controlling image help show that, for Taylor, the earthly and the heavenly are one and the same?

COMPOSITION

Analyzing a Title

■ Write a brief essay in which you discuss the title of Taylor's poem. First tell what the title means. Then explain how the title helps to explain the poem itself. Finally tell whether you think the title is appropriate, and give reasons to support your opinion.

Using a Controlling Image

■ Write a poem that uses a conceit, or controlling image. Follow the format of Taylor's "Huswifery" or of Bradstreet's "To My Dear and Loving Husband" (page 31), keeping the same basic sentence structure but changing the key words. You may want to begin, for example, by completing this line: "Make me, _____, your _____ complete."

COMPARING WRITERS

In William Bradford, Anne Bradstreet, and Edward Taylor we find a quest for heavenly joy meeting face to face the real world of flesh and blood. Even the selections by Christopher Columbus and John Smith reveal a contrast between Eden-like dreams and the unavoidable realities of earth. This contrast between the real and the ideal is one of the most American of themes, one that will appear in every unit of this book.

■ Find passages from at least two writers in this unit that demonstrate an awareness of both the real world and an ideal one. Describe each writer's attitude toward that contrast.

William Byrd   *1674–1744*

The New England Puritans wrote so much and so vividly that they tend to dominate early American literature. We should remind ourselves that not all early American settlers were Puritans. In the southern colonies, especially, other English settlers had founded prosperous plantations and communities with a style of life quite unlike that of New England.

William Byrd was one of the most brilliant of the southern landowning aristocracy. These southern gentry modeled themselves on the English upper classes, taking pride in stately homes furnished with fine china, paintings, and books. Though hard-working and religious, they were not afraid of some of the worldly pleasures that the Puritans shunned.

Byrd was born in Jamestown, which John Smith had helped establish sixty-seven years earlier. When Byrd was only seven years old, his rich father sent him to England for his education. Byrd lived in London more than half of his life, enjoying the city's society and its theaters. He was fifty-two before he returned to Virginia. There he read his Greek and Latin classics every day; owned the second largest library in America, numbering 3,600 books; entertained and visited his neighbors; and managed his huge 180,000-acre estate, upon which he founded the city of Richmond.

Byrd's writings include diaries, travel books, and poems. One of his best-known works, *The History of the Dividing Line,* recounts his experiences on a surveying trip that defined the Virginia–North Carolina border. *A Progress to the Mines* (1732), another well-known work, is Byrd's account of a trip to the iron-mining territory of western Virginia, where he visited the estate of former governor Spotswood. The Spotswoods' elegant "enchanted castle," with its pet deer leaping around and smashing the china, provides a striking contrast to New England earnestness and plain living.

William Byrd

from **A Progress to the Mines**

September 27, 1732 I rode eight miles together over a stony road and had on either side continual poisoned fields, with nothing but saplings growing on them. Then I came into the main county road that leads from Fredericksburg to Germanna, which last place I reached in ten miles more.

This famous town consists of Colonel Spotswood's enchanted castle on one side of the street and a baker's dozen[1] of ruinous tenements on the other, where so many German families had dwelt some years ago, but are now removed ten miles higher, in the fork of Rappahannock,[2] to land of their own. There had also been a chapel about a bowshot from the colonel's house, at the end of an avenue of cherry trees, but some pious people had lately burned it down, with intent to get another built nearer to their own homes.

Here I arrived about three o'clock and found only Mrs. Spotswood at home, who received her old acquaintance with many a gra-

cious smile. I was carried into a room elegantly set off with pier glasses,[3] the largest of which came soon after to an odd misfortune. Amongst other favorite animals that cheered this lady's solitude, a brace[4] of tame deer ran familiarly about the house, and one of them came to stare at me as a stranger; but, unluckily spying his own figure in the glass, he made a spring over the tea table that stood under it and shattered the glass to pieces and, falling back upon the tea table, made a terrible fracas among the china. This exploit was so sudden, and accompanied with such noise, that it surprised me and perfectly frightened Mrs. Spotswood. But 'twas worth all the damage to show the moderation and good humor with which she bore this disaster.

In the evening the noble colonel came home from his mines, who saluted me very civilly, and Mrs. Spotswood's sister, Miss Theky, who had been to meet him *en cavalier*,[5] was so kind too as to bid me welcome. We talked

---

1. **baker's dozen:** thirteen.
2. **Rappahannock:** river flowing through northeastern Virginia.

3. **pier glasses:** tall mirrors.
4. **brace:** pair.
5. *en cavalier* [än ka va lyä′]: French for "on horseback."

over a legend of old stories, supped about nine, and then prattled with the ladies till 'twas time for a traveler to retire. In the meantime, I observed my old friend to be very uxorious[6] and exceedingly fond of his children. This was so opposite to the maxims he used to preach up before he was married that I could not forbear rubbing up the memory of them. But he gave a very good-natured turn to his change of sentiments by alleging that whoever brings a poor gentlewoman into so solitary a place, from all her friends and acquaintance, would be ungrateful not to use her and all that belongs to her with all possible tenderness.

September 28   We all kept snug in our several apartments till nine, except Miss Theky, who was the housewife of the family. At that hour we met over a pot of coffee, which was not quite strong enough to give us the palsy.

After breakfast the colonel and I left the ladies to their domestic affairs and took a turn in the garden, which has nothing beautiful but three terrace walks that fall in slopes one below another. I let him understand that besides the pleasure of paying him a visit I came to be instructed by so great a master in the mystery of making iron, wherein he had led the way and was the Tubal-cain[7] of Virginia. He corrected me a little there by assuring me he was not only the first in this country but the first in North America who had erected a regular furnace. That they ran altogether upon bloomeries[8] in New England and Pennsylvania till his example had made them attempt greater works. But in this last colony, they have so few ships to carry their iron to Great Britain that they must be content to make it only for their own use, and must be obliged to manufacture it when they have done. That he hoped he had done the country very great service by setting so good an example. . . .

Then I inquired after his own mines, and hoped, as he was the first that engaged in this great undertaking, that he had brought them to the most perfection. He told me he had iron in several parts of his great tract of land, consisting of forty-five thousand acres. But that the mine he was at work upon was thirteen miles below Germanna. That his ore (which was very rich) he raised a mile from his furnace and was obliged to cart the iron, when it was made, fifteen miles to Massaponax, a plantation he had upon Rappahannock River; but that the road was exceeding good, gently declining all the way, and had no more than one hill to go up in the whole journey. . . .

But at the same time he gave me to understand that his furnace had done no great feats lately, because he had been taken up in building an air furnace at Massaponax, which he had now brought to perfection and should be thereby able to furnish the whole country with all sorts of cast iron as cheap and as good as ever came from England. I told him he must do one thing more to have a full vent for those commodities: he must keep a *chaloupe*[9] running into all the rivers to carry his wares home to people's own doors. And if he would do that I would set a good example and take off a whole ton of them.

Our conversation on this subject continued till dinner, which was both elegant and plentiful. The afternoon was devoted to the ladies, who showed me one of their most beautiful walks. They conducted me through a shady lane to the landing and by the way made me drink some very fine water that issued from a marble fountain and ran incessantly.

September 29   Having employed about two hours in retirement, I sallied out at the first summons to breakfast, where our conversation with the ladies, like whip sillabub,[10] was

---

6. **uxorious** [uk sôr′ē əs]: fond of his wife.
7. **Tubal-cain:** master ironworker and toolmaker described in the Bible, Genesis 4 : 22.
8. **bloomeries:** formerly, furnaces where iron was made directly from iron ore.

9. **chaloupe** [shə lōōp′]: French for "shallop," a small boat.
10. **whip sillabub:** light, frothy dessert made of sweetened milk or cream.

very pretty but had nothing in it. This it seems was Miss Theky's birthday, upon which I made her my compliments and wished she might live twice as long a married woman as she had lived a maid. I did not presume to pry into the secret of her age, nor was she forward to disclose it, for this humble reason, lest I should think her wisdom fell short of her years. She contrived to make this day of her birth a day of mourning, for, having nothing better at present to set her affections upon, she had a dog that was a great favorite. It happened that very morning the poor cur had done something very uncleanly upon the colonel's bed, for which he was condemned to die. However, upon her entreaty, she got him a reprieve, but was so concerned that so much severity should be intended on her birthday that she was not to be comforted; and lest such another accident might oust the poor cur of his clergy, she protested she would board out her dog at a neighbor's house, where she hoped he would be more kindly treated.

Then the colonel and I took another turn in the garden to discourse farther on the subject of iron.

We had a Michaelmas[11] goose for dinner, of Miss Theky's own raising, who was now good-natured enough to forget the jeopardy of her dog. In the afternoon we walked in a meadow by the riverside, which winds in the form of a horseshoe about Germanna, making it a peninsula containing about four hundred acres.

_____

11. **Michaelmas:** September 29, the feast of Saint Michael.

Rappahannock forks about fourteen miles below this place, the northern branch being the larger and consequently must be the river that bounds My Lord Fairfax's grant of the Northern Neck.

September 30   The sun rose clear this morning, and so did I, and finished all my little affairs by breakfast. It was then resolved to wait on the ladies on horseback, since the bright sun, the fine air, and the wholesome exercise all invited us to it. We forded the river a little above the ferry and rode six miles up the neck to a fine level piece of rich land, where we found about twenty plants of ginseng, with the scarlet berries growing on the top of the middle stalk. The root of this is of wonderful virtue in many cases, particularly to raise the spirits and promote perspiration, which makes it a specific in colds and coughs. The colonel complimented me with all we found in return for my telling him the virtues of it. We were all pleased to find so much of this king of plants so near the colonel's habitation and growing, too, upon his own land, but were, however, surprised to find it upon level ground, after we had been told it grew only upon the north side of stony mountains. I carried home this treasure with as much joy as if every root had been a graft of the tree of life, and washed and dried it carefully.

This airing made us as hungry as so many hawks, so that, between appetite and a very good dinner, 'twas difficult to eat like a philosopher.

STUDY QUESTIONS

Recalling

1. With what two words is Colonel Spotswood's home described in paragraph 2? List three details from the description of the house in paragraph 3.

2. What two related topics do Byrd and Colonel Spotswood discuss on September 28?

3. Name at least four activities described in paragraphs 4, 9, and 13 that the men and women share.

Interpreting

4. Based on Byrd's description, make three generalizations that characterize life on the Spotswood plantation.
5. What aspect of southern life does the discussion between Byrd and Colonel Spotswood illustrate?

Extending

6. How does life on Spotswood's plantation contrast with life in New England as described in the writings of the Puritans?

LITERARY FOCUS

Analogy, Simile, and Metaphor

Few things are more basic to an appreciation of literature than a sense of analogy. An **analogy** compares two things or groups of things that are similar in some ways but not in all ways. A writer uses an analogy to make an experience more vivid for the reader or to explain something unfamiliar by comparing it to something familiar.

The two most common ways in which writers make analogies are simile and metaphor. A **simile** states a comparison by using a word or phrase that clearly indicates the comparison. Most similes use *like* or *as* to indicate the comparison.

When Byrd tells us that his breakfast conversation was *"like* whip sillabub," he uses a simile. He presents an image—something we can perceive with our senses—to reinforce his abstract statement that the conversation was "very pretty but had nothing in it." The image of something light and frothy makes his abstract statement vivid and concrete.

A **metaphor** makes a comparison by identifying one thing with another. If Byrd had said that his conversation *was* whip sillabub, he would have been using a metaphor. Metaphors do not use signal words, such as *like* or *as,* to identify the comparisons they make. They are direct identifications and one of the most powerful of imaginative devices.

Using a simile or a metaphor is an imaginative act. It is a creative attempt to make an experience more intense or more universal or simply clearer. It is the kind of imaginative act that can take a journal or a history and help turn it into literature.

Thinking About Simile and Metaphor

■ What two similes occur in the last sentence of the selection? What abstract word does the first simile make concrete? What does the second simile mean? Rewrite the sentence making the first simile into a metaphor.

VOCABULARY

Antonyms

Antonyms are words that have opposite or nearly opposite meanings, such as *temporary* and *permanent*. The words in capitals are from *A Progress to the Mines*. Choose the word that is an antonym of each word in capitals, *as it is used in this selection*. Write the number of each item and the letter of your choice on a separate sheet.

1. INCESSANTLY: (a) never (b) always (c) now (d) later
2. REPRIEVE: (a) pardon (b) revise (c) remake (d) condemn
3. OUST: (a) eject (b) hurt (c) keep (d) joust
4. JEOPARDY: (a) gloom (b) danger (c) safety (d) authority
5. RESOLVED: (a) doubted (b) solved (c) decided (d) finished

COMPOSITION

Writing a Comparison/Contrast

■ Compare and contrast the Plain Style of the Puritans with the more casual and decorative writing style of Byrd. First describe the Plain Style, and cite specific examples of it. Then describe Byrd's style, and cite specific examples of it. Conclude by describing how the two styles compare or contrast. *For help with this assignment, refer to Lesson 2 in the Writing About Literature Handbook at the back of this book.*

Writing a Persuasive Advertisement

■ Write an advertisement persuading eighteenth-century Europeans to come to the southern colonies. Be sure to specify the attractions of the land and the life, as John Smith does in his *Description of New England* (page 20). Use comparison and contrast to draw for your audience a picture of how they would be able to change their lives.

Jonathan Edwards   *1703–1758*

Jonathan Edwards and William Byrd are the first two writers in this book who were actually born in America. In fact, Edwards is the first major American writer who was educated and lived his entire life in the New World.

Edwards was an extraordinary child who, at the age of eleven or twelve, wrote scientific essays on insects, colors, and rainbows. When he was thirteen, he entered Yale, where he experienced a religious conversion. In 1729 he succeeded his grandfather as minister in Northampton, Massachusetts. Edwards became a leading figure in the movement known as the Great Awakening, a fervent revival of religious feeling that swept America from New England to the South from about 1734 to 1749. His sermon *Sinners in the Hands of an Angry God* remains the most famous literary monument to the Great Awakening.

In 1750 some of the Northampton Puritans began to disagree with their famous minister and removed Edwards from his post. He moved, in a kind of exile, to the frontier village of Stockbridge. There he preached to the Indians and wrote many of the works that made him the most influential American writer before Franklin.

Edwards is best known, even notorious, for his sermon *Sinners in the Hands of an Angry God,* which he preached to a congregation at Enfield, Connecticut, in 1741. The Enfield sermon shows Edwards as the hell-fire preacher, but it is unfair to this learned and complex religious thinker to allow *Sinners* totally to represent him. After all, sermons such as this had been traditional for hundreds of years. Edwards' other writings appeal to his readers' reason as well as to their emotions. The lovely and equally devout essay-meditation "The Beauty of the World" shows him in a softer light. It helps to give us a more balanced view of this intense and devoted man.

Yet on that famous Sunday in 1741, Edwards' purpose was not to be gentle or easy on his audience. His words smoke with fire and brimstone as he makes his people not only think about their own sinful nature and the all-powerful God they served but *feel* these things as well.

Model for Active Reading

In this selection, and in one selection in each unit, you will find notes in the right-hand margin that highlight parts of the selection. These notes point out important ideas of the literary period and draw your attention to literary elements and techniques covered in the Literary Focuses. Page numbers in the notes will refer you to more extensive discussions of these important ideas and elements.

Jonathan Edwards

from Sinners in the Hands of an Angry God

The occasion (p. 22): In this persuasive speech, Edwards chooses the most appropriate occasion to deliver his message: a Sunday church service.

So that thus it is that natural men are held in the hand of God over the pit of Hell; they have deserved the fiery pit, and are already sentenced to it; and God is dreadfully provoked. His anger is as great towards them as to those that are actually suffering the executions of the fierceness of his wrath in Hell, and they have done nothing in the least to appease or abate that anger.

Puritan idea: The Puritans kept reminding themselves that the soul was a constant battleground between the forces of good and evil (p. 2).

Neither is God in the least bound by any promise to hold 'em up one moment. The Devil is waiting for them; Hell is gaping for them; the flames gather and flash about them, and would fain[1] lay hold on them and swallow them up. The fire pent up in their own hearts is struggling to break out, and they have no interest in any mediator; there are no means within reach that can be any security to them. In short, they have no refuge, nothing to take hold of. All that preserves them every moment is the mere arbitrary will and uncovenanted unobliged forbearance of an incensed God.[2]

The use of this awful subject may be of awakening unconverted persons in this congregation. This that you have heard is the case of every one of you that are out of Christ.[3] That world of mercy, that lake of burning brimstone, is extended abroad under you. There is a dreadful pit of the glowing flames of the wrath of God; there is Hell's wide gaping mouth open; and you have nothing to stand upon, nor anything to take hold of. There is nothing between you and Hell but the air; it is only the power and mere pleasure of God that holds you up.

The audience (p. 22): Edwards speaks directly to the congregation he wants to persuade and emphasizes that his words apply to members of the congregation.

You probably are not sensible of this; you find you are kept out of Hell, but don't see the hand of God in it, but look at other things, as the good state of your bodily constitution, your care of your own life, and the means you use for your own preservation. But indeed these things are nothing; if God should withdraw his hand, they would avail no more to keep you from falling than the thin air to hold up a person that is suspended in it.

Your wickedness makes you as it were heavy as lead and to tend downwards with great weight and pressure towards Hell. And if God should let you go, you would immediately sink and

---

1. **fain:** gladly.
2. **uncovenanted . . . God:** self-control of an angry God who, Edwards says, has not promised, and is under no obligation, to grant salvation to any individual. The idea of the Covenant, a binding pact between God and his people, was much debated among the Puritans.
3. **out of Christ:** out of God's grace.

swiftly descend and plunge into the bottomless gulf, and your healthy constitution, and your own care and prudence and best contrivance,[4] and all your righteousness would have no more influence to uphold you and keep you out of Hell than a spider's web would have to stop a falling rock. . . .

The bow of God's wrath is bent, and the arrow made ready on the string, and justice bends the arrow at your heart, and strains the bow, and it is nothing but the mere pleasure of God, and that of an angry God, without any promise or obligation at all, that keeps the arrow one moment from being made drunk with your blood.

Thus are all you that never passed under a great change of heart, by the mighty power of the spirit of God upon your souls; all that were never born again, and made new creatures, and raised from being dead in sin to a state of new, and before altogether unexperienced, light and life (however you may have reformed your life in many things, and may have had religious affections, and may keep up a form of religion in your families and closets[5] and in the house of God, and may be strict in it), you are thus in the hands of an angry God. 'Tis nothing but his mere pleasure that keeps you from being this moment swallowed up in everlasting destruction.

The God that holds you over the pit of Hell, much as one holds a spider or some loathsome insect over the fire, abhors you, and is dreadfully provoked. His wrath towards you burns like fire; he looks upon you as worthy of nothing else but to be cast into the fire; he is of purer eyes than to bear to have you in his sight; you are ten thousand times so abominable in his eyes as the most hateful venomous serpent is in ours. . . . .

O sinner! Consider the fearful danger you are in: 'Tis a great furnace of wrath, a wide and bottomless pit, full of the fire of wrath, that you are held over in the hand of that God, whose wrath is provoked and incensed as much against you as against many of the damned in Hell. You hang by a slender thread, with the flames of divine wrath flashing about it, and ready every moment to singe it and burn it asunder; and you have no interest in any mediator, and nothing to lay hold of to save yourself, nothing to keep off the flames of wrath, nothing of your own, nothing that you ever have done, nothing that you can do, to induce God to spare you one moment. . . .

There is reason to think that there are many in this congregation now hearing this discourse that will actually be the subjects of this very misery to all eternity. We know not who they are, or in what seats they sit, or what thoughts they now have: It may be they are now at ease, and hear all these things without much dis-

---

4. **contrivance:** effort.
5. **closets:** small rooms, especially for meditation.

Puritan idea: Puritans exhibited "care," "prudence," and "righteousness" in their daily lives to show that they possessed grace and would be granted salvation (p. 2).

Controlling image (p. 34): The dominant image in this paragraph is of the wrathful God as an archer.

Simile and metaphor (p. 39): Comparisons to a spider, fire, and the "hateful venomous serpent" are similes because they are directly stated with *as* or *like*. Comparisons of Hell to a "furnace" and a "bottomless pit" are metaphors. Both devices add vividness.

Repetition and rhythm (p. 14): These devices of oral recitation make the sermon more forceful.

turbance, and are now flattering themselves that they are not the persons, promising themselves that they shall escape. If we knew that there was one person, and but one, in the whole congregation that was to be the subject of this misery, what an awful thing would it be to think of! If we knew who it was, what an awful sight would it be to see such a person! How might all the rest of the congregation lift up a lamentable and bitter cry over him! But alas! instead of one, how many is it likely will remember this discourse in Hell?

And it would be a wonder if some that are now present should not be in Hell in a very short time, before this year is out. And it would be no wonder if some person that now sits here in some seat of this meetinghouse in health, and quiet and secure, should be there before tomorrow morning. Those of you that finally continue in a natural condition, that shall keep out of Hell longest, will be there in a little time! Your damnation does not slumber; it will come swiftly, and in all probability very suddenly upon many of you. You have reason to wonder that you are not already in Hell. 'Tis doubtless the case of some that heretofore you have seen and known, that never deserved Hell more than you, and that heretofore appeared as likely to have been now alive as you: Their case is past all hope. They are crying in extreme misery and perfect despair. But here you are in the land of the living, and in the house of God, and have an opportunity to obtain salvation. What would not those poor damned, helpless souls give for one day's such opportunity as you now enjoy!

And now you have an extraordinary opportunity, a day wherein Christ has flung the door of mercy wide open, and stands in the door calling and crying with a loud voice to poor sinners; á day, wherein many are flocking to him, and pressing into the kingdom of God. Many are daily coming from the east, west, north and south; many that were very lately in the same miserable condition that you are in, are in now a happy state, with their hearts filled with love to Him that has loved them and washed them from their sins in His own blood, and rejoicing in hope of the Glory of God. How awful is it to be left behind at such a day! To see so many others feasting, while you are pining and perishing! To see so many rejoicing and singing for joy of heart, while you have cause to mourn for sorrow of heart and howl for vexation of spirit! How can you rest one moment in such a condition? . . .

Therefore let everyone that is out of Christ now awake and fly from the wrath to come. The wrath of Almighty God is now undoubtedly hanging over a great part of this congregation: Let everyone fly out of Sodom! *Haste and escape for your lives, look not behind you, escape to the mountain, lest you be consumed.*[6]

Puritan idea: Puritans watched closely over one another, judging every act according to whether or not it truly glorified God (p. 2).

Plain Style (p. 3): Puritans tried to communicate ideas as clearly as possible, as Edwards does in the last part of this paragraph.

Allusion (p. 29): The reference to the biblical story of Sodom emphasizes the wrath of God.

---

6. *Haste . . . consumed:* In Genesis 19 : 17 the angels warn Lot, the only virtuous inhabitant of the sinful city of Sodom, to flee the city before they destroy it.

Needlework from a chair, New England, c. 1725.

Jonathan Edwards

The Beauty of the World

The beauty of the world consists wholly of sweet mutual consents,[1] either within itself or with the Supreme Being. As to the corporeal[2] world, though there are many other sorts of consents, yet the sweetest and most charming beauty of it is its resemblance of spiritual beauties. The reason is that spiritual beauties are infinitely the greatest, and bodies being but the shadows of beings, they must be so much the more charming as they shadow forth spiritual beauties. This beauty is peculiar to[3] natural things, surpassing the art of man.

Thus there is the resemblance of a decent trust, dependence, and acknowledgment in the planets continually moving around the sun, receiving his influences by which they are made happy, bright, and beautiful: a decent attendance in the secondary planets, an image of majesty, power, glory, and beneficence in the sun in the midst of all, and so in terrestrial[4] things, as I have shown in another place.

It is very probable that that wonderful suitableness of green for the grass and plants, the blues of the sky, the white of the clouds, the colors of flowers, consists in a complicated proportion that these colors make one with another, either in their magnitude of the rays, the number of vibrations that are caused in the atmosphere, or some other way. So there is a great suitableness between the objects of different sense, as between sounds, colors, and smells; as between colors of the woods and flowers and the smells and the singing of birds, which it is probable consist in a certain proportion of the vibrations that are made in the different organs. So there are innumerable other agreeablenesses of motions, figures, etc. The gentle motions of waves, of the lily, [are] agreeable to other things that represent calmness, gentleness, and benevolence. The fields and woods seem to rejoice, and how joyful do the birds seem to be in it. How much a resemblance is there of every grace in the field covered with plants and flowers when the sun shines serenely and undisturbedly upon them; how a resemblance, I say, of every grace and beautiful disposition of mind, of an inferior towards a superior cause, preserver, benevolent benefactor, and a fountain of happiness.

How great a resemblance of a holy and virtuous soul is a calm, serene day. What an infinite number of such like beauties is there in that one thing, the light, and how complicated a harmony and proportion is it probable belongs to it.

. . . Hence the reason why almost all men, and those that seem to be very miserable, love life—because they cannot bear to lose sight of such a beautiful and lovely world. The idea, that every moment whilst we live has a beauty that we take not distinct notice of, brings a pleasure that, when we come to the trial, we had rather live in much pain and misery than lose.

---

1. **consents:** agreements and harmonies.
2. **corporeal:** material, physical.
3. **peculiar to:** characteristic of.
4. **terrestrial:** earthly.

STUDY QUESTIONS

Sinners in the Hands of an Angry God

Recalling

1. According to the first paragraph, over what does God hold "natural men"? What is the only thing that "preserves" them?
2. Name three things that will *not* keep them from Hell, according to the third and fourth paragraphs.
3. What opportunity do people facing Hell have, according to Edwards?

Interpreting

4. What concrete images in the first paragraph make Hell vivid? Describe the general tone of this paragraph.
5. At what point in the sermon is there a marked change in tone and topic? Describe that change. Why is the new tone appropriate to the new topic?
6. In your opinion, how effective is Edwards' sermon as an example of persuasion? Give at least two specific reasons (other than those discussed in the marginal annotations) to support your opinion.

Extending

7. What are the advantages and the disadvantages of making such an emotional appeal rather than a cool and reasoned argument? What are some occasions when an emotional appeal is best? When is reason more effective?

The Beauty of the World

Recalling

1. Of what does the beauty of the world consist, according to the first sentence?
2. According to the first paragraph, what is the "sweetest and most charming beauty" of the corporeal (material) world? To what is this beauty "peculiar"?
3. Give at least five examples of "suitableness" in nature, according to paragraph 3.
4. According to the final paragraph, why do almost all people love life?

Interpreting

5. Explain the comparison that Edwards draws in paragraph 4. What more general harmony does the comparison suggest?
6. In your own words, explain fully why the natural world is beautiful to Edwards.

Extending

7. Do you agree with Edwards' explanation of why people love life? Are there other reasons that Edwards does not mention?

VIEWPOINT

Perry Miller, a specialist on Puritans, says:

The truth is, Edwards was infinitely more than a theologian. He was one of America's five or six major artists, who happened to work with ideas instead of with poems or novels. He was much more a psychologist and a poet than a logician.

—*Jonathan Edwards*

■ Find several passages in *Sinners* or in "The Beauty of the World" that show Edwards relying more on psychology or on poetic images than on logic or reason to make his point.

COMPOSITION

Citing Evidence

■ In a short essay defend or attack this proposition: "It is difficult to believe that the same man who delivered *Sinners in the Hands of an Angry God* also wrote 'The Beauty of the World.'" If you defend the statement, cite specific passages defining the conflict between the two selections. If you attack it, cite specific passages showing how the ideas and the emotions in the two selections can be harmonized. *For help with this assignment, refer to Lesson 3 in the Writing About Literature Handbook at the back of this book.*

Writing a Description

■ Write a description of a miserable place, as Edwards does in *Sinners,* using concrete details of sight, sound, smell, and touch. Use several similes and metaphors. If you prefer, write about an inviting place instead, describing it so vividly that your reader will not want to miss it.

READING FOR APPRECIATION

The Historical Imagination

Reading literature offers us an *experience,* but to have the experience, to make the words come alive, we must read actively. We must use our imaginations, participating with the writer in producing or reproducing the experience of the literature. That experience, which is never exactly the same for all readers, or for the same reader on all occasions, is only a potential until we ourselves release it.

One kind of imagination we must bring to literature is *historical.* After all, why should we limit ourselves to the experiences of twentieth-century Americans? In many ways, we share the same basic values and emotions that people had in Homer's Greece, Shakespeare's London, and Bradford's Plymouth. Yet at other times and in other places, people also had different ideas and feelings. As we learn to read literature with an active historical imagination, we release ourselves into those other times and places, illuminating our own time and our own place.

We certainly do not have to *agree* with the world views of other people, or with the opinions of any particular writer, in order to share imaginatively the experience of literature. We do not have to agree with the beliefs of Jonathan Edwards to feel the shiver of terror that ran down the spines of those who listened to him that Sunday. We do not have to be a Puritan poet like Anne Bradstreet to know what it means to love someone. Yet the poet's expression of what it means to her helps us to see what it can mean to us. In just such a way, by using our historical imagination, we can make the past speak to us through literature.

Literature is not always an escape from our own time, nor should it be. It offers us the pleasure of learning about ourselves by learning about others. How are we different, say, from the Puritans of seventeenth-century New England? What do they still have to offer us in the way of wisdom? How can they, as people, expand our sense of the complexity and variety of human nature?

Reading the Puritan writers is not easy. They challenge us to penetrate their time and place, their minds and hearts. The task is difficult not simply because our language has changed or because the Puritans did not share our modern ideas. The task is difficult because the past *is* the past. With the aid of the historical imagination, however, we can make the past live again.

THE AMERICAN VOICE

A Natural Paradise

The writers who appear in this unit have at least one thing in common: They all lived and wrote at a time when the New World was truly new. A place of possibility, America seemed to provide a second birth to anyone who desired to build a community, establish a church, gain fame and honor, or make a new life.

The initial awe and excitement of the early Americans, however, always seemed to focus on the land itself—an enormous garden, an untouched natural paradise. Words like the following, all examples of the American voices we have heard in this unit, are a part of that myth of the American Eden:

Columbus

During that time I walked among the trees which was the most beautiful thing which I had ever seen.

Smith

Here nature and liberty afford us that freely which in England we want. . . .

Edwards

Hence the reason why almost all men, and those that seem to be very miserable, love life—because they cannot bear to lose sight of such a beautiful and lovely world.

Columbus was writing of the Caribbean, Smith of New England, and Edwards of the whole world, yet they were all inspired by the American abundance before their eyes. They saw in America a dream come true, a vision made real. As this book continues, we will hear other American writers voicing these same ideas and emotions. The abundant land is one American theme to keep in mind throughout our entire literary history.

Key to Illustrations on Page 1 and Facing Page.

1. Captain John Smith. Nineteenth-century engraving.

2. Columbus setting sail for the New World, engraving by Theodor de Bry, 1594.

3. Portrait of Mrs. Elizabeth Freake and Baby Mary, unknown artist, c. 1670.

4. Landing at Jamestown, Virginia, 1607.

5. Colonial hornbook, a small board with the alphabet, numbers, etc., used by early American schoolchildren.

6. A chief of the Ojibwa, painting by George Catlin, 1832.

7. Pilgrims signing the Mayflower Compact, 1620. Nineteenth-century engraving.

8. *Whirling Rainbow People,* 1948 sand painting (an ancient art form still practiced by American Indians).

9. Jonathan Edwards. Nineteenth-century engraving.

10. Embroidered chair seat cover, attributed to Anne Bradstreet, seventeenth century.

Key to Illustrations appears on page 97.

REASON
AND
REVOLUTION

1750–1800

A New Nation

On April 19, 1775, a group of American Minutemen faced British redcoats across the little bridge outside the village of Concord, Massachusetts. Suddenly someone—no one knows who—fired a musket shot, "the shot heard round the world," and the American Revolution began. That shot was the climax of years of frustration, anger, and preparation among the colonists.

During the half-century before the Revolution, the thirteen colonies had begun to prosper and to seem less and less like perilous settlements on the edge of a wilderness. They had begun to communicate more with one another and to grow aware of their mutual problems and feelings. They shared their anger over the oppressive political and economic policies of the British government. No one at that time, however, was thinking of revolution—not yet.

Then came a series of infuriating laws and taxes. The Stamp Act in 1765 required that the colonists buy special stamps for newspapers, licenses, pamphlets, and many other documents. The Quartering Act in 1765 forced colonists to feed and house British soldiers in their own homes. The Townshend Acts in 1767 taxed tea, glass, lead, and paper. When some of the colonial assemblies refused to abide by the new laws, the

Title page from the revolutionary pamphlet
Common Sense, Thomas Paine, 1776.

COMMON SENSE;

ADDRESSED TO THE

INHABITANTS

OF

AMERICA,

On the following interesting

SUBJECTS.

I. Of the Origin and Design of Government in general, with concise Remarks on the English Constitution.

II. Of Monarchy and Hereditary Succession.

III. Thoughts on the present State of American Affairs.

IV. Of the present Ability of America, with some miscellaneous Reflections.

Man knows no Master save creating Heaven, Or those whom choice and common good ordain.
THOMSON.

PHILADELPHIA:
Printed, and Sold, by R. BELL, in Third-Street.
MDCCLXXVI.

British government declared those assemblies "dissolved." Violence was not far away: The Boston Massacre erupted in 1770 when British troops fired on a taunting mob. In 1773 the British Parliament insisted again on its right and power to tax Americans. The tax on tea became a symbol, and the famous Boston Tea Party became a symbol too—a symbol of American resistance—as colonists dressed as Indians dumped a shipment of British tea into Boston Harbor.

Americans protested and petitioned King George III for "no taxation without representation." They wanted only what was reasonable, they said. They wanted to share in their own government. Britain replied with the Intolerable Acts of 1774, designed to punish Massachusetts for the Boston Tea Party. Many more rights that had been granted to the colonists in their charters were revoked. Then, when Paul Revere spotted the redcoats on their way to seize American arms at Concord, Americans responded with force.

Yet it was not until January 1776 that a widely heard public voice demanded complete separation from England. The voice was that of Thomas Paine, whose pamphlet *Common Sense,* with its heated language, increased the growing demand for separation. It pointed the way toward the Declaration of Independence in July. If ever writing affected public affairs, *Common Sense* did.

We will not be surprised to find that most American literature in the eighteenth century was political. Through newspapers, magazines, pamphlets, broadsides, and letters, colonial leaders discussed their ideas of human nature and of government. They began forging a new sense of national identity. Battles had to be fought before the thirteen colonies achieved independence. Nevertheless, for years before the first shot was fired, *language* was the source of growing American power. For those Americans it was language that connected reason and revolution. By the time the Revolutionary War was over in 1783, Americans were well on their way to establishing a literary heritage as extraordinary as their political one.

The Age of Reason

Thomas Jefferson once said that a rational society is one that "informs the mind, sweetens the temper, cheers our spirits, and promotes health." Jefferson's attitude—a firm belief in progress, common sense, and the pursuit of happiness—is typical of the period we now call the Age of Reason.

Some historians say we oversimplify the complex eighteenth century in suggesting it was a time when everyone was "reasonable." Of course everyone was not reasonable. The century was marked by fiery emotion as much as by cool logic. But it was a time when people believed in the *possibilities* of reason. It is that hope, that optimism, that gives the age its character.

Americans at this time were influenced by the European movement called the Enlightenment. Followers of Enlightenment ideas believed that people could discover truth by the light of reason alone. They shed the light of reason on the darkness of ignorance, superstition, social injustice, and political tyranny—all in a quest to build the perfect society. Through science and rational government, they thought, order could be established in the world. Above all, followers of Enlightenment ideas stressed the importance of resisting arbitrary limitations on their own free thoughts.

Enlightened Americans, like Europeans, came to trust in human potential. They began to rely on the power of their own minds to shape their own destinies, and the power of their own *language* to express what

Detail from *Boy with a Squirrel*, John Singleton Copley, 1766.

that destiny should be. They thought, wrote, and spoke with a greater self-confidence than a young nation had ever done before. Jefferson once commented that one evening spent at Ben Franklin's house in Philadelphia in the company of musicians, lawyers, and politicians was worth a whole week in Paris.

Writing and Revolution

During the 1770s no one in America could claim to be a professional novelist, poet, or playwright. Yet a great number of Americans expressed themselves on the subjects of liberty, government, law, reason, and individual and national freedom. Throughout the land, weekly "Poet's Corners" in American newspapers never lacked locally written poems, songs, and satires. Americans filled pamphlets with anonymous poems on the issues of the day. They produced a great number of political **broadsides**—sheets of paper covered with anonymous poems, songs, and essays—that could be tacked up around the city, left on doorsteps, or even read to groups on street corners. This writing was not sophisticated, but it was the writing of people whose lives were touched by the events of a turbulent time.

The policies of Great Britain helped make writers—even poets—out of many colonials. Furor over the Stamp Act of 1765 brought out poems every-where: in political pamphlets, in newspapers, nailed to trees, slipped under doors. When British soldiers killed several Boston citizens in 1770, a flurry of broadsides protested the senseless deaths. The awkward, naive verses—written by people who were not professional writers—suggest that the pain and shock of the events were intense enough to stir even in nonliterary people the need to express their feelings.

Gradually, negative protests turned into more positive expressions. Besides petitioning against "taxation without representation," more and more Americans started calling for more self-government. Paine's pamphlet *Common Sense* sold an extraordinary 100,000 copies in three months. The Declaration of Independence—the culmination of the writing of this period—carries the voice not of an individual but of a whole people. It is more than writing of the period; it defined the meaning of the Revolution.

Toward a National Literature

Americans of the eighteenth century produced a great variety of unusual forms of literature: ballads, skits, broadsides, newspaper poems, editorials, essays, private and public letters, satires, pamphlets—written by people of every social class and almost every degree of skill. The energy of the age did not express itself in the usual forms with great original poetry, fiction, drama, music, or art. Nevertheless, there were some writers, composers, and painters of note.

Joel Barlow, an urbane and sophisticated man, produced a mock-epic poem called *The Hasty Pudding*. Phillis Wheatley, a former slave, produced highly praised religious and patriotic verses; in 1773 she published what was probably the first book by a black American. Philip Freneau wrote bitter satires and fiery political poems, earning the title "Poet of the American Revolution." The composer William Billings and the painter John Singleton Copley demonstrated that music and art could also flourish in America, even though these artists imitated the formal, balanced, restrained classical style of European artists.

It would be some time before America would learn to be itself artistically, but it did make a beginning. The new nation had the desire to be new in every way possible. Political indepen-

Noah Webster, nationalist and scholar, who standardized American spelling and wrote the *American Dictionary.*

dence brought with it a desire for literary and artistic independence. In 1783 Noah Webster, a literary nationalist, declared: "America must be as independent in literature as she is in politics, as famous for the arts as for arms."

What would make an *American* book? Many writers thought that the new nation possessed at least two unique subjects, two things no European had experienced: the natural wilderness and the Revolution. They believed that the majestic, awe-inspiring landscape provided a setting and even an antagonist that would be the basis of a great literature. They also believed that the Revolution provided stories of great human experiences and the beginning of an American mythology. They began to see the possibility of typical American characters in literature: The first American comedy, Royall Tyler's *The Contrast* (1787), gave the public a homespun American who outsmarts the more "sophisticated" characters. The Yankee hero was born.

If Columbus "discovered" America, then patriots such as Franklin, Paine, and Jefferson, in the words of one historian, "invented" it. That invention of an American self and society, an American *identity,* was the greatest single imaginative creation of this period. The writing in this unit can give us some idea of the complexity and the excitement of trying to answer the question that was once posed by Jean de Crèvecoeur: "What then is the American, this new man?"

TIME LINE

1733–1758	Benjamin Franklin, *Poor Richard's Almanack*			
1750	First playhouse in America opens in New York City		1750	Germany: Death of composer Johann Sebastian Bach
1751	First sugar cane in America grown in Louisiana		1751	France: Denis Diderot, *Encyclopédie*
1752	Franklin performs electricity experiment with kite and key			
1754	Columbia University founded in New York City		1755	England: Samuel Johnson completes *Dictionary of the English Language*
1757	First streetlights in America used in Philadelphia		1759	France: Voltaire, *Candide*
1761	*The Complete Housewife,* early American cookbook		1761	Austria: Wolfgang Amadeus Mozart begins writing minuets at age five
			1762	France: Jean Jacques Rousseau, *The Social Contract*
			1764	England: Practice of numbering houses begun in London
1765	British Parliament imposes Stamp Act on colonies		1765	Scotland: James Watt invents steam engine
	Chocolate is first produced in America: Dorchester, Mass.			
1766	John Singleton Copley's painting *Boy with Squirrel* a great success in London			
1767	Daniel Boone first explores west of Appalachians		1769	France: Nicolas-Joseph Cugnot builds first automobile with steam-powered engine
1770	Boston Massacre		1770	Germany: Birth of composer Ludwig van Beethoven
	William Billings, first important American composer, publishes *The New England Psalm-Singer*			

Daniel Boone

1772   Charles Wilson Peale completes life-size portrait of George Washington

1773   Boston Tea Party

Phillis Wheatley's *Poems on Various Subjects, Religious and Moral* published in London

1774   First Continental Congress meets in Philadelphia

First museum in America established in Philadelphia

1775   Patrick Henry delivers Speech in Virginia Convention

Revolutionary War begins

1776   Thomas Paine, *American Crisis*

Thomas Jefferson writes Declaration of Independence

1777   France: Chemist Antoine Lavoisier coins term *oxygen*

1778   Captain Cook discovers Hawaii

1780   American Academy of Arts and Sciences established in Boston

1781   England: William Herschel discovers planet Uranus

1782   Jean de Crèvecoeur, *Letters from an American Farmer*

1783   Revolution ends

Noah Webster publishes *American Spelling Book*, standardizing spelling of American English

First American edition of *Mother Goose Rhymes*

1784   Franklin invents bifocal lenses

1786   First commercially made ice cream sold in New York City

1787	Royall Tyler, *The Contrast,* first American comedy
1788	Constitution ratified
1789	Washington inaugurated as first President
	Thanksgiving first celebrated as national holiday
	William Hill Brown, *The Power of Sympathy,* first American novel
1790	First national census of U.S. population: 4 million
	Capital of U.S. moved from New York to Philadelphia
1791	Franklin, *Autobiography*
	Bill of Rights ratified
	William Bartram, *Travels*
1792	New York Stock Exchange organized
1793	Eli Whitney invents cotton gin
1796	Washington delivers his Farewell Address
	Joel Barlow's poem, *The Hasty Pudding*
1798	Yellow fever epidemic kills 2086 people in New York City
	Robert Fulton invents the *Nautilus,* a hand-operated, four-man submarine
1800	Jefferson elected President
	Capital of U.S. moved from Philadelphia to Washington
	Library of Congress founded
	John Chapman ("Johnny Appleseed") wanders the Ohio valley

1789   Germany: Physicist Martin Klaproth discovers uranium

France: Bastille stormed; Revolution begins

England: Poet William Blake, *Songs of Innocence*

1793   France: Monarchy abolished; King Louis XVI and Marie Antoinette executed

1798   England: Edward Jenner publishes results of successful inoculation against smallpox

England: Poet Samuel Taylor Coleridge, "The Rime of the Ancient Mariner"

1799   Egypt: Rosetta Stone found, enabling deciphering of hieroglyphics

1800   Italy: Allessandro Volta invents electric battery

England: Poet William Wordsworth publishes Romantic manifesto, the Preface to *Lyrical Ballads*

Benjamin Franklin   *1706–1790*

Benjamin Franklin was born in Boston, the son of a poor craftsman who could not afford to keep him long in school. He educated himself by reading widely. As a teenager he learned the printing trade and published his first essay in his brother's newspaper. Proud, ambitious, and independent, Franklin left Boston at the age of seventeen and arrived penniless in Philadelphia. He soon established himself as a printer and a civic leader, became rich, and retired from business at the age of forty-two.

Such an outline of Franklin's life, however, does not do justice to his extraordinary range of accomplishments. After retiring from business, Franklin intended to devote the rest of his life to his deepest interest—science—the only thing, it was said, about which he was not ironic. He did make substantial contributions to the scientific knowledge of his time. In fact, his work on lightning rods, earthquakes, bifocal lenses, and electricity made him world famous, and the Franklin stove is still used in some homes. Nevertheless, it was public affairs that dominated the last half of his life.

Franklin spent many years in England and France, where he was a popular figure among intellectuals and aristocrats. Before the Revolution he represented the colonies in London, trying to persuade the British government to modify its oppressive tax policies in America. In 1776, at age seventy, he joined Thomas Jefferson, John Adams, and others on the committee that drafted the Declaration of Independence. Later he served as the American representative in Paris and helped negotiate the peace treaty with England. In his final years he was a delegate to the Constitutional Convention and worked for the ratification of the Constitution.

At the time of his death, no other American was better known or more respected. In both the Old World and the New World, Franklin was seen as a representative American: the clever, prudent, self-made man, the thrifty Yankee who works hard, who knows how to take advantage of an opportunity, and who "gets ahead." His energy, curiosity, tact, charm, and practicality brought him many successes in business, literature, science, and government.

Franklin's life was full; he lived with intensity and imagination. Even his death, according to his plan, would reflect his feeling for life. This is the **epitaph**, or tombstone inscription, he wrote for himself:

> The Body of B. Franklin, printer; Like the cover of an old Book, Its contents torn out, and stripped of its Lettering and Gilding, Lies here, Food for Worms. But the work shall not be wholly Lost: For it will, as he believed, appear once more. In a new and more perfect Edition. Corrected and amended by the Author. He was born Jan. 6, 1706. Died 17—.

Franklin published *Poor Richard's Almanack* every year for twenty-five years (1733–1758), pretending the attitudes and observations were those of one "Richard Saunders." An **almanac** is an annual collection of statistics, weather forecasts, current events, and other useful or entertaining information. Franklin enlivened his almanac with Poor Richard's **proverbs** and **aphorisms**, short sayings memorable for their wit and wisdom, which he later collected into a book titled *The Way to Wealth*.

Benjamin Franklin

from **Poor Richard's Almanack**

God helps them that help themselves.

Fish and Visitors stink after three days.

Beware of little Expenses: a small Leak will sink a great Ship.

No gains without pains.

Love your Neighbor; yet don't pull down your Hedge.

There are no ugly loves, nor handsome prisons.

At the working man's house hunger looks in, but dares not enter.

To err is human, to repent divine; to persist, devilish.

Keep thy shop, and thy shop will keep thee.

You may be too cunning for One, but not for All.

The Cat in Gloves catches no Mice.

Dost thou love Life? Then do not squander Time; for that's the Stuff Life is made of.

He that falls in love with himself, will have no rivals.

For want of a Nail the Shoe is lost; for want of a Shoe the Horse is lost; for want of a Horse the Rider is lost.

What you would seem to be, be really.

STUDY QUESTIONS

Interpreting

1. According to the second aphorism, why do fish and visitors have a common characteristic? According to the third aphorism, why can little expenses be compared to a leak in a ship?
2. Why are there "no ugly loves, nor handsome prisons"?

3. Which of the aphorisms stress the importance of hard work? Of thrift? Of honesty?
4. What recommendations and observations about human behavior do the other aphorisms make?

Extending

5. Which of these sayings do you find applicable today? Which do you think are amusing? Why?

When he was sixty-five, Franklin, already internationally famous, began writing his autobiography. An **autobiography** is the story of a person's life told by the person who lived it; Franklin told his story in the form of a letter to his son. Franklin never completed his autobiography, never reaching his account of the Declaration of Independence. Yet Franklin was able to make clear that he enjoyed creating in himself "the American, this new man."

Benjamin Franklin

from **The Autobiography**

My Brother had in 1720 or 21, begun to print a Newspaper. It was the second that appeared in America, and was called the *New England Courant.* The only one before it was the *Boston News Letter.* I remember his being dissuaded by some of his Friends from the Undertaking, as not likely to succeed, one Newspaper being in their Judgment enough for America. At this time (1771) there are not less than five and twenty. He went on, however, with the Undertaking, and after having worked in composing the Types and printing off the Sheets, I was employed to carry the Papers through the Streets to the Customers. He had some ingenious Men among his Friends who amused themselves by writing little Pieces for this Paper, which gained it Credit, and made it more in Demand; and these Gentlemen often visited us. Hearing their Conversations, and their Accounts of the Approbation[1] their Papers were received with, I was excited to try my Hand among them. But being still a Boy, and suspecting that my Brother would object to printing any Thing of mine in his Paper if he knew it to be mine, I contrived to disguise my Hand, and writing an anonymous Paper, I put it in at Night under the Door of the Printing House. It was found in the Morning and communicated to his Writing Friends when they called in as usual. They read it, commented on it in my Hearing, and I had the exquisite Pleasure of finding it met with their Approbation, and that in their different Guesses at the Author none were named but Men of some Character among us for Learning and Ingenuity.

I suppose now that I was rather lucky in my Judges: And that perhaps they were not really so very good ones as I then esteemed them. Encouraged, however, by this, I wrote and conveyed in the same Way to the Press several more Papers,[2] which were equally approved, and I kept my Secret till my small Fund of Sense for such Performances was pretty well exhausted, and then I discovered[3] it; when I began to be considered a little more by my Brother's Acquaintance, and in a manner that did not quite please him, as he thought, probably with reason, that it tended to make me too vain. . . .

One of the Pieces in our Newspaper, on some political Point which I have now forgotten, gave Offense to the Assembly. He was taken up, censured and imprisoned for a Month by the Speaker's Warrant, I suppose because he would not discover his Author. I too was taken up and examined before the Council; but though I did not give them any satisfaction, they contented themselves with admonishing

---

1. **Approbation:** approval.

2. **Papers:** articles.
3. **discovered:** revealed.

me, and dismissed me; considering me perhaps as an Apprentice who was bound to keep his Master's Secrets. During my Brother's Confinement, which I resented a good deal, notwithstanding our private Differences, I had the Management of the Paper, and I made bold to give our Rulers some Rubs in it, which my Brother took very kindly, while others began to consider me in an unfavorable Light, as a young Genius that had a Turn for Libeling and Satyr.[4] My Brother's Discharge was accompanied with an Order of the House (a very odd one) *that James Franklin should no longer print the Paper called the New England Courant.* There was a Consultation held in our Printing House among his Friends what he should do in this Case. Some proposed to evade the Order by changing the Name of the Paper; but my Brother seeing Inconveniences in that, it was finally concluded on as a better Way, to let it be printed for the future under the Name of *Benjamin Franklin.* And to avoid the Censure of the Assembly that might fall on him, as still printing it by his Apprentice, the Contrivance was that my old Indenture[5] should be returned to me with a full Discharge on the Back of it, to be shown on Occasion; but to secure to him the Benefit of my Service, I was to sign new Indentures for the Remainder of the Term, which were to be kept private. A very flimsy Scheme it was, but, however, it was immediately executed, and the Paper went on accordingly under my Name for several Months. At length a fresh Difference arising between my Brother and me, I took upon me to assert my Freedom, presuming that he would not venture to produce the new Indentures. It was not fair in me to take this Advantage, and this I therefore reckon one of the first Errata[6] of my Life: But the Unfairness of it weighed little with me, when under the Impressions of Resentment for the Blows his Passion too often urged him to bestow upon me. Though he was

otherwise not an ill-natured Man: Perhaps I was too saucy[7] and provoking.

When he found I would leave him, he took care to prevent my getting Employment in any other Printing House of the Town, by going round and speaking to every Master, who accordingly refused to give me Work. I then thought of going to New York as the nearest Place where there was a Printer; and I was the rather inclined to leave Boston when I reflected that I had already made myself a little obnoxious to the governing Party; and from the arbitrary Proceedings of the Assembly in my Brother's Case it was likely I might if I stayed soon bring myself into Scrapes. . . .

Selling some of his books to raise money, Franklin journeys first to New York, and then to Philadelphia. After sailing through a storm, walking about fifty miles, and finally rowing a small boat, he arrives on a Sunday morning in October 1723.

I was in my Working Dress, my best Clothes being to come round by Sea. I was dirty from my Journey; my Pockets were stuffed out with Shirts and Stockings; I knew no Soul, nor where to look for Lodging. I was fatigued with Traveling, Rowing and Want of Rest. I was very hungry, and my whole Stock of Cash consisted of a Dutch Dollar[8] and about a Shilling[9] in Copper. The latter I gave the People of the Boat for my Passage, who at first refused it on Account of my Rowing; but I insisted on their taking it, a Man being sometimes more generous when he has but a little Money than when he has plenty, perhaps through Fear of being thought to have but little.

Then I walked up the Street, gazing about, till near the Market House I met a Boy with Bread. I had made many a Meal on Bread, and inquiring where he got it, I went immediately to the Baker's he directed me to in Second

---

4. **Satyr** [sat′ĭr]: satire.
5. **Indenture:** contract that binds one person to work for another, sometimes as an apprentice.
6. **Errata** [ə rā′tə]: errors.

7. **saucy:** disrespectful.
8. **Dutch Dollar:** unit of currency in circulation before the U.S. dollar was established.
9. **Shilling:** British coin equal to one-twentieth of a pound.

Street; and asked for Biscuit, intending such as we had in Boston, but they it seems were not made in Philadelphia; then I asked for a three-penny Loaf, and was told they had none such; so not considering or knowing the Difference of Money and the greater Cheapness nor the Names of his Bread, I bade him give me three-penny worth of any sort. He gave me accordingly three great Puffy Rolls. I was surprised at the Quantity, but took it, and having no room in my Pockets, walked off, with a Roll under each Arm, and eating the other. Thus I went up Market Street as far as Fourth Street, passing by the Door of Mr. Read, my future Wife's Father, when she standing at the Door saw me, and thought I made, as I certainly did, a most awkward ridiculous Appearance. Then I turned and went down Chestnut Street and part of Walnut Street, eating my Roll all the Way, and coming round, found my self again at Market Street Wharf, near the Boat I came in, to which I went for a Draft[10] of the River Water, and being filled with one of my Rolls, gave the other two to a Woman and her Child that came down the River in the Boat with us and were waiting to go farther. Thus refreshed, I walked again up the Street, which by this time had many clean dressed People in it who were all walking the same Way; I joined them, and thereby was led into the great Meetinghouse of the Quakers[11] near the Market. I sat down among them, and after looking round a while and hearing nothing said,[12] being very drowsy through Labor and want of Rest the preceding Night, I fell fast asleep, and continued so till the Meeting broke up, when one was kind enough to rouse me. This was therefore the first House I was in or slept in, in Philadelphia. . . .

During the next several years Franklin becomes a successful printer and businessman.

10. **Draft:** drink.
11. **Quakers:** the Society of Friends, a Christian religious group founded in the seventeenth century.
12. **hearing . . . said:** Quaker religious meetings include long periods of silence.

In the following section of his Autobiography, *he tells how he put his practical instincts to work to achieve spiritual "success" as well.*

It was about this time that I conceived the bold and arduous Project of arriving at moral Perfection. I wished to live without committing any Fault at any time; I would conquer all that either Natural Inclination, Custom, or Company might lead me into. As I knew, or thought I knew, what was right and wrong, I did not see why I might not *always* do the one and avoid the other. But I soon found I had undertaken a Task of more Difficulty than I had imagined. While my Attention was taken up in guarding against one Fault, I was often surprised by another. Habit took the Advantage of Inattention. Inclination was sometimes too strong for Reason. I concluded at length that the mere speculative Conviction that it was our Interest to be completely virtuous was not sufficient to prevent our Slipping, and that the contrary Habits must be broken and good ones acquired and established, before we can have any Dependence on a steady uniform Rectitude of Conduct. For this purpose I therefore contrived the following Method.

In the various Enumerations of the moral Virtues I had met with in my Reading, I found the Catalogue more or less numerous, as different Writers included more or fewer Ideas under the same Name. Temperance, for Example, was by some confined to Eating and Drinking, while by others it was extended to mean the moderating every other Pleasure, Appetite, Inclination or Passion, bodily or mental, even to our Avarice and Ambition. I proposed to myself, for the sake of Clearness, to use rather more Names with fewer Ideas annexed to each, than a few Names with more Ideas; and I included under Thirteen Names of Virtues all that at that time occurred to me as necessary or desirable, and annexed to each a short Precept,[13] which fully expressed the Extent I gave to its Meaning.

13. **Precept:** rule.

Benjamin Franklin's Experiment, June 1752, print by Currier and Ives, 1876.

These Names of Virtues with their Precepts were

1. TEMPERANCE

Eat not to Dullness.
Drink not to Elevation.

2. SILENCE

Speak not but what may benefit others or yourself. Avoid trifling Conversation.

3. ORDER

Let all your Things have their Places. Let each Part of your Business have its Time.

4. RESOLUTION

Resolve to perform what you ought. Perform without fail what you resolve.

5. FRUGALITY

Make no Expense but to do good to others or yourself: i.e., Waste nothing.

6. INDUSTRY

Lose no Time. Be always employed in something useful. Cut off all unnecessary Actions.

7. SINCERITY

Use no hurtful Deceit.
Think innocently and justly; and, if you speak, speak accordingly.

8. JUSTICE

Wrong none by doing Injuries or omitting the Benefits that are your Duty.

9. MODERATION

Avoid Extremes. Forbear resenting Injuries so much as you think they deserve.

10. CLEANLINESS

Tolerate no Uncleanness in Body, Clothes or Habitation.

11. TRANQUILITY

Be not disturbed at Trifles or at Accidents common or unavoidable.

12. CHASTITY

13. HUMILITY

Imitate Jesus and Socrates.[14]

• • •

I made a little Book in which I allotted a Page for each of the Virtues. I ruled each Page with red Ink, so as to have seven Columns, one for each Day of the Week, marking each Column with a Letter for the Day. I crossed these Columns with thirteen red Lines, marking the Beginning of each Line with the first Letter of one of the Virtues, on which Line and in its proper Column I might mark by a little black Spot every Fault I found upon Examination to have been committed respecting that Virtue upon that Day.

TEMPERANCE							
	S	M	T	W	T	F	S
T							
S	••	•			•		•
O	•	•	•			•	•	•
R			•			•	
F		•			•		
I			•				
S							
J							
M							
Cl.							
T							
Ch.							
H							

I determined to give a Week's strict Attention to each of the Virtues successively. Thus in the first Week my great Guard was to avoid every the least Offense against Temperance, leaving the other Virtues to their ordinary Chance, only marking every Evening the Faults of the Day. Thus if in the first Week I could keep my first Line marked *T* clear of Spots, I supposed the Habit of that Virtue so much strengthened and its opposite weakened, that I might venture extending my Attention to include the next, and for the following Week keep both Lines clear of Spots. Proceeding thus to the last, I could go through a Course complete in Thirteen Weeks, and four Courses in a

---

14. **Socrates** [sok′rə tēz]: Greek philosopher and teacher (470?–399 B.C.).

Year. And like him who having a Garden to weed does not attempt to eradicate all the bad Herbs at once, which would exceed his Reach and his Strength, but works on one of the Beds at a time, and having accomplished the first proceeds to a Second; so I should have (I hoped) the encouraging Pleasure of seeing on my Pages the Progress I made in Virtue, by clearing successively my Lines of their Spots, till in the End, by a Number of Courses, I should be happy in viewing a clean Book after a thirteen Weeks' daily Examination.

The Precept of *Order* requiring that *every Part of my Business should have its allotted Time,* one Page in my little Book contained the following Scheme of Employment for the Twenty-four Hours of a natural Day:

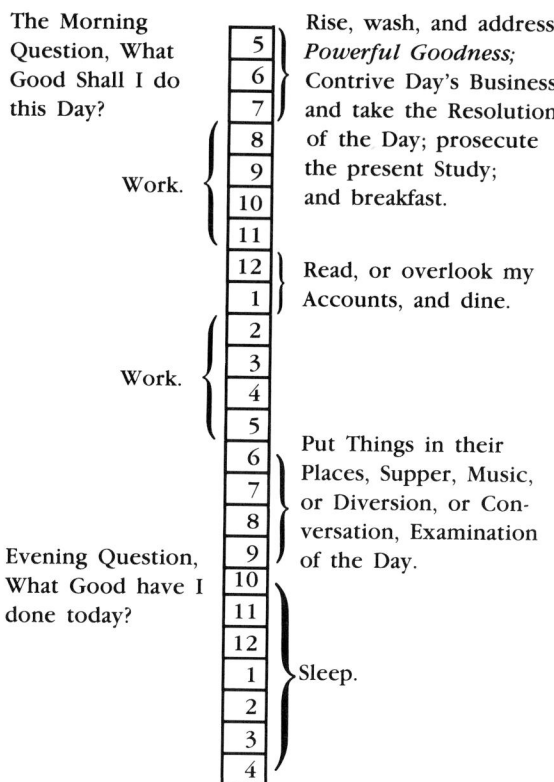

The Morning Question, What Good Shall I do this Day?

Work.

Evening Question, What Good have I done today?

5
6
7
8
9
10
11
12
1
2
3
4
5
6
7
8
9
10
11
12
1
2
3
4

Rise, wash, and address *Powerful Goodness;* Contrive Day's Business and take the Resolution of the Day; prosecute the present Study; and breakfast.

Read, or overlook my Accounts, and dine.

Put Things in their Places, Supper, Music, or Diversion, or Conversation, Examination of the Day.

Sleep.

I entered upon the Execution of this Plan for Self-Examination, and continued it with occasional Intermissions for some time. I was sur-

prised to find myself so much fuller of Faults than I had imagined, but I had the Satisfaction of seeing them diminish. To avoid the Trouble of renewing now and then my little Book, which, by scraping out the Marks on the Paper of old Faults to make room for new Ones in a new Course, became full of Holes, I transferred my Tables and Precepts to the Ivory Leaves of a Memorandum Book on which the Lines were drawn with red Ink that made a durable Stain, and on those Lines I marked my Faults with a black Lead Pencil, which Marks I could easily wipe out with a wet Sponge. After a while I went through one Course only in a Year, and afterwards only one in several Years, till at length I omitted them entirely, being employed in Voyages and Business abroad with a Multiplicity of Affairs that interfered; but I always carried my little Book with me.

My Scheme of *Order* gave me the most Trouble, and I found that though it might be practicable where a Man's Business was such as to leave him the Disposition of his Time, that of a Journeyman Printer,[15] for instance, it was not possible to be exactly observed by a Master, who must mix with the World and often receive People of Business at their own Hours. *Order* too, with regard to Places for Things, Papers, etc., I found extremely difficult to acquire. I had not been early accustomed to *Method,* and having an exceeding good Memory, I was not so sensible of the Inconvenience attending Want of Method. This Article therefore cost me much painful Attention, and my Faults in it vexed me. . . .

In Truth I found myself incorrigible with respect to *Order;* and now I am grown old, and my Memory bad, I feel very sensibly the want of it. But on the whole, though I never arrived at the Perfection I had been so ambitious of obtaining, but fell far short of it, yet I was by the Endeavor a better and a happier Man than I otherwise should have been if I had not attempted it.

---

15. **Journeyman Printer:** worker who has completed an apprenticeship and works for a master printer.

STUDY QUESTIONS

Recalling

1. How does Ben Franklin submit his articles to the *Courant?*
2. Why does the government try to close down the *Courant?* What does Ben's brother do to evade the government order?
3. According to the third paragraph, how does Ben take advantage of his brother? For what reasons does Ben leave Boston?
4. What three adjectives in the fifth paragraph describe how Ben looked and felt when he arrived in Philadelphia? What becomes of the puffy rolls he bought?
5. According to the seventh paragraph, why does Franklin create his "Method" for "moral perfection"? Summarize the method.
6. What surprises Franklin when he begins to follow his plan for self-examination (page 63)? What satisfaction does he have? What gives him the most trouble?

Interpreting

7. State three or more dominant characteristics of Ben Franklin as a young man. Cite an incident to illustrate each characteristic.
8. Find three examples of humor or worldly wisdom that help illustrate why Franklin was regarded as one of the wittiest Americans of the eighteenth century.

Extending

9. How can writing an autobiography contribute to self-knowledge? By way of example, explain what Ben Franklin the autobiographer comes to see about Ben Franklin the young man.

VIEWPOINT

In one of his novels, Herman Melville, the nineteenth-century American writer, described Franklin in this way:

Having carefully weighed the world, Franklin could act any part in it. By nature turned to knowledge, his mind was often grave, but never serious.

—*Israel Potter*

■ Discuss Melville's distinction between *grave* and *serious.* Find one example in the selection where Franklin deals with a grave issue in a light manner.

VOCABULARY

Synonyms

A **synonym** is a word that has the same or nearly the same meaning as another word. *Journey* and *voyage* are synonyms. The words in capital letters are from the *Autobiography.* Choose the word that is *nearest* the meaning of each word in capitals, *as it is used in the selection.* Write the number of each item and the letter of your choice on a separate sheet.

1. INGENUITY: (a) approbation (b) cleverness (c) innocence (d) disturbance
2. ADMONISH: (a) finish (b) scold (c) require (d) admire
3. CENSURE: (a) freedom (b) vote (c) count (d) disapproval
4. RECTITUDE: (a) uprightness (b) custom (c) cowardice (d) indigestion
5. INCORRIGIBLE: (a) confused (b) courageous (c) unable to be reformed (d) easy

COMPOSITION

Writing About Autobiography

■ Choose one paragraph from the *Autobiography,* and write a short composition in which you show how Franklin tells his story using both objective facts and subjective feelings. First identify the facts that Franklin provides. Then describe the feelings he suggests. Conclude by explaining the total impression Franklin creates.

Writing Aphorisms

■ Write contemporary adaptations of two of the sayings of Poor Richard. First write a paraphrase, or short summary in your own words, of each of the two Poor Richard sayings. Then create a modern aphorism that conveys the same meaning.

Patrick Henry   *1736–1799*

"If this be treason, make the most of it!" Outcries like this one opposing the Stamp Act have assured Patrick Henry a place of honor among orators of the American Revolution. Born in Virginia, Henry worked as a storekeeper but ran hopelessly into debt because of his poor business sense. When he began to practice law, however, his talent as an orator won him wide recognition. Eventually, he held various positions in the public service: member of the Virginia House of Burgesses and of the Continental Congress, commander of Virginia's military forces, and governor of the new Commonwealth of Virginia from 1776 to 1779. Henry was also the major voice in the drafting of the Bill of Rights.

After his years of public service, Henry was badly in debt again, and so he returned to his law practice in 1788. Though a major figure in the Revolution, he turned down George Washington's invitations to become secretary of state and Chief Justice of the Supreme Court. A fellow Virginian said that in private Henry was "modest, mild, and in religious matters, a saint." Yet when he spoke in public, he became the "Son of Thunder."

We hear that thunder in the following speech, which he delivered in 1775 to the Virginia Convention. The delegates had assembled to discuss the British military buildup in America. Gathered in St. John's Church in Richmond on that mild March day were Virginia's greatest men, including Washington and Jefferson. The first speakers urged moderation and compromise with the British. But Henry spoke strongly, dramatically, defiantly. We have come to see his speech as a masterpiece of clear, skillful oratory, a forceful blend of argument and emotion. As we know now, Henry's speech, which begins on the following page, won the day. The Declaration of Independence was only a few months away.

Patrick Henry delivering a speech. Nineteenth-century engraving.

Patrick Henry

Speech in the Virginia Convention

Mr. President: No man thinks more highly than I do of the patriotism, as well as abilities, of the very worthy gentlemen who have just addressed the house. But different men often see the same subject in different lights; and, therefore, I hope it will not be thought disrespectful to those gentlemen, if, entertaining, as I do, opinions of a character very opposite to theirs, I shall speak forth my sentiments freely and without reserve. This is no time for ceremony. The question before the house is one of awful moment[1] to this country. For my own part, I consider it as nothing less than a question of freedom or slavery. And in proportion to the magnitude of the subject ought to be the freedom of the debate. It is only in this way that we can hope to arrive at truth, and fulfill the great responsibility which we hold to God and our country. Should I keep back my opinions at such a time, through fear of giving

_____

1. **awful moment:** dreadful importance.

offense, I should consider myself as guilty of treason toward my country, and of an act of disloyalty toward the Majesty of Heaven, which I revere above all earthly kings.

Mr. President, it is natural to man to indulge in the illusions of hope. We are apt to shut our eyes against a painful truth, and listen to the song of that siren till she transforms us into beasts.[2] Is this the part of wise men, engaged in a great and arduous struggle for liberty? Are we disposed to be of the number of those who having eyes see not, and having ears hear not,[3] the things which so nearly concern their temporal[4] salvation? For my part, whatever anguish of spirit it may cost, I am willing to know the whole truth; to know the worst and to provide for it.

I have but one lamp by which my feet are guided, and that is the lamp of experience. I know of no way of judging of the future but by the past. And judging by the past, I wish to know what there has been in the conduct of the British ministry for the last ten years to justify those hopes with which gentlemen have been pleased to solace themselves and the house? Is it that insidious smile with which our petition has been lately received? Trust it not, sir; it will prove a snare to your feet. Suffer not yourselves to be betrayed with a kiss.[5] Ask yourselves how this gracious reception of our petition comports with those warlike preparations which cover our waters and darken our land. Are fleets and armies necessary to a work of love and reconciliation? Have we shown ourselves so unwilling to be reconciled that force must be called in to win back our love? Let us not deceive ourselves, sir. These are the implements of war and subjugation—the last arguments to which kings resort.

I ask gentlemen, sir, what means this martial array, if its purpose be not to force us to submission? Can gentlemen assign any other possible motive for it? Has Great Britain any enemy in this quarter of the world, to call for all this accumulation of navies and armies? No, sir, she has none. They are meant for us: they can be meant for no other. They are sent over to bind and rivet upon us those chains which the British ministry have been so long forging.

And what have we to oppose to them? Shall we try argument? Sir, we have been trying that for the last ten years. Have we anything new to offer upon the subject? Nothing. We have held the subject up in every light of which it is capable; but it has been all in vain. Shall we resort to entreaty and humble supplication? What terms shall we find which have not been already exhausted? Let us not, I beseech you, sir, deceive ourselves longer.

Sir, we have done everything that could be done to avert the storm which is now coming on. We have petitioned; we have remonstrated; we have supplicated; we have prostrated ourselves before the throne, and have implored its interposition[6] to arrest the tyrannical hands of the ministry and Parliament. Our petitions have been slighted; our remonstrances have produced additional violence and insult; our supplications have been disregarded; and we have been spurned with contempt from the foot of the throne! In vain, after these things, may we indulge the fond[7] hope of peace and reconciliation. There is no longer any room for hope. If we wish to be free, if we mean to preserve inviolate those inestimable privileges for which we have been so long contending, if we mean not basely to abandon the noble struggle in which we have been so long engaged, and which we have pledged ourselves never to abandon until the glorious object of our contest shall be obtained—we must fight! I repeat it, sir, we must fight! An appeal to arms and to the God of Hosts is all that is left us!

---

2. **listen . . . beasts:** In Homer's *Odyssey* the enchantress Circe charms men with her song and then turns them into swine.
3. **having eyes . . . hear not:** In Ezekiel 12 : 2 the prophet addresses those "who have eyes to see, but see not, who have ears to hear, but hear not."
4. **temporal:** earthly.
5. **betrayed . . . kiss:** In Luke 22 : 47–48 Judas betrays Jesus with a kiss.

---

6. **interposition:** intervention.
7. **fond:** foolish.

They tell us, sir, that we are weak—unable to cope with so formidable an adversary. But when shall we be stronger? Will it be the next week, or the next year? Will it be when we are totally disarmed, and when a British guard shall be stationed in every house? Shall we gather strength by irresolution and inaction? Shall we acquire the means of effectual resistance by lying supinely on our backs and hugging the delusive phantom of hope until our enemies shall have bound us hand and foot? Sir, we are not weak, if we make a proper use of those means which the God of nature hath placed in our power. Three millions of people, armed in the holy cause of liberty, and in such a country as that which we possess, are invincible by any force which our enemy can send against us. Besides, sir, we shall not fight our battles alone. There is a just God who presides over the destinies of nations and who will raise up friends to fight our battles for us. The battle, sir, is not to the strong alone;[8] it is to the vig-ilant, the active, the brave. Besides, sir, we have no election.[9] If we were base enough to desire it, it is now too late to retire from the contest. There is no retreat but in submission and slavery! Our chains are forged! Their clanging may be heard on the plains of Boston! The war is inevitable—and let it come! I repeat it, sir, let it come!

It is in vain, sir, to extenuate the matter. Gentlemen may cry, "Peace, peace"—but there is no peace. The war is actually begun! The next gale that sweeps from the north[10] will bring to our ears the clash of resounding arms! Our brethren are already in the field! Why stand we here idle? What is it that gentlemen wish? What would they have? Is life so dear, or peace so sweet, as to be purchased at the price of chains and slavery? Forbid it, Almighty God! I know not what course others may take; but as for me, give me liberty or give me death!

---

8. **battle . . . strong alone:** "The race is not to the swift, nor the battle to the strong" (Ecclesiastes 9:11).

9. **election:** choice.
10. **next gale . . . north:** In Massachusetts some colonists had already begun to show open resistance against the British.

STUDY QUESTIONS

Recalling
1. Why is Henry stating his opinion at this time?
2. According to the third and fourth paragraphs, what does Henry believe is Britain's purpose in America?
3. According to the sixth paragraph, what have the colonists already done "to avert the storm"? What does Henry say they must do now?
4. According to the seventh paragraph, why is the American army "invincible"?
5. As Henry concludes, what does he say has already begun?

Interpreting
6. What does Henry accomplish through his series of questions in paragraph 7?

7. Which evidence that Henry cites in support of his argument is factual, or provable? Which evidence is opinion?
8. When Henry says, "I know not what course others may take," how is he trying to make his listeners feel? Identify at least two more instances where he appeals to his audience's emotions.

Extending
9. In what ways do you think Henry's speech illustrates the beliefs of the Age of Reason?

LITERARY FOCUS

Oratory
Oratory, the art of public speaking, played a crucial part in the American past. In an age long before radio and television, commanding the at-

tention of an audience with a powerful address was the surest way to win an election, debate public issues, sell products, and, as the sermon of Jonathan Edwards in the preceding unit illustrates, spread a religious message.

Oratory flourished in ancient Greek and Roman times, when speakers were judged by the power of their words and the way those words were presented to the public. Reasoned arguments and emotional appeals were both important. Classical orators developed intricate systems of rules and devices for speaking properly. Three of these oratorical devices, found in Henry's speech and still used today, are rhetorical questions, repetition, and improvisation.

A **rhetorical question** is a question that the speaker really does not intend as a question, or one that he means to answer himself. Henry asks, "Is this the part of wise men, engaged in a great and arduous struggle for liberty?" He expects his audience to be so sure of the answer that no one will need to think twice about the response. A rhetorical question can give a speaker a tone of confidence or a biting satiric edge. It can also act as a bridge between a speaker and an audience, implying that they understand each other perfectly.

Repetition can be as effective in oratory as it is in poetry. Henry says, "We have petitioned; we have remonstrated; we have supplicated; we have prostrated ourselves before the throne." His repetitions add force to what he says; they add the weight of accumulated evidence.

Improvisation is the skill of speaking without reading word for word from a written text. No original manuscript of Henry's speech exists, although he certainly would have prepared his speech in his mind. He probably had a scheme or outline and may even have memorized some of the best of his sentences. Yet he could not have known in advance what previous speakers were going to say, and his speech does sound like a direct reply. William Wirt, who wrote a biography of Henry, reconstructed the text of the speech from outside sources and accounts given by other delegates at the convention. The speech we now read as a finished piece of oratory was probably created in large part as it was being delivered, by a master of improvisation.

Thinking About Oratory
Find another rhetorical question and another example of repetition in Henry's speech.

COMPOSITION

Writing About Oratory
What is Henry's purpose in his speech? Cite with examples the particular techniques that Henry uses to accomplish that purpose. You may consider his use of facts, statistics, examples, and opinions. *For help with this assignment, refer to Lesson 4 in the Writing About Literature Handbook at the back of this book.*

Writing a Guest Editorial
Many local television and radio stations invite their audiences to express their opinions on the air. Write an editorial on a subject that is important to you or your community. Limit yourself to a speech that you can deliver in two minutes. State your case clearly, using facts, statistics, and examples wherever appropriate. Be sure your audience knows where you stand on the issue and what action you think should be taken.

Anonymous Broadside

"The Bold Americans" was circulated as an anonymous broadside, a large printed sheet of paper, in late 1775 or early 1776. While other songs of the time, such as "Yankee Doodle," sang out wholeheartedly for complete independence, "The Bold Americans" offered a compromise. It reminds us that those who called for complete separation from Britain were actually few in number and that a large percentage of Americans wanted *both* a measure of liberty and continued affiliation with England.

Anonymous

The Bold Americans

Come all you bold young Bostonians, come listen unto me:
I will sing you a song concerning liberty.
Concerning liberty, my boys, the truth I will unfold,
Of the bold Americans, who scorn to be controlled.

5 We'll honor George,[1] our sovereign, on any reasonable terms,
But if he don't grant us liberty, we'll all lay down our arms.
But if he will grant us liberty, so plainly shall you see,
We are the boys that fear no noise! Success to liberty!

We'll honor George, our sovereign, while he sits on the throne.
10 If he grants us liberty, no other king we'll own.
If he will grant us liberty, so plainly shall you see,
We are the boys that fear no noise! Success to liberty!

Come all you sparkling landladies, come fill the other bowl,
We'll drink a health to those brave boys who scorn to be controlled,
15 Another to George Washington, who fought so manfully.
So now we end our ditty, boys: Success to liberty!

---

1. **George:** George III (1738–1820), who was king of Great Britain, 1760–1820.

The Boston Tea Party, 1773. Nineteenth-century engraving.

STUDY QUESTIONS

Recalling

1. What do the bold Americans "scorn"?
2. For what reason will the bold Americans lay down their arms and refuse to defend the British government?
3. Whom do the bold Americans toast in the last stanza?

Interpreting

4. Describe the mixed attitude toward rebellion displayed in this song.
5. Which details make the bold Americans seem reasonable and open-minded?

Extending

6. How can songs reflect the attitudes and beliefs of a particular time and place?

Dekanawida

Centuries before the American colonists banded together to set up
an independent government, a large group of Native Americans had
established a unified government of their own called the Five
Nations, also known as the Iroquois Confederacy. The Five
Nations—Mohawk, Seneca, Onondaga, Oneida, and Cayuga—
admitted the Tuscarora in 1724 and became the Six Nations (still
commonly called the Iroquois Confederacy).

The Iroquois Confederacy, covering much of the area that is now
New York State, brought together tribes with similar customs and
languages. These tribes had often warred against one another and
had weakened themselves against outside enemies. A great chief,
Dekanawida, united the tribes and created the code of laws upon
which the federation rested. What we now call the Iroquois
Constitution was the remarkable civil and social system Dekanawida
named the Great Binding Law.

Dekanawida traveled from tribe to tribe, organizing the
confederacy, establishing the Great Peace, and persuading tribes to
subscribe to the Great Law. The Great Law was a comprehensive
and efficient system to protect the Five Nations from outside
enemies and from themselves. It covered membership in the league,
council procedures, rules for debate and decision making, and the
rights and responsibilities of leaders, as well as laws relating to
marriage, emigration, treason, and festivals.

In this selection Dekanawida invests the chief of the Onondaga
with the responsibility of keeping the Council Fire. He then goes on
to enumerate some of the aspects of the system that made the
Iroquois a dominant power. The Iroquois Constitution takes its
place with the other political statements in this unit: Benjamin
Franklin used the Iroquois Confederacy as an example when trying
to persuade American colonists to unite. It is even said that Thomas
Jefferson studied the Iroquois code in his efforts to interpret the
Constitution of the United States.

An Iroquois wampum belt made of polished beads, commemorating the unification of the Five Nations.

Dekanawida

from **The Iroquois Constitution**

The Tree of the Great Peace

I am Dekanawida and with the Five Nations' Confederate Lords I plant the Tree of the Great Peace. I plant it in your territory, Adodarho, and the Onondaga Nation, in the territory of you who are Firekeepers.

I name the tree the Tree of the Great Long Leaves. Under the shade of this Tree of the Great Peace we spread the soft white feathery down of the globe thistle as seats for you, Adodarho, and your cousin Lords.

We place you upon those seats, spread soft with the feathery down of the globe thistle, there beneath the shade of the spreading branches of the Tree of Peace. There shall you sit and watch the Council Fire of the Confederacy of the Five Nations, and all the affairs of the Five Nations shall be transacted at this place.

Roots have spread out from the Tree of the Great Peace, one to the north, one to the east, one to the south and one to the west. The name of these roots is the Great White Roots and their nature is Peace and Strength.

If any man or any nation outside the Five Nations shall obey the laws of the Great Peace and make known their disposition to the Lords of the Confederacy, they may trace the Roots to the Tree and if their minds are clean and they are obedient and promise to obey the wishes of the Confederate Council, they shall be welcomed to take shelter beneath the Tree of the Long Leaves.

We place at the top of the Tree of the Long Leaves an Eagle who is able to see afar. If he sees in the distance any evil approaching or any danger threatening, he will at once warn the people of the Confederacy.

The Care of the Fire

The Smoke of the Confederate Council Fire shall ever ascend and pierce the sky so that other nations who may be allies may see the Council Fire of the Great Peace.

You, Adodarho, and your thirteen cousin Lords shall faithfully keep the space about the Council Fire clean and you shall allow neither dust nor dirt to accumulate. I lay a Long Wing before you as a broom. As a weapon against a crawling creature I lay a staff with you so that you may thrust it away from the Council Fire.

The Laws of the Council

Whenever the Confederate Lords shall assemble for the purpose of holding a council, the Onondaga Lords shall open it by expressing their gratitude to their cousin Lords and greeting them, and they shall make an address and offer thanks to the earth where men dwell, to the streams of water, the pools, the springs and the lakes, to the maize and the fruits, to the medicinal herbs and trees, to the forest trees for their usefulness, to the animals that serve as food and give their pelts for clothing, to the great winds and the lesser winds, to the Thunderers, to the Sun, the mighty warrior, to the moon, to the messengers of the Creator who reveal his wishes and to the Great Creator who dwells in the heavens above, who gives all the things useful to men, and who is the source and the ruler of health and life.

All the business of the Five Nations' Confederate Council shall be conducted by the two combined bodies of Confederate Lords. First the question shall be passed upon by the Mohawk and Seneca Lords; then it shall be discussed and passed by the Oneida and Cayuga Lords. Their decisions shall then be referred to the Onondaga Lords (Firekeepers) for final judgment.

When the Council of the Five Nation Lords shall convene, they shall appoint a speaker for the day. He shall be a Lord of either the Mohawk, Onondaga, or Seneca Nation.

No individual or foreign nation interested in a case, question or proposition shall have any voice in the Confederate Council except to answer a question put to him or them by the speaker for the Lords.

If the conditions which shall arise at any future time call for an addition to or change of this law, the case shall be carefully considered, and if a new beam seems necessary or beneficial, the proposed change shall be voted upon and, if adopted, it shall be called, "Added to the Rafters."

The Clans

Among the Five Nations and their posterity there shall be the following original clans: Great Name Bearer, Ancient Name Bearer, Great Bear, Ancient Bear, Turtle, Painted Turtle, Standing Rock, Large Plover, Little Plover, Deer, Pigeon Hawk, Eel, Ball, Opposite-Side-of-the-Hand, and Wild Potatoes. These clans, distributed through their respective Nations, shall be the sole owners and holders of the soil of the country, and in them is it vested as a birthright.

People of the Five Nations [who are] members of a certain clan shall recognize every other member of that clan, irrespective of the Nation, as relatives.

The lineal descent of the people of the Five Nations shall run in the female line. Women shall be considered the progenitors of the Nation. They shall own the land and the soil. Men and women shall follow the status of the mother.

The Leaders

The Lords of the Confederacy of the Five Nations shall be mentors of the people for all time. The thickness of their skin shall be seven spans—which is to say that they shall be proof against anger, offensive actions, and criticism. Their hearts shall be full of peace and good will and their minds filled with a yearning for the welfare of the people of the Confederacy. With endless patience they shall carry out their duty, and their firmness shall be tempered with a tenderness for their people. Neither anger nor fury shall find lodgment in their minds, and all their words and actions shall be marked by calm deliberation.

The Festivals

The rites and festivals of each Nation shall remain undisturbed and shall continue as before because they were given by the people of old times as useful and necessary for the good of men.

The recognized festivals of Thanksgiving shall be the Midwinter Thanksgiving, the Maple or Sugar Making Thanksgiving, the Raspberry Thanksgiving, the Strawberry Thanksgiving, the Corn Planting Thanksgiving, the Corn Hoeing Thanksgiving, the Little Festival of Green Corn, the Great Festival of Ripe Corn, and the complete Thanksgiving for the Harvest.

The Symbols

A large bunch of shell strings, in the making of which the Five Nations' Confederate Lords have equally contributed, shall symbolize the completeness of the union and certify the pledge of the Nations represented by the Confederate Lords of the Mohawk, the Oneida, the Onondaga, the Cayuga, and the Seneca, that all are united and formed into one body or union called the Union of the Great Law, which they have established.

Five arrows shall be bound together very strong, and each arrow shall represent one nation. As the five arrows are strongly bound, this shall symbolize the complete union of the nations. Thus are the Five Nations united completely and enfolded together, united into one head, one body, and one mind. Therefore they shall labor, legislate, and council together for the interest of future generations.

STUDY QUESTIONS

Recalling

1. What tree does Dekanawida plant in the first section? What does he say the eagle at the top will do?
2. According to the second section, what is the purpose of the Council Fire? What qualities, according to "The Leaders," should all Lords of the Five Nations possess?
3. According to "The Festivals," why should the rites and festivals of each nation remain undisturbed?
4. What two symbols of the complete union of the Five Nations Confederacy are described in the final section?

Interpreting

5. Why is a tree an appropriate symbol for peace achieved through a unification such as the Iroquois Confederacy?
6. What is Dekanawida suggesting about laws when he describes them as beams and rafters?
7. Find the part of the Iroquois Constitution that suggests each of these modern ideas: national holidays, legislative houses, parliamentary procedure, constitutional amendments.

Extending

8. Tell how the flag of the United States, like the five arrows, represents a nation "united completely and enfolded together."

Thomas Jefferson *1743–1826*

Thomas Jefferson wanted John Adams to draft the Declaration of Independence. "I will not," said Adams. "What can be your reasons?" Jefferson asked. Adams replied, "You can write ten times better than I can." "Well," said Jefferson, "if you are decided, I will do as well as I can."

The author of the most famous statement of American principles was born and raised in Virginia, where he studied law, became both an excellent horseman and a competent violinist, and began his public life as a member of the Virginia House of Burgesses. Jefferson was devoted to the growth of both the American land and the American mind. This man of many talents cultivated ten thousand acres of land and built a library of ten thousand volumes, the books that were ultimately the beginning of the Library of Congress. He was a philosopher, scientist, farmer, architect, and inventor (he invented a plow that revolutionized farming); he was governor of Virginia, ambassador to France, and third President of the United States.

Despite his sophistication as a scholar and a gentleman, Jefferson put all the force of his personality behind the drive to build a society based upon equality. He refused to allow his birthday to become a national holiday or to allow coins to be stamped with his image. Democracy was a genuine way of life for him, and his vision of America was a nation in which every family would live freely, independently, and close to the land. His only published book, *Notes on the State of Virginia* (1785), is one of the most important books of its time, a record of Jefferson's beliefs, especially that "those who labor in the earth are the chosen people of God."

In the Declaration of Independence, Jefferson addresses not only his fellow Americans but the rest of the world as well. He wants "to place before mankind the common sense of the subject, in terms so plain and firm as to command their assent."

Thomas Jefferson

Declaration of Independence

When in the Course of human events it becomes necessary for one people to dissolve the political bands which have connected them with another, and to assume among the powers of the earth the separate and equal station to which the Laws of Nature and of Nature's God entitle them, a decent respect to the opinions of mankind requires that they should declare the causes which impel them to the separation.

We hold these truths to be self-evident: that all men are created equal; that they are endowed by their Creator with certain unalienable[1] Rights; that among these are Life, Liberty and the pursuit of Happiness; That to secure these rights, Governments are instituted among Men, deriving their just powers from the consent of the governed; That whenever any Form of Government becomes destructive of these ends, it is the Right of the People to alter or to abolish it, and to institute new Government, laying its foundation on such principles, and organizing its powers in such form, as to them shall seem most likely to effect their Safety and Happiness. Prudence, indeed, will dictate that Governments long established should not be changed for light and transient causes; and accordingly all experience hath shown that mankind are more disposed to suffer while evils are sufferable than to right themselves by abolishing the forms to which they are accustomed. But when a long train of abuses and usurpations,[2] pursuing invariably the same Objects, evinces a design to reduce them under absolute Despotism,[3] it is their right, it is their duty, to throw off such Government, and to provide new Guards for their future security. Such has been the patient suf-

ferance of these Colonies; and such is now the necessity which constrains[4] them to alter their former Systems of Government. The history of the present King of Great Britain is a history of repeated injuries and usurpations, all having in direct object the establishment of an absolute Tyranny over these States. To prove this, let Facts be submitted to a candid[5] world.

He has refused his Assent to Laws the most wholesome and necessary for the public good.

He has forbidden his Governors to pass Laws of immediate and pressing importance, unless suspended in their operation till his Assent should be obtained; and when so suspended, he has utterly neglected to attend to them.

He has refused to pass other Laws for the accommodation of large districts of people, unless those people would relinquish the right of Representation in the Legislature, a right inestimable to them and formidable to tyrants only.

He has called together legislative bodies at places unusual, uncomfortable, and distant from the depository of their public records, for the sole purpose of fatiguing them into compliance with his measures.

He has dissolved Representative Houses repeatedly, for opposing with manly firmness his invasions on the rights of the people.

He has refused for a long time after such dissolutions to cause others to be elected, whereby the Legislative powers, incapable of Annihilation, have returned to the People at large for their exercise, the State remaining in the mean time exposed to all the dangers of invasions from without and convulsions within.

He has endeavored to prevent the population of these States; for that purpose obstructing the Laws for Naturalization of Foreigners,

---

1. **unalienable:** that cannot be taken away.
2. **usurpations:** unlawful seizures of power.
3. **Despotism:** tyranny.

4. **constrains:** forces.
5. **candid:** impartial.

refusing to pass others to encourage their migration hither, and raising the conditions of new Appropriations of Lands.

He has obstructed the Administration of Justice, by refusing his Assent to Laws for establishing Judiciary powers.

He has made Judges dependent on his Will alone for the tenure of their offices, and the amount and payment of their salaries.

He has erected a multitude of New Offices, and sent hither swarms of Officers to harass our people and eat out their substance.

He has kept among us, in times of peace, Standing Armies, without the Consent of our legislatures.

He has affected to render the Military independent of, and superior to, the Civil power.

He has combined with others to subject us to a jurisdiction foreign to our constitutions and unacknowledged by our laws; giving his Assent to their Acts of pretended Legislation:

For quartering large bodies of armed troops among us;

For protecting them, by a mock Trial, from punishment for any Murders which they should commit on the Inhabitants of these States;

For cutting off our Trade with all parts of the world;

For imposing Taxes on us without our Consent;

For depriving us, in many cases, of the benefits of Trial by Jury;

For transporting us beyond Seas to be tried for pretended offenses;

For abolishing the free System of English Laws in a neighboring Province,[6] establishing therein an Arbitrary government, and enlarging its Boundaries, so as to render it at once an example and fit instrument for introducing the same absolute rule into these Colonies;

For taking away our Charters, abolishing our most valuable Laws, and altering, fundamentally, the Forms of our Governments;

For suspending our own Legislatures, and declaring themselves invested with Power to legislate for us in all cases whatsoever.

He has abdicated Government here, by declaring us out of his Protection and waging War against us.

He has plundered our seas, ravaged our Coasts, burned our towns, and destroyed the lives of our people.

He is at this time transporting large Armies of foreign Mercenaries to complete the works of death, desolation and tyranny, already begun with circumstances of Cruelty and perfidy[7] scarcely paralleled in the most barbarous ages, and totally unworthy the Head of a civilized nation.

He has constrained our fellow Citizens taken Captive on the high Seas to bear Arms against their Country, to become the executioners of their friends and Brethren, or to fall themselves by their Hands.

He has excited domestic insurrections amongst us, and has endeavored to bring on the inhabitants of our frontiers the merciless Indian Savages whose known rule of warfare is an undistinguished destruction of all ages, sexes, and conditions.

In every stage of these Oppressions We have Petitioned for Redress[8] in the most humble terms. Our repeated Petitions have been answered only by repeated injury. A Prince whose character is thus marked by every act which may define a Tyrant is unfit to be the ruler of a free people.

Nor have We been wanting in attentions to our British brethren. We have warned them from time to time of attempts by their legislature[9] to extend an unwarrantable jurisdiction over us. We have reminded them of the circumstances of our emigration and settlement here. We have appealed to their native justice and magnanimity, and we have conjured[10]

---

6. **abolishing . . . neighboring Province:** In 1774 the British, having captured Quebec, forced strict laws on colonists there.

7. **perfidy** [pur'fi dē]: betrayal of trust.
8. **Redress** [ri dres']: just compensation for a wrong done.
9. **their legislature:** British Parliament.
10. **conjured:** solemnly appealed to.

The Declaration of Independence, John Trumbull, 1786.

them by the ties of our common kindred to disavow these usurpations, which would inevitably interrupt our connections and correspondence. They too have been deaf to the voice of justice and of consanguinity.[11] We must therefore acquiesce in the necessity which denounces[12] our Separation and hold them, as we hold the rest of mankind, Enemies in War, in Peace Friends.

We, therefore, the Representatives of the United States of America in General Congress Assembled, appealing to the Supreme Judge of the world for the rectitude of our intentions, do in the Name and by the Authority of the good People of these Colonies, solemnly publish and declare that these United Colonies are and of right ought to be Free and Independent States; that they are Absolved from all Allegiance to the British Crown, and that all political connection between them and the State of Great Britain is and ought to be totally dissolved, and that as Free and Independent States, they have full Power to levy War, conclude Peace, contract Alliances, establish Commerce, and to do all other Acts and Things which Independent States may of right do.

And for the support of this Declaration, with a firm reliance on the protection of Divine Providence, we mutually pledge to each other our Lives, our Fortunes, and our sacred Honor.

---

11. **consanguinity** [kon′sang gwin′ə tē]: blood relationship.
12. **denounces:** here, announces.

Thomas Jefferson **79**

STUDY QUESTIONS

Recalling

1. According to the first paragraph, what does "a decent respect to the opinions of mankind" require?
2. According to the second paragraph, what truths are self-evident? What is the purpose of government, and when should a government be replaced?
3. Moving from a theory of government to the situation in 1776, what does Jefferson claim King George's "direct object" has been in the colonies? How does Jefferson set out to prove his claim?
4. What does Jefferson say the Americans have done "in every stage of these Oppressions"? To what does he say "our British brethren" have been deaf?
5. What does the final paragraph "publish and declare"?

Interpreting

6. Why does including Jefferson's bill of particulars make the Declaration more effective?
7. How is the faith in reason characteristic of the eighteenth century reflected in the opening paragraph? In Jefferson's remarks about Prudence in the second paragraph? In the description of the colonists' peaceful attempts to redress their grievances?

Extending

8. In the final sentence of the Declaration, the signers pledge their "Fortunes," or fate. What do you think their fate would have been if Britain had been the victor in the Revolution?

VIEWPOINT

The historian Garry Wills explains the following about the Declaration of Independence:

> When Jefferson spoke of pursuing happiness, he had nothing vague or private in mind. He meant a public happiness which is measurable, which is, indeed, the test and justification of any government.
> —*Inventing America: Jefferson's Declaration of Independence*

■ List three statements from the Declaration that suggest what Jefferson's idea of "public happiness" was.

VOCABULARY

Loaded Words

A **loaded word** has a particularly strong set of associations for the reader. Such a word arouses strong feelings and appeals to the emotions. A writer often deliberately uses loaded words to move people to action by appealing to their feelings, to their fears and prejudices, or to their hopes and illusions.

Jefferson uses very strong, loaded nouns when describing the behavior of King George. For example, he writes about *usurpations, despotism,* and *tyranny.* Jefferson also selects verbs with very negative associations. He says, for example, that King George "has refused" and "has endeavored to prevent."

■ Find five more verbs that describe the king's actions in such a way as to rouse Jefferson's audience to anger.

COMPOSITION

Citing Evidence

■ Write a brief composition in which you give three reasons why you think the Declaration of Independence is a successful political statement. Is it its clarity, its reasonableness, its passion, its rhetoric? State your opinion, and then cite specific examples to support it. *For help with this assignment, refer to Lesson 3 in the Writing About Literature Handbook at the back of this book.*

Writing a Letter to the Editor

■ Assume that you are writing a letter to the editor of your local newspaper. Using the Declaration of Independence as a basis, address the people of your community. First list three things that the Declaration means to you, and then tell what it can continue to mean for your community. Be sure to indicate in your letter the specific Age of Reason ideas and principles that are still valid and can be carried over into the twentieth century.

Thomas Paine   *1737–1809*

America's most effective revolutionary propagandist failed at many jobs before he became a journalist. While he was growing up in England, he tried life as a corset maker, a grocer, a sailor, a teacher, and a tax collector. By the time he left England for America, he was thirty-seven years old and well acquainted with poverty, disappointment, and sorrow: His first wife had died after less than one year of marriage.

Paine came to America because he had met Benjamin Franklin in London. Franklin gave Paine the encouragement he desperately needed, as well as a letter of introduction praising him as an "ingenious, worthy young man." Franklin's insight certainly paid off. Within two years Tom Paine became a successful journalist, publishing anonymously the pamphlet *Common Sense* in January of 1776, the first American cry for complete independence. *Common Sense* sold almost a half million copies. Nothing that had been written in America was so widely read or so influential.

The rest of Paine's life was marked by career failures, private disappointments, and public controversies. Nevertheless, he persisted in writing against tyranny and monarchy. *The Rights of Man* (1791–1792), for example, is the work of a man who combined clear thinking with an intense feeling for human possibilities.

The American Crisis, Number 1 is the first of sixteen pamphlets Paine wrote beginning in December 1776. At that time, five months after the Declaration of Independence, Washington's forces were retreating, their morale low. The American commander had these stirring words, which begin on the following page, read to his men just before they crossed the Delaware to fight at Trenton.

Thomas Paine

from **The American Crisis**

These are the times that try men's souls. The summer soldier and the sunshine patriot will, in this crisis, shrink from the service of their country; but he that stands it *now,* deserves the love and thanks of man and woman. Tyranny, like hell, is not easily conquered; yet we have this consolation with us, that the harder the conflict, the more glorious the triumph. What we obtain too cheap, we esteem too lightly: it is dearness only that gives every thing its value. Heaven knows how to put a proper price upon its goods; and it would be strange indeed if so celestial an article as *freedom* should not be highly rated. Britain, with an army to enforce her tyranny, has declared that she has a right not only to *tax* but "to

bind us in *all cases whatsoever*"; and if being *bound in that manner* is not slavery, then is there not such a thing as slavery upon earth. Even the expression is impious; for so unlimited a power can belong only to God. . . .

I have as little superstition in me as any man living, but my secret opinion has ever been, and still is, that God Almighty will not give up a people to military destruction, or leave them unsupportedly to perish, who have so earnestly and so repeatedly sought to avoid the calamities of war, by every decent method which wisdom could invent. Neither have I so much of the infidel[1] in me as to suppose that

---

1. **infidel:** unbeliever.

First Blow for Liberty, A. H. Ritchie. Nineteenth-century engraving.

He has relinquished the government of the world, and given us up to the care of devils; and as I do not, I cannot see on what grounds the king of Britain can look up to heaven for help against us: a common murderer, a highwayman, or a housebreaker, has as good a pretense as he. . . .

I once felt all that kind of anger which a man ought to feel against the mean[2] principles that are held by the Tories:[3] a noted one, who kept a tavern at Amboy, was standing at his door, with as pretty a child in his hand, about eight or nine years old, as I ever saw, and after speaking his mind as freely as he thought was prudent, finished with this unfatherly expression, "Well! give me peace in my day." Not a

man lives on the continent but fully believes that a separation must some time or other finally take place, and a generous parent should have said, "If there must be trouble, let it be in my day, that my child may have peace"; and this single reflection, well applied, is sufficient to awaken every man to duty. Not a place upon earth might be so happy as America. Her situation is remote from all the wrangling world, and she has nothing to do but to trade with them. A man can distinguish himself between temper and principle, and I am as confident, as I am that God governs the world, that America will never be happy till she gets clear of foreign dominion. Wars, without ceasing, will break out till that period arrives, and the continent must in the end be conqueror; for though the flame of liberty may sometimes cease to shine, the coal can never expire. . . .

---

2. **mean:** small-minded.
3. **Tories:** colonists loyal to Great Britain.

STUDY QUESTIONS

Recalling
1. According to the first paragraph, whom is Paine criticizing? Whom is he praising?
2. According to the first paragraph, what is the purpose of Britain's army? What has Britain declared?
3. What "secret opinion" does Paine state in his second paragraph?
4. What does the third paragraph state about the possibility of happiness in America? What does it say must be accomplished before America can be happy?

Interpreting
5. What is the price of freedom, according to Paine? For what is Paine, therefore, criticizing the "summer soldiers," the "sunshine patriots," and the tavernkeeper in Amboy?
6. To what emotions does Paine appeal when he describes the king of Britain? Where in this se-

lection does Paine rely on reason rather than emotion?

Extending
7. The "crisis" Paine speaks of was nothing less than the potential defeat of the American armies. Do you think Paine's words have a more general application as well?

VIEWPOINT

Tom Paine himself once said that his purpose as a writer was to use plain language

to make those who can scarcely read understand . . . [and] to fit the powers of thinking and the turn of language to the subject, so as to bring out a clear conclusion that shall hit the point in question and nothing else.

◾ Cite at least one sentence from *Crisis* in which you think Paine achieves this purpose.

LITERARY FOCUS

Methods of Persuasion

Paine's *Crisis* is a superb example of persuasive writing (see page 22). To persuade colonial men and women to stand firm, take courage, and continue fighting, he uses a number of methods:

Concrete examples. Good persuasion supports general statements with facts, quotations, and other examples to convince the audience that the general statements are true. In paragraph 1 Paine declares that Britain's army "enforces tyranny"; to support this statement, he quotes directly from the British themselves.

Vivid language. Vivid language and images appeal to the audience's emotions and make persuasive writing powerful. Consider how much weaker Paine's opening statement would be if he merely said, "These are bad times."

Exaggeration. Persuasive writers often exaggerate in order to rouse the emotions of their audiences. Paine says, for example, that Americans have sought to avoid war "by every decent method which wisdom could invent." By overstating, he makes his point.

Repetition. By repeating words and ideas, the persuasive writer emphasizes their importance and lodges them even more firmly in the minds of the audience. When Paine wants to say that King George has committed crimes against the Americans, he combines exaggeration and repetition: He compares the king to "a common murderer, a highwayman, or a housebreaker."

Parallelism. **Parallelism** is the repeating of phrases or sentences so that the repeated parts are alike in structure or in meaning. By using balanced sentences with parallel structures, a persuasive writer creates a rhythm that reinforces the message. Paine says, "The harder the conflict, the more glorious the triumph." Parallel structures add a feeling of completeness and sureness of thought to what the writer has to say.

Thinking About Methods of Persuasion

■ What concrete example in the third paragraph illustrates Paine's feelings about the Tories? Where in the third paragraph does Paine repeat words and sentence structures? What makes his final sentence so forceful?

COMPOSITION

Writing About Persuasion

■ Write a short essay in which you first state the purpose of either Henry's speech (page 66) or the Declaration of Independence (page 77). Then cite with examples the particular techniques that Henry or Jefferson uses to accomplish his purpose. *For help with this assignment, refer to Lesson 4 in the Writing About Literature Handbook at the back of this book.*

Writing Persuasion

■ Compose a short speech, a newspaper editorial, or a radio or television commercial intended to persuade someone to take action on a matter of urgent public interest. You may want to analyze a few examples from today's media before writing your own. Include concrete examples, vivid language, exaggeration, repetition, and parallel structure to make your argument more persuasive.

COMPARING WRITERS

■ If you had been indecisive about America's role in the years before the Revolution, which would have influenced you more to join the Revolution—Henry's speech, Jefferson's Declaration, or Paine's pamphlet? Compare at least two of these selections, citing specific examples of the arguments each uses and the emotional responses each calls up. Tell how the attitude and style of each author affects his argument, making it more or less persuasive.

Phillis Wheatley   *1754?–1784*

Phillis Wheatley's life remains a testament to the triumph of talent over difficult circumstances. When she was about eight years old, she was taken from her home in Africa, brought on a slave ship to Boston, and sold to a wealthy family, the Wheatleys, who gave her their name and their religion. They also recognized her extraordinary talents. Within two years she had learned English and was reading the Bible. Soon she was reading the great English poets, such as Milton and Pope, as well as Latin writers, such as Virgil and Terence.

Wheatley was only sixteen when she published her first poem. It made her famous, and at nineteen she went to London, where she became a celebrity and where her *Poems on Various Subjects, Religious and Moral* was published in 1773. Back in Boston she continued to write, but her last years were sad ones, marked by obscurity and poverty.

"To His Excellency, General Washington" is typical of Wheatley's verse: modeled on the conventions of the English poetry of the time, formal, elegant, making frequent use of classical allusions. Thomas Paine was the first to publish the poem in his *Philadelphia Magazine* in 1775. Washington himself liked the poem so much that he wrote to Wheatley and invited her to visit him. She did meet Washington in Cambridge, Massachusetts, in 1776, but unfortunately no record exists of what these two Americans from such different backgrounds said to each other.

Phillis Wheatley

To His Excellency, General Washington

Celestial choir! enthron'd in realms of light,
  Columbia's[1] scenes of glorious toils I write.
While freedom's cause her anxious breast alarms,
She flashes dreadful in refulgent[2] arms.
5 See mother earth her offspring's fate bemoan,
And nations gaze at scenes before unknown!

---

1. **Columbia:** goddess personifying America.
2. **refulgent** [ri ful′jənt]: brightly shining.

See the bright beams of heaven's revolving light
Involved in sorrows and the veil of night!

    The goddess comes, she moves divinely fair,
10 Olive and laurel binds her golden hair:
Wherever shines this native of the skies,
Unnumber'd charms and recent graces rise.

    Muse!³ bow propitious while my pen relates
How pour her armies through a thousand gates,
15 As when Eolus⁴ heaven's fair face deforms,
Enwrapp'd in tempest and a night of storms;
Astonish'd ocean feels the wild uproar,
The refluent⁵ surges beat the sounding shore;
Or thick as leaves in Autumn's golden reign,
20 Such, and so many, moves the warrior's train.
In bright array they seek the work of war,
Where high unfurl'd the ensign⁶ waves in air.
Shall I to Washington their praise recite?
Enough thou know'st them in the fields of fight.
25 Thee, first in peace and honors—we demand
The grace and glory of thy martial band.
Fam'd for thy valor, for thy virtues more,
Hear every tongue thy guardian aid implore!

    One century scarce perform'd its destined round,
30 When Gallic⁷ powers Columbia's fury found;
And so may you, whoever dares disgrace
The land of freedom's heaven-defended race!
Fix'd are the eyes of nations on the scales,
For in their hopes Columbia's arm prevails.
35 Anon Britannia⁸ droops the pensive head,
While round increase the rising hills of dead.
Ah! cruel blindness to Columbia's state!
Lament thy thirst of boundless power too late.

    Proceed, great chief, with virtue on thy side,
40 Thy ev'ry action let the goddess guide.
A crown, a mansion, and a throne that shine,
With gold unfading, WASHINGTON! be thine.

---

3. **Muse:** Wheatley asks the aid of the goddess who presides over the creation of poetry.
4. **Eolus** [ē′ə ləs]: in Greek mythology, god of the winds.
5. **refluent** [ref′lo͞o ənt]: flowing back.
6. **ensign:** flag.
7. **Gallic:** French. Washington fought the French during the French and Indian War (1754–1763).
8. **Britannia:** goddess personifying Great Britain.

STUDY QUESTIONS

Recalling

1. What phrases does Wheatley use in lines 3–4 to describe the goddess Columbia? In lines 10–13?
2. What does Wheatley call George Washington in line 25? What does he have on his side, according to line 39?
3. According to lines 29–32, what defends America? What will happen to anyone who disgraces America?

Interpreting

4. Identify at least three positive qualities of America in Wheatley's portrait.
5. How are Washington's virtues tied to Wheatley's portrait of America? What, ultimately, makes him noble?
6. In what ways can this poem be seen as a warning? What is Wheatley suggesting about the American forces when she uses the images of the storm (lines 15–18) and the leaves (lines 19–20)?

Extending

7. Explain how Wheatley is continuing an American tradition, begun by Puritan writers, when she calls Americans a "heaven-defended race."

LITERARY FOCUS

The Heroic Couplet

Phillis Wheatley wrote most of her verse in the form that dominated English poetry in the eighteenth century, the heroic couplet. A **heroic couplet** is a pair of rhymed lines in iambic pentameter. Each line, therefore, has ten syllables and five beats, or accents:

Anón Británnia dróops the pénsive héad
While róund incréase the rísing hílls of
  dréad

To keep the regular pattern of ten syllables and five beats, however, some words give up a syllable (for example, *Britannia,* pronounced as *Bri tan'yə*).

Literary taste changes from age to age. For over two centuries poets and readers enjoyed heroic couplets and accepted them as a standard of English verse. Skillful poets have been able to make this pattern sound natural and have used it to create great poetry. The English poets Geoffrey Chaucer and Alexander Pope were masters of the heroic couplet. To the ears of some modern readers, however, the couplet may sound too regular when used for more than a few lines at a time. Nevertheless, even though this form is now mainly used for a humorous or a deliberately archaic effect, we can still hear in poems like Wheatley's the noble accents and attitudes of a time past.

Thinking About the Heroic Couplet

■ Anne Bradstreet's "To My Dear and Loving Husband" (page 31) uses the heroic couplet. Choose two of Bradstreet's couplets and point out the accented syllables and the end rhymes.

VOCABULARY

Sentence Completions

Each of the following sentences contains a blank with four possible words for completing the sentence. The words are from "To His Excellency, General Washington." Choose the word that completes each sentence correctly, using the word *as it is used in this selection.* Write the number of each item and the letter of your choice on a separate sheet.

1. Since the boss is in a generous mood, it seems a ____ time to ask him for a raise.
   (a) celestial   (c) pensive
   (b) propitious   (d) martial
2. The troops are in battle ____.
   (a) array   (c) reign
   (b) ensign   (d) laurel
3. The expression on the girl's face was ____ as she thought through her dilemma.
   (a) destined   (c) unfurled
   (b) pensive   (d) celestial
4. I call upon the ____ of poetry to inspire my song.
   (a) Britannia   (c) Eolus
   (b) Columbia   (d) Muse
5. His ____ spirit was expressed in the belligerent thrust of his jaw.
   (a) pensive   (c) celestial
   (b) martial   (d) propitious

William Bartram   *1739–1823*

William Bartram virtually grew up in the botanical garden built by his father in Philadelphia. John Bartram, the first American botanist, took William with him on explorations and scientific expeditions in search of America's plants and flowers. William's interest in observing and describing nature remained strong all his life.

In 1773 Bartram set out alone on a two-year journey through the Carolinas, Georgia, Florida, and Mississippi. He collected specimens of plants and animals, made careful drawings, observed life on the frontier, and took a special interest in the American Indians he met. As a mark of honor, the Seminole Indians of Florida named him the Flower Hunter.

Bartram's record of the journey was published in 1791 with a typical, meticulous, Age of Reason title: *Travels Through North and South Carolina, Georgia, East and West Florida, the Cherokee Country, the Extensive Territories of the Muscogulges, or Creek Confederacy, and the Country of the Chactaws.* The book was especially popular in Europe and was praised by the English poets Wordsworth and Coleridge. Like Crèvecoeur's essays (see page 93), published at about the same time, Bartram's book presented an image of America as a place truly appropriate for the "pursuit of happiness."

Bartram was a scientist, an Enlightenment man in America, but he was also something of a poet himself. His writing combines observation and adventure, objectivity and excitement. Bartram communicates his sense of the sheer *wonder* of what he saw— things few Americans had ever seen.

William Bartram's drawing of the alligators of east Florida.

William Bartram

from Travels

The Alligators of East Florida

The noise of the crocodiles[1] kept me awake the greater part of the night, but when I arose in the morning, contrary to my expectations, there was perfect peace; very few of them to be seen, and those were asleep on the shore. Yet I was not able to suppress my fears and apprehensions of being attacked by them in future; and indeed yesterday's combat with them, notwithstanding I came off in a manner victorious, or at least made a safe retreat, had left sufficient impression on my mind to damp my courage; and it seemed too much for one of my strength, being alone in a very small boat, to encounter such collected danger.

To pursue my voyage up the river, and be obliged every evening to pass such dangerous defiles,[2] appeared to me as perilous as running the gauntlet[3] betwixt two rows of Indians armed with knives and firebrands. I however resolved to continue my voyage one day longer, if I possibly could with safety, and then return down the river, should I find the like difficulties to oppose. Accordingly I got everything on board, charged my gun, and set sail, cautiously, along shore. As I passed by Battle Lagoon, I began to tremble and keep a good lookout; when suddenly a huge alligator rushed out of the reeds, and with a tremendous roar came up and darted as swift as an arrow under my boat, emerging upright on my lee quarter,

---

1. **crocodiles:** Bartram uses *crocodile* and *alligator* interchangeably.

2. **defiles** [de fīlz′]: narrow passages.
3. **running the gauntlet:** punishment in which an offender was beaten while running between two rows of people.

with open jaws, and belching water and smoke that fell upon me like rain in a hurricane. I laid soundly about his head with my club, and beat him off; and after plunging and darting about my boat, he went off on a straight line through the water, seemingly with the rapidity of lightning, and entered the cape of the lagoon. I now employed my time to the very best advantage in paddling close along shore, but could not forbear looking now and then behind me, and presently perceived one of them coming up again. The water of the river hereabouts was shoal[4] and very clear; the monster came up with the usual roar and menaces, and passed close by the side of my boat, when I could distinctly see a young brood of alligators, to the number of one hundred or more, following after her in a long train. They kept close together in a column, without straggling off to the one side or the other; the young appeared to be of an equal size, about fifteen inches in length, almost black, with pale yellow transverse-waved clouds or blotches, much like rattlesnakes in color. I now lost sight of my enemy again.

Still keeping close along shore, on turning a point or projection of the riverbank, at once I beheld a great number of hillocks or small pyramids, resembling haycocks,[5] ranged like an encampment along the banks. They stood fifteen or twenty yards distant from the water, on a high marsh, about four feet perpendicular above the water. I knew them to be the nests of the crocodile, having had a description of them before, and now expected a furious and general attack, as I saw several large crocodiles swimming abreast of these buildings. These nests being so great a curiosity to me, I was determined at all events immediately to land and examine them. Accordingly, I ran my bark[6] on shore at one of their landing places, which was a sort of nick, or little dock, from which ascended a sloping path or road up to the edge of the meadow, where their nests were; most of them were deserted, and the great thick whitish eggshells lay broken and scattered upon the ground round about them.

The nests, or hillocks, are of the form of an obtuse[7] cone, four feet high and four or five feet in diameter at their bases; they are constructed with mud, grass, and herbage. At first they lay a floor of this kind of tempered mortar on the ground, upon which they deposit a layer of eggs, and upon this a stratum of mortar, seven or eight inches in thickness, and then another layer of eggs; and in this manner, one stratum upon another, nearly to the top. I believe they commonly lay from one to two hundred eggs in a nest. These are hatched, I suppose, by the heat of the sun; and perhaps the vegetable substances mixed with the earth, being acted upon by the sun may cause a small degree of fermentation, and so increase the heat in those hillocks. The ground for several acres about these nests showed evident marks of a continual resort[8] of alligators; the grass was everywhere beaten down, hardly a blade or straw was left standing; whereas, all about, at a distance, it was five or six feet high, and as thick as it could grow together.

The female, as I imagine, carefully watches her own nest of eggs until they are all hatched; or perhaps while she is attending her own brood, she takes under her care and protection as many as she can get at one time, either from her own particular nest or others; but certain it is that the young are not left to shift for themselves; for I have had frequent opportunities of seeing the female alligator leading about the shores her train of young ones, just as a hen does her brood of chickens; and she is equally assiduous and courageous in defending the young, which are under her care, and providing for their subsistence; and when she is basking upon the warm banks, with her brood around her, you may hear the young ones con-

---

4. **shoal** [shōl]: shallow.
5. **haycocks:** small, cone-shaped haystacks.
6. **bark:** small boat.

7. **obtuse** [əb tōos']: blunt on top.
8. **resort:** movement.

tinually whining and barking like young puppies. I believe but few of a brood live to the years of full growth and magnitude, as the old feed on the young as long as they can make prey of them.

The alligator when full grown is a very large and terrible creature, and of prodigious strength, activity, and swiftness in the water. I have seen them twenty feet in length, and some are supposed to be twenty-two or twenty-three feet. Their body is as large as that of a horse; their shape exactly resembles that of a lizard, except their tail, which is flat or cuneiform,[9] being compressed on each side and gradually diminishing from the abdomen to the extremity, which, with the whole body, is covered with horny plates or squamae,[10] impenetrable when on the body of the live animal, even to a rifle ball, except about their head and just behind their forelegs or arms, where it is said they are only vulnerable. The head of a full-grown one is about three feet, and the mouth opens nearly the same length; their eyes are small in proportion, and seem sunk deep in the head, by means of the prominency of the brows; the nostrils are large, inflated, and

prominent on the top, so that the head in the water resembles, at a distance, a great chunk of wood floating about. Only the upper jaw moves, which they raise almost perpendicular, so as to form a right angle with the lower one. In the forepart of the upper jaw, on each side, just under the nostrils, are two very large, thick, strong teeth, or tusks, not very sharp, but rather the shape of a cone: These are as white as the finest polished ivory, and are not covered by any skin or lips, and always in sight, which gives the creature a frightful appearance. In the lower jaw are holes opposite to these teeth, to receive them: When they clap their jaws together it causes a surprising noise, like that which is made by forcing a heavy plank with violence upon the ground, and may be heard at a great distance.

But what is yet more surprising to a stranger is the incredible loud and terrifying roar which they are capable of making, especially in the spring season, their breeding time. It most resembles very heavy distant thunder, not only shaking the air and waters, but causing the earth to tremble; and when hundreds and thousands are roaring at the same time, you can scarcely be persuaded but that the whole globe is violently and dangerously agitated.

---

9. **cuneiform** [kū nē′ə fôrm]: wedge-shaped.
10. **squamae** [skwā′mē]: scales.

STUDY QUESTIONS

Recalling

1. What "fears and apprehensions" does Bartram mention in the first paragraph? What happened as he passed Battle Lagoon?
2. According to the third paragraph, what did Bartram expect when he saw the alligator nests? What did he do?
3. What description of the nests does Bartram provide in the fourth paragraph? Of a female alligator in the fifth paragraph?
4. What basic facts about the alligator does Bartram provide in the sixth paragraph?

5. According to the last paragraph, what is the most "surprising" thing about alligators?

Interpreting

6. Find two sentences where Bartram writes objectively, scientifically reporting the facts of his experience. Find two sentences where he writes subjectively, attempting to convey his feelings about his experience.
7. What does Bartram reveal about the kind of person he was with the statement, "I was determined at all events to immediately land and examine them [the nests]"? Consider the context of the first two paragraphs.

Extending

8. Bartram's work no longer has scientific value because modern scientists have made more thorough studies of alligators. In your opinion, what value does his writing have today?

LITERARY FOCUS

Description

Description is writing that creates an impression of a person, a place, or a thing. Bartram uses description in this passage from his *Travels*. He uses some narrative here too, especially when he tells of rising in the morning and continuing his journey up the river, but the emphasis is on clear and vivid description. He makes it possible for us to imagine what he saw. To do so, he uses the following techniques:

Specific sensory language. Bartram gives many concrete and specific sensory details. For example, notice his precise visual description of the nests: "the form of an obtuse cone, four feet high and four or five feet in diameter at their bases; they are constructed with mud, grass and herbage." He does *not* say, "They looked like medium-sized mounds of dirt," which would give us a much less valuable picture.

Bartram's language appeals to other senses besides sight. We can almost hear the alligators as "hundreds and thousands are roaring at the same time."

Selected and organized details. In the sixth paragraph Bartram does not attempt to tell everything about the alligator at once. He separates the parts of the animal and describes them in detail in a spatial order we can follow clearly: overall size and shape, tail, hide, head. In this way he avoids a vague or jumbled impression.

Comparisons. Few of Bartram's readers had seen alligators, but all had seen horses. To emphasize the bulk of the alligators' torsos, Bartram says "their body is as large as that of a horse." He uses the familiar to help describe the unfamiliar.

Thinking About Description

In this selection from Bartram, find another example of sensory language, of organized details, and of comparison with another animal.

VOCABULARY

Words from Latin

People who write scientific reports in English often use words derived from Latin. For example, both *penicillin* and *coronary* are medical terms that come from Latin. In his report about alligators, Bartram uses the Latin word *squamae* to refer to the scalelike parts of the animals.

In addition to supplying us with scientific terms, Latin has greatly influenced the everyday vocabulary of English speakers and writers. Look up the following words from Bartram's report, and give each word's original form and Latin meaning.

1. stratum
2. magnitude
3. prodigious
4. cuneiform
5. vulnerable

COMPOSITION

Analyzing Descriptive Writing

Choose one of Bartram's comparisons or one of his descriptive images, and tell why you think it is appropriate or inappropriate. First make sure you tell your audience what Bartram is describing. Then explain whether the description helps you picture the item clearly. Tell why or why not.

Writing a Description

Using the three methods Bartram uses—specific sensory language, selected and organized details, and comparisons (see preceding Literary Focus)—write a description of an animal. Assume that your reader has *never seen* the animal you choose to write about. You may want to follow Bartram's example and combine your description with a narrative of your own encounter with the animal.

Jean de Crèvecoeur *1735–1813*

Michel-Guillaume-Jean de Crèvecoeur spent the first nineteen years of his life in France. After living in England and Canada, and traveling throughout the American colonies as a surveyor, he settled on a farm near Chester, New York, in 1769. There he began writing his *Letters from an American Farmer,* published in London in 1782.

Like most literary letters, Crèvecoeur's were addressed to a particular person—a "Mr. F. B."—but were actually intended for a large audience. In fact, Crèvecoeur's letters reached a much larger audience than he had anticipated. Europeans were eager for information about the New World, and Crèvecoeur's *Letters,* translated into several languages, made him famous. His idealized vision of a "new man" living in a land of boundless opportunities, free from the restraints and class structure of Europe, was extremely influential in shaping the Old World's image of America.

Most Americans, of course, were well aware that the human race had not escaped all its problems merely by crossing the Atlantic. George Washington, for one, thought Crèvecoeur's picture "too flattering." Yet Crèvecoeur's excitement at the *possibilities* for freedom, equality, and prosperity was genuine—and that enthusiasm is communicated in his writing, which begins on the following page.

Model for Active Reading

In this selection, and in one selection in each unit, you will find notes in the right-hand margin that highlight parts of the selection. These notes point out important ideas of the period—in this case, the Enlightenment—and draw your attention to literary elements and techniques covered in the Literary Focuses. Page numbers in the notes will refer you to more extensive discussions of these important ideas and elements.

Jean de Crèvecoeur

from **Letters from an American Farmer**

"What then is the American?"

I wish I could be acquainted with the feelings and thoughts which must agitate the heart and present themselves to the mind of an enlightened Englishman, when he first lands on this continent. . . . Here he beholds fair cities, substantial villages, extensive fields, an immense country filled with decent houses, good roads, orchards, meadows, and bridges, where a hundred years ago all was wild, woody, and uncultivated! What a train of pleasing ideas this fair spectacle must suggest; it is a prospect which must inspire a good citizen with the most heartfelt pleasure.

The difficulty consists in the manner of viewing so extensive a scene. He is arrived on a new continent; a modern society offers itself to his contemplation, different from what he had hitherto seen. It is not composed, as in Europe, of great lords who possess everything, and of a herd of people who have nothing. Here are no aristocratical families, no courts, no kings, no bishops, no ecclesiastical dominion, no invisible power giving to a few a very visible one, no great manufacturers employing thousands, no great refinements of luxury. The rich and the poor are not so far removed from each other as they are in Europe. . . .

What then is the American, this new man? He is either a European or the descendant of a European, hence that strange mixture of blood, which you will find in no other country. I could point out to you a family whose grandfather was an Englishman, whose wife was Dutch, whose son married a French woman, and whose present four sons have now four wives of different nations. *He* is an American who, leaving behind him all his ancient prejudices and manners, receives new ones from the new mode of life he has embraced, the new government he obeys, and the new rank he holds. He becomes an American by being received in the broad lap of our great *Alma Mater*.[1] Here individuals of all nations are melted into a new race of men whose labors and posterity will one day cause great changes in the world.

Americans are the western pilgrims who are carrying along with them that great mass of arts, sciences, vigor, and industry which began long since in the east; they will finish the great circle. The Americans were once scattered all over Europe; here they are incorporated into one of the finest systems of population which has

Enlightenment idea: Crèvecoeur refers to enlightened people and notes that belief in progress and hope were typical of the time (p. 50).

Selected and organized details (p. 92) and Repetition (p. 69): In this *description* Crèvecoeur provides a catalogue of Old World injustices and uses repetition to stress their absence in America.

Rhetorical question (p. 69): Crèvecoeur answers his question himself.

---

1. *Alma Mater* [äl′mə mät′ər]: Latin for "foster mother," referring here to America.

ever appeared, and which will hereafter become distinct by the power of the different climates they inhabit.

The American ought therefore to love this country much better than that wherein either he or his forefathers were born. Here the rewards of his industry follow with equal steps the progress of his labor; his labor is founded on the basis of nature, *self-interest*; can it want a stronger allurement? Wives and children, who before in vain demanded of him a morsel of bread, now, fat and frolicsome, gladly help their father to clear those fields whence exuberant crops are to arise to feed and to clothe them all, without any part being claimed either by a despotic prince, a rich abbot,[2] or a mighty lord. Here religion demands but little of him—a small voluntary salary to the minister and gratitude to God; can he refuse these? The American is a new man, who acts upon new principles; he must therefore entertain new ideas and form new opinions. From involuntary idleness, servile dependence, penury,[3] and useless labor, he has passed to toils of a very different nature, rewarded by ample subsistence.[4]—This is an American.

---

2. **abbot:** man who heads an abbey of monks.
3. **penury** [pen′yər ē]: extreme poverty.
4. **subsistence:** livelihood.

> **Enlightenment idea:**
> Crèvecoeur stresses that Americans use their own powers to shape their destinies (p. 50).

> **Specific sensory language** (p. 92): Crèvecoeur adds specific details and sensory images to his *description*.

STUDY QUESTIONS

Recalling

1. According to the first two paragraphs, what does an Englishman behold when he arrives in America? What does he *not* behold?
2. According to the third paragraph, what does the American leave behind? What does the American embrace, obey, and hold?
3. According to the last paragraph, what was the result of labor in the Old World? For what do people work in America?
4. Why must Americans "entertain new ideas and form new opinions"?

Interpreting

5. What is the effect of the long lists of details describing Europe and America in paragraphs 1 and 2?
6. What, in your own words, is Crèvecoeur's definition of an American?
7. In addition to the rhetorical question that opens the third paragraph, what other rhetorical questions does Crèvecoeur ask? Where does he exaggerate?

Extending

8. In what way is Crèvecoeur's description of America reminiscent of the writing of the earliest visitors from Europe, such as Columbus (page 15), John Smith (page 19), and William Bradford (page 23)?

COMPOSITION

Writing a Comparison/Contrast

■ Write a short essay summarizing the characteristics of an American as described by Crèvecoeur. For each characteristic that you mention, compare Crèvecoeur's "new man" to today's American. Be sure to show both what they have in common and what makes them different.

Writing a Literary Letter

■ Compose your own literary letter, addressing it to a public figure or to a fictitious character, but actually aiming it at a wider audience. First comment on a current event. Then describe your version of an ideal America and tell how you feel the event and the ideal compare.

READING FOR APPRECIATION

The Sound of Prose

Since so much of the literature in this unit is oratory, or public statement, we should remind ourselves that prose makes a *sound.* In other words, most literature begins with a speaking voice. Some people say they read mostly with their eyes, that they do not hear anything as they read. It may not matter that we do not hear a voice behind a newspaper article, an advertisement, or a legal document. Yet with any writing we call literature, the language itself is a large part of the pleasure of reading, and we will miss much of that pleasure, miss the experience, if we do not find a voice for what we read.

Reading aloud is one way not to miss that pleasure. However, most of the time we read silently. (At least we do in the modern world. A few centuries ago, silent reading was considered an amazing feat!) So we need, as always, to be imaginative and to read *aloud silently* or *silently aloud.* This technique means hearing in our mind's ear the rise and fall of a human voice, pausing, emphasizing, shifting tone. Literature is, after all, human communication. It is someone speaking to us.

There is no tape recording of how Patrick Henry delivered his speech at the Virginia Convention. Yet when we read we must give that speech a voice.

Where did Henry pause? Which words did he emphasize? Where did he drop his voice, or raise it, for greater effect? We can imagine his emphases in one possible "script":

What *is* it that gentlemen wish? [Voice rising, slightly louder:] What would they *have?* Is life so *dear* [slight pause], or peace so *sweet* [slight pause], as to be purchased [with rising indignation] at the price of *chains* and *slavery?* For*bid* it, Almighty *God!* [Then more quietly, rising to the conclusion] I know not what course *others* may take; but as for *me* [pause], give me *liberty* [long pause] or give me *death!*

There is no single "correct" way of reading a sentence. In addition, prose writers have very few devices available to help readers hear their voices. They can use *italics,* exclamation points (!), or CAPITALS for emphasis. The can use commas, parentheses, or dashes for pauses. However, these devices are limited and quickly become tiresome if overused. It is up to each reader's active participation in the experience of literature if he or she is going to hear the amused voice of Franklin remembering his youth or the warm voice of Crèvecoeur filled with love of country.

THE AMERICAN VOICE

Liberty

Most of the American voices in this unit, from the famous to the anonymous, carry the message of the Declaration of Independence. They are Age of Reason voices that are strongly emotional, talking about matters of life and death, yet still logical, coherent, and organized. In particular, they share a vision of the liberty and the freedom that would allow Americans to think and feel as independent individuals long after the Revolution:

Franklin
I took upon me to assert my Freedom. . . .

Henry
If we wish to be free, if we mean to preserve inviolate those inestimable privileges . . . we must fight!

Anonymous
I will sing you a song concerning liberty.
Concerning liberty, my boys, the truth I will unfold,
Of the bold Americans, who scorn to be controlled.

Jefferson
We hold these truths to be self-evident, that all men are created equal, that they are endowed by their Creator with certain unalienable Rights, that among these are Life, Liberty and the pursuit of Happiness.

Paine
For though the flame of liberty may sometimes cease to shine, the coal can never expire.

Crèvecoeur
The American ought therefore to love this country much better than that wherein either he or his forefathers were born. Here the rewards of his industry follow with equal steps the progress of his labor; his labor is founded on the basis of nature, self-interest; can it want a stronger allurement?

Freedom in American literary expression had helped to create the American political system. Writing about liberty helped to make liberty possible. The literature in this unit helped to found the nation on the basis of private and public independence.

As the new United States continued to grow, American literature also continued to grow. Literature helped the nation to achieve an identity by defining its characteristics, its problems, and its goals. Liberty is one of those characteristics. It is part of the answer to Crèvecoeur's question, "What then is the American, this new man?" The American is someone free to create a new literature, to found a new tradition, to speak in a new voice.

Key to Illustrations on Pages 48–49.

1. Baltimore, Maryland, c. 1750.
2. American Continental dollar, 1776.
3. Betsy Ross sewing the first American flag, illustration by Elizabeth Moore Hallowell.
4. *The Battle of Lexington, April 19, 1775.* Early twentieth-century engraving.
5. William Bartram. Nineteenth-century engraving.
6. *The Spirit of '76,* lithograph from a painting by Archibald M. Willard.
7. *Benjamin Franklin,* David Martin, 1766.
8. *The Midnight Ride of Paul Revere,* Grant Wood, 1931.
9. Phillis Wheatley, engraved frontispiece to her *Poems on Various Subjects, Religious and Moral,* 1773.
10. *Daniel Boone Escorting Settlers Through the Cumberland Gap,* George Caleb Bingham, 1852.

Key to Illustrations appears on page 151.

NATIVE GROUNDS

1800–1840

Growth and Prosperity

In 1789 George Washington, not only an American hero, but an international hero of freedom, was inaugurated as first President of the United States. The American Revolution had been a success. Would the new nation be equally successful? Many questions remained to be answered. Could a modern republic—a nation without a king or a hereditary aristocracy—withstand the tensions of a large and varied population? Would there be economic prosperity? Would there be real democracy? Would the new Constitution stand the test of time? In short, would the American experiment work?

Many of the nation's first problems were physical ones. In an age of few good roads and no rapid and reliable means of transportation or communication, it was difficult for the thirteen states to conceive of themselves and act as a single nation. Regional rivalries and even separate cultures had to be reconciled. As Lincoln asked years later, could a nation "conceived in liberty and dedicated to the proposition that all men are created equal . . . long endure"?

In fact the nation did prosper, did expand, and did overcome the dangers it faced. Jefferson's Louisiana Purchase in 1803 vastly enlarged the territory. The War of 1812 offered a challenge to the proud new nation, and the victory reasserted American independence. By 1821

Illustration (detail) from a French edition of Edgar Allan Poe's "The Raven," Edouard Manet. 1875.

ten new states had joined the original thirteen. Settlers moved west; roads and waterways improved. Steamships created a new network of trade and communication. New factories and mills began to move the nation away from a largely agricultural economy toward a more urban and industrialized society.

"Our Own Books"

As Americans continued to build the nation, they came increasingly to feel less like transported Europeans. The native grounds of the Old World—the European environment, its traditions and customs, its languages and literatures—gave way to the native grounds of the New World. A new culture and a new literature had to be created. With an increasing nationalism, a sense of national pride, Americans began to call for a literature that would be less dependent upon European models, one that would express their Americanism. The playwright Royall Tyler saw what was needed: "that we write our own books . . . and that they exhibit our own manners."

During the first decades of the American republic, a great deal of *writing* was done, but very little of it possessed that mysterious vitality that made it *literature*. For example, not many people today have heard of Mrs. Susannah Rowson. Yet her novel *Charlotte Temple,* published in the United States in 1794, sold fifty thousand copies

by 1810 and appeared in two hundred editions before it settled into near oblivion. Better known is Charles Brockden Brown, perhaps the most original of early American novelists. Brown's *Wieland* (1798) was quite successful. He often used American locales in his tales, and he established some subjects that were to become common in American writing: settlers, Indians, forests, madness, sin, and guilt. With greater artistry, Poe, Hawthorne, Melville, and Faulkner would develop the material Brown used in the eighteenth century.

In 1820 it was still possible for a British critic, Sydney Smith, to ask, "Who reads an American book?" Smith, like many other Europeans, wondered why any intelligent person would want to bother reading books from such an unformed, uncultured, unsophisticated place as America. Yet in the same year that Smith asked his mocking question, Washington Irving's *Sketch Book* was published in England. American literature of lasting value

was beginning to be created. The next year William Cullen Bryant gained fame for his poem "Thanatopsis." James Fenimore Cooper brought out the first of the Leatherstocking novels, *The Pioneers,* in 1823. Edgar Allan Poe published his first volume of poetry in 1827.

Who were the people who produced this first American literature, and what made their work unmistakably American? In the first place they were *writers,* not soldiers of fortune like John Smith (page 19), business leaders like Ben Franklin (page 56), or government leaders like Thomas Jefferson (page 76). Though they sometimes had to do other things to make a living, they thought of themselves as writers, and they were thought of as writers by their growing public.

Second, they began writing about American people in American places dealing with American problems. This accomplishment may seem like something to take for granted, but it is important to remember that no one had ever done it before. Their characters and settings were not *always* American, and their forms were usually British, but they did take the first steps. They wrote about the American wilderness, the Revolution, pioneers, American town and city life. They praised American heroes and American artists and told American tales. Their subjects were freedom, expansion, the individual—definitely not European subjects.

Natty Bumppo and the Indian chieftain Chingachgook, from an 1872 edition of *The Last of the Mohicans* by Cooper.

The Romantic Writers

We cannot think about Irving, Cooper, Bryant, and Poe—the writers represented in this unit—as if they were all writing about the same things in the same way. We should recognize, however, that all four writers shared some of the characteristics of Romanticism, a literary movement that began in Europe in the late eighteenth century and dominated literature on both sides of the Atlantic in the first half of the nineteenth century.

Romanticism was a reaction to **Classicism,** the Age of Reason movement in the arts that attempted to duplicate the order and balance in the art of Greece and Rome. While Classicism stressed reason over emotion and social concerns over personal ones, Romantic writers stressed personal experience and were often highly emotional. Among the earliest Romantic writers were the British poet William Wordsworth and the German poet Johann Wolfgang von Goethe.

The qualities of Romanticism vary from place to place, and few Romantic writers exhibit all of them. But there are six characteristics that can give us a general definition of **Romanticism:** (1) a profound love of nature; (2) a focus on the self and the individual; (3) a fascination with the supernatural, the mysterious, and the gothic; (4) a yearning for the picturesque and the exotic; (5) a deep-rooted idealism; and (6) a passionate nationalism, or love of country.

One quality of Romantic writers, then, is a deep feeling for nature. Close observation of the natural world usually gives a Romantic writer an insight into all life, especially human life. We can find this kind of detailed observation of nature in Irving, Cooper, and Bryant—particularly in Bryant's poems and in Cooper's breadth of feeling for the unspoiled wilderness.

Romantic writers also reveal with emotion their own personal visions and delve deeply into the individual personalities of their characters. Poe is the best representative of this strain of Romanticism, for he often displays the tortured minds and hearts of inward-looking characters. It is Poe also who demonstrates a fascination with the **gothic**—the dark, irrational side of the imagination.

One generalization about Romantic writing fits all four of the authors in this unit. Romantic writers were often interested in the picturesque and the exotic, in times and places other than their own, especially the past. Sometimes this interest in the past offers an escape from an oppressive or unromantic present. Irving's "Devil and Tom Walker" is set in and around a Boston that had vanished a century before the tale was written, and the story is wrapped in legend, rumor, suggestion, and fantasy. Cooper's hero, the frontiersman Natty Bumppo, lived in an America that was already a legendary past for Cooper's readers. Bryant's "Thanatopsis" moves deep into the past of the human race. Poe's story, "The Fall of the House of Usher," is not set in any country at all or in any time that we can easily recognize.

Irving, Cooper, and Bryant often wrote with a fervent idealism, a belief in a heroic mode of behavior that would make life worthwhile. Nationalism, too, was a part of the imaginative lives of these writers—men who were completely aware of the importance of establishing an *American* literary art.

These four writers of the first half of the nineteenth century began an American Romantic tradition that would be developed by Emerson, Hawthorne, Melville, Whitman, and Faulkner, writers you will meet later in this book. We continue to read the four writers in this unit, however, not only because of their historical importance but because they still offer exciting and meaningful imaginative experiences.

TIME LINE

1803 U.S. negotiates Louisiana Purchase from France

Lewis and Clark explore west of Mississippi River

1807 Robert Fulton launches steamboat *Clermont* on Hudson River

1812 War of 1812 against Great Britain begins

First lead pencils manufactured (Concord, Mass.)

1814 Francis Scott Key writes "The Star-Spangled Banner"

First school in U.S. for higher education of women (Middlebury, Conn.)

1817 William Cullen Bryant, "Thanatopsis"

1820 Washington Irving, *The Sketch Book*

First canning factory in U.S. (Boston, Mass.)

1800 England: Poet William Wordsworth publishes Romantic manifesto, the Preface to *Lyrical Ballads*

1804 France: Napoleon crowns himself Emperor

1805 England: William Wordsworth completes *The Prelude*

1808 Austria: German composer Ludwig van Beethoven, *Symphony No. 5*

1812 Germany: Jacob and Wilhelm Grimm, *Fairy Tales*

1813 England: Jane Austen, *Pride and Prejudice*

1815 Belgium: Napoleon defeated at Battle of Waterloo

1818 England: Mary Shelley, *Frankenstein*

1820 England: Sir Walter Scott, *Ivanhoe*

England: John Keats, "Ode on a Grecian Urn"

1823 James Fenimore Cooper, first of the Leatherstocking Tales	**1823** England: Lord Byron, *Don Juan*
President Monroe issues Monroe Doctrine	
1825 Erie Canal opens	**1825** Russia: Bolshoi Ballet established
1826 First overland route to California blazed	
1827 James Audubon, *Birds of America*	
1828 Noah Webster, *American Dictionary of the English Language*	
1830 U.S. population: 12.6 million	
1831 First regularly scheduled steam locomotive service	**1831** France: Victor Hugo, *The Hunchback of Notre Dame*
Joseph Henry builds first electric motor	Germany: Johann Wolfgang von Goethe completes *Faust*
Edgar Allan Poe, *Poems*	
1832 First clipper ship, *Ann McKim,* launched at Baltimore	**1832** Russia: Alexander Pushkin, *Eugene Onegin*
	1833 Slavery abolished in British Empire
1834 Americans begin to eat tomatoes, previously considered poisonous	
Cyrus McCormick patents reaper	
	1835 Denmark: Hans Christian Andersen, *Fairy Tales*
1836 Texas declares independence from Mexico	
Ralph Waldo Emerson, *Nature*	
1837 Nathaniel Hawthorne, *Twice-Told Tales*	**1837** England: Charles Dickens, *Oliver Twist*
1839 First baseball diamond laid out (Cooperstown, N.Y.)	
1840 Edgar Allan Poe, *Tales of the Grotesque and Arabesque*	
Richard Dana, *Two Years Before the Mast*	
Samuel Morse patents telegraph	

Washington Irving   *1783–1859*

Washington Irving, born during the Revolution and named after George Washington, was the first American storyteller to be internationally recognized as a man of letters. A member of a wealthy New York family, Irving reluctantly studied law and even managed to pass his bar examination. However, he preferred reading, roaming the countryside, and listening to the old tales told by the villagers in New York's Hudson Valley.

Like Ben Franklin in the preceding unit, Irving had begun to publish witty and satiric letters in a newspaper edited by his brother. By the time he was twenty-four, he was publishing a satiric magazine appropriately named after a spicy appetizer, *Salmagundi.* *Salmagundi* carried essays and sketches making fun of everything from Thomas Jefferson's politics to the latest fashions. Irving was fond of using pen names, and he signed his articles with such names as William Wizard and Anthony Evergreen.

In 1809 Irving created another pseudonym, Diedrich Knickerbocker, and published Knickerbocker's *History of New York from the Beginning of the World to the End of the Dutch Dynasty.* Knickerbocker was supposed to be an eccentric old historian who often confused fact with folklore, giving Irving an opportunity to mix old tales and satiric opinions with a bit of history. The *History* entertained its readers with hilarious sketches of the customs, manners, families, and "history" of old New York. It was enormously popular and established Irving as a celebrity.

In 1815 Irving went to Europe and spent the next seventeen years in Britain, France, Germany, Italy, and Spain, exploring local traditions, customs, and folklore. "My native country was full of youthful promise: Europe was rich in the accumulated treasures of age," he wrote in his 1820 *Sketch Book.* An elegant English gentleman named Geoffrey Crayon was supposedly the author of some of the stories in the Sketch Book, but the two most famous stories—"Rip Van Winkle" and "The Legend of Sleepy Hollow"—are told by old Knickerbocker. Both tales have become American classics even though Irving borrowed their plots from two traditional German tales before placing them in the Hudson Valley setting. In fact, it is this ability to blend European sophistication and American flavor that is the most distinctive characteristic of Irving's writing.

Irving finally settled down at Sunnyside, his estate on the bank of the Hudson. There he continued writing travel books, histories, biographies of Columbus and Washington, more tales and sketches. Combining elegance and folklore, humor and history, nostalgia and satire, Irving achieved what no American writer had done before: He became an American writer admired and accepted by Europe.

The English novelist Thackeray summed up Irving's accomplishments when he called him "the first Ambassador from the New World of Letters to the Old."

"The Devil and Tom Walker" is one of the stories in Irving's *Tales of a Traveler* (1824). It is Irving's version of the old German legend of Faust, the man who sold his soul to the devil. Irving set the tale in New England in the 1720s—a time when Puritanism was fading and commercialism was growing. He placed it, appropriately, in the section of the book called "The Money Diggers."

Washington Irving

The Devil and Tom Walker

A few miles from Boston in Massachusetts, there is a deep inlet, winding several miles into the interior of the country from Charles Bay, and terminating in a thickly wooded swamp or morass. On one side of this inlet is a beautiful dark grove; on the opposite side the land rises abruptly from the water's edge into a high ridge, on which grow a few scattered oaks of great age and immense size. Under one of these gigantic trees, according to old stories, there was a great amount of treasure buried by Kidd the pirate.[1] The inlet allowed a facility to bring the money in a boat secretly and at night to the very foot of the hill; the elevation of the place permitted a good lookout to be kept that no one was at hand; while the remarkable trees formed good landmarks by which the place might easily be found again. The old stories add, moreover, that the Devil presided at the hiding of the money, and took it under his guardianship; but this, it is well known, he always does with buried treasure, particularly when it has been ill-gotten. Be that as it may, Kidd never returned to recover his wealth, being shortly after seized at Boston, sent out to England, and there hanged for a pirate.

About the year 1727, just at the time that earthquakes were prevalent in New England and shook many tall sinners down upon their knees, there lived near this place a meager, miserly fellow, of the name of Tom Walker. He had a wife as miserly as himself: they were so miserly that they even conspired to cheat each other. Whatever the woman could lay hands on she hid away; a hen could not cackle but she was on the alert to secure the new-laid egg. Her husband was continually prying about to detect her secret hoards, and many and fierce were the conflicts that took place about what ought to have been common property. They lived in a forlorn-looking house that stood alone and had an air of starvation. A few straggling savin trees, emblems of sterility, grew near it; no smoke ever curled from its chimney; no traveler stopped at its door. A miserable horse, whose ribs were as articulate as the bars of a gridiron, stalked about a field, where a thin carpet of moss, scarcely covering the ragged beds of puddingstone,[2] tantalized and balked his hunger; and sometimes he would lean his head over the fence, look piteously at the passerby, and seem to petition deliverance from this land of famine.

---

1. **Kidd the pirate:** Captain William Kidd (1645–1701).

2. **puddingstone:** kind of rock in which pebbles are embedded like plums in a pudding.

The house and its inmates had altogether a bad name. Tom's wife was a tall termagant, fierce of temper, loud of tongue, and strong of arm. Her voice was often heard in wordy warfare with her husband; and his face sometimes showed signs that their conflicts were not confined to words. No one ventured, however, to interfere between them. The lonely wayfarer shrunk within himself at the horrid clamor and clapperclawing;[3] eyed the den of discord askance; and hurried on his way, rejoicing, if a bachelor, in his celibacy.

One day that Tom Walker had been to a distant part of the neighborhood, he took what he considered a shortcut homeward, through the swamp. Like most shortcuts, it was an ill-chosen route. The swamp was thickly grown with great gloomy pines and hemlocks, some of them ninety feet high, which made it dark at noonday, and a retreat for all the owls of the neighborhood. It was full of pits and quagmires, partly covered with weeds and mosses, where the green surface often betrayed the traveler into a gulf of black, smothering mud; there were also dark and stagnant pools, the abodes of the tadpole, the bullfrog, and the water snake, where the trunks of pines and hemlocks lay half drowned, half rotting, looking like alligators sleeping in the mire.

Tom had long been picking his way cautiously through this treacherous forest; stepping from tuft to tuft of rushes and roots, which afforded precarious footholds among deep sloughs; or pacing carefully, like a cat, along the prostrate trunks of trees; startled now and then by the sudden screaming of the bittern, or the quacking of a wild duck rising on the wing from some solitary pool. At length he arrived at a firm piece of ground, which ran out like a peninsula into the deep bosom of the swamp. It had been one of the strongholds of the Indians during their wars with the first colonists. Here they had thrown up a kind of fort, which they had looked upon as almost impregnable, and had used as a place of refuge for their squaws and children. Nothing remained of the old Indian fort but a few embankments, gradually sinking to the level of the surrounding earth, and already overgrown in part by oaks and other forest trees, the foliage of which formed a contrast to the dark pines and hemlocks of the swamp.

It was late in the dusk of evening when Tom Walker reached the old fort, and he paused there awhile to rest himself. Anyone but he would have felt unwilling to linger in this lonely, melancholy place, for the common people had a bad opinion of it from the stories handed down from the time of the Indian wars, when it was asserted that the savages held incantations here and made sacrifices to the evil spirit.

Tom Walker, however, was not a man to be troubled with any fears of the kind. He reposed himself for some time on the trunk of a fallen hemlock, listening to the boding cry of the tree toad, and delving with his walking staff into a mound of black mold at his feet. As he turned up the soil unconsciously, his staff struck against something hard. He raked it out of the vegetable mold, and lo! a cloven[4] skull, with an Indian tomahawk buried deep in it, lay before him. The rust on the weapon showed the time that had elapsed since this deathblow had been given. It was a dreary memento of the fierce struggle that had taken place in this last foothold of the Indian warriors.

"Humph!" said Tom Walker, as he gave it a kick to shake the dirt from it.

"Let that skull alone!" said a gruff voice. Tom lifted up his eyes and beheld a great black man seated directly opposite him, on the stump of a tree. He was exceedingly surprised, having neither heard nor seen anyone approach; and he was still more perplexed on observing, as well as the gathering gloom would permit, that the stranger was neither Negro nor Indian. It is true he was dressed in a rude half-Indian garb, and had a red belt or sash swathed round his body; but his face was

---

3. **clapperclawing:** scratching, clawing.

4. **cloven** [klō′vən]: split.

neither black nor copper color, but swarthy and dingy, and begrimed with soot, as if he had been accustomed to toil among fires and forges. He had a shock of coarse black hair that stood out from his head in all directions, and bore an ax on his shoulder.

He scowled for a moment at Tom with a pair of great red eyes.

"What are you doing on my grounds?" said the black man, with a hoarse growling voice.

"Your grounds!" said Tom, with a sneer. "No more your grounds than mine; they belong to Deacon Peabody."

"Deacon Peabody be d——d," said the stranger, "as I flatter myself he will be, if he does not look more to his own sins and less to those of his neighbors. Look yonder, and see how Deacon Peabody is faring."

Tom looked in the direction that the stranger pointed and beheld one of the great trees, fair and flourishing without, but rotten at the core, and saw that it had been nearly hewn through, so that the first high wind was likely to blow it down. On the bark of the tree was scored the name of Deacon Peabody, an eminent man, who had waxed wealthy by driving shrewd bargains with the Indians. He now looked around, and found most of the tall trees marked with the name of some great man of the colony, and all more or less scored by the ax. The one on which he had been seated, and which had evidently just been hewn down, bore the name of Crowninshield; and he recollected a mighty rich man of that name, who made a vulgar display of wealth, which it was whispered he had acquired by buccaneering.

"He's just ready for burning!" said the black man, with a growl of triumph. "You see I am likely to have a good stock of firewood for winter."

"But what right have you," said Tom, "to cut down Deacon Peabody's timber?"

"The right of a prior claim," said the other. "This woodland belonged to me long before one of your whitefaced race put foot upon the soil."

"And pray, who are you, if I may be so bold?" said Tom.

"Oh, I go by various names. I am the wild huntsman in some countries; the black miner in others. In this neighborhood I am known by the name of the black woodsman. I am he to whom the red men consecrated this spot, and in honor of whom they now and then roasted a white man, by way of sweet-smelling sacrifice. Since the red men have been exterminated by you white savages, I amuse myself by presiding at the persecutions of Quakers and Anabaptists;[5] I am the great patron and prompter of slave dealers, and the grandmaster of the Salem witches."

"The upshot of all which is that, if I mistake not," said Tom, sturdily, "you are he commonly called Old Scratch."

"The same, at your service!" replied the black man, with a half-civil nod.

Such was the opening of this interview, according to the old story; though it has almost

---

5. **Quakers and Anabaptists:** two religious groups that were often persecuted for their beliefs.

too familiar an air to be credited. One would think that to meet with such a singular personage, in this wild, lonely place, would have shaken any man's nerves; but Tom was a hard-minded fellow, not easily daunted, and he had lived so long with a termagant wife that he did not even fear the Devil.

It is said that after this commencement they had a long and earnest conversation together as Tom returned homeward. The black man told him of great sums of money buried by Kidd the pirate under the oak trees on the high ridge, not far from the morass. All these were under his command, and protected by his power, so that none could find them but such as propitiated[6] his favor. These he offered to place within Tom Walker's reach, having conceived an especial kindness for him; but they were to be had only on certain conditions. What these conditions were may be easily surmised, though Tom never disclosed them publicly. They must have been very hard, for he required time to think of them, and he was not a man to stick at trifles when money was in view. When they had reached the edge of the swamp, the stranger paused. "What proof have I that all you have been telling me is true?" said Tom. "There's my signature," said the black man, pressing his finger on Tom's forehead. So saying, he turned off among the thickets of the swamp and seemed, as Tom said, to go down, down, down into the earth, until nothing but his head and shoulders could be seen, and so on, until he totally disappeared.

When Tom reached home, he found the black print of a finger burned, as it were, into his forehead, which nothing could obliterate.

The first news his wife had to tell him was the sudden death of Absalom Crowninshield, the rich buccaneer. It was announced in the papers with the usual flourish that "a great man had fallen in Israel."[7]

Tom recollected the tree which his black friend had just hewn down, and which was ready for burning. "Let the freebooter roast," said Tom. "Who cares!" He now felt convinced that all he had heard and seen was no illusion.

He was not prone to let his wife into his confidence; but as this was an uneasy secret, he willingly shared it with her. All her avarice was awakened at the mention of hidden gold, and she urged her husband to comply with the black man's terms and secure what would make them wealthy for life. However Tom might have felt disposed to sell himself to the Devil, he was determined not to do so to oblige his wife; so he flatly refused, out of the mere spirit of contradiction. Many and bitter were the quarrels they had on the subject; but the more she talked, the more resolute was Tom not to be damned to please her.

At length she determined to drive the bargain on her own account, and if she succeeded, to keep all the gain to herself. Being of the

---

6. **propitiated** [prə pish′ē āt id]: earned, gained.
7. **Israel:** II Samuel 3 : 38. The Puritans traditionally called New England "Israel," their Promised Land.

same fearless temper as her husband, she set off for the old Indian fort towards the close of a summer's day. She was many hours absent. When she came back, she was reserved and sullen in her replies. She spoke something of a black man, whom she had met about twilight hewing at the root of a tall tree. He was sulky, however, and would not come to terms: she was to go again with a propitiatory offering, but what it was she forbore to say.

The next evening she set off again for the swamp, with her apron heavily laden. Tom waited and waited for her, but in vain; midnight came, but she did not make her appearance: morning, noon, night returned, but still she did not come. Tom now grew uneasy for her safety, especially as he found she had carried off in her apron the silver teapot and spoons, and every portable article of value. Another night elapsed, another morning came; but no wife. In a word, she was never heard of more.

What was her real fate nobody knows, in consequence of so many pretending to know. It is one of those facts which have become confounded by a variety of historians. Some asserted that she lost her way among the tangled mazes of the swamp and sank into some pit or slough; others, more uncharitable, hinted that she had eloped with the household booty and made off to some other province; while others surmised that the tempter had decoyed her into a dismal quagmire, on the top of which her hat was found lying. In confirmation of this, it was said a great black man, with an ax on his shoulder, was seen late that very evening coming out of the swamp, carrying a bundle tied in a check apron, with an air of surly triumph.

The most current and probable story, however, observes that Tom Walker grew so anxious about the fate of his wife and his property that he set out at length to seek them both at the Indian fort. During a long summer's afternoon he searched about the gloomy place, but no wife was to be seen. He called her name repeatedly, but she was nowhere to be heard. The bittern alone responded to his voice as he

flew screaming by; or the bullfrog croaked dolefully from a neighboring pool. At length, it is said, just in the brown hour of twilight, when the owls began to hoot, and the bats to flit about, his attention was attracted by the clamor of carrion crows hovering about a cypress tree. He looked up and beheld a bundle tied in a check apron and hanging in the branches of the tree, with a great vulture perched hard by, as if keeping watch upon it. He leaped with joy; for he recognized his wife's apron, and supposed it to contain the household valuables.

"Let us get hold of the property," said he consolingly to himself, "and we will endeavor to do without the woman."

As he scrambled up the tree, the vulture spread its wide wings and sailed off, screaming, into the deep shadows of the forest. Tom seized the checked apron, but, woeful sight! found nothing but a heart and liver tied up in it!

Such, according to this most authentic old story, was all that was to be found of Tom's wife. She had probably attempted to deal with the black man as she had been accustomed to deal with her husband; but though a female scold is generally considered a match for the Devil, yet in this instance she appears to have had the worst of it. She must have died game, however; for it is said Tom noticed many prints of cloven feet deeply stamped about the tree, and found handfuls of hair that looked as if they had been plucked from the coarse black shock of the woodman. Tom knew his wife's prowess by experience. He shrugged his shoulders, as he looked at the signs of a fierce clapperclawing. "Egad," said he to himself, "Old Scratch must have had a tough time of it!"

Tom consoled himself for the loss of his property with the loss of his wife, for he was a man of fortitude. He even felt something like gratitude towards the black woodman, who, he considered, had done him a kindness. He sought, therefore, to cultivate a further acquaintance with him, but for some time without success; the old blacklegs played shy, for whatever people may think, he is not always to be had for calling for: he knows how to play his cards when pretty sure of his game.

At length, it is said, when delay had whetted Tom's eagerness to the quick and prepared him to agree to anything rather than not gain the promised treasure, he met the black man one evening in his usual woodman's dress, with his ax on his shoulder, sauntering along the swamp and humming a tune. He affected to receive Tom's advances with great indifference, made brief replies, and went on humming his tune.

By degrees, however, Tom brought him to business, and they began to haggle about the terms on which the former was to have the pirate's treasure. There was one condition which need not be mentioned, being generally understood in all cases where the Devil grants favors; but there were others about which, though of less importance, he was inflexibly obstinate. He insisted that the money found through his means should be employed in his service. He proposed, therefore, that Tom should employ it in the black traffic; that is to say, that he should fit out a slave ship. This, however, Tom resolutely refused: he was bad enough in all conscience, but the Devil himself could not tempt him to turn slave trader.

Finding Tom so squeamish on this point, he did not insist upon it, but proposed, instead, that he should turn usurer,[8] the Devil being extremely anxious for the increase of usurers, looking upon them as his peculiar[9] people.

To this no objections were made, for it was just to Tom's taste.

"You shall open a broker's shop in Boston next month," said the black man.

"I'll do it tomorrow, if you wish," said Tom Walker.

"You shall lend money at two per cent a month."

"Egad, I'll charge four!" replied Tom Walker.

"You shall extort bonds, foreclose mortgages, drive the merchants to bankruptcy—"

"I'll drive them to the d——l," cried Tom Walker.

"You are the usurer for my money!" said blacklegs with delight. "When will you want the rhino?"[10]

"This very night."

"Done!" said the Devil.

"Done!" said Tom Walker. So they shook hands and struck a bargain.

A few days' time saw Tom Walker seated behind his desk in a countinghouse in Boston.

His reputation for a ready-moneyed man who would lend money out for a good consideration soon spread abroad. Everybody remembers the time of Governor Belcher,[11] when money was particularly scarce. It was a time of paper credit. The country had been deluged with government bills; the famous Land Bank[12] had been established; there had been a rage for speculating; the people had run mad with schemes for new settlements, for building cities in the wilderness; land jobbers[13] went about with maps of grants and townships and El Dorados,[14] lying nobody knew where, but which everybody was ready to purchase. In a word, the great speculating fever which breaks out every now and then in the country had raged to an alarming degree, and everybody was dreaming of making sudden fortunes from nothing. As usual the fever had subsided; the dream had gone off, and the imaginary fortunes with it; the patients were left in doleful plight, and the whole country resounded with the consequent cry of "hard times."

At this propitious time of public distress did Tom Walker set up as usurer in Boston.

8. **usurer** [ū′zhər ər]: one who lends money at an unfair interest rate.
9. **peculiar**: special.

10. **rhino** [rī′nō]: slang for "money."
11. **Governor Belcher**: Jonathan Belcher, governor of Massachusetts and New Hampshire from 1730 to 1741.
12. **Land Bank**: bank that loaned money to people based on mortgages controlled by the bank.
13. **land jobbers**: people who bought and sold undeveloped land as a speculation.
14. **El Dorados** [el′də rä′dōs]: places of fabulous wealth. Explorers had searched for the legendary place the Spanish called El Dorado, "the golden one."

His door was soon thronged by customers. The needy and adventurous, the gambling speculator, the dreaming land jobber, the thriftless tradesman, the merchant with cracked credit, in short, everyone driven to raise money by desperate means and desperate sacrifices hurried to Tom Walker.

Thus Tom was the universal friend of the needy, and acted like a "friend in need"; that is to say, he always exacted good pay and good security. In proportion to the distress of the applicant was the hardness of his terms. He accumulated bonds and mortgages, gradually squeezed his customers closer and closer, and sent them at length, dry as a sponge, from his door.

In this way he made money hand over hand, became a rich and mighty man, and exalted his cocked hat upon 'Change.[15] He built himself, as usual, a vast house, out of ostentation; but left the greater part of it unfinished and unfurnished, out of parsimony. He even set up a carriage in the fullness of his vainglory, though he nearly starved the horses which drew it; and as the ungreased wheels groaned and screeched on the axletrees, you would have thought you heard the souls of the poor debtors he was squeezing.

As Tom waxed old, however, he grew thoughtful. Having secured the good things of this world, he began to feel anxious about those of the next. He thought with regret on the bargain he had made with his black friend, and set his wits to work to cheat him out of the conditions. He became, therefore, all of a sudden, a violent churchgoer. He prayed loudly and strenuously, as if heaven were to be taken by force of lungs. Indeed, one might always tell when he had sinned most during the week by the clamor of his Sunday devotion. The quiet Christians who had been modestly and steadfastly traveling Zionward[16] were struck with self-reproach at seeing themselves so suddenly outstripped in their career by this new-made convert. Tom was as rigid in religious as in money matters; he was a stern supervisor and censurer of his neighbors, and seemed to think every sin entered up to their account became a credit on his own side of the page. He even talked of the expediency of reviving the persecution of Quakers and Anabaptists. In a word, Tom's zeal became as notorious as his riches.

Still, in spite of all this strenuous attention to forms, Tom had a lurking dread that the Devil, after all, would have his due. That he might not be taken unawares, therefore, it is said he always carried a small Bible in his coat pocket. He had also a great folio Bible on his countinghouse desk, and would frequently be found reading it when people called on business; on such occasions he would lay his green spectacles in the book, to mark the place, while he turned round to drive some usurious bargain.

Some say that Tom grew a little crack-brained in his old days, and that, fancying his end approaching, he had his horse new shod, saddled and bridled, and buried with his feet uppermost; because he supposed that at the last day the world would be turned upside down, in which case he should find his horse standing ready for mounting, and he was determined at the worst to give his old friend a run for it. This, however, is probably a mere old wives' fable. If he really did take such a precaution, it was totally superfluous; at least so says the authentic old legend, which closes his story in the following manner.

One hot summer afternoon in the dog days, just as a terrible black thunder-gust was coming up, Tom sat in his countinghouse, in his white linen cap and India silk morning gown. He was on the point of foreclosing a mortgage, by which he would complete the ruin of an unlucky land speculator for whom he had professed the greatest friendship. The poor land jobber begged him to grant a few months' indulgence. Tom had grown testy and irritated, and refused another day.

"My family will be ruined, and brought

---

15. **'Change:** the Exchange, where merchants and bankers met to do business.
16. **Zionward:** toward Heaven.

upon the parish," said the land jobber. "Charity begins at home," replied Tom; "I must take care of myself in these hard times."

"You have made so much money out of me," said the speculator.

Tom lost his patience and his piety. "The Devil take me," said he, "if I have made a farthing!"

Just then there were three loud knocks at the street door. He stepped out to see who was there. A black man was holding a black horse, which neighed and stamped with impatience.

"Tom, you're come for," said the black fellow gruffly. Tom shrank back, but too late. He had left his little Bible at the bottom of his coat pocket, and his big Bible on the desk buried under the mortgage he was about to foreclose: never was sinner taken more unawares. The black man whisked him like a child into the saddle, gave the horse the lash, and away he galloped, with Tom on his back, in the midst of the thunderstorm. The clerks stuck their pens behind their ears and stared after him from the windows. Away went Tom Walker, dashing down the streets, his white

cap bobbing up and down, his morning gown fluttering in the wind, and his steed striking fire out of the pavement at every bound. When the clerks turned to look for the black man, he had disappeared.

Tom Walker never returned to foreclose the mortgage. A countryman who lived on the border of the swamp reported that in the height of the thunder-gust he had heard a great clattering of hoofs and a howling along the road, and, running to the window, caught sight of a figure such as I have described, on a horse that galloped like mad across the fields, over the hills, and down into the black hemlock swamp towards the old Indian fort; and that shortly after a thunderbolt falling in that direction seemed to set the whole forest in a blaze.

The good people of Boston shook their heads and shrugged their shoulders, but had been so much accustomed to witches and goblins and tricks of the Devil, in all kinds of shapes, from the first settlement of the colony, that they were not so much horror-struck as might have been expected. Trustees were appointed to take charge of Tom's effects. There was nothing, however, to administer upon. On searching his coffers, all his bonds and mortgages were found reduced to cinders. In place of gold and silver, his iron chest was filled with chips and shavings; two skeletons lay in his stable instead of his half-starved horses, and the very next day his great house took fire and was burned to the ground.

Such was the end of Tom Walker and his ill-gotten wealth. Let all griping money brokers lay this story to heart. The truth of it is not to be doubted. The very hole under the oak trees, whence he dug Kidd's money, is to be seen to this day; and the neighboring swamp and old Indian fort are often haunted in stormy nights by a figure on horseback, in morning gown and white cap, which is doubtless the troubled spirit of the usurer. In fact, the story has resolved itself into a proverb, and is the origin of that popular saying, so prevalent throughout New England, of "The Devil and Tom Walker."

Recalling

1. What adjectives in the second paragraph describe Tom and his wife?
2. Why does Tom refuse the Devil's offer at first? As a result, what does Tom's wife do? What does Tom find when he looks for her?
3. In addition to the "one condition which need not be mentioned," what does Tom agree to do in return for the treasure?
4. According to page 111, what sort of man does Tom become after his pact with the Devil? Why does he build a big house? Why does he leave it unfinished?
5. As Tom grows old, about what does he grow anxious?
6. What does Tom say to the poor land jobber? What are Tom's last words? What becomes of his possessions?

Interpreting

7. What character trait of the Walkers is reinforced by the descriptions of their house and horse in the second paragraph? Does this trait later change? Explain.
8. What is the "one condition which need not be mentioned" (page 110)?
9. Why are Tom's last words ironic?
10. Identify in the story two elements of Romanticism described in the introduction to this unit. Which details make the story an American tale, despite its age-old theme?

Extending

11. What would you say are some of the positive human traits not possessed by Tom and his wife that Irving wants us to think about?

VIEWPOINT

Literary critic Lewis Leary points out that although Irving spent many years in other countries, he saw his own country clearly.

With quick eye, ready tongue, and alert recognition of absurdities, he sits quietly at both ends of the American literary spectrum—an expatriate seeking reverently in Europe for sources of culture, but . . . most effective in realizing American characters enmeshed in American ideals.

—*Washington Irving*

What qualities of Tom and his wife seem to you to be common to people of all places? What qualities seem to be particularly American? What do you think makes these two characters become victims of their "ideals"?

LITERARY FOCUS

Narration

Narration is writing that tells a story, moving from event to event, usually in chronological order. A narrative may be factual, like William Bradford's *Of Plymouth Plantation* (which appears on page 24), or fictional, like "The Devil and Tom Walker."

Sometimes a fictional narrative will have elements that make it seem factual. In "The Devil and Tom Walker" Irving uses the narrator of the story, Diedrich Knickerbocker, to help make his fictional narrative seem like fact.

Knickerbocker is supposed to be a historian, and so his reputation lends the story believability. He uses expressions like "this most authentic old story" to make us believe that this outlandish tale actually happened. He cites his sources of information and even tells us that there are a few details of which he is not quite sure (implying that everything else is absolutely correct). These devices give the narrative the ring of truth.

Thinking About Narration

■ Find two other examples in the story of "evidence" presented by the narrator to make us believe that his fictional narrative is a true story.

COMPOSITION

Summarizing a Narrative

■ Tell the story of Tom Walker and his wife in one paragraph. Include all the major events in the story and omit unimportant details. Make your sentences move smoothly from event to event, creating one connected narrative.

Retelling from a Different Point of View

■ Retell the story of Tom Walker using Mrs. Walker as the narrator. Cover only the events up to the point of her disappearance. Remember to consider her personality, the events she witnesses, her relationship to Tom, and her final meeting with Old Scratch.

James Fenimore Cooper 1789–1851

Although James Fenimore Cooper is best remembered for his novels of the American frontier, he himself never experienced the danger and struggle of pioneer life. The son of a wealthy judge, Cooper grew up in Cooperstown, a settlement established by his father in New York State. By 1789, however, the frontier had moved farther west, and there were few pioneers left. "I was never among the Indians," Cooper admitted. "All that I know of them is from reading, and from hearing my father speak of them." From his home Cooper watched wagon trains heading west; he left the rest up to his imagination.

After several years as a sailor and then as an officer, Cooper married and settled down to the life of a gentleman farmer with money inherited from his father. Tradition says that one day he tossed aside the British novel he was reading and exclaimed to his wife, "I could write a better book myself." She challenged him to do so, and Cooper produced a sentimental novel, *Precaution.* Determined to improve, he wrote a tale of the Revolution, *The Spy,* which became a great success in America and Europe.

In 1823 Cooper published *The Pioneers,* the first of the Leatherstocking Tales, five novels centering around the career of the frontiersman Natty Bumppo. Natty has many names—Leatherstocking, Deerslayer, Pathfinder—but his character never changes. He is strong, brave, resourceful, independent, and absolutely honorable, with a profound understanding of nature. The five novels—*The Deerslayer, The Last of the Mohicans, The Pathfinder, The Prairie,* and *The Pioneers*—make up an American epic, chronicling the westward march of civilization and the destruction of the wilderness.

Cooper went on to write over thirty novels, including eleven exciting adventures of the sea. His plots were often improbable and his language unrealistic, but he charged his works with an energy that made them immensely popular. He created the American historical novel, using authentic American subjects. He infused those subjects with a spirit of chivalry and romanticism like that of the British novelist Sir Walter Scott—complete with heroes and villains, picturesque settings, extraordinary adventures, and a profound love of country.

In Natty Bumppo, Cooper did what few writers ever succeed in doing: He created a character so original and so influential that it became a myth. Natty is the title character in *The Deerslayer.* At the time of the story, he is an untried youth, but one who already possesses qualities that would become typical of the American hero.

James Fenimore Cooper

from **The Deerslayer**

The incidents of this tale occurred between the years 1740 and 1745, when the settled portions of the colony of New York were confined to the four Atlantic counties, a narrow belt of country on each side of the Hudson, extending from its mouth to the falls near its head, and to a few advanced "neighborhoods" on the Mohawk and the Schoharie. Broad belts of the virgin wilderness not only reached the shores of the first river, but they even crossed it, stretching away into New England, and affording forest covers to the noiseless moccasin of the native warrior as he trod the secret and bloody warpath. A bird's-eye view of the whole region east of the Mississippi must then have offered one vast expanse of woods, relieved by a comparatively narrow fringe of cultivation along the sea, dotted by the glittering surfaces of lakes, and intersected by the waving lines of rivers. In such a vast picture of solemn solitude, the district of country we design to paint sinks into insignificance, though we feel encouraged to proceed by the conviction that, with slight and immaterial distinctions, he who succeeds in giving an accurate idea of any portion of this wild region must necessarily convey a tolerably correct notion of the whole.

Whatever may be the changes produced by man, the eternal round of the seasons is unbroken. Summer and winter, seedtime and harvest, return in their stated order with a sublime precision, affording to man one of the noblest of all the occasions he enjoys of proving the high powers of his far-reaching mind, in compassing[1] the laws that control their exact uniformity, and in calculating their never-ending revolutions. Centuries of summer suns had warmed the tops of the same noble oaks and pines, sending their heats even to the te-

nacious roots, when voices were heard calling to each other in the depths of a forest, of which the leafy surface lay bathed in the brilliant light of a cloudless day in June, while the trunks of the trees rose in gloomy grandeur in the shades beneath. The calls were in different tones, evidently proceeding from two men who had lost their way and were searching in different directions for their path. At length a shout proclaimed success, and presently a man of gigantic mold broke out of the tangled labyrinth of a small swamp, emerging into an opening that appeared to have been formed partly by the ravages of the wind, and partly by those of fire. This little area, which afforded a good view of the sky, although it was pretty well filled with dead trees, lay on the side of one of the high hills, or low mountains, into which nearly the whole surface of the adjacent country was broken.

"Here is room to breathe in!" exclaimed the liberated forester as soon as he found himself under a clear sky, shaking his huge frame like a mastiff[2] that has just escaped from a snowbank: "Hurrah! Deerslayer; here is daylight at last, and yonder is the lake."

These words were scarcely uttered when the second forester dashed aside the bushes of the swamp and appeared in the area. After making a hurried adjustment of his arms and disordered dress, he joined his companion, who had already begun his dispositions for a halt.

"Do you know this spot?" demanded the one called Deerslayer, "or do you shout at the sight of the sun?"

"Both, lad, both; I know the spot, and am not sorry to see so useful a friend as the sun. Now we have got the p'ints of the compass in our minds once more, and 'twill be our own

---

1. **compassing:** understanding.

2. **mastiff:** large, powerful dog.

faults if we let anything turn them topsy-turvy ag'in as has just happened. My name is not Hurry Harry, if this be not the very spot where the land hunters 'camped the last summer and passed a week. See, yonder are the dead bushes of their bower, and here is the spring. Much as I like the sun, boy, I've no occasion for it to tell me it is noon; this stomach of mine is as good a timepiece as is to be found in the colony, and it already p'ints to half-past twelve. So open the wallet,[3] and let us wind up for another six hours' run."

At this suggestion, both set themselves about making the preparations necessary for their usual frugal but hearty meal. We will profit by this pause in the discourse to give the reader some idea of the appearance of the men, each of whom is destined to enact no insignificant part in our legend. It would not have been easy to find a more noble specimen of vigorous manhood than was offered in the person of him who called himself Hurry Harry. His real name was Henry March; but the frontiermen having caught the practice of giving *sobriquets*[4] from the Indians, the appellation of Hurry was far oftener applied to him than his proper designation, and not infrequently he was termed Hurry Skurry, a nickname he had obtained from a dashing, reckless, offhand manner, and a physical restlessness that kept him so constantly on the move as to cause him to be known along the whole line of scattered habitations that lay between the province and the Canadas. The stature of Hurry Harry exceeded six feet four, and, being unusually well-proportioned, his strength fully realized the idea created by his gigantic frame. The face did no discredit to the rest of the man, for it was both good-humored and handsome. His air was free, and, though his manner necessarily partook of the rudeness of a border life, the grandeur that pervaded so noble a physique prevented it from becoming altogether vulgar.

Deerslayer, as Hurry called his companion, was a very different person in appearance, as well as in character. In stature he stood about six feet in his moccasins, but his frame was comparatively light and slender, showing muscles, however, that promised unusual agility, if not unusual strength. His face would have had little to recommend it except youth, were it not for an expression that seldom failed to win upon those who had leisure to examine it and to yield to the feeling of confidence it created. This expression was simply that of guileless truth, sustained by an earnestness of purpose and a sincerity of feeling that rendered it remarkable. At times this air of integrity seemed to be so simple as to awaken the suspicion of a want of the usual means to discriminate between artifice and truth; but few came in serious contact with the man without losing this distrust in respect for his opinions and motives.

Both these frontiermen were still young, Hurry having reached the age of six- or eight-and-twenty, while Deerslayer was several years his junior. Their attire needs no particular description, though it may be well to add that it was composed in no small degree of dressed deerskins, and had the usual signs of belonging to those who pass their time between the skirts of civilized society and the boundless forests. There was, notwithstanding, some attention to smartness and the picturesque in the arrangements of Deerslayer's dress more particularly in the part connected with his arms and accouterments. His rifle was in perfect condition, the handle of his hunting knife was neatly carved, his powder horn was ornamented with suitable devices lightly cut into the material, and his shot pouch was decorated with wampum. On the other hand, Hurry Harry, either from constitutional recklessness or from a secret consciousness how little his appearance required artificial aids, wore everything in a careless, slovenly manner, as if he felt a noble scorn for the trifling accessories of dress and ornaments. Perhaps the peculiar effect of his

---

3. **wallet:** knapsack.
4. *sobriquets* [sō′ brə kā′]: French for "nicknames."

fine form and great stature was increased, rather than lessened, by this unstudied and disdainful air of indifference.

"Come, Deerslayer, fall to, and prove that you have a Delaware[5] stomach, as you say you have had a Delaware edication," cried Hurry, setting the example by opening his mouth to receive a slice of cold venison steak that would have made an entire meal for a European peasant; "fall to, lad, and prove your manhood on this poor devil of a doe with your teeth, as you've already done with your rifle."

"Nay, nay, Hurry, there's little manhood in killing a doe, and that too out of season; though there might be some in bringing down a painter[6] or a catamount,[7] returned the other, disposing himself to comply. "The Delawares have given me my name not so much on account of a bold heart, as on account of a quick eye and an active foot. There may not be any cowardice in overcoming a deer, but sartain it is, there's no great valor."

"The Delawares themselves are no heroes," muttered Hurry through his teeth, the mouth being too full to permit it to be fairly opened, "or they would never have allowed them loping vagabonds, the Mingos,[8] to make them women."

"That matter is not rightly understood—has never been rightly explained," said Deerslayer earnestly, for he was as zealous a friend as his companion was dangerous as an enemy; "the Mengwe[9] fill the woods with their lies, and misconstruct words and treaties. I have now lived ten years with the Delawares, and know them to be as manful as any other nation when the proper time to strike comes."

------

5. **Delaware:** Indian of the Delaware River Valley.
6. **painter:** in Deerslayer's dialect, a panther or cougar.
7. **catamount** [kat′ə mount]: wild cat, such as a puma.
8. **Mingos:** Delaware name for the Iroquois, meaning "the treacherous."
9. **Mengwe:** variant of *Mingo.*

"Harkee, Master Deerslayer, since we are on the subject, we may as well open our minds to each other in a man-to-man way; answer me one question. You have had so much luck among the game as to have gotten a title, it would seem, but did you ever hit anything human or intelligible: did you ever pull trigger on an inimy that was capable of pulling one upon you?"

This question produced a singular collision between mortification and correct feeling in the bosom of the youth that was easily to be traced in the workings of his ingenuous countenance. The struggle was short, however, uprightness of heart soon getting the better of false pride and frontier boastfulness.

"To own the truth, I never did," answered Deerslayer, "seeing that a fitting occasion never offered. The Delawares have been peaceable since my sojourn with 'em, and I hold it to be onlawful to take the life of man, except in open and generous warfare."

"What! did you never find a fellow thieving among your traps and skins, and do the law on him, with your own hands, by way of saving the magistrates trouble in the settlements, and the rogue himself the cost of the suit?"

"I am no trapper, Hurry," returned the young man proudly: "I live by the rifle, a we'pon at which I will not turn my back on any man of my years atween the Hudson and the St. Lawrence. I never offer a skin that has not a hole in its head besides them which natur' made to see with or to breathe through."

". . . I shall not frequent your society long, friend Natty, unless you look higher than four-footed beasts to practice your rifle on."

"Our journey is nearly ended, you say, Master March, and we can part tonight, if you see occasion. I have a fri'nd waiting for me who will think it no disgrace to consort with a fellow creatur' that has never yet slain his kind."

STUDY QUESTIONS

Recalling

1. What "bird's-eye view" of the region east of the Mississippi does the first paragraph provide? In the second paragraph locate a description that tells of the timeless, unspoiled environment in which the narrative takes place.
2. In paragraphs 3–6 who are the two characters we find in the woods and what do they set about doing?
3. According to the seventh paragraph, what kind of "specimen" is Harry? According to the eighth paragraph, how is Deerslayer different from Harry? What makes Deerslayer's expression "remarkable"?
4. Who educated Deerslayer? How did he acquire his nickname?
5. On what three subjects do Harry and Deerslayer disagree in the last nine paragraphs?

Interpreting

6. Who killed the doe that Deerslayer and Harry eat? What is that marksman's attitude toward slaying a doe?
7. Identify at least three character traits that make Deerslayer admirable or heroic. In comparison, what sort of person is Harry?
8. Judging from the first two paragraphs, what is the author's attitude toward nature? Identify the other elements of Romanticism the narrative contains (see the Introduction to this unit).

Extending

9. Most of Cooper's readers lived in towns and cities. Why would a romance of the wilderness such as The Deerslayer appeal to them?

LITERARY FOCUS

The American Language: Dialect

A few years after Cooper began his Leatherstocking Tales, Noah Webster published the first specifically American dictionary, The American Dictionary of the English Language (1828). Americans were becoming aware that their language was beginning to differ from the English written and spoken in England.

Today British and American English differ somewhat in both pronunciation and vocabulary. For example, when the British speak of the "bonnet" of a car, they mean what we call the "hood."

Similarly, differences in vocabulary and pronunciation grew up within different regions of the United States.

These various ways of speaking and writing particular to a specific region of the country are called **dialects.** Some people, for example, say skillet, while others say frying pan. Some pronounce root to rhyme with toot; some pronounce it to rhyme with foot.

American writers have always taken pleasure in recording American dialects. In The Deerslayer Cooper writes atween for between, and p'ints for points. In later units of this book, Mark Twain, Bret Harte, and Willa Cather use dialects very effectively in their short stories. The use of written dialects helps us to imagine speaking voices more accurately and to understand characters more fully. It brings characters to life, even though we may occasionally need a footnote to tell us that a painter is a panther.

Thinking About Dialect

Find three other words in The Deerslayer that are examples of Deerslayer's and Harry's dialect. Tell what the words mean, and indicate which words you would use in their places if you were speaking.

COMPOSITION

Writing About a Quotation

In The Deerslayer Natty says, "I hold it to be onlawful to take the life of man, except in open and generous warfare." Write a composition discussing what this quotation tells about the hero. First tell why it is significant that Deerslayer cares about what is unlawful and what is not. Then discuss the meaning of the unusual phrase "generous warfare." Conclude with a general statement of how this sentence reflects Natty's whole character. For help with this assignment, refer to Lesson 5 in the Writing About Literature Handbook at the back of this book.

Writing a Description of a Hero

Write a description of a contemporary American hero. Take your hero from literature or from real life. You may want to organize your description by asking these questions: What does the hero look like? What is the hero's personality? What qualities make him or her a hero?

William Cullen Bryant   *1794–1878*

William Cullen Bryant, the "father of American poetry," grew up in a small village in western Massachusetts. He began writing when he was very young, composing devout religious poems and even publishing one when he was thirteen. Bryant's father encouraged him to continue writing poetry but recommended that he become a lawyer in order to make a living.

After a short time as a lawyer, however, Bryant began a career as one of the nation's most distinguished journalists. He became the editor-in-chief of the influential *New York Evening Post* and used his position to put forth his strong political and social views. He supported the early labor movement, free speech, a free press, and the abolition of slavery. He was instrumental in Lincoln's election to the presidency; in fact, it was Bryant who introduced Lincoln to the voters of New York. For the last thirty years of his life, Bryant was New York City's most prominent citizen, yet he continued to write poetry. His noble and romantic verses, often based on the American landscape, established him as the first American poet to have an enduring reputation. At his death, New York City's flags flew at half-mast.

Bryant probably wrote "Thanatopsis" when he was about nineteen. Several years later his father sent it to the *North American Review,* an important Boston literary magazine. When it was published—anonymously, according to the custom of the magazine—readers could not believe that it had been written by a young man, or even by an American. Even the editors of the magazine thought that Bryant's father had actually written it. As successful as the poem was, Bryant later revised it. He added the beginning section (lines 1–17) and the ending (lines 66–81).

The title of the poem is a Greek word meaning "view of death." The poem is, however, much more than that. "Thanatopsis," which begins on the following page, is a Romantic poet's vision of what it means to be a human being—to be both a mortal individual and a part of enduring nature.

William Cullen Bryant

Thanatopsis

To him who in the love of Nature holds
Communion with her visible forms, she speaks
A various language; for his gayer hours
She has a voice of gladness, and a smile
5 And eloquence of beauty, and she glides
Into his darker musings, with a mild
And healing sympathy, that steals away
Their sharpness, ere[1] he is aware. When thoughts
Of the last bitter hour come like a blight
10 Over thy spirit, and sad images
Of the stern agony, and shroud, and pall,
And breathless darkness, and the narrow house,[2]
Make thee to shudder, and grow sick at heart—
Go forth, under the open sky, and list
15 To Nature's teachings, while from all around—
Earth and her waters, and the depths of air—
Comes a still voice.

      Yet a few days, and thee
The all-beholding sun shall see no more
In all his course; nor yet in the cold ground,
20 Where thy pale form was laid, with many tears,
Nor in the embrace of ocean, shall exist
Thy image. Earth, that nourished thee, shall claim
Thy growth, to be resolved to earth again,
And, lost each human trace, surrendering up
25 Thine individual being, shalt thou go
To mix forever with the elements,
To be a brother to the insensible rock
And to the sluggish clod, which the rude swain[3]
Turns with his share[4] and treads upon. The oak
30 Shall send his roots abroad, and pierce thy mold.

 Yet not to thine eternal resting place
Shalt thou retire alone, nor couldst thou wish
Couch[5] more magnificent. Thou shalt lie down
With patriarchs of the infant world—with kings,

---

1. **ere** [âr]: before.
2. **narrow house:** coffin.
3. **swain:** country youth.
4. **share:** plowshare.
5. **Couch:** bed.

Kindred Spirits, 1849, Asher B. Durand.
Bryant and the painter Thomas Cole share
their Romantic awe of nature.

35　The powerful of the earth—the wise, the good,
　　Fair forms, and hoary seers of ages past,
　　All in one mighty sepulcher. The hills
　　Rock-ribbed and ancient as the sun—the vales
　　Stretching in pensive quietness between;
40　The venerable woods—rivers that move
　　In majesty, and the complaining brooks
　　That make the meadows green; and, poured round all,
　　Old Ocean's gray and melancholy waste—
　　Are but the solemn decorations all
45　Of the great tomb of man. The golden sun,
　　The planets, all the infinite host of heaven,
　　Are shining on the sad abodes of death,
　　Through the still lapse of ages. All that tread
　　The globe are but a handful to the tribes
50　That slumber in its bosom. Take the wings
　　Of morning,[6] pierce the Barcan wilderness,[7]
　　Or lose thyself in the continuous woods
　　Where rolls the Oregon[8] and hears no sound,
　　Save his own dashings—yet the dead are there:
55　And millions in those solitudes, since first
　　The flight of years began, have laid them down
　　In their last sleep—the dead reign there alone.
　　So shalt thou rest, and what if thou withdraw
　　In silence from the living, and no friend
60　Take note of thy departure? All that breathe
　　Will share thy destiny. The gay will laugh
　　When thou art gone, the solemn brood of care
　　Plod on, and each one as before will chase
　　His favorite phantom; yet all these shall leave
65　Their mirth and their employments, and shall come
　　And make their bed with thee. As the long train
　　Of ages glides away, the sons of men,
　　The youth in life's fresh spring, and he who goes
　　In the full strength of years, matron and maid,
70　The speechless babe, and the gray-headed man—

---

6. **Take . . . morning:** from Psalm 139 : 9, in which
the psalmist sings of flying away to distant places.
7. **Barcan** [bär′kən] **wilderness:** the deserts of Barca
in North Africa.
8. **Oregon:** American Indian name for the Columbia
River.

William Cullen Bryant **121**

Shall one by one be gathered to thy side,
By those, who in their turn shall follow them.

So live, that when thy summons comes to join
The innumerable caravan, which moves
75 To that mysterious realm where each shall take
His chamber in the silent halls of death,
Thou go not, like the quarry-slave at night,
Scourged to his dungeon, but, sustained and soothed
By an unfaltering trust, approach thy grave,
80 Like one who wraps the drapery of his couch
About him, and lies down to pleasant dreams.

STUDY QUESTIONS

Recalling

1. According to lines 1–8, to whom does nature speak? To what two different human moods does nature respond?

2. What do lines 14–17 recommend to those who "grow sick at heart" when they think of death?

3. According to lines 22–30, what will happen to all people? What two points should people remember, according to lines 31–33?

4. What do lines 61–66 tell the readers will happen after their own deaths?

5. What simile does Bryant use in lines 80–81 to suggest the way the reader should "approach thy grave"?

Interpreting

6. What lesson about death does the poet expect us to learn from closely observing nature? What is the overall relationship between human beings and nature, according to the poet?

7. What comforting observation about human experience does the poet make repeatedly throughout the poem (lines 31–32, 48–50, 60–61, 64–66, 70–72, and 75–76)?

8. With what emotion does Bryant suggest people face death?

9. In what way does the subject matter of the poem reflect the Romantic interest in the self, or the individual?

Extending

10. Poets often use the image of the *seasons of human life.* Tell in your own words what this expression means. How does the image of human seasons reflect the central idea of Bryant's poem?

VIEWPOINT

In his biography of Bryant, critic Charles H. Brown writes:

> To him, as he said in his lectures on poetry, "the great spring of poetry is emotion." . . . Nevertheless, Bryant's practice in composition was not to warble as a bird does, for he held that poetry not only appeals to "the passions and the imagination" but also to the understanding.   —*William Cullen Bryant*

■ Find at least two passages in "Thanatopsis" that show how Bryant blends emotions and ideas. First find a controlled and thoughtful presentation of a feeling; then find an emotional presentation of an idea.

LITERARY FOCUS

Meter

All writing has rhythm. Rhythm simply means the arrangement of stressed and unstressed syllables in a work. Only poetry, however, has meter. **Meter** is a regular rhythm—that is, stressed and unstressed syllables in an arrangement that has a pattern. Meter is an important element of most poetry written before the twentieth century, and studying a poem's meter can help us appreciate the craft and tone of the poet.

The basic unit of meter is the **foot.** Usually a foot consists of one stressed syllable and one or two unstressed syllables. The most common foot in English-language poetry is the **iambic foot,** an unstressed syllable followed by a stressed syllable. There are five iambic feet in this line from Shakespeare's *Julius Caesar:*

Yŏnd Ca̒ssiŭs ha̒s ă le̒an aňd hu̒ngrў lo̒ok.

The stressed syllables are marked (′); the unstressed syllables are marked (˘).

A **trochaic foot** is an iambic foot in reverse: a stressed syllable followed by an unstressed syllable. This line from Poe's "Raven" illustrates eight trochaic feet:

Oňce ŭpoň ă midnight drearў, while Ῐ pŏn-

dered, weak aňd wearў.

An **anapestic foot** consists of two unstressed syllables followed by one stressed syllable. It is often used to capture swift movement, as in this line from "The Destruction of Sennacherib" by the British Romantic poet Lord Byron:

The Ăssy̆riăn ca̒me dowň li̒ke ă wo̒lf ŏn the̒

fo̒ld.

A **dactylic foot** is an anapestic foot in reverse: a stressed syllable followed by two unstressed syllables. Dactylic feet have a jingly, nursery-rhyme quality, illustrated in this line from a poem by E. E. Cummings:

a̒ny̆oňe li̒ved iň ă pretty̆ hŏw to̒wn

Notice that Cummings ends the line without completing the final foot. Poets may also vary the feet within a line. Sometimes they use a **spondaic foot,** consisting of two stressed syllables alone, for emphasis. Spondaic feet often occur at the end of a line of poetry, as in this line from "Thanatopsis":

Iň a̒ll hi̒s course; nŏr ye̒t iň the̒ co̒ld gro̒und.

When we describe the meter of a poem, we must consider not only the kinds of feet it contains but also the number of feet in each line. We use the prefixes mono- (one), di- (two), tri- (three), tetra- (four), penta- (five), and hex- (six) to identify the number of feet in a line. The meter of "Thanatopsis," for example, is iambic pentameter: It has five iambic feet in each line.

Unrhymed iambic pentameter is sometimes called **blank verse,** one of the most common meters in British and American poetry. Blank verse attempts to sound like English as it is spoken, and so every line need not be perfectly regular. A poet using iambic pentameter will deliberately vary the stresses to avoid monotony and to use the sound of the verse to support the meaning. The line quoted above from "Thanatopsis" shows Bryant using two heavy stresses—a spondee—at the end of the line to reinforce the idea of death and finality that is in the meaning of the words themselves.

Emerson's "Concord Hymn" is written in a simpler meter, iambic tetrameter:

Oň thi̒s green ba̒nk, by̆ thi̒s sŏft stre̒am,

We̒ se̒t tŏda̒y ă vo̒tiv̆e sto̒ne.

This meter seems perfect for the subject and the occasion of the poem: Emerson chose a meter that would lend itself to hymnlike singing.

Just as poets may vary types of feet, they may vary the number of feet in their lines, as Emily Dickinson does in this stanza:

The̒ So̒ul sĕle̒cts hĕr own So̒ciĕty̆—

Theň—shu̒ts the̒ Do̒or—

To̒ her di̒viňe Maj̆o̒rĭty̆—

Pre̒sent nŏ mo̒re—

When we mark a poem with stressed and unstressed marks to determine its meter, we are **scanning** the poem. **Scansion** is a useful tool for analyzing the rhythmic patterns of poems written in standard meters.

Thinking About Meter

1. Choose four lines from Bryant's "Thanatopsis," and scan them. Account for every syllable.
2. Choose another poem that you have read in this book. Scan four lines from the poem, and give the name of the meter the poet uses.

VOCABULARY

Antonyms

Antonyms are words that have opposite or nearly opposite meanings. The following words in capitals are from "Thanatopsis." Choose the word that is an antonym of each word in capitals, *as the word is used in this selection.* Write the number of each item and the letter of your choice on a separate sheet.

1. BLIGHT: (a) disease (b) light (c) health (d) darkness

2. VALES: (a) dreams (b) hills (c) valleys (d) laughter

3. PALL: (a) boredom (b) paleness (c) brightness (d) shroud

4. INSENSIBLE: (a) aware (b) stupid (c) mighty (d) unconscious

5. HOARY: (a) elderly (b) white (c) frosted (d) youthful

COMPOSITION

Writing About Theme

■ Write a composition about the theme of "Thanatopsis." Begin by stating the theme. Then discuss lines 1–17 and 66–81, which Bryant added during a revision. Tell what those lines add to the poem's theme. Show how Bryant illuminates his theme through setting, through the specific events that he discusses, and through the kinds of people he refers to. *For help with this assignment, refer to Lesson 6 in the Writing About Literature Handbook at the back of this book.*

Writing About Nature

■ Like Bryant, many artists have heard the "voice" of nature. Write a paragraph describing one natural phenomenon—for example, the seasons, a storm, plants, or animals—and tell what you think the "voice" of nature seems to be saying about life itself.

Edgar Allan Poe   *1809–1849*

The short, unhappy life of Edgar Allan Poe was marked by poverty, restlessness, and feverish creative activity. Nevertheless, this struggling, sometimes overwhelmingly lonely man became, after his death, one of the most widely read and influential American writers.

Edgar Poe was born in Boston, the son of traveling actors. His mother died when he was still an infant, and a wealthy Virginia couple, the Allans, became his foster parents. He received a good education and seemed to be headed for the life of a gentleman when he entered the University of Virginia. However, heavy gambling debts and a wild life forced him to drop out.

Refusing to join his foster father's business, Poe fled to Boston and, under an assumed name, joined the United States Army. At the age of eighteen, he published his first book of poetry and, in 1829, a second book. His foster father helped him win an appointment to the U.S. Military Academy at West Point, but once again a rigid life seemed incompatible with the writing Poe wanted to do. He deliberately broke rules and behaved in a way that made it necessary for West Point to expel him. His third book of poems, published soon after his expulsion, was dedicated to "the U.S. Corps of Cadets."

Poe knew that he was not going to inherit the Allans' fortune and that he would have to make his own way in the world. He moved from city to city, from job to job, usually as an editor or journalist, continuing to write poems, short stories, and reviews. His steadiest income came as the editor of a newly founded magazine, the *Southern Literary Messenger.*

In 1838 Poe published his only novel, *The Narrative of Arthur Gordon Pym,* a mysterious sea adventure. His *Tales of the Grotesque and Arabesque* came out in 1840, as he continued to contribute stories and poems to an assortment of journals. Nevertheless, Poe was unable to escape his spirit-breaking poverty. Even "The Raven," his most popular work, brought him little money. When his beloved wife, Virginia, died in 1847, Poe found his deep sorrow difficult to bear. He died in 1849, as completely "alone" as any American artist has ever been.

A few writers have found Poe's writing unpolished and juvenile: Emerson called him "the jingle man," and Mark Twain said he would read Poe only if someone paid him to do so. Yet most writers and critics, especially Europeans, have admired Poe more than any other American writer. The Irish poet W. B. Yeats considered Poe "certainly the greatest of American poets." Poe is still praised for his extraordinary ability to create moods and atmospheres, his unforgettable images, the music of his language, and his awareness of universal human fears.

Poe said that when he set out to write a poem with a melancholy effect, the word *nevermore* was the first word that came into his mind, both for its sound and for its meaning. The subject of the poem, he decided, had to be the death of a beautiful woman, "unquestionably, the most poetical topic in the world." His first thought was to have *nevermore* repeated by a parrot, but he saw greater possibilities in a raven, "the bird of ill omen," an emblem of "Mournful and Never-ending Remembrance."

Edgar Allan Poe

The Raven

Once upon a midnight dreary, while I pondered, weak and weary,
Over many a quaint and curious volume of forgotten lore—
While I nodded, nearly napping, suddenly there came a tapping,
As of someone gently rapping, rapping at my chamber door—
5 "'Tis some visitor," I muttered, "tapping at my chamber door—
    Only this and nothing more."

Ah, distinctly I remember it was in the bleak December;
And each separate dying ember wrought its ghost upon the floor.
Eagerly I wished the morrow—vainly I had sought to borrow
10 From my books surcease of sorrow—sorrow for the lost Lenore—
For the rare and radiant maiden whom the angels name Lenore—
    Nameless *here* for evermore.

And the silken, sad, uncertain rustling of each purple curtain
Thrilled me—filled me with fantastic terrors never felt before;
15 So that now, to still the beating of my heart, I stood repeating
"'Tis some visitor entreating entrance at my chamber door—
Some late visitor entreating entrance at my chamber door—
    This it is and nothing more."

Presently my soul grew stronger; hesitating then no longer,
20 "Sir," said I, "or Madam, truly your forgiveness I implore;
But the fact is I was napping, and so gently you came rapping,
And so faintly you came tapping, tapping at my chamber door,
That I scarce was sure I heard you"—here I opened wide the door—
    Darkness there and nothing more.

This lithograph was made by painter Edouard Manet (1832–1883) for a French translation of "The Raven."

25 Deep into that darkness peering, long I stood there wondering, fearing,
Doubting, dreaming dreams no mortal ever dared to dream before;
But the silence was unbroken, and the stillness gave no token,
And the only word there spoken was the whispered word, "Lenore?"
This I whispered, and an echo murmured back the word, "Lenore!"
30   Merely this and nothing more.

Back into the chamber turning, all my soul within me burning,
Soon again I heard a tapping somewhat louder than before.
"Surely," said I, "surely that is something at my window lattice;
Let me see, then, what thereat is, and this mystery explore—
35 Let my heart be still a moment and this mystery explore—
       'Tis the wind and nothing more!"

Open here I flung the shutter, when, with many a flirt and flutter,
In there stepped a stately Raven of the saintly days of yore.
Not the least obeisance made he; not a minute stopped or stayed he;
40 But, with mien of lord or lady, perched above my chamber door—
Perched upon a bust of Pallas[1] just above my chamber door—
       Perched, and sat, and nothing more.

Then this ebony bird beguiling my sad fancy into smiling,
By the grave and stern decorum of the countenance it wore,
45 "Though thy crest be shorn and shaven, thou," I said, "art sure no craven,
Ghastly grim and ancient Raven wandering from the Nightly shore—
Tell me what thy lordly name is on the Night's Plutonian[2] shore!"
       Quoth the Raven "Nevermore."

Much I marveled this ungainly fowl to hear discourse so plainly,
50 Though its answer little meaning—little relevancy bore;
For we cannot help agreeing that no living human being
Ever yet was blessed with seeing bird above his chamber door—
Bird or beast upon the sculptured bust above his chamber door,
       With such name as "Nevermore."

55 But the Raven, sitting lonely on the placid bust, spoke only
That one word, as if his soul in that one word he did outpour.
Nothing farther then he uttered—not a feather then he fluttered—
Till I scarcely more than muttered "Other friends have flown before—
On the morrow *he* will leave me, as my Hopes have flown before."
60   Then the bird said "Nevermore."

---

1. **Pallas** [pal′əs]: in Greek mythology Pallas Athena, the goddess of wisdom.
2. **Plutonian** [ploo tō′nē ən]: dark; referring to Pluto, Greek god of the underworld.

Startled at the stillness broken by reply so aptly spoken,
"Doubtless," said I, "what it utters is its only stock and store
Caught from some unhappy master whom unmerciful Disaster
Followed fast and followed faster till his songs one burden bore—
65 Till the dirges of his Hope that melancholy burden bore
　　　　Of 'Never—nevermore.' "

But the Raven still beguiling my sad fancy into smiling,
Straight I wheeled a cushioned seat in front of bird and bust and door;
Then, upon the velvet sinking, I betook myself to linking
70 Fancy unto fancy, thinking what this ominous bird of yore—
What this grim, ungainly, ghastly, gaunt, and ominous bird of yore
　　　　Meant in croaking "Nevermore."

This I sat engaged in guessing, but no syllable expressing
To the fowl whose fiery eyes now burned into my bosom's core;
75 This and more I sat divining, with my head at ease reclining
On the cushion's velvet lining that the lamplight gloated o'er,
But whose velvet violet lining with the lamplight gloating o'er,
　　　　She shall press, ah, nevermore!

Then, methought, the air grew denser, perfumed from an unseen censer
80 Swung by seraphim[3] whose footfalls tinkled on the tufted floor.
"Wretch," I cried, "thy God hath lent thee—by these angels he hath sent thee
Respite—respite and nepenthe[4] from thy memories of Lenore;
Quaff, oh quaff this kind nepenthe and forget this lost Lenore!"
　　　　Quoth the Raven "Nevermore."

85 "Prophet!" said I, "thing of evil!—prophet still, if bird or devil!—
Whether Tempter sent, or whether tempest tossed thee here ashore,
Desolate yet all undaunted, on this desert land enchanted—
On this home by Horror haunted—tell me truly, I implore—
Is there—*is* there balm in Gilead?[5]—tell me—tell me, I implore!"
90 　　　　Quoth the Raven "Nevermore."

"Prophet!" said I, "thing of evil!—prophet still, if bird or devil!
By that Heaven that bends above us—by that God we both adore—
Tell this soul with sorrow laden if, within the distant Aidenn,[6]
It shall clasp a sainted maiden whom the angels name Lenore—
95 Clasp a rare and radiant maiden whom the angels name Lenore."
　　　　Quoth the Raven "Nevermore."

---

3. **seraphim** [ser′ə fim′]: angels.
4. **nepenthe** [ni pen′thē]: in classical mythology a drink that banishes sorrow.
5. **balm in Gilead** [gil′ē əd]: Poe's version of "Is there no balm in Gilead?"
(Jeremiah 8 : 22), referring to a healing ointment made in Gilead in ancient
Palestine; therefore, a relief from suffering.
6. **Aidenn** [ā′dən]: Arabic for "Eden" or heaven.

"Be that word our sign of parting, bird or fiend!" I shrieked, upstarting—
"Get thee back into the tempest and the Night's Plutonian shore!
Leave no black plume as a token of that lie thy soul hath spoken!
100 Leave my loneliness unbroken!—quit the bust above my door!
Take thy beak from out my heart, and take thy form from off my door!"
       Quoth the Raven "Nevermore."

And the Raven, never flitting, still is sitting, *still* is sitting
On the pallid bust of Pallas just above my chamber door;
105 And his eyes have all the seeming of a demon's that is dreaming,
And the lamplight o'er him streaming throws his shadow on the floor;
And my soul from out that shadow that lies floating on the floor
       Shall be lifted—nevermore!

STUDY QUESTIONS

Recalling

1. In stanzas 1–3 what is the speaker doing when he first hears the tapping? What does he seek "to borrow"? What does he say "to still the beating" of his heart?
2. In stanzas 4–5 what does the speaker see when he opens the door? What does he whisper?
3. What does the speaker hope is making the tapping noise in stanza 6? What happens when he opens the shutter?
4. What is the only word the raven speaks? In stanza 9 to what does the speaker think the word relates? How does he explain the word when the raven first repeats it (lines 62–66)?
5. About what does the speaker begin to think when he wheels his chair in front of the raven (lines 69–72)?
6. What question does the speaker ask in lines 88–90? In lines 93–95? What does the raven reply? What does it say when ordered to leave?
7. Where is the raven now? What will never be lifted from the raven's shadow?

Interpreting

8. Does the speaker believe the words he says in lines 16–18 and line 36? How do you know?
9. Who is "she" in line 78? Who is the "wretch" in line 81? Trace the speaker's thoughts in lines 78–83.
10. What does the speaker interpret "nevermore" in line 84 and in line 96 to mean? What do you know about the raven's answers that the speaker does not realize?
11. What does the raven come to represent for the speaker? What does "Plutonian shore" (line 98) suggest about the speaker's final evaluation of the raven? Of himself?
12. Evaluate the speaker's emotional state at the beginning of the poem, in the next-to-the-last stanza, and in the last stanza. What does the future probably hold for the speaker?
13. Describe the mood of the poem. Which expressions in stanzas 1–2 help establish the mood?

Extending

14. Poe felt the death of a beautiful woman was "the most poetical topic in the world." What do you think makes a topic "poetical"? Name at least three topics you find poetical, and tell why they are suitable for poetry.

LITERARY FOCUS

Poe and the Single Effect

In a review of *Twice-Told Tales* by his contemporary, Nathaniel Hawthorne, Poe asserted that a work of literature must arrange all of its elements so that they combine to achieve a single effect. In fact, Poe believed that a poet or a short story writer must begin with an idea of a single effect and then create the characters and incidents to produce that effect. He said, "In the whole composition there should be no word written, of which the tendency, direct or indirect, is not to the one preestablished design." He added, "If [an author's] very initial sentence tend not to the outbringing of this [single] effect, then he has failed in his first step."

Poe believed, in other words, that one clear, powerfully felt emotion should carry the reader through the work. Of course, literature may display many different emotions, but Poe believed they must all ultimately combine into one overwhelming feeling for the reader.

Thinking About Single Effect

1. What is the single effect of "The Raven"?
2. Discuss the first sentence of "The Raven," pointing out how each element of it contributes to the single effect.

Sound Devices

Poe's use of sound devices in poetry is as important as his subject matter. The particular music of his verses creates mood, reveals character, and conveys ideas, in addition to providing that pleasure in sound that only poetry can provide.

Most sound devices are kinds of **repetition. Alliteration,** for example, is the repetition of consonant sounds at the beginnings of words and of sounds within words. Poe uses alliteration to create an almost hypnotic effect in phrases like "weak and weary" and "silken, sad, uncertain rustling." (**Consonance** is the repetition in nearby words of similar consonant sounds preceded by different accented vowels.)

Assonance is the repetition of vowel sounds, and Poe uses assonance mainly to create mood. The most conspicuous example in "The Raven" is the open *o* sound, with its deep mournful effect: "sorrow—sorrow for the lost Lenore."

Poe uses the assonance of the *o* sound as the basis for the poem's most common rhyme. **Rhyme** is a kind of repetition, and it also can be used to create mood. Notice, for example, how many times the poet rhymes that long moaning sound: "nevermore," "door," "Lenore," "implore," "yore," "bore," and so on. Rhyme can reinforce meaning; the poet emphasizes the absence of his beloved when he rhymes *Lenore* with *nevermore.*

Internal rhyme is rhyme that occurs within a single line:

Ah, distinctly I *remember* it was in the bleak *December.*

Poe uses internal rhyme as another kind of repeated sound, like alliteration or assonance, for hypnotic effect, for mood, and simply for the pleasure of the repetition itself.

Poe also employs **onomatopoeia,** the use of words with sounds that suggest their meanings. For example, the words *tapping* and *rapping,* in addition to meaning "knocking," actually suggest the sound of someone or something knocking at the door. Poe repeats the words in the first stanza, just as a knock at the door is repeated.

Thinking About Sound Devices

■ Find at least two more examples in "The Raven" of alliteration, assonance, internal rhyme, and onomatopoeia. Tell how Poe's use of each of these sound devices contributes to the meaning or the mood of the poem.

"To Helen" shows how a Romantic poet can use classical images for his own purposes. Inspired by the beauty of the mother of one of his friends, Poe uses Helen of Troy—"the face that launched a thousand ships"—to represent that beauty. Helen may also be an allusion to the Greek goddess of light, but whatever the specific reference Poe intended, she is clearly the poet's timeless ideal of pure beauty.

Edgar Allan Poe

To Helen

Helen, thy beauty is to me
    Like those Nicéan[1] barks of yore,
That gently, o'er a perfumed sea,
    The weary, way-worn wanderer bore
5   To his own native shore.

On desperate seas long wont[2] to roam,
    Thy hyacinth[3] hair, thy classic face,
Thy Naiad[4] airs have brought me home
    To the glory that was Greece,
10 And the grandeur that was Rome.

Lo! in yon brilliant window niche
    How statue-like I see thee stand,
    The agate lamp within thy hand!
Ah, Psyche,[5] from the regions which
15   Are Holy Land!

---

1. **Nicéan** [nī sē′ən] **barks:** Poe may be referring to boats from the shipbuilding city of Nicea in Asia Minor. It is likely, however, that he created the phrase for its melodious sound.
2. **wont** [wônt]: accustomed.
3. **hyacinth** [hī′ə sinth′]: wavy and perfumed.
4. **Naiad** [nī′ad]: in classical mythology, a water nymph.
5. **Psyche** [sī′kē]: goddess of the soul.

In this early poem, Poe directs all his details toward a single effect—his vision of a terrible, lifelong loneliness.

In this selection, and in one selection in each unit, you will find notes in the right-hand margin that highlight parts of the selection. These notes point out important ideas of the period—in this case, the Romantic movement—and draw your attention to literary elements and techniques covered in the Literary Focuses. Page numbers in the notes will refer you to more extensive discussions of these important ideas and elements.

Alone

From childhood's hour I have not been
As others were—I have not seen
As others saw—I could not bring
My passions from a common spring—
5 From the same source I have not taken
My sorrow—I could not awaken
My heart to joy at the same tone—
And all I lov'd—*I* lov'd alone—
Then—in my childhood—in the dawn
10 Of a most stormy life—was drawn
From ev'ry depth of good and ill
The mystery which binds me still—
From the torrent, or the fountain—
From the red cliff of the mountain—
15 From the sun that 'round me roll'd
In its autumn tint of gold—
From the lightning in the sky
As it pass'd me flying by—
From the thunder, and the storm—
20 And the cloud that took the form
(When the rest of Heaven was blue)
Of a demon in my view—

Romantic idea: The poem focuses on the self, common in Romantic poetry (p. 101).

Alliteration, Assonance, and Rhyme (p. 131): The *l* sounds in line 8 and the *o* sounds of lines 7–8 add to the "music" of the poem. By rhyming "alone" with "tone," Poe stresses the title.

Romantic idea: The Romantic writer is often fascinated by mystery (p. 101).

Meter (p. 122): The first eight lines of the poem are iambic tetrameter. From line 11 to the end, the poem becomes trochaic, reversing its rhythm.

STUDY QUESTIONS

To Helen

Recalling

1. To what does the poet compare Helen's beauty in the first stanza? Who is brought "to his own native shore"?
2. What images describe Helen in the second stanza? Who is brought home in this stanza? To what is he brought home?
3. What is Helen doing in the third stanza? With whom is she associated in line 14? From where does she come?

Interpreting

4. State in your own words the condition the speaker was in before encountering Helen.
5. Considering the places to which Helen brings the speaker and the place from which she comes, name the three kinds of joys or comforts she seems to provide. What might the agate lamp represent? What has Helen done for the speaker to explain why he calls her Psyche?
6. In what way is this poem idealistic? Which of the other characteristics of Romanticism (listed in the Introduction to this unit) does this poem display?

Alone

Recalling

1. In what three ways is the speaker set apart, according to lines 1–4? From when do these differences exist?
2. What does the speaker say arose "in the dawn" of a "most stormy life"?
3. What, according to line 22, has the speaker seen in all places?

Interpreting

4. Summarize the main idea of the first eight lines in one sentence. What characteristics of the speaker are implied in these lines?
5. Do we ever learn exactly what "mystery" binds the speaker? What do lines 20–22 suggest about the speaker? About the mystery?

Extending

6. What are the insights and the positive results that may come from a poet's suffering?

COMPOSITION

Writing About Poetry

■ Write a composition in which you show how the specific techniques used in "To Helen" contribute to the meaning of the poem. First state the poem's meaning. Next identify the poem's images and allusions, and tell why they are appropriate to the meaning. Then discuss the rhythm and the rhyme, describing the overall feeling they suggest. Conclude with a general statement about the poet's effectiveness in using these devices. *For help with this assignment, refer to Lesson 7 in the Writing About Literature Handbook at the back of this book.*

Writing with Classical Allusions

■ Write a brief description of a person or a place using at least one of the following classical names to help describe your subject. You may want to look up the names in a dictionary or encyclopedia to add details to your description.

Zeus	Hercules
Olympus	Odysseus
Athena	Elysium
Penelope	Achilles
Hermes	

"The Fall of the House of Usher" is one of Poe's most famous tales. Like many gothic stories, it is set in an old mansion that suggests the terrible events that will take place there. Setting, characterization, plot, theme, and style all contribute to the single effect of terror. The story, however, is much more than a tale of terror: It is a portrait of an isolated and suffering human being.

Edgar Allan Poe

The Fall of the House of Usher

Son coeur est un luth suspendu;
Sitôt qu'on le touche il résonne.[1]

De Béranger

During the whole of a dull, dark, and soundless day in the autumn of the year, when the clouds hung oppressively low in the heavens, I had been passing alone, on horseback, through a singularly dreary tract of country, and at length found myself, as the shades of the evening drew on, within view of the melancholy House of Usher. I know not how it was—but, with the first glimpse of the building, a sense of insufferable gloom pervaded my spirit. I say insufferable, for the feeling was unrelieved by any of that half-pleasurable, because poetic, sentiment with which the mind usually receives even the sternest natural images of the desolate or terrible. I looked upon the scene before me—upon the mere house and the simple landscape features of the domain—upon the bleak walls—upon the vacant eyelike windows—upon a few rank sedges[2]—and upon a few white trunks of decayed trees—with an utter depression of soul which I can compare to no earthly sensation more properly than to the afterdream of the reveler upon opium—the bitter lapse into everyday life—the hideous dropping off of the veil. There was an iciness, a sinking, a sickening of the heart—an unredeemed dreariness of thought which no goading of the imagination could torture into aught[3] of the sublime. What was it—I paused to think—what was it that so unnerved me in the contemplation of the House of Usher? It was a mystery all insoluble; nor could I grapple with the shadowy fancies that crowded upon me as I pondered. I was forced to fall back upon the unsatisfactory conclusion that while, beyond doubt, there *are* combinations of very simple natural objects which have the power of thus affecting us, still the analysis of this power lies among considerations beyond our depth. It was possible, I reflected, that a mere different arrangement of the particulars of the scene, of the details of the picture, would be sufficient to modify, or perhaps to annihilate, its capacity for sorrowful impression; and, acting upon this idea, I reined my horse to the precipitous brink of a black

---

1. *Son . . . resonné:* "His heart is a suspended lute; as soon as one touches it, it resounds." From "Le Refus" by French poet Pierre-Jean Béranger (1780–1857).
2. **sedges:** grasslike plants that grow in swampy ground.

3. **aught:** anything.

and lurid tarn[4] that lay in unruffled luster by the dwelling, and gazed down—but with a shudder even more thrilling than before—upon the remodeled and inverted images of the gray sedge, and the ghastly tree stems, and the vacant and eyelike windows.

Nevertheless, in this mansion of gloom I now proposed to myself a sojourn of some weeks. Its proprietor, Roderick Usher, had been one of my boon companions in boyhood; but many years had elapsed since our last meeting. A letter, however, had lately reached me in a distant part of the country—a letter from him—which, in its wildly importunate nature, had admitted of no other than a personal reply. The MS.[5] gave evidence of nervous agitation. The writer spoke of acute bodily illness—of a mental disorder which oppressed him—and of an earnest desire to see me, as his best and indeed his only personal friend, with a view of attempting, by the cheerfulness of my society, some alleviation of his malady. It was the manner in which all this, and much more, was said—it was the apparent *heart* that went with his request—which allowed me no room for hesitation; and I accordingly obeyed forthwith what I still considered a very singular summons.

Although as boys we had been even intimate associates, yet I really knew little of my friend. His reserve had been always excessive and habitual. I was aware, however, that his very ancient family had been noted, time out of mind, for a peculiar sensibility of temperament, displaying itself, through long ages, in many works of exalted art, and manifested, of late, in repeated deeds of munificent[6] yet unobtrusive charity, as well as in a passionate devotion to the intricacies, perhaps even more than to the orthodox and easily recognizable beauties, of musical science. I had learned, too, the very remarkable fact that the stem of the Usher race, all time-honored as it was, had

put forth at no period any enduring branch; in other words, that the entire family lay in the direct line of descent, and had always, with very trifling and very temporary variation, so lain. It was this deficiency, I considered, while running over in thought the perfect keeping of the character of the premises with the accredited character of the people, and while speculating upon the possible influence which the one, in the long lapse of centuries, might have exercised upon the other—it was this deficiency, perhaps, of collateral[7] issue, and the consequent undeviating transmission from sire to son of the patrimony[8] with the name, which had at length so identified the two as to merge the original title of the estate in the quaint and equivocal appellation of the "House of Usher"—an appellation which seemed to include, in the minds of the peasantry who used it, both the family and the family mansion.

I have said that the sole effect of my somewhat childish experiment—that of looking down within the tarn—had been to deepen the first singular impression. There can be no doubt that the consciousness of the rapid increase of my superstition—for why should I not so term it?—served mainly to accelerate the increase itself. Such, I have long known, is the paradoxical law of all sentiments having terror as a basis. And it might have been for this reason only that, when I again uplifted my eyes to the house itself, from its image in the pool, there grew in my mind a strange fancy—a fancy so ridiculous, indeed, that I but mention it to show the vivid force of the sensations which oppressed me. I had so worked upon my imagination as really to believe that about the whole mansion and domain there hung an atmosphere peculiar to themselves and their immediate vicinity—an atmosphere which had no affinity with the air of heaven, but which had reeked up from the decayed trees, and the gray wall, and the silent tarn—a pes-

---

4. **tarn:** small lake.
5. **MS.:** manuscript.
6. **munificent:** generous.

7. **collateral** [kə lat′ər əl]: descended from common ancestors, but in a different line.
8. **patrimony** [pat′rə mō′nē]: inheritance.

tilent and mystic vapor, dull, sluggish, faintly discernible, and leaden-hued.

Shaking off from my spirit what *must* have been a dream, I scanned more narrowly the real aspect of the building. Its principal feature seemed to be that of an excessive antiquity. The discoloration of ages had been great. Minute fungi overspread the whole exterior, hanging in a fine tangled webwork from the eaves. Yet all this was apart from any extraordinary dilapidation. No portion of the masonry had fallen; and there appeared to be a wild inconsistency between its still perfect adaptation of parts, and the crumbling condition of the individual stones. In this there was much that reminded me of the specious totality[9] of old woodwork which has rotted for long years in some neglected vault, with no disturbance from the breath of the external air. Beyond this indication of extensive decay, however, the fabric gave little token of instability. Perhaps the eye of a scrutinizing observer might have discovered a barely perceptible fissure, which, extending from the roof of the building in front, made its way down the wall in a zigzag direction, until it became lost in the sullen waters of the tarn.

Noticing these things, I rode over a short causeway to the house. A servant-in-waiting took my horse, and I entered the Gothic[10] archway of the hall. A valet, of stealthy step, thence conducted me, in silence, through many dark and intricate passages in my progress to the studio of his master. Much that I encountered on the way contributed, I know not how, to heighten the vague sentiments of which I have already spoken. While the objects around me—while the carvings of the ceilings, the somber tapestries of the walls, the ebon blackness of the floors, and the phantasmagoric[11] armorial trophies which rattled as I strode, were but matters to which, or to such as which, I

9. **specious totality:** giving the illusion of being in one piece.
10. **Gothic:** tall and pointed.
11. **phantasmagoric** [fan taz′mə gôr′ik]: fantastic; dreamlike.

had been accustomed from my infancy—while I hesitated not to acknowledge how familiar was all this—I still wondered to find how unfamiliar were the fancies which ordinary images were stirring up. On one of the staircases, I met the physician of the family. His countenance, I thought, wore a mingled expression of low cunning and perplexity. He accosted me with trepidation and passed on. The valet now threw open a door and ushered me into the presence of his master.

The room in which I found myself was very large and lofty. The windows were long, narrow, and pointed, and at so vast a distance from the black oaken floor as to be altogether inaccessible from within. Feeble gleams of encrimsoned light made their way through the trellised panes and served to render sufficiently distinct the more prominent objects around; the eye, however, struggled in vain to reach the remoter angles of the chamber, or the recesses of the vaulted and fretted[12] ceiling. Dark draperies hung upon the walls. The general furniture was profuse, comfortless, antique, and tattered. Many books and musical instruments lay scattered about, but failed to give any vitality to the scene. I felt that I breathed an atmosphere of sorrow. An air of stern, deep, and irredeemable gloom hung over and pervaded all.

Upon my entrance, Usher arose from a sofa on which he had been lying at full length and greeted me with a vivacious warmth which had much in it, I at first thought, of an overdone cordiality—of the constrained effort of the *ennuyé*[13] man of the world. A glance, however, at his countenance convinced me of his perfect sincerity. We sat down; and for some moments, while he spoke not, I gazed upon him with a feeling half of pity, half of awe. Surely, man had never before so terribly altered, in so brief a period, as had Roderick Usher! It was with difficulty that I could bring myself to admit the identity of the wan being

before me with the companion of my early boyhood. Yet the character of his face had been at all times remarkable. A cadaverousness of complexion; an eye large, liquid, and luminous beyond comparison; lips somewhat thin and very pallid, but of a surpassingly beautiful curve; a nose of a delicate Hebrew model, but with a breadth of nostril unusual in similar formations; a finely molded chin, speaking, in its want of prominence, of a want of moral energy; hair of a more than weblike softness and tenuity; these features, with an inordinate expansion above the regions of the temple, made up altogether a countenance not easily to be forgotten. And now, in the mere exaggeration of the prevailing character of these features, and of the expression they were wont to convey, lay so much of change that I doubted to whom I spoke. The now ghastly pallor of the skin, and the now miraculous luster of the eye, above all things startled and even awed me. The silken hair, too, had been suffered to grow all unheeded, and as, in its wild gossamer texture, it floated rather than fell about the face, I could not, even with effort, connect its Arabesque[14] expression with any idea of simple humanity.

In the manner of my friend I was at once struck with an incoherence—an inconsistency; and I soon found this to arise from a series of feeble and futile struggles to overcome a habitual trepidancy—an excessive nervous agitation. For something of this nature I had indeed been prepared, no less by his letter, than by reminiscences of certain boyish traits, and by conclusions deduced from his peculiar physical conformation and temperament. His action was alternately vivacious and sullen. His voice varied rapidly from a tremulous indecision (when the animal spirits seemed utterly in abeyance) to that species of energetic concision—that abrupt, weighty, unhurried, and hollow-sounding enunciation—that leaden, self-balanced and perfectly modulated guttural ut-

---

12. **fretted:** ornamented.
13. *ennuyé* [än nwē ā′]: French for "bored."

14. **Arabesque** [ar′ə besk′]: fantastic and complex, like the designs on Arab architecture.

terance, which may be observed in the lost drunkard, or the irreclaimable eater of opium, during the periods of his most intense excitement.

It was thus that he spoke of the object of my visit, of his earnest desire to see me, and of the solace he expected me to afford him. He entered, at some length, into what he conceived to be the nature of his malady. It was, he said, a constitutional and a family evil, and one for which he despaired to find a remedy— a mere nervous affection,[15] he immediately added, which would undoubtedly soon pass. It displayed itself in a host of unnatural sensations. Some of these, as he detailed them, interested and bewildered me; although, perhaps, the terms and the general manner of the narration had their weight. He suffered much from a morbid acuteness of the senses; the most insipid food was alone endurable; he could wear only garments of certain texture; the odors of all flowers were oppressive; his eyes were tortured by even a faint light; and there were but peculiar sounds, and these from stringed instruments, which did not inspire him with horror.

To an anomalous[16] species of terror I found him a bounden slave. "I shall perish," said he, "I *must* perish in this deplorable folly. Thus, thus, and not otherwise, shall I be lost. I dread the events of the future, not in themselves, but in their results. I shudder at the thought of any, even the most trivial, incident which may operate upon this intolerable agitation of soul. I have, indeed, no abhorrence of danger, except in its absolute effect—in terror. In this unnerved—in this pitiable condition—I feel that the period will sooner or later arrive when I must abandon life and reason together, in some struggle with the grim phantasm, FEAR."

I learned, moreover, at intervals, and through broken and equivocal hints, another singular feature of his mental condition. He was enchained by certain superstitious impressions in regard to the dwelling which he tenanted, and whence, for many years, he had never ventured forth—in regard to an influence whose supposititious[17] force was conveyed in terms too shadowy here to be restated—an influence which some peculiarities in the mere form and substance of his family mansion had, by dint of long sufferance, he said, obtained over his spirit—an effect which the physique of the gray walls and turrets, and of the dim tarn into which they all looked down had, at length, brought about upon the morale of his existence.

He admitted, however, although with hesitation, that much of the peculiar gloom which thus afflicted him could be traced to a more natural and far more palpable origin—to the severe and long-continued illness—indeed to the evidently approaching dissolution—of a tenderly beloved sister—his sole companion for long years—his last and only relative on earth. "Her decease," he said, with a bitterness which I can never forget, "would leave him (him the hopeless and the frail) the last of the ancient race of the Ushers." While he spoke, the lady Madeline (for so was she called) passed slowly through a remote portion of the apartment, and, without having noticed my presence, disappeared. I regarded her with an utter astonishment not unmingled with dread—and yet I found it impossible to account for such feelings. A sensation of stupor oppressed me as my eyes followed her retreating steps. When a door at length closed upon her, my glance sought instinctively and eagerly the countenance of the brother—but he had buried his face in his hands, and I could only perceive that a far more than ordinary wanness had overspread the emaciated fingers through which trickled many passionate tears.

The disease of the lady Madeline had long baffled the skill of her physicians. A settled apathy, a gradual wasting away of the person, and frequent although transient affections of a par-

---

15. **affection:** affliction.
16. **anomalous** [ə nom′ə ləs]: abnormal.

17. **supposititious** [sə poz′ə tish′əs]: supposed.

tially cataleptical[18] character were the unusual diagnosis. Hitherto she had steadily borne up against the pressure of her malady, and had not betaken herself finally to bed; but on the closing in of the evening of my arrival at the house, she succumbed (as her brother told me at night with inexpressible agitation) to the prostrating power of the destroyer, and I learned that the glimpse I had obtained of her person would thus probably be the last I should obtain—that the lady, at least while living, would be seen by me no more.

For several days ensuing, her name was unmentioned by either Usher or myself, and during this period I was busied in earnest endeavors to alleviate the melancholy of my friend. We painted and read together; or I listened, as if in a dream, to the wild improvisations of his speaking guitar. And thus, as a closer and still closer intimacy admitted me more unreservedly into the recesses of his spirit, the more bitterly did I perceive the futility of all attempt at cheering a mind from which darkness, as if an inherent positive quality, poured forth upon all objects of the moral and physical universe in one unceasing radiation of gloom.

I shall ever bear about me a memory of the many solemn hours I thus spent alone with the master of the House of Usher. Yet I should fail in any attempt to convey an idea of the exact character of the studies, or of the occupations, in which he involved me, or led me the way. An excited and highly distempered ideality[19] threw a sulfureous[20] luster over all. His long improvised dirges will ring forever in my ears. Among other things, I hold painfully in mind a certain singular perversion and amplification of the wild air of the last waltz of von Weber.[21] From the paintings over which his elaborate fancy brooded, and which grew, touch by touch, into vaguenesses at which I shuddered

---

18. **cataleptical** [kat′əl ep′tik əl]: state marked by loss of consciousness and deathlike muscular rigidity.
19. **distempered ideality:** feverish unreality.
20. **sulfureous:** greenish-yellow.
21. **von Weber:** Karl Maria von Weber (1786–1826), German Romantic composer.

the more thrillingly, because I shuddered knowing not why—from these paintings (vivid as their images now are before me) I would in vain endeavor to educe more than a small portion which should lie within the compass of merely written words. By the utter simplicity, by the nakedness of his designs, he arrested and overawed attention. If ever mortal painted an idea, that mortal was Roderick Usher. For me at least—in the circumstances then surrounding me—there arose out of the pure abstractions which the hypochondriac contrived to throw upon his canvas, an intensity of intolerable awe, no shadow of which felt I ever yet in the contemplation of the certainly glowing yet too concrete reveries of Fuseli.[22]

One of the phantasmagoric conceptions of my friend, partaking not so rigidly of the spirit of abstraction, may be shadowed forth, although feebly, in words. A small picture presented the interior of an immensely long and rectangular vault or tunnel, with low walls, smooth, white, and without interruption or device. Certain accessory points of the design served well to convey the idea that this excavation lay at an exceeding depth below the surface of the earth. No outlet was observed in any portion of its vast extent, and no torch or other artificial source of light was discernible; yet a flood of intense rays rolled throughout and bathed the whole in a ghastly and inappropriate splendor.

I have just spoken of that morbid condition of the auditory nerve which rendered all music intolerable to the sufferer with the exception of certain effects of stringed instruments. It was, perhaps, the narrow limits to which he thus confined himself upon the guitar which gave birth, in great measure, to the fantastic character of his performances. But the fervid facility of his impromptus could not be so accounted for. They must have been, and were, in the notes as well as in the words of his wild fantasias (for he not unfrequently accompanied himself with rhymed verbal improvisations),

the result of that intense mental collectedness and concentration to which I have previously alluded as observable only in particular moments of the highest artificial excitement. The words of one of these rhapsodies I have easily remembered. I was, perhaps, the more forcibly impressed with it as he gave it because, in the under or mystic current of its meaning, I fancied that I perceived, and for the first time, a full consciousness on the part of Usher of the tottering of his lofty reason upon her throne. The verses, which were entitled "The Haunted Palace," ran very nearly, if not accurately, thus:

I

In the greenest of our valleys,
  By good angels tenanted,
Once a fair and stately palace—
  Radiant palace—reared its head.
In the monarch Thought's dominion—
  It stood there!
Never seraph spread a pinion
  Over fabric half so fair.

II

Banners yellow, glorious, golden,
  On its roof did float and flow;
(This—all this—was in the olden
  Time long ago)
And every gentle air that dallied,
  In that sweet day,
Along the ramparts plumed and pallid,
  A wingèd odor went away.

III

Wanderers in that happy valley
  Through two luminous windows saw
Spirits moving musically
  To a lute's well-tunèd law,
Round about a throne, where sitting
  (Porphyrogene!)[23]
In state his glory well befitting,
  The ruler of the realm was seen.

---

22. **Fuseli:** John Henry Fuseli (1742–1825), Swiss-born English Romantic painter.

23. **Porphyrogene** [pôr fə ro′je nē]: born to the purple—that is, to royalty.

IV

And all with pearl and ruby glowing
  Was the fair palace door,
Through which came flowing, flowing, flowing,
  And sparkling evermore,
A troop of Echoes whose sweet duty
  Was but to sing,
In voices of surpassing beauty,
  The wit and wisdom of their king.

V

But evil things, in robes of sorrow,
  Assailed the monarch's high estate;
(Ah, let us mourn, for never morrow
  Shall dawn upon him, desolate!)
And, round about his home, the glory
  That blushed and bloomed
Is but a dim-remembered story
  Of the old time entombed.

VI

And travelers now within that valley,
  Through the red-litten[24] windows, see
Vast forms that move fantastically
  To a discordant melody;
While, like a rapid ghastly river,
  Through the pale door,
A hideous throng rush out forever,
  And laugh—but smile no more.

I well remember that suggestions arising from this ballad led us into a train of thought wherein there became manifest an opinion of Usher's which I mention not so much on account of its novelty (for other men have thought thus) as on account of the pertinacity with which he maintained it. This opinion, in its general form, was that of the sentience[25] of all vegetable things. But, in his disordered fancy the idea had assumed a more daring character and trespassed, under certain conditions, upon the kingdom of inorganization.[26] I

lack words to express the full extent or the earnest abandon of his persuasion. The belief, however, was connected (as I have previously hinted) with the gray stones of the home of his forefathers. The conditions of the sentience had been here, he imagined, fulfilled in the method of collocation of these stones—in the order of their arrangement, as well as in that of the many fungi which overspread them and of the decayed trees which stood around—above all, in the long undisturbed endurance of this arrangement and in its reduplication in the still waters of the tarn. Its evidence—the evidence of the sentience—was to be seen, he said (and I here started as he spoke), in the gradual yet certain condensation of an atmosphere of their own about the waters and the walls. The result was discoverable, he added, in that silent yet importunate and terrible influence which for centuries had molded the destinies of his family, and which made *him* what I now saw him—what he was. Such opinions need no comment, and I will make none.

Our books—the books which, for years, had formed no small portion of the mental existence of the invalid—were, as might be supposed, in strict keeping with this character of phantasm. We pored together over such works as the *Ververt et Chartreuse*[27] of Gresset; the *Belphegor* of Machiavelli; the *Heaven and Hell* of Swedenborg; the *Subterranean Voyage of Nicholas Klimm* by Holberg; the *Chiromancy* of Robert Flud, of Jean D'Indaginé, and of De la Chambre; the *Journey into the Blue Distance* of Tieck; and the *City of the Sun* of Campanella. One favorite volume was a small octavo edition of the *Directorium Inquisitorum* by the Dominican Eymeric de Gironne; and there were passages in Pomponius Mela, about the old African Satyrs and Aegipans, over which Usher would sit dreaming for hours. His chief

---

24. **litten:** lighted.
25. **sentience** [sen′shəns]: capacity for feeling.
26. **inorganization:** inanimate objects.

27. ***Ververt et Chartreuse,*** etc.: Actual titles of obscure books of magic and mysticism. The last one in the paragraph is a book of "vigils for the dead."

delight, however, was found in the perusal of an exceedingly rare and curious book in quarto Gothic—the manual of a forgotten church—the *Vigiliae Mortuorum secundum Chorum Ecclesiae Maguntinae.*

I could not help thinking of the wild ritual of this work, and of its probable influence upon the hypochondriac, when one evening, having informed me abruptly that the lady Madeline was no more, he stated his intention of preserving her corpse for a fortnight (previously to its final interment) in one of the numerous vaults within the main walls of the building. The worldly reason, however, assigned for this singular proceeding was one which I did not feel at liberty to dispute. The brother had been led to his resolution (so he told me) by consideration of the unusual character of the malady of the deceased, of certain obtrusive and eager inquiries on the part of her medical men, and of the remote and exposed situation of the burial ground of the family. I will not deny that when I called to mind the sinister countenance of the person whom I met upon the staircase on the day of my arrival at the house, I had no desire to oppose what I regarded as at best but a harmless, and by no means an unnatural, precaution.

At the request of Usher, I personally aided him in the arrangements for the temporary entombment. The body having been encoffined, we two alone bore it to its rest. The vault in which we placed it (and which had been so long unopened that our torches, half smothered in its oppressive atmosphere, gave us little opportunity for investigation) was small, damp, and entirely without means of admission for light, lying, at great depth, immediately beneath that portion of the building in which was my own sleeping apartment. It had been used, apparently in remote feudal times, for the worst purposes of a donjon keep and in later days as a place of deposit for powder or some other highly combustible substance, as a portion of its floor and the whole interior of a long archway through which we reached it were carefully sheathed with copper. The door, of massive iron, had been also similarly protected. Its immense weight caused an unusually sharp grating sound as it moved upon its hinges.

Having deposited our mournful burden upon trestles within this region of horror, we partially turned aside the yet unscrewed lid of the coffin and looked upon the face of the tenant. A striking similitude between the brother and sister now first arrested my attention; and Usher, divining, perhaps, my thoughts, murmured out some few words from which I learned that the deceased and himself had been twins, and that sympathies of a scarcely intelligible nature had always existed between them. Our glances, however, rested not long upon the dead—for we could not regard her unawed. The disease which had thus entombed the lady in the maturity of youth had left, as usual in all maladies of a strictly cataleptical character, the mockery of a faint blush upon the bosom and the face, and that suspiciously lingering smile upon the lip which is so terrible in death. We replaced and screwed down the lid, and, having secured the door of iron, made our way, with toil into the scarcely less gloomy apartments of the upper portion of the house.

And now, some days of bitter grief having elapsed, an observable change came over the features of the mental disorder of my friend. His ordinary manner had vanished. His ordinary occupations were neglected or forgotten. He roamed from chamber to chamber with hurried, unequal, and objectless step. The pallor of his countenance had assumed, if possible, a more ghastly hue—but the luminousness of his eye had utterly gone out. The once occasional huskiness of his tone was heard no more; and a tremulous quaver, as if of extreme terror, habitually characterized his utterance. There were times, indeed, when I thought his unceasingly agitated mind was laboring with some oppressive secret, to divulge which he struggled for the necessary courage. At times, again, I was obliged to resolve all into the mere inexplicable vagaries of madness, for I beheld him gazing upon vacancy for long hours, in an attitude of the profoundest attention, as if listening to some imaginary sound. It was no wonder that his condition terrified—that it infected me. I felt creeping upon me by slow yet certain degrees, the wild influences of his own fantastic yet impressive superstitions.

It was, especially, upon retiring to bed late in the night of the seventh or eighth day after the placing of the lady Madeline within the donjon, that I experienced the full power of such feelings. Sleep came not near my couch—while the hours waned and waned away. I struggled to reason off the nervousness which had dominion over me. I endeavored to believe that much, if not all, of what I felt was due to the bewildering influence of the gloomy furniture of the room—of the dark and tattered draperies, which, tortured into motion by the breath of a rising tempest, swayed fitfully to and fro upon the walls, and rustled uneasily about the decorations of the bed. But my efforts were fruitless. An irrepressible tremor gradually pervaded my frame; and at length there sat upon my very heart an incubus[28] of utterly causeless alarm. Shaking this off with a gasp and a struggle, I uplifted myself upon the pillows, and, peering earnestly within the intense darkness of the chamber, harkened—I know not why, except that an instinctive spirit prompted me—to certain low and indefinite sounds which came, through the pauses of the storm, at long intervals, I knew not whence. Overpowered by an intense sentiment of horror, unaccountable yet unendurable, I threw on my clothes with haste (for I felt that I should sleep no more during the night), and endeavored to arouse myself from the pitiable condition into which I had fallen by pacing rapidly to and fro through the apartment.

I had taken but few turns in this manner when a light step on an adjoining staircase arrested my attention. I presently recognized it as that of Usher. In an instant afterward he rapped, with a gentle touch, at my door, and entered, bearing a lamp. His countenance was, as usual, cadaverously wan—but, moreover, there was a species of mad hilarity in his eyes—an evidently restrained hysteria in his whole demeanor. His air appalled me—but anything was preferable to the solitude which I had so long endured, and I even welcomed his presence as a relief.

"And you have not seen it?" he said abruptly, after having stared about him for some moments in silence—"you have not then seen it?—but, stay! you shall." Thus speaking, and having carefully shaded his lamp, he hurried to one of the casements and threw it freely open to the storm.

The impetuous fury of the entering gust nearly lifted us from our feet. It was, indeed, a tempestuous yet sternly beautiful night, and one wildly singular in its terror and its beauty. A whirlwind had apparently collected its force in our vicinity, for there were frequent and violent alterations in the direction of the wind; and the exceeding density of the clouds (which hung so low as to press upon the turrets of the house) did not prevent our perceiving the lifelike velocity with which they flew careering from all points against each other, without passing away into the distance. I say that even their exceeding density did not prevent our perceiving this—yet we had no glimpse of the moon or stars—nor was there any flashing forth of the lightning. But the under surfaces of the huge masses of agitated vapor, as well as all terrestrial objects immediately around us, were glowing in the unnatural light of a faintly luminous and distinctly visible gaseous exhalation which hung about and enshrouded the mansion.

"You must not—you shall not behold this!" said I, shudderingly, to Usher, as I led him, with a gentle violence, from the window to a seat. "These appearances, which bewilder you, are merely electrical phenomena not uncommon—or it may be that they have their ghastly origin in the rank miasma of the tarn. Let us

---

28. **incubus** [ing'kyə bəs]: nightmare.

close this casement; the air is chilling and dangerous to your frame. Here is one of your favorite romances. I will read, and you shall listen; and so we will pass away this terrible night together."

The antique volume which I had taken up was the "Mad Trist"[29] of Sir Launcelot Canning; but I had called it a favorite of Usher's more in sad jest than in earnest; for in truth there is little in its uncouth and unimaginative prolixity which could have had interest for the lofty and spiritual ideality of my friend. It was, however, the only book immediately at hand; and I indulged a vague hope that the excitement which now agitated the hypochondriac might find relief (for the history of mental disorder is full of similar anomalies) even in the extremeness of the folly which I should read. Could I have judged, indeed, by the wild overstrained air of vivacity with which he harkened, or apparently harkened, to the words of the tale, I might well have congratulated myself upon the success of my design.

I had arrived at that well-known portion of the story where Ethelred, the hero of the Trist, having sought in vain for peaceable admission into the dwelling of the hermit, proceeds to make good an entrance by force. Here, it will be remembered, the words of the narrative run thus:

"And Ethelred, who was by nature of a doughty[30] heart, and who was now mighty withal, on account of the powerfulness of the wine which he had drunken, waited no longer to hold parley with the hermit, who, in sooth, was of an obstinate and maliceful turn, but, feeling the rain upon his shoulders, and fearing the rising of the tempest, uplifted his mace outright, and, with blows, made quickly room in the plankings of the door for his gauntleted hand; and now pulling therewith sturdily, he so cracked, and ripped, and tore all asunder, that the noise of the dry and hollow-sounding

wood alarumed and reverberated throughout the forest."

At the termination of this sentence I started and, for a moment, paused; for it appeared to me (although I at once concluded that my excited fancy had deceived me)—it appeared to me that, from some very remote portion of the mansion, there came, indistinctly to my ears, what might have been, in its exact similarity of character, the echo (but a stifled and dull one certainly) of the very cracking and ripping sound which Sir Launcelot had so particularly described. It was, beyond doubt, the coincidence alone which had arrested my attention; for, amid the rattling of the sashes of the casements and the ordinary commingled noises of the still increasing storm, the sound in itself had nothing, surely, which should have interested or disturbed me. I continued the story:

"But the good champion Ethelred, now entering within the door, was sore enraged and amazed to perceive no signal of the maliceful hermit; but, in the stead thereof, a dragon of a scaly and prodigious demeanor, and of a fiery tongue, which sat in guard before a palace of gold, with a floor of silver; and upon the wall there hung a shield of shining brass with this legend enwritten—

Who entereth herein, a conqueror hath bin;
Who slayeth the dragon, the shield he
    shall win.

And Ethelred uplifted his mace, and struck upon the head of the dragon, which fell before him, and gave up his pesty breath with a shriek so horrid and harsh, and withal so piercing, that Ethelred had fain to close his ears with his hands against the dreadful noise of it, the like whereof was never before heard."

Here again I paused abruptly, and now with a feeling of wild amazement—for there could be no doubt whatever that, in this instance, I did actually hear (although from what direction it proceeded I found it impossible to say) a low and apparently distant, but harsh, protracted, and most unusual screaming or grating

---

29. **"Mad Trist"**: The book and its author are fictional. A *trist* is a meeting.
30. **doughty** [dou′tē]: brave.

sound—the exact counterpart of what my fancy had already conjured up for the dragon's unnatural shriek as described by the romancer.

Oppressed, as I certainly was, upon the occurrence of this second and most extraordinary coincidence, by a thousand conflicting sensations, in which wonder and extreme terror were predominant, I still retained sufficient presence of mind to avoid exciting, by any observation, the sensitive nervousness of my companion. I was by no means certain that he had noticed the sounds in question; although, assuredly, a strange alteration had, during the last few minutes, taken place in his demeanor. From a position fronting my own, he had gradually brought round his chair, so as to sit with his face to the door of the chamber; and thus I could but partially perceive his features, although I saw that his lips trembled as if he were murmuring inaudibly. His head had dropped upon his breast—yet I knew that he was not asleep from the wide and rigid opening of the eye as I caught a glance of it in profile. The motion of his body, too, was at variance with this idea—for he rocked from side to side with a gentle yet constant and uniform sway. Having rapidly taken notice of all this, I resumed the narrative of Sir Launcelot, which thus proceeded:

"And now the champion, having escaped from the terrible fury of the dragon, bethinking himself of the brazen shield and of the breaking up of the enchantment which was upon it, removed the carcass from out of the way before him, and approached valorously over the silver pavement of the castle to where the shield was upon the wall, which in sooth tarried not for his full coming, but fell down at his feet upon the silver floor with a mighty great and terrible ringing sound."

No sooner had these syllables passed my lips, than—as if a shield of brass had indeed, at the moment, fallen heavily upon the floor of silver—I became aware of a distinct, hollow, metallic, and clangorous, yet apparently muffled, reverberation. Completely unnerved, I leaped to my feet; but the measured rocking movement of Usher was undisturbed. I rushed to the chair in which he sat. His eyes were bent fixedly before him, and throughout his whole countenance there reigned a stony rigidity. But, as I placed my hand upon his shoulder, there came a strong shudder over his whole person; a sickly smile quivered about his lips; and I saw that he spoke in a low, hurried, and gibbering murmur, as if unconscious of my presence. Bending closely over him, I at length drank in the hideous import of his words.

"Not hear it?—yes, I hear it, and *have* heard it. Long—long—long—many minutes, many hours, many days have I heard it—yet I dared not—oh, pity me, miserable wretch that I am!—I dared not—I *dared* not speak! *We have put her living in the tomb!* Said I not that my senses were acute? I *now* tell you that I heard her first feeble movements in the hollow coffin. I heard them—many, many days ago—yet I dared not—*I dared not speak!* And now—tonight—Ethelred—ha!ha!—the breaking of the hermit's door, and the death cry of the dragon, and the clangor of the shield!—say, rather, the rending of her coffin, and the grating of the iron hinges of her prison, and her struggles within the coppered archway of the vault! Oh whither shall I fly? Will she not be here anon? Is she not hurrying to upbraid me for my haste? Have I not heard her footstep on the stair? Do I not distinguish that heavy and horrible beating of her heart? Madman!"—here he sprang furiously to his feet, and shrieked out his syllables as if in the effort he were giving up his soul—*"Madman! I tell you that she now stands without the door!"*

As if in the superhuman energy of his utterance there had been found the potency of a spell—the huge antique panels to which the speaker pointed threw slowly back, upon the instant, their ponderous and ebony jaws. It was the work of the rushing gust—but then without those doors there *did* stand the lofty and enshrouded figure of the lady Madeline of Usher. There was blood upon her white robes, and the evidence of some bitter struggle upon every portion of her emaciated frame. For a moment she remained trembling and reeling to and fro upon the threshold—then, with a low moaning cry, fell heavily inward upon the person of her brother, and in her violent and now final death agonies, bore him to the floor a corpse, and a victim to the terrors he had anticipated.

From that chamber, and from that mansion, I fled aghast. The storm was still abroad in all its wrath as I found myself crossing the old causeway. Suddenly there shot along the path a wild light, and I turned to see whence a gleam so unusual could have issued; for the vast house and its shadows were alone behind me. The radiance was that of the full, setting, and blood-red moon, which now shone vividly through that once barely discernible fissure, of which I have before spoken as extending from the roof of the building, in a zigzag direction, to the base. While I gazed, this fissure rapidly widened—there came a fierce breath of the whirlwind—the entire orb of the satellite burst at once upon my sight—my brain reeled as I saw the mighty walls rushing asunder—there was a long tumultuous shouting sound like the voice of a thousand waters—and the deep and dank tarn at my feet closed sullenly and silently over the fragments of the *"House of Usher."*

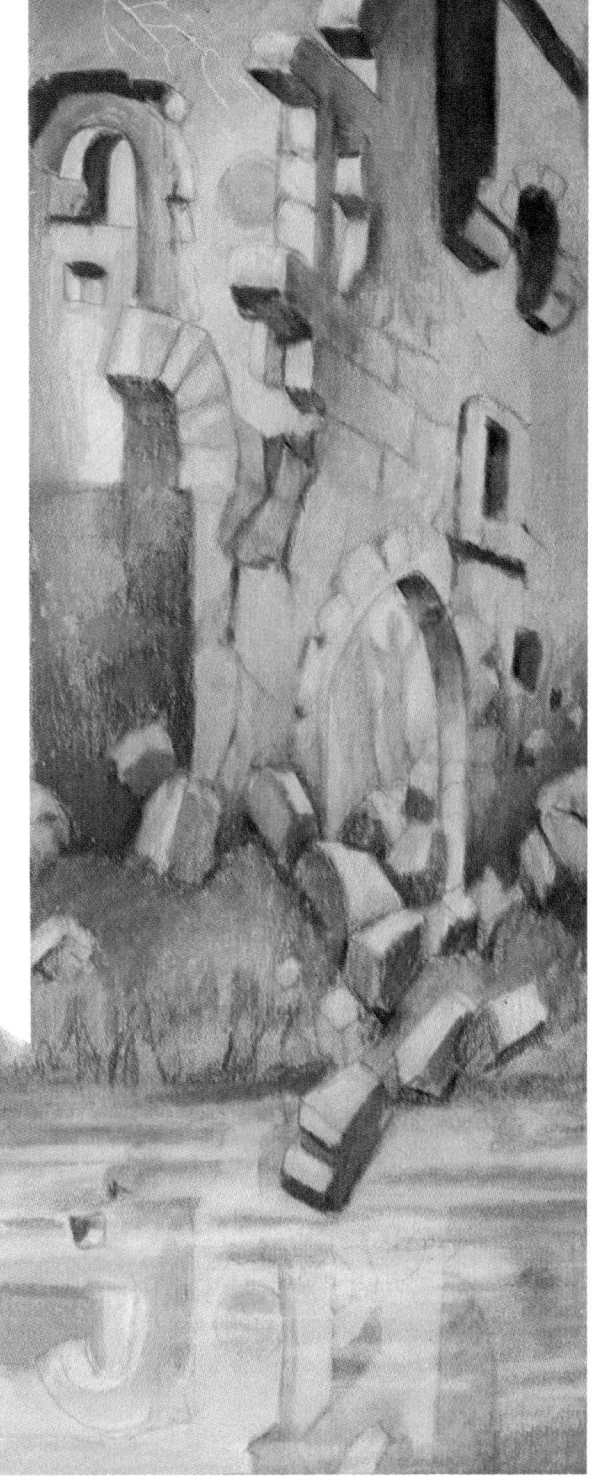

STUDY QUESTIONS

Recalling

1. What adjective does the narrator first use to describe the house of Usher? According to the third paragraph, what do the peasants mean when they say "House of Usher"?

2. Upon meeting the narrator, what does Roderick say about the nature of his "malady"? To what terror is he a "slave"? What does he admit is the natural cause of his gloomy condition?

3. What three things does the narrator do in an attempt to alleviate Roderick's melancholy (page 140)? What does the narrator understand for the first time when he hears Roderick perform "The Haunted Palace"?

4. What does the narrator notice while turning aside the lid of Madeline's coffin? What does Roderick explain?

5. What "observable change" comes over Roderick after the entombment of Madeline? What does his condition do to the narrator?

6. What interruptions occur when the narrator reads passages from "Mad Trist" to Roderick? What does Roderick reveal about Madeline's entombment?

7. What does the narrator see when the doors open "their ponderous and ebony jaws"? What happens to Roderick?

8. What happens to the house in the last paragraph?

Interpreting

9. What does Roderick's condition when the narrator arrives reveal about his relationship with his sister? Why is it significant that they are twins?

10. Why might Roderick have put Madeline in the tomb while she was alive? What other mysteries or supernatural elements does the story contain?

11. Name at least three character traits the narrator reveals about Roderick, either directly or indirectly. Does the narrator really understand his friend? How do you know?

12. Try to explain Roderick's deterioration. What in his own behavior might be the cause of his destruction?

13. What is the dual meaning of the story's title? Why is it significant that the Usher family has no "collateral issue" (paragraph 3)?

Extending

14. The English Romantic writer, Samuel Taylor Coleridge, said that we experience a "willing suspension of disbelief" when we read literature. In other words, we ignore our doubts about the possibility of events happening and willingly accept what the author tells us. Did you suspend your disbelief as you read "The Fall of the House of Usher"? Do you think the suspension of disbelief is necessary for the full enjoyment of a work of fiction? Why or why not?

VIEWPOINT

An expert on Poe, Arthur Hobson Quinn, writes of this story:

One of the most common errors in Poe criticism lies in the assumption of the absence of heart in his characters. But the narrator has come a long distance simply because the appeal of Roderick Usher has clutched at his friendship through that quality—"It was the apparent *heart* that went with his request."

—Edgar Allan Poe

■ Do you agree that the narrator and Roderick are believable characters with genuine, heartfelt emotions? Or do you find the characters artificial and mechanical? Support your opinion with details from the story itself.

LITERARY FOCUS

Setting: Atmosphere and Mood

In "The Fall of the House of Usher" the **setting**—the time and place in which the events occur—is as important as the characters themselves. It would be impossible, for example, to imagine the Ushers living anywhere else than in their ancient house near the black tarn. If they did, they would not be the same people we find in this story. As characters, they not only contribute to the setting, but they are created in part *by* the setting.

In what country is the story set? It is certainly not America, for in Poe's time the United States was not old enough to have produced this ancient family and crumbling mansion. Where is the House of Usher? Nowhere, except within the pages of the story itself. Yet the setting seems "real," with highly specific details about the rooms and the furnishings. The setting is a combination of reality and unreality that contributes to the unearthly effect of the story.

Notice, too, how Poe uses the setting to control the atmosphere, or mood—the general feeling—of the story by surrounding almost every object with adjectives piled upon adjectives: *dull, dark, dreary, bleak, decayed, pestilent, leaden-hued.* Each adjective has a separate meaning, of course, but more important is the way they merge, building an atmosphere of gloom and unreality. That atmosphere conveys not only the physical appearance of the house, but the Ushers' mental and spiritual condition as well.

Thinking About Setting
▨ Choose a passage in the story—the description of Usher's studio, for example—and point out the adjectives that create the atmosphere and mood.

VOCABULARY

Recognizing Shades of Meaning
Though several adjectives can combine to create a single effect, it is equally important to be aware of the shades of meanings of individual adjectives. *Dull* and *bleak,* for example, do not mean exactly the same thing. *Dull* suggests a quality of light; *bleak* suggests a wider picture of emptiness and hopelessness.

▨ Use your dictionary to define the following words from "The Fall of the House of Usher," paying special attention to the differences in meaning among the words in each group.

Group 1: decayed, morbid, pestilent
Group 2: pallid, ghastly, insipid
Group 3: dreary, somber, grim

COMPOSITION

Writing About the Total Effect
▨ Describe the total effect of "The Fall of the House of Usher." How does Poe use the following literary elements to achieve this effect: (1) the setting, (2) the characters, (3) the plot, and (4) the theme of the story? *For help with this assignment, refer to Lesson 8 in the Writing About Literature Handbook at the back of this book.*

Describing a Setting
▨ Write a paragraph describing a house or another place that has its own special atmosphere. Like Poe, use strings of adjectives to help convey the atmosphere. Assume that you are creating the setting for a mystery, a science fiction story, a humorous story, or a serious contemporary story.

COMPARING WRITERS

Washington Irving, James Fenimore Cooper, William Cullen Bryant, and Edgar Allan Poe are America's early Romantic writers. They share many of the characteristics of Romanticism (see the Introduction to this unit), yet they also differ greatly from one another.

1. Compare and contrast the profound love of nature in Bryant and Cooper. What does each author think should be the relationship between people and the natural world?
2. Compare and contrast the focus on the self and the individual in Irving, Cooper, Bryant, and Poe. What does each author reveal about the effects of this intense self-concern?
3. Compare and contrast the fascination with the supernatural in Irving and Poe. What effect does each author try to achieve?

READING FOR APPRECIATION

Significant Detail

Our greatest delight as readers lies in the details of what we are reading. In fact, the pleasure of reading literature comes from responding to the actual words as they appear before our eyes. If we fully respond to the details of "The Devil and Tom Walker," "Thanatopsis," "The Raven," or "The Fall of the House of Usher," we will sense some of the pleasure that Irving, Bryant, and Poe had as they created their texts. If we read too quickly, without attention, looking only for some abstract "meaning," reading is likely to become a chore rather than a pleasure. We must attend to the details. In fact, it is only from the details that the specific meaning arises.

Each good story or poem is different from all others, even if it shares its themes, its forms, its language with thousands of other works. That difference, that unique sound and texture, is what we try to capture as we read. We might try to sum up "Thanatopsis," for example, in this way: "We will all die, but we should be comforted by the thought that we will all be gathered into nature with every man and woman who lived before

us." Here we have the main idea of the poem but none of its pleasure. If we are to enjoy "Thanatopsis," or any poem, it will be because we give ourselves up to the specific movements of its verse, to the sound carrying us from line to line, to the details and images that make us feel the thought. Our pleasure is not always in "happy" thoughts, but in the perfection, the rightness of the language:

To be a brother to the insensible rock
And to the sluggish clod, which the rude swain
Turns with his share and treads upon. The oak
Shall send his roots abroad, and pierce thy mold.

From this feeling of negation, we move *with* and *in* the language of the poem toward a more positive and comforting feeling:

So live, that when thy summons comes to join
The innumerable caravan . . .
Thou go not, like the quarry-slave at night,
Scourged to his dungeon, but, sustained and soothed
By an unfaltering trust. . . .

To take just one detail, ask yourself why *innumerable* is so right here. For one thing, *innumerable caravan* suggests a long and stately procession moving toward a definite goal, rather than a disorderly or panic-driven mob. For another, *innumerable* is the only word in the poem with as many as five syllables, and the sense that many syllables suddenly come together in one word supports the sense that many (in fact, *innumerable*) people are moving together in this caravan. In itself, *innumerable* is not a particularly interesting word at all. Yet placed within its context in this poem, it becomes a source of delight.

Consider the gridiron ribs of Tom Walker's horse. From that detail we see that Tom is so greedy that he feeds his poor horse only enough to keep it alive. Think about the doors to Roderick's room in Poe's story. They open like "ponderous and ebony jaws." That detail—jaws—continues the suggestion made at the beginning of the story—with "vacant eyelike windows"—that the house itself is almost human. Such details are sources of *meaning* and part of the *pleasure* of a text.

THE AMERICAN VOICE

Other Times, Other Places

One of the paradoxes of Romantic literature is that it can be passionately nationalistic and still long for foreign places and ancient ages. Romantic authors, like those in this unit, insist on the value of their own land, their own customs and language, their own time in history. Yet these same authors often dream of old tales and exotic settings, as the following quotations reveal:

Irving
Under one of these gigantic trees, according to old stories, there was a great amount of treasure buried by Kidd the pirate. The inlet allowed a facility to bring the money in a boat secretly and at night to the very foot of the hill; the elevation of the place permitted a good lookout to be kept that no one was at hand; while the remarkable trees formed good landmarks by which the place might easily be found again.

Cooper
The incidents of this tale occurred between the years 1740 and 1745, when the settled portions of the colony of New York were confined to the four Atlantic counties. . . . A bird's-eye view of the whole region east of the Mississippi must then have offered one vast expanse of woods, relieved by a comparatively narrow fringe of cultivation along the sea, dotted by the glittering surfaces of lakes, and intersected by the waving lines of rivers. In such a vast picture of solemn solitude, the district of country we design to paint sinks into insignificance. . . .

Bryant
*. . . Thou shalt lie down
With patriarchs of the infant
    world—with kings,
The powerful of the earth—the
    wise, the good,
Fair forms, and hoary seers of
    ages past. . . .*

Poe
*Thy Naiad airs have brought
    me home
  To the glory that was Greece,
And the grandeur that was
    Rome.*

These writers established a national identity for American literature in the first part of the nineteenth century. They helped define the character of the New World, but they never gave up the marvels of the past.

Key to Illustrations on Pages 98–99.

1		2		8
3	4	5		9
6	7			10

1. *Fur Traders Descending the Missouri,* George Caleb Bingham, 1851.
2. Women operating looms in a New England mill, early nineteenth century.
3. Monticello, the Virginia home of Thomas Jefferson, designed by Jefferson himself.
4. Edgar Allan Poe, daguerreotype (early photograph) by Mathew Brady.
5. *Baltimore Oriole,* colored engraving from *Birds of America* (1827–1838), John James Audubon.
6. James Fenimore Cooper, engraving, 1831.
7. *The Old House of Representatives,* Samuel F. B. Morse, 1822.
8. *Pat Lyon at the Forge,* John Neagle, 1826.
9. William Cullen Bryant. Nineteenth-century engraving.
10. The steamboat *Clermont,* built by Robert Fulton, 1807.

Key to Illustrations appears on page 215.

NEW ENGLAND RENAISSANCE

1840–1855

During the colonial and revolutionary periods American culture struggled for survival. During the early nineteenth century it struggled for individuality. By mid-century it was struggling for greatness.

A remarkable outburst of creativity marked this time, especially the years 1840 to 1855. Two famous books about this time—*American Renaissance* and *The Flowering of New England*—suggest in their titles the extraordinary quality of this period. A *renaissance* is a rebirth, a vital period in a culture, a ripeness that calls forth a concentration of great writers and artists. Such flowering periods took place in ancient Athens, in fifteenth- and sixteenth-century Italy, and in Elizabethan England. The United States, by mid-nineteenth century, began to flower. It had achieved self-confidence, prosperity, and a settled and mature culture. American expansiveness and the assertion of individualism seemed to demand a great literature to celebrate and explain—and to criticize as well—the mysterious uniqueness of American life.

As the nation consolidated and grew, its problems grew too: Slavery, materialism, child labor, and political corruption had become crucial dilemmas in America, and the Mexican-American War (1846–1848) provoked heated debates about American expansion. Yet as most Americans looked about them, they saw new states joining the union, a great movement into the central plains of the

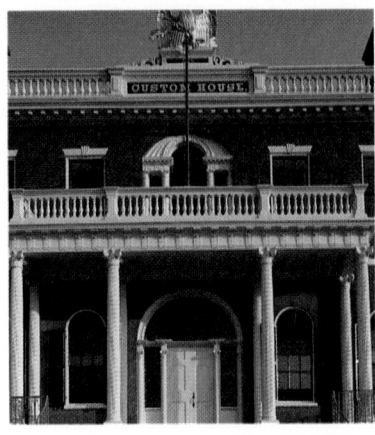

The Custom House in Salem, Massachusetts, where Nathaniel Hawthorne once worked.

continent, and a conspicuous growth of industry, invention, technology, and trade that produced a general prosperity, pride, and confidence in the nation's future.

Democracy, a concept that in the eighteenth century few people thought would actually work, was indeed working. The election of Andrew Jackson in 1828, the first real "man of the people" to become President, dramatized the democratic spirit and the new, easy, not always graceful ways of Americans, freed from European constraints of class and tradition.

The Literary Response

Americans had always produced a vital literary response to their experience: the Native Americans, the Puritans, the planters, the revolutionaries, the early Romantics. Yet many American writers—even Irving and Cooper—seemed to be still a bit provincial, still under the influence of English and other European writers. The first steps taken by Irving, Cooper, Bryant, and Poe had to be lengthened, and now came the giant strides. A convenient historical marker is Emerson's stirring lecture *The American Scholar* (1837), often called America's intellectual declaration of independence. Emerson exclaimed, "We will walk on our own feet; we will work with our own hands; we will speak our own minds." The na-

tion listened and took the words to heart.

Increasingly, American writers, many of them directly inspired by Emerson, began to free themselves from European models. During a relatively few years, concentrating around Boston and the village of Concord, a number of writers appeared whom we now think of as "classic." Some of them, such as Emerson and Hawthorne, were well known in their time; others, like Thoreau, were uncelebrated until years after their deaths. Their influence, especially Emerson's, reached Walt Whitman in New York and Emily Dickinson in western Massachusetts. We say these writers are great because their work has for many readers a vitality and originality that endures, that transcends time and place. They produced work that has a scope and a depth that still reach us, still inspire us, still make us ask the great questions and face the most mysterious of realities. At times this literature celebrates

the American, even the human, spirit. At times it criticizes the easy optimism that also marked the first half of the nineteenth century.

The Transcendentalists

Transcendentalism is a formidable term describing the movement in American culture that energized much of the literature of this period. To *transcend* something is to rise above it, to pass beyond its limits.

Transcendentalism is based on the belief that the most fundamental truths about life and death can be reached only by going beyond the world of the senses. The Transcendentalists believed—democratically—that each and every man and woman, living as a true individual, free from restraining dogma and dull habits of thought, could rise above the material world. They believed that each human mind could know something of the ultimate spiritual reality but could not know it through logic or the data of the senses. Rather, that knowledge came through a deep, free *intuition,* which they recognized as the "highest power of the Soul."

Transcendentalist is a fairly loose term referring to a large group of men and women who were very different from one another both as individuals and as writers. They did not have a strict doctrine or code to which they all subscribed. Transcendentalism is more of a tendency,

The rhodora, a flower that symbolized for Emerson the transcendental beauty and power of nature.

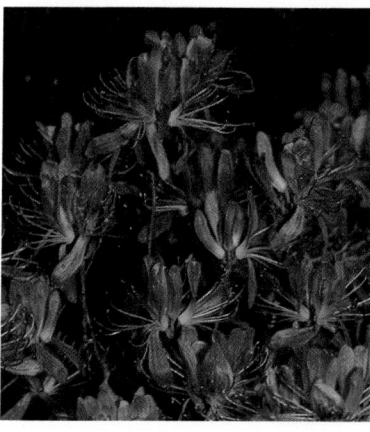

an attitude, than it is a philosophy in any well-defined way. Nevertheless, we are able to define some aspects of it.

Nature played an important role in the Transcendentalist view. Nature was divine, alive with spirit; the human mind could *read* nature, find truths in it. To live in harmony with nature, to allow one's deepest intuitive being to communicate with nature, was a source of goodness and inspiration. We hear Emerson, in his rhapsodic essay *Nature,* an emotional outpouring, trying to capture in words the experience of that communication with nature:

"Standing on the bare ground— my head bathed by the blithe air and uplifted into infinite space—all mean egotism vanishes. I become a transparent eyeball; I am nothing; I see all; the currents of the Universal Being circulate through me; I am part or particle of God."

The Transcendentalists believed that this deep intuition of a spiritual reality is available to us only if we allow ourselves to be individuals, and Transcendentalist writing places a strong emphasis on *individualism.* Transcendentalism is also very *democratic,* asserting that the powers of the individual mind and soul are equally available to all people. These powers are not dependent upon wealth or background or education. We all have a potential equality as spiritual beings, and the divinity

within each of us can be realized by the laborer and the farmer as well as by the learned minister and the scholar. For Emerson, every person can be a kind of poet, releasing individual imaginative power.

Such thoughts and feelings led the Transcendentalists to intense *moral enthusiasm* and concerns. Society, with its emphasis on material success, is often seen as a source of corruption. The Transcendentalist wants to do the right thing, the moral thing. That desire brought many Transcendentalists into efforts to *reform society,* to create a utopia—a perfect social and political system. They worked toward their ideal through utopian communities such as Brook Farm, through the antislavery movement, and through a sometimes vigorous feminism. The tone of Transcendentalist writing is often intensely optimistic and aspiring. It frequently suggests that the individual, in harmony with the divine universe, can transform the world.

The Darker Visions

The optimism of the Transcendentalists was not shared by all the great writers of the time. There were those—Hawthorne and Melville are the outstanding examples—who saw the universe as a more confusing and difficult place. Nature, they thought, is ambiguous, not easy to read, interpret, and harmonize. Evil and suffering had to be accounted for and were not to be brushed airily aside. Human nature was obstinate. Life was, as it always had been and always would be, mysterious.

Emerson could not read Hawthorne with pleasure, for he found Hawthorne's tales too gloomy. Hawthorne admired Emerson but thought him "a mystic, stretching his hand out of cloud-land, in vain search for something real." Melville had no use at all for Transcendentalism and the optimism of Emerson. To him it was all "nonsense," a much too easy dismissal of life's "disagreeable facts." For Melville life was a matter of compromises, not ideals—a spectacle of disappointment and illusion.

It is our privilege, as readers, not to need to take sides. Each of us will have preferences, perhaps recognizing part of the truth in one writer, part in another, perhaps seeing different parts at different times of our lives. Two elements, however, are common to all these writers: the power of their writing and the sincerity of their search.

Nathaniel Hawthorne's study and writing table in The Old Manse, Salem, Massachusetts.

The American Romance

An important development in American writing began to take shape with the writing of Hawthorne and Melville. This was the idea of the *romance*.

"Native Grounds" (pages 98–151) contains works of the early American Romantic writers—Irving, Cooper, Bryant, and Poe. These writers certainly exemplify many of the characteristics of the large movement called Romanticism. But it is with Hawthorne that an American writer began to make a critical distinction between a *novel* and a *romance*. This important distinction is useful in helping us to define just what it is that makes an American narrative different from a European narrative.

Hawthorne described what he meant by romance in the Preface to *The House of the Seven Gables* (1851):

"When a writer calls his work a Romance, it need hardly be observed that he wishes to claim a certain latitude, both as to its fashion and material, which he would not have felt himself entitled to assume, had he professed to be writing a Novel. The latter form of composition is presumed to aim at a very minute fidelity, not merely to the possible, but to the probable and ordinary course of man's experience. The former—while, as a work of art, it must rigidly subject itself to laws, and while it sins unpardonably so far

as it may swerve aside from the truth of the human heart—has fairly a right to present that truth under circumstances, to a great extent, of the writer's own choosing or creation."

Hawthorne's statement makes clear that he thought a romance need not be totally faithful to reality. A romance can make greater use of the marvelous, the improbable, the eccentric, even the completely unbelievable. A romance need not tie itself to an accurate portrait of real people in the real social and physical world—as a novel does—as long as it is true to the human heart. Hawthorne's story "The Minister's Black Veil" is built on a highly improbable situation, but it remains faithful to larger human emotions. Melville's *Moby-Dick* contains characters and events that we never would expect to find in the real world, yet this great novel never fails to strike a reader as a voyage into authentic human experience.

As Hawthorne wrote, it would be a great mistake for a

reader to try to bring "his fancy-pictures almost into positive contact with the realities of the moment." For Hawthorne—and for many of the American novelists to follow him—an American "novel" should only be judged as a romance.

The Fireside Poets

The Fireside Poets—Henry Wadsworth Longfellow, Oliver Wendell Holmes, James Russell Lowell, and John Greenleaf Whittier—also began writing during the time of Emerson, Hawthorne, and Melville. Their visions, however, were neither strictly Transcendental nor difficult and bleak. They did not form an organized group, but history has linked them for what they had in common.

The Fireside Poets were often concerned with ordinary American people, history, and values. Their poems were inspiring and easy to read; they made the reading of poetry immensely popular. The name *Fireside Poets* suggests their honored place in American homes during the 1800s. Together these poets forged a kind of national mythology—creating American scenes, telling American tales, putting into poetry a romanticized image of the American way of life. Though now they bow to the greatness of Emerson, Thoreau, Hawthorne, and Melville, they did spread an awareness of poetry throughout the country and contribute to the American Renaissance.

TIME LINE

1840 *The Dial,* Transcendentalist magazine, begins publication

Brook Farm, utopian community, established

1841 Ralph Waldo Emerson, *Self-Reliance* and *Essays*

1841 Antarctica: Englishman James Ross explores the continent

1842 New York Philharmonic Symphony Orchestra established

U.S. and Seminole Indians sign peace treaty

1843 John Greenleaf Whittier, *Lays of My Home and Other Poems*

1843 England: Charles Dickens, *A Christmas Carol*

1844 France: Alexander Dumas *père, The Three Musketeers*

1845 First written examinations given in Boston public schools

1845 Ireland: Failure of potato crop causes famine

1846 Oliver Wendell Holmes, *Poems*

Herman Melville, *Typee*

Smithsonian Institution established in Washington

Mexican-American War begins

1846 Germany: Astronomers discover planet Neptune

Belgium: Adolphe Sax patents saxophone

1847 First adhesive postage stamp used in America

1847 England: Charlotte Brontë, *Jane Eyre*

England: Emily Brontë, *Wuthering Heights*

1848 James Russell Lowell, *The Biglow Papers* and *A Fable for Critics*

California Gold Rush begins

Mexican-American War ends: U.S. adds much territory to its borders

1849 Elizabeth Blackwell becomes first woman in U.S. to receive a medical degree

Francis Parkman, *The Oregon Trail*

1850 Nathaniel Hawthorne, *The Scarlet Letter*

Congress enacts Compromise of 1850

U.S. population 23.1 million

1851 Herman Melville, *Moby-Dick*

Nathaniel Hawthorne, *The House of the Seven Gables*

The *New York Times* first published

Isaac Singer patents first continuous-stitch sewing machine

1852 Harriet Beecher Stowe, *Uncle Tom's Cabin*

1853 U.S. purchases southern New Mexico and Arizona from Mexico

1854 Henry David Thoreau, *Walden*

1855 Henry Wadsworth Longfellow, *The Song of Hiawatha*

1848 Belgium: Karl Marx and Friedrich Engels, *The Communist Manifesto*

1849 France: Realism movement in art begins

1850 England: Charles Dickens, *David Copperfield*

1851 Italy: Giuseppe Verdi composes the opera *Rigoletto*

1852 Europe: Crimean War begins

France: Henry Gifford makes successful flight in steam-powered airship

1854 England: Alfred, Lord Tennyson, "The Charge of the Light Brigade"

1855 Africa: David Livingstone discovers Victoria Falls

THE ESSAY: *Emerson and Thoreau*

Ralph Waldo Emerson   *1803–1882*

Outwardly Ralph Waldo Emerson's life was quiet and well ordered, but inwardly it overflowed with new ideas. Emerson was born in Boston, the son of a Unitarian minister who died when Waldo, as he preferred to be called, was eight years old. He attended Harvard, studied theology, and became a Unitarian minister himself in 1829. In that year he was also married, but his beloved wife, Ellen, died only sixteen months later.

In 1832, for reasons of conscience, Emerson felt obliged to resign his ministry. After a trip to Europe, where he met the English writers Wordsworth, Coleridge, and Carlyle, he settled in the village of Concord, Massachusetts. He remarried and began his lifelong career as lecturer and writer. At Concord he became a member of the Transcendental Club and was surrounded by a remarkable group of men and women, including Henry David Thoreau, Bronson Alcott, and Margaret Fuller.

It was at Concord that Emerson composed his first book, *Nature* (1836). His address called *The American Scholar* (1837) has been an inspiration to generations of young Americans, but Emerson did not achieve national fame until his *Essays* appeared in 1841. Then came *Essays: Second Series* (1844), *Representative Men* (1849), and *The Conduct of Life* (1860).

When he was a young man, Emerson began writing what he called his "Savings Bank," the remarkable journals and notebooks that were not published in full until almost a century after his death. He would "deposit" in these journals his daily thoughts and observations as well as notes on his wide reading. From them he would "withdraw" the language and ideas for lectures. As he became increasingly famous as an American "prophet," he traveled widely throughout the country, delivering the lectures in a rich and beautiful voice. The lectures, polished and improved with many deliveries, often became the basis for the essays that were important influences upon so many American writers, including Thoreau, Whitman, Dickinson, and Frost. Yet Emerson's great influence extended beyond the literary community to the American people at large. His optimism, his belief in the vast possibilities of mind and spirit, and his doctrine of self-reliance well suited a democratic, progressive nation.

No single essay of Emerson's can give an adequate sense of his range of thought and mood. If at times he appears to contradict himself, it is because he wished himself and all of us to grow and to become aware of the mystery and richness of experience. "I wish to say what I think and feel today," he declared, "with the proviso that tomorrow perhaps I shall contradict it all. Freedom boundless I wish." Emerson continually redefined his own vision and fought to inspire others to have the noblest conceptions of themselves and of the "God in us."

It is easy to find oversimplified, watered-down versions of Emersonian aspiration, optimism, and individualism. Simplifications of his thought often lead toward the very opposite of what he meant. When Emerson spoke, for example, of the potential powers of the self-reliant individual—"A man is stronger than a city"—he did not mean that we should become irresponsibly obsessed with our selves. He did not mean that individualism is a license to do as we wish as we grasp for power and wealth. For Emerson, individualism is idealistic. He would have us trust in "divine providence," live in harmony with nature and with what he called the Oversoul, the universal spirit that is the source of all unity and growth. Emerson believed that if we "see truly" we will "live truly."

Nature and "Self-Reliance" are two of Emerson's best-known and most influential essays. *Nature* is a lyrical expression of the harmony Emerson felt between himself and nature. "Self-Reliance" is also at the core of Emerson's ideas—what one of his biographers calls "a twenty-one gun salute to self-reliance."

Spring Blossoms, George Inness, 1889.

Ralph Waldo Emerson

from **Nature**

To go into solitude, a man needs to retire as much from his chamber as from society. I am not solitary whilst I read and write, though nobody is with me. But if a man would be alone, let him look at the stars. The rays that come from those heavenly worlds will separate between him and what he touches. One might think the atmosphere was made transparent with this design, to give man, in the heavenly bodies, the perpetual presence of the sublime. Seen in the streets of cities, how great they are! If the stars should appear one night in a thousand years, how would men believe and adore, and preserve for many generations the remembrance of the city of God which had been shown! But every night come out these envoys of beauty, and light the universe with their admonishing smile.

The stars awaken a certain reverence because, though always present, they are inaccessible; but all natural objects make a kindred impression when the mind is open to their influence. Nature never wears a mean[1] appearance. Neither does the wisest man extort her secret and lose his curiosity by finding out all her perfection. Nature never became a toy to a wise spirit. The flowers, the animals, the mountains reflected the wisdom of his best hour, as much as they had delighted the simplicity of his childhood. . . .

To speak truly, few adult persons can see nature. Most persons do not see the sun. At least they have a very superficial seeing. The sun illuminates only the eye of the man, but shines into the eye and the heart of the child. The lover of nature is he whose inward and outward senses are still truly adjusted to each other, who has retained the spirit of infancy even into the era of manhood. His intercourse with heaven and earth becomes part of his daily food. In the presence of nature a wild delight runs through the man, in spite of real sorrows. Nature says: He is my creature, and maugre[2] all his impertinent griefs, he shall be glad with me. Not the sun or the summer alone, but every hour and season yields its tribute of delight; for every hour and change corresponds to and authorizes a different state of the mind, from breathless noon to grimmest midnight. Nature is a setting that fits equally well a comic or a mourning piece. In good health, the air is a cordial[3] of incredible virtue. Crossing a bare common,[4] in snow puddles, at twilight, under a clouded sky, without having in my thoughts any occurrence of special good fortune, I have enjoyed a perfect exhilaration. I am glad to the brink of fear. In the woods, too, a man casts off his years, as the snake his slough, and at what period soever of life is always a child. In the woods is perpetual youth. Within these plantations of God, a decorum[5] and sanctity reign; a perennial festival is dressed, and the guest sees not how he should tire of them in a thousand years. In the woods, we return to reason and faith. There I feel that nothing can befall me in life—no disgrace, no calamity (leaving me my eyes), which nature cannot repair. Standing on the bare ground—my head bathed by the blithe air and uplifted into infinite space—all mean egotism vanishes. I become a transparent eyeball; I am nothing; I see all; the currents of the Universal Being circulate through me; I am part or particle of God. The name of the nearest friend sounds then foreign and accidental: to be brothers, to be acquaintances, master or servant, is then a trifle and a disturbance. I am the lover of uncontained and immortal beauty.

---

1. **mean:** shabby; miserly; ignoble.
2. **maugre** [môʹgər]: in spite of.
3. **cordial:** stimulating medicine or drink.
4. **common:** area of open public land.
5. **decorum:** rightness; harmony.

In the wilderness, I find something more dear and connate[6] than in streets or villages. In the tranquil landscape, and especially in the distant line of the horizon, man beholds somewhat as beautiful as his own nature.

The greatest delight which the fields and woods minister is the suggestion of an occult relation between man and the vegetable. I am not alone and unacknowledged. They nod to me, and I to them. The waving of the boughs in the storm is new to me and old. It takes me by surprise, and yet is not unknown. Its effect is like that of a higher thought or a better emotion coming over me, when I deemed I was thinking justly or doing right.

---

6. **connate** [kon'āt]: closely related.

Yet it is certain that the power to produce this delight does not reside in nature, but in man, or in a harmony of both. It is necessary to use these pleasures with great temperance. For nature is not always tricked[7] in holiday attire; but the same scene which yesterday breathed perfume and glittered as for the frolic of the nymphs is overspread with melancholy today. Nature always wears the colors of the spirit. To a man laboring under calamity, the heat of his own fire hath sadness in it. Then there is a kind of contempt of the landscape felt by him who has just lost by death a dear friend. The sky is less grand as it shuts down over less worth in the population. . . .

---

7. **tricked:** dressed.

STUDY QUESTIONS

Recalling

1. According to paragraph 1, what does Emerson say would happen if the stars appeared one night in a thousand years?
2. According to paragraph 2, why does Emerson believe the stars awaken a reverence in people? When do natural objects make a similar impression of reverence?
3. According to paragraph 3, how does Emerson describe the lover of nature?
4. Summarize the first sentence of paragraph 4. Be sure to use your own words in the summary.

Interpreting

5. Near the end of paragraph 3, what does Emerson mean when he describes himself as "a transparent eyeball" when in the woods? How does this state of mind affect his relationship with God?
6. Where does Emerson believe the power for a true relationship between man and God comes from, according to paragraph 5?

Extending

7. What do you think is the difference between the kind of meaning Emerson finds in nature and the meaning a botanist, a geographer, or an astrophysicist finds in nature?

Ralph Waldo Emerson

from **Self-Reliance**

Trust thyself: every heart vibrates to that iron string. Accept the place the divine providence has found for you, the society of your contemporaries, the connection of events. Great men have always done so, and confided themselves childlike to the genius[1] of their age, betraying their perception that the absolutely trustworthy was seated at their heart, working through their hands, predominating in all their being. And we are now men, and must accept in the highest mind the same transcendent destiny; and not minors and invalids in a protected corner, not cowards fleeing before a revolution, but guides, redeemers, and benefactors, obeying the Almighty effort and advancing on Chaos and the Dark. . . .

A foolish consistency is the hobgoblin of little minds, adored by little statesmen and philosophers and divines. With consistency a great soul has simply nothing to do. He may as well concern himself with his shadow on the wall. Speak what you think now in hard words, and tomorrow speak what tomorrow thinks in hard words again, though it contradict everything you said today. "Ah, so you shall be sure to be misunderstood." Is it so bad then to be misunderstood? Pythagoras was misunderstood, and Socrates, and Jesus, and Luther, and Copernicus, and Galileo, and Newton,[2] and every pure and wise spirit that ever took flesh. To be great is to be misunderstood. . . .

Man is timid and apologetic; he is no longer upright; he dares not say, "I think," "I am," but quotes some saint or sage. He is ashamed before the blade of grass or the blowing rose. These roses under my window make no reference to former roses or to better ones; they are for what they are; they exist with God today. There is no time to them. There is simply the rose; it is perfect in every moment of its existence. Before a leaf bud has burst, its whole life acts; in the full-blown flower there is no more; in the leafless root there is no less. Its nature is satisfied and it satisfies nature in all moments alike. But man postpones or remembers; he does not live in the present, but with reverted[3] eye laments the past, or, heedless of the riches that surround him, stands on tiptoe to foresee the future. He cannot be happy and strong until he too lives with nature in the present, above time.

This should be plain enough. Yet see what strong intellects dare not yet hear God himself unless he speak the phraseology of I know not what David, or Jeremiah, or Paul.[4] We shall not always set so great a price on a few texts, on a few lives. We are like children who repeat by rote the sentences of grandames and tutors and, as they grow older, of the men of talents and character they chance to see— painfully recollecting the exact words they spoke. Afterwards, when they come into the point of view which those had who uttered these sayings, they understand them and are willing to let the words go, for at any time they can use words as good when occasion comes. If we live truly, we shall see truly. It is as easy for the strong man to be strong as it is for the weak to be weak. When we have new perception, we shall gladly disburden the memory of its hoarded treasures as old rubbish. When a man lives with God, his voice shall be as sweet as the murmur of the brook and the rustle of the corn. . . .

---

1. **genius:** spirit.
2. **Pythagoras . . . Newton:** Individuals who made an extraordinary contribution to scientific, philosophical, or religious thinking.

3. **reverted:** backward-looking.
4. **David . . . Paul:** biblical writers.

STUDY QUESTIONS

Recalling

1. According to paragraph 1, to what "iron string" does every heart vibrate?
2. According to paragraph 2, what is "the hobgoblin of little minds"? What does the paragraph say about Pythagoras, Socrates, and Jesus?
3. At the beginning of paragraph 3, how is man described? According to the end of the paragraph, under what conditions will man be "happy and strong"?
4. According to the last paragraph, what will happen if we live truly?

Interpreting

5. Explain two lessons that great figures of the past teach us about the concept of self-reliance.
6. Explain two lessons that nature teaches about self-reliance.
7. In your opinion does Emerson express optimism or pessimism about human nature and human potential? What seems to be the basis of his belief? Support your answer to this question with specific references to the essay.

Extending

8. Explain to what extent the concept of self-reliance can be considered a fundamental American idea. Support your answer with references to works that you have read in this book as well as to other aspects of American life and history.

LITERARY FOCUS

Figurative Language

Literal language is language that means exactly what it says, word for word—for example, "I stand on tiptoe to reach the shelf." **Figurative language** is language that is not meant to be taken literally. For example, Emerson describes someone who "stands on tiptoe to foresee the future." Phrases using figurative language, such as similes and metaphors, are often called **figures of speech.**

The origin of *figure* is the Latin word for "form" or "shape," and figurative language gives to an idea a familiar form or shape. When Emerson says, for instance, that he becomes a "transparent eyeball," he uses figurative language. He presents a concrete image—something we can perceive with our senses—to help us understand the abstract idea of wonder.

Figurative language can also make commonplace ideas fresh and vivid. When Emerson says, "I am glad to the *brink* of fear," or when he tells us, "a man casts off his years, *as the snake his slough,*" he provides vivid pictures of emotions that otherwise might not seem unusual. By using figurative language throughout the third paragraph of *Nature,* Emerson underscores the extraordinary exhilaration he experiences in nature.

Thinking About Figurative Language

■ Find at least three examples of figurative language in "Self-Reliance." Tell why each image is appropriate to the idea it makes concrete.

On July 4, 1837, a monument was unveiled in Concord, at the spot where the American Minutemen had first done battle with British troops in 1775. At the request of the Monument Committee, Emerson wrote the words to this hymn, which was sung at the memorial ceremony.

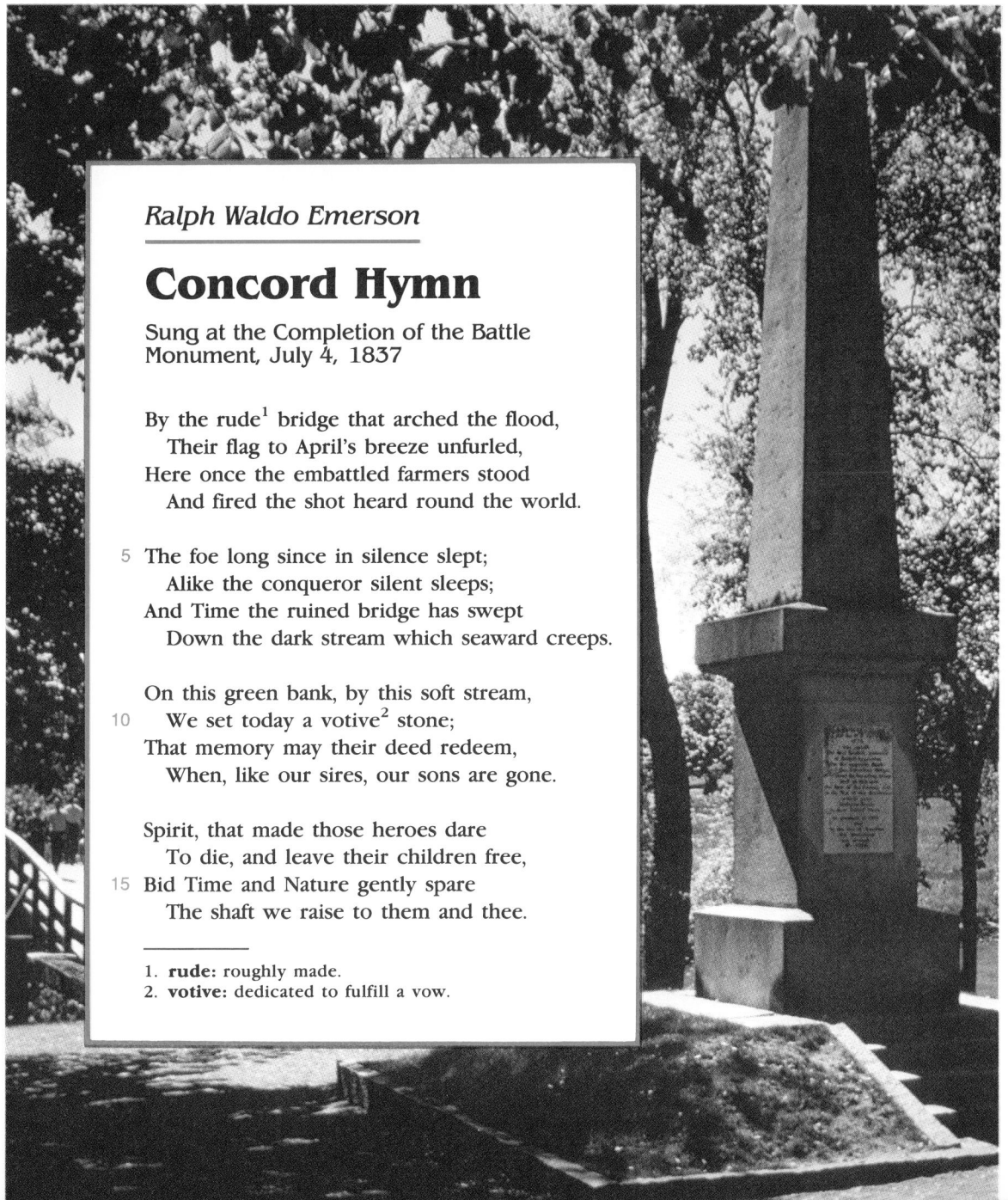

Ralph Waldo Emerson

Concord Hymn

Sung at the Completion of the Battle
Monument, July 4, 1837

By the rude[1] bridge that arched the flood,
   Their flag to April's breeze unfurled,
Here once the embattled farmers stood
   And fired the shot heard round the world.

5 The foe long since in silence slept;
   Alike the conqueror silent sleeps;
And Time the ruined bridge has swept
   Down the dark stream which seaward creeps.

On this green bank, by this soft stream,
10   We set today a votive[2] stone;
That memory may their deed redeem,
   When, like our sires, our sons are gone.

Spirit, that made those heroes dare
   To die, and leave their children free,
15 Bid Time and Nature gently spare
   The shaft we raise to them and thee.

1. **rude:** roughly made.
2. **votive:** dedicated to fulfill a vow.

Written while the idea for the essay *Nature* (page 161) was developing in Emerson's mind, this poem expresses the same intimacy between human nature and the surrounding world. Here the poet stops to address the rhodora, a shrub that often flowers in spring before its leaves appear.

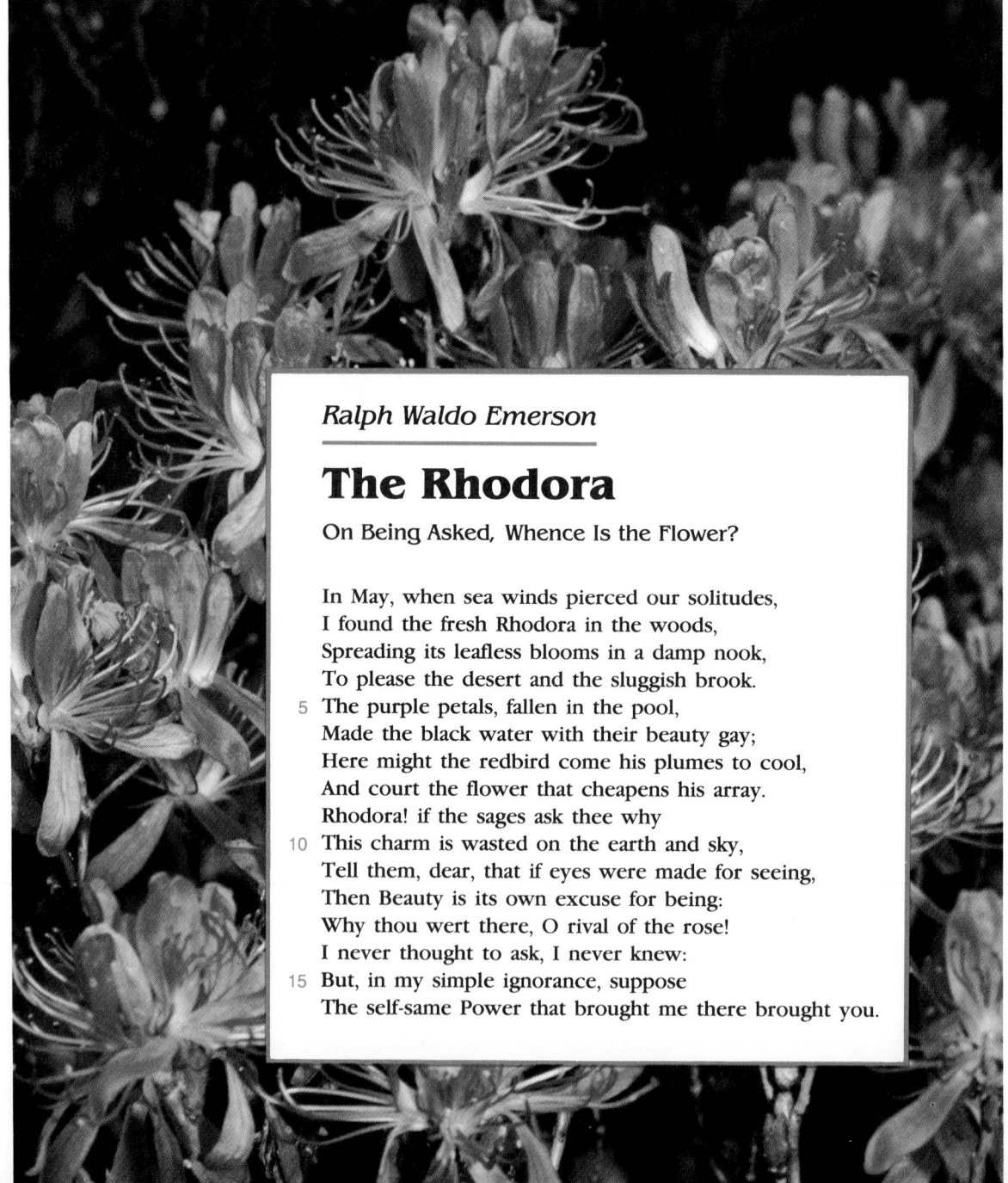

Ralph Waldo Emerson

The Rhodora

On Being Asked, Whence Is the Flower?

In May, when sea winds pierced our solitudes,
I found the fresh Rhodora in the woods,
Spreading its leafless blooms in a damp nook,
To please the desert and the sluggish brook.
5 The purple petals, fallen in the pool,
Made the black water with their beauty gay;
Here might the redbird come his plumes to cool,
And court the flower that cheapens his array.
Rhodora! if the sages ask thee why
10 This charm is wasted on the earth and sky,
Tell them, dear, that if eyes were made for seeing,
Then Beauty is its own excuse for being:
Why thou wert there, O rival of the rose!
I never thought to ask, I never knew:
15 But, in my simple ignorance, suppose
The self-same Power that brought me there brought you.

Concord Hymn

Recalling

1. According to stanzas 1 and 2, what was fired at Concord Bridge, and what has since happened to the bridge?
2. According to stanza 3, what will redeem the deaths of the heroes?
3. What is the poet's request in the last stanza?

Interpreting

4. In what sense was the shot fired at Concord Bridge "heard round the world"?
5. What ideals is the poet celebrating in lines 13–14?

The Rhodora

Recalling

1. What question prompts the poet to write?
2. What question does Emerson say the sages might ask? What answer does he say should be given to the sages?
3. According to the last four lines, what had always been the poet's own response to the rhodora?

Interpreting

4. In a larger sense, what does the rhodora represent?
5. How does the poet contrast himself with the sages? What does this contrast suggest about the kind of attitude needed to understand nature?
6. What do you think the poet really means by his "simple ignorance"?
7. Explain the meaning of line 16. What harmony does the line imply?

Extending

8. Do you agree that "Beauty is its own excuse for being"? Tell why or why not.

VIEWPOINT

Van Wyck Brooks, a well-known literary critic, summarizes the effect of Emerson's ideas:

He addressed himself . . . especially to students and beginners in life. . . . [He] stirred them to take life strivingly in full belief that what man had done man could do, that the world was all opportunities. . . . All art was yet to be created, all literature yet to be written. All nature was new and undescribed.

—*The Flowering of New England*

■ Do you think Emerson's ideas are practical as well as noble? Are they impossible ideals, or could they work in today's world?

LITERARY FOCUS

Stanza Forms

A **stanza** is a grouping together of lines of poetry into a fixed number of lines. Commonly used stanzas include:

the couplet	(2 lines)
the tercet	(3 lines)
the quatrain	(4 lines)
the cinquain	(5 lines)
the sestet	(6 lines)
the octave	(8 lines)

Groups of lines not in fixed numbers, such as those in Bryant's "Thanatopsis" (page 120), are called **verse paragraphs.**

Stanzas organize a poem into thoughts or sections, much as paragraphs help to organize prose. In using stanzas, a poet usually establishes a meter (see page 122) and a **rhyme scheme,** or pattern of end rhymes. The rhyme scheme of a poem is indicated by assigning a different letter of the alphabet to each new rhyming sound. For example, the rhyme scheme of the first stanza of "Concord Hymn" is *abab.*

Throughout the history of poetry, some special combinations of meters and rhyme schemes have proved popular with poets and readers, including:

the **heroic couplet**—two rhymed lines of iambic pentameter

the **triplet**—three rhymed lines of iambic pentameter

the **heroic stanza**—four lines of iambic pentameter with alternate lines rhyming *(abab)*

the **ballad stanza**—four lines in which tetrameter and trimeter lines alternate and only the second and fourth lines rhyme *(abcb).*

Emerson's "Concord Hymn" was originally written to be set to music, and like most songs, it employs a strict stanza pattern. Emerson uses a stanza appropriate to his subject: the **hymnal stanza**—four lines of iambic tetrameter rhyming either *abcb* or *abab*. The hymnal stanza is one of the most common poetic stanzas, largely because of its regularity; in fact, it is sometimes called **common measure.**

Emerson is skillful, however, in avoiding too much regularity. Notice, for example, how he varies the meter in line 8 and uses some rhymes that are not exact, such as *flood* and *stood.* These variations help to avoid monotony.

Thinking About Stanza Forms

1. What stanza form does Edgar Allan Poe use in the poem "To Helen" (page 132)?
2. Although Emerson's "Rhodora" is written as one stanza, indicate how you would divide the poem into separate stanzas, and tell why you would divide it in that way.

VOCABULARY

Abstract Words

Emerson was both a poet and a philosopher, expressing his ideas and feelings in a language both abstract and concrete. He often uses examples and images taken from the real world and from nature to support his concepts. His writing, though it deals with difficult ideas, thus has an immediacy that philosophical writing often does not have.

Each of the following abstract words appears in Emerson's *Nature.* Look up each word in a dictionary, and then define it in your own words. Give a concrete example to make the definition more complete.

1. sublime
2. exhilaration
3. decorum
4. egotism
5. harmony
6. infinite

COMPOSITION

Writing About a Sentence

Emerson's individual sentences often capture his thought and convey it with intensity and clarity. Choose one of Emerson's sentences, and write a short essay showing how that one sentence carries a large measure of his meaning. First define the important words in the sentence. Then summarize the main idea of Emerson's essay, and tell how the sentence expresses that idea. *For help with this assignment, refer to Lesson 5 in the Writing About Literature Handbook at the back of this book.*

Writing a Persuasive Essay

The Transcendentalists were sure that society could and should be improved. Write a persuasive essay on an improvement you would make in society. First clearly propose your improvement, and tell why it is important. Then detail the specific practical measures you would take to put it into effect. Conclude with an appeal to your audience to support your proposal.

Henry David Thoreau *1817–1862*

Thoreau lived a deliberately unconventional life. "His virtues," his friend Emerson said, "sometimes ran into extremes." Thoreau marched to his own tune, or as he put it, to the beat of "a different drummer." He knew that "most men think differently from myself," but he never regretted that he did not think like his neighbors.

Of all the writers associated with Concord, Massachusetts, Thoreau was the only one born there. He attended Harvard but refused all the careers his education prepared him for, such as minister, lawyer, or merchant. To many people he appeared "irresponsible" all his life. He hated joining any organization or movement or cooperating with institutions. After graduation he came back to Concord, where he supported himself by odd jobs that left him the freedom he desired.

He tried teaching school but did not like it. His father owned a small pencil factory, and for a while Thoreau worked there; but then, so he said, one day he found that he had made "the perfect pencil." After that he wondered why he should do the same thing over and over.

For two years Thoreau lived in Emerson's house, paying for his room and board by taking care of the house while Emerson was away on lecture tours. Sometimes he worked as a land surveyor, but he did not want to own land himself: It would have tied him down.

Thoreau's actions were the actions of an individual: To whatever extent he wanted to reform society, he would do so by changing the individual lives of men and women. One year he refused to pay a small tax, making a symbolic gesture against the policies of the federal government, especially the Mexican-American War and slavery. He spent a night in jail before his aunt paid the tax for him and had him released. From that experience he wrote the great essay *Civil Disobedience,* which years later affected the course of history through its strong influence on Gandhi in India and Martin Luther King, Jr., in the United States.

Thoreau died young, and most people thought him an interesting failure. Emerson said that he lacked ambition. He published only two books during his lifetime (together with a few poems and essays), *A Week on the Concord and Merrimack Rivers* (1849) and *Walden* (1854). He had to pay for the publication of both books himself, and neither sold many copies during his lifetime. His reputation was a local one. The townsfolk who knew him as a talented but difficult friend would have been astonished to know that in the twentieth century Thoreau would be more widely read than the great Emerson himself.

Thoreau's most memorable gesture was his move to Walden Pond. He lived for two years and two months in a cabin he built with his own hands on a piece of land owned by Emerson. (The cabin, he figured, cost him exactly 28 dollars and 12 1/2 cents.) That experience gave him the material for one of the greatest of American classics, *Walden*. Much of *Walden* is Thoreau's observation of nature, Emersonian in spirit but more sharply drawn than Emerson's observations. "It was a pleasure and a privilege to walk with him," wrote Emerson of the man he always thought of as a somewhat thorny disciple. "He knew the country like a fox or a bird. . . . The depth of his perception found likeness throughout Nature, and I know not any genius who so swiftly inferred universal law from the single fact." *Walden,* in fact, is not so much about living in the woods as it is about living itself.

Walden Pond, Concord, Massachusetts.

In this selection, and in one selection in each unit, you will find notes in the right-hand margin that highlight parts of the selection. These notes point out important ideas of the period—in this case, the Transcendentalist movement—and draw your attention to literary elements and techniques covered in the Literary Focuses. Page numbers in the notes will refer you to more extensive discussions of these important ideas and elements.

Henry David Thoreau

from **Walden**

from Economy

When I wrote the following pages, or rather the bulk of them, I lived alone, in the woods, a mile from any neighbor, in a house which I had built myself, on the shore of Walden Pond, in Concord, Massachusetts, and earned my living by the labor of my hands only. I lived there two years and two months. At present I am a sojourner[1] in civilized life again.

I should not obtrude my affairs so much on the notice of my readers if very particular inquiries had not been made by my townsmen concerning my mode of life, which some would call impertinent,[2] though they do not appear to me at all impertinent, but, considering the circumstances, very natural and pertinent. Some have asked what I got to eat; if I did not feel lonesome; if I was not afraid; and the like. Others have been curious to learn what portion of my income I devoted to charitable purposes; and some, who have large families, how many poor children I maintained. I will therefore ask those of my readers who feel no particular interest in me to pardon me if I undertake to answer some of these questions in this book. In most books, the *I*, or first person, is omitted; in this it will be retained; that, in respect to egotism, is the main difference. We commonly do not remember that it is, after all, always the first person that is speaking. I should not talk so much about myself if there were anybody else whom I knew as well. . . .

Persuasion (p. 22): Thoreau calls upon his personal experience to give greater support to his observations.

The mass of men lead lives of quiet desperation. What is called resignation is confirmed desperation. From the desperate city you go into the desperate country, and have to console yourself with the bravery of minks and muskrats. A stereotyped but unconscious

---

1. **sojourner:** visitor.
2. **impertinent:** irrelevant; inappropriate.

despair is concealed even under what are called the games and amusements of mankind. There is no play in them, for this comes after work. But it is a characteristic of wisdom not to do desperate things.

When we consider what, to use the words of the catechism,[3] is the chief end of man,[4] and what are the true necessaries and means of life, it appears as if men had deliberately chosen the common mode of living because they preferred it to any other. Yet they honestly think there is no choice left. But alert and healthy natures remember that the sun rose clear. It is never too late to give up our prejudices. No way of thinking or doing, however ancient, can be trusted without proof. What everybody echoes or in silence passes by as true today may turn out to be falsehood tomorrow, mere smoke of opinion, which some had trusted for a cloud that would sprinkle fertilizing rain on their fields. What old people say you cannot do, you try and find that you can. Old deeds for old people, and new deeds for new. . . .

One young man of my acquaintance, who has inherited some acres, told me that he thought he should live as I did, *if he had the means.* I would not have anyone adopt *my* mode of living on any account; for, beside that before he has fairly learned it I may have found out another for myself, I desire that there may be as many different persons in the world as possible; but I would have each one be very careful to find out and pursue *his own* way, and not his father's or his mother's or his neighbor's instead. The youth may build or plant or sail, only let him not be hindered from doing that which he tells me he would like to do. It is by a mathematical point only that we are wise, as the sailor or the fugitive slave keeps the polestar[5] in his eye; but that is sufficient guidance for all our life. We may not arrive at our port within a calculable period, but we would preserve the true course.

> Transcendentalist idea: Freedom from dull habit can lead to the discovery of spiritual truths (p. 154).

from Where I Lived, and What I Lived For

As I have said, I do not propose to write an ode to dejection, but to brag as lustily as chanticleer[6] in the morning, standing on his roost, if only to wake my neighbors up.

When first I took up my abode in the woods, that is, began to spend my nights as well as days there, which, by accident, was on Independence Day, or the Fourth of July, 1845, my house was not finished for winter, but was merely a defense against the rain, without plastering or chimney, the walls being of rough weatherstained

---

3. **catechism** [kat′ə kiz′əm]: handbook that teaches the principles of a religion through questions and answers.
4. **chief . . . man:** "What is the chief end of man?" is a question from the Shorter Catechism in the New England Primer.
5. **polestar:** Polaris, the North Star, used for navigation.
6. **chanticleer** [chan′tə klēr′]: literally, "the loud singer": a rooster.

boards, with wide chinks, which made it cool at night. The upright white hewn studs and freshly planed door and window casings gave it a clean and airy look, especially in the morning, when its timbers were saturated with dew, so that I fancied that by noon some sweet gum would exude from them. To my imagination it retained throughout the day more or less of this auroral[7] character, reminding me of a certain house on a mountain which I had visited the year before. This was an airy and unplastered cabin, fit to entertain a traveling god, and where a goddess might trail her garments. The winds which passed over my dwelling were such as sweep over the ridges of mountains, bearing the broken strains, or celestial parts only, of terrestrial music. The morning wind forever blows, the poem of creation is uninterrupted, but few are the ears that hear it. Olympus[8] is but the outside of the earth everywhere. . . .

I went to the woods because I wished to live deliberately, to front[9] only the essential facts of life, and see if I could not learn what it had to teach, and not, when I came to die, discover that I had not lived. I did not wish to live what was not life, living is so dear; nor did I wish to practice resignation, unless it was quite necessary. I wanted to live deep and suck out all the marrow of life, to live so sturdily and Spartan-like[10] as to put to rout all that was not life, to cut a broad swath and shave close, to drive life into a corner, and reduce it to its lowest terms, and, if it proved to be mean, why then to get the whole and genuine meanness of it, and publish its meanness to the world; or if it were sublime, to know it by experience, and be able to give a true account of it in my next excursion. For most men, it appears to me, are in a strange uncertainty about it, whether it is of the devil or of God, and have *somewhat hastily* concluded that it is the chief end of man here to "glorify God and enjoy him forever."[11]

Still we live meanly, like ants; though the fable tells us that we were long ago changed into men;[12] like pygmies we fight with cranes;[13] it is error upon error, and clout upon clout, and our best virtue has for its occasion a superfluous and evitable[14] wretchedness. Our life is frittered away by detail. An honest man has hardly need to count more than his ten fingers, or in extreme

Description (p. 92): Thoreau uses language that appeals to the senses to make his description concrete and vivid.

Transcendentalist idea: Living in harmony with nature is a source of inspiration (p. 155).

Simile (p. 39): Thoreau compares human life to the life of ants to underscore what he means by "meanly."

---

7. **auroral** [ə rôr′əl]: resembling the dawn.
8. **Olympus**: in Greek mythology, the mountain home of the gods.
9. **front:** face.
10. **Spartan-like:** simple, hardy, and disciplined, like the life of the Spartans of ancient Greece.
11. **"glorify . . . forever":** answer to the question "What is the chief end of man?" in the New England Primer.
12. **fable . . . men:** in a Greek fable Zeus transforms ants into men.
13. **pygmies . . . cranes:** in the *Iliad* the Trojans are compared to cranes battling pygmies.
14. **evitable:** avoidable.

cases he may add his ten toes, and lump the rest. Simplicity, simplicity, simplicity! I say, let your affairs be as two or three, and not a hundred or a thousand; instead of a million count half a dozen, and keep your accounts on your thumbnail. In the midst of this chopping sea of civilized life, such are the clouds and storms and quicksands and thousand-and-one items to be allowed for, that a man has to live, if he would not founder and go to the bottom and not make his port at all, by dead reckoning,[15] and he must be a great calculator indeed who succeeds. Simplify, simplify. Instead of three meals a day, if it be necessary eat but one; instead of a hundred dishes, five; and reduce other things in proportion. . . .

For my part, I could easily do without the post office. I think that there are very few important communications made through it. To speak critically, I never received more than one or two letters in my life—I wrote this some years ago—that were worth the postage. The penny post is, commonly, an institution through which you seriously offer a man that penny for his thoughts which is so often safely offered in jest. And I am sure that I never read any memorable news in a newspaper. If we read of one man robbed, or murdered, or killed by accident, or one house burned, or one vessel wrecked, or one steamboat blown up, or one cow run over on the Western Railroad, or one mad dog killed, or one lot of grasshoppers in the winter—we never need read of another. One is enough. If you are acquainted with the principle, what do you care for a myriad instances and applications? To a philosopher all *news,* as it is called, is gossip, and they who edit and read it are old women over their tea. Yet not a few are greedy after this gossip. . . .

Time is but the stream I go a-fishing in. I drink at it; but while I drink, I see the sandy bottom and detect how shallow it is. Its thin current slides away, but eternity remains. I would drink deeper; fish in the sky, whose bottom is pebbly with stars. I cannot count one. I know not the first letter of the alphabet. I have always been regretting that I was not as wise as the day I was born. The intellect is a cleaver; it discerns and rifts its way into the secret of things. I do not wish to be any more busy with my hands than is necessary. My head is hands and feet. I feel all my best faculties concentrated in it. My instinct tells me that my head is an organ for burrowing, as some creatures use their snout and forepaws, and with it I would mine and burrow my way through these hills. I think that the richest vein is somewhere hereabouts; so by the divining rod[16] and thin rising vapors I judge; and here I will begin to mine.

Transcendentalist idea: Only by simplifying our material lives and rising above the material world can we discover spiritual reality (p. 154).

Methods of persuasion (p. 84): Thoreau uses exaggeration and repetition to persuade the reader that his opinion of the post office and newspapers is justified.

Figurative language (p. 164): Thoreau compares time to a stream, using a figure of speech to make his abstract idea concrete.

---

15. **dead reckoning:** navigating without sighting the stars.
16. **divining rod:** forked stick that supposedly reveals the presence of underground minerals or water.

from Conclusion

I left the woods for as good a reason as I went there. Perhaps it seemed to me that I had several more lives to live, and could not spare any more time for that one. It is remarkable how easily and insensibly we fall into a particular route, and make a beaten track for ourselves. I had not lived there a week before my feet wore a path from my door to the pondside; and though it is five or six years since I trod it, it is still quite distinct. It is true, I fear that others may have fallen into it, and so helped to keep it open. The surface of the earth is soft and impressible by the feet of men; and so with the paths which the mind travels. How worn and dusty, then, must be the highways of the world, how deep the ruts of tradition and conformity! I did not wish to take a cabin passage, but rather to go before the mast and on the deck of the world, for there I could best see the moonlight amid the mountains. I do not wish to go below now.

I learned this, at least, by my experiment: that if one advances confidently in the direction of his dreams, and endeavors to live the life which he has imagined, he will meet with a success unexpected in common hours. He will put some things behind, will pass an invisible boundary; new, universal, and more liberal laws will begin to establish themselves around and within him; or the old laws be expanded, and interpreted in his favor in a more liberal sense, and he will live with the license of a higher order of beings. In proportion as he simplifies his life, the laws of the universe will appear less complex, and solitude will not be solitude, nor poverty poverty, nor weakness weakness. If you have built castles in the air, your work need not be lost; that is where they should be. Now put the foundations under them. . . .

Why should we be in such desperate haste to succeed, and in such desperate enterprises? If a man does not keep pace with his companions, perhaps it is because he hears a different drummer. Let him step to the music which he hears, however measured or far away. It is not important that he should mature as soon as an apple tree or an oak. Shall he turn his spring into summer? If the condition of things which we were made for is not yet, what were any reality which we can substitute? We will not be shipwrecked on a vain reality. Shall we with pains erect a heaven of blue glass over ourselves, though when it is done we shall be sure to gaze still at the true ethereal heaven far above, as if the former were not? . . .

However mean your life is, meet it and live it; do not shun it and call it hard names. It is not so bad as you are. It looks poorest when you are richest. The faultfinder will find faults even in paradise. Love your life, poor as it is. You may perhaps have some pleasant, thrilling, glorious hours, even in a poorhouse. The setting sun is reflected from the windows of the almshouse as brightly as

Transcendentalist idea: Spiritual reality is available only to people living as true individuals (p. 155).

from the rich man's abode; the snow melts before its door as early in the spring. I do not see but a quiet mind may live as contentedly there, and have as cheering thoughts, as in a palace. The town's poor seem to me often to live the most independent lives of any. Maybe they are simply great enough to receive without misgiving. Most think that they are above being supported by the town; but it oftener happens that they are not above supporting themselves by dishonest means, which should be more disreputable. Cultivate poverty like a garden herb, like sage. Do not trouble yourself much to get new things, whether clothes or friends. Turn the old; return to them. Things do not change; we change. Sell your clothes and keep your thoughts. God will see that you do not want society. If I were confined to a corner of a garret all my days, like a spider, the world would be just as large to me while I had my thoughts about me. . . .

The life in us is like the water in the river. It may rise this year higher than man has ever known it, and flood the parched uplands; even this may be the eventful year, which will drown out all our muskrats. It was not always dry land where we dwell. I see far inland the banks which the stream anciently washed, before science began to record its freshets. Everyone has heard the story, which has gone the rounds of New England, of a strong and beautiful bug which came out of the dry leaf of an old table of apple tree wood which had stood in a farmer's kitchen for sixty years, first in Connecticut, and afterward in Massachusetts—from an egg deposited in the living tree many years earlier still, as appeared by counting the annual layers beyond it— which was heard gnawing out for several weeks, hatched perchance by the heat of an urn. Who does not feel his faith in a resurrection and immortality strengthened by hearing of this? Who knows what beautiful and winged life, whose egg has been buried for ages under many concentric layers of woodenness in the dead dry life of society, deposited at first in the alburnum[17] of the green and living tree, which has been gradually converted into the semblance of its well-seasoned tomb—heard perchance gnawing out now for years by the astonished family of man, as they sat round the festive board—may unexpectedly come forth from amidst society's most trivial and handseled furniture, to enjoy its perfect summer life at last!

I do not say that John or Jonathan[18] will realize all this; but such is the character of that morrow which mere lapse of time can never make to dawn. The light which puts out our eyes is darkness to us. Only that day dawns to which we are awake. There is more day to dawn. The sun is but a morning star.

Aphorism (p. 57): Throughout *Walden*, Thoreau offers short, memorable recommendations to the reader.

Transcendentalist idea: Society can be and should be improved (p. 155).

17. **alburnum** [al bur′nəm]: youngest part of the wood in a tree, through which the sap moves.
18. **John or Jonathan:** the average person. Thoreau is using the popular names for the average Englishman (John Bull) and the average American (Brother Jonathan).

Recalling

1. In paragraph 3 of "Economy," what does Thoreau say most people lead?
2. According to paragraph 5 of "Economy," what are Thoreau's reasons for not wanting the young man to adopt his way of life?
3. From paragraph 3 of "Where I Lived," list at least five reasons that Thoreau gives for going to live in the woods.
4. According to paragraph 4 of "Where I Lived," by what is life "frittered away"? What does the exclamation in this paragraph call for?
5. In paragraph 1 of "Conclusion," why does Thoreau say he left the woods?
6. According to paragraph 2 of "Conclusion," what does Thoreau say he learned by his "experiment"?
7. In paragraph 4 of "Conclusion," what does Thoreau tell the reader to do, "however mean your life is"?
8. Summarize the story that has "gone the rounds of New England," which Thoreau relates in paragraph 5 of "Conclusion." According to Thoreau, what does hearing this story strengthen?

Interpreting

9. Describe in your own words what you think Thoreau means by "lives of quiet desperation."
10. Explain in your own words what Thoreau means, in paragraph 3 of "Conclusion," by hearing a "different drummer."
11. What emotions might Thoreau want to arouse in his reader with the story of the "beautiful bug"?
12. Summarize the central message Thoreau conveys in *Walden.*

Extending

13. What are some of the things that surround us in America today about which Thoreau might cry, "Simplify, simplify"?

VIEWPOINT

One of the finest essays on Thoreau is the personal one by Emerson. Defining Thoreau's greatness, Emerson also has one regret:

Had his genius been only contemplative, he had been fitted to his life, but with his energy and practical ability he seemed born for great enterprise and for command; and I so much regret the loss of his rare powers of action, that I cannot help counting it a fault in him that he had no ambition. Wanting this, instead of engineering for all America, he was the captain of a huckleberry-party.

—"Thoreau"

Do you agree that a person with such practical ability as Thoreau ought to take on "great enterprise"? Was the Walden "huckleberry-party" a sufficiently "great enterprise"? In what way is *Walden* itself an example of "engineering for all America"?

COMPOSITION

Writing About Nonfiction

Write a composition discussing the purpose of *Walden.* Cite techniques Thoreau uses to accomplish the purpose. Discuss sensory details, facts, statistics, examples, and opinions. *For help with this assignment, refer to Lesson 4 in the Writing About Literature Handbook at the back of this book.*

Writing a Personal Essay

Write a short personal essay keeping your style informal and directly addressing the reader. Use a sentence from *Walden* as a starting point ("Things do not change; we change," for example), or start with your own original thought. Then apply that idea to several different situations, and comment upon them. End by drawing one clear conclusion.

COMPARING WRITERS

Emerson and Thoreau were personal friends, shared many of the same ideas, and wrote about many of the same subjects. Yet their approaches to their experiences were quite different. Try to define the differences between these two writers. What relationship did each have to nature? What did each believe to be the most important things in life? How would you describe the tone of each?

FICTION: *Hawthorne and Melville*

Nathaniel Hawthorne   *1804–1864*

The same New England that gave birth to the hopeful visions of the Transcendentalists also brought forth the troubled vision of Nathaniel Hawthorne. Hawthorne, son of a sea captain, was born in Salem, Massachusetts, and raised by his mother. One of Hawthorne's ancestors had been among the judges who condemned the "witches" of Salem in 1692, and Hawthorne felt that the traits of his Puritan ancestors had "intertwined themselves" with his own character. After graduating from Bowdoin College in Maine, he was drawn back to Salem.

Yet Hawthorne was no Puritan. He looked back with distaste upon "the whole dismal severity of the Puritanic code of law." For twelve years he lived in his mother's house in Salem, a semirecluse, studying the American past, teaching himself to write. In 1837 *Twice-Told Tales,* his first collection of stories, appeared, and Hawthorne left his lonely chamber.

He worked at the Boston Custom House and then lived for a while among the Transcendental reformers and visionaries at the utopian community, Brook Farm. Later he turned the Brook Farm experience into a brilliant satiric book, *The Blithedale Romance.* In 1842 he married Sophia Peabody and moved to the Old Manse at Concord, where Emerson had lived. In 1846 he published *Mosses from an Old Manse,* another collection of stories. Unable to support himself and his wife, Hawthorne returned once again to Salem, where he received a political appointment as Surveyor of the Port.

Removed from office by a change of administrations, he began *The Scarlet Letter,* a subtle study of guilt and retribution in Puritan Boston. Published in 1850, *The Scarlet Letter* became a sensation. Hawthorne followed it with *The House of the Seven Gables.* When his college friend Franklin Pierce became President, Hawthorne was appointed American consul at Liverpool, England. After many years in Europe, he returned to America but, with the exception of *The Marble Faun* in 1860, he was unable to complete any major work during his later years.

Hawthorne listened to conversations at Emerson's house and went boating with Thoreau, but his spirit was very different from theirs. As Emerson and Thoreau assert human freedom, Hawthorne reminds us of human limitations. He called his tales "allegories of the heart." An **allegory** is a story with a symbolic meaning used to teach a moral principle. Hawthorne's allegories are stories of how pride and isolation frustrate our capacity for love and sympathy. Among the most characteristic of Hawthorne's "allegories of the heart" is "The Minister's Black Veil," which takes place in a small New England town one hundred years before Hawthorne's time.

Nathaniel Hawthorne

The Minister's Black Veil

A Parable

The sexton stood in the porch of Milford meetinghouse, pulling lustily at the bellrope. The old people of the village came stooping along the street. Children, with bright faces, tripped merrily beside their parents, or mimicked a graver gait, in the conscious dignity of their Sunday clothes. Spruce bachelors looked sidelong at the pretty maidens and fancied that the sabbath sunshine made them prettier than on weekdays. When the throng had mostly streamed into the porch, the sexton began to toll the bell, keeping his eye on the Reverend Mr. Hooper's door. The first glimpse of the clergyman's figure was the signal for the bell to cease its summons.

"But what has good Parson Hooper got upon his face?" cried the sexton in astonishment.

All within hearing immediately turned about and beheld the semblance of Mr. Hooper, pacing slowly his meditative way towards the meetinghouse. With one accord they started, expressing more wonder than if some strange minister were coming to dust the cushions of Mr. Hooper's pulpit.

"Are you sure it is our parson?" inquired Goodman[1] Gray of the sexton.

"Of a certainty it is good Mr. Hooper," replied the sexton. "He was to have exchanged pulpits with Parson Shute of Westbury; but Parson Shute sent to excuse himself yesterday, being to preach a funeral sermon."

The cause of so much amazement may appear sufficiently slight. Mr. Hooper, a gentlemanly person of about thirty, though still a bachelor, was dressed with due clerical neatness, as if a careful wife had starched his band and brushed the weekly dust from his Sunday's garb. There was but one thing remarkable in his appearance. Swathed about his forehead, and hanging down over his face, so low as to be shaken by his breath, Mr. Hooper had on a black veil. On a nearer view, it seemed to consist of two folds of crape,[2] which entirely concealed his features, except the mouth and chin, but probably did not intercept his sight, farther than to give a darkened aspect to all living and inanimate things. With this gloomy shade before him, good Mr. Hooper walked onward, at a slow and quiet pace, stooping somewhat and looking on the ground, as is customary with abstracted[3] men, yet nodding kindly to those of his parishioners who still waited on the meetinghouse steps. But so wonderstruck were they, that his greeting hardly met with a return.

"I can't really feel as if good Mr. Hooper's face was behind that piece of crape," said the sexton.

"I don't like it," muttered an old woman, as she hobbled into the meetinghouse. "He has changed himself into something awful, only by hiding his face."

"Our parson has gone mad!" cried Goodman Gray, following him across the threshhold.

A rumor of some unaccountable phenomenon had preceded Mr. Hooper into the meetinghouse, and set all the congregation astir. Few could refrain from twisting their heads towards the door; many stood upright and turned directly about; while several little boys clambered upon the seats and came down again with a terrible racket. There was a general bustle, a rustling of the women's gowns and shuffling of the men's feet, greatly at variance with that hushed repose which should attend the

---

1. **Goodman:** a title similar to *Mister*.

2. **crape** [krāp]: black, crinkled cloth often worn as a sign of mourning.

3. **abstracted:** withdrawn and preoccupied.

entrance of the minister. But Mr. Hooper appeared not to notice the perturbation of his people. He entered with an almost noiseless step, bent his head mildly to the pews on each side, and bowed as he passed his oldest parishioner, a white-haired great-grandsire, who occupied an armchair in the center of the aisle. It was strange to observe how slowly this venerable man became conscious of something singular in the appearance of his pastor. He seemed not fully to partake of the prevailing wonder till Mr. Hooper had ascended the stairs and showed himself in the pulpit, face to face with his congregation, except for the black veil. That mysterious emblem was never once withdrawn. It shook with his measured breath as he gave out the psalm; it threw its obscurity between him and the holy page as he read the Scriptures; and while he prayed, the veil lay heavily on his uplifted countenance. Did he seek to hide it from the dread Being whom he was addressing?

Such was the effect of this simple piece of crape, that more than one woman of delicate nerves was forced to leave the meetinghouse. Yet perhaps the pale-faced congregation was almost as fearful a sight to the minister as his black veil to them.

Mr. Hooper had the reputation of a good preacher, but not an energetic one: he strove to win his people heavenward by mild persuasive influences, rather than to drive them thither by the thunders of the Word. The sermon which he now delivered was marked by the same characteristics of style and manner, as the general series of his pulpit oratory. But there was something, either in the sentiment of the discourse itself or in the imagination of the auditors, which made it greatly the most powerful effort that they had ever heard from their pastor's lips. It was tinged, rather more darkly than usual, with the gentle gloom of Mr. Hooper's temperament. The subject had reference to secret sin, and those sad mysteries which we hide from our nearest and dearest, and would

fain conceal from our own consciousness, even forgetting that the Omniscient[4] can detect them. A subtle power was breathed into his words. Each member of the congregation, the most innocent girl, and the man of hardened breast, felt as if the preacher had crept upon them, behind his awful veil, and discovered their hoarded iniquity of deed or thought. Many spread their clasped hands on their bosoms. There was nothing terrible in what Mr. Hooper said—at least, no violence; and yet, with every tremor of his melancholy voice, the hearers quaked. An unsought pathos came hand in hand with awe. So sensible were the audience of some unwonted attribute in their minister that they longed for a breath of wind to blow aside the veil, almost believing that a stranger's visage would be discovered, though the form, gesture, and voice were those of Mr. Hooper.

At the close of the services, the people hurried out with indecorous confusion, eager to communicate their pent-up amazement, and conscious of lighter spirits the moment they lost sight of the black veil. Some gathered in little circles, huddled closely together, with their mouths all whispering in the center; some went homeward alone, wrapped in silent meditation; some talked loudly, and profaned the Sabbath day with ostentatious laughter. A few shook their sagacious heads, intimating that they could penetrate the mystery; while one or two affirmed that there was no mystery at all, but only that Mr. Hooper's eyes were so weakened by the midnight lamp as to require a shade. After a brief interval, forth came good Mr. Hooper also, in the rear of his flock. Turning his veiled face from one group to another, he paid due reverence to the hoary heads, saluted the middle-aged with kind dignity, as their friend and spiritual guide, greeted the young with mingled authority and love, and laid his hands on the little children's heads to bless them. Such was always his custom on the Sabbath day. Strange and bewildered looks repaid him for his courtesy. None, as on former occasions, aspired to the honor of walking by

---

4. **Omniscient** [om nish′ ənt]: God; the all-knowing.

their pastor's side. Old Squire Saunders, doubtless by an accidental lapse of memory, neglected to invite Mr. Hooper to his table, where the good clergyman had been wont to bless the food almost every Sunday since his settlement. He returned, therefore, to the parsonage and, at the moment of closing the door, was observed to look back upon the people, all of whom had their eyes fixed upon the minister. A sad smile gleamed faintly from beneath the black veil and flickered about his mouth, glimmering as he disappeared.

"How strange," said a lady, "that a simple black veil such as any woman might wear on her bonnet should become such a terrible thing on Mr. Hooper's face!"

"Something must surely be amiss with Mr. Hooper's intellects," observed her husband, the physician of the village. "But the strangest part of the affair is the effect of this vagary, even on a sober-minded man like myself. The black veil, though it covers only our pastor's face, throws its influence over his whole person, and makes

him ghostlike from head to foot. Do you not feel it so?"

"Truly do I," replied the lady; "and I would not be alone with him for the world. I wonder he is not afraid to be alone with himself!"

"Men sometimes are so," said her husband.

The afternoon service was attended with similar circumstances. At its conclusion, the bell tolled for the funeral of a young lady. The relatives and friends were assembled in the house, and the more distant acquaintances stood about the door, speaking of the good qualities of the deceased, when their talk was interrupted by the appearance of Mr. Hooper, still covered with his black veil. It was now an appropriate emblem. The clergyman stepped into the room where the corpse was laid, and bent over the coffin to take a last farewell of his deceased parishioner. As he stooped, the veil hung straight down from his forehead, so that, if her eyelids had not been closed for ever, the dead maiden might have seen his face. Could Mr. Hooper be fearful of her glance, that he so hastily caught back the black veil? A person who watched the interview between the dead and living scrupled not to affirm that, at the instant when the clergyman's features were disclosed, the corpse had slightly shuddered, rustling the shroud and muslin cap, though the countenance retained the composure of death. A superstitious old woman was the only witness of this prodigy. From the coffin, Mr. Hooper passed into the chambers of the mourners, and thence to the head of the staircase to make the funeral prayer. It was a tender and heart-dissolving prayer, full of sorrow, yet so imbued with celestial hopes that the music of a heavenly harp, swept by the fingers of the dead, seemed faintly to be heard among the saddest accents of the minister. The people trembled, though they but darkly understood him, when he prayed that they, and himself, and all of mortal race, might be ready, as he trusted this young maiden had been, for the dreadful hour that should snatch the veil from their faces. The bearers went heavily forth, and the mourners followed, saddening all the street, with the dead before them, and Mr. Hooper in his black veil behind.

"Why do you look back?" said one in the procession to his partner.

"I had a fancy," replied she, "that the minister and the maiden's spirit were walking hand in hand."

"And so had I, at the same moment," said the other.

That night, the handsomest couple in Milford village were to be joined in wedlock. Though reckoned a melancholy man, Mr. Hooper had a placid cheerfulness for such occasions, which often excited a sympathetic smile where livelier merriment would have been thrown away. There was no quality of his disposition which made him more beloved than this. The company at the wedding awaited his arrival with impatience, trusting that the strange awe which had gathered over him throughout the day would now be dispelled. But such was not the result. When Mr. Hooper came, the first thing that their eyes rested on was the same horrible black veil, which had added deeper gloom to the funeral, and could portend nothing but evil to the wedding. Such was its immediate effect on the guests that a cloud seemed to have rolled duskily from beneath the black crape, and dimmed the light of the candles. The bridal pair stood up before the minister. But the bride's cold fingers quivered in the tremulous hand of the bridegroom, and her deathlike paleness caused a whisper that the maiden who had been buried a few hours before was come from her grave to be married. If ever another wedding were so dismal, it was that famous one where they tolled the wedding knell.[5] After performing the ceremony, Mr. Hooper raised a glass of wine to his lips, wishing happiness to the new-married couple, in a strain of mild pleasantry that ought to have brightened the features of the guests, like a cheerful gleam from the hearth. At that instant, catching a glimpse of his figure in the looking glass, the black veil involved his own spirit in the horror with which it overwhelmed all others. His frame shuddered—his lips grew white—he spilt the untasted wine upon the carpet—and rushed forth into the darkness. For the Earth, too, had on her Black Veil.

The next day, the whole village of Milford talked of little else than Parson Hooper's black veil. That, and the mystery concealed behind it, supplied a topic of discussion between acquaintances meeting in the street and good women gossiping at their open windows. It was the first item of news that the tavernkeeper told to his guests. The children babbled of it on their way to school. One imitative little imp covered his face with an old black handkerchief, thereby so affrighting his playmates that the panic seized himself, and he well nigh lost his wits by his own waggery.

It was remarkable that, of all the busybodies and impertinent people in the parish, not one ventured to put the plain question to Mr.

---

5. **If . . . knell:** Hawthorne is referring to his own short story, "The Wedding Knell." A *knell* usually describes the sound of a bell at a funeral.

Hooper, wherefore he did this thing. Hitherto, whenever there appeared the slightest call for such interference, he had never lacked advisers, nor shown himself averse to be guided by their judgment. If he erred at all, it was by so painful a degree of self-distrust that even the mildest censure would lead him to consider an indifferent action as a crime. Yet, though so well acquainted with this amiable weakness, no individual among his parishioners chose to make the black veil a subject of friendly remonstrance. There was a feeling of dread, neither plainly confessed nor carefully concealed, which caused each to shift the responsibility upon another, till at length it was found expedient to send a deputation of the church, in order to deal with Mr. Hooper about the mystery before it should grow into a scandal. Never did an embassy so ill discharge its duties. The minister received them with friendly courtesy, but became silent after they were seated, leaving to his visitors the whole burden of introducing their important business. The topic, it might be supposed, was obvious enough. There was the black veil, swathed round Mr. Hooper's forehead, and concealing every feature above his placid mouth, on which, at times, they could perceive the glimmering of a melancholy smile. But that piece of crape, to their imagination, seemed to hang down before his heart, the symbol of a fearful secret between him and them. Were the veil but cast aside, they might speak freely of it, but not till then. Thus they sat a considerable time, speechless, confused, and shrinking uneasily from Mr. Hooper's eye, which they felt to be fixed upon them with an invisible glance. Finally, the deputies returned abashed to their constituents, pronouncing the matter too weighty to be handled, except by a council of the churches if, indeed, it might not require a general synod.[6]

But there was one person in the village unappalled by the awe with which the black veil had impressed all beside herself. When the deputies returned without an explanation, or even venturing to demand one, she, with the calm energy of her character, determined to chase away the strange cloud that appeared to be settling round Mr. Hooper, every moment more darkly than before. As his plighted wife,[7] it should be her privilege to know what the black veil concealed. At the minister's first visit, therefore, she entered upon the subject with a direct simplicity, which made the task easier both for him and her. After he had seated himself, she fixed her eyes steadfastly upon the veil, but could discern nothing of the dreadful gloom that had so overawed the multitude: it was but a double fold of crape, hanging down from his forehead to his mouth, and slightly stirring with his breath.

"No," said she aloud, and smiling, "there is nothing terrible in this piece of crape, except that it hides a face which I am always glad to look upon. Come, good sir, let the sun shine from behind the cloud. First lay aside your black veil: then tell me why you put it on."

Mr. Hooper's smile glimmered faintly.

"There is an hour to come," said he, "when all of us shall cast aside our veils. Take it not amiss, beloved friend, if I wear this piece of crape till then."

"Your words are a mystery too," returned the young lady. "Take away the veil from them, at least."

"Elizabeth, I will," said he, "so far as my vow may suffer me. Know, then, this veil is a type and a symbol, and I am bound to wear it ever, both in light and darkness, in solitude and before the gaze of multitudes, and as with strangers, so with my familiar friends. No mortal eye will see it withdrawn. This dismal shade must separate me from the world: even you, Elizabeth, can never come behind it!"

"What grievous affliction hath befallen you," she earnestly inquired, "that you should thus darken your eyes forever?"

"If it be a sign of mourning," replied Mr. Hooper, "I, perhaps, like most other mortals,

---

6. **synod** [sin′əd]: meeting of the governing body of all the churches.

7. **plighted wife:** betrothed; fiancée.

have sorrows dark enough to be typified by a black veil."

"But what if the world will not believe that it is the type of an innocent sorrow?" urged Elizabeth. "Beloved and respected as you are, there may be whispers that you hide your face under the consciousness of secret sin. For the sake of your holy office, do away this scandal!"

The color rose into her cheeks as she intimated the nature of the rumors that were already abroad in the village. But Mr. Hooper's mildness did not forsake him. He even smiled again—that same sad smile, which always appeared like a faint glimmering of light, proceeding from the obscurity beneath the veil.

"If I hide my face for sorrow, there is cause enough," he merely replied; "and if I cover it for secret sin, what mortal might not do the same?"

And with this gentle but unconquerable obstinacy did he resist all her entreaties. At length Elizabeth sat silent. For a few moments she appeared lost in thought, considering, probably, what new methods might be tried to withdraw her lover from so dark a fantasy, which, if it had no other meaning, was perhaps a symptom of mental disease. Though of a firmer character than his own, the tears rolled down her cheeks. But in an instant, as it were, a new feeling took the place of sorrow: her eyes were fixed insensibly on the black veil when, like a sudden twilight in the air, its terrors fell around her. She arose, and stood trembling before him.

"And do you feel it then at last?" said he mournfully.

She made no reply, but covered her eyes with her hand, and turned to leave the room. He rushed forward and caught her arm.

"Have patience with me, Elizabeth!" cried he passionately. "Do not desert me, though this veil must be between us here on earth. Be mine, and hereafter there shall be no veil over my face, no darkness between our souls! It is but a mortal veil—it is not for eternity! Oh, you know not how lonely I am and how frightened to be alone behind my black veil.

Do not leave me in this miserable obscurity forever!"

"Lift the veil but once, and look me in the face," said she.

"Never! It cannot be!" replied Mr. Hooper.

"Then, farewell!" said Elizabeth.

She withdrew her arm from his grasp and slowly departed, pausing at the door to give one long, shuddering gaze that seemed almost to penetrate the mystery of the black veil. But even amid his grief, Mr. Hooper smiled to think that only a material emblem had separated him from happiness, though the horrors which it shadowed forth must be drawn darkly between the fondest of lovers.

From that time no attempts were made to remove Mr. Hooper's black veil or, by a direct appeal, to discover the secret which it was supposed to hide. By persons who claimed a superiority to popular prejudice, it was reckoned merely an eccentric whim, such as often mingles with the sober actions of men otherwise rational and tinges them all with its own semblance of insanity. But with the multitude, good Mr. Hooper was irreparably a bugbear.[8] He could not walk the street with any peace of mind, so conscious was he that the gentle and timid would turn aside to avoid him, and that others would make it a point of hardihood to throw themselves in his way. The impertinence of the latter class compelled him to give up his customary walk at sunset to the burial ground; for when he leaned pensively over the gate, there would always be faces behind the gravestones, peeping at his black veil. A fable went the rounds that the stare of the dead people drove him thence. It grieved him, to the very depth of his kind heart, to observe how the children fled from his approach, breaking up their merriest sports while his melancholy figure was yet afar off. Their instinctive dread caused him to feel, more strongly than aught else, that a preternatural[9]

---

8. **bugbear:** something dreaded.
9. **preternatural:** supernatural.

horror was interwoven with the threads of the black crape. In truth, his own antipathy to the veil was known to be so great that he never willingly passed before a mirror nor stooped to drink at a still fountain, lest, in its peaceful bosom, he should be affrighted by himself. This was what gave plausibility to the whispers that Mr. Hooper's conscience tortured him for some great crime, too horrible to be entirely concealed or otherwise than so obscurely intimated. Thus, from beneath the black veil, there rolled a cloud into the sunshine, an ambiguity of sin or sorrow, which enveloped the poor minister, so that love or sympathy could never reach him. It was said that ghost and fiend consorted with him there. With self-shudderings and outward terrors, he walked continually in its shadow, groping darkly within his own soul, or gazing through a medium that saddened the whole world. Even the lawless wind, it was believed, respected his dreadful secret and never blew aside the veil. But still good Mr. Hooper sadly smiled at the pale visages of the worldly throng as he passed by.

Among all its bad influences, the black veil had the one desirable effect of making its wearer a very efficient clergyman. By the aid of his mysterious emblem—for there was no other apparent cause—he became a man of awful power over souls that were in agony for sin. His converts always regarded him with a dread peculiar to themselves, affirming, though but figuratively, that, before he brought them to celestial light, they had been with him behind the black veil. Its gloom, indeed, enabled him to sympathize with all dark affections.[10] Dying sinners cried aloud for Mr. Hooper, and would not yield their breath till he appeared; though ever, as he stooped to whisper consolation, they shuddered at the veiled face so near their own. Such were the terrors of the black veil, even when death had bared his visage! Strangers came long distances to attend service at his church, with the mere idle purpose of gazing at his figure, because it was forbidden them to behold his face. But many were made to quake ere they departed! Once, during Governor Belcher's[11] administration, Mr. Hooper was appointed to preach the election sermon.[12] Covered with his black veil, he stood before the chief magistrate, the council, and the representatives, and wrought so deep an impression that the legislative measures of that year were characterized by all the gloom and piety of our earliest ancestral sway.

In this manner Mr. Hooper spent a long life, irreproachable in outward act, yet shrouded in dismal suspicions; kind and loving, though unloved and dimly feared; a man apart from men, shunned in their health and joy, but ever summoned to their aid in mortal anguish. As years wore on, shedding their snows above his sable veil, he acquired a name throughout the New England churches, and they called him Father Hooper. Nearly all his parishioners, who were of mature age when he was settled, had been borne away by many a funeral: he had one congregation in the church, and a more crowded one in the churchyard; and having wrought so late into the evening, and done his work so well, it was now good Father Hooper's turn to rest.

Several persons were visible by the shaded candlelight in the death-chamber of the old clergyman. Natural connections[13] he had none. But there was the decorously grave, though unmoved physician, seeking only to mitigate the last pangs of the patient whom he could not save. There were the deacons, and other eminently pious members of his church. There also was the Reverend Mr. Clark of Westbury, a young and zealous divine, who had ridden in haste to pray by the bedside of the expiring minister. There was the nurse, no hired handmaiden of death, but one whose calm affection had endured thus long in secrecy, in solitude,

10. **affections:** emotions.

11. **Governor Belcher:** Jonathan Belcher, governor of Massachusetts and New Hampshire from 1730 to 1744.
12. **election sermon:** Mr. Hooper was given the honor of preaching at the governor's inaugural ceremony.
13. **natural connections:** relatives.

amid the chill of age, and would not perish, even at the dying hour. Who but Elizabeth! And there lay the hoary head of good Father Hooper upon the death-pillow, with the black veil still swathed about his brow and reaching down over his face, so that each more difficult gasp of his faint breath caused it to stir. All through life that piece of crape had hung between him and the world: It had separated him from cheerful brotherhood and woman's love, and kept him in that saddest of all prisons, his own heart; and still it lay upon his face, as if to deepen the gloom of his darksome chamber and shade him from the sunshine of eternity.

For some time previous, his mind had been confused, wavering doubtfully between the past and the present, and hovering forward, as it were, at intervals, into the indistinctness of the world to come. There had been feverish turns, which tossed him from side to side and wore away what little strength he had. But in his most convulsive struggles, and in the wildest vagaries of his intellect, when no other thought retained its sober influence, he still showed an awful solicitude lest the black veil should slip aside. Even if his bewildered soul could have forgotten, there was a faithful woman at his pillow, who, with averted eyes, would have covered that aged face, which she had last beheld in the comeliness of manhood. At length the death-striken old man lay quietly in the torpor of mental and bodily exhaustion, with an imperceptible pulse, and breath that grew fainter and fainter, except when a long, deep, and irregular inspiration seemed to prelude the flight of his spirit.

The minister of Westbury approached the bedside.

"Venerable Father Hooper," said he, "the moment of your release is at hand. Are you ready for the lifting of the veil that shuts in time from eternity?"

Father Hooper at first replied merely by a feeble motion of his head; then, apprehensive, perhaps, that his meaning might be doubtful, he exerted himself to speak.

"Yea," said he, in faint accents, "my soul hath a patient weariness until that veil be lifted."

"And is it fitting," resumed the Reverend Mr. Clark, "that a man so given to prayer, of such a blameless example, holy in deed and thought so far as mortal judgment may pronounce; is it fitting that a father in the church should leave a shadow on his memory that may seem to blacken a life so pure? I pray you, my venerable brother, let not this thing be! Suffer us to be gladdened by your triumphant aspect as you go to your reward. Before the veil of eternity be lifted, let me cast aside this black veil from your face!"

And thus speaking, the Reverend Mr. Clark bent forward to reveal the mystery of so many years. But, exerting a sudden energy that made all the beholders stand aghast, Father Hooper snatched both his hands from beneath the bedclothes and pressed them strongly on the black veil, resolute to struggle if the minister of Westbury would contend with a dying man.

"Never!" cried the veiled clergyman. "On earth, never!"

"Dark old man!" exclaimed the affrighted minister, "with what horrible crime upon your soul are you now passing to the judgment?"

Father Hooper's breath heaved; it rattled in his throat; but, with a mighty effort, grasping forward with his hands, he caught hold of life, and held it back till he should speak. He even raised himself in bed; and there he sat, shivering with the arms of death around him, while the black veil hung down, awful, at that last moment, in the gathered terrors of a lifetime. And yet the faint, sad smile, so often there, now seemed to glimmer from its obscurity and linger on Father Hooper's lips.

"Why do you tremble at me alone?" cried he, turning his veiled face round the circle of pale spectators. "Tremble also at each other! Have men avoided me, and women shown no pity, and children screamed and fled, only for my black veil? What, but the mystery which it obscurely typifies, has made this piece of crape so awful? When the friend shows his inmost heart to his friend; the lover to his best-beloved; when man does not vainly shrink from the eye of his Creator, loathsomely treasuring up the secret of his sin; then deem me a monster, for the symbol beneath which I have lived, and die! I look around me, and lo! on every visage a black veil!"

While his auditors shrank from one another in mutual affright, Father Hooper fell back upon his pillow, a veiled corpse, with a faint smile lingering on the lips. Still veiled, they laid him in his coffin, and a veiled corpse they bore him to the grave. The grass of many years has sprung up and withered on that grave, the burial stone is moss-grown, and good Mr. Hooper's face is dust; but awful is still the thought, that it moldered beneath the black veil!

STUDY QUESTIONS

Recalling

1. What is the subject of Mr. Hooper's sermon on the first day he wears the black veil?
2. What does Reverend Hooper tell Elizabeth the veil is? What two possible explanations for wearing the veil do they discuss?
3. What reasons does Hooper give Elizabeth not to desert him? For what reason does he smile after Elizabeth breaks their engagement and leaves?
4. What does the author say is "the one desirable effect" the black veil has?
5. On his deathbed, what does Reverend Hooper say men, women, and children have done? What does he say he sees on every face?

Interpreting

6. What human emotions are shown to fail between Elizabeth and Reverend Hooper as a result of the veil?
7. What is the chief effect that the veil has on Reverend Hooper? Support your answer with evidence from the story.
8. What might Reverend Hooper mean when he says that everyone wears a black veil?
9. List at least four possible reasons Reverend Hooper might have for wearing the veil. Why is it appropriate that we never learn the precise reason?
10. Hawthorne purposely leaves the meaning of the veil ambiguous and up to the reader. What do you think the veil means? Why?

VIEWPOINT

Critic Marius Bewley, in a study of classic American writers, writes about "The Minister's Black Veil":

> The fullness of life . . . can only come about through self-surrender, through a refusal to withhold oneself, or any part of one's personality, in a human relationship.
>
> In the last analysis, this was what Hawthorne believed was the essence of human reality. The most compelling truth of all that Mr. Hooper tried to teach by means of his dismal veil is the necessity of self-surrender.
>
> —*The Eccentric Design*

■ Do you agree that self-surrender is central to the story? Support your opinion by discussing Mr. Hooper's intended marriage and the marriage of "the handsomest couple in Milford village" in the light of this statement.

LITERARY FOCUS

Symbol

A **symbol** is something that conveys two kinds of meaning: It is simply itself, *and* it stands for something other than itself. The American eagle, for example, is an actual bird; it also represents the power and individualism of America. A symbol, in other words, is both literal and figurative. People, places, things, and even events can be used symbolically.

Hawthorne centers "The Minister's Black Veil" on the veil and what it means to the characters. If the meaning of a symbol is obscure, that obscurity may also be part of the meaning.

A symbol is a way of telling a story and a way of conveying meaning. The best symbols are those that are believable in the lives of the characters and also convincing as they convey a meaning beyond the literal level of the story.

Thinking About Symbols

■ Discuss the veil in "The Minister's Black Veil" by considering the following questions: What do the characters think and say about it? What do they never say about it? What does the author say about it? What does the author not say about it? Is the obscurity of the symbol itself part of its meaning?

Ambiguity

Ambiguity is a way of expressing something so that its meaning is uncertain. An ambiguous statement is one that can be understood in two or more ways.

Usually, in our everyday lives, we strive for clear and unambiguous statements: "I want that sweater." Occasionally, it is useful or at least prudent to be ambiguous: "Oh, what an unusual sweater!" Writers, however, are often deliberately ambiguous—not because they want to confuse us but because they want to open up our minds to the possibilities of multiple meanings.

"The Minister's Black Veil" is an excellent example of a story in which ambiguity has been deliberately used. Hawthorne delicately hangs between one interpretation and another. To get the most from the story, we should relish the many possibilities, not resist them in favor of one limited response, one "definite" meaning.

Thinking About Ambiguity

■ Because of the veil in "The Minister's Black Veil," many of Mr. Hooper's actions seem ambiguous. Discuss the ambiguity of his final speech and of the "faint, sad smile" lingering on his lips. Tell what the story gains because of its multiple meanings.

COMPOSITION

Developing a Thesis Statement

■ Good critical writing does more than retell a story or paraphrase a poem: A thesis statement often defines a question and then attempts to answer it. For example, "Why does Mr. Hooper do what he does?" Write an interpretive essay answering this question or asking a question of your own about "The Minister's Black Veil." Develop your answer with material from the story. Conclude with a paragraph about how the question and the answer help in understanding the story. *For help with this assignment, refer to Lesson 1 in the Writing About Literature Handbook at the back of this book.*

Describing a Symbol

■ Choose a person, place, thing, or event to serve as a symbol. Then write a short composition (or a story, if you wish) describing how that symbol can mean different things to different people at different times. For example, a cane: To a boy it may symbolize his father's authority; to the father it may symbolize old age; to the mother it may symbolize elegance. Remember that the best symbols are not only universal but also a natural part of the lives of people.

Herman Melville   *1819–1891*

"NO! in thunder." This, according to Melville, is what the true writer, the great writer, says. With his own great "NO!" Melville set himself against the optimism of Emerson and the Transcendentalists, challenged conformity, and rejected the idea of progress and prosperity that dominated the American mind in the 1800s.

Born in New York City, Melville was the son of a prosperous merchant who died when Herman was eleven. The boy was forced to leave school when he was twelve; later, unable to find a profession, he became a sailor. His sailing years gave him the background of ships and mutinies and exotic islands that served him well in his early successes, *Typee* (1846) and *Omoo* (1847).

He quickly became a literary celebrity in both England and America, but he refused to continue producing the sort of adventure books the public wanted. At the age of thirty, Melville began a new kind of book, *Moby-Dick,* a whaling story of great complexity and power, meant to rival the work of Shakespeare. Yet it took almost a century before the novel was recognized by more than a handful of readers. The tale of the obsessed hero-villain Captain Ahab and his doomed search for the white whale, Moby Dick, is now regarded as one of the most vital stories available to the American imagination.

However, with the incomprehension that met *Moby-Dick* and the commercial failure of his next two works, *Pierre* and *The Confidence Man,* Melville saw that he could not support his family by writing. Bitter, at times acting in ways that made people think him insane, he was forced to spend twenty years at a routine job in the Custom House in New York City. Even other American writers hardly remembered him, and once when a British admirer tried to find him in New York, no one knew if he was alive or dead. He published some poems, which were ignored by the public, and at his death he left the manuscript of his short novel *Billy Budd.* Generations later, readers began to discover Melville.

Moby-Dick, often considered the greatest American novel, is a masterpiece with many layers. It is a sea adventure, an exciting chase after a destructive and mysterious creature. It is an encyclopedia of the concrete details of nineteenth-century whaling life. It is a psychological portrait of a bitter, crusty, brilliant man aching for vengeance and searching for truth. It is a myth about the place of humankind in the universe.

The portrait of Ahab given here is a sketch of the main character, Captain Ahab, in action. Ishmael, the young sailor who narrates the book, has signed aboard the *Pequod* without ever having met its captain. In this scene Ahab's striking appearance and his Shakespearean oratory reveal his extraordinary purpose—to turn a commercial voyage for whale oil into a personal voyage of vengeance.

Herman Melville

from **Moby-Dick**

Ahab

For several days after leaving Nantucket, nothing above hatches[1] was seen of Captain Ahab. The mates regularly relieved each other at the watches, and for aught that could be seen to the contrary, they seemed to be the only commanders of the ship; only they sometimes issued from the cabin with orders so sudden and peremptory that, after all, it was plain they but commanded vicariously. Yes, their supreme lord and dictator was there, though hitherto unseen by any eyes not permitted to penetrate into the now sacred retreat of the cabin. . . .

Now, it being Christmas when the ship shot from out her harbor, for a space we had biting polar weather, though all the time running away from it to the southward; and by every degree and minute of latitude which we sailed, gradually leaving that merciless winter and all its intolerable weather behind us. It was one of those less lowering, but still gray and gloomy enough mornings of the transition, when with a fair wind the ship was rushing through the water with a vindictive sort of leaping and melancholy rapidity, that as I mounted to the deck at the call of the forenoon watch, so soon as I leveled my glance towards the taffrail, foreboding shivers ran over me. Reality outran apprehension; Captain Ahab stood upon his quarter-deck.[2]

There seemed no sign of common bodily illness about him, nor of the recovery from

---

1. **above hatches:** on deck.

2. **quarter-deck:** rear upper deck, reserved for officers.

any. He looked like a man cut away from the stake, when the fire has overrunningly wasted all the limbs without consuming them or taking away one particle from their compacted aged robustness. His whole high, broad form seemed made of solid bronze and shaped in an unalterable mold, like Cellini's cast Perseus.[3] Threading its way out from among his gray hairs and continuing right down one side of his tawny scorched face and neck, till it disappeared in his clothing, you saw a slender rod-like mark, lividly whitish. It resembled that perpendicular seam sometimes made in the straight, lofty trunk of a great tree when the upper lightning tearingly darts down it, and, without wrenching a single twig, peels and grooves out the bark from top to bottom ere running off into the soil, leaving the tree still greenly alive, but branded. Whether that mark was born with him, or whether it was the scar left by some desperate wound, no one could certainly say. By some tacit consent, throughout the voyage little or no allusion was made to it, especially by the mates. But once Tashtego's senior, an old Gayhead Indian[4] among the crew, superstitiously asserted that not till he was full forty years old did Ahab become that way branded, and then it came upon him, not in the fury of any mortal fray, but in an elemental strife at sea. Yet this wild hint seemed inferentially negatived by what a gray Manxman[5] insinuated, an old sepulchral man who, having never before sailed out of Nantucket, had never ere this laid eye upon wild Ahab. Nevertheless, the old sea traditions, the immemorial credulities, popularly invested this old Manxman with preternatural powers of discernment. So that no white sailor seriously contradicted him when he said that if ever Captain Ahab should be tranquilly laid out—which might hardly come to pass, so he muttered—then whoever should do that last office for the dead would find a birthmark on him from crown to sole.

So powerfully did the whole grim aspect of Ahab affect me, and the livid brand which streaked it, that for the first few moments I hardly noted that not a little of this overbearing grimness was owing to the barbaric white leg upon which he partly stood. It had previously come to me that this ivory leg had at sea been fashioned from the polished bone of the sperm whale's jaw. "Aye, he was dismasted off Japan," said the old Gayhead Indian once; "but like his dismasted craft, he shipped another mast without coming home for it. He has a quiver of 'em."

I was struck with the singular posture he maintained. Upon each side of the *Pequod's* quarter-deck, and pretty close to the mizzen shrouds,[6] there was an auger hole bored about half an inch or so into the plank. His bone leg steadied in that hole, one arm elevated, and holding by a shroud, Captain Ahab stood erect, looking straight out beyond the ship's ever-pitching prow. There was an infinity of firmest fortitude, a determinate, unsurrenderable willfulness, in the fixed and fearless forward dedication of that glance. Not a word he spoke; nor did his officers say aught to him, though by all their minutest gestures and expressions, they plainly showed the uneasy, if not painful, consciousness of being under a troubled master-eye. And not only that, but moody stricken Ahab stood before them with a crucifixion in his face, in all the nameless regal overbearing dignity of some mighty woe.

Ere long, from his first visit in the air, he withdrew into his cabin. But after that morning, he was every day visible to the crew, either standing in his pivot hole, or seated upon an ivory stool he had, or heavily walking the deck. As the sky grew less gloomy, indeed, began to grow a little genial, he became still less and less a recluse, as if, when the ship had

---

3. **Cellini's** [chə lē′nēz] **cast Perseus** [pur′sē əs]: bronze-cast statue of Perseus, a hero of Greek mythology, by Italian sculptor Benvenuto Cellini.
4. **Gayhead Indian:** Indian from Gayhead, a town in Martha's Vineyard, Massachusetts.
5. **Manxman:** native of the Isle of Man, one of the British Isles.

6. **shrouds:** sails.

sailed from home, nothing but the dead wintry bleakness of the sea had then kept him so secluded. And, by and by, it came to pass that he was almost continually in the air; but, as yet, for all that he said, or perceptibly did, on the at last sunny deck, he seemed as unnecessary there as another mast. But the *Pequod* was only making a passage now, not regularly cruising; nearly all whaling preparatives needing supervision the mates were fully competent to, so that there was little or nothing out of himself to employ or excite Ahab now, and thus chase away, for that one interval, the clouds that layer upon layer were piled upon his brow, as ever all clouds choose the loftiest peaks to pile themselves upon.

Nevertheless, ere long, the warm, warbling persuasiveness of the pleasant holiday weather we came to seemed gradually to charm him from his mood. For, as when the red-cheeked dancing girls, April and May, trip home to the wintry, misanthropic woods, even the barest, ruggedest, most thunder-cloven old oak will at least send forth some few green sprouts to welcome such glad-hearted visitants; so Ahab did, in the end, a little respond to the playful allurings of that girlish air. More than once did he put forth the faint blossom of a look which, in any other man, would have soon flowered out in a smile.

One morning shortly after breakfast, Ahab, as was his wont, ascended the cabin gangway to the deck. There most sea captains usually walk at that hour, as country gentlemen, after the same meal, take a few turns in the garden.

Soon his steady ivory stride was heard, as to and fro he paced his old rounds, upon planks so familiar to his tread that they were all over dented, like geological stones, with the peculiar mark of his walk. Did you fixedly gaze, too, upon that ribbed and dented brow, there also, you would see still stranger footprints—the footprints of his one unsleeping, ever-pacing thought.

But on the occasion in question, those dents looked deeper, even as his nervous step that morning left a deeper mark. And so full of his thought was Ahab, that at every uniform turn that he made, now at the mainmast and now at the binnacle, you could almost see that thought turn in him as he turned, and pace in him as he paced; so completely possessing him, indeed, that it all but seemed the inward mold of every outer movement.

"D'ye mark him, Flask?" whispered Stubb; "the chick that's in him pecks the shell. 'Twill soon be out."

The hours wore on—Ahab now shut up within his cabin; anon, pacing the deck, with the same intense bigotry of purpose[7] in his aspect.

It drew near the close of day. Suddenly he came to a halt by the bulwarks and, inserting his bone leg into the auger hole there, and with one hand grasping a shroud, he ordered Starbuck to send everybody aft.[8]

"Sir!" said the mate, astonished at an order seldom or never given on shipboard except in some extraordinary case.

"Send everybody aft," repeated Ahab. "Mast-heads, there! come down!"

When the entire ship's company were assembled, and with curious and not wholly un-apprehensive faces were eyeing him, for he looked not unlike the weather horizon when a storm is coming up, Ahab, after rapidly glancing over the bulwarks and then darting his eyes among the crew, started from his standpoint; and as though not a soul were nigh him resumed his heavy turns upon the deck. With bent head and half-slouched hat he continued to pace, unmindful of the wondering whispering among the men; till Stubb cautiously whispered to Flask that Ahab must have summoned them there for the purpose of witnessing a pedestrian feat. But this did not last long. Vehemently pausing, he cried:

"What do ye do when ye see a whale, men?"

---

7. **bigotry of purpose:** total singlemindedness.
8. **aft:** rear section of a ship.

"Sing out for him!" was the impulsive rejoinder from a score of clubbed voices.

"Good!" cried Ahab, with a wild approval in his tones, observing the hearty animation into which his unexpected question had so magnetically thrown them.

"And what do ye next, men?"

"Lower away, and after him!"

"And what tune is it ye pull to, men?"

"A dead whale or a stove[9] boat!"

More and more strangely and fiercely glad and approving grew the countenance of the old man at every shout; while the mariners began to gaze curiously at each other, as if marveling how it was that they themselves became so excited at such seemingly purposeless questions.

But they were all eagerness again as Ahab, now half revolving in his pivot hole, with one hand reaching high up a shroud and tightly, almost convulsively, grasping it, addressed them thus:

"All ye mastheaders have before now heard me give orders about a white whale. Look ye! d'ye see this Spanish ounce of gold?"—holding up a broad bright coin to the sun—"It is a sixteen dollar piece, men—a doubloon. D'ye see it? Mr. Starbuck, hand me yon topmaul."

While the mate was getting the hammer, Ahab, without speaking, was slowly rubbing the gold piece against the skirts of his jacket, as if to heighten its luster, and without using any words was meanwhile lowly humming to himself, producing a sound so strangely muffled and inarticulate that it seemed the mechanical humming of the wheels of his vitality in him.

Receiving the topmaul from Starbuck, he advanced towards the mainmast with the hammer uplifted in one hand, exhibiting the gold with the other, and with a high raised voice exclaiming: "Whosoever of ye raises me a white-headed whale with a wrinkled brow and a crooked jaw; whosoever of ye raises me that white-headed whale, with three holes punctured in his starboard fluke[10]—look ye, whosoever of ye raises me that same white whale, he shall have this gold ounce, my boys!"

"Huzza! huzza!" cried the seamen, as with swinging tarpaulins they hailed the act of nailing the gold to the mast.

"It's a white whale, I say," resumed Ahab, as he threw down the topmaul; "a white whale. Skin your eyes for him, men; look sharp for white water; if ye see but a bubble, sing out."

All this while Tashtego, Daggoo, and Queequeg had looked on with even more intense interest and surprise than the rest, and at the mention of the wrinkled brow and crooked jaw they had started as if each was separately touched by some specific recollection.

"Captain Ahab," said Tashtego, "that white whale must be the same that some call Moby Dick."

"Moby Dick?" shouted Ahab. "Do ye know the white whale then, Tash?"

"Does he fantail[11] a little curious, sir, before he goes down?" said the Gayheader deliberately.

"And has he a curious spout, too," said Daggoo, "very bushy, even for a parmacetty,[12] and mighty quick, Captain Ahab?"

"And he have one, two, tree—oh! good many iron in him hide, too, Captain," cried Queequeg disjointedly, "all twiske-tee be-twisk, like him—him—" faltering hard for a word, and screwing his hand round and round as though uncorking a bottle—"like him—him—"

"Corkscrew!" cried Ahab. "Aye, Queequeg, the harpoons lie all twisted and wrenched in him; aye, Daggoo, his spout is a big one, like a whole shock of wheat, and white as a pile of our Nantucket wool after the great annual sheepshearing; aye, Tashtego, and he fantails like a split jib[13] in a squall. Death and devils!

---

9. **stove:** smashed.

10. **starboard fluke:** right half of a whale's tail.
11. **fantail:** spread out the tail like a fan.
12. **parmacetty:** dialect for *spermaceti,* a waxlike substance taken from oil in the head of a sperm whale; used to make cosmetics, candles, and other items.
13. **jib:** triangular sail ahead of the mainmast.

men, it is Moby Dick ye have seen—Moby Dick—Moby Dick!"

"Captain Ahab," said Starbuck, who, with Stubb and Flask, had thus far been eyeing his superior with increasing surprise, but at last seemed struck with a thought which somewhat explained all the wonder. "Captain Ahab, I have heard of Moby Dick—but it was not Moby Dick that took off thy leg?"

"Who told thee that?" cried Ahab; then pausing, "Aye, Starbuck; aye, my hearties all round; it was Moby Dick that dismasted me; Moby Dick that brought me to this dead stump I stand on now. Aye, aye," he shouted with a terrific, loud, animal sob, like that of a heart-stricken moose; "Aye, aye! it was that accursed white whale that razeed[14] me; made a poor pegging lubber[15] of me for ever and a day!" Then tossing both arms, with measureless imprecations he shouted out: "Aye, aye! and I'll chase him round Good Hope, and round the Horn,[16] and round the Norway Maelstrom, and round perdition's flames before I give him up. And this is what ye have shipped for, men! to chase that white whale on both sides of land, and over all sides of earth, till he spouts black blood and rolls fin out. What say ye, men, will ye splice hands on it, now? I think ye do look brave."

"Aye, aye!" shouted the harpooners and seamen, running closer to the excited old man: "A sharp eye for the White Whale; a sharp lance for Moby Dick!"

"God bless ye," he seemed to half sob and half shout. "God bless ye, men. Steward! go draw the great measure of grog. But what's this long face about, Mr. Starbuck; wilt thou not chase the white whale? art not game for Moby Dick?"

"I am game for his crooked jaw, and for the jaws of Death too, Captain Ahab, if it fairly comes in the way of the business we follow; but I came here to hunt whales, not my commander's vengeance. How many barrels will thy vengeance yield thee even if thou gettest it, Captain Ahab? it will not fetch thee much in our Nantucket market."

"Nantucket market! Hoot! But come closer, Starbuck; thou requirest a little lower layer. If money's to be the measurer, man, and the accountants have computed their great counting-house the globe, by girdling it with guineas, one to every three parts of an inch; then let me tell thee that my vengeance will fetch a great premium *here!*"

"He smites his chest," whispered Stubb. "What's that for? methinks it rings most vast, but hollow."

"Vengeance on a dumb brute!" cried Starbuck, "that simply smote thee from blindest instinct! Madness! To be enraged with a dumb thing, Captain Ahab, seems blasphemous."

"Hark ye yet again—the little lower layer. All visible objects, man, are but as pasteboard masks. But in each event—in the living act, the undoubted deed—there some unknown but still reasoning thing puts forth the moldings of its features from behind the unreasoning mask. If man will strike, strike through the mask! How can the prisoner reach outside except by thrusting through the wall? To me, the white whale is that wall, shoved near to me. Sometimes I think there's naught beyond. But 'tis enough. He tasks me; he heaps me; I see in him outrageous strength, with an inscrutable malice sinewing it. That inscrutable thing is chiefly what I hate; and be the white whale agent, or be the white whale principal, I will wreak that hate upon him. Talk not to me of blasphemy, man; I'd strike the sun if it insulted me. For could the sun do that, then could I do the other; since there is ever a sort of fair play herein, jealousy presiding over all creations. But not my master, man, is even that fair play. Who's over me? Truth hath no confines. Take off thine eye! More intolerable than fiends'

---

14. **razeed** [rā zēd′]: removed the upper deck of a ship; here, referring to Ahab's leg.
15. **lubber:** slow, clumsy person.
16. **Good Hope . . . Horn:** the Cape of Good Hope at the southern tip of Africa and Cape Horn at the southern tip of South America.

glarings is a doltish stare! So, so; thou reddenest and palest; my heat has melted thee to anger-glow. But look ye, Starbuck, what is said in heat, that thing unsays itself. There are men from whom warm words are small indignity. I meant not to incense thee. Let it go. Look! see yonder Turkish cheeks of spotted tawn—living, breathing pictures painted by the sun. The Pagan leopards—the unrecking and unworshipping things that live and seek and give no reasons for the torrid life they feel! The crew, man, the crew! Are they not one and all with Ahab in this matter of the whale? See Stubb! he laughs! See yonder Chilean! he snorts to think of it. Stand up amid the general hurricane, thy one tossed sapling cannot, Starbuck! And what is it? Reckon it. 'Tis but to help strike a fin; no wondrous feat for Starbuck. What is it more? From this one poor hunt, then, the best lance out of all Nantucket, surely he will not hang back when every foremast hand has clutched a whetstone? Ah! constrainings seize thee; I see! the billow lifts thee! Speak, but speak!—Aye, aye! thy silence, then, *that* voices thee. *(Aside)* Something shot from my dilated nostrils, he has inhaled it in his lungs. Starbuck now is mine, cannot oppose me now without rebellion."

"God keep me!—keep us all!" murmured Starbuck, lowly. But in his joy at the enchanted, tacit acquiescence of the mate, Ahab did not hear his foreboding invocation; nor yet the low laugh from the hold; nor yet the presaging vibrations of the winds in the cordage; nor yet the hollow flap of the sails against the masts, as for a moment their hearts sank in. For again Starbuck's downcast eyes lighted up with the stubbornness of life; the subterranean laugh died away; the winds blew on; the sails filled out; the ship heaved and rolled as before. Ah, ye admonitions and warnings! why stay ye not when ye come? But rather are ye predictions than warnings, ye shadows! Yet not so much predictions from without, as verifications of the foregoing things within. For with little external to constrain us, the innermost necessities in our being, these still drive us on.

STUDY QUESTIONS

Recalling

1. What does Ishmael, the narrator, call Captain Ahab in paragraph 1? How does he describe Ahab's "form" in paragraph 3?
2. What incentive does Ahab offer his crew for sighting the white whale?
3. According to Ahab, what did Moby Dick do to him? What does Ahab claim is the purpose of their voyage?
4. What is Starbuck's first objection to the hunt for Moby Dick? What does he then say seems "blasphemous"?
5. What two qualities does Ahab say he sees in the whale? What does he say about blasphemy?
6. In the last paragraph, what "foreboding invocation" does Ahab not hear? What does Ishmael ask of "admonitions and warnings"?

Interpreting

7. Identify three dominant traits of Ahab's.
8. What do we learn about Ahab's character from his statement, "I'd strike the sun if it insulted me"?
9. What deeper meaning is suggested by Ahab's desire to "strike through the mask" of things?
10. What distinction does Ahab make when he speaks of the whale as "agent" or "principal"? What does he mean by each of these terms?
11. Explain in your own words the observation about human nature that Ishmael makes in the last paragraph.

Extending

12. Why do you think the ocean and its creatures have so often provided writers with material for serious thoughts about time, evil, life, and death?

VIEWPOINT

The literary critic Richard Chase sees *Moby-Dick* in the light of Emerson's idea of self-reliance:

> It is a book about the alienation from life that results from an excessive . . . self-dependence. . . . As Newton Arvin [another critic] demonstrates, there is some reason to think of Ahab as guilty of *hubris,* in the Greek sense, or of excessive pride, in the Christian sense; but there is more reason to think of him as guilty of or victimized by a distorted "self-reliance."
>
> —*The American Novel and Its Tradition*

▤ Discuss Ahab's "distorted 'self-reliance.'" What elements of self-reliance does Ahab take to an extreme? What elements of self-reliance play no part in Ahab's character?

LITERARY FOCUS

Diction

One element of *Moby-Dick* that contributes to its success as a work of art is its extraordinary diction. **Diction** is word choice: It is the use of exactly the right word to fit the character, the meaning, and the tone the writer is trying to achieve.

To define Ahab's remarkable character, Melville gives the captain the vocabulary of a sailor *and* the vocabulary of a Shakespearean hero. Ahab says:

> Aye, Starbuck; aye, my hearties all round; it was Moby Dick that dismasted me. . . . What say ye, men, will ye splice hands on it, now?

Yet Ahab also says:

> All visible objects, man, are but as pasteboard masks. But in each event—in the living act, the undoubted deed—there some unknown but still reasoning thing puts forth the moldings of its features from behind the unreasoning mask.

Ahab's diction reflects his whaler's occupation *(aye, hearties, splice)* and his philosopher's mental struggles *(visible objects, unreasoning mask).*

Thinking About Diction

▤ Find two other examples in the selection from *Moby-Dick* in which diction tells something about a character.

VOCABULARY

Denotation and Connotation

Words have both **denotations,** their dictionary definitions, and **connotations,** the associations that they take on in context.

The following phrases are from *Moby-Dick.* Indicate which meaning is suggested, or *connoted,* by each italicized word as it is used in the selection.

1. an old *sepulchral* man:
   - (a) entombed
   - (b) deadly
   - (c) gray
   - (d) grim

2. the *barbaric* white leg:
   - (a) pagan
   - (b) crude
   - (c) elemental
   - (d) ornate

3. moody *stricken* Ahab:
   - (a) wounded
   - (b) slapped
   - (c) crippled
   - (d) tormented

4. like *geological* stones:
   - (a) scientific
   - (b) old
   - (c) elemental
   - (d) hard

5. vast, but *hollow:*
   - (a) loud
   - (b) empty
   - (c) heartless
   - (d) large

COMPOSITION

Writing About Character

▤ Write a short composition about Ahab or another literary character. Organize your composition by first telling what we learn about the character *directly* from the author. Then tell what we learn *indirectly* from what the character and other characters say and do. Conclude with a general statement about the character.

Writing a Character Sketch

▤ Write a brief character sketch of another character in this book or one of your own creation. Allow the character to be revealed both *directly,* by what you tell the reader, and *indirectly,* by the character's own words and actions.

POETRY: *Longfellow, Holmes, Lowell, Whittier*

Henry Wadsworth Longfellow
1807–1882

Longfellow was the best-known of the Fireside Poets and the most successful American poet of his age. *Hiawatha* (1855), for instance, sold about one million copies in his lifetime—a rare achievement for a book of verse. Longfellow was so revered that his seventy-fifth birthday was celebrated in schoolrooms across the land. When he died, a memorial bust was placed in the Poet's Corner of Westminster Abbey in England. He is still the only American so honored.

Born in Maine, Longfellow attended Bowdoin College, where one of his classmates was Nathaniel Hawthorne. He loved languages and became so skilled in them that for most of his life, first at Bowdoin, later at Harvard, he taught a great variety of languages and literatures, even writing his own language textbooks. As a result of his attachment to languages and his broad knowledge of European literature, and through his work as a teacher, anthologist, and poet, Longfellow did much to bring European culture to America.

Longfellow wrote poems on a wide range of subjects, contemporary and historical, and he used many different verse forms and meters with great technical skill. His most famous works, however, are those that bring to life stories from the American past: *Evangeline* (1847), *The Courtship of Miles Standish* (1858), and "Paul Revere's Ride" (1861). Late in life, grieving over his wife's death, Longfellow also translated *The Divine Comedy,* the fourteenth-century epic by the Italian poet Dante. Throughout his life Longfellow wrote noble and elevated verse built around romanticized characters and heroic sentiments. His versatility and enthusiasm won him a large audience, but, more important, he helped to popularize poetry itself in America.

Both "A Psalm of Life" and "The Tide Rises, the Tide Falls" offer large views of life. However, the tone, or poet's attitude, is different in the two poems. In the first the young Longfellow urges us to live vigorously in spite of hardships. In the second the same poet, now older, gazes back on life with a sense of melancholy.

Henry Wadsworth Longfellow

A Psalm of Life

What the Heart of the Young Man Said
    to the Psalmist

Tell me not, in mournful numbers,[1]
    Life is but an empty dream!—
For the soul is dead that slumbers,
    And things are not what they seem.

5 Life is real! Life is earnest!
    And the grave is not its goal;
Dust thou art, to dust returnest,
    Was not spoken of the soul.

Not enjoyment, and not sorrow,
10 Is our destined end or way;
But to act, that each tomorrow
    Find us farther than today.

Art is long, and Time is fleeting,
    And our hearts, though stout and brave,
15 Still, like muffled drums, are beating
    Funeral marches to the grave.

In the world's broad field of battle,
    In the bivouac[2] of Life,
Be not like dumb, driven cattle!
20 Be a hero in the strife!

Trust no Future, howe'er pleasant!
    Let the dead Past bury its dead!
Act—act in the living Present!
    Heart within, and God o'erhead!

25 Lives of great men all remind us
    We can make our lives sublime,
And, departing, leave behind us
    Footprints on the sands of time;

Footprints that perhaps another,
30 Sailing o'er life's solemn main,[3]
A forlorn and shipwrecked brother,
    Seeing, shall take heart again.

---

1. **numbers:** verses.
2. **bivouac:** temporary camp.
3. **main:** ocean.

Henry Wadsworth Longfellow

The Tide Rises,
The Tide Falls

The tide rises, the tide falls,
The twilight darkens, the curlew[1] calls;
Along the seasands damp and brown
The traveler hastens toward the town,
5   And the tide rises, the tide falls.

Darkness settles on roofs and walls,
But the sea, the sea in the darkness calls;
The little waves, with their soft white hands,
Efface the footprints in the sands,
10   And the tide rises, the tide falls.

The morning breaks; the steeds in their stalls
Stamp and neigh as the hostler[2] calls;
The day returns, but nevermore
Returns the traveler to the shore,
15   And the tide rises, the tide falls.

---

1. **curlew** [kur′lōo̅]: large wading bird whose call is
associated with evening.
2. **hostler** [hos′lər]: person who takes care of horses.

STUDY QUESTIONS

A Psalm of Life

Recalling

1. What demand does the speaker make in lines
1–2? What opinion does he proclaim in line 5?
2. According to stanza 3, what is "our destined
end or way"?
3. According to stanza 6, when should we act?
4. What do we learn from the lives of the great,
according to stanza 7?

Interpreting

5. In your own words summarize the speaker's
advice for living.
6. Why is the image in stanza 5 of a "field of battle" appropriate to the speaker's view of life?

7. Based on the last two stanzas, explain how the speaker feels we can help future generations. To what, specifically, might the image in line 28 refer?

Extending
8. In what respects is Emerson's ideal of self-reliance echoed by the speaker?

The Tide Rises, the Tide Falls

Recalling
1. According to stanza 1, what is the setting (time and place) of the poem?
2. According to stanza 2, what evidence does the traveler leave behind? What happens to this evidence?
3. What line is repeated throughout the poem?
4. What returns in the third stanza? What never returns?

Interpreting
5. Does the action of the tide suggest permanence or impermanence? Explain.
6. What does the poet suggest about nature and about human life in lines 13 –14?
7. How does repetition underscore the meaning of the poem?

Extending
8. Longfellow wrote "A Psalm of Life" when he was young and "The Tide Rises, the Tide Falls" when he was old. How do you think the first poem represents the visions and ideals of a young person? What elements in the second poem indicate the view of a mature and experienced person looking back and assessing life?

LITERARY FOCUS

Repetition in Poetry
The most basic device of poetry—the one that gives poetry most of its musical quality—is repetition. It includes not only the repetition of sounds (see page 131) and rhythms but the repetition of words and lines.

Often individual words are repeated in a poem for emphasis. For example, in "The Tide Rises, the Tide Falls " Longfellow repeats the words *tide* and *sea* a number of times, suggesting the importance of these words to the meaning of the poem.

Entire lines may also be repeated in a poem. A repeated line or group of lines is called a **refrain.** Like a musical refrain—the chorus of a song, for example—a poetic refrain occurs at regular intervals. "The tide rises, the tide falls" is both the title and the refrain of Longfellow's poem.

Thinking About Repetition
Find and discuss at least two examples of word repetition in "A Psalm of Life." Tell what the repetition contributes to the meaning of the poem.

Rhythm
Rhythm is the arrangement of stressed and unstressed syllables in a poem. When the rhythm forms a regular pattern, it is called **meter** (see page 122).

The rhythm of "The Tide Rises, the Tide Falls" is irregular. For example, the first two lines of the poem swing forward and backward like a pendulum:

The tide rises, the tide falls,
The twilight darkens, the curlew calls.

This rhythm suits the meaning, suggesting the rise and fall of the tide itself.

The "rising-falling" rhythm is created in part by punctuation, usually a comma, that interrupts certain lines, such as line 1. The resulting pause, a **caesura,** accentuates the "rising" and the "falling" of the line.

Lines 3 – 4 of the poem have a more regular rhythm, and no comma interrupts their flow:

Along the seasands damp and brown
The traveler hastens toward the town.

The contrast between the rhythms of the first two lines and the rhythm of the next two lines echoes the contrast between the tide and the traveler that the poet wishes to make.

Sometimes the sense and the grammatical structure of a line flow into the next line, as line 3 flows into line 4. This is a **run-on** line. If a line does not flow on to another line, it is called an **end-stopped line.**

Thinking About Rhythm
How does the regular rhythm, or meter, of "A Psalm of Life" echo the meaning of the poem?

Oliver Wendell Holmes *1809–1894*

Like the other Fireside Poets, Oliver Wendell Holmes was a man of extraordinary vitality and versatility. Remembered now as a man of letters, he was also a doctor, a teacher, dean of Harvard Medical School, a lecturer, a reformer, and one of America's greatest conversationalists.

Holmes, a descendant of the Puritan poet Anne Bradstreet (page 30), was born in Cambridge, Massachusetts. He was the class poet at Harvard. He studied law there but grew devoted to medicine, which he traveled to Paris to learn. In 1836, the year he received his M.D., he also published his first collection of poems. Holmes became a professor of medicine at Harvard, where he was immensely popular with his students and deeply respected by his peers as well. Among his many scientific publications was a work that helped lower the fearfully high mortality rate among newborn children.

Many people would be content with such a full and distinguished life. However, Holmes made a second career of literature. He wrote novels and published poetry in periodicals. He helped organize the Saturday Club, a group of writers and scientists who met regularly for conversation. With James Russell Lowell and John Greenleaf Whittier, he helped found the *Atlantic Monthly,* an important literary magazine that printed humorous essays by Holmes and serialized one of his most popular works, *The Autocrat of the Breakfast-Table,* a marvelous collection of wise and witty conversations.

Holmes's lyric poem "Old Ironsides" was inspired by plans to demolish the frigate *Constitution,* which had won an important naval battle in the War of 1812. Its sides were not made of iron, but it had so gallantly withstood the assaults of British warships that it had won the nickname Old Ironsides. The poem, published in a Boston newspaper, aroused such protest that Old Ironsides was saved.

"The Chambered Nautilus" reveals Holmes the poet-scientist. The chambered nautilus is a sea mollusk that builds its own pearly shell, chamber by chamber, as it grows. *Nautilus* means "sailor," an appropriate term for this creature: It was once thought to send out a membrane that acted as a sail, enabling it to float across the water in the wind.

Oliver Wendell Holmes

Old Ironsides

Ay, tear her tattered ensign[1] down!
  Long has it waved on high,
And many an eye has danced to see
  That banner in the sky;
5 Beneath it rung the battle shout,
  And burst the cannon's roar—
The meteor of the ocean air
  Shall sweep the clouds no more.

Her deck, once red with heroes' blood,
10 Where knelt the vanquished foe,
When winds were hurrying o'er the flood,
  And waves were white below,

No more shall feel the victor's tread,
  Or know the conquered knee—
15 The harpies[2] of the shore shall pluck
  The eagle of the sea!

Oh, better that her shattered hulk
  Should sink beneath the wave;
Her thunders shook the mighty deep,
20 And there should be her grave;
Nail to the mast her holy flag,
  Set every threadbare sail,
And give her to the god of storms,
  The lightning and the gale!

---

1. **ensign:** flag.

2. **harpies:** in Greek mythology, hideous winged creatures that carry off the souls of the dead.

U.S.S. Constitution vs. H.M.S. Guerriere, 19 July 1812, Thomas Birch.

Oliver Wendell Holmes

The Chambered Nautilus

This is the ship of pearl, which, poets feign,
    Sails the unshadowed main—
    The venturous bark that flings
On the sweet summer wind its purpled wings
5 In gulfs enchanted, where the Siren[1] sings,
    And coral reefs lie bare,
Where the cold sea-maids rise to sun their streaming hair.

Its webs of living gauze no more unfurl;
    Wrecked is the ship of pearl!
10   And every chambered cell,
Where its dim dreaming life was wont to dwell,
As the frail tenant shaped his growing shell,
    Before thee lies revealed—
Its irised[2] ceiling rent,[3] its sunless crypt unsealed!

15 Year after year beheld the silent toil
    That spread his lustrous coil;
    Still, as the spiral grew,
He left the past year's dwelling for the new,
Stole with soft step its shining archway through,
20   Built up its idle door,
Stretched in his last-found home, and knew the old no more.

Thanks for the heavenly message brought by thee,
    Child of the wandering sea,
    Cast from her lap, forlorn!
25 From thy dead lips a clearer note is born
Than ever Triton[4] blew from wreathèd horn!
    While on mine ear it rings,
Through the deep caves of thought I hear a voice that sings:

Build thee more stately mansions, O my soul,
30   As the swift seasons roll!
    Leave thy low-vaulted past!
Let each new temple, nobler than the last,
Shut thee from heaven with a dome more vast,
    Till thou at length art free,
35 Leaving thine outgrown shell by life's unresting sea!

---

1. **Siren:** in Greek mythology, a sea goddess whose songs lured sailors to their deaths.
2. **irised:** rainbow-colored.
3. **rent:** torn apart.
4. **Triton** [trī′tən]: in Greek mythology, a sea god with the body of a man and the tail of a fish, usually pictured carrying a conch-shell trumpet.

Shell, photograph by Edward Weston.

STUDY QUESTIONS

Old Ironsides

Recalling

1. What image does the poet use to describe Old Ironsides in line 7? In line 16? With what was the deck of the ship once red, according to line 9?
2. According to stanza 3, what does the poet consider a better end for the old battleship?

Interpreting

3. What qualities does the ship seem to symbolize for the poet?
4. Why does the poet oppose the demolition of Old Ironsides?
5. What advice about human life is suggested by the poet's preferred end to the battleship?

The Chambered Nautilus

Recalling

1. Find two phrases in stanza 1 that describe the chambered nautilus.
2. What "lies revealed" in stanza 2?
3. According to stanza 3, what did the nautilus leave year after year? Summarize the process it followed.
4. According to stanzas 4 and 5, what does the voice from the "deep caves of thought" tell the poet's soul to build?

Interpreting

5. What qualities are attributed to the chambered nautilus through the images of stanza 1?
6. What has happened to the nautilus in stanza 2?
7. According to stanza 5, what lessons about human life does the poet learn by observing the nautilus?
8. Do the details in stanza 3 prepare the reader for the comparison made in the last stanza? Explain.

LITERARY FOCUS

Personification and Apostrophe

Personification is a figure of speech in which human qualities are given to objects, animals, and ideas. Holmes personifies Old Ironsides when he says that it "No more shall feel the victor's tread." Of course, he does not mean this literally; a ship cannot really feel anything. However, through personification, Holmes convinces us for a moment that this old battleship has courage, pride, and, probably, emotions as well. We believe with him that Old Ironsides has undergone the struggles of war and deserves the respect we would give a hero.

Personification can be a powerful and moving device, because it appeals to our *human* nature. Naturally, we sympathize more readily with something that is human—and therefore like us—than with something nonhuman. Personification enables the poet to bring us one step closer to the subject. Often this device makes reading the poem a more dramatic and compelling experience.

A literary device related to personification is **apostrophe,** in which a poet directly addresses an inanimate object, an idea, or an absent person. Holmes's address to the chambered nautilus is an example of apostrophe. For centuries the most common apostrophe was the poet's address to the Muse of Poetry.

Thinking About Personification and Apostrophe

1. Find an example of personification in "The Chambered Nautilus."
2. Find an example of apostrophe in one of Emerson's poems. Does Emerson also personify the thing he addresses? Explain.

COMPOSITION

Writing About Personification

Write a short essay discussing Holmes's use of personification in "The Chambered Nautilus." First identify the human qualities given to the nautilus. Then tell why they are appropriate to the poet's subject. Conclude with your comments on the emotions aroused in the reader by this use of personification.

Writing a Personification

Select an object—something you own or see around you—and compose a short essay or poem in which you personify that object. You might, for example, tell what the object "sees," "hears," "feels," what it "thinks" or "regrets" or "desires."

James Russell Lowell   *1819–1891*

James Russell Lowell was perhaps the most gifted of the Fireside Poets. He was a critic, journalist, reformer, teacher, editor, lecturer, and diplomat, as well as a poet and a wit. With Longfellow and Holmes, Lowell was one of the "Brahmins"—the name of the highest caste of Indian society, which Holmes applied to the Boston aristocracy.

Like the other Fireside Poets, Lowell lived long and accomplished much. He grew up in Cambridge, Massachusetts. A student of law at Harvard, he discovered that he greatly preferred literature. Two collections of poetry, a volume of literary essays, and some journalistic work supporting the antislavery movement established him as a noted writer by the age of twenty-seven.

Three of Lowell's best-known poetic works appeared in 1848. *The Vision of Sir Launfal* is a romantic epic about knighthood, influenced by the King Arthur legends. *A Fable for Critics* contains sharp satiric portraits of the writers of the day, including Lowell himself. *The Biglow Papers* is a collection of poems and letters, featuring a down-to-earth character named Hosea Biglow, whose clever observations are delivered in a humorous rural New England dialect.

In 1855 Lowell succeeded Longfellow as professor of modern languages at Harvard, where he taught until 1872. With Holmes and others he helped found the *Atlantic Monthly,* serving as its first editor, and co-edited the *North American Review.* Under his guidance both of these publications gained literary and intellectual prominence. Later, as the U.S. ambassador to Spain, and then to Great Britain, Lowell became a popular spokesperson for democracy.

"Auspex", which appears on the following page, reveals Lowell's lyric gift. In it he draws an extended comparison between nature's songbirds and his own poems. An "auspex," in Ancient Rome, was someone who watched for omens in the flights of birds.

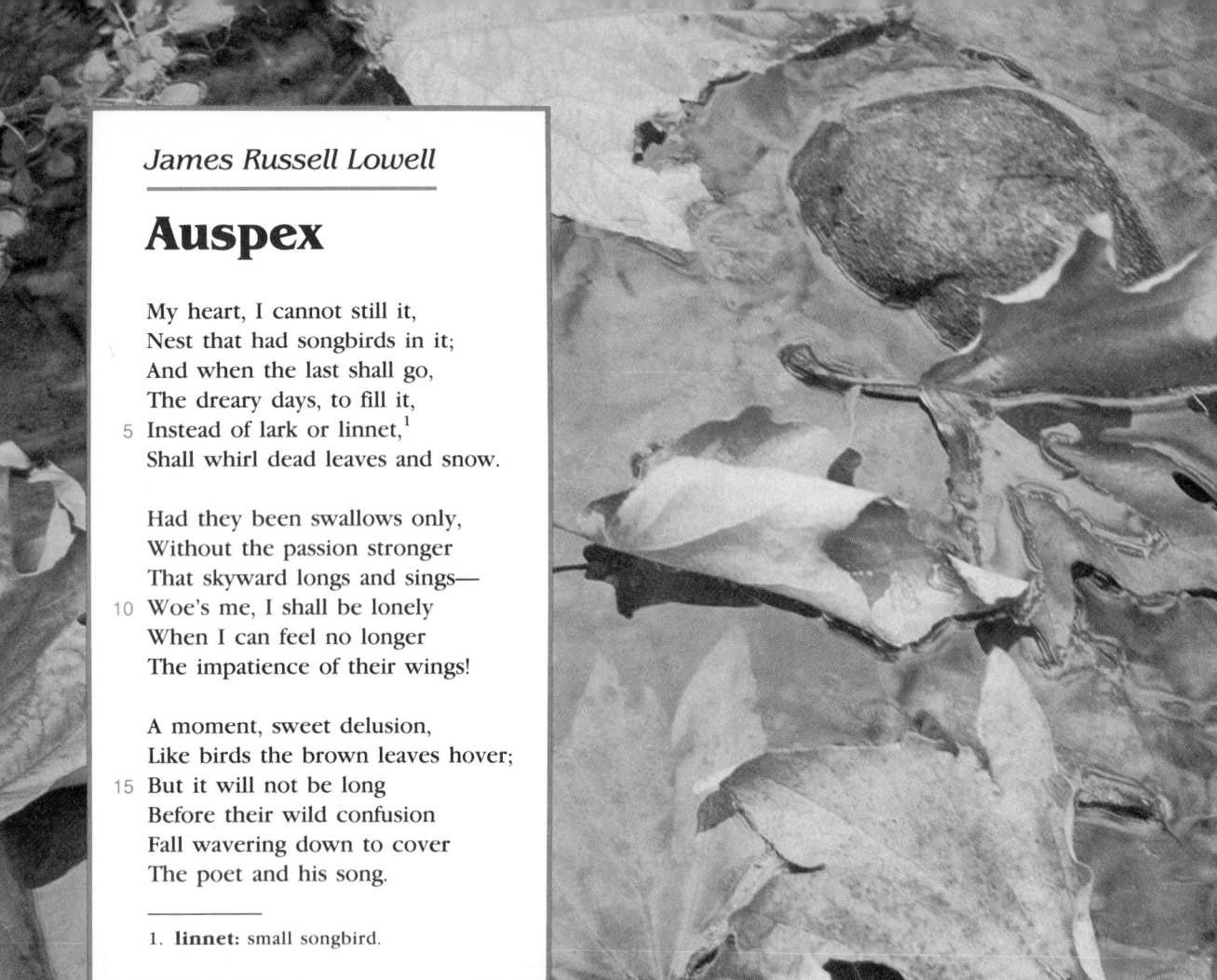

James Russell Lowell

Auspex

My heart, I cannot still it,
Nest that had songbirds in it;
And when the last shall go,
The dreary days, to fill it,
5 Instead of lark or linnet,[1]
Shall whirl dead leaves and snow.

Had they been swallows only,
Without the passion stronger
That skyward longs and sings—
10 Woe's me, I shall be lonely
When I can feel no longer
The impatience of their wings!

A moment, sweet delusion,
Like birds the brown leaves hover;
15 But it will not be long
Before their wild confusion
Fall wavering down to cover
The poet and his song.

_____

1. **linnet:** small songbird.

STUDY QUESTIONS

Recalling

1. To what does the poet compare his heart in lines 1–2?
2. According to stanza 1, what will whirl in the poet's heart when the last bird has gone?
3. According to stanza 2, what birds do not fill the poet's heart? What will make the poet "lonely"?
4. What does the poet call the moment in which the birds hover? What does he say "will not be long" in happening?

Interpreting

5. What do the songbirds represent? What does the auspex represent? What is suggested by the image of the songbirds leaving the nest in the first stanza?
6. Why does the poet say that he wishes his "birds" had been ordinary swallows instead of songbirds? Does he really mean what he says? Explain.
7. Explain the "sweet delusion" in line 13. What does the poet say will occur to dispel his delusion?

John Greenleaf Whittier 1807–1892

Like the other Fireside Poets—Longfellow, Holmes, and Lowell—
John Greenleaf Whittier won fame and reverence during a long
career. He was not only honored by his peers but also beloved by
the nation at large. His poems were recited by students, and his
books were found on the shelves of countless American homes. In
1877 the *Atlantic Monthly* celebrated Whittier's seventieth birthday
with a dinner attended by virtually every noteworthy living
American author. His eightieth birthday was the occasion for a
national celebration.

Unlike the other Fireside Poets, however, Whittier rose from
markedly humble beginnings. He grew up on a Massachusetts farm,
situated on land an ancestor had cleared in 1648. Although he later
idealized his boyhood in his most famous poem, *Snow-Bound,* his
life on the farm was often difficult. Hard work took its toll on his
health, and he later suffered from periodic physical breakdowns. His
upbringing was modest in another way: His family were Quakers,
whose basic principles were piety, plainness, simplicity, and love of
social justice. These ideals were ever after the hallmarks of
Whittier's life and his poetry.

Whittier vigorously opposed slavery. Encouraged by his lifelong
friend, the abolitionist William Lloyd Garrison, he threw himself into
the antislavery movement with uncommon devotion—principally as
a newspaper writer and editor. In 1835 he and another abolitionist
were attacked during a lecture tour in New Hampshire. Miraculously,
they made their way through a barrage of gunfire and escaped
unhurt.

As a poet Whittier matured late in life. Having remained a simple
man with down-to-earth tastes, he wrote increasingly about what he
loved best: rural America, with its local traditions, customs, and
close-knit family life. *Snow-Bound* (1866), in which the poet recalls
his boyhood on the farm, takes place before the time of telephones,
snowplows, and snowmobiles. When a blizzard struck, the farm was
instantly isolated. Outdoors was a world transformed by the miracle
of snow; inside were warmth and family life, with its deep affections
and simple pleasures. *Snow-Bound* is a poem of memory, a vision
of youth, suggesting that the poet was remembering a kind of life
that, even then, was passing away. Parts of *Snow-Bound* appear on
the following pages.

The engravings on pages 210–212 are from an 1874 edition of *Snow-Bound.*

John Greenleaf Whittier

from **Snow-Bound**

The Storm

The sun that brief December day
Rose cheerless over hills of gray,
And, darkly circled, gave at noon
A sadder light than waning moon.
5 Slow tracing down the thickening sky
Its mute and ominous prophecy,
A portent seeming less than threat,
It sank from sight before it set.
A chill no coat, however stout,
10 Of homespun stuff could quite shut out,
A hard, dull bitterness of cold,
    That checked, mid-vein, the circling race
    Of lifeblood in the sharpened face,
The coming of the snowstorm told.

· · ·

15 Unwarmed by any sunset light
The gray day darkened into night,
A night made hoary[1] with the swarm

And whirl-dance of the blinding storm,
As zigzag wavering to and fro
20 Crossed and recrossed the wingèd snow:
And ere the early bedtime came
The white drift piled the window frame,
And through the glass the clothesline posts
Looked in like tall and sheeted ghosts.

The First Morning

25 So all night long the storm roared on:
The morning broke without a sun;
In tiny spherule[2] traced with lines
Of Nature's geometric signs,
In starry flake, and pellicle,[3]
30 All day the hoary meteor fell;
And, when the second morning shone,
We looked upon a world unknown,
On nothing we could call our own.
Around the glistening wonder bent
35 The blue walls of the firmament,
No cloud above, no earth below—
A universe of sky and snow!
The old familiar sights of ours
Took marvelous shapes; strange domes and towers

---

1. **hoary** [hôr′ē]: white.

2. **spherule** [sfer′o̅o̅l]: small sphere.
3. **pellicle:** thin film.

40　Rose up where sty or corncrib stood,
　　Or garden wall, or belt of wood;
　　A smooth white mound the brushpile showed,
　　A fenceless drift what once was road;
　　The bridle post an old man sat
45　With loose-flung coat and high cocked hat;
　　The well curb had a Chinese roof;
　　And even the long sweep,[4] high aloof,
　　In its slant splendor, seemed to tell
　　Of Pisa's leaning miracle.[5]
50　A prompt, decisive man, no breath
　　Our father wasted: "Boys, a path!"
　　Well pleased (for when did farmer boy
　　Count such a summons less than joy?)
　　Our buskins[6] on our feet we drew;
55　　With mittened hands, and caps drawn low,
　　　To guard our necks and ears from snow,
　　We cut the solid whiteness through.
　　And, where the drift was deepest, made
　　A tunnel walled and overlaid
60　With dazzling crystal: we had read

　　Of rare Aladdin's[7] wondrous cave,
　　And to our own his name we gave,
　　With many a wish the luck were ours
　　To test his lamp's supernal[8] powers.

The Hearth at Night

65　The moon above the eastern wood
　　Shone at its full; the hill range stood
　　Transfigured in the silver flood,
　　Its blown snows flashing cold and keen,
　　Dead white, save where some sharp ravine
70　Took shadow, or the somber green
　　Of hemlocks turned to pitchy black
　　Against the whiteness at their back.
　　For such a world and such a night
　　Most fitting that unwarming light,
75　Which only seemed where'er it fell
　　To make the coldness visible.
　　Shut in from all the world without,
　　We sat the clean-winged hearth[9] about.
　　Content to let the north wind roar

---

4. **sweep:** pole with a bucket at one end, used to raise water from a well.
5. **Pisa's** [pē′zəz] **leaning miracle:** the famous Leaning Tower of Pisa, Italy.
6. **buskins:** high, laced, leather boots.

7. **Aladdin:** boy in the *Arabian Nights* who found treasures in a cave with the aid of a magic lamp.
8. **supernal:** supernatural.
9. **clean-winged hearth:** The hearth was cleaned with a broom made from a turkey's wing.

80 In baffled rage at pane and door,
While the red logs before us beat
The frost line back with tropic heat;
And ever, when a louder blast
Shook beam and rafter as it passed,
85 The merrier up its roaring draft
The great throat of the chimney laughed.
The house dog on his paws outspread
Laid to the fire his drowsy head,
The cat's dark silhouette on the wall
90 A couchant[10] tiger's seemed to fall;
And, for the winter fireside meet,
Between the andirons' straddling feet,
The mug of cider simmered slow,
The apples sputtered in a row,
95 And, close at hand, the basket stood
With nuts from brown October's wood.
What matter how the night behaved?
What matter how the north wind raved?
Blow high, blow low, not all its snow
100 Could quench our hearthfire's ruddy glow.
O Time and Change!—with hair as gray

As was my sire's that winter day,
How strange it seems, with so much gone
Of life and love, to still live on!
105 Ah, brother![11] only I and thou
Are left of all that circle now—
The dear home faces whereupon
That fitful firelight paled and shone.

•   •   •

Yet Love will dream, and Faith will trust,
110 (Since He who knows our need is just)
That somehow, somewhere, meet we must.
Alas for him who never sees
The stars shine through his cypress trees!
Who, hopeless, lays his dead away,
115 Nor looks to see the breaking day
Across the mournful marbles[12] play!
Who hath not learned, in hours of faith,
The truth to flesh and sense unknown,
That Life is ever lord of Death,
120 And Love can never lose its own!

----

10. **couchant** [kou′chənt]: lying down.

11. **brother:** the poet's brother, Matthew
Whittier (1812–1883).
12. **marbles:** marble tombstones.

STUDY QUESTIONS

Recalling

1. In the section "The Storm," what details of the sunrise and the sunset foretell the storm?
2. How does the poet describe his father in the section "The First Morning"? What does the father tell the boys to do?
3. According to lines 98–100, what can the north wind not quench?
4. What does the poet address in line 101? What does he say seems strange?
5. According to the last three lines, what truth does the poet say he has learned?

Interpreting

6. What can you tell about the father's relationship to the children from lines 50–53?
7. In the section "The Hearth at Night," what emotions does Whittier suggest his family felt as they sat around the hearth?
8. State in your own words the poet's ideas about life, death, and change expressed in the final lines of the poem.

Extending

9. Whittier's memory of his boyhood is primarily a happy one. Do you think Whittier is justified in omitting the dangerous and more difficult aspects of a great winter blizzard?

LITERARY FOCUS

Imagery

Imagery is a collection of mental pictures. Although visual imagery is the most common, it is important to remember that an image can appeal to any of our physical senses. For example, Whittier uses many images of what the storm looks like. But when he writes that "all night long the storm roared on," he also suggests what the storm sounds like—perhaps a menacing beast.

A poet can suggest to our imagination a particular sight, sound, smell, taste, or feeling. Much of the pleasure of reading poetry comes from our enjoyment of images, which may be astonishing and lovely in themselves. Moreover, effective images stimulate us to consider familiar things in new ways.

Thinking About Imagery

Find three other images in this selection from *Snow-Bound.* At least one of these images should appeal to a sense other than sight. Describe each image in your own words, and tell what purpose it serves in the poem.

VOCABULARY

Vivid Adjectives

The beauty of Whittier's images stems in part from his careful choice of adjectives. Define each of these adjectives, *as it is used in the poem.* Then write an original sentence for each, in which you use the adjective to create an image.

1. waning (line 4)
2. ominous (line 6)
3. hoary (line 17)
4. supernal (line 64)
5. ruddy (line 100)

COMPOSITION

Writing About Imagery

Snow-Bound encompasses in its imagery many changes of scene and a variety of moods. In an essay tell how Whittier evokes contrasting emotions by using contrasting images. First tell which images describe light, which images describe darkness, and what emotional response the poet has to each image. Then do the same thing for the images of cold and warmth. Conclude with a comment about your own response to the images.

Writing a Remembrance

In either prose or verse, compose your own recollection of an experience or a time that was important in your life. Fill your description with sharp images that suggest what the experience or time meant to you then. End your composition, as Whittier does, with a comment about it from your point of view today.

COMPARING WRITERS

In the selections in this unit, Longfellow, Holmes, Lowell, and Whittier reveal their profound concern with the passage of time. Based on the poems you have read, tell what at least two of these poets have to say about time. What attitudes and emotions do these poets share?

READING FOR APPRECIATION

The Sound of Poetry

Poems began with the human voice singing or chanting. Now that we *see* most poems in print rather than *hear* them recited, we can easily forget that one of the pleasures of poetry is the sound it makes.

Perhaps we should say: the sound we make *for* it, or *of* it. A printed poem, like a musical score, is only an indication of what can happen in "performance," even if we are reading silently. Yet the sound of poetry is not pure like the sound of a piano: It is part of the words. When we read a poem, we do not want the sense to overwhelm the verse; we do not want the verse to overwhelm the sense.

Look at the rhythm of Whittier's *Snow-Bound,* for example. Possible heavy or long pauses are marked with //, and light or short pauses with /. Try these lines, taking no pause at all or just the hint of a pause at the ends of lines, unless a pause is indicated:

The moon / above the eastern
    wood /
Shone at its full; // the hill range
    stood
Transfigured in the silver flood, /
Its blown snows flashing / cold
    and keen, /
Dead white, // save where some
    sharp ravine
Took shadow, / or the somber
    green
Of hemlocks turned to pitchy
    black /
Against the whiteness at their
    back. //

You may disagree with this phrasing; the point, however, is that we can avoid a monotonous sing-song:

The   MOON   aBOVE   the
    EASTern WOOD
Shone AT its FULL; the HILL
    range STOOD

—and so forth. There are subtler and more pleasant rhythms than that. At the same time we do not want to turn the poem into prose. Whittier did not write: "The moon above the eastern wood shone at its full; the hill range stood transfigured in the silver flood. . . ."

All poems do not sound alike, although the poems of a single poet do sometimes take on the "voice" of that poet. Find a "music" appropriate to some poems. Lowell's "Auspex" would be a good candidate. Allow the English language to have its natural way, but allow the verse to have its way as well.

THE AMERICAN VOICE

Self-Reliance

Self-reliance in all its forms seems always to have been a part of American culture. During the New England Renaissance, however, it was given special attention and special expression.

Emerson

Trust thyself: every heart vibrates to that iron string. Accept the place the divine providence has found for you. . . . Speak what you think now in hard words, and tomorrow speak what tomorrow thinks in hard words again, though it contradict everything you said today. . . . To be great is to be misunderstood.

Thoreau

In most books, the I, or first person, is omitted; in this it will be retained; that, in respect to egotism, is the main difference. We commonly do not remember that it is, after all, always the first person that is speaking. I should not talk so much about myself if there were anybody else whom I knew as well. . . . If a man does not keep pace with his companions, perhaps it is because he hears a different drummer. Let him step to the music which he hears, however measured or far away.

Hawthorne

"Oh, you know not how lonely I am and how frightened to be alone behind my black veil."

Melville

"He tasks me; he heaps me; I see in him outrageous strength, with an inscrutable malice sinewing it. That inscrutable thing is chiefly what I hate; and be the white whale agent, or be the white whale principal, I will wreak that hate upon him. Talk not to me of blasphemy, man; I'd strike the sun if it insulted me."

Longfellow

Be not like dumb, driven cattle! Be a hero in the strife!

As a true American idea self-reliance has withstood the extremes of optimism and pessimism. It has lifted some people to glorious visions and, when distorted, isolated some people to the point of destruction. It has been the basis for a great variety of philosophical ideas, and it has inspired many political thinkers. Every period of American literature, every unit in this book, reveals in some way that self-reliance is an idea continually defining and redefining the American imagination.

Key to Illustrations on Pages 152–153.

1. Ralph Waldo Emerson, photographer unknown, c. 1855.
2. *Gold Mining in California*, print by Currier and Ives, 1871.
3. Inventor Isaac Singer demonstrating his sewing machine, engraving, c. 1853.
4. The power of newspapers, painting, artist unknown, c. 1846.
5. Nineteenth-century weather vane in the form of Columbia, personification of America.
6. *The Whale Fishery*, print by Currier and Ives, c. 1845.
7. *Nathaniel Hawthorne*, Charles Osgood, 1840.
8. Illustration from the title page of Henry David Thoreau's *Walden*, original 1854 edition.
9. Henry David Thoreau, daguerreotype (early photograph) by Benjamin D. Maxham, 1856.

Key to Illustrations appears on page 293.

CONFLICT AND CELEBRATION

1855–1880

MARK TWAIN

KNOWN TO EVERYONE – LIKED BY ALL

Near the middle of the nineteenth century, the American showman P. T. Barnum returned from a tour of Europe. The young poet Walt Whitman, then working as a reporter for the Brooklyn *Eagle,* interviewed Barnum and asked him if seeing Europe made him less impressed with America. "No! Not a bit of it!" cried Barnum. "Why, sir, you can't imagine the difference. There everything is frozen—kings and *things*—formal, but absolutely frozen: here it is *life.*"

Like so many other Americans, Barnum was aware that America was indeed flourishing and full of life. The transplantings from Europe of people, customs, and ideas had been successful. The roots had taken hold; what had been foreign had become native. Full of confidence, Americans were envisioning a nation that would reach from sea to sea. The explorations of Lewis and Clark had spurred the idea of that destiny, and thousands of men and women moved westward to homestead, enduring hardship and danger because they saw the limitless possibilities of making new lives on the American land.

At the same time that the westward expansion was beginning, the United States and the Constitution met their sternest test. That test, the Civil War, divided America against itself for the first time. It tore apart the carefully woven fabric of the *united* states.

Cartoon of Mark Twain riding his "Celebrated Jumping Frog," Frederick Waddy, 1872.

A Nation Divided

By the middle of the century, the North had secured prosperity through manufacturing and commerce. Factories flourished; industry sought protective tariffs and a strong federal government. Cities boomed with plenty of work and plenty of workers. In the South, on the other hand, the economy had remained agricultural, depending on cotton exports, the slave system, and low tariffs. For Southerners the agrarian way of life and the rights of the individual states were cherished as the foundations of Jeffersonian democracy. As the century wore on, the Northern and the Southern ways of life seemed more and more irreconcilable. Just as Americans have always had to face the question of the place of the individual person within the whole society, so Americans before the Civil War had to face the question of the rights of individual states within a democratic union.

Every year the debates grew fiercer. Abolitionists became more and more vocal. William Lloyd Garrison attacked slavery every week in his newspaper, *The Liberator.* Harriet Beecher Stowe moved the emotions of many people with *Uncle Tom's Cabin* (1852). As each new western state entered the Union, a decision had to be made: would the state be slave or free? Compromise after compromise was reached until the tension

became too great. When Abraham Lincoln was elected President in 1860, the Southern states took action. In December of 1860, South Carolina seceded from the Union; within a month six more states followed, and four others joined the new Confederacy soon after. With the firing at Fort Sumter on April 12, 1861, the Civil War began.

It is difficult to express what a civil war means to a nation: "Cousin against cousin" is a tired phrase, but it tells the truth. The young Mark Twain of Hannibal, Missouri, joined a Confederate militia; his brother accepted a Union appointment and moved to the Nevada Territory. In Maryland thousands enlisted in the Confederacy, and thousands more with the Union Army. Throughout the nation families were divided and friends became enemies.

The Civil War was fought on a scale that America had never before seen. On land and sea, in the Mississippi Valley and in the Virginia Wilderness, across

Pennsylvania, Tennessee, and Georgia, in massive battles and unrecorded skirmishes—people fought and died. Bull Run, Shiloh, Chancellorsville, Gettysburg, Vicksburg, Atlanta—early Southern victories eventually gave way to Northern ones. On April 9, 1865, after a long and bitter war that some people had thought would take only a few weeks, Robert E. Lee, General of the Confederate Armies, surrendered to the Union Commander, General Ulysses S. Grant, at Appomattox Court House.

For the new nation, the Civil War, or War Between the States, was a tragedy of the greatest magnitude. The war decimated a generation and left the nation its most painful legacy.

Expansion and Celebration

The South, caught in a struggle for new power after the war, had to endure the long and painful Reconstruction Period. Elsewhere, however, the end of the war was cause for celebration. The nation had been preserved and could get on with its business. In the North cities opened their gates again.

This postwar period was named the Gilded Age by Mark Twain. It was an age that seemed to have lost some of its ideals in the chaos and hatred of war, and it filled that void with an intense materialism. The two decades after the war were a time of rapid technological progress: They witnessed the

Walt Whitman Urging the Bird of Freedom to Soar, caricature by Max Beerbohm, 1904.

completion of the transcontinental railroad and the invention of the typewriter, the ticker tape, the telephone, the light bulb, and the "horseless carriage." They were even more a time of profit, economic development, and financial wheeling-and-dealing—the age of the Robber Barons. The nation had found strength through the war, but it had lost some innocence.

The great new source of joy and inspiration, however, was the West. The West was "wild," exciting, new: It was still a frontier, with all the possibilities of an unspoiled place. Few people thought of the plight of the Indians; all that mattered was the great frontier where dreams were fulfilled and fortunes made. The newspaper editor Horace Greeley was credited with the words that symbolized the spirit of the time: "Go west, young man!"

The toil of the slaves, the bloodshed of battle, the celebration of a reunited America, the boom in technology, the populating of the American frontier, and the displacement of the Indian cultures were dramatic experiences. Out of such experiences came memorable contributions to our literature.

Three Americans

During these turbulent years three writers emerged who used the American language in new ways and who would prove to be among America's liter-

ary giants—Walt Whitman, Emily Dickinson, and Mark Twain.

Whitman. "I sound my barbaric yawp over the roofs of the world." So Walt Whitman cried out in *Song of Myself.* There was indeed something elemental, unmannered and unmannerly, in the new language American writers found themselves using. The American experience could only be described with new expressions: Whitman invented them. A new literature demanded using new rhythms and new forms: Whitman generated them. Whitman absorbed America. He became the country in his poetry, and his songs became America's new self-portrait.

Dickinson. The American language shaped the sound of Emily Dickinson's poetry as well, but it is the quieter, drier, crisper tone of New England speech we hear in her poems. Most of our early poets wrote in a language close to the "literary" style of England, but the poems of Dickinson—like those of

Whitman—take on the characteristic turns and twists of American speech. Her poems deal with the profound matters that New England writers had always explored, but her voice takes on an irony and reveals a sensibility that still seems modern today.

Mark Twain. We can never think of Mark Twain as anything but a product of the American frontier. A child of the Mississippi River, the great dividing line between East and West, he sought his fortune in California. He was able to tell the world about mining camps and backwater towns, daring riverboat pilots, braggarts and adventurers, country children and their dreams—and he told of these things in the language of the people who experienced them. Steeped in his time and place, a master of dialect and rural humor, Mark Twain wrote in a language that opened a new mine of American literature.

Wherever Americans were going after the war, they were not returning to the past. The old forms and many of the old ideals had died in the war. New ones were not easily found. Perhaps Mark Twain's Huckleberry Finn best sums up the direction many Americans felt they had to take:

"But I reckon I got to light out for the Territory ahead of the rest, because Aunt Sally she's going to adopt me and sivilize me and I can't stand it. I been there before."

TIME LINE

1855 Walt Whitman, *Leaves of Grass*	**1855** Russia: Ivan Turgenev, *A Month in the Country*
Frederick Douglass, *My Bondage and My Freedom*	
1857 Dred Scott case rules Missouri Compromise unconstitutional	**1857** France: Gustave Flaubert, *Madame Bovary*
E. G. Otis installs first safety elevator	England: Thomas Hughes, *Tom Brown's Schooldays*
1858 Oliver Wendell Holmes, *Autocrat of the Breakfast Table*	
First transatlantic telegraph cable laid	
1859 First oil well in U.S. drilled (Titusville, Pa.)	
1860 Abraham Lincoln elected President	**1860** England: Florence Nightingale founds world's first nursing school
Pony Express established	
1861 Civil War begins	**1861** England: Charles Dickens, *Great Expectations*
Federal income tax instituted	
1862 Civil War battles of Shiloh, Antietam, and Fredericksburg	**1862** Russia: Ivan Turgenev, *Fathers and Sons*
1863 Lincoln issues Emancipation Proclamation	
Lincoln delivers Gettysburg Address	
	1864 Russia: Leo Tolstoy begins *War and Peace*
	France: Louis Pasteur develops pasteurization method
1865 Civil War ends	**1865** England: Lewis Carroll, *Alice in Wonderland*
Lincoln assassinated	Austria: Franz Schubert (died 1828), first performance of *Unfinished Symphony*
1866 Cholera epidemic strikes many American cities	**1866** Russia: Feodor Dostoevsky, *Crime and Punishment*
1867 U.S. buys Alaska from Russia for two cents per acre	**1867** France: Pierre Michaux begins to manufacture bicycles
Mark Twain, "The Celebrated Jumping Frog of Calaveras County"	Sweden: Alfred Nobel patents dynamite

1868 First professional baseball team, Cincinnati Red Stockings, founded

Louisa May Alcott, *Little Women*

1869 National Women Suffrage Association organized

First transcontinental railroad line completed

1870 John D. Rockefeller founds Standard Oil Company

1871 P. T. Barnum opens "The Greatest Show on Earth" in New York

1872 James Whistler paints *The Artist's Mother*

1874 First U.S. zoo established (Philadelphia, Pa.)

1875 Thomas Eakins paints realistic masterpiece, *The Gross Clinic*

1876 Alexander Graham Bell invents telephone

Mark Twain, *The Adventures of Tom Sawyer*

American Centennial Exposition held in Philadelphia

1877 Thomas Edison invents phonograph

1878 Henry James, *Daisy Miller*

1879 Thomas Edison invents electric light bulb

Frank W. Woolworth opens his first store

1880 *The Dial* magazine founded

U.S. population estimate: 50 million

1868 Japan: Shogunate abolished; power returns to emperor

1869 England: Jules Verne, *Twenty Thousand Leagues Under the Sea*

Suez Canal opens, connecting Mediterranean Sea and Red Sea

1870 Franco-Prussian War begins

1871 England: George Eliot, *Middlemarch*

1872 First international soccer game played, Scotland versus England

1874 France: Impressionist painting first exhibited

1876 Russia: Peter Tchaikovsky composes *Swan Lake*

1878 England: Thomas Hardy, *The Return of the Native*

1879 England: Gilbert and Sullivan, *Pirates of Penzance*

Russia: Feodor Dostoevsky, *The Brothers Karamazov*

1880 France: Auguste Rodin exhibits *The Thinker*

Spirituals

Spirituals reflect the two deepest concerns of the black slaves who gave them birth: earthly bondage and religious faith. In fact, many of these songs have their origins in religious hymns, transformed by memories of African music. Spirituals were also taken up and sung by white Americans in camp meetings and other religious gatherings in the nineteenth century. They were collected in such books as *The Southern Harmony* (1835) and *The Sacred Harp* (1844), yet no printed version can fully convey to us now the power and the emotion of the original sound of "the sorrow songs," as they were called.

Many spirituals had double meanings and were used to transmit secret messages, especially about escape. "Go Down, Moses," for example, is based on the biblical account of the bondage of the Jews in Egypt. However, it probably also refers to Harriet Tubman, a former slave who was known as "Moses." Tubman repeatedly risked her life to help slaves escape.

"Follow the Drinking Gourd" told escaped slaves that the Big Dipper in the sky pointed to the North Star—the direction of freedom. The spiritual is based on an old gospel hymn, "Follow the Risen Lord," and was sung by those using the Underground Railroad, the network of escape that carried many slaves to freedom. The "old man" of the song may refer to a man called Peg Leg Joe, one of the "conductors," or guides, on the Underground Railroad. "Old Man," however, has also long been a nickname for the Mississippi River.

Go Down, Moses

When Israel was in Egypt land,
  Let my people go!
Oppressed so hard they could not stand,
  Let my people go!

Chorus
5 Go down, Moses,
  Way down in Egypt land
Tell ole Pharaoh,
  Let my people go!

Thus say the Lord, bold Moses said,
10   Let my people go!
If not I'll smite your first-born dead,
  Let my people go!

Chorus
Go down, Moses,
  Way down in Egypt land
15 Tell ole Pharaoh,
  Let my people go!

No more shall they in bondage toil,
  Let my people go!
Let them come out with Egypt's spoil,
20   Let my people go!

Chorus
Go down, Moses,
  Way down in Egypt land
Tell ole Pharaoh,
  Let my people go!

STUDY QUESTIONS

Recalling
1. In stanza 1 how are the people of Israel in Egypt described?
2. In the Chorus what specifically is Moses asked to do?
3. With what words does Moses threaten Pharaoh in stanza 2?

Interpreting
4. Who does *my* refer to in the repeated line "Let my people go"? Who tells Moses to "Go down . . . in Egypt's land"?
5. What does this spiritual show about the condition and faith of the slaves who sang it? What emotions would have inspired a spiritual such as this?

Extending
6. Why do you think slaves in America sang about the captivity of the Jews in Egypt? Might there have been practical reasons for doing so?

Follow the Drinking Gourd

When the sun comes back and the first quail calls,
    Follow the drinking gourd,
For the old man is a-waiting for to carry you to freedom
    If you follow the drinking gourd.

5 Follow the drinking gourd,
    Follow the drinking gourd,
For the old man is a-waiting for to carry you to freedom
    If you follow the drinking gourd.

The river bank will make a very good road,
10   The dead trees show you the way,
Left foot, peg foot traveling on
    Follow the drinking gourd.

The river ends between two hills
    Follow the drinking gourd.
15 There's another river on the other side,
    Follow the drinking gourd.

Where the little river meets the great big river,
    Follow the drinking gourd.
The old man is a-waiting for to carry you to freedom,
20   If you follow the drinking gourd.

STUDY QUESTIONS

Recalling

1. According to stanza 1, when is the right time to begin to "follow the drinking gourd"?
2. According to stanza 3, which road should the slave take first? What landmarks show the way?
3. According to the last stanza, where is the old man waiting? For what or for whom is the old man waiting?

Interpreting

4. What larger spiritual meaning might a slave have added to the literal meaning of crossing a river to "the other side"?
5. What emotions do you think this song could have inspired in the slaves who sang it as they escaped?

Extending

6. Do people still write and sing songs to give each other courage and hope in desperate situations? Name one such song, and tell its message in your own words.

VIEWPOINT

In his autobiography the modern black poet James Weldon Johnson observes about the spirituals that

so many of these songs contain more than mere melody; there is sounded in them that elusive undertone, the note in music which is not heard with the ears.

■ Describe in your own words "that elusive undertone" of the spirituals. How would you define the music "not heard with the ears"?

Frederick Douglass   *c. 1817–1895*

Frederick Douglass was born into slavery. He learned to read in the Auld household in Baltimore, at first with the support of his master's wife and later against her orders. What he read made him long for freedom.

In 1838 Douglass succeeded in his second attempt at escape. A few years later he attended a meeting of the Massachusetts Anti-Slavery Society and gave an extemporaneous speech that was so inspiring that he was engaged to be one of the society's agents. Douglass was a brilliant orator. His speeches and his 1845 autobiography, *Narrative of the Life of Frederick Douglass,* were powerful fuel for the Abolitionist cause. However, he was still a fugitive slave, and by naming names and places in his autobiography he placed himself in great danger. He went abroad, where in 1847 some English friends purchased his freedom.

Returning to America, Douglass published an antislavery magazine that urged political solutions until the war came. He also wrote an updated version of his autobiography entitled *My Bondage and My Freedom* (1855). After the war he remained committed to his people and his country, holding important positions such as that of Minister to Haiti. A final version of his autobiography, *Life and Times of Frederick Douglass,* was published in 1882.

As a writer Douglass makes his points with characteristic simplicity and dignity through the simple recitation of the facts of his life. In *My Bondage and My Freedom* Douglass tells his story plainly, letting his experience speak for itself.

Frederick Douglass

from **My Bondage and My Freedom**

I lived in the family of Master Hugh, at Baltimore, seven years, during which time—as the almanac makers say of the weather—my condition was variable. The most interesting feature of my history here was my learning to read and write, under somewhat marked disadvantages. In attaining this knowledge, I was compelled to resort to indirections by no means congenial to my nature and which were really humiliating to me. My mistress—who had begun to teach me—was suddenly checked in her benevolent design by the strong advice of her husband. In faithful compliance with this advice, the good lady had not only ceased to instruct me herself, but had set her face as a flint against my learning to read by any means. It is due, however, to my mistress to say that she did not adopt this course in all its stringency at the first. She either thought it unnecessary or she lacked the depravity indispensable to shutting me up in mental darkness. It was at least necessary for her to have some training and some hardening in the exercise of the slaveholder's prerogative to make her equal to forgetting my human nature and character, and to treating me as a thing destitute of a moral or an intellectual nature. Mrs. Auld—my mistress—was a most kind and tenderhearted woman; and, in the humanity of her heart and the simplicity of her mind, she set out, when I first went to live with her, to treat me as she supposed one human being ought to treat another.

It is easy to see that, in entering upon the duties of a slaveholder, some little experience is needed. Nature has done almost nothing to prepare men and women to be either slaves or slaveholders. Nothing but rigid training, long persisted in, can perfect the character of the one or the other. One cannot easily forget to love freedom; and it is as hard to cease to respect that natural love in our fellow creatures.

On entering upon the career of a slaveholding mistress, Mrs. Auld was singularly deficient; nature, which fits nobody for such an office, had done less for her than any lady I had known. It was no easy matter to induce her to think and to feel that the curly-headed boy who stood by her side and even leaned on her lap, who was loved by little Tommy and who loved little Tommy in turn, sustained to her only the relation of a chattel. I was *more* than that, and she felt me to be more than that. I could talk and sing; I could laugh and weep; I could reason and remember; I could love and hate. I was human, and she, dear lady, knew and felt me to be so. How could she then treat me as a brute, without a mighty struggle with all the noble powers of her own soul. That struggle came, and the will and power of the husband was victorious. Her noble soul was overthrown; but he that overthrew it did not himself escape the consequences. He, not less than the other parties, was injured in his domestic peace by the fall.

When I went into their family, it was the abode of happiness and contentment. The mistress of the house was a model of affection and tenderness. Her fervent piety and watchful uprightness made it impossible to see her without thinking and feeling—"that woman is a Christian." There was no sorrow nor suffering for which she had not a tear, and there was no innocent joy for which she had not a smile. She had bread for the hungry, clothes for the naked, and comfort for every mourner that came within her reach. Slavery soon proved its ability to divest her of these excellent qualities and her home of its early happiness. Conscience cannot stand much violence. Once thoroughly broken down, *who* is he that can repair the damage? It may be broken toward the slave on Sunday, and toward the master on Monday. It cannot endure such shocks. It must stand entire, or it does not stand at all. If my condition waxed bad, that of the family waxed not better. The first step, in the wrong direction, was the violence done to nature and to conscience in arresting the benevolence that would have enlightened my young mind. In ceasing to instruct me, she must begin to justify herself *to* herself; and, once consenting to take sides in such a debate, she was riveted to her position. One needs very little knowledge of moral philosophy to see *where* my mistress now landed. She finally became even more violent in her opposition to my learning to read than was her husband himself. She was not satisfied with simply doing as *well* as her husband had commanded her, but seemed resolved to better his instruction. Nothing appeared to make my poor mistress—after her turning toward the downward path—more angry than seeing me, seated in some nook or corner, quietly reading a book or a newspaper. I have had her rush at me with the utmost fury, and snatch from my hand such newspaper or book, with something of the wrath and consternation which a traitor might be supposed to feel on being discovered in a plot by some dangerous spy.

Mrs. Auld was an apt woman, and the advice of her husband, and her own experience, soon demonstrated to her entire satisfaction that education and slavery are incompatible with each other. When this conviction was thoroughly established, I was most narrowly watched in all my movements. If I remained in a separate room from the family for any considerable length of time, I was sure to be suspected of having a book, and was at once called upon to give an account of myself. All this, however, was entirely *too late.* The first, and never to be retraced, step had been taken. In teaching me the alphabet, in the days of her simplicity and kindness, my mistress had given me the "inch," and now, no ordinary precaution could prevent me from taking the "ell."[1]

---

1. **"ell"**: former English measure of length, used mainly for cloth, equal to forty-five inches.

Seized with a determination to learn to read at any cost, I hit upon many expedients to accomplish the desired end. The plea which I mainly adopted, and the one by which I was most successful, was that of using my young white playmates, whom I met in the street, as teachers. I used to carry, almost constantly, a copy of Webster's spelling book in my pocket; and, when sent on errands, or when play time was allowed me, I would step, with my young friends, aside, and take a lesson in spelling. I generally paid my *tuition fee* to the boys with bread, which I also carried in my pocket. For a single biscuit, any of my hungry little comrades would give me a lesson more valuable to me than bread. Not every one, however, demanded this consideration, for there were those who took pleasure in teaching me whenever I had a chance to be taught by them. I am strongly tempted to give the names of two or three of those little boys as a slight testimonial of the gratitude and affection I bear them, but prudence forbids; not that it would injure me, but it might possibly embarrass them; for it is almost an unpardonable offense to do any thing, directly or indirectly, to promote a slave's freedom in a slave state. It is enough to say of my warm-hearted little playfellows that they lived on Philpot street very near Durgin & Bailey's shipyard.

Although slavery was a delicate subject, and very cautiously talked about among grownup people in Maryland, I frequently talked about it—and that very freely—with the white boys. I would sometimes say to them, while seated on a curb stone or a cellar door, "I wish I could be free, as you will be when you get to be men." "You will be free, you know, as soon as you are twenty-one and can go where you like, but I am a slave for life. Have I not as good a right to be free as you have?" Words like these, I observed, always troubled them; and I had no small satisfaction in wringing from the boys, occasionally, that fresh and bitter condemnation of slavery that springs from nature, unseared and unperverted. Of all consciences, let me have those to deal with which have not been bewildered by the cares of life. I do not remember ever to have met with a *boy,* while I was in slavery, who defended the slave system; but I have often had boys to console me with the hope that something would yet occur by which I might be made free. Over and over again, they have told me that "they believed *I* had as good a right to be free as *they* had," and that "they did not believe God ever made anyone to be a slave." The reader will easily see that such little conversations with my playfellows had no tendency to weaken my love of liberty nor to render me contented with my condition as a slave.

When I was about thirteen years old and had succeeded in learning to read, every increase of knowledge, especially respecting the free states, added something to the almost intolerable burden of the thought—"I am a slave for life." To my bondage I saw no end. It was a terrible reality, and I shall never be able to tell how sadly that thought chafed my young spirit. Fortunately, or unfortunately, about this time in my life, I had made enough money to buy what was then a very popular schoolbook, the *Columbian Orator.* I bought this addition to my library of Mr. Knight on Thames street, Fell's Point, Baltimore, and paid him fifty cents for it. I was first led to buy this book by hearing some little boys say that they were going to learn some little pieces out of it for the Exhibition. This volume was indeed a rich treasure, and every opportunity afforded me, for a time, was spent in diligently perusing it. . . . The dialogue and the speeches were all redolent of the principles of liberty, and poured floods of light on the nature and character of slavery. . . . I was no longer the light-hearted, gleesome boy, full of mirth and play, as when I landed first at Baltimore. Knowledge had come. . . .

This knowledge opened my eyes to the horrible pit and revealed the teeth of the frightful dragon that was ready to pounce upon me, but it opened no way for my escape. I have often wished myself a beast or a bird—anything, rather than a slave. I was wretched and gloomy

beyond my ability to describe. I was too thoughtful to be happy. It was this everlasting thinking which distressed and tormented me; and yet there was no getting rid of the subject of my thoughts. All nature was redolent of it. Once awakened by the silver trump[2] of knowledge, my spirit was roused to eternal wakefulness. Liberty! the inestimable birthright of every man had for me converted every object into an asserter of this great right. It was heard

---

2. **trump:** trumpet.

ment adopted by my once kind mistress toward me. I can easily believe that my leaden, downcast, and discontented look was very offensive to her. Poor lady! She did not know my trouble, and I dared not tell her. Could I have freely made her acquainted with the real state of my mind and given her the reasons therefor, it might have been well for both of us. Her abuse of me fell upon me like the blows of the false prophet upon his ass; she did not know that an *angel* stood in the way;[3] and—such is the relation of master and slave—I could not tell her. Nature had made us *friends;* slavery made us *enemies.* My interests were in a direction opposite to hers, and we both had our private thoughts and plans. She aimed to keep me ignorant; and I resolved to know, although knowledge only increased my discontent. My feelings were not the result of any marked cruelty in the treatment I received; they sprung from the consideration of my being a slave at all. It was *slavery*—not its mere *incidents*—that I hated. I had been cheated. I saw through the attempt to keep me in ignorance; I saw that slaveholders would have gladly made me believe that they were merely acting under the authority of God in making a slave of me and in making slaves of others, and I treated them as robbers and deceivers. The feeding and clothing me well could not atone for taking my liberty from me. The smiles of my mistress could not remove the deep sorrow that dwelt in my young bosom. Indeed these, in time, came only to deepen my sorrow. She had changed; and the reader will see that I had changed too. We were both victims to the same overshadowing evil—*she* as mistress, *I* as slave. I will not censure her harshly; she cannot censure me, for she knows I speak but the truth, and have acted in my opposition to slavery, just as she herself would have acted in a reverse of circumstances.

in every sound and beheld in every object. It was ever present to torment me with a sense of my wretched condition. The more beautiful and charming were the smiles of nature, the more horrible and desolate was my condition. I saw nothing without seeing it, and I heard nothing without hearing it. I do not exaggerate when I say that it looked from every star, smiled in every calm, breathed in every wind, and moved in every storm.

I have no doubt that my state of mind had something to do with the change in the treat-

---

3. **blows . . . way:** The reference is to the biblical tale (Numbers 22 : 21–35) in which an ass, despite being beaten by her master, Balaam, cannot obey and move on because an angel blocks her way.

STUDY QUESTIONS

Recalling

1. At the beginning of the selection, what does Douglass call "the most interesting feature" of his history in the Auld household?
2. What was Mrs. Auld like when Douglass first met her? Was she "trained" in being a slaveholder?
3. Who told Mrs. Auld to stop teaching Douglass to read? Eventually, what was her attitude toward Douglass' reading?
4. After Mrs. Auld stopped instructing him, what was Douglass' chief means for continuing his education? What "tuition fee" did he usually pay?
5. What book, in particular, does Douglass call a "rich treasure"? Of what principles does he say it was redolent?

Interpreting

6. Why was learning to read so important to Douglass?
7. What does Douglass mean when he says in the last paragraph that he and Mrs. Auld were "victims of the same overshadowing evil"?
8. What is Douglass' overall attitude toward his experiences? Does he seem bitter or sympathetic toward the Aulds and others?

LITERARY FOCUS

Autobiography

A **biography** is an account of a person's life that is factual, or at least claims to be so. It is not, however, a mere chronicle of days or events; rather, it is an overview, an attempt to place the subject in time and to explain the meaning or importance of his or her life.

An **autobiography** is also an account of a person's life, but here the subject is the author as well. The autobiographer believes that his or her life is interesting enough, important enough, or exemplary enough to merit consideration. The best autobiographies give a cogent view of the author's world and his or her place in it.

Frederick Douglass' three versions of his autobiography were written for a cause: to show the world that a black man, a slave, was a human being in the complete sense of "human"—at a time when there were those who said otherwise. Beyond what Douglass says directly about slavery, the quality of his writing, the sensitivity he displays, and the simple facts of his life are eloquent in themselves. In writing more than an antislavery tract, Douglass became not only a leader but a symbol who helped change American history.

Thinking About Autobiography

Where in Douglass' account does the author directly state his opinion of slavery? Where does he let the facts of his life speak for themselves?

COMPOSITION

Writing About Nonfiction

Write a brief essay in which you discuss Douglass' purpose in writing his autobiography. First state his purpose in your own words. Then cite examples of the techniques he uses to accomplish his purpose—for example, sensory details, facts, examples, and opinions. *For help with this assignment, refer to Lesson 4 in the Writing About Literature Handbook at the back of this book.*

Writing a Review

Place yourself in the days before the Civil War, and compose a short review of Douglass' *My Bondage and My Freedom* that might have appeared in a newspaper or a magazine of the time. Your review should contain quotations and examples from the extract as well as your comments on the author's style. Conclude by telling why you recommend the book or why you do not.

National Portrait Gallery, Smithsonian

Mary Chesnut   *1822–1886*

Mary Boykin Chesnut grew up with the daughters of Southern planters amid all the elegance that attended such surroundings. Her father was a proslavery politician who served as both governor of and senator from South Carolina; her mother came from an old established Carolina family.

At seventeen Mary married her childhood sweetheart, James Chesnut, Jr., a wealthy Carolina lawyer. James was elected senator from South Carolina in 1858, and though he was a moderate who did not favor secession, he stood with the Southern delegation as war approached. Later he served under General Beauregard and advised Confederate President Jefferson Davis. Thus Mary Chesnut had the advantage of personal contact with many of the leading Southern figures during the Civil War.

Mary Chesnut feared the war, and she hated to see it come. Yet when it came she was loyal to her friends and family. She visited hospitals, rejoiced in Confederate victories, and wept at Confederate defeats. Nevertheless, even in victory, her joy was tinged by grief and bitterness at the agonies and evils of warfare.

The pages of Chesnut's journal sparkle with humor and tears, for Mary Chesnut was a keen observer and a moving one. Her journal is one of the most valuable documents to come down to us from the war period: It grants us the privilege of seeing history from the point of view, not of a soldier or a politician, but simply of a sympathetic person who was there.

A Cotton Plantation on the Mississippi,
1884, Currier and Ives lithograph.

Mary Chesnut

from **A Wartime Journal**

March 1861

"Now this is positive," they say. "Fort Sumter[1] is to be relieved, and we are to have no war." Poor Sumter—not half as much as we would be!

After all, far too good to be true.

If there be no war, how triumphant Mr. Chesnut will be. He is the only man who has persisted from the first that his would be a *peaceful* revolution. Heaven grant it may prove so.

April 7, 1861

Things are happening so fast.

My husband has been made an aide-de-camp[2] of General Beauregard.

Three hours ago we were quietly packing to go home. The convention has adjourned.

Now he tells me the attack upon Fort Sumter may begin tonight. Depends upon Anderson and the fleet outside. The *Herald* says that this show of war outside of the bar is intended for Texas.

John Manning came in with his sword and red sash. Pleased as a boy to be on Beauregard's staff while the row goes on. He has gone with Wigfall to Captain Hartstene with instructions.

Mr. Chesnut is finishing a report he had to make to the convention.

Mrs. Hayne called. She had, she said, "but one feeling, pity for those who are not here."

Jack Preston, Willie Alston—"the take-life-easys," as they are called—with John Green, "the big brave," have gone down to the island—volunteered as privates.

Seven hundred men were sent over. Ammunition wagons rumbling along the streets all night. Anderson burning blue lights—signs and signals for the fleet outside, I suppose.

Today at dinner there was no allusion to things as they stand in Charleston Harbor. There was an undercurrent of intense excitement. There could not have been a more brilliant circle. In addition to our usual quartet (Judge Withers, Langdon Cheves, and Trescot), our two governors dined with us, Means and Manning.

These men all talked so delightfully. For once in my life I listened.

That over, business began. In earnest, Governor Means rummaged a sword and red sash from somewhere and brought it for Colonel Chesnut, who has gone to demand the surrender of Fort Sumter.

And now, patience—we must wait.

Why did that green goose Anderson go into Fort Sumter? Then everything began to go wrong.

Now they have intercepted a letter from him, urging them to let him surrender. He paints the horrors likely to ensue if they will not.

He ought to have thought of all that before he put his head in the hole.

April 12, 1861

Anderson will not capitulate.

Yesterday was the merriest, maddest dinner we have had yet. Men were more audaciously wise and witty. We had an unspoken foreboding it was to be our last pleasant meeting. Mr. Miles dined with us today. Mrs. Henry King rushed in: "The news, I come for the latest

---

1. **Fort Sumter:** fort in Charleston Harbor, southeastern South Carolina, occupied in early 1861 by Union troops under the command of Major Robert Anderson.
2. **aide-de-camp** [ād′də kamp′]: an officer who serves as an assistant to a superior officer.

news—all of the men of the King family are on the island"—of which fact she seemed proud.

While she was here, our peace negotiator—or envoy—came in. That is, Mr. Chesnut returned—his interview with Colonel Anderson had been deeply interesting—but was not inclined to be communicative, wanted his dinner. Felt for Anderson. Had telegraphed to President Davis[3] for instructions.

What answer to give Anderson, etc., etc. He has gone back to Fort Sumter with additional instructions.

When they were about to leave the wharf, A. H. Boykin sprang into the boat in great excitement; thought himself ill-used. A likelihood of fighting—and he to be left behind!

I do not pretend to go to sleep. How can I? If Anderson does not accept terms—at four—the orders are—he shall be fired upon.

I count four—St. Michael chimes. I begin to hope. At half-past four, the heavy booming of a cannon.

I sprang out of bed. And on my knees—prostrate—I prayed as I never prayed before.

There was a sound of stir all over the house—pattering of feet in the corridor—all seemed hurrying one way. I put on my double gown and a shawl and went too. It was to the housetop.

The shells were bursting. In the dark I heard a man say, "waste of ammunition."

I knew my husband was rowing about in a boat somewhere in that dark bay. And that the shells were roofing it over—bursting toward the fort. If Anderson was obstinate—he was to order the forts on our side to open fire. Certainly fire had begun. The regular roar of the cannon—there it was. And who could tell what each volley accomplished of death and destruction.

The women were wild, there on the housetop. Prayers from the women and imprecations from the men, and then a shell would light up

The Metropolitan Museum of Art

Southern women making uniforms for Confederate soldiers.

the scene. Tonight, they say, the forces are to attempt to land.

The *Harriet Lane* had her wheelhouse[4] smashed and put back to sea.

We watched up there—everybody wondered. Fort Sumter did not fire a shot.

Today Miles and Manning, colonels now—aides to Beauregard—dined with us. The latter hoped I would keep the peace. I give him only good words, for he was to be under fire all day and night, in the bay carrying orders, etc.

Last night—or this morning truly—up on the housetop I was so weak and weary I sat down on something that looked like a black stool. "Get up, you foolish woman—your dress is on fire," cried a man. And he put me out. It was a chimney, and the sparks caught my clothes. Susan Preston and Mr. Venable then

---

3. **President Davis:** Jefferson Davis (1808–1889), president of the Confederacy from 1861 to 1865.

4. **wheelhouse:** enclosed area on the deck of a ship that shelters the steering equipment and the pilot.

Mary Chesnut   **233**

came up. But my fire had been extinguished before it broke out into a regular blaze.

Do you know, after all that noise and our tears and prayers, nobody has been hurt. Sound and fury, signifying nothing.[5] A delusion and a snare. . . .

April 13, 1861

Nobody hurt, after all. How gay we were last night.

Reaction after the dread of all the slaughter we thought those dreadful cannons were making such a noise in doing.

Not even a battery[6] the worse for wear.

Fort Sumter has been on fire. He has not yet silenced any of our guns. So the aides—still with swords and red sashes by way of uniform—tell us.

But the sound of those guns makes regular meals impossible. None of us go to table. But tea trays pervade the corridors, going everywhere.

Some of the anxious hearts lie on their beds and moan in solitary misery. Mrs. Wigfall and I solace ourselves with tea in my room.

These women have all a satisfying faith. . . .

But our men could not tarry with us in these cool shades and comfortable quarters—water unlimited, excellent table, etc., etc. They have gone back to Manassas,[7] and the faithful Brewster with them, to bring us the latest news. They left us in excellent spirits, which we shared until they were out of sight. We went with them to Warrenton and there heard that General Johnston was in full retreat and that a column was advancing upon Beauregard.

So we came back, all forlorn. If our husbands are taken prisoners, what will they do with them? . . .

Lincoln wants four hundred millions of money—and men in proportion.
Can he get them?
He will find us a heavy handful.

July 9, 1861

Our battle summer. May it be our first and our last. So-called.

After all, we have not had any of the horrors of war. Could there have been a gayer or pleasanter life than we led in Charleston? And Montgomery, how exciting it all was there. So many clever men and women congregated from every part of the South.

Flies and mosquitoes and a want of neatness and a want of good things to eat did drive us away.

In Richmond the girls say it is perfectly delightful. We find it so, too, but the bickering and quarreling has begun there.

July 14, 1861

Mr. C remained closeted with them—the president and General Lee[8] etc., etc.—all the afternoon. The news does not seem pleasant. At least, he is not inclined to tell me any of it. Satisfied himself with telling me how sensible and soldierly this handsome General Lee is. General Lee's military sagacity was his theme. Of course, the president dominated the party—as well by his weight of brain as by his position.

I did not care a fig for a description of the war council. I wanted to know what is in the wind now.

July 16, 1861

. . . I did not know there was such a "bitter cry" left in me. But I wept my heart away today when my husband went off. . . .

---

5. **Sound . . . nothing:** from *Macbeth*, Act V, Scene v, lines 26–28; part of Macbeth's description of life's tragedy.
6. **battery:** artillery unit.
7. **Manassas** [mə nas′es]: a town in northeastern Virginia.

8. **General Lee:** Robert Edward Lee (1807–1870), commander in chief of the Confederate Army.

July 22, 1861

Mrs. Davis came in so softly that I did not know she was here until she leaned over me, kissed me, and said:

"A great battle has been fought—Jeff Davis led the center, Joe Johnston the right wing, Beauregard the left wing of the army. Your husband is all right. Wade Hampton is wounded. Colonel Johnson of the Legion killed—so are Colonel Bee and Colonel Bartow. Kirby Smith is wounded or killed."

I had no heart to speak. She went on in that desperate calm way to which people betake themselves when under greatest excitement. "Bartow was rallying his men, leading them into the hottest of the fight—died gallantly, at the head of his regiment.

"The president telegraphs me only that 'it is a great victory.' General Cooper has all the other telegrams." Still I said nothing. I was stunned. Then I was so grateful. Those nearest and dearest to me were safe still.

Then she began in the same concentrated voice to read from a paper she held in her hand.

"Dead and dying cover the field. Sherman's[9] battery taken, Lynchburg regiment cut to pieces. Three hundred of the Legion[10] wounded."

They got me up. Times were too wild with excitement to stay in bed. We went into Mrs. Preston's room.

She made me lie down on her bed. Men, women, and children streamed in. Every living soul had a story to tell. "Complete victory" you heard everywhere.

We had been such anxious wretches! The revulsion of feeling was almost too much to bear.

Scene in a Confederate army hospital.

August 23, 1861

But oh, such a day! since I wrote this morning.

Have been with Mrs. Randolph to all the hospitals.

I can never again shut out of view the sights I saw of human misery. I sit thinking, shut my eyes, and see it all. Thinking—yes, and there is enough to think about now, God knows. Gillands was the worst. Long rows of ill men on cots. Ill of typhoid fever, of every human ailment—dinner tables, eating, drinking, wounds being dressed—all horrors, to be taken in at one glance. . . .

Then we went to the St. Charles. Horrors upon horrors again—want of organization. Long rows of them dead, dying. Awful smells, awful sights.

A boy from home had sent for me. He was lying in a cot, ill of fever. Next him a man died in convulsions while we stood there.

I was making arrangements with a nurse, hiring him to take care of this lad. I do not remember any more, for I fainted. . . .

---

9. **Sherman's:** referring to William Tecumseh Sherman (1820–1891), a colonel during the first battle of Manassas; later, a Union general.
10. **Legion:** Hampton Legion, formed and equipped by the wealthy Wade Hampton of South Carolina.

Mary Chesnut **235**

Women who come before the public are in a bad box now. False hair is taken off and searched for papers. Pistols are sought for [under] "cotillons renversés."[11] Bustles are "suspect." All manner of things, they say, come over the border under the huge hoops now worn. So they are ruthlessly torn off. Not legs but arms are looked for under hoops. And sad to say, found. Then women are used as detectives and searchers to see that no men come over in petticoats.

So the poor creatures coming this way are humiliated to the deepest degree.

February 11, 1862

Confederate affairs in a blue way. Roanoke taken, Fort Henry on the Tennessee River open to them, and we fear the Mississippi River, too. We have evacuated Romney—wherever that is. New armies, new fleets, swarming and threatening everywhere.

We ought to have as good a conceit of ourselves as they have of us—and to be willing to do as much to save ourselves from a nauseous union with them as they are willing to do by way of revengeful coercion in forcing us back.

You'll never win us back, no never—etc., etc.

England's eye is scornful and scoffing as she turns it toward us—and on our miseries. I have nervous chills every day. Bad news is killing me. . . .

March 10, 1862

Congaree House. Second year. Confederate independence. I write daily for my own distractions. These memoirs *pour servir*[12] may some future day afford dates, facts, and prove useful to more important people than I am. I do not wish to do any harm or to hurt any-

one. If any scandalous stories creep in, they are easily burned. It is hard, in such a hurry as things are in, to separate wheat from chaff.

Now I have made my protest and written down my wishes. I can scribble on with a free will and free conscience. . . .

Medea—when asked: "Country, wealth, husband, children—all gone. What remains?" "Medea remains." . . .[13]

"There is a time in most men's lives when they resemble Job, sitting among the ashes[14] and drinking in the full bitterness of complicated misfortune." . . .

May 13, 1862

Read Beverley Tucker's *Partisan*.[15]

Just such a rosewater revolution he imagines as we fancied we were to have—and now the reality is hideous and an agony.

The color of slaves—that is all—the misery of poverty, alike everywhere, only a person can be beaten with many stripes by his own family—his father or mother—or schoolmaster or superior officer by land or sea, or master, if he is an apprentice, *or* her husband, if she is a woman—everybody who chooses, if she be a child.

Wherever there is a cry of pain, I am on the side of the one who cries.

June 11, 1862

General Scott on Southern soldiers. He says we have élan, courage, woodcraft, consummate horsemanship, endurance of pain equal to the Indians, but that we will not submit to discipline. We will not take care of things or husband our resources. Where we are, there is waste and destruction. If it could all be done

---

11. **"cotillons renversés"** [cō tē yon′ rän ver sā′]: petticoats.
12. *pour servir* [pōōr′ ser vēr′]: French for "in order to serve."

13. **"Medea remains"**: from Act 2 of *Medea* by Seneca, a Roman dramatist. Medea was a suffering, tragic figure.
14. **sitting . . . ashes:** the reference is to Job 2 : 8. Job suffered greatly but retained his faith in God.
15. *Partisan: The Partisan Leader: A Tale of the Future,* an 1836 tale about a war to found a southern Confederacy.

by one wild desperate dash, we would do it. But he does not think we can stand the long blank months between the acts—waiting! We can bear pain without a murmur, but we will not submit to be bored. . . .

I know how it feels to die—I have felt it again and again.

For instance. Someone calls out, "Albert Sidney Johnston is killed." My heart stands still. I feel no more. I am for so many seconds, so many minutes—I know not how long—I am utterly without sensation of any kind—dead. And then there is that great throb, that keen agony of physical pain—the works are wound up again, the ticking of the clock begins anew, and I take up the burden of life once more. Someday it will stop too long, or my feeble heart will be too worn out to make that awakening jar, and all will be over. I know not—think when the end comes that there will be any difference except the miracle of the new wind up, throb. And now good news is just as bad—"Hurrah—Stonewall[16] has saved us!" Pleasure that is almost pain—

Soldiers in the streets of Richmond.

June 29, 1862

Victory! Victory heads every telegram now, one reads on the bulletin board.

It is the anniversary of the battle of Fort Moultrie.[17]

They went off so quickly. I wonder if it is not a trap laid for us, to lead us away from Richmond—to some place where they can manage to do us more harm.

And now comes the list of killed and wounded.

Victory does not seem to soothe the sore hearts. Mrs. Haskell has five sons before the enemy's illimitable cannon. Mrs. Preston two.

A call from that dark-eyed one—Mrs. C. She has adopted a languid and helpless man-

ner. She has taken her belle-mère example to heart, but the latter has been found out. She may talk in as silly a manner as she pleases, she will never deceive anybody into thinking her a fool anymore.

This fair one rejoices that her sons were too young to be soldiers. "Of course, one fretted and worried about one's husband—but then, everyone knew husbands had a way of taking care of themselves. But, oh—the heartbreak and misery if one's son was there."

Then she gave us details of the fight. "McClellan is routed. And we have 12,000 prisoners."

"Prisoners! And what are we to do with them? We can't feed our own people."

July 26, 1864

When I remember all the truehearted, the lighthearted, the gay and gallant boys who have come laughing, singing, dancing in my way in the three years past, I have looked into their

---

16. **Stonewall:** Thomas Jonathan (Stonewall) Jackson (1824–1863), Confederate general.
17. **battle . . . Moultrie:** a battle of the Revolutionary War.

brave young eyes and helped them as I could every way and then seen them no more forever. They lie stark and cold, dead upon the battlefield or moldering away in hospitals or prisons—which is worse. I think, if I consider the long array of those bright youths and loyal men who have gone to their deaths almost before my very eyes, my heart might break, too.

Is anything worth it? This fearful sacrifice—this awful penalty we pay for war?

STUDY QUESTIONS

Recalling

1. What historic event occurred on the night of April 12? What is Chesnut's assessment of the event?
2. According to the entry for July 16, what did Mary Chesnut do when her husband went off to the war? How did she react on July 22 when Mrs. Davis told her of the battle?
3. Where did Chesnut go on August 23? What did she see there? What happened to her?
4. On March 10 for what reason does Chesnut say she kept her journal?
5. What does Chesnut say about the reality of war on May 13, 1862?

Interpreting

6. What concerns does Chesnut express about her husband and friends?
7. Briefly describe Chesnut's attitude toward the war and toward the Confederacy. Are her feelings consistent?
8. Identify at least three characteristics of Mary Chesnut's journal that make it different from histories or memoirs by important politicians or generals of the time.

Extending

9. Do you think Chesnut is honest about her feelings? Why or why not?

LITERARY FOCUS

The Journal

A **journal,** like a **diary,** is a day-to-day account that a person writes of his or her life. Millions of people keep diaries; most of them are never seen by anyone other than the writer. Some journals are written self-consciously, with an eye to readers. Some preserve ordinary thoughts in ordinary language and so have little worth to anyone other than the writer. Some preserve extraordinary thoughts in language that is alive and permanent.

The special quality of a journal is that it plunges us into the midst of life. If it sounds too self-conscious, too "literary," it loses the flavor of an immediate, spontaneous response to daily events as they are happening. However, if it merely lists dull details, it will be of little interest to anyone except perhaps a historian.

Mary Chesnut's journal is successful both as a diary and as literature. She is a moving and gifted writer whose experiences we are able to share over a hundred years after they were recorded.

Thinking About the Journal

What do you think are the advantages of writing down ideas and impressions in a journal day by day, as the events take place? What are the limitations of this method?

COMPOSITION

Writing About a Diary

Write a brief essay describing the variations in Chesnut's attitude toward war as her journal progresses. Begin by describing her initial attitude. Then tell how she changes, citing examples and details from the journal. Consider especially the entries for April 12 and 13 and those following July 22, 1861.

Writing a Journal Entry

Imagine that you have witnessed a public event that involved many people. Write a journal entry describing the event. Begin by giving a "bird's-eye view" of the whole event, including some objective facts. Then make the event personal, as Mary Chesnut does, by focusing on your own experience of the event.

Robert E. Lee *1807–1870*

Robert Edward Lee was born at Stratford Hall, Virginia, into one of the oldest and most esteemed families in the nation. Thomas Lee had been a royal governor of Virginia; Richard Henry Lee was the delegate to the Continental Congress who in 1776 proposed that the colonies "are, and of right ought to be" independent. Robert's father, Light-Horse Harry Lee, was a hero of the Revolution and a governor of Virginia.

Following in his father's footsteps, Lee chose a career in the military, graduating with high honors from the United States Military Academy at West Point. During the Mexican-American War he rose to the rank of colonel and was praised as "the greatest military genius in America." In 1852 he became superintendent of West Point.

The War Between the States presented Lee with a heart-breaking dilemma. Although he supported neither slavery nor secession, he knew he could not fight against family and neighbors in his beloved Virginia. Offered the command of the Federal Army, he refused and resigned his commission. He joined the Confederate forces and took command of the Army of Northern Virginia. After brilliant victories at Manassas, Fredericksburg, and Chancellorsville, he was made general-in-chief of the Confederate armies.

On April 9, 1865, with the collapse of Confederate forces, Lee surrendered to Ulysses S. Grant at Appomattox. He told his army: "Men, we have fought through the war together. I have done my best for you; my heart is too full to say more." After the war Lee attempted to repair the damage that had been done and urged fellow Southerners to put their bitterness behind them. Adored by his troops and respected by his enemies, Lee remains a symbol of not only Southern but American dignity.

Lee was an able writer. His letters are of interest for the light they throw on historic events and for the revelations they give us into the mind and heart of a great statesman. In the following letter, written to his sister, Lee explains his reason for resigning from the Federal Army.

Robert E. Lee

Letter to His Sister

To Mrs. Anne Marshall
Baltimore, Maryland

Arlington, Virginia
April 20, 1861

My Dear Sister:

I am grieved at my inability to see you. I have been waiting for a more convenient season, which has brought to many before me deep and lasting regret. Now we are in a state of war which will yield to nothing. The whole South is in a state of revolution, into which Virginia, after a long struggle, has been drawn; and though I recognize no necessity for this state of things, and would have forborne and pleaded to the end for redress of grievances, real or supposed, yet in my own person I had to meet the question whether I should take part against my native State.

With all my devotion to the Union, and the feeling of loyalty and duty of an American citizen, I have not been able to make up my mind to raise my hand against my relatives, my children, my home. I have, therefore, resigned my commission in the Army, and, save in defense of my native State (with the sincere hope that my poor services may never be needed), I hope I may never be called upon to draw my sword.

I know you will blame me, but you must think as kindly as you can, and believe that I have endeavored to do what I thought right. To show you the feeling and struggle it has cost me I send you a copy of my letter of resignation. I have no time for more. May God guard and protect you and yours and shower upon you everlasting blessings, is the prayer of

Your devoted brother,
R. E. Lee

STUDY QUESTIONS

Recalling
1. According to the first paragraph, what question did Lee have to meet?
2. According to the second paragraph, what did Lee feel toward the Union and as an American citizen? What could he nevertheless *not* do? What decision did he therefore make?

3. Why does Lee say he enclosed the copy of his letter of resignation?

Interpreting
4. Briefly describe in your own words Lee's state of mind in making the decision to resign his commission from the Federal Army.
5. What kind of person does this letter reveal Lee to have been?

Abraham Lincoln   *1809–1865*

"We cannot escape history," Abraham Lincoln once said. Lincoln himself was caught in history and proved to be one of history's greatest and most tragic personalities.

Born in a log cabin in Kentucky, Lincoln spent his boyhood in Indiana where he struggled to get an education, taking every opportunity to read the books that were available to him. In 1830 his family, plagued by poverty, moved to Illinois where Lincoln became interested in politics. Two years later he ran for the Illinois state legislature—and lost. He continued to pursue a political career, however, and moved steadily into public view. In 1858 he debated Stephen Douglas, his opponent in the Illinois Senate race, and became nationally known as a brilliant, compelling speaker.

Elected the nation's sixteenth President in 1860, Lincoln saw as his chief duty the preservation of the Union. In speech after speech, he inspired Americans at a time of dark despair. His dream was that the nation be reunited "with malice toward none; and charity for all." But five days after Lee's surrender at Appomattox, Lincoln was shot in a Washington theater, and his plans for a harmonious reunion died with him.

Lincoln's speeches were written to express his convictions and convince others to share them. His language is masterful: plain, powerful, dignified, as in the Gettysburg Address. On November 19, 1863, Lincoln attended the dedication of a national cemetery at Gettysburg, the site of a great but costly Union victory. The main speaker was Edward Everett, one of the most admired orators in the country. Everett gave a lengthy address, and Lincoln's aim was to make a few pertinent remarks following Everett's performance. Afterward, however, Everett wrote to Lincoln: "I should be glad if I could flatter myself that I came as near to the central idea of the occasion in two hours, as you did in two minutes." In the ten sentences that appear on the following page, Lincoln gave the world a masterpiece of oratory and one of the greatest speeches ever written by an American.

Abraham Lincoln

The Gettysburg Address

Four score and seven years ago our fathers brought forth on this continent, a new nation, conceived in Liberty, and dedicated to the proposition that all men are created equal.

Now we are engaged in a great civil war, testing whether that nation, or any nation so conceived and so dedicated, can long endure. We are met on a great battlefield of that war. We have come to dedicate a portion of that field, as a final resting place for those who here gave their lives that that nation might live. It is altogether fitting and proper that we should do this.

But, in a larger sense, we can not dedicate—we can not consecrate—we can not hallow—this ground. The brave men, living and dead, who struggled here, have consecrated it, far above our poor power to add or detract. The world will little note, nor long remember what we say here, but it can never forget what they did here. It is for us the living, rather, to be dedicated here to the unfinished work which they who fought here have thus far so nobly advanced. It is rather for us to be here dedicated to the great task remaining before us—that from these honored dead we take increased devotion to that cause for which they gave the last full measure of devotion—that we here highly resolve that these dead shall not have died in vain—that this nation, under God, shall have a new birth of freedom—and that government of the people, by the people, for the people, shall not perish from the earth.

STUDY QUESTIONS

Recalling

1. What happened "four score and seven years ago"?
2. What is happening "now," according to paragraph 2?
3. According to paragraph 3, what is the "great task remaining before us"?

Interpreting

4. State in your own words the kind of nation that Lincoln says is having its endurance tested by the Civil War.
5. In your own words, state the main point of Lincoln's speech. For what does he argue?
6. To what chief emotion or feeling does Lincoln's speech appeal?

Extending

7. Do you think the Gettysburg Address is more powerful as a written document or an oral presentation? Explain your answer.

VOCABULARY

Diction and Style

Diction, or word choice, has a significant effect on a writer's style. The words a writer chooses to use must be appropriate to the audience, the occasion, the subject, the speaker, and the tone. How different, how unmemorable, would have been Lincoln's address if he had chosen words appropriate to a casual style: "Eighty-seven years ago some folks set up a government so that everybody could be free and equal." Instead he used a formal vocabulary, noble, dignified, worthy of its subject.

Choose five words from the Gettysburg Address, and tell why Lincoln's use of each is appropriate. Define each word precisely, and give at least one synonym that would not be as fitting as the word Lincoln chose to use.

COMPOSITION

Analyzing Coherence

In a brief essay analyze Lincoln's methods for creating coherence in the Gettysburg Address. Begin by describing how Lincoln uses transition words such as *but* and *rather*. Then tell how he uses pronouns that refer to things said earlier, words that indicate a sequence in time, and repetitions of words. Show how these devices tie the sentences together and help structure the address.

Writing an Oral Tribute

Choose one of the people you have encountered thus far in this unit, and write a speech in which you pay tribute to him or her. The speech may be a funeral oration or a tribute to be made at a present-day ceremony. Like Lincoln, keep your speech to ten sentences. Remember that it is a *speech,* to be read aloud.

Chief Joseph   *c. 1840–1904*

Chief Joseph succeeded his father as leader of the Nez Perce tribe in 1873. At that time, under a treaty of 1863, the tribal lands in the Wallowa Valley of Oregon had been ceded to the United States Government. Chief Joseph considered the treaty illegal and refused to recognize it. When the government attempted to remove the Nez Perce by force, Chief Joseph decided to fight.

Though his warriors won several battles, they were heavily outnumbered by the U.S. Army. Chief Joseph's strategy was to attempt to march across the Canadian border to join forces with the Sioux. The march was a brilliantly conducted retreat across Idaho and Montana, punctuated by battles between the Indians and federal troops. However, after traveling over a thousand miles, the band of men, women, and children were on the brink of collapse. Forty miles from the Canadian border, Chief Joseph was forced to surrender. He was taken to Leavenworth prison and, after his release, to the Indian Territory in what is now Oklahoma. He spent the last years of his life on the Colville Indian Reservation in the state of Washington.

Chief Joseph never ceased to strive for the betterment of conditions for Native Americans. In 1879 he wrote "An Indian's View of Indian Affairs" for the *North American Review;* in 1903 he made an impressive visit to Washington, D.C., on behalf of his people.

The following extract is from Chief Joseph's speech of surrender, made in October of 1877. Its natural nobility of spirit and simple language make a powerful statement about the horrors of warfare.

Chief Joseph

I Will Fight No More Forever

Tell General Howard I know his heart. What he told me before, I have in my heart. I am tired of fighting. Our chiefs are killed. Looking Glass is dead. Toohoolhoolzote is dead. The old men are all dead. It is the young men who say yes and no. He who led on the young men is dead. It is cold and we have no blankets. The little children are freezing to death. My people, some of them, have run away to the hills and have no blankets, no food; no one knows where they are—perhaps freezing to death. I want to have time to look for my children and see how many I can find. Maybe I shall find them among the dead. Hear me, my chiefs. I am tired; my heart is sick and sad. From where the sun now stands I will fight no more forever.

Detail from *Chief Joseph's Surrender,* Olaf C. Seltzer.

Thomas Gilcrease Institute

STUDY QUESTIONS

Recalling

1. Name five of the conditions that cause Chief Joseph to surrender.
2. What promise does Chief Joseph make in the last sentence?

Interpreting

3. Near the end of the speech, to whom does Chief Joseph refer when he says "my children"? What does this reference suggest about Chief Joseph's role?
4. What purpose other than surrender do you think is served by Chief Joseph's speech? How would you characterize the tone of the speech?

Extending

5. Because war is one of the most terrible of human experiences, it is one of the most difficult to write about. What qualities do you think a writer should possess to be able to communicate to readers the reality of war?

COMPARING WRITERS

■ All the people whose works appear in this section were caught in the web of history. How, in his or her own way, did each person rise above the suffering? What evidence in the writings of Douglass, Lee, Lincoln, and Chief Joseph explains why they have come to be regarded as symbols of noble ideals?

THREE MAJOR WRITERS

Walt Whitman   *1819–1892*

In 1855 Ralph Waldo Emerson, the most famous literary figure of his day, received a book from an unknown poet. The book was called *Leaves of Grass,* and the poet's name was Walt Whitman. A picture of the author appeared on the title page: bearded, in work pants, shirt open, wide-brimmed hat cocked at a jaunty angle. He seemed at once inviting and distanced, friendly and yet somehow alone. He seemed, indeed, as he described himself, "one of the roughs." Emerson thought the book was "the most extraordinary piece of wit and wisdom that America has yet contributed." Here was the new American voice he had been calling for. However, when he wrote to Whitman in a private letter, "I greet you at the beginning of a great career," he was startled by the young man's response. Whitman, without Emerson's permission, quoted Emerson's praise-filled remark on the cover of the next edition of *Leaves of Grass.*

Such audacity was a mark of the spirit of the man whom many now consider America's greatest poet. A great reader, he was nurtured by the Transcendentalists, yet he was no country-dwelling New Englander contemplating the quiet joys of nature. He had spent his early manhood in New York City, soaking up its sights and sounds. Later he traveled down the Mississippi, absorbing the variety of America. He listened to the talk of street gangs and working people, of farmers and soldiers, and saw in them the essence of America. He loved his country and its democracy, which allowed all forms of human spirit to flourish. His poetry extends the Transcendentalists' joy in nature to a love for humanity in all its manifestations. Whitman's verse became a sweeping catalogue of America, pouring forth like the operatic arias of which he was so fond.

Whitman was born on Long Island, New York, into a devout Quaker family. He grew up in Brooklyn, where he left school at eleven to become, in turn, an office boy, a doctor's helper, a printer's assistant, a journalist, a typesetter, and a printer. At twenty-seven he became editor of the *Brooklyn Eagle,* but he left the job when the paper took a proslavery stand. Later he taught in country schools. When in 1855 he came out with the first edition of *Leaves of Grass* (containing twelve poems), he had to set the type himself and pay for the book's publication.

Acceptance by the American public came slowly. Most readers—and there were few enough of them—were shocked by the unconventional subject matter, the unusual forms, and the break with standard rhyme and meter that Whitman's "free verse"

17

These are really the thoughts of all men in all ages and lands, they
    are not original with me,
If they are not yours as much as mine they are nothing, or next to
    nothing,
If they are not the riddle and the untying of the riddle they are nothing,
If they are not just as close as they are distant they are nothing.

5 This is the grass that grows wherever the land is and the water is,
This the common air that bathes the globe.

42

. . .

This is the city and I am one of the citizens,
Whatever interests the rest interests me, politics, wars, markets,
    newspapers, schools,
The mayor and councils, banks, tariffs, steamships, factories, stocks,
    stores, real estate and personal estate.

The little plentiful manikins[2] skipping around in collars and tailed coats,
5 I am aware who they are, (they are positively not worms or fleas,)
I acknowledge the duplicates of myself, the weakest and shallowest is
    deathless with me,
What I do and say the same waits for them,
Every thought that flounders in me the same flounders in them.

I know perfectly well my own egotism,
10 Know my omnivorous[3] lines and must not write any less,
And would fetch you whoever you are flush with myself.

Not words of routine this song of mine,
But abruptly to question, to leap beyond yet nearer bring; . . .

51

The past and present wilt—I have filled them, emptied them,
And proceed to fill my next fold of the future.

Listener up there! what have you to confide to me?
Look in my face while I snuff the sidle of evening,[4]
5 (Talk honestly, no one else hears you, and I stay only a minute longer.)

---

2. **manikins:** little men.
3. **omnivorous** [om niv′ər əs]: taking in everything; here, covering all subjects.
4. **snuff . . . evening:** put out the light of day, which is moving sideways across
the sky.

Do I contradict myself?
Very well then I contradict myself,
(I am large, I contain multitudes.)

I concentrate toward them that are nigh,[5] I wait on the door-slab.
10 Who has done his day's work? who will soonest be through with his
supper?
Who wishes to walk with me?

Will you speak before I am gone? will you prove already too late?

52

The spotted hawk swoops by and accuses me, he complains of my
gab and my loitering.

I too am not a bit tamed, I too am untranslatable,
I sound my barbaric yawp over the roofs of the world.

The last scud[6] of day holds back for me,
5 It flings my likeness after the rest and true as any on the shadow'd
wilds,
It coaxes me to the vapor and the dusk.

I depart as air, I shake my white locks at the runaway sun,
I effuse[7] my flesh in eddies, and drift it in lacy jags.

I bequeath myself to the dirt to grow from the grass I love,
10 If you want me again look for me under your boot soles.

You will hardly know who I am or what I mean,
But I shall be good health to you nevertheless,
And filter and fiber your blood.

Failing to fetch me at first keep encouraged,
15 Missing me one place search another,
I stop somewhere waiting for you.

---

5. **nigh:** near.
6. **scud:** low, dark, wind-driven clouds.
7. **effuse:** pour forth.

STUDY QUESTIONS

Recalling

1. According to line 1 of section 1, who is the poet celebrating? Whom do lines 2–3 also include in the celebration?
2. What facts about himself does Whitman reveal in lines 6–9 of section 1? With what adjectives does Whitman describe himself in section 4?
3. Who fetches the grass in section 6? What does Whitman guess the grass might be? What does the "smallest sprout" show?
4. According to section 17, are Whitman's thoughts original? Whose thoughts are they?
5. What does Whitman say he knows "perfectly well" in section 42? What does he say his song is *not*? According to this section, what *is* the purpose of his song?
6. In section 51 what explanation does the poet give for contradicting himself?
7. To what animal does Whitman compare himself in section 52? What does he sound "over the roofs of the world"? Where does he tell us to look for him if we want him again?

Interpreting

8. Describe the relationship Whitman sets up with the reader in the first section.
9. Name as many characteristics of Whitman's "self" as you can. Which characteristics seem the most prominent?
10. Consider the image of the grass in sections 6 and 52. What does the grass have to do with life and death?
11. By associating himself with the grass, what does the poet suggest about himself? Summarize Whitman's attitude toward nature.

Extending

12. Why might Whitman have called his volume of poetry *Leaves of Grass?*

LITERARY FOCUS

Free Verse

Free verse is poetry that has an irregular rhythm and line length and that attempts to avoid any predetermined verse structure; instead, it uses the cadences of natural speech. While it alternates stressed and unstressed syllables as stricter verse forms do, free verse does so in a looser way.

Whitman's poetry is an example of free verse at its most impressive. Listen, for instance, to a line from "Song of Myself":

> A child said *What is the grass?* fetching it to me with full hands;

Here, question and answer create a rising and falling effect, ending in a stop.

Whitman continues:

> How could I answer the child? I do not know what it is any more than he.

The same question-and-answer pattern is repeated, the same rising and falling effect. This is not prose but poetry. It is arranged rhythmically, tightened and loosened by the poet. It has a plan, although the plan seems to "grow" organically— like its subjects, nature and human beings.

Although free verse had been used before Whitman—notably in Italian opera and in the King James translation of the Bible—it was Whitman who pioneered the form and made it acceptable in American poetry. It has since been used by Ezra Pound, T. S. Eliot, William Carlos Williams, Wallace Stevens, and other major American poets of the twentieth century.

Thinking About Free Verse

■ Why is free verse particularly suited to Whitman's ideas? How do you think it relates to Whitman's democratic principles?

Walt Whitman

I Hear America Singing

I hear America singing, the varied carols I hear,
Those of mechanics, each one singing his as it should be blithe and
    strong,
The carpenter singing his as he measures his plank or beam,
The mason singing his as he makes ready for work, or leaves off
    work,
5 The boatman singing what belongs to him in his boat, the deckhand
    singing on the steamboat deck,
The shoemaker singing as he sits on his bench, the hatter singing as
    he stands,
The woodcutter's song, the plowboy's on his way in the morning, or
    at noon intermission or at sundown,
The delicious singing of the mother, or of the young wife at work, or
    of the girl sewing or washing,
Each singing what belongs to him or her and to none else,
10 The day what belongs to the day—at night the party of young
    fellows, robust, friendly,
Singing with open mouths their strong melodious songs.

Cradling Wheat,
Thomas Hart Benton, 1939.

When the Union army was defeated at the first battle of Bull Run in 1861, many Americans suddenly realized that the war was going to be longer and more terrible than they had thought. Whitman responded with this poem.

Beat! Beat! Drums!

Beat! beat! drums!—blow! bugles! blow!
Through the windows—through doors—burst like a ruthless force,
Into the solemn church, and scatter the congregation,
Into the school where the scholar is studying;
5 Leave not the bridegroom quiet—no happiness must he have now
    with his bride,
Nor the peaceful farmer any peace, plowing his field or gathering his
    grain,
So fierce you whirr and pound you drums—so shrill you bugles
    blow.

Beat! beat! drums!—blow! bugles! blow!
Over the traffic of cities—over the rumble of wheels in the streets;
10 Are beds prepared for sleepers at night in the houses? no sleepers
    must sleep in those beds,
No bargainers' bargains by day—no brokers or speculators[1]—would
    they continue?
Would the talkers be talking? would the singer attempt to sing?
Would the lawyer rise in the court to state his case before the judge?
Then rattle quicker, heavier drums—you bugles wilder blow.

15 Beat! beat! drums!—blow! bugles! blow!
Make no parley—stop for no expostulation,
Mind not the timid—mind not the weeper or prayer,
Mind not the old man beseeching the young man,
Let not the child's voice be heard, nor the mother's entreaties,
20 Make even the trestles to shake the dead where they lie awaiting the
    hearses,
So strong you thump O terrible drums—so loud you bugles blow.

---

1. **speculators:** people who take large risks in business transactions hoping to make large, quick profits.

Walt Whitman

When I Heard the Learn'd Astronomer

When I heard the learn'd astronomer,
When the proofs, the figures, were ranged in columns before me,
When I was shown the charts and diagrams, to add, divide, and
    measure them,
When I sitting heard the astronomer where he lectured with much
    applause in the lecture room,
5 How soon unaccountable I became tired and sick,
Till rising and gliding out I wandered off by myself,
In the mystical moist night air, and from time to time,
Looked up in perfect silence at the stars.

This Dust Was Once the Man

This dust was once the man,
Gentle, plain, just and resolute, under whose cautious hand,
Against the foulest crime in history known in any land or age,
Was saved the Union of these States.

A Noiseless Patient Spider

A noiseless patient spider,
I marked where on a little promontory[1] it stood isolated,
Marked how to explore the vacant vast surrounding,
It launched forth filament,[2] filament, filament, out of itself,
5 Ever unreeling them, ever tirelessly speeding them.

And you O my soul where you stand,
Surrounded, detached, in measureless oceans of space,
Ceaselessly musing, venturing, throwing, seeking the spheres to
    connect them,
Till the bridge you will need be formed, till the ductile[3] anchor hold,
10 Till the gossamer thread you fling catch somewhere, O my soul.

---

1. **promontory:** high portion of land extending out into a body of water.
2. **filament:** slender fiber or thread.
3. **ductile** [dukt'əl]: pliant; easily bent.

STUDY QUESTIONS

I Hear America Singing

Recalling

1. According to line 1, what does Whitman hear?
2. Name eight of the people that Whitman hears, according to lines 2–8.
3. According to line 9, what does each person sing?

Interpreting

4. What one word could describe in general what each person sings about?
5. What aspects of American life are being celebrated in this poem? Is the description of America "singing" literal, figurative, or both? Explain.

Beat! Beat! Drums!

Recalling

1. What people do the drums and bugles disturb in each of stanzas 1, 2, and 3?
2. What verbs and adjectives are used to describe the sounds of the drums and bugles?

Interpreting

3. Based on the description of the drums and bugles and the effect they have, what do they seem to represent? What does the simile in line 2 imply?
4. Are the people in stanzas 1 and 2 doing anything out of the ordinary? Why is this significant?
5. Why might the people in stanza 3 be praying, beseeching, and so on? What do the drums and bugles do to their prayers and pleas?
6. Explain how rhythm and repetition reinforce the meaning of the poem. In particular, consider the effect of lines 1, 8, and 15.

Extending

7. What images other than drums and bugles might Whitman have used to make his point?

When I Heard the Learn'd Astronomer

Recalling

1. What aids does the astronomer use to supplement his lecture?
2. What does the poet become as he listens?
3. Where does the poet go when he wanders off? What does he do?

Interpreting

4. What is the effect of the parallel structure and repetition in lines 1–4?
5. How does the poet contrast himself with the astronomer? What wisdom does he find that the astronomer and his audience do not have?

Extending

6. What does this poem have in common with Romantic or Transcendentalist poetry that you have read? In what ways is it different?

This Dust Was Once the Man

Recalling

1. What four adjectives describe the man?
2. What did the man save?

Interpreting

3. To what major event does "the foulest crime in history" refer?
4. Who is the man referred to in the poem?

A Noiseless Patient Spider

Recalling

1. According to stanza 1, where and how is the spider standing? What is it doing?
2. According to stanza 2, where and how is the poet's "soul" standing? What is it doing? What three things is it waiting for?

Interpreting

3. What two things are being compared in this poem? What specific similarities between the two does the poet draw?
4. Why does the soul need to form a "bridge"? To what will the bridge connect it?

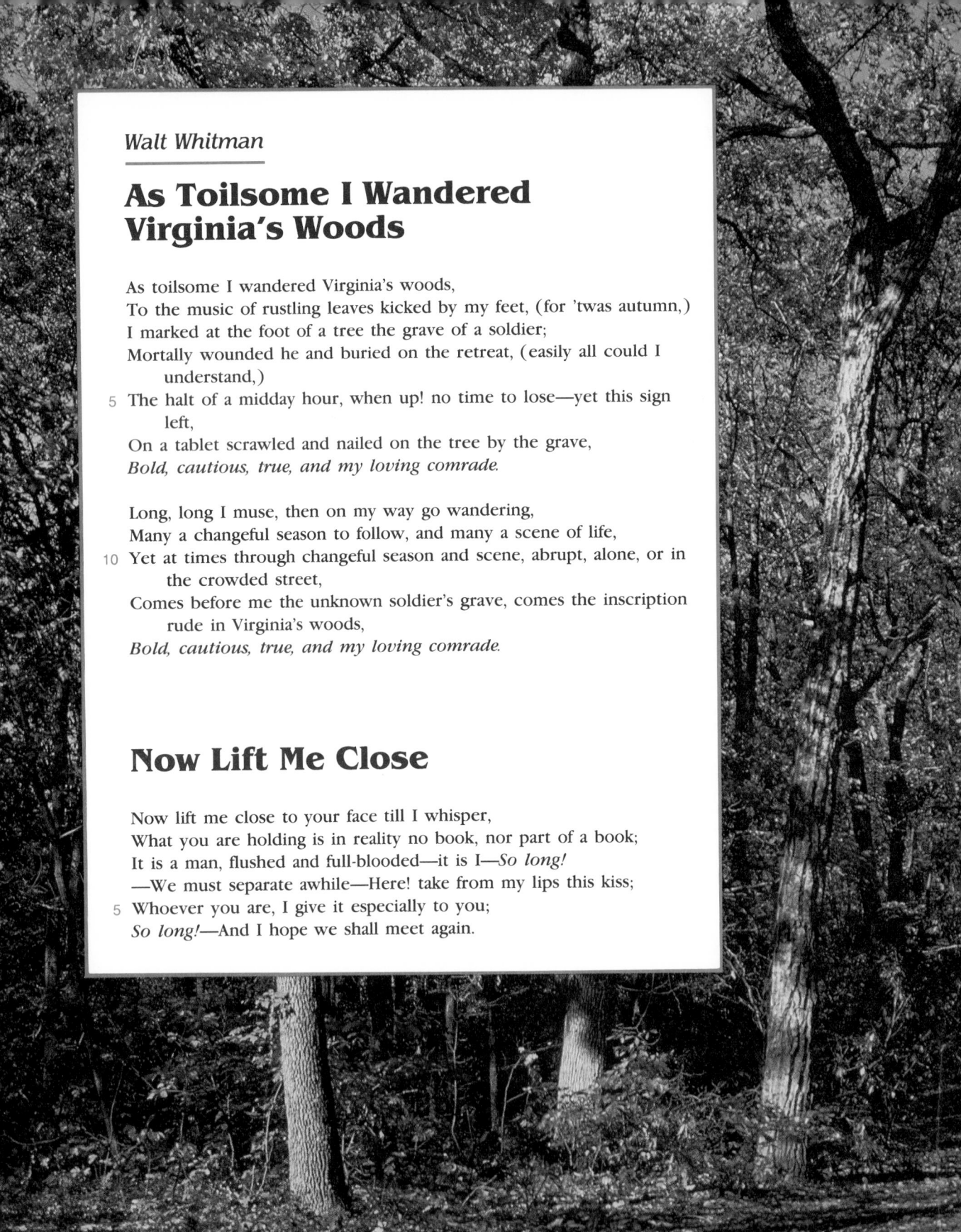

Walt Whitman

As Toilsome I Wandered Virginia's Woods

As toilsome I wandered Virginia's woods,
To the music of rustling leaves kicked by my feet, (for 'twas autumn,)
I marked at the foot of a tree the grave of a soldier;
Mortally wounded he and buried on the retreat, (easily all could I
    understand,)
5 The halt of a midday hour, when up! no time to lose—yet this sign
    left,
On a tablet scrawled and nailed on the tree by the grave,
Bold, cautious, true, and my loving comrade.

Long, long I muse, then on my way go wandering,
Many a changeful season to follow, and many a scene of life,
10 Yet at times through changeful season and scene, abrupt, alone, or in
    the crowded street,
Comes before me the unknown soldier's grave, comes the inscription
    rude in Virginia's woods,
Bold, cautious, true, and my loving comrade.

Now Lift Me Close

Now lift me close to your face till I whisper,
What you are holding is in reality no book, nor part of a book;
It is a man, flushed and full-blooded—it is I—*So long!*
—We must separate awhile—Here! take from my lips this kiss;
5 Whoever you are, I give it especially to you;
So long!—And I hope we shall meet again.

STUDY QUESTIONS

As Toilsome I Wander'd Virginia's Woods

Recalling

1. In stanza 1 what does the poet encounter as he wanders through Virginia's woods?
2. What is written on the tablet?
3. According to stanza 2, what does the poet do before he wanders away? When does he think of the inscription again?

Interpreting

4. Why is it significant that the encounter takes place in autumn?
5. What is ironic about the word *cautious* on the tablet? With what word does *cautious* contrast? Does this paradox make sense? Explain your answer.
6. Whose "comrade" was the dead man originally? Whose comrade does the dead man become? Why?

Extending

7. Have you ever had a similar experience of years later remembering an event "abrupt, alone, or in the crowded street"?

Now Lift Me Close

Recalling

1. According to lines 2–3, what "in reality" is the "book" the poet says "you" are holding?
2. With what words does Whitman say good-by? What does he hope?

Interpreting

3. Who is the "you" addressed in the poem? What kind of relationship does the poet establish with "you"?
4. What is the poet's attitude toward "you"?

Extending

5. This poem looks toward Whitman's old age, when he would face death. Does knowing this deepen or change your reaction to the poem?

Model for Active Reading

In this selection, and in one selection in each unit, you will find notes in the right-hand margin that highlight parts of the selection. These notes point out important ideas of the period—in this case, the democratic idea—and draw your attention to literary elements and techniques covered in the Literary Focuses. Page numbers in the notes will refer you to more extensive discussions of these important ideas and elements.

Walt Whitman

Souvenirs of Democracy

The business man, the acquirer vast,
After assiduous years, surveying results, preparing for departure,
Devises houses and lands to his children—bequeaths stocks,
    goods—funds for a school or hospital,
Leaves money to certain companions to buy tokens, souvenirs
    of gems and gold;
5 Parceling out with care—And then, to prevent all cavil,[1]
His name to his testament[2] formally signs.

> **Democratic idea:** Whitman suggests the widespread prosperity and material success of the Gilded Age (page 218).

But I, my life surveying,
With nothing to show, to devise, from its idle years,
Nor houses, nor lands—nor tokens of gems or gold for my
    friends,
10 Only these Souvenirs of Democracy—In them—in all my
    songs—behind me leaving,
To You, whoever you are, (bathing, leavening[3] this leaf
    especially with my breath—pressing on it a moment with
    my own hands;
—Here! feel how the pulse beats in my wrists!—how my heart's
    blood is swelling, contracting!)
I will You, in all, Myself, with promise to never desert you,
To which I sign my name,

> **Autobiography** (p. 230): Whitman offers his poems as a verse autobiography, the story of his life.

> **Apostrophe** (p. 206): Whitman addresses the reader directly.

> **Free verse** (p. 251): Whitman approximates natural speech while maintaining poetic rhythms.

> **Democratic idea:** Whitman asserts his selfhood and independence even while he remains a part of a great nation (page 219).

Walt Whitman

---

1. **cavil:** trivial objections.
2. **testament:** last will and testament.
3. **leavening** [lev′ə ning]: raising.

STUDY QUESTIONS

Recalling

1. According to the first stanza, what does the "business man" leave? To whom does he leave it?
2. According to lines 10–13, what does Whitman bequeath? To whom does he bequeath it?
3. What is the poet's final promise?

Interpreting

4. What does stanza 2 suggest about the businessman of stanza 1?
5. What are the "Souvenirs of Democracy" to which Whitman refers? Why is that term appropriate?
6. Based on the evidence in stanza 2, does Whitman really believe that he has "nothing to show" for his life? Explain how he actually seems to feel about his life and work.
7. What is the effect of Whitman's unusual gesture of actually signing the poem?

Extending

8. What would you say is Whitman's greatest legacy? Which of his ideas is most appealing to you, and why?

VIEWPOINT

In the Preface to the first edition of his poems, Walt Whitman boldly says:

The Americans of all nations at any time upon the earth have probably the fullest poetical nature. The United States themselves are essentially the greatest poem.

—*Leaves of Grass*

■ What quality of American culture is Whitman trying to describe? In what sense is his statement true? In what sense can a nation be a "poem"?

VOCABULARY

Americanisms

An **Americanism** is a word or phrase that has originated in America. Americans have always been practical about language, and when a word has been needed to name a new experience or object or idea, we have invented it. Indian names, new scientific terms, brand names, slang, modified words from other languages, and colloquialisms are common sources of Americanisms.

Many dictionaries recognize this vital element of our speech and point out Americanisms: For example, *woodchuck, trick or treat, Sun Belt, clobber, megaphone, powderkeg, radar,* and *overcoat* are all Americanisms. Whitman uses the Americanism *loaf* in "Song of Myself."

■ Use your dictionary to find at least five Americanisms. Tell what each means, and identify its origin.

COMPOSITION

Writing About Poetry

■ In a brief essay examine Whitman's use of free verse, rhythm, repetition, and punctuation in one of the poems you have read. Begin by showing the ways in which certain lines capture the quality of everyday speech. Then explain how Whitman's style relates to the meaning of the poem. *For help with this assignment, refer to Lesson 7 in the Writing About Literature Handbook at the back of this book.*

Using Free Verse

■ Try writing a short poem in free verse. Remember that although rhythm and line length will be irregular, you should not lose sight of rhythm altogether. If you have difficulty in deciding on a topic for your poem, you might write an updated version of "I Hear America Singing."

Emily Dickinson   *1830–1886*

Only seven of Emily Dickinson's poems were published during her lifetime, and even those were published anonymously. Yet after her death people found in her home many small packages of her poems. Some of the poems had been carefully revised and neatly tied with ribbons; others had been scrawled on scraps of paper. In all, 1,775 poems were preserved. One of the great poets of the English language had lived and died unknown to the public.

Dickinson was born in her father's house in Amherst, Massachusetts. She attended the Mount Holyoke Female Seminary in nearby South Hadley and visited Boston, Washington, and Philadelphia when she was young. The last time she left home was in 1864, to travel to Boston for an eye examination. As she grew older, she communicated with fewer and fewer people. She dressed all in white, and her neighbors knew there was something extraordinary about this radiant yet isolated woman. At the age of fifty-six Dickinson died in the house in which she had been born.

Dickinson's poems, however, survived her. On April 15, 1862, Thomas Wentworth Higginson, a kindly but undistinguished literary critic, had received a letter from Dickinson. Higginson did not know her. Dickinson enclosed four of her poems, wondering whether they were good poems, whether they "breathed." Higginson saw that the poems had quality, but he thought they were "not for publication." They were too informal, too abrupt; even their punctuation was peculiar. Later editors of Dickinson's work were equally unperceptive. Deeming her style "not correct," they rewrote what Dickinson had written in order to make it "proper." It was not until 1955 that *The Complete Poems* were printed exactly as Dickinson had written them so that readers could discover the measure of her achievement.

Like Whitman's, Dickinson's was a totally dedicated art, though a private one. Through her poetry she wrote what she called her "letter to the World," even though she chose to live most of her life isolated from the world. Her personality, her self—the Soul she so often writes about—was so strong and independent that she was able to write poems of genuine originality. She was influenced by the Bible, classical myths, Shakespeare, the English Romantic poet John Keats, and Ralph Waldo Emerson, but no influence over-shadowed her own spirit.

Dickinson presents her poems in a wry voice, with sharp, unusual images, and a highly expressive method of punctuation. Her subjects are the great subjects—life, death, nature, God—and her special talent is to express her lofty thoughts using concrete images from everyday experience. Her simplicity is deceptive: This is a poet who shows us that life is simultaneously joyful and tragic, mysterious and crystal clear.

Emily Dickinson

This is my letter to the World

This is my letter to the World
That never wrote to Me—
The simple News that Nature told—
With tender Majesty

5 Her Message is committed
To Hands I cannot see—
For love of Her—Sweet—countrymen—
Judge tenderly—of Me

STUDY QUESTIONS

Recalling
1. According to stanza 1, to whom is the poet's letter addressed? What "News" does it contain?
2. In stanza 2, what does the poet ask her "countrymen" to do?

Interpreting
3. To what is Dickinson referring when she uses the phrase "my letter to the World"?
4. How is nature related to the poet's "letter"?
5. What does the fact that the world never wrote back suggest about Dickinson's life?
6. To what does "Her" refer in lines 5 and 7?
7. What attitude about herself and her poetry does Dickinson reveal in stanza 2? Explain your answer.

Emily Dickinson's home, Amherst, Massachusetts.

Emily Dickinson

I dwell in Possibility—

I dwell in Possibility—
A fairer House than Prose—
More numerous of Windows—
Superior—for Doors—

5 Of Chambers as the Cedars—
Impregnable of Eye—
And for an Everlasting Roof
The Gambrels[1] of the Sky—

Of Visitors—the fairest—
10 For Occupation—This—
The spreading wide my narrow Hands
To gather Paradise—

---

1. **Gambrels:** angled roofs.

STUDY QUESTIONS

Recalling
1. What "House" is "Possibility" fairer than?
2. Name the four parts of the "Houses" the poet compares.
3. What is the poet's "Occupation" in the "House" of "Possibility"?

Interpreting
4. Considering the contrast in line 2, identify the thing that Dickinson is equating with "Possibility." What does line 1 therefore mean? What does the use of the word *possibility* imply?
5. What is implied by the more numerous windows? By the superior number of doors? Does this seem to be a contradiction? Explain.
6. What is the "Occupation" in the last stanza? What do lines 11–12 imply about this occupation?

Extending
7. Why do you think people write poetry?

Emily Dickinson

"Nature" is what we see—

"Nature" is what we see—
The Hill—the Afternoon—
Squirrel—Eclipse—the Bumble bee—
Nay—Nature is Heaven—
5 Nature is what we hear—
The Bobolink[1]—the Sea—
Thunder—the Cricket—
Nay—Nature is Harmony—
Nature is what we know—
10 Yet have no art to say—
So impotent Our Wisdom is
To her Simplicity.

---

1. **Bobolink:** variety of songbird.

I never saw a Moor—

I never saw a Moor[1]—
I never saw the Sea—
Yet know I how the Heather looks
And what a Billow[2] be.

5 I never spoke with God
Nor visited in Heaven—
Yet certain am I of the spot
As if the Checks[3] were given—

---

1. **Moor:** open, rolling land often swampy and covered with heather.
2. **Billow:** a large wave.
3. **Checks:** probably the seat checks, indicating destination, that are issued to train passengers when their tickets are collected.

STUDY QUESTIONS

"Nature" is what we see—

Recalling
1. What does the poet say nature is in line 1? In line 4?
2. What does the poet say nature is in line 5? In line 8?
3. What do lines 9–10 say nature is?
4. Compared with what is our wisdom impotent, according to lines 11–12?

Interpreting
5. Explain the relationship between the definitions of nature in lines 1 and 4 and between the definitions in lines 5 and 8. What word in line 4 and 8 makes the relationship clear?
6. In your own words explain what the last four lines suggest about nature.

I never saw a Moor—

Recalling
1. According to stanza 1, what two things has the poet never seen? What does she nevertheless know about them?
2. According to stanza 2, where has the poet never visited? Of what is she nevertheless certain?

Interpreting
3. What specific type of belief is suggested by the poet in stanza 2?
4. In what way does the poet's argument in stanza 1 affect her argument in stanza 2? Explain.
5. Where does parallel structure occur within the poem? How does this organized structure affect the poet's argument?

Extending
6. Dickinson's early editors rewrote line 4 as "And what a wave must be" and line 8 as "As if the chart were given." Do you think these changes improved the poem? Do you think editors should rewrite a poet's original compositions? Explain your answers.

Emily Dickinson

Apparently with no surprise

Apparently with no surprise
To any happy Flower
The Frost beheads it at its play—
In accidental power—
5 The blonde Assassin passes on—
The Sun proceeds unmoved
To measure off another Day
For an Approving God.

My life closed twice before its close—

My life closed twice before its close—
It yet remains to see
If Immortality unveil
A third event to me

5 So huge, so hopeless to conceive
As these that twice befell.
Parting is all we know of heaven,
And all we need of hell.

STUDY QUESTIONS

Apparently with no surprise

Recalling

1. According to lines 3−4, what happens to the flower?
2. According to lines 6−8, how does the sun react, and how does God feel about the incident?

Interpreting

3. What might the "accidental" aspect of the frost's power suggest about nature? What might the flower's apparent lack of surprise suggest about nature?
4. Beyond the death of one flower, what is this poem about? Explain the significance of God's reaction to these events.
5. According to what the poem implies, who *is* surprised by the flower's death? Why?

Extending

6. One of Dickinson's greatest talents was her ability to find universal meanings in everyday events. Why do you think all great literature must be able to do this?

My life closed twice before its close—

Recalling

1. According to stanza 1, what has happened twice to the poet? What does she say remains to be seen?
2. How does the poet define parting in stanza 2?

Interpreting

3. What happened to cause the poet's life to "close twice before its close"? In what line is this made clear?
4. What is the "third event"? In comparing it to the first two events, what does the poet reveal about her feelings regarding the first two?
5. In what sense might parting be "all we know of heaven"? How might it be "all we need of hell"?

Extending

6. Many biographers of Dickinson have suggested that this poem was prompted by the departures of two men in whom the poet had a romantic interest. Does knowing this add to your appreciation of the poem? Do you think Dickinson might be referring to another kind of departure? Explain your answers.

Emily Dickinson

There's a certain Slant of light

There's a certain Slant of light,
Winter Afternoons—
That oppresses, like the Heft
Of Cathedral Tunes—

5 Heavenly Hurt, it gives us—
We can find no scar,
But internal difference,
Where the Meanings, are—

None may teach it—Any—
10 'Tis the Seal Despair—
An imperial affliction
Sent us of the Air—

When it comes, the Landscape listens—
Shadows—hold their breath—
15 When it goes, 'tis like the Distance
On the look of Death—

STUDY QUESTIONS

Recalling
1. According to stanza 1, what does the certain slant of light do? When does it come?
2. What does the slant of light give us, according to stanza 2?
3. What two things is the slant of light called in stanza 3?
4. According to stanza 4, what happens when the slant of light comes? What is it like when it goes?

Interpreting
5. Why is it significant that the light occurs on *winter* afternoons? What might winter suggest?
6. Describe the mood or feeling that the slant of light brings.
7. What does the light seem to represent to the poet? Explain how lines 15–16 reinforce this meaning.

Extending
8. Why do you think certain seasons evoke certain moods and emotions?

Emily Dickinson

The Soul selects her own Society—

Success is counted sweetest

The Soul selects her own Society—
Then—shuts the Door—
To her divine Majority—
Present no more—

5 Unmoved—she notes the Chariots—pausing—
At her low Gate—
Unmoved—an Emperor be kneeling
Upon her Mat—

I've known her—from an ample nation—
10 Choose One—
Then—close the Valves of her attention—
Like Stone—

Success is counted sweetest
By those who ne'er succeed.
To comprehend a nectar
Requires sorest need.

5 Not one of all the purple Host
Who took the Flag today
Can tell the definition
So clear of Victory

As he defeated—dying—
10 On whose forbidden ear
The distant strains of triumph
Burst agonized and clear!

STUDY QUESTIONS

The Soul selects her own Society—

Recalling

1. According to stanza 1, what does the "Soul" select? What does she do then?
2. What two things leave the soul unmoved, according to stanza 2?
3. According to stanza 3, what does the soul choose? What does she do then?

Interpreting

4. What does the phrase "I've known her" in line 9 suggest about the identity of the soul?
5. What do the images in lines 2 and 9–10 suggest about this soul? What other lines in the poem reinforce this meaning?
6. What can we infer about this soul from her attitude toward the images of royalty in stanza 2?

Success is counted sweetest

Recalling

1. According to stanza 1, to whom is success "sweetest"? What is required to "comprehend a nectar"?
2. What does "the purple Host" achieve? What is it unable to do, according to stanza 2?

Interpreting

3. Restate the observation made in lines 1–2 in your own words. How are lines 3–4 related to this observation?
4. How is the observation about soldiers and armies in stanzas 2 and 3 related to lines 1–2?

Extending

5. Do you agree with the observation about success and human nature expressed in this poem? Why or why not?

Emily Dickinson

I felt a Funeral, in my Brain

I felt a Funeral, in my Brain,
And Mourners to and fro
Kept treading—treading—till it seemed
That Sense was breaking through—

5 And when they all were seated,
A Service, like a Drum—
Kept beating—beating—till I thought
My Mind was going numb—

And then I heard them lift a Box
10 And creak across my Soul
With those same Boots of Lead, again,
Then Space—began to toll,

As all the Heavens were a Bell,
And Being, but an Ear,
15 And I, and Silence, some strange Race
Wrecked, solitary, here—

And then a Plank in Reason, broke,
And I dropped down, and down—
And hit a World, at every plunge,
20 And Finished knowing—then—

The Bustle in a House

The Bustle in a House
The Morning after Death
Is solemnest of industries
Enacted upon Earth—

5 The Sweeping up the Heart
And putting Love away
We shall not want to use again
Until Eternity.

I felt a Funeral, in my Brain

Recalling
1. Where does the "Funeral" take place? Who keeps treading to and fro?
2. What keeps beating? What do the mourners lift?
3. According to stanza 3, what begins to toll after the mourners leave?
4. What breaks, according to stanza 5? What happens then?

Interpreting
5. What is the "Service" in line 6? What is the "Box" in line 9?
6. Whose funeral is the speaker envisioning? What might the last two stanzas be describing?
7. Compare the images beginning in line 12 with the images of the funeral presented in lines 1–11. Which group of images is clearer? Why?

The Bustle in a House

Recalling
1. According to stanza 1, when and where does the bustle described in the poem occur?
2. According to stanza 2, what is swept up? What is put away? Until when won't we want to use the love?

Interpreting
3. What analogy does the poet make in this poem? In what line does the analogy become clear?
4. What do the images in lines 5 and 6 suggest about human reactions and needs after a death?
5. Can the first stanza be interpreted on a literal level? Explain your answer.

Emily Dickinson

Because I could not stop for Death—

Because I could not stop for Death—
He kindly stopped for me—
The Carriage held but just Ourselves—
And Immortality.

5 We slowly drove—He knew no haste
And I had put away
My labor and my leisure too,
For His Civility—

We passed the School, where Children strove
10 At Recess—in the Ring—
We passed the Fields of Gazing Grain—
We passed the Setting Sun—

Or rather—He passed Us—
The Dews drew quivering and chill—
15 For only Gossamer, my Gown—
My Tippet[1]—only Tulle[2]—

We paused before a House that seemed
A Swelling of the Ground—
The Roof was scarcely visible—
20 The Cornice[3]—in the Ground—

Since then—'tis Centuries—and yet
Feels shorter than the Day
I first surmised the Horses' Heads
Were toward Eternity—

---

1. **Tippet:** scarf for the neck and shoulders,
hanging down in front.
2. **Tulle** [tool]: fine netting used for scarves and
veils.
3. **Cornice** [kôr′ nis]: the projecting decorative
molding along the top of a building.

I heard a Fly buzz—when I died—

I heard a Fly buzz—when I died—
The Stillness in the Room
Was like the Stillness in the Air—
Between the Heaves of Storm—

5 The Eyes around—had wrung them dry—
And Breaths were gathering firm
For that last Onset—when the King
Be witnessed—in the Room—

I willed my Keepsakes—Signed away
10 What portion of me be
Assignable—and then it was
There interposed a Fly—

With Blue—uncertain stumbling Buzz—
Between the light—and me—
15 And then the Windows failed—and then
I could not see to see—

This World is not Conclusion

This World is not Conclusion.
A Species stands beyond—
Invisible, as Music—
But positive, as Sound—
5 It beckons, and it baffles—
Philosophy—don't know—
And through a Riddle, at the last—
Sagacity, must go—
To guess it, puzzles scholars—
10 To gain it, Men have borne
Contempt of Generations
And Crucifixion, shown—
Faith slips—and laughs, and rallies—
Blushes, if any see—
15 Plucks at a twig of Evidence—
And asks a Vane, the way—
Much Gesture, from the Pulpit—
Strong Hallelujahs roll—
Narcotics cannot still the Tooth
20 That nibbles at the soul—

STUDY QUESTIONS

Because I could not stop for Death—

Recalling
1. According to stanza 1, why did Death stop for the speaker? What did Death's carriage hold?
2. What three things did the speaker and Death pass in stanza 3? Where did they pause in stanza 5?
3. According to stanza 6, how much time has passed since the day of Death's visit? What does that time feel shorter than?

Interpreting
4. Is the speaker in this poem alive or dead? What day is she describing?
5. What do lines 1–2 suggest about human behavior?

6. What might the three things the speaker passed in stanza 3 represent?
7. What is the "House" in the ground in stanza 5? Is this the speaker's final destination? Explain.
8. Why does the day described seem so long to the speaker?

I heard a Fly buzz—when I died—

Recalling
1. What does the speaker hear in stanza 1? When does she hear it?
2. According to stanza 2, what are the "Eyes" and "Breaths" doing?
3. According to stanzas 3–4, what interposes between the light and the speaker? What happens then?

Interpreting

4. What is happening to the speaker? Who are the other people in the room?
5. What is unusual about the description of the people in lines 5–6? From whose point of view are they being described?
6. Why is the fly's appearance somewhat ironic? What basic message about death is suggested to the poet by the appearance of the fly?

This World is not Conclusion

Recalling

1. What two adjectives in lines 1–4 describe the "Species" that stands beyond this world? What does this species do in line 5?
2. According to lines 7–8, where must "Sagacity" go?
3. What comes "from the Pulpit" in line 17?
4. According to the last two lines, what can narcotics not still?

Interpreting

5. What baffling question is this poem about?
6. Identify two ways through which human beings have tried to answer the question, according to the poet. What do the last two lines suggest about these answers?

Extending

7. What elements of Dickinson's poetry seem most modern to you? Does she seem old-fashioned, or does she seem like one of our contemporaries? Explain your answer.

VIEWPOINT

The scholar who edited the definitive texts of Dickinson's poems, Thomas H. Johnson, tells us:

Emily Dickinson loved words ardently. Her feeling about them amounted to veneration and her selection of them was ritualistic.

■ What evidence do you find to support Johnson's contention? What unusual or well-chosen words add power to the poems you have read? How does Dickinson's use of everyday words help make her abstract ideas more concrete?

LITERARY FOCUS

Slant Rhyme

In **perfect,** or **exact, rhyme,** the consonants change but the vowel sounds stay the same: *be/*

see, talking/walking, history/mystery. In **slant rhyme**—also called **off rhyme, near rhyme, approximate rhyme,** and **imperfect rhyme**—the vowel sounds are similar but not identical: *be/ sigh, talking/working, history/mastery.*

Emily Dickinson is noted for her use of slant rhyme to achieve special effects. Consider, for example, her poem "This is my letter to the World." The first stanza builds tension because the reader expects a perfect rhyme that never comes. In the concluding line of the poem, however, it does come: "see" and "Me" rhyme exactly.

On the other hand, in "The Soul selects her own Society— " Dickinson wants to end on a jarring note. She uses the slant rhyme "One"/ "Stone." The overall effect of all the slant rhymes in this poem is to create a discordant quality that mirrors the abrupt, unsociable actions of the Soul.

The jarring effect of a slant rhyme can also underscore a word's importance. In "The Bustle in a House " the importance of "Eternity" is stressed by the imperfect rhyme it completes: "away"/"Eternity."

Thinking About Slant Rhyme

■ What slant rhymes occur in "I heard a Fly buzz—when I died—" and "Apparently with no surprise"? What effects do they have? How are the slant rhymes related to the meaning of each poem?

Types of Poetry

Poetry is often classified as narrative, dramatic, or lyric. These categories are more clearcut in some poems than in others. The category in which we place a poem will often depend on what we consider the main purpose of the poem to be.

The main purpose of a **narrative poem** is to tell a story. Narrative poetry includes the **epic,** a long poem that recounts the adventures of heroic figures in polished, elevated language. Narrative poetry also includes the **mock-epic,** a poem about a comical or foolhardy hero that parodies epic grandeur. The **ballad** is a shorter narrative poem.

The main purpose of a **dramatic poem** is to reveal character through dialogue and monologue. A dramatic poem may contain narrative elements, but it usually presents characters in a particular situation rather than in a series of events. The focus of the dramatic poem is on character, not events.

The main purpose of a **lyric poem** is to communicate the emotions of the poet. Lyric poems are generally short and attempt to achieve a single, unified effect. By far, most poetry falls into this category. Lyric poems, too, may contain narrative or dramatic elements, but the focus of the lyric is on the personal feelings of the poet.

Thinking About Types of Poetry

1. In which category—narrative, dramatic, or lyric—would you place Dickinson's poems? Why?
2. Note any examples in Dickinson of a blend of the elements of more than one type of poetry.

VOCABULARY

Analogies

Analogies are comparisons that point out relationships between items. Analogy items on vocabulary tests are usually written as two pairs of words. The words in the first pair are related to each other in the same way as those in the second pair: for example, WORD : SENTENCE : : PAGE : BOOK.

The words in capitals in the following analogies appear in Emily Dickinson's poems. Complete the analogies by choosing the pair of words that is related in the same way as the pair in capital letters.

1. ONSET : CONCLUSION : :
   (a) end : beginning   (c) grief : sorrow
   (b) numbness : cold   (d) plodding : dancing
2. TREADING : BEATING : :
   (a) sticks : stones   (c) feet : heart
   (b) ears : eyes   (d) desert : mountain
3. HEATHER : BILLOW : :
   (a) fixed : moving   (c) land : ocean
   (b) rising : falling   (d) grow : decline
4. HEFT : HANDS : :
   (a) jumping : legs   (c) brightness : eyes
   (b) learning : reading   (d) thirst : water
5. MUSIC : SOUND : :
   (a) cake : bread   (c) wind : air
   (b) poetry : language   (d) dancing : jumping

COMPOSITION

Analyzing Slant Rhyme

Choose one of Dickinson's poems, and write an analysis of the effect of the poet's use of exact and slant rhyme. Begin by telling what the rhymes are. Then explain how the rhymes work (sometimes along with capitalization and punctuation) to emphasize certain words and meanings. Conclude with a comment about the overall relationship between the rhymes and the poem's meaning.

Writing About an Abstract Idea

Like all great writers, Dickinson often uses concrete words to make abstract ideas clearer. In a poem or a short composition describe or explain an abstract idea or emotion. Use concrete words to create the clearest possible impression for your reader. Some abstractions you might write about are poetry, nature, joy, or success.

COMPARING WRITERS

Both Walt Whitman and Emily Dickinson were poets of great originality and intense emotion. Yet in temperament and life style they were almost exactly opposite. What do Whitman's and Dickinson's poems suggest about the sources of poetic inspiration? Where do they suggest the truly imaginative life can be found? What do you think made the poetry of these writers so fresh and original?

Mark Twain   *1835–1910*

Mark Twain, who was born Samuel Langhorne Clemens, spent his early life in Missouri, chiefly in the river town of Hannibal. Here he became a journeyman printer and later a riverboat pilot. So much did he love the life on the Mississippi River that he later chose a pen name that would link him with the river forever: "Mark twain!" was a river call meaning "two fathoms" and indicating that the water was deep enough for safe passage.

When the Civil War closed the Mississippi River, Sam Clemens headed for Nevada, where he dreamed of striking it rich. He did not. Instead he supported himself by newspaper reporting, specializing in humorous feature stories. Soon the pseudonym "Mark Twain" was well-known in California and Nevada and with the publication of "The Celebrated Jumping Frog of Calaveras County" (1865) in the East as well. In 1867, as a correspondent for the *Alta California,* Clemens set out for Europe and the Middle East. This journey provided the material for *Innocents Abroad* (1869), a sharp-tongued look at raw American travelers that quickly became a best seller. Another huge success, *Roughing It* (1872), recounted Clemens' experiences in the "Wild West."

By now the rough-edged westerner had married a wealthy eastern lady, and the family settled in Hartford, Connecticut, where Clemens met Charles Dudley Warner and William Dean Howells, the most influential literary critic of the day. With Warner Twain collaborated on *The Gilded Age* (1874), a satire that gave its name to the era of corrupt materialism that followed the Civil War. In Howells' *Atlantic Monthly* Twain recounted his experiences as a riverboat pilot in a series, "Old Times on the Mississippi," later called *Life on the Mississippi* (1883). *The Adventures of Tom Sawyer* (1876) established Twain as a master of fiction, and its sequel, *The Adventures of Huckleberry Finn* (1883), as one of the greatest novelists America has ever produced.

Mark Twain did not write a story; he told it. His mastery of American speech—the native vernacular—and his ability "to spin a yarn" are unrivaled; and whether his yarn spinning is aimed at pure entertainment or at social satire, his humor is irresistible. His realism and detail influenced many later writers of American fiction: Ernest Hemingway once said that "all modern American literature comes from one book by Mark Twain called *Huckleberry Finn.*"

Plagued by financial misfortunes and the deaths of loved ones, Twain's later years saw him frequently embittered, his work given to dark satire and philosophic brooding. *A Connecticut Yankee in King Arthur's Court* (1889) is a biting satire set in the Middle Ages; *Pudd'nhead Wilson* (1894) is an attack on racial discrimination. *The Man That Corrupted Hadleyburg* (1900) is probably the best of his powerful pessimistic tales.

Though Mark Twain first achieved fame as a western humorist, his greatest works—*The Adventures of Huckleberry Finn, The Adventures of Tom Sawyer,* and *Life on the Mississippi*—are set on the long river that divided the nation. Sam Clemens' boyhood dreams and memories are the sources of *Life on the Mississippi,* which begins with a vivid description of the arrival of a riverboat in Hannibal, Missouri.

Mark Twain

from **Life on the Mississippi**

A Boy's Ambition

When I was a boy, there was but one permanent ambition among my comrades in our village on the west bank of the Mississippi River. That was, to be a steamboatman. We had transient ambitions of other sorts, but they were only transient. When a circus came and went, it left us all burning to become clowns; the first Negro minstrel show that came to our section left us all suffering to try that kind of life; now and then we had a hope that if we lived and were good, God would permit us to be pirates. These ambitions faded out, each in its turn; but the ambition to be a steamboatman always remained.

Once a day a cheap, gaudy packet[1] arrived upward from St. Louis, and another downward from Keokuk.[2] Before these events had transpired, the day was glorious with expectancy; after they had transpired, the day was a dead and empty thing. Not only the boys, but the whole village, felt this. After all these years I can picture that old time to myself now, just as it was then: the white town drowsing in the sunshine of a summer's morning; the streets empty, or pretty nearly so; one or two clerks sitting in front of the Water Street stores, with their splint-bottomed chairs tilted back against the wall, chins on breasts, hats slouched over their faces, asleep—with shingle-shavings enough around to show what broke them down; a sow and a litter of pigs loafing along the sidewalk, doing a good business in watermelon rinds and seeds; two or three lonely little freight piles scattered about the levee;[3] a pile of skids[4] on the slope of the stone-paved wharf, and the fragrant town drunkard asleep in the shadow of them; two or three wood flats[5] at the head of the wharf, but nobody to listen to the peaceful lapping of the wavelets against them; the great Mississippi, the majestic, the magnificent Mississippi, rolling its mile-wide tide along, shining in the sun; the dense forest away on the other side; the "point" above the town, and the "point" below, bounding the river-glimpse and turning it into a sort of sea, and withal a very still and brilliant and lonely one. Presently a film of dark smoke appears above one of those remote "points"; instantly a Negro drayman,[6] famous for his quick

---

1. **packet:** boat that carries mail, passengers, and freight at fixed times over a fixed route.
2. **Keokuk** [kē′ə kuk′]: Mississippi River town at the southeastern tip of Iowa.

3. **levee** [lev′ ē]: landing place along the river.
4. **skids:** low, movable wooden platforms.
5. **wood flats:** small flat-bottomed boats.
6. **drayman:** driver of a dray, a low, sturdy cart with removable sides.

eye and prodigious voice, lifts up the cry, "S-t-e-a-m-boat a-comin'!" and the scene changes! The town drunkard stirs, the clerks wake up, a furious clatter of drays follows, every house and store pours out a human contribution, and all in a twinkling the dead town is alive and moving. Drays, carts, men, boys, all go hurrying from many quarters to a common center, the wharf. Assembled there, the people fasten their eyes upon the coming boat as upon a wonder they are seeing for the first time.

And the boat *is* rather a handsome sight, too. She is long and sharp and trim and pretty; she has two tall, fancy-topped chimneys, with a gilded device of some kind swung between them; a fanciful pilothouse, all glass and "gingerbread," perched on top of the texas deck[7] behind them; the paddleboxes are gorgeous with a picture or with gilded rays above the boat's name; the boiler deck, the hurricane deck, and the texas deck are fenced and ornamented with clean white railings; there is a flag gallantly flying from the jackstaff; the furnace doors are open and the fires glaring bravely; the upper decks are black with passengers; the captain stands by the big bell, calm, imposing, the envy of all; great volumes of the blackest smoke are rolling and tumbling out of the chimneys—a husbanded grandeur created with a bit of pitch pine just before arriving at a town; the crew are grouped on the forecastle;[8] the broad stage[9] is run far out over the port bow, and an envied deckhand stands picturesquely on the end of it with a coil of rope in his hand; the pent steam is screaming through the gaugecocks; the captain lifts his hand, a bell rings, the wheels stop; then they turn back, churning the water to foam, and the steamer is at rest. Then such a scramble as there is to get aboard, and to get ashore, and to take in freight and to discharge freight, all

at one and the same time; and such a yelling and cursing as the mates facilitate it all with! Ten minutes later the steamer is under way again, with no flag on the jackstaff and no black smoke issuing from the chimneys. After ten more minutes the town is dead again, and the town drunkard asleep by the skids once more.

A Cub Pilot's Experience: Learning the River

Years later, while on a trip down the Mississippi, Twain felt his boyhood ambition surface again, and he signed on as apprentice to the pilot of the Paul Jones, *Mr. Bixby.*

The *Paul Jones* was now bound for St. Louis. I planned a siege against my pilot, and at the end of three hard days he surrendered. He agreed to teach me the Mississippi River from New Orleans to St. Louis for five hundred dollars, payable out of the first wages I should receive after graduating. I entered upon the small enterprise of "learning" twelve or thirteen hundred miles of the great Mississippi River with the easy confidence of my time of life. If I had really known what I was about to require of my faculties, I should not have had the courage to begin. I supposed that all a pilot had to do was to keep his boat in the river, and I did not consider that that could be much of a trick, since it was so wide.

The boat backed out from New Orleans at four in the afternoon, and it was "our watch" until eight. Mr. Bixby, my chief, "straightened her up," plowed her along past the sterns of the other boats that lay at the levee, and then said, "Here, take her; shave those steamships as close as you'd peel an apple." I took the wheel, and my heart went down into my boots; for it seemed to me that we were about to scrape the side off every ship in the line, we were so close. I held my breath and began to claw the boat away from the danger; and I had my own opinion of the pilot who had known no better than to get us into such peril, but I was too wise to express it. In half a minute I had a

---

7. **texas deck:** On a Mississippi River steamboat the deck adjoining the officers' cabins was called texas because the cabins there were the largest on the ship.
8. **forecastle** [fōk′səl]: upper deck.
9. **stage:** plank for loading and unloading cargo and passengers.

Steamboats on the Mississippi.

wide margin of safety intervening between the *Paul Jones* and the ships; and within ten seconds more I was set aside in disgrace, and Mr. Bixby was going into danger again and flaying me alive with abuse of my cowardice. I was stung, but I was obliged to admire the easy confidence with which my chief loafed from side to side of his wheel, and trimmed the ships so closely that disaster seemed ceaselessly imminent. When he had cooled a little he told me that the easy water was close ashore and the current outside, and therefore we must hug the bank, upstream, to get the benefit of the former, and stay well out, downstream, to take advantage of the latter. In my own mind I resolved to be a downstream pilot and leave the upstreaming to people dead to prudence.

Now and then Mr. Bixby called my attention to certain things. Said he, "This is Six-Mile Point." I assented. It was pleasant enough information, but I could not see the bearing of it. I was not conscious that it was a matter of any interest to me. Another time he said, "This is Nine-Mile Point." Later he said, "This is Twelve-Mile Point." They were all about level with the water's edge; they all looked about alike to me; they were monotonously unpicturesque. I hoped Mr. Bixby would change the subject. But no; he would crowd up around a point, hugging the shore with affection, and then say: "The slack water ends here, abreast this bunch of China-trees; now we cross over." So he crossed over. He gave me the wheel once or twice, but I had no luck. I either came near chipping off the edge of a sugar plantation, or else I yawed[10] too far from shore, and so I dropped back into disgrace again and got abused.

The watch was ended at last, and we took supper and went to bed. At midnight the glare of a lantern shone in my eyes, and the night watchman said:

"Come! turn out!"

---

10. **yawed:** unintentionally swerved outside the planned route.

And then he left. I could not understand this extraordinary procedure; so I presently gave up trying to, and dozed off to sleep. Pretty soon the watchman was back again, and this time he was gruff. I was annoyed. I said:

"What do you want to come bothering around here in the middle of the night for? Now as like as not I'll not get to sleep again tonight."

The watchman said:

"Well, if this ain't good, I'm blessed."

The "off-watch" was just turning in, and I heard some brutal laughter from them, and such remarks as, "Hello, watchman! ain't the new cub turned out yet? He's delicate, likely. Give him some sugar in a rag and send for the chambermaid to sing rock-a-by-baby to him."

About this time Mr. Bixby appeared on the scene. Something like a minute later I was climbing the pilot-house steps with some of my clothes on and the rest in my arms. Mr. Bixby was close behind, commenting. Here was something fresh—this thing of getting up in the middle of the night to go to work. It was a detail in piloting that had never occurred to me at all. I knew that boats ran all night, but somehow I had never happened to reflect that somebody had to get up out of a warm bed to run them. I began to fear that piloting was not quite so romantic as I had imagined it was; there was something very real and worklike about this new phase of it.

It was a rather dingy night, although a fair number of stars were out. The big mate was at the wheel, and he had the old tub pointed at a star and was holding her straight up the middle of the river. The shores on either hand were not much more than a mile apart, but they seemed wonderfully far away and ever so vague and indistinct. The mate said:

"We've got to land at Jones's plantation, sir."

The vengeful spirit in me exulted. I said to myself, I wish you joy of your job, Mr. Bixby; you'll have a good time finding Mr. Jones's plantation such a night as this; and I hope you never *will* find it as long as you live.

Mr. Bixby said to the mate:

"Upper end of the plantation, or the lower?"

"Upper."

"I can't do it. The stumps there are out of water at this stage. It's no great distance to the lower, and you'll have to get along with that."

"All right, sir. If Jones don't like it he'll have to lump it, I reckon."

And then the mate left. My exultation began to cool and my wonder to come up. Here was a man who not only proposed to find this plantation on such a night, but to find either end of it you preferred. I dreadfully wanted to ask a question, but I was carrying about as many short answers as my cargo room would admit of, so I held my peace. All I desired to ask Mr. Bixby was the simple question whether he was ass enough to really imagine he was going to find that plantation on a night when all plantations were exactly alike and all the same color. But I held in. I used to have fine inspirations of prudence in those days.

Mr. Bixby made for the shore and soon was scraping it, just the same as if it had been daylight. And not only that, but singing

"Father in heaven the day is declining," etc.

It seemed to me that I had put my life in the keeping of a peculiarly reckless outcast. Presently he turned on me and said:

"What's the name of the first point above New Orleans?"

I was gratified to be able to answer promptly, and I did. I said I didn't know.

"Don't *know?*"

This manner jolted me. I was down at the foot again, in a moment. But I had to say just what I had said before.

"Well, you're a smart one," said Mr. Bixby. "What's the name of the *next* point?"

Once more I didn't know.

"Well this beats anything. Tell me the name of *any* point or place I told you."

I studied a while and decided that I couldn't.

"Look-a-here! What do you start out from, above Twelve-Mile Point, to cross over?"

"I—I—don't know."

"You—you—don't know?" mimicking my drawling manner of speech. "What *do* you know?"

"I—I—nothing, for certain."

"By the great Caesar's ghost I believe you! You're the stupidest dunderhead I ever saw or ever heard of, so help me Moses! The idea of *you* being a pilot—*you!* Why, you don't know enough to pilot a cow down a lane."

Oh, but his wrath was up! He was a nervous man, and he shuffled from one side of his wheel to the other as if the floor was hot. He would boil a while to himself, and then overflow and scald me again.

"Look-a-here! What do you suppose I told you the names of those points for?"

I tremblingly considered a moment, and then the devil of temptation provoked me to say:

"Well—to—to—be entertaining, I thought."

This was a red rag to the bull. He raged and stormed so (he was crossing the river at the time) that I judge it made him blind, because he ran over the steering oar of a trading scow.[11] Of course the traders sent up a volley of red-hot profanity. Never was a man so grateful as Mr. Bixby was: because he was brim full, and here were subjects who would *talk back*. He threw open a window, thrust his head out, and such an irruption followed as I never had heard before. The fainter and farther away the scowmen's curses drifted, the higher Mr. Bixby lifted his voice and the weightier his adjectives grew. When he closed the window he was empty. You could have drawn a seine[12] through his system and not caught curses enough to disturb your mother with. Presently he said to me in the gentlest way:

"My boy, you must get a little memorandum book, and every time I tell you a thing,

---

11. **trading scow:** a large, flat-bottomed boat with square ends used for carrying coal and other cargo.
12. **seine** [sān]: large fishing net.

put it down right away. There's only one way to be a pilot, and that is to get this entire river by heart. You have to know it just like A B C."

That was a dismal revelation to me; for my memory was never loaded with anything but blank cartridges. . . .

By the time we had gone seven or eight hundred miles up the river, I had learned to be a tolerably plucky upstream steersman, in daylight, and before we reached St. Louis I had made a trifle of progress in night work, but only a trifle. I had a notebook that fairly bristled with the names of towns, "points," bars, islands, bends, reaches, etc.; but the information was to be found only in the notebook—none of it was in my head. It made my heart ache to think I had only got half of the river set down; for as our watch was four hours off and four hours on, day and night, there was a long four-hour gap in my book for every time I had slept since the voyage began.

My chief was presently hired to go on a big New Orleans boat, and I packed my satchel and went with him. She was a grand affair. When I stood in her pilothouse I was so far above the water that I seemed perched on a mountain; and her decks stretched so far away, fore and aft, below me, that I wondered how I could ever have considered the little *Paul Jones* a large craft. There were other differences, too. The *Paul Jones*'s pilothouse was a cheap, dingy, battered rattletrap, cramped for room: but here was a sumptuous glass temple; room enough to have a dance in; showy red and gold window curtains; an imposing sofa; leather cushions and a back to the high bench where visiting pilots sit, to spin yarns and "look at the river"; bright, fanciful "cuspadors"[13] instead of a broad wooden box filled with sawdust; nice new oilcloth on the floor; a hospitable big stove for winter; a wheel as high as my head, costly with inlaid work; a wire tiller rope; bright brass knobs for the bells; and a tidy, white-aproned, black "texas tender,"[14]

13. "cuspadors" [kus′pə dôrz′]: spittoons.
14. "texas tender": a servant of the officers on texas deck.

to bring up tarts and ices and coffee during midwatch, day and night. Now this was "something like"; and so I began to take heart once more to believe that piloting was a romantic sort of occupation after all. The moment we were under way I began to prowl about the great steamer and fill myself with joy. She was as clean and as dainty as a drawing room; when I looked down her long, gilded saloon, it was like gazing through a splendid tunnel; she had an oil picture, by some gifted sign painter, on every stateroom door; she glittered with no end of prism-fringed chandeliers; the clerk's office was elegant, the bar was marvelous, and the barkeeper had been barbered and upholstered at incredible cost. The boiler deck (i.e., the second story of the boat, so to speak) was as spacious as a church, it seemed to me; so with the forecastle; and there was no pitiful handful of deckhands, firemen, and roustabouts[15] down there, but a whole battalion of men. The fires were fiercely glaring from a long row of furnaces, and over them were eight huge boilers! This was unutterable pomp. The mighty engines—but enough of this. I had never felt so fine before. And when I found that the regiment of natty servants respectfully "sir'd" me, my satisfaction was complete.

When I returned to the pilothouse St. Louis was gone and I was lost. Here was a piece of river which was all down in my book, but I could make neither head nor tail of it: you understand, it was turned around. I had seen it, when coming upstream, but I had never faced about to see how it looked when it was behind me. My heart broke again, for it was plain that I had got to learn this troublesome river *both ways.*

A Dangerous Crossing

My late voyage's notebooking was but a confusion of meaningless names. It had tangled me all up in a knot every time I had looked at it in the daytime. I now hoped for respite in sleep; but no, it reveled all through my head

15. **roustabouts**: laborers on a ship.

Levee at St. Louis, photo by Oscar Kuehn, 1904.

till sunrise again, a frantic and tireless nightmare.

Next morning I felt pretty rusty and low-spirited. We went booming along, taking a good many chances, for we were anxious to "get out of the river" (as getting out to Cairo[16] was called) before night should overtake us. But Mr. Bixby's partner, the other pilot, presently grounded the boat, and we lost so much time getting her off that it was plain the darkness would overtake us a good long way above the mouth. This was a great misfortune, especially to certain of our visiting pilots, whose boats would have to wait for their return, no matter how long that might be. It sobered the

pilothouse talk a good deal. Coming upstream, pilots did not mind low water or any kind of darkness; nothing stopped them but fog. But downstream work was different; a boat was too nearly helpless, with a stiff current pushing behind her; so it was not customary to run downstream at night in low water.

There seemed to be one small hope, however: if we could get through the intricate and dangerous Hat Island crossing before night, we could venture the rest, for we would have plainer sailing and better water. But it would be insanity to attempt Hat Island at night. So there was a deal of looking at watches all the rest of the day, and a constant ciphering upon the speed we were making; Hat Island was the eternal subject; sometimes hope was high and sometimes we were delayed in a bad crossing,

16. **Cairo:** Mississippi River town at the southern tip of Illinois.

Mark Twain **281**

and down it went again. For hours all hands lay under the burden of this suppressed excitement; it was even communicated to me, and I got to feeling so solicitous about Hat Island, and under such an awful pressure of responsibility, that I wished I might have five minutes on shore to draw a good, full, relieving breath, and start over again. We were standing no regular watches. Each of our pilots ran such portions of the river as he had run when coming upstream, because of his greater familiarity with it; but both remained in the pilothouse constantly.

An hour before sunset, Mr. Bixby took the wheel and Mr. W——— stepped aside. For the next thirty minutes every man held his watch in his hand and was restless, silent, and uneasy. At last somebody said, with a doomful sigh:

"Well, yonder's Hat Island—and we can't make it."

All the watches closed with a snap, everybody sighed and muttered something about its being "too bad, too bad—ah, if we could *only* have got here half an hour sooner!" and the place was thick with the atmosphere of disappointment. Some started to go out, but loitered, hearing no bell tap to land. The sun dipped behind the horizon, the boat went on. Inquiring looks passed from one guest to another; and one who had his hand on the doorknob, and had turned it, waited, then presently took away his hand and let the knob turn back again. We bore steadily down the bend. More looks were exchanged, and nods of surprised admiration—but no words. Insensibly the men drew together behind Mr. Bixby as the sky darkened and one or two dim stars came out. The dead silence and sense of waiting became oppressive. Mr. Bixby pulled the cord, and two deep, mellow notes from the big bell floated off on the night. Then a pause, and one more note was struck. The watchman's voice followed, from the hurricane deck:

"Labboard[17] lead, there! Stabboard[18] lead!"

The cries of the leadsmen[19] began to rise out of the distance, and were gruffly repeated by the wordpassers on the hurricane deck.

"M-a-r-k[20] three! M-a-r-k three! Quarter-less-three! Half twain! Quarter twain! M-a-r-k twain! Quarter-less"—

Mr. Bixby pulled two bellropes, and was answered by faint jinglings far below in the engineroom, and our speed slackened. The steam began to whistle through the gaugecocks. The cries of the leadsmen went on—and it is a weird sound, always, in the night. Every pilot in the lot was watching, now, with fixed eyes, and talking under his breath. Nobody was calm and easy but Mr. Bixby. He would put his wheel down and stand on a spoke, and as the steamer swung into her (to me) utterly invisible marks—for we seemed to be in the midst of a wide and gloomy sea—he would meet and fasten her there. Talk was going on, now, in low voices:

"There; she's over the first reef all right!"

After a pause, another subdued voice:

"Her stern's coming down just *exactly* right, by *George!* Now she's in the marks;[21] over she goes!"

Somebody else muttered:

"Oh, it was done beautiful—*beautiful!*"

Now the engines were stopped altogether, and we drifted with the current. Not that I could see the boat drift, for I could not, the stars being all gone by this time. This drifting was the dismalest work; it held one's heart still. Presently I discovered a blacker gloom than that which surrounded us. It was the head of the island. We were closing right down upon it. We entered its deeper shadow, and so imminent seemed the peril that I was likely to suffocate; and I had the strongest impulse to do *something*, anything, to save the vessel. But still Mr. Bixby stood by his wheel, silent, intent

---

17. **labboard:** larboard, the left side of the ship.
18. **stabboard:** starboard, the right side of the ship.

19. **leadsmen** [ledz'mən]: men who use a lead line, a weighted line for measuring water depth.
20. **Mark:** one of the markers on a lead line to indicate depth in fathoms (a fathom equals six feet). "Mark twain" indicates two fathoms.
21. **marks:** safe water.

as a cat, and all the pilots stood shoulder to shoulder at his back.

"She'll not make it!" somebody whispered.

The water grew shoaler[22] and shoaler by the leadsmen's cries, till it was down to—

"Eight-and-a-half! E-i-g-h-t feet! E-i-g-h-t feet! Seven-and"—

Mr. Bixby said warningly through his speaking tube to the engineer:

"Stand by, now!"

"Aye-aye, sir."

"Seven-and-a-half! Seven feet! *Six*-and"—

We touched bottom! Instantly Mr. Bixby set a lot of bells ringing, shouted through the tube, "*Now* let her have it—every ounce you've got!" then to his partner, "Put her hard down! snatch her! snatch her!" The boat rasped and ground her way through the sand, hung upon the apex of disaster a single tremendous instant, and then over she went! And such a shout as went up at Mr. Bixby's back never loosened the roof of a pilothouse before!

_____
22. **shoaler:** shallower.

There was no more trouble after that. Mr. Bixby was a hero that night; and it was some little time, too, before his exploit ceased to be talked about by river men.

Fully to realize the marvelous precision required in laying the great steamer in her marks in that murky waste of water, one should know that not only must she pick her intricate way through snags and blind reefs, and then shave the head of the island so closely as to brush the overhanging foliage with her stern, but at one place she must pass almost within arm's reach of a sunken and invisible wreck that would snatch the hull timbers from under her if she should strike it, and destroy a quarter of a million dollars' worth of steamboat and cargo in five minutes, and maybe a hundred and fifty human lives into the bargain.

The last remark I heard that night was a compliment to Mr. Bixby, uttered in soliloquy and with unction by one of our guests. He said:

"By the Shadow of Death, but he's a lightning pilot!"

STUDY QUESTIONS

Recalling

1. According to the opening paragraphs, what was the one permanent ambition of the writer and all his childhood friends? What daily events did all Hannibal look forward to?
2. What adjectives does Twain use to describe the Mississippi River in the second paragraph?
3. According to the section "A Cub Pilot's Experience," upon what enterprise did Twain enter with the "easy confidence" of youth? Who agreed to train him?
4. What is the method that Mr. Bixby recommended for learning to be a pilot?
5. Identify five differences between the *Paul Jones* and the New Orleans boat on which Twain traveled back from St. Louis. What "heart-breaking" realization did he have as he headed downstream?

Interpreting

6. Describe Twain's attitude as a boy toward the Mississippi River and toward the profession of riverboat pilot.
7. What is Twain's general attitude toward himself as a youth as evidenced by the tone of this selection? Cite details to support your answer.
8. Who is the "hero" of this selection? What details lead you to this conclusion?
9. What clues does this selection give you toward understanding why Samuel Clemens chose the pen name "Mark Twain"?

Extending

10. What aspects of Twain's excitement about learning a new skill seem authentic?

"The Celebrated Jumping Frog of Calaveras County" is Mark Twain's most famous western tale. It is actually a story within a frame story: The first narrator introduces us to a second narrator, Simon Wheeler, who then tells the tale. Our pleasure is in the company of Wheeler himself, a man who loves to talk and who could, as we see at the end, go on spinning his tall tales forever.

Mark Twain

The Celebrated Jumping Frog of Calaveras County

In compliance with the request of a friend of mine, who wrote me from the East, I called on good-natured, garrulous old Simon Wheeler, and inquired after my friend's friend, Leonidas W. Smiley, as requested to do, and I hereunto append the result. I have a lurking suspicion that *Leonidas W.* Smiley is a myth; that my friend never knew such a personage; and that he only conjectured that if I asked old Wheeler about him, it would remind him of his infamous *Jim* Smiley, and he would go to work and bore me to death with some exasperating reminiscence of him as long and as tedious as it should be useless to me. If that was the design, it succeeded.

I found Simon Wheeler dozing comfortably by the barroom stove of the dilapidated tavern in the decayed mining camp of Angel's, and I noticed that he was fat and baldheaded, and had an expression of winning gentleness and simplicity upon his tranquil countenance. He roused up, and gave me good day. I told him that a friend of mine had commissioned me to make some inquiries about a cherished companion of his boyhood named *Leonidas W.* Smiley—*Rev. Leonidas W.* Smiley, a young minister of the gospel, who he had heard was at one time a resident of Angel's Camp. I added that if Mr. Wheeler could tell me anything about this Rev. Leonidas W. Smiley, I would feel under many obligations to him.

Simon Wheeler backed me into a corner and blockaded me there with his chair, and then sat down and reeled off the monotonous narrative which follows this paragraph. He never smiled, he never frowned, he never changed his voice from the gentle-flowing key to which he tuned his initial sentence, he never betrayed the slightest suspicion of enthusiasm; but all through the interminable narrative there ran a vein of impressive earnestness and sincerity, which showed me plainly that, so far from his imagining that there was anything ridiculous or funny about his story, he regarded it as a really important matter, and admired its two heroes as men of transcendent genius in *finesse.* I let him go on in his own way, and never interrupted him once.

"Rev. Leonidas W. H'm, Reverend Le—well, there was a feller here once by the name of *Jim* Smiley, in the winter of '49—or maybe it was the spring of '50—I don't recollect exactly, somehow, though what makes me think it was one or the other is because I remember the big flume[1] warn't finished when he first come to the camp; but anyway, he was the curiousest man about always betting on anything that turned up you ever see, if he could get anybody to bet on the other side; and if he couldn't he'd change sides. Any way that suited the other man would suit *him*—any way just so's he got a bet, *he* was satisfied. But still he was lucky, uncommon lucky; he most always come out winner. He was always ready and laying for a chance; there couldn't be no solit'ry thing mentioned but that feller'd offer to bet on it, and take ary side you please, as I was just telling you. If there was a horse race, you'd find him flush or you'd find him busted at the end of it; if there was a dog fight, he'd bet on it; if there was a cat fight, he'd bet on it; if there was a chicken fight, he'd bet on it; why, if there was two birds setting on a fence, he would bet you which one would fly first; or if there was a camp meeting,[2] he would be there reg'lar to bet on Parson Walker, which he judged to be the best exhorter about here, and so he was too, and a good man. If he even see a straddle bug[3] start to go anywheres, he would bet you how long it would take him to get to—to wherever he was going to, and if you took him up, he would foller that straddle bug to Mexico but what he would find out where he was bound for and how long he was on the road. Lots of the boys here has seen that Smiley, and can tell you about him. Why, it never made no difference to *him*—he'd bet on *any* thing—the dangdest feller. Parson Walker's wife laid very sick once, for a good while, and it seemed as if they warn't going to save her; but one morning he come in, and Smiley up and asked him how she was, and he said she was considerable better—thank the Lord for his inf'nite mercy—and coming on so smart that with the blessing of Prov'dence she'd get well yet; and Smiley, before he

thought, says, 'Well, I'll resk two-and-a-half she don't anyway.'

"Thish-yer Smiley had a mare—the boys called her the fifteen-minute nag, but that was only in fun, you know, because of course she was faster than that—and he used to win money on that horse, for all she was so slow and always had the asthma, or the distemper, or the consumption, or something of that kind. They used to give her two or three hundred yards' start, and then pass her underway; but always at the fag end[4] of the race she'd get excited and desperate like, and come cavorting and straddling up, and scattering her legs around limber, sometimes in the air, and sometimes out to one side among the fences, and kicking up m-o-r-e dust and raising m-o-r-e racket with her coughing and sneezing and blowing her nose—and *always* fetch up at the stand just about a neck ahead, as near as you could cipher it down.

"And he had a little small bull pup, that to look at him you'd think he warn't worth a cent but to set around and look ornery and lay for a chance to steal something. But as soon as money was up on him he was a different dog; his underjaw'd begin to stick out like the fo'castle[5] of a steamboat, and his teeth would uncover and shine like the furnaces. And a dog might tackle him and bullyrag him, and bite him, and throw him over his shoulder two or three times, and Andrew Jackson[6]—which was the name of the pup—Andrew Jackson would never let on but what *he* was satisfied, and hadn't expected nothing else—and the bets being doubled and doubled on the other side all the time, till the money was all up; and then all of a sudden he would grab that other dog jest by the j'int of his hind leg and freeze to it—not chaw, you understand, but only just grip and hang on till they throwed up the sponge, if it was a year. Smiley always come out winner on that pup, till he harnessed a dog

1. **flume** [floom]: artificial inclined channel for conducting water to provide power and transport objects.
2. **camp meeting:** religious meeting and service held in the mining camp.
3. **straddle bug:** long-legged beetle.

4. **fag end:** last part.
5. **fo'castle:** forecastle; upper deck.
6. **Andrew Jackson:** after the general and seventh President of the United States.

once that didn't have no hind legs, because they'd been sawed off in a circular saw, and when the thing had gone along far enough, and the money was all up, and he come to make a snatch for his pet holt,[7] he see in a minute how he'd been imposed on, and how the other dog had him in the door, so to speak, and he 'peared surprised, and then he looked sorter discouraged-like, and didn't try no more to win the fight, and so he got shucked out bad. He give Smiley a look, as much as to say his heart was broke, and it was *his* fault, for putting up a dog that hadn't no hind legs for him to take holt of, which was his main dependence in a fight, and then he limped off a piece and laid down and died. It was a good pup, was that Andrew Jackson, and would have made a name for hisself if he'd lived, for the stuff was in him and he had genius—I know it, because he hadn't no opportunities to speak of, and it don't stand to reason that a dog could make such a fight as he could under them circumstances if he hadn't no talent. It always makes me feel sorry when I think of that last fight of his'n, and the way it turned out.

"Well, thish-yer Smiley had rat terriers[8] and chicken cocks[9] and tomcats and all them kind of things, till you couldn't rest, and you couldn't fetch nothing for him to bet on but he'd match you. He ketched a frog one day, and took him home, and said he cal'lated to educate him; and so he never done nothing for three months but set in his back yard and learn that frog to jump. And you bet you he *did* learn him, too. He'd give him a little punch behind, and the next minute you'd see that frog whirling in the air like a doughnut—see him turn one summerset, or maybe a couple, if he got a good start, and come down flatfooted and all right, like a cat. He got him up so in the matter of ketching flies, and kep' him in practice so constant, that he'd nail a fly every time as fur as he could see him. Smiley said all a

frog wanted was education, and he could do 'most anything—and I believe him. Why, I've seen him set Dan'l Webster[10] down here on this floor—Dan'l Webster was the name of the frog—and sing out, 'Flies, Dan'l, flies!' and quicker'n you could wink he'd spring straight up and snake a fly off'n the counter there, and flop down on the floor ag'in as solid as a gob of mud, and fall to scratching the side of his head with his hind foot as indifferent as if he hadn't no idea he'd been doin' any more'n any frog might do. You never see a frog so modest and straightfor'ard as he was, for all he was so gifted. And when it come to fair and square jumping on a dead level, he could get over more ground at one straddle than any animal of his breed you ever see. Jumping on a dead level was his strong suit, you understand; and when it come to that, Smiley would ante up money on him as long as he had a red.[11] Smiley was monstrous proud of his frog, and well he might be, for fellers that had traveled and been everywheres all said he laid over any frog that ever *they* see.

"Well, Smiley kep' the beast in a little lattice box, and he used to fetch him downtown sometimes and lay for a bet. One day a feller—a stranger in the camp, he was—come acrost him with his box, and says:

" 'What might it be that you've got in the box?'

"And Smiley says, sorter indifferent-like, 'It might be a parrot, or it might be a canary, maybe, but it ain't—it's only just a frog.'

"And the feller took it, and looked at it careful, and turned it round this way and that, and says, 'H'm—so 'tis. Well, what's *he* good for?'

" 'Well,' Smiley says, easy and careless, 'he's good enough for *one* thing, I should judge—he can outjump any frog in Calaveras County.'

"The feller took the box again, and took another long, particular look, and give it back to Smiley, and says, very deliberate, 'Well,' he

---

7. **holt:** hold.
8. **rat terriers:** dogs skilled in catching rats.
9. **chicken cocks:** here, roosters trained for fights on which bets were made.

10. **Dan'l Webster:** after Daniel Webster, the American statesman and orator.
11. **a red:** a red cent; any money.

says, 'I don't see no p'ints about that frog that's any better'n any other frog.'

" 'Maybe you don't,' Smiley says. 'Maybe you understand frogs and maybe you don't understand 'em; maybe you've had experience, and maybe you ain't only a amature, as it were. Anyways, I've got *my* opinion, and I'll resk forty dollars that he can outjump any frog in Calaveras County.'

"And the feller studied a minute, and then says, kinder sad-like, 'Well, I'm only a stranger here, and I ain't got no frog; but if I had a frog, I'd bet you.'

"And then Smiley says, 'That's all right—that's all right—if you'll hold my box a minute, I'll go and get you a frog.' And so the feller took the box, and put up his forty dollars along with Smiley's, and set down to wait.

"So he set there a good while thinking and thinking to himself, and then he got the frog out and prized his mouth open and took a teaspoon and filled him full of quailshot[12]—filled him pretty near up to his chin—and set him on the floor. Smiley he went to the swamp and slopped around in the mud for a long time, and finally he ketched a frog, and fetched him in, and give him to this feller, and says:

" 'Now, if you're ready, set him alongside of Dan'l, with his fore paws just even with Dan'l's, and I'll give the word.' Then he says, 'One—two—three—*git!*' and him and the feller touched up the frogs from behind, and the new frog hopped off lively, but Dan'l give a heave, and hysted up his shoulders—so—like a

_____

12. **quailshot:** small lead pellets used for shooting quail.

Frenchman, but it warn't no use—he couldn't budge; he was planted as solid as a church, and he couldn't no more stir than if he was anchored out. Smiley was a good deal surprised, and he was disgusted too, but he didn't have no idea what the matter was, of course.

"The feller took the money and started away; and when he was going out at the door, he sorter jerked his thumb over his shoulder—so—at Dan'l, and says again, very deliberate, 'Well,' he says, 'I don't see no p'ints about that frog that's any better'n any other frog.'

"Smiley he stood scratching his head and looking down at Dan'l a long time, and at last he says, 'I do wonder what in the nation that frog throw'd off for—I wonder if there ain't something the matter with him—he 'pears to look mighty baggy, somehow.' And he ketched Dan'l by the nap of the neck, and hefted him, and says, 'Why blame my cats if he don't weigh five pound!' and turned him upside down and he belched out a double handful of shot. And then he see how it was, and he was

the maddest man—he set the frog down and took out after that feller, but he never ketched him. And—"

Here Simon Wheeler heard his name called from the front yard, and got up to see what was wanted. And turning to me as he moved away, he said: "Just set where you are, stranger, and rest easy—I ain't going to be gone a second."

But, by your leave, I did not think that a continuation of the history of the enterprising vagabond *Jim* Smiley would be likely to afford me much information concerning the Rev. *Leonidas W.* Smiley, and so I started away.

At the door I met the sociable Wheeler returning, and he buttonholed me and recommenced:

"Well, thish-yer Smiley had a yaller one-eyed cow that didn't have no tail, only just a short stump like a bannanner, and—"

However, lacking both time and inclination, I did not wait to hear about the afflicted cow, but took my leave.

STUDY QUESTIONS

Recalling
1. With what adjectives does the narrator describe Wheeler and Wheeler's reminiscences in the first paragraph?
2. About whom does the narrator ask Wheeler? About whom does Wheeler speak?
3. According to Wheeler's opening paragraph, about what was Jim Smiley "the curiousest man"?
4. How did Smiley's bullpup surprise people? What eventually became of the dog?
5. What did Smiley train his frog to do? Summarize what the stranger did to the frog and Smiley's reaction.

Interpreting
6. The narrator tells us that Wheeler bored him to death. Do you think Twain expects the reader to have the same reaction? How can you tell?
7. Does Wheeler's account of what happened to Smiley's dog make sense? Does it matter? Why or why not?
8. What kind of person is Jim Smiley, as Wheeler presents him?
9. Who is really the main character in this story, and why?

Extending
10. Why do you think people love to tell tall tales—and to listen to them?

A **fable** is a tale in which animals behave as if they were human beings; it usually ends with a moral. Here Mark Twain adopts the traditional fable format and in the simple language of fables gives us his view of art and our ways of experiencing it.

Mark Twain

A Fable

Once upon a time an artist who had painted a small and very beautiful picture placed it so that he could see it in the mirror. He said, "This doubles the distance and softens it, and it is twice as lovely as it was before."

The animals out in the woods heard of this through the housecat, who was greatly admired by them because he was so learned, and so refined and civilized, and so polite and high-bred, and could tell them so much which they didn't know before, and were not certain about afterward. They were much excited about this new piece of gossip, and they asked questions, so as to get at a full understanding of it. They asked what a picture was, and the cat explained.

"It is a flat thing," he said; "wonderfully flat, marvelously flat, enchantingly flat and elegant. And, oh, so beautiful!"

That excited them almost to a frenzy, and they said they would give the world to see it. Then the bear asked:

"What is it that makes it so beautiful?"

"It is the looks of it," said the cat.

This filled them with admiration and uncertainty, and they were more excited than ever. Then the cow asked:

"What is a mirror?"

"It is a hole in the wall," said the cat. "You look in it, and there you see the picture, and it is so dainty and charming and ethereal and inspiring in its unimaginable beauty that your head turns round and round, and you almost swoon with ecstasy."

The ass had not said anything as yet; he now began to throw doubts. He said there had never been anything as beautiful as this before, and probably wasn't now. He said that when it took a whole basketful of sesquipedalian[1] adjectives to whoop up a thing of beauty, it was time for suspicion.

It was easy to see that these doubts were having an effect upon the animals, so the cat went off offended. The subject was dropped for a couple of days, but in the meantime curiosity was taking a fresh start, and there was a revival of interest perceptible. Then the animals assailed the ass for spoiling what could possibly have been a pleasure to them, on a mere suspicion that the picture was not beautiful, without any evidence that such was the case. The ass was not troubled; he was calm, and said there was one way to find out who was in the right, himself or the cat: he would go and look in that hole, and come back and tell what he found there. The animals felt relieved and grateful, and asked him to go at once—which he did.

But he did not know where he ought to stand; and so, through error, he stood between the picture and the mirror. The result was that the picture had no chance, and didn't show up. He returned home and said:

"The cat lied. There was nothing in that

_____

1. **sesquipedalian** [ses′ kwi pi dā′lē ən]: having many syllables.

hole but an ass. There wasn't a sign of a flat thing visible. It was a handsome ass, and friendly, but just an ass, and nothing more."

The elephant asked:

"Did you see it good and clear? Were you close to it?"

"I saw it good and clear, O Hathi, King of Beasts. I was so close that I touched noses with it."

"This is very strange," said the elephant; "the cat was always truthful before—as far as we could make out. Let another witness try. Go, Baloo, look in the hole, and come and report."

So the bear went. When he came back, he said:

"Both the cat and the ass have lied; there was nothing in the hole but a bear."

Great was the surprise and puzzlement of the animals. Each was now anxious to make the test himself and get at the straight truth. The elephant sent them one at a time.

First, the cow. She found nothing in the hole but a cow.

The tiger found nothing in it but a tiger.

The lion found nothing in it but a lion.

The leopard found nothing in it but a leopard.

The camel found a camel, and nothing more.

Then Hathi was wroth,[2] and said he would have the truth, if he had to go and fetch it himself. When he returned, he abused his whole subjectry for liars, and was in an unappeasable fury with the moral and mental blindness of the cat. He said that anybody but a nearsighted fool could see that there was nothing in the hole but an elephant.

MORAL, BY THE CAT

You can find in a text whatever you bring, if you will stand between it and the mirror of your imagination. You may not see your ears, but they will be there.

---

2. **wroth** [rôth]: very angry.

STUDY QUESTIONS

Recalling

1. What adjectives in the first paragraph describe the artist's picture? What does the artist say is the effect of viewing his picture in a mirror?
2. Who tells the animals in the woods about the picture? According to the second paragraph, why is this newsbearer admired by the other animals?
3. Who does not believe that such a beautiful picture exists? What reason does he give for his suspicions?
4. What does each animal see when he looks in the mirror?
5. According to the cat, what is the moral?

Interpreting

6. What criticism of the housecat may be inferred from the second paragraph? Of the forest animals?

7. Explain the donkey's statement in your own words. Do you agree with him? Why or why not?
8. What does the cat's moral suggest about the chief necessity for appreciating art? Why, then, can the forest animals not appreciate the beautiful picture?

Extending

9. How would you describe the purpose of a work of art, for example a painting, a story, a poem, or a song?

VIEWPOINT

Justin Kaplan, one of Twain's biographers, tells us that Twain's "preferred form" is

the oral, humorous story, which . . . relies for its effectiveness on the manner of the telling instead of the outcome. . . . It is delivered gravely and unsuspectingly, with no overt cues for laughter, and it may wander around as much as it pleases.

—Introduction to *The Great Short Works of Mark Twain*

◼ According to Kaplan's definition, which selection by Twain most clearly illustrates an "oral, humorous story," and why? Does the same "grave delivery" apply to the humor in the other selections? If so, where?

LITERARY FOCUS

Colloquial Language

Colloquial language is the everyday language we use in our conversation. It is sometimes ungrammatical, and it may contain slang words and phrases. It varies from place to place and among ethnic groups.

Rendering colloquial speech in print is an art, an art that Mark Twain mastered. Not only was he able to capture dialect realistically, but he had a knack for knowing when to use colloquial language and when to avoid it. The first narrator in "The Celebrated Jumping Frog of Calaveras County" has an educated, slightly pompous way of speaking: "I hereunto append," "personage," "conjectured." His language is not colloquial; it is quite formal English. Simon Wheeler, on the other hand, speaks in colloquial language; he uses a western dialect: "fellers," "curiousest," "This-yer." Wheeler's language is especially delightful to us because we see that Twain and his narrator enjoy it so much themselves.

Twain is also careful not to overdo the colloquial language. Wheeler's speech has the *suggestion* of western dialect; it is not an accurate recording. If it were, it would bore and confuse the reader, who would find it largely unintelligible. Twain's aim is to capture the colloquial American voice, not to make a study of it. He succeeds so well in "The Jumping Frog" that Wheeler's speech not only makes the tale, it *is* the tale.

Thinking About Colloquial Language

◼ Find instances of colloquial language in *Life on the Mississippi*. How does Twain's use of colloquial conversation make his memories seem more realistic and exciting?

COMPOSITION

Analyzing Contrasting Tones

◼ Write a brief essay contrasting the romantic or nostalgic parts of *Life on the Mississippi* with the more realistic ones. Begin by defining the two different tones of the selection. Then give examples of each. Conclude with a comment on how Twain uses language to achieve these different tones.

Writing a Fable

◼ Write a fable of your own in which you use animal characters to make a point about human nature. Try to get something of Twain's graceful humor and simplicity of language into your writing. Like Twain, you might begin your fable with "Once upon a time. . . ."

COMPARING WRITERS

◼ Whitman, Dickinson, and Twain all helped develop American literature as a singular expression of American life. How do the styles and subjects of these three writers differ from those of the American authors who preceded them? What do you think makes Whitman, Dickinson, and Twain so distinctly American?

READING FOR APPRECIATION

Meaning

As we read, most of us ask some version of the question, "What does it mean?" But in order to get the most out of what we read, we ought to first stop and ask ourselves the odd question, "What do we *mean* by 'mean'?" It will help to make a few distinctions.

To begin with, we should recognize the fact that no statement *about* a poem or a story, no summary of it, can take the place of the work itself. For convenience we sometimes make such statements and summaries. To do so is fine as long as we know that they are not the same as the poem or story *as it is written.*

Surely, we want to interpret a work so that as many of its multiple meanings as possible are brought to light. These meanings will include much more than whatever "message" we may find—and we must not turn ourselves exclusively into "message seekers." The meanings of a work will also include the way the specific language works, the tone of a work, its shape, its movements. In short, the complete meaning of a work of literature is its *total effect.*

As we read we must ask not only *what does this say,* but also *how does this work,* and *what happens in it?* For the way the poem or story happens is part of its meaning. We may say, for example, that Whitman's "As Toilsome I Wander'd Virginia's Woods" can be paraphrased, or restated, as follows: "The poet remembers coming across the grave of an unknown soldier in the woods and an inscription nailed to a nearby tree. Long after that incident he still sees the grave and the inscription. The memory comes back to him suddenly." Compare this version of the poem with the poem itself. You will sense at once how much of the *meaning* is missing.

In the paraphrase, for one thing, the repeated refrain is missing—the important line that makes its effect by its very repetition. All the poem's rhythms disappear in a paraphrase, and you can hear at once how the phrasing of the words creates the poem's effect. In the refrain, for example, there are three short words—"Bold," "cautious," "true"—followed by a long phrase—"and my loving comrade"—which suggests the sudden rush of emotion that sprang into the poet's heart. If you are moved by the way that phrase is positioned twice within the poem, then you will see how hard it is to isolate meaning from the total effect of the work. The meaning is what happens in the poem *as it happens.*

THE AMERICAN VOICE

The Shadow of War

The writers in this unit lived through a turbulent time in American history. The Civil War brought many Americans face to face with suffering and death. It also shocked many people into an intense awareness of the value of human life itself. Whether they faced war's violence publicly as soldiers or privately as poets, the writers in this unit confronted the harsh facts of war with honesty and courage. They found strength and refuge in a larger vision of the compassionate individual.

Chesnut

I think, if I consider the long array of those bright youths and loyal men who have gone to their deaths almost before my very eyes, my heart might break, too.

Lee

I hope I may never be called upon to draw my sword.

Lincoln

It is rather for us to be here dedicated to the great task remaining before us—that from these honored dead we take increased devotion to that cause for which they gave the last full measure of devotion—that we here highly resolve that these dead shall not have died in vain.

Chief Joseph

Hear me, my chiefs. I am tired; my heart is sick and sad. From where the sun now stands I will fight no more forever.

Whitman

*Beat! beat! drums!—blow! bu-
    gles! blow!*
*Through the windows—through
    doors—burst like a ruthless
    force,*
*Into the solemn church, and
    scatter the solemn congrega-
    tion*
*Into the school where the
    scholar is studying.*

Dickinson

*Not one of all the purple Host
Who took the Flag today
Can tell the definition
So clear of Victory*

*As he defeated—dying—
On whose forbidden ear
The distant strains of triumph
Burst agonized and clear!*

Americans endured the war with a combination of realism and idealism. The American voice spoke of victory and of defeat, of compassion deeply felt, and of hard lessons learned. The period to come would reflect in its realistic literature both that surviving compassion and the effects of those hard lessons.

Key to Illustrations on Pages 216–217.

1	2		8
3		4	9
5	6	7	10

1. Photograph of Emily Dickinson, 1847.

2. *Coming and Going of the Pony Express,* Frederick Remington, 1906.

3. *Bombardment of Island Number Ten in the Mississippi River,* print by Currier and Ives, 1862.

4. *Portrait of the Artist's Mother,* James Abbott McNeill Whistler, 1871.

5. *Frederick Douglass,* Elisha Hammond, 1844.

6. An early typewriter, from a 1908 advertisement.

7. *Manhantango Valley Farm,* artist unknown, c. 1860.

8. Drawing of Mark Twain, from an early twentieth-century box label.

9. *Across the Continent—Westward the Course of Empire Takes Its Way,* print by Currier and Ives, 1868.

10. *Walt Whitman,* Thomas Eakins, 1887.

Key to Illustrations appears on page 427.

REGIONALISM AND REALISM

1880–1910

In the decades around the turn of the century, America continued its energetic expansion and its growth in population, wealth, and military power. The Civil War had challenged the nation's self-confidence and had put an end to the optimism of the mid-nineteenth century. After the war a new, more varied, bewildering America emerged. In the Puritan age, in the revolutionary age, in the age of the western frontier, America seemed to have a single, clear direction. Now it seemed to be moving in many different directions at once.

The war had devastated the nation. Throughout the South people suffered from the continued effects of economic collapse. In the North industry flourished, having been spurred by the production demands of the war. The movement west continued as established American families and new immigrants searching for a better life spread out and populated new territories. The isolated frontier was becoming only a memory as railroads continued to crisscross the continent.

The great cities, too, expanded rapidly: The population of Philadelphia tripled between 1870 and 1910; that of New York quadrupled. Chicago's population multiplied an astounding twenty times as the new capital of the Midwest became, in the poet Carl Sandburg's words, "the Nation's Freight Handler."

Affluence—its origins as well as its effects on Americans—was frequently a subject of the writing of this time.

Thomas Jefferson's dream of an agrarian America, with small towns and family farms, was vanishing. The United States was becoming a wealthy industrial nation.

By the 1890s there were over four thousand American millionaires, and some whose wealth greatly exceeded a mere million dollars—men like Andrew Carnegie, who made his fortune in iron and steel; J. P. Morgan, the great financier; and John D. Rockefeller, founder of the Standard Oil Company. The Gilded Age, as Mark Twain called it in a satirical novel, was a time of fabulous display of wealth, larger and larger corporations and industrial monopolies, and a widening gap between haves and have-nots among the American people.

Indeed, as wealth grew more conspicuous, poverty became more visible. In the Midwest a series of natural disasters forced farmers to move from state to state in order to eke from the soil the barest means of existence. In the West wheat growers battled the railroads, whose owners were condemned in works such as Frank Norris' *The Octopus* (1901). Drawing the most criticism were the burgeoning urban centers: Journalist Lincoln Steffens called poverty and slums "the shame of the cities," attacking too the urban phenomenon of political corruption and "bossism." Other "muckraking" journalists, such as Upton Sinclair and Ida Tar-

bell, criticized corrupt business practices and urged governmental reforms.

The literature of the decades just before and after 1900 responded to the new conditions of American life by turning from Romanticism and Transcendental optimism toward a franker portrayal of society and of human nature. The major literary movements of this period were Realism, Regionalism, and an offshoot of Realism called Naturalism.

Realism

The elements of Realism are so familiar to us today that we may have difficulty in seeing Realism as a specific movement in literature. What, then, did Realism mean to the writers for whom it was something new?

In part, Realism was a reaction against Romanticism. Realism turned from an emphasis on the strange toward a faithful rendering of the ordinary, a slice of life as it is really lived. The Realist writers avoided the improba-

bilities of such Romantic tales as Washington Irving's "Devil and Tom Walker" (page 105) and Edgar Allan Poe's "Fall of the House of Usher" (page 135). As the American novelist Frank Norris said: "Realism is the kind of fiction that confines itself to the type of normal life." Or as William Dean Howells, one of the earliest exponents of Realism, put it: "Let fiction cease to lie about life; let it portray men and women as they are."

Realism frequently provided an outlet for a writer's democratic sympathies. Middle- and lower-class people were often its subjects, and the Realist writers took their characters' lives as seriously as they took the lives of the rich and powerful. For example, Stephen Crane's *Red Badge of Courage* focused on an ordinary soldier; earlier war stories dealt not with common soldiers but with kings, nobles, and generals.

Yet if things are *too* normal, *too* ordinary, there may be no imaginative lure to the writing. It is more accurate to say that Realist literature finds the drama and the tension beneath the ordinary surface of life. A Realist writer is more objective than subjective, more descriptive than symbolic. A Realist writer gets to the heart of human experience without ever swerving too far from verisimilitude, or lifelikeness. Realists looked for Truth in everyday truths.

Many Realist writers found the greatest sources for litera-

Poverty—its causes and its effects—was also a fundamental subject for American Realist writers.

ture in the daily life that immediately surrounded them. Some were called Regional writers: They set their literature in the region they knew best, the area where they lived.

Regionalism

In an age when transportation and communication were not what they are today, Regional literature was especially popular, for it satisfied Americans' demand to know how people lived in other parts of the country. Mark Twain and Bret Harte illustrated for the whole nation the rough excitement of the "Wild West." Kate Chopin's stories portrayed the colorful mixture of languages and cultures in Louisiana. Sarah Orne Jewett wrote quiet, well-observed sketches of rural New England life.

However, in reading Regional literature, Americans found more than a travel guide. The aim of most Regional fiction was to capture the special atmosphere, the "local color," of the area and people it portrayed. As the midwestern writer Hamlin Garland, in an essay called "Local Color in Art," explains:

". . . I am using local color to mean something more than a forced study of the picturesque scenery of a state. Local color in a novel means that it has such quality and background that it could not have been written in any other place, or by anyone [other] than a native."

Like Realist fiction, Regional literature generally deals with the lives of ordinary people. Accurate descriptions of the characters' activities and realistic use of dialect are important in capturing the local color of the region. Equally important are accurate descriptions of nature, of the physical appearance of the environment being portrayed. Good Regionalist writing used all the elements of the local scene to extend insights and observations to the universal.

Naturalism

Environment also plays an important role in Naturalism, an outgrowth of Realism that responded to theories in science, psychology, human behavior, and social thought current in the late nineteenth century.

In Naturalist fiction people are often caught within forces of nature or society that are beyond their understanding or control. For instance, the hero of Jack London's "To Build a Fire" is crushed by the over-

whelming force of the Arctic cold. Tim Haskins, a farmer in Hamlin Garland's "Under the Lion's Paw," suffers beneath an economic force that he is not equipped to fight. In *The Red Badge of Courage* Henry Fleming, the young soldier, usually must act under the shadow of larger forces that he cannot know or understand; in Theodore Dreiser's novels the characters' actions are determined by uncontrollable social and physical factors.

Naturalist writing uses a facts-only approach, a style made of detailed observation of the "truth" of human experiences. Romantic illusions, sentiments, and idealistic solutions to problems are all absent from Naturalistic writing. Poets as well as novelists participated in this movement: Edwin Arlington Robinson, for example, showed his characters in the harsh light of day, unromanticized, often unhappy and unfulfilled.

Although Naturalist literature described the world with sometimes brutal realism, it sometimes also aimed at bettering the world through social reform. For example, Frank Norris and Hamlin Garland, in portraying the plight of the western and midwestern farmer, hoped to bring a desperate situation to the eyes of the American public and so to improve it. This combination of grim reality and desire for improvement is typical of America as it moved into the twentieth century.

TIME LINE

1880   Andrew Carnegie begins establishing libraries

      Sidney Lanier, *Science of English Verse*

1881   Henry James, *Portrait of a Lady* and *Washington Square*

      Booker T. Washington founds Tuskegee Institute (Alabama)

      Clara Barton founds American Red Cross

1883   Sidney Lanier, "Song of the Chattahoochee"

      Thomas Edison discovers that electric current can be sent through space

      "Buffalo Bill" Cody opens his first Wild West show

1884   Mark Twain, *The Adventures of Huckleberry Finn*

1885   William Dean Howells, *The Rise of Silas Lapham*

1886   Sarah Orne Jewett, "A White Heron"

      Statue of Liberty dedicated

1889   Reporter Nellie Bly begins record trip around the world (72 days, 6 hours, 11 minutes)

1890   William James, *Principles of Psychology*

      Ladybugs imported from Australia to save California citrus crop

1891   Hamlin Garland, *Main-Travelled Roads*

      James A. Naismith invents game of basketball

1880   Russia: Peter Ilyich Tchaikovsky, "1812 Overture"

1881   Cuba: Doctor Carlos Finlay discovers that mosquitoes transmit yellow fever

1883   England: Robert Louis Stevenson, *Treasure Island*

      Paris–Istanbul: Orient Express train makes first run

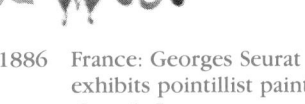

1886   France: Georges Seurat exhibits pointillist painting, *La Grande Jatte*

1887   Italy: Giuseppe Verdi, *Otello*

      England: Arthur Conan Doyle, *A Study in Scarlet,* first Sherlock Holmes novel

1889   Japan: Physician Shibasabura Kitasato isolates the bacillus that causes tetanus

1890   Norway: Henrik Ibsen, *Hedda Gabler*

1893 World's Columbian Exposition opens in Chicago

Katherine Lee Bates writes "America the Beautiful"

Colorado first state to grant women right to vote

Henry Ford builds his first automobile

1894 Kate Chopin, *Bayou Folk*

1895 Stephen Crane, *The Red Badge of Courage*

1896 Sarah Orne Jewett, *The Country of the Pointed Firs*

Paul Laurence Dunbar, *Lyrics of a Lowly Life*

1897 Edwin Arlington Robinson, "Richard Cory"

Klondike Gold Rush begins

1898 Henry James, *The Turn of the Screw*

Spanish-American War

1899 Frank Norris, *McTeague*

Scott Joplin, "Maple Leaf Rag"

1900 L. Frank Baum, *The Wonderful Wizard of Oz*

Theodore Dreiser, *Sister Carrie*

1901 Frank Norris, *The Octopus*

1902 Muckraking movement begins

1893 Ireland: W. B. Yeats, *The Celtic Twilight*

1894 Germany: Rudolf Diesel invents diesel engine

England: Rudyard Kipling, *The Jungle Book*

1895 France: Lumière brothers project moving pictures on screen for first time

Italy: Guglielmo Marconi invents wireless telegraph

England: Oscar Wilde, *The Importance of Being Earnest*

1897 England: H. G. Wells, *The Invisible Man*

England: Irish-born playwright George Bernard Shaw, *Candida*

Ireland: Bram Stoker, *Dracula*

1898 France: Polish-born physicist Marie Curie discovers radium

1900 Austria: Sigmund Freud, *The Interpretation of Dreams*

China: Boxer Rebellion against foreign influence

1901 Russia: Anton Chekhov, *The Three Sisters*

1903 Orville and Wilbur Wright make first successful flight in motorized airplane

First World Series played

Henry James, *The Ambassadors*

Jack London, *The Call of the Wild*

1906 Charles Ives composes "The Unanswered Question"

First musical radio program broadcast in U.S.

1907 Mother's Day first celebrated

Commercial plastic produced

1908 Jack London, "To Build a Fire"

1909 First animated cartoon, *Gertie the Dinosaur,* produced

Explorers Robert Peary and Matthew Henson are first to reach North Pole

Frank Lloyd Wright designs Robie House in Chicago

1910 Edwin Arlington Robinson, "Miniver Cheevy"

Halley's Comet does not destroy the earth as many people had expected

U.S. population: 92 million

1903 Beginning of Russo-Japanese War

1905 Germany: Physicist Albert Einstein proposes special theory of relativity and equation $E=mc^2$

1906 John Galsworthy begins *The Forsyte Saga*

1907 France: Pablo Picasso paints *Les Demoiselles d'Avignon,* beginning of Cubism

1908 France: Marcel Proust begins *Remembrance of Things Past*

1910 China: Slavery abolished

Russia: Composer Igor Stravinsky completes ballet *The Firebird*

MATTHEW HENSON

FICTION

Bret Harte   *1836–1902*

Bret Harte was born an Easterner, yet in a handful of stories, he captured much of the humor and romance that make up our myth of the American West. Although his finest stories were written during the 1860s, Harte stands as the first writer of the local color movement that continued until approximately the turn of the century.

Harte was born in Albany, New York, but he ventured west in 1854, when he was only eighteen. In California he tried prospecting, rode "shotgun" on a stagecoach, and then found work in journalism, first as a typesetter, then as an editor, and finally as a writer.

In the 1850s California was a booming, turbulent, and colorful frontier. The discovery of gold in 1848 had drawn prospectors and adventurers from all over the United States and the rest of the world. Mining towns had sprung up; small towns had turned into cities; fortunes had been made and lost; and people from all walks of life had been thrown together in rough, sometimes violent circumstances. History was being made, and a whole new way of life was being forged. The colorful incidents of western life and vivid anecdotes of "old-timers" fired the imagination of Bret Harte, who began to turn this material into fiction.

While serving as editor of the *Overland Monthly,* a literary magazine, Harte wrote a story that made him famous across the land, "The Luck of Roaring Camp" (1868). Soon after came "The Outcasts of Poker Flat." These stories were spectacularly successful both here and in England, among readers eager for descriptions of California and the Wild West. As a result, the prestigious Boston literary magazine the *Atlantic Monthly* offered Harte a special contract for any twelve selections he would like to contribute. The return east was a disappointment, however: Harte's later stories did not match the early ones in quality and were less successful with readers. Harte spent most of his remaining years abroad, in Germany, Scotland, and England, continuing to write and working as a diplomat.

Yet in those early stories, particularly in "The Outcasts of Poker Flat," Harte painted a romantic portrait of the West that has endured. The local color of the West, its particular time and place, are described as well as in many of Mark Twain's sketches. Characters like John Oakhurst, the gambler with nerves of steel, have become fixtures in America's collective imagination.

Main street in a western town, c. 1870.

Bret Harte

The Outcasts of Poker Flat

As Mr. John Oakhurst, gambler, stepped into the main street of Poker Flat on the morning of the twenty-third of November, 1850, he was conscious of a change in its moral atmosphere from the preceding night. Two or three men, conversing earnestly together, ceased as he approached, and exchanged significant glances. There was a Sabbath lull in the air, which, in a settlement unused to Sabbath influences, looked ominous.

Mr. Oakhurst's calm, handsome face betrayed small concern of these indications. Whether he was conscious of any predisposing cause, was another question. "I reckon they're after somebody," he reflected; "likely it's me." He returned to his pocket the handkerchief with which he had been whipping away the red dust of Poker Flat from his neat boots, and

quietly discharged his mind of any further conjecture.

In point of fact, Poker Flat was "after somebody." It had lately suffered the loss of several thousand dollars, two valuable horses, and a prominent citizen. It was experiencing a spasm of virtuous reaction, quite as lawless and ungovernable as any of the acts that had provoked it. A secret committee[1] had determined to rid the town of all improper persons. This was done permanently in regard of two men who were then hanging from the boughs of a sycamore in the gulch, and temporarily in the banishment of certain other objectionable char-

---

1. **secret committee:** vigilance committee, a group of citizens that bands together to punish criminals when usual law enforcement agencies are lacking.

acters. I regret to say that some of these were ladies. It is but due to the sex, however, to state that their impropriety was professional, and it was only in such easily established standards of evil that Poker Flat ventured to sit in judgment.

Mr. Oakhurst was right in supposing that he was included in this category. A few of the committee had urged hanging him as a possible example, and a sure method of reimbursing themselves from his pockets of the sums he had won from them. "It's agin[2] justice," said Jim Wheeler, "to let this yer young man from Roaring Camp—an entire stranger—carry away our money." But a crude sentiment of equity residing in the breasts of those who had been fortunate enough to win from Mr. Oakhurst, overruled this narrower local prejudice.

Mr. Oakhurst received his sentence with philosophic calmness, none the less coolly that he was aware of the hesitation of his judges. He was too much of a gambler not to accept Fate. With him life was at best an uncertain game, and he recognized the usual percentage in favor of the dealer.

A body of armed men accompanied the deported wickedness of Poker Flat to the outskirts of the settlement. Besides Mr. Oakhurst, who was known to be a coolly desperate man, and for whose intimidation the armed escort was intended, the expatriated party consisted of a young woman familiarly known as "The Duchess"; another, who had gained the infelicitous title of "Mother Shipton";[3] and "Uncle Billy," a suspected sluice-robber[4] and confirmed drunkard. The cavalcade provoked no comments from the spectators, nor was any word uttered by the escort. Only when the gulch which marked the uttermost limit of Poker Flat was reached, the leader spoke briefly and to the point. The exiles were forbidden to return at the peril of their lives.

As the escort disappeared, their pent-up feelings found vent in a few hysterical tears from the Duchess, some bad language from Mother Shipton, and a Parthian[5] volley of expletives from Uncle Billy. The philosophic Oakhurst alone remained silent. He listened calmly to Mother Shipton's desire to cut somebody's heart out, to the repeated statements of the Duchess that she would die in the road, and to the alarming oaths that seemed to be bumped out of Uncle Billy as he rode forward. With the easy good humor characteristic of his class, he insisted upon exchanging his own riding horse, "Five Spot," for the sorry mule which the Duchess rode. But even this act did not draw the party into any closer sympathy. The young woman readjusted her somewhat draggled plumes with a feeble, faded coquetry; Mother Shipton eyed the possessor of "Five Spot" with malevolence, and Uncle Billy included the whole party in one sweeping anathema.

The road to Sandy Bar—a camp that not having as yet experienced the regenerating influences of Poker Flat, consequently seemed to offer some invitation to the emigrants—lay over a steep mountain range. It was distant a day's severe journey. In that advanced season, the party soon passed out of the moist, temperate regions of the foothills, into the dry, cold, bracing air of the Sierras.[6] The trail was narrow and difficult. At noon the Duchess, rolling out of her saddle upon the ground, declared her intention of going no further, and the party halted.

The spot was singularly wild and impressive. A wooded amphitheater, surrounded on three sides by precipitous cliffs of naked granite, sloped gently toward the crest of another precipice that overlooked the valley. It was undoubtedly the most suitable spot for a camp, had camping been advisable. But Mr. Oakhurst knew that scarcely half the journey to Sandy

---

2. **agin** [ə gin']: dialect variation of *against.*
3. **"Mother Shipton"**: English woman accused of witchcraft (1488–1560).
4. **sluice** [sloōs]-**robber:** one who steals from sluices. A sluice is a long sloping trough used for washing gold ore.

5. **Parthian** [pär'thē ən]: referring to an ancient people of southwest Asia, whose cavalry was noted for shooting at an enemy while retreating or pretending to retreat.
6. **Sierras** [sē er'əz]: Sierra Nevada mountain range in eastern California.

Bar was accomplished, and the party were not equipped or provisioned for delay. This fact he pointed out to his companions curtly, with a philosophic commentary on the folly of "throwing up their hand before the game was played out." But they were furnished with liquor, which in this emergency stood them in place of food, fuel, rest and prescience. In spite of his remonstrances, it was not long before they were more or less under its influence. Uncle Billy passed rapidly from a bellicose state into one of stupor, the Duchess became maudlin, and Mother Shipton snored. Mr. Oakhurst alone remained erect, leaning against a rock, calmly surveying them.

Mr. Oakhurst did not drink. It interfered with a profession which required coolness, impassiveness and presence of mind, and, in his own language, he "couldn't afford it." As he gazed at his recumbent fellow exiles, the loneliness begotten of his pariah trade,[7] his habits of life, his very vices, for the first time seriously oppressed him. He bestirred himself in dusting his black clothes, washing his hands and face, and other acts characteristic of his studiously neat habits, and for a moment forgot his annoyance. The thought of deserting his weaker and more pitiable companions never perhaps occurred to him. Yet he could not help feeling the want of that excitement, which singularly enough was most conducive to that calm equanimity for which he was notorious. He looked at the gloomy walls that rose a thousand feet sheer above the circling pines around him; at the sky, ominously clouded; at the valley below, already deepening into shadow. And doing so, suddenly he heard his own name called.

A horseman slowly ascended the trail. In the fresh, open face of the newcomer, Mr. Oakhurst recognized Tom Simson, otherwise known as "The Innocent" of Sandy Bar. He had met him some months before over a "little game," and had, with perfect equanimity, won

the entire fortune—amounting to some forty dollars—of that guileless youth. After the game was finished, Mr. Oakhurst drew the youthful speculator behind the door and thus addressed him: "Tommy, you're a good little man, but you can't gamble worth a cent. Don't try it over again." He then handed him his money back, pushed him gently from the room, and so made a devoted slave of Tom Simson.

There was a remembrance of this in his boyish and enthusiastic greeting of Mr. Oakhurst. He had started, he said, to go to Poker Flat to seek his fortune. "Alone?" No, not exactly alone; in fact—a giggle—he had run away with Piney Woods. Didn't Mr. Oakhurst remember Piney? She that used to wait on the table at the Temperance House? They had been engaged a long time, but old Jake Woods had objected, and so they had run away, and were going to Poker Flat to be married, and here they were. And they were tired out, and how lucky it was they had found a place to camp and company. All this the Innocent delivered rapidly, while Piney—a stout, comely damsel of fifteen—emerged from behind the pine tree, where she had been blushing unseen, and rode to the side of her lover.

Mr. Oakhurst seldom troubled himself with sentiment. Still less with propriety. But he had a vague idea that the situation was not felicitous. He retained, however, his presence of mind sufficiently to kick Uncle Billy, who was about to say something, and Uncle Billy was sober enough to recognize in Mr. Oakhurst's kick a superior power that would not bear trifling. He then endeavored to dissuade Tom Simson from delaying further, but in vain. He even pointed out the fact that there was no provision nor means of making a camp. But, unluckily, the Innocent met this objection by assuring the party that he was provided with an extra mule loaded with provisions, and by the discovery of a rude attempt at a log house near the trail. "Piney can stay with Mrs. Oakhurst," said the Innocent, pointing to the Duchess, "and I can shift for myself."

Nothing but Mr. Oakhurst's admonishing

---

7. **pariah** [pə riˈə]**trade:** despicable occupation. A pariah is one who is despised; an outcast.

foot saved Uncle Billy from bursting into a roar of laughter. As it was, he felt compelled to retire up the cañon[8] until he could recover his gravity. There he confided the joke to the tall pine trees, with many slaps of his leg, contortions of his face, and the usual profanity. But when he returned to the party, he found them seated by a fire—for the air had grown strangely chill and the sky overcast—in apparently amicable conversation. Piney was actually talking in an impulsive, girlish fashion to the Duchess, who was listening with an interest and animation she had not shown for many days. The Innocent was holding forth, apparently with equal effect, to Mr. Oakhurst and Mother Shipton, who was actually relaxing into amiability. "Is this yer a d——d picnic?" said Uncle Billy, with inward scorn, as he surveyed the sylvan[9] group, the glancing firelight and the tethered animals in the foreground. Suddenly an idea mingled with the alcoholic fumes that disturbed his brain. It was apparently of a jocular nature, for he felt impelled to slap his leg again and cram his fist into his mouth.

As the shadows crept slowly up the mountain, a slight breeze rocked the tops of the pine trees, and moaned through their long and gloomy aisles. The ruined cabin, patched and covered with pine boughs, was set apart for the ladies. As the lovers parted, they unaffectedly exchanged a parting kiss, so honest and sincere that it might have been heard above the swaying pines. The frail Duchess and the malevolent Mother Shipton were probably too stunned to remark upon this last evidence of simplicity, and so turned without a word to the hut. The fire was replenished, the men lay down before the door, and in a few minutes were asleep.

Mr. Oakhurst was a light sleeper. Toward morning he awoke benumbed and cold. As he stirred the dying fire, the wind, which was now blowing strongly, brought to his cheek that which caused the blood to leave it—snow!

He started to his feet with the intention of awakening the sleepers, for there was no time to lose. But turning to where Uncle Billy had been lying he found him gone. A suspicion leaped to his brain and a curse to his lips. He ran to the spot where the mules had been tethered; they were no longer there. The tracks were already rapidly disappearing in the snow.

The momentary excitement brought Mr. Oakhurst back to the fire with his usual calm. He did not waken the sleepers. The Innocent slumbered peacefully, with a smile on his good-humored, freckled face; the virgin Piney slept beside her frailer sisters as sweetly as though attended by celestial guardians, and Mr. Oakhurst, drawing his blanket over his shoulders, stroked his mustachios and waited for the dawn. It came slowly in a whirling mist of snowflakes that dazzled and confused the eye. What could be seen of the landscape appeared magically changed. He looked over the valley, and summed up the present and future in two words—"Snowed in!"

A careful inventory of the provisions, which, fortunately for the party, had been stored within the hut, and so escaped the felonious fingers of Uncle Billy, disclosed the fact that with care and prudence they might last ten days longer. "That is," said Mr. Oakhurst, *sotto voce*[10] to The Innocent, "if you're willing to board us. If you aint—and perhaps you'd better not—you can wait till Uncle Billy gets back with provisions." For some occult reason, Mr. Oakhurst could not bring himself to disclose Uncle Billy's rascality, and so offered the hypothesis that he had wandered from the camp and had accidentally stampeded the animals. He dropped a warning to the Duchess and Mother Shipton, who of course knew the facts of their associate's defection. "They'll find out the truth about us *all,* when they find out anything," he added, significantly, "and there's no good frightening them now."

Tom Simson not only put all his worldly

---

8. **cañon** [kan′yən]: variant of *canyon*.
9. **sylvan** [sil′vən]: characteristic of the woods.

10. *sotto voce* [sot′ō vō′chē]: Italian for "under the voice"; in an undertone.

store at the disposal of Mr. Oakhurst, but seemed to enjoy the prospect of their enforced seclusion. "We'll have a good camp for a week, and then the snow'll melt, and we'll all go back together." The cheerful gaiety of the young man and Mr. Oakhurst's calm infected the others. The Innocent, with the aid of pine boughs, extemporized a thatch for the roofless cabin, and the Duchess directed Piney in the rearrangement of the interior with a taste and tact that opened the blue eyes of that provincial maiden to their fullest extent. "I reckon now you're used to fine things at Poker Flat," said Piney. The Duchess turned away sharply to conceal something that reddened her cheeks through its professional tint, and Mother Shipton requested Piney not to "chatter." But when Mr. Oakhurst returned from a weary search for the trail, he heard the sound of happy laughter echoed from the rocks. He stopped in some alarm, and his thoughts first naturally reverted to the whiskey—which he had prudently cachéd.[11] "And yet it don't somehow sound like whiskey," said the gambler. It was not until he caught sight of the blazing fire through the still blinding storm, and the group around it, that he settled to the conviction that it was "square fun."

Whether Mr. Oakhurst had cachéd his cards with the whiskey as something debarred the free access of the community, I cannot say. It was certain that, in Mother Shipton's words, he "didn't say cards once" during that evening. Haply the time was beguiled by an accordion, produced somewhat ostentatiously by Tom Simson, from his pack. Notwithstanding some difficulties attending the manipulation of this instrument, Piney Woods managed to pluck several reluctant melodies from its keys, to an accompaniment by the Innocent on a pair of bone castanets. But the crowning festivity of the evening was reached in a rude camp meeting hymn, which the lovers, joining hands, sang with great earnestness and vociferation. I fear that a certain defiant tone and Covenanter's

swing[12] to its chorus, rather than any devotional quality, caused it to speedily infect the others, who at last joined in the refrain:

I'm proud to live in the service of the Lord,
And I'm bound to die in His army.[13]

The pines rocked, the storm eddied and whirled above the miserable group, and the flames of their altar leaped heavenward, as if in token of the vow.

At midnight the storm abated, the rolling clouds parted, and the stars glittered keenly above the sleeping camp. Mr. Oakhurst, whose professional habits had enabled him to live on the smallest possible amount of sleep, in dividing the watch with Tom Simson, somehow managed to take upon himself the greater part of that duty. He excused himself to the Innocent, by saying that he had "often been a week without sleep." "Doing what?" asked Tom. "Poker!" replied Oakhurst, sententiously; "when a man gets a streak of luck, he don't get tired. The luck gives in first. Luck," continued the gambler, reflectively, "is a mighty queer thing. All you know about it for certain is that it's bound to change. And it's finding out when it's going to change that makes you. We've had a streak of bad luck since we left Poker Flat— you come along and slap you get into it, too. If you can hold your cards right along you're all right. For," added the gambler, with cheerful irrelevance,

I'm proud to live in the service of the Lord,
And I'm bound to die in His army.

The third day came, and the sun, looking through the white-curtained valley, saw the outcasts divide their slowly decreasing store of provisions for the morning meal. It was one of the peculiarities of that mountain climate that its rays diffused a kindly warmth over the wintry landscape, as if in regretful commiseration

---

11. *cachéd* [ka shād′]: modified French for "hidden."

12. **Covenanter's** [kuv′ə nan′tərz] **swing:** implying a lively rhythm. Covenanters were Scottish Presbyterians who demanded separation from the Church of England.
13. **"I'm . . . army":** The lines are from "Service of the Lord," an early American spiritual.

of the past. But it revealed drift on drift of snow, piled high around the hut; a hopeless, uncharted, trackless sea of white lying below the rocky shores to which the castaways still clung. Through the marvelously clear air, the smoke of the pastoral village of Poker Flat rose miles away. Mother Shipton saw it, and from a remote pinnacle of her rocky fastness, hurled in that direction a final malediction. It was her last vituperative attempt, and perhaps for that reason was invested with a certain degree of sublimity. It did her good, she privately informed the Duchess. "Just you go out there and cuss, and see." She then set herself to the task of amusing "the child," as she and the Duchess were pleased to call Piney. Piney was no chicken, but it was a soothing and ingenious theory of the pair to thus account for the fact that she didn't swear and wasn't improper.

When night crept up again through the gorges, the reedy notes of the accordion rose and fell in fitful spasms and long-drawn gasps by the flickering campfire. But music failed to fill entirely the aching void left by insufficient food, and a new diversion was proposed by Piney —storytelling. Neither Mr. Oakhurst nor his female companions caring to relate their personal experiences, this plan would have failed, too, but for the Innocent. Some months before he had chanced upon a stray copy of Mr. Pope's[14] ingenious translation of the *Iliad*.[15] He now proposed to narrate the principal incidents of that poem—having thoroughly mastered the argument and fairly forgotten the words—in the current vernacular of Sandy Bar. And so for the rest of that night the Homeric demigods again walked the earth. Trojan bully and wily Greek wrestled in the winds, and the great pines in the cañon seemed to bow to the wrath of the son of Peleus.[16] Mr. Oakhurst lis-

tened with quiet satisfaction. Most especially was he interested in the fate of "Ash-heels,"[17] as the Innocent persisted in denominating the "swift-footed Achilles."

So with small food and much of Homer and the accordion, a week passed over the heads of the outcasts. The sun again forsook them, and again from leaden skies the snowflakes were sifted over the land. Day by day closer around them drew the snowy circle, until at last they looked from their prison over drifted walls of dazzling white, that towered twenty feet above their heads. It became more and more difficult to replenish their fires, even from the fallen trees beside them, now half-hidden in the drifts. And yet no one complained. The lovers turned from the dreary prospect and looked into each other's eyes, and were happy. Mr. Oakhurst settled himself coolly to the losing game before him. The Duchess, more cheerful than she had been, assumed the care of Piney. Only Mother Shipton—once the strongest of the party—seemed to sicken and fade. At midnight on the tenth day she called Oakhurst to her side. "I'm going," she said, in a voice of querulous weakness, "but don't say anything about it. Don't waken the kids. Take the bundle from under my head and open it." Mr. Oakhurst did so. It contained Mother Shipton's rations for the last week, untouched. "Give 'em to the child," she said, pointing to the sleeping Piney. "You've starved yourself," said the gambler. "That's what they call it," said the woman querulously, as she lay down again, and turning her face to the wall, passed quietly away.

The accordion and the bones were put aside that day, and Homer was forgotten. When the body of Mother Shipton had been committed to the snow, Mr. Oakhurst took the Innocent aside, and showed him a pair of snowshoes, which he had fashioned from the old pack saddle. "There's one chance in a hundred to save her yet," he said, pointing to Piney; "but it's there," he added, pointing toward

---

14. **Mr. Pope's:** referring to Alexander Pope (1688–1744), an English poet.
15. *Iliad* [il′ē əd]: Greek epic poem by Homer, describing the war between the Trojans, natives of ancient Troy, and the Greeks.
16. **son of Peleus** [pēl′yōōs]: Achilles [ə kil′ēz], Greek warrior hero in the Trojan War.

17. **"Ash-heels":** mispronunciation of *Achilles*, emphasizing his one vulnerable spot, his heel.

Poker Flat. "If you can reach there in two days she's safe." "And you?" asked Tom Simson. "I'll stay here," was the curt reply.

The lovers parted with a long embrace. "You are not going, too," said the Duchess, as she saw Mr. Oakhurst apparently waiting to accompany him. "As far as the cañon," he replied. He turned suddenly, and kissed the Duchess, leaving her pallid face aflame, and her trembling limbs rigid with amazement.

Night came, but not Mr. Oakhurst. It brought the storm again and the whirling snow. Then the Duchess, feeding the fire, found that some one had quietly piled beside the hut enough fuel to last a few days longer. The tears rose to her eyes, but she hid them from Piney.

The women slept but little. In the morning, looking into each other's faces, they read their fate. Neither spoke; but Piney, accepting the position of the stronger, drew near and placed her arm around the Duchess's waist. They kept this attitude for the rest of the day. That night the storm reached its greatest fury, and rending asunder the protecting pines, invaded the very hut.

Toward morning they found themselves unable to feed the fire, which gradually died away. As the embers slowly blackened, the Duchess crept closer to Piney, and broke the silence of many hours: "Piney, can you pray?" "No, dear," said Piney, simply. The Duchess, without knowing exactly why, felt relieved, and putting her head upon Piney's shoulder, spoke no more. And so reclining, the younger and purer pillowing the head of her soiled sister upon her virgin breast, they fell asleep.

The wind lulled as if it feared to waken them. Feathery drifts of snow, shaken from the long pine boughs, flew like white-winged birds, and settled about them as they slept. The moon through the rifted clouds looked down upon what had been the camp. But all human stain, all trace of earthly travail, was hidden beneath the spotless mantle mercifully flung from above.

They slept all that day and the next, nor did they waken when voices and footsteps broke the silence of the camp. And when pitying fingers brushed the snow from their wan faces, you could scarcely have told from the equal peace that dwelt upon them, which was she that had sinned. Even the Law of Poker Flat recognized this, and turned away, leaving them still locked in each other's arms.

But at the head of the gulch, on one of the largest pine trees, they found the deuce of clubs[18] pinned to the bark with a bowie knife. It bore the following, written in pencil, in a firm hand:

---

†

BENEATH THIS TREE

LIES THE BODY

OF

JOHN OAKHURST,

WHO STRUCK A STREAK OF BAD LUCK

ON THE 23D OF NOVEMBER, 1850,

AND

HANDED IN HIS CHECKS

ON THE 7TH DECEMBER, 1850

†

And pulseless and cold, with a Derringer[19] by his side and a bullet in his heart, though still calm as in life, beneath the snow, lay he who was at once the strongest and yet the weakest of the outcasts of Poker Flat.

---

18. **deuce of clubs:** two of clubs, considered to have the lowest value in a deck of cards.
19. **Derringer** [der′in jər]: small short-barreled pistol, named after Henry Deringer (1806–1868), an American gunsmith.

Recalling

1. As the story opens, what has the secret committee of Poker Flat decided to do? Who is directly affected by the committee's decision?
2. What is John Oakhurst's "profession"? How does he receive his "sentence," according to the fifth paragraph?
3. Why are Tom Simson and Piney Woods going to Poker Flat? What natural event puts them and the outcasts in danger?
4. What does Mother Shipton do to help Piney? Why does Tom leave the group?
5. When the rescue party arrives, what do they find?

Interpreting

6. Briefly describe John Oakhurst and his attitude toward life. Explain how his final actions relate to his philosophy of life.
7. What are Tom and Piney like? What effect do they have on Mother Shipton and on Oakhurst?
8. What forces do all the characters have to face? How do all of them except Uncle Billy behave in this crisis?

Extending

9. Which elements of this story are common elements of western fiction that you have encountered in films, TV shows, or other works about the West?

LITERARY FOCUS

The Short Story

A **short story** is a brief prose fiction, usually one that can be read in a single sitting. It generally contains the six major elements of fiction—characterization, setting, theme, plot, point of view, and style.

Characterization refers to the way an author develops the personalities of the characters. In a short story there is usually only one character whose personality is fully developed; there are rarely more than two or three. The main character is often called the **protagonist.**

The **setting** is the time and place in which the events occur. Most short stories have only one setting that is described in great detail and rarely more than two or three settings.

The **theme** is the main idea that the writer communicates to the reader. In a short story there is usually one theme.

The **plot** is the series of events that takes us from a beginning to an end. Each event in the plot is related to the **conflict,** the struggle that the main character undergoes. Traditionally, the short story opens with **exposition,** background information vital to our understanding of what will follow. The events in the story follow a **rising action** until they reach a **climax**—the point of highest dramatic tension or excitement. After the climax a **falling action** leads to a **resolution**—a conclusion in which the conflict is resolved and the "knot" of the plot is untied. The resolution of the story is sometimes called the **denouement** (dā'noo̅ män'), a French word meaning "untying."

Thinking About the Short Story

■ Trace the structure of "The Outcasts of Poker Flat." First identify the exposition, the events that make up the rising action, and the climax. Then identify the events that make up the falling action and the resolution. What is the chief conflict in the story?

Flat and Round Characters

The English novelist E. M. Forster described fictional characters as either flat or round. A **flat character** is built around a single trait, quality, or idea. This type of character is immediately recognizable and never changes or surprises us. Flat characters include **stereotypes,** or **stock characters,** such as the noble hero, the innocent young lover, the fiendish villain, and the faithful friend. Stories of hard-boiled detectives and dashing secret agents involve flat characters; they may of course be wonderfully entertaining stories, but they are still predictable.

A round character, on the other hand, satisfies our sense of the actual richness and complexity of human nature. **Round characters** are developed by the author; they change and grow. They often exhibit contradictory traits, and, like real human beings, frequently surprise us. The greatest characters in literature are those that are most "round."

"The Outcasts of Poker Flat" is an example of an effective story with several flat characters. For example, Uncle Billy is dishonest, devious, and selfish throughout. Some of the characters are "rounder" than Uncle Billy, but all the characters are clearly defined types.

Thinking About Flat and Round Characters

1. In what way are Tom and Piney flat characters?
2. Mother Shipton and the Duchess may be considered "rounder" because they begin with one set of traits and end with another. Describe the change in these two characters.
3. What seems contradictory in Oakhurst? Comment on the last sentence of the story.
4. Select one flat character and one round character from other stories you have read. Describe the characters, and tell why they are flat or round.

VOCABULARY

Regionalisms

A **regionalism** is a word or phrase peculiar to a particular region of the country. Every region invents its own words and phrases, and sometimes these new expressions are so unusual that they can be understood only by the people who live in the region.

A writer will use regionalisms to make his characters' speech more vivid, more believable, and more closely tied to the time and place of the story. When Oakhurst, for example, reflects, "I reckon they're after somebody," we know from his expression that he is a man of the West.

Thinking About Regionalisms

1. Find another regionalism in "The Outcasts of Poker Flat."

2. Make a list of expressions that are part of the speech of your own region. Which ones do you think would not be easily understood by someone living somewhere else? Which ones do you think would be universally understood? Why?

COMPOSITION

Applying a Statement About Literature

The Regionalist Hamlin Garland said that local color in a story "means that it has such quality and background that it could not have been written in any other place" (see page 297). Write an essay applying this statement to "The Outcasts of Poker Flat." First cite the details of setting, or background, in the story. Then explain how this background is particularly fitting for these characters and, therefore, for the story. *For help with this assignment, refer to Lesson 9 in the Writing About Literature Handbook at the back of this book.*

Writing a Character Sketch

Write a short character sketch of a real or a fictional person. Begin by describing one or two traits of the person. Then illustrate the traits by showing the character in action, participating in an event or performing a specific action. Make the character as "round" as possible; that is, give the character enough qualities and complexity to make him or her genuinely human. Remember that round characters, like people, often experience many emotions.

Sarah Orne Jewett   *1849–1909*

Sarah Orne Jewett wrote compassionately and gracefully about the part of the world she knew best—her native New England. Jewett was born in the village of South Berwick, on the Maine coast. As a young girl she accompanied her father, a local doctor, on his visits to remote farms and small fishing towns. Her imagination was stirred by the life styles and personalities she encountered and by her father's anecdotes. Soon she set out to collect local legends, examine the family histories of nearby fishermen and farmers, and study their manners and speech.

At the age of fourteen, she started writing sketches with the material she had gathered. By the time she was twenty, her stories were polished enough for the pages of the *Atlantic Monthly,* America's most distinguished literary journal. *Deephaven* (1877), a collection of her tales and sketches, was the first of more than twenty works, including her masterpiece, *The Country of the Pointed Firs* (1896).

In her stories and novels Sarah Orne Jewett sought to preserve a way of life that was passing and a natural landscape that was changing. She reveals in "A White Heron" her extraordinary sensitivity to the natural world and her kinship with those who live close to it.

Sarah Orne Jewett

A White Heron

The woods were already filled with shadows one June evening, just before eight o'clock, though a bright sunset still glimmered faintly among the trunks of the trees. A little girl was driving home her cow, a plodding, dilatory, provoking creature in her behavior, but a valued companion for all that. They were going away from the western light, and striking deep into the dark woods, but their feet were familiar with the path, and it was no matter whether their eyes could see it or not.

There was hardly a night the summer through when the old cow could be found waiting at the pasture bars; on the contrary, it was her greatest pleasure to hide herself away among the high huckleberry bushes, and though she wore a loud bell she had made the discovery that if one stood perfectly still it would not ring. So Sylvia had to hunt for her until she found her, and call "Co'! Co'!" with never an answering "Moo," until her childish patience was quite spent. If the creature had not given good milk and plenty of it, the case would have seemed very different to her owners. Besides, Sylvia had all the time there was, and very little use to make of it. Sometimes in pleasant weather it was a consolation to look upon the cow's pranks as an intelligent attempt to play hide and seek, and as the child had no playmates she lent herself to this amusement with a good deal of zest. Though this chase had been so long that the wary animal herself had given an unusual signal of her where-abouts, Sylvia had only laughed when she came upon Mistress Moolly at the swampside, and urged her affectionately homeward with a twig of birch leaves. The old cow was not inclined to wander farther, she even turned in the right direction for once as they left the pasture, and stepped along the road at a good pace. She was quite ready to be milked now, and seldom stopped to browse. Sylvia wondered what her grandmother would say because they were so late. It was a great while since she had left home at half past five o'clock, but everybody knew the difficulty of making this errand a short one. Mrs. Tilley had chased the horned torment too many summer evenings herself to blame anyone else for lingering, and was only thankful as she waited that she had Sylvia, now-adays, to give such valuable assistance. The good woman suspected that Sylvia loitered oc-casionally on her own account; there never was such a child for straying about out-of-doors since the world was made! Everybody said that it was a good change for a little maid who had tried to grow for eight years in a crowded manufacturing town, but, as for Sylvia herself, it seemed as if she never had been alive at all before she came to live at the farm. She thought often with wistful compassion of a wretched dry geranium that belonged to a town neighbor.

" 'Afraid of folks,' " old Mrs. Tilley said to herself, with a smile, after she had made the unlikely choice of Sylvia from her daughter's houseful of children, and was returning to the farm. " 'Afraid of folks,' they said! I guess she won't be troubled no great with 'em up to the old place!" When they reached the door of the lonely house and stopped to unlock it, and the cat came to purr loudly, and rub against them, a deserted pussy, indeed, but fat with young robins, Sylvia whispered that this was a beau-tiful place to live in, and she never should wish to go home.

The companions followed the shady wood-road, the cow taking slow steps, and the child very fast ones. The cow stopped long at the brook to drink, as if the pasture were not half a swamp, and Sylvia stood still and waited, let-ting her bare feet cool themselves in the shoal water, while the great twilight moths struck softly against her. She waded on through the brook as the cow moved away, and listened to the thrushes with a heart that beat fast with pleasure. There was a stirring in the great boughs overhead. They were full of little birds and beasts that seemed to be wide awake, and going about their world, or else saying good-night to each other in sleepy twitters. Sylvia herself felt sleepy as she walked along. How-ever, it was not much farther to the house, and the air was soft and sweet. She was not often in the woods so late as this, and it made her feel as if she were a part of the gray shadows and the moving leaves. She was just thinking how long it seemed since she first came to the farm a year ago, and wondering if everything went on in the noisy town just the same as when she was there; the thought of the great red-faced boy who used to chase and frighten her made her hurry along the path to escape from the shadow of the trees.

Suddenly this little woods girl is horror stricken to hear a clear whistle not very far away. Not a bird's whistle, which would have a sort of friendliness, but a boy's whistle, deter-mined, and somewhat aggressive. Sylvia left the cow to whatever sad fate might await her, and stepped discreetly aside into the bushes, but she was just too late. The enemy had discov-ered her, and called out in a very cheerful and persuasive tone, "Halloa, little girl, how far is it to the road?" and trembling Sylvia answered almost inaudibly, "A good ways."

She did not dare to look boldly at the tall young man, who carried a gun over his shoul-der, but she came out of her bush and again followed the cow, while he walked alongside.

"I have been hunting for some birds," the stranger said kindly, "and I have lost my way, and need a friend very much. Don't be afraid," he added gallantly. "Speak up and tell me what your name is, and whether you think I can spend the night at your house, and go out gunning early in the morning."

Sylvia was more alarmed than before. Would not her grandmother consider her much to blame? But who could have foreseen such an accident as this? It did not appear to be her fault, and she hung her head as if the stem of it were broken, but managed to answer "Sylvy," with much effort when her companion again asked her name.

Mrs. Tilley was standing in the doorway when the trio came into view. The cow gave a loud moo by way of explanation.

"Yes, you'd better speak up for yourself, you old trial! Where'd she tuck herself away this time, Sylvy?" Sylvia kept an awed silence; she knew by instinct that her grandmother did not comprehend the gravity of the situation. She must be mistaking the stranger for one of the farmer lads of the region.

The young man stood his gun beside the door, and dropped a heavy game bag beside it; then he bade Mrs. Tilley good evening, and repeated his wayfarer's story, and asked if he could have a night's lodging.

"Put me anywhere you like," he said. "I must be off early in the morning, before day; but I am very hungry, indeed. You can give me some milk at any rate, that's plain."

"Dear sakes, yes," responded the hostess,

whose long slumbering hospitality seemed to be easily awakened. "You might fare better if you went out on the main road a mile or so, but you're welcome to what we've got. I'll milk right off, and you make yourself at home. You can sleep on husks or feathers," she proffered graciously. "I raised them all myself. There's good pasturing for geese just below here towards the ma'sh. Now step round and set a plate for the gentleman, Sylvy!" And Sylvia promptly stepped. She was glad to have something to do, and she was hungry herself.

It was a surprise to find so clean and comfortable a little dwelling in this New England wilderness. The young man had known the horrors of its most primitive housekeeping, and the dreary squalor of that level of society which does not rebel at the companionship of hens. This was the best thrift of an old-fashioned farmstead, though on such a small scale that it seemed like a hermitage.[1] He listened eagerly to the old woman's quaint talk, he watched Sylvia's pale face and shining gray eyes with ever growing enthusiasm, and insisted that this was the best supper he had eaten for a month; then, afterward, the new-made friends sat down in the doorway together while the moon came up.

Soon it would be berry time, and Sylvia was a great help at picking. The cow was a good milker, though a plaguy[2] thing to keep track of, the hostess gossiped frankly, adding presently that she had buried four children, so that Sylvia's mother, and a son (who might be dead) in California were all the children she had left. "Dan, my boy, was a great hand to go gunning," she explained sadly. "I never wanted for pa'tridges or gray squer'ls while he was to home. He's been a great wand'rer, I expect, and he's no hand to write letters. There, I don't blame him, I'd ha' seen the world myself if it had been so I could.

"Sylvia takes after him," the grandmother continued affectionately, after a minute's pause. "There ain't a foot o' ground she don't know her way over, and the wild creatures counts her one o' themselves. Squer'ls she'll tame to come an' feed right out o' her hands, and all sorts o' birds. Last winter she got the jaybirds to bangeing[3] here, and I believe she'd 'a' scanted herself of her own meals to have plenty to throw out amongst 'em, if I hadn't kep' watch. Anything but crows, I tell her, I'm willin' to help support—though Dan he went an' tamed one o' them that did seem to have reason same as folks. It was round here a good spell after he went away. Dan an' his father they didn't hitch[4]—but he never held up his head ag'in after Dan had dared him an' gone off."

The guest did not notice this hint of family sorrows in his eager interest in something else.

"So Sylvy knows all about birds, does she?" he exclaimed, as he looked round at the little girl who sat, very demure but increasingly sleepy, in the moonlight. "I am making a collection of birds myself. I have been at it ever since I was a boy." (Mrs. Tilley smiled.) "There are two or three very rare ones I have been hunting for these five years. I mean to get them on my own ground if they can be found."

"Do you cage 'em up?" asked Mrs. Tilley doubtfully, in response to this enthusiastic announcement.

"Oh, no, they're stuffed and preserved, dozens and dozens of them," said the ornithologist,[5] "and I have shot or snared every one myself. I caught a glimpse of a white heron three miles from here on Saturday, and I have followed it in this direction. They have never been found in this district at all. The little white heron, it is," and he turned again to look at Sylvia with the hope of discovering that the rare bird was one of her acquaintances.

But Sylvia was watching a hoptoad in the narrow footpath.

"You would know the heron if you saw it," the stranger continued eagerly. "A queer tall

---

1. **hermitage:** home of a hermit, someone who lives alone in an isolated place, often for religious reasons.
2. **plaguy** [plā′gē]: annoying.
3. **bangeing** [ban′jing]: lounging about.
4. **hitch:** get along well with each other.
5. **ornithologist** [ôr′nə thol′ə jist]: expert on birds.

white bird with soft feathers and long thin legs. And it would have a nest perhaps in the top of a high tree, made of sticks, something like a hawk's nest.''

Sylvia's heart gave a wild beat; she knew that strange white bird, and had once stolen softly near where it stood in some bright green swamp grass, away over at the other side of the woods. There was an open place where the sunshine always seemed strangely yellow and hot, where tall, nodding rushes grew, and her grandmother had warned her that she might sink in the soft black mud underneath and never be heard of more. Not far beyond were the salt marshes and beyond those was the sea, the sea which Sylvia wondered and dreamed about, but never had looked upon, though its great voice could often be heard above the noise of the woods on stormy nights.

"I can't think of anything I should like so much as to find that heron's nest," the handsome stranger was saying. "I would give ten dollars to anybody who could show it to me," he added desperately, "and I mean to spend my whole vacation hunting for it if need be. Perhaps it was only migrating, or had been chased out of its own region by some bird of prey."

Mrs. Tilley gave amazed attention to all this, but Sylvia still watched the toad, not divining, as she might have done at some calmer time, that the creature wished to get to its hole under the doorstep, and was much hindered by the unusual spectators at that hour of the evening. No amount of thought, that night, could decide how many wished-for treasures the ten dollars, so lightly spoken of, would buy.

The next day the young sportsman hovered about the woods, and Sylvia kept him company, having lost her first fear of the friendly lad, who proved to be most kind and sympathetic. He told her many things about the birds and what they knew and where they lived and what they did with themselves. And he gave her a jackknife, which she thought as great a treasure as if she were a desert islander. All day long he did not once make her troubled or

afraid except when he brought down some unsuspecting singing creature from its bough. Sylvia would have liked him vastly better without his gun; she could not understand why he killed the very birds he seemed to like so much. But as the day waned, Sylvia still watched the young man with loving admiration. She had never seen anybody so charming and delightful; the woman's heart, asleep in the child, was vaguely thrilled by a dream of love. Some premonition of that great power stirred and swayed these young foresters who traversed the solemn woodlands with soft-footed silent care. They stopped to listen to a bird's song; they pressed forward again eagerly, parting the branches, speaking to each other rarely and in whispers; the young man going first and Sylvia following, fascinated, a few steps behind, with her gray eyes dark with excitement.

She grieved because the longed-for white heron was elusive, but she did not lead the guest, she only followed, and there was no such thing as speaking first. The sound of her own unquestioned voice would have terrified her—it was hard enough to answer yes or no when there was need of that. At last evening began to fall, and they drove the cow home together, and Sylvia smiled with pleasure when they came to the place where she heard the whistle and was afraid only the night before.

Half a mile from home, at the farther edge of the woods, where the land was highest, a great pine tree stood, the last of its generation. Whether it was left for a boundary mark, or for what reason, no one could say; the woodchoppers who had felled its mates were dead and gone long ago, and a whole forest of sturdy trees, pines and oaks and maples, had grown again. But the stately head of this old pine towered above them all and made a landmark for sea and shore miles and miles away. Sylvia knew it well. She had always believed that whoever climbed to the top of it could see the ocean; and the little girl had often laid her hand on the great rough trunk and looked up wistfully at those dark boughs that the wind always stirred, no matter how hot and still the air might be below. Now she thought of the tree with a new excitement, for why, if one climbed it at break of day, could not one see all the world, and easily discover whence the white heron flew, and mark the place, and find the hidden nest?

What a spirit of adventure, what wild ambition! What fancied triumph and delight and glory for the later morning when she could make known the secret! It was almost too real and too great for the childish heart to bear.

All night the door of the little house stood open, and the whippoorwills came and sang upon the very step. The young sportsman and his old hostess were sound asleep, but Sylvia's great design kept her broad awake and watching. She forgot to think of sleep. The short summer night seemed as long as the winter darkness, and at last when the whippoorwills ceased, and she was afraid the morning would after all come too soon, she stole out of the house and followed the pasture path through the woods, hastening toward the open ground beyond, listening with a sense of comfort and companionship to the drowsy twitter of a half-awakened bird, whose perch she had jarred in passing. Alas, if the great wave of human interest which flooded for the first time this dull little life should sweep away the satisfactions of an existence heart to heart with nature and the dumb[6] life of the forest!

There was the huge tree asleep yet in the paling moonlight, and small and hopeful Sylvia began with utmost bravery to mount to the top of it, with tingling, eager blood coursing the channels of her whole frame, with her bare feet and fingers, that pinched and held like bird's claws to the monstrous ladder reaching up, up, almost to the sky itself. First she must mount the white oak tree that grew alongside, where she was almost lost among the dark branches and the green leaves heavy and wet with dew; a bird fluttered off its nest, and a red squirrel ran to and fro and scolded pettishly at the harmless housebreaker. Sylvia felt her way easily. She had often climbed there,

and knew that higher still one of the oak's upper branches chafed against the pine trunk, just where its lower boughs were set close together. There, when she made the dangerous pass from one tree to the other, the great enterprise would really begin.

She crept out along the swaying oak limb at last, and took the daring step across into the old pine tree. The way was harder than she thought; she must reach far and hold fast, the sharp dry twigs caught and held her and scratched her like angry talons, the pitch made her thin little fingers clumsy and stiff as she went round and round the tree's great stem, higher and higher upward. The sparrows and robins in the woods below were beginning to wake and twitter to the dawn, yet it seemed much lighter there aloft in the pine tree, and the child knew that she must hurry if her project were to be of any use.

The tree seemed to lengthen itself out as she went up, and to reach farther and farther upward. It was like a great mainmast to the voyaging earth; it must truly have been amazed that morning through all its ponderous frame as it felt this determined spark of human spirit creeping and climbing from higher branch to branch. Who knows how steadily the least twigs held themselves to advantage this light, weak creature on her way! The old pine must have loved his new dependent. More than all the hawks, and bats, and moths, and even the sweet-voiced thrushes, was the brave, beating heart of the solitary gray-eyed child. And the tree stood still and held away the winds that June morning while the dawn grew bright in the east.

Sylvia's face was like a pale star, if one had seen it from the ground when the last thorny bough was past, and she stood trembling and tired but wholly triumphant, high in the tree-top. Yes, there was the sea with the dawning sun making a golden dazzle over it, and toward that glorious east flew two hawks with slow-moving pinions.[7] How low they looked in the

---

6. **dumb:** silent.

7. **pinions** [pin′yənz]: wings.

air from that height when before one had only seen them far up, and dark against the blue sky. Their gray feathers were as soft as moths; they seemed only a little way from the tree, and Sylvia felt as if she too could go flying away among the clouds. Westward, the woodlands and farms reached miles and miles into the distance; here and there were church steeples, and white villages; truly it was a vast and awesome world.

The birds sang louder and louder. At last the sun came up bewilderingly bright. Sylvia could see the white sails of ships out at sea, and the clouds that were purple and rose-colored and yellow at first began to fade away. Where was the white heron's nest in the sea of green branches, and was this wonderful sight and pageant of the world the only reward for having climbed to such a giddy height? Now look down again, Sylvia, where the green marsh is set among the shining birches and dark hemlocks; there where you saw the white heron once you will see him again; look, look! a white spot of him like a single floating feather comes up from the dead hemlock and grows larger, and rises, and comes close at last, and goes by the landmark pine with steady sweep of wing and outstretched slender neck and crested head. And wait! wait! do not move a foot or finger, little girl, do not send an arrow of light and consciousness from your two eager eyes, for the heron has perched on a pine bough not far beyond yours, and cries back to his mate on the nest, and plumes his feathers for the new day!

The child gives a long sigh a minute later when a company of shouting catbirds comes also to the tree, and vexed by their fluttering and lawlessness the solemn heron goes away. She knows his secret now, the wild, light, slender bird that floats and wavers, and goes back like an arrow presently to his home in the green world beneath. Then Sylvia, well satisfied, makes her perilous way down again, not daring to look far below the branch she stands on, ready to cry sometimes because her fingers ache and her lamed feet slip. Wondering over and over again what the stranger would say to her, and what he would think when she told him how to find his way straight to the heron's nest.

"Sylvy, Sylvy!" called the busy old grandmother again and again, but nobody answered, and the small husk bed was empty, and Sylvia had disappeared.

The guest waked from a dream, and remembering his day's pleasure hurried to dress himself that it might sooner begin. He was sure from the way the shy little girl looked once or twice yesterday that she had at least seen the white heron, and now she must really be persuaded to tell. Here she comes now, paler than ever, and her worn old frock is torn and tattered, and smeared with pine pitch. The grandmother and the sportsman stand in the door together and question her, and the splendid moment has come to speak of the dead hemlock tree by the green marsh.

But Sylvia does not speak after all, though the old grandmother fretfully rebukes her, and the young man's kind appealing eyes are looking straight in her own. He can make them rich with money; he has promised it, and they are poor now. He is so well worth making happy, and he waits to hear the story she can tell.

No, she must keep silence! What is it that suddenly forbids her and makes her dumb? Has she been nine years growing, and now, when the great world for the first time puts out a hand to her, must she thrust it aside for a bird's sake? The murmur of the pine's green branches is in her ears, she remembers how the white heron came flying through the golden air and how they watched the sea and the morning together, and Sylvia cannot speak; she cannot tell the heron's secret and give its life away.

Dear loyalty, that suffered a sharp pang as the guest went away disappointed later in the day, that could have served and followed him and loved him as a dog loves! Many a night Sylvia heard the echo of his whistle haunting the pasture path as she came home with the loitering cow. She forgot even her sorrow at the sharp report of his gun and the piteous sight of thrushes and sparrows dropping silent to the ground, their songs hushed and their pretty feathers stained and wet with blood. Were the birds better friends than their hunter might have been—who can tell? Whatever treasures were lost to her, woodlands and summertime, remember! Bring your gifts and graces and tell your secrets to this lonely country child.

STUDY QUESTIONS

Recalling

1. How did Sylvia's family describe Sylvia to her grandmother, according to the third paragraph? What does the author call Sylvia in the fifth paragraph?
2. How does Sylvia react when she first hears the young man's whistle? In what kind of voice does she answer his question in the fifth paragraph?
3. What is the young man's hobby? What does he offer to give Sylvia if she helps him find the white heron?
4. How does Sylvia finally sight the white heron? Does she tell the young man of her discovery?
5. What question does the author ask in the last paragraph?

Interpreting

6. Identify Sylvia's chief character trait, as de-

veloped in the opening paragraphs of the story. In what ways is Sylvia like the white heron?

7. Consider the meaning of the name *Sylvia* or the word *sylvan*. How does Sylvia feel about nature? How do her feelings compare to the young man's?

8. What new senses are awakened in Sylvia as a result of her friendship? What ideas come into conflict in this story?

9. In making her choice at the end of the story, what new experience is Sylvia ending? In more general terms, between what is she choosing?

Extending

10. Do you think Sylvia had an obligation to help her new friend by telling him what he wanted to know, or to help her grandmother by taking the money?

VIEWPOINT

In a discussion of Sarah Orne Jewett's work, the twentieth-century author Willa Cather writes:

Miss Jewett wrote of the people who grew out of the soil and the life of the country near her heart, not about exceptional individuals at war with their environment.
—Preface to *The Country of the Pointed Firs*

▦ How would you describe the relationship between Sylvia and her environment? What are the advantages and limitations of such a relationship? Do you think Sylvia is nevertheless an "exceptional individual"? Why or why not?

LITERARY FOCUS

Point of View

The writer of fiction must decide from which point of view to tell a story. A story has a **first-person point of view** if one of the characters tells the tale in his or her own words, using the first-person pronoun *I*. A story has a **third-person point of view** if the narrator stands back from the events and uses the third-person pronouns *he* and *she* to refer to the characters. A narrator who tells us the thoughts of many characters and who also tells us things that no character could know uses the **omniscient** ("all-knowing") **third-person point of view.**

In "A White Heron" Jewett could have employed a first-person point of view by having Sylvia tell us in her own voice what happened to her and what she was thinking. This point of view might have made Sylvia's dilemma more immediate and realistic, but we could then know only what Sylvia herself knew and felt; we could not learn, for example, that the young man thinks Sylvia is "pale," "tattered," and "dirty" and that he suspects she knows the home of the heron.

By using the omniscient third-person point of view, the narrator of "A White Heron" can tell us the thoughts of all the characters and can jump out of the characters' heads to describe them objectively. The narrator can even *intrude* on the story with personal opinion, as on page 316 ("Alas, if . . . ").

Thinking about Point of View

1. Find another instance where the narrator reveals the young man's thoughts. What do his thoughts reveal about his character?

2. Find another instance where the narrator intrudes on the story. What does the intrusion suggest about the narrator's attitude toward Sylvia and her secret?

COMPOSITION

Writing About a Symbol

▦ In an essay discuss what you think the white heron symbolizes. First discuss what the color white suggests about the bird, and tell why it is important that the bird is unusual and rarely seen. Go on to tell what qualities of Sylvia herself the heron represents. Then discuss the significance of the white heron in the work as a whole, explaining how it relates to the theme of the work. *For help with this assignment, refer to Lesson 5 in the Writing About Literature Handbook at the back of this book.*

Creating a Setting

▦ In a paragraph or two describe a place about which you have strong feelings, as Jewett obviously has for the Maine wilderness. First describe the general area you want your reader to see. Then fill out your description with details of sights and sounds and any other physical impressions that can make the setting vivid. Conclude by telling how you feel about the setting.

Kate Chopin   *1851–1904*

Delicate, objective, and *poignant* are words often used to describe the local color stories of Kate Chopin. Born in St. Louis, Missouri, Kate O'Flaherty Chopin married at nineteen and went to live in New Orleans, Louisiana. During the more than ten years she spent there, she became fascinated by the variety of Louisiana life, the rich mixture of cultures, and the many languages and dialects. After her husband's death in 1882, she returned to St. Louis with her six children and began to write.

Just as Bret Harte gave the world a vision of the American West and Sarah Orne Jewett wrote delicate sketches of rural New England, Kate Chopin was chiefly interested in Louisiana. The characters who inhabit Chopin's world are generally Louisiana Creoles, descendants of the original French and Spanish colonists, and Cajuns, descendants of Louisiana's French Canadian settlers. While Chopin is interested in capturing the flavor of Louisiana life as she knew it—as she does in her collection of stories, *Bayou Folk* (1894)—she moves beyond local color to explore the characters of her time and place.

Chopin cared deeply about the roles of women in society and she often writes about a woman's responsibilities to her family, her community, and herself. It is this theme that dominates her most famous novel, *The Awakening* (1899). "A Pair of Silk Stockings" offers a sensitive portrait of another woman who also cares deeply about her responsibilities.

Kate Chopin

A Pair of Silk Stockings

Little Mrs. Sommers one day found herself the unexpected possessor of fifteen dollars. It seemed to her a very large amount of money, and the way in which it stuffed and bulged her worn old *porte-monnaie*[1] gave her a feeling of importance such as she had not enjoyed for years.

The question of investment was one that occupied her greatly. For a day or two she walked about apparently in a dreamy state, but really absorbed in speculation and calculation. She did not wish to act hastily, to do anything she might afterward regret. But it was during the still hours of the night when she lay awake revolving plans in her mind that she seemed to see her way clearly toward a proper and judicious use of the money.

A dollar or two should be added to the price usually paid for Janie's shoes, which would insure their lasting an appreciable time longer than they usually did. She would buy so and so many yards of percale for new shirtwaists for the boys and Janie and Mag. She had intended to make the old ones do by skillful patching. Mag should have another gown. She had seen some beautiful patterns, veritable bargains in the shop windows. And still there would be left enough for new stockings—two pairs apiece—and what darning that would save for a while! She would get caps for the boys and sailor hats for the girls. The vision of her little brood looking fresh and dainty and new for once in their lives excited her and made her restless and wakeful with anticipation.

The neighbors sometimes talked of certain "better days" that little Mrs. Sommers had known before she had ever thought of being Mrs. Sommers. She herself indulged in no such morbid retrospection. She had no time—no second of time to devote to the past. The needs of the present absorbed her every faculty. A vision of the future like some dim, gaunt monster sometimes appalled her, but luckily tomorrow never comes.

Mrs. Sommers was one who knew the value of bargains; who could stand for hours making her way inch by inch toward the desired object that was selling below cost. She could elbow her way if need be; she had learned to clutch a piece of goods and hold it and stick to it with persistence and determination till her turn came to be served, no matter when it came.

But that day she was a little faint and tired. She had swallowed a light luncheon—no! when she came to think of it, between getting the children fed and the place righted, and preparing herself for the shopping bout, she had actually forgotten to eat any luncheon at all!

She sat herself upon a revolving stool before a counter that was comparatively deserted, trying to gather strength and courage to charge through an eager multitude that was besieging breastworks[2] of shirting[3] and figured lawn.[4] An all-gone limp feeling had come over her and she rested her hand aimlessly upon the counter. She wore no gloves. By degrees she grew aware that her hand had encountered something very soothing, very pleasant to touch. She looked down to see that her hand lay upon a pile of silk stockings. A placard nearby announced that they had been reduced in price from two dollars and fifty cents to one dollar and ninety-eight cents; and a young girl who stood behind the counter asked her if she wished to examine their line of silk hosiery.

---

1. ***porte-monnaie*** [pôrt mō nā′]: French for "change purse."

2. **breastworks:** low, hastily built defense walls; here, merchandise displays.
3. **shirting:** material for making shirts.
4. **figured lawn:** fine, sheer, patterned cloth.

She smiled, just as if she had been asked to inspect a tiara[5] of diamonds with the ultimate view of purchasing it: But she went on feeling the soft, sheeny luxurious things—with both hands now, holding them up to see them glisten, and to feel them glide serpent-like through her fingers.

Two hectic blotches came suddenly into her pale cheeks. She looked up at the girl.

"Do you think there are any eights-and-a-half among these?"

There were any number of eights-and-a-half. In fact, there were more of that size than any other. Here was a light blue pair; there were some lavender, some all black and various shades of tan and gray. Mrs. Sommers selected a black pair and looked at them very long and closely. She pretended to be examining their texture, which the clerk assured her was excellent.

"A dollar and ninety-eight cents," she mused aloud. "Well, I'll take this pair." She handed the girl a five-dollar bill and waited for her change and for her parcel. What a very small parcel it was! It seemed lost in the depths of her shabby old shopping bag.

Mrs. Sommers after that did not move in the direction of the bargain counter. She took the elevator, which carried her to an upper floor into the region of the ladies' waiting rooms. Here, in a retired corner, she exchanged her cotton stockings for the new silk ones which she had just bought. She was not going through any acute mental process or reasoning with herself, nor was she striving to explain to her satisfaction the motive of her action. She was not thinking at all. She seemed for the time to be taking a rest from that laborious and fatiguing function and to have abandoned herself to some mechanical impulse that directed her actions and freed her of responsibility.

How good was the touch of the raw silk to her flesh! She felt like lying back in the cushioned chair and reveling for a while in the luxury of it. She did for a little while. Then she replaced her shoes, rolled the cotton stockings together and thrust them into her bag. After doing this she crossed straight over to the shoe department and took her seat to be fitted.

She was fastidious. The clerk could not make her out; he could not reconcile her shoes with her stockings, and she was not too easily pleased. She held back her skirts and turned her feet one way and her head another way as she glanced down at the polished, pointed-tipped boots. Her foot and ankle looked very pretty. She could not realize that they belonged to her and were a part of herself. She wanted an excellent and stylish fit, she told the young fellow who served her, and she did not mind the difference of a dollar or two more in the price so long as she got what she desired.

It was a long time since Mrs. Sommers had been fitted with gloves. On rare occasions when she had bought a pair they were always bargains, so cheap that it would have been preposterous and unreasonable to have expected them to be fitted to the hand.

Now she rested her elbow on the cushion of the glove counter, and a pretty, pleasant young creature, delicate and deft of touch, drew a long-wristed kid[6] over Mrs. Sommers' hand. She smoothed it down over the wrist and buttoned it neatly, and both lost themselves for a second or two in admiring contemplation of the little symmetrical gloved hand. But there were other places where money might be spent.

There were books and magazines piled up in the window of a stall a few paces down the street. Mrs. Sommers bought two high-priced magazines such as she had been accustomed to read in the days when she had been accustomed to other pleasant things. She carried them without wrapping. As well as she could she lifted her skirts at the crossings. Her stockings and boots and well fitting gloves had

---

5. **tiara** [tē ar′ə]: woman's crownlike headdress.

6. **kid:** soft glove made of goatskin.

worked marvels in her bearing—had given her a feeling of assurance, a sense of belonging to the well-dressed multitude.

She was very hungry. Another time she would have stilled the cravings for food until reaching her own home, where she would have brewed herself a cup of tea and taken a snack of anything that was available. But the impulse that was guiding her would not suffer her to entertain any such thought.

There was a restaurant at the corner. She had never entered its doors; from the outside she had sometimes caught glimpses of spotless damask[7] and shining crystal, and soft-stepping waiters serving people of fashion.

When she entered her appearance created no surprise, no consternation, as she had half feared it might. She seated herself at a small table alone, and an attentive waiter at once approached to take her order. She did not want a profusion; she craved a nice and tasty bite— a half dozen blue-points,[8] a plump chop with cress, a something sweet—a crème-frappée,[9] for instance; a glass of Rhine wine, and after all a small cup of black coffee.

While waiting to be served she removed her gloves very leisurely and laid them beside her. Then she picked up a magazine and glanced through it, cutting the pages with a blunt edge of her knife.[10] It was all very agreeable. The damask was even more spotless than it had seemed through the window, and the crystal more sparkling. There were quiet ladies and gentlemen, who did not notice her, lunching at the small tables like her own. A soft, pleasing strain of music could be heard, and a gentle breeze was blowing through the window. She tasted a bite, and she read a word or two, and she sipped the amber wine and wiggled her toes in the silk stockings. The price of it made no difference. She counted the money out to the waiter and left an extra coin on his tray, whereupon he bowed before her as before a princess of royal blood.

There was still money in her purse, and her next temptation presented itself in the shape of a matinee poster.

It was a little later when she entered the theater, the play had begun and the house seemed to her to be packed. But there were vacant seats here and there, and into one of them she was ushered, between brilliantly dressed women who had gone there to kill time and eat candy and display their gaudy attire. There were many others who were there solely for the play and acting. It is safe to say there was no one present who bore quite the attitude which Mrs. Sommers did to her surroundings. She gathered in the whole—stage and players and people in one wide impression, and absorbed it and enjoyed it. She laughed at the comedy and wept—she and the gaudy woman next to her wept over the tragedy. And they talked a little together over it. And the gaudy woman wiped her eyes and sniffled on a tiny square of filmy, perfumed lace and passed little Mrs. Sommers her box of candy.

The play was over, the music ceased, the crowd filed out. It was like a dream ended. People scattered in all directions. Mrs. Sommers went to the corner and waited for the cable car.

A man with keen eyes, who sat opposite to her, seemed to like the study of her small, pale face. It puzzled him to decipher what he saw there. In truth, he saw nothing—unless he were wizard enough to detect a poignant wish, a powerful longing that the cable car would never stop anywhere, but go on and on with her forever.

---

7. **damask** [dam′əsk]: durable, lustrous, reversible fabric, often used for table linen.

8. **blue-points:** oysters.

9. **crème-frappée** [krem fra pā′]: French for "whipped cream."

10. **cutting . . . knife:** The pages of certain elegant magazines had to be slit open at the outer edges by the reader.

Recalling

1. How does Mrs. Sommers feel about unexpectedly possessing fifteen dollars, according to the opening paragraph? According to the third paragraph, how does she plan to spend the money?
2. What do the neighbors say about Mrs. Sommers, according to the fourth paragraph? Why does Mrs. Sommers not indulge in such "morbid retrospection"?
3. On the day on which this story takes place, how does Mrs. Sommers feel (paragraph 6)? How is she resting her hand on the counter when "an all-gone limp feeling" comes over her (paragraph 7)?
4. How does Mrs. Sommers spend the fifteen dollars? As Mrs. Sommers takes the cable car home, what is her "poignant wish"?

Interpreting

5. Describe Mrs. Sommers' life as a wife and mother. Does her life seem to have been different before she married? If so, how was it different?
6. Does Mrs. Sommers buy the silk stockings deliberately—that is, calmly and with forethought? Explain.
7. Why is this day special for Mrs. Sommers? Why does she long for the cable car to "go on and on with her forever"? Why is this wish called "poignant"?

Extending

8. Do you consider Mrs. Sommers justified in thinking of her own needs and desires? Why or why not?

LITERARY FOCUS

Character Motivation

In order for fictional characters to appear true to life and to be interesting, they must act in ways that we can understand. That is, the writer must supply adequate **motivation**, stating or implying the reasons for their behavior. A character may surprise us, may act in an unexpected or inconsistent way, but we must be convinced that the action is plausible.

At the beginning of "A Pair of Silk Stockings," we are told that Mrs. Sommers is careful about the "proper and judicious use of money." Her entire past life leads us to expect her to act in a certain way—specifically, to spend her extra fifteen dollars on buying things for her children. We are surprised to discover that she spends the money on herself instead.

Kate Chopin never states *directly* why Mrs. Sommers changes her mind. Rather, the motivation is *implied*. For instance, we learn that Mrs. Sommers is tired and has eaten no lunch. "An all-gone limp feeling" overwhelms her just as she rests her hand upon a pile of silk stockings. At this point, her original plans for the money seem to vanish; her weariness and the smooth, pleasant sensation of the silk against her skin suddenly make her think of herself and her own wishes.

Since we have probably had similar experiences, we can imagine why Mrs. Sommers acts as she does. Although Kate Chopin does not name the reasons, she makes us feel that Mrs. Sommers is adequately motivated.

Thinking About Character Motivation

■ Choose another character from a story you have read in this book. What are the character's motives for action? Are they believable? Do any of the motives conflict with others?

COMPOSITION

Writing About Character

■ Write an essay about the character of Mrs. Sommers. Begin by discussing whether she is a flat character or a round one (see page 309). Then tell what we learn about the character by what she says, does, thinks, and feels. Describe her motivations and what they tell about the kind of woman she is. Conclude with your own opinion of the character.

Describing a Character's Movements

■ Much of this story depends on detailed descriptions of Mrs. Sommers' actions. Imagine a character in a situation. Then describe in detail the character's physical movements as he or she performs a single, specific action, such as painting a picture, watering a plant, or eating a meal.

Hamlin Garland   *1860–1940*

Hamlin Garland grew up among poor farmers in the Midwest. He watched his family and friends move from farm to farm, from state to state, trying to make a living despite harsh economic conditions and a series of natural disasters. Garland himself fled the Midwest when he was in his twenties and settled in Boston to complete his education. On a visit home he was struck again by the poverty of rural America, and this world became the backdrop for most of his writing.

Working for East Coast journals, he produced from his memories of youth a series of stories depicting the everyday lives of simple midwestern farmers. The stories were gathered together in 1891 and published under the title *Main-Travelled Roads.* Other, similar collections followed soon after.

Garland was firmly convinced that fiction should be realistic and drawn from personal experience. In *Crumbling Idols* (1894), a collection of essays, he argues that truth in literature is best achieved by writers who flavor their stories with the "local color" of the region they know best. Many of Garland's later works are biographical. They include his autobiography, *A Son of the Middle Border* (1917), and the story of his wife's family, *A Daughter of the Middle Border* (1921), which won Garland the Pulitzer Prize.

Hand in hand with his concern for truth in literature was Garland's belief that literature could be a means of achieving economic and social reform. "Under the Lion's Paw," his most famous story, is written with a sense of outrage at the plight of the midwestern farmer. The tale is a far cry from the Romantic writings of Washington Irving and James Fenimore Cooper. With almost brutal realism, Garland brings to life the desperate situation of the struggling farmers and casts the harsh light of reality on the relationship between Americans and the land.

Model for Active Reading

In this selection, and in one selection in each unit, you will find notes in the right-hand margin that highlight parts of the selection. These notes point out important ideas of the period—in this case, Realist, Regionalist, and Naturalist ideas—and draw your attention to literary elements and techniques covered in the Literary Focuses. Page numbers in the notes will refer you to more extensive discussions of these important ideas and elements.

Hamlin Garland

Under the Lion's Paw

I

It was the last of autumn and first day of winter coming together. All day long the plowmen on their prairie farms had moved to and fro in their wide level fields through the falling snow, which melted as it fell, wetting them to the skin—all day, notwithstanding the frequent squalls of snow, the dripping, desolate clouds, and the muck of the furrows, black and tenacious as tar.

Mood (p. 148): Strings of adjectives help establish an atmosphere for the setting of the story.

Under their dripping harness the horses swung to and fro silently, with that marvelous uncomplaining patience which marks the horse. All day the wild geese, honking wildly, as they sprawled sidewise down the wind, seemed to be fleeing from an enemy behind, and with neck outthrust and wings extended, sailed down the wind, soon lost to sight.

Yet the plowman behind his plow, though the snow lay on his ragged greatcoat, and the cold clinging mud rose on his heavy boots, fettering him like gyves,[1] whistled in the very beard of the gale. As day passed, the snow, ceasing to melt, lay along the plowed land, and lodged in the depth of the stubble, till on each slow round the last furrow stood out black and shining as jet[2] between the plowed land and the gray stubble.

When night began to fall, and the geese, flying low, began to alight invisibly in the near cornfield, Stephen Council was still at work "finishing a land."[3] He rode on his sulky plow[4] when going with the wind, but walked when facing it. Sitting bent and cold but cheery under his slouch hat, he talked encouragingly to his four-in-hand.[5]

Regionalist idea: Accurate descriptions of the characters' activities are important in capturing the "local color" of the region (p. 297).

Dialect (p. 297): Characters' conversation is written in the dialect of the region to support the "local color."

"Come round there, boys!—Round agin! We got t' finish this land. Come in there, Dan! *Stiddy,* Kate,—stiddy! None o' y'r tantrums, Kittie. It's purty tuff, but got a be did. *Tchk! tchk!* Step along, Pete! Don't let Katie git y'r single-tree[6] on the wheel. *Once more!*"

They seemed to know what he meant, and that this was the last round, for they worked with greater vigor than before.

"Once more, boys, an' then, sez I, oats an' a nice warm stall, an' sleep f'r all."

By the time the last furrow was turned on the land it was too dark to see the house, and the snow was changing to rain again.

---

1. **gyves** [jīvz]: shackles, chains.
2. **jet:** velvet black, coallike mineral.
3. **"finishing a land":** completing work on a section of a farm.
4. **sulky plow:** plow having wheels and a driver's seat.
5. **four-in-hand:** team of four horses driven by one person.

The tired and hungry man could see the light from the kitchen shining through the leafless hedge, and he lifted a great shout, "Supper f'r a half a dozen!"

It was nearly eight o'clock by the time he had finished his chores and started for supper. He was picking his way carefully through the mud, when the tall form of a man loomed up before him with a premonitory cough.

"Waddy ye want?" was the rather startled question of the farmer.

"Well, ye see," began the stranger, in a deprecating tone, "we'd like t' git in f'r the night. We've tried every house f'r the last two miles, but they hadn't any room f'r us. My wife's jest about sick, 'n' the children are cold and hungry—"

"Oh, y' want 'o stay all night, eh?"

"Yes, sir; it 'ud be a great accom—"

"Waal, I don't make it a practice t' turn anybuddy way hungry, not on sech nights as this. Drive right in. We ain't got much, but sech as it is—"

But the stranger had disappeared. And soon his steaming, weary team, with drooping heads and swinging single-trees, moved past the well to the block beside the path. Council stood at the side of the schooner[7] and helped the children out—two little half-sleeping children—and then a small woman with a babe in her arms.

"There ye go!" he shouted jovially, to the children. "*Now* we're all right! Run right along to the house there, an' tell Mam' Council you wants sumpthin' t' eat. Right this way, Mis'—keep right off t' the right there. I'll go an' git a lantern. Come," he said to the dazed and silent group at his side.

"Mother," he shouted, as he neared the fragrant and warmly lighted kitchen, "here are some wayfarers an' folks who need sumpthin' t' eat an' a place t' snooze." He ended by pushing them all in.

Mrs. Council, a large, jolly, rather coarse-looking woman, took the children in her arms. "Come right in, you little rabbits. 'Most asleep, hey? Now here's a drink o' milk f'r each o' ye. I'll have s'm tea in a minute. Take off y'r things and set up t' the fire."

While she set the children to drinking milk, Council got out his lantern and went out to the barn to help the stranger about his team, where his loud, hearty voice could be heard as it came and went between the haymow and the stalls.

The woman came to light as a small, timid, and discouraged-looking woman, but still pretty, in a thin and sorrowful way.

"Land sakes! An' you've traveled all the way from Clear Lake

---

6. **single-tree:** pivoted swinging bar to which the traces of a harness are fastened and by which a vehicle is pulled.

7. **schooner:** prairie schooner, a broad-wheeled covered wagon.

t'-day in this mud! Waal! waal! No wonder you're all tired out. Don't wait f'r the men, Mis'—" She hesitated, waiting for the name.

"Haskins."

"Mis' Haskins, set right up to the table an' take a good swig o' tea whilst I make y' s'm toast. It's green tea, an' it's good. I tell Council as I git older I don't seem to enjoy Young Hyson n'r Gunpowder.[8] I want the reel green tea, jest as it comes off'n the vines. Seems t'have more heart in it, some way. Don't s'pose it has. Council says it's all in m' eye." Going on in this easy way, she soon had the children filled with bread and milk and the woman thoroughly at home, eating some toast and sweetmelon pickles, and sipping the tea.

"See the little rats!" she laughed at the children. "They're full as they can stick now, and they want to go to bed. Now, don't git up, Mis' Haskins; set right where you are an' let me look after 'em. I know all about young ones, though I'm all alone now. Jane went an' married last fall. But, as I tell Council, it's lucky we keep our health. Set right there, Mis' Haskins; I won't have you stir a finger."

It was an unmeasured pleasure to sit there in the warm, homely kitchen, the jovial chatter of the housewife driving out and holding at bay the growl of the impotent, cheated wind.

Realist idea: Realistic fiction turned from the Romantic emphasis on the strange toward a faithful rendering of the ordinary (p. 296).

The little woman's eyes filled with tears which fell down upon the sleeping baby in her arms. The world was not so desolate and cold and hopeless, after all.

"Now I hope Council won't stop out there and talk politics all night. He's the greatest man to talk politics an' read the *Tribune*— How old is it?"

She broke off and peered down at the face of the babe.

"Two months 'n' five days," said the mother, with a mother's exactness.

"Ye don't say! I want 'o know! The dear little pudzy-wudzy!" she went on, stirring it up in the neighborhood of the ribs with her fat forefinger. "Pooty tough on 'oo to go galivant'n' 'cross lots this way—"

"Yes, that's so; a man can't lift a mountain," said Council, entering the door. "Mother, this is Mr. Haskins, from Kansas. He's been eat up 'n' drove out by grasshoppers."

"Glad t' see yeh!—Pa, empty that washbasin 'n' give him a chance t' wash."

Haskins was a tall man, with a thin, gloomy face. His hair was a reddish brown, like his coat, and seemed equally faded by the wind and sun, and his sallow face, though hard and set, was pathetic somehow. You would have felt that he had suffered much by the line of his mouth showing under his thin, yellow mustache.

---

8. **Young Hyson . . . Gunpowder:** types of Chinese green tea.

"Hain't Ike got home yet, Sairy?"

"Hain't seen 'im."

"W-a-a-l, set right up, Mr. Haskins; wade right into what we've got; 'tain't much, but we manage to live on it—she gits fat on it," laughed Council, pointing his thumb at his wife.

After supper, while the women put the children to bed, Haskins and Council talked on, seated near the huge cooking stove, the steam rising from their wet clothing. In the Western fashion Council told as much of his own life as he drew from his guest. He asked but few questions, but by and by the story of Haskins' struggles and defeat came out. The story was a terrible one, but he told it quietly, seated with his elbows on his knees, gazing most of the time at the hearth.

"I didn't like the looks of the country, anyhow," Haskins said, partly rising and glancing at his wife. "I was ust t' northern Ingyannie,[9] where we have lots o' timber 'n' lots o' rain, 'n' I didn't like the looks o' that dry prairie. What galled me the worst was goin' s' far away acrosst so much fine land layin' all through here vacant."

"And the 'hoppers eat ye four years, hand runnin', did they?"

"Eat! They wiped us out. They chawed everything that was green. They jest set around waitin' f'r us to die t' eat us, too. My God! I ust t' dream of 'em sittin' 'round on the bedpost, six feet long, workin' their jaws. They eet the fork handles. They got worse 'n' worse till they jest rolled on one another, piled up like snow in winter. Well, it ain't no use. If I was t' talk all winter I couldn't tell nawthin'. But all the while I couldn't help thinkin' of all that land back here that nobuddy was usin' that I ought 'o had 'stead o' bein' out there in that cussed country."

"Waal, why didn't ye stop an' settle here?" asked Ike, who had come in and was eating his supper.

"Fer the simple reason that you fellers wantid ten 'r fifteen dollars an acre fer the bare land, and I hadn't no money fer that kind o' thing."

"Yes, I do my own work," Mrs. Council was heard to say in the pause that followed. "I'm a-gettin' purty heavy t' be on m' laigs all day, but we can't afford t' hire, so I keep rackin' around somehow, like a foundered horse. S' lame—I tell Council he can't tell how lame I am, f'r I'm jest as lame in one laig as t' other." And the good soul laughed at the joke on herself as she took a handful of flour and dusted the biscuit board to keep the dough from sticking.

"Well, I hain't *never* been very strong," said Mrs. Haskins. "Our folks was Canadians an' small-boned, and then since my last child I hain't got up again fairly. I don't like t' complain. Tim has about all he can bear now—but they was days this week when I jes wanted to lay right down an' die."

---

9. **Ingyannie** [in' gē an'ē]: dialect form of *Indiana.*

"Waal, now, I'll tell ye," said Council, from his side of the stove, silencing everybody with his good-natured roar, "I'd go down and *see* Butler, *anyway,* if I was you. I guess he'd let you have his place purty cheap; the farm's all run down. He's ben anxious t' let t' somebuddy next year. It 'ud be a good chance fer you. Anyhow, you go to bed and sleep like a babe. I've got some plowin' t' do, anyhow, an' we'll see if somethin' can't be done about your case. Ike, you go out an' see if the horses is all right, an' I'll show the folks t' bed."

When the tired husband and wife were lying under the generous quilts of the spare bed, Haskins listened a moment to the wind in the eaves, and then said, with a slow and solemn tone, "There are people in this world who are good enough t' be angels, an' only haff t' die to *be* angels."

II

Jim Butler was one of those men called in the West "land poor."[10] Early in the history of Rock River he had come into the town and started in the grocery business in a small way, occupying a small building in a mean[11] part of the town. At this period of his life he earned all he got, and was up early and late sorting beans, working over butter, and carting his goods to and from the station. But a change came over him at the end of the second year, when he sold a lot of land for four times what he paid for it. From that time forward he believed in land speculation[12] as the surest way of

> **Flat character** (p. 309): Butler is "one of those men"—that is, he is a stereotype.

10. **"land poor"**: owning land but having little money.
11. **mean**: poor.
12. **land speculation**: buying and selling land for a profit.

getting rich. Every cent he could save or spare from his trade he put into land at forced sale,[13] or mortgages on land, which were "just as good as the wheat," he was accustomed to say.

Farm after farm fell into his hands, until he was recognized as one of the leading landowners of the county. His mortgages were scattered all over Cedar County, and as they slowly but surely fell in he sought usually to retain the former owner as tenant.

He was not ready to foreclose; indeed, he had the name of being one of the "easiest" men in the town. He let the debtor off again and again, extending the time whenever possible.

"I don't want y'r land," he said. "All I'm after is the int'rest on my money—that's all. Now, if y' want 'o stay on the farm, why, I'll give y' a good chance. I can't have the land layin' vacant." And in many cases the owner remained as tenant.

In the meantime he had sold his store; he couldn't spend time in it; he was mainly occupied now with sitting around town on rainy days smoking and "gassin' with the boys," or in riding to and from his farms. In fishing time he fished a good deal. Doc Grimes, Ben Ashley, and Cal Cheatham were his cronies on these fishing excursions or hunting trips in the time of chickens or partridges. In winter they went to northern Wisconsin to shoot deer.

In spite of all these signs of easy life Butler persisted in saying he "hadn't enough money to pay taxes on his land," and was careful to convey the impression that he was poor in spite of his twenty farms. At one time he was said to be worth fifty thousand dollars, but land had been a little slow of sale of late, so that he was not worth so much.

A fine farm, known as the Higley place, had fallen into his hands in the usual way the previous year, and he had not been able to find a tenant for it. Poor Higley, after working himself nearly to death on it in the attempt to lift the mortgage, had gone off to Dakota, leaving the farm and his curse to Butler. This was the farm which Council advised Haskins to apply for; and the next day Council hitched up his team and drove down town to see Butler.

"You jest let *me* do the talkin'," he said. "We'll find him wearin' out his pants on some salt barrel somew'ers; and if he thought you *wanted* a place he'd sock it to you hot and heavy. You jest keep quiet; I'll fix 'im."

Butler was seated in Ben Ashley's store telling fish yarns when Council sauntered in casually.

"Hello, But; lyin' agin, hey!"

"Hello, Steve! how goes it?"

"Oh, so-so. Too dang much rain these days. I thought it was goin' t' freeze up f'r good last night. Tight squeak if I get m' plowin' done. How's farmin' with *you* these days?"

Round character (p. 309): Stephen Council is a "rounder" character than Butler, with more facets to his personality.

---

13. **forced sale:** buying cheaply from someone who is forced to sell.

"Bad. Plowin' ain't half done."

"It 'ud be a religious idee f'r you t' go out an' take a hand y'rself."

"I don't haff to," said Butler, with a wink.

"Got anybody on the Higley place?"

"No. Know anybody?"

"Waal, no; not eggsackly. I've got a relation back t' Michigan who's ben hot an' cold on the idee o' comin' West f'r some time. *Might* come if he could get a good layout. What do you talk on the farm?"

"Well, I d'know. I'll rent it on shares or I'll rent it money rent."

"Waal, how much money, say?"

"Well, say ten per cent, on the price—two-fifty."

"Waal, that ain't bad. Wait on 'im till 'e thrashes?"[14]

Haskins listened eagerly to his important question, but Council was coolly eating a dried apple which he had speared out of a barrel with his knife. Butler studied him carefully.

"Well, knocks me out of twenty-five dollars interest."

"My relation'll need all he's got t' git his crops in," said Council, in the safe, indifferent way.

"Well, all right; *say* wait," concluded Butler.

"All right; this is the man. Haskins, this is Mr. Butler—no relation to Ben—the hardest-working man in Cedar County."

On the way home Haskins said: "I ain't much better off. I'd like that farm; it's a good farm, but it's all run down, an' so 'm I. I could make a good farm of it if I had half a show. But I can't stock it n'r seed it."

"Waal, now, don't you worry," roared Council in his ear. "We'll pull y' through somehow till next harvest. He's agreed t' hire it plowed, an' you can earn a hundred dollars plowin' an' y' c'n git the seed o' me, an' pay me back when y' can."

Haskins was silent with emotion, but at last he said, "I ain't got nothin' t' live on."

"Now, don't you worry 'bout that. You jest make your headquarters at ol' Steve Council's. Mother'll take a pile o' comfort in havin' y'r wife an' children 'round. Y' see, Jane's married off lately, an' Ike's away a good 'eal, so we'll be darn glad t' have y' stop with us this winter. Nex' spring we'll see if y' can't git a start agin." And he chirruped to the team, which sprang forward with the rumbling, clattering wagon.

"Say, looky here, Council, you can't do this. I never saw—" shouted Haskins in his neighbor's ear.

Council moved about uneasily in his seat and stopped his stammering gratitude by saying: "Hold on now: don't make such a fuss over a little thing. When I see a man down, an' things all on top

Point of view (p. 319): Garland uses the omniscient point of view, and so the narrator has the freedom to tell how any of the characters are reacting.

---

14. **Wait . . . thrashes:** await rent payment until the harvest is in.

of'm, I jest like t' kick 'em off an' help 'm up. That's the kind of religion I got, an' it's about the *only* kind."

They rode the rest of the way home in silence. And when the red light of the lamp shone out into the darkness of the cold and windy night, and he thought of this refuge for his children and wife, Haskins could have put his arm around the neck of his burly companion and squeezed him like a lover. But he contented himself with saying, "Steve Council, you'll git y'r pay f'r this some day."

"Don't want any pay. My religion ain't run on such business principles."

The wind was growing colder, and the ground was covered with a white frost, as they turned into the gate of the Council farm, and the children came rushing out, shouting, "Papa's come!" They hardly looked like the same children who had sat at the table the night before. Their torpidity, under the influence of sunshine and Mother Council, had given way to a sort of spasmodic cheerfulness, as insects in winter revive when laid on the hearth.

III

Haskins worked like a fiend, and his wife, like the heroic woman that she was, bore also uncomplainingly the most terrible burdens. They rose early and toiled without intermission till the darkness fell on the plain, then tumbled into bed, every bone and muscle aching with fatigue, to rise with the sun next morning to the same round of the same ferocity of labor.

The eldest boy drove a team all through the spring, plowing and seeding, milked the cows, and did chores innumerable, in most ways taking the place of a man.

An infinitely pathetic but common figure, this boy on the American farm, where there is no law against child labor. To see him in his coarse clothing, his huge boots, and his ragged cap, as he staggered with a pail of water from the well, or trudged in the cold and cheerless dawn out into the frosty field behind his team, gave the city-bred visitor a sharp pang of sympathetic pain. Yet Haskins loved his boy, and would have saved him from this if he could, but he could not.

By June the first year the result of such Herculean[15] toil began to show on the farm. The yard was cleaned up and sown to grass, the garden plowed and planted, and the house mended.

Council had given them four of his cows.

"Take 'em an' run 'em on shares. I don't want 'o milk s' many. Ike's away s' much now, Sat'd'ys an' Sund'ys, I can't stand the bother anyhow."

Point of view (p. 319): The omniscient narrator can intrude on the story with a general comment, as Garland does here.

---

15. **Herculean** [hur'kyə lē'ən]: requiring great strength; referring to the Greek hero Hercules.

Other men, seeing the confidence of Council in the newcomer, had sold him tools on time; and as he was really an able farmer, he soon had round him many evidences of his care and thrift. At the advice of Council he had taken the farm for three years, with the privilege of re-renting or buying at the end of the term.

"It's a good bargain, an' y' want 'o nail it," said Council. "If you have any kind ov a crop, you c'n pay y'r debts, an' keep seed an' bread."

The new hope which now sprang up in the heart of Haskins and his wife grew great almost as a pain by the time the wide field of wheat began to wave and swirl in the winds of July. Day after day he would snatch a few moments after supper to go and look at it.

"Have ye seen the wheat t'-day, Nettie?" he asked one night as he rose from supper.

"No, Tim, I ain't had time."

"Well, take time now. Le's go look at it."

She threw an old hat on her head—Tommy's hat—and looking almost pretty in her thin, sad way, went out with her husband to the hedge.

"Ain't it grand, Nettie? Just look at it."

It was grand. Level, russet here and there, heavy-headed, wide as a lake, and full of multitudinous whispers and gleams of wealth, it stretched away before the gazers like the fabled field of the cloth of gold.[16]

"Oh, I think—I *hope* we'll have a good crop, Tim; and oh, how good the people have been to us!"

"Yes; I don't know where we'd be t'-day if it hadn't ben f'r Council and his wife."

"They're the best people in the world," said the little woman, with a great sob of gratitude.

"We'll be in the field on Monday, sure," said Haskins, gripping the rail on the fence as if already at the work of the harvest.

The harvest came, bounteous, glorious, but the winds came and blew it into tangles, and the rain matted it here and there close to the ground, increasing the work of gathering it threefold.

Oh, how they toiled in those glorious days! Clothing dripping with sweat, arms aching, filled with briers, fingers raw and bleeding, backs broken with the weight of heavy bundles, Haskins and his man toiled on. Tommy drove the harvester, while his father and a hired man bound on the machine. In this way they cut ten acres every day, and almost every night after supper, when the hand went to bed, Haskins returned to the field shocking the bound grain in the light of the moon. Many a night he worked till his anxious wife came out at ten o'clock to call him in to rest and lunch.

Realist idea: Middle- and lower-class people are often the subjects of Realistic fiction, and the writer takes their lives as seriously as the lives of the rich and powerful (p. 296).

---

16. **field . . . gold:** place in France where French King François I met the English King Henry VIII in 1520; a magnificent spectacle.

At the same time she cooked for the men, took care of the children, washed and ironed, milked the cows at night, made the butter, and sometimes fed the horses and watered them while her husband kept at the shocking.

No slave in the Roman galleys[17] could have toiled so frightfully and lived, for this man thought himself a free man, and that he was working for his wife and babes.

When he sank into his bed with a deep groan of relief, too tired to change his grimy, dripping clothing, he felt that he was getting nearer and nearer to a home of his own, and pushing the wolf of want a little farther from his door.

There is no despair so deep as the despair of a homeless man or woman. To roam the roads of the country or the streets of the city, to feel there is no rood of ground on which the feet can rest, to halt weary and hungry outside lighted windows and hear laughter and song within—these are the hungers and rebellions that drive men to crime and women to shame.

It was the memory of this homelessness, and the fear of its coming again, that spurred Timothy Haskins and Nettie, his wife, to such ferocious labor during that first year.

Character motivation (p. 325): Garland explains why Tim Haskins works so hard.

IV

" 'M, yes; 'm, yes; first rate," said Butler, as his eye took in the neat garden, the pigpen, and the well-filled barnyard. "You're gitt'n quite a stock around yeh. Done well, eh?"

Haskins was showing Butler around the place. He had not seen it for a year, having spent the year in Washington and Boston with Ashley, his brother-in-law, who had been elected to Congress.

"Yes, I've laid out a good deal of money durin' the last three years. I've paid out three hundred dollars f'r fencin'."

"Um—h'm! I see, I see," said Butler while Haskins went on:

"The kitchen there costs two hundred; the barn ain't cost much in money, but I've put a lot o' time on it. I've dug a new well, and I—".

"Yes, yes, I see. You've done well. Stock worth a thousand dollars," said Butler, picking his teeth with a straw.

"About that," said Haskins, modestly. "We begin to feel 's if we was gitt'n a home f'r ourselves; but we've worked hard. I tell you we begin to feel it, Mr. Butler, and we're goin' t' begin to ease up purty soon. We've been kind o' plannin' a trip back t' *her* folks after the fall plowin's done."

"*Eggs*-actly!" said Butler, who was evidently thinking of something else. "I suppose you've kind o' calc'lated on stayin' here three years more?"

---

17. **Roman galleys:** ancient ships propelled by slaves chained to rows of oars.

"Well, yes. Fact is, I think I c'n buy the farm this fall, if you'll give me a reasonable show."

"Um—m! What do you call a reasonable show?"

"Well, say a quarter down and three years' time."

Butler looked at the huge stacks of wheat, which filled the yard, over which the chickens were fluttering and crawling, catching grasshoppers, and out of which the crickets were singing innumerably. He smiled in a peculiar way as he said, "Oh, I won't be hard on yeh. But what did you expect to pay f'r the place?"

"Why, about what you offered it for before, two thousand, five hundred, or *possibly* three thousand dollars," he added quickly as he saw the owner shake his head.

"This farm is worth five thousand and five hundred dollars," said Butler, in a careless and decided voice.

"What!" almost shrieked the astounded Haskins. "What's this? Five thousand? Why that's double what you offered it for three years ago."

"Of course, and it's worth it. It was all run down then; now it's in good shape. You've laid out fifteen hundred dollars in improvements, according to your own story."

"But *you* had nothin' t' do about that. It's my work an' my money."

"You bet it was; but it's my land."

"But what's to pay me for all my—"

"Ain't you had the use of 'em?" replied Butler, smiling calmly into his face.

Haskins was like a man struck on the head with a sandbag; he couldn't think; he stammered as he tried to say: "But—I never'd git the use—You'd rob me! More'n that: you agreed—you promised that I could buy or rent at the end of three years at—"

"That's all right. But I didn't say I'd let you carry off the improvements, nor that I'd go on renting the farm at two-fifty. The land is doubled in value, it don't matter how; it don't enter into the question; an' now you can pay me five hundred dollars a year rent, or take it on your own terms at fifty-five hundred, or—git out."

He was turning away when Haskins, the sweat pouring from his face, fronted him, saying again:

"But *you've* done nothing to make it so. You hain't added a cent. I put it all there myself, expectin' to buy. I worked an' sweat to improve it. I was workin' for myself an' babes—"

"Well, why didn't you buy when I offered to sell? What y' kickin' about?"

"I'm kickin' about payin' you twice f'r my own things—my own fences, my own kitchen, my own garden."

Butler laughed. "You're too green t'eat, young feller. *Your* improvements! The law will sing another tune."

Regionalist idea: Accurate descriptions of the physical environment are important in capturing "local color," (p. 297).

"But I trusted your word."

"Never trust anybody, my friend. Besides, I didn't promise not to do this thing. Why, man, don't look at me like that. Don't take me for a thief. It's the law. The reg'lar thing. Everybody does it."

"I don't care if they do. It's stealin' jest the same. You take three thousand dollars of my money—the work o' my hands and my wife's." He broke down at this point. He was not a strong man mentally. He could face hardship, ceaseless toil, but he could not face the cold and sneering face of Butler.

"But I don't take it," said Butler, coolly. "All you've got to do is to go on jest as you've been a-doin', or give me a thousand dollars down, and a mortgage at ten per cent on the rest."

Haskins sat down blindly on a bundle of oats near by, and with staring eyes and drooping head went over the situation. He was under the lion's paw. He felt a horrible numbness in his heart and limbs. He was hid in a mist, and there was no path out.

Butler walked about, looking at the huge stacks of grain, and pulling now and again a few handfuls out, shelling the heads in his hands and blowing the chaff away. He hummed a little tune as he did so. He had an accommodating air of waiting.

Haskins was in the midst of the terrible toil of the last year. He was walking again in the rain and the mud behind his plow; he felt the dust and dirt of the threshing. The ferocious husking time, with its cutting wind and biting, clinging snows, lay hard upon him. Then he thought of his wife, how she had cheerfully cooked and baked, without holiday and without rest.

"Well, what do you think of it?" inquired the cool, mocking, insinuating voice of Butler.

"I think you're a thief and a liar!" shouted Haskins, leaping up. "A blackhearted houn'!" Butler's smile maddened him; with a sudden leap he caught a fork in his hands, and whirled it in the air. "You'll never rob another man!" he grated through his teeth, a look of pitiless ferocity in his accusing eyes.

Butler shrank and quivered, expecting the blow; stood, held hypnotized by the eyes of the man he had a moment before despised—a man transformed into an avenging demon. But in the deadly hush between the lift of the weapon and its fall there came a gush of faint, childish laughter and then across the range of his vision, far away and dim, he saw the sunbright head of his baby girl, as with the pretty, tottering run of a two-year-old, she moved across the grass of the dooryard. His hands relaxed; the fork fell to the ground; his head lowered.

"Make out y'r deed an' mor'gage, an' git off'n my land, an' don't ye never cross my line again; if y' do, I'll kill ye."

Butler backed away from the man in wild haste, and climbing into his buggy with trembling limbs drove off down the road, leaving Haskins seated dumbly on the sunny piles of sheaves, his head sunk into his hands.

Naturalist idea: In Naturalist fiction people are often caught within forces of society that are beyond their understanding and control (p. 297).

STUDY QUESTIONS

Recalling

1. According to the opening paragraph, under what conditions do the plowmen work all day? Whom does Stephen Council encounter as he picks his way home through the mud for dinner?

2. What natural disaster drove the Haskins family from Kansas?

3. Why does Stephen Council take Haskins to meet Jim Butler? How does Council attempt to outsmart Butler?

4. Who helps Tim Haskins work the farm? In what ways does Stephen Council give assistance?

5. When Butler sees the improvements that the Haskins family have made on the farm, what does he do?

6. What does Haskins do when he realizes that he is "under the lion's paw" (page 338)? What makes him abandon his violent impulses, and, consequently, what does he say and do?

Interpreting

7. What do the adjectives in the first four paragraphs of the story suggest about the realities of turn-of-the-century midwestern farming? What do the descriptions of the horse and geese help emphasize?

8. Why does Council help the Haskins family? Why does Butler help them?

9. In what struggle common in Naturalist literature (see page 297) is Haskins finally victorious? In what struggle is he the loser?

Extending

10. Can you identify with the characters of this story despite its Regionalism? In what way are the problems of turn-of-the-century midwestern farmers similar to many peoples' problems today?

VIEWPOINT

Robert E. Spiller, writing of Hamlin Garland's *Main-Travelled Roads* and its sequel, *Prairie Folks*, says that the stories

> tell of the unadorned hardships, lightened by occasional small pleasures and made meaningful by the power of nature, that fill the lives of the people of . . . the prairie.

— *Literary History of the United States*

■ Find instances in "Under the Lion's Paw" of small pleasures that lighten the burden of the farmers. Do you agree that the power of nature makes the farmers' hardships more meaningful? Why or why not?

COMPOSITION

Writing About Literature and Its Period

■ Write a brief essay that begins with this statement: "'Under the Lion's Paw' typifies the literature of its period." List at least three reasons (consider the content, the style, and the tone of the story), and support them with quotations and specific details from the story. *For help with this assignment, refer to Lesson 10 in the Writing About Literature Handbook at the back of this book.*

Writing an Editorial

■ Many of the economic practices that Garland attacks were also criticized by the "muckraking" journalists of his day. Write a newspaper editorial in which you condemn a specific economic or social practice that you feel is unjust. Support your opinion with facts and examples, and end with a recommendation of how the situation should be remedied. You might examine editorials in a local newspaper for ideas. Be sure to balance the emotional appeal of your editorial with a clear, logical, and persuasive argument.

Jack London   *1876–1916*

Few American writers knew working-class life as well as Jack London did, and few have written about it with London's immediacy. London's early years were spent in poverty. He had little formal education and worked at a series of odd jobs as he wandered about America and the rest of the world. Arrested for vagrancy near Buffalo, New York, London spent a month in jail. This was the turning point in his life.

London decided that he must have an education, and he worked hard to complete high school. He then attended the University of California for a few months but was lured away by the great Klondike Gold Rush of 1897–1898. Returning from Alaska empty-handed, London attempted to earn a living by setting his adventures down on paper. With the publication of *The Call of the Wild* in 1903, his fortunes changed dramatically: The struggling young writer suddenly became the highest-paid author in America. *The Sea Wolf* (1904) and *White Fang* (1906) were equally successful and, like *The Call of the Wild,* are still widely read today.

London's reading, and his sympathies with what he saw as an oppressed working class, made him an ardent believer in the necessity of social reform. Many of his books reflect his political ideas and deal with the struggle between opposing forces. Often London sets his conflicts in the great outdoors, where a human being struggles against the harsh laws of nature.

From his youth Jack London had learned that life is a struggle for survival; he never felt obliged to make life seem prettier or more romantic than he himself had found it. There have been many romantic tales of the Gold Rush in the Yukon, but "To Build a Fire" is not one of them. In this story, a lone man is pitted against a relentless Yukon winter. London's realism is sometimes quite grim, but it reflects his view of human life in an inhospitable universe.

Jack London

To Build a Fire

Day had broken cold and gray, exceedingly cold and gray, when the man turned aside from the main Yukon trail[1] and climbed the high earth-bank, where a dim and little-traveled trail led eastward through the fat spruce timberland. It was a steep bank, and he paused for breath at the top, excusing the act to himself by looking at his watch. It was nine o'clock. There was no sun nor hint of sun, though there was not a cloud in the sky. It was a clear day, and yet there seemed an intangible pall over the face of things, a subtle gloom that made the day dark, and that was due to the absence of sun. This fact did not worry the man. He was used to the lack of sun. It had been days since he had seen the sun, and he knew that a few more days must pass before that cheerful orb, due south, would just peep above the skyline and dip immediately from view.

The man flung a look back along the way he had come. The Yukon lay a mile wide and hidden under three feet of ice. On top of this ice were as many feet of snow. It was all pure white, rolling in gentle undulations where the ice jams of the freeze-up had formed. North and south, as far as his eye could see, it was unbroken white, save for a dark hairline that curved and twisted from around the spruce-covered island to the south, and that curved and twisted away into the north, where it disappeared behind another spruce-covered island. This dark hairline was the trail—the main trail—that led south five hundred miles to the Chilcoot Pass, Dyea,[2] and salt water; and that

---

1. **Yukon** [yōō′kon] **trail**: trail extending from southeastern Alaska through the Yukon territory of northwestern Canada and along the Yukon River through central Alaska to the Bering Sea.

2. **Dyea** [dī′a]: former town at the start of the trail.

led north seventy miles to Dawson, and still on to the north a thousand miles to Nulato,[3] and finally to St. Michael on Bering Sea, a thousand miles and half a thousand more.

But all this—the mysterious, far-reaching hairline trail, the absence of sun from the sky, the tremendous cold, and the strangeness and weirdness of it all—made no impression on the man. It was not because he was long used to it. He was a newcomer in the land, a *checha-quo*,[4] and this was his first winter. The trouble with him was that he was without imagination. He was quick and alert in the things of life, but only in the things, and not in the significances. Fifty degrees below zero meant eighty-odd degrees of frost. Such fact impressed him as being cold and uncomfortable, and that was all. It did not lead him to meditate upon his frailty as a creature of temperature, and upon man's frailty in general, able only to live within certain narrow limits of heat and cold; and from there on it did not lead him to the conjectural field of immortality and man's place in the universe. Fifty degrees below zero stood for a bite of frost that hurt and that must be guarded against by the use of mittens, earflaps, warm moccasins, and thick socks. Fifty degrees below zero was to him just precisely fifty degrees below zero. That there should be anything more to it than that was a thought that never entered his head.

As he turned to go on, he spat speculatively. There was a sharp, explosive crackle that startled him. He spat again. And again, in the air, before it could fall to the snow, the spittle crackled. He knew that at fifty below spittle crackled on the snow, but this spittle had crackled in the air. Undoubtedly it was colder than fifty below—how much colder he did not know. But the temperature did not matter. He was bound for the old claim on the left fork of Henderson Creek, where the boys were already. They had come over across the

divide from the Indian Creek country, while he had come the roundabout way to take a look at the possibilities of getting out logs in the spring from the islands in the Yukon. He would be in to camp by six o'clock; a bit after dark, it was true, but the boys would be there, a fire would be going, and a hot supper would be ready. As for lunch, he pressed his hand against the protruding bundle under his jacket. It was also under his shirt, wrapped up in a handkerchief and lying against the naked skin. It was the only way to keep the biscuits from freezing. He smiled agreeably to himself as he thought of those biscuits, each cut open and sopped in bacon grease, and each enclosing a generous slice of fried bacon.

He plunged in among the big spruce trees. The trail was faint. A foot of snow had fallen since the last sled had passed over, and he was glad he was without a sled, traveling light. In fact, he carried nothing but the lunch wrapped in the handkerchief. He was surprised, however, at the cold. It certainly was cold, he concluded, as he rubbed his numb nose and cheekbones with his mittened hand. He was a warm-whiskered man, but the hair on his face did not protect the high cheekbones and the eager nose that thrust itself aggressively into the frosty air.

At the man's heels trotted a dog, a big native husky, the proper wolf-dog, gray-coated and without any visible or temperamental difference from its brother, the wild wolf. The animal was depressed by the tremendous cold. It knew that it was no time for traveling. Its instinct told it a truer tale than was told to the man by the man's judgment. In reality, it was not merely colder than fifty below zero; it was colder than sixty below, than seventy below. It was seventy-five below zero. Since the freezing point is thirty-two above zero, it meant that one hundred and seven degrees of frost obtained. The dog did not know anything about thermometers. Possibly in its brain there was no sharp consciousness of a condition of very cold such as was in the man's brain. But the brute had its instinct. It experienced a vague

3. **Dawson** and **Nulato:** former goldmining centers in the Yukon.
4. *chechaquo* [chē chä′kō]: In the Pacific Northwest, slang for "a newcomer."

but menacing apprehension that subdued it and made it slink along at the man's heels, and that made it question eagerly every unwonted[5] movement of the man as if expecting him to go into camp or to seek shelter somewhere and build a fire. The dog had learned fire, and it wanted fire, or else to burrow under the snow and cuddle its warmth away from the air.

The frozen moisture of its breathing had settled on its fur in a fine powder of frost, and especially were its jowls, muzzle, and eyelashes whitened by its crystalled breath. The man's red beard and mustache were likewise frosted, but more solidly, the deposit taking the form of ice and increasing with every warm, moist breath he exhaled. Also, the man was chewing tobacco, and the muzzle of ice held his lips so rigidly that he was unable to clear his chin when he expelled the juice. The result was that a crystal beard of the color and solidity of amber was increasing its length on his chin. If he fell down it would shatter itself, like glass, into brittle fragments. But he did not mind the appendage. It was the penalty all tobacco chewers paid in that country, and he had been out before in two cold snaps. They had not been so cold as this, he knew, but by the spirit thermometer[6] at Sixty Mile he knew they had been registered at fifty below and at fifty-five.

He held on through the level stretch of woods for several miles, crossed a wide flat, and dropped down a bank to the frozen bed of a small stream. This was Henderson Creek, and he knew he was ten miles from the forks. He looked at his watch. It was ten o'clock. He was making four miles an hour, and he calculated that he would arrive at the forks at half past twelve. He decided to celebrate that event by eating his lunch there.

The dog dropped in again at his heels, with a tail drooping discouragement, as the man swung along the creekbed. The furrow of the old sled trail was plainly visible, but a dozen

---

5. **unwonted** [un wôn′tid]: unusual.
6. **spirit thermometer:** thermometer that contains alcohol instead of mercury and is used in extreme cold.

inches of snow covered the marks of the last runners. In a month no man had come up or down that silent creek. The man held steadily on. He was not much given to thinking, and just then particularly he had nothing to think about save that he would eat lunch at the forks and that at six o'clock he would be in camp with the boys. There was nobody to talk to; and, had there been, speech would have been impossible because of the ice muzzle on his mouth. So he continued monotonously to chew tobacco and to increase the length of his amber beard.

Once in a while the thought reiterated itself that it was very cold and that he had never experienced such cold. As he walked along he rubbed his cheekbones and nose with the back of his mittened hand. He did this automatically, now and again changing hands. But rub as he would, the instant he stopped his cheekbones went numb, and the following instant the end of his nose went numb. He was sure to frost his cheeks; he knew that, and experienced a pang of regret that he had not devised a nose strap of the sort Bud wore in cold snaps. Such a strap passed across the cheeks, as well, and saved them. But it didn't matter much, after all. What were frosted cheeks? A bit painful, that was all; they were never serious.

Empty as the man's mind was of thoughts, he was keenly observant, and he noticed the changes in the creek, the curves and bends and timber jams, and always he sharply noted where he placed his feet. Once, coming around a bend, he shied abruptly, like a startled horse, curved away from the place where he had been walking, and retreated several paces back along the trail. The creek he knew was frozen clear to the bottom—no creek could contain water in that arctic winter—but he knew also that there were springs that bubbled out from the hillsides and ran along under the snow and on top the ice of the creek. He knew that the coldest snaps never froze these springs, and he knew likewise their danger. They were traps. They hid pools of water under the snow that might be three inches deep, or three feet.

Sometimes a skin of ice half an inch thick covered them, and in turn was covered by the snow. Sometimes there were alternate layers of water and ice skin, so that when one broke through he kept on breaking through for a while, sometimes wetting himself to the waist.

That was why he had shied in such panic. He had felt the give under his feet and heard the crackle of a snow-hidden ice skin. And to get his feet wet in such a temperature meant trouble and danger. At the very least it meant delay, for he would be forced to stop and build a fire, and under its protection to bare his feet while he dried his socks and moccasins. He stood and studied the creek bed and its banks, and decided that the flow of water came from the right. He reflected a while, rubbing his nose and cheeks, then skirted to the left, stepping gingerly and testing the footing for each step. Once clear of the danger, he took a fresh chew of tobacco and swung along at his four-mile gait.

In the course of the next two hours he came upon several similar traps. Usually the snow above the hidden pools had a sunken, candied appearance that advertised the danger. Once again, however, he had a close call; and once, suspecting danger, he compelled the dog to go on in front. The dog did not want to go. It hung back until the man shoved it forward, and then it went quickly across the white, unbroken surface. Suddenly it broke through, floundered to one side, and got away to firmer footing. It had wet its forefeet and legs, and almost immediately the water that clung to it turned to ice. It made quick efforts to lick the ice off its legs, then dropped down in the snow and began to bite out the ice that had formed between the toes. This was a matter of instinct. To permit the ice to remain would mean sore feet. It did not know this, it merely obeyed the mysterious prompting that arose from the deep crypts of its being. But the man knew, having achieved a judgment on the subject, and he removed the mitten from his right hand and helped tear out the ice particles. He did not expose his fingers more than a minute, and was astonished at the swift numbness that smote them. It certainly was cold. He pulled on the mitten hastily, and beat the hand savagely across his chest.

At twelve o'clock the day was at its brightest. Yet the sun was too far south on its winter journey to clear the horizon. The bulge of the earth intervened between it and Henderson Creek, where the man walked under a clear sky at noon and cast no shadow. At half past twelve, to the minute, he arrived at the forks of the creek. He was pleased at the speed he had made. If he kept it up, he would certainly be with the boys by six. He unbuttoned his jacket and shirt and drew forth his lunch. The action consumed no more than a quarter of a minute, yet in that brief moment the numbness laid hold of the exposed fingers. He did not put the mitten on, but instead struck the fingers a dozen sharp smashes against his leg. Then he sat down on a snow-covered log to eat. The sting that followed upon the striking of his fingers against his leg ceased so quickly that he was startled. He had had no chance to take a bite of biscuit. He struck the fingers repeatedly and returned them to the mitten, baring the other hand for the purpose of eating. He tried to take a mouthful, but the ice muzzle prevented. He had forgotten to build a fire and thaw out. He chuckled at his foolishness, and as he chuckled he noted the numbness creeping into the exposed fingers. Also, he noted that the stinging which had first come to his toes when he sat down was already passing away. He wondered whether the toes were warm or numb. He moved them inside the moccasins and decided that they were numb.

He pulled the mitten on hurriedly and stood up. He was a bit frightened. He stamped up and down until the stinging returned into the feet. It certainly was cold, was his thought. That man from Sulphur Creek had spoken the truth when telling how cold it sometimes got in the country. And he had laughed at him at the time! That showed one must not be too sure of things. There was no mistake about it, it *was* cold. He strode up and down, stamping his feet and threshing his arms, until reassured by the returning warmth. Then he got out matches and proceeded to make a fire. From the undergrowth, where high water of the previous spring had lodged a supply of seasoned twigs, he got his firewood. Working carefully from a small beginning, he soon had a roaring fire, over which he thawed the ice from his face and in the protection of which he ate his biscuits. For the moment the cold of space was outwitted. The dog took satisfaction in the fire, stretching out close enough for warmth and far enough away to escape being singed.

When the man had finished, he filled his pipe and took his comfortable time over a smoke. Then he pulled on his mittens, settled the earflaps of his cap firmly about his ears, and took the creek trail up the left fork. The dog was disappointed and yearned back toward the fire. This man did not know cold. Possibly all the generations of his ancestry had been ignorant of cold, of real cold, of cold one hundred and seven degrees below freezing point. But the dog knew; all its ancestry knew, and it had inherited the knowledge. And it knew that it was not good to walk abroad in such fearful cold. It was the time to lie snug in a hole in the snow and wait for a curtain of cloud to be drawn across the face of outer space whence this cold came. On the other hand, there was no keen intimacy between the dog and the man. The one was the toil slave of the other, and the only caresses it had ever received were the caresses of the whiplash and of harsh and menacing throat-sounds that threatened the whiplash. So the dog made no effort to communicate its apprehension to the man. It was not concerned in the welfare of the man; it was for its own sake that it yearned back toward the fire. But the man whistled, and spoke to it with the sound of whiplashes, and the dog swung in at the man's heel and followed after.

The man took a chew of tobacco and proceeded to start a new amber beard. Also, his moist breath quickly powdered with white his mustache, eyebrows, and lashes. There did not seem to be so many springs on the left fork of the Henderson, and for half an hour the man saw no signs of any. And then it happened. At a place where there were no signs, where the soft, unbroken snow seemed to advertise solidity beneath, the man broke through. It was not deep. He wet himself halfway to the knees before he floundered out to the firm crust.

He was angry, and cursed his luck aloud. He had hoped to get into camp with the boys at six o'clock, and this would delay him an hour, for he would have to build a fire and dry out his footgear. This was imperative at that low temperature—he knew that much; and he turned aside to the bank, which he climbed. On top, tangled in the underbrush about the trunks of several small spruce trees, was a high-water deposit of dry firewood—sticks and twigs, principally, but also larger portions of seasoned branches and fine, dry, last-year's grasses. He threw down several large pieces on top of the snow. This served for a foundation and prevented the young flame from drowning itself in the snow it otherwise would melt. The flame he got by touching a match to a small shred of birch bark that he took from his pocket. This burned even more readily than paper. Placing it on the foundation, he fed the young flame with wisps of dry grass and with the tiniest dry twigs.

He worked slowly and carefully, keenly aware of his danger. Gradually, as the flame grew stronger, he increased the size of the twigs with which he fed it. He squatted in the snow, pulling the twigs out from their entanglement in the brush and feeding directly to the flame. He knew there must be no failure. When it is seventy-five below zero, a man must not fail in his first attempt to build a fire—that is, if his feet are wet. If his feet are dry, and he fails, he can run along the trail for half a mile and restore his circulation. But the circulation of wet and freezing feet cannot be restored by running when it is seventy-five below. No matter how fast he runs, the wet feet will freeze the harder.

All this the man knew. The old-timer on

Sulphur Creek had told him about it the previous fall, and now he was appreciating the advice. Already all sensation had gone out of his feet. To build the fire he had been forced to remove his mittens, and the fingers had quickly gone numb. His pace of four miles an hour had kept his heart pumping blood to the surface of his body and to all the extremities. But the instant he stopped, the action of the pump eased down. The cold of space smote the unprotected tip of the planet, and he, being on that unprotected tip, received the full force of the blow. The blood of his body recoiled before it. The blood was alive, like the dog, and like the dog it wanted to hide away and cover itself up from the fearful cold. So long as he walked four miles an hour, he pumped that blood, willy-nilly,[7] to the surface; but now it ebbed away and sank down into the recesses of his body. The extremities were the first to feel its absence. His wet feet froze the faster, and his exposed fingers numbed the faster, though they had not yet begun to freeze. Nose and cheeks were already freezing, while the skin of all his body chilled as it lost its blood.

But he was safe. Toes and nose and cheeks would be only touched by the frost, for the fire was beginning to burn with strength. He was feeding it with twigs the size of his finger. In another minute he would be able to feed it with branches the size of his wrist, and then he could remove his wet footgear, and, while it dried, he could keep his naked feet warm by the fire, rubbing them at first, of course, with snow. The fire was a success. He was safe. He remembered the advice of the old-timer on Sulphur Creek, and smiled. The old-timer had been very serious in laying down the law that no man must travel alone in the Klondike[8] after fifty below. Well, here he was; he had had the accident; he was alone; and he had saved himself. Those old-timers were rather womanish, some of them, he thought. All a man had to do was to keep his head; and he was all right. Any man who was a man could travel alone. But it was surprising, the rapidity with which his cheeks and nose were freezing. And he had not thought his fingers could go lifeless in so short a time. Lifeless they were, for he could scarcely make them move together to grip a twig, and they seemed remote from his body and from him. When he touched a twig, he had to look and see whether or not he had hold of it. The wires were pretty well down between him and his finger ends.

All of which counted for little. There was the fire, snapping and crackling and promising life with every dancing flame. He started to untie his moccasins. They were coated with ice; the thick German socks were like sheaths of iron halfway to the knees; and the moccasin strings were like rods of steel all twisted and knotted as by some conflagration.[9] For a moment he tugged with his numb fingers, then, realizing the folly of it, he drew his sheath knife.

But before he could cut the strings, it happened. It was his own fault or, rather, his mistake. He should not have built the fire under the spruce tree. He should have built it in the open. But it had been easier to pull the twigs from the brush and drop them directly on the fire. Now the tree under which he had done this carried a weight of snow on its boughs. No wind had blown for weeks, and each bough was fully freighted. Each time he had pulled a twig he had communicated a slight agitation to the tree—an imperceptible agitation, so far as he was concerned, but an agitation sufficient to bring about the disaster. High up in the tree one bough capsized its load of snow. This fell on the boughs beneath, capsizing them. This process continued, spreading out and involving the whole tree. It grew like an avalanche, and it descended without warning upon the man and the fire, and the fire was blotted out! Where it had burned was a mantle of fresh and disordered snow.

The man was shocked. It was as though he

---

7. **willy-nilly:** inevitably.
8. **Klondike** [klon′dīk]: Yukon gold-mining region.

9. **conflagration:** big, destructive fire.

had just heard his own sentence of death. For a moment he sat and stared at the spot where the fire had been. Then he grew very calm. Perhaps the old-timer on Sulphur Creek was right. If he had only had a trailmate he would have been in no danger now. The trailmate could have built the fire. Well, it was up to him to build the fire over again, and this second time there must be no failure. Even if he succeeded, he would most likely lose some toes. His feet must be badly frozen by now, and there would be some time before the second fire was ready.

Such were his thoughts, but he did not sit and think them. He was busy all the time they were passing through his mind. He made a new foundation for a fire, this time in the open, where no treacherous tree could blot it out. Next, he gathered dry grasses and tiny twigs from the high-water flotsam. He could not bring his fingers together to pull them out, but he was able to gather them by the handful. In this way he got many rotten twigs and bits of green moss that were undesirable, but it was the best he could do. He worked methodically, even collecting an armful of the larger branches to be used later when the fire gathered strength. And all the while the dog sat and watched him, a certain yearning wistfulness in its eyes, for it looked upon him as the fire provider, and the fire was slow in coming.

When all was ready, the man reached in his pocket for a second piece of birch bark. He knew the bark was there, and, though he could not feel it with his fingers, he could hear its crisp rustling as he fumbled for it. Try as he would, he could not clutch hold of it. And all the time, in his consciousness, was the knowledge that each instant his feet were freezing. This thought tended to put him in a panic, but he fought against it and kept calm. He pulled on his mittens with his teeth, and threshed his arms back and forth, beating his hands with all his might against his sides. He did this sitting down, and he stood up to do it; and all the while the dog sat in the snow, its wolf-brush of a tail curled around warmly over its forefeet,

its sharp wolf ears pricked forward intently as it watched the man. And the man, as he beat and threshed with his arms and hands, felt a great surge of envy as he regarded the creature that was warm and secure in its natural covering.

After a time he was aware of the first far-away signals of sensation in his beaten fingers. The faint tingling grew stronger till it evolved into a stinging ache that was excruciating, but which the man hailed with satisfaction. He stripped the mitten from his right hand and fetched forth the birch bark. The exposed fingers were quickly going numb again. Next he brought out his bunch of sulphur matches. But the tremendous cold had already driven the life out of his fingers. In his effort to separate one match from the others, the whole bunch fell in the snow. He tried to pick it out of the snow, but failed. The dead fingers could neither touch nor clutch. He was very careful. He drove the thought of his freezing feet, and nose, and cheeks, out of his mind, devoting his whole soul to the matches. He watched, using the sense of vision in place of touch, and when he saw his fingers on each side the bunch, he closed them—that is, he willed to close them, for the wires were down, and the fingers did not obey. He pulled the mitten on the right hand, and beat it fiercely against his knee. Then, with both mittened hands, he scooped the bunch of matches, along with much snow, into his lap. Yet he was no better off.

After some manipulation he managed to get the bunch between the heels of his mittened hands. In this fashion he carried it to his mouth. The ice crackled and snapped when by a violent effort he opened his mouth. He drew the lower jaw in, curled the upper lip out of the way, and scraped the bunch with his upper teeth in order to separate a match. He succeeded in getting one, which he dropped on his lap. He was no better off. He could not pick it up. Then he devised a way. He picked it up in his teeth and scratched it on his leg. Twenty times he scratched before he succeeded in lighting it. As it flamed he held it with his teeth to the birch bark. But the burning brimstone went up his nostrils and into his lungs, causing him to cough spasmodically. The match fell into the snow and went out.

The oldtimer on Sulphur Creek was right, he thought in the moment of controlled despair that ensued: after fifty below, a man should travel with a partner. He beat his hands, but failed in exciting any sensation. Suddenly he bared both hands, removing the mittens with his teeth. He caught the whole bunch between the heels of his hands. His arm-muscles not being frozen enabled him to press the hand heels tightly against the matches. Then he scratched the bunch along his leg. It flared into flame, seventy sulphur matches at once! There was no wind to blow them out. He kept his head to one side to escape the strangling fumes, and held the blazing bunch to the birch bark. As he so held it, he became aware of sensation in his hand. His flesh was burning. He could smell it. Deep down below the surface he could feel it. The sensation developed into pain that grew acute. And still he endured it, holding the flame of the matches clumsily to the bark that would not light readily because his own burning hands were in the way, absorbing most of the flame.

At last, when he could endure no more, he jerked his hands apart. The blazing matches fell sizzling into the snow, but the birch bark was alight. He began laying dry grasses and the tiniest twigs on the flame. He could not pick and choose, for he had to lift the fuel between the heels of his hands. Small pieces of rotten wood and green moss clung to the twigs, and he bit them off as well as he could with his teeth. He cherished the flame carefully and awkwardly. It meant life, and it must not perish. The withdrawal of blood from the surface of his body now made him begin to shiver, and he grew more awkward. A large piece of green moss fell squarely on the little fire. He tried to poke it out with his fingers, but his shivering frame made him poke too far, and he disrupted the nucleus of the little fire, the burning grasses and tiny twigs separating and scattering. He

tried to poke them together again, but in spite of the tenseness of the effort, his shivering got away with him, and the twigs were hopelessly scattered. Each twig gushed a puff of smoke and went out. The fire provider had failed. As he looked apathetically about him, his eyes chanced on the dog, sitting across the ruins of the fire from him, in the snow, making restless, hunching movements, slightly lifting one forefoot and then the other, shifting its weight back and forth on them with wistful eagerness.

The sight of the dog put a wild idea into his head. He remembered the tale of the man, caught in a blizzard, who killed a steer and crawled inside the carcass, and so was saved. He would kill the dog and bury his hands in the warm body until the numbness went out of them. Then he could build another fire. He spoke to the dog, calling it to him; but in his voice was a strange note of fear that frightened the animal, who had never known the man to speak in such way before. Something was the matter, and its suspicious nature sensed danger—it knew not what danger, but somewhere, somehow, in its brain arose an apprehension of the man. It flattened its ears down at the sound of the man's voice, and its restless, hunching movements and the liftings and shiftings of its forefeet became more pronounced; but it would not come to the man. He got on his hands and knees and crawled toward the dog. This unusual posture again excited suspicion, and the animal sidled mincingly away.

The man sat up in the snow for a moment and struggled for calmness. Then he pulled on his mittens, by means of his teeth, and got upon his feet. He glanced down at first in order to assure himself that he was really standing up, for the absence of sensation in his feet left him unrelated to the earth. His erect position in itself started to drive the webs of suspicion from the dog's mind; and when he spoke peremptorily,[10] with the sound of whip-lashes in his voice, the dog rendered its customary allegiance and came to him. As it came

---

10. **peremptorily**: dictatorially.

within reaching distance, the man lost his control. His arms flashed out to the dog, and he experienced genuine surprise when he discovered that his hands could not clutch, that there was neither bend nor feeling in the fingers. He had forgotten for the moment that they were frozen and that they were freezing more and more. All this happened quickly, and before the animal could get away, he encircled its body with his arms. He sat down in the snow, and in this fashion held the dog, while it snarled and whined and struggled.

But it was all he could do, hold its body encircled in his arms and sit there. He realized that he could not kill the dog. There was no way to do it. With his helpless hands he could neither draw nor hold his sheath knife nor throttle the animal. He released it, and it plunged wildly away, with tail between its legs, and still snarling. It halted forty feet away and surveyed him curiously, with ears sharply pricked forward. The man looked down at his hands in order to locate them, and found them hanging on the ends of his arms. It struck him as curious that one should have to use his eyes in order to find out where his hands were. He began threshing his arms back and forth, beating the mittened hands against his sides. He did this for five minutes, violently, and his heart pumped enough blood up to the surface to put a stop to his shivering. But no sensation was aroused in the hands. He had an impression that they hung like weights on the ends of his arms, but when he tried to run the impression down, he could not find it.

A certain fear of death, dull and oppressive, came to him. This fear quickly became poignant as he realized that it was no longer a mere matter of freezing his fingers and toes, or of losing his hands and feet, but that it was a matter of life and death with the chances against him. This threw him into a panic, and he turned and ran up the creekbed along the old, dim trail. The dog joined in behind and kept up with him. He ran blindly, without intention, in fear such as he had never known in his life. Slowly, as he plowed and floundered through the snow, he began to see things again—the banks of the creeks, the old timber jams, the leafless aspens, and the sky. The running made him feel better. He did not shiver. Maybe, if he ran on, his feet would thaw out; and, anyway, if he ran far enough, he would reach camp and the boys. Without doubt he would lose some fingers and toes and some of his face; but the boys would take care of him, and save the rest of him when he got there. And at the same time there was another thought in his mind that said he would never get to the camp and the boys; that it was too many miles away, that the freezing had too great a start on him, and that he would soon be stiff and dead. This thought he kept in the background and refused to consider. Sometimes it pushed itself forward and demanded to be heard, but he thrust it back and strove to think of other things.

It struck him as curious that he could run at all on feet so frozen that he could not feel them when they struck the earth and took the weight of his body. He seemed to himself to skim along above the surface, and to have no connection with the earth. Somewhere he had once seen a winged Mercury,[11] and he wondered if Mercury felt as he felt when skimming over the earth.

His theory of running until he reached camp and the boys had one flaw in it: he lacked the endurance. Several times he stumbled, and finally he tottered, crumpled up, and fell. When he tried to rise, he failed. He must sit and rest, he decided, and next time he would merely walk and keep on going. As he sat and regained his breath, he noted that he was feeling quite warm and comfortable. He was not shivering, and it even seemed that a warm glow had come to his chest and trunk. And yet, when he touched his nose or cheeks,

there was no sensation. Running would not thaw them out. Nor would it thaw out his hands and feet. Then the thought came to him that the frozen portions of his body must be extending. He tried to keep this thought down, to forget it, to think of something else; he was aware of the panicky feeling that it caused, and he was afraid of the panic. But the thought asserted itself, and persisted, until it produced a vision of his body totally frozen. This was too much, and he made another wild run along the trail. Once he slowed down to a walk, but the thought of the freezing extending itself made him run again.

And all the time the dog ran with him, at his heels. When he fell down a second time, it curled its tail over its forefeet and sat in front of him, facing him, curiously eager and intent. The warmth and security of the animal angered him, and he cursed it till it flattened down its ears appeasingly. This time the shivering came more quickly upon the man. He was losing in his battle with the frost. It was creeping into his body from all sides. The thought of it drove him on, but he ran no more than a hundred feet, when he staggered and pitched headlong. It was his last panic. When he had recovered his breath and control, he sat up and entertained in his mind the conception of meeting death with dignity. However, the conception did not come to him in such terms. His idea of it was that he had been making a fool of himself, running around like a chicken with its head cut off—such was the simile that occurred to him. Well, he was bound to freeze anyway, and he might as well take it decently. With this newfound peace of mind came the first glimmerings of drowsiness. A good idea, he thought, to sleep off to death. It was like taking an anaesthetic.[12] Freezing was not so bad as people thought. There were lots worse ways to die.

He pictured the boys finding his body next day. Suddenly he found himself with them,

---

11. **Mercury:** in Roman mythology, messenger of the gods; considered to have winged feet.

12. **anaesthetic:** something that produces a loss of sensation.

coming along the trail and looking for himself. And, still with them, he came around a turn in the trail and found himself lying in the snow. He did not belong with himself any more, for even then he was out of himself, standing with the boys and looking at himself in the snow. It certainly was cold, was his thought. When he got back to the States he could tell the folks what real cold was. He drifted on from this to a vision of the old-timer on Sulphur Creek. He could see him quite clearly, warm and comfortable, and smoking a pipe.

"You were right, old hoss; you were right," the man mumbled to the old-timer of Sulphur Creek.

Then the man drowsed off into what seemed to him the most comfortable and satisfying sleep he had ever known. The dog sat facing him and waiting. The brief day drew to a close in a long, slow twilight. There were no signs of a fire to be made, and, besides, never in the dog's experience had it known a man to sit like that in the snow and make no fire. As the twilight drew on, its eager yearning for the fire mastered it, and with a great lifting and shifting of forefeet, it whined softly, then flattened its ears down in anticipation of being chidden[13] by the man. But the man remained silent. Later, the dog whined loudly. And still later it crept close to the man and caught the scent of death. This made the animal bristle and back away. A little longer it delayed, howling under the stars that leaped and danced and shone brightly in the cold sky. Then it turned and trotted up the trail in the direction of the camp it knew, where were the other food providers and fire providers.

---

13. **chidden:** scolded.

STUDY QUESTIONS

Recalling

1. According to the third paragraph, what four things make no impression on the man as he navigates the wilderness? What is the "trouble" with the man?
2. What does the dog have that "tells" it a truer tale than the man's judgment (paragraph 6)?
3. Describe the "traps" that the man tries to avoid (page 343). Why does the man compel the dog to go in front on page 344?
4. The man builds his first fire after lunch. Why must he later build another fire?
5. When the man tries to build the second fire, his fires fail twice. What causes the first failure? The second?
6. What happens to the man at the end of the story? What happens to the dog?

Interpreting

7. Against what force does the man struggle in this story? What is the outcome of that struggle?

8. What two qualities of the dog and of the man contrast? What does the ending suggest about London's view of these qualities and their relationship to survival in the natural world?
9. Describe the mood or atmosphere of the story. What elements of Naturalism does it contain?

Extending

10. Do you think the man could have used his judgment and survived? What different decisions might he have made? What might he have done if he had not been lacking in imagination?

LITERARY FOCUS

Conflict

The **conflict** in a work of fiction is the battle that the main character must wage against an opposing force. Usually the events of the story are all related to the conflict, and the conflict is resolved in some way by the story's end.

A battle with nature is a common conflict in literature, particularly Naturalist literature. Other common types are conflict between two characters; conflict between a character and the laws of society; conflict between a character and chance or fate; and inner conflict, in which a character struggles with personal weaknesses, illusions, or desires.

Thinking About Conflict
▪ Consider the other stories you have read in this book. Find at least one example of each of the five kinds of conflict.

VOCABULARY

Vivid Action Words; Antonyms
A story about a man alone freezing to death seems an unlikely source for vivid verbs. Yet it is the masterful use of these words that gives this story much of its descriptive power. London shows us ice that "curved" and "twisted," a man who "stamped" and "strode," a dog that "whined" and "trotted."

A good way to understand exactly what a word means is to name its antonym, or opposite. The verbs in capitals are from "To Build a Fire." Choose the verb that is an antonym of each verb in capitals, *as it is used in this selection.*

1. CRACKLED: (a) popped (b) puffed (c) sparked (d) whispered
2. PLUNGED: (a) approached (b) entered (c) hung back (d) recoiled
3. SKIRTED: (a) circled (b) covered (c) went through (d) went back
4. FREIGHTED: (a) clear of (b) lightened (c) stiffened (d) strengthened
5. SKIM: (a) float (b) fly (c) plod (d) sink

COMPOSITION

Writing About a Quotation
▪ The old-timer in "To Build a Fire" warns that "after fifty below, a man should travel with a partner." In a brief essay first explain the literal meaning of the warning. Then explain the deeper significance that the unheeded warning might have for the main character. Relate the quotation to the theme of the work. *For help with this assignment, refer to Lesson 5 in the Writing About Literature Handbook at the back of this book.*

Describing a Conflict
▪ In a few paragraphs describe a struggle with nature that you or someone you know has experienced. Provide details to make the description vivid and build suspense by reminding the reader of the consequences of the struggle. Be sure to explain how the conflict was resolved.

COMPARING WRITERS

1. Both Sarah Orne Jewett, in "A White Heron," and Kate Chopin, in "A Pair of Silk Stockings," concentrate on their main characters' thoughts and feelings. In both stories the main character faces a certain choice and must make a decision. How are the choices facing the two characters different? How are they similar? How do the characters' decisions differ?
2. The writers in this unit do not use Regionalist techniques in the same way or to the same degree. Compare the use of local color in "The Outcasts of Poker Flat," "A White Heron," and "A Pair of Silk Stockings." Which story emphasizes local color the most? Which of the stories seem rooted in a particular time and place? Which one could perhaps have taken place somewhere else? Why?
3. Both the farmers in Garland's "Under the Lion's Paw" and the man in London's "To Build a Fire" battle nature. In what ways are their battles the same? How are they different? Compare the ideas about nature in these stories with the ideas about nature expressed by Emerson (pages 161–163) and Thoreau (pages 171–176).

POETRY

Sidney Lanier 1842–1881

Sidney Lanier (lə nir′) grew up in the pre–Civil War South, but he greeted the new age of industrialism and scientific progress by writing some of the most advanced and daring poetry of his time.

Lanier was born in Macon, Georgia. At the outbreak of the Civil War, he enlisted in the Confederate Army as a private. Four months before the end of the war, he was captured by Union troops and sent to a federal prison, where he contracted the tuberculosis that would afflict him for the rest of his short life. His first published work, the novel *Tiger Lilies* (1867), was based on his Civil War experiences.

Lanier was primarily a poet and a musician. In fact, he played the flute well enough to join the Peabody Symphony Orchestra in Baltimore as first flutist. He sought to apply some of the rules of musical composition to the composition of poetry; his theories about the relationship of music to verse are contained in *The Science of English Verse* (1880). In "The Song of the Chattahoochee" Lanier applies his theories about poetry and music to demonstrate that the sound and the sense of a poem are inseparable.

Sidney Lanier

Song of the Chattahoochee

Out of the hills of Habersham,
Down the valleys of Hall,[1]
I hurry amain[2] to reach the plain,
Run the rapid and leap the fall,
5 Split at the rock and together again,
Accept my bed, or narrow or wide,
And flee from folly on every side
With a lover's pain to attain the plain
  Far from the hills of Habersham,
10 Far from the valleys of Hall.

All down the hills of Habersham,
All through the valleys of Hall,

---

1. **Habersham . . . Hall:** two mountainous counties in northern Georgia, through which the Chattahoochee River flows.
2. **amain** [ə mān′]: at full speed.

The rushes cried, *Abide, abide,*
The willful waterweeds held me thrall,
15 The laving[3] laurel turned my tide,
The ferns and the fondling grass said *Stay,*
The dewberry dipped for to work delay,
And the little reeds sighed, *Abide, abide,*
　　Here in the hills of Habersham,
20　　*Here in the valleys of Hall.*

High o'er the hills of Habersham,
　Veiling the valleys of Hall,
The hickory told me manifold
Fair tales of shade, the poplar tall
25 Wrought me her shadowy self to hold,
The chestnut, the oak, the walnut, the pine,
Overleaning, with flickering meaning and sign,
Said, *Pass not, so cold, these manifold*
　　Deep shades of the hills of Habersham,
30　　*These glades in the valleys of Hall.*

And oft in the hills of Habersham,
　And oft in the valleys of Hall,
The white quartz shone, and the smooth brook-stone
Did bar me of passage with friendly brawl,
35 And many a luminous jewel lone
　— Crystals clear or a-cloud with mist
Ruby, garnet and amethyst —
Made lures with the lights of streaming stone
　　In the clefts of the hills of Habersham,
40　　In the beds of the valleys of Hall.

But oh, not the hills of Habersham,
　And oh, not the valleys of hall
Avail: I am fain[4] for to water the plain.
Downward the voices of Duty call —
45 Downward, to toil and be mixed with the main,[5]
The dry fields burn, and the mills are to turn,
And a myriad flowers mortally yearn,
And the lordly main from beyond the plain
　　Calls o'er the hills of Habersham,
50　　Calls through the valleys of Hall.

---

3. **laving:** washing up against.
4. **fain:** compelled by circumstances.
5. **main:** the open sea.

STUDY QUESTIONS

Recalling

1. Who is the speaker of this poem, according to the title?
2. According to the first stanza, to what does the river hurry? From what does it flee?
3. What do the ferns and grasses "say" to the river in the second stanza? What do the reeds "sigh"?
4. What "toil" must the river perform before it mixes with "the main," according to the last stanza? What calls the river in the last three lines?

Interpreting

5. To what two basic uses is the river put when it reaches the plain?
6. Basically, what lures the river to the hills of Habersham and the valleys of Hall?
7. What figurative device does the poet use in the title and throughout the poem? To what is the poet comparing the river?
8. On the figurative level what might the course of the river represent? "The folly on either side" (stanza 1)? The "duty" of the plain?
9. What do you think "the main" represents?

10. What poetic devices make the poem musical? How is the music related to the subject and the theme of the poem?

COMPOSITION

Writing About Sound and Meaning in Poetry

■ Lanier believed poetry should be as much like music as possible. Write a short composition describing the "music" you find in "The Song of the Chattahoochee." Begin by discussing the length of the lines and their regularity or irregularity. Then point out how the poet seems to be trying to reflect in sound the subject matter of the poem. Conclude with your opinion of the value of writing poetry in this way and your reasons for thinking as you do.

Writing an Extended Personification

■ In "Song of the Chattahoochee" Lanier personifies a river and has it speak for itself. Imagine that you are the wind, an ocean, a tree, or some other element of nature. Write a paragraph (or a poem, if you wish) in which you describe in detail your movements, thoughts, and sensations.

Edwin Arlington Robinson
1869–1935

Edwin Arlington Robinson was a New Englander who never forgot his regional ties. Born in Head Tide, a tiny village in Maine, Robinson grew up in Gardiner, Maine, on which he modeled Tilbury Town, the fictional setting for many of his most famous poems.

At twenty-eight Robinson moved to New York City, where he lived in semipoverty and wrote without much of a readership. His life was made somewhat easier in 1902 when President Theodore Roosevelt, an admirer of his work, appointed him to a post in the New York Custom House where Herman Melville had once been employed. However, Robinson's first real success did not come until 1910, with the publication of *The Town Down the River*. In time he was awarded three Pulitzer Prizes and found himself one of America's favorite poets.

In technique Robinson is a traditionalist whose tightly structured verse may, on first inspection, appear to be simpler than it really is. For if Robinson is traditional in style, he is daringly realistic in his subject matter. Most of his poems attempt to tell the "truth" about Tilbury Town. To a Realist like Robinson, that truth includes not only love and tranquillity, but also sadness, tragedy, frustration, and waste. The particular flavor of Robinson's best poems springs from his mixture of realism with irony and even humor. Richard Cory and Miniver Cheevy, two of Tilbury Town's most famous inhabitants, are keenly observed human beings, full of contradictions, living what Thoreau would have called "lives of quiet desperation."

Edwin Arlington Robinson

Richard Cory

Whenever Richard Cory went down town,
We people on the pavement looked at him:
He was a gentleman from sole to crown,
Clean favored, and imperially slim.

5 And he was always quietly arrayed,
And he was always human when he talked;
But still he fluttered pulses when he said,
"Good morning," and he glittered when he walked.

And he was rich—yes, richer than a king—
10 And admirably schooled in every grace:
In fine,[1] we thought that he was everything
To make us wish that we were in his place.

So on we worked, and waited for the light,
And went without the meat, and cursed the bread;
15 And Richard Cory, one calm summer night,
Went home and put a bullet through his head.

---

1. **In fine:** in brief.

STUDY QUESTIONS

Recalling

1. Which line in the poem identifies the speaker? Which lines tell you about the economic condition of the speaker?
2. What is Richard Cory "from sole to crown"? What effect does he have when he says "Good morning"?
3. What, "in fine," do the people think of Richard Cory (stanza 3)?
4. What is the "surprise" ending?

Interpreting

5. How are the "we" of the poem different from Richard Cory?
6. What do "crown" (line 3) and "imperially" (line 4) indicate about the speaker's impression of Richard Cory?
7. What effect does Cory's final action seem to have on everyone in Tilbury Town? What does Tilbury Town's reaction to Cory's life and death suggest about human understanding?

Edwin Arlington Robinson

Miniver Cheevy

Miniver Cheevy, child of scorn,
　　Grew lean while he assailed the seasons;
He wept that he was ever born,
　　And he had reasons.

5 Miniver loved the days of old
　　When swords were bright and steeds were prancing;
The vision of a warrior bold
　　Would set him dancing.

Miniver sighed for what was not,
10　　And dreamed, and rested from his labors;
He dreamed of Thebes[1] and Camelot,[2]
　　And Priam's[3] neighbors.

Miniver mourned the ripe renown
　　That made so many a name so fragrant;
15 He mourned Romance, now on the town,[4]
　　And Art, a vagrant.

Miniver loved the Medici,[5]
　　Albeit[6] he had never seen one;
He would have sinned incessantly
20　　Could he have been one.

Miniver cursed the commonplace
　　And eyed a khaki suit with loathing;
He missed the medieval grace
　　Of iron clothing.

25 Miniver scorned the gold he sought,
　　But sore annoyed was he without it;
Miniver thought, and thought, and thought,
　　And thought about it.

Miniver Cheevy, born too late,
30　　Scratched his head and kept on thinking;
Miniver coughed, and called it fate,
　　And kept on drinking.

---

1. **Thebes** [thēbz]: leading city-state of ancient Greece.
2. **Camelot:** legendary site in England of King Arthur's court and Round Table.
3. **Priam** [prī′əm]: King of Troy during the Trojan War.
4. **on the town:** on welfare.
5. **Medici** [med′i chē]: rich, powerful family of Florence, Italy, in the fourteenth, fifteenth, and sixteenth centuries.
6. **Albeit** [ôl bē′it]: although.

STUDY QUESTIONS

Recalling

1. For what does Cheevy sigh and mourn in the first five stanzas? What does Cheevy curse in the sixth stanza?
2. What are Cheevy's feelings about gold, according to the seventh stanza?
3. To what does Cheevy attribute his unhappiness in line 31? What does he keep on doing, according to the last line of the poem?

Interpreting

4. What do lines 9–10 reveal about Cheevy's character? Lines 17–18? Lines 25–26?
5. Basically, how does Cheevy see himself? How do we see him? What really causes his unhappiness?

Extending

6. Could Richard Cory and Miniver Cheevy be found only in a small Maine town at the turn of the century? Explain your answer.

LITERARY FOCUS

Irony

Irony is a contrast or a difference between the way things seem and the way they really are. In literature there are three kinds of irony. **Verbal irony** occurs when words that appear to be saying one thing are really saying something quite different. **Situational irony** occurs when what is expected to happen is not what actually comes to pass. **Dramatic irony** occurs when events that mean one thing to the characters mean something quite different to the reader.

Irony is often accompanied by a grim humor. There is an element of dark humor, for example, in the mistaken ideas that the townspeople have of Richard Cory, while Miniver Cheevy is almost comical in his hypocrisy and self-delusion.

Thinking About Irony

1. How is the use of the adjective "calm" in the next-to-last line of "Richard Cory" an example of verbal irony?
2. Explain the situational irony in "Richard Cory."
3. Tell why "Miniver Cheevy" is an example of dramatic irony.

COMPOSITION

Writing a Comparison/Contrast

■ Write a brief essay comparing and contrasting "Richard Cory" and "Miniver Cheevy." Begin with a statement of each poem's theme. Then show what the characters have in common and how they differ. Conclude by discussing the tone of each poem and the general impression each leaves with the reader. *For help with this assignment, refer to Lesson 2 in the Writing About Literature Handbook at the back of this book.*

Using Situational or Dramatic Irony

■ Write a character study in poem or paragraph form in which an ironic "surprise" ending throws new light on the character you are describing. For example, you might write about a person who seems popular but who is actually quite lonely, or about someone who seems kind but in the end proves false and calculating. The irony may be situational or dramatic.

Paul Laurence Dunbar   *1872–1906*

Paul Laurence Dunbar was the first black American writer to make his living entirely by writing. Born in Dayton, Ohio, the son of former slaves, Dunbar became interested in writing verse when, as a child, he heard a poem by the English writer William Wordsworth. By the age of fourteen, Dunbar was reciting his own poems before school assemblies; in high school, the only black student in his class, he was editor in chief of the school newspaper.

Nevertheless, despite his school successes, Dunbar graduated into a world with few prospects for a poet. With the help of former schoolmates Orville and Wilbur Wright, he started a small newspaper for the black community, but the venture failed. Dunbar was forced to take a job as an elevator operator to support himself and his widowed mother.

In 1892 a former teacher arranged for Dunbar to read before the Western Association of Writers. His reading impressed the members so much that the poet soon found himself on the road to national recognition. His poetry collection *Majors and Minors* was published in 1895 to widespread critical acclaim, and *Lyrics of a Lowly Life* (1896) sold over twelve thousand copies.

Dunbar was a prolific writer, producing poems, stories, and novels. Many of his poems and stories are written in the dialect of the black community, but in "Douglass" Dunbar dispenses with dialect. To pay tribute to the black leader Frederick Douglass (1817?–1895), Dunbar adopts the grand language and formal speech of the sonnet.

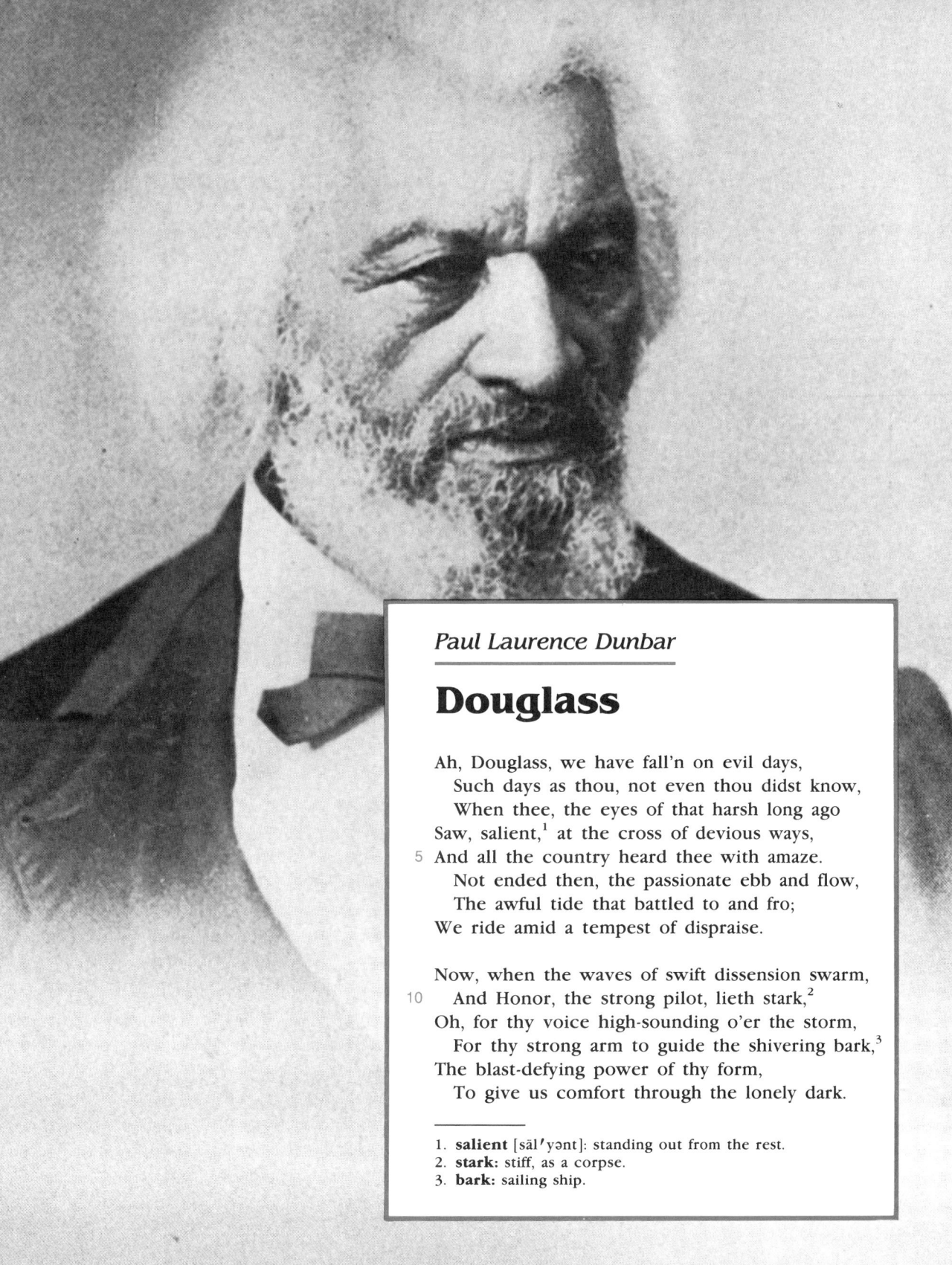

Paul Laurence Dunbar

Douglass

Ah, Douglass, we have fall'n on evil days,
  Such days as thou, not even thou didst know,
  When thee, the eyes of that harsh long ago
Saw, salient,[1] at the cross of devious ways,
5 And all the country heard thee with amaze.
  Not ended then, the passionate ebb and flow,
  The awful tide that battled to and fro;
We ride amid a tempest of dispraise.

Now, when the waves of swift dissension swarm,
10   And Honor, the strong pilot, lieth stark,[2]
Oh, for thy voice high-sounding o'er the storm,
  For thy strong arm to guide the shivering bark,[3]
The blast-defying power of thy form,
  To give us comfort through the lonely dark.

---

1. **salient** [sāl′yənt]: standing out from the rest.
2. **stark:** stiff, as a corpse.
3. **bark:** sailing ship.

STUDY QUESTIONS

Recalling

1. How do Dunbar's days compare to Douglass' earlier days, according to lines 1–3 and 6–8?
2. How had the country reacted to Douglass' insights, according to line 5? What three qualities of Douglass' does the speaker then call for in lines 11–14?

Interpreting

3. What image does the poem introduce in lines 6–8, and how is that image developed in lines 9–14?

Extending

4. Since Douglass was already dead when Dunbar wrote this poem, why do you think the poet calls upon him?
5. Which of Douglass' qualities or virtues suggested in this poem are evident from his autobiography on pages 226–229?

LITERARY FOCUS

The Sonnet

A **sonnet** is a lyric poem of fourteen lines written in **iambic pentameter**—five feet to a line, each foot made up of an unstressed syllable followed by a stressed one.

English sonnets, sometimes called **Shakespearean sonnets** (after the greatest poet to use them), have three quatrains (groups of four lines) followed by a rhymed couplet, with the rhyme scheme *abab cdcd efef gg.*

Italian sonnets, sometimes called **Petrarchan sonnets** (after the fourteenth-century Italian poet Francesco Petrarch), divide into a group of eight lines, or **octave,** followed by a group of six lines, or **sestet.** The octave has the rhyme scheme *abbaabba;* the sestet usually rhymes *cdcdee* or *cdecde.* The octave usually states a single thought, and the sestet usually expands upon that thought, contradicts it, or develops it in some other way.

Sonnets were immensely popular during the European Renaissance; poets wrote sonnet sequences, dozens of sonnets linked together by the same themes and often addressed to the same person. Sonnets usually dealt with lofty themes—love, faith, honor—and they enabled a poet to express deep emotions within conventional forms. They remained in fashion until the early nineteenth century. Some poets of our time use the sonnet form but often modify it to suit their own poetic needs.

Thinking About Sonnets

■ Which type of sonnet is "Douglass"? Why? How does Dunbar's use of the sonnet form contribute to the effectiveness of his poem?

COMPARING WRITERS

■ Sidney Lanier, Edwin Arlington Robinson, and Paul Laurence Dunbar had very different backgrounds, yet all three felt strongly about their roots and chose to express their feelings through poetry. Which of the poems in this section seems to you the most strongly rooted in the poet's native soil? Which poem includes historic facts? Which, despite regional settings, seem to be about human beings anywhere? Support your answers with evidence from the poems.

THE AMERICAN NOVEL

Unlike poetry and drama, novels are a relatively modern invention. A **novel** can best be defined as a book-length prose fiction. Early novels in English fall into three categories: the **picaresque novel,** a loose series of episodes recounting the adventures of wanderers and lovable rogues, often with a satiric aim; the **novel of sentiment,** a highly emotional tale of romance and tears that ends with a moral message; and the **gothic novel,** a tale of mystery and fear that includes elements of the supernatural as well as the romantic.

The earliest American novels also fell into these categories. Hugh Henry Brackenridge's *Modern Chivalry* (1792) is a picaresque adventure story that pokes fun at political problems during George Washington's presidency; Susanna Rowson's *Charlotte Temple* (1790) is a sentimental moral tale; and Charles Brockden Brown's *Wieland* (1798) and *Ormond* (1799) are tales of gothic horror that incidentally explore the psychological motivations of their characters.

It was not until the nineteenth century that America produced major novelists who are still widely read today. In 1823 James Fenimore Cooper (page 114) published the first of his Leatherstocking Tales, romantic adventures chronicling the exploits of Natty Bumppo, a noble frontiersman who became the model for the classic American hero. At about the same time William Gilmore Simms of South Carolina was writing similar Romantic adventure tales, earning for himself the nickname "the southern Cooper."

Another major novelist of the pre–Civil War period is Nathaniel Hawthorne (page 178), who published his masterpiece, *The Scarlet Letter,* in 1850. *The Scarlet Letter* is a tightly woven tale that explores the nature of sin; it is a work of complex symbolism and profound insights into its characters' minds and hearts. The nature of good and evil is also probed in *Moby-Dick* (1851), a tale of whales and whalers by Herman Melville (page 189). *Moby-Dick*'s profound philosophical questioning and its almost Shakespearean language place it among the outstanding novels of the nineteenth century.

After confronting the realities of the Civil War, American novelists turned more and more toward Realistic fiction. In the works of Mark Twain (page 274), local color makes for true-to-life adventure, and Twain as a satirist never shirks from depicting the real world in all its folly. Twain's use of dialect and colloquial language had a strong impact on almost all American writers to follow him; novels with adolescent heroes like Twain's *Huckleberry Finn* (1884) appear again and again in American fiction.

HAWTHORNE

MELVILLE

CATHER   **FAULKNER**

William Dean Howells set forth the principles of Realism in the 1890s, and if his *Rise of Silas Lapham* (1885) only partially reflects his theories, his ideas are masterfully realized in the novels of his friend Henry James. James explores the realities of society and the nature of the human mind in such works as *The American* (1877), *The Portrait of a Lady* (1881), and *The Turn of the Screw* (1898). His novel *The Ambassadors* (1903) is considered to be a masterpiece of **psychological realism,** writing that probes deeply into the complexities of characters' thoughts and motivations.

Realism is carried one step further in the Naturalistic novels of Stephen Crane (page 366), Theodore Dreiser, and Frank Norris. In the grim world of Dreiser's *Sister Carrie* (1900) and *An American Tragedy* (1925), characters are trapped by overwhelming forces that they cannot control or even understand. Norris' *McTeague* (1899) is a brutally frank portrait of greed, while *The Octopus* (1901) tells of the grim life of western ranchers battling the railroads.

Regionalism and Realism work hand in hand in the novels of Edith Wharton, which include *Ethan Frome* (1911), a portrait of New England farm life, and *The Age of Innocence* (1920). Ole Rolvaag's *Giants in the Earth* (1927) describes the life of Norwegian immigrants in South Dakota, while Willa Cather (page 541) offers a poetical portrait of the Nebraska frontier in *My Ántonia* (1918) and celebrates America's past in the equally lyrical *Death Comes for the Archbishop* (1927). Lyricism is also an element of Thomas Wolfe's autobiographical novel *Look Homeward, Angel* (1929), while Ellen Glasgow offers powerful pictures of the changing South in *Barren Ground* (1925) and *Vein of Iron* (1935).

Sinclair Lewis (page 511), the first American to win the Nobel Prize for Literature, was a sharp social critic, writing about small-town America in *Main Street* (1920), businessmen in *Babbitt*

STEINBECK HEMINGWAY

TWAIN

JAMES

(1922), and the medical profession in *Arrowsmith* (1925). American social values between the two world wars are also explored by F. Scott Fitzgerald (page 525) in *The Great Gatsby* (1925), by John Dos Passos in his trilogy *U.S.A.,* and by Nathanael West in *Day of the Locust* (1939).

Probably the three most outstanding novelists of pre–World War II America are Ernest Hemingway (page 517), William Faulkner (page 666), and John Steinbeck (page 617). Hemingway further develops the American hero in such works as *A Farewell to Arms* (1929), a tale of love during World War I, and *For Whom the Bell Tolls* (1940), a story of an American who fights in the Spanish Civil War. Hemingway's detached, journalistic prose style has been much imitated. Faulkner writes lyrical "stream-of-consciousness" novels set in his native South, including *The Sound and the Fury* (1929), a portrait of a once aristocratic family, and *Light in August* (1932). Steinbeck draws warm, human portraits in such novels as *Of Mice and Men* (1937) and *The Grapes of Wrath* (1939), a saga of a dust-bowl family driven to find a new life in California. Other important writers of fiction before World War II include Katherine Anne Porter (page 603), Eudora Welty (page 642), William Saroyan (page 781), and Thornton Wilder (page 696).

Novelists writing since World War II have turned more and more toward experimental fiction. Ralph Ellison's powerful novel *Invisible Man* (1952) is complex in its symbolism and its structure, while Joseph Heller explores World War II itself in his fragmentary dark comedy *Catch-22* (1961). Other postwar American novelists to achieve international recognition include Carson McCullers (page 689), John Updike (page 802), Bernard Malamud (page 772), Truman Capote (page 793), and Saul Bellow (page 831), the most recent American winner of the Nobel Prize for Literature.

Stephen Crane   *1871–1900*

Stephen Crane's amazing achievements within his short life—he died of tuberculosis at twenty-eight—show that he developed very early his extraordinary gift for writing. Crane left Syracuse University after only one semester, a period during which he spent more time playing baseball than studying. Yet during that semester he had already begun work on his first novel, *Maggie: A Girl of the Streets.*

After leaving Syracuse Crane moved to New York City and found work as a journalist. He was only twenty when he heard Hamlin Garland (page 326) lecture on Realism in fiction. Inspired, Crane resumed work on *Maggie,* a harsh, uncompromising picture of life among New York City's poor. The book was rejected by several editors, who felt the American public was not ready for so un-Romantic a tale. Apparently they were right: When in 1893 Crane borrowed money from his brother to have *Maggie* published, a few writers praised the book, but it did not sell.

Nevertheless, Crane began work on another novel. He called it *The Red Badge of Courage: An Episode of the American Civil War,* and it would prove to be his finest literary achievement. Hamlin Garland gave Crane the money to have the book typed; it was serialized in 1894 and published in book form one year later. *The Red Badge* was a resounding success and has become one of America's classic novels.

Crane, of course, was too young to have experienced the Civil War firsthand. He was strongly influenced, however, by the realistic novels of the Russian master Leo Tolstoy, and he also met and talked with Civil War veterans in order to get a sense of the "reality" of battle. Later, when he was working as a newspaper correspondent, he covered the Greco-Turkish War in 1897 and the Spanish-American War in 1898. These experiences proved to him that the feelings he had portrayed chiefly from his imagination in *The Red Badge* were indeed accurate descriptions of what it felt like to be in battle.

Most of Crane's other fiction and nonfiction is grounded in personal experience. His short story "The Blue Hotel" (1898) is set in the American West, which he visited in the course of his career as journalist; "The Open Boat" (1897) is based on his experience of being shipwrecked while traveling to Cuba. Crane also wrote some poetry, collected in two volumes—*The Black Riders* (1895) and *War Is Kind* (1899). These short, bitter poems reveal a man whose life had been filled with pain and hardship but who refused to shut his eyes to the grim truths he saw. Crane's later work declined in power, but *The Red Badge* will always hold a high place in the history of the American novel.

Introducing **The Red Badge of Courage**

The Red Badge of Courage has been called a "flowering of pure Naturalism." There is no denying the Naturalist elements in *The Red Badge*. In portraying the grim war experiences of a bewildered young farmer-turned-soldier, Crane's novel tells a story of struggle and survival with uncompromising clarity. Nevertheless, Crane does not adopt the flat, factual style of most Naturalist literature, for he also has a poet's imagination.

Crane studied the remarkable Civil War photographs of Mathew Brady for help with the details of battles, and he read a number of books about the war. But he wanted to give one soldier's impression of the war, not a journalistic account. As he wrote, he filtered many of the experiences through the mind of his character Henry Fleming, creating a literary style that is sometimes called impressionism. **Impressionism** is a style of writing that presents an author's or a character's impressions of an experience, rather than a more realistic description of it. Crane anticipated the style of the French impressionist painters, and one Crane expert, Robert W. Stallman, describes his style this way:

> It is composed of disconnected images which, like the blobs of color in a French impressionist painting, coalesce [unite, or merge] one with another. . . . Every seemingly disconnected detail [is part of the] pattern of the whole. The intensity of a Crane tale is due to this patterned coalescence of disconnected things, everything at once fluid and precise.

Consider, for example, the opening sentence of *The Red Badge:*

> The cold passed reluctantly from the earth, and the retiring fogs revealed an army stretched out on the hills, resting.

Here rhythm and alliteration work hand in hand with careful word placement to create the effect of a curtain rising upon a vivid drama about to begin or the unveiling of a painting.

It would be a mistake to read *The Red Badge of Courage* as a Civil War novel. It is an "episode" of the war, and the war provides a background, but we never find out much about the war itself. We do not learn what battle is being described nor when it took place nor what role it had in the outcome of the war. Like the soldiers in the novel, we see only a fragment of the total picture. Our full view is of a young man swinging wildly between confidence and fear, between understanding and bewilderment, as he seeks to forge a self that will see him through not only a war but a lifetime.

Soldiers, Union and Confederate. Historical photographs throughout this novel bring to life the wartime experiences of both sides.

Stephen Crane

The Red Badge of Courage

Chapter 1

The cold passed reluctantly from the earth, and the retiring fogs revealed an army stretched out on the hills, resting. As the landscape changed from brown to green, the army awakened, and began to tremble with eagerness at the noise of rumors. It cast its eyes upon the roads, which were growing from long troughs of liquid mud to proper thoroughfares. A river, amber-tinted in the shadow of its banks, purled[1] at the army's feet; and at night, when the stream had become of a sorrowful blackness, one could see across it the red, eye-like gleam of hostile campfires set in the low brows of distant hills.

Once a certain tall soldier developed virtues and went resolutely to wash a shirt. He came flying back from a brook waving his garment bannerlike. He was swelled with a tale he had heard from a reliable friend, who had heard it from a truthful cavalryman,[2] who had heard it from his trustworthy brother, one of the orderlies at division headquarters. He adopted the important air of a herald[3] in red and gold.

"We're goin' t' move t'morrah—sure," he said pompously to a group in the company street. "We're goin' 'way up the river, cut across, an' come around in behint 'em."

To his attentive audience he drew a loud and elaborate plan of a very brilliant campaign.

---

1. **purled:** rippled.

2. **cavalryman:** horse soldier.
3. **herald:** formerly, official who carried messages between sovereigns and announced state proclamations.

When he had finished, the blue-clothed[4] men scattered into small arguing groups between the rows of squat brown huts. Smoke drifted lazily from a multitude of quaint chimneys.

"It's a lie! that's all it is—a thunderin' lie!" said another private loudly. His smooth face was flushed, and his hands were thrust sulkily into his trousers' pockets. He took the matter as an affront to him. "I don't believe the derned old army's ever going to move. We're set. I've got ready to move eight times in the last two weeks, and we ain't moved yet."

The tall soldier felt called upon to defend the truth of a rumor he himself had introduced. He and the loud one came near to fighting over it.

A corporal began to swear before the assemblage. He had just put a costly board floor in his house, he said. During the early spring he had refrained from adding extensively to the comfort of his environment because he had felt that the army might start on the march at any moment. Of late, however, he had been impressed that they were in a sort of eternal camp.

Many of the men engaged in a spirited debate. One outlined in a peculiarly lucid manner all the plans of the commanding general. He was opposed by men who advocated that there were other plans of campaign. Meanwhile, the soldier who had fetched the rumor bustled about with much importance. He was continually assailed by questions.

"What's up, Jim?"

"Th' army's goin' t' move."

"Ah, what yeh talkin' about? How yeh know it is?"

"Well, yeh kin b'lieve me er not, jest as yeh like. I don't care a hang."

There was much food for thought in the manner in which he replied. He came near to convincing them by disdaining to produce proofs. They grew much excited over it.

There was a youthful private who listened with eager ears to the words of the tall soldier and to the varied comments of his comrades. After receiving a fill of discussions concerning marches and attacks, he went to his hut and crawled through an intricate hole that served it as a door. He wished to be alone with some new thoughts that had lately come to him.

The youth was in a little trance of astonishment. So they were at last going to fight. On the morrow, perhaps, there would be a battle, and he would be in it. For a time he was obliged to labor to make himself believe. He could not accept with assurance an omen that he was about to mingle in one of those great affairs of the earth.

He had burned several times to enlist. Tales of great movements shook the land. He had read of marches, sieges, conflicts, and he had longed to see it all. His busy mind had drawn for him large pictures extravagant in color, lurid with breathless deeds.

But his mother had discouraged him. She had affected to look with some contempt upon the quality of his war ardor and patriotism. She could calmly seat herself, and with no apparent difficulty give him many hundreds of reasons why he was of vastly more importance on the farm than on the field of battle. She had had certain ways of expression that told him that her statements on the subject came from a deep conviction.

At last, however, he had made firm rebellion against this yellow light thrown upon the color of his ambitions. The newspapers, the gossip of the village, his own picturings, had aroused him to an uncheckable degree. They were in truth fighting finely down there. Almost every day the newspapers printed accounts of a decisive victory.

One night, as he lay in bed, the winds had carried to him the clangoring of the church bell as some enthusiast jerked the rope frantically to tell the twisted news of a great battle. This voice of the people rejoicing in the night had made him shiver in a prolonged ecstasy of excitement. Later, he had gone down to his mother's room and had spoken thus: "Ma, I'm going to enlist."

---

4. **blue-clothed:** In the Civil War, Union soldiers of the North wore blue uniforms; Confederate soldiers of the South, gray.

"Henry, don't you be a fool," his mother had replied. She had then covered her face with the quilt. There was an end to the matter for that night.

Nevertheless, the next morning he had gone to a town that was near his mother's farm and had enlisted in a company that was forming there. When he had returned home, his mother was milking the brindle cow. Four others stood waiting. "Ma, I've enlisted," he had said to her diffidently. There was a short silence. "The Lord's will be done, Henry," she had finally replied, and had then continued to milk the brindle cow.

When he had stood in the doorway with his soldier's clothes on his back, and with the light of excitement and expectancy in his eyes almost defeating the glow of regret for the home bonds, he had seen two tears leaving their trails on his mother's scarred cheeks.

Still, she had disappointed him by saying nothing whatever about returning with his shield or on it.[5] He had privately primed himself for a beautiful scene. He had prepared certain sentences which he thought could be used with touching effect. But her words destroyed his plans. She had doggedly peeled potatoes and addressed him as follows: "You watch out, Henry, an' take good care of yerself. Don't go a-thinkin' you can lick the hull rebel army at the start, because yeh can't. Yer jest one little feller amongst a hull lot of others, and yeh've got to keep quiet an' do what they tell yeh. I know how you are, Henry.

"I've knet yeh eight pair of socks, Henry, and I've put in all yer best shirts, because I want my boy to be jest as warm and comf'able as anybody in the army. Whenever they get holes in 'em, I want yeh to send 'em right-away back to me, so's I kin dern 'em.

"Don't forgit about the socks and the shirts, child; and I've put a cup of blackberry jam with yer bundle, because I know yeh like it above all things. Goodbye, Henry. Watch out, and be a good boy."

He had, of course, been impatient under the ordeal of this speech. It had not been quite what he expected, and he had borne it with an air of irritation. He departed feeling vague relief.

Still, when he had looked back from the gate, he had seen his mother kneeling among the potato parings. Her brown face, upraised, was stained with tears, and her spare form was quivering. He bowed his head and went on, feeling suddenly ashamed of his purposes.

From his home he had gone to the seminary[6] to bid adieu[7] to many schoolmates. They had thronged about him with wonder and admiration. He had felt the gulf now between them and had swelled with calm pride. He and some of his fellows who had donned blue were quite overwhelmed with privileges for all of one afternoon, and it had been a very delicious thing. They had strutted.

A certain light-haired girl had made vivacious fun at his martial spirit, but there was another and darker girl whom he had gazed at steadfastly, and he thought she grew demure and sad at sight of his blue and brass.[8] As he had walked down the path between the rows of oaks, he had turned his head and detected her at a window watching his departure. As he perceived her, she had immediately begun to stare up through the high tree branches at the sky. He had seen a good deal of flurry and haste in her movement as she changed her attitude. He often thought of it.

On the way to Washington his spirit had soared. The regiment was fed and caressed at station after station until the youth had believed that he must be a hero. There was a lavish expenditure of bread and cold meats, coffee, and pickles and cheese. As he basked in the smiles of the girls and was patted and complimented by the old men, he had felt growing

---

5. **with . . . it:** Spartan warriors were said to have been told by their wives and mothers to return from battle either with their shields or upon them—that is, either victorious or dead.

6. **seminary:** here, school.

7. **adieu** [ə dōō′]: French for "good-by."

8. **blue and brass:** brass buttons and trimming on his blue uniform.

within him the strength to do mighty deeds of arms.

After complicated journeyings with many pauses, there had come months of monotonous life in a camp. He had had the belief that real war was a series of death struggles with small time in between for sleep and meals; but since his regiment had come to the field, the army had done little but sit still and try to keep warm.

He had grown to regard himself merely as a part of a vast blue demonstration. His province was to look out, as far as he could, for his personal comfort. For recreation he could twiddle his thumbs and speculate on the thoughts which must agitate the minds of the generals. Also, he was drilled and drilled and reviewed, and drilled and drilled and reviewed.

The only foes he had seen were some pickets[9] along the river bank. They were a sun-tanned, philosophical lot, who sometimes shot reflectively at the blue pickets. When reproached for this afterwards, they usually expressed sorrow, and swore by their gods that the guns had exploded without their permission. The youth, on guard duty one night, conversed across the stream with one of them. He was a slightly ragged man, who spat skillfully between his shoes and possessed a great fund of bland and infantile assurance. The youth liked him personally.

"Yank," the other had informed him, "yer a right dum good feller." This sentiment, floating to him upon the still air, had made him temporarily regret war.

Various veterans had told him tales. Some talked of gray, bewhiskered hordes who were advancing with unspeakable valor. Others spoke of tattered and eternally hungry men who fired despondent powders. "They'll charge through fire an' brimstone t' git a holt on a haversack,[10] an' sech stomachs ain't a-last-in' long," he was told.

However, he perceived now that it did not greatly matter what kind of soldiers he was going to fight, so long as they fought. There was a more serious problem. He lay in his bunk pondering upon it. He tried to mathematically prove to himself that he would not run from a battle.

Previously he had never felt obliged to wrestle too seriously with this question. But here he was confronted with a thing of moment. It had suddenly appeared to him that perhaps in a battle he might run. He was forced to admit that as far as war was concerned, he knew nothing of himself.

A little panic-fear grew in his mind. As his imagination went forward to a fight, he saw hideous possibilities. He contemplated the lurking menaces of the future, and failed in an effort to see himself standing stoutly in the midst of them.

He sprang from the bunk and began to pace nervously to and fro. "Good Lord, what's th' matter with me?" he said aloud.

He felt that in this crisis his laws of life were useless. Whatever he had learned of himself was here of no avail. He was an unknown quantity. He must accumulate information of himself, and meanwhile he resolved to remain close upon his guard lest those qualities of which he knew nothing should everlastingly disgrace him.

After a time the tall soldier slid dexterously through the hole. The loud private followed. They were wrangling.

"That's all right," said the tall soldier as he entered. He waved his hand expressively. "You can believe me or not, jest as you like. All you got to do is to sit down and wait as quiet as you can. Then pretty soon you'll find out I was right."

His comrade grunted stubbornly. For a moment he seemed to be searching for a formidable reply. Finally he said: "Well, you don't know everything in the world, do you?"

"Didn't say I knew everything in the world," retorted the other sharply. He began to stow various articles snugly into his knapsack.

---

9. **pickets:** guards, sentries.
10. **haversack:** a canvas shoulder bag for carrying rations or provisions.

A Confederate camp scene in 1861.

The youth, pausing in his nervous walk, looked down at the busy figure. "Going to be a battle, sure, is there, Jim?" he asked.

"Of course there is," replied the tall soldier. "Of course there is. You jest wait 'til tomorrow, and you'll see one of the biggest battles ever was. You jest wait."

"Huh!" said the loud one from a corner.

"Well," remarked the youth, "like as not this story'll turn out jest like them others did."

"Not much it won't," replied the tall soldier, exasperated. "Not much it won't. Didn't the cavalry all start this morning?" He glared about him. No one denied his statement. "The cavalry started this morning," he continued. "They say there ain't hardly any cavalry left in camp. They're going to Richmond, or some place, while we fight all the Johnnies.[11] It's some dodge like that. The regiment's got orders, too. A feller what seen 'em go to headquarters told me a little while ago. And they're raising blazes all over camp—anybody can see that."

"Shucks!" said the loud one.

The youth remained silent for a time. At last he spoke to the tall soldier. "Jim!"

"What?"

"How do you think the reg'ment'll do?"

"Oh, they'll fight all right, I guess, after they once get into it," said the other, with cold judgment.

"Think any of the boys'll run?" persisted the youth.

"Oh, there may be a few of 'em run, but there's them kind in every regiment, 'specially when they first goes under fire," said the other in a tolerant way. "Of course it might happen that the hull kit-and-boodle[12] might start and run, if some big fighting came first off. But I think most of 'em'll fight like sin after they oncet git shootin'," he added, with a mighty emphasis on the last four words.

"Oh, you think you know—" began the loud soldier with scorn.

The other turned savagely upon him. They had a rapid altercation, in which they fastened

---

11. **Johnnies:** Confederate soldiers were called "Johnny Rebs"; Union soldiers, "Billy Yanks."

12. **kit-and-boodle:** everybody; a variation of *kit and caboodle.*

upon each other various strange epithets.[13]

The youth at last interrupted them. "Did you ever think you might run yourself, Jim?" he asked. On concluding the sentence he laughed as if he had meant to aim a joke. The loud soldier also giggled.

The tall private waved his hand. "Well," said he profoundly, "I've thought it might get too hot for Jim Conklin in some of them scrimmages, and if a whole lot of the boys started and run, why, I s'pose I'd start and run. And if I once started to run, I'd run like the devil, and no mistake. But if everybody was a-standing and a-fighting, why, I'd stand and fight. Be jiminey, I would. I'll bet on it."

The youth of this tale felt gratitude for these words of his comrade. He had feared that all of the untried men possessed a great and correct confidence. He now was in a measure reassured.

Chapter 2

The next morning the youth discovered that his tall comrade had been the fast-flying messenger of a mistake. There was much scoffing at the latter by those who had yesterday been firm adherents of his views, and there was even a little sneering by men who had never believed the rumor.

The youth felt, however, that his problem was in no wise lifted from him. There was, on the contrary, an irritating prolongation. The tale had created in him a great concern for himself. Now, with the newborn question in his mind, he was compelled to sink back into his old place as part of a blue demonstration.

For days he made ceaseless calculations, but they were all wondrously unsatisfactory. He found that he could establish nothing. He finally concluded that the only way to prove himself was to go into the blaze, and then figuratively to watch his legs to discover their merits and faults. He reluctantly admitted that he could not sit still and with a mental slate

and pencil derive an answer. To gain it, he must have blaze, blood, and danger, even as a chemist requires this, that, and the other. So he fretted for an opportunity.

Meanwhile he continually tried to measure himself by his comrades. The youth would have liked to have discovered another who suspected himself. A sympathetic comparison of mental notes would have been a joy to him.

He occasionally tried to fathom[14] a comrade with seductive sentences. He looked about to find men in the proper mood. All attempts failed to bring forth any statement which looked in any way like a confession to those doubts which he privately acknowledged in himself.

In his great anxiety his heart was continually clamoring at what he considered the intolerable slowness of the generals. They seemed content to perch tranquilly on the riverbank, and leave him bowed down by the weight of a great problem. He wanted it settled forthwith. He could not long bear such a load, he said. Sometimes his anger at the commanders reached an acute stage, and he grumbled about the camp like a veteran.

One morning, however, he found himself in the ranks of his prepared regiment. The men were whispering speculations and recounting the old rumors. In the gloom before the break of the day their uniforms glowed a deep purple hue. From across the river the red eyes were still peering. In the eastern sky there was a yellow patch like a rug laid for the feet of the coming sun; and against it, black and pattern-like, loomed the gigantic figure of the colonel on a gigantic horse.

From off in the darkness came the trampling of feet. The youth could occasionally see dark shadows that moved like monsters. The regiment stood at rest for what seemed a long time. The youth grew impatient. It was unendurable the way these affairs were managed. He wondered how long they were to be kept

---

13. **epithets** [ep′ə thets]: here, abusive names.

14. **fathom**: probe.

waiting. He turned toward the colonel and saw him lift his gigantic arm and calmly stroke his mustache.

At last he heard from along the road at the foot of the hill the clatter of a horse's galloping hoofs. It must be the coming of orders. He bent forward, scarce breathing. The exciting clickety-click, as it grew louder and louder, seemed to be beating upon his soul. Presently a horseman with jangling equipment drew rein before the colonel of the regiment. The two held a short, sharp-worded conversation. The men in the foremost ranks craned their necks.

As the horseman wheeled his animal and galloped away, he turned to shout over his shoulder. "Don't forget that box of cigars!" The colonel mumbled in reply. The youth wondered what a box of cigars had to do with war.

A moment later the regiment went swinging off into the darkness. It was now like one of those moving monsters wending with many feet. The air was heavy, and cold with dew. A mass of wet grass, marched upon, rustled like silk.

The men stumbled along still muttering speculations. There was a subdued debate. Once a man fell down, and as he reached for his rifle a comrade, unseeing, trod upon his hand. He of the injured fingers swore bitterly and aloud. A low, tittering laugh went among his fellows.

Presently they passed into a roadway and marched forward with easy strides. A dark regiment moved before them, and from behind also came the tinkle of equipments on the bodies of marching men.

The rushing yellow of the developing day went on behind their backs. When the sunrays at last struck full and mellowingly upon the earth, the youth saw that the landscape was streaked with two long, thin, black columns which disappeared on the brow of a hill in front, and rearward vanished in a wood. They were like two serpents crawling from the cavern of the night.

The youth was engaged with his own eternal debate. He was despondent and sullen, and threw shifting glances about him. He studied the faces of his companions, ever on the watch to detect kindred emotions. He suffered disappointment. Some ardor of the air which was causing the veteran commands to move with glee—almost with song—had infected the new regiment. The men began to speak of victory as of a thing they knew.

The youth, considering himself as separated from the others, was saddened by the blithe and merry speeches that went from rank to rank. The company wags[15] all made their best endeavors. The regiment tramped to the tune of laughter.

A rather fat soldier attempted to pilfer a horse from a dooryard. He was escaping with his prize when a young girl rushed from the house and grabbed the animal's mane. There followed a wrangle. The young girl, with pink cheeks and shining eyes, stood like a dauntless statue.

The observant regiment, standing at rest in the roadway, whooped at once, and entered whole-souled upon the side of the maiden. The men became so engrossed in this affair that they entirely ceased to remember their own large war.

At nightfall the column broke into regimental pieces, and the fragments went into the fields to camp. Tents sprang up like strange plants. Campfires, like red, peculiar blossoms, dotted the night.

The youth kept from his companions as much as circumstances would allow him. In the evening he wandered a few paces into the gloom. From this little distance the many fires, with the black forms of men passing to and fro before the crimson rays, made weird and satanic effects.

He lay down in the grass. The blades pressed tenderly against his cheek. The moon had been lighted and was hung in a treetop. The liquid stillness of the night enveloping him made him feel vast pity for himself.

---

15. **wags:** jokers.

He wished that he was at home again making the endless rounds from the house to the barn, from the barn to the fields, from the fields to the barn, from the barn to the house. He remembered he had often cursed the brindle cow and her mates, and had sometimes flung milking stools. But, from his present point of view, there was a halo of happiness about each of their heads, and he would have sacrificed all the brass buttons on the continent to have been enabled to return to them. He told himself that he was not formed for a soldier. And he mused seriously upon the radical differences between himself and those men who were dodging implike around the fires.

As he mused thus, he heard the rustle of grass, and, upon turning his head, discovered the loud soldier. He called out, "Oh, Wilson!"

The latter approached and looked down. "Why hello, Henry; is it you? What you doing here?"

"Oh, thinking," said the youth.

The other sat down and carefully lighted his pipe. "You're getting blue, my boy. You're looking thundering peeked.[16] What the dickens is wrong with you?"

"Oh, nothing," said the youth.

The loud soldier launched then into the subject of the anticipated fight. "Oh, we've got 'em now!" As he spoke his boyish face was wreathed in a gleeful smile, and his voice had an exultant ring. "We've got 'em now. At last, by the eternal thunders, we'll lick 'em good!"

"If the truth was known," he added more soberly, *"they've* licked *us* about every clip up to now; but this time—this time—we'll lick 'em good!"

"Well, Jim Conklin says we'll get a-plenty of fighting this time."

"He's right for once, I guess, though I can't see how it come. This time we're in for a big battle, and we've got the best end of it, certain sure."

He arose and began to pace to and fro excitedly. The thrill of his enthusiasm made him walk with an elastic step. He was sprightly, vigorous, fiery in his belief in success. He looked into the future with clear, proud eye, and he swore with the air of an old soldier.

"How do you know you won't run when the time comes?" asked the youth.

"Run?" said the loud one; "run?—of course not!" He laughed.

"Well," continued the youth, "lots of good-a-'nough men have thought they was going to do great things before the fight, but when the time come they skedaddled."

"Oh, that's all true, I s'pose," replied the other; "but I'm not going to skedaddle. The man that bets on my running will lose his money, that's all." He nodded confidently.

"Oh, shucks!" said the youth. "You ain't the bravest man in the world, are you?"

"No, I ain't," exclaimed the loud soldier indignantly; "and I didn't say I was the bravest man in the world, neither. I said I was going to do my share of fighting—that's what I said. And I am, too. Who are you, anyhow? You talk as if you thought you was Napoleon Bonaparte."[17] He glared at the youth for a moment, and then strode away.

The youth called in a savage voice after his comrade: "Well, you needn't git mad about it!" But the other continued on his way and made no reply.

He felt alone in space when his injured comrade had disappeared. His failure to discover any mite of resemblance in their viewpoints made him more miserable than before. No one seemed to be wrestling with such a terrific personal problem. He was a mental outcast.

He went slowly to his tent and stretched himself on a blanket by the side of the snoring tall soldier. In the darkness he saw visions of a thousand-tongued fear that would babble at his back and cause him to flee, while others were going coolly about their country's business. He

---

16. **peeked** [pē′kid]: variant of *peaked;* sickly.

17. **Napoleon Bonaparte** [nə pō′lē ən bō′nə pärt′]: (1769–1821) French general with extraordinary military skill and aggressiveness who later became emperor.

admitted that he would not be able to cope with this monster. He felt that every nerve in his body would be an ear to hear the voices, while other men would remain stolid and deaf.

He stared at the red, shivering reflection of a fire on the white wall of his tent until, exhausted and ill from the monotony of his suffering, he fell asleep.

Chapter 3

When another night came the columns, changed to purple streaks, filed across two pontoon bridges.[18] Upon the other shore a dark and mysterious range of hills was curved against the sky. The insect voices of the night sang solemnly.

After this crossing the youth assured himself that at any moment they might be suddenly and fearfully assaulted from the caves of the lowering woods. He kept his eyes watchfully upon the darkness.

But his regiment went unmolested to a camping place, and its soldiers slept the brave sleep of wearied men. In the morning they were routed out with early energy, and hustled along a narrow road that led deep into the forest.

It was during this rapid march that the regiment lost many of the marks of a new command.

The men had begun to count the miles upon their fingers, and they grew tired. There was perspiration and grumblings. After a time they began to shed their knapsacks. Men extricated themselves from thick shirts. Presently few carried anything but their necessary clothing, blankets, haversacks, canteens, and arms and ammunition. "You can now eat and shoot," said the tall soldier to the youth. "That's all you want to do."

There was sudden change from the ponderous infantry[19] of theory to the light and speedy infantry of practice. The regiment, relieved of a burden, received a new impetus. But there was much loss of valuable knapsacks and, on the whole, very good shirts.

Presently the army again sat down to think. The odor of the peaceful pines was in the men's nostrils. The sounds of monotonous axe blows rang through the forest, and the insects, nodding upon their perches, crooned like old women. The youth returned to his theory of a blue demonstration.

One gray dawn, however, he was kicked in the leg by the tall soldier, and then, before he was entirely awake, he found himself running down a wood road in the midst of men who were panting from the first effects of speed. His canteen banged rhythmically upon his thigh, and his haversack bobbed softly. His musket bounced a trifle from his shoulder at each stride and made his cap feel uncertain upon his head. From the distance came a sudden spatter of firing.

He was bewildered. As he ran with his comrades he strenuously tried to think, but all he knew was that if he fell down those coming behind would tread upon him. All his faculties seemed to be needed to guide him over and past obstructions. He felt carried along by a mob.

The sun spread disclosing rays, and, one by one, regiments burst into view like armed men just born of the earth. The youth perceived that the time had come. He was about to be measured. For a moment he felt in the face of his great trial like a babe, and the flesh over his heart seemed very thin. He seized time to look about him calculatingly.

But he instantly saw that it would be impossible for him to escape from the regiment. It enclosed him. And there were iron laws of tradition and law on four sides. He was in a moving box.

As he perceived this fact it occurred to him that he had never wished to come to the war. He had not enlisted of his free will. He had been dragged by the merciless government. And now they were taking him out to be slaughtered.

18. **pontoon bridges:** temporary bridges supported by a number of flat-bottomed boats or floating hollow cylinders (pontoons).
19. **infantry:** foot soldiers.

The regiment slid down a bank and wallowed across a little stream. As they climbed the hill on the farther side artillery began to boom. Here the youth forgot many things as he felt a sudden impulse of curiosity. He scrambled up the bank with a speed that could not be exceeded by a bloodthirsty man.

He expected a battle scene.

There were some little fields girted and squeezed by a forest. Spread over the grass and in among the tree trunks, he could see knots and waving lines of skirmishers who were running hither and thither and firing at the landscape. A dark battle line lay upon a sun struck clearing that gleamed orange color. A flag fluttered.

Other regiments floundered up the bank. The brigade was formed in line of battle, and after a pause started slowly through the woods in the rear of the receding skirmishers, who were continually melting into the scene to appear again farther on. They were always busy as bees, deeply absorbed in their little combats.

The youth tried to observe everything. He was aware that these battalions with their commotions were woven red and startling into the gentle fabric of softened greens and browns. It looked to be a wrong place for a battlefield.

The skirmishers in advance fascinated him. Their shots into thickets and at distant and prominent trees spoke to him of tragedies—hidden, mysterious, solemn.

Once the line encountered the body of a dead soldier. He lay upon his back staring at the sky. He was dressed in an awkward suit of yellowish brown. The youth could see that the soles of his shoes had been worn to the thinness of writing paper, and from a great rent in one the dead foot projected piteously. And it was as if fate had betrayed the soldier. In death it exposed to his enemies that poverty which in life he had perhaps concealed from his friends.

The ranks opened covertly to avoid the corpse. The invulnerable dead man forced a way for himself. The youth looked keenly at the ashen face. The wind raised the tawny beard. It moved as if a hand were stroking it. He vaguely desired to walk around and around

A Union camp scene, outside General McClellan's tent.

the body and stare; the impulse of the living to try to read in dead eyes the answer to the Question.

During the march the ardor which the youth had acquired when out of view of the field rapidly faded to nothing. His curiosity was quite easily satisfied. If an intense scene had caught him with its wild swing as he came to the top of the bank, he might have gone roaring on. This advance upon Nature was too calm. He had opportunity to reflect. He had time in which to wonder about himself and to attempt to probe his sensations.

Absurd ideas took hold upon him. He thought that he did not relish the landscape. The shadows of the woods were formidable. He was certain that in this vista there lurked fierce-eyed hosts. The swift thought came to him that the generals did not know what they were about. It was all a trap. The enemy would presently swallow the whole command. He glared about him, expecting to see the stealthy approach of his death.

He thought that he must break from the ranks and harangue his comrades. They must not all be killed like pigs; and he was sure it would come to pass unless they were informed of these dangers. The generals were idiots to send them marching into a regular pen. There was but one pair of eyes in the corps. He would step forth and make a speech. Shrill and passionate words came to his lips.

The line, broken into moving fragments by the ground, went calmly on through fields and woods. The youth looked at the men nearest him, and saw, for the most part, expressions of deep interest, as if they were investigating something that had fascinated them. One or two stepped with overvaliant airs as if they were already plunged into war. Others walked as upon thin ice. The greater part of the untested men appeared quiet and absorbed. They were going to look at war, the red animal— war, the blood-swollen god. And they were deeply engrossed in this march.

As he looked the youth gripped his outcry at his throat. He saw that even if the men were tottering with fear they would laugh at his warning. They would jeer him, and, if practicable, pelt him with missiles.

He assumed, then, the demeanor of one who knows that he is doomed alone to unwritten responsibilities. He lagged, with tragic glances at the sky. He was surprised presently by the young lieutenant of his company, who began heartily to beat him with a sword, calling out in a loud and insolent voice: "Come, young man, get up into the ranks there. No skulking'll do here." He mended his pace with suitable haste. And he hated the lieutenant, who had no appreciation of fine minds. He was a mere brute.

After a time the brigade was halted in the cathedral light of a forest. The busy skirmishers were still popping. Through the aisles of the wood could be seen the floating smoke from their rifles. Sometimes it went up in little balls, white and compact.

During this halt many men in the regiment began erecting tiny hills in front of them. They used stones, sticks, earth, and anything they thought might turn a bullet. Some built comparatively large ones, while others seemed content with little ones. Directly, however, they were ordered to withdraw from that place.

This astounded the youth. He forgot his stewing over the advance movement. "Well, then, what did they march us out here for?" he demanded of the tall soldier. The latter with calm faith began a heavy explanation, although he had been compelled to leave a little protection of stones and dirt to which he had devoted much care and skill.

When the regiment was aligned in another position each man's regard for his safety caused another line of small entrenchments. They ate their noon meal behind a third one. They were moved from this one also. They were marched from place to place with apparent aimlessness.

The youth had been taught that a man became another thing in a battle. He saw his salvation in such a change. Hence this waiting was an ordeal to him. He was in a fever of impatience. He considered that there was denoted a lack of purpose on the part of the generals. He began to complain to the tall soldier. "I can't stand this much longer," he cried. "I don't see what good it does to make us wear out our legs for nothin'."

The philosophical tall soldier measured a sandwich of cracker and pork and swallowed it in a nonchalant manner. "Oh, I suppose we must go reconnoitering around the country jest to keep 'em from getting too close, or to develop 'em, or something."

In the afternoon the regiment went out over the same ground it had taken in the morning. The landscape then ceased to threaten the youth. He had been close to it and become familiar with it.

When, however, they began to pass into a new region, his old fears of stupidity and incompetence reassailed him, but this time he doggedly let them babble. He was occupied with his problem, and in his desperation he concluded that the stupidity did not greatly matter.

Once he thought he had concluded that it would be better to get killed directly and end his troubles. Regarding death thus out of the corner of his eye, he conceived it to be nothing but rest, and he was filled with a momentary astonishment that he should have made an extraordinary commotion over the mere matter of getting killed. He would die; he would go to some place where he would be understood. It was useless to expect appreciation of his profound and fine senses from such men as the lieutenant. He must look to the grave for comprehension.

The skirmish fire increased to a long clattering sound. With it was mingled faraway cheering. A battery spoke.

Directly the youth would see the skirmishers running. They were pursued by the sound of musketry fire. After a time the hot, dangerous flashes of the rifles were visible. Smoke clouds went slowly and insolently across the fields like observant phantoms. The din became crescendo, like the roar of an oncoming train.

A brigade ahead of them and on the right went into action with a rending roar. It was as if it had exploded. And thereafter it lay stretched in the distance behind a long gray wall, that one was obliged to look twice at to make sure that it was smoke.

The youth, forgetting his neat plan of getting killed, gazed spellbound. His eyes grew wide and busy with the action of the scene. His mouth was a little ways open.

Of a sudden he felt a heavy and sad hand laid upon his shoulder. Awakening from his trance of observation, he turned and beheld the loud soldier.

"It's my first and last battle, old boy," said the latter, with intense gloom. "Something tells me—"

"What?"

"I'm a gone coon this first time and—and I w-want you to take these here things—to—my—folks." He ended in a quavering sob of pity for himself. He handed the youth a little packet done up in a yellow envelope.

"Why, what the devil—" began the youth again.

But the other gave him a glance as from the depths of a tomb, and raised his limp hand in a prophetic manner and turned away.

Chapter 4

The brigade was halted in the fringe of a grove. The men crouched among the trees and pointed their restless guns out at the fields. They tried to look beyond the smoke.

Out of this haze they could see running men. Some shouted information and gestured as they hurried.

The men of the new regiment watched and listened eagerly, while their tongues ran on in gossip of the battle. They mouthed rumors that had flown like birds out of the unknown.

"They say Perry has been driven in with big loss."

"Yes, Carrott went t' th' hospital. He said he was sick. That smart lieutenant is commanding 'G' Company. Th' boys say they won't be under Carrott no more if they all have t' desert."

"Hannises' batt'ry is took."

"It ain't either. I saw Hannises' batt'ry off on th' left not more'n fifteen minutes ago."

A Union battery in action, June 1864.

"Th' general, he ses he is goin' t' take th' hull command of th' 304th when we go inteh action, an' then he ses we'll do sech fightin' as never another one reg'ment done."

The din in front swelled to a tremendous chorus. The youth and his fellows were frozen to silence. They could see a flag that tossed in the smoke angrily. Near it were the blurred and agitated forms of troops. There came a turbulent stream of men across the fields. A battery changing positions at a frantic gallop scattered the stragglers right and left.

A shell screaming like a storm banshee[20] went over the huddled heads of the reserves. It landed in the grove, and exploding redly flung the brown earth. There was a little shower of pine needles.

Bullets began to whistle among the branches and nip at the trees. Twigs and leaves came sailing down. It was as if a thousand axes, wee and invisible, were being wielded. Many of the men were constantly dodging and ducking their heads.

The lieutenant of the youth's company was shot in the hand. He began to swear so wondrously, that a nervous laugh went along the regimental line. The officer's profanity sounded conventional. It relieved the tightened senses of the new men. It was as if he had hit his fingers with a tack hammer at home.

He held the wounded member carefully away from his side so that the blood would not drip upon his trousers.

The captain of the company, tucking his sword under his arm, produced a handkerchief and began to bind with it the lieutenant's wound. And they disputed as to how the binding should be done.

The battle flag in the distance jerked about madly. It seemed to be struggling to free itself from an agony. The billowing smoke was filled with horizontal flashes.

Men running swiftly emerged from it. They grew in numbers until it was seen that the whole command was fleeing. The flag suddenly

20. **banshee** [ban′shē]: in Scottish and Irish folklore, a spirit whose wailing foretells an approaching death.

sank down as if dying. Its motion as it fell was a gesture of despair.

Wild yells came from behind the walls of smoke. A sketch in gray and red dissolved into a moblike body of men who galloped like wild horses.

The youth achieved one little thought in the midst of this chaos. The composite monster which had caused the other troops to flee had not then appeared. He resolved to get a view of it, and then, he thought he might very likely run better than the best of them.

Chapter 5

There were moments of waiting. The youth thought of the village street at home before the arrival of the circus parade on a day in the spring. He remembered how he had stood, a small, thrillful boy, prepared to follow the dingy lady upon the white horse, or the band in its faded chariot. He saw the yellow road, the lines of expectant people, and the sober houses.

Someone cried, "Here they come!"

There was rustling and muttering among the men. They displayed a feverish desire to have every possible cartridge ready to their hands. The boxes were pulled around into various positions, and adjusted with great care. It was as if seven hundred new bonnets were being tried on.

"Here they come! Here they come!" Gun locks clicked.

Across the smoke-infested fields came a brown swarm of running men who were giving shrill yells. They came on, stooping and swinging their rifles at all angles. A flag, tilted forward, sped near the front.

As he caught sight of them, the youth was momentarily startled by a thought that perhaps his gun was not loaded. He stood trying to rally his faltering intellect so that he might recollect the moment when he had loaded, but he could not.

A hatless general pulled his dripping horse to a stand near the colonel of the 304th. He shook his fist in the other's face. "You've got to hold 'em back!" he shouted savagely; "you've got to hold 'em back!"

In his agitation the colonel began to stammer. "A-all r-right, General, all right! We-we'll do our—we-we'll d-d-do—do our best, General."

The man at the youth's elbow was mumbling, as if to himself: "Oh, we're in for it now! oh, we're in for it now!"

Perspiration streamed down the youth's face, which was soiled like that of a weeping urchin. He frequently, with a nervous movement, wiped his eyes with his coat sleeve. His mouth was still a little way open.

He got the one glance at the foe-swarming field in front of him, and instantly ceased to debate the question of his piece being loaded. Before he was ready to begin—before he had announced to himself that he was about to fight—he threw the obedient, well-balanced rifle into position and fired a first wild shot.

He suddenly lost concern for himself, and forgot to look at a menacing fate. He became not a man but a member. He felt that something of which he was a part—a regiment, an army, a cause, or a country—was in a crisis. He was welded into a common personality which was dominated by a single desire. For some moments he could not flee no more than a little finger can commit a revolution from a hand.

There was a consciousness always of the presence of his comrades about him. He felt the subtle battle brotherhood more potent even than the cause for which they were fighting. It was a mysterious fraternity born of the smoke and danger of death.

He was at a task. He was like a carpenter who has made many boxes, making still another box, only there was furious haste in his movements. He, in his thought, was careering off in other places, even as the carpenter who as he works whistles and thinks of his friend or his enemy, his home or a saloon. And these jilted dreams were never perfect to him afterward, but remained a mass of blurred shapes.

Presently he began to feel the effects of the war atmosphere—a blistering sweat, a sensation that his eyeballs were about to crack like hot stones. A burning roar filled his ears.

Following this came a red rage. He developed the acute exasperation of a pestered animal, a well-meaning cow worried by dogs. He had a mad feeling against his rifle, which could only be used against one life at a time. He wished to rush forward and strangle with his fingers.

Buried in the smoke of many rifles, his anger was directed not so much against the men whom he knew were rushing toward him as against the swirling battle phantoms which were choking him.

There was a blare of heated rage mingled with a certain expression of intentness on all faces. Many of the men were making low-toned noises with their mouths, and these subdued cheers, snarls, imprecations, prayers, made a wild, barbaric song, strange and chantlike, with the resounding chords of the war march. The man at the youth's elbow was babbling. The tall soldier was swearing in a loud voice. Of a sudden another broke out in a querulous way, like a man who has mislaid his hat. "Well, why don't they support us? Why don't they send supports? Do they think—"

The youth in his battle sleep heard this as one who dozes hears.

There was a singular absence of heroic poses. The men bending and surging in their haste and rage were in every impossible attitude. The steel ramrods clanked and clanged with incessant din as the men pounded them furiously into the hot rifle barrels. The flaps of the cartridge boxes were all unfastened, and bobbed idiotically with each movement. The rifles, once loaded, were jerked to the shoulder and fired without apparent aim into the smoke or at one of the blurred and shifting forms which upon the field before the regiment had been growing larger and larger, like puppets under a magician's hands.

The officers, at their intervals, rearward, neglected to stand in picturesque attitudes. They were bobbing to and fro roaring directions and encouragements. The dimensions of their howls were extraordinary. And often they nearly stood upon their heads in their anxiety to observe the enemy on the other side of the tumbling smoke.

The lieutenant of the youth's company had encountered a soldier who had fled screaming at the first volley of his comrades. Behind the lines these two were acting a little isolated scene. The man was blubbering and staring with sheeplike eyes at the lieutenant, who had seized him by the collar and was pommeling him. He drove him back into the ranks with many blows. The soldier went mechanically, dully, with his animal-like eyes upon the officer. Perhaps there was to him a divinity expressed in the voice of the other—stern, hard, with no reflection of fear in it. He tried to reload his gun, but his shaking hands prevented. The lieutenant was obliged to assist him.

The men dropped here and there like bundles.

The captain of the youth's company had been killed in an early part of the action. His body lay stretched out in the position of a tired man resting, but upon his face there was an astonished and sorrowful look, as if he thought some friend had done him an ill turn. The babbling man was grazed by a shot that made the blood stream widely down his face. He clasped both hands to his head. "Oh!" he said, and ran. Another grunted suddenly as if he had been struck by a club in the stomach. He sat down and gazed ruefully. In his eyes there was mute, indefinite reproach. Further up the line a man, standing behind a tree, had had his knee joint splintered by a ball. Immediately he had dropped his rifle and gripped the tree with both arms. And there he remained, clinging desperately and crying for assistance, that he might withdraw his hold upon the tree.

At last an exultant yell went along the quivering line. The firing dwindled from an uproar to a last vindictive popping. As the smoke slowly eddied away, the youth saw that the charge had been repulsed. The enemy were scattered into reluctant groups.

Some in the regiment began to whoop frenziedly. Many were silent. Apparently they were trying to contemplate themselves.

After the fever had left his veins, the youth thought that at last he was going to suffocate. He became aware of the foul atmosphere in which he had been struggling. He was grimy and dripping like a laborer in a foundry. He grasped his canteen and took a long swallow of the warmed water.

A sentence with variations went up and down the line. "Well, we've helt 'em back. We've helt 'em back; derned if we haven't." The men said it blissfully, leering at each other with dirty smiles.

The youth turned to look behind him and off to the right and off to the left. He experienced the joy of a man who at last finds leisure in which to look about him.

Underfoot there were a few ghastly forms motionless. They lay twisted in fantastic contortions. Arms were bent and heads were turned in incredible ways. It seemed that the dead men must have fallen from some great height to get into such positions. They looked to be dumped out upon the ground from the sky.

A small procession of wounded men were going drearily toward the rear. It was a flow of blood from the torn body of the brigade.

As he gazed around him, the youth felt a flash of astonishment at the blue, pure sky and the sun gleaming on the trees and fields. It was surprising that Nature had gone tranquilly on with her golden process in the midst of so much devilment.

Chapter 6

The youth awakened slowly. He came gradually back to a position from which he could regard himself. For moments he had been scrutinizing his person in a dazed way as if he had never before seen himself. Then he picked up his cap from the ground. He wriggled in his jacket to make a more comfortable fit, and kneeling, relaced his shoe. He thoughtfully mopped his reeking[21] features.

So it was all over at last! The supreme trial had been passed. The red, formidable difficulties of war had been vanquished.

He went into an ecstasy of self-satisfaction. He had the most delightful sensations of his life. Standing as if apart from himself, he viewed that last scene. He perceived that the man who had fought thus was magnificent.

He felt that he was a fine fellow. He saw himself even with those ideals which he had considered as far beyond him. He smiled in deep gratification.

There were some handshakings and deep speeches with men whose features were familiar, but with whom the youth now felt the bonds of tied hearts. He helped a cursing comrade to bind up a wound of the shin.

But, of a sudden, cries of amazement broke out along the ranks of the new regiment. "Here they come ag'in! Here they come ag'in!"

The youth turned quick eyes upon the field. He discerned forms begin to swell in masses out of a distant wood. He again saw the tilted flag speeding forward.

The shells, which had ceased to trouble the regiment for a time, came swirling again, and exploded in the grass or among the leaves of the trees. They looked to be strange war flowers bursting into fierce bloom.

The men groaned. The luster faded from their eyes. Their smudged countenances now expressed a profound dejection. They moved their stiffened bodies slowly, and watched in sullen mood the frantic approach of the enemy.

The youth stared. Surely, he thought, this impossible thing was not about to happen. He waited as if he expected the enemy to suddenly stop, apologize, and retire bowing. It was all a mistake.

---

21. **reeking:** here, sweating.

But the firing began somewhere on the regimental line and ripped along in both directions. The level sheets of flame developed great clouds of smoke that tumbled and tossed in the mild wind near the ground for a moment, and then rolled through the ranks as through a gate.

Into the youth's eyes there came a look that one can see in the orbs[22] of a jaded horse. His neck was quivering with nervous weakness, and the muscles of his arms felt numb and bloodless. His hands, too, seemed large and awkward, as if he was wearing invisible mittens. And there was a great uncertainty about his knee joints.

He slowly lifted his rifle and catching a glimpse of the thick spread field he blazed at a cantering cluster. He stopped then and began to peer as best he could through the smoke. He caught changing views of the ground covered with men who were all running and yelling.

To the youth it was an onslaught of redoubtable dragons. He became like the man who lost his legs at the approach of the red and green monster. He waited in a sort of a horrified, listening attitude. He seemed to shut his eyes and wait to be gobbled.

A man near him who up to this time had been working feverishly at his rifle suddenly stopped and ran with howls. A lad whose face had borne an expression of exalted courage, the majesty of he who dares give his life, was, at an instant, smitten abject.[23] He blanched like one who has come to the edge of a cliff at midnight and is suddenly made aware. There was a revelation. He, too, threw down his gun and fled. There was no shame in his face. He ran like a rabbit.

Others began to scamper away through the smoke. The youth turned his head, shaken from his trance by this movement as if the regiment was leaving him behind. He saw the few fleeing forms.

He yelled then with fright and swung about. For a moment, in the great clamor, he was like a proverbial chicken.[24] He lost the direction of safety. Destruction threatened him from all points.

Directly he began to speed toward the rear in great leaps. His rifle and cap were gone. His unbuttoned coat bulged in the wind. The flap of his cartridge box bobbed wildly, and his canteen, by its slender cord, swung out behind. On his face was all the horror of those things which he imagined.

The lieutenant sprang forward bawling. The youth saw his features wrathfully red, and saw him make a dab with his sword. His one thought of the incident was that the lieutenant was a peculiar creature to feel interested in such matters upon this occasion.

He ran like a blind man. Two or three times he fell down. Once he knocked his shoulder so heavily against a tree that he went headlong.

Since he had turned his back upon the fight, his fears had been wondrously magnified. Death about to thrust him between the shoulderblades was far more dreadful than death about to smite him between the eyes.

As he ran on, he mingled with others. He dimly saw men on his right and on his left, and he heard footsteps behind him. He thought that all the regiment was fleeing, pursued by these ominous crashes.

In his flight the sound of these following footsteps gave him his once meager relief. He felt vaguely that death must make a first choice of the men who were nearest; the initial morsels for the dragons would be those who were following him. So he displayed the zeal of an insane sprinter in his purpose to keep them in the rear. There was a race.

As he, leading, went across a little field, he found himself in a region of shells. They hurtled over his head with long wild screams. As he listened, he imagined them to have rows of

---

22. **orbs:** eyes.
23. **smitten abject:** struck low.

24. **like . . . chicken:** that is, like a chicken with its head cut off; frantic.

The "stolid and undaunted" guns of a Union battery, 1863.

cruel teeth that grinned at him. Once one lit before him and the livid lightning of the explosion effectually barred the way in his chosen direction. He groveled on the ground and then springing up went careering off through some bushes.

He experienced a thrill of amazement when he came within view of a battery in action. The men there seemed to be in conventional moods, altogether unaware of the impending annihilation. The battery was disputing with a distant antagonist and the gunners were wrapped in admiration of their shooting. They were continually bending in coaxing postures over the guns. They seemed to be patting them on the back and encouraging them with words. The guns, stolid and undaunted, spoke with dogged valor.

He came upon a general of division seated upon a horse that pricked its ears in an interested way at the battle. Sometimes the general was surrounded by horsemen and at other times he was quite alone. He looked to be much harassed. He had the appearance of a businessman whose market is swinging up and down.

The youth went as near as he dared, trying to overhear words. Perhaps the general, unable to comprehend chaos, might call upon him for information. And he could tell him. He knew all concerning it. Of a surety the force was in a fix, and any fool could see that if they did not retreat while they had opportunity—why—

He felt that he would like to thrash the general, or at least approach and tell him in plain words exactly what he thought him to be. It was criminal to stay calmly in one spot and make no effort to stay destruction. He loitered in a fever of eagerness for the division commander to apply to him.

As he warily moved about, he heard the general call out irritably: "Tompkins, go over an' see Taylor, an' tell him not t' be in such an all-fired hurry; tell him t' halt his brigade in th' edge of th' woods; tell him t' detach a reg'ment—say I think th' center'll break if we don't help it out some; tell him t' hurry up."

A slim youth on a fine chestnut horse caught these swift words from the mouth of his superior. He made his horse bound into a gallop almost from a walk in his haste to go upon his mission. There was a cloud of dust.

A moment later the youth saw the general bounce excitedly in his saddle.

"Yes, by heavens, they have!" The officer leaned forward. His face was aflame with excitement. "Yes, by heavens, they've held 'im! They've held 'im!"

He began blithely to roar at his staff: "We'll wallop 'im now. We'll wallop 'im now. We've got 'em sure." He turned suddenly upon an aid: "Here—you—Jones—quick—ride after Tompkins—see Taylor—tell him t' go in—everlastingly—like blazes—anything."

As another officer sped his horse after the first messenger, the general beamed upon the earth like a sun. In his eyes was a desire to chant a paean.[25] He kept repeating, "They've held 'em, by heavens!"

His excitement made his horse plunge, and he merrily kicked and swore at it. He held a little carnival of joy on horseback.

---

25. **paean** [pē′ən]: song of joy or triumph.

STUDY QUESTIONS

Recalling

1. According to page 369, what sort of pictures did the youth have of war before he enlisted? As what has the youth grown to regard himself (page 371)?
2. With what serious problem does the youth grapple as he lies in his bunk after hearing the tall soldier's rumor (page 371)?
3. What is the tall soldier's name? The loud soldier's? The youth's? Where do we discover this information?
4. Identify four thoughts or feelings that Henry has as he runs on page 376.
5. As Henry gets his first glimpse of the "foe-swarming field" (page 381), what does he do? What does he lose? What does he become?
6. During the second exchange of gunfire (Chapter 6), what does Henry see the men doing? What does he do soon after?

Interpreting

7. What does this section imply about the new recruits' understanding of the events in which they participate? What is suggested by the fact that Crane withholds the names of his characters until well into the story?
8. What is Henry's great fear in the first two chapters? Why does he begin running in Chapter 3, firing in Chapter 5, and fleeing from battle in Chapter 6?
9. Are Henry's thoughts about war and his own place in the war consistent? Explain the irony of his thinking, just before the battle, that "he never wished to come to the war."
10. Based on your answers to questions 8 and 9, characterize Henry Fleming.

Extending

11. How are the main characters in this novel similar to and different from the soldiers you have read about elsewhere or seen in war films?

Chapter 7

The youth cringed as if discovered in a crime. By heavens, they had won after all! The imbecile[1] line had remained and become victors. He could hear cheering.

He lifted himself upon his toes and looked in the direction of the fight. A yellow fog lay wallowing on the treetops. From beneath it came the clatter of musketry. Hoarse cries told of an advance.

He turned away amazed and angry. He felt that he had been wronged.

He had fled, he told himself, because annihilation approached. He had done a good part in saving himself, who was a little piece of the army. He had considered the time, he said, to be one in which it was the duty of every little piece to rescue itself if possible. Later the officers could fit the little pieces together again, and make a battle front. If none of the little pieces were wise enough to save themselves from the flurry of death at such a time, why, then, where would be the army? It was all plain that he had proceeded according to very correct and commendable rules. His actions had been sagacious things. They had been full of strategy. They were the work of a master's legs.

Thoughts of his comrades came to him. The brittle blue line had withstood the blows and won. He grew bitter over it. It seemed that the blind ignorance and stupidity of those little pieces had betrayed him. He had been overturned and crushed by their lack of sense in holding the position, when intelligent deliberation would have convinced them that it was impossible. He, the enlightened man who looks afar in the dark, had fled because of his superior perceptions and knowledge. He felt a great anger against his comrades. He knew it could be proved that they had been fools.

He wondered what they would remark when later he appeared in camp. His mind heard howls of derision. Their density would not enable them to understand his sharper point of view.

He began to pity himself acutely. He was ill-used. He was trodden beneath the feet of an iron injustice. He had proceeded with wisdom and from the most righteous motives under heaven's blue only to be frustrated by hateful circumstances.

A dull, animal-like rebellion against his fellows, war in the abstract, and fate grew within him. He shambled along with bowed head, his brain in a tumult of agony and despair. When he looked lowering up, quivering at each sound, his eyes had the expression of those of a criminal who thinks his guilt little and his punishment great, and knows that he can find no words.

He went from the fields into a thick wood, as if resolved to bury himself. He wished to get out of hearing of the crackling shots which were to him like voices. So he went far, seeking dark and intricate places.

After a time the sound of musketry grew faint and the cannon boomed in the distance. The sun, suddenly apparent, blazed among the trees. The insects were making rhythmical noises. They seemed to be grinding their teeth in unison. A woodpecker stuck his impudent head around the side of a tree. A bird flew on lighthearted wing.

Off was the rumble of death. It seemed now that Nature had no ears.

This landscape gave him assurance. A fair field holding life. It was the religion of peace. It would die if its timid eyes were compelled to see blood. He conceived Nature to be a woman with a deep aversion to tragedy.

He threw a pine cone at a jovial squirrel, and he ran with chattering fear. High in a treetop he stopped, and poking his head cautiously from behind a branch, looked down with an air of trepidation.

The youth felt triumphant at this exhibition. There was the law, he said. Nature had given him a sign. The squirrel, immediately upon recognizing danger, had taken to his legs without ado. He did not stand stolidly baring his furry

---

1. **imbecile:** here, weak.

belly to the missile, and die with an upward glance at the sympathetic heavens. On the contrary, he had fled as fast as his legs could carry him; and he was but an ordinary squirrel, too—doubtless no philosopher of his race. The youth wended, feeling that Nature was of his mind. She reinforced his argument with proofs that lived where the sun shone.

The youth went again into the deep thickets. The brushed branches made a noise that drowned the sounds of cannon. He walked on, going from obscurity into promises of a greater obscurity.

At length he reached a place where the high, arching boughs made a chapel. He softly pushed the green doors aside and entered. Pine needles were a gentle brown carpet. There was a religious half light.

Near the threshold he stopped, horror-stricken at the sight of a thing.

He was being looked at by a dead man, who was seated with his back against a columnlike tree. The corpse was dressed in a uniform that once had been blue, but was now faded to a melancholy shade of green. The eyes, staring at the youth, had changed to the dull hue to be seen on the side of a dead fish. The mouth was open. Its red had changed to an appalling yellow. Over the gray skin of the face ran little ants. One was trundling some sort of a bundle along the upper lip.

The youth gave a shriek as he confronted the thing. He was for moments turned to stone before it. He remained staring into the liquid-looking eyes. The dead man and the living man exchanged a long look. Then the youth cautiously put one hand behind him and brought it against a tree. Leaning upon this, he retreated, step by step, with his face still toward the thing. He feared that if he turned his back, the body might spring up and stealthily pursue him.

The branches, pushing against him, threatened to throw him over upon it. His unguided feet, too, caught aggravatingly in brambles; and with it all he received a subtle suggestion to touch the corpse. As he thought of his hand upon it, he shuddered profoundly.

At last he burst the bonds which had fastened him to the spot and fled, unheeding the underbrush. He was pursued by a sight of the blank ants swarming greedily upon the gray face and venturing horribly near to the eyes.

After a time he paused, and, breathless and panting, listened. He imagined some strange voice would come from the dead throat and squawk after him in horrible menaces.

The trees about the portal of the chapel moved soughingly in a soft wind. A sad silence was upon the little guarding edifice.

Chapter 8

The trees began softly to sing a hymn of twilight. The sun sank until slanted bronze rays struck the forest. There was a lull in the noises of insects, as if they had bowed their beaks and were making a devotional pause. There was silence save for the chanted chorus of the trees.

Then, upon this stillness, there suddenly broke a tremendous clangor of sounds. A crimson roar came from the distance.

The youth stopped. He was transfixed by this terrific medley of all noises. It was as if worlds were being rended. There was the ripping sound of musketry and the breaking crash of the artillery.

It suddenly occurred to the youth that the fight in which he had been was, after all, but perfunctory popping. In the hearing of this present din he was doubtful if he had seen real battle scenes. This uproar explained a celestial battle; it was tumbling hordes a-struggle in the air.

Reflecting, he saw a sort of a humor in the point of view of himself and his fellows during the late encounter. They had taken themselves and the enemy very seriously and had imagined that they were deciding the war. Individuals must have supposed that they were cutting the letters of their names deep into everlasting tablets of brass, or enshrining their reputations forever in the hearts of their countrymen, while, as to fact, the affair would appear in printed reports under a meek and immaterial title. But he saw that it was good, else, he said, in battle everyone would surely run save forlorn hopes[2] and their ilk.

He proceeded again on his forward way. The battle was like the grinding of an immense and terrible machine to him. Its complexities and powers, its grim processes, fascinated him. He must go close and see it produce corpses.

He came to a fence and clambered over it. On the far side, the ground was littered with clothes and guns. A newspaper, folded up, lay in the dirt. A dead soldier was stretched with his face hidden in his arm. Farther off there was a group of four or five corpses keeping mournful company. A hot sun had blazed upon the spot.

He came finally to a road from which he could see in the distance dark and agitated bodies of troops, smoke-fringed. In the lane was a bloodstained crowd streaming to the rear. The wounded men were cursing, groaning, and wailing.

One of the wounded men had a shoeful of blood. He hopped like a schoolboy in a game. He was laughing hysterically.

Another had the gray seal of death already upon his face. His lips were curled in hard lines and his teeth were clenched. His hands were bloody from where he had pressed them upon his wound. He seemed to be awaiting the moment when he should pitch headlong. He stalked like the specter of a soldier, his eyes burning with the power of a stare into the unknown.

There were some who proceeded sullenly, full of anger at their wounds, and ready to turn upon anything as an obscure cause.

The youth joined this crowd and marched along with it. The torn bodies expressed the awful machinery in which the men had been entangled.

There was a tattered man, fouled with dust, blood and powder stain from hair to shoes, who trudged quietly at the youth's side. He was listening with eagerness and much humility to the lurid descriptions of a bearded sergeant. His lean features wore an expression of awe and admiration. He was like a listener in a

---

2. **forlorn hopes:** groups of soldiers detached from the main group for perilous missions.

A young Confederate soldier helps a wounded comrade, 1863.

country store to wondrous tales told among the sugar barrels.

After a time he began to sidle near to the youth, and in a diffident way try to make him a friend. His voice was gentle as a girl's voice and his eyes were pleading. The youth saw with surprise that the soldier had two wounds, one in the head, bound with a blood-soaked rag, and the other in the arm, making that member dangle like a broken bough.

After they had walked together for some time, the tattered man mustered sufficient courage to speak. "Was pretty good fight, wa'n't it?" he timidly said. The youth, deep in thought, glanced up at the bloody and grim figure with its lamblike eyes. "What?"

"Was pretty good fight, wa'n't it?"

"Yes," said the youth shortly. He quickened his pace.

But the other hobbled industriously after him. There was an air of apology in his manner, but he evidently thought that he needed only to talk for a time, and the youth would perceive that he was a good fellow.

"Was pretty good fight, wa'n't it?" he began in a small voice, and then he achieved the fortitude to continue. "Dern me if I ever see fellers fight so. I knowed th' boys'd lick when they oncet got square at it. Th' boys ain't had no fair chancet up t' now, but this time they showed what they was. I knowed it'd turn out this way. Yeh can't lick them boys. No, sir! They're fighters, they be."

His homely face was suffused with a light of love for the army which was to him all things beautiful and powerful.

After a time he turned to the youth. "Where yeh hit, ol' boy?" he asked in a brotherly tone.

The youth felt instant panic at this question, although at first its full import was not borne in upon him.

"What?" he asked.

"Where yeh hit?" repeated the tattered man.

"Why," began the youth, "I—I—that is—why—I—"

He turned away suddenly and slid through the crowd. His brow was heavily flushed, and his fingers were picking nervously at one of his buttons. He bent his head and fastened his eyes studiously upon the button as if it were a little problem.

The tattered man looked after him in astonishment.

Chapter 9

The youth fell back in the procession until the tattered soldier was not in sight. Then he started to walk on with the others.

But he was amid wounds. The mob of men was bleeding. Because of the tattered soldier's question he now felt that his shame could be viewed. He was continually casting sidelong glances to see if the men were contemplating the letters of guilt he felt burned into his brow.

At times he regarded the wounded soldiers in an envious way. He conceived persons with torn bodies to be peculiarly happy. He wished that he, too, had a wound, a red badge of courage.

The spectral soldier was at his side like a stalking reproach. The man's eyes were still fixed in a stare into the unknown. His gray, appalling face had attracted attention in the crowd, and men, slowing to his dreary pace, were walking with him. They were discussing his plight, questioning him and giving him advice. In a dogged way he repelled them, signing to them to go on and leave him alone. The shadows of his face were deepening and his tight lips seemed holding in check the moan of great despair. There could be seen a certain stiffness in the movements of his body, as if he were taking infinite care not to arouse the passion of his wounds. As he went on, he seemed always looking for a place, like one who goes to choose a grave.

Something in the gesture of the man as he waved the bloody and pitying soldiers away made the youth start as if bitten. He yelled in horror. Tottering forward, he laid a quivering hand upon the man's arm. As the latter slowly turned his waxlike features toward him, the youth screamed:

"Jim Conklin!"

The tall soldier made a little commonplace smile. "Hello, Henry," he said.

The youth swayed on his legs and glared strangely. He stuttered and stammered. "Oh, Jim—oh, Jim—oh, Jim—"

The tall soldier held out his gory hand. There was a curious red and black combination of new blood and old blood upon it. "Where yeh been, Henry?" he asked. He continued in a monotonous voice. "I thought mebbe yeh got keeled over. There's been thunder t' pay t'day. I was worryin' about it a good deal."

The youth still lamented. "Oh, Jim—oh, Jim—oh, Jim—"

"Yeh know," said the tall soldier, "I was out there." He made a careful gesture. "An' what a circus! An' b'jiminey, I got shot—I got shot. Yes, b'jiminey, I got shot." He reiterated this fact in a bewildered way, as if he did not know how it came about.

The youth put forth anxious arms to assist him, but the tall soldier went firmly on as if propelled. Since the youth's arrival as a guardian for his friend, the other wounded men had ceased to display much interest. They occupied themselves again in dragging their own tragedies toward the rear.

Suddenly, as the two friends marched on, the tall soldier seemed to be overcome by terror. His face turned to a semblance of gray paste. He clutched the youth's arm and looked all about him, as if dreading to be overheard. Then he began to speak in a shaking whisper:

"I tell yeh what I'm 'fraid of, Henry—I'll tell yeh what I'm 'fraid of. I'm 'fraid I'll fall down—an' then yeh know—them artillery wagons—they like as not'll run over me. That's what I'm 'fraid of—"

The youth cried out to him hysterically: "I'll take care of yeh, Jim! I'll take care of yeh! I swear I will!"

"Sure—will yeh, Henry?" the tall soldier beseeched.

"Yes—yes—I tell yeh—I'll take care of yeh, Jim!" protested the youth. He could not speak accurately because of the gulpings in his throat.

But the tall soldier continued to beg in a lowly way. He now hung babelike to the youth's arm. His eyes rolled in the wildness of his terror. "I was allus a good friend t' yeh, wa'n't I, Henry? I've allus been a pretty good feller, ain't I? An' it ain't much t' ask, is it? Jest t' pull me along outer th' road? I'd do it fer you, wouldn't I, Henry?"

He paused in piteous anxiety to await his friend's reply.

The youth had reached an anguish where the sobs scorched him. He strove to express his loyalty, but he could only make fantastic gestures.

However, the tall soldier seemed suddenly to forget all those fears. He became again the grim, stalking specter of a soldier. He went stonily forward. The youth wished his friend to lean upon him, but the other always shook his head and strangely protested. "No—no—no—leave me be—leave me be—"

His look was fixed again upon the unknown. He moved with mysterious purpose, and all of the youth's offers he brushed aside. "No—no—leave me be—leave me be—"

The youth had to follow.

Presently the latter heard a voice talking softly near his shoulder. Turning he saw that it belonged to the tattered soldier. "Ye'd better take 'im outa th' road, pardner. There's a batt'ry comin' down th' road an' he'll git runned over. He's a goner anyhow in about five minutes—yeh kin see that. Ye'd better take 'im outa th' road. Where th' blazes does he git his stren'th from?"

"Lord knows!" cried the youth. He was shaking his hands helplessly.

He ran forward presently and grasped the tall soldier by the arm. "Jim! Jim!" he coaxed, "come with me."

The tall soldier weakly tried to wrench himself free. "Huh," he said vacantly. He stared at the youth for a moment. At last he spoke as if dimly comprehending. "Oh! Inteh th' fields? Oh!"

He started blindly through the grass.

The youth turned once to look at the lashing riders and jouncing guns of the battery. He was startled from this view by a shrill outcry from the tattered man.

"He's runnin'!"

Turning his head swiftly, the youth saw his friend running in a staggering and stumbling way toward a little clump of bushes. His heart seemed to wrench itself almost free from his body at this sight. He made a noise of pain. He and the tattered man began a pursuit. There was a singular race.

When he overtook the tall soldier he began to plead with all the words he could find. "Jim—Jim—what are you doing—what makes you do this way—you'll hurt yerself."

The tall soldier faced about as upon relentless pursuers. In his eyes there was a great appeal. "Leave me be, can't yeh? Leave me be fer a minnit."

The youth recoiled. "Why, Jim," he said, in a dazed way, "what's the matter with you?"

The tall soldier turned and, lurching dangerously, went on. The youth and the tattered soldier followed, sneaking as if whipped, feeling unable to face the stricken man if he should again confront them. They began to have thoughts of a solemn ceremony. There was something ritelike in these movements of the doomed soldier. And there was a resemblance in him to a devotee of a mad religion, blood-sucking, muscle-wrenching, bone-crushing. They were awed and afraid. They hung back lest he have at command a dreadful weapon.

At last, they saw him stop and stand motionless. Hastening up, they perceived that his face wore an expression telling that he had at last found the place for which he had struggled. His spare figure was erect; his bloody hands were quietly at his side. He was waiting with patience for something that he had come to meet. He was at the rendezvous. They paused and stood, expectant.

Confederate private, a "youth" of the war.

There was a silence.

Finally, the chest of the doomed soldier began to heave with a strained motion. It increased in violence until it was as if an animal was within and was kicking and tumbling furiously to be free.

This spectacle of gradual strangulation made the youth writhe, and once as his friend rolled his eyes, he saw something in them that made him sink wailing to the ground. He raised his voice in a last supreme call.

"Jim—Jim—Jim—"

The tall soldier opened his lips and spoke. He made a gesture. "Leave me be—don't tech me—leave me be—"

There was another silence while he waited.

Suddenly, his form stiffened and straightened. Then it was shaken by a prolonged ague.[3] He stared into space. To the two watchers there was a curious and profound dignity in the firm lines of his awful face.

He was invaded by a creeping strangeness that slowly enveloped him. For a moment the tremor of his legs caused him to dance a sort of hideous hornpipe.[4] His arms beat wildly

---

3. **ague** [ā′gyoo]: a fit of shivering.
4. **hornpipe**: lively folk dance.

about his head in expression of implike enthusiasm.

His tall figure stretched itself to its full height. There was a slight rending sound. Then it began to swing forward, slow and straight, in the manner of a falling tree. A swift muscular contortion made the left shoulder strike the ground first. The body seemed to bounce a little way from the earth.

The youth had watched, spellbound, this ceremony at the place of meeting. His face had been twisted into an expression of every agony he had imagined for his friend.

He now sprang to his feet and, going closer, gazed upon the pastelike face. The mouth was open and the teeth showed in a laugh.

As the flap of the blue jacket fell away from the body, he could see that the side looked as if it had been chewed by wolves.

The youth turned, with sudden, livid rage, toward the battlefield. He shook his fist.

The red sun was pasted in the sky like a wafer.

Chapter 10

The tattered man stood musing.

"Well, he was reg'lar jim-dandy fer nerve, wa'n't he," said he finally in a little awestruck voice. "A reg'lar jim-dandy." He thoughtfully poked one of the docile hands with his foot. "I wonner where he got 'is stren'th from? I never seen a man do like that before. It was a funny thing. Well, he was a reg'lar jim-dandy."

The youth desired to screech out his grief. He was stabbed, but his tongue lay dead in the tomb of his mouth. He threw himself again upon the ground and began to brood.

The tattered man stood musing.

"Look-a-here, pardner," he said after a time. He regarded the corpse as he spoke. "He's up an' gone, ain't 'e, an' we might as well begin t' look out fer ol' number one. This here thing is all over. An' I must say I ain't enjoying any great health m'self these days."

The youth, awakened by the tattered soldier's tone, looked quickly up. He saw that he was swinging uncertainly on his legs and that

his face had turned to a shade of blue.

"Good Lord!" he cried, "you ain't goin' t'—not you, too."

The tattered man waved his hand. "Nary die," he said. "All I want is some pea soup an' a good bed. Some pea soup," he repeated dreamfully.

The youth arose from the ground. "I wonder where he came from. I left him over there." He pointed. "And now I find 'im here. And he was coming from over there, too." He indicated a new direction. They both turned toward the body as if to ask of it a question.

"Well," at length spoke the tattered man, "There ain't no use in our stayin' here an' tryin' t' ask him anything."

The youth nodded an assent wearily.

As they plodded on, the tattered soldier continued to talk.

"Yeh know Tom Jamison, he lives next door t' me up home. He's a nice feller, he is, and we was allus good friends. Smart, too. Smart as a steel trap. Well, when we was a-fightin' this afternoon, all of a sudden he begin t' rip up an' beller at me. 'Yer shot,' he ses t' me. I put up m' hand t' m' head an' when I looked at m' fingers, I seen, sure 'nough, I was shot. I give a holler an' begin t' run, but b'fore I could git away another one hit me in th' arm an' whirl' me clean 'round. I got skeared when they was all a-shootin' b'hind me an' I run t' beat all, but I cotch it pretty bad. I've an idee I'd 'a' been fightin' yit, if 'twasn't fer Tom Jamison."

Then he made a calm announcement: "There's two of 'em—little ones—but they're beginnin' t' have fun with me now. I don't b'lieve I kin walk much furder."

They went slowly on in silence. "Yeh look pretty peek-ed yerself," said the tattered man at last. "I bet yeh've got a worser one than yeh think. Ye'd better take keer of yer hurt. It don't do t' let sech things go. It might be inside mostly, an' them plays thunder. Where is it located?"

The youth had been wriggling since the introduction of this topic. He now gave a cry of exasperation and made a furious motion with his hand. "Oh, don't bother me!" he said. He was enraged against the tattered man, and could have strangled him. His companions seemed ever to play intolerable parts. They were ever upraising the ghost of shame on the stick of their curiosity. He turned toward the tattered man as one at bay. "Now, don't bother me," he repeated with desperate menace.

"Well, Lord knows I don't wanta bother anybody," said the other. There was a little accent of despair in his voice as he replied, "Lord knows I've gota 'nough m' own t' tend to."

The youth, who had been holding a bitter debate with himself and casting glances of hatred and contempt at the tattered man, here spoke in a hard voice. "Goodbye," he said.

The tattered man looked at him in gaping amazement. "Why—why, pardner, where yeh goin'?" he asked unsteadily. The youth, looking at him, could see that he, too, like that other one, was beginning to act dumb and animal-like. His thoughts seemed to be floundering about in his head. "Now—now—look—a— here, you Tom Jamison—now—I won't have this—this here won't do. Where—where yeh goin'?"

The youth pointed vaguely. "Over there," he replied.

"Well, now look—a—here—now," said the tattered man, rambling on in idiot fashion. His head was hanging forward and his words were slurred. "This thing won't do, now, Tom Jamison. It won't do. I know yeh, yeh pig-headed devil. Yeh wanta go trompin' off with a bad hurt. It ain't right—now—Tom Jamison—it ain't. Yeh wanta leave me take keer of yeh, Tom Jamison. It ain't—right—it ain't—fer yeh t' go—trompin' off—with a bad hurt—it ain't— ain't—ain't right—it ain't."

The youth went on. Turning at a distance he saw the tattered man wandering about helplessly in the field.

He now thought that he wished he was dead. He believed that he envied those men whose bodies lay strewn over the grass of the fields and on the fallen leaves of the forest.

The simple questions of the tattered man had been knife thrusts to him. They asserted a society that probes pitilessly at secrets until all is apparent. His late companion's chance persistency made him feel that he could not keep his crime concealed in his bosom. It was sure to be brought plain by one of those arrows which cloud the air and are constantly pricking, discovering, proclaiming those things which are willed to be forever hidden. He admitted that he could not defend himself against this agency.[5] It was not within the power of vigilance.

Chapter 11

He became aware that the furnace roar of the battle was growing louder. Great brown clouds had floated to the still heights of air before him. The noise, too, was approaching. The woods filtered men and the fields became dotted.

As he rounded a hillock, he perceived that the roadway was now a crying mass of wagons, teams, and men. From the heaving tangle issued exhortations, commands, imprecations. Fear was sweeping it all along. The cracking whips bit and horses plunged and tugged. The white-topped wagons strained and stumbled in their exertions like fat sheep.

The youth felt comforted in a measure by this sight. They were all retreating. Perhaps, then, he was not so bad after all. He seated himself and watched the terror-stricken wagons.

Presently the calm head of a forward-going column of infantry appeared in the road. It came swiftly on. Avoiding the obstructions gave it the sinuous movements of a serpent. The men at the head butted mules with their musket stocks. They prodded teamsters,[6] indifferent to all howls.

The commands to make way had the ring of

---

5. **agency:** force.
6. **teamsters:** those whose work it is to drive teams of horses or other animals.

a great importance in them. The men were going forward to the heart of the din. They were to confront the eager rush of the enemy. This importance made their faces grave and stern. And the backs of the officers were very rigid.

As the youth looked at them the black weight of his woe returned to him. He felt that he was regarding a procession of chosen beings. He could never be like them. He could have wept in his longings.

As he watched his envy grew until he thought that he wished to change lives with one of them. He would have liked to have used a tremendous force, he said, throw off himself and become a better. Swift pictures of himself, apart, yet in himself, came to him—a blue desperate figure leading lurid charges with one knee forward and a broken blade high—a blue, determined figure standing before a crimson and steel assault, getting calmly killed on a high place before the eyes of all. He thought of the magnificent pathos of his dead body.

These thoughts uplifted him. He felt the quiver of war desire. In his ears, he heard the ring of victory. He knew the frenzy of a rapid successful charge. The music of the trampling feet, the sharp voices, the clanking arms of the column near him made him soar on the red wings of war. For a few moments he was sublime.

He thought that he was about to start for the front. Indeed, he saw a picture of himself, dust-stained, haggard, panting, flying to the front at the proper moment to seize and throttle the dark, leering witch of calamity.

Then the difficulties of the thing began to drag at him. He hesitated, balancing awkwardly on one foot.

He had no rifle; he could not fight with his hands, said he resentfully to his plan. Well, rifles could be had for the picking. They were extraordinarily profuse.

Also, he continued, it would be a miracle if he found his regiment. Well, he could fight with any regiment.

He started forward slowly. He stepped as if he expected to tread upon some explosive thing. Doubts and he were struggling.

He would truly be a worm if any of his comrades should see him returning thus, the marks of his flight upon him. His tireless fate would bring forth, when the strife lulled for a moment, a man to ask of him an explanation. In imagination he felt the scrutiny of his companions as he painfully labored through some lies.

Eventually, his courage expended itself upon these objections. The debates drained him of his fire.

Furthermore, various ailments had begun to cry out. He discovered that he had a scorching thirst. His face was so dry and grimy that he thought he could feel his skin crackle. Each bone of his body had an ache in it, and seemingly threatened to break with each movement. His feet were like two sores. Also, his body was calling for food, and, when he tried to walk, his head swayed and he tottered. He could not see with distinctness. Small patches of green mist floated before his vision.

While he had been tossed by many emotions, he had not been aware of ailments. Now they beset him and made clamor. As he was at last compelled to pay attention to them, his capacity for self-hate was multiplied. In despair, he declared that he was not like those others. He now conceded it to be impossible that he should ever become a hero. He was a craven loon.[7] Those pictures of glory were piteous things. He groaned from his heart and went staggering off.

A certain mothlike quality within him kept him in the vicinity of the battle. He had a great desire to see, and to get news. He wished to know who was winning.

He told himself that, despite his unprecedented suffering, he had never lost his greed for a victory. Yet, he said, in a half-apologetic manner to his conscience, he could not but know that a defeat for the army this time might mean many favorable things for him. The

---

7. **craven loon:** cowardly, worthless person.

blows of the enemy would splinter regiments into fragments. Thus, many men of courage, he considered, would be obliged to desert the colors[8] and scurry like chickens. He would appear as one of them. They would be sullen brothers in distress, and he could then easily believe he had not run any farther or faster than they.

In a defeat there would be roundabout vindication of himself. He thought it would prove, in a manner, that he had fled early because of his superior powers of perception. A serious prophet upon predicting a flood should be the first man to climb a tree. This would demonstrate that he was indeed a seer.

As these thoughts went rapidly through his mind, he turned upon them and tried to thrust them away. He denounced himself as a villain. He said that he was the most unutterably selfish man in existence. His mind pictured the soldiers who would place their defiant bodies before the spear of the yelling battle fiend, and as he saw their dripping corpses on an imagined field, he said that he was their murderer.

Again he thought that he wished he was dead. He believed that he envied a corpse. Thinking of the slain, he achieved a great contempt for some of them, as if they were guilty for thus becoming lifeless. They might have been killed by lucky chances, he said, before they had had opportunities to flee or before they had been really tested. Yet they would receive laurels[9] from tradition. He cried out bitterly that their crowns were stolen and their robes of glorious memories were shams. However, he still said that it was a great pity he was not as they.

A defeat of the army had suggested itself to him as a means of escape from the consequences of his fall. He considered now, however, that it was useless to think of such a possibility. His education had been that success for that mighty blue machine was certain; that

---

8. **colors:** flag of a regiment or country.
9. **laurels:** honors. Ancient Greeks crowned the victors of various contests with wreaths made from the leaves of laurel trees.

it would make victories as a contrivance turns out buttons. He presently discarded all his speculations in the other direction. He returned to the creed of soldiers.

When he perceived again that it was not possible for the army to be defeated, he tried to bethink him of a fine tale which he could take back to his regiment, and with it turn the expected shafts of derision.

But it became impossible for him to invent a tale he felt he could trust. He experimented with many schemes, but threw them aside one by one as flimsy. He was quick to see vulnerable places in them all.

Furthermore, he was much afraid that some arrow of scorn might lay him mentally low before he could raise his protecting tale.

He imagined the whole regiment saying: "Where's Henry Fleming? He run, didn't 'e? Oh, my!" He recalled various persons who would be quite sure to leave him no peace about it. They would doubtless question him with sneers, and laugh at his stammering hesitation. In the next engagement they would try to keep watch of him to discover when he would run.

Wherever he went in camp, he would encounter insolent and lingeringly cruel stares. As he imagined himself passing near a crowd of comrades, he could hear some one say, "There he goes!" He seemed to hear some one make a humorous remark in a low tone. At it the others all crowed and cackled. He was a slang phrase.

Chapter 12

The column that had butted stoutly at the obstacles in the roadway was barely out of the youth's sight before he saw dark waves of men come sweeping out of the woods and down through the fields. He knew at once that the steel fibers had been washed from their hearts.

The youth was horror-stricken. He stared in agony and amazement. He forgot that he was engaged in combating the universe.

The fight was lost. The dragons were coming with invincible strides. The army, helpless

A squad of Union soldiers, 1863.

in the matted thickets and blinded by the overhanging night, was going to be swallowed. War, the red animal, war, the blood-swollen god, would have bloated fill.

Within him something bade to cry out. He had the impulse to make a rallying speech, to sing a battle hymn, but he could only get his tongue to call into the air: "Why—why—what—what's th' matter?"

Soon he was in the midst of them. They were leaping and scampering all about him. Their blanched faces shone in the dusk.

The youth, after rushing about and throwing interrogations at the heedless bands of retreating infantry, finally clutched a man by the arm. They swung around face to face.

"Why—why—" stammered the youth, struggling with his balking tongue.

The man screamed, "Let go me! Let go me!" His face was livid and his eyes were rolling uncontrolled. He was heaving and panting. He still grasped his rifle, perhaps having forgotten to release his hold upon it. He tugged franti-

cally, and the youth being compelled to lean forward was dragged several paces.

"Let go me! Let go me!"

"Why—why—" stuttered the youth.

"Well, then!" bawled the man in a lurid rage. He adroitly and fiercely swung his rifle. It crushed upon the youth's head. The man ran on.

The youth's fingers had turned to paste upon the other's arm. The energy was smitten from his muscles. He saw the flaming wings of lightning flash before his vision. There was a deafening rumble of thunder within his head.

Suddenly his legs seemed to die. He sank writhing to the ground. He tried to arise. In his efforts against the numbing pain he was like a man wrestling with a creature of the air.

There was a sinister struggle.

Sometimes he would achieve a position half erect, battle with the air for a moment, and then fall again, grabbing at the grass. His face was of a clammy pallor. Deep groans were wrenched from him.

Stephen Crane **397**

At last, with a twisting movement, he got upon his hands and knees, and from thence, like a babe trying to walk, to his feet. Pressing his hands to his temples, he went lurching over the grass.

He fought an intense battle with his body. His dulled senses wished him to swoon and he opposed them stubbornly, his mind portraying unknown dangers and mutilations if he should fall upon the field. He went tall-soldier fashion. He imagined secluded spots where he could fall and be unmolested. To search for one he strove against the tide of his pain.

Once he put his hand to the top of his head and timidly touched the wound. The scratching pain of the contact made him draw a long breath through his clenched teeth. His fingers were dabbled with blood. He regarded them with a fixed stare.

Around him he could hear the grumble of jolted cannon as the scurrying horses were lashed toward the front. Once, a young officer on a besplashed charger nearly ran him down. He turned and watched the mass of guns, men, and horses sweeping in a wide curve toward a gap in a fence.

The blue haze of evening was upon the field. The lines of forest were long purple shadows. One cloud lay along the western sky partly smothering the red.

As the youth left the scene behind him, he heard the guns suddenly roar out. He imagined them shaking in black rage.

He hurried on in the dusk. The day had faded until he could barely distinguish place for his feet.

The little narrow roadway now lay lifeless. There were overturned wagons like sun-dried boulders. The bed of the former torrent was choked with the bodies of horses and splintered parts of war machines.

It had come to pass that his wound pained him but a little. He was afraid to move rapidly, however, for a dread of disturbing it. He held his head very still and took many precautions against stumbling. He was filled with anxiety, and his face was pinched and drawn in antici-

pation of the pain of any sudden mistake of his feet in the gloom.

The new silence of his wound made much worriment. The little blistering voices of pain that had called out from his scalp were, he thought, definite in their expression of danger. By them he believed that he could measure his plight. But when they remained ominously silent he became frightened and imagined terrible fingers that clutched into his brain.

Amid it he began to reflect upon various incidents and conditions of the past. He bethought him of certain meals his mother had cooked at home, in which those dishes of which he was particularly fond had occupied prominent positions. He saw the spread table. The pine walls of the kitchen were glowing in the warm light from the stove. Too, he remembered how he and his companions used to go from the schoolhouse to the bank of a shaded pool. He felt the swash of the fragrant water upon his body. The leaves of the overhanging maple rustled with melody in the wind of youthful summer.

He was overcome presently by a dragging weariness. His head hung forward and his shoulders were stooped as if he were bearing a great bundle. His feet shuffled along the ground.

He held continuous arguments as to whether he should lie down and sleep at some near spot, or force himself on until he reached a certain haven. He often tried to dismiss the question, but his body persisted in rebellion and his senses nagged at him like pampered babies.

At last he heard a cheery voice near his shoulder: "Yeh seem t' be in a pretty bad way, boy?"

The youth did not look up, but he assented with thick tongue. "Uh!"

The owner of the cheery voice took him firmly by the arm. "Well," he said, with a round laugh, "I'm goin' your way. Th' hull gang is goin' your way. An' I guess I kin give yeh a lift."

As they went along, the man questioned the

youth, and assisted him with the replies like one manipulating the mind of a child. "What reg'ment do yeh b'long teh? Eh? What's that? Th' 304th N' York? Why, what corps is that in? Oh, it is? Why, I thought they wasn't engaged t'-day—they're 'way over in th' center. Oh, they was, eh? Well, pretty nearly everybody got their share 'a fightin' t'-day. By dad, I give myself up fer dead any number 'a times. How did yeh git 'way over here, anyhow? Your reg'ment is a long way from here, ain't it? Well, I guess we can find it."

In the search which followed, the man of the cheery voice seemed to the youth to possess a wand of a magic kind. He threaded the mazes of the tangled forest with a strange fortune. In encounters with guards and patrols he displayed the keenness of a detective and the valor of a gamin.[10] Obstacles fell before him and became of assistance. The youth, with his chin still on his breast, stood woodenly by while his companion beat ways and means out of sullen things.

The forest seemed a vast hive of men buzzing about in frantic circles, but the cheery man conducted the youth without mistakes, until at last he began to chuckle with glee and self-satisfaction. "Ah, there yeh are! See that fire?"

The youth nodded stupidly.

"Well, there's where your reg'ment is. An' now goodbye, ol' boy, good luck t' yeh."

A warm and strong hand clasped the youth's languid fingers for an instant, and then he heard a cheerful and audacious whistling as the man strode away. As he who had so befriended him was thus passing out of his life, it suddenly occurred to the youth that he had not once seen his face.

Chapter 13

The youth went slowly toward the fire indicated by his departed friend. As he reeled, he bethought him of the welcome his comrades

---

10. **gamin** [gam′in]: neglected child of the streets who survives by means of aggressiveness and ingenuity.

would give him. He had a conviction that he would soon feel in his sore heart the barbed missiles of ridicule. He had no strength to invent a tale; he would be a soft target.

He made vague plans to go off into the deeper darkness and hide, but they were all destroyed by the voices of exhaustion and pain from his body. His ailments, clamoring, forced him to seek the place of food and rest, at whatever cost.

He swung unsteadily toward the fire. He could see the forms of men throwing black shadows in the red light, and as he went nearer it became known to him in some way that the ground was strewn with sleeping men.

Of a sudden he confronted a black and monstrous figure. A rifle barrel caught some glinting beams. "Halt! halt!" He was dismayed for a moment, but he presently thought that he recognized the nervous voice. As he stood tottering before the rifle barrel, he called out: "Why, hello, Wilson, you—you here?"

The rifle was lowered to a position of caution and the loud soldier came slowly forward. He peered into the youth's face. "That you, Henry?"

"Yes, it's—it's me."

"Well, well, ol' boy," said the other, "by ginger, I'm glad t' see yeh! I give yeh up fer a goner. I thought yeh was dead sure enough." There was husky emotion in his voice.

The youth found that now he could barely stand upon his feet. There was a sudden sinking of his forces. He thought he must hasten to produce his tale to protect him from the missiles already at the lips of his redoubtable comrades. So, staggering before the loud soldier, he began: "Yes, yes. I've—I've had an awful time. I've been all over. Way over on th' right. Ter'ble fightin' over there. I had an awful time. I got separated from th' reg'ment. Over on th' right I got shot. In th' head. I never see sech fightin'. Awful time. I don't see how I could'a got separated from th' reg'ment. I got shot, too."

His friend had stepped forward quickly. "What? Got shot? Why didn't yeh say so first?

Poor ol' boy, we must—hol' on a minnit; what am I doin'. I'll call Simpson."

Another figure at that moment loomed in the gloom. They could see that it was the corporal. "Who yeh talkin' to, Wilson?" he demanded. His voice was anger-toned. "Who yeh talkin' to? Yeh th' derndest sentinel—why— hello, Henry, you here? Why, I thought you was dead four hours ago! Great Jerusalem, they keep turnin' up every ten minutes or so! We thought we'd lost forty-two men by straight count, but if they keep on a-comin' this way, we'll git th' comp'ny all back by mornin' yit. Where was yeh?"

"Over on th' right. I got separated—" began the youth with considerable glibness.

But his friend had interrupted hastily. "Yes, an' he got shot in th' head an' he's in a fix, an' we must see t' him right away." He rested his rifle in the hollow of his left arm and his right around the youth's shoulder.

"Gee, it must hurt like thunder!" he said.

The youth leaned heavily upon his friend. "Yes, it hurts—hurts a good deal," he replied. There was a faltering in his voice.

"Oh," said the corporal. He linked his arm in the youth's and drew him forward. "Come on, Henry. I'll take keer 'a yeh."

As they went on together the loud private called out after them: "Put 'im t' sleep in my blanket, Simpson. Look at his head by th' fire an' see how it looks. Maybe it's a pretty bad un. When I git relieved in a couple 'a minnits, I'll be over an' see t' him."

The youth's senses were so deadened that his friend's voice sounded from afar and he could scarcely feel the pressure of the corporal's arm. He submitted passively to the latter's directing strength. His head was hanging forward upon his breast. His knees wobbled.

The corporal led him into the glare of the fire. "Now, Henry," he said, "Let's have a look at yer ol' head."

The youth sat down obediently and the corporal, laying aside his rifle, began to fumble in the bushy hair of his comrade. He was obliged to turn the other's head so that the full flush of the firelight would beam upon it. He puckered his mouth with a critical air. He drew back his lips and whistled through his teeth when his fingers came in contact with the splashed blood and the rare wound.

"Ah, here we are!" he said. He awkwardly made further investigations. "Jest as I thought," he added presently. "Yeh've been grazed by a ball. It's raised a queer lump jest as if some feller had lammed yeh on th' head with a club. It stopped a-bleedin' long time ago. Th' most about it is that in th' mornin' yeh'll feel that a number ten hat wouldn't fit yeh. An' your head'll be all het up an' feel as dry as burnt pork. An' yeh may git a lot 'a other sicknesses, too, by mornin'. Now, you jest sit here an' don't move, while I go rout out th' relief. Then I'll send Wilson t' take keer 'a yeh."

The corporal went away. The youth remained on the ground like a parcel. He stared with a vacant look into the fire.

The fire crackled musically. From it swelled light smoke. Overhead the foliage moved softly. The leaves, with their faces turned toward the blaze, were colored shifting hues of silver, often edged with red. Far off to the right, through a window in the forest could be seen a handful of stars lying, like glittering pebbles, on the black level of the night.

The youth sat in a forlorn heap until his friend the loud young soldier came, swinging two canteens by their light strings. "Well, now, Henry, ol' boy, we'll have yeh fixed up in jest about a minnit."

The loud young soldier produced an extensive handkerchief from his pocket. He folded it into a manner of bandage and soused water upon the middle of it. This crude arrangement he bound over the youth's head, tying the ends in a queer knot at the back of the neck.

"There," he said, moving off and surveying his deed, "yeh look like th' devil, but I bet yeh feel better."

The youth contemplated his friend with grateful eyes. Upon his aching and swelling head the cold cloth was like a tender woman's hand.

"Yeh don't holler ner say nothin'," remarked his friend approvingly. "I know I'm a blacksmith at takin' kerr 'a sick folks, an' yeh never squeaked. Yer a good un, Henry. Most 'a men would 'a' been in th' hospital long ago. A shot in th' head ain't foolin' business."

The youth made no reply, but began to fumble with the buttons of his jacket.

"Well, come, now," continued his friend, "come on. I must put yeh t' bed an' see that yeh git a good night's rest."

The other got carefully erect, and the loud young soldier led him among the sleeping forms lying in groups and rows. Presently he stooped and picked up his blankets. He spread the rubber one upon the ground and placed the woollen one about the youth's shoulders.

"There now," he said, "lie down and git some sleep."

The youth got carefully down. He stretched out with a murmur of relief and comfort. The ground felt like the softest couch.

But of a sudden he ejaculated: "Hol' on a minnit! Where you goin' t' sleep?"

His friend waved his hand impatiently. "Right down there."

"Well, but hol' on a minnit," continued the youth. "What yeh goin' t' sleep in? I've got your—"

The loud young soldier snarled: "Shet up an' go t' sleep. Don't be makin' a fool 'a yerself," he said severely.

After the reproof the youth said no more. An exquisite drowsiness had spread through him. The warm comfort of the blanket enveloped him. His head fell forward on his crooked arm and his weighted lids went softly down over his eyes. Hearing a splatter of musketry from the distance, he wondered indifferently if those men sometimes slept.

STUDY QUESTIONS

Recalling

1. What rationalization for his flight from battle does Henry make in the fourth paragraph of Chapter 7, and what "sign" from nature comforts him on page 387? What sight leaves him horror-stricken at the end of Chapter 7?
2. What is the "red badge of courage" that Henry envies (Chapter 9)?
3. Who is the spectral soldier, and what happened to him before Henry meets him? What does he say when he refuses to lean on Henry, and what are his last words before he dies?
4. What question does the tattered soldier ask Henry before Henry abandons him (Chapter 10)?
5. How is Henry wounded (Chapter 12)? How does he get back to his regiment? How does he explain his wound to Wilson (Chapter 13)?

Interpreting

6. What comforting message does Henry discern from the behavior of the squirrel? In light of the message, why is Henry's encounter with the dead man ironic, and what view of nature is suggested by this incident?
7. What does Conklin's death scene suggest about friendship and understanding?
8. What is ironic about Henry's wound? Why does he not reveal the truth to Wilson?
9. Contrast Henry's treatment of the tattered soldier with the cheerful soldier's treatment of Henry.

Extending

10. The term *pathetic fallacy* is often used to describe the human belief that nature mirrors human emotions and behavior. *Pathetic* comes from *pathos*, the Greek word for "feeling." Why would a Naturalist call this belief a pathetic fallacy? Would a Romantic or a Transcendentalist use this term? Explain.

Wounded Union soldiers in camp.

Chapter 14

When the youth awoke it seemed to him that he had been asleep for a thousand years, and he felt sure that he opened his eyes upon an unexpected world. Gray mists were slowly shifting before the first efforts of the sun rays. An impending splendor could be seen in the eastern sky. An icy dew had chilled his face, and immediately upon arousing he curled farther down into his blanket. He stared for a while at the leaves overhead, moving in a heraldic wind of the day.

The distance was splintering and blaring with the noise of fighting. There was in the sound an expression of a deadly persistency, as if it had not begun and was not to cease.

About him were the rows and groups of men that he had dimly seen the previous night. They were getting a last draught of sleep before the awakening. The quaint light at the dawning dressed the skin of the men in corpselike hues and made the tangled limbs appear pulseless and dead. The youth started up with a little cry when his eyes first swept over this motionless mass of men, thick-spread upon the ground, pallid, and in strange postures. He believed for an instant that he was in the house of the dead, and he did not dare to move lest these corpses start up, squalling and squawking. In a second, however, he achieved his proper mind. He saw that this somber picture was not a fact of the present, but a mere prophecy.

He heard then the noise of a fire crackling briskly in the cold air, and, turning his head, he saw his friend pottering busily about a small blaze. A few other figures moved in the fog, and he heard the hard cracking of axe blows.

Suddenly there was a hollow rumble of drums. A distant bugle sang faintly. Similar sounds, varying in strength, came from near and far over the forest. The bugles called to each other like brazen gamecocks.[1] The near thunder of the regimental drums rolled.

The body of men in the woods rustled. There was a general uplifting of heads. A mur-

---

1. **gamecocks:** roosters specially bred and trained for fighting.

muring of voices broke upon the air. In it there was much bass of grumbling oaths. An officer's peremptory tenor rang out and quickened the stiffened movement of the men. The tangled limbs unravelled. The corpse-hued faces were hidden behind fists that twisted slowly in the eye sockets.

The youth sat up and gave vent to an enormous yawn. His friend, perceiving him to be awake, came from the fire. "Well, Henry, ol' man, how do yeh feel this mornin'?" he demanded.

The youth yawned again. Then he puckered his mouth to a little pucker. His head, in truth, felt precisely like a melon, and there was an unpleasant sensation at his stomach.

"I feel pretty bad," he said.

"Thunder!" exclaimed the other. "Let's see th' bandage—I guess it's slipped." He began to tinker at the wound in rather a clumsy way until the youth exploded.

"Dern it!" he said in sharp irritation. "Why in good thunderation can't you be more easy? I'd rather you'd stand off an' throw guns at it. Now, go slow, an' don't act as if you was nailing down carpet."

He glared with insolent command at his friend, but the latter answered soothingly. "Well, well, come an' git some grub," he said. "Then, maybe, yeh'll feel better."

At the fireside the loud young soldier watched over his comrade's wants with tenderness and care. He had some fresh meat, which he roasted hurriedly upon a stick. He sat down then and contemplated the youth's appetite with glee.

The youth took note of a remarkable change in his comrade since those days of camp life upon the riverbank. He was not furious at small words that pricked his conceits. He was no more a loud young soldier. There was about him now a fine reliance. He showed a quiet belief in his purposes and his abilities. And this inward confidence evidently enabled him to be indifferent to little words of other men aimed at him.

The youth wondered where had been born those new eyes; when his comrade had made the great discovery that there were many men who would refuse to be subjected by him. Apparently, the other had now climbed a peak of wisdom from which he could perceive himself as a very wee thing. And the youth saw that ever after it would be easier to live in his friend's neighborhood.

His comrade balanced his cup on his knee. "Well, Henry," he said, "what d'yeh think th' chances are? D'yeh think we'll wallop 'em?"

The youth considered for a moment. "Day b'fore yesterday," he finally replied, with boldness, "you would 'a' bet you'd lick the hull kit-an'-boodle all by yourself."

His friend looked a trifle amazed. "Would I?" he asked. He pondered. "Well, perhaps I would," he decided at last. He stared humbly at the fire.

The youth was quite disconcerted at this surprising reception of his remarks. "Oh, no, you wouldn't either," he said hastily trying to retrace.

But the other made a deprecating gesture. "Oh, yeh needn't mind, Henry," he said. "I believe I was a pretty big fool in those days." He spoke as after a lapse of years.

There was a pause.

"All th' officers say we've got th' rebs in a pretty tight box," said the friend, clearing his throat in a commonplace way. "They all seem t' think we've got 'em jest where we want 'em."

"I don't know about that," the youth replied. "What I seen over on th' right makes me think it was th' other way about. From where I was, it looked as if we was gettin' a good poundin' yestirday."

"D'yeh think so?" inquired the friend. "I thought we handled 'em pretty rough yestirday."

"Not a bit," said the youth. "Why, man, you didn't see nothing of the fight. Why!" Then a sudden thought came to him. "Oh! Jim Conklin's dead."

His friend started. "What? Is he? Jim Conklin?"

The youth spoke slowly. "Yes. He's dead. Shot in th' side."

"Yeh don't say so. Jim Conklin . . . poor cuss!"

There was another little pause.

"Th' reg'ment lost over half th' men yestirday," remarked the friend eventually. "I thought 'a course they was all dead, but, they kep' a-comin' back last night until it seems, after all, we didn't lost but a few. They'd been scattered all over, wanderin' around in th' woods, fightin' with other reg'ments, an' everything. Jest like you done."

"So?" said the youth.

Chapter 15

The regiment was standing at order arms at the side of a lane, waiting for the command to march, when suddenly the youth remembered the little packet enwrapped in a faded yellow envelope which the loud young soldier had entrusted to him. It made him start. He uttered an exclamation and turned toward his comrade.

"Wilson!"

"What?"

His friend, at his side in the ranks, was thoughtfully staring down the road. From some cause his expression was at that moment very meek. The youth, regarding him with sidelong glances, felt impelled to change his purpose. "Oh, nothing," he said.

His friend turned his head in some surprise. "Why, what was yeh goin' t' say?"

"Oh, nothing," repeated the youth.

He resolved not to deal the little blow. It was sufficient that the fact made him glad. It was not necessary to knock his friend on the head with the misguided packet.

He had been possessed of much fear of his friend, for he felt certain that during the first period of leisure his friend would ask him to relate his adventures of the previous day.

He now rejoiced in the possession of a small weapon with which he could prostrate his comrade at the first signs of a cross-examination. He was master. It would now be he who could laugh and shoot the shafts of derision.

The friend had, in a weak hour, spoken with sobs of his own death. But he had not died, and thus he had delivered himself into the hands of the youth.

The latter felt immensely superior to his friend.

His self-pride was now restored. In the shade of its flourishing growth he stood with braced and self-confident legs. Since nothing could now be discovered he did not shrink from an encounter with the eyes of judges, and allowed no thoughts of his own to keep him from an attitude of manfulness. He had performed his mistakes in the dark, so he was still a man.

He had been taught that many obligations of a life were easily avoided. The lessons of yesterday had been that retribution was a laggard and blind. There was a little flower of confidence growing within him. He was now a man of experience. He had been out among the dragons, he said, and he assured himself that they were not so hideous as he had imagined them.

He remembered how some of the men had run from the battle. As he recalled their terror-struck faces, he felt a scorn for them. They had surely been more fleet and more wild than was absolutely necessary. They were weak mortals. As for himself, he had fled with discretion and dignity.

He was aroused from his reverie by his friend, who, having hitched about nervously and blinked at the trees for a time, suddenly coughed in an introductory way, and spoke.

"Fleming!"

"What?"

The friend put his hand up to his mouth and coughed again. He fidgeted in his jacket.

"Well," he gulped at last, "I guess yeh might as well give me back them letters." Dark, prickling blood had flushed into his cheeks and brow.

"All right, Wilson," said the youth. He loosened two buttons of his coat, thrust in his hand, and brought forth the packet. As he extended it to his friend, the latter's face was turned from him.

His friend at his side seemed suffering great shame. As he contemplated him, the youth felt his heart grow more strong and stout. He had never been compelled to blush in such manner for his acts; he was an individual of extraordinary virtues.

He reflected, with condescending pity: "Too bad! Too bad! The poor devil, it makes him feel tough!"

After this incident, and as he reviewed the battle pictures he had seen, he felt quite competent to return home and make the hearts of the people glow with stories of war. He could see himself in a room of warm tints telling tales to listeners. He could exhibit laurels. They were insignificant; still, in a district where laurels were infrequent, they might shine.

He saw his gaping audience picturing him as the central figure in blazing scenes. And he imagined the consternation of his mother and the young lady at the seminary as they drank his recitals. Their vague feminine formula for beloved ones doing brave deeds on the field of battle without risk of life would be destroyed.

Chapter 16

A sputtering of musketry was always to be heard. Later, the cannon had entered the dispute. In the fog-filled air their voices made a thudding sound. The reverberations were continued. This part of the world led a strange, battleful existence.

The youth's regiment was marched to relieve a command that had lain long in some damp trenches. The men took positions behind a curving line of rifle pits that had been turned up, like a large furrow, along the line of woods. Before them was a level stretch, peopled with short, deformed stumps. From the woods beyond came the dull popping of the skirmishers and pickets, firing in the fog. From the right came the noise of a terrific fracas.

The men cuddled behind the small embankment and sat awaiting their turn.

Before the gray mists had been totally obliterated by the sun rays, the regiment was marching in a spread column carefully through the woods. The disordered, hurrying lines of the enemy could sometimes be seen down through the groves and little fields. They were yelling, shrill and exultant.

At this sight the youth forgot many personal matters and became greatly enraged. He began a long and intricate denunciation of the commander of the forces.

"Mebbe it wa'n't all his fault—not all together. He did th' best he knowed. It's our luck t' git licked often," said his friend in a weary tone. He was trudging along with stooped shoulders and shifting eyes, like a man who has been caned and kicked.

"Well, don't we fight like the devil? Don't we do all that men can?" demanded the youth loudly.

He was secretly dumbfounded at this sentiment when it came from his lips. For a moment his face lost its valor, and he looked guiltily about him. But no one questioned his right to deal in such words, and presently he recovered his air of courage. He went on to repeat a statement he had heard going from group to group at the camp that morning. "The brigadier said he never saw a new reg'ment fight the way we fought yestirday, didn't he? And we didn't do better than many another reg'ment, did we? Well, then, you can't say it's th' army's fault, can you?"

In his reply, the friend's voice was stern. "'A course not," he said. "No man dare say we don't fight like th' devil. No man will ever dare say it. But still—still, we don't have no luck."

"Well, then, if we fight like the devil an' don't ever whip, it must be the general's fault," said the youth grandly and decisively. "And I don't see any sense in fighting and fighting and fighting, yet always losing through some old lunkhead of a general."

A sarcastic man who was tramping at the

youth's side, then spoke lazily. "Mebbe yeh think yeh fit th' hull battle yestirday, Fleming," he remarked.

The speech pierced the youth. Inwardly he was reduced to an abject pulp by these chance words. His legs quaked privately. He cast a frightened glance at the sarcastic man.

"Why, no," he hastened to say in a conciliating voice, "I don't think I fought the whole battle yesterday."

But the other seemed innocent of any deeper meaning. Apparently, he had no information.

The youth, nevertheless, felt a threat. His mind shrank from going near to the danger, and thereafter he was silent. The significance of the sarcastic man's words took from him all loud moods that would make him appear prominent. He became suddenly a modest person.

There was low-toned talk among the troops. The officers were impatient and snappy. The troops, sifting through the forest, were sullen. In the youth's company once a man's laugh rang out. A dozen soldiers turned their faces quickly toward him and frowned with vague displeasure.

The noise of firing dogged their footsteps. Sometimes, it seemed to be driven a little way, but it always returned again with increased insolence. The men muttered and cursed, throwing black looks in its direction.

In a clear space the troops were at last halted. Regiments and brigades, broken and detached through their encounters with thickets, grew together again, and lines were faced toward the pursuing bark of the enemy's infantry.

This noise, following like the yellings of eager, metallic hounds, increased to a loud and joyous burst, and then, as the sun went serenely up the sky throwing illuminating rays into the gloomy thickets, it broke forth into prolonged pealings. The woods began to crackle as if afire.

"Whoop-a-dadee," said a man, "here we are! Everybody fightin'. Blood an' destruction."

"I was willin' t' bet they'd attack as soon as th' sun got fairly up," savagely asserted the lieutenant who commanded the youth's company. He jerked without mercy at his little moustache. He strode to and fro with dark dignity in the rear of his men, who were lying down behind whatever protection they had collected.

The day had grown more white, until the sun shed his full radiance upon the thronged forest. A sort of a gust of battle came sweeping toward that part of the line where lay the youth's regiment. The front shifted a trifle to meet it squarely. There was a wait. In this part of the field there passed slowly the intense moments that precede the tempest.

A single rifle flashed in a thicket before the regiment. In an instant it was joined by many others. There was a mighty song of clashes and crashes that went sweeping through the woods. The guns in the rear, aroused and enraged by shells that had been thrown burrlike at them, suddenly involved themselves in a hideous altercation with another band of guns. The battle roar settled to a rolling thunder, which was a single, long explosion.

In the regiment there was a peculiar kind of hesitation denoted in the attitudes of the men. They were worn, exhausted, having slept but little and labored much. They rolled their eyes toward the advancing battle as they stood awaiting the shock. Some shrank and flinched. They stood as men tied to stakes.

Chapter 17

This advance of the enemy had seemed to the youth like a ruthless hunting. He began to fume with rage and exasperation. He beat his foot upon the ground, and scowled with hate at the swirling smoke that was approaching like a phantom flood. There was a maddening quality in this seeming resolution of the foe to give him no rest, to give him no time to sit down and think. Yesterday he had fought and had fled rapidly. There had been many adventures. For today he felt that he had earned opportunities for contemplative repose. He could have enjoyed portraying to uninitiated listeners var-

Wartime journalists who brought the news to "uninitiated listeners."

ious scenes at which he had been a witness or ably discussing the processes of war with other proved men. Too, it was important that he should have time for physical recuperation. He was sore and stiff from his experiences. He had received his fill of all exertions, and he wished to rest.

But those other men seemed never to grow weary; they were fighting with their old speed. He had a wild hate for the relentless foe. Yesterday, when he had imagined the universe to be against him, he had hated it; today he hated the army of the foe with the same great hatred. He was not going to be badgered of his life, like a kitten chased by boys, he said. It was not well to drive men into final corners; at those moments they could all develop teeth and claws.

His fingers twined nervously about his rifle. He wished that it was an engine of annihilating power. He felt that he and his companions were being taunted and derided. The tormentors were flies sucking insolently at his blood,

and he thought that he would have given his life for a revenge of seeing their faces in pitiful plights.

The winds of battle had swept all about the regiment, until the one rifle, instantly followed by others, flashed in its front. A moment later the regiment roared forth its sudden and valiant retort. A dense wall of smoke settled slowly down. It was furiously slit and slashed by the knifelike fire from the rifles.

To the youth the fighters resembled animals tossed for a death struggle into a dark pit. There was a sensation that he and his fellows, at bay, were pushing back, always pushing fierce onslaughts of creatures who were slippery. Their beams of crimson seemed to get no purchase upon[2] the bodies of their foes; the latter seemed to evade them with ease, and come through, between, around, and about with unopposed skill.

When, in a dream, it occurred to the youth

---

2. **to get . . . upon:** unable to hit.

that his rifle was an impotent stick, he lost sense of everything but his hate, his desire to smash into pulp the glittering smile of victory which he could feel upon the faces of his enemies.

The youth was not conscious that he was erect upon his feet. He did not know the direction of the ground. Indeed, once he even lost the habit of balance and fell heavily. He was up again immediately. One thought went through the chaos of his brain at the time. He wondered if he had fallen because he had been shot. But the suspicion flew away at once. He did not think more of it.

He had taken up a first position behind the little tree, with a direct determination to hold it against the world. He had not deemed it possible that his army could that day succeed, and from this he felt the ability to fight harder. But the throng had surged in all ways, until he lost directions and locations, save that he knew where lay the enemy.

The flames bit him, and the hot smoke broiled his skin. His rifle barrel grew so hot that ordinarily he could not have borne it upon his palms; but he kept on stuffing cartridges into it, and pounding them with his clanking, bending ramrod. If he aimed at some charging form through the smoke, he pulled his trigger with a fierce grunt, as if he were dealing a blow of the fist with all his strength.

When the enemy seemed falling back before him and his fellows, he went instantly forward, like a dog who, seeing his foes lagging, turns and insists upon being pursued. And when he was compelled to retire again, he did it slowly, sullenly, taking steps of wrathful despair.

Once he, in his intense hate, was almost alone, and was firing when all those near him had ceased. He was so engrossed in his occupation that he was not aware of a lull.

He was recalled by a hoarse laugh and a sentence that came to his ears in a voice of contempt and amazement. "Yeh infernal fool, don't yeh know enough t' quit when there ain't anything t' shoot at?"

He turned then and, pausing with his rifle thrown half into position, looked at the blue line of his comrades. During this moment of leisure they seemed all to be engaged in staring with astonishment at him. They had become spectators. Turning to the front again, he saw, under the lifted smoke, a deserted ground.

He looked bewildered for a moment. Then there appeared upon the glazed vacancy of his eyes a diamond point of intelligence. "Oh," he said, comprehending.

He returned to his comrades and threw himself upon the ground. He sprawled like a man who had been thrashed. His flesh seemed strangely on fire, and the sounds of the battle continued in his ears. He groped blindly for his canteen.

The lieutenant was crowing. He called out to the youth: "By heavens, if I had ten thousand wildcats like you, I could tear th' stomach outa this war in less'n a week!"

Some of the men muttered and looked at the youth in awestruck ways. It was plain that as he had gone on loading and firing and cursing without the proper intermission, they had found time to regard him. And they now looked upon him as a war devil.

The friend came staggering to him. There was some fright and dismay in his voice. "Are yeh all right, Fleming? There ain't nothin' th' matter with yeh, Henry, is there?"

These incidents made the youth ponder. It was revealed to him that he had been a barbarian, a beast. He had fought like a pagan who defends his religion. Regarding it, he saw that it was fine, wild, and in some ways, easy. He had been a tremendous figure, no doubt. By this struggle he had overcome obstacles which he had admitted to be mountains. They had fallen like paper peaks, and he was now what he called a hero. And he had not been aware of the process. He had slept and, awakening, found himself a knight.

He lay and basked in the occasional stares of his comrades. Their faces were varied in degrees of blackness from the burned powder. Some were utterly smudged. They were reeking with perspiration, and their breaths came hard and wheezing. And from these soiled expanses they peered at him.

"Hot work! Hot work!" cried the lieutenant deliriously. He walked up and down, restless and eager. Sometimes his voice could be heard in a wild, incomprehensible laugh.

When he had a particularly profound thought upon the science of war, he always unconsciously addressed himself to the youth.

The forest still bore its burden of clamor. From off under the trees came the rolling clatter of the musketry. Each distant thicket seemed a strange porcupine with quills of flame. A cloud of dark smoke, as from smoldering ruins, went up toward the sun, now bright and gay in the blue, enameled sky.

Chapter 18

The ragged line had respite for some minutes, but during its pause the struggle in the forest became magnified until the trees seemed to quiver from the firing and the ground to shake. It seemed difficult to live in such an atmosphere. The chests of the men strained for a bit of freshness, and their throats craved water.

The youth's friend had a geographical illusion concerning a stream, and he obtained permission to go for some water. Immediately canteens were showered upon him. "Fill mine, will yeh?" "Bring me some, too." "And me, too." He departed, laden. The youth went with his friend, feeling a desire to throw his heated body into the stream and, soaking there, drink quarts.

They made a hurried search for the supposed stream, but did not find it. "No water here," said the youth. They turned without delay and began to retrace their steps.

Down an aisle of the grove, the youth and his companion saw a jangling general and his staff. A moment later the small cavalcade was directly in front of the two soldiers. Another officer, riding with the skillful abandon of a cowboy, galloped his horse to a position before the general. The two unnoticed foot soldiers made a little show of going on, but they lin-

gered near in the desire to overhear the conversation. Perhaps they thought some great inner historical things would be said.

The general, whom the boys knew as the commander of their division, looked at the other officer and spoke coolly, as if he were criticizing his clothes. "Th' enemy's formin' over there for another charge," he said. "They'll break through there unless we work like thunder t' stop them."

Then he began to talk rapidly and in a lower tone. He frequently illustrated his words with a pointing finger. The two infantrymen could hear nothing until finally he asked: "What troops can you spare?"

The officer who rode like a cowboy reflected for an instant. "Well," he said, "I had to order in th' 12th to help th' 76th, an' I haven't really got any. But there's th' 304th. They fight like a lot 'a mule drivers. I can spare them best of any."

The youth and his friend exchanged glances of astonishment.

The general spoke sharply. "Get 'em ready, then. I'll watch developments from here, an' send you word when t' start them. It'll happen in five minutes."

As the other officer tossed his fingers toward his cap and, wheeling his horse, started away, the general called out to him in a sober voice: "I don't believe many of your mule drivers will get back."

The other shouted something in reply. He smiled.

With scared faces, the youth and his companion hurried back to the line.

These happenings had occupied an incredibly short time, yet the youth felt that he had been made aged. New eyes were given to him. And the most startling thing was to learn suddenly that he was very insignificant. The officer spoke of the regiment as if he referred to a broom. Some part of the woods needed sweeping, perhaps, and he merely indicated a broom in a tone properly indifferent to its fate. It was war, no doubt, but it appeared strange.

As the two boys approached the line, the

lieutenant perceived them and swelled with wrath. "Fleming—Wilson—how long does it take yeh to git water, anyhow—where yeh been to?"

But his oration ceased as he saw their eyes, which were large with great tales. "We're goin' t' charge—we're goin' t' charge!" cried the youth's friend, hastening with his news.

"Charge?" said the lieutenant. "Charge? Well, this is real fightin'!" Over his soiled countenance there went a boastful smile.

A little group of soldiers surrounded the two youths. "Are we, sure 'nough? Well, I'll be derned! Charge? What fer? What at?"

A moment later the officers began to bustle among the men, pushing them into a more compact mass and into a better alignment. They chased those that straggled and fumed at a few men who seemed to show by their attitudes that they had decided to remain at that spot. They were like critical shepherds struggling with sheep.

Presently, the regiment seemed to draw it-self up and heave a deep breath. None of the men's faces were mirrors of large thoughts. The soldiers were bended and stooped like sprinters before a signal. Many pairs of glinting eyes peered from the grimy faces toward the curtains of the deeper woods. They seemed to be engaged in deep calculations of time and distance.

They were surrounded by the noises of the monstrous altercation between the two armies. The world was fully interested in other matters. Apparently the regiment had its small affair to itself.

The youth, turning, shot a quick inquiring glance at his friend. The latter returned to him the same manner of look. They were the only ones who possessed an inner knowledge. "Mule drivers—don't believe many will get back." It was an ironical secret. Still, they saw no hesitation in each other's faces, and they nodded a mute and unprotesting assent when a shaggy man near them said in a meek voice, "We'll git swallowed."

Union forces on the move, 1862.

Chapter 19

The youth stared at the land in front of him. Its foliages now seemed to veil powers and horrors. He was unaware of the machinery of orders that started the charge, although from the corners of his eyes he saw an officer, who looked like a boy a-horseback, come galloping, waving his hat. Suddenly he felt a straining and heaving among the men. The line fell slowly forward like a toppling wall, and, with a convulsive gasp that was intended for a cheer, the regiment began its journey. The youth was pushed and jostled for a moment before he understood the movement at all, but directly he lunged ahead and began to run.

He fixed his eye upon a distant and prominent clump of trees where he had concluded the enemy were to be met, and he ran toward it as toward a goal. He had believed throughout that it was a mere question of getting over an unpleasant matter as quickly as possible, and he ran desperately, as if pursued for a murder. His face was drawn hard and tight with the stress of his endeavor. His eyes were fixed in a lurid glare. And with his soiled and disordered dress, his red and inflamed features surmounted by the dingy rag with its spot of blood, his wildly swinging rifle and banging accouterments,[3] he looked to be an insane soldier.

As the regiment swung from its position out into a cleared space, the woods and thickets before it awakened. Yellow flames leaped toward it from many directions. The forest made a tremendous objection.

The line lurched straight for a moment. Then the right wing swung forward; it in turn was surpassed by the left. Afterward the center careered to the front until the regiment was a wedge-shaped mass, but an instant later the opposition of the bushes, trees, and uneven places on the ground split the command and scattered it into detached clusters.

The youth, light-footed, was unconsciously in advance. His eyes still kept note of the clump of trees. From all places near it the clannish yell of the enemy could be heard. The little flames of rifles leaped from it. The song of the bullets was in the air and shells snarled among the treetops. One tumbled directly into the middle of a hurrying group and exploded in crimson fury. There was an instant's spectacle of a man, almost over it, throwing up his hands to shield his eyes.

Other men, punched by bullets, fell in grotesque agonies. The regiment left a coherent trail of bodies.

It seemed to the youth that he saw everything. Each blade of the green grass was bold and clear. The brown or gray trunks of the trees showed each roughness of their surfaces. And the men of the regiment, with their starting eyes and sweating faces, running madly, or falling, as if thrown headlong, to queer, heaped-up corpses—all were comprehended. His mind took a mechanical but firm impression, so that afterward everything was pictured and explained to him, save why he himself was there.

But there was a frenzy made from this furious rush. The men, pitching forward insanely, had burst into cheerings, moblike and barbaric, but tuned in strange keys that can arouse the dullard and the stoic.[4] It made a mad enthusiasm that, it seemed, would be incapable of checking itself before granite and brass. There was the delirium that encounters despair and death, and is heedless and blind to the odds. It is a temporary but sublime absence of selfishness. And because it was of this order was the reason, perhaps, why the youth wondered, afterward, what reasons he could have had for being there.

Presently the straining pace ate up the energies of the men. As if by agreement, the leaders began to slacken their speed. The volleys directed against them had had a seeming windlike effect. The regiment snorted and blew. Among some stolid trees it began to fal-

---

3. **accouterments** [ə koo′tər mənts]: soldier's equipment, other than arms and clothing.

4. **stoic** [stō′ik]: person unaffected by pain or pleasure.

ter and hesitate. The men, staring intently, began to wait for some of the distant walls of smoke to move and disclose to them the scene. Since much of their strength and their breath had vanished, they returned to caution. They were become men again.

The youth had a vague belief that he had run miles, and he thought, in a way, that he was now in some new and unknown land.

The moment the regiment ceased its advance the protesting splutter of musketry became a steadied roar. Long and accurate fringes of smoke spread out. From the top of a small hill came level belchings of yellow flame that caused an inhuman whistling in the air.

The men, halted, had opportunity to see some of their comrades, dropping with moans and shrieks. A few lay under foot, still or wailing. And now for an instant the men stood, their rifles slack in their hands, and watched the regiment dwindle. They appeared dazed and stupid. This spectacle seemed to paralyze them, overcome them with a fatal fascination. They stared woodenly at the sights, and lowering their eyes, looked from face to face. It was a strange pause, and a strange silence.

Then, above the sounds of the outside commotion, arose the roar of the lieutenant. He strode suddenly forth, his infantile features black with rage.

"Come on, yeh fools!" he bellowed. "Come on! Yeh can't stay here. Yeh must come on." He said more, but much of it could not be understood.

He started rapidly forward, with his head turned toward the men. "Come on," he was shouting. The men stared with blank eyes at him. He was obliged to halt and retrace his steps. He stood then with his back to the enemy and delivered gigantic curses into the faces of the men. His body vibrated from the weight and force of his imprecations. And he could string oaths with the facility of a maiden who strings beads.

The friend of the youth aroused. Lurching suddenly forward and dropping to his knees, he fired an angry shot at the persistent woods.

This action awakened the men. They huddled no more like sheep. They seemed suddenly to bethink them of their weapons, and at once commenced firing. Belabored by their officers, they began to move forward. The regiment, involved like a cart involved in mud and muddle, started unevenly with many jolts and jerks. The men stopped now every few paces to fire and load, and in this manner moved slowly on from trees to trees.

The command went painfully forward until an open space interposed between them and the lurid lines. Here, crouching and cowering behind some trees, the men clung with desperation, as if threatened by a wave. They looked wild-eyed, and as if amazed at this furious disturbance they had stirred. The whole affair seemed incomprehensible to many of them.

As they halted thus the lieutenant again began to bellow profanely. Regardless of the vindictive threats of the bullets, he went about coaxing, berating. His lips, that were habitually in a soft and childlike curve, were now writhed into unholy contortions. He swore by all possible deities.

Once he grabbed the youth by the arm. "Come on, yeh lunkhead!" he roared. "Come on! We'll all git killed if we stay here. We've on'y got t' go across that lot. An' then"—the remainder of his idea disappeared in a blue haze of curses.

The youth stretched forth his arm. "Cross there?" His mouth was puckered in doubt and awe.

"Certainly. Jest 'cross th' lot! We can't stay here," screamed the lieutenant. He poked his face close to the youth and waved his bandaged hand. "Come on!" Presently he grappled with him as if for a wrestling bout.

The private felt a sudden unspeakable indignation against his officer. He wrenched fiercely and shook him off.

"Come on yerself, then," he yelled. There was a bitter challenge in his voice.

They galloped together down the regimental front. The friend scrambled after them. In front of the colors the three men began to bawl: "Come on! come on!" They danced and gyrated like tortured savages.

The flag, obedient to these appeals, bended its glittering form and swept toward them. The men wavered in indecision for a moment, and then with a long, wailful cry the dilapidated regiment surged forward and began its new journey.

Over the field went the scurrying mass. It was a handful of men splattered into the faces of the enemy. Toward it instantly sprang the yellow tongues. A vast quantity of blue smoke hung before them. A mighty banging made ears valueless.

The youth ran like a madman to reach the woods before a bullet could discover him. He ducked his head low, like a football player. In his haste his eyes almost closed, and the scene was a wild blur. Pulsating saliva stood at the corners of his mouth.

Within him, as he hurled himself forward, was born a love, a despairing fondness for this flag which was near him. It was a creation of beauty and invulnerability. Because no harm could come to it he endowed it with power. He kept near, as if it could be a saver of lives.

In the mad scramble he was aware that the color sergeant[5] flinched suddenly, as if struck by a bludgeon. He faltered, and then became motionless, save for his quivering knees.

He made a spring and a clutch at the pole. At the same instant his friend grabbed it from the other side. They jerked at it, stout and furious, but the color sergeant was dead, and the corpse would not relinquish its trust. For a moment there was a grim encounter. The dead man, swinging with bended back, seemed to be obstinately tugging, in ludicrous and awful ways, for the possession of the flag.

It was past in an instant of time. They wrenched the flag furiously from the dead man, and, as they turned again, the corpse swayed forward with bowed head. One arm swung high, and the curved hand fell with heavy protest on the friend's unheeding shoulder.

Chapter 20

When the two youths turned with the flag they saw that much of the regiment had crumbled away, and the dejected remnant was coming slowly back. The men, having hurled themselves in projectile fashion, had presently expended their forces. They slowly retreated, with their faces still toward the spluttering woods, and their hot rifles still replying to the din. Several officers were giving orders, their voices keyed to screams.

"Where yeh goin'?" the lieutenant was asking in a sarcastic howl. And a red-bearded officer, whose voice of triple brass[6] could plainly be heard, was commanding: "Shoot into 'em! Shoot into 'em." There was a melee[7] of screeches, in which the men were ordered to do conflicting and impossible things.

The youth and his friend had a small scuffle over the flag. "Give it t' me!" "No, let me keep it!" Each felt satisfied with the other's possession of it, but each felt bound to declare, by an offer to carry the emblem, his willingness to further risk himself. The youth roughly pushed his friend away.

The regiment fell back to the stolid trees. There it halted for a moment to blaze at some dark forms that had begun to steal upon its track. Presently it resumed its march again, curving among the tree trunks. By the time the depleted regiment had again reached the first open space they were receiving a fast and merciless fire. There seemed to be mobs all about them.

The greater part of the men, discouraged, their spirits worn by the turmoil, acted as if stunned. They accepted the pelting of the bullets with bowed and weary heads. It was of no purpose to strive against walls. It was of no use to batter themselves against granite.

The youth went along with slipping, uncertain feet. He kept watchful eyes rearward. A scowl of mortification and rage was upon his

---

5. **color sergeant:** flag bearer.

6. **triple brass:** great strength and power.
7. **melee** [mā′lā′]: noisy, confused fight.

face. He had thought of a fine revenge upon the officer who had referred to him and his fellows as mule drivers. But he saw that it could not come to pass. His dreams had collapsed when the mule drivers, dwindling rapidly, had wavered and hesitated on the little clearing, and then had recoiled. And now the retreat of the mule drivers was a march of shame to him.

A dagger-pointed gaze from without his blackened face was held toward the enemy, but his greater hatred was riveted upon the man, who, not knowing him, had called him a mule driver.

He presently wrapped his heart in the cloak of his pride and kept the flag erect. He harangued his fellows, pushing against their chests with his free hand. To those he knew well he made frantic appeals, beseeching them by name. Between him and the lieutenant, scolding and near to losing his mind with rage, there was felt a subtle fellowship and equality. They supported each other in all manner of hoarse, howling protests.

But the regiment was a machine run down. The two men babbled at a forceless thing. The soldiers who had heart to go slowly were continually shaken in their resolves by a knowledge that comrades were slipping with speed back to the lines. It was difficult to think of reputation when others were thinking of skins. Wounded men were left crying on this black journey.

The smoke fringes and flames blustered always. The youth, peering once through a sudden rift in a cloud, saw a brown mass of troops, interwoven and magnified until they appeared to be thousands. A fierce-hued flag[8] flashed before his vision.

Immediately, as if the uplifting of the smoke had been prearranged, the troops burst into a rasping yell, and a hundred flames jetted toward the retreating band. A rolling gray cloud again interposed as the regiment doggedly replied. Men ran hither and thither, seeking with

their eyes roads of escape. With serene regularity, as if controlled by a schedule, bullets buffed into men.

The youth walked stolidly into the midst of the mob, and with his flag in his hands took a stand as if he expected an attempt to push him to the ground. He unconsciously assumed the attitude of the color bearer in the fight of the preceding day. He passed over his brow a hand that trembled. His breath did not come freely. He was choking during this small wait for the crisis.

His friend came to him. "Well, Henry, I guess this is goodbye."

"Oh, shut up," replied the youth, and he would not look at the other.

The officers labored like politicans to beat the mass into a proper circle to face the menaces. The ground was uneven and torn. The men curled into depressions and fitted themselves snugly behind whatever would frustrate a bullet.

Some lazy and ignorant smoke curled slowly. The men, hiding from the bullets, waited anxiously for it to lift and disclose the plight of the regiment.

The silent ranks were suddenly thrilled by the eager voice of the youthful lieutenant bawling out: "Here they come! Right onto us!" His further words were lost in a roar of wicked thunder from the men's rifles.

The youth's eyes had instantly turned in the direction indicated by the agitated lieutenant, and he had seen the haze of treachery disclosing a body of soldiers of the enemy. They were so near that he could see their features. There was a recognition as he looked at the types of faces. Also he perceived with dim amazement that their uniforms were rather gay in effect, being light gray, accented with a brilliant-hued facing. Moreover, the clothes seemed new.

These troops had apparently been going forward with caution, their rifles held in readiness, when the youthful lieutenant had discovered them and their movement had been interrupted by the volley from the blue regiment. From the moment's glimpse, it was derived

---

8. **fierce-hued flag:** bright flag; that is, the red flag of the Confederate troops.

that they had been unaware of the proximity of their dark-suited foes, or had mistaken the direction. Almost instantly they were shut utterly from the youth's sight by the smoke from the energetic rifles of his companions. He strained his vision to learn the accomplishment of the volley, but the smoke hung before him.

The two bodies of troops exchanged blows in the manner of a pair of boxers. The fast angry firings went back and forth. The men in blue were intent with the despair of their circumstances, and they seized upon the revenge to be had at close range. Their thunder swelled loud and valiant. Their curving front bristled with flashes and the place resounded with the clangor of their ramrods. The youth ducked and dodged for a time and achieved a few unsatisfactory views of the enemy. There appeared to be many of them and they were replying swiftly. They seemed moving toward the blue regiment, step by step. He seated himself gloomily on the ground with his flag between his knees.

As he noted the vicious, wolflike temper of his comrades he had a sweet thought that if the enemy was about to swallow the regimental broom as a large prisoner, it could at least have the consolation of going down with bristles forward.

But the blows of the antagonist began to grow more weak. Fewer bullets ripped the air, and finally, when the men slackened to learn of the fight, they could see only dark, floating smoke. The regiment lay still and gazed. Presently some chance whim came to the pestering blur, and it began to coil heavily away. The men saw a ground vacant of fighters. It would have been an empty stage if it were not for a few corpses that lay thrown and twisted into fantastic shapes upon the sward.

At sight of this tableau,[9] many of the men in blue sprang from behind their covers and made an ungainly dance of joy. Their eyes burned and a hoarse cheer of elation broke from their dry lips.

---

9. **tableau** [tab lō′]: silent, motionless representation of a scene.

Union troops prepare for battle, May 1862.

It had begun to seem to them that events were trying to prove that they could not fight well. When on the verge of submission to these opinions, the small duel had showed them that the proportions were not impossible, and by it they had revenged themselves upon their misgivings and upon the foe.

The impetus of enthusiasm was theirs again. They gazed about them with looks of uplifted pride, feeling new trust in the grim, always confident weapons in their hands. And they were men.

Chapter 21

Presently they knew that no firing threatened them. All ways seemed once more opened to them. The dusty blue lines of their friends were disclosed a short distance away. In the distance there were many colossal noises, but in all this part of the field there was a sudden stillness.

They perceived that they were free. The depleted band drew a long breath of relief and gathered itself into a bunch to complete its trip.

In this last length of journey the men began to show strange emotions. They hurried with nervous fear. Some who had been dark and unfaltering in the grimmest moments now could not conceal an anxiety that made them frantic. It was perhaps that they dreaded to be killed in insignificant ways after the times for proper military deaths had passed. Or, perhaps, they thought it would be too ironical to get killed at the portals of safety. With backward looks of perturbation, they hastened.

As they approached their own lines there was some sarcasm exhibited on the part of a gaunt and bronzed regiment that lay resting in the shade of trees. Questions were wafted to them.

"Where yeh been?"
"What yeh comin' back fer?"
"Why didn't yeh stay there?"
"Was it warm out there, sonny?"
"Goin' home now, boys?"

The youth's tender flesh was deeply stung by these remarks. From under his creased brows he glowered with hate at the mockers. He meditated upon a few revenges. Still, many in the regiment hung their heads in criminal fashion, so that it came to pass that the men trudged with sudden heaviness, as if they bore upon their bended shoulders the coffin of their honor.

They turned when they arrived at their old position to regard the ground over which they had charged.

The youth in this contemplation was smitten with a large astonishment. He discovered that the distances, as compared with the brilliant measurings of his mind, were trivial and ridiculous. The stolid trees, where much had taken place, seemed incredibly near. The time, too, now that he reflected, he saw to have been short. He wondered at the number of emotions and events that had been crowded into such little spaces. Elfin[10] thoughts must have exaggerated and enlarged everything, he said.

It seemed, then, that there was bitter justice in the speeches of the gaunt and bronzed veterans. He veiled a glance of disdain at his fellows who strewed the ground, choking with dust, red from perspiration, misty-eyed, disheveled.

However, to the youth there was a considerable joy in musing upon his performances during the charge. He had had very little time previously in which to appreciate himself, so that there was now much satisfaction in quietly thinking of his actions.

As the regiment lay heaving from its hot exertions, the officer who had named them as mule drivers came galloping along the line. He had lost his cap. His tousled hair streamed wildly, and his face was dark with vexation and wrath. His temper was displayed with more clearness by the way in which he managed his horse. He jerked and wrenched savagely at his bridle, stopping the hard-breathing animal with

---

10. **elfin:** small.

a furious pull near the colonel of the regiment. He immediately exploded in reproaches which came unbidden to the ears of the men. They were suddenly alert, being always curious about black words between officers.

"Oh, thunder, MacChesnay, what an awful bull[11] you made of this thing!" began the officer. He attempted low tones, but his indignation caused certain of the men to learn the sense of his words. "What an awful mess you made! Good Lord, man, you stopped about a hundred feet this side of a very pretty success! If your men had gone a hundred feet farther you would have made a great charge, but as it is—what a lot of mud diggers you've got anyway!"

The men, listening with bated breath, now turned their curious eyes upon the colonel. They had a ragamuffin interest in this affair.

The colonel was seen to straighten his form and put one hand forth in oratorical fashion. He wore an injured air; it was as if a deacon[12] had been accused of stealing. The men were wiggling in an ecstasy of excitement.

But of a sudden the colonel's manner changed. He shrugged his shoulders. "Oh, well, general, we went as far as we could," he said calmly.

"As far as you could?" snorted the other. "Well, that wasn't very far, was it?" He wheeled his horse and rode stiffly away.

The lieutenant, who had listened with an air of impotent rage to the interview, spoke suddenly in firm and undaunted tones. "I don't care what a man is—whether he is a general or what—if he says th' boys didn't put up a good fight out there he's a fool."

"Lieutenant," began the colonel severely, "this is my own affair, and I'll trouble you—"

The lieutenant made an obedient gesture. "All right, colonel, all right," he said. He sat down with an air of being content with himself.

<hr>

11. **bull:** slang for blunder or mess.
12. **deacon:** person who assists a priest or minister in some Christian churches.

The news that the regiment had been reproached went along the line. For a time the men were bewildered by it. They conceived it to be a huge mistake.

Presently, however, they began to believe that in truth their efforts had been called light. The youth could see this conviction weigh upon the entire regiment until the men were like cuffed and cursed animals, but withal rebellious.

The friend, with a grievance in his eye, went to the youth. "I wonder what he does want," he said. "He must think we went out there an' played marbles! I never see sech a man!"

The youth exclaimed with sudden exasperation: "He's a lunkhead! I wish he'd come along next time. We'd show 'im what—"

He ceased because several men had come hurrying up. Their faces expressed a bringing of great news.

"O Flem, yeh jest oughta heard!" cried one, eagerly.

"Heard what?" said the youth. The others made an excited circle. "Well, sir, th' colonel met your lieutenant right by us, an' he ses: 'Ahem! ahem!' he ses. 'Mr. Hasbrouck!' he ses, 'by th' way, who was that lad what carried th' flag?' he ses. There, Flemin', what d' yeh think 'a that? 'Who was th' lad what carried th' flag?' he ses, an' th' lieutenant, he speaks up right away: 'That's Flemin', an' he's a jimhickey,' he ses, right away. 'A jimhickey,' he ses—those 'r his words. He did, too. I say he did. If you kin tell this story better than I kin, go ahead an' tell it. Well, then, keep yer mouth shet. Th' lieutenant, he ses: 'He's a jimhickey,' an' th' colonel, he ses: 'Ahem! ahem! he is, indeed, a very good man t' have, ahem! He kep' th' flag 'way t' th' front. I saw 'im. He's a good un,' ses th' colonel. 'You bet,' ses th' lieutenant, 'he an' a feller named Wilson was at th' head 'a th' charge, howlin' all th' time,' he ses. 'Head 'a th' charge all th' time,' he ses. 'A feller named Wilson,' he ses. There, Wilson, m' boy, put that in a letter an' send it hum t' yer mother, hey? 'A feller named Wilson,' he ses. An' th' colonel, he ses: 'Were they, indeed? Ahem! ahem! My sakes!' he ses. 'At th' head 'a th' reg'ment?' he ses. 'They were,' says the lieutenant. 'My sakes!' ses th' colonel. He ses: 'Well, well, well,' he ses, 'those two babies?' 'They were,' ses th' lieutenant. 'Well, well,' ses th' colonel, 'they deserve t' be major generals,' he ses. 'They deserve t' be major generals.'"

The youth and his friend had said: "Huh!" "Yer lyin', Thompson," "He never sed it." "Oh, what a lie!" But despite these youthful scoffings and embarrassments, they knew that their faces were deeply flushing from thrills of pleasure. They exchanged a secret glance of joy and congratulation.

They speedily forgot many things. The past held no pictures of error and disappointment. They were very happy, and their hearts swelled with grateful affection for the colonel and the youthful lieutenant.

Chapter 22

When the woods again began to pour forth the dark-hued masses of the enemy the youth felt serene self-confidence. He smiled briefly when he saw men dodge and duck at the long screechings of shells that were thrown in giant handfuls over them. He stood, erect and tranquil, watching the attack begin against a part of the line that made a blue curve along the side of an adjacent hill. His vision being unmolested by smoke from the rifles of his companions, he had opportunities to see parts of the hard fight.

Off a short way he saw two regiments fighting a little separate battle with two other regiments. It was in a cleared space, wearing a set-apart look. The firings were incredibly fierce and rapid. These intent regiments apparently were oblivious of all larger purposes of war, and were slugging each other as if at a matched game.

In another direction he saw a magnificent brigade going with the evident intention of driving the enemy from a wood. They passed in out of sight and presently there was a most awe-inspiring racket. Having stirred this prodigious uproar, and, apparently, finding it too prodigious, the brigade, after a little time, came marching airily out again with its fine formation in nowise disturbed. There were no traces of speed in its movements. The brigade was jaunty.

On a slope to the left there was a long row of guns, gruff and maddened, denouncing the enemy. The round red discharges from the guns made a crimson flare and a high, thick smoke.

Presently there was a stillness, pregnant with meaning. The blue lines shifted and changed a trifle and stared expectantly at the silent woods and fields before them. The hush was solemn and churchlike.

Of a sudden the guns on the slope roared out a message of warning. A spluttering sound had begun in the woods. It swelled with amazing speed to a profound clamor that involved the earth in noises. The splitting crashes swept along the lines until an interminable roar was developed. To those in the midst of it, it became a din fitted to the universe. It was the whirring and thumping of gigantic machinery, complications among the smaller stars. The youth's ears were filled up. They were incapable of hearing more.

On an incline over which a road wound he saw wild and desperate rushes of men perpetually backward and forward in riotous surges. These parts of the opposing armies were two long waves that pitched upon each other madly at dictated points. To and fro they swelled. Sometimes, one side by its yells and cheers would proclaim decisive blows, but a moment later the other side would be all yells and cheers. And always in their swift and deadly rushes to and fro the men screamed and yelled like maniacs.

Particular pieces of fence or secure positions behind collections of trees were wrangled over, as gold thrones or pearl bedsteads. The youth could not tell from the battle-flags flying like crimson foam in many directions which color of cloth was winning.

His emaciated[13] regiment bustled forth with undiminished fierceness when its time came.

---

13. **emaciated** [i mā′shē ā′tid]: here, thinned-out.

When assaulted again by bullets, the men burst out in a barbaric cry of rage and pain. They bent their heads in aims of intent hatred behind the projected hammers of their guns. Their ramrods clanged loud with fury as their eager arms pounded the cartridges into the rifle barrels.

The lieutenant produced from a hidden receptacle of his mind new and portentous oaths suited to the emergency. Strings of expletives he swung lashlike over the backs of his men, and it was evident that his previous efforts had in nowise impaired his resources.

The youth, still the bearer of the colors, did not feel his idleness. He was deeply absorbed as a spectator. The crash and swing of the great drama made him lean forward, intent-eyed, his face working in small contortions. Sometimes he prattled, words coming unconsciously from him in grotesque exclamations. He did not know that he breathed; that the flag hung silently over him, so absorbed was he.

A formidable line of the enemy came within dangerous range. They could be seen plainly—tall, gaunt men with excited faces running with long strides toward a wandering fence.

At sight of this danger the men fired a plumping volley at the foes. There had been no order given; the men, upon recognizing the menace, had immediately let drive their flock of bullets without waiting for word of command.

But the enemy were quick to gain the protection of the wandering line of fence. They slid down behind it with remarkable celerity, and from this position they began briskly to slice up the blue men.

These latter braced their energies for a great struggle. Those behind the fence frequently shouted and yelped in taunts and gibelike cries, but the regiment maintained a stressed silence. Perhaps, at this new assault the men recalled the fact that they had been named mud diggers, and it made their situation thrice bitter. They were breathlessly intent upon keeping the ground and thrusting away

President Abraham Lincoln visits Union officers in the field, 1862.

the rejoicing body of the enemy. They fought swiftly and with a despairing savageness denoted in their expressions.

The youth had resolved not to budge whatever should happen. Some arrows of scorn that had buried themselves in his heart had generated strange and unspeakable hatred. It was clear to him that his final and absolute revenge was to be achieved by his dead body lying, torn and guttering,[14] upon the field. This was to be a poignant retaliation upon the officer who had said "mule drivers," and later "mud diggers," for in all the wild graspings of his mind for a unit responsible for his sufferings and commotions he always seized upon the man who had dubbed him wrongly. And it was his idea, vaguely formulated, that his corpse would be for those eyes a great and salt[15] reproach.

The regiment bled extravagantly. Grunting bundles of blue began to drop. The orderly sergeant of the youth's company was shot through the cheeks.

Others fell down about the feet of their companions. Some of the wounded crawled out and away, but many lay still, their bodies twisted into impossible shapes.

The youth looked once for his friend. He saw a vehement young man, powder-smeared and frowzled, whom he knew to be him. The lieutenant, also, was unscathed in his position at the rear. He had continued to curse, but it was now with the air of a man who was using his last box of oaths.

For the fire of the regiment had begun to wane and drip. The robust voice, that had come strangely from the thin ranks, was growing rapidly weak.

Chapter 23

The colonel came running along back of the line. There were other officers following him. "We must charge 'm!" they shouted. "We must charge 'm!" they cried with resentful voices, as if anticipating a rebellion against this plan by the men.

The youth, upon hearing the shouts, began to study the distance between him and the enemy. He made vague calculations. He saw that to be firm soldiers they must go forward. It would be death to stay in the present place, and with all the circumstances to go backward would exalt too many others. Their hope was to push the galling foes away from the fence.

He expected that his companions, weary and stiffened, would have to be driven to this assault, but as he turned toward them he perceived with a certain surprise that they were giving quick and unqualified expressions of assent. There was an ominous, clanging overture to the charge when the shafts of the bayonets rattled upon the rifle barrels. At the yelled words of command the soldiers sprang forward in eager leaps. It was a blind and despairing rush by the collection of men in dusty and tattered blue, over a green sward and under a sapphire sky, toward a fence, dimly outlined in smoke, from behind which spluttered the fierce rifles of enemies.

The youth kept the bright colors to the front. He was waving his free arm in furious circles, the while shrieking mad calls and appeals, urging on those that did not need to be urged, for it seemed that the mob of blue men hurling themselves on the dangerous group of rifles were again grown suddenly wild with an enthusiasm of unselfishness. From the many firings starting toward them, it looked as if they would merely succeed in making a great sprinkling of corpses on the grass between their former position and the fence. But they were in a state of frenzy, and it made an exhibition of sublime recklessness.

He himself felt daring spirit. He was capable of profound sacrifices, a tremendous death. He had no time for dissections, but he knew that he thought of the bullets only as things that could prevent him from reaching the place of his endeavor. There were subtle flashings of joy within him that thus should be his mind.

He strained all his strength. His eyesight

---

14. **guttering:** here, bleeding.
15. **salt:** bitter.

was shaken and dazzled by the tension of thought and muscle. He did not see anything excepting the mist of smoke gashed by the little knives of fire, but he knew that in it lay the aged fence of a vanished farmer protecting the snuggled bodies of the gray men.

As he ran a thought of the shock of contact gleamed in his mind. He expected a great concussion when the two bodies of troops crashed together. This became a part of his wild battle madness. He could feel the onward swing of the regiment about him and he conceived of a thunderous, crushing blow that would prostrate the resistance and spread consternation and amazement for miles. This dream made him run faster among his comrades, who were giving vent to hoarse and frantic cheers.

But presently he could see that many of the men in gray did not intend to abide the blow. The smoke, rolling, disclosed men who ran, their faces still turned. These grew to a crowd, who retired stubbornly. Individuals wheeled frequently to send a bullet at the blue wave.

But at one part of the line there was a grim and obdurate group that made no movement. They were settled firmly down behind posts and rails. A flag, ruffled and fierce, waved over them, and their rifles dinned fiercely.

The blue whirl of men got very near, until it seemed that in truth there would be a close and frightful scuffle. There was an expressed disdain in the opposition of the little group, that changed the meaning of the cheers of the men in blue. They became yells of wrath, directed, personal. The cries of the two parties were now in sound an interchange of scathing insults.

The youth had centered the gaze of his soul upon that other flag. Its possession would be high pride. It would express bloody minglings, near blows. He had a gigantic hatred for those who made great difficulties and complications. They caused it to be as a craved treasure of mythology, hung amid tasks and contrivances of danger.

He plunged like a mad horse at it. He was resolved it should not escape if wild blows and darings of blows could seize it. His own emblem, quivering and aflare, was winging toward the other. It seemed there would shortly be an encounter of strange beaks and claws, as of eagles.

The youth, in his leapings, saw, as through a mist, a picture of four or five men writhing upon their knees with bowed heads as if they had been stricken by bolts from the sky. Tottering among them was the rival color bearer, whom the youth saw had been bitten vitally by the bullets of the last formidable volley. He perceived this man fighting a last struggle, the struggle of one whose legs are grasped by demons. It was a ghastly battle. Over his face was the bleach of death, but set upon it was the dark and hard lines of desperate purpose. With this terrible grin of resolution he hugged his precious flag to him and was stumbling and staggering in his design to go the way that led to safety for it.

Those in advance of the scampering blue men, howling cheers, leaped at the fence. The despair of the lost was in his eyes as he glanced back at them.

The youth's friend went over the obstruction in a tumbling heap and sprang at the flag as a panther at prey. He pulled at it and, wrenching it free, swung up its red brilliancy with a mad cry of exultation even as the color bearer, gasping, lurched over in a final throe and, stiffening convulsively, turned his dead face to the ground. There was much blood upon the grass blades.

At the place of success there began more wild clamorings of cheers. The men gesticulated and bellowed in an ecstasy. When they spoke it was as if they considered their listener to be a mile away. What hats and caps were left to them they often slung high in the air.

After the men had celebrated sufficiently they settled down behind the old rail fence, on the opposite side to the one from which their foes had been driven. A few shot perfunctorily at distant marks.

There was some long grass. The youth nestled in it and rested, making a convenient rail support the flag. His friend, jubilant and glorified, holding his treasure with vanity, came to him there. They sat side by side and congratulated each other.

Chapter 24

The roarings that had stretched in a long line of sound across the face of the forest began to grow intermittent and weaker. The stentorian[16] speeches of the artillery continued in some distant encounter, but the crashes of the musketry had almost ceased. The youth and his friend of a sudden looked up, feeling a deadened form of distress at the waning of these noises, which had become a part of life. They could see changes going on among the troops. There were marchings this way and that way. A battery wheeled leisurely. On the crest of a small hill was the thick gleam of many departing muskets.

The youth rose. "Well, what now, I wonder?" he said. By his tone he seemed to be preparing to resent some new monstrosity in the way of dins and smashes.

They waited, watching. Within a little while the regiment received orders to retrace its way. The men got up grunting from the grass. They jerked their stiffened legs, and stretched their arms over their heads. They all groaned. They had as many objections to this change as they would have had to a proposal for a new battle.

They trampled slowly back over the field across which they had run in a mad scamper.

The regiment marched until it had joined its fellows. The reformed brigade, in column, aimed through a wood at the road. Directly they were in a mass of dust-covered troops, and were trudging along in a way parallel to the enemy's lines as these had been defined by the previous turmoil.

They passed within view of a stolid white house, and at this point the division curved away from the field and went winding off in the direction of the river. When the signifi-

cance of this movement had impressed itself upon the youth he breathed a breath of new satisfaction. He finally nudged his friend. "Well, it's all over," he said to him.

His friend gazed backward. They mused.

For a time the youth was obliged to reflect in a puzzled and uncertain way. His mind was undergoing a subtle change. It took moments for it to cast off its battleful ways and resume its accustomed course of thought. Gradually his brain emerged from the clogged clouds, and at last he was enabled to more closely comprehend himself and circumstance.

He understood then that the existence of shot and counter-shot was in the past. He had dwelt in a land of strange, squalling upheavals and had come forth. He had been where there was red of blood and black of passion, and he was escaped. His first thoughts were given to rejoicings at this fact.

Later he began to study his deeds, his failures, and his achievements. Regarding his procession of memory he felt gleeful and unregretting, for in it his public deeds were paraded in great and shining prominence. Those performances which had been witnessed by his fellows marched now in wide purple and gold. They went gaily with music. It was pleasure to watch these things. He spent delightful minutes viewing the gilded images of memory.

He saw that he was good. He recalled with a thrill of joy the respectful comments of his fellows upon his conduct.

Nevertheless, the ghost of his flight from the first engagement appeared to him and danced. There were small shoutings in his brain about these matters. For a moment he blushed, and the light of his soul flickered with shame.

A specter of reproach came to him. There loomed the dogging memory of the tattered soldier—he who, gored by bullets and faint for blood, had fretted concerning an imagined wound in another; he who had loaned his last of strength and intellect for the tall soldier; he who, blind with weariness and pain, had been deserted in the field.

---

16. **stentorian:** resounding.

As he marched along the little branch-hung roadway among his prattling companions this vision of cruelty brooded over him. It clung near him always and darkened his view of these deeds in purple and gold. Whichever way his thoughts turned they were followed by the somber phantom of the desertion in the fields. He looked stealthily at his companions, feeling sure that they must discern in his face evidences of this pursuit. But they were plodding in ragged array, discussing with quick tongues the accomplishments of the late battle.

For a time this pursuing recollection of the tattered man took all elation from the youth's veins. He saw his vivid error, and he was afraid that it would stand before him all his life. He took no share in the chatter of his comrades, nor did he look at them or know them, save when he felt sudden suspicion that they were seeing his thoughts and scrutinizing each detail of the scene with the tattered soldier.

Yet gradually he mustered force to put the sin at a distance. And at last his eyes seemed to be opened to some new ways. He found that he could look back upon the brass and bombast of his earlier gospels[17] and see them truly. He was gleeful when he discovered that he now despised them.

With this conviction came a store of assur-

17. **gospels:** here, personal beliefs.

ance. He felt a quiet manhood, nonassertive but of sturdy and strong blood. He knew that he would no more quail before his guides wherever they should point. He had been to touch the great death, and found that, after all, it was but the great death. He was a man.

So it came to pass that as he trudged from the place of blood and wrath his soul changed. He came from hot plowshares[18] to prospects of clover tranquilly, and it was as if hot plowshares were not. Scars faded as flowers.

It rained. The procession of weary soldiers became a bedraggled train, despondent and muttering, marching with churning effort in a trough of liquid brown mud under a low, wretched sky. Yet the youth smiled, for he saw that the world was a world for him, though many discovered it to be made of oaths and walking sticks. He had rid himself of the red sickness of battle. The sultry nightmare was in the past. He had been an animal blistered and sweating in the heat and pain of war. He turned now with a lover's thirst to images of tranquil skies, fresh meadows, cool brooks—an existence of soft and eternal peace.

Over the river a golden ray of sun came through the hosts of leaden rain clouds.

18. **hot plowshares:** reference to Isaiah 2 : 4, " . . . and they shall beat their swords into plowshares . . . ," which describes an end to warfare. Thus, *hot plowshares* are swords, or war in general.

STUDY QUESTIONS

Recalling

1. What change does Henry observe in Wilson on page 403? What incident in Wilson's past makes Henry feel superior to him?
2. In Chapter 17 what does Henry do when everyone else has stopped firing? What is his lieutenant's reaction?
3. Whom do Henry and Wilson overhear when they go in search of water (Chapter 18)?

What term used to describe their regiment do they find especially insulting?
4. During the next charge (Chapter 19), how do Henry and Wilson distinguish themselves? Over what do they have a "small scuffle," and what are their feelings during this scuffle (Chapter 20)? Who "wins"?
5. For what reason does the officer on horseback reproach the colonel of the regiment on page 417? Despite this criticism, what do Henry and Wilson hear that prompts them to

exchange a "secret glance of joy and congratulation" (page 418)?

6. What heroic act is performed by Wilson in
   Chapter 23?

7. What gives Henry a "thrill of joy" in the final
   chapter (page 422)? What "sin" does he put
   at a distance? What does Henry now feel he
   is, having touched "the great death"?

Interpreting

8. What does Henry's attitude toward Wilson's
   mistake reveal about Henry's character at
   that point? Trace the subsequent change in
   Henry's attitude toward Wilson.

9. What causes Henry to continue firing in
   Chapter 17? Does he distinguish himself from
   the "blue demonstration" here? Why or why
   not?

10. What effect does the insult to the regiment
    seem to have on Henry? What effect does
    the praise he earns from his comrades have?

11. On a figurative level, what battle has Henry
    won by the novel's end? What positive quali-
    ties has he displayed to warrant his final
    evaluation of himself?

Extending

12. The theme of initiation into adulthood is a
    common one in American fiction. What are
    some of the definitions of being an adult that
    The Red Badge of Courage makes you think
    about? Why is the war setting of the novel
    appropriate for dealing with the initiation
    theme?

LITERARY FOCUS

The Elements of Fiction

No one has ever come up with a totally acceptable measure of where a short story ends
and a novel begins. Yet since the novel is longer,
it provides the writer with more time and space to
introduce and develop all the elements of fiction:
characterization, plot, setting, point of view,
theme, and style.

The **characterization** in a novel—that is, the
depiction of the personalities of the tale—is invariably more complex than that of most short stories. While some of the minor characters in *The
Red Badge of Courage* are rather flat, interme-
diate characters such as Conklin and Wilson are
rounder. That is, the "tall soldier" and the "loud

soldier" that we meet in the first chapter are not
the same when we meet them later. And of
course the main character, or **protagonist,** of the
novel, Private Henry Fleming, is someone we get
to know very well indeed: We are privileged to
learn his most secret thoughts and feelings;
sometimes we even know more about Henry than
he knows himself.

The **plot** of a novel is the series of incidents
that takes us from a "beginning" to an "end." In
The Red Badge of Courage the plot concerns the
incidents of the war: the long wait for battle, the
first exchange of gunfire, Henry's flight and return
and his final acts of bravery. These are not a
hodgepodge of unrelated episodes; the **conflict**
in the novel—the battle that the protagonist must
wage—gives a focus to the events of the plot. In
The Red Badge the chief conflict is between
Henry and his own weaknesses, and the incidents
of the plot mark Henry's development from an un-
proven "youth" to a self-confident "man." The
events of the plot move in a clear direction.

The **setting** is the time and place in which the
events of the novel occur. In *The Red Badge of
Courage* the overall setting is the American Civil
War, although it is certainly not developed with
the wealth of information that we would find in a
historical novel. Crane tells us nothing about the
history of the war itself, but instead gives us the
details of the war as seen through a young private's eyes: the blue uniforms and the gray, the
pickets across the river, the ramrods and the cartridge boxes and the muskets. The specific settings—the banks of a river, a nighttime forest, a
road at dawn, a smoky battlefield—are painted in
an impressionistic style: We are not given a list of
everything in the scene but Henry Fleming's personal impression of what is immediately around
him.

Setting, plot, and characterization are thus all
tied to **point of view,** the position from which the
characters and the action are seen by the author.
In *The Red Badge of Courage* Crane uses the
third-person point of view, but the narrator does
not jump in and out of all his characters' heads
as an **omniscient** ("all-knowing") **narrator** does.
Instead, the narrator limits himself to one character's mind, Henry Fleming's. By writing in the
limited third-person point of view, Crane
achieves an intimacy that adds impact to the
events of his story, but he can still jump out of

his character's head when he wishes to, unlike a first-person narrator. For example, Crane can call Henry "the youthful private," something Henry would never call himself, and thereby distance Henry from the reader so that the ironies of Henry's character are more apparent.

The **theme** is the main idea or message that the writer communicates to the reader. Many readers feel that *The Red Badge of Courage* makes a statement about maturity and adulthood; others find a spiritual message; some discover a statement about the ironies of war; still others feel that Crane is stressing the indifference of environment to human misery. Obviously, a novel may contain more than one theme.

The **style** of a novel refers to the words the writer chooses and the way the words are put together. For example, Crane chooses words that are concrete and vivid; he uses strong images and figurative language; his sentences show a keen awareness of rhythm and alliteration. He also includes realistic dialect in sharp contrast to the complexity of his narrative prose.

Style also refers to a writer's characteristic way of writing: We speak, for example, of Crane's poetic, impressionistic style and compare it to the "facts only" style of Jack London (page 340).

Thinking About the Elements of Fiction

1. Are most of the officers in *The Red Badge of Courage* flat or round characters? How does this relate to the point of view of the novel?
2. In addition to the protagonist's battle with himself and his own weaknesses, what other conflicts are present in the novel? Against what else must Henry struggle?
3. Consider the keen awareness of rhythm that is part of Crane's style. What paragraphs in Chapter 23 seem to best capture the rhythm of the soldiers' actions? Explain the effect that sentence length has on the rhythm of these paragraphs.

VIEWPOINT

One viewpoint on the conclusion of the novel is that

Henry has matured as an individual and a member of society. Henry has learned the nature of fear and battle. . . . More important, he has learned the essence of man's duty to man, as well as the fact that life (like war) is not a romantic dream but a matter of compromises.

—Eric Solomon, "The Structure of *The Red Badge of Courage*"

■ Do you agree with Solomon's evaluation of the novel's ending? Do you think his statement adequately describes *The Red Badge of Courage*? If not, what would you add to it?

VOCABULARY

Concrete Language

Realistic novels and stories achieve part of their effect through the use of concrete, down-to-earth language. They do not attempt to portray life as it is really lived by describing it with flowery, ornate, obscure, or self-consciously "literary" words. They do not use abstractions when concrete words will do.

Crane chooses his words with great care, and sometimes his straightforwardness and simplicity escape our notice. Notice how often Crane uses words like *mud, noise, earth, sun, blood, grass, teeth, fire.* He deliberately keeps his language in tune with the flesh-and-blood story he tells.

Thinking About Concrete Language

■ Find at least five other examples of words or expressions in *The Red Badge of Courage* that show Crane's down-to-earth language.

COMPOSITION

Applying a Statement About Literature

■ The Roman historian Livy (59 B.C.–A.D. 17) wrote, "The event corresponds less to expectations in war than in any other case whatever." Explain the comment by Livy. Then demonstrate how it fits *The Red Badge of Courage. For help with this assignment, refer to Lesson 9 in the Writing About Literature Handbook at the back of this book.*

Researching a Topic

■ Most historians agree that the "episode of the Civil War" on which Crane bases his story is the Battle of Chancellorsville. Write a report on this battle, researching the topic in encyclopedias, history books, and first hand accounts if available. Tell when and where the battle was fought, which side was victorious, and the damage done to both sides.

READING FOR APPRECIATION

The Emotional Imagination

At the end of the first unit of this book (page 46), we talked about the need each reader has to bring an active imagination to literature. This is especially important as we read about the lives of people who lived in times and places different from our own. We called this the historical imagination. Yet there is another aspect of imaginative reading that we must learn to exercise as well—the *emotional imagination.*

It is true that we like to see people like ourselves mirrored in art. We take pleasure in seeing a familiar reality portrayed in a painting or in a story. Most literature, however, cannot limit itself to our reality.

Truly active reading means opening ourselves to ways of thinking, feeling, and seeing that are different from our own. We shut ourselves off from a great deal of pleasure and knowledge if we resist what is strange or unfamiliar. As we read, we need to give ourselves up to the language, reading slowly, carefully, allowing the language to guide us, to take us beyond ourselves and into the lives of characters different from ourselves—and into the minds of the writers, too.

For example, we may take two attitudes while reading Paul Laurence Dunbar's poem "Douglass" (page 361). We may stand apart from it, looking at what Dunbar said about Douglass and about the world that he, Dunbar, saw around him, a time of "dispraise," "dissension," and "lonely dark." Or we may exercise, while we read, a greater imagination, allowing ourselves to enter the spirit of a young black poet looking back upon a hero of an earlier time, crying out for the help that might come with Douglass' "high-sounding" voice and "blast-defying power." The "we" and "us" of the poem become all of us, black and white, male and female, as we read.

In the stories and poems in this unit, we are asked to become for a while a great many men and women. In Kate Chopin's "Pair of Silk Stockings" we imagine what it is like to feel restricted and to allow ourselves a few moments filled with the excitement of wider horizons. We share the frustrated anger and sense of injustice of a struggling midwestern farmer in Garland's "Under the Lion's Paw." Yet, paradoxically, what we often find as we read, giving ourselves up to "strange" experiences, is that after all there is something of ourselves in all of these characters. They are "what we might have been" or "what we might be."

The greatest challenge to our emotional imaginations in this unit is Stephen Crane's *Red Badge of Courage.* Here we are asked to share the inner life of Henry Fleming for a relatively long period of time and to move with him through many changes of his own emotional development. Is Henry Fleming inconsistent? Yes, he is—as we all are to some extent. Is "living with him" in these pages to put ourselves on an emotional roller coaster? Indeed it is. As we live moment to moment in the language of the novel, we find ourselves moving from uncertainty to exultation to shame, and then back through a "great calmness" to a dizzying sense that "in the space-whirl of events no grain like him would be lost."

Yet it is possible to deny ourselves so much wisdom, so much experience, by blocking our emotional imaginations as we read. By doing so we impoverish ourselves. Our emotional imaginations enable us to engage in the very lives of literary characters—an imaginative act that connects literature and the world of real people in which we live. How much wiser and richer we may be, and how much pleasure we may find in reading, if we are willing for an hour or two to enter—through language—the lives of others.

THE AMERICAN VOICE

Down to Earth

The writers of the Realist period in American literature often shocked their contemporaries. In our own time we still see them as breaking away from some long-standing American traditions.

The Realists and Naturalists no longer took comfort from the religious vision that had supported the Puritan writers. They did not share the sense of new possibilities that had fired the imaginations of the writers of the Revolution. They did not exult with the optimism of the Transcendentalists.

Instead, they brought their ideas and emotions out of the clouds and down to earth. They took long, hard looks at what living in the world was really like in their time—without flinching from the suffering, without explaining away or softening the *struggle* of being human.

London
There was no sun nor hint of sun, though there was not a cloud in the sky. It was a clear day, and yet there seemed an intangible pall over the face of things.

Garland
Haskins worked like a fiend, and his wife, like the heroic woman that she was, bore also uncomplainingly the most terrible burdens. They rose early and toiled without intermission till the darkness fell on the plain.

Robinson
So on we worked, and waited for the light.

Dunbar
*Ah, Douglass, we have fall'n on evil days
Such days as thou, not even thou didst know.*

Crane
He had been to touch the great death, and found that, after all, it was but the great death. He was a man. . . .

It rained. The procession of weary soldiers became a bedraggled train, despondent and muttering, marching with churning effort in a trough of liquid brown mud under a low, wretched sky. Yet the youth smiled, for he saw that the world was a world for him, though many discovered it to be made of oaths and walking sticks.

The writers in this unit reported what they saw: There were joys and times of happiness—but they were scattered within a world of struggle.

Key to Illustrations on Pages 294–295.

1	2	3		8
4		5		9
6	7			10

1. Paul Laurence Dunbar, detail of a postage stamp.
2. Alexander Graham Bell speaking at the opening of the New York–Chicago telephone circuit, 1892.
3. A Red Cross nurse tends a patient, from a calendar, 1899.
4. Wright brothers' first airplane flight at Kitty Hawk, North Carolina, December 17, 1903.
5. Stephen Crane, photographer unknown, c. 1895.
6. *Bret Harte,* John Pettie, 1884.
7. *The Wagon Boss,* Charles M. Russell, late nineteenth century.
8. Detail of *Country School,* Winslow Homer, 1871.
9. Sarah Orne Jewett, engraving.
10. Detail from *Northeaster,* Winslow Homer, 1895.

Key to Illustrations appears on Page 565.

NEW DIRECTIONS

1910–1930

The Era of Modernism

The English novelist Virginia Woolf once said that "on or about December 1910, human nature changed." Of course, human nature did not change, and Woolf knew it. What she meant was that the perception of human nature and of the human condition changed, and that the new perceptions were often expressed in startling and bewildering ways.

Life in the early twentieth century seemed suddenly different. New inventions allowed people to travel from place to place with a speed that was never before possible. The telephone, the radio, and the widespread availability of books, newspapers, and magazines all made people more aware of how others lived and thought. A person living in a remote village learned more about the variety and complexity of life on this planet than even a well-educated person living in a big city had known in the last century. The modern mind found this new knowledge exciting, but it was also bewildered by all the conflicting philosophies and ways of life.

The years from 1910 to 1930 are often called the Era of Modernism, for there seems to have been in both Europe and America a strong awareness of some sort of "break" with the past. Movements in all the arts overlapped and succeeded one another with amazing speed—Imagism, Cubism, Dadaism, Vorticism, and many others. The new

Paris scene during the 1920s, when people often met at sidewalk cafés.

artists shared a desire to capture the complexity of modern life, to focus on the variety and confusion of the twentieth century by reshaping and sometimes discarding the ideas and habits of the nineteenth century. The Era of Modernism was indeed the era of the New.

The Lost Generation

The pivotal event of the Modernist era was World War I (1914–1918). Before the war the attitude toward the new century was one of great optimism. America was emerging from nineteenth-century isolation: The Spanish-American War and the opening of the Panama Canal made America a world power; millions of immigrants brought new ideas and ways of life to American shores. Improved communications and transportation made Europe and the East more accessible, and American artists were able to exchange views and share ideas with their colleagues abroad.

Many American writers of this period lived in Europe for part if not all of their lives. Ezra Pound went to London in 1908; Robert Frost visited England a few years later; Gertrude Stein settled in Paris; poet Langston Hughes and playwright Eugene O'Neill traveled the world as merchant seamen. In part because of their widening experience—and in part because of their extraordinary talents— Americans for the first time

were in the vanguard of the arts: Pound and T. S. Eliot shaped the poetry of the Modernist era; Stein fostered the early careers of Pablo Picasso and other modern painters.

The European and American artistic communities drew closer together. Pound acted as the London representative of *Poetry: A Magazine of Verse,* an experimental publication begun in Chicago by Harriet Monroe in 1912. The Imagist poems that Pound sent back to Chicago had their effect on Carl Sandburg in the Midwest and Amy Lowell in New England, and in Chicago poets such as Sandburg, Edgar Lee Masters, and Vachel Lindsay now had an influential magazine in which their voices could be heard. O'Neill returned to New York City's Greenwich Village to see his experimental plays performed. Hughes became a leading figure in the burst of creativity called the Harlem Renaissance. Pound encouraged Frost, influenced John Crowe Ransom, and exchanged views

with his old college friend William Carlos Williams. Hilda Doolittle published the first volume of Marianne Moore's poetry. Stein assisted Sherwood Anderson and the young Ernest Hemingway. Artists and writers taught one another, learned from one another, paid one another's bills, and helped one another bring new works before the public. The travelers came home from Europe and spread the Modernist message throughout America.

Those American writers who did not go abroad before the war visited Europe during and after the war. E. E. Cummings worked as an ambulance driver in World War I and was taken prisoner in France. Ernest Hemingway was wounded in action. Archibald MacLeish spent five years in Paris during the 1920s. Countee Cullen went there on a Guggenheim fellowship in 1928.

It was not simply going abroad, however, that made the greatest difference to Americans in Europe: It was the outrage of the war itself. World War I was the key event in early twentieth-century experience, an event that had a profound effect on the optimism that had preceded it. World War I was war on a scale that the world had never seen, war that destroyed a generation in Europe and led tens of thousands of Americans to early graves. To many, World War I was a tragic failure of old values, of old politics, of old ideas. Now more than ever peo-

Gertrude Stein in her Paris home, meeting place for writers and artists.

ple felt they must cast off the traditions of the nineteenth century; the need for change was deep, and the mood was often one of confusion and despair.

Gertrude Stein once told the young Ernest Hemingway, "You are all a lost generation," and the term has been used again and again to describe the people of the postwar years. It describes the Americans who remained in Paris as a colony of "expatriates," or exiles: Writers like Hemingway lived in semi-poverty on the Left Bank of the river Seine and went to Gertrude Stein's salon as a safe refuge in stormy seas. It describes the Americans who returned to their native land with an intense awareness of living in an unfamiliar, changing world.

Yet, on the surface the mood in America during the 1920s did not seem desperate. Many Americans returned to their previous belief in isolation, their contempt for Europe reconfirmed by the war and the Treaty of Versailles that ended it. The open door was closed to immigrants, and America did not join the League of Nations, an association—later succeeded by the United Nations—established to promote peace. Instead Americans entered a decade of prosperity and exhibitionism that Prohibition, the legal ban against alcoholic beverages, did more to encourage than to curb. Fashions were extravagant; more and more automobiles crowded the roads; advertising flourished; and

nearly every American home had a radio in it. Fads swept the nation: People danced the Charleston, and they sat upon flagpoles. In 1927 Charles Lindbergh piloted an airplane across the Atlantic and became everyone's hero.

This was the Jazz Age, when New Orleans musicians moved "up the river" to Chicago, and the theaters of New York's Harlem pulsed with the music that had become a symbol of the times. These were the Roaring Twenties.

The roaring of the decade served to mask a quiet pain, the sense of loss that Gertrude Stein had observed in Paris. Carl Sandburg's poetic jazz rhythms might be hopeful, but Langston Hughes's are often bitter. F. Scott Fitzgerald portrays the Jazz Age as a generation of "the beautiful and damned," drowning in their pleasures. From England Eliot spoke of the "immense panorama of futility and anarchy which is contemporary history," and he gave a name to

the modern world in the title of his most famous poem—*The Waste Land.*

The task of the Modernist writers was, however, not only to express the waste and futility they experienced. They took up the burden of attempting to make some sense of that experience.

Modernist Literature

When we speak of Modernist literature, we speak of a broad range of artists and movements all seeking, in varying degrees, to break with the style, form, and content of the nineteenth century. Old ways of seeing, old ways of making sense of experience, just did not seem to work anymore for twentieth-century writers. "Make it new" was the cry of Ezra Pound, and most other writers of the time worked vigorously and self-consciously to make their poems and plays and novels new and different.

Modern psychology had a profound impact on the literature of the early twentieth century, and most great Modernist writers were interested in the workings of the human mind. Ordinary discourse had always put thoughts in a linear, cause-and-effect order: "If this is true and that is true, then this must be true." Now came the recognition that the human mind does not always follow this straight-line pattern; we often think by leaping from association to association in what the psychologist William James called the "stream of conscious-ness."

Gertrude Stein, a pupil of James's, tried to capture this "stream" through such devices as repetition and run-on sentences. The greatest practitioner of the Modernist style, however, was the Irish novelist James Joyce, whose *Ulysses* (1922) is sometimes said to be the last novel ever written because it took prose narrative to its most extreme point. Joyce's influence was extraordinary, and although novels are of course still being written all over the world, they are written with a heightened awareness of the experiments of Joyce.

Modernists took risks as they wrote in new forms and styles. Eugene O'Neill uses a number of experimental devices to reveal the flow of his characters' thoughts on stage. Ernest Hemingway opens most of his stories in the middle of the "stream," revealing background information as it comes up naturally and not in the long expository sections standard in nineteenth-century fiction. In "The Love Song of J. Alfred Prufrock" T. S. Eliot attempts to duplicate the "stream" of Prufrock's thoughts in a dramatic monologue. The result is a series of fragments that the reader must piece together.

Modernist literature is often experimental in form and in content. Poetry usually discards the nineteenth-century traditions of meter and rhyme. Free verse is the tool of most Modernist poets, and even if a poem retains some rhymes, the poet rarely puts them in the usual places. The visual appearance of poetry is also a significant factor, another means of breaking with traditions. The poems of E. E. Cummings, for example, are noted for lowercase letters in strange places and words spaced oddly on a page. For his poems William Carlos Williams chooses everyday subjects that would seem highly unusual by nine-teenth-century standards—a raid on the refrigerator, for instance, or a red wheelbarrow.

Modernist literature is often fragmentary, reflecting not only the "stream of consciousness" but the Modernist perception of the twentieth century as a jumble of conflicting ideas. Sometimes we are presented with only one fragment, the manner of presentation implying that there is no larger whole; the fragment "is what it is." This is true of Pound's and Doolittle's Imagist poetry, and of most of the poems of Gertrude Stein. It is also true of many poems by William Carlos Williams: In "This Is Just to Say," for example, Williams presents only a tiny piece of someone's life, but the poem is nevertheless satisfy-ingly complete; the fragment is enough.

Modernists often insist that their readers participate and draw their own conclusions. Direct statements of abstract ideas or emotions are usually avoided. The Modernist *shows* rather than *tells.* In Imagist poetry, for example, an image is used to capture an emotion; the poet does not tell us, "This is how I felt." In Hemingway's stories painful and moving experiences are coolly recounted by a detached narrator; the reader supplies the emotions and decides why the experiences are signifi-cant.

In the attempt to capture the bewilderment of modern life, Modernist literature is some-times intentionally puzzling. We may sometimes miss the eso-teric allusions in the poetry of Pound and Eliot, and we can never be sure why "so much de-pends" on Williams' red wheel-barrow. The point may be that the mystery itself is the "mes-sage." If there is something we do not know, we may not be meant to know it but rather to be puzzled by it and so to think about the mystery again and again.

American street scene during the 1920s, a time of progress and prosperity.

The degrees to which writers of this period adapted Modernist techniques vary greatly. Some writers did take comfort in the pattern and discipline of nineteenth-century literary forms. Edna St. Vincent Millay, for example, continued to write sonnets; much of Robert Frost's poetry is traditionally rhymed and patterned. In content, however, these writers are part of the Modernist era: Their subject matter shows that they could not have been writing at any other time. In fact, one of the most fascinating aspects of Modernist literature is the way each individual writer comes to terms with the changes of the time. Each poet or novelist seems to ask, "What does being 'new' mean to me?" The responses of these creative individuals produced the great variety of Modernist literature.

The Modernist Achievement

What did the Modernists accomplish? They took the first great steps in the search for a new art. They broke out of old forms and styles and generated new ones. They studied the elements of the past that could still be used and showed why the rest had to be put aside. Pound demonstrated the value of ancient Chinese literature; Eliot used the tradition of the English metaphysical poets of the seventeenth century. They and those who followed them used the past to create a new relationship with a new world. Wallace Stevens called this relationship "the supreme fiction," a way of living in the world, creating it anew every day, and being open to change even as the world itself changes. The Modernist achievement—in poetry, fiction, drama, in music and painting, in sculpture and architecture, in psychology and philosophy—lies largely in throwing open for us the doors of possibility.

TIME LINE

1910   First electric washing machines introduced

1911   Edith Wharton, *Ethan Frome*

Pulitzer Prizes established

Songwriter Irving Berlin, "Alexander's Ragtime Band"

1912   Harriet Monroe founds *Poetry: A Magazine of Verse*

Edna St. Vincent Millay, *Renascence and Other Poems*

1913   Henry Ford pioneers assembly line, producing 1,000 Model T automobiles a day

1914   Gertrude Stein, *Tender Buttons*

Robert Frost, *North of Boston*

1915   Edgar Lee Masters, *Spoon River Anthology*

1916   Norman Rockwell begins illustrating covers for *Saturday Evening Post*

Carl Sandburg, *Chicago Poems*

1917   U.S. declares war on Germany

Jeanette Rankin is first woman elected to House of Representatives

T. S. Eliot, *Prufrock and Other Observations*

1911   Antarctica: Norwegian explorer Roald Amundsen reaches South Pole

China: Manchu dynasty overthrown; republic established with Sun Yat-Sen as president

1912   Atlantic Ocean: *Titanic*, British ocean liner, sinks on its maiden voyage

England: George Bernard Shaw, *Pygmalion*

Sweden: Jim Thorpe, Native American, outstanding athlete at Olympic Games

1913   England: D. H. Lawrence, *Sons and Lovers*

Germany: Thomas Mann, *Death in Venice*

France: Premiere of *The Rite of Spring*, ballet by Russian composer Igor Stravinsky

1914   Beginning of World War I

Central America: Panama Canal opened

1915   Germany: Albert Einstein announces his general theory of relativity

1917   Russia: Revolution begins; Bolsheviks seize power

Switzerland: Carl Jung, *Psychology of the Unconscious*

France: Poet Paul Valéry, "La Jeune Parque"

Jim Thorpe

Robert Frost

Norman Rockwell

1918 U.S. population: 103.5 million	**1918** Worldwide influenza epidemic—approximately 20 million die by 1920
Willa Cather, *My Ántonia*	
1919 Sherwood Anderson, *Winesburg, Ohio*	**1919** France: Treaty of Versailles signed, ending World War I
1920 Women gain right to vote	**1920** League of Nations established
Sinclair Lewis, *Main Street*	
Beginning of Prohibition Era	
Eugene O'Neill, *Beyond the Horizon*	
1921 Marianne Moore, *Poems*	**1921** France: Pablo Picasso, *Three Musicians*
Rudolph Valentino stars in *The Sheik*	Ireland: W. B. Yeats, *Michael Robartes and the Dancer*
1922 T. S. Eliot, *The Waste Land*	**1922** Germany: Herman Hesse, *Siddhartha*
Sinclair Lewis, *Babbitt*	France: *Ulysses,* by Irish novelist James Joyce, published in Paris
William Carlos Williams, *Spring and All*	Egypt: ancient tomb of Tutankhamen discovered
	Italy: Benito Mussolini becomes dictator
1923 E. E. Cummings, *tulips and chimneys*	**1923** Germany: Adolph Hitler writes *Mein Kampf* while in jail
Robert Frost, *New Hampshire*	Germany: Arnold Schönberg composes *Piano Suite,* first work based on twelve-tone system
Wallace Stevens, *Harmonium*	
Time magazine first published	
1924 George Gershwin, *Rhapsody in Blue*	**1924** Germany: Thomas Mann, *The Magic Mountain*
Congress makes all native-born American Indians citizens	
1925 Nellie Taylor Ross of Wyoming becomes first woman governor	**1925** Austria: *The Trial,* by Czech writer Franz Kafka, published after his death
F. Scott Fitzgerald, *The Great Gatsby*	England: Scot John Baird televises images of moving objects for first time
The Gold Rush with Charlie Chaplin produced	Austria: Composer Alban Berg, *Wozzeck,* an opera
Theodore Dreiser, *An American Tragedy*	

1926 Ernest Hemingway, *The Sun Also Rises*

Langston Hughes, *The Weary Blues*

1927 *The Jazz Singer* with Al Jolson: first "talkie"

Charles Lindbergh makes first solo nonstop transatlantic flight

Babe Ruth hits sixty home runs for New York Yankees

Carl Sandburg, *The American Songbag*

1928 Stephen Vincent Benét, *John Brown's Body*

Anthropologist Margaret Mead, *Coming of Age in Samoa*

1929 William Faulkner, *The Sound and the Fury*

Ernest Hemingway, *A Farewell to Arms*

Stock Market crashes; beginning of Great Depression

1930 Grant Wood paints *American Gothic*

Sinclair Lewis first American to win Nobel Prize for Literature

1926 England: A. A. Milne, *Winnie the Pooh*

1927 Russia: Igor Pavlov, *Conditioned Reflexes*

England: Virginia Woolf, *To the Lighthouse*

1928 England: Sir Alexander Fleming discovers penicillin

Holland: Women participate in Olympics for first time

China: Chiang Kai-shek forms united government

France: Kellogg-Briand Pact signed, outlawing war

1929 Germany: Erich Maria Remarque, *All Quiet on the Western Front*

1930 Germany: Nazi party wins majority in national election

India: Mahatma Gandhi leads protests against British rule

POETRY

Ezra Pound   *1885–1972*

Ezra Pound—whose expression "Make it new" served as a rallying cry for the writers of his time—was the driving force behind Modernist literature. For more than fifty years his restless mind busied itself seeking new discoveries and innovations in the art of poetry. Yet this self-styled "revolutionist" of the arts was also profoundly conservative, searching history for the "best" and most useful things he could find among the world's literature, religions, philosophies, and social systems. Pound wished to change the world's governments and economics. In this he failed, but he did change the face of literature in his time.

Pound was born in a small town in Idaho, grew up in a suburb of Philadelphia, and after attending the University of Pennsylvania, left America for Europe, where he remained until 1945. His early years in London and Paris were a whirlwind of Modernist activity as he invented Imagism (see page 441) and worked hard at "modernizing" his own poetry. As the London representative of *Poetry* magazine, Pound helped nurture the careers of many new talents. He championed the Irish novelist James Joyce, became a close friend of T. S. Eliot, and influenced the prose of the young American novelist Ernest Hemingway.

After 1925 Pound made his home in Rapallo, Italy. Here he devoted his life to social-economic thought and to his long poem the *Cantos,* one of the most beautiful but puzzling poems ever written by a great poet.

In Italy Pound became an admirer of Benito Mussolini, and his idealistic but misplaced trust in that dictator had devastating consequences. During World War II he broadcast over the Italian radio, foolishly thinking that he was contributing to peace and to a better world society. After the war he was arrested and imprisoned by American troops in Pisa, an experience reflected in what is perhaps his greatest poetic achievement, *The Pisan Cantos.*

Judged mentally incapable of standing trial, Pound spent thirteen years in a hospital for the insane in Washington, D.C., where he continued to write some of his finest work. In 1958 he was allowed to return to his beloved Italy to live out a troubled old age.

The following poems are all from Pound's early years in London and Paris. "L'Art, 1910" ("Art, 1910") expresses his excitement for the "new" in painting and all the arts. "In a Station of the Metro" is a classic Imagist poem, presenting a quick, sharp image of people seen in the darkness of the Paris subway (the Metro). "Erat Hora" ("There Was an Hour") is Pound at his most lyrical, and "The River-Merchant's Wife" is a translation from the Chinese. All are written in the free verse that Pound worked hard to promote.

Ezra Pound

L'Art, 1910

Green arsenic[1] smeared on an egg-white cloth,
Crushed strawberries! Come, let us feast our eyes.

---

1. **arsenic** [är′sə nik]: poisonous chemical compound, often
used as an ingredient in paint.

In a Station
of the Metro

The apparition of these faces in the crowd;
Petals on a wet, black bough.

Erat Hora

"Thank you, whatever comes." And then she turned
And, as the ray of sun on hanging flowers
Fades when the wind hath lifted them aside,
Went swiftly from me. Nay, whatever comes
5 One hour was sunlit and the most high gods
May not make boast of any better thing
Than to have watched that hour as it passed.

The River-Merchant's Wife: A Letter

While my hair was still cut straight across my forehead
I played about the front gate, pulling flowers.
You came by on bamboo stilts, playing horse,
You walked about my seat, playing with blue plums.
5 And we went on living in the village of Chokan:[1]
Two small people, without dislike or suspicion.

At fourteen I married My Lord you.
I never laughed, being bashful.
Lowering my head, I looked at the wall.
10 Called to, a thousand times, I never looked back.

At fifteen I stopped scowling,
I desired my dust to be mingled with yours
Forever and forever and forever.
Why should I climb the look out?

15 At sixteen you departed,
You went into far Ku-to-yen,[2] by the river of swirling eddies,
And you have been gone five months.
The monkeys make sorrowful noise overhead.

You dragged your feet when you went out.
20 By the gate now, the moss is grown, the different mosses,
Too deep to clear them away!
The leaves fall early this autumn, in wind.
The paired butterflies are already yellow with August
Over the grass in the West garden;
25 They hurt me. I grow older.
If you are coming down through the narrows of the river Kiang,[3]
Please let me know beforehand,
And I will come out to meet you
                As far as Cho-fu-Sa.[4]

---

1. **Chokan** [chō′kän′]: suburb of Nanking, city in the People's Republic of China.
2. **Ku-to-yen** [kōō′tō′yen′]: island in the Yangtze Kiang [yäng′tsē kyang] River, largest river in China.
3. **river Kiang:** referring to the Yangtze Kiang River.
4. **Cho-fu-Sa** [chō′fōō′sä′]: beach along the Yangtze Kiang River, a few hundred miles above Nanking.

STUDY QUESTIONS

L'Art, 1910

Recalling

1. According to the title, what is being described?
2. What colors does the poem mention? What invitation does it include?

Interpreting

3. What does the combination of colors suggest about the physical appearance of the painting? What does "smeared" suggest? Why is "feast" especially well chosen?
4. Is the painting traditional or modern? Explain your opinion with examples from the poem.
5. Does Pound seem to like the painting? Can we be sure? Explain your opinion.

Extending

6. Do you think you would like the painting? Why or why not?

In a Station of the Metro

Recalling

1. Where does this poem take place?
2. What two images are juxtaposed, or placed next to each other, in the poem?

Interpreting

3. Does the poet supply you with any information about how you should think or feel about the poem? What does the poem consist of? What makes it "poetic"?
4. Why does the poet use the word *apparition* rather than *appearance*? (Consider the connotations of *apparition*.)

Erat Hora

Recalling

1. What simile describes the woman's departure?
2. What adjective describes the one hour that the speaker spent with the woman?

Interpreting

3. How does the speaker feel about the woman? Is he sorry that she leaves? What does he nevertheless feel about the hour they spent together?
4. Who probably speaks the words in quotation marks?
5. Explain how the poem's title relates to its content. What does the poem suggest about human experience and the passing of time?

Extending

6. What sharp images do this poem and the two preceding poems produce in your mind? How are the poems different from nineteenth-century poetry that you have read? Which two of these three poems by Pound are more radical departures? Explain your choice.

The River-Merchant's Wife

Recalling

1. What form does the poem take? Who is writing it?
2. At what age did the river-merchant's wife marry? What did she stop doing at fifteen, and what did she desire? What happened when the wife was sixteen?
3. What do the monkeys do in line 18? What do the butterflies do in line 25? What does the wife do in line 25?
4. If her husband tells her when he is coming through the narrows of the river Kiang, what will the wife do?

Interpreting

5. How have the wife's feelings for her husband changed since she married him? How does she feel about her husband's absence?
6. Is monkeys' chattering usually described as it is here? What do the negative descriptions of the monkeys and butterflies reflect?
7. Is the tone of this poem sentimental or matter-of-fact? Cite lines to support your answer.

Extending

8. How is the attitude of the wife in this poem different from the attitude expressed in nineteenth-century Romantic poetry that you have read? Compare this poem to Poe's "To Helen" or "Alone" (pages 132–133).

VIEWPOINT

Ezra Pound's own comment on "In a Station of the Metro" shows the poet at work:

Three years ago in Paris I got out of a "metro" train at La Concorde, and saw suddenly a beautiful face, and then another and another, and then a beautiful child's face, and then another beautiful woman, and I tried all day to find words for what this had meant to me, and I could not find any words that seemed to me worthy, or as lovely as that sudden emotion. And that evening, as I went home . . . I was still trying and I found, suddenly, the expression. I do not mean that I found words, but there came an equation . . . not in speech, but in little splotches of color. . . . That is to say, my experience in Paris should have gone into paint.

■ What does Pound mean when he says that an "equation" can be a poetic experience? Do you think "In a Station of the Metro" would have made a good painting? Why or why not?

LITERARY FOCUS

Imagism

The literary movement **Imagism** was begun by Ezra Pound and a few friends who wanted to rid poetry of the "bad habits" that they felt nineteenth-century poets had fallen into: the use of too many words; the use of words no longer in actual speech; repetitious subject matter; and the use of tired poetic patterns, especially traditional stanzas and meters. The Imagists wanted "direct treatment of the 'thing' " and a rhythm like that of a musical phrase. Instead of having the poet tell us what we should be feeling, Pound and his colleagues wanted an image to produce the emotion, to "speak for itself."

In "In a Station of the Metro" Pound attempts to produce the emotion he felt when he walked down into a Paris subway station and suddenly saw a number of faces in the dim light. To capture the emotion, Pound uses the image of petals on a wet, black bough. The image is not decoration: It is central to the poem's meaning. In fact, it *is* the poem's meaning.

Imagist poems are usually written in **free verse**—verse with no fixed rhythm—and are often quite short. They use one quick image to capture an emotion, to freeze one moment in time. Imagists took some of their inspiration from the highly disciplined Japanese verse form **haiku:** The first line of a haiku contains five syllables; the second line, seven; and the third line, five.

Imagism was a movement that came and went: Few pure Imagist poems were written after 1920. Nevertheless, the ideas of Imagism have had a great impact on modern poetry and on the way we read it.

Thinking About Imagism

■ Why is "L'Art, 1910" an Imagist poem? What elements of Imagism does "Erat Hora" contain?

COMPOSITION

Writing About Poetry

■ Although longer and more narrative than a pure Imagist poem, "The River-Merchant's Wife" uses many of the devices of Imagist poetry. In a brief essay discuss these devices and their relation to the poem's subject matter. First explain the meaning of the poem. Then consider the poem's use of (a) simple, direct language; (b) free verse; and (c) sharp images to convey emotions. *For help with this assignment, refer to Lesson 7 in the Writing About Literature Handbook at the back of this book.*

Writing an Imagist Poem

■ Write your own Imagist poem of two to five lines. Use one central image to capture a mood or emotion. You might reexamine "In a Station of the Metro" before you begin. To begin, think of a scene that has interested you, and think of an object or action to which your scene can be compared. Write the poem by stating the relationship in simple terms. Read your poem aloud to decide where it can be broken into lines most naturally.

T. S. Eliot   *1888–1965*

Born into a prominent St. Louis family and educated at Harvard, Thomas Stearns Eliot first met Ezra Pound in England in 1914. The two men were outwardly different—Pound rough, wild, Bohemian; Eliot the image of a polite, conservatively dressed gentleman—yet together, both as critics and as poets, they did more than anyone else to revolutionize literary tastes in the twentieth century.

Eliot's long poem *The Waste Land*, which appeared in 1922, ranks with James Joyce's novel *Ulysses* as the greatest success of the Modernist movement in Anglo-American literature. It became instantly famous among literary people, many of whom thought that it spoke for the postwar generation in its suggestion that the twentieth century was a fragmented, emotionally and spiritually arid period. Few at the time saw the poem's deeply religious concerns, nor did they recognize that in defining the condition of the modern "waste land," Eliot was searching for something better.

The crisis marked by *The Waste Land* was resolved for Eliot when he became a devout member of the Church of England. In 1927 he described himself as "classicist in literature, royalist in politics, and Anglo-Catholic in religion"—a remarkable turnaround, for as a Modernist, Eliot was "supposed" to be none of these. His spiritual journey can be traced through his poetry from *Gerontion* (1919), *The Hollow Men* (1925), and *Ash Wednesday* (1930) to one of the most profound religious poems in English, *Four Quartets* (1943).

In his later years Eliot worked for a large British publishing house. He also wrote plays, many of them in verse, and contributed a substantial body of literary criticism. He was awarded the Nobel Prize for Literature in 1948. In the years that followed, Eliot achieved a personal happiness that at last matched the pleasure he derived from his public life as the leading man of letters of his time.

"The Love Song of J. Alfred Prufrock" is an early poem but is marked by an assurance in phrasing that has made many of its lines almost proverbial in our century. It is a dramatic monologue spoken by one J. Alfred Prufrock, whose very name seems to combine the dignity and absurdity of his public and private selves. These two selves are probably the "you and I" of the first line—a person who outwardly is a "proper" member of the "best" society, but who inwardly is lost, lonely, and suffering, not unlike the poet himself at the time the poem was written.

The Love Song of J. Alfred Prufrock

S'io credesse che mia risposta fosse
A persona che mai tornasse al mondo,
Questa fiamma staria senza piu scosse.
Ma perciocche giammai di questo fondo
Non torno vivo alcun, s'i'odo il vero,
Senza tema d'infamia ti rispondo.[1]

Let us go then, you and I,
When the evening is spread out against the sky
Like a patient etherized[2] upon a table;
Let us go, through certain half-deserted streets,
5 The muttering retreats
Of restless nights in one-night cheap hotels
And sawdust restaurants with oyster-shells:
Streets that follow like a tedious argument
Of insidious[3] intent
10 To lead you to an overwhelming question . . .
Oh, do not ask, "What is it?"
Let us go and make our visit.

    In the room the women come and go
Talking of Michelangelo.[4]

15   The yellow fog that rubs its back upon the windowpanes,
The yellow smoke that rubs its muzzle on the windowpanes
Licked its tongue into the corners of the evening,
Lingered upon the pools that stand in drains,
Let fall upon its back the soot that falls from chimneys,
20 Slipped by the terrace, made a sudden leap,
And seeing that it was a soft October night,
Curled once about the house, and fell asleep.

---

1. *S'io credesse . . . ti rispondo:* "If I believed my reply were being made to one who would ever return to the world, this flame [his soul] would shake no more; but since, if what I hear is true, none ever did return alive from this depth, I answer you without fear of dishonor." One of the condemned spirits in Hell confesses his sins to the poet Dante in the *Inferno,* Chapter XXVII, lines 61–66. The spirit believed—wrongly—that Dante would be unable to return to the world from Hell.
2. **etherized** [ē'thə rīzd]: made insensitive to pain; anesthetized with ether, as before an operation.
3. **insidious** [in sid'ē əs]: waiting to entrap, or trick; deceitful.
4. **Michelangelo** [mi'kəl an'jə lō]: The great Italian artist Michelangelo Buonarroti [bwō nä rô'tē] (1475–1564).

And indeed there will be time
For the yellow smoke that slides along the street,
25 Rubbing its back upon the windowpanes;
There will be time, there will be time
To prepare a face to meet the faces that you meet;
There will be time to murder and create,
And time for all the works and days of hands
30 That lift and drop a question on your plate;
Time for you and time for me,
And time yet for a hundred indecisions,
And for a hundred visions and revisions,
Before the taking of a toast and tea.

35   In the room the women come and go
Talking of Michelangelo.

   And indeed there will be time
To wonder, "Do I dare?" and, "Do I dare?"
Time to turn back and descend the stair,
40 With a bald spot in the middle of my hair—
(They will say: "How his hair is growing thin!")
My morning coat, my collar mounting firmly to the chin,
My necktie rich and modest, but asserted by a simple pin—
(They will say: "But how his arms and legs are thin!")
45 Do I dare
Disturb the universe?
In a minute there is time
For decisions and revisions which a minute will reverse.

   For I have known them all already, known them all—
50 Have known the evenings, mornings, afternoons,
I have measured out my life with coffee spoons;
I know the voices dying with a dying fall
Beneath the music from a farther room.
   So how should I presume?

55   And I have known the eyes already, known them all—
The eyes that fix you in a formulated phrase,
And when I am formulated, sprawling on a pin,
When I am pinned and wriggling on the wall,
Then how should I begin
60 To spit out all the butt-ends of my days and ways?
   And how should I presume?

   And I have known the arms already, known them all—
Arms that are braceleted and white and bare
(But in the lamplight, downed with light brown hair!)

65 Is it perfume from a dress
  That makes me so digress?
  Arms that lie along a table, or wrap about a shawl.
   And should I then presume?
   And how should I begin?

     . . . . .

70 Shall I say, I have gone at dusk through narrow streets
  And watched the smoke that rises from the pipes
  Of lonely men in shirtsleeves, leaning out of windows? . . .

   I should have been a pair of ragged claws
  Scuttling across the floors of silent seas.

     . . . . .

75 And the afternoon, the evening, sleeps so peacefully!
  Smoothed by long fingers,
  Asleep . . . tired . . . or it malingers,[5]
  Stretched on the floor, here beside you and me.
  Should I, after tea and cakes and ices,
80 Have the strength to force the moment to its crisis?
  But though I have wept and fasted, wept and prayed,
  Though I have seen my head (grown slightly bald) brought in
   upon a platter,[6]
  I am no prophet—and here's no great matter;
  I have seen the moment of my greatness flicker,
85 And I have seen the eternal Footman[7] hold my coat, and snicker,
  And in short, I was afraid.

   And would it have been worth it, after all,
  After the cups, the marmalade, the tea,
  Among the porcelain, among some talk of you and me,
90 Would it have been worthwhile,
  To have bitten off the matter with a smile,
  To have squeezed the universe into a ball
  To roll it toward some overwhelming question,
  To say: "I am Lazarus,[8] come from the dead,
95 Come back to tell you all, I shall tell you all"—
  If one, settling a pillow by her head,
   Should say: "That is not what I meant at all.
   That is not it, at all."

---

5. **malingers** [mə ling′gərz]: pretends to be sick.
6. **head . . . platter:** The reference is to the prophet John the Baptist, whose head was delivered on a platter to Salome as a reward for her dancing (Matthew 14 : 1–11).
7. **eternal Footman:** Death.
8. **Lazarus** [laz′ə rəs]: The reference is to John 11:1–44, in which Jesus resurrected Lazarus from the dead.

And would it have been worth it, after all,
100 Would it have been worthwhile,
After the sunsets and the dooryards and the sprinkled streets,
After the novels, after the teacups, after the skirts that trail
along the floor—
And this, and so much more?—
It is impossible to say just what I mean!
105 But as if a magic lantern⁹ threw the nerves in patterns on
a screen:
Would it have been worthwhile
If one, settling a pillow or throwing off a shawl,
And turning toward the window, should say:
"That is not it at all,
110 That is not what I meant, at all."

· · · · ·

No! I am not Prince Hamlet,¹⁰ nor was meant to be;
Am an attendant lord, one that will do
To swell a progress,¹¹ start a scene or two,
Advise the prince; no doubt, an easy tool,
115 Deferential, glad to be of use,
Politic, cautious, and meticulous;
Full of high sentence,¹² but a bit obtuse;
At times, indeed, almost ridiculous—
Almost, at times, the Fool.

120 I grow old . . . I grow old . . .
I shall wear the bottoms of my trousers rolled.

Shall I part my hair behind? Do I dare to eat a peach?
I shall wear white flannel trousers, and walk upon the beach.
I have heard the mermaids singing, each to each.

125 I do not think that they will sing to me.

I have seen them riding seaward on the waves
Combing the white hair of the waves blown back
When the wind blows the water white and black.

We have lingered in the chambers of the sea
130 By sea-girls wreathed with seaweed red and brown
Till human voices wake us, and we drown.

---

9. **magic lantern:** machine for projecting images.
10. **Prince Hamlet:** tragic hero of Shakespeare's play *Hamlet.*
11. **to swell a progress:** take part in a royal procession.
12. **high sentence:** flowery, fancy speech full of proverbs and advice,
like that of the old counselor Polonius in *Hamlet.*

STUDY QUESTIONS

Recalling

1. According to lines 1–14, what are "you and I" going out to "make"? To what do the streets lead? For what does Prufrock say there will be time in line 27? In lines 32–34?

2. According to lines 37–46, what would Prufrock "disturb" if he dared to ask his question? Why "in short" doesn't Prufrock "force the moment to its crisis" (lines 75–86)? What remark by someone "settling a pillow" would make asking the question not worthwhile (lines 87–98)?

3. After he fails to ask his question, who does Prufrock say he is and is not (lines 111–119)?

4. Whom has Prufrock heard singing, according to lines 124–131? What does he think these creatures will not do?

Interpreting

5. What do the opening quotation from Dante, the descriptions of the fog, and the simile in line 3 suggest about Prufrock's mood or feelings?

6. Reread lines 10–11, 45–46, 80, and 93–94. What do these lines suggest about Prufrock's opinion of the question he considers asking? What does the title suggest about the question? What is Prufrock trying to avoid when he keeps saying "there will be time" in lines 23–48?

7. Why would Prufrock think of himself as "you and I," or "we"? What do the following lines reveal about Prufrock's view of his life and his self-image: the opening quotation, lines 51, 73–74, 82, and 85?

8. How would Prufrock be like Lazarus if he asked the question? In not asking the question, why is he unlike Hamlet?

9. What do the images in lines 121–123 suggest about the future Prufrock foresees for himself? Is this future different from his past?

10. How are the mermaids unlike the women Prufrock visits? Why is it significant that Prufrock hears the mermaids? That they will not sing for him?

Extending

11. In what ways are we all like Prufrock some of the time? Why might a middle-aged person in particular identify with him?

12. Tell how this poem helps explain why the young Eliot called the modern world a "waste land" and why Gertrude Stein called the young generation who had fought in World War I a "lost generation."

VIEWPOINT

Although Prufrock says he is not Hamlet, the Eliot critic Grover Smith believes that

> Eliot's Prufrock is a tragic figure. . . . The plight of this hesitant, inhibited man, an aging dreamer trapped in decayed, shabby-genteel surroundings, aware of beauty and faced with sordidness, mirrors the plight of the sensitive in the presence of the dull.
>
> —*T. S. Eliot's Poetry and Plays*

■ What evidence supports Smith's view? What evidence suggests that Prufrock is not tragic but comic? Do you believe he is either one or the other? Explain.

LITERARY FOCUS

Dramatic Monologue

In plays we often encounter **monologues**, long speeches by one character that reveal his or her thoughts to the audience and to other characters. In a poem that is a **dramatic monologue**, we have, in a sense, the monologue without the rest of the play. The poet creates a character who does the talking and who, through speech, reveals something about his or her life and feelings. The poet who used dramatic monologue most often was the nineteenth-century English poet Robert Browning.

Eliot's "Love Song of J. Alfred Prufrock" is a dramatic monologue. Prufrock is not T. S. Eliot, although of course he has something of Eliot in him. He is a character created by Eliot, and he speaks directly to us. He tells us his thoughts in leaps and bounds, jumping from one image to another, just as a human mind does. As we listen to his monologue and make the connections that are not spelled out, we come to understand the essence of the man, the private self that Prufrock hides from acquaintances.

Thinking About Dramatic Monologue

■ In which of the poems by Ezra Pound does a character speak directly to us? What does this character reveal about himself or herself?

VOCABULARY

Word Origins and Overtones

Musical notes have overtones, reverberations that are part of the richness of the sound. Words, too, have overtones—the richness of meaning that comes from their origins and that is part of the "heritage" of the word.

In line 9 of "The Love Song of J. Alfred Prufrock," for example, Prufrock uses the word *insidious*. We may know that *insidious* means "secretly dangerous," but it is even more helpful to know that the word comes from Latin *in-* + *sedere*, "to lie in wait in order to ambush." Eliot has chosen the perfect word to suggest Prufrock's terror as he walks the streets.

Look up the origins of the following words in a dictionary, and tell how the origin of the word reflects its use by Eliot in "The Love Song of J. Alfred Prufrock:

1. revisions
2. presume
3. malingers
4. deferential
5. meticulous

COMPOSITION

Writing About Poetry

■ Although "The Love Song of J. Alfred Prufrock" is written in free verse, some sections have distinct rhythms, and there is a good deal of rhyme. In a brief essay discuss the use of rhyme and rhythm in the poem. First show how Eliot prevents his rhymes and rhythms from falling into a predictable pattern. Then explain how the lack of pattern relates to the tone and content of the poem. *For help with this assignment, refer to Lesson 7 in the Writing About Literature Handbook at the back of this book.*

Writing a Dramatic Monologue

■ Write a dramatic monologue in poetry or prose. Use the voice of the woman Prufrock loves or the voice of one of Prufrock's gentleman friends. Try to let the character's personality come through the monologue, and allow the character to include his or her impressions of Prufrock. You may begin by describing the character's first meeting with Prufrock.

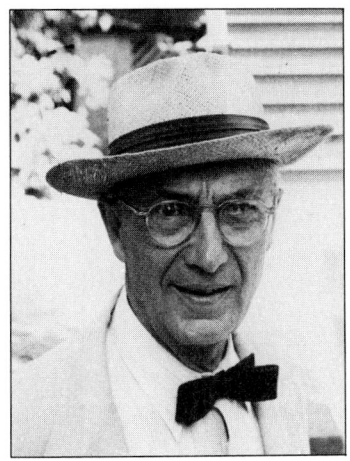

William Carlos Williams   *1883–1963*

Ezra Pound and T. S. Eliot left America because they thought that they could not thrive artistically in their native land. William Carlos Williams, who had been Pound's friend since college days, stayed home in New Jersey. He had an international background himself: His father was English; his mother, Puerto Rican. Williams wanted his poetry to be very American, made out of the American language, reflecting American sights and sounds and ways of life.

Williams was born in New Jersey and attended the University of Pennsylvania Medical School. He published his first volume of poetry in 1909, while still in college. These early poems were Romantic verses in the style of traditional nineteenth-century English poetry. When Williams sent Pound a copy of an early book of his verse, Pound wrote back from London with kindly but severe criticism: "Your book," he said, "would not attract even passing attention here. There are fine lines in it, but nowhere I think do you add anything to the poets you have used as models."

Within a few years, however, Williams found his own voice, and he was never again an imitator. He became a Modernist and initially an Imagist, but, unlike Pound and Eliot, he celebrated the world before his eyes and scorned allusions to history, religion, and ancient literature. Returning to New Jersey to raise a family and set up a medical practice, he fell in love with everyday American life. He wrote often of his patients and neighbors, working-class men and women in the industrialized section of New Jersey near the town of Paterson. His observations are contained in *Paterson* (1946–1958), a poem of epic length filled with delightful glimpses of urban American life. Another major work, *In the American Grain* (1925), explores the mythic greatness of famous Americans.

Williams' poetry is noted for its precision; in his best work he makes us think that a poem is just right—neither a word too few nor a word too many. His great gift is his ability to make poetry from the most ordinary objects and experiences. In the following poems he makes wonderful poetic moments out of the appearance of a wheelbarrow in the rain, peasants dancing, unusual behavior in a neighbor, a fire truck racing through the city, and a trip to the icebox.

William Carlos Williams

The Red Wheelbarrow

so much depends
upon

a red wheel
barrow

5 glazed with rain
water

beside the white
chickens.

The Dance

In Breughel's[1] great picture, The Kermess,[2]
the dancers go round, they go round and
around, the squeal and the blare and the
tweedle of bagpipes, a bugle and fiddles
5 tipping their bellies (round as the thick-
sided glasses whose wash they impound[3])
their hips and their bellies off balance
to turn them. Kicking and rolling about
the Fair Grounds, swinging their butts, those
10 shanks must be sound to bear up under such
rollicking measures, prance as they dance
in Breughel's great picture, The Kermess.

1. **Breughel's** [brōō′gəlz]: referring to Pieter Brueghel
the Elder (1522–1569), Flemish painter noted for his
scenes of peasant life.
2. **The Kermess** [kur′mis]: Breughel's 1568 painting
of a peasant kermess, or fair.
3. **wash they impound:** liquid they drink.

Detail from *Peasant Dance,*
Pieter Brueghel, c. 1568.

The Artist

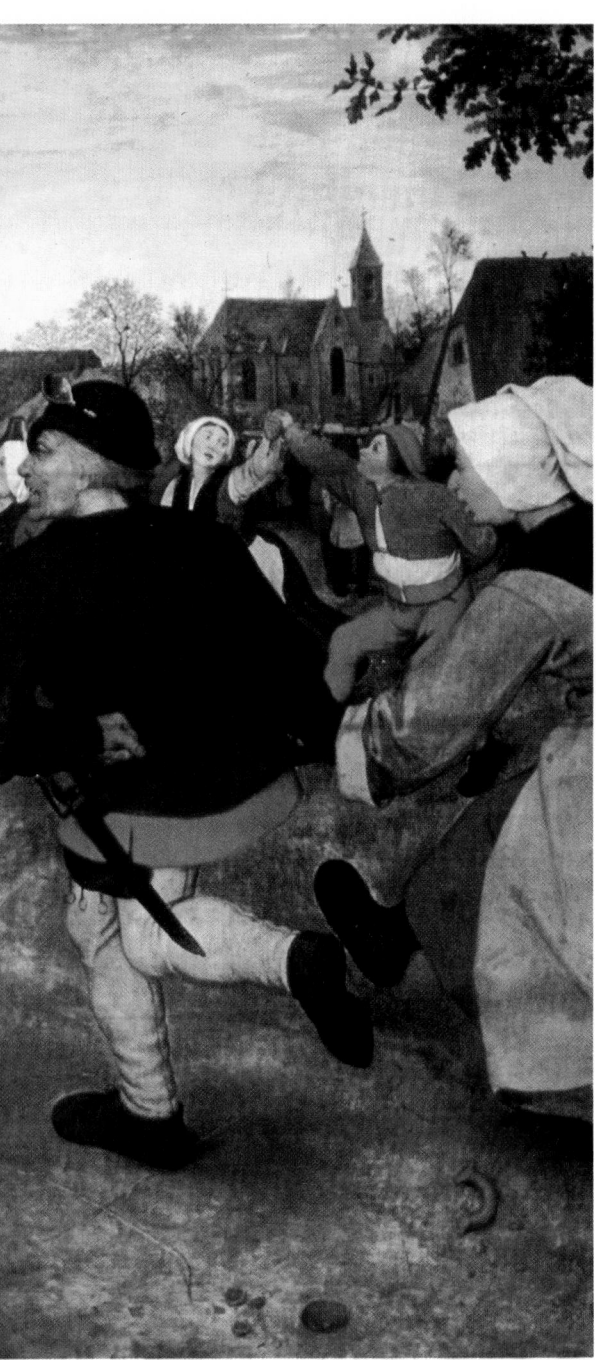

Kunsthistorisches Museum, Vienna

Mr. T.
        bareheaded
               in a soiled undershirt
his hair standing out
5   on all sides
               stood on his toes
heels together
        arms gracefully
               for the moment
10 curled above his head.
        Then he whirled about
               bounded
into the air
        and with an *entrechat*[1]
15   perfectly achieved
completed the figure.
        My mother
               taken by surprise
where she sat
20   in her invalid's chair
               was left speechless.
Bravo! she cried at last
        and clapped her hands.
               The man's wife
25 came from the kitchen:
        What goes on here? she said.
               But the show was over.

---

1. *entrechat* [än′trə shä′]: in ballet, a leap in which dancers cross their legs or strike their heels together several times.

William Carlos Williams

The Great Figure

Among the rain
and lights
I saw the figure 5
in gold
on a red
firetruck
moving
tense
unheeded
to gong clangs
siren howls
and wheels rumbling
through the dark city.

This Is Just to Say

I have eaten
the plums
that were in
the icebox

and which
you were probably
saving
for breakfast

Forgive me
they were delicious
so sweet
and so cold

I Saw the Figure 5 in Gold,
Charles Demuth, 1928.

STUDY QUESTIONS

The Red Wheelbarrow

Recalling

1. What three items are mentioned in the poem? What does the first line tell us about them?

Interpreting

2. Why might the objects in the poem be very important? Can we be sure? Explain.

3. What elements of Imagism, described on page 441, does this poem exhibit? What elements of Modernist literature in general, described on pages 431–433, does the poem display?

The Dance

Recalling

1. In what direction do the dancers in Breughel's picture move?

2. What three words name the sounds of the bagpipes?

Interpreting

3. Is the music to which the people dance professional and melodious? Is their dancing professional? How do we know?

4. Identify six poetic devices that help the poet capture the dancing or its musical accompaniment.

5. What does the poet seem to admire about Breughel's painting?

Extending

6. Compare the painting by Breughel with the description in "The Dance." What visual details has the poet captured in words?

The Artist

Recalling

1. What is Mr. T. wearing? What does he do?

2. What does the speaker's mother say when she sees Mr. T.'s "performance"? What does Mr. T.'s wife say?

Interpreting

3. What is the contrast between the speaker's mother and Mr. T.'s wife? Between the speaker's mother and Mr. T.?

4. Besides the speaker's mother, who else appreciates "the show"? Explain.

5. Is it usual for Mr. T. to act as he does? How do we know? Who or what makes Mr. T. an artist?

The Great Figure

Recalling

1. According to the title, what sort of figure is the figure 5?
2. On what is the figure 5 printed? What color is it?
3. How is the figure 5 moving? Through what is it moving?

Interpreting

4. Explain how the figure 5 can literally be "moving tense."
5. Why is it significant that the figure 5 is "in gold"? That the city is "dark"?
6. By whom is the figure 5 "unheeded"? Is it really unheeded? Explain.
7. What does this poem suggest about beauty? About modern life?

Extending

8. Based on the poems by Williams that you have read, what generalization would you make about his subject matter? Do you find his poems "poetic"? Why or why not?

This Is Just to Say

Recalling

1. What has the speaker eaten? For what were these things probably being saved?

Interpreting

2. How important is the incident described in this poem? Why do you think Williams chose an incident of this sort for his poem?
3. What do the last four lines suggest about the objects being saved and the reason that the speaker expects to be forgiven?
4. What does the title have to do with the rest of the poem?

LITERARY FOCUS

Free Verse

T. S. Eliot once said that "free verse is a contradiction in terms." Eliot meant that a poet is never "free" to write down anything at all, break it into lines, and call it "verse," or poetry. There must be some reason for using **free verse**—verse with no fixed rhythm—some relationship between form and meaning.

Whitman (see page 246), Pound, and Eliot are all masters of free verse, and so is William Carlos

Williams. In "The Red Wheelbarrow" Williams demonstrates how lines of free verse can be broken to direct the reader's attention to important words, images, or ideas. For example, he forces us to realize that the barrow indeed has a wheel by breaking up "wheelbarrow" on two lines:

> a red wheel
> barrow

Williams does the same with "rainwater," another familiar word we might rush over:

> glazed with rain
> water

Williams also keeps to a pattern when he breaks up his lines: A three-word line is followed by a one-word line to form a "stanza"; the "stanza" is repeated three times. Thus, while the poem has an irregular *rhythmic* pattern (the number of syllables in each line varies), it does have a strict *visual* pattern. We can see that Williams is writing "freely," but—as Eliot suggests—not as freely as we think at first.

Thinking About Free Verse

1. Describe the strict visual pattern of "The Artist." How is the pattern related to the poem's subject?
2. How do line breaks help emphasize thoughts and images in "This Is Just to Say" and "The Great Figure"?

COMPOSITION

Writing About Free Verse

■ Choose any one of Williams' poems, and write a brief analysis of the effects of the poet's use of free verse. First discuss the positions of specific words and the line breaks. Then describe the overall visual appearance of the poem. Consider how the arrangement of words on the page relates to the poem's content.

Writing Free Verse

■ Write a short free-verse poem in which the words form a visual pattern, as they do in "The Red Wheelbarrow" and "The Dancer." Try to use the line breaks to emphasize important thoughts and images, as Williams does. If you wish, you might follow the model of "The Red Wheelbarrow": a three-word line followed by a one-word line repeated three times.

H. D. (Hilda Doolittle)   *1886–1961*

Hilda Doolittle, who signed her poetry H. D., was born in Bethlehem, Pennsylvania. As a student at Bryn Mawr College, she knew both Ezra Pound and William Carlos Williams, and she later renewed her acquaintance with Pound in London. One day, in the British Museum tearoom, she was showing some of her poems to Pound and to Richard Aldington, an English poet whom she later married. Pound took a blue pencil to the poems, deleting what he thought were unnecessary words—and Imagism was invented.

Pound sent three of Doolittle's poems to *Poetry* magazine, where they appeared over the name "H. D., Imagiste," and in time Doolittle became one of the leading Imagist poets. An admirer of Greek lyrics, she attempted to capture their simplicity and precision in her own work. Her first collection of poetry, *Sea Garden,* was published in 1916; her *Collected Poems,* in 1925. In "Sea Rose" Doolittle rigorously avoids the sentimentality that usually accompanied the rose in poetry. In "Oread" she imagines herself a Greek mountain nymph experiencing the beauty of nature.

H. D.

Sea Rose

Rose, harsh rose,
marred and with stint of petals,
meager flower, thin,
sparse of leaf,

5 more precious
than a wet rose
single on a stem—
you are caught in the drift.

Stunted, with small leaf,
10 you are flung on the sand,
you are lifted
in the crisp sand
that drives in the wind.

Can the spice-rose
15 drip such acrid fragrance
hardened in a leaf?

H. D.

Oread

Whirl up, sea—
whirl your pointed pines,
splash your great pines
on our rocks,
5 hurl your green over us,
cover us with your pools of fir.

STUDY QUESTIONS

Sea Rose

Recalling
1. What words and phrases describe the sea rose in lines 1–4?
2. What is the rose "more precious than"?
3. What happens to the sea rose in lines 9–13? To what rose is it compared in lines 14–15?

Interpreting
4. What elements of Imagism, as described on page 441, does this poem display?
5. What makes the sea rose more precious than the usual hothouse rose—that is, the "wet rose / single on a stem"?

6. In addition to a sea rose, what is this poem about?

Oread

Recalling
1. To whom or what is this poem addressed, according to the first line?

Interpreting
2. Since an oread is a *mountain* nymph, what is the "sea" in line 1?
3. Who is the speaker in this poem? How does the speaker seem to feel about being splashed by pines and green?
4. Why is this considered an Imagist poem (see page 441)?

Gertrude Stein   *1874–1946*

Gertrude Stein is known as much for her influence on other artists as for her own contribution to literature. Wealthy, brilliant, and unconventional, Stein was a leading patron of Modernism and a good friend to the artists Pablo Picasso and Henri Matisse and the writers Ernest Hemingway and Sherwood Anderson.

Stein was born in Pennsylvania and grew up in Europe and California. As a student at Radcliffe, she met the psychologist William James and became interested in his theories about the workings of the human mind. She went on to study medicine at Johns Hopkins, but in 1902 abandoned her studies and abruptly moved to Paris, which became the capital of Modernism in all the arts. Here Stein was famous for her wit and hospitality; after World War I her home became the haven to which all American "expatriates" flocked. She returned only once to America, on a triumphant lecture tour in the early thirties, and after enduring the Nazi occupation of France, she died in 1946.

Stein was an early admirer of Picasso and Matisse—respected painters today, but considered shocking in their youth, when they broke with most of the conventions of the art world. Stein wanted her writing to be as revolutionary as the art she purchased and championed—and it was. Her first major work, *Three Lives* (1905), tries to present its characters' thinking patterns, but it still retains recognizable characters and a plot of sorts. With *The Making of Americans* (1925), plot and character disappear altogether, just as recognizable objects had begun to disappear from the paintings of the abstract artists.

Surprisingly, after these avant-garde ventures Stein showed herself capable of pleasing a wide audience: Her autobiography, published in 1933, was a great popular success. It is typical of the oddness and freshness of Stein's work that she called the book *The Autobiography of Alice B. Toklas,* naming it not for herself, but for her lifelong friend.

"I Am Rose" and "A Sound" are two short, experimental poems. The first, a bit like a nursery rhyme and a bit like Emily Dickinson, reminds us of Stein's famous utterance, "Rose is a rose is a rose is a rose." The second is from *Tender Buttons* (1914), a series of "portraits" of familiar objects rendered unfamiliar in an attempt to duplicate in words what the Cubists were doing in their paintings. Stein's purpose is to encourage us to take delight in the words as we find them.

Gertrude Stein

I Am Rose

I am a Rose my eyes are blue
I am a Rose and who are you
I am a Rose and when I sing
I am a Rose like anything

A Sound

Elephant beaten with candy and little pops and
chews all bolts and reckless rats, this is this.

Chinese Restaurant,
a Cubist painting by
Max Weber, 1915.

Collection Whitney Museum of American Art

STUDY QUESTIONS

I Am Rose

Recalling

1. According to the poem, when is the speaker most roselike?

Interpreting

2. Do you think this poem has a meaning? Why or why not?
3. What does this poem force the reader to do?
4. What sort of phrase is "like anything"? Are such phrases generally found in traditional nineteenth-century poetry? Explain your answer.
5. What elements of Modernism, as described on pages 431–433, does this poem display?

Extending

6. What might the roses in this poem and in H. D.'s "Sea Rose" (page 455) have in common? What might they have in common with Emerson's rhodora (page 166)? What does Emerson tell us about the rhodora that neither H. D. nor Stein tells us about her rose?

A Sound

Recalling

1. According to the title, what does this poem describe? What words in the poem seem to relate to the title?

Interpreting

2. Why do you think Stein does not tell us what the sound is? What does "this is this" imply?

3. What does this poem force the reader to do? What elements of Modernism, as described on pages 431–433, does it contain?

Extending

4. How is this poem like the painting in "L'Art, 1910"? Do you find Stein's poetry even more radical than Pound's? Why or why not?

VIEWPOINT

"A Sound" is from Stein's book *Tender Buttons*. Richard Bridgeman writes:

For Gertrude Stein, *Tender Buttons* represented her full-scale break out of the prison of conventional form into the colorful realm of the sensitized imagination. But it did not signal an abandonment of control.
—*Gertrude Stein in Pieces*

■ What makes "A Sound" unconventional? How does it express Stein's "sensitized imagination"? Do you agree that control has not been abandoned? Why or why not?

COMPARING WRITERS

■ Pound, Eliot, Williams, H. D., and Stein—all but one lived abroad for most of their lives, yet all helped revolutionize American poetry in the twentieth century. What did each of these writers have to say about modern life? How in his or her own way did each poet throw new light on the objects and phenomena of twentieth-century living?

Carl Sandburg   *1878–1967*

Although influenced by Pound and the Imagists, Carl Sandburg wanted to reach a wider audience—and he did. From the 1916 publication of *Chicago Poems* until his death in 1967, Sandburg was one of America's most popular and successful poets.

Sandburg was the son of Swedish immigrants who settled in Galesburg, Illinois. As a young man he fought in the Spanish-American War, traveled the country working a wide variety of jobs, and finally settled in Chicago. Here he found employment as a newspaper reporter and began to contribute poems to *Poetry* magazine.

From 1912 to 1925, Chicago was an exciting residence for a poet. It was home not only to the influential *Poetry* magazine but also to such notable writers as Theodore Dreiser, Sherwood Anderson, Vachel Lindsay, and Edgar Lee Masters. With the publication of *Chicago Poems,* Sandburg became one of Chicago's literary giants. Dubbed "the Bard of the Midwest," he soon wrote three more highly successful volumes of poetry, *Cornhuskers* (1918), *Smoke and Steel* (1920), and *Slabs of the Sunburnt West* (1922).

Sandburg was a great admirer of Walt Whitman and in his enthusiasm for America might be considered Whitman's successor. He also admired Abraham Lincoln, as Whitman had, and wrote what is considered the definitive Lincoln biography. He frequently lectured on the lives of Whitman and Lincoln, and he also performed folk songs throughout the United States—folk songs that expressed the American spirit and that he collected in *The American Songbag* (1927).

Sandburg won the Pulitzer Prize for his Lincoln biography in 1940 and for his *Complete Poems* in 1951. He was decorated by the king of Sweden, and he addressed a joint session of Congress on the 150th anniversary of Lincoln's birth. He continued to write through his final years, which he spent on his farm in North Carolina.

If in such popular poems as "Fog" we can see the effect of the Imagists on Sandburg's poetry, the influence of Walt Whitman is even more marked. Sandburg's exuberant free verse is reminiscent of Whitman's style; his celebration of America reminds us of Whitman's themes. "Chicago," which originally appeared in *Poetry* magazine, is a catalogue of details describing the bustling city. "Jazz Fantasia" captures the sounds of the Jazz Age and displays Sandburg's fondness for American slang: A fantasia is a musical composition that does not follow a strict form. *The People, Yes*, a long poem published in 1936, is a declaration of faith in American workers and the American system.

Carl Sandburg

from **The People, Yes**

       The people will live on.
The learning and blundering people will live on.
       They will be tricked and sold and again sold
And go back to the nourishing earth for rootholds,
5   The people so peculiar in renewal and comeback,
       You can't laugh off their capacity to take it.
The mammoth[1] rests between his cyclonic dramas.

The people so often sleepy, weary, enigmatic,
is a vast huddle with many units saying:
10   "I earn my living.
      I make enough to get by
      and it takes all my time.
      If I had more time
      I could do more for myself
15   and maybe for others.
      I could read and study
      and talk things over
      and find out about things.
      It takes time.
20 I wish I had the time."

               • • •

       The people know the salt of the sea
       and the strength of the winds
       lashing the corners of the earth.
       The people take the earth
25   as a tomb of rest and a cradle of hope.
       Who else speaks for the Family of Man?
       They are in tune and step
       with constellations of universal law.

               • • •

In the darkness with a great bundle of grief
      the people march.
30 In the night, and overhead a shovel of stars for
      keeps, the people march:
               "Where to? what next?"

---

1. **mammoth** [mam′əth]: extinct prehistoric elephant; anything
of enormous size and strength.

Carl Sandburg

Chicago

Hog Butcher for the World,
Tool Maker, Stacker of Wheat,
Player with Railroads and the Nation's Freight Handler;
Stormy, husky, brawling,
5   City of the Big Shoulders:

They tell me you are wicked and I believe them, for I have seen
    your painted women under the gas lamps luring the farm boys.
And they tell me you are crooked and I answer: Yes, it is true I have
    seen the gunman kill and go free to kill again.
And they tell me you are brutal and my reply is: On the faces of
    women and children I have seen the marks of wanton hunger.
And having answered so I turn once more to those who sneer at this
    my city, and I give them back the sneer and say to them:
10 Come and show me another city with lifted head singing so proud to
    be alive and coarse and strong and cunning.
Flinging magnetic curses amid the toil of piling job on job, here is a
    tall bold slugger set vivid against the little soft cities;
Fierce as a dog with tongue lapping for action, cunning as a savage
    pitted against the wilderness,
       Bareheaded,
       Shoveling,
15   Wrecking,
       Planning,
       Building, breaking, rebuilding,
Under the smoke, dust all over his mouth, laughing with white teeth,
Under the terrible burden of destiny laughing as a young man laughs,
20 Laughing even as an ignorant fighter laughs who has never lost a
    battle,
Bragging and laughing that under his wrist is the pulse, and under his
    ribs the heart of the people,
         Laughing!
Laughing the stormy, husky, brawling laughter of Youth, half-naked,
    sweating, proud to be Hog Butcher, Tool Maker, Stacker of
    Wheat, Player with Railroads and Freight Handler to the Nation.

Jazz Fantasia

Drum on your drums, batter on your banjoes,
sob on the long cool winding saxophones.
Go to it, O jazzmen.

Sling your knuckles on the bottoms of the happy
5   tin pans, let your trombones ooze, and go husha-
husha-hush with the slippery sandpaper.

Moan like an autumn wind high in the lonesome treetops, moan soft
like you wanted somebody terrible, cry like a racing car slipping
away from a motorcycle cop, bang-bang! you jazzmen, bang
10   altogether drums, traps, banjoes, horns, tin cans—make two people
fight on the top of a stairway and scratch each other's eyes in a
clinch tumbling down the stairs.

Can the rough stuff . . . now a Mississippi steamboat pushes up the
night river with a hoo-hoo-hoo-oo . . . and the green lanterns calling
15   to the high soft stars . . . a red moon rides on the humps of the low
river hills . . . go to it, O jazzmen.

STUDY QUESTIONS

The People, Yes

Recalling

1. According to lines 1–8, what will the "learning and blundering" people do? In what are the people "so peculiar"? According to lines 8–20, what would the people do if they had more time? What do they wish?
2. According to lines 21–28, what do the people know? With what are they "in tune and step"?
3. According to lines 29–31, with what bundle do the people march? What do they ask?

Interpreting

4. Citing details to support your answer, tell what kind or class of people this poem is about. What aspects of "the people" are celebrated?

(Consider especially lines 2, 5, 25, and the questions the people ask in the final line.)
5. Explain the "yes" in the poem's title.

Extending

6. This poem was written during the Great Depression of the 1930s. Explain how knowing this affects your interpretation of the poem.

Chicago

Recalling

1. What is Chicago called in the first three lines?
2. What three things do "they" tell the speaker in lines 6–8? What does the speaker say Chicago is like in line 10? In lines 13–17?
3. How does Chicago laugh in line 19? In line 20? What does it laugh in line 22?

Carl Sandburg **463**

Interpreting

4. What does the poet like about Chicago? What negative aspects does he recognize? Explain how the good and bad are related.
5. In what ways does the form of the poem relate to its content?

Extending

6. What qualities of Sandburg's Chicago do you think are still reflected in urban life? Do you find big, bustling cities like Chicago as exciting as Sandburg does? Why or why not?

Jazz Fantasia

Recalling

1. According to lines 1–3, to whom is this poem addressed?
2. Identify at least five musical instruments named in this poem.
3. According to line 7, how should the musicians "moan"? How should they "cry"? According to line 8, like what boat should they sound?

Interpreting

4. What makes this poem a "fantasia"? Identify at least three words or phrases that are slang or ungrammatical. Why is the use of such words or phrases appropriate?
5. What human emotions and human situations does the poet feel jazz expresses?
6. Explain the transition, or change, that "Can the rough stuff" signals.

Extending

7. What would you say is Sandburg's attitude toward America and Americans, based on "Chicago" and this poem? What would you say is his attitude toward modern life and the whirlwind of changes that occurred at the beginning of this century? How are his attitude and his outlook different from J. Alfred Prufrock's (page 443)?

VIEWPOINT

In his biography of Sandburg, Professor Richard Crowder comments:

> Whether consciously or not, Sandburg sensed that the spirit of Chicago could not be expressed totally in the confines of the usual lyric verse. . . . "Chicago" unlocked both language, form, and subject matter in a way that some critics found distasteful, some puzzling, and some invigorating.
>
> —Carl Sandburg

■ How does Sandburg's free-verse form relate to the spirit of Chicago that he wishes to convey? Why do you think some critics in Sandburg's day might have found the language and subject matter of "Chicago" distasteful or puzzling?

LITERARY FOCUS

Jazz Rhythms and Onomatopoeia

When someone once asked him what jazz was, Louis Armstrong replied, "If you have to ask, you'll never know." Armstrong was one of many New Orleans artists who relocated in Chicago after 1919, making that city the center of jazz for a decade. And not just any decade—the twenties were the Jazz Age, when the originally black American music became music for all Americans and a symbol of the "roaring" times.

Jazz has a "feel" to it that cannot be well described in writing. If other music is usually *on* the beat, jazz is usually a bit *off* the beat, or *syncopated.* If the main aspect of most western music is its tune, the main feature of jazz is its rhythm. If most musicians follow their music to the note, jazz musicians do not: They *improvise.*

In "Jazz Fantasia" Sandburg not only wants to write about jazz, he wants to suggest something of its sound and rhythm:

> let your TROMbones OOZE, and go HUSHa-HUSHa-HUSH with the slippery SANDpaper.

The **onomatopoeia,** or use of words to imitate sounds, helps capture the rhythm: The stressed *hush-* followed by the unstressed *-a* and then repeated imitates the sandpaper's sound.

Thinking About Jazz Rhythms and Onomatopoeia

■ What other instances of onomatopoeia does "Jazz Fantasia" contain? How do they help capture jazz rhythms?

Edna St. Vincent Millay   *1892–1950*

Edna St. Vincent Millay wrote of the rebellious spirit of her generation in the traditional language and style of Romantic poetry, and so achieved popularity with Modernist and Traditionalist alike.

Millay was born in Rockland, Maine, and educated at Vassar College. She began writing poetry in early youth; in fact, her popular poem *Renascence,* published when she was still at Vassar, had been written when she was in high school.

After college Millay headed straight for Greenwich Village, the section of New York City that had become the center for artists, intellectuals, and a Bohemian life style. The beautiful Edna Millay was a popular member of Greenwich Village society: She knew all sorts of people, acted in "experimental" theaters, and was the envy of hundreds of young Americans who read her poetry. Among her early volumes are *A Few Figs from Thistles* (1920), *Second April* (1921), and *The Harp-Weaver and Other Poems* (1923), for which she won the Pulitzer Prize.

Millay married in 1923 and lived the rest of her life on a farm in upstate New York. Nevertheless, she continued writing. During the Depression her poetry became more socially aware, and with the approach of World War II, she wrote many attacks on the Fascist regimes in Europe.

Most of Millay's poetry expresses personal joys and sorrows in sonnets and other strict verse forms. "Recuerdo," which means "I remember" in Spanish, dates from her Greenwich Village years. It is a melodious expression of the fun of being young and in love in the middle of New York City.

Edna St. Vincent Millay

Recuerdo

We were very tired, we were very merry—
We had gone back and forth all night on the ferry.
It was bare and bright, and smelled like a stable—
But we looked into a fire, we leaned across a table,
5 We lay on a hilltop underneath the moon;
And the whistles kept blowing, and the dawn came soon.

We were very tired, we were very merry—
We had gone back and forth all night on the ferry;
And you ate an apple, and I ate a pear,
10 From a dozen of each we had bought somewhere;
And the sky went wan, and the wind came cold,
And the sun rose dripping, a bucketful of gold.

We were very tired, we were very merry,
We had gone back and forth all night on the ferry.
15 We hailed, "Good morrow, mother!" to a shawl-covered head,
And bought a morning paper, which neither of us read;
And she wept, "God bless you!" for the apples and pears,
And we gave her all our money but our subway fares.

STUDY QUESTIONS

Recalling
1. What did the speaker and her companion do all night?
2. What did the speaker and her companion buy from a "shawl-covered head"? What did they give to the woman?

Interpreting
3. Who is "you" in line 9? Describe the speaker's relationship with this person.

4. Did the appearance of the ferry (line 2) and the weather conditions (line 11) matter to the speaker and her companion? Explain. What is suggested by the purchase of a paper "which neither of us read" and by the gifts to the old woman?
5. Why are the repetitions in the poem appropriate to its content?
6. What qualities of the speaker's way of life encourage her generosity? What does line 12 suggest about the source of the poet's real wealth?

Edgar Lee Masters   *1869–1950*

Edgar Lee Masters considered his midwestern childhood restrictive, but although he became a prosperous Chicago lawyer, his poetic imagination remained in the town where he had grown up. Masters was born in Garnett, Kansas, and spent most of his youth in southern Illinois, in the same rural area where Abraham Lincoln had spent his early years. In 1892 Masters moved to Chicago, where despite a thriving practice as a criminal lawyer, he began to contribute to *Poetry* magazine. Although he wrote a number of novels and plays, he is best remembered for *Spoon River Anthology* (1915), a poetic examination of small-town life in the Midwest.

The stories of the people who lived on the fictitious Spoon River are told in free verse like that popularized by Carl Sandburg. In subject matter *Spoon River* bears a similarity to the Tilbury Town poems of Edwin Arlington Robinson.

The people of Spoon River are now in the town cemetery. They "speak" from their graves, summing up their lives.

Edgar Lee Masters

Cassius Hueffer

They have chiseled on my stone the words:
"His life was gentle, and the elements so mixed in him
That nature might stand up and say to all the world,
This was a man."[1]
5 Those who knew me smile
As they read this empty rhetoric.

My epitaph[2] should have been:
"Life was not gentle to him,
And the elements so mixed in him
10 That he made warfare on life,
In the which he was slain."
While I lived I could not cope with slanderous tongues,
Now that I am dead I must submit to an epitaph
Graven by a fool!

---

1. **"His life . . . man"**: from Mark Antony's eulogy of Brutus
in Shakespeare's *Julius Caesar* (Act V, Scene v, lines 73–75).
2. **epitaph** [ep′ ə taf]: inscription on a tombstone.

Edgar Lee Masters

Lucinda Matlock

I went to the dances at Chandlerville,
And played snap-out[1] at Winchester.
One time we changed partners,
Driving home in the moonlight of middle June,
And then I found Davis.
We were married and lived together for seventy years,
Enjoying, working, raising the twelve children,
Eight of whom we lost
Ere I had reached the age of sixty.
I spun, I wove, I kept the house, I nursed the sick,
I made the garden, and for holiday
Rambled over the fields where sang the larks,
And by Spoon River gathering many a shell,
And many a flower and medicinal weed—
Shouting to the wooded hills, singing to the green valleys.
At ninety-six I had lived enough, that is all,
And passed to a sweet repose.
What is this I hear of sorrow and weariness,
Anger, discontent and drooping hopes?
Degenerate sons and daughters,
Life is too strong for you—
It takes life to love Life.

---

1. **snap-out:** game in which players hold hands in a long line and those at the end of the line are flung off when the leader makes a sudden turn.

STUDY QUESTIONS

Cassius Hueffer

Recalling

1. According to the epitaph on his grave, what was Hueffer's life?
2. According to Hueffer, how did "life" treat him?
3. What must Hueffer "submit to" now that he is dead, according to the last two lines?

Interpreting

4. Is the actual epitaph on Hueffer's grave a complimentary one? Why do people who knew Hueffer smile?
5. Does Hueffer blame himself for his unhappy life? Explain.
6. What does Hueffer's anger at the false epitaph reveal about his attitude during his life?

Extending

7. What do you think Lucinda Matlock would have told Hueffer? What might he have told her?

Lucinda Matlock

Recalling

1. How did Lucinda Matlock meet Davis? Who was Davis?
2. For how long did Lucinda Matlock live with her husband? How many children did they have? What happened to eight of them?
3. How old was Lucinda Matlock when she "had lived enough"?
4. What question does Lucinda Matlock ask? What does Lucinda Matlock say it takes "to love Life"?

Interpreting

5. What details of Lucinda Matlock's life would most people in the twentieth century find remarkable? Based on lines 6–9 and 10–17, does Lucinda Matlock think her life was remarkable?
6. Whom in particular is Lucinda Matlock addressing in this poem? Why does she address these people? What, basically, is she telling them?

Extending

7. Do you think Lucinda Matlock has a message for people today? Of what people from America's past does she remind you? Explain your answers.

COMPOSITION

Writing About Character

In a brief essay describe either Lucinda Matlock or Cassius Hueffer. Begin by stating what you believe were the person's significant characteristics, and then support your statement with details from the poem.

Writing an Epitaph

Write a poem in which a character you create speaks his or her own epitaph. Try to have your character clearly display some aspect of human nature; for example, he or she might be bitter, devout, ambitious, or hypocritical. Use free verse, as Masters does.

COMPARING WRITERS

Just as writers are often affected by the literary movements of their day, they are usually influenced by those who wrote before them. How is Sandburg reminiscent of Whitman? What aspects of traditional nineteenth-century poetry does Millay's poem exhibit? What do the poems of Edgar Lee Masters and Edwin Arlington Robinson have in common?

Jean Toomer   *1894–1967*

During the 1920s black literature flourished, particularly among writers in the Harlem section of New York City. This important flowering of black arts and letters became known as the Harlem Renaissance, and Jean Toomer was one of its most talented figures.

Toomer was born in Washington, D.C., and attended college in several parts of the United States. He then went to teach school in Georgia, where he absorbed the sights and sounds that went into *Cane* (1923). After settling in Harlem and contributing to a variety of literary journals, Toomer's interests turned to religion and philosophy, and he wrote a number of essays on these subjects. Like Melville, he was an almost forgotten writer for many years. His works were rediscovered in the 1960s.

Cane has since become one of the classics of black American literature. An unusual book, it combines prose sketches of black Southerners with poetry that expresses Toomer's feelings about identity and southern life. As a series of fragments meant to be brought together in the reader's mind, it resembles Eliot's *Waste Land* and Hemingway's *In Our Time* and reflects the Modernist experimentation of the period. In the following poem from *Cane,* Toomer captures the surprise of unseasonable weather in rural Georgia.

Jean Toomer

November Cotton Flower

Boll weevil's[1] coming, and the winter's cold,
Made cotton stalks look rusty, seasons old,
And cotton, scarce as any southern snow,
Was vanishing; the branch,[2] so pinched and slow,
5 Failed in its function as the autumn rake;
Drought fighting soil had caused the soil to take
All water from the streams; dead birds were found
In wells a hundred feet below the ground—
Such was the season when the flower bloomed.
10 Old folks were startled, and it soon assumed
Significance. Superstition saw
Something it had never seen before:
Brown eyes that loved without a trace of fear,
Beauty so sudden for that time of year.

---

1. **boll weevil** [bōl′wē′vəl]: long-beaked beetle whose larvae
eat and destroy cotton bolls.
2. **branch:** here, a small stream.

STUDY QUESTIONS

Recalling

1. What two things, according to line 1, make the cotton stalks look rusty and old? What happens to the cotton in lines 3–4?
2. What event startles the "old folks," according to lines 9–11?
3. What does the poet say this unexpected event soon assumes?
4. What two things has "Superstition" never seen before?

Interpreting

5. In what season does this poem take place? What do the details of lines 1–8 imply about the human emotions this season usually arouses? What event makes this year different?
6. How does Toomer make the sudden bloom come as a surprise to the reader as well as to the people of Georgia?
7. Who is superstitious? What does the final couplet suggest about the effects of the sudden bloom on most human beings?

Countee Cullen 1903–1946

Countee Cullen was a central figure in New York's black literary circles at the time of the Harlem Renaissance. He began to publish poetry while still a student at New York University, and after getting his master's degree from Harvard, became an editor of *Opportunity,* an influential black journal. His first poetry collection, *Color,* was published in 1925 and was rapidly followed by *Copper Sun* and *The Ballad of the Brown Girl.*

In 1928 Cullen went to Paris on a Guggenheim fellowship. After his return he taught French in New York City public schools and continued to write and edit. In his later years he published two books for children, *The Lost Zoo* (1940) and *My Lives and How I Lost Them* (1942).

"Any Human to Another" shows that Cullen resisted the influence of the Modernists. His favorite poet was the English Romantic John Keats, and his style retains the nineteenth-century traditions of stanza, rhyme, and direct statement.

Tombstones,
Jacob Lawrence, 1942.

Countee Cullen

Any Human to Another

The ills I sorrow at
Not me alone
Like an arrow,
Pierce to the marrow,
5 Through the fat
And past the bone.

Your grief and mine
Must intertwine
Like sea and river,
10 Be fused and mingle,
Diverse yet single,
Forever and forever.

Let no man be so proud
And confident,
15 To think he is allowed
A little tent
Pitched in a meadow
Of sun and shadow
All his little own.

20 Joy may be shy, unique,
Friendly to a few,
Sorrow never scorned to speak
To any who
Were false or true.

25 Your every grief
Like a blade
Shining and unsheathed
Must strike me down.
Of bitter aloes[1] wreathed,
30 My sorrow must be laid
On your head like a crown.

_____
1. **aloes** [al′ōz]: spiny plants of the lily family,
native to South Africa. The medicinal
juice of the plant has a very bitter taste.

STUDY QUESTIONS

Recalling
1. According to the title, who is speaking to whom?
2. What does the speaker not do alone, according to the first stanza? What two things must intertwine, according to the second stanza?
3. What is no one allowed, according to the third stanza?
4. According to the fourth stanza, what may joy be? To whom does sorrow never scorn to speak?

Interpreting
5. Restate the idea expressed in the third stanza without using figurative language.
6. Basically, why does the speaker feel we must share his sorrow? Precisely whose sorrow does he feel we must share?

Extending
7. Why is this a traditional poem by nineteenth-century standards? (See the explanation of Imagism on page 441 and of Modernism on pages 431–433.)

Langston Hughes *1902–1967*

Langston Hughes was the most accomplished poet of the Harlem Renaissance. A true "Renaissance man," he wrote drama, fiction, popular songs, and movie screenplays; worked on anthologies and translations; and generously helped the careers of many younger writers. He is, however, best noted for his poetry.

Hughes was born in Missouri and went to high school in Cleveland, Ohio, where he began writing poetry for a school magazine. He went on to Columbia University in New York City but a year later left to go to sea. After traveling as a merchant seaman to Africa and Europe, he returned to America and continued writing poetry. His work appeared in a number of prominent black journals and in the chief anthology of the Harlem Renaissance, *The New Negro* (1925).

The poet Vachel Lindsay helped Hughes publish his first volume of poetry, *The Weary Blues* (1926). His literary reputation secure, Hughes decided to complete his formal education. After graduating from Lincoln University, he returned to New York City, where he continued to write and was active in the theater. His later books of poems include *The Dream Keeper* (1932), *Fields of Wonder* (1947), and *Montage of a Dream Deferred* (1951). He wrote two autobiographical volumes, *The Big Sea* (1940) and *I Wonder as I Wander* (1956).

Much of Hughes's best writing appeared in newspapers. Especially popular were the sketches he wrote for the Chicago *Defender* during the 1940s. These short tales chronicle the adventures of a character named Simple, whose innocent but shrewd observations of the world gave Hughes many opportunities for sharp satire and social criticism.

"Dream Variations" demonstrates how well Hughes had absorbed the international Modernist techniques and adapted them to his subject matter and to jazz and blues rhythms.

Langston Hughes

Dream Variations

To fling my arms wide
In some place of the sun,
To whirl and to dance
Till the white day is done.
5 Then rest at cool evening
Beneath a tall tree
While night comes on gently,
    Dark like me—
That is my dream!

10 To fling my arms wide
In the face of the sun,
Dance! Whirl! Whirl!
Till the quick day is done.
Rest at pale evening . . .
15 A tall, slim tree . . .
Night coming tenderly
    Black like me.

STUDY QUESTIONS

Recalling

1. Where does the speaker want to fling his arms wide, according to the first stanza? According to the second stanza?
2. What is night called in line 8? In line 17?

Interpreting

3. What does the speaker associate with day and night?
4. What are the variations in the poem, as suggested by the title?

5. Which two lines make a slight shift in the poem's meter, or regular rhythm? Which line breaks the meter completely? What does the irregular rhythm of these lines suggest, or what effect does it seem to create?

COMPARING WRITERS

■ Toomer, Cullen, and Hughes all wrote of the experience of being black. What comments do their poems make about the black experience? What elements in their poems are also universal?

John Crowe Ransom   *1888–1974*

John Crowe Ransom was one of the most influential critics of his time, as well as a poet in his own right. Born in Tennessee, Ransom first taught at Vanderbilt University, from which he had graduated before going on to Oxford University in England. At Vanderbilt, and later at Kenyon College in Ohio, Professor Ransom was at the center of an important circle of critics who brought about a revolution in the way we read literature.

Ransom's critical theories are contained in *The New Criticism* (1941), a work whose title gave a name to the revolution in critical thinking that Ransom helped lead. The New Critics give scrupulous attention to the *text* of a literary work, looking at what the text actually does instead of seeking its meaning in the author's biography or in ideas external to the work. In emphasizing that a literary work should "stand alone," the New Critics were obviously influenced by Pound and the Imagists (see page 441).

Ransom's background as professor and critic is apparent in his poetry: A self-conscious critical intelligence seems always to be looking over the poet's shoulder. His poems are noted for their craftsmanship and for their poised irony; they are extremely non-Romantic in tone but often formal in style.

In "Janet Waking" Ransom takes a subject that can easily lead to sentimentality—the death of a child's pet—and treats it in an unsentimental way. He achieves this lack of sentiment through a highly structured format and by shifting from childish to "adult" language, thereby distancing himself from the child's emotions with his characteristic aloofness.

John Crowe Ransom

Janet Waking

Beautifully Janet slept
Till it was deeply morning. She woke then
And thought about her dainty-feathered hen,
To see how it had kept.

5 One kiss she gave her mother.
Only a small one gave she to her daddy
Who would have kissed each curl of his
    shining baby;
No kiss at all for her brother.

"Old Chucky, old Chucky!" she cried,
10 Running across the world upon the grass
To Chucky's house, and listening. But alas,
Her Chucky had died.

It was a transmogrifying[1] bee
Came droning down to Chucky's old bald head
15 And sat and put the poison. It scarcely bled,
But how exceedingly

And purply did the knot
Swell with the venom and communicate
Its rigor![2] Now the poor comb[3] stood
    up straight
20 But Chucky did not.

So there was Janet
Kneeling on the wet grass, crying her
    brown hen
(Translated[4] far beyond the daughters of men)
To rise and walk upon it.

25 And weeping fast as she had breath
Janet implored us, "Wake her from her sleep!"
And would not be instructed in how deep
Was the forgetful kingdom of death.

---

1. **transmogrifying** [trans mog′rə fī′ing]: transforming
in a grotesque manner.
2. **rigor:** severity; here, referring to *rigor mortis,*
the stiffening of body tissues after death.
3. **comb:** red, fleshy outgrowth on a chicken's head.
4. **translated:** transported.

STUDY QUESTIONS

Recalling
1. What does Janet think about when she wakes up? What does she discover?
2. What does Janet cry for the pet to do in the sixth stanza? What does she ask "us" in the last stanza? In what will she not be "instructed"?

Interpreting
3. Describe the tone of lines 19–20. What is the effect of these lines?
4. What is childish about Janet's actions in the second stanza? Is her reaction to Chucky's death equally childish? From what is Janet "waking"?

Extending
5. If you were Janet's parents, what would you do after providing the "instruction" in the last lines?

COMPOSITION

Writing About Poetry
In a brief essay analyze the structure of "Janet Waking." First describe the strict stanza form and rhyme scheme. Then discuss any breaks in meter and any slant rhymes that vary the strict form. Finally consider how the structure of the poem relates to its tone and content.

Writing a Narrative
Write a short narrative composition, or a poem if you wish, about an ordinary, everyday event. Describe the event in such a way, however, that it does not seem ordinary. Point out its causes and effects. Give details that bring out the drama or the suspense of the event. Conclude with a statement of the meaning of the event to those who experienced it.

Archibald MacLeish   *1892–1982*

Archibald MacLeish attended Yale and the Harvard Law School, but he soon gave up law for literature. During the 1920s he spent five years in Paris, home to many American artists for whom experimentation was the order of the day. Two of his early volumes of poetry, *The Happy Marriage* (1924) and *Streets in the Moon* (1926), reflect the influence of Pound and Eliot.

When MacLeish returned to America, however, he departed from his Paris Modernism, seeking to reach a wider audience by making his poetry more accessible. He turned toward public speech, reciting his poetry before large gatherings and earning a reputation as a fine orator. He also held a series of important government posts during and after World War II. His *Collected Poems* appeared in 1950; in 1959 he won a Pulitzer Prize for *J. B., A Play in Verse,* a modern version of the biblical Book of Job.

In later years MacLeish taught rhetoric at Harvard and often appeared on television. Like Carl Sandburg and Robert Frost, he became one of America's best known and most revered poets. He was often called upon to write poems commemorating landmark American events.

The famous "Ars Poetica" is a product of MacLeish's Paris days, when he had abandoned traditional poetic forms. Its much-quoted final lines, "A poem should not mean / But be," sum up one of the chief doctrines of Imagism.

Plant Forms,
Arthur Dove, 1915.

Archibald MacLeish

Ars Poetica

A poem should be palpable[1] and mute
As a globed fruit,

Dumb
As old medallions to the thumb,

5 Silent as the sleeve-worn stone
Of casement ledges where the moss
    has grown—

A poem should be wordless
As the flight of birds.

A poem should be motionless in time
10 As the moon climbs,

Leaving, as the moon releases
Twig by twig the night-entangled trees,

Leaving, as the moon behind the winter leaves,
Memory by memory the mind—

15 A poem should be motionless in time
As the moon climbs.

A poem should be equal to:
Not true.

For all the history of grief
20 An empty doorway and a maple leaf.

For love
The leaning grasses and two lights
    above the sea—

A poem should not mean
But be.

---

1. **palpable:** tangible; able to be touched and felt.

STUDY QUESTIONS

Recalling
1. What five adjectives in the first eight lines describe what a poem should be?
2. According to the second section, what should a poem be?
3. Rather than be "true," what should a poem be? Rather than "mean," what should it do?

Interpreting
4. How are the adjectives in lines 3, 5, and 7 related to "mute" in line 1? How can a poem be "palpable and mute"? What does "globed" suggest about the poem?
5. Is the statement in line 1 abstract or concrete? How does the simile in line 2 help explain it? Do lines 3–4, 5–6, and 7–8 follow the same logic?
6. What might line 9 mean? Why does the poet repeat lines 9–10 at the end of the second section?
7. What do lines 19–22 suggest a poet should do to capture "the history of grief" or "love"? What does MacLeish therefore mean in lines 17–18? Why would he single out "the history of grief" or "love"?
8. Explain in your own words the basic rule of Imagism stated in lines 23–24. Why is "Ars Poetica" *not* a pure Imagist poem?

VIEWPOINT

Archibald MacLeish was not the first poet to attempt to define his art; poets have done so throughout the centuries. In a 1923 article in the *Atlantic Monthly* Carl Sandburg said:

> poetry is the achievement of the synthesis
> of hyacinths and biscuits.
> —"Poetry Considered"

▪ How is Sandburg's definition like MacLeish's in its *means* of conveying information? How is the "message" itself different? What are the implications of the word *biscuits*, and how do "biscuits" differ from the images MacLeish chooses?

Marianne Moore   *1887–1972*

Marianne Moore is among the most delightful of American poets. Her witty, sharp, and strangely fascinating poems offer sparkling surfaces that quickly grasp her readers' attention and keep them alert.

Moore was born in Missouri, studied biology at Bryn Mawr College in Pennsylvania, and later moved to Brooklyn, New York. Her interest in science never left her, and it is apparent in both the subject matter and the precision of her verse. For a time she edited the influential New York literary journal *The Dial,* but she gained a large measure of popularity for a completely different reason: She was a passionate baseball fan.

In 1919 Moore sent some of her poetry to Ezra Pound, from whom she received much encouragement. She became widely admired by other poets, yet she herself was shy about publishing her work. Her first volume of poetry was published in England in 1921—without her knowledge and much to her annoyance—by H. D. and another admirer. Later volumes include *Observations* (1924) and *Selected Poems* (1935). Moore is also noted for her delightful translations of the French writer La Fontaine's *Fables* (1954).

Moore's poetry is refreshingly original; her vision is precise but rather eccentric. The brilliant and oblique surfaces of her poems are filled with observations of animals and nature, even as she cryptically tosses in mysterious quotations from her reading. Moore darts out with lines that move us immediately, but no sooner has her more direct self appeared than it disappears again, withdrawn behind her famous reticence.

"Poetry" is Moore's most frequently reprinted poem, a playful yet thoughtful reply to someone who seems to have told the poet that he or she did not "like" poetry. "Arthur Mitchell" describes the dancer and founder of the Dance Theater of Harlem, perhaps in his most famous role, that of Puck in Mendelssohn's ballet *A Midsummer Night's Dream.*

Marianne Moore

Poetry

I, too, dislike it: there are things that are important beyond all this fiddle.
   Reading it, however, with a perfect contempt for it, one discovers in
   it after all, a place for the genuine.
      Hands that can grasp, eyes
5   that can dilate, hair that can rise
         if it must, these things are important not because a

high-sounding interpretation can be put upon them but because they are
   useful. When they become so derivative[1] as to become unintelligible,
   the same thing may be said for all of us, that we
10   do not admire what
      we cannot understand: the bat
         holding on upside down or in quest of something to

eat, elephants pushing, a wild horse taking a roll, a tireless wolf under
   a tree, the immovable critic twitching his skin like a horse that feels a flea, the base-
15   ball fan, the statistician—
      nor is it valid
         to discriminate against "business documents and

schoolbooks"; all these phenomena are important. One must make a distinction
   however: when dragged into prominence by half poets, the result is not poetry,
20   nor till the poets among us can be
      "literalists of
      the imagination"—above
         insolence and triviality and can present

for inspection, "imaginary gardens with real toads in them," shall we have
25   it. In the meantime, if you demand on the one hand,
   the raw material of poetry in
      all its rawness and
      that which is on the other hand
         genuine, you are interested in poetry.

---

1. **derivative:** arrived at through complex reasoning and deduction.

Marianne Moore

Arthur Mitchell

Slim dragonfly
too rapid for the eye
    to cage—
contagious gem of virtuosity—
5 make visible, mentality.
Your jewels of mobility

reveal
  and veil
    a peacock-tail.

Dancer Arthur Mitchell at home.

STUDY QUESTIONS

Poetry

Recalling

1. What does the poet call poetry in line 1? What does she say one discovers when reading poetry "with a perfect contempt for it"?
2. According to the poet, why are the things in lines 4–5 important? Why are they *not* important? When poems "become so derivative as to become unintelligible," what is our reaction?
3. What "distinction" must we make about poetry, according to lines 18–19? What would ideal poets be, according to lines 21–22, and what would they "present for inspection"?

Interpreting

4. What do lines 4–5 suggest about the elements that make good poetry "genuine"? What kind of poetry does Moore *dis*like?
5. What does Moore mean by "imaginary gardens with real toads in them"?
6. Why is the argument of the poem made more effective by the poet's pretending to agree with someone who dislikes poetry?

Arthur Mitchell

Recalling

1. For what is Mitchell "too rapid"? What sort of "gem" is he? What does he "make visible"?
2. What do Mitchell's "jewels of mobility" do?

Interpreting

3. What does "virtuosity" suggest about Mitchell's talents as a dancer?
4. In what way might Mitchell's art be "contagious"? What has it prompted in Moore?
5. What is a peacock's tail like when it opens? When it closes? What do the last three lines therefore imply about Mitchell's art?
6. In addition to Mitchell's art, what art does this poem seem to be about? What might the last three lines therefore imply?

VOCABULARY

Synonyms

A **synonym** is a word that has the same or nearly the same meaning as another word. *Joy* and *exaltation* are synonyms. The words in capital letters are from "Poetry." Choose the word that is nearest the meaning of each word in capitals, *as it is used in the selection.*

1. INSOLENCE: (a) pride (b) insomnia (c) privacy (d) insult
2. TRIVIALITY: (a) pot holder (b) temptation (c) something unimportant (d) surface
3. CONTEMPT: (a) relief (b) scorn (c) amazement (d) pity
4. PHENOMENA: (a) trifles (b) happenings (c) phantoms (d) eons
5. DISCRIMINATE: (a) let go (b) cheat (c) show anger (d) show preference

COMPARING WRITERS

For centuries poets have felt a need to keep defining, describing, and defending their art. Compare the definitions and the defenses of poetry in MacLeish's "Ars Poetica" and Moore's "Poetry." How do the poets differ in the images they use to define poetry? What does each say is the purpose of poetry? On what aspects of poetry do you think these two poets would agree?

E. E. Cummings   *1894–1962*

Edward Estlin Cummings, as a poet and as a painter, spent his artistic life in pursuit of one of the most American of goals—individuality. Cummings was born in Cambridge, Massachusetts, the son of a prominent New England clergyman. After graduating from Harvard, he served as an ambulance driver in World War I. He was held in a prison camp in France, an experience that resulted in his powerful book, *The Enormous Room* (1922). He lived briefly in Paris during the early twenties and upon returning to America settled in Greenwich Village, New York's artistic community. His career flourished, and he became one of Greenwich Village's most famous residents.

Both his poetry and his painting reflect Cummings' concern with the need to be independent in our modern age of technology. The first things we notice about his poems are the distinctive arrangements of the words on the page and the use of lowercase letters where earlier poets and more conventional writers use capitals. In fact, the poet liked to sign his work "e. e. cummings" and even had his name legally changed to this lowercase form. He also liked to play with words, to break them apart or use them in unusual ways.

The small letters, the unconventional syntax, and the unusual spacing of words were Cummings' way of expressing individuality and participating in what he called "The New Art." Yet beneath the unconventional Modernist surfaces, Cummings' poetry is a lyrical celebration of the most traditional of poetic subjects: the joy of living ("since feeling is first"), the wonders of nature ("r-p-o-p-h-e-s-s-a-g-r"), and love itself ("your little voice").

E. E. Cummings

since feeling is first

since feeling is first
who pays any attention
to the syntax[1] of things
will never wholly kiss you;
5 wholly to be a fool
while Spring is in the world

my blood approves,
and kisses are a better fate
than wisdom
10 lady i swear by all flowers. Don't cry
—the best gesture of my brain is less than
your eyelids' flutter which says

we are for each other: then
laugh, leaning back in my arms
15 for life's not a paragraph

And death i think is no parenthesis

---

1. **syntax:** systematic arrangement.

r-p-o-p-h-e-s-s-a-g-r

                         r-p-o-p-h-e-s-s-a-g-r
                  who
a)s w(e loo)k
upnowgath
5   PPEGORHRASS
                              eringint(o-
aThe):l
          eA
             !p:
10 S   a
                    (r
rIvInG   .gRrEaPsPhOs)
                                        to
rea(be)rran(com)gi(e)ngly
15 ,grasshopper;

E. E. Cummings

your little voice

your little voice
                    Over the wires came leaping
and i felt suddenly
dizzy
        With the jostling and shouting of merry flowers
wee skipping high-heeled flames
5 courtesied before my eyes
                            or twinkling over to my side
Looked up
with impertinently exquisite faces
floating hands were laid upon me
I was whirled and tossed into delicious dancing
10 up
Up
with the pale important
                        stars and the Humorous
                                                    moon
dear girl
How i was crazy how i cried when i heard
                                        over time
15 and tide and death
leaping
Sweetly
            your voice

STUDY QUESTIONS

since feeling is first

Recalling

1. What will a person "who pays attention to the syntax of things" never do?
2. Of what does the speaker's "blood" approve? What is a better fate than wisdom?
3. What is more than the "best gesture" of the speaker's brain? What does the flutter of the lady's eyelids say?
4. Why should the lady laugh?

Interpreting

5. With what is "syntax" contrasted? What does it represent? With what is "wisdom" contrasted? What is the relationship between the flutter of the lady's eyelids and "feeling"?
6. Basically, what is the speaker saying to the reader? To the lady?

r-p-o-p-h-e-s-s-a-g-r

Interpreting

1. How does the overall shape of the poem relate to its subject?
2. Why are the letters in the words jumbled?

your little voice

Recalling

1. Over what does the "dear girl's" voice come leaping in the first line? How does the speaker suddenly feel when the voice comes leaping?
2. Identify at least three images that the speaker associates with his dizziness.
3. Over what does the "dear girl's" little voice come leaping in the last five lines?

Interpreting

4. What ordinary experience of modern life does the poem make extraordinary?
5. How does the speaker feel about the "dear girl"?

Extending

6. What aspect of each of Cummings' poems makes it original and refreshing?

LITERARY FOCUS

The Shape of Poems

E. E. Cummings was among the first generation of poets who composed on the typewriter, and this instrument had a strong influence on his work. Poets composing on the typewriter found that they could visualize ways of spacing their lines and words that they would not have considered if their manuscripts were handwritten.

"r-p-o-p-h-e-s-s-a-g-r" is a classic example of a poem that is basically visual. It cannot be read aloud; its attempt is to capture, through word juggling, strange spacing, and surprising punctuation, the effect of a grasshopper gathering, leaping, and rearranging itself. The shape of the poem is a large part of its meaning.

In "The Artist" (page 451) William Carlos Williams also considers the shape of his poem on the printed page. The lines are divided into three groups of words of approximately the same lengths so that each line makes visual the dance step performed by Mr. T. with its final, abrupt end. The shape reflects the meaning.

Since playing with the shape of a poem was another means of breaking with the traditional conventions of stanza and meter, the practice became popular with many Modernist poets. As time passed, however, these visual games began to be less and less surprising.

Thinking About the Shape of Poems

▮ How does the shape of "your little voice" reflect the content of the poem? Why does "up" appear as the only word on line 11 and line 12? Why is the second "up" capitalized?

COMPOSITION

Writing a Paraphrase

▮ Rewrite the three poems by Cummings in prose paragraph form, using conventional English. Use correct punctuation, capitalization, and spellings, and add or change words for clarity where necessary. Conclude by telling what you think the poems gain and what they lose in paraphrases.

Writing a Poem with Shape

▮ Choose an object or a creature that has a characteristic motion, and write a poem in which you capture that motion by playing with words and their visual appearance on the page, as "r-p-o-p-h-e-s-s-a-g-r" does. If a typewriter is unavailable, print your poem so that the spacing is clear. You might write about a basketball, a diver, a toaster, or a kangaroo.

Wallace Stevens   *1879–1955*

Stevens wrote, "The greatest poverty is not to live in a physical world." As a poet Stevens never stopped emphasizing the relationship between the concrete, physical world and the shaping power of the human imagination. He spent a lifetime putting into words the joy that comes from looking at "things as they are" and thinking about them.

Stevens was born in Pennsylvania and attended Harvard before moving to New York City, where he attended law school. In New York he mingled with other young writers, among them William Carlos Williams and Marianne Moore. His poems began to appear in magazines in 1914. Two years later Stevens and his wife moved to Hartford, Connecticut, where he worked as a lawyer; eventually he became vice-president of a large insurance company. He wrote his poetry on evenings and weekends, just as his friend Williams wrote after a busy day as a family doctor.

For most of his life Stevens drew a line, he said, between poetry and business. He kept his comfortable life quite uneventful, especially as compared to the lives of contemporary poets who fought in wars, sailed the oceans, and lived in Paris and Greenwich Village. On the other hand, his imaginative life was full: He wrote poems overflowing with ideas, striking images, and brilliant colors that moved him into the ranks of Pound, Eliot, and Frost as one of America's major poets.

Stevens' first volume, *Harmonium,* attracted little attention when it was published in 1923. So great, however, was his reputation among some poets and critics that *Harmonium* was republished in 1931. He did not publish again for more than a decade, but he then began to produce a lush and maturing body of work in *Ideas of Order* (1935), *The Man with the Blue Guitar* (1937), *Parts of a World* (1942), *Transport to Summer* (1947), and *The Auroras of Autumn* (1950). In his later years he began to break down the line between poetry and business, making some public appearances and receiving the honors of a younger generation who had grown up reading Stevens' verse and who had come to see him as a poetic "ancestor."

Living, as Stevens saw it, means to transform reality—what we experience "as and where we live"—by the power of the imagination. His early poems show the imagination in action, changing ordinary subjects into exotic, witty, and elegant lyrics. As he grew in poetic mastery, his poems became more philosophical, taking up the great subjects that Emerson, Whitman, and Dickinson also dealt with: nature, death, joy, the real and the ideal. He explored ways of thinking about reality so that we might find happiness within it, reconciling ourselves to the world we live in and changing with it, finding our way among its confusions. As he says in his greatest poem, *Notes Toward a Supreme Fiction,* "The freshness of transformation is the freshness of a world. It is our own, it is ourselves."

"The Load of Sugar Cane" offers a scene that would be an everyday experience to the unimaginative vision but one that becomes a bright and magical pleasure as Stevens presents and transforms it. "Anecdote of the Jar" also demonstrates the imagination at work, shaping the world around it.

Wallace Stevens

The Load of Sugar Cane

The going of the glade boat[1]
Is like water flowing;

Like water flowing
Through the green saw grass,
5 Under the rainbows;

Under the rainbows
That are like birds,
Turning, bedizened,[2]

While the wind still whistles
10 As kildeer[3] do,

When they rise
At the red turban
Of the boatman.

---

1. **glade boat:** boat specially constructed for gliding through swampland.
2. **bedizened** [bi dī′ zənd]: brilliantly dressed or decorated.
3. **kildeer:** small wading birds with piercing cries.

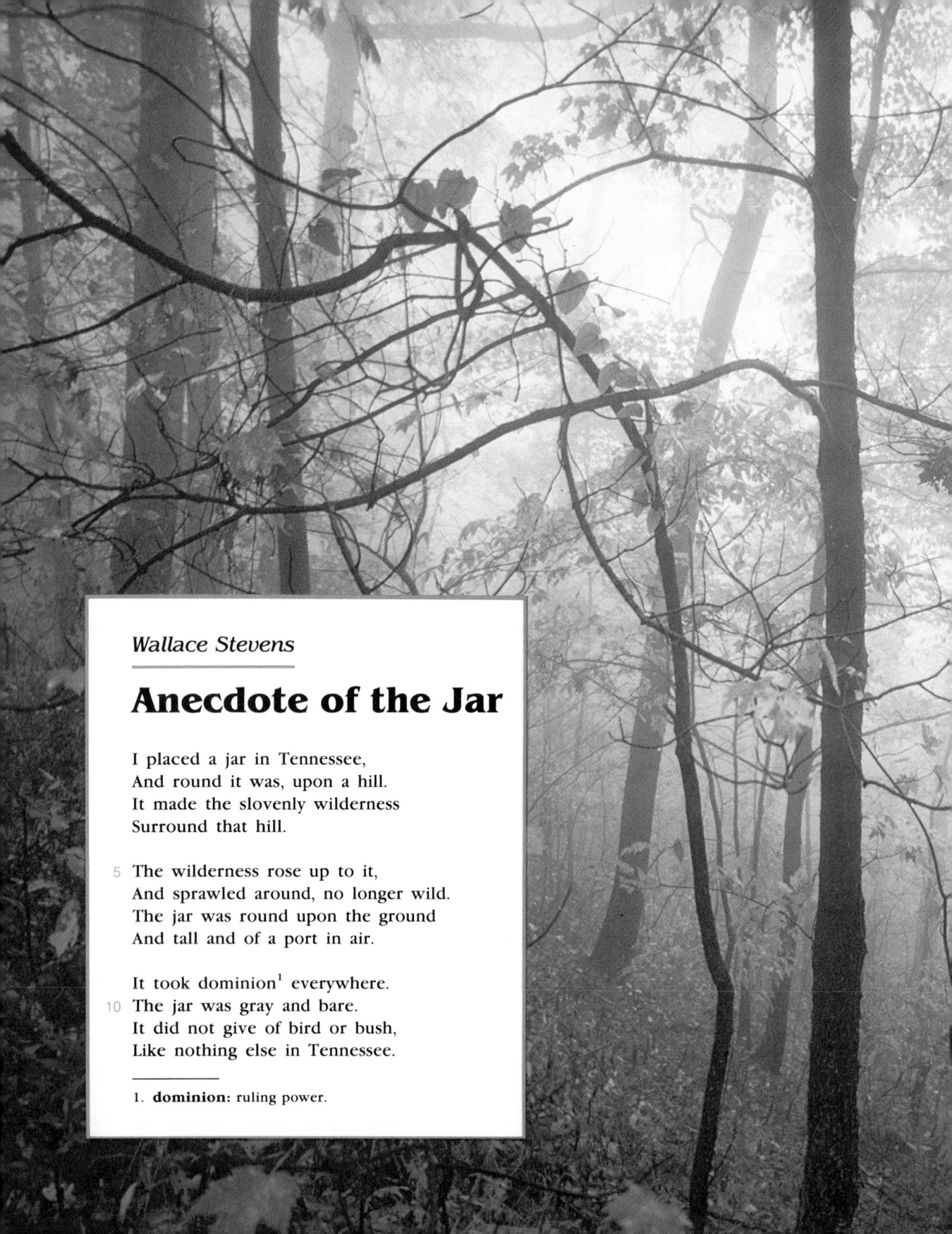

Wallace Stevens

Anecdote of the Jar

I placed a jar in Tennessee,
And round it was, upon a hill.
It made the slovenly wilderness
Surround that hill.

5   The wilderness rose up to it,
And sprawled around, no longer wild.
The jar was round upon the ground
And tall and of a port in air.

It took dominion[1] everywhere.
10 The jar was gray and bare.
It did not give of bird or bush,
Like nothing else in Tennessee.

---

1. **dominion:** ruling power.

STUDY QUESTIONS

The Load of Sugar Cane

Recalling

1. To what is the going of the glade boat likened?
2. Where does the water flow?
3. To what are the rainbows compared?
4. When do the birds turn? In what way does the wind whistle?
5. When do the kildeer whistle? At what do they rise?

Interpreting

6. Consider your answers for questions 1–5, and tell what the "events" in the poem form. That is, where does the poem begin; where does it move to in lines 2–5 and then in lines 6–10; where does the poem end?
7. What poetic devices contribute to the musical effect of this poem?

Anecdote of the Jar

Recalling

1. What shape is the jar? Where does the speaker place it?
2. According to the second stanza, what happens to the wilderness around the jar?
3. What does the jar "take" everywhere? Of what does it "not give"?

Interpreting

4. Explain in your own words the effect of the jar on the Tennessee wilderness. Does its effect seem positive in the first two stanzas? In the third? Why is *jar* an appropriate word?
5. How is a jar different from the wilderness? What might the jar represent?

Extending

6. Do you think ambiguity makes a poem more memorable? More effective? What do you think Marianne Moore (page 480) would have said about this poem?

VIEWPOINT

Lucy Beckett writes that the first lines of Stevens' "Anecdote of the Jar"

> define lightly but as well as any he ever wrote Stevens' hope for poetry, his belief that through it the slovenly wilderness of the modern world can be made, for however transient a time, to yield modern man something that will satisfy his need.
>
> —*Wallace Stevens*

■ Tell in your own words what need it is that the poem attempts to satisfy. Describe how poetry and all the arts attempt to meet that need.

COMPOSITION

Writing About Poetry

■ In a brief essay discuss the use of colors in "The Load of Sugar Cane." First describe the picture the poet tries to paint. Then tell how the colors blend and contrast. Conclude with a statement about the visual impression the poem leaves on the reader.

Writing a Description

■ Write a paragraph or a short poem describing an object or a scene. Use colors to give your reader a vivid impression of what you see. You may want to blend colors, contrast them, or even invent new names for some unusual colors.

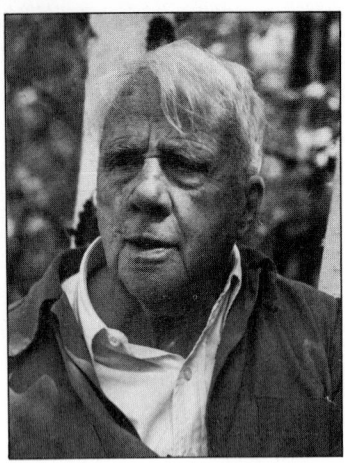

Robert Frost *1874–1963*

Robert Frost—a poet of dignity, simplicity, and ambiguity—has proved to be one of the most popular American poets of the twentieth century. A four-time winner of the Pulitzer Prize, Frost received special recognition by Congress in 1960 and the following January, at age eighty-six, had the honor of reciting at President John F. Kennedy's inauguration.

Frost was born in San Francisco but in early youth returned with his family to the area of the country with which he is closely associated—New England. His mother, who wrote poetry herself, introduced him to the works of the English Romantic writers, the New England Transcendentalists, and the poets of her native Scotland. After briefly attending Dartmouth and Harvard colleges and working as a journalist and a schoolteacher, Frost purchased a farm in New Hampshire. Here, between farm chores, he began his career as a poet.

Frost wrote not only of the natural world but also of his struggle to raise a family against a backdrop of financial hardship and of the bleak bouts of depression that would assail him all his life. In 1912, unable to get his poems published in America, he sold his farm and took his family to England.

In London Frost became acquainted with Ezra Pound and his associates, and he was able to publish his first volume, *A Boy's Will,* in 1913. Another volume, *North of Boston,* followed soon after. Through the influence of Pound and other critics, Frost became known on this side of the Atlantic, so that, by the time he returned to America in 1915, he was well on the road to fame.

Despite the debt of gratitude he owed Pound and the Modernists, Frost never subscribed to all the tenets of Modernism. To be sure, he was familiar with the ideas of William James and other modern psychologists, but he was equally familiar with the works of William Cullen Bryant, Ralph Waldo Emerson, and other nineteenth-century masters. In Frost's work we find traces of the Romantic love of nature that marked the literature of the nineteenth century coupled with a modern sense of irony. We find in Frost's poems some of Thoreau's love of isolation, Hawthorne's dark vision, Longfellow's traditional craftsmanship, Dickinson's dry humor, and Robinson's realistic characterization.

Eclectic in many ways, Frost is nevertheless able to achieve a quiet, reflective New England voice all his own. He speaks a common speech, unaffected, a modern Plain Style. His voice rings in poems that puzzle over many of the same thought-provoking questions that American poets have always explored, but Frost's poems display a twentieth-century poet's uncertainty about what the answers to those questions may be.

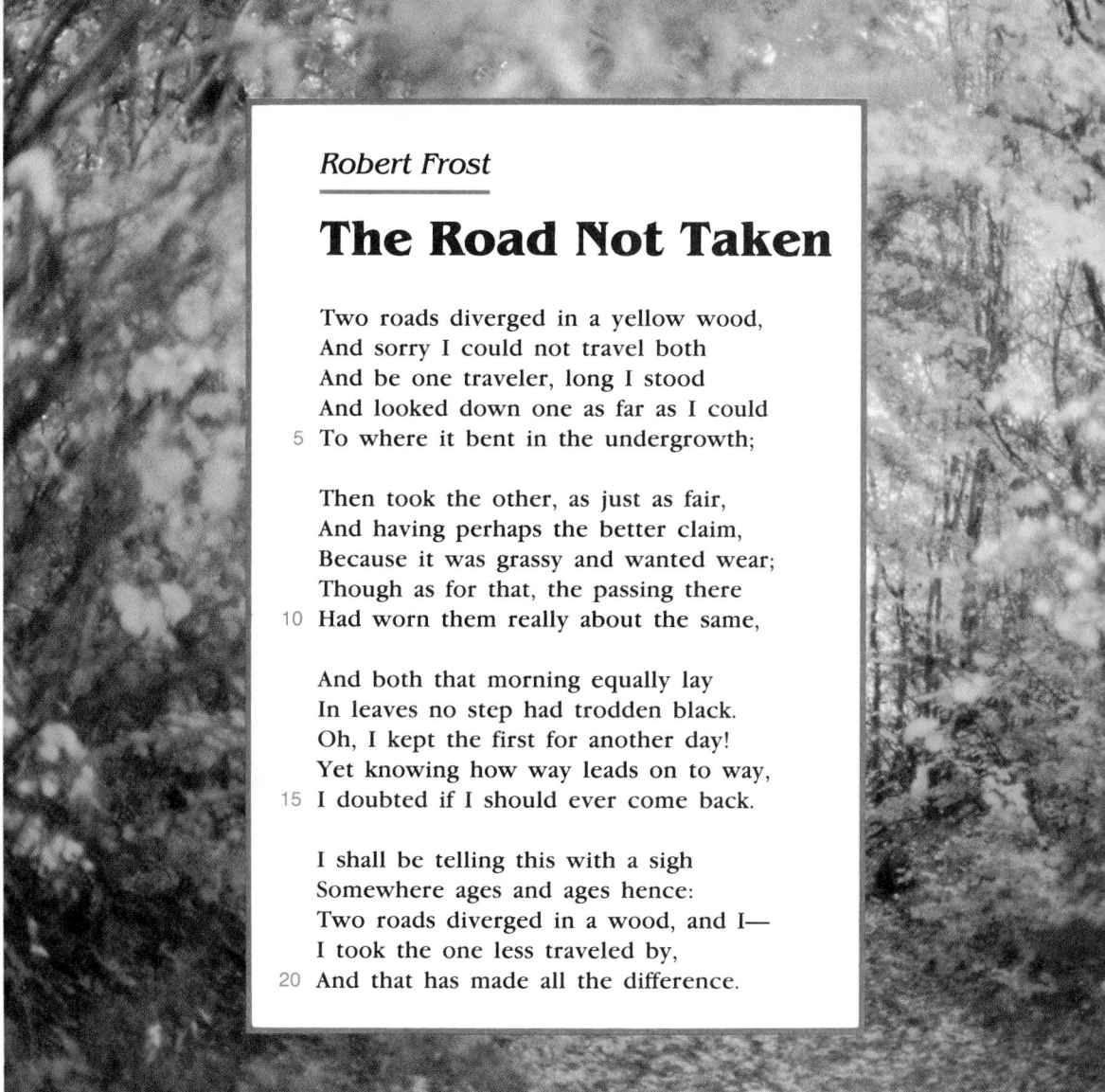

Robert Frost

The Road Not Taken

Two roads diverged in a yellow wood,
And sorry I could not travel both
And be one traveler, long I stood
And looked down one as far as I could
5 To where it bent in the undergrowth;

Then took the other, as just as fair,
And having perhaps the better claim,
Because it was grassy and wanted wear;
Though as for that, the passing there
10 Had worn them really about the same,

And both that morning equally lay
In leaves no step had trodden black.
Oh, I kept the first for another day!
Yet knowing how way leads on to way,
15 I doubted if I should ever come back.

I shall be telling this with a sigh
Somewhere ages and ages hence:
Two roads diverged in a wood, and I—
I took the one less traveled by,
20 And that has made all the difference.

STUDY QUESTIONS

Recalling

1. What diverged in the yellow wood? About what was the speaker sorry in the first stanza? Where does the speaker stand and look?
2. According to line 7, why did the second road have the better claim?
3. For what did the speaker "keep" the first road? What did he doubt?
4. How does the speaker think he will be telling this story "ages and ages hence"? What has "made all the difference"?

Interpreting

5. Considering lines 9–10 and 11–12, how different were the two roads? What is Frost therefore saying?
6. What might the roads represent? What does his choice indicate about the speaker?
7. Does the speaker think he made the wrong choice? Why or why not? How is his attitude related to the title?

Extending

8. Suggest other dilemmas comparable to the speaker's.

Robert Frost

Fire and Ice

Some say the world will end in fire,
Some say in ice.
From what I've tasted of desire
I hold with those who favor fire.
5 But if it had to perish twice,
I think I know enough of hate
To say that for destruction ice
Is also great
And would suffice.

Acquainted with the Night

I have been one acquainted with the night.
I have walked out in rain—and back in rain.
I have outwalked the furthest city light.

I have looked down the saddest city lane.
5 I have passed by the watchman on his beat
And dropped my eyes, unwilling to explain.

I have stood still and stopped the sound of feet
When far away an interrupted cry
Came over houses from another street,

10 But not to call me back or say good-by;
And further still at an unearthly height
One luminary clock against the sky

Proclaimed the time was neither wrong nor right.
I have been one acquainted with the night.

Nothing Gold Can Stay

Nature's first green is gold,
Her hardest hue to hold.
Her early leaf's a flower;
But only so an hour.
5 Then leaf subsides to leaf.
So Eden sank to grief,
So dawn goes down to day.
Nothing gold can stay.

Fire and Ice

Recalling

1. What are the two things "some say" the world will end in, according to the speaker?
2. What emotion does the speaker associate with each element that could end the world?

Interpreting

3. What does the poet suggest that the two emotions have in common?
4. What other kinds of destruction besides destruction of the world might the poem be about?
5. Is this poem written in free verse? Explain.

Acquainted with the Night

Recalling

1. When and where has the speaker walked in lines 1–3? What has he seen in line 4? What has he heard in lines 7–10?
2. What did the clock proclaim?

Interpreting

3. What is the night in this poem like? What does line 13 tell you about the speaker's mood on the night being described?

4. What might the speaker mean in a larger sense by "night"?
5. What effect or meaning does Frost achieve by repeating line 1 as line 14?

Extending

6. Compare the speaker of this poem with J. Alfred Prufrock (page 443).

Nothing Gold Can Stay

Recalling

1. According to the poem, what happens to "nature's first green"? To "her early leaf"? To Eden? To dawn?

Interpreting

2. To what might "green" and "gold" in line 1 refer?
3. What do Eden, dawn, and a flower have in common? What might "gold" therefore represent in the poem as a whole?
4. In light of your interpretation of "gold" in question 3, explain the possible meanings of the title and last line of this poem.

Extending

5. Do you agree with the ideas suggested in this poem? Why or why not?

Robert Frost

Stopping by Woods on a Snowy Evening

Whose woods these are I think I know.
His house is in the village, though;
He will not see me stopping here
To watch his woods fill up with snow.

5 My little horse must think it queer
To stop without a farmhouse near
Between the woods and frozen lake
The darkest evening of the year.

He gives his harness bells a shake
10 To ask if there is some mistake.
The only other sound's the sweep
Of easy wind and downy flake.

The woods are lovely, dark, and deep,
But I have promises to keep,
15 And miles to go before I sleep,
And miles to go before I sleep.

STUDY QUESTIONS

Interpreting

4. What causes the speaker to stop?
5. What do the owner and the horse have in common? How do they differ from the speaker?
6. Why does the speaker leave the woods? Does he regret leaving?
7. What might the incident in the woods represent? What might lines 15–16, especially "sleep," mean?
8. Describe the rhyme scheme of the poem. How is the poem "knit" to a close?

Recalling

1. Where does the owner of the woods live? What will he not see, according to the first stanza?
2. According to the speaker, what must the horse think? According to the second stanza, when is the event in the poem taking place?
3. According to the final stanza, what must the speaker do before he sleeps? What does the speaker say he must keep?

Desert Places

Snow falling and night falling fast, oh, fast
In a field I looked into going past,
And the ground almost covered smooth in snow,
But a few weeds and stubble showing last.

5 The woods around it have it—it is theirs.
All animals are smothered in their lairs.
I am too absent-spirited to count;
The loneliness includes me unawares.

And lonely as it is, that loneliness
10 Will be more lonely ere it will be less—
A blanker whiteness of benighted[1] snow
With no expression, nothing to express.

They cannot scare me with their empty spaces
Between stars—on stars where no human race is.
15 I have it in me so much nearer home
To scare myself with my own desert places.

---

1. **benighted:** surrounded by darkness.

STUDY QUESTIONS

Recalling

1. What does the speaker see in lines 1–4 of the poem?
2. What mood, created by the scene, affects the speaker, too, in lines 5–8?
3. Once in this mood, what does the speaker claim the future will bring, according to lines 9–12?
4. What does the speaker admit about the stars in lines 13–14?

Interpreting

5. Would you characterize the snow scene as a negative or a positive picture? Why?
6. How do you explain the jump to a discussion of stars in lines 13–14? How would you characterize the speaker of the poem?

Extending

7. How are the experiences described in this poem and in "Stopping by Woods on a Snowy Evening" alike? How are the moods created by these experiences different? How would Emerson (page 159) explain this difference?

Robert Frost

Mending Wall

Something there is that doesn't love a wall,
That sends the frozen-ground-swell under it
And spills the upper boulders in the sun,
And makes gaps even two can pass abreast.
5 The work of hunters is another thing:
I have come after them and made repair
Where they have left not one stone on a stone,
But they would have the rabbit out of hiding,
To please the yelping dogs. The gaps I mean,
10 No one has seen them made or heard them made,
But at spring mending-time we find them there.
I let my neighbor know beyond the hill;
And on a day we meet to walk the line
And set the wall between us once again.
15 We keep the wall between us as we go.
To each the boulders that have fallen to each.
And some are loaves and some so nearly balls
We have to use a spell to make them balance:
"Stay where you are until our backs are turned!"
20 We wear our fingers rough with handling them.
Oh, just another kind of outdoor game,

One on a side. It comes to little more:
There where it is we do not need the wall:
He is all pine and I am apple orchard.
25 My apple trees will never get across
And eat the cones under his pines, I tell him.
He only says, "Good fences make good neighbors."
Spring is the mischief in me, and I wonder
If I could put a notion in his head:
30 *"Why* do they make good neighbors? Isn't it
Where there are cows? But here there are no cows.
Before I built a wall I'd ask to know
What I was walling in or walling out,
And to whom I was like to give offense.
35 Something there is that doesn't love a wall,
That wants it down." I could say "Elves" to him,
But it's not elves exactly, and I'd rather
He said it for himself. I see him there,
Bringing a stone grasped firmly by the top
40 In each hand, like an old-stone savage armed.
He moves in darkness as it seems to me,
Not of woods only and the shade of trees.
He will not go behind his father's saying,
And he likes having thought of it so well
45 He says again, "Good fences make good neighbors."

Robert Frost

Birches

When I see birches bend to left and right
Across the lines of straighter darker trees,
I like to think some boy's been swinging them.
But swinging doesn't bend them down to stay
5 As ice storms do. Often you must have seen them
Loaded with ice a sunny winter morning
After a rain. They click upon themselves
As the breeze rises, and turn many-colored
As the stir cracks and crazes their enamel.
10 Soon the sun's warmth makes them shed crystal shells
Shattering and avalanching on the snow crust—
Such heaps of broken glass to sweep away
You'd think the inner dome of heaven had fallen.
They are dragged to the withered bracken by the load,
15 And they seem not to break; though once they are bowe
So low for long, they never right themselves:
You may see their trunks arching in the woods
Years afterwards, trailing their leaves on the ground
Like girls on hands and knees that throw their hair
20 Before them over their heads to dry in the sun.
But I was going to say when Truth broke in
With all her matter of fact about the ice storm,
I should prefer to have some boy bend them
As he went out and in to fetch the cows—
25 Some boy too far from town to learn baseball,
Whose only play was what he found himself,
Summer or winter, and could play alone.
One by one he subdued his father's trees

By riding them down over and over again
30 Until he took the stiffness out of them,
And not one but hung limp, not one was left
For him to conquer. He learned all there was
To learn about not launching out too soon
And so not carrying the tree away
35 Clear to the ground. He always kept his poise
To the top branches, climbing carefully
With the same pains you use to fill a cup
Up to the brim, and even above the brim.
Then he flung outward, feet first, with a swish,
40 Kicking his way down through the air to the ground.
So was I once myself a swinger of birches.
And so I dream of going back to be.
It's when I'm weary of considerations,
And life is too much like a pathless wood
45 Where your face burns and tickles with the cobwebs
Broken across it, and one eye is weeping
From a twig's having lashed across it open.
I'd like to get away from earth awhile
And then come back to it and begin over.
50 May no fate willfully misunderstand me
And half grant what I wish and snatch me away
Not to return. Earth's the right place for love:
I don't know where it's likely to go better.
I'd like to go by climbing a birch tree,
55 And climb black branches up a snow-white trunk
Toward heaven, till the tree could bear no more,
But dipped its top and set me down again.
That would be good both going and coming back.
One could do worse than be a swinger of birches.

STUDY QUESTIONS

Mending Wall

Recalling

1. According to lines 1–9, what happens because "Something there is that doesn't love a wall"? What other kind of destruction to the wall, described in lines 5–9, is not as significant to the speaker?
2. Describe how the speaker and his neighbor go about fixing the wall at spring mending-time (lines 12–22).
3. According to the speaker in lines 24–36, why do he and his neighbor not need a wall? What does the neighbor say?

Interpreting

4. Describe the character of the neighbor as seen by the speaker.
5. Does the speaker definitely want the wall torn down? How do you know?

Birches

Recalling

1. According to lines 1–5, what does the speaker like to think has caused the birches to bend? What bends them "down to stay"?
2. According to lines 25–27, what is the "only play" of some boy "too far from town to learn baseball"?
3. Of what does the speaker dream, according to lines 41–42? From what would he like to get away for a while? What does he not want fate to do?
4. Toward what does the speaker want to climb? What does he want the tree to do when it can "bear no more"?

Interpreting

5. What sort of childhood does a boy who lives "too far from town to learn baseball" have? In describing the boy, whom is the speaker really describing?
6. Restate lines 43–48 in your own words, explaining why the speaker wants to get away from earth. According to lines 52–53, what is one reason he does *not* want to escape from earth?
7. What kinds of activities might swinging on birches represent? What might "could bear no more" signify?

Extending

8. What general statement, based on the poems you have read, can you make about Frost's relationship with nature? Explain how many of Frost's poems are traditional and Romantic in both form and content.

VIEWPOINT

Frost himself once wrote:

There are two types of realist—the one who offers a good deal of dirt with his potato to show that it is a real one; and the one who is satisfied with the potato brushed clean. I'm inclined to be the second kind. . . . To me, the thing that art does for life is to strip it to form.

—*Selected Prose of Robert Frost*

1. Explain in your own words the two types of realist Frost describes. How would Frost's poems be different if he were the first kind of realist?
2. Do you agree with Frost's statement about what art does? Why or why not?

LITERARY FOCUS

Tone

Tone in literature is the author's attitude. An author can demonstrate an attitude toward characters, toward subjects, and toward the reader.

Some tones are clearly defined and easy to notice, such as a humorous tone or an angry tone. Some tones are more complicated, reflecting a combination of emotions in the writer. An ironic tone, for example, can suggest that a writer is both sympathetic toward and critical of a character or a subject.

Tone is often crucial to understanding a poem or a story. It is sometimes necessary to read a passage several times, sometimes aloud, to try to hear the voice of the author and decide what tone is being conveyed. Mark Twain's stories, for example, convey much of their wry humor and irony only through the tone adopted by the author.

Robert Frost's tone undergoes many subtle changes from poem to poem. In "Birches" his tone seems serene and celebratory. In "Fire and Ice" he mixes his own brand of pessimism with a combination of objectivity and amusement.

Thinking About Tone

1. Describe in your own words the tone in any other of Frost's poems. Is the tone simple and clear, or does it seem to signal a combination of emotions in the poet?
2. Describe the tone in one poem by each of the following: Edwin Arlington Robinson (page 356), Ezra Pound (page 437), T. S. Eliot (page 442), and Wallace Stevens (page 488). Which tone seems most like the tone of a poem by Frost? Why?

COMPOSITION

Writing About Theme and Tone

■ Write a brief essay analyzing the relationship between the theme and the tone in one of Robert Frost's poems. Begin with a statement of the theme. Then describe the tone, and show how the tone supports or brings out the theme.

Writing a Description

■ Write a brief description in prose or poetry of some aspect of the natural world, using common speech as does Robert Frost. Keep your statements simple by reducing them to the clearest, most meaningful words that convey your ideas. You may choose to write about the weather, a storm, a season, or even the simplicity of the natural world itself.

COMPARING WRITERS

1. Try to find some common ground in Frost poems as different in content as "The Road Not Taken," "Stopping by Woods on a Snowy Evening," "Acquainted with the Night," "Mending Wall," and "Birches." As you answer, consider what these poems all seem to suggest about compromise and about moving on. Then compare Frost's message with the ideas of other poets of this period. Do any of the others also see the world as a confusing place?
2. Hughes, Ransom, MacLeish, Moore, Cummings, Stevens, and even Frost were all affected by the Imagists in one way or another. Which of their poems use modern free verse? Which poems make frequent use of images to capture emotions?

FICTION

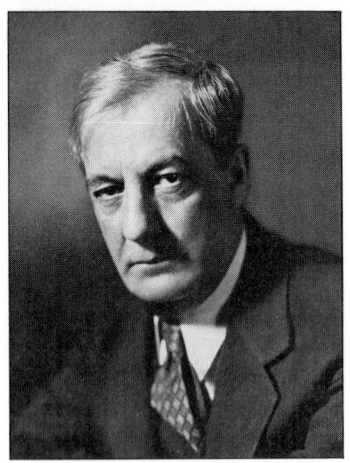

Sherwood Anderson   *1876–1941*

Sherwood Anderson's stories of American life reflect what he believed were the most important qualities for a modern writer: honesty, simplicity, and straightforwardness. Anderson grew up in Camden and Clyde, small Ohio towns much like the one he invented as the setting of his most famous work, *Winesburg, Ohio.* Camden and Clyde were prosperous farming communities, but the Anderson family did not prosper, and the young Anderson longed for the variety and opportunities of city life. He moved to Cleveland and later to Chicago, where he pursued an unsatisfying career in advertising. In 1912 he made a dramatic change in his life with his decision to write.

Anderson began to associate with Carl Sandburg, Theodore Dreiser, Edgar Lee Masters, and other writers living in Chicago. Influenced by the poems of Masters' *Spoon River Anthology,* Anderson began to record, in prose, his own feelings about life in small-town America. These tales of Winesburg were collected as a volume in 1919, and they made Anderson famous. He continued his explorations of small-town life in *The Triumph of the Egg* (1921), *Horses and Men* (1923), and *Death in the Woods and Other Stories* (1933), but he was never again as successful as he had been with the Winesburg stories.

Like Masters, Anderson did not believe that village life was the rose-colored picture that so many other writers painted. His characters are often lonely and isolated, dissatisfied with their world and frustrated in their attempts to find something better. Anderson treated them realistically, in the simple language that Gertrude Stein, his friend and champion, did much to encourage and that would, in turn, influence the styles of Ernest Hemingway and William Faulkner, two writers whose early careers Anderson helped nurture. "Sophistication" is typical of the Winesburg stories in its realism, its characters' honest longings, and its poetic evocation of the sights and sounds of turn-of-the-century life.

Sherwood Anderson

Sophistication

It was early evening of a day in the late fall and the Winesburg County Fair had brought crowds of country people into town. The day had been clear and the night came on warm and pleasant. On the Trunion Pike, where the road after it left town stretched away between berry fields now covered with dry brown leaves, the dust from passing wagons arose in clouds. Children, curled into little balls, slept on the straw scattered on wagon beds. Their hair was full of dust and their fingers black and sticky. The dust rolled away over the fields and the departing sun set it ablaze with colors.

In the main street of Winesburg crowds filled the stores and the sidewalks. Night came on, horses whinnied, the clerks in the stores ran madly about, children became lost and cried lustily, an American town worked terribly at the task of amusing itself.

Pushing his way through the crowds in Main Street, young George Willard concealed himself in the stairway leading to Doctor Reefy's office and looked at the people. With feverish eyes he watched the faces drifting past under the store lights. Thoughts kept coming into his head and he did not want to think. He stamped impatiently on the wooden steps and looked sharply about. "Well, is she going to stay with him all day? Have I done all this waiting for nothing?" he muttered.

George Willard, the Ohio village boy, was fast growing into manhood and new thoughts had been coming into his mind. All that day, amid the jam of people at the Fair, he had gone about feeling lonely. He was about to leave Winesburg to go away to some city where he hoped to get work on a city newspaper and he felt grown-up. The mood that had taken possession of him was a thing known to men and unknown to boys. He felt old and a little tired. Memories awoke in him. To his mind his new sense of maturity set him apart, made of him a half-tragic figure. He wanted someone to understand the feeling that had taken possession of him after his mother's death.

There is a time in the life of every boy when he for the first time takes the backward view of life. Perhaps that is the moment when he crosses the line into manhood. The boy is walking through the street of his town. He is thinking of the future and of the figure he will cut in the world. Ambitions and regrets awake within him. Suddenly something happens; he stops under a tree and waits as for a voice calling his name. Ghosts of old things creep into his consciousness; the voices outside of himself whisper a message concerning the limitations of life. From being quite sure of himself and his future he becomes not at all sure. If he be an imaginative boy a door is torn open and for the first time he looks out upon the world, seeing, as though they marched in procession before him, the countless figures of men who before his time have come out of nothingness into the world, lived their lives and again disappeared into nothingness. The sadness of sophistication has come to the boy. With a little gasp he sees himself as merely a leaf blown by the wind through the streets of his village. He knows that in spite of all the stout[1] talk of his fellows he must live and die in uncertainty, a thing blown by the winds, a thing destined like corn to wilt in the sun. He shivers and looks eagerly about. The eighteen years he has lived seem but a moment, a breathing space in the long march of humanity. Already he hears death calling. With all his heart he wants to come close to some other human, touch someone with his hands, be touched by the hand of another. If he prefers that the other be a woman, that is because he believes that a

---

1. **stout:** tough.

Scene at a traditional American county fair, about 1910.

woman will be gentle, that she will understand. He wants, most of all, understanding.

When the moment of sophistication came to George Willard his mind turned to Helen White, the Winesburg banker's daughter. Always he had been conscious of the girl growing into womanhood as he grew into manhood. Once on a summer night when he was eighteen, he had walked with her on a country road and in her presence had given way to an impulse to boast, to make himself appear big and significant in her eyes. Now he wanted to see her for another purpose. He wanted to tell her of the new impulses that had come to him. He had tried to make her think of him as a man when he knew nothing of manhood and now he wanted to be with her and to try to make her feel the change he believed had taken place in his nature.

As for Helen White, she also had come to a period of change. What George felt, she in her young woman's way felt also. She was no longer a girl and hungered to reach into the grace and beauty of womanhood. She had come home from Cleveland, where she was attending college, to spend a day at the Fair. She also had begun to have memories. During the day she sat in the grandstand with a young man, one of the instructors from the college, who was a guest of her mother's. The young man was of a pedantic[2] turn of mind and she felt at once he would not do for her purpose. At the Fair she was glad to be seen in his company as he was well dressed and a stranger. She knew that the fact of his presence would create an impression. During the day she was

2. **pedantic:** scholarly but trivial.

happy, but when night came on she began to grow restless. She wanted to drive the instructor away, to get out of his presence. While they sat together in the grandstand and while the eyes of former schoolmates were upon them, she paid so much attention to her escort that he grew interested. "A scholar needs money. I should marry a woman with money," he mused.

Helen White was thinking of George Willard even as he wandered gloomily through the crowds thinking of her. She remembered the summer evening when they had walked together and wanted to walk with him again. She thought that the months she had spent in the city, the going to theaters and the seeing of great crowds wandering in lighted thoroughfares, had changed her profoundly. She wanted him to feel and be conscious of the change in her nature.

The summer evening together that had left its mark on the memory of both the young man and the woman had, when looked at quite sensibly, been rather stupidly spent. They had walked out of town along a country road. Then they had stopped by a fence near a field of young corn and George had taken off his coat and let it hang on his arm. "Well, I've stayed here in Winesburg—yes—I've not yet gone away but I'm growing up," he had said. "I've been reading books and I've been thinking. I'm going to try to amount to something in life.

"Well," he explained, "that isn't the point. Perhaps I'd better quit talking."

The confused boy put his hand on the girl's arm. His voice trembled. The two started to walk back along the road toward town. In his desperation George boasted, "I'm going to be a big man, the biggest that ever lived here in Winesburg," he declared. "I want you to do something, I don't know what. Perhaps it is none of my business. I want you to try to be different from other women. You see the point. It's none of my business, I tell you. I want you to be a beautiful woman. You see what I want."

The boy's voice failed and in silence the two came back into town and went along the street to Helen White's house. At the gate he tried to say something impressive. Speeches he had thought out came into his head, but they seemed utterly pointless. "I thought—I used to think—I had it in my mind you would marry Seth Richmond. Now I know you won't," was all he could find to say as she went through the gate and toward the door of her house.

On the warm fall evening as he stood in the stairway and looked at the crowd drifting through Main Street, George thought of the talk beside the field of young corn and was ashamed of the figure he had made of himself. In the street the people surged up and down like cattle confined in a pen. Buggies and wagons almost filled the narrow thoroughfare. A band played and small boys raced along the sidewalk, diving between the legs of men. Young men with shining red faces walked awkwardly about with girls on their arms. In a room above one of the stores, where a dance was to be held, the fiddlers tuned their instruments. The broken sounds floated down through an open window and out across the murmur of voices and the loud blare of the horns of the band. The medley of songs got on young Willard's nerves. Everywhere, on all sides, the sense of crowding, moving life closed in about him. He wanted to run away by himself and think. "If she wants to stay with that fellow she may. Why should I care? What difference does it make to me?" he growled and went along Main Street and through Hern's Grocery into a side street.

George felt so utterly lonely and dejected that he wanted to weep but pride made him walk rapidly along, swinging his arms. He came to Wesley Moyer's livery barn[3] and stopped in the shadows to listen to a group of men who talked of a race Wesley's stallion, Tony Tip, had won at the Fair during the afternoon. A crowd had gathered in front of the barn and before the crowd walked Wesley, prancing up

---

3. **livery barn:** barn or stable from which horses and carriages can be hired.

and down and boasting. He held a whip in his hand and kept tapping the ground. Little puffs of dust arose in the lamplight. "Quit your talking," Wesley exclaimed. "I wasn't afraid, I knew I had 'em beat all the time. I wasn't afraid."

Ordinarily George Willard would have been intensely interested in the boasting of Moyer, the horseman. Now it made him angry. He turned and hurried away along the street. "Old windbag," he sputtered. "Why does he want to be bragging? Why don't he shut up?"

George went into a vacant lot, and as he hurried alone, fell over a pile of rubbish. A nail protruding from an empty barrel tore his trousers. He sat down on the ground and swore. With a pin he mended the torn place and then arose and went on. "I'll go to Helen White's house, that's what I'll do. I'll walk right in. I'll say that I want to see her. I'll walk right in and sit down, that's what I'll do," he declared, climbing over a fence and beginning to run.

On the veranda of Banker White's house Helen was restless and distraught. The instructor sat between the mother and daughter. His talk wearied the girl. Although he had also been raised in an Ohio town, the instructor began to put on the airs of the city. He wanted to appear cosmopolitan.[4] "I like the chance you have given me to study the background out of which most of our girls come," he declared. "It was good of you, Mrs. White, to have me down for the day." He turned to Helen and laughed. "Your life is still bound up with the life of this town?" he asked. "There are people here in whom you are interested?" To the girl his voice sounded pompous and heavy.

Helen arose and went into the house. At the door leading to a garden at the back she stopped and stood listening. Her mother began to talk. "There is no one here fit to associate with a girl of Helen's breeding," she said.

Helen ran down a flight of stairs at the back of the house and into the garden. In the darkness she stopped and stood trembling. It seemed to her that the world was full of meaningless people saying words. Afire with eagerness she ran through the garden gate and, turning a corner by the banker's barn, went into a little side street. "George! Where are you, George?" she cried, filled with nervous excitement. She stopped running, and leaned against a tree to laugh hysterically. Along the dark little street came George Willard, still saying words. "I'm going to walk right into her house. I'll go right in and sit down," he declared as he came up to her. He stopped and stared stupidly. "Come on," he said and took hold of her hand. With hanging heads they walked away along the street under the trees. Dry leaves rustled underfoot. Now that he had found her George wondered what he had better do and say.

At the upper end of the Fair Ground, in Winesburg, there is a half-decayed old grandstand. It has never been painted and the boards are all warped out of shape. The Fair Ground stands on top of a low hill rising out of the valley of Wine Creek and from the grandstand one can see at night, over a cornfield, the lights of the town reflected against the sky.

George and Helen climbed the hill to the Fair Ground, coming by the path past Waterworks Pond. The feeling of loneliness and isolation that had come to the young man in the crowded streets of his town was both broken and intensified by the presence of Helen. What he felt was reflected in her.

In youth there are always two forces fighting in people. The warm unthinking little animal struggles against the thing that reflects and remembers, and the older, the more sophisticated thing had possession of George Willard. Sensing his mood, Helen walked beside him filled with respect. When they got to the grandstand they climbed up under the roof and sat down on one of the long bench-like seats.

There is something memorable in the experience to be had by going into a fairground

---

4. **cosmopolitan:** worldly; experienced.

that stands at the edge of a Middle Western town on a night after the annual fair has been held. The sensation is one never to be forgotten. On all sides are ghosts, not of the dead, but of living people. Here, during the day just passed, have come the people pouring in from the town and the country around. Farmers with their wives and children and all the people from the hundreds of little frame houses have gathered within these board walls. Young girls have laughed and men with beards have talked of the affairs of their lives. The place has been filled to overflowing with life. It has itched and squirmed with life and now it is night and the life has all gone away. The silence is almost terrifying. One conceals oneself standing silently beside the trunk of a tree and what there is of a reflective tendency in his nature is intensified. One shudders at the thought of the meaninglessness of life while at the same instant, and if the people of the town are his people, one lives life so intensely that tears come into the eyes.

In the darkness under the roof of the grandstand, George Willard sat beside Helen White and felt very keenly his own insignificance in the scheme of existence. Now that he had come out of town where the presence of the people stirring about, busy with a multitude of affairs, had been so irritating, the irritation was all gone. The presence of Helen renewed and refreshed him. It was as though her woman's hand was assisting him to make some minute readjustment of the machinery of his life. He began to think of the people in the town where he had always lived with something like reverence. He had reverence for Helen. He wanted to love and to be loved by her, but he did not want at the moment to be confused by her womanhood. In the darkness he took hold of her hand and when she crept close put a hand on her shoulder. A wind began to blow and he shivered. With all his strength he tried to hold and to understand the mood that had come upon him. In that high place in the darkness the two oddly sensitive human atoms held each other tightly and waited. In the mind of each was the same thought. "I have come to this lonely place and here is this other," was the substance of the thing felt.

In Winesburg the crowded day had run itself out into the long night of the late fall. Farm horses jogged away along lonely country roads pulling their portion of weary people. Clerks began to bring samples of goods in off the sidewalks and lock the doors of stores. In the Opera House a crowd had gathered to see a show and further down Main Street the fiddlers, their instruments tuned, sweated and worked to keep the feet of youth flying over a dance floor.

In the darkness in the grandstand Helen White and George Willard remained silent. Now and then the spell that held them was broken and they turned and tried in the dim light to see into each other's eyes. They kissed but that impulse did not last. At the upper end of the Fair Ground a half-dozen men worked over horses that had raced during the afternoon. The men had built a fire and were heating kettles of water. Only their legs could be seen as they passed back and forth in the light. When the wind blew, the little flames of the fire danced crazily about.

George and Helen arose and walked away into the darkness. They went along a path past a field of corn that had not yet been cut. The wind whispered among the dry corn blades. For a moment during the walk back into town the spell that held them was broken. When they had come to the crest of Waterworks Hill they stopped by a tree and George again put his hands on the girl's shoulders. She embraced him eagerly and then again they drew quickly back from that impulse. They stopped kissing and stood a little apart. Mutual respect grew big in them. They were both embarrassed and to relieve their embarrassment dropped into the animalism of youth. They laughed and began to pull and haul at each other. In some way chastened and purified by the mood they had been in, they became, not man and woman, not boy and girl, but excited little animals.

It was so they went down the hill. In the darkness they played like two splendid young things in a young world. Once, running swiftly forward, Helen tripped George and he fell. He squirmed and shouted. Shaking with laughter, he rolled down the hill. Helen ran after him. For just a moment she stopped in the darkness. There is no way of knowing what woman's thoughts went through her mind but, when the bottom of the hill was reached and she came up to the boy, she took his arm and walked beside him in dignified silence. For some reason they could not have explained they had both got from their silent evening together the thing needed. Man or boy, woman or girl, they had for a moment taken hold of the thing that makes the mature life of men and women in the modern world possible.

STUDY QUESTIONS

Recalling

1. As the story opens, what event is being celebrated in Winesburg? At what does Winesburg work, according to the second paragraph?

2. For whom is George looking? What did he do when he walked with her down a country road "once on a summer night" (page 506)? What does he want to do now?

3. Of whom was Helen thinking "even as he wandered gloomily through the crowds thinking of her" (page 507)? What does Helen want to communicate about her nature (page 507)?

4. How do George and Helen finally meet? Where do they go? What is the "substance of the thing" they feel there (page 509)? According to the last paragraph, what have Helen and George done "for a moment"?

Interpreting

5. Briefly describe the kind of town Anderson creates as Winesburg, Ohio.

6. What do George and Helen have in common? What do they want to share? What does Anderson suggest about adolescents in general?

7. In the fifth paragraph, what does Anderson suggest is the "sadness of sophistication"? What does he later suggest is "the thing that makes the mature life of men and women in the modern world possible"?

8. What is inconclusive about the ending, or resolution, of the story? Does the inconclusive ending make the story more true to life? Does the story follow the standard short story format described in the Literary Focus on page 309? Explain your answers.

9. Looking at the story as a whole, does the title have a positive or negative connotation?

Extending

10. The twentieth century saw a tremendous shift in population as many young Americans left their rural communities for big cities. Does this story give you any insights into why they left? Do you think adolescents like George Willard were happy with the life they found in big cities? Explain.

COMPOSITION

Citing Evidence

In a brief essay illustrate with evidence from the story that George feels isolated from his community. You might proceed by tracing George's activities from the beginning to the end of the story. *For help with this assignment, refer to Lesson 3 in the Writing About Literature Handbook at the back of this book.*

Writing a Continuation of a Story

Write an additional page to the story of George and Helen. Follow one or both of the characters as they act upon the decision or discovery they make as Anderson ends the story. You may want to allow some time to pass, perhaps picking up the characters years later. Be sure to tie their lives to the character motivations in the story.

Sinclair Lewis   *1885–1951*

Like Edgar Lee Masters and Sherwood Anderson, Sinclair Lewis wrote about the world of small-town America, a world that he too had found confining. Like Mark Twain, however, he looked with a satiric eye, and his dark humor and keen powers of observation made him one of the most popular novelists of the post–World War I era and the first American to receive the Nobel Prize for Literature.

Lewis was born in Sauk Centre, Minnesota, the son of a country doctor. His childhood was introspective and virtually friendless, and early in life he turned to writing as a means of escaping personal unhappiness. Lewis' early manhood was spent in various attempts to "find himself." He went to Yale but soon left. He lived briefly in a utopian community set up by the social critic Upton Sinclair; he traveled to Central America to seek work building the Panama Canal; he attempted to support himself as a writer in New York City. Eventually he completed his education at Yale and returned to New York, where he wrote industriously but with little financial success.

Everything changed in 1920 with *Main Street,* Lewis' fifth novel. A sharply observed satire, *Main Street* was a runaway best seller. Lewis' next novel, *Babbitt* (1922), was equally popular; in fact, the word *babbitt* has entered our language, synonymous with the type of conventional, conforming businessman the novel portrays. In 1930, after the publication of *Arrowsmith* (1925), *Elmer Gantry* (1927), and *Dodsworth* (1929), Lewis was awarded the Nobel Prize.

Like all great satirists, Lewis' intention was to liberate his readers from ideas that he found shallow and foolish. His hope was to reveal to Americans the foibles of their time and place, to hold up a mirror to the smug materialism that he saw around him, and, through laughter, to move Americans from the complacent attitudes into which they had fallen. His novels are often mercilessly hilarious, but in many he displays a deep sympathy for his characters. In "The Hack Driver" Lewis tells a tale of a "city slicker" on a rural errand.

Sinclair Lewis

The Hack Driver

When I graduated from law school I suppose I was about as artificial and idiotic and ambitious as most youngsters. I wanted to climb, socially and financially. I wanted to be famous and dine at large houses with men who shuddered at the Common People who don't dress for dinner. You see, I hadn't learned that the only thing duller than a polite dinner is the conversation afterward, when the victims are digesting the dinner and accumulating enough strength to be able to play bridge. Oh, I was a fine young calf! I even planned a rich marriage. Imagine then how I felt when, after taking honors and becoming fifteenth assistant clerk in the magnificent law firm of Hodgins, Hodgins,

Berkman and Taupe, I was set not at preparing briefs[1] but at serving summonses![2] Like a cheap private detective! Like a mangy sheriff's officer! They told me I had to begin that way and, holding my nose, I feebly went to work. I was kicked out of actresses' dressing rooms, and from time to time I was righteously beaten by large and indignant litigants.[3] I came to know, and still more to hate, every dirty and shadowy corner of the city. I thought of fleeing to my

---

1. **briefs:** short reports summarizing the main point in a legal case.
2. **serving summonses:** delivering official orders to appear in court.
3. **litigants:** people involved in a lawsuit.

home town, where I could at once become a full-fledged attorney at law. I rejoiced one day when they sent me out forty miles or so to a town called New Mullion, to serve a summons on one Oliver Lutkins. This Lutkins had worked in the Northern Woods, and he knew the facts about a certain timberland boundary agreement. We needed him as a witness, and he had dodged service.

When I got off the train at New Mullion, my sudden affection for sweet and simple villages was dashed by the look of the place, with its mud-gushing streets and its rows of shops either paintless or daubed with a sour brown. Though it must have numbered eight or nine thousand inhabitants, New Mullion was as littered as a mining camp. There was one agreeable-looking man at the station—the expressman. He was a person of perhaps forty, red-faced, cheerful, thick; he wore his overalls and denim jumper as though they belonged to him, he was quite dirty and very friendly and you knew at once he liked people and slapped them on the back out of pure easy affection.

"I want," I told him, "to find a fellow named Oliver Lutkins."

"Him? I saw him 'round here 'twan't an hour ago. Hard fellow to catch, though—always chasing around on some phony business or other. Probably trying to get up a poker game in the back of Fritz Beinke's harness shop. I'll tell you, boy—Any hurry about locating Lutkins?"

"Yes. I want to catch the afternoon train back." I was as impressively secret as a stage detective.

"I'll tell you. I've got a hack. I'll get out the bone-shaker and we can drive around together and find Lutkins. I know most of the places he hangs out."

He was so frankly friendly, he so immediately took me into the circle of his affection, that I glowed with the warmth of it. I knew, of course, that he was drumming up business, but his kindness was real, and if I had to pay hack fare in order to find my man, I was glad that the money would go to this good fellow. I got

him down to two dollars an hour; he brought from his cottage, a block away, an object like a black piano box on wheels.

He didn't hold the door open, certainly he didn't say, "Ready, sir." I think he would have died before calling anybody "sir." When he gets to Heaven's gate he'll call St. Peter "Pete," and I imagine the good saint will like it. He remarked, "Well, young fellow, here's the handsome equipage,"[4] and his grin—well, it made me feel that I had always been his neighbor. They're so ready to help a stranger, those villagers. He had already made it his own task to find Oliver Lutkins for me.

He said, and almost shyly: "I don't want to butt in on your private business, young fellow, but my guess is that you want to collect some money from Lutkins—he never pays anybody a cent; he still owes me six bits[5] on a poker game I was fool enough to get into. He ain't a bad sort of a Yahoo[6] but he just naturally hates to loosen up on a coin of the realm. So if you're trying to collect any money off him, we better kind of you might say creep up on him and surround him. If you go asking for him—anybody can tell you come from the city, with that trick Fedora[7] of yours—he'll suspect something and take a sneak. If you want me to, I'll go into Fritz Beinke's and ask for him, and you can keep out of sight behind me."

I loved him for it. By myself I might never have found Lutkins. Now, I was an army with reserves. In a burst I told the hack driver that I wanted to serve a summons on Lutkins; that the fellow had viciously refused to testify in a suit where his knowledge of a certain conversation would clear up everything. The driver listened earnestly—and I was still young enough to be grateful at being taken seriously

---

4. **equipage** [ekʹwə pij]: fancy carriage.
5. **six bits:** *Bit* is a colloquial term for 12.5 cents; six bits is therefore 75 cents.
6. **Yahoo** [yäʹhoo]: term for "man" deriving from brutish, manlike creatures in Jonathan Swift's *Gulliver's Travels.*
7. **Fedora** [fi dôrʹə]: Soft felt hat with a slightly curved brim.

by any man of forty. At the end he pounded my shoulder (very painfully) and chuckled: "Well, we'll spring a little surprise on Brer[8] Lutkins."

"Let's start, driver."

"Most folks around here call me Bill. Or Magnuson. William Magnuson, fancy carting and hauling."

"All right, Bill. Shall we tackle this harness shop—Beinke's?"

"Yes, jus' likely to be there as anywheres. Plays a lot of poker and a great hand at bluffing!" Bill seemed to admire Mr. Lutkins's ability as a scoundrel; I fancied that if he had been sheriff he would have caught Lutkins with fervor and hanged him with affection.

At the somewhat gloomy harness shop we descended and went in. The room was odorous with the smell of dressed leather. A scanty sort of a man, presumably Mr. Beinke, was selling a horse collar to a farmer.

"Seen Nolly Lutkins around today? Friend of his looking for him," said Bill, with treacherous heartlessness.

Beinke looked past him at my shrinking alien self; he hesitated and owned: "Yuh, he was in here a little while ago. Guess he's gone over to the Swede's to get a shave."

"Well, if he comes in, tell him I'm looking for him. Might get up a little game of poker. I've heard tell that Lutkins plays these here immoral games of chance."

"Yuh, I believe he's known to sit in on Authors,[9]" Beinke growled.

We sought the barber shop of "the Swede." Bill was again good enough to take the lead, while I lurked at the door. He asked not only the Swede but two customers if they had seen Lutkins. The Swede decidedly had not; he raged: "I ain't seen him, and I don't want to, but if you find him you can just collect the dollar thirty-five he owes me." One of the customers thought he had seen Lutkins "hiking down Main Street, this side of the hotel."

"Well, then," Bill concluded, as we labored up into the hack, "his credit at the Swede's being ausgewent,[10] he's probably getting a scrape at Heinie Gray's. He's too darn lazy to shave himself."

At Gray's barber shop we missed Lutkins by only five minutes. He had just left—presumably for the poolroom. At the poolroom it appeared that he had merely bought a pack of cigarettes and gone on. Thus we pursued him, just behind him but never catching him, for an hour, till it was past one and I was hungry. Village born as I was, and in the city often lonely for good coarse country wit, I was so delighted by Bill's cynical opinions on the barbers and clergymen and doctors and draymen of New Mullion that I scarcely cared whether I found Lutkins or not.

"How about something to eat?" I suggested. "Let's go to a restaurant and I'll buy you a lunch."

"Well, ought to go home to the old woman. And I don't care much for these restaurants—ain't but four of 'em and they're all rotten. Tell you what we'll do. Like nice scenery? There's an elegant view from Wade's Hill. We'll get the old woman to put us up a lunch—she won't charge you but a half dollar, and it'd cost you that for a greasy feed at the cafe—and we'll go up there and have a Sunday-school picnic."

I knew that my friend Bill was not free from guile; I knew that his hospitality to the Young Fellow from the City was not altogether a matter of brotherly love. I was paying him for his time; in all I paid him for six hours (including the lunch hour) at what was then a terrific price. But he was no more dishonest than I, who charged the whole thing up to the Firm, and it would have been worth paying him myself to have his presence. His country serenity, his natural wisdom, was a refreshing bath to the city-twitching youngster. As we sat on the hilltop, looking across orchards and a creek which slipped among the willows, he talked of New Mullion, gave a whole gallery of portraits. He was cynical yet tender. Nothing had escaped him, yet there was nothing, no

---

8. **Brer** [brur]: southern dialect for "brother."
9. **Authors:** simple children's card game.

10. **ausgewent** [ous'ge went]: made-up, German-sounding word meaning "used up."

matter how ironically he laughed at it, which was beyond his understanding and forgiveness. In ruddy color he painted the rector's wife who when she was most in debt most loudly gave the responses at which he called the "Episcopalopian church." He commented on the boys who came home from college in "ice cream pants," and on the lawyer who, after years of torrential argument with his wife, would put on either a linen collar or a necktie, but never both. He made them live. In that day I came to know New Mullion better than I did the city, and to love it better.

If Bill was ignorant of universities and of urban ways, yet much had he traveled in the realm of jobs. He had worked on railroad section gangs, in harvest fields and contractors' camps, and from his adventures he had brought back a philosophy of simplicity and laughter. He strengthened me. Nowadays, thinking of Bill, I know what people mean (though I abominate the simpering phrase) when they yearn over "real he-men."

We left that placid place of orchards and resumed the search for Oliver Lutkins. We could not find him. At last Bill cornered a friend of Lutkins and made him admit that "he guessed Oliver'd gone out to his ma's farm, three miles north."

We drove out there, mighty with strategy.

"I know Oliver's ma. She's a terror. She's a cyclone," Bill sighed. "I took a trunk out for her once, and she pretty near took my hide off because I didn't treat it like it was a crate of eggs. She's somewheres about nine feet tall and four feet thick and quick's a cat, and she sure manhandles the Queen's English. I'll bet Oliver has heard that somebody's on his trail and he's sneaked out there to hide behind his ma's skirts. Well, we'll try bawling her out. But you better let me do it, boy. You may be great at Latin and geography, but you ain't educated in cussing."

We drove into a poor farmyard; we were faced by an enormous and cheerful old woman. My guardian stockily stood before her and snarled, "Remember me? I'm Bill Magnuson, the expressman. I want to find your son Oliver.

Friend of mine here from the city's got a present for him."

"I don't know anything about Oliver and I don't want to," she bellowed.

"Now you look here. We've stood for just about enough plenty nonsense. This young man is the attorney general's provost,[11] and we got legal right to search any and all premises for the person of one Oliver Lutkins."

Bill made it seem terrific, and the Amazon[12] seemed impressed. She retired into the kitchen and we followed. From the low old range, turned by years of heat into a dark silvery gray, she snatched a sadiron,[13] and she marched on us, clamoring, "You just search all you want to—providin' you don't mind getting burnt to a cinder!" She bellowed, she swelled, she laughed at our nervous retreat.

"Let's get out of this. She'll murder us," Bill groaned and, outside: "Did you see her grin? She was making fun of us. Can you beat that for nerve?"

I agreed that it was lese majesty.[14]

We did, however, make adequate search. The cottage had but one story. Bill went round it, peeking in at all the windows. We explored the barn and the stable; we were reasonably certain that Lutkins was not there. It was nearly time for me to catch the afternoon train, and Bill drove me to the station. On the way to the city I worried very little over my failure to find Lutkins. I was too absorbed in the thought of Bill Magnuson. Really, I considered returning to New Mullion to practice law. If I had found Bill so deeply and richly human might I not come to love the yet uncharted Fritz Beinke and the Swede barber and a hundred other slow-spoken, simple, wise neighbors? I saw a candid and happy life beyond the neat learnings of universities' law firms. I was excited, as one who has found a treasure.

But if I did not think much about Lutkins, the office did. I found them in a state next morning;

---

11. **provost** [prō′vəst]: official in charge.
12. **Amazon** [am′ə zon′]: here, a large, strong woman.
13. **sadiron** [sad′ī′ərn]: heavy iron for pressing clothes.
14. **lese majesty** [lēz′maj′is tē]: rude behavior toward someone, especially someone in authority, who should be treated with respect.

the suit was ready to come to trial; they had to have Lutkins; I was a disgrace and a fool. That morning my eminent career almost came to an end. The Chief did everything but commit mayhem; he somewhat more than hinted that I would do well at ditchdigging. I was ordered back to New Mullion, and with me they sent an ex-lumbercamp clerk who knew Lutkins. I was rather sorry, because it would prevent my loafing again in the gorgeous indolence of Bill Magnuson.

When the train drew in at New Mullion, Bill was on the station platform, near his dray. What was curious was that the old dragon, Lutkins's mother, was there talking to him, and they were not quarreling but laughing.

From the car steps I pointed them out to the lumbercamp clerk, and in young hero worship I murmured: "There's a fine fellow, a real man."

"Meet him here yesterday?" asked the clerk.

"I spent the day with him."

"He help you hunt for Oliver Lutkins?"

"Yes, he helped me a lot."

"He must have! He's Lutkins himself!"

But what really hurt was that when I served the summons Lutkins and his mother laughed at me as though I were a bright boy of seven, and with loving solicitude they begged me to go to a neighbor's house and take a cup of coffee.

"I told 'em about you, and they're dying to have a look at you," said Lutkins joyfully. "They're about the only folks in town that missed seeing you yesterday."

STUDY QUESTIONS

Recalling

1. When he first graduated from law school, where did the narrator work? What was his "title," according to the opening paragraph?
2. Why did the narrator visit New Mullion?
3. What did the expressman at the station offer to do? What did he say his name was?
4. In what places did the hack driver and the narrator search for Oliver Lutkins? How did Lutkins' mother chase them from her farm?
5. Why was "the Chief" at the law firm angry with the narrator (page 516)?
6. With whom did the narrator return to New Mullion? What did the narrator discover on this second trip?

Interpreting

7. Why did the narrator like "Bill Magnuson"? What sort of character is Oliver Lutkins? Is Lutkins basically likable?
8. At the end of the story, why were Lutkins' neighbors "dying to have a look" at the young lawyer?
9. What sort of irony—verbal, situational, or dramatic—is the basis of this story? Are the narrator's evaluations of "Bill Magnuson" and of New Mullion humorous in retrospect? Which evaluation of New Mullion is especially inaccurate?

Extending

10. What other characters in this book or in films remind you of Oliver Lutkins, and why? Why do you think amusing tales of "country bumpkins" who outsmart "city slickers" have always been so popular in America?

VIEWPOINT

In introducing a collection of Lewis' short stories, his biographer Mark Schorer tells us:

"The Hack Driver," . . . besides being an amusing comedy in its own right, expresses quite directly Lewis' own lifelong impulse to break out of the bondage of respectability.
—Introduction to *I'm a Stranger Here Myself and Other Stories*

■ How might "The Hack Driver" express this "lifelong impulse" of Sinclair Lewis'? Which events or details in the story support Schorer's view?

Ernest Hemingway   *1899–1961*

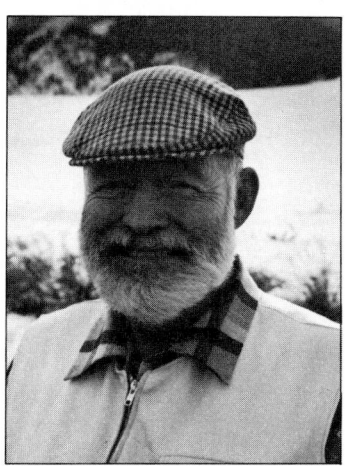

Literature, for Ernest Hemingway, was "just writing as well as you can and finishing what you start." This simple understatement characterizes the style of the writer whom many now consider one of the masters of twentieth-century prose.

Hemingway was born in Oak Park, Illinois, began writing in high school, and later worked for a Kansas City newspaper. On family trips to the Michigan woods he was introduced to the outdoor adventures that would remain a part of his life and his writing. During World War I he served in the ambulance corps of the Italian army and was wounded in battle. The experiences of war and of being wounded were traumatic; Hemingway returns to them in one way or another in all his later writing.

After the war Hemingway went to Paris, then considered the literary capital of the world. Here, in an effort to perfect his craft, he read widely and sought the advice of more experienced writers. Gertrude Stein and Ezra Pound had a profound effect on his style: From Stein he learned to control sentence rhythms with plain words and repetition; from Pound, to use precise language, sharp images, and as few words as possible.

Hemingway's novel *The Sun Also Rises* (1926) brilliantly captures his years in Paris as one of the "lost generation"; his posthumous memoir *A Moveable Feast* (1964) contains vivid portraits of Pound, Stein, F. Scott Fitzgerald, and the other American artists who formed a colony of "expatriates" in those postwar years. His first major work, *In Our Time* (1925), is a series of thematically related stories that, in Modernist fashion, must be pieced together in the reader's mind. His other novels include *A Farewell to Arms* (1929), a love story set during World War I; *For Whom the Bell Tolls* (1940), an epic story set against the Spanish Civil War of the 1930s; and *The Old Man and the Sea* (1952), an allegorical tale of a fisherman off the coast of Cuba. In 1954 Hemingway received the Nobel Prize for Literature.

Like the author himself, the Hemingway hero lives a life of great adventure. Whether big-game hunting, deep-sea fishing, boxing, bullfighting, or soldiering, he displays what Hemingway called "grace under pressure." Yet this "tough-guy" image is in some ways a mask disguising an extremely sensitive nature. That sensitivity is apparent in his story "In Another Country," where the narrator reports with characteristic matter-of-factness events so sad and terrible that they need no comment.

Ernest Hemingway

In Another Country

In the fall the war[1] was always there, but we did not go to it any more. It was cold in the fall in Milan[2] and the dark came very early. Then the electric lights came on, and it was pleasant along the streets looking in the windows. There was much game hanging outside the shops, and the snow powdered in the fur of the foxes and the wind blew their tails. The deer hung stiff and heavy and empty, and small birds blew in the wind and the wind turned their feathers. It was a cold fall and the wind came down from the mountains.

We were all at the hospital every afternoon, and there were different ways of walking across the town through the dusk to the hospital. Two of the ways were alongside canals, but they were long. Always, though, you crossed a bridge across a canal to enter the hospital. There was a choice of three bridges. On one of them a woman sold roasted chestnuts. It was warm, standing in front of her charcoal fire, and the chestnuts were warm afterward in your pocket. The hospital was very old and very beautiful, and you entered through a gate and walked across a courtyard and out a gate on the other side. There were usually funerals starting from the courtyard. Beyond the old hospital were the new brick pavilions, and there we met every afternoon and were all very polite and interested in what was the matter, and sat in the machines that were to make so much difference.

The doctor came up to the machine where I was sitting and said: "What did you like best to do before the war? Did you practice a sport?"

Modernist idea: Instead of beginning with the *exposition* standard in traditional short stories (p. 309), Hemingway starts his story in the middle of the narrator's memory of the war.

Point of view (p. 319): The story is told in the first person; the narrator uses the pronoun *I* and is limited to suggesting the attitudes and thoughts of other characters.

1. **the war:** World War I (1914–1918).
2. **Milan** [Mi lan′]: city in northern Italy.

I said: "Yes, football."

"Good," he said. "You will be able to play football again better than ever."

My knee did not bend and the leg dropped straight from the knee to the ankle without a calf, and the machine was to bend the knee and make it move as in riding a tricycle. But it did not bend yet, and instead the machine lurched when it came to the bending part. The doctor said: "That will all pass. You are a fortunate young man. You will play football again like a champion."

In the next machine was a major who had a little hand like a baby's. He winked at me when the doctor examined his hand, which was between two leather straps that bounced up and down and flapped the stiff fingers, and said: "And will I too play football, captain-doctor?" He had been a very great fencer, and before the war the greatest fencer in Italy.

The doctor went to his office in the back room and brought a photograph which showed a hand that had been withered almost as small as the major's, before it had taken a machine course, and after was a little larger. The major held the photograph with his good hand and looked at it very carefully. "A wound?" he asked.

"An industrial accident," the doctor said.

"Very interesting, very interesting," the major said, and handed it back to the doctor.

"You have confidence?"

"No," said the major.

There were three boys who came each day who were about the same age I was. They were all three from Milan, and one of them was to be a lawyer, and one was to be a painter, and one had intended to be a soldier, and after we were finished with the machines, sometimes we walked back together to the Café Cova, which was next door to the Scala.[3] We walked the short way through the communist quarter because we were four together. The people hated us because we were officers, and from a wineshop some one would call out, "A basso gli ufficiali!"[4] as we passed. Another boy who walked with us sometimes and made us five wore a black silk handkerchief across his face because he had no nose then and his face was to be rebuilt. He had gone out to the front from the military academy and been wounded within an hour after he had gone into the front line for the first time. They rebuilt his face, but he came from a very old family and they could never get the nose exactly right. He went to South America and worked in a bank. But this was a long time ago, and then we did not any of us know how it was going to be afterward. We only

Diction (p. 197): Hemingway chooses simple words to achieve a matter-of-fact tone.

Modernist idea: The author makes no direct statement about the tragedies of war but merely uses a verb tense *(was to be/had intended to be)* that forces his readers to draw their own conclusions (p. 432).

Tone (p. 502): Hemingway's characteristically matter-of-fact tone does not falter, even in reporting the most terrible facts.

3. **the Scala** [ska′la]: famous opera house in Milan.
4. **"A basso gli ufficiali!"** [a ba′sō lyē o͞o fē cha′lē]: "Down with officers!"

Scene in a Red Cross hospital, 1914.

knew then that there was always the war, but that we were not going to it any more.

We all had the same medals, except the boy with the black silk bandage across his face, and he had not been at the front long enough to get any medals. The tall boy with a very pale face who was to be a lawyer had been a lieutenant of Arditi[5] and had three medals of the sort we each had only one of. He had lived a very long time with death and was a little detached. We were all a little detached, and there was nothing that held us together except that we met every afternoon at the hospital. Although, as we walked to the Cova through the tough part of town, walking in the dark, with light and singing coming out of the wine-shops, and sometimes having to walk into the street when the men and women would crowd together on the sidewalk so that we would have had to jostle them to get by, we felt held together by there being something that had happened that they, the people who disliked us, did not understand.

Modernist idea: Detachment and disillusionment with warfare were common among the "lost generation" (p. 431).

5. **Arditi** [ar dē′tē]: corps of soldiers specially selected for dangerous operations.

We ourselves all understood the Cova, where it was rich and warm and not too brightly lighted, and noisy and smoky at certain hours, and there were always girls at the tables and the illustrated papers on a rack on the wall. The girls at the Cova were very patriotic, and I found that the most patriotic people in Italy were the café girls—and I believe they are still patriotic.

The boys at first were very polite about my medals and asked me what I had done to get them. I showed them the papers, which were written in very beautiful language and full of *fratellanza* and *abnegazione*,[6] but which really said, with the adjectives removed, that I had been given the medals because I was an American. After that their manner changed a little toward me, although I was their friend against outsiders. I was a friend, but I was never really one of them after they had read the citations, because it had been different with them and they had done very different things to get their medals. I had been wounded, it was true; but we all knew that being wounded, after all, was really an accident. I was never ashamed of the ribbons, though, and sometimes, after the cocktail hour, I would imagine myself having done all the things they had done to get their medals; but walking home at night through the empty streets with the cold wind and all the shops closed, trying to keep near the street lights, I knew that I would never have done such things, and I was very much afraid to die, and often lay in bed at night by myself, afraid to die and wondering how I would be when I went back to the front again.

The three with the medals were like hunting-hawks; and I was not a hawk, although I might seem a hawk to those who had never hunted; they, the three, knew better and so we drifted apart. But I stayed good friends with the boy who had been wounded his first day at the front, because he would never know now how he would have turned out; so he could never be accepted either, and I liked him because I thought perhaps he would not have turned out to be a hawk either.

The major, who had been the great fencer, did not believe in bravery, and spent much time while we sat in the machines correcting my grammar. He had complimented me on how I spoke Italian, and we talked together very easily. One day I had said that Italian seemed such an easy language to me that I could not take a great interest in it; everything was so easy to say. "Ah, yes," the major said. "Why, then, do you not take up the use of grammar?" So we took up the use of grammar, and soon Italian was such a difficult language that I was afraid to talk to him until I had the grammar straight in my mind.

The major came very regularly to the hospital. I do not think

Round character (p. 309): The narrator is a complex, well-developed character whose thoughts, when we learn them, reveal conflicting emotions and attitudes.

Irony (p. 359): Both verbal and situational irony are abundant, but readers must perceive the irony on their own.

6. *fratellanza* [fra tāl an′za] **and** *abnegazione* [ab nā ga tzyō′nā]: Italian for ''brotherhood'' and ''self-denial.''

he ever missed a day, although I am sure he did not believe in the machines. There was a time when none of us believed in the machines, and one day the major said it was all nonsense. The machines were new then and it was we who were to prove them. It was an idiotic idea, he said, "a theory, like another." I had not learned my grammar, and he said I was a stupid impossible disgrace, and he was a fool to have bothered with me. He was a small man and he sat straight up in his chair with his right hand thrust into the machine and looked straight ahead at the wall while the straps thumped up and down with his fingers in them.

"What will you do when the war is over if it is over?" he asked me. "Speak grammatically!"

"I will go to the States."

"Are you married?"

"No, but I hope to be."

"The more of a fool you are," he said. He seemed very angry. "A man must not marry."

"Why, Signor Maggiore?"[7]

"Don't call me 'Signor Maggiore.'"

"Why must not a man marry?"

"He cannot marry. He cannot marry," he said angrily. "If he is to lose everything, he should not place himself in a position to lose that. He should not place himself in a position to lose. He should find things he cannot lose."

He spoke very angrily and bitterly, and looked straight ahead while he talked.

"But why should he necessarily lose it?"

"He'll lose it," the major said. He was looking at the wall. Then he looked down at the machine and jerked his little hand out from between the straps and slapped it hard against his thigh. "He'll lose it," he almost shouted. "Don't argue with me!" Then he called to the attendant who ran the machines. "Come and turn this thing off."

He went back into the other room for the light treatment and the massage. Then I heard him ask the doctor if he might use his telephone and he shut the door. When he came back into the room, I was sitting in another machine. He was wearing his cape and had his cap on, and he came directly toward my machine and put his arm on my shoulder.

"I am so sorry," he said, and patted me on the shoulder with his good hand. "I would not be rude. My wife has just died. You must forgive me."

"Oh—" I said, feeling sick for him. "I am *so* sorry."

Symbolism (p. 187): The machines *are* machines in the story, but they also come to represent something else.

---

7. **Signor Maggiore** [sēn yôr′ maj jō′rä]: Italian for "Mr. Major." In Italy it was a sign of respect to say *Signor* before an officer's rank.

He stood there biting his lower lip. "It is very difficult," he said. "I cannot resign myself."

He looked straight past me and out through the window. Then he began to cry. "I am utterly unable to resign myself," he said and choked. And then crying, his head up looking at nothing, carrying himself straight and soldierly, with tears on both his cheeks and biting his lips, he walked past the machines and out the door.

The doctor told me that the major's wife, who was very young and whom he had not married until he was definitely invalided out of the war, had died of pneumonia. She had been sick only a few days. No one expected her to die. The major did not come to the hospital for three days. Then he came at the usual hour, wearing a black band on the sleeve of his uniform. When he came back, there were large framed photographs around the wall, of all sorts of wounds before and after they had been cured by the machines. In front of the machine the major used were three photographs of hands like his that were completely restored. I do not know where the doctor got them. I always understood we were the first to use the machines. The photographs did not make much difference to the major because he only looked out of the window.

> **Modernist idea:** The lack of a traditional *climax* or *resolution* (p. 309) reflects the Modernist experimentation with standard forms and perception of the modern world as fragmentary and confusing (p. 432).

STUDY QUESTIONS

Recalling

1. Where does the narrator go every afternoon, according to the second paragraph?
2. What had the major been before the war, and in what part of the body has he been injured? When was the boy with the silk handkerchief injured? What had been the career plans of the three others who accompany the narrator to the cafe each afternoon?
3. According to the narrator, why do the three Italians change in their attitude toward him? What does the narrator say the "three with the medals" are like? Does the narrator feel he is like this?
4. Near the end of the story, what does the major say "a man must not" do? What has happened to the major's wife?
5. What do the pictures described in the last paragraph show? What does the narrator "not know" about these pictures? What has he "always understood"?

Interpreting

6. Why might the narrator feel different from the three boys from Milan? Why might he feel kinship with the boy with the silk handkerchief?
7. Why does the major tell the narrator not to marry?
8. How are the narrator's and the major's wounds more than merely physical injuries? Do the narrator and the major believe that the machines will work? What might the machines come to represent to the wounded soldiers by the story's end?
9. The story takes place in Italy, and the narrator is the only American. Is this the only reason for the title? Explain.

Extending

10. How does this story help explain the attitude of the "lost generation" after World War I? Do you think all the characters are "lost"? Why or why not?

VIEWPOINT

Hugh Kenner, an expert in modern literature, has remarked that Ernest Hemingway

> developed the knack of telling simultaneously an overt story and a hidden one.

Kenner suggests that the real center of a Hemingway story is not the direct statements on the "surface" of the story but the concerns that the writer communicates indirectly. How would you distinguish the "overt" story from the "hidden" one in "In Another Country"? What does the narrator never say that the reader nevertheless understands?

LITERARY FOCUS

Prose Style

Ernest Hemingway was as concerned about style as any poet would be. The simplicity of his prose is deceptive, for each word in carefully chosen and placed to create a rhythm that moves the reader along.

Reread the first paragraph of "In Another Country." Notice how the sentences get longer in the middle and how the last sentence is the shortest. There is a sense of conclusion to the last sentence, enhanced by the repetition of words from earlier sentences: "cold," "fall," "wind." The paragraph is circular: It returns us to the ideas with which it began. The repetition of *I* sounds makes it roll to its perfect conclusion. No word, no syllable, no sound is accidental or arbitrary.

At the same time, Hemingway's simple language mirrors the matter-of-fact point of view that he wishes to achieve. Hemingway writes in a **journalistic prose style,** observing from a detached point of view, presenting the facts as a journalist would and forcing the reader to draw the conclusions. When in the last paragraph of "In Another Country" the narrator tells us "I do not know where the doctor got them," we know

he is implying with quiet irony that the pictures have been faked. Yet the sentence itself could have been written by a child. The simple language underscores Hemingway's desire to observe the facts without elaboration so that his readers are forced to draw the conclusions and perceive the irony for themselves.

Thinking About Prose Style

How do the sentence rhythms in the last paragraph reflect the finality of the death of the major's wife? How does the language underscore the narrator's matter-of-fact attitude toward the death? What do we conclude that the narrator never tells us?

COMPOSITION

Writing a Comparison/Contrast

Find a passage from "In Another Country" that illustrates the main characteristics of Hemingway's prose style. Then find a passage from another story in this volume that strikes you as very different in style. You might consider the stories of Poe, Crane, or Jewett. Make notes on word choice, sentence length, sound, and point of view in the two selections, and then arrange your notes in a logical order. Based on your notes, write a brief essay in which you compare and contrast the two prose styles. *For help with this assignment, refer to Lesson 2 in the Writing About Literature Handbook at the back of this book.*

Writing a Narrative

Choose an actual historical event, or invent a significant event. In a few paragraphs tell what happened using a detached, journalistic style similar to Ernest Hemingway's. Narrate the story of what happened in simple language; use dialogue if appropriate. Omit any direct statements about the significance of the event. Force your readers to draw their own conclusions by including hints about the event's importance.

F. Scott Fitzgerald   *1896–1940*

When F. Scott Fitzgerald wrote "There are no second acts in American life," he might have been describing his own career. The spokesman of the Roaring Twenties, Fitzgerald achieved great success early in life but was unable to sustain that success into middle age. Burned out by personal and financial disasters, he died of a heart attack at forty-four.

Fitzgerald was born in St. Paul, Minnesota, into a family of little wealth but great social ambitions. After attending Princeton and serving as an officer in World War I, he settled in New York City, walking the streets in cardboard shoes and wondering where his next meal would come from. Such worries ended in 1920 with the publication of *This Side of Paradise.* The book was an overnight success, and Fitzgerald was able to marry Zelda Sayre, the southern belle with whom he had fallen in love, and to live glamorously in Europe and America.

Throughout the twenties Fitzgerald mingled with the rich and fashionable, maintaining a high style of living. When the frantic twenties ended in the great stock market crash of 1929, Fitzgerald's private life and lucrative career crashed also: His wife suffered a series of nervous breakdowns; his high-paying magazine market evaporated; and although he had made vast amounts of money, he found that he had spent it all. In a desperate attempt to pay for his wife's hospitalization, he spent his last years turning out undistinguished screenplays in Hollywood.

Yet Fitzgerald was also a serious artist, and he produced a body of work that captures the Jazz Age as only an insider could capture it. His masterpiece, *The Great Gatsby* (1925), is a vivid and moving portrait of Jazz Age characters whose talents and dignity are distorted by false values. His semiautobiographical short stories and novels *Tender Is the Night* (1934) and *The Last Tycoon* (1941) reflect a sharp awareness of the tragic attachment to wealth and "society" from which Fitzgerald, like his heroes, suffered.

Basil Lee, the hero of "He Thinks He's Wonderful," bears a striking resemblance to Fitzgerald as a teen-ager. Basil is viewed with Fitzgerald's characteristic blend of satire and sympathy.

F. Scott Fitzgerald

He Thinks He's Wonderful

1

After the college board examinations in June, Basil Duke Lee and five other boys from St. Regis School boarded the train for the West. Two got out at Pittsburgh, one slanted south toward St. Louis and two stayed in Chicago; from then on Basil was alone. It was the first time in his life that he had ever felt the need of tranquillity, but now he took long breaths of it; for, though things had gone better toward the end, he had had an unhappy year at school.

He wore one of those extremely flat derbies[1] in vogue during the twelfth year of the century, and a blue business suit become a little too short for his constantly lengthening body. Within he was by turns a disembodied spirit, almost unconscious of his person and moving in a mist of impressions and emotions, and a fiercely competitive individual trying desperately to control the rush of events that were the steps in his own evolution from child

to man. He believed that everything was a matter of effort—the current principle of American education—and his fantastic ambition was continually leading him to expect too much. He wanted to be a great athlete, popular, brilliant and always happy. During this year at school, where he had been punished for his "freshness," for fifteen years of thorough spoiling at home, he had grown uselessly introspective, and this interfered with that observation of others which is the beginning of wisdom. It was apparent that before he obtained much success in dealing with the world he would know that he'd been in a fight.

He spent the afternoon in Chicago, walking the streets and avoiding members of the underworld. He bought a detective story called "In the Dead of the Night," and at five o'clock recovered his suitcase from the station check room and boarded the Chicago, Milwaukee and St. Paul. Immediately he encountered a contemporary, also bound home from school.

---

1. **derbies:** stiff hats with round crowns and curved brims.

Margaret Torrence was fourteen; a serious girl, considered beautiful by a sort of tradition, for she had been beautiful as a little girl. A year and a half before, after a breathless struggle, Basil had succeeded in kissing her on the forehead. They met now with extraordinary joy; for a moment each of them to the other represented home, the blue skies of the past, the summer afternoons ahead.

He sat with Margaret and her mother in the dining car that night. Margaret saw that he was no longer the ultraconfident boy of a year before; his brightness was subdued, and the air of consideration in his face—a mark of his recent discovery that others had wills as strong as his, and more power—appeared to Margaret as a charming sadness. The spell of peace after a struggle was still upon him. Margaret had always liked him—she was of the grave, conscientious type who sometimes loved him and whose love he could never return—and now she could scarcely wait to tell people how attractive he had grown.

After dinner they went back to the observation car and sat on the deserted rear platform while the train pulled them visibly westward between the dark wide farms. They talked of people they knew, of where they had gone for Easter vacation, of the plays they had seen in New York.

"Basil, we're going to get an automobile," she said, "and I'm going to learn to drive."

"That's fine." He wondered if his grandfather would let him drive the electric[2] sometimes this summer.

The light from inside the car fell on her young face, and he spoke impetuously, borne on by the rush of happiness that he was going home: "You know something? You know you're the prettiest girl in the city?"

At the moment when the remark blurred with the thrilling night in Margaret's heart, Mrs. Torrence appeared to fetch her to bed.

Basil sat alone on the platform for a while, scarcely realizing that she was gone, at peace with himself for another hour and content that everything should remain patternless and shapeless until tomorrow.

2

Fifteen is of all ages the most difficult to locate—to put one's fingers on and say, "That's the way I was." The melancholy Jacques[3] does not select it for mention, and all one can know is that somewhere between thirteen, boyhood's majority, and seventeen, when one is a sort of counterfeit young man, there is a time when youth fluctuates hourly between one world and another—pushed ceaselessly forward into unprecedented experiences and vainly trying to struggle back to the days when nothing had to be paid for. Fortunately none of our contemporaries remember much more than we do of how we behaved in those days; nevertheless the curtain is about to be drawn aside for an inspection of Basil's madness that summer.

To begin with, Margaret Torrence, in one of those moods of idealism which overcome the most matter-of-fact girls, gave it as her rapt opinion that Basil was wonderful. Having practised believing things all year at school, and having nothing much to believe at that moment, her friends accepted the fact. Basil suddenly became a legend. There were outbreaks of giggling when girls encountered him on the street, but he suspected nothing at all.

One night, when he had been home a week, he and Riply Buckner went on to an after dinner gathering on Imogene Bissel's veranda. As they came up the walk Margaret and two other girls suddenly clung together, whispered convulsively and pursued one another around the yard, uttering strange cries—an inexplicable business that ended only when Gladys Van Schellinger, tenderly and impressively accompanied by her mother's maid, arrived in a limousine.

---

2. **electric:** early type of automobile powered by an electric battery.

3. **the melancholy Jacques** [jäʹkwēz]: a character in Shakespeare's *As You Like It* who philosophizes about the stages of life.

All of them were a little strange to one another. Those who had been East at school felt a certain superiority, which, however, was more than counterbalanced by the fact that romantic pairings and quarrels and jealousies and adventures, of which they were lamentably ignorant, had gone on while they had been away.

After the ice cream at nine they sat together on the warm stone steps in a quiet confusion that was halfway between childish teasing and adolescent coquetry.[4] Last year the boys would have ridden their bicycles around the yard; now they had all begun to wait for something to happen.

They knew it was going to happen, the plainest girls, the shyest boys; they had begun to associate with others the romantic world of summer night that pressed deeply and sweetly on their senses. Their voices drifted in a sort of broken harmony in to Mrs. Bissel, who sat reading beside an open window.

"No, look out. You'll break it. Bay-zil!"

"Rip-lee!"

"Sure I did!"

Laughter.

"—on Moonlight Bay
We could hear their voices call—"

"Did you see—"

"Connie, don't—don't! You tickle. Look out!"

Laughter.

"Going to the lake tomorrow?"

"Going Friday."

"Elwood's home."

"Is Elwood home?"

"—you have broken my heart—"

"Look out now!"

"Look out!"

Basil sat beside Riply on the balustrade,[5] listening to Joe Gorman singing. It was one of the griefs of his life that he could not sing "so people could stand it," and he conceived a sudden admiration for Joe Gorman, reading into his personality the thrilling clearness of those sounds that moved so confidently through the dark air.

They evoked for Basil a more dazzling night than this, and other more remote and enchanted girls. He was sorry when the voice died away, and there was a rearranging of seats and a businesslike quiet—the ancient game of Truth had begun.

"What's your favorite color, Bill?"

"Green," supplies a friend.

"Sh-h-h! Let him alone."

Bill says, "Blue."

"What's your favorite girl's name?"

"Mary," says Bill.

"Mary Haupt! Bill's got a crush on Mary Haupt!"

She was a cross-eyed girl, a familiar personification of repulsiveness.

"Who would you rather kiss than anybody?"

Across the pause a snicker stabbed the darkness.

"My mother."

"No, but what girl?"

"Nobody."

"That's not fair. Forfeit! Come on, Margaret."

"Tell the truth, Margaret."

She told the truth and a moment later Basil looked down in surprise from his perch; he had just learned that he was her favorite boy.

"Oh, yes-s!" he exclaimed sceptically. "Oh, yes-s! How about Hubert Blair?"

He renewed a casual struggle with Riply Buckner and presently they both fell off the balustrade. The game became an inquisition into Gladys Van Schellinger's carefully chaperoned heart.

"What's your favorite sport?"

"Croquet."[6]

The admission was greeted by a mild titter.

"Favorite boy."

---

4. **coquetry** [kō′kə trē]: flirting.
5. **balustrade** [bal′əs trād′]: railing supported by posts.

6. **croquet** [krō kā′]: outdoor game in which mallets are used to drive a wooden ball through small hoops.

"Thurston Kohler."

A murmur of disappointment.

"Who's he?"

"A boy in the East."

This was manifestly an evasion.

"Who's your favorite boy here?"

Gladys hesitated. "Basil," she said at length.

The faces turned up to the balustrade this time were less teasing, less jocular. Basil depreciated the matter with "Oh, yes-s! Sure! Oh, yes-s!" But he had a pleasant feeling of recognition, a familiar delight.

Imogene Bissel, a dark little beauty and the most popular girl in their crowd, took Gladys' place. The interlocutors[7] were tired of gastronomic[8] preferences—the first question went straight to the point.

"Imogene, have you ever kissed a boy?"

"No." A cry of wild unbelief. "I have not!" she declared indignantly.

"Well, have you ever been kissed?"

Pink but tranquil, she nodded, adding, "I couldn't help it."

"Who by?"

"I won't tell."

"Oh-h-h! How about Hubert Blair?"

"What's your favorite book, Imogene?"

"Beverly of Graustark."

"Favorite girl?"

"Passion Johnson."

"Who's she?"

"Oh, just a girl at school."

Mrs. Bissel had fortunately left the window.

"Who's your favorite boy?"

Imogene answered steadily, "Basil Lee."

This time an impressed silence fell. Basil was not surprised—we are never surprised at our own popularity—but he knew that these were not those ineffable girls, made up out of books and faces momentarily encountered, whose voices he had heard for a moment in Joe Gorman's song. And when, presently, the first telephone rang inside, calling a daughter home, and the girls, chattering like birds, piled all together into Gladys Van Schellinger's limousine, he lingered back in the shadow so as not to seem to be showing off. Then, perhaps because he nourished a vague idea that if he got to know Joe Gorman very well he would get to sing like him, he approached him and asked him to go to Lambert's for a soda.

Joe Gorman was a tall boy with white eyebrows and a stolid face who had only recently become one of their "crowd." He did not like Basil, who, he considered, had been "stuck up" with him last year, but he was acquisitive of useful knowledge and he was momentarily overwhelmed by Basil's success with girls.

It was cheerful in Lambert's, with great moths batting against the screen door and languid couples in white dresses and suits spread about the little tables. Over their sodas, Joe proposed that Basil come home with him to spend the night; Basil's permission was obtained over the telephone.

Passing from the gleaming store into the darkness, Basil was submerged in an unreality in which he seemed to see himself from the outside, and the pleasant events of the evening began to take on fresh importance.

Disarmed by Joe's hospitality, he began to discuss the matter.

"That was a funny thing that happened tonight," he said, with a disparaging little laugh.

"What was?"

"Why, all those girls saying I was their favorite boy." The remark jarred on Joe. "It's a funny thing," went on Basil. "I was sort of unpopular at school for a while, because I was fresh,[9] I guess. But the thing must be that some boys are popular with boys and some are popular with girls."

He had put himself in Joe's hands, but he was unconscious of it; even Joe was only aware of a certain desire to change the subject.

"When I get my car," suggested Joe, up in his room, "we could take Imogene and Margaret and go for rides."

---

7. **interlocutors** [in'tər lok′yə tərz]: people participating in a conversation.

8. **gastronomic:** relating to food and fine eating.

9. **fresh:** unmannerly.

"All right."

"You could have Imogene and I'd take Margaret, or anybody I wanted. Of course I know they don't like me as well as they do you."

"Sure they do. It's just because you haven't been in our crowd very long yet."

Joe was sensitive on that point and the remark did not please him. But Basil continued: "You ought to be more polite to the older people if you want to be popular. You didn't say how do you do to Mrs. Bissel tonight."

"I'm hungry," said Joe quickly. "Let's go down to the pantry and get something to eat."

Clad only in their pajamas, they went downstairs. Principally to dissuade Basil from pursuing the subject, Joe began to sing in a low voice:

"Oh, you beautiful doll,
You great—big—"

But the evening, coming after the month of enforced humility at school, had been too much for Basil. He got a little awful. In the kitchen, under the impression that his advice had been asked, he broke out again:

"For instance, you oughtn't to wear those white ties. Nobody does that that goes East to school." Joe, a little red, turned around from the ice box and Basil felt a slight misgiving. But he pursued with: "For instance, you ought to get your family to send you East to school. It'd be a great thing for you. Especially if you want to go East to college, you ought to first go East to school. They take it out of you."

Feeling that he had nothing special to be taken out of him, Joe found the implication distasteful. Nor did Basil appear to him at that moment to have been perfected by the process.

"Do you want cold chicken or cold ham?" They drew up chairs to the kitchen table. "Have some milk?"

"Thanks."

Intoxicated by the three full meals he had had since supper, Basil warmed to his subject. He built up Joe's life for him little by little,

transformed him radiantly from what was little more than a Midwestern bumpkin[10] to an Easterner bursting with *savoir-faire*[11] and irresistible to girls. Going into the pantry to put away the milk, Joe paused by the open window for a breath of quiet air; Basil followed. "The thing is if a boy doesn't get it taken out of him at school, he gets it taken out of him at college," he was saying.

Moved by some desperate instinct, Joe opened the door and stepped out onto the back porch. Basil followed. The house abutted on the edge of the bluff occupied by the residential section, and the two boys stood silent for a moment, gazing at the scattered lights of the lower city. Before the mystery of the unknown human life coursing through the streets below, Basil felt the purport of his words grow thin and pale.

He wondered suddenly what he had said and why it had seemed important to him, and when Joe began to sing again softly, the quiet mood of the early evening, the side of him that was best, wisest and most enduring, stole over him once more. The flattery, the vanity, the fatuousness of the last hour moved off, and when he spoke it was almost in a whisper:

"Let's walk around the block."

The sidewalk was warm to their bare feet. It was only midnight, but the square was deserted save for their whitish figures, inconspicuous against the starry darkness. They snorted with glee at their daring. Once a shadow, with loud human shoes, crossed the street far ahead, but the sound served only to increase their own unsubstantiality. Slipping quickly through the clearings made by gas lamps among the trees, they rounded the block, hurrying when they neared the Gorman house as though they had been really lost in a midsummer night's dream.

Up in Joe's room, they lay awake in the darkness.

10. **bumpkin:** awkward person.
11. ***savoir-faire*** [sav′wär fär′]: ability to behave appropriately in any situation.

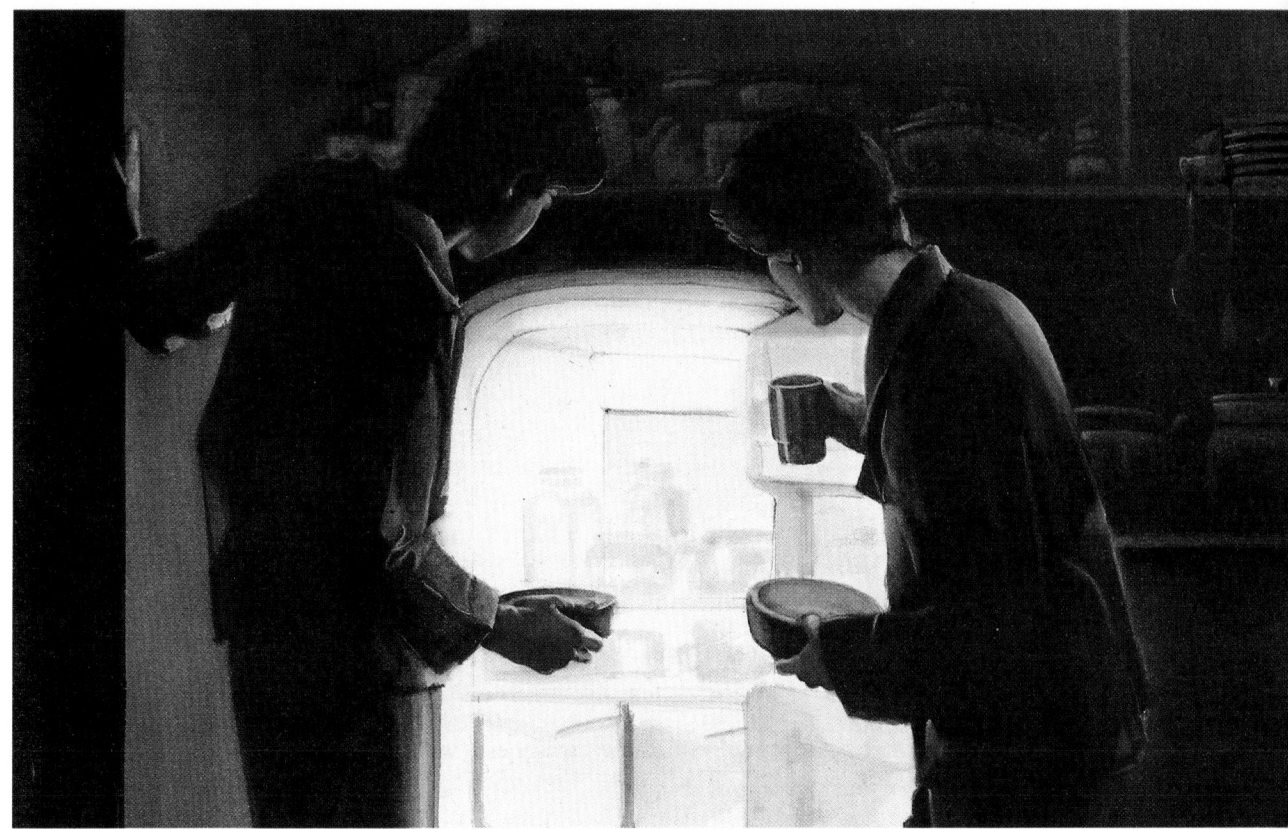

"I talked too much," Basil thought. "I probably sounded pretty bossy and maybe I made him sort of mad. But probably when we walked around the block he forgot everything I said."

Alas, Joe had forgotten nothing—except the advice by which Basil had intended him to profit.

"I never saw anybody as stuck up," he said to himself wrathfully. "He thinks he's wonderful. He thinks he's so darn popular with girls."

3

An element of vast importance had made its appearance with the summer; suddenly the great thing in Basil's crowd was to own an automobile. Fun no longer seemed available save at great distances, at suburban lakes or remote country clubs. Walking downtown ceased to be a legitimate pastime. On the contrary, a single block from one youth's house to another's must be navigated in a car. Dependent groups formed around owners and they began to wield what was, to Basil at least, a disconcerting power.

On the morning of a dance at the lake he called up Riply Buckner.

"Hey, Rip, how you going out to Connie's tonight?"

"With Elwood Leaming."

"Has he got a lot of room?"

Riply seemed somewhat embarrassed. "Why, I don't think he has. You see, he's taking Margaret Torrence and I'm taking Imogene Bissel."

"Oh!"

Basil frowned. He should have arranged all this a week ago. After a moment he called up Joe Gorman.

"Going to the Davies' tonight, Joe?"

"Why, yes."

"Have you got room in your car—I mean, could I go with you?"

"Why, yes, I suppose so."

There was a perceptible lack of warmth in his voice.

"Sure you got plenty of room?"

"Sure. We'll call for you quarter to eight."

Basil began preparations at five. For the second time in his life he shaved, completing the operation by cutting a short straight line under his nose. It bled profusely, but on the advice of Hilda, the maid, he finally stanched the flow with little pieces of toilet paper. Quite a number of pieces were necessary; so, in order to facilitate breathing, he trimmed it down with a scissors, and with this somewhat awkward mustache of paper and gore clinging to his upper lip, wandered impatiently around the house.

At six he began working on it again, soaking off the tissue paper and dabbing at the persistently freshening crimson line. It dried at length, but when he rashly hailed his mother it opened once more and the tissue paper was called back into play.

At quarter to eight, dressed in blue coat and white flannels, he drew one last bar of powder across the blemish, dusted it carefully with his handkerchief and hurried out to Joe Gorman's car. Joe was driving in person, and in front with him were Lewis Crum and Hubert Blair. Basil got in the big rear seat alone and they drove without stopping out of the city onto the Black Bear Road, keeping their backs to him and talking in low voices together. He thought at first that they were going to pick up other boys; now he was shocked, and for a moment he considered getting out of the car, but this would imply that he was hurt. His spirit, and with it his face, hardened a little and he sat without speaking or being spoken to for the rest of the ride.

After half an hour the Davies' house, a huge rambling bungalow occupying a small peninsula in the lake, floated into sight. Lanterns outlined its shape and wavered in gleaming lines on the gold-and-rose colored water, and as they came near, the low notes of bass horns and drums were blown toward them from the lawn.

Inside Basil looked about for Imogene. There was a crowd around her seeking dances, but she saw Basil; his heart bounded at her quick intimate smile.

"You can have the fourth, Basil, and the eleventh and the second extra. . . . How did you hurt your lip?"

"Cut it shaving," he said hurriedly. "How about supper?"

"Well, I have to have supper with Riply because he brought me."

"No, you don't," Basil assured her.

"Yes, she does," insisted Riply, standing close at hand. "Why don't you get your own girl for supper?"

—but Basil had no girl, though he was as yet unaware of the fact.

After the fourth dance, Basil led Imogene down to the end of the pier, where they found seats in a motorboat.

"Now what?" she said.

He did not know. If he had really cared for her he would have known. When her hand rested on his knee for a moment he did not notice it. Instead, he talked. He told her how he had pitched on the second baseball team at school and had once beaten the first in a five-inning game. He told her that the thing was that some boys were popular with boys and some boys were popular with girls—he, for instance, was popular with girls. In short, he unloaded himself.

At length, feeling that he had perhaps dwelt disproportionately on himself, he told her suddenly that she was his favorite girl.

Imogene sat there, sighing a little in the moonlight. In another boat, lost in the darkness beyond the pier, sat a party of four. Joe Gorman was singing:

> "My little love—
> —in honey man,
> He sure has won my—"

"I thought you might want to know," said Basil to Imogene. "I thought maybe you thought I liked somebody else. The truth game didn't get around to me the other night."

"What?" asked Imogene vaguely. She had forgotten the other night, all nights except this, and she was thinking of the magic in Joe Gorman's voice. She had the next dance with him; he was going to teach her the words of a new song. Basil was sort of peculiar, telling her all this stuff. He was good-looking and attractive and all that, but—she wanted the dance to be over. She wasn't having any fun.

The music began inside—"Everybody's Doing It," played with many little nervous jerks on the violins.

"Oh, listen!" she cried, sitting up and snapping her fingers. "Do you know how to rag?"[12]

"Listen, Imogene"—He half realized that something had slipped away—"let's sit out this dance—you can tell Joe you forgot."

She rose quickly. "Oh, no, I can't!"

Unwillingly Basil followed her inside. It had not gone well—he had talked too much again. He waited moodily for the eleventh dance so that he could behave differently. He believed now that he was in love with Imogene. His self-deception created a tightness in his throat, a counterfeit of longing and desire.

Before the eleventh dance he was aware that some party was being organized from which he was purposely excluded. There were whisperings and arguings among some of the boys, and unnatural silences when he came near. He heard Joe Gorman say to Riply Buckner, "We'll just be gone three days. If Gladys can't go, why don't you ask Connie? The chaperons'll—" he changed his sentence as he saw Basil—"and we'll all go to Smith's for ice cream soda."

Later, Basil took Riply Buckner aside but failed to elicit any information: Riply had not forgotten Basil's attempt to rob him of Imogene tonight.

"It wasn't about anything," he insisted. "We're going to Smith's, honest. . . . How'd you cut your lip?"

"Cut it shaving."

When his dance with Imogene came she was even vaguer than before, exchanging mysterious communications with various girls as they moved around the room, locked in the convulsive grip of the Grizzly Bear.[13] He led her out to the boat again, but it was occupied, and they walked up and down the pier while he tried to talk to her and she hummed:

"My little lov-in honey man—"

"Imogene, listen. What I wanted to ask you when we were on the boat before was about the night we played Truth. Did you really mean what you said?"

"Oh, what do you want to talk about that silly game for?"

It had reached her ears, not once but several times, that Basil thought he was wonderful—news that was flying about with as much volatility as the rumor of his graces two weeks before. Imogene liked to agree with everyone—and she had agreed with several impassioned boys that Basil was terrible. And it was difficult not to dislike him for her own disloyalty.

But Basil thought that only ill luck ended the intermission before he could accomplish his purpose; though what he had wanted he had not known.

Finally, during the intermission, Margaret Torrence, whom he had neglected, told him the truth.

"Are you going on the touring party up to the St. Croix River?" she asked. She knew he was not.

"What party?"

"Joe Gorman got it up. I'm going with Elwood Leaming."

"No, I'm not going," he said gruffly. "I couldn't go."

"Oh!"

---

12. **rag:** type of dance popular in the early 1900s.

13. **Grizzly Bear:** popular dance of the period.

"I don't like Joe Gorman."

"I guess he doesn't like you much either."

"Why? What did he say?"

"Oh, nothing."

"But what? Tell me what he said."

After a minute she told him, as if reluctantly: "Well, he and Hubert Blair said you thought—you thought you were wonderful." Her heart misgave her.

But she remembered he had asked her for only one dance. "Joe said you told him that all the girls thought you were wonderful."

"I never said anything like that," said Basil indignantly, "never!"

He understood—Joe Gorman had done it all, taken advantage of Basil's talking too much—an affliction which his real friends had always allowed for—in order to ruin him. The world was suddenly compact of villainy. He decided to go home.

In the coat room he was accosted by Bill Kampf: "Hello, Basil, how did you hurt your lip?"

"Cut it shaving."

"Say, are you going to this party they're getting up next week?"

"No."

"Well, look, I've got a cousin from Chicago coming to stay with us and mother said I could have a boy out for the weekend. Her name is Minnie Bibble."

"Minnie Bibble?" repeated Basil, vaguely revolted.

"I thought maybe you were going to that party, too, but Riply Buckner said to ask you and I thought—"

"I've got to stay home," said Basil quickly.

"Oh, come on, Basil," he pursued. "It's only for two days, and she's a nice girl. You'd like her."

"I don't know," Basil considered. "I'll tell you what I'll do, Bill. I've got to get the street car home. I'll come out for the weekend if you'll take me over to Wildwood now in your car."

"Sure I will."

Basil walked out on the veranda and approached Connie Davies.

"Goodbye," he said. Try as he might, his voice was stiff and proud. "I had an awfully good time."

"I'm sorry you're leaving so early, Basil." But she said to herself: "He's too stuck up to have a good time. He thinks he's wonderful."

From the veranda he could hear Imogene's laughter down at the end of the pier. Silently he went down the steps and along the walk to meet Bill Kampf, giving strollers a wide berth as though he felt the sight of him would diminish their pleasure.

It had been an awful night.

Ten minutes later Bill dropped him beside the waiting trolley. A few last picnickers sauntered aboard and the car bobbed and clanged through the night toward St. Paul.

Presently two young girls sitting opposite Basil began looking over at him and nudging each other, but he took no notice—he was thinking how sorry they would all be—Imogene and Margaret, Joe and Hubert and Riply.

"Look at him now!" they would say to themselves sorrowfully. "President of the United States at twenty-five! Oh, if we only hadn't been so bad to him that night!"

He thought he was wonderful!

4

Ermine Gilberte Labouisse Bibble was in exile. Her parents had brought her from New Orleans to Southampton[14] in May, hoping that the active outdoor life proper to a girl of fifteen would take her thoughts from love. But North or South, a storm of sapling arrows flew about her. She was "engaged" before the first of June.

Let it not be gathered from the foregoing that the somewhat hard outlines of Miss Bibble at twenty had already begun to appear. She was of a radiant freshness; her head had reminded otherwise not illiterate young men of damp blue violets, pierced with blue windows that looked into a bright soul, with today's new roses showing through.

---

14. **Southampton:** resort town along the southern shore of Long Island in New York State.

She was in exile. She was going to Glacier National Park[15] to forget. It was written[16] that in passage she would come to Basil as a sort of initiation, turning his eyes out from himself and giving him a first dazzling glimpse into the world of love.

She saw him first as a quiet handsome boy with an air of consideration in his face, which was the mark of his recent re-discovery that others had wills as strong as his, and more power. It appeared to Minnie—as a few months back it had appeared to Margaret Torrence, like a charming sadness. At dinner he was polite to Mrs. Kampf in a courteous way that he had from his father, and he listened to Mr. Bibble's discussion of the word "Creole"[17] with such evident interest and appreciation that Mr. Bibble thought, "Now here's a young boy with something *to* him."

After dinner, Minnie, Basil and Bill rode into Black Bear village to the movies, and the slow diffusion of Minnie's charm and personality presently became the charm and personality of the affair itself.

It was thus that all Minnie's affairs for many years had a family likeness. She looked at Basil, a childish open look; then opened her eyes wider as if she had some sort of comic misgivings, and smiled—she smiled—

For all the candor of this smile, its effect, because of the special contours of Minnie's face and independent of her mood, was of sparkling invitation. Whenever it appeared Basil seemed to be suddenly inflated and borne upward, a little farther each time, only to be set down when the smile had reached a point where it must become a grin, and chose instead to melt away. It was like a drug. In a little while he wanted nothing except to watch it with a vast buoyant delight.

Then he wanted to see how close he could get to it.

There is a certain stage of an affair between young people when the presence of a third party is a stimulant. Before the second day had well begun, before Minnie and Basil had progressed beyond the point of great gross compliments about each other's surpassing beauty and charm, both of them had begun to think about the time when they could get rid of their host, Bill Kampf.

In the late afternoon, when the first cool of the evening had come down and they were fresh and thin-feeling from swimming, they sat in a cushioned swing, piled high with pillows and shaded by the thick veranda vines; Basil put his arm around her and leaned toward her cheek and Minnie managed it that he touched her fresh lips instead. And he had always learned things quickly.

They sat there for an hour, while Bill's voice reached them, now from the pier, now from the hall above, now from the pagoda[18] at the end of the garden, and three saddled horses chafed their bits in the stable and all around them the bees worked faithfully among the flowers. Then Minnie reached up to reality, and they allowed themselves to be found—

"Why, we were looking for you too."

And Basil, by simply waving his arms and wishing, floated miraculously upstairs to brush his hair for dinner.

"She certainly is a wonderful girl. Oh, gosh, she certainly is a wonderful girl!"

He mustn't lose his head. At dinner and afterward he listened with unwavering deferential attention while Mr. Bibble talked of the boll weevil.

"But I'm boring you. You children want to go off by yourselves."

"Not at all, Mr. Bibble. I was very interested—honestly."

"Well, you all go on and amuse yourselves. I didn't realize time was getting on. Nowadays it's so seldom you meet a young man with good manners and good common sense in his

---

15. **Glacier National Park:** national park in northwest Montana.
16. **written:** fated.
17. **"Creole"** [krē′ōl]: referring to the descendants of French and Spanish settlers in Louisiana.

18. **pagoda** [pə gō′də]: small summer house resembling a Far Eastern temple.

head, that an old man like me is likely to go along forever."

Bill walked down with Basil and Minnie to the end of the pier. "Hope we'll have a good sailing tomorrow. Say, I've got to drive over to the village and get somebody for my crew. Do you want to come along?"

"I reckon I'll sit here for a while and then go to bed," said Minnie.

"All right. You want to come, Basil?"

"Why—why, sure, if you want me, Bill."

"You'll have to sit on a sail I'm taking over to be mended."

"I don't want to crowd you."

"You won't crowd me. I'll go get the car."

When he had gone they looked at each other in despair. But he did not come back for an hour—something happened about the sail or the car that took a long time. There was only the threat, making everything more poignant and breathless, that at any minute he *would* be coming.

By and by they got into the motorboat and sat close together murmuring: "This fall—" "When you come to New Orleans—" "When I go to Yale year after next—" "When I come North to school—" "When I get back from Glacier Park—" "Kiss me once more." . . . "You're terrible. Do you know you're terrible? . . . You're absolutely terrible—"

The water lapped against the posts; sometimes the boat bumped gently on the pier; Basil undid one rope and pushed, so that they swung off and way from the pier, and became a little island in the night. . . .

Next morning, while he packed his bag, she opened the door of his room and stood beside him. Her face shone with excitement; her dress was starched and white.

"Basil, listen! I have to tell you: Father was talking after breakfast and he told Uncle George that he'd never met such a nice, quiet, level-headed boy as you, and Cousin Bill's got to tutor this month, so father asked Uncle George if he thought your family would let you go to Glacier Park with us for two weeks so I'd have some company." They took hands and danced excitedly around the room. "Don't say anything about it, because I reckon he'll have to write your mother and everything. Basil, isn't it wonderful?"

So when Basil left at eleven, there was no misery in their parting. Mr. Bibble, going into the village for a paper, was going to escort Basil to his train, and till the motorcar moved away the eyes of the two young people shone and there was a secret in their waving hands.

Basil sank back in the seat, replete with happiness. He relaxed—to have made a success of the visit was so nice. He loved her—he loved even her father sitting beside him, her father who was privileged to be so close to her, to fuddle[19] himself at that smile.

Mr. Bibble lit a cigar. "Nice weather," he said. "Nice climate up to the end of October."

"Wonderful," agreed Basil. "I miss October now that I go East to school."

"Getting ready for college?"

"Yes, sir; getting ready for Yale." A new pleasurable thought occurred to him. He hesitated, but he knew that Mr. Bibble, who liked him, would share his joy. "I took my preliminaries this spring and I just heard from them—I passed six out of seven."

"Good for you!"

Again Basil hesitated, then he continued: "I got A in ancient history and B in English history and English A. And I got C in algebra A and Latin A and B. I failed French A."

"Good!" said Mr. Bibble.

"I should have passed them all," went on Basil, "but I didn't study hard at first. I was the youngest boy in my class and I had a sort of swelled head about it."

It was well that Mr. Bibble should know he was taking no dullard to Glacier National Park. Mr. Bibble took a long puff of his cigar.

On second thought, Basil decided that his last remark didn't have the right ring and he amended it a little.

"It wasn't exactly a swelled head, but I never had to study very much, because in En-

---

19. **fuddle:** intoxicate.

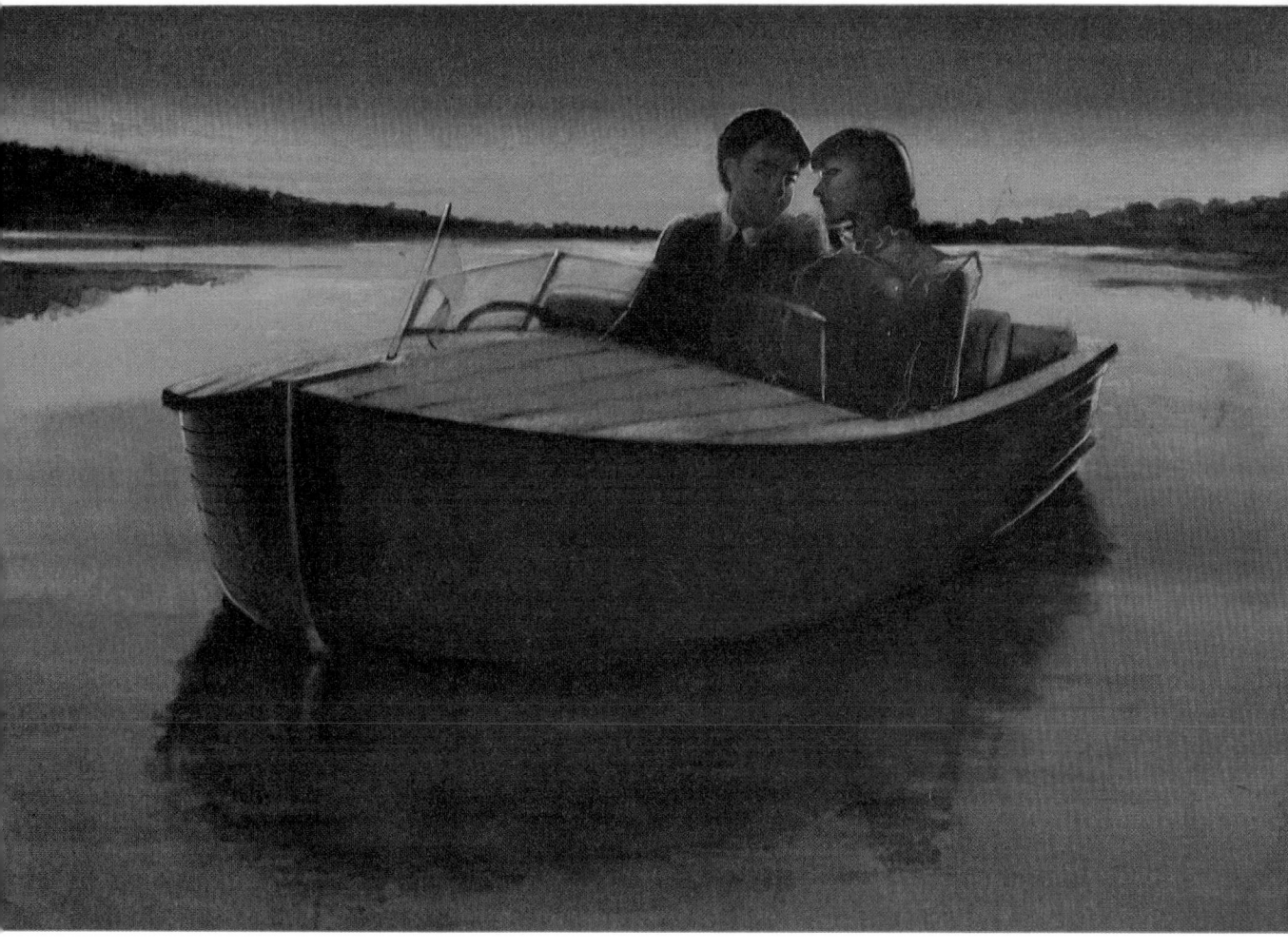

glish I'd usually read most of the books before, and in history I'd read a lot too." He broke off and tried again: "I mean, when you say swelled head you think of a boy just going around with his head swelled, sort of, saying, 'Oh, look how much I know!' Well, I wasn't like that. I mean, I didn't think I knew everything, but I was sort of—"

As he searched for the elusive word, Mr. Bibble said, "H'm!" and pointed with his cigar at a spot in the lake.

"There's a boat," he said.

"Yes," agreed Basil. "I don't know much about sailing. I never cared for it. Of course I've been out a lot, just tending boards and all

that, but most of the time you have to sit with nothing to do. I like football."

"H'm!" said Mr. Bibble. "When I was your age I was out in the Gulf in a catboat every day."

"I guess it's fun if you like it," conceded Basil.

"Happiest days of my life."

The station was in sight. It occurred to Basil that he should make one final friendly gesture.

"Your daughter certainly is an attractive girl, Mr. Bibble," he said. "I usually get along with girls all right, but I don't usually like them very much. But I think your daughter is the most attractive girl I ever met." Then, as the car stopped, a faint misgiving overtook him and he was impelled to add with a disparaging little laugh, "Goodbye. I hope I didn't talk too much."

"Not at all," said Mr. Bibble. "Good luck to you. Goo'-bye."

A few minutes later, when Basil's train had pulled out, Mr. Bibble stood at the newsstand buying a paper and already drying his forehead against the hot July day.

"Yes, sir! That was a lesson not to do anything in a hurry," he was saying to himself vehemently. "Imagine listening to that fresh kid gabbling about himself all through Glacier Park! Thank the good Lord for that little ride!"

On his arrival home, Basil literally sat down and waited. Under no pretext would he leave the house save for short trips to the drug store for refreshments, whence he returned on a full run. The sound of the telephone or the doorbell galvanized him into the rigidity of the electric chair.

That afternoon he composed a wondrous geographical poem, which he mailed to Minnie:

Of all the fair flowers of Paris
  Of all the red roses of Rome,
Of all the deep tears of Vienna
  The sadness wherever you roam,
I think of that night by the lakeside,
  The beam of the moon and stars,
And the smell of an aching like perfume,
  The tune of the Spanish guitars.

But Monday passed and most of Tuesday and no word came. Then, late in the afternoon of the second day, as he moved vaguely from room to room looking out of different windows into a barren lifeless street, Minnie called him on the phone.

"Yes?" His heart was beating wildly.

"Basil, we're going this afternoon."

"Going!" he repeated blankly.

"Oh, Basil, I'm so sorry. Father changed his mind about taking anybody West with us."

"Oh!"

"I'm so sorry, Basil."

"I probably couldn't have gone."

There was a moment's silence. Feeling her presence over the wire, he could scarcely breathe, much less speak.

"Basil, can you hear me?"

"Yes."

"We may come back this way. Anyhow, remember we're going to meet this winter in New York."

"Yes," he said, and he added suddenly: "Perhaps we won't ever meet again."

"Of course we will. They're calling me, Basil. I've got to go. Goodbye."

He sat down beside the telephone, wild with grief. The maid found him half an hour later bowed over the kitchen table. He knew what had happened as well as if Minnie had told him. He had made the same old error, undone the behavior of three days in half an hour. It would have been no consolation if it had occurred to him that it was just as well. Somewhere on the trip he would have let go and things might have been worse—though perhaps not so sad. His only thought now was that she was gone.

He lay on his bed, baffled, mistaken, miserable but not beaten. Time after time, the same vitality that had led his spirit to a scourging made him able to shake off the blood like water not to forget, but to carry his wounds with him to new disasters and new atonements—toward his unknown destiny.

Two days later his mother told him that on condition of his keeping the batteries on charge, and washing it once a week, his grandfather had consented to let him use the electric whenever it was idle in the afternoon. Two hours later he was out in it, gliding along Crest Avenue at the maximum speed permitted by the gears and trying to lean back as if it were a Stutz Bearcat.[20] Imogene Bissel waved at him from in front of her house and he came to an uncertain stop.

"You've got a car!"

---

20. **Stutz Bearcat:** luxury car of the 1910s and 1920s, built very low to the ground.

"It's grandfather's," he said modestly. "I thought you were up on that party at the St. Croix."

She shook her head. "Mother wouldn't let me go—only a few girls went. There was a big accident over in Minneapolis and mother won't even let me ride in a car unless there's someone over eighteen driving."

"Listen, Imogene, do you suppose your mother meant electrics?"

"Why, I never thought—I don't know. I could go and see."

"Tell your mother it won't go over twelve miles an hour," he called after her.

A minute later she ran joyfully down the walk. "I can go, Basil," she cried. "Mother never heard of any wrecks in an electric. What'll we do?"

"Anything," he said in a reckless voice. "I didn't mean that about this bus making only twelve miles an hour—it'll make fifteen. Listen, let's go down to Smith's and have a claret lemonade."

"Why, Basil Lee!"

STUDY QUESTIONS

Recalling

1. What opinion does Margaret spread about town when Basil returns from school (page 527)? What do Margaret, Gladys, and Imogene say about Basil when they play "Truth" (page 529)?

2. What does Basil tell Imogene at the dance at the lake (Section 3)? After Imogene abandons Basil to dance with Joe Gorman, what does Basil believe he feels for Imogene? What "truth" does Margaret tell Basil?

3. Where does Basil go when he is excluded from his friends' touring party? With whom does he now "fall in love"?

4. What does Basil expect Mr. Bibble to do? Does he do it? What are Mr. Bibble's last words about Basil (page 538)?

5. At the end of the story, what does Basil's grandfather let Basil use?

Interpreting

6. What makes Basil "think he's wonderful"? Why does he talk so much about himself? Does his outward confidence mask inner doubts? Explain.

7. Why does Margaret tell everyone that Basil is wonderful? Why do so many girls say that Basil is their "favorite boy"? Noting that their opinions change, what is Fitzgerald suggesting about adolescent behavior with these events?

8. How does Basil feel when Mr. Bibble fails to invite him to Glacier National Park? What does the ending of the story, in which Imogene goes for a ride with Basil, suggest about the depth of Basil's feelings?

9. Do you think Fitzgerald is making fun of Basil? Is he fond of Basil? Does he sympathize with Basil's problems? Explain.

Extending

10. Do you agree with any of Fitzgerald's observations about adolescence? Do you think Sherwood Anderson (page 504) or Mark Twain (page 274) would agree? Explain your opinion and give your reasons.

VIEWPOINT

Basil Lee appears in a series of stories by Fitzgerald, about which Jackson R. Bryer and John Kuehl write:

> Another recurrent motif or symbol is that of the automobile and the kind of romantic promise and social prestige its possession conveys.
>
> —Introduction to *The Basil and Josephine Stories*

▪ Do you agree that in "He Thinks He's Wonderful" the automobile represents romance and social prestige? Why or why not? What other details of the story underscore Basil's romantic and social values?

F. Scott Fitzgerald **539**

LITERARY FOCUS

Characterization

Characterization refers to the personality of a character and the ways in which the writer creates and develops that personality. Characterization can be direct or indirect.

With **direct characterization** a writer directly states facts about a character's personality. Fitzgerald does this in the second paragraph of "He Thinks He's Wonderful" when he tells us, among other things, that Basil was "a mist of impressions and emotions" but also "a fiercely competitive person."

With **indirect characterization** a writer reveals a character's personality indirectly through descriptions of characters, their thoughts, words, and actions. A writer may indirectly reveal a character through physical description. When we learn that Basil is wearing a derby "in vogue" and a blue business suit, we recognize that he is a conformist who wants to impress others with his appearance; when we learn that the suit is "a little too short," we realize that he is awkward and not so impressive.

A second way of revealing character indirectly is through action. When Basil tries so hard to mask the cut he made shaving, we see again how concerned he is with his appearance.

We also learn about Basil from his thoughts. When Margaret tells Basil about the rumors Joe Gorman has been spreading, Fitzgerald shows us how upset and persecuted Basil feels by telling us (page 534) exactly what Basil is thinking.

A character may also be revealed through speech. Basil's final conversation with Mr. Bibble underscores his tendency to talk too much and helps explain why others find him conceited.

Finally, a character may be revealed through the perceptions of other characters. Mr. Bibble gives us one evaluation of Basil when he exclaims, "Imagine listening to that fresh kid gabbling about himself all through Glacier Park!"

Thinking About Characterization

■ Find at least one more example of each of the six methods of characterization—direct and in-direct—that help create the character of Basil Lee. Is Basil a round character (see page 309)? Explain.

VOCABULARY

Slang

Slang is very informal language that is not considered standard usage. Slang words are usually coined by groups of people who want to find new, fresh expressions or give new meanings to old expressions. Groups also coin words in order to give the members of the group a feeling of belonging to a special community of "insiders."

Some words in standard usage take on different meanings when they are used as slang. In "He Thinks He's Wonderful," for example, *freshness* describes a lovely, unspoiled girl. *Fresh,* when applied to Basil, however, is a slang word for impertinent or unmannerly.

■ Find at least one other slang expression in the story. Tell what it means in standard English.

COMPOSITION

Writing About Character

■ Choose one of the characters besides Basil in "He Thinks He's Wonderful" and, in a brief essay, examine the means by which he or she is characterized. Begin with a general statement about the character's personality. Then consider the various methods of characterization that Fitzgerald uses, citing examples from the story. Conclude by explaining whether the character is flat or round.

Writing a Description

■ Write a paragraph in which you describe a popular literary or television character by using only *direct description* of that character's personality. Then, in a few paragraphs or a short story, capture the same character using any or all of the five methods of indirect characterization. Which of your efforts more effectively captures your character's personality, and why?

Willa Cather   *1873–1947*

Willa Cather's stories and novels breathe with the spirit of the American land. They also often present one of the most difficult subjects in fiction: the celebration of the life of a good person, a life "complete and beautiful."

Willa Cather was born in Virginia, but her family moved to a farm in Nebraska when she was ten years old. She began to write while still at the University of Nebraska, but later turned to editing, working first in Pittsburgh and then in New York City. In 1912 she turned her full attention to producing fiction.

The great prairie lands on which Cather spent her girlhood and the pioneering spirit of her Nebraska neighbors, many of them European immigrants, gave her material for much of her best writing. Unlike Sherwood Anderson and Sinclair Lewis, Cather loved the rural world of her youth. Her feeling for the land and its people was very deep; long after she had left Nebraska, she remembered it in such moving works as *O Pioneers!* (1913), *My Ántonia* (1918), and "Neighbor Rosicky" (1928). Other novels, such as *The Song of the Lark* (1915) and *Death Comes for the Archbishop* (1927), reveal her interest in the American Southwest, while *Shadows on the Rock* (1931), is a historical novel of seventeenth-century Quebec.

Cather's work is filled with bold strokes of the imagination and rises to moments of passionate intensity, but it never strives for oddness or eccentric effects. Cather's is a quiet art that disguises itself, so that the reader is more aware of the subject than of the technique. *Death Comes for the Archbishop,* for example, appears to be traditional in its beautiful recreation of the lives of two European priests in early New Mexico, but it is actually quite experimental in its loose construction and abandonment of a traditional plot.

In "Neighbor Rosicky" Cather celebrates a good person. The great Russian novelist Leo Tolstoy once declared that "Happy families are all alike"—implying that troubled lives and troubled people make better material for fiction. Yet in her portrait of Neighbor Rosicky, Cather demonstrates that happy families are not all alike. Rosicky is portrayed with such rich affection that he never becomes a type. He stands forth as an individual in harmony with himself, an individual who displays the human values that Willa Cather most admired.

Willa Cather

Neighbor Rosicky

I

When Doctor Burleigh told neighbor Rosicky he had a bad heart, Rosicky protested.

"So? No, I guess my heart was always pretty good. I got a little asthma, maybe. Just a awful short breath when I was pitchin' hay last summer, dat's all."

"Well now, Rosicky, if you know more about it than I do, what did you come to me for? It's your heart that makes you short of breath, I tell you. You're sixty-five years old, and you've always worked hard, and your heart's tired. You've got to be careful from now on, and you can't do heavy work any more. You've got five boys at home to do it for you."

The old farmer looked up at the Doctor with a gleam of amusement in his queer triangular-shaped eyes. His eyes were large and lively, but the lids were caught up in the middle in a curious way, so that they formed a triangle. He did not look like a sick man. His brown face was creased but not wrinkled, he had a ruddy color in his smooth-shaven cheeks and in his lips, under his long brown moustache. His hair was thin and ragged around his ears, but very little gray. His forehead, naturally high and crossed by deep parallel lines, now ran all the way up to his pointed crown. Rosicky's face had the habit of looking interested—suggested a contented disposition and a reflective quality that was gay rather than grave. This gave him a certain detachment, the easy manner of an onlooker and observer.

"Well, I guess you ain't got no pills fur a bad heart, Doctor Ed. I guess the only thing is fur me to git me a new one."

Doctor Burleigh swung round in his desk-chair and frowned at the old farmer. "I think if I were you, I'd take a little care of the old one, Rosicky."

Rosicky shrugged. "Maybe I don't know how. I expect you mean fur me not to drink my coffee no more."

"I wouldn't, in your place. But you'll do as you choose about that. I've never yet been able to separate a Bohemian[1] from his coffee or his pipe. I've quit trying. But the sure thing is you've got to cut out farm work. You can feed the stock and do chores about the barn, but you can't do anything in the fields that makes you short of breath."

"How about shelling corn?"

"Of course not!"

Rosicky considered with puckered brows.

"I can't make my heart go no longer'n it wants to, can I, Doctor Ed?"

"I think it's good for five or six years yet, maybe more, if you'll take the strain off it. Sit around the house and help Mary. If I had a good wife like yours, I'd want to stay around the house."

His patient chuckled. "It ain't no place fur a man. I don't like no old man hanging round the kitchen too much. An' my wife, she's a awful hard worker her own self."

"That's it; you can help her a little. My heavens, Rosicky, you are one of the few men I know who has a family he can get some comfort out of; happy dispositions, never quarrel among themselves, and they treat you right. I want to see you live a few years and enjoy them."

"Oh, they're good kids, all right," Rosicky assented.

The Doctor wrote him a prescription and asked him how his oldest son, Rudolph, who had married in the spring, was getting on. Rudolph had struck out for himself, on rented land. "And how's Polly? I was afraid Mary mightn't like an American daughter-in-law, but it seems to be working out all right."

"Yes, she's a fine girl. Dat widder[2] woman bring her daughters up very nice. Polly got lots of spunk, an' she got some style, too. Da's nice, for young folks to have some style." Rosicky inclined his head gallantly. His voice and his twinkly smile were an affectionate compliment to his daughter-in-law.

"It looks like a storm, and you'd better be getting home before it comes. In town in the car?" Doctor Burleigh rose.

"No, I'm in de wagon. When you got five boys, you ain't got much chance to ride round in de Ford. I ain't much for cars, noway."

"Well, it's a good road out to your place; but I don't want you bumping around in a wagon much. And never again on a hayrake, remember!"

Rosicky placed the Doctor's fee delicately behind the desk telephone, looking the other way, as if this were an absent-minded gesture. He put on his plush cap and his corduroy jacket with a sheepskin collar, and went out.

The Doctor picked up his stethoscope and frowned at it as if he were seriously annoyed with the instrument. He wished it had been telling tales about some other man's heart, some old man who didn't look the Doctor in the eye so knowingly, or hold out such a warm brown hand when he said goodbye. Doctor Burleigh had been a poor boy in the country before he went away to medical school; he had known Rosicky almost ever since he could remember, and he had a deep affection for Mrs. Rosicky.

Only last winter he had had such a good breakfast at Rosicky's, and that when he needed it. He had been out all night on a long, hard confinement[3] case at Tom Marshall's—a big rich farm where there was plenty of stock and plenty of feed and a great deal of expensive farm machinery of the newest model, and no comfort whatever. The woman had too many

---

1. **Bohemian** [bō hē′mē ən]: person from Bohemia, a region of western Czechoslovakia.

2. **widder:** Rosicky's pronunciation of *widow*.
3. **confinement:** childbirth.

children and too much work, and she was no manager. When the baby was born at last, and handed over to the assisting neighbor woman, and the mother was properly attended to, Burleigh refused any breakfast in that slovenly house, and drove his buggy—the snow was too deep for a car—eight miles to Anton Rosicky's place. He didn't know another farmhouse where a man could get such a warm welcome and such good strong coffee with rich cream. No wonder the old chap didn't want to give up his coffee!

He had driven in just when the boys had come back from the barn and were washing up for breakfast. The long table, covered with a bright oilcloth, was set out with dishes waiting for them, and the warm kitchen was full of the smell of coffee and hot biscuit and sausage. Five big handsome boys, running from twenty to twelve, all with what Burleigh called natural good manners—they hadn't a bit of the painful self-consciousness he himself had to struggle with when he was a lad. One ran to put his horse away, another helped him off with his fur coat and hung it up, and Josephine, the youngest child and the only daughter, quickly set another place under her mother's direction.

With Mary, to feed creatures was the natural expression of affection—her chickens, the calves, her big hungry boys. It was a rare pleasure to feed a young man whom she seldom saw and of whom she was as proud as if he belonged to her. Some country housekeepers would have stopped to spread a white cloth over the oilcloth, to change the thick cups and plates for their best china, and the wooden-handled knives for plated ones. But not Mary.

"You must take us as you find us, Doctor Ed. I'd be glad to put out my good things for you if you was expected, but I'm glad to get you any way at all."

He knew she was glad—she threw back her head and spoke out as if she were announcing him to the whole prairie. Rosicky hadn't said anything at all; he merely smiled his twinkling smile, put some more coal on the fire, and went into his own room to pour the Doctor a little drink in a medicine glass. When they were all seated, he watched his wife's face from his end of the table and spoke to her in Czech. Then, with the instinct of politeness which seldom failed him, he turned to the Doctor and said slyly, "I was just tellin' her not to ask you no questions about Mrs. Marshall till you eat some breakfast. My wife, she's terrible fur to ask questions."

The boys laughed, and so did Mary. She watched the Doctor devour her biscuit and sausage, too much excited to eat anything herself. She drank her coffee and sat taking in everything about her visitor. She had known him when he was a poor country boy, and was boastfully proud of his success, always saying: "What do people go to Omaha for, to see a doctor, when we got the best one in the state right here?" If Mary liked people at all, she felt physical pleasure in the sight of them, personal exultation in any good fortune that came to them. Burleigh didn't know many women like that, but he knew she was like that.

When his hunger was satisfied, he did, of course, have to tell them about Mrs. Marshall, and he noticed what a friendly interest the boys took in the matter.

Rudolph, the oldest one (he was still living at home then), said: "The last time I was over there, she was lifting them big heavy milk cans, and I knew she oughtn't to be doing it."

"Yes, Rudolph told me about that when he come home, and I said it wasn't right," Mary put in warmly. "It was all right for me to do them things up to the last, for I was terrible strong, but that woman's weakly. And do you think she'll be able to nurse it, Ed?" She sometimes forgot to give him the title she was so proud of. "And to think of your being up all night and then not able to get a decent breakfast! I don't know what's the matter with such people."

"Why, Mother," said one of the boys, "if Doctor Ed had got breakfast there, we wouldn't have him here. So you ought to be glad."

"He knows I'm glad to have him, John, any time. But I'm sorry for that poor woman, how bad she'll feel the Doctor had to go away in the cold without his breakfast."

"I wish I'd been in practice when these were getting born." The doctor looked down the row of close-clipped heads. "I missed some good breakfasts by not being."

The boys began to laugh at their mother because she flushed so red, but she stood her ground and threw up her head. "I don't care, you wouldn't have got away from this house without breakfast. No doctor ever did. I'd have had something ready fixed that Anton could warm up for you."

The boys laughed harder than ever, and exclaimed at her: "I'll bet you would!" "She would, that!"

"Father, did you get breakfast for the doctor when we were born?"

"Yes, and he used to bring me my breakfast, too, mighty nice. I was always awful hungry!" Mary admitted with a guilty laugh.

While the boys were getting the Doctor's horse, he went to the window to examine the house plants. "What do you do to your geraniums to keep them blooming all winter, Mary? I never pass this house that from the road I don't see your windows full of flowers."

She snapped off a dark red one, and a ruffled new green leaf, and put them in his buttonhole. "There, that looks better. You look too solemn for a young man, Ed. Why don't you git married? I'm worried about you. Settin' at breakfast, I looked at you real hard, and I seen you've got some gray hairs already."

"Oh, yes! They're coming. Maybe they'd come faster if I married."

"Don't talk so. You'll ruin your health eating at the hotel. I could send your wife a nice loaf of nut bread, if you only had one. I don't like to see a young man getting gray. I'll tell you something, Ed; you make some strong black tea and keep it handy in a bowl, and every morning just brush it into your hair, an' it'll keep the gray from showin' much. That's the way I do!"

Sometimes the Doctor heard the gossipers in the drugstore wondering why Rosicky didn't get on faster. He was industrious, and so were his boys, but they were rather free and easy, weren't pushers, and they didn't always show good judgment. They were comfortable, they were out of debt, but they didn't get much ahead. Maybe, Doctor Burleigh reflected, people as generous and warmhearted and affectionate as the Rosickys never got ahead much; maybe you couldn't enjoy your life and put it into the bank, too.

II

When Rosicky left Doctor Burleigh's office he went into the farm implement store to light his pipe and put on his glasses and read over the list Mary had given him. Then he went into the general merchandise place next door and stood about until the pretty girl with the plucked eyebrows, who always waited on him, was free. Those eyebrows, two thin India-ink strokes, amused him, because he remembered how they used to be. Rosicky always prolonged his shopping by a little joking; the girl knew the old fellow admired her, and she liked to chaff[4] with him.

"Seems to me about every other week you buy ticking, Mr. Rosicky, and always the best quality," she remarked as she measured off the heavy bolt[5] with red stripes.

"You see, my wife is always makin' goose-fedder pillows, an' de thin stuff don't hold in dem little down fedders."

"You must have lots of pillows at your house."

"Sure. She makes quilts of dem, too. We sleeps easy. Now she's makin' a fedder quilt for my son's wife. You know Polly, that married my Rudolph. How much my bill, Miss Pearl?"

"Eight eighty-five."

"Chust make it nine, and put in some candy fur de women."

"As usual. I never did see a man buy so

---

4. **chaff:** to tease and joke in a good-natured way.
5. **bolt:** roll of cloth of a specific length.

much candy for his wife. First thing you know, she'll be getting too fat."

"I'd like dat. I ain't much fur all dem slim women like what de style is now."

"That's one for me, I suppose, Mr. Bohunk!" Pearl sniffed and elevated her India-ink strokes.

When Rosicky went out to his wagon, it was beginning to snow—the first snow of the season, and he was glad to see it. He rattled out of town and along the highway through a wonderfully rich stretch of country, the finest farms in the county. He admired this High Prairie, as it was called, and always liked to drive through it. His own place lay in a rougher territory, where there was some clay in the soil and it was not so productive. When he bought his land, he hadn't the money to buy on High Prairie; so he told his boys, when they grumbled, that if their land hadn't some clay in it, they wouldn't own it at all. All the same, he enjoyed looking at these fine farms, as he enjoyed looking at a prize bull.

After he had gone eight miles, he came to the graveyard, which lay just at the edge of his own hayland. There he stopped his horses and sat still on his wagon seat, looking about at the snowfall. Over yonder on the hill he could see his own house, crouching low, with the clump of orchard behind and the windmill before, and all down the gentle hillslope the rows of pale gold cornstalks stood out against the white field. The snow was falling over the cornfield and the pasture and the hayland, steadily, with very little wind—a nice dry snow. The graveyard had only a light wire fence about it and was all overgrown with long red grass. The fine snow, settling into this red grass and upon the few little evergreens and the headstones, looked very pretty.

It was a nice graveyard, Rosicky reflected, sort of snug and homelike, not cramped or mournful—a big sweep all round it. A man could lie down in the long grass and see the complete arch of the sky over him, hear the wagons go by; in summer the mowing machine rattled right up to the wire fence. And it was so near home. Over there across the cornstalks his own roof and windmill looked so good to him that he promised himself to mind the Doctor and take care of himself. He was awful fond of his place, he admitted. He wasn't anxious to leave it. And it was a comfort to think that he would never have to go farther than the edge of his own hayfield. The snow, falling over his barnyard and the graveyard, seemed to draw things together like. And they were all old neighbors in the graveyard, most of them friends; there was nothing to feel awkward or embarrassed about. Embarrassment was the most disagreeable feeling Rosicky knew. He didn't often have it—only with certain people whom he didn't understand at all.

Well, it was a nice snowstorm; a fine sight to see the snow falling so quietly and graciously over so much open country. On his cap and shoulders, on the horses' backs and manes, light, delicate, mysterious it fell; and with it a dry cool fragrance was released into the air. It meant rest for vegetation and men and beasts, for the ground itself; a season of long nights for sleep, leisurely breakfasts, peace by the fire. This and much more went through Rosicky's mind, but he merely told himself that winter was coming, clucked to his horses, and drove on.

When he reached home, John, the youngest boy, ran out to put away his team for him, and he met Mary coming up from the outside cellar with her apron full of carrots. They went into the house together. On the table, covered with oilcloth figured with clusters of blue grapes, a place was set, and he smelled hot coffeecake of some kind. Anton never lunched in town; he thought that extravagant, and anyhow he didn't like the food. So Mary always had something ready for him when he got home.

After he was settled in his chair, stirring his coffee in a big cup, Mary took out of the oven a pan of *kolache*[6] stuffed with apricots, exam-

---

6. *kolache* [kō′lä chē]: buns made of sweet dough filled with jam or fruit.

ined them anxiously to see whether they had got too dry, put them beside his plate, and then sat down opposite him.

Rosicky asked her in Czech if she wasn't going to have any coffee.

She replied in English, as being somehow the right language for transacting business: "Now what did Doctor Ed say, Anton? You tell me just what."

"He said I was to tell you some compliments, but I forgot 'em." Rosicky's eyes twinkled.

"About you, I mean. What did he say about your asthma?"

"He says I ain't got no asthma." Rosicky took one of the little rolls in his broad brown fingers. The thickened nail of his right thumb told the story of his past.

"Well, what is the matter? And don't try to put me off."

"He don't say nothing much, only I'm a little older, and my heart ain't so good like it used to be."

Mary started and brushed her hair back from her temples with both hands as if she were a little out of her mind. From the way she glared, she might have been in a rage with him.

"He says there's something the matter with your heart? Doctor Ed says so?"

"Now don't yell at me like I was a hog in de garden, Mary. You know I always did like to hear a woman talk soft. He didn't say anything de matter wid my heart, only it ain't so young like it used to be, an' he tell me not to pitch hay or run de corn-sheller."

Mary wanted to jump up, but she sat still. She admired the way he never under any circumstances raised his voice or spoke roughly. He was city-bred, and she was country-bred; she often said she wanted her boys to have their papa's nice ways.

"You never have no pain there, do you? It's your breathing and your stomach that's been wrong. I wouldn't believe nobody but Doctor Ed about it. I guess I'll go see him myself. Didn't he give you no advice?"

"Chust to take it easy like, an' stay round de house dis winter. I guess you got some carpenter work for me to do. I kin make some new shelves for you, and I want dis long time to build a closet in de boys' room and make dem two little fellers keep dere clo'es hung up."

Rosicky drank his coffee from time to time, while he considered. His moustache was of the soft long variety and came down over his mouth like the teeth of a buggy-rake over a bundle of hay. Each time he put down his cup, he ran his blue handkerchief over his lips. When he took a drink of water, he managed very neatly with the back of his hand.

Mary sat watching him intently, trying to find any change in his face. It is hard to see anyone who has become like your own body to you. Yes, his hair had got thin, and his high forehead had deep lines running from left to right. But his neck, always clean shaved except in the busiest seasons, was not loose or baggy. It was burned a dark reddish brown, and there were deep creases in it, but it looked firm and full of blood. His cheeks had a good color. On either side of his mouth there was a half-moon down the length of his cheek, not wrinkles, but two lines that had come there from his habitual expression. He was shorter and broader than when she married him; his back had grown broad and curved, a good deal like the shell of an old turtle, and his arms and legs were short.

He was fifteen years older than Mary, but she had hardly ever thought about it before. He was

her man, and the kind of man she liked. She was rough, and he was gentle—city-bred, as she always said. They had been shipmates on a rough voyage and had stood by each other in trying times. Life had gone well with them because, at bottom, they had the same ideas about life. They agreed, without discussion, as to what was most important and what was secondary. They didn't often exchange opinions, even in Czech—it was as if they had thought the same thought together. A good deal had to be sacrificed and thrown overboard in a hard life like theirs, and they had never disagreed as to the things that could go. It had been a hard life, and a soft life, too. There wasn't anything brutal in the short, broad-backed man with the three-cornered eyes and the forehead that went on to the top of his skull. He was a city man, a gentle man, and though he had married a rough farm girl, he had never touched her without gentleness.

They had been at one accord not to hurry through life, not to be always skimping and saving. They saw their neighbors buy more land and feed more stock than they did, without discontent. Once when the creamery agent came to the Rosickys to persuade them to sell him their cream, he told them how much money the Fasslers, their nearest neighbors, had made on their cream last year.

"Yes," said Mary, "and look at them Fassler children! Pale, pinched little things, they look like skimmed milk. I'd rather put some color into my children's faces than put money into the bank."

The agent shrugged and turned to Anton.

"I guess we'll do like she says," said Rosicky.

III

Mary very soon got into town to see Doctor Ed, and then she had a talk with her boys and set a guard over Rosicky. Even John, the youngest, had his father on his mind. If Rosicky went to throw hay down from the loft, one of the boys ran up the ladder and took the fork from him. He sometimes complained that though he was getting to be an old man, he wasn't an old woman yet.

That winter he stayed in the house in the afternoons and carpentered, or sat in the chair between the window full of plants and the wooden bench where the two pails of drinking water stood. This spot was called "Father's corner," though it was not a corner at all. He had a shelf there, where he kept his Bohemian papers and his pipes and tobacco, and his shears and needles and thread and tailor's thimble. Having been a tailor in his youth, he couldn't bear to see a woman patching at his clothes, or at the boys'. He liked tailoring, and always patched all the overalls and jackets and work-shirts. Occasionally he made over a pair of pants one of the older boys had outgrown, for the little fellow.

While he sewed, he let his mind run back over his life. He had a good deal to remember, really; life in three countries. The only part of his youth he didn't like to remember was the two years he had spent in London, in Cheapside,[7] working for a German tailor who was wretchedly poor. Those days, when he was nearly always hungry, when his clothes were dropping off him for dirt, and the sound of a strange language kept him in continual bewilderment, had left a sore spot in his mind that wouldn't bear touching.

He was twenty when he landed at Castle Garden[8] in New York, and he had a protector[9] who got him work in a tailor shop in Vesey Street, down near the Washington Market. He looked upon that part of his life as very happy. He became a good workman, he was industrious, and his wages were increased from time to time. He minded his own business and envied nobody's good fortune. He went to night school and learned to read English. He often did overtime work and was well paid for it,

but somehow he never saved anything. He couldn't refuse a loan to a friend, and he was self-indulgent. He liked a good dinner, and a little went for beer, a little for tobacco; a good deal went to the girls. He often stood through an opera on Saturday nights; he could get standing room for a dollar. Those were the great days of opera in New York, and it gave a fellow something to think about for the rest of the week. Rosicky had a quick ear, and a child-ish love of all the stage splendor; the scenery, the costumes, the ballet. He usually went with a chum, and after the performance they had beer and maybe some oysters somewhere. It was a fine life; for the first five years or so it satisfied him completely. He was never hungry or cold or dirty, and everything amused him: a fire, a dog fight, a parade, a storm, a ferry ride. He thought New York the finest, richest, friendliest city in the world.

Moreover, he had what he called a happy home life. Very near the tailor shop was a small furniture factory, where an old Austrian, Loeffler, employed a few skilled men and made unusual furniture, most of it to order, for the rich German housewives uptown. The top floor of Loeffler's five-story factory was a loft, where he kept his choice lumber and stored the odd pieces of furniture left on his hands. One of the young workmen he employed was a Czech, and he and Rosicky became fast friends. They persuaded Loeffler to let them have a sleeping-room in one corner of the loft. They bought good beds and bedding and had their pick of the furniture kept up there. The loft was low-pitched, but light and airy, full of windows, and good-smelling by reason of the fine lumber put up there to season. Old Loeffler used to go down to the docks and buy wood from South America and the East from the sea captains. The young men were as foolish about their house as a bridal pair. Zichec, the young cabi-netmaker, devised every sort of convenience, and Rosicky kept their clothes in order. At night and on Sundays, when the quiver of ma-chinery underneath was still, it was the quiet-est place in the world, and on summer nights

---

7. **Cheapside:** working-class area in the East End of London.
8. **Castle Garden:** chief immigrant station of the United States between 1855 and 1890.
9. **protector:** friend or relative who helps a new immigrant.

all the sea winds blew in. Zichec often practiced on his flute in the evening. They were both fond of music and went to the opera together. Rosicky thought he wanted to live like that forever.

But as the years passed, all alike, he began to get a little restless. When spring came round, he would begin to feel fretted, and he got to drinking. He was likely to drink too much of a Saturday night. On Sunday he was languid and heavy, getting over his spree. On Monday he plunged into work again. So he never had time to figure out what ailed him, though he knew something did. When the grass turned green in Park Place, and the lilac hedge at the back of Trinity churchyard put out its blossoms, he was tormented by a longing to run away. That was why he drank too much; to get a temporary illusion of freedom and wide horizons.

Rosicky, the old Rosicky, could remember as if it were yesterday the day when the young Rosicky found out what was the matter with him. It was on a Fourth of July afternoon, and he was sitting in Park Place in the sun. The lower part of New York was empty. Wall Street, Liberty Street, Broadway, all empty. So much stone and asphalt with nothing going on, so many empty windows. The emptiness was intense, like the stillness in a great factory when the machinery stops and the belts and bands cease running. It was too great a change, it took all the strength out of one. Those blank buildings, without the stream of life pouring through them, were like empty jails. It struck young Rosicky that this was the trouble with big cities; they built you in from the earth itself, cemented you away from any contact with the ground. You lived in an unnatural world, like the fish in an aquarium, who were probably much more comfortable than they ever were in the sea.

On that very day he began to think seriously about the articles he had read in the Bohemian papers, describing prosperous Czech farming communities in the West. He believed he would like to go out there as a farm hand; it was hardly possible that he could ever have land of his own. His people had always been workmen; his father and grandfather had worked in shops. His mother's parents had lived in the country, but they rented their farm and had a hard time to get along. Nobody in his family had ever owned any land—that belonged to a different station of life altogether. Anton's mother died when he was little, and he was sent into the country to her parents. He stayed with them until he was twelve, and formed those ties with the earth and the farm animals and growing things which are never made at all unless they are made early. After his grandfather died, he went back to live with his father and stepmother, but she was very hard on him, and his father helped him to get passage to London.

After that Fourth of July day in Park Place, the desire to return to the country never left him. To work on another man's farm would be all he asked; to see the sun rise and set and to plant things and watch them grow. He was a very simple man. He was like a tree that has not many roots, but one taproot that goes down deep. He subscribed for a Bohemian paper printed in Chicago, then for one printed in Omaha. His mind got farther and farther west. He began to save a little money to buy his liberty. When he was thirty-five, there was a great meeting in New York of Bohemian athletic societies, and Rosicky left the tailor shop and went home with the Omaha delegates to try his fortune in another part of the world.

IV

Perhaps the fact that his own youth was well over before he began to have a family was one reason why Rosicky was so fond of his boys. He had almost a grandfather's indulgence for them. He had never had to worry about any of them—except, just now, a little about Rudolph.

On Saturday night the boys always piled

into the Ford, took little Josephine, and went to town to the moving-picture show. One Saturday morning they were talking at the breakfast table about starting early that evening, so that they would have an hour or so to see the Christmas things in the stores before the show began. Rosicky looked down the table.

"I hope you boys ain't disappointed, but I want you to let me have de car tonight. Maybe some of you can go in with de neighbors."

Their faces fell. They worked hard all week, and they were still like children. A new jackknife or a box of candy pleased the older ones as much as the little fellow.

"If you and Mother are going to town," Frank said, "maybe you could take a couple of us along with you, anyway."

"No, I want to take de car down to Rudolph's, and let him an' Polly go in to de show. She don't git into town enough, an' I'm afraid she's gettin' lonesome, an' he can't afford no car yet."

That settled it. The boys were a good deal dashed. Their father took another piece of applecake and went on: "Maybe next Saturday night de two little fellers can go along wid dem."

"Oh, is Rudolph going to have the car every Saturday night?"

Rosicky did not reply at once; then he began to speak seriously: "Listen, boys; Polly ain't lookin' so good. I don't like to see nobody lookin' sad. It comes hard fur a town girl to be a farmer's wife. I don't want no trouble to start in Rudolph's family. When it starts, it ain't so easy to stop. An American girl don't git used to our ways all at once. I like to tell Polly she and Rudolph can have the car every Saturday night till after New Year's, if it's all right with you boys."

"Sure it's all right, Papa," Mary cut in. "And it's good you thought about that. Town girls is used to more than country girls. I lay awake nights, scared she'll make Rudolph discontented with the farm."

The boys put as good a face on it as they could. They surely looked forward to their Saturday nights in town. That evening Rosicky drove the car the half-mile down to Rudolph's new, bare little house.

Polly was in a short-sleeved gingham dress, clearing away the supper dishes. She was a trim, slim little thing, with blue eyes and shingled[10] yellow hair, and her eyebrows were reduced to a mere brush-stroke, like Miss Pearl's.

"Good evening, Mr. Rosicky. Rudolph's at the barn, I guess." She never called him father or Mary mother. She was sensitive about having married a foreigner. She never in the world would have done it if Rudolph hadn't been such a handsome, persuasive fellow and such a gallant lover. He graduated in her class in the high school in town, and their friendship began in the ninth grade.

Rosicky went in, though he wasn't exactly asked. "My boys ain't goin' to town tonight, an' I brought de car over fur you two to go in to de picture show."

Polly, carrying dishes to the sink, looked over her shoulder at him. "Thank you. But I'm late with my work tonight, and pretty tired. Maybe Rudolph would like to go in with you."

"Oh, I don't go to de shows! I'm too old-fashioned. You won't feel so tired after you ride in de air a ways. It's a nice clear night, an' it ain't cold. You go an' fix yourself up, Polly, an' I'll wash de dishes an' leave everything nice fur you."

Polly blushed and tossed her bob.[11] "I couldn't let you do that, Mr. Rosicky. I wouldn't think of it."

Rosicky said nothing. He found a bib apron on a nail behind the kitchen door. He slipped it over his head and then took Polly by her two elbows and pushed her gently toward the door of her own room. "I washed up de

---

10. **shingled:** woman's short haircut in which the hair over the nape of the neck is shaped close to the head.
11. **bob:** short hair.

kitchen many times for my wife, when de babies was sick or somethin'. You go an' make
yourself look nice. I like you to look prettier'n
any of dem town girls when you go in. De
young folks must have some fun, an' I'm goin'
to look out fur you, Polly."

That kind, reassuring grip on her elbows,
the old man's funny bright eyes, made Polly
want to drop her head on his shoulder for a
second. She restrained herself, but she lingered
in his grasp at the door of her room, murmuring tearfully: "You always lived in the city
when you were young, didn't you? Don't you
ever get lonesome out here?"

As she turned round to him, her hand fell
naturally into his, and he stood holding it and
smiling into her face with his peculiar, knowing, indulgent smile without a shadow of reproach in it. "Dem big cities is all right fur de
rich, but dey is terrible hard fur de poor."

"I don't know. Sometimes I think I'd like to
take a chance. You lived in New York, didn't
you?"

"An' London. Da's bigger still. I learned my
trade dere. Here's Rudolph comin', you better
hurry."

"Will you tell me about London some
time?"

"Maybe. Only I ain't no talker, Polly. Run
an' dress yourself up."

The bedroom door closed behind her, and
Rudolph came in from the outside, looking
anxious. He had seen the car and was sorry
any of his family should come just then. Supper
hadn't been a very pleasant occasion. Halting
in the doorway, he saw his father in a kitchen
apron, carrying dishes to the sink. He flushed
crimson and something flashed in his eye. Rosicky held up a warning finger.

"I brought de car over fur you an' Polly to
go to de picture show, an' I made her let me
finish here so you won't be late. You go put on
a clean shirt, quick!"

"But don't the boys want the car, Father?"

"Not tonight dey don't." Rosicky fumbled
under his apron and found his pants pocket. He
took out a silver dollar and said in hurried

whisper: "You go an' buy dat girl some ice
cream an' candy tonight, like you was courtin'.
She's awful good friends wid me."

Rudolph was very short of cash, but he
took the money as if it hurt him. There had
been a crop failure all over the county. He had
more than once been sorry he'd married this
year.

In a few minutes the young people came
out, looking clean and a little stiff. Rosicky hurried them off, and then he took his own time
with the dishes. He scoured the pots and pans
and put away the milk and swept the kitchen.
He put some coal in the stove and shut off the
drafts, so the place would be warm for them
when they got home late at night. Then he sat
down and had a pipe and listened to the clock
tick.

Generally speaking, marrying an American
girl was certainly a risk. A Czech should marry
a Czech. It was lucky that Polly was the daughter of a poor widow woman; Rudolph was
proud, and if she had a prosperous family to
throw up at him, they could never make it go.
Polly was one of four sisters, and they all
worked; one was bookkeeper in the bank, one
taught music, and Polly and her younger sister
had been clerks, like Miss Pearl. All four of
them were musical, had pretty voices, and sang
in the Methodist choir, which the eldest sister
directed.

Polly missed the sociability of a store position. She missed the choir, and the company of
her sisters. She didn't dislike housework, but
she disliked so much of it. Rosicky was a little
anxious about this pair. He was afraid Polly
would grow so discontented that Rudy would
quit the farm and take a factory job in Omaha.
He had worked for a winter up there, two
years ago, to get money to marry on. He had
done very well, and they would always take
him back at the stockyards. But to Rosicky that
meant the end of everything for his son. To be
a landless man was to be a wage earner, a
slave, all your life; to have nothing, to be
nothing.

Rosicky thought he would come over and

do a little carpentering for Polly after the New Year. He guessed she needed jollying. Rudolph was a serious sort of chap, serious in love and serious about his work.

Rosicky shook out his pipe and walked home across the fields. Ahead of him the lamplight shone from his kitchen windows. Suppose he were still in a tailor shop on Vesey Street, with a bunch of pale, narrow-chested sons working on machines, all coming home tired and sullen to eat supper in a kitchen that was a parlor also; with another crowded, angry family quarreling just across the dumbwaiter[12] shaft, and squeaking pulleys at the windows where dirty washings hung on dirty lines above a court full of old brooms and mops and ash-cans. . . .

He stopped by the windmill to look up at the frosty winter stars and draw a long breath before he went inside. That kitchen with the shining windows was dear to him; but the sleeping fields and bright stars and the noble darkness were dearer still.

V

On the day before Christmas the weather set in very cold; no snow, but a bitter, biting wind that whistled and sang over the flat land and lashed one's face like fine wires. There was baking going on in the Rosicky kitchen all day, and Rosicky sat inside, making over a coat that Albert had outgrown into an overcoat for John. Mary had a big red geranium in bloom for Christmas, and a row of Jerusalem cherry trees, full of berries. It was the first year she had ever grown these; Doctor Ed brought her the seeds from Omaha when he went to some medical convention. They reminded Rosicky of plants he had seen in England; and all afternoon, as he stitched, he sat thinking about those two years in London, which his mind usually shrank from even after all this while.

He was a lad of eighteen when he dropped

---

12. **dumbwaiter:** small elevator used to send food, trash, etc., from one floor to another.

down into London, with no money and no connections except the address of a cousin who was supposed to be working at a confectioner's. When he went to the pastry shop, however, he found that the cousin had gone to America. Anton tramped the streets for several days, sleeping in doorways and on the Embankment,[13] until he was in utter despair. He knew no English, and the sound of the strange language all about him confused him. By chance he met a poor German tailor who had learned his trade in Vienna,[14] and could speak a little Czech. This tailor, Lifschnitz, kept a repair shop in a Cheapside basement, underneath a cobbler. He didn't much need an apprentice, but he was sorry for the boy and took him in for no wages but his keep and what he could pick up. The pickings were supposed to be coppers given you when you took work home to a customer. But most of the customers called for their clothes themselves, and the coppers that came Anton's way were very few. He had, however, a place to sleep. The tailor's family lived upstairs in three rooms; a kitchen, a bedroom, where Lifschnitz and his wife and five children slept, and a livingroom. Two corners of this living room were curtained off for lodgers; in one Rosicky slept on an old horsehair sofa, with a feather quilt to wrap himself in. The other corner was rented to a wretched, dirty boy, who was studying the violin. He actually practiced there. Rosicky was dirty, too. There was no way to be anything else. Mrs. Lifschnitz got the water she cooked and washed with from a pump in a brick court, four flights down. There were bugs in the place, and multitudes of fleas, though the poor woman did the best she could. Rosicky knew she often went empty to give another potato or a spoonful of dripping to the two hungry, sad-eyed boys who lodged with her. He used to think he would never get out of there, never get a clean shirt to his back again. What would he do, he wondered, when his clothes actually dropped to pieces and the worn cloth wouldn't hold patches any longer?

It was still early when the old farmer put aside his sewing and his recollections. The sky had been a dark gray all day, with not a gleam of sun, and the light failed at four o'clock. He went to shave and change his shirt while the turkey was roasting. Rudolph and Polly were coming over for supper.

After supper they sat round in the kitchen, and the younger boys were saying how sorry they were it hadn't snowed. Everybody was sorry. They wanted a deep snow that would lie long and keep the wheat warm, and leave the ground soaked when it melted.

"Yes, sir!" Rudolph broke out fiercely; "if we have another dry year like last year, there's going to be hard times in this country."

Rosicky filled his pipe. "You boys don't know what hard times is. You don't owe nobody, you got plenty to eat an' keep warm, an' plenty water to keep clean. When you got them, you can't have it very hard."

Rudolph frowned, opened and shut his big right hand, and dropped it clenched upon his knee. "I've got to have a good deal more than that, Father, or I'll quit this farming gamble. I can always make good wages railroading, or at the packing house,[15] and be sure of my money."

"Maybe so," his father answered dryly.

Mary, who had just come in from the pantry and was wiping her hands on the roller towel, thought Rudy and his father were getting too serious. She brought her darning basket and sat down in the middle of the group.

"I ain't much afraid of hard times, Rudy," she said heartily. "We've had a plenty, but we've always come through. Your father wouldn't never take nothing very hard, not even hard times. I got a mind to tell you a story on him. Maybe you boys can't hardly remember the year we had that terrible hot wind, that burned everything up on the Fourth

---

13. **Embankment:** part of the north bank of the Thames River in London.
14. **Vienna** [vē en′ə]: capital city of Austria, near the Czechoslovakian border.

15. **packing house:** plant where meat is processed and packed.

of July? All the corn an' the gardens. An' that was in the days when we didn't have alfalfa yet—I guess it wasn't invented.

"Well, that very day your father was out cultivatin' corn, and I was here in the kitchen makin' plum preserves. We had bushels of plums that year. I noticed it was terrible hot, but it's always hot in the kitchen when you're preservin', an' I was too busy with my plums to mind. Anton come in from the field about three o'clock, an' I asked him what was the matter.

" 'Nothin',' he says, 'but it's pretty hot, an' I think I won't work no more today.' He stood round for a few minutes, an' then he says: 'Ain't you near through? I want you should git up a nice supper for us tonight. It's Fourth of July.'

"I told him to git along, that I was right in the middle of preservin', but the plums would taste good on hot biscuit. 'I'm goin' to have fried chicken, too,' he says, and he went off an' killed a couple. You three oldest boys was little fellers, playin' round outside, real hot an' sweaty, an' your father took you to the horse tank down by the windmill an' took off your clothes an' put you in. Them two box elder trees was little then, but they made shade over the tank. Then he took off all his own clothes, an' got in with you. While he was playin' in the water with you, the Methodist preacher drove into our place to say how all the neighbors was goin' to meet at the schoolhouse that night, to pray for rain. He drove right to the windmill, of course, and there was your father and you three with no clothes on. I was in the kitchen door, an' I had to laugh, for the preacher acted like he ain't never seen a naked man before. He surely was embarrassed, an' your father couldn't git to his clothes; they was all hangin' up on the windmill to let the sweat dry out of 'em. So he laid in the tank where he was, an' put one of you boys on top of him to cover him up a little, an' talked to the preacher.

"When you got through playin' in the water, he put clean clothes on you and a clean shirt on himself, an' by that time I'd begun to get supper. He says: 'It's too hot in here to eat comfortable. Let's have a picnic in the orchard. We'll eat our supper behind the mulberry hedge, under them linden trees.'

"So he carried our supper down, an' a bottle of my wild grape wine, an' everything tasted good, I can tell you. The wind got cooler as the sun was goin' down, and it turned out pleasant, only I noticed how the leaves was curled up on the linden trees. That made me think, an' I asked your father if that hot wind all day hadn't been terrible hard on the gardens an' the corn.

" 'Corn,' he says, 'there ain't no corn.'

" 'What you talkin' about?' I said. 'Ain't we got forty acres?'

" 'We ain't got an ear,' he says, 'nor nobody else ain't got none. All the corn in this country was cooked by three o'clock today, like you'd roasted it in an oven.'

" 'You mean you won't get no crop at all?' I asked him. I couldn't believe it, after he'd worked so hard.

" 'No crop this year,' he says. 'That's why we're havin' a picnic. We might as well enjoy what we got.'

"An' that's how your father behaved, when all the neighbors was so discouraged they couldn't look you in the face. An' we enjoyed ourselves that year, poor as we was, an' our neighbors wasn't a bit better off for bein' miserable. Some of 'em grieved till they got poor digestions and couldn't relish what they did have."

The younger boys said they thought their father had the best of it. But Rudolph was thinking that, all the same, the neighbors had managed to get ahead more, in the fifteen years since that time. There must be something wrong about his father's way of doing things. He wished he knew what was going on in the back of Polly's mind. He knew she liked his father, but he knew, too, that she was afraid of something. When his mother sent over coffeecake or prune tarts or a loaf of fresh bread, Polly seemed to regard them with a certain suspicion. When she observed to him that his brothers had nice manners, her tone implied that it was remarkable they should have. With his mother she was stiff and on her guard. Mary's hearty frankness and gusts of good humor irritated her. Polly was afraid of being unusual or conspicuous in any way, of being "ordinary," as she said!

When Mary had finished her story, Rosicky laid aside his pipe.

"You boys like me to tell you about some of dem hard times I been through in London?" Warmly encouraged, he sat rubbing his forehead along the deep creases. It was bothersome to tell a long story in English (he nearly always talked to the boys in Czech), but he wanted Polly to hear this one.

"Well, you know about dat tailor shop I worked in in London? I had one Christmas dere I ain't never forgot. Times was awful bad before Christmas; de boss ain't got much work, an' have it awful hard to pay his rent. It ain't so much fun, bein' poor in a big city like London, I'll say! All de windows is full of good t'ings to eat, an' all de pushcarts in de streets is full, an' you smell 'em all de time, an' you ain't got no money—not a bit. I didn't mind de cold so much, though I didn't have no overcoat, chust a short jacket I'd outgrowed so it wouldn't meet on me, an' my hands was chapped raw. But I always had a good appetite, like you all know, an' de sight of dem pork pies in de windows was awful fur me!

"Day before Christmas was terrible foggy dat year, an' dat fog gits into your bones and makes you all damp like. Mrs. Lifschnitz didn't give us nothin' but a little bread an' drippin' for supper, because she was savin' to try for to give us a good dinner on Christmas Day. After supper de boss say I can go an' enjoy myself, so I went into de streets to listen to de Christmas singers. Dey sing old songs an' make very nice music, an' I run round after dem a good ways, till I got awful hungry. I t'ink maybe if I go home, I can sleep till morning an' forget my belly.

"I went into my corner real quiet, and roll up in my fedder quilt. But I ain't got my head down, till I smell somet'ing good. Seem like it git stronger an' stronger, an' I can't git to sleep noway. I can't understand dat smell. Dere was a gas light in a hall across de court, dat always shine in at my window a little. I got up an' look round. I got a little wooden box in my corner fur a stool, 'cause I ain't got no chair. I picks up dat box, and under it dere is a roast goose on a platter! I can't believe my eyes. I carry it to de window where de light comes in, an' touch it and smell it to find out, an' den I taste it to be sure. I say, I will eat chust one little bite of dat goose, so I can go to sleep, and tomorrow I won't eat none at all. But I tell you, boys, when I stop, one half of dat goose was gone!"

The narrator bowed his head, and the boys shouted. But little Josephine slipped behind his chair and kissed him on the neck beneath his ear.

"Poor little Papa, I don't want him to be hungry!"

"Da's long ago, child. I ain't never been hungry since I had your mudder to cook fur me."

"Go on and tell us the rest, please," said Polly.

"Well, when I come to realize what I done, of course, I felt terrible. I felt better in de stomach, but very bad in de heart. I set on my bed wid dat platter on my knees, an' it all come to me; how hard dat poor woman save to buy dat goose, and how she get some neighbor to cook it dat got more fire, an' how she put it in my corner to keep it away from dem hungry children. Dey was a old carpet hung up to shut my corner off, an' de children wasn't allowed to go in dere. An' I know she put it in my corner because she trust me more'n she did de violin boy. I can't stand it to face her after I spoil de Christmas. So I put on my shoes and go out into de city. I tell myself I better throw myself in de river; but I guess I ain't dat kind of a boy.

"It was after twelve o'clock, an' terrible cold, an' I start out to walk about London all night. I walk along de river awhile, but dey was lots of drunks all along; men, and women too. I chust move along to keep away from de police. I git onto de Strand, an' den over to New Oxford Street, where dere was a big German restaurant on de ground floor, wid big windows all fixed up fine, an' I could see de people havin' parties inside. While I was lookin' in, two men and two ladies come out, laughin' and talkin' and feelin' happy about all dey been eatin' an' drinkin', and dey was speakin' Czech—not like de Austrians, but like de home folks talk it.

"I guess I went crazy, an' I done what I ain't never done before nor since. I went right up to dem gay people an' begun to beg dem: 'Fellow-countrymen, *please* give me money enough to buy a goose!'

"Dey laugh, of course, but de ladies speak awful kind to me, an' dey take me back into de restaurant and give me hot coffee and cakes, an' make me tell all about how I happened to come to London, an' what I was doin' dere. Dey take my name and where I work down on paper, an' both of dem ladies give me ten shillings.[16]

"De big market at Covent Garden ain't very far away, an' by dat time it was open. I go dere an' buy a big goose an' some pork pies, an' potatoes and onion, an' cakes an' oranges fur de children—all I could carry! When I git home, everybody is still asleep. I pile all I bought on de kitchen table, an' go in an' lay down on my bed, an' I ain't waken up till I hear dat woman scream when she come out into her kitchen. My goodness, but she was surprise! She laugh an' cry at de same time, an' hug me and waken all de children. She ain't stop fur no breakfast; she git de Christmas dinner ready dat morning, and we all sit down an' eat all we can hold. I ain't never seen dat violin boy have all he can hold before.

"Two three days after dat, de two men come to hunt me up, an' dey ask my boss, and

he give me a good report an' tell dem I was a steady boy all right. One of dem Bohemians was very smart an' run a Bohemian newspaper in New York, an' de odder was a rich man, in de importing business, an' dey been traveling togedder. Dey told me how t'ings was easier in New York, an' offered to pay my passage when dey was goin' home soon on a boat. My boss say to me: 'You go. You ain't got no chance here, an' I like to see you git ahead, fur you always been a good boy to my woman, and fur dat fine Christmas dinner you give us all.' An' da's how I got to New York."

That night when Rudolph and Polly, arm in arm, were running home across the fields with the bitter wind at their backs, his heart leaped for joy when she said she thought they might have his family come over for supper on New Year's Eve. "Let's get up a nice supper, and not let your mother help at all; make her be company for once."

"That would be lovely of you, Polly," he said humbly. He was a very simple, modest boy, and he, too, felt vaguely that Polly and her sisters were more experienced and worldly than his people.

VI

The winter turned out badly for farmers. It was bitterly cold, and after the first light snows before Christmas there was no snow at all— and no rain. March was as bitter as February. On those days when the wind fairly punished the country, Rosicky sat by his window. In the fall he and the boys had put in a big wheat planting, and now the seed had frozen in the ground. All that land would have to be ploughed up and planted over again, planted in corn. It had happened before, but he was younger then, and he never worried about what had to be. He was sure of himself and of Mary; he knew they could bear what they had to bear, that they would always pull through somehow. But he was not so sure about the young ones, and he felt troubled because Rudolph and Polly were having such a hard start.

Sitting beside his flowering window while

---

16. **shillings:** In the British monetary system before 1971, the shilling was a coin worth 1/20 of a pound. Ten shillings would have been a fairly generous gift at the time the story takes place.

the panes rattled and the wind blew in under the door, Rosicky gave himself to reflection as he had not done since those Sundays in the loft of the furniture factory in New York, long ago. Then he was trying to find what he wanted in life for himself; now he was trying to find what he wanted for his boys, and why it was he so hungered to feel sure they would be here, working this very land, after he was gone.

They would have to work hard on the farm, and probably they would never do much more than make a living. But if he could think of them as staying here on the land, he wouldn't have to fear any great unkindness for them. Hardships, certainly; it was a hardship to have the wheat freeze in the ground when seed was so high; and to have to sell your stock because you had no feed. But there would be other years when everything came along right, and you caught up. And what you had was your own. You didn't have to choose between bosses and strikers, and go wrong either way. You didn't have to do with dishonest and cruel people. They were the only things in his experience he had found terrifying and horrible; the look in the eyes of a dishonest and crafty man, of a scheming and rapacious[17] woman.

In the country, if you had a mean neighbor, you could keep off his land and make him keep off yours. But in the city, all the foulness and misery and brutality of your neighbors was part of your life. The worst things he had come upon in his journey through the world were human—depraved and poisonous specimens of man. To this day he could recall certain terrible faces in the London streets. There were mean people everywhere, to be sure, even in their own country town here. But they weren't tempered, hardened, sharpened, like the treacherous people in cities who live by grinding or cheating or poisoning their fellow men. He had helped to bury two of his fellow workmen in the tailoring trade, and he was distrustful of the organized industries that see one

out of the world in big cities. Here, if you were sick, you had Doctor Ed to look after you; and if you died, fat Mr. Haycock, the kindest man in the world, buried you.

It seemed to Rosicky that for good, honest boys like his, the worst they could do on the farm was better than the best they would be likely to do in the city. If he'd had a mean boy, now, one who was crooked and sharp and tried to put anything over on his brothers, then town would be the place for him. But he had no such boy. As for Rudolph, the discontented one, he would give the shirt off his back to anyone who touched his heart. What Rosicky really hoped for his boys was that they could get through the world without ever knowing much about the cruelty of human beings. "Their mother and me ain't prepared them for that," he sometimes said to himself.

These thoughts brought him back to a grateful consideration of his own case. What an escape he had had, to be sure! He, too, in his time, had had to take money for repair work from the hand of a hungry child who let it go so wistfully; because it was money due his boss. And now, in all these years, he had never had to take a cent from anyone in bitter need—never had to look at the face of a woman become like a wolf's from struggle and famine. When he thought of these things, Rosicky would put on his cap and jacket and slip down to the barn and give his workhorses a little extra oats, letting them eat it out of his hand in their slobbery fashion. It was his way of expressing what he felt, and made him chuckle with pleasure.

The spring came warm, with blue skies—but dry, dry as a bone. The boys began ploughing up the wheat fields to plant them over in corn. Rosicky would stand at the fence corner and watch them, and the earth was so dry it blew up in clouds of brown dust that hid the horses and the sulky plough and the driver. It was a bad outlook.

The big alfalfa field that lay between the home place and Rudolph's came up green, but Rosicky was worried because during that open

---

17. **rapacious** [rə pā′shəs]: greedy.

windy winter a great many Russian thistle plants had blown in there and lodged. He kept asking the boys to rake them out; he was afraid their seed would root and "take the alfalfa." Rudolph said that was nonsense. The boys were working so hard planting corn, their father felt he couldn't insist about the thistles, but he set great store by that big alfalfa field. It was a feed you could depend on—and there was some deeper reason, vague, but strong. The peculiar green of that clover woke early memories in old Rosicky, went back to something in his childhood in the old world. When he was a little boy, he had played in fields of that strong blue-green color.

One morning, when Rudolph had gone to town in the car, leaving a work team idle in his barn, Rosicky went over to his son's place, put the horses to the buggy rake, and set about quietly raking up those thistles. He behaved with guilty caution, and rather enjoyed stealing a march on Doctor Ed, who was just then taking his first vacation in seven years of practice and was attending a clinic in Chicago. Rosicky

got the thistles raked up, but did not stop to burn them. That would take some time, and his breath was pretty short, so he thought he had better get the horses back to the barn.

He got them into the barn and to their stalls, but the pain had come on so sharp in his chest that he didn't try to take the harness off. He started for the house, bending lower with every step. The cramp in his chest was shutting him up like a jackknife. When he reached the windmill, he swayed and caught at the ladder. He saw Polly coming down the hill, running with the swiftness of a slim greyhound. In a flash she had her shoulder under his armpit.

"Lean on me, Father, hard! Don't be afraid. We can get to the house all right."

Somehow they did, though Rosicky became blind with pain; he could keep on his legs, but he couldn't steer his course. The next thing he was conscious of was lying on Polly's bed, and Polly bending over him wringing out bath towels in hot water and putting them on his chest. She stopped only to throw coal into the stove, and she kept the teakettle and the black pot going. She put these hot applications on him for nearly an hour, she told him afterwards, and all that time he was drawn up stiff and blue, with the sweat pouring off him.

As the pain gradually loosed its grip, the stiffness went out of his jaws, the black circles round his eyes disappeared, and a little of his natural color came back. When his daughter-in-law buttoned his shirt over his chest at last, he sighed.

"Da's fine, de way I feel now, Polly. It was a awful bad spell, an' I was so sorry it all come on you like it did."

Polly was flushed and excited. "Is the pain really gone? Can I leave you long enough to telephone over to your place?"

Rosicky's eyelids fluttered. "Don't telephone, Polly. It ain't no use to scare my wife. It's nice and quiet here, an' if I ain't too much trouble to you, just let me lay still till I feel like myself. I ain't got no pain now. It's nice here."

Polly bent over him and wiped the moisture from his face. "Oh, I'm so glad it's over!" she broke out impulsively. "It just broke my heart to see you suffer so, Father."

Rosicky motioned her to sit down on the chair where the teakettle had been, and looked up at her with that lively affectionate gleam in his eyes. "You was awful good to me, I won't never forget dat. I hate it to be sick on you like dis. Down at de barn I say to myself, dat young girl ain't had much experience in sickness, I don't want to scare her, an' maybe she's got a baby comin' or somet'ing."

Polly took his hand. He was looking at her so intently and affectionately and confidingly; his eyes seemed to caress her face, to regard it with pleasure. She frowned with her funny streaks of eyebrows, and then smiled back at him.

"I guess maybe there is something of that kind going to happen. But I haven't told anyone yet, not my mother or Rudolph. You'll be the first to know."

His hand pressed hers. She noticed that it was warm again. The twinkle in his yellow-brown eyes seemed to come nearer.

"I like mighty well to see dat little child, Polly," was all he said. Then he closed his eyes and lay half-smiling. But Polly sat still, thinking hard. She had a sudden feeling that nobody in the world, not her mother, not Rudolph, or anyone, really loved her as much as old Rosicky did. It perplexed her. She sat frowning and trying to puzzle it out. It was as if Rosicky had a special gift for loving people, something that was like an ear for music or an eye for color. It was quiet, unobtrusive; it was merely there. You saw it in his eyes—perhaps that was why they were merry. You felt it in his hands, too. After he dropped off to sleep, she sat holding his warm, broad, flexible brown hand. She had never seen another in the least like it. She wondered if it wasn't a kind of gypsy hand, it was so alive and quick and light in its communications—very strange in a farmer. Nearly all the farmers she knew had huge lumps of fists, like mauls, or they were knotty and bony and uncomfortable-looking, with stiff fingers. But Rosicky's was like quicksilver,[18] flexible, muscular, about the color of a pale cigar, with deep, deep creases across the palm. It wasn't nervous, it wasn't a stupid lump; it was a warm brown human hand, with some cleverness in it, a great deal of generosity, and something else which Polly could only call "gypsy-like"— something nimble and lively and sure, in the way that animals are.

Polly remembered that hour long afterwards; it had been like an awakening to her. It seemed to her that she had never learned so much about life from anything as from old Rosicky's hand. It brought her to herself; it communicated some direct and untranslatable message.

When she heard Rudolph coming in the car, she ran out to meet him.

"Oh, Rudy, your father's been awful sick!

---

18. **quicksilver:** fluid and moving, like mercury.

He raked up those thistles he's been worrying about, and afterwards he could hardly get to the house. He suffered so I was afraid he was going to die."

Rudolph jumped to the ground. "Where is he now?"

"On the bed. He's asleep. I was terribly scared, because, you know, I'm so fond of your father." She slipped her arm through his and they went into the house. That afternoon they took Rosicky home and put him to bed, though he protested that he was quite well again.

The next morning he got up and dressed and sat down to breakfast with his family. He told Mary that his coffee tasted better than usual to him, and he warned the boys not to bear any tales to Doctor Ed when he got home. After breakfast he sat down by his window to do some patching and asked Mary to thread several needles for him before she went to feed her chickens—her eyes were better than his, and her hands steadier. He lit his pipe and took up John's overalls. Mary had been watching him anxiously all morning, and as she went out of the door with her bucket of scraps, she saw that he was smiling. He was thinking, indeed, about Polly, and how he might never have known what a tender heart she had if he hadn't got sick over there. Girls nowadays didn't wear their heart on their sleeve. But now he knew Polly would make a fine woman after the foolishness wore off. Either a woman had that sweetness at her heart or she hadn't. You couldn't always tell by the look of them; but if they had that, everything came out right in the end.

After he had taken a few stitches, the cramp began in his chest, like yesterday. He put his pipe cautiously down on the windowsill and bent over to ease the pull. No use—he had better try to get to his bed if he could. He rose and groped his way across the familiar floor, which was rising and falling like the deck of a ship. At the door he fell. When Mary came in, she found him lying there, and the moment she touched him she knew that he was gone.

Doctor Ed was away when Rosicky died, and for the first few weeks after he got home he was hard driven. Every day he said to himself that he must get out to see that family that had lost their father. One soft, warm moonlight night in early summer he started for the farm. His mind was on other things, and not until his road ran by the graveyard did he realize that Rosicky wasn't over there on the hill where the red lamplight shone, but here, in the moonlight. He stopped his car, shut off the engine, and sat there for a while.

A sudden hush had fallen on his soul. Everything here seemed strangely moving and significant, though signifying what, he did not know. Close by the wire fence stood Rosicky's mowing machine, where one of the boys had been cutting hay that afternoon; his own workhorses had been going up and down there. The new-cut hay perfumed all the night air. The moonlight silvered the long, billowy grass that grew over the graves and hid the fence; the few little evergreens stood out black in it, like shadows in a pool. The sky was very blue and soft, the stars rather faint because the moon was full.

For the first time it struck Doctor Ed that this was really a beautiful graveyard. He thought of city cemeteries, acres of shrubbery and heavy stone, so arranged and lonely and unlike anything in the living world. Cities of the dead, indeed; cities of the forgotten, of the "put away." But this was open and free, this little square of long grass which the wind forever stirred. Nothing but the sky overhead, and the many-colored fields running on until they met that sky. The horses worked here in summer; the neighbors passed on their way to town; and over yonder, in the cornfield, Rosicky's own cattle would be eating fodder as winter came on. Nothing could be more undeathlike than this place; nothing could be more right for a man who had helped to do the work of great cities and had always longed for the open country and had got to it at last. Rosicky's life seemed to him complete and beautiful.

STUDY QUESTIONS

Recalling

1. According to the opening paragraph, what is Doctor Ed's diagnosis of Anton Rosicky? What does the doctor say Rosicky must stop doing?

2. According to page 548, why had life gone well for Rosicky and his wife? Why do they not often exchange opinions?

3. Who are Rudolph and Polly, and what is Rosicky afraid will happen to them, according to page 551?

4. For what does Rosicky "hunger to feel sure" (page 558)? Where does he not want his children to live?

5. How does Rosicky bring on his first heart attack? Who helps him to recover?

6. Who is buried in the graveyard when Doctor Ed stops there near the end of the story? To what does the doctor compare the graveyard? How does he describe the graveyard?

Interpreting

7. Basically, why is the Rosicky farm adequate but not prosperous?

8. Describe the relationship between Mr. and Mrs. Rosicky. How is their relationship different from the relationship between Rudolph and Polly when we first meet them? What changes do we see in Polly in the course of the story?

9. Why is land so important to Rosicky? What are some of the positive values he equates with living off the land?

10. What has Rosicky achieved in his lifetime? What has he achieved in the course of this story—that is, from the time Doctor Ed tells him he has heart trouble until the time of his death?

Extending

11. How is Cather's attitude toward rural life different from that of Sherwood Anderson (page 504) or Edgar Lee Masters (page 467)? What attitude does Cather project about city life? Do you agree, and why?

VIEWPOINT

The literary critic Granville Hicks once wrote:

From the first, it is clear, the one theme that seemed to Miss Cather worth writing about was heroic idealism, the joyous struggle against nature sustained by a confidence in the ultimate beneficence of that nature against which it fought.

—"The Case Against Willa Cather"

■ Where in the story does Rosicky struggle against nature? Where does he display confidence that nature is ultimately "beneficent," or kind? In what ways is the immigrant hero of "Neighbor Rosicky" like the Puritans and pioneers of early America?

LITERARY FOCUS

Theme

A work of fiction always tells us a story—about people, where they lived, what they thought, what adventures they encountered. In "Neighbor Rosicky," for example, we become interested in Rosicky and his whole family. We are interested in Rosicky's health, in his farm, in how the marriage of Rudolph and Polly will work out, and so on.

Yet the "story" is only half the story: The other half is its meaning, its ideas, the significance the author gives it. The main idea of a story is its **theme.**

When we state a theme, we are only indicating our own sense of what gives the story importance or meaning. We are not "summing up" the story itself or reducing it to some commonplace thought. For example, if we were merely to say that "Neighbor Rosicky" shows that "if you lead a good life, you may die content," we would be leaving out everything that makes the story interesting.

We must also recognize that there is no one theme to the exclusion of all others. A complex story like "Neighbor Rosicky" has many themes. It is not only about the life and death of a good man; it is also about rural life as opposed to city life and about the fulfillment of the American dream in the lives of pioneers and immigrants. Exactly what we decide is the theme will often depend on our own perceptions, on what *we* think is important in the world.

Thinking About Theme

1. State in your own words what "Neighbor Rosicky" has to say about life and death, about rural versus city life, and about the American dream.

2. What other themes do you find in the story? What, for example, does the story say about love and marriage? About family and neighbors? Why is the title significant?

VOCABULARY

Sentence Completions

Each of the following sentences contains a blank with four possible words for completing the sentence. The words are from "Neighbor Rosicky." Choose the word that completes each sentence correctly, using the word *as it is used in the selection.*

1. We keep shovels, axes, a plow, and other _____ in the shed in the backyard.
   (a) implements   (c) dispositions
   (b) resources   (d) trifles
2. The log split in half with the last blow of the _____ on the wedge.
   (a) broom   (c) saw
   (b) drill   (d) maul
3. The clerk cut three yards from the _____ of silk.
   (a) ream   (c) bolt
   (b) ticking   (d) loom
4. His classmates loved to _____ him about the pretty girl.
   (a) renounce   (c) chastise
   (b) chaff   (d) reproach

COMPOSITION

Writing About Theme

Choose one story or poem you have read in this book, and tell what you think is its theme. Write an essay in which you begin by stating the theme. Then show how the author illuminates this theme through characterization, setting, events, point of view, and tone. *For help with this assignment, refer to Lesson 6 in the Writing About Literature Handbook .*

Writing About Character

Some of the characters you have encountered in this unit are unhappy or confused about their lives. Choose one of these characters— Cassius Hueffer (page 467), Basil Lee (page 526), George Willard, or Helen White (page 505), for example—and show how he or she might have benefited from an encounter with Anton Rosicky, as Polly did. Describe the encounter in the first person, in the form of a diary entry written by the character you choose, or in the third person, in short story form.

COMPARING WRITERS

One effect of the Modernist movement was to encourage writers to demand more participation from their audiences. In what ways does each of the stories in this unit involve you in the lives and thoughts of its characters?

READING FOR APPRECIATION

Making Inferences

The words *imply* and *infer* are sometimes confused. To *imply* something is to suggest without stating it directly. For example, a person who asks, "Are you going to be using the car tonight?" is usually implying, "I'd like to use the car." To *infer* is to "draw out" a meaning or a suggestion that is not stated directly; the person who is asked if he or she is going to be using the car *infers* that the person asking wants to use it.

A speaker or an author can *imply;* a listener or a reader can *infer.* Both of these processes are at work, or should be at work, in much modern literature. When a writer and a reader are both participating in these actions with attention and imagination, the experience of literature can be its most creative and satisfying.

Of course not everything in literature demands that we make inferences. Often things are what they are, and statements can be taken for just what they say. When someone once asked Ezra Pound what the frogs "meant" in one of his poems, Pound replied that sometimes "frogs is frogs." When Doctor Ed, at the end of "Neighbor Rosicky," says that Rosicky's life was "complete and beautiful," Willa Cather would like us to infer nothing beyond that simple and sublime statement, complete in itself, and see Rosicky's life as the doctor and Cather herself see it.

Yet the selections in this unit often do demand that we make inferences. Marianne Moore's "Poetry" (page 481), for example, begins, "I, too, dislike it." It becomes clear, however, by the time we have finished the poem, that Moore wants us to infer that in fact she *does* like poetry—only, of course, when it is "genuine."

In "The Road Not Taken" (page 493) we soon infer that the poem is about more than a walk Robert Frost once took in the woods. The poet implies that the roads in the wood are in some sense "the roads of life" when he tells us that he will be "telling this with a sigh" at some time in the future and says that his choice of road has made "all the difference." The clues are so strong that we know we must make some inferences about these "roads."

Hemingway's "In Another Country" forces us to make many inferences. When the gentle Italian major suddenly acts strangely, speaking "angrily and bitterly" and telling the narrator that a man "cannot marry," it is at first impossible to infer the major's motives. However, by the end of the story we can infer that the major knew his wife to be in great danger of dying and that he loves his wife so much that the thought of losing her is more than he can bear.

Making inferences is a vital part of reading literature. An author can imply a great deal in a story or a poem, but if we do not infer from what is there and participate as we read, we leave the experience of literature incomplete.

THE AMERICAN VOICE

"Make It New"

When Ezra Pound said, "Make it new," he expressed what so many American artists felt. The twentieth century, so vastly different from what had come before it, presented a whole world that had to be re-seen, re-evaluated, and re-imagined. The writers in this unit built into their poems and stories the surprise of the new, the shock of the new. It inspired some to celebrate; it left some with confusion and a sense of loss. Their works contained unusual images, desperate questions, and experiments in reordering the world. "What now would make sense?" they asked. "How should we face the future?" These artists reshaped literature to try to arrive at new relationships between people and the *new* New World.

Eliot
Do I dare
Disturb the universe? . . .

Williams
            Then he whirled about
                    bounded
into the air
and with an entrechat
            perfectly achieved
completed the figure. . . .
        What goes on here? she said.

Stein
. . . this is this.

MacLeish
A poem should be wordless
As the flight of birds.

Stevens
I placed a jar in Tennessee,
And round it was, upon a hill.
It made the slovenly wilderness
Surround that hill.

Anderson
Man or boy, woman or girl, they had for a moment taken hold of the thing that makes the mature life of men and women in the modern world possible.

Hemingway
He stood there biting his lower lip. "It is very difficult," he said. "I cannot resign myself."

Fitzgerald
. . . not to forget, but to carry his wounds with him to new disasters and new atonements—toward his unknown destiny.

Whether the modern age inspired them or dispirited them, the writers grouped here affirmed the power of the imagination. The act of writing itself was a way of ordering a disordered time and place, an authentic source of delight. Through literature life still offered meaning, beauty, and a measure of joy.

Key to Illustrations on Pages 428–429.

1. Detail of *American Gothic,* Grant Wood, 1930.
2. United States Army poster, World War I.
3. Detail of *Allies Day,* Childe Hassam, 1917.
4. Detail of *Morning News,* Francis Luis Mora, 1912.
5. Detail of *Gertrude Stein,* Pablo Picasso, 1906.
6. Lamp, designed by Louis Tiffany, c. 1910.
7. F. Scott Fitzgerald, photographer unknown.
8. Robert Frost, photograph by Tom Hollyman.
9. *I Saw the Figure 5 in Gold,* Charles Demuth, 1928.
10. Ernest Hemingway, photograph by John Bryson.

U·S·AIR MAIL
8c
AMELIA EARHART

Photograph © 1982 by Jill Krementz

Key to Illustrations appears on page 741.

MIDCENTURY VOICES

1930–1960

The Great Depression

The vibrant, experimental, roaring 1920s ended with a bang—the great stock market crash of 1929. Not only the United States but all the industrial nations of the world found themselves suddenly cast into a disastrous economic depression. The collapse of Wall Street meant terrible times: Businesses failed; factories closed down. Millions of Americans found themselves out of work, their homes or farms lost, their hopes abandoned.

As the Great Depression deepened, the cities of America could no longer be celebrated as Carl Sandburg had celebrated Chicago (page 462)—laughing as a "fighter laughs who has never lost a battle." The American landscape saw armies of wandering men and women searching for jobs. Soup kitchens and bread lines were a constant reminder of how many Americans were forced to accept the charity of others.

The poverty and despair of the 1930s brought forth a new attitude toward government and society. President Franklin Roosevelt called for a "New Deal" for the American people, and his administrations began many programs of direct and indirect assistance to those who had lost not only their jobs but faith in their own future. Americans confronted a decade of self-doubt that was all the more shocking because of the vivid decade that had preceded it.

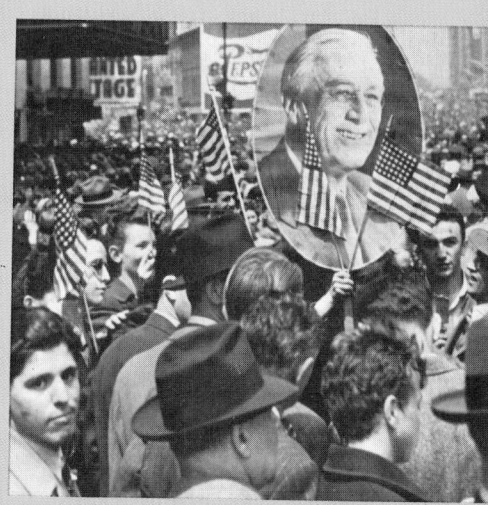

The Literature of Crisis

In the world of literature, as in all the arts, a period of great freedom and experimentation came to an end with the Depression. Many of the great artists of the early twentieth century had years to live and some of their greatest works still to produce—painters such as Pablo Picasso, composers such as Igor Stravinsky and Arnold Schoenberg, and writers such as Pound, Eliot, Yeats, Stevens, and Joyce. Yet these artists had done their shocking work, their influential work, in the first decades of the century.

The next generation, the writers in this unit, absorbed the lessons of the Modernists: They grew up in an atmosphere of Modernism and incorporated into their own work the discoveries and experiments, the new styles and forms, of Modernism. Yet they also witnessed the hard lessons of a nation's poverty and suffering. These writers—striving for both artistic excellence *and* social commitment—produced what critic Alfred Kazin has called the literature of crisis.

In order to put these writers to work, the federal government, through such agencies as the Works Progress Administration, commissioned books, pamphlets, brochures, and other writing of a largely documentary nature. This literature was intended not only to give writers a chance to make a living but also to put America on record for itself, to remind it of its greatness in a time of trouble.

American photographers like Walker Evans documented the country's struggle through the 1930s.

This documentary literature included descriptions and histories of American places—landmarks, towns, cities, and rivers. Writers prepared a detailed guidebook for each state. Writers also collaborated with photographers such as Margaret Bourke-White and Dorothea Lange to produce journalistic and photographic records of the ways America lived. The greatest of these documents is *Let Us Now Praise Famous Men*—a study of Alabama sharecroppers—by writer James Agee and photographer Walker Evans.

The major fiction writers of the time produced novels closely tied to the lives of ordinary people, literature in which style and experiment stepped aside in favor of human stories told with emotion and social commitment. These were the kind of books produced by John Steinbeck, John Dos Passos, and James T. Farrell. Dos Passos' trilogy *U.S.A.* (completed 1936) used journalistic techniques and a style imitating newsreels to tell an epi-sodic story of social unrest and the decline of individuality. The undoubted masterpiece of this type of novel is Steinbeck's *Grapes of Wrath* (1939), the gripping story of the Joads, Oklahoma farmers driven by poverty to find a new natural paradise in California. Ma Joad's outcry sums up the sense of the times: "We ain' gonna die out. People is goin' on—changin' a little, maybe, but goin' right on."

In contrast to the documentary and Realist writers of the time, two novelists combined a feeling for the people with a continued reliance on the American Romantic tradition. Thomas Wolfe's novels—including *Of Time and the River* (1935) and *You Can't Go Home Again* (1940)—are highly autobiographical, lyrical journeys into the artist's own self. William Faulkner's large, complex novels are Romantic in another sense: They create a whole world of their own. *The Sound and the Fury* (1929), *Absalom, Absalom!* (1936), and *The Hamlet* (1940) are among the Faulkner novels that detail the decline of southern aristocratic families and the rise of the opportunistic people who replace them. In a style often demanding, often a kind of modern gothic, Faulkner's novels raise his characters to mythic proportions. Modern and Romantic, both Wolfe and Faulkner reflect a profound understanding of the common people and of their time and place. In a time of social crisis, they emphasized the individual.

Postwar America

During the 1930s Americans watched the rise of Fascism in Europe, as Mussolini came to power in Italy, Hitler in Germany, and Franco in Spain. They watched Russia labor under the dictatorship of Stalin. In 1939 they watched World War II break out and Europe once again become an enormous battleground.

Many Americans had long felt free of Europe's troubles. In the modern world, however, every country is tied to every other country through economics, trade, political alliances, or beliefs and principles. In a time of rapid transportation and communication, in the age of modern warfare, Americans could not remain uninvolved. Democracy itself seemed threatened, as the world appeared to be falling to fascist expansion. After the attack at Pearl Harbor on December 7, 1941, Americans entered the war, suffered through it, and helped to win the most devastating conflict the world had ever seen.

The effect of World War II on American culture and literature, however, was quite different from the effect of World War I. After World War I Americans had abandoned their old beliefs and optimism and threw themselves headlong into whatever was new and exciting, breaking boundaries and estab-

Four Darks in Red, Mark Rothko, 1958.

lished forms. After World War II Americans did not seem as disillusioned, as much a "lost generation," as they had been during the 1920s. There were crises of course—for example, the anti-Communist McCarthy hearings and the Cold War with the Soviet Union. Overall, however, the country entered a period of prosperity, growth, and a generally contented peacefulness. The greatest reason for anxiety seemed to sink beneath the surface of daily life: With the development of atomic warfare, the world, it was clear, would never be quite the same again.

Postwar Literature

Some postwar literature directly confronts the events of the time. Randall Jarrell's "Death of the Ball Turret Gunner" recalls the violence of aerial warfare. W. H. Auden's "Unknown Citizen" por-

trays an individual dwarfed by the State. Yet much of the literature seems to respond *indirectly* to its own time, turning away as if in self-protection. Thornton Wilder's *Our Town,* which seems the most peaceful and untroubled of works, was already, at its first production in 1938, a nostalgic celebration of a world that had vanished. In Steinbeck's "Leader of the People" and in James Agee's "Knoxville: Summer, 1915" we find a nostalgia for vanished worlds. In Walter Van Tilburg Clark's "Portable Phonograph" the world looks longingly back to a time before its most destructive war. Faulkner's "Bear" takes its characters back to an almost mythological past.

The literature of 1930–1960 is so varied that it is difficult to make generalizations about it. Indeed, generalizations about periods of literature are always dangerous and must be taken only as indications of tendencies. Yet we do notice in postwar writing a trend toward poems and stories that celebrate private experiences, memories of childhood (as in Theodore Roethke), or moments of private happiness (as in Sylvia Plath's "Blackberrying" and Jack Kerouac's "Alone on a Mountaintop"). Literature reflects the world in which it is created—even if that reflection is a withdrawal from public concerns into private experience.

TIME LINE

1930–1960 AMERICAN EVENTS

1930   Katherine Anne Porter, *Flowering Judas and Other Stories*

1931   Empire State Building, 102 stories, completed

1932   William Faulkner, *Light in August*

        Amelia Earhart first woman to fly solo across Atlantic Ocean

1933   Congress passes anti-Depression acts, founds National Recovery Administration (NRA), and begins many public works projects

1934   Clarinetist Benny Goodman organizes band and becomes "King of Swing"

1935   George and Ira Gershwin, opera *Porgy and Bess*

1936   Jesse Owens, black American track star, wins four Olympic gold medals in Berlin

1937   John Dos Passos, *U.S.A.*

1938   Thornton Wilder, *Our Town*

        Orson Welles's radio broadcast *Invasion from Mars* causes panic

1939   John Steinbeck, *The Grapes of Wrath*

1940   Richard Wright, *Native Son*

        Carson McCullers, *The Heart Is a Lonely Hunter*

        Thomas Wolfe, *You Can't Go Home Again*

1941   U.S. enters World War II

        Eudora Welty, *A Curtain of Green and Other Stories*

WORLD EVENTS 1930–1960

1930   Worldwide economic depression

1932   England: Aldous Huxley, *Brave New World*

1933   Germany: Adolf Hitler appointed chancellor

        Ireland: W. B. Yeats, *Collected Poems*

1934   Germany: Engineer Werner von Braun launches two experimental rockets

1936   Spain: Civil War begins

1937   France: Spaniard Pablo Picasso paints *Guernica*

1938   England: Graham Greene, *Brighton Rock*

        Hungary: Lajos Biro invents ballpoint pen

1939   France: Irish novelist James Joyce, *Finnegans Wake*

        Beginning of World War II

1942   William Faulkner, "The Bear"

1944   Tennessee Williams, *The Glass Menagerie*

1945   Frank Lloyd Wright designs Guggenheim Museum

John Steinbeck, *The Red Pony*

1946   Benjamin Spock, M.D., *Baby and Child Care*

1948   W. H. Auden, *The Age of Anxiety*

Delmore Schwartz, *In Dreams Begin Responsibilities*

Transistor invented

1949   William Faulkner wins Nobel Prize for Literature

Arthur Miller, *Death of a Salesman*

1950   Jackson Pollock paints *Lavender Mist,* first "drip" painting

1951   Marianne Moore, *Collected Poems*

UNIVAC, first mass-produced computer

1952   Ernest Hemingway, *The Old Man and the Sea*

Ralph Ellison, *Invisible Man*

1942   France: Albert Camus, *The Stranger*

1943   France: Oceanographer Jacques Cousteau invents aqualung

1944   France: Jean-Paul Sartre, *No Exit*

1945   Japan: Atomic bombs dropped on Hiroshima and Nagasaki

England: George Orwell, *Animal Farm*

1946   Greece: Nikos Kazantzakis, *Zorba the Greek*

1947   Holland: *Diary of a Young Girl,* by Anne Frank, discovered and published

1948   Israel established by United Nations

South Africa: Alan Paton, *Cry the Beloved Country*

1949   China: Communists, led by Mao Zedung, defeat Nationalists; establish People's Republic

England: George Orwell, *Nineteen Eighty-Four*

1950   Korea: War begins between North and South Korea

Japan: Akira Kurosawa's film *Rashomon* gains world renown

1952   Albert Schweitzer, German humanitarian and physician, receives Nobel Peace Prize

Wales: Dylan Thomas, *Collected Poems*

Ireland: Samuel Beckett, *Waiting for Godot*

1953   Theodore Roethke, *The Waking*

Arthur Miller, *The Crucible*

1955   Elizabeth Bishop, *North and South—A Cold Spring*

1956   John F. Kennedy, *Profiles in Courage*

1957   Leonard Bernstein and Stephen Sondheim, *West Side Story*

1958   First commercial copying machine is produced

1959   Alaska and Hawaii become forty-ninth and fiftieth states

Robert Lowell, *Life Studies*

1960   Jack Kerouac, *Lonesome Traveler*

Gwendolyn Brooks, *The Bean Eaters*

1953   Tibet: Edmund Hillary of New Zealand and Tenzing Norgay of Nepal climb Mount Everest

1954   England: William Golding, *The Lord of the Flies*

1956   Sweden: Filmmaker Ingmar Bergman, *The Seventh Seal*

1957   U.S.S.R.: *Sputnik I,* first satellite, launched

1958   U.S.S.R.: Boris Pasternak, *Dr. Zhivago*

1959   Germany: Günter Grass, *The Tin Drum*

France: Eugene Ionesco, *Rhinoceros*

1960   England: Playwright Harold Pinter, *The Caretaker*

POETRY

W. H. Auden   *1907–1973*

Wystan Hugh Auden was one of the master craftsmen of English verse. In many ways he wrote against the grain of Modernism, basing his poems upon a wide knowledge of traditional meters and forms. His poems are not afraid of sentiment or nostalgia, but they characteristically surprise us with reminders of realities.

Auden was born an Englishman, and it was as an English poet that he made a dazzling, youthful reputation. After 1939, however, he lived mostly in America, becoming an American citizen in 1946. As the titles of two collections of his verse suggest, there is *The English Auden* and *The American Auden*.

The English Auden made a reputation for himself while still an undergraduate at Oxford University. His first volume, *Poems*, appeared in 1930. Throughout the thirties he continued to amaze the reading public with his brash verses that reflected an interest in science, industrial landscapes, and modern psychology. With such comrades as novelist Christopher Isherwood and poet Stephen Spender, he plunged into politics. He saw Nazi Germany at first hand, and he worked with the Republican side against the Fascists in Spain. Some of Auden's fine early poems are marred by a heavy insistence on his political ideas.

In 1939 he began a new life and freed himself from the restrictions of Europe. He came to New York, where he produced some of his finest works. In America he felt a revival of his Christianity, which grew stronger as he grew older. He taught at Swarthmore College during World War II, and in 1948 he won the Pulitzer Prize for *The Age of Anxiety,* a long poem that uses Old English alliterations as it follows the lives of four people through a postwar world of uncertainty and isolation. His other major volumes are *Nones* (1951), *The Shield of Achilles* (1955), and *Homage to Clio* (1960). A prolific and versatile writer, Auden also collaborated with the great modern composer Igor Stravinsky on an opera, *The Rake's Progress,* in addition to producing lively literary criticism.

In his later years Auden lived in a house he bought in Kirchstetten, Austria. He died in Vienna in 1973 and was buried near his beloved house. On his memorial plaque in London's Westminster Abbey are words from the poem he wrote in memory of the Irish poet W. B. Yeats—"In the prison of his days / Teach the free man how to praise"—words that sum up his own life as well.

Auden's poems are marked by exquisite craft, wise observation of history, and trust in the value of art. Like "The Unknown Citizen" they can sharply describe the relationships between people and the governments they create. Like "If I Could Tell You" they can brim with a deeply moving human sympathy.

W. H. Auden

If I Could Tell You

Time will say nothing but I told you so,
Time only knows the price we have to pay;
If I could tell you I would let you know.

If we should weep when clowns put on their show,
5 If we should stumble when musicians play,
Time will say nothing but I told you so.

There are no fortunes to be told, although,
Because I love you more than I can say,
If I could tell you I would let you know.

10 The winds must come from somewhere when they blow,
There must be reasons why the leaves decay;
Time will say nothing but I told you so.

Perhaps the roses really want to grow,
The vision seriously intends to stay;
15 If I could tell you I would let you know.

Suppose the lions all get up and go,
And all the brooks and soldiers run away;
Will Time say nothing but I told you so?
If I could tell you I would let you know.

STUDY QUESTIONS

Recalling

1. According to the poem, what is the only thing that time will say? What would the speaker do if he could? Why would he do this, according to the third stanza?
2. What does the fourth stanza say about the winds and the leaves? What does the fifth stanza say about the roses and the vision?

Interpreting

3. What seems to be the relationship between the speaker and the person he addresses? Which images in the poem suggest this relationship?

4. What does the speaker fear will happen to the roses and the vision? What does he therefore fear will happen to his relationship with the person he addresses? Is he certain about the future?
5. Might this poem be about more than the relationship between the speaker and the person he addresses? Explain.

Extending

6. In what ways is this poem reminiscent of poetry of previous centuries? (Consider both the form and content of the poem.) In what way is it a "modern" poem? (Consider the tone, or attitude, of the poet.)

The Unknown Citizen

(To JS/07/M/378
This Marble Monument
Is Erected by the State)

He was found by the Bureau of Statistics to be
One against whom there was no official complaint,
And all the reports on his conduct agree
That, in the modern sense of an old-fashioned word, he was a saint,
5 For in everything he did he served the Greater Community.
Except for the War till the day he retired
He worked in a factory and never got fired,
But satisfied his employers, Fudge Motors Inc.
Yet he wasn't a scab[1] or odd in his views,
10 For his Union reports that he paid his dues,
(Our report on his Union shows it was sound)
And our Social Psychology workers found
That he was popular with his mates and liked a drink.
The Press are convinced that he bought a paper every day
15 And that his reactions to advertisements were normal in every way.
Policies taken out in his name prove that he was fully insured,
And his Health-card shows he was once in hospital but left it cured.
Both Producers Research and High-Grade Living declare
He was fully sensible to the advantages of the Installment Plan
20 And had everything necessary to the Modern Man,
A phonograph, a radio, a car and a frigidaire.
Our researchers into Public Opinion are content
That he held the proper opinions for the time of year;
When there was peace, he was for peace; when there was war, he
    went.
25 He was married and added five children to the population,
Which our Eugenist[2] says was the right number for a parent of his
    generation,
And our teachers report that he never interfered with their
    education.
Was he free? Was he happy? The question is absurd:
Had anything been wrong, we should certainly have heard.

---

1. **scab:** worker who refuses to strike or replaces a striker.
2. **Eugenist** [ū jen′ist]: specialist in eugenics, the movement to improve
inherited traits in humans.

STUDY QUESTIONS

Recalling

1. According to the inscription under the title, on what does this poem appear? Who has erected it?
2. According to lines 1–5, in what sense was the unknown citizen a "saint"?
3. Identify at least four organizations or groups of people who have passed positive judgments on the unknown citizen. Except for the war, where did the unknown citizen work until he retired (line 7)?
4. What questions are asked in the last two lines of the poem? According to the poem, why are these questions absurd?

Interpreting

5. What kind of "State," or government, has erected this monument? Why would a government erect a public monument to an "unknown citizen"?
6. Describe at least four ways in which the unknown citizen was found to be "ideal." Does the *poet* find such behavior ideal?
7. What is ironic about the last two lines of the poem?
8. Basically, what is this poem criticizing?

Extending

9. What aspects of the modern world does this poem make you think about? Do you agree with the poet's opinion of everything he criticizes? Why or why not?

VIEWPOINT

Hayden Carruth, a critic of Auden, has written:

Auden was a profoundly emotional writer, and I fail to see how any reader can miss that quality in his writing, that force, that humility, even when the knowledge is specialized—Auden was fond of scientific writing and by no means unschooled in it—and the thought is complex or quirky. For me, the poet who shows me his mind as well as his heart . . . is always more interesting than the one who shows me his heart alone.

■ Where in Auden's poems do you find the poet "showing his mind"? Where do you find him "showing his heart"?

LITERARY FOCUS

Satire

Auden's "Unknown Citizen" is a popular modern satire. **Satire** is a kind of writing that holds up someone or something to ridicule or serious criticism. It is an attitude, not a form. Satirists see something they think is wrong with another person, with a group of people, with an institution, or with society at large. They attempt to correct the follies or errors of the world by holding those errors up for inspection in a way that allows us to laugh at them.

Some satires are gentle, poking good-natured fun; others are harsh, attacking serious evils. In either case, satire is a public art: It intends to make society better by showing the excesses and imbalances of human nature. It assumes that there is a rational norm of behavior, and it makes us laugh, even if that laughter is bitter, at departures from the norm.

Auden's "Unknown Citizen" is a serious poem with bitter overtones, although we may not see at first how serious it is. Auden pushes his vision of the modern bureaucratic state to an extreme, hoping that his comic excess will make each of us realize that we, too, are in danger of becoming "unknown citizens."

Thinking About Satire

1. How would you describe the norm of a good government and a good society that Auden wants to bring about?
2. Do you think satires are really effective in bringing about changes in the world? Why or why not?

Theodore Roethke   *1908–1963*

Theodore Roethke was a much loved and honored poet during his lifetime, winning the Pulitzer Prize, the National Book Award, and the Bollingen Prize. However, many of his poems have received a higher honor than any official prize can bestow: They have become favorite poems with many readers.

Roethke fashioned his poems from intense memories of his childhood and boyhood in Michigan. His father and grandfather were florists, and Roethke grew up in a world of flowers, plants, and large commercial greenhouses. Images of growth and decay can be found in all of his books, including *Open House* (1941), *The Lost Son* (1948), *The Waking* (1953), and *Words for the Wind* (1958).

Roethke's poems are closely observed lyrics. He details the processes of the natural world and, like Emerson and Whitman, almost mystically identifies with nature: "In my veins, in my bones I feel it." In the free verse of "Big Wind" he recaptures a struggle to keep his flowers alive as a great storm lashes his greenhouse. Like Auden, Roethke was also a master of the stricter forms of poetry, and in "The Waking" he puts some thoroughly modern ideas into a thoroughly old-fashioned form.

Theodore Roethke

Big Wind

Where were the greenhouses going,
Lunging into the lashing
Wind driving water
So far down the river
5 All the faucets stopped?—
So we drained the manure machine
For the steam plant,
Pumping the stale mixture
Into the rusty boilers,
10 Watching the pressure gauge
Waver over to red,
As the seams hissed
And the live steam
Drove to the far
15 End of the rose-house,
Where the worst wind was,
Creaking the cypress window frames,
Cracking so much thin glass
We stayed all night,
20 Stuffing the holes with burlap;
But she rode it out,
That old rose-house,
She hove¹ into the teeth of it,
The core and pith² of that ugly storm,
25 Ploughing with her stiff prow,
Bucking into the wind-waves
That broke over the whole of her,
Flailing her sides with spray,
Flinging long strings of wet across the rooftop,
30 Finally veering, wearing themselves out, merely
Whistling thinly under the wind-vents;
She sailed until the calm morning,
Carrying her full cargo of roses.

---

1. **hove:** heaved.
2. **pith:** vital force.

The Waking

I wake to sleep, and take my waking slow.
I feel my fate in what I cannot fear.
I learn by going where I have to go.

We think by feeling. What is there to know?
5 I hear my being dance from ear to ear.
I wake to sleep, and take my waking slow.

Of those so close beside me, which are you?
God bless the Ground! I shall walk softly there,
And learn by going where I have to go.

10 Light takes the Tree; but who can tell us how?
The lowly worm climbs up a winding stair;
I wake to sleep, and take my waking slow.

Great Nature has another thing to do
To you and me; so take the lively air,
15 And, lovely, learn by going where to go.

This shaking keeps me steady. I should know.
What falls away is always. And is near.
I wake to sleep, and take my waking slow.
I learn by going where I have to go.

STUDY QUESTIONS

Big Wind

Recalling
1. What question does the first line ask? What are the greenhouses doing in lines 2–3?
2. What do the speaker and his companion do in lines 6–9? What is the pressure gauge for the boilers doing?
3. What outcome does the speaker report in lines 20–21? In lines 32–33?

Interpreting
4. What is the controlling image (see page 34) in this poem?

5. What might the storm have done to the green-houses and the roses?
6. Who or what saved the rose-house? What could have happened to the speaker and his companions?
7. How does the speaker seem to feel about the old rose-house? What more general message might there be in the rose-house's endurance?

Extending
8. What do you think a Naturalist writer like Jack London (page 340) or Stephen Crane (page 366) might have said about this poem? What qualities of the poem reflect the tradition of American nature poetry? What qualities are especially modern?

The Waking

Recalling

1. According to the poem, to what does the speaker wake? In what does he feel his fate (line 2)? How does he learn? How does he think we all think (line 4)?
2. What does the speaker hear in line 5? What does he say about nature in line 13? What advice does he give in lines 14–15?

Interpreting

3. What might the speaker mean by the waking? By the sleeping? What is "another thing" that nature has to do "to you and me," in addition to the waking described in stanzas 1–4?
4. Why would the speaker "take his waking slow"?
5. Explain the advice we are given in line 14. How is it related to the refrain "I learn by going where I have to go"?

Extending

6. In what ways is the attitude toward life expressed in this poem different from the attitude expressed in Eliot's "The Love Song of J. Alfred Prufrock" on page 443.

LITERARY FOCUS

The Villanelle

W. H. Auden's "If I Could Tell You" (page 574) and Theodore Roethke's "Waking" are written in the strict form known as the villanelle. A **villanelle** is a poem of nineteen lines divided into five tercets (three-line stanzas) and a final quatrain, using only two rhymes throughout. It was a favorite verse form of French poets four hundred years ago, and some modern poets such as Auden, Roethke, and the Welsh poet Dylan Thomas have accepted its challenge in our century.

The most unusual characteristic of the villanelle is its use of refrains, or repeated lines. The first line of the poem becomes the final line of the second and fourth stanzas, and the third line becomes the final line of the third and fifth stanzas. Both refrains are brought together in the final two lines.

While Auden and Roethke adhere to the demands of the villanelle, they also vary the form slightly to avoid stiffness. Both poets vary their refrains. Auden keeps his two rhymes pure: All the lines rhyme with "so" and "pay." Roethke, however, uses some slant rhymes: "Slow" is made to rhyme with "you" and "how"; "fear" is made to rhyme with "there," "stair," and "air."

Why would modern poets choose to write in so limited and demanding a form as the villanelle? We may suggest two answers. First, good poets are skilled in a craft and sometimes they want to challenge themselves. The Irish poet W. B. Yeats wrote of the "fascination of what's difficult," and clearly Auden and Roethke were fascinated with the sheer difficulty of the villanelle. The poem gives pleasure to both poet and reader when the form "comes out right." Second, the circling form of the villanelle can be a reflection of the subject matter of the poem: It suggests, for example, the circling and repeating questions about life asked in Auden's "If I Could Tell You."

Thinking About the Villanelle

1. How does Auden vary the refrain in "If I Could Tell You"? How does Roethke vary the refrain in "The Waking"?
2. Why is the villanelle form appropriate to the subject of Roethke's "Waking"?

COMPOSITION

Writing About a Quotation

In a brief essay explain the importance of Roethke's refrain, "I learn by going where I have to go." Begin by telling precisely what the line means. Then discuss how the line adds to the meaning of other lines in the poem. Conclude with your own reflections on the value of what the poem says. *For help with this assignment, refer to Lesson 5 in the Writing About Literature Handbook at the back of this book.*

Writing a Villanelle

After studying Auden's and Roethke's villanelles, try writing one of your own. Think of it as an exercise in craft, a puzzle to be solved. You may want to begin by choosing the rhymes you want to use and then planning the final words of all your lines. Then "fill in" each line, keeping in mind that although Auden and Roethke have used five beats in each line (pentameter), you need not.

Robert Lowell   *1917–1977*

Robert Lowell was born into one of the oldest and most distinguished of Boston families: Two well-known American poets, James Russell Lowell (page 207) and Amy Lowell, were among his ancestors. Yet from an early age Lowell turned away from the comfortable life, writing poetry that seemed haunted by a sense of the past, by a mysterious burden of guilt, by an urgent and inescapable seriousness.

The need to perform a symbolic act made Lowell leave the East, with all its reminders of the past, and attend college in Ohio, where he studied under the poet John Crowe Ransom (page 476). Immensely talented and thoughtful, Lowell achieved early success as a poet, winning the Pulitzer Prize for *Lord Weary's Castle* (1946) before he was thirty. In that book and in *The Mills of the Kavanaughs* (1951) he examined his own world-weariness in verse that is highly crafted, heavy, and dense with symbols. In this style, he seemed to have achieved a permanent reputation.

In mid-life, however, Lowell suddenly and drastically changed his style. He had discovered the poetry of some younger Americans, in particular Allen Ginsberg, who were writing in a much more open and direct style. Lowell's own poetry, the poetry that had brought him such early fame, no longer pleased him. It sounded to his ears "willfully difficult," with a "stiff, humorless, and even impenetrable surface." He began working on a new sort of poetry that has come to be called confessional poetry.

In these **confessional poems** Lowell began to speak with a sometimes embarrassing openness and frankness about his own life. He broke radically with the dominant critical tradition of his generation, a tradition that taught that we are never to think of the "I" in a poem as the actual person of the poet himself. In Lowell's later poems the "I" is clearly to be taken as Robert Lowell himself. The volume in which Lowell's new, personal poems appeared was *Life Studies* (1959), and it became immensely influential, giving rise to a group of talented confessional poets that included John Berryman, Sylvia Plath, and Anne Sexton. Following their example, lesser poets all over America began to write poems about "I"—talky poems that recounted their personal problems, few of which were as interesting as the spiritual quest of Robert Lowell.

"Hawthorne" is typical of Lowell in many ways. It is personal yet it deals with the past. Carefully crafted yet casual, it offers a portrait of an artist in search of the sources of art.

Robert Lowell

Hawthorne

Follow its lazy main street lounging
from the alms house to Gallows Hill[1]
along a flat, unvaried surface
covered with wooden houses
5 aged by yellow drain
like the unhealthy hair of an old dog.
You'll walk to no purpose
in Hawthorne's Salem.

I cannot resilver the smudged plate.[2]

10 I drop to Hawthorne, the customs officer,[3]
measuring coal and mostly trying to keep
        warm—
to the stunted black schooner,
the dismal South-end dock,
the wharf-piles with their fungus of ice.
15 On State Street[4]
a steeple with a glowing dial-clock
measures the weary hours,
the merciless march of professional feet.

Even this shy distrustful ego
20 sometimes walked on top of the blazing roof,

and felt those flashes
that char the discharged cells of the brain.

Look at the faces—
Longfellow, Lowell, Holmes and Whittier![5]
25 Study the grizzled silver of their beards.
Hawthorne's picture,
however, has a blond mustache
and golden General Custer scalp.[6]
He looks like a Civil War officer.
30 He shines in the firelight. His hard
survivor's smile is touched with fire.

Leave him alone for a moment or two,
and you'll see him with his head
bent down, brooding, brooding,
35 eyes fixed on some chip,
some stone, some common plant,
the commonest thing,
as if it were the clue.
The disturbed eyes rise,
40 furtive, foiled, dissatisfied
from meditation on the true
and insignificant.

---

1. **Gallows Hill:** site in Salem, Massachusetts, where
people who were believed to be witches were hanged.
2. **resilver . . . plate:** referring to early photographs,
which were taken on a metal plate coated with silver.
3. **customs officer:** Hawthorne worked as a customs
officer in Salem.
4. **State Street:** main street in Boston's business district.

5. **Longfellow . . . Whittier!:** Fireside Poets, who
lived in New England.
6. **golden . . . scalp:** referring to the long blond
hair of George Armstrong Custer (1839–1876), who
served as a general in the Civil War and was later
killed by the Sioux Indians in the Battle of Little
Big Horn.

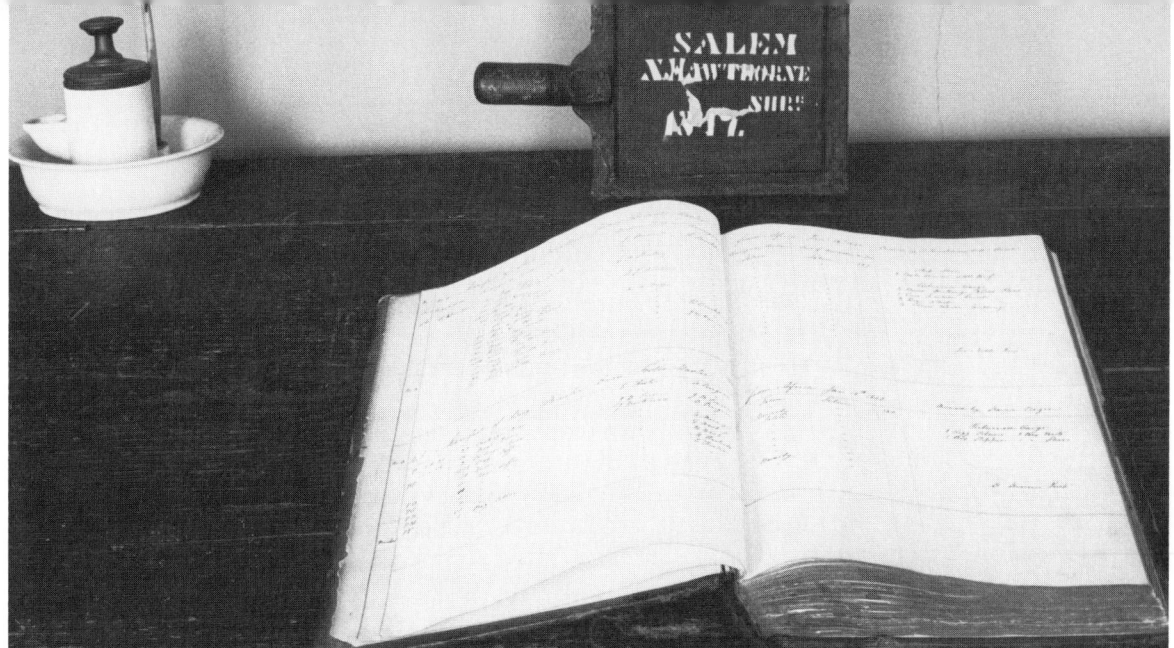

STUDY QUESTIONS

Recalling

1. According to lines 1–8, if "you" follow the lazy main street of Hawthorne's Salem, how will you walk? What can the speaker not do, according to line 9?
2. What description is given of Hawthorne's duties as a customs officer? How is Hawthorne described in line 19? What does the speaker say Hawthorne sometimes did and felt?
3. With what four other New England writers is Hawthorne contrasted in lines 23–31? What does Hawthorne's picture show in contrast to the other writers' grizzled beards?
4. According to lines 32–42, how will "you" see Hawthorne if you "leave him alone for a moment or two"? On what do his eyes seem to be fixed? What makes them "furtive, foiled, dissatisfied"?

Interpreting

5. What is the speaker trying to find as he walks the streets of Hawthorne's Salem? What does line 9 suggest?
6. What aspects of Hawthorne's job as a customs officer are captured in lines 10–11? What aspect of Hawthorne is captured in lines 20–22?
7. Why is it significant that Hawthorne does *not* have a grizzled beard, as the other New England writers do?

8. What qualities does the speaker seem to admire in Hawthorne?

Extending

9. What are some of the things you might learn about a writer and his work by visiting the places where he lived and learning about his jobs and background? Why do you think another writer—such as Robert Lowell—might be especially interested in paying such a visit?

COMPOSITION

Writing About a Work and Its Author

Write a brief essay telling what light Lowell's "Hawthorne" throws on Hawthorne's story "The Minister's Black Veil" (page 179). Discuss Lowell's claim that Hawthorne looked for meaning in "the commonest thing," and tell how that search for meaning relates to the story. Why might Hawthorne, after having written the story, appear to Lowell "foiled, dissatisfied"?

Writing About the Past

Write a short composition or a poem in which you take a close look at some event or person in America's past and tell what that event or person means to you. Describe your subject fully in its own time and place. Then indicate why it is still important and valuable to you.

Kenneth Fearing *1902–1961*

Kenneth Fearing was both a poet and a novelist, but he made his living by writing articles for magazines. Like Auden, he wrote several verse satires of contemporary life, including *Dead Reckoning* (1938) and *Stranger at Coney Island* (1949).

Fearing liked to fill his poems with common American speech, slang, clichés, urban landscapes, and images drawn from objects Americans use in their everyday life. With such "unpoetic" materials he created compassionate portraits of people who often seem buried beneath trivial objects, unclear thoughts, and abused language. "Cracked Record Blues" raises some very large questions from a casual encounter with an everyday object.

Kenneth Fearing

Cracked Record Blues

If you watch it long enough you can see the clock move,
If you try hard enough you can hold a little water in the palm of
　　your hand,
If you listen once or twice you know it's not the needle, or the tune,
　　but a crack in the record when sometimes a phonograph falters
　　and repeats, and repeats, and repeats, and repeats—

And if you think about it long enough, long enough, long enough,
　　long enough then everything is simple and you can understand
　　the times,
5 You can see for yourself that the Hudson[1] still flows, that the seasons
　　change as ever, that love is always love,
Words still have a meaning, still clear and still the same;
You can count upon your fingers that two plus two still equals, still
　　equals, still equals, still equals—
There is nothing in this world that should bother the mind.

Because the mind is a common sense affair filled with common sense
　　answers to common sense facts,
10 It can add up, can add up, can add up, can add up earthquakes and
　　subtract them from fires,
It can bisect an atom or analyze the planets—
All it has to do is to, do is to, do is to, do is to start at the beginning
　　and continue to the end.

---

1. **Hudson:** Hudson River in New York.

STUDY QUESTIONS

Recalling

1. According to line 3, what will we know if we listen once or twice? According to line 4, what can we understand if we think about it long enough?
2. According to lines 9–11, why is there "nothing in this world" that should bother the mind? What are the three things the mind can do? According to the last line, what must the mind do to perform these three things?

Interpreting

3. Considering the parallel structure of lines 3 and 4, determine what the poet is equating with the cracked record.

4. To what aspect of modern life do lines 10 and 11 refer? What do the things in these lines have in common with a phonograph record? How is the last line of the poem related to a phonograph record?
5. Does the poet really believe that "everything is simple" and that the mind can understand everything if it starts at the beginning and continues to the end? What does the crack in the record suggest?
6. How does the poem's sound echo its sense?

Extending

7. What are some of the things in modern life that this poem makes you think about? What specific things are suggested by lines 10 and 11, for example?

© Rollie McKenna

Elizabeth Bishop   *1911–1980*

Elizabeth Bishop's verse is warm and personal, with an elegance that reflects the personality and reputation of the poet herself. Bishop was born in Massachusetts, grew up in Nova Scotia, Canada, and attended Vassar College. She took inspiration from the poems of Marianne Moore (page 480), particularly Moore's meticulous observation of nature. Bishop traveled a great deal during her life, and themes of home and exile are often to be found in her poems. For sixteen years she lived in Brazil, before returning to her native Massachusetts in the later part of her life. She received many honors, including the Pulitzer Prize and National Book Award.

"The Fish," one of her relatively early poems, has become one of the more reprinted American poems of this century. It describes a moment in which observation is transformed into revelation.

Elizabeth Bishop

The Fish

I caught a tremendous fish
and held him beside the boat
half out of water, with my hook
fast in a corner of his mouth.
5 He didn't fight.
He hadn't fought at all.
He hung a grunting weight,
battered and venerable
and homely. Here and there
10 his brown skin hung in strips
like ancient wallpaper,
and its pattern of darker brown
was like wallpaper:
shapes like full-blown roses
15 stained and lost through age.
He was speckled with barnacles,[1]
fine rosettes[2] of lime,
and infested
with tiny white sea-lice,

---

1. **barnacles** [bär′nə kəlz]: small saltwater shellfish that attach themselves to underwater objects and other animals.
2. **rosettes** [rō zets′]: rose-shaped patterns.

20 and underneath two or three
rags of green weed hung down.
While his gills were breathing in
the terrible oxygen
—the frightening gills,
25 fresh and crisp with blood,
that can cut so badly—
I thought of the coarse white flesh
packed in like feathers,
the big bones and the little bones,
30 the dramatic reds and blacks
of his shiny entrails,[3]
and the pink swim-bladder[4]
like a big peony.
I looked into his eyes
35 which were far larger than mine
but shallower, and yellowed,
the irises backed and packed
with tarnished tinfoil
seen through the lenses
40 of old scratched isinglass.[5]
They shifted a little, but not
to return my stare.
—It was more like the tipping
of an object toward the light.
45 I admired his sullen face,
the mechanism of his jaw,
and then I saw
that from his lower lip
—if you could call it a lip—
50 grim, wet, and weaponlike,
hung five old pieces of fish line,
or four and a wire leader[6]
with the swivel still attached,
with all their five big hooks
55 grown firmly in his mouth.
A green line, frayed at the end
where he broke it, two heavier lines,
and a fine black thread
still crimped from the strain and snap

60 when it broke and he got away.
Like medals with their ribbons
frayed and wavering,
a five-haired beard of wisdom
trailing from his aching jaw.
65 I stared and stared
and victory filled up
the little rented boat,
from the pool of bilge[7]
where oil had spread a rainbow
70 around the rusted engine
to the bailer[8] rusted orange,
the sun-cracked thwarts,[9]
the oarlocks on their strings,
the gunnels[10]—until everything
75 was rainbow, rainbow, rainbow!
And I let the fish go.

---

7. **bilge** [bilj]: dirty, stagnant water that collects
in the bottom of a boat.
8. **bailer:** device for removing water from a boat.
9. **thwarts:** seats for rowers.
10. **gunnels:** upper edges of the sides of a boat.

---

3. **entrails:** inner organs.
4. **swim-bladder:** gas-filled sac in most bony fishes
that enables them to maintain or change depth
in water.
5. **isinglass** [ī′zin glas′]: thin sheets of transparent
mica, a crystallized mineral.
6. **leader:** short piece of line used to attach a
hook to fish line.

STUDY QUESTIONS

Recalling

1. What does the speaker catch? What does line 6 report about the difficulty of catching it?
2. What three adjectives describe the fish in lines 8–9? What simile describes its skin? What are its gills breathing, according to line 23?
3. After studying the fish's eyes and face, what does the speaker see hanging from its lower "lip"? With what does she compare these things in line 61? In line 63?
4. What does the speaker say fills the little rented boat in line 66? What does everything become, according to line 75? What does the speaker then do?

Interpreting

5. What do the five hooks with their broken lines indicate about the fish? How do they contrast with the information in lines 5–6?
6. Is the description of the fish basically emotional, or is it precise and scientific? Why does the poet call the oxygen "terrible"?
7. What conflict within the speaker might your answers to question 6 reflect? What is the outcome of that conflict? Why does the speaker let the fish go?

Extending

8. What other "conflicts" or dilemmas of modern life does this poem make you think about?

VOCABULARY

Analogies

Analogies are comparisons that point out relationships between items. Analogy items on vocabulary tests are usually written as two pairs of words. The words in the first pair are related to each other in the same way as those in the second pair: for example,

HOT : COLD : : BRIGHT : DARK.

The first word in capitals in each of the following analogies is from "The Fish." Complete the analogies by choosing the pair of words that is related in the same way as the pair in capital letters.

1. BATTERED : BRUISED : :
   (a) beaten : rubbed   (c) wounded : cut
   (b) scorched : flame   (d) wrecked : injured

2. VENERABLE : SAINTLY : :
   (a) impressive : holy   (c) ancient : modern
   (b) novel : new   (d) animal : human

3. BARNACLES : OYSTERS : :
   (a) rocks : crabs   (c) unwanted : wanted
   (b) dandruff : scalp   (d) rotten : fresh

4. INFESTED : FILLED : :
   (a) ruinous : lucrative   (c) permeable : porous
   (b) poisoned : cured   (d) saturated : soaked

5. GILLS : LUNGS : :
   (a) water : land   (c) oxygen : air
   (b) fish : mammal   (d) before : after

Randall Jarrell   *1914–1965*

Tennessee-born Randall Jarrell was one of the most versatile writers of his generation: poet, teacher, translator, novelist, essayist, and highly respected literary critic.

Jarrell's interest in literature was stimulated by the poet-critic John Crowe Ransom (page 476), who was teaching at Tennessee's Vanderbilt University, where Jarrell went to college. Jarrell too became a teacher, a profession he loved: He once said that even if he were rich enough not to have to work, he would want to go on teaching. His books of poetry include *Losses* (1948) and *The Woman at the Washington Zoo* (1960). Jarrell also became one of the most influential critics of poetry in his time. Some of his best essays appear in *Poetry and the Age* (1953).

The only interruption to Jarrell's life as teacher-critic-poet came during World War II, when he served in the Army Air Force. His war experiences provided him with some of his best poems, such as the memorable "Death of the Ball Turret Gunner," for which Jarrell himself provided this note:

> A ball turret was a plexiglass sphere set into the belly of a B-17 or B-24, and inhabited by two .50 caliber machine-guns and one man, a short small man. When this gunner tracked with his machine-guns a fighter attacking his bomber from below, he revolved with the turret; hunched upside-down in his little sphere, he looked like the fetus in the womb. The fighters which attacked him were armed with cannon firing explosive shells. The hose was a steam hose.

Randall Jarrell

The Death of the Ball Turret Gunner

From my mother's sleep I fell into the State,
And I hunched in its belly till my wet fur froze.
Six miles from earth, loosed from its dream of life,
I woke to black flak[1] and the nightmare fighters.
5 When I died they washed me out of the turret with a hose.

---

1. **flak:** anti-aircraft fire.

Margaret Walker   *born 1915*

Margaret Walker's work is aimed at bringing to the attention of readers the strengths and trials of black Americans. Born in Birmingham, Alabama, where her father was a Methodist preacher, Walker gained success with her first book, *For My People,* winning the Yale Younger Poets prize in 1942. She studied at Northwestern University and the University of Iowa and then embarked upon a life of writing and teaching. For many years she taught at Jackson State College in Mississippi.

"Lineage" indicates one of Walker's most passionate concerns. It is also a reflection on a subject common in the poems of other poets in this unit, especially Auden and Lowell—the strength of the past and the strength of the present.

Margaret Walker

Lineage

My grandmothers were strong.
They followed plows and bent to toil.
They moved through fields sowing seed.
They touched earth and grain grew.
5 They were full of sturdiness and singing.
My grandmothers were strong.

My grandmothers are full of memories
Smelling of soap and onions and wet clay
With veins rolling roughly over quick hands
10 They have many clean words to say.
My grandmothers were strong.
Why am I not as they?

Gwendolyn Brooks   *born 1917*

The first black writer to win a Pulitzer Prize (for *Annie Allen* in 1949), Gwendolyn Brooks is recognized as one of America's most steadily productive and distinguished poets. Brooks grew up in Chicago, where she has spent most of her life and where she often sets her poems. She began writing poetry that was quite formal and traditional, but in her later work she often adopted free verse and more open forms. Her later work also became more outspoken as she turned to problems of social and racial justice. Her volumes include *A Street in Bronzeville* (1945) and *The Bean Eaters* (1960).

"Strong Men, Riding Horses" is an urban poem. It is a twentieth-century look at the past, a past now alive perhaps only through the movies.

Gwendolyn Brooks

Strong Men, Riding Horses

Lester after the Western

Strong Men, riding horses. In the West
On a range five hundred miles. A Thousand. Reaching
From dawn to sunset. Rested blue to orange.
From hope to crying. Except that Strong Men are
5 Desert-eyed. Except that Strong Men are
Pasted to stars already. Have their cars
Beneath them. Rentless, too. Too broad of chest
To shrink when the Rough Man hails. Too flailing
To redirect the Challenger, when the challenge
10 Nicks; slams; buttonholes. Too saddled.

I am not like that. I pay rent, am addled
By illegible landlords, run, if robbers call.

What mannerisms I present, employ,
Are camouflage, and what my mouths remark
15 To word-wall off that broadness of the dark
Is pitiful.
I am not brave at all.

STUDY QUESTIONS *(Jarrell)*

Recalling

1. Into what did the ball turret gunner fall? From what was he loosed? To what did he wake?
2. What happened when he died?

Interpreting

3. Why is it significant that the gunner falls where he falls in line 1?
4. What does the poem suggest about war?

Extending

5. Does the ball turret gunner have anything in common with the unknown citizen in Auden's poem on page 575? Why or why not?

STUDY QUESTIONS *(Walker)*

Recalling

1. What were the speaker's "grandmothers," according to line 1? What happened when they touched earth?
2. What are the speaker's grandmothers now, according to line 7?
3. What does the speaker ask in the final line?

Interpreting

4. State in your own words the qualities that the speaker seems to admire in her grandmothers. What does she mean by "grandmothers"?
5. What does the last line imply about the speaker's wishes?
6. Describe the diction, or word choice, in the poem. How is it related to the poem's content?

Extending

7. How would you answer the speaker's final question? Do you agree that modern Americans are not as strong as their ancestors? What are some of the things we have today that our "grandmothers" might have desired?

STUDY QUESTIONS *(Brooks)*

Recalling

1. What sort of men are riding horses in the West, according to line 1? For what are these men "too broad of chest"?
2. According to lines 11–12, how is the speaker unlike the strong men of the West? What are his "mannerisms," according to line 14? What adjective describes the remarks he makes to "word-wall off that broadness of the dark"?
3. What does the speaker conclude about himself in the final line?

Interpreting

4. What characters from American life is this poem about? What do "broad of chest," "desert-eyed," and "rentless" suggest about these characters?
5. What do "camouflage" and "word-wall" suggest about the speaker's methods of "fighting"? How would these methods differ from the fighting methods of a traditional western hero?
6. What two things does the speaker find wrong with the strong men? (Consider the fact that they are "desert-eyed" and "rentless" and that they are "*too* broad of chest.") What one quality does he particularly envy? (Consider the last two lines of the poem.)

Extending

7. What aspects of modern civilization does this poem make you think about? What are the rewards of being "civilized"? What might we envy about the less "civilized" heroes of the American West?

VOCABULARY *(Brooks)*

Compound Words

When Gwendolyn Brooks creates the compound word *word-wall,* she is doing what English speakers have been doing for centuries: putting old words together to describe something new. For example, *landlord,* another compound Brooks uses, was originally used by medieval farmers to describe the *lord,* or nobleman, who owned the *land* they farmed.

Using a dictionary, explain the origins of each of the following compound words, as well as the current meaning or meanings.

1. aboveboard
2. aftermath
3. barnstorm
4. bigwig
5. turtleneck
6. catercorner
7. crestfallen
8. foolscap
9. pinafore
10. turnpike

Reed Whittemore   *born 1919*

Reed Whittemore, though best known for his lyric poems, has also written stories and essays, taught English in college, and co-edited one of America's "little magazines," *Furioso,* from 1939 to 1953. His books include *Heroes and Heroines* (1946), *An American Takes a Walk* (1956), and *The Boy from Iowa* (1962).

"The Fall of the House of Usher" is a good example of the importance of tone in a work of literature. Whittemore retells the story of Edgar Allan Poe's famous gothic tale (page 135). His modern rendition, however, produces an unexpected effect, an effect quite different from Poe's frightening original.

Reed Whittemore

The Fall of the House of Usher

It was a big boxy wreck of a house
Owned by a classmate of mine named Rod Usher,
Who lived in the thing with his twin sister.
He was a louse and she was a souse.

5 While I was visiting them one wet summer, she died.
We buried her,
Or rather we stuck her in a back room for a bit, meaning to
   bury her
When the graveyard dried.

But the weather got wetter.
10 One night we were both waked by a twister,
Plus a screeching and howling outside that turned out to be sister
Up and dying again, making it hard for Rod to forget her.

He didn't. He and she died in a heap, and I left quick,
Which was lucky since the house fell in right after,

15   Like a ton of brick.

STUDY QUESTIONS

Recalling

1. How is the House of Usher described in line 1? Who is living in "the thing," according to lines 2–3?
2. What happens to the sister "one wet summer"? Where do "Rod" and the narrator "stick" the sister?
3. What wakes "Rod" and the narrator one night? What happens to "Rod" and his sister in line 13? What does the narrator do?
4. According to line 15, how does the House of Usher "fall in"?

Interpreting

5. How is the diction, or word choice, of this poem different from that in Poe's "Fall of the House of Usher"? How is the poet's overall style different from that of Poe?
6. What is the tone, or writer's attitude, in this poem? How do style, diction, and rhyme contribute to that tone?
7. What sort of phrase is the last line of the poem? When is this phrase usually used? What comment about Poe's story does this phrase seem to make?

Extending

8. Could any masterpiece—a play by Shakespeare, for example—be made to sound funny if presented in a shorthand version of the plot alone? In what way does this poem pay a compliment to Poe?

LITERARY FOCUS

Parody

Parody is humorous imitation. A writer can parody another writer's plot, characters, setting, theme, or style, usually by means of exaggeration.

Parody is almost as old as literature itself. It seems that as soon as people began writing, there was someone ready to make fun of what they had written. One of the oldest parodies is *The Clouds,* a comedy by the Greek playwright Aristophanes. It pokes fun at the thinking of the great philosopher Socrates. In another play, *The Frogs,* Aristophanes mocks the styles of two of the greatest writers of all time, the Greek tragedians Sophocles and Euripides.

We should not assume, however, that a parodist hates or even dislikes the author being parodied. In a sense, parody is a form of tribute. It is impossible or pointless to parody an unknown writer or a mediocre writer. Every good writer has mannerisms, and those mannerisms are what make the writer's style unique. Cooper, Emerson, Thoreau, Whitman, Twain, Eliot, Hemingway, Fitzgerald—all have been the subject of parodies.

"The Fall of the House of Usher" by Reed Whittemore does not parody Poe's style: Poe's narrator, as you may recall, speaks in a most elaborate English, and if there is any joke on style in this poem, it is a joke on the inarticulateness of much modern American speech. Whittemore's parody is actually aimed at Poe's plot, and indeed Poe skirts the absurd in his famous story. It is an "unbelievable" story, made great by Poe's style, which wraps the tale in a language that makes it not only believable but unforgettable.

Whittemore's parody, therefore, allows us to laugh at the absurd aspects of "The Fall of the House of Usher" at the same time that our admiration for Poe is enhanced. After all, if Poe's story were not a *great* story, Whittemore would never have written his parody.

Thinking About Parody

Which lines in Whittemore's poem do you think are the funniest? Which expressions contrast most vividly with Poe's original words?

Richard Wilbur *born 1921*

Richard Wilbur has established himself as a poet working steadily within the traditional forms and approaches of English poetry. His poems are elegant without calling attention to themselves. They are thoughtful, fresh, and carefully crafted.

Wilbur was born in New York City but has lived most of his adult life in New England. He has taught at several New England colleges. His first volume, *The Beautiful Changes* (1947), won him the solid recognition that has increased with *Things of This World* (1956), *Advice to a Prophet* (1961), *Walking to Sleep* (1969), and *The Mind-Reader* (1976). He has also produced superb verse translations of the French dramatist Molière and written essays that have been collected as *Responses* (1976).

Wilbur is a master of stanza forms, as he shows in "Year's End." He adopts an unusual but effective rhyme scheme and then maintains it gracefully for the length of the poem. Like Robert Frost, an early master of Wilbur's, he likes to work against the challenge of a form rather than in free verse. (Frost has said that, to him, writing free verse was like playing tennis without a net.) "Year's End" is typical of Wilbur's meditative lyrics: not flashy, not a confession of the author's personal problems, but simply deriving pleasure from its moving images and its imaginative use of language. The shape of the poem is a common one in Romantic and post-Romantic poetry: We see the speaker walking in a landscape, and we overhear the thoughts that the landscape produces within him.

Richard Wilbur

Year's End

Now winter downs[1] the dying of the year,
And night is all a settlement of snow;
From the soft street the rooms of houses show
A gathered light, a shapen[2] atmosphere,
5 Like frozen-over lakes whose ice is thin
And still allows some stirring down within.

I've known the wind by water banks to shake
The late leaves down, which frozen where they fell
And held in ice as dancers in a spell
10 Fluttered all winter long into a lake;
Graved[3] on the dark in gestures of descent,
They seemed their own most perfect monument.

There was perfection in the death of ferns
Which laid their fragile cheeks against the stone
15 A million years. Great mammoths overthrown
Composedly have made their long sojourns,
Like palaces of patience, in the gray
And changeless lands of ice. And at Pompeii[4]

The little dog lay curled and did not rise
20 But slept the deeper as the ashes rose
And found the people incomplete, and froze
The random hands, the loose unready eyes
Of men expecting yet another sun
To do the shapely thing they had not done.

25 These sudden ends of time must give us pause.
We fray[5] into the future, rarely wrought[6]
Save in the tapestries of afterthought.
More time, more time. Barrages of applause
Come muffled from a buried radio.
30 The New-year bells are wrangling with the snow.

---

1. **downs:** covers in white, as with feathers ("down").
2. **shapen:** shaped.
3. **graved:** engraved.
4. **Pompeii** [pom pā′]: city of ancient Rome, partly preserved in lava from a volcanic eruption that destroyed it in A.D. 79
5. **fray:** battle; here, also unravel.
6. **wrought:** shaped.

STUDY QUESTIONS

Recalling

1. According to the title, when does this poem take place? What does winter "down" in the first stanza?
2. In the second stanza what happens to the leaves where they fall? With what are the leaves held in ice compared?
3. What perfection does the poet note in lines 13–15? With what does he compare great mammoths in the gray and changeless lands of ice?
4. What do the ashes find in the fourth stanza? What did the people frozen by the ashes in Pompeii expect, according to lines 23–24?
5. What must give us pause, according to line 25? What is "wrangling with the snow" in the last line?

Interpreting

6. What do the frozen leaves, the fern fossils, the mammoths, and the dog and people of Pompeii have in common? What do the "perfect monument" of the frozen leaves, the "perfection" of the fern fossils, and the description of the mammoths suggest about the poet's view of these things?
7. According to the poet, did the people of Pompeii achieve perfection before they died? Did they expect to? When do lines 26–27 suggest that human beings become perfectly "shaped"?
8. What human attitude toward life do the bells of the new year represent, and why are the bells "wrangling" with the snow? Does the poet suggest that the bells will win the "wrangle"? Explain.
9. What aspect of our own lives does the poet suggest we think about when we pause to consider "these sudden ends of time"?

Extending

10. What are some of the thoughts you have had on New Year's Eve? Do you find the last day of the year happy, sad, or both? Why do you suppose so many people throughout the world celebrate in some way on their respective new years?

© Rollie McKenna

Sylvia Plath   *1932–1963*

Sylvia Plath was born in Boston and published her first poems and fiction when she was only seventeen. Her interest in writing continued while she was a student at Smith College. Plath's poetry and her autobiographical novel, *The Bell Jar,* show, however, that she lived an intense and often troubled inner life.

She graduated from Smith in 1955 with highest honors and won a scholarship to Cambridge University in England. There she met and married Ted Hughes, who was to become one of the leading British poets of his generation. Plath and Hughes lived in America for a while but then returned to England, where she wrote most of the poems for which she is best known.

Plath was influenced by her friend Robert Lowell (page 581), whose *Life Studies* (1959) had begun a fashion for "confessional" poetry. Plath adopted the confessional mode, writing, she said, at "top speed, as one might write an urgent letter." These late poems, published by her husband after her death, appeared in the volume *Ariel* (1965). In recent years, interest in Plath's life has occasioned the publication of most of the poems she left in manuscript, as well as her letters and diaries.

Most of Plath's poems are deeply personal, but they do not all record her sufferings. "Blackberrying," though with a violent undercurrent, is in the tradition of Romantic nature poetry that began in America with William Cullen Bryant.

Sylvia Plath

Blackberrying

Nobody in the lane, and nothing, nothing but blackberries,
Blackberries on either side, though on the right mainly,
A blackberry alley, going down in hooks, and a sea
Somewhere at the end of it, heaving. Blackberries
5 Big as the ball of my thumb, and dumb as eyes
Ebon[1] in the hedges, fat
With blue-red juices. These they squander on my fingers.
I had not asked for such a blood sisterhood; they must love me.
They accommodate themselves to my milkbottle, flattening their
        sides.

10 Overhead go the choughs[2] in black, cacophonous[3] flocks—
Bits of burnt paper wheeling in a blown sky.
Theirs is the only voice, protesting, protesting.
I do not think the sea will appear at all.
The high, green meadows are glowing, as if lit from within.
15 I come to one bush of berries so ripe it is a bush of flies,
Hanging their blue-green bellies and their wing panes in a Chinese
        screen.[4]
The honey-feast of the berries has stunned them; they believe in
        heaven.
One more hook, and the berries and bushes end.

The only thing to come now is the sea.
20 From between two hills a sudden wind funnels at me,
Slapping its phantom laundry in my face.
These hills are too green and sweet to have tasted salt.
I follow the sheep path between them. A last hook brings me
To the hills' northern face, and the face is orange rock
25 That looks out on nothing, nothing but a great space
Of white and pewter[5] lights, and a din like silversmiths
Beating and beating at an intractable metal.

---

1. **Ebon** [eb′ən]: black.
2. **choughs** [chufs]: birds with glossy black feathers and red legs and beak.
3. **cacophonous** [kə kof′ə nəs]: harsh sounding.
4. **Chinese screen:** folding screen of wood and silk, covered with scenes
painted in brilliant colors.
5. **pewter** [pū′tər]: dull, silvery-gray.

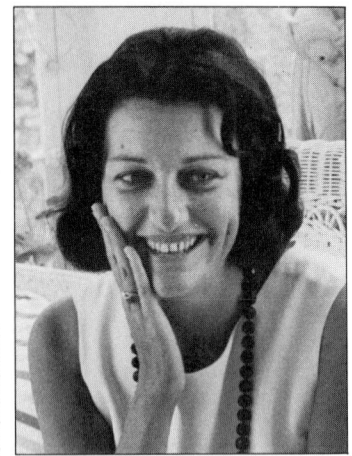
© Rollie McKenna

Anne Sexton   *1928–1972*

Like Sylvia Plath, Anne Sexton was a student of Robert Lowell's. She studied poetry with Lowell at Boston University, and most of her poems are written in the "confessional" mode, recording some of life's most painful experiences—such as the loss of loved ones and the breakdown of relationships—with a raw directness. Sexton once said that poetry should be a "shock to the senses. It should almost hurt." Certainly the material of her poetry is the life of a woman who felt a great deal of hurt in her life.

Sexton was born in Newton, Massachusetts. For a while, she taught high school, and later she taught at Boston University. Her life was troubled with recurring mental illness, a struggle that forms the basis for some of her finest poems. Her books include *To Bedlam and Part Way Back* (1960), *All My Pretty Ones* (1962), *Live or Die* (for which she won the Pulitzer Prize in 1967), *Love Poems* (1969), and *The Book of Folly* (1972).

"What's That" is a beautifully mysterious poem, filled with delicate expression and hidden anxiety. If we are never sure exactly what the "it" is that is the subject of the poem, we are sure that it is a reality different from that represented by the cars going by on the street.

Model for Active Reading

In this selection, and in one selection in each unit, you will find notes in the right-hand margin that highlight parts of the selection. These notes point out important ideas of the period—in this case, postwar ideas—and draw your attention to literary elements and techniques covered in the Literary Focuses. Page numbers in the notes will refer you to more extensive discussions of these important ideas and elements.

Anne Sexton

What's That

Before it came inside
I had watched it from my kitchen window,
watched it swell like a new balloon,
watched it slump and then divide,
5 like something I know I know—
a broken pear or two halves of the moon,
or round white plates floating nowhere
or fat hands waving in the summer air
until they fold together like a fist or a knee.
10 After that it came to my door. Now it lives here.
And of course: it is a soft sound, soft as a seal's ear,
that was caught between a shape and a shape and then
        returned to me.

You know how parents call
from sweet beaches anywhere, *come in come in,*
15 and how you sank under water to put out
the sound, or how one of them touched in the hall
at night: the rustle and the skin
you couldn't know, but heard, the stout
slap of tides and the dog snoring. It's here
20 now, caught back from time in my adult year—
the image we did forget: the cranking shells on our feet
or the swing of the spoon in soup. It is as real
as splinters stuck in your ear. The noise we steal
is half a bell. And outside cars whisk by on the
        suburban street

25 and are there and are true.
What else is this, this intricate shape of air?
calling me, calling you.

Free verse (p. 454): The poem does not employ a regular rhythm, or meter.

Rhyme scheme (p. 167): Despite the irregular rhythm, a strict pattern of rhymes in the first stanza is repeated in the second.

Postwar idea: Many midcentury poets deal with intimate personal experiences (p. 569).

Diction and tone (p. 197 and p. 502): Twentieth-century American poets often use contractions and colloquial English, achieving an informal tone.

Postwar idea: Many midcentury writers have more questions than they have answers (p. 569).

STUDY QUESTIONS (Plath)

Recalling

1. What is in the lane, according to line 1? To what do they go down "in hooks"? What do they "squander" on the speaker's fingers? What does she conclude in line 8?
2. In line 13 what does the speaker not think will appear? What happens in line 18?
3. What funnels at the speaker in line 20? What does the poet decide about the hills in line 22? To what has the last "hook" brought her in line 24? On what does the orange rock "look out"?

Interpreting

4. What sort of experience is the speaker's encounter with the blackberries?
5. What does the speaker think will never happen? Does it happen? Is this ironic?
6. What words in line 25 have we heard earlier in the poem? Explain how the repetition relates to the poem's irony.
7. What does the poem suggest about human emotions or emotional experiences?

LITERARY FOCUS (Plath)

Imagery

We cannot read "Blackberrying" without sensing its intense feeling. It is a highly emotional poem, and as we read, word by word, line by line, we share the poet's emotional adventure.

Yet notice how seldom, if ever, the poet tells us *directly* what she is feeling. Rather, she makes the *images* project the feeling. She does not tell us *about* the experience: She recreates it for us, largely through the imagery, so that we may experience it ourselves.

Most of the imagery in this poem is visual, made of vivid pictures. These are not just any paths, but paths that twist like a series of "hooks," forcing us to see this particular landscape. "Green meadows" is in itself not a remarkable image, but it becomes one when described as "glowing, as if lit from within." The image tells us, indirectly, that the poet, too, must be somehow "lit from within" as she shares, becomes a part of, this landscape.

Thinking About Imagery

◼ Identify the images of sound, taste, and touch in "Blackberrying." Tell what each contributes to an understanding of the poet's emotions.

STUDY QUESTIONS (Sexton)

Recalling

1. From where did the poet watch "it" before it came inside? How did it swell? Like what did it slump and then divide?
2. What happened after the poet watched it, according to line 10? Where does it now live?
3. Identify three images the poet remembers in lines 13–19. According to lines 20–21, what is here *now,* and from what was it caught back? To what is it compared in lines 22–23?
4. According to line 25, what are the cars whisking by on the suburban street? With what question does the poem end?

Interpreting

5. How does the poem communicate the reality of "it"? How does the poem communicate the vagueness of "it"?
6. What do the cars on the street represent? With what are they contrasted?
7. Why does the poet never explain precisely what "it" is?
8. Explain what the final question may mean.

Extending

9. Have you ever had an experience similar to the one described in this poem—an experience of *déjà vu,* for example? Discuss how the poet captures that experience in this poem.

COMPARING WRITERS

The concern with the problems of society at large that marked much of the literature of the Great Depression and the World War II years gave way, in the fifties, to more personal concerns. Nevertheless, in writing about themselves, modern writers also express attitudes and problems of modern life that we all share.

1. Which of the poems you have read in this unit exhibit primarily social concerns? What are their concerns?
2. Which of the poems in this unit deal with highly personal feelings or experiences? What are some of the modern attitudes or dilemmas they reflect?
3. Which of the poems suggest that modern Americans can learn something from America's past? What values do they suggest can be learned from the past?

FICTION

Katherine Anne Porter   *1890–1980*

Katherine Anne Porter wrote very little in the course of a long lifetime. Yet almost everything she wrote was so polished, so well-crafted, that she is considered among the finest of American prose writers.

Porter was born in Indian Creek, Texas, and her family had roots in the Old South. Many of her stories reflect her adolescent life in the Southwest and the family tales she heard when a girl. She worked on newspapers and then lived, for a significant period of her youth, in Mexico, which she called "my familiar country." Some of her most famous tales have a Mexican background. In later years Porter taught in American universities.

Porter excelled in the short story and novella, forms that reflect her talent for concentration and discipline. Her first book, which included "The Jilting of Granny Weatherall," was *Flowering Judas,* published in 1930. Her other major works were *Noon Wine* (1937), *Pale Horse, Pale Rider* (1939), *The Leaning Tower* (1944), and the novel *Ship of Fools* (1962).

Porter writes often of the passing of the old order and of the confusion and guilt that accompany change. However, she deals with these large subjects in very confined forms. In "The Jilting of Granny Weatherall" every phrase that runs through Granny's mind counts toward the total effect. The story's disjointed "stream-of-consciousness" style, still experimental at the time it was written, reflects the Modernist break with traditional narrative that Porter saw in the works of James Joyce, Virginia Woolf, and Ernest Hemingway.

Katherine Anne Porter

The Jilting of Granny Weatherall

She flicked her wrist neatly out of Doctor Harry's pudgy careful fingers and pulled the sheet up to her chin. The brat ought to be in knee breeches. Doctoring around the country with spectacles on his nose! "Get along now, take your schoolbooks and go. There's nothing wrong with me."

Doctor Harry spread a warm paw like a cushion on her forehead where the forked green vein danced and made her eyelids twitch. "Now, now, be a good girl, and we'll have you up in no time."

"That's no way to speak to a woman nearly eighty years old just because she's down. I'd have you respect your elders, young man."

"Well, Missy, excuse me." Doctor Harry patted her cheek. "But I've got to warn you, haven't I? You're a marvel, but you must be careful or you're going to be good and sorry."

"Don't tell me what I'm going to be. I'm on my feet now, morally speaking. It's Cornelia. I had to go to bed to get rid of her."

Her bones felt loose, and floated around in her skin, and Doctor Harry floated like a balloon around the foot of the bed. He floated and pulled down his waistcoat and swung his glasses on a cord. "Well, stay where you are, it certainly can't hurt you."

"Get along and doctor your sick," said Granny Weatherall. "Leave a well woman alone. I'll call for you when I want you. . . . Where were you forty years ago when I pulled through milk leg[1] and double pneumonia? You weren't even born. Don't let Cornelia lead you on," she shouted, because Doctor Harry ap-

---

1. **milk leg:** painful swelling of the leg, usually as a result of infection during childbirth.

peared to float up to the ceiling and out. "I pay my own bills, and I don't throw my money away on nonsense!"

She meant to wave goodbye, but it was too much trouble. Her eyes closed of themselves, it was like a dark curtain drawn around the bed. The pillow rose and floated under her, pleasant as a hammock in a light wind. She listened to the leaves rustling outside the window. No, somebody was swishing newspapers: no, Cornelia and Doctor Harry were whispering together. She leaped broad awake, thinking they whispered in her ear.

"She was never like this, *never* like this!" "Well, what can we expect?" "Yes, eighty years old. . . ."

Well, and what if she was? She still had ears. It was like Cornelia to whisper around doors. She always kept things secret in such a public way. She was always being tactful and kind. Cornelia was dutiful; that was the trouble with her. Dutiful and good: "So good and dutiful," said Granny, "that I'd like to spank her." She saw herself spanking Cornelia and making a fine job of it.

"What'd you say, Mother?"

Granny felt her face tying up in hard knots. "Can't a body think, I'd like to know?"

"I thought you might want something."

"I do. I want a lot of things. First off, go away and don't whisper."

She lay and drowsed, hoping in her sleep that the children would keep out and let her rest a minute. It had been a long day. Not that she was tired. It was always pleasant to snatch a minute now and then. There was always so much to be done, let me see: tomorrow.

Tomorrow was far away and there was nothing to trouble about. Things were finished somehow when the time came; thank God there was always a little margin over for peace: then a person could spread out the plan of life and tuck in the edges orderly. It was good to have everything clean and folded away, with the hair brushes and tonic bottles sitting

straight on the white embroidered linen: the day started without fuss and the pantry shelves laid out with rows of jelly glasses and brown jugs and white stone-china jars with blue whirligigs[2] and words painted on them: coffee, tea, sugar, ginger, cinnamon, allspice: and the bronze clock with the lion on top nicely dusted off. The dust that lion could collect in twenty-four hours! The box in the attic with all those letters tied up, well, she'd have to go through that tomorrow. All those letters— George's letters and John's letters and her letters to them both—lying around for the children to find afterwards made her uneasy. Yes, that would be tomorrow's business. No use to let them know how silly she had been once.

While she was rummaging around she found death in her mind and it felt clammy and unfamiliar. She had spent so much time preparing for death there was no need for bringing it up again. Let it take care of itself now. When she was sixty she had felt very old, finished, and went around making farewell trips to see her children and grandchildren, with a secret in her mind: This is the very last of your mother, children! Then she made her will and came down with a long fever. That was all just a notion like a lot of other things, but it was lucky too, for she had once for all got over the idea of dying for a long time. Now she couldn't be worried. She hoped she had better sense now. Her father had lived to be one hundred and two years old and had drunk a noggin of strong hot toddy on his last birthday. He told the reporters it was his daily habit, and he owed his long life to that. He had made quite a scandal and was very pleased about it. She believed she'd just plague Cornelia a little.

"Cornelia! Cornelia!" No footsteps, but a sudden hand on her cheek. "Bless you, where have you been?"

"Here, Mother."

"Well, Cornelia, I want a noggin of hot toddy."

---

2. **whirligigs:** circular patterns; swirls.

"Are you cold, darling?"

"I'm chilly, Cornelia. Lying in bed stops the circulation. I must have told you that a thousand times."

Well, she could just hear Cornelia telling her husband that Mother was getting a little childish and they'd have to humor her. The thing that most annoyed her was that Cornelia thought she was deaf, dumb, and blind. Little hasty glances and tiny gestures tossed around her and over her head saying, "Don't cross her, let her have her way, she's eighty years old," and she sitting there as if she lived in a thin glass cage. Sometimes Granny almost made up her mind to pack up and move back to her own house where nobody could remind her every minute that she was old. Wait, wait, Cornelia, till your own children whisper behind your back!

In her day she had kept a better house and had got more work done. She wasn't too old yet for Lydia to be driving eighty miles for advice when one of the children jumped the track, and Jimmy still dropped in and talked things over: "Now, Mammy, you've a good business head, I want to know what you think of this? . . ." Old. Cornelia couldn't change the furniture around without asking. Little things, little things! They had been so sweet when they were little. Granny wished the old days were back again with the children young and everything to be done over. It had been a hard pull, but not too much for her. When she thought of all the food she had cooked, and all the clothes she had cut and sewed, and all the gardens she had made—well, the children showed it. There they were, made out of her, and they couldn't get away from that. Sometimes she wanted to see John again and point to them and say, Well, I didn't do so badly, did I? But that would have to wait. That was for tomorrow. She used to think of him as a man, but now all the children were older than their father, and he would be a child beside her if she saw him now. It seemed strange and there was something wrong in the idea. Why, he couldn't possibly recognize her. She had fenced in a hundred acres once, digging the post holes herself and clamping the wires with just a boy to help. That changed a woman. John would be looking for a young woman with the peaked Spanish comb in her hair and the painted fan. Digging post holes changed a woman. Riding country roads in the winter when women had their babies was another thing: sitting up nights with sick horses and sick children and hardly ever losing one. John, I hardly ever lost one of them! John would see that in a minute, that would be something he could understand, she wouldn't have to explain anything!

It made her feel like rolling up her sleeves and putting the whole place to rights again. No matter if Cornelia was determined to be everywhere at once, there were a great many things left undone on this place. She would start tomorrow and do them. It was good to be strong enough for everything, even if all you made melted and changed and slipped under your hands, so that by the time you finished you almost forgot what you were working for. What was it I set out to do? she asked herself intently, but she could not remember. A fog rose over the valley, she saw it marching across the creek swallowing the trees and moving up the hill like an army of ghosts. Soon it would be at the near edge of the orchard, and then it was time to go in and light the lamps. Come in, children, don't stay out in the night air.

Lighting the lamps had been beautiful. The children huddled up to her and breathed like little calves waiting at the bars in the twilight. Their eyes followed the match and watched the flame rise and settle in a blue curve, then they moved away from her. The lamp was lit, they didn't have to be scared and hang on to Mother any more. Never, never, never more. God, for all my life I thank Thee. Without Thee, my God, I could never have done it. Hail, Mary, full of grace.[3]

I want you to pick all the fruit this year and see that nothing is wasted. There's always

---

3. **Hail . . . grace:** beginning of a Roman Catholic prayer to the Virgin Mary.

someone who can use it. Don't let good things rot for want of using. You waste life when you waste good food. Don't let things get lost. It's bitter to lose things. Now, don't let me get to thinking, not when I am tired and taking a little nap before supper. . . .

The pillow rose about her shoulders and pressed against her heart and the memory was being squeezed out of it: oh, push down the pillow, somebody: it would smother her if she tried to hold it. Such a fresh breeze blowing and such a green day with no threats in it. But he had not come, just the same. What does a woman do when she has put on the white veil and set out the white cake for a man and he doesn't come? She tried to remember. No, I swear he never harmed me but in that. He never harmed me but in that . . . and what if he did? There was the day, the day, but a whirl of dark smoke rose and covered it, crept up and over into the bright field where everything was planted so carefully in orderly rows. That was hell, she knew hell when she saw it. For sixty years she had prayed against remembering him and against losing her soul in the deep pit of hell, and now the two things were mingled in one and the thought of him was a smoky cloud from hell that moved and crept in her head when she had just got rid of Doctor Harry and was trying to rest a minute. Wounded vanity, Ellen, said a sharp voice in the top of her mind. Don't let your wounded vanity get the upper hand of you. Plenty of girls get jilted. You were jilted, weren't you? Then stand up to it. Her eyelids wavered and let in streamers of blue-gray light like tissue paper over her eyes. She must get up and pull the shades down or she'd never sleep. She was in bed again and the shades were not down. How could that happen? Better turn over, hide from the light, sleeping in the light gave you nightmares. "Mother, how do you feel now?" and a stinging wetness on her forehead. But I don't like having my face washed in cold water!

Hapsy? George? Lydia? Jimmy? No, Cornelia, and her features were swollen and full of little puddles. "They're coming, darling, they'll all be here soon." Go wash your face, child, you look funny.

Instead of obeying, Cornelia knelt down and put her head on the pillow. She seemed to be talking but there was no sound. "Well, are you tongue-tied? Whose birthday is it? Are you going to have a party?"

Cornelia's mouth moved urgently in strange shapes. "Don't do that, you bother me, daughter."

"Oh, no, Mother. Oh, no. . . ."

Nonsense. It was strange about children. They disputed your every word. "No what, Cornelia?"

"Here's Doctor Harry."

"I won't see that boy again. He just left five minutes ago."

"That was this morning, Mother. It's night now. Here's the nurse."

"This is Doctor Harry, Mrs. Weatherall. I never saw you look so young and happy!"

"Ah, I'll never be young again—but I'd be happy if they'd let me lie in peace and get rested."

She thought she spoke up loudly, but no one answered. A warm weight on her forehead, a warm bracelet on her wrist, and a breeze went on whispering, trying to tell her something. A shuffle of leaves in the everlasting hand of God. He blew on them and they danced and rattled. "Mother, don't mind, we're going to give you a little hypodermic." "Look here, daughter, how do ants get in this bed? I saw sugar ants yesterday." Did you send for Hapsy too?

It was Hapsy she really wanted. She had to go a long way back through a great many rooms to find Hapsy standing with a baby on her arm. She seemed to herself to be Hapsy also, and the baby on Hapsy's arm was Hapsy and himself and herself, all at once, and there was no surprise in the meeting. Then Hapsy melted from within and turned flimsy as gray gauze and the baby was a gauzy shadow, and Hapsy came up close and said, "I thought you'd never come," and looked at her very searchingly and said, "You haven't changed a bit!" They leaned forward to kiss, when Cornelia began whispering from a long way off, "Oh, is there anything you want to tell me? Is there anything I can do for you?"

Yes, she had changed her mind after sixty years and she would like to see George. I want you to find George. Find him and be sure to tell him I forgot him. I want him to know I had my husband just the same and my children and my house like any other woman. A good house too and a good husband that I loved and fine children out of him. Better than I hoped for even. Tell him I was given back everything he took away and more. Oh, no, oh, no, there was something else besides the house and the man and the children. Oh, surely they were not all? What was it? Something not given back. . . . Her breath crowded down under her ribs and grew into a monstrous frightening shape with cutting edges; it bored up into her head, and the agony was unbelievable: Yes, John, get the doctor now, no more talk, my time has come.

When this one was born it should be the last. The last. It should have been born first, for it was the one she had truly wanted. Everything came in good time. Nothing left out, left over. She was strong, in three days she would be as well as ever. Better. A woman needed milk in her to have her full health.

"Mother, do you hear me?"

"I've been telling you—"

"Mother, Father Connolly's here."

"I went to Holy Communion only last week. Tell him I'm not so sinful as all that."

"Father just wants to speak to you."

He could speak as much as he pleased. It was like him to drop in and inquire about her soul as if it were a teething baby, and then stay on for a cup of tea and a round of cards and gossip. He always had a funny story of some sort, usually about an Irishman who made his little mistakes and confessed them, and the point lay in some absurd thing he would blurt out in the confessional showing his struggles between native piety and original sin. Granny felt easy about her soul. Cornelia, where are your manners? Give Father Connolly a chair. She had her secret comfortable understanding with a few favorite saints who cleared a straight road to God for her. All as surely signed and sealed as the papers for the new Forty Acres. Forever . . . heirs and assigns[4] forever. Since the day the wedding cake was not cut, but thrown out and wasted. The whole bottom dropped out of the world, and there she was blind and sweating with nothing under feet and the walls falling away. His hand had caught her under the breast, she had not fallen, there was the freshly polished floor with the green rug on it, just as before. He had cursed like a sailor's parrot and said, "I'll kill him for you." Don't lay a hand on him, for my sake leave something to God. "Now, Ellen, you must believe what I tell you. . . ."

So there was nothing, nothing to worry about any more, except sometimes in the night one of the children screamed in a nightmare, and they both hustled out shaking and hunting for the matches and calling, "There, wait a minute, here we are!" John, get the doctor now, Hapsy's time has come. But there was Hapsy standing by the bed in a white cap. "Cornelia, tell Hapsy to take off her cap. I can't see her plain."

Her eyes opened very wide and the room stood out like a picture she had seen somewhere. Dark colors with the shadows rising towards the ceiling in long angles. The tall black dresser gleamed with nothing on it but John's picture, enlarged from a little one, with John's eyes very black when they should have been blue. You never saw him, so how do you know how he looked? But the man insisted the copy was perfect, it was very rich and handsome. For a picture, yes, but it's not my husband. The table by the bed had a linen cover and a candle and a crucifix. The light was blue from Cornelia's silk lampshades. No sort of light at all, just frippery.[5] You had to live forty years with kerosene lamps to appreciate honest elec-

---

4. **assigns:** people to whom property is legally transferred.

5. **frippery:** showy, useless display of elegance.

tricity. She felt very strong and she saw Doctor Harry with a rosy nimbus[6] around him.

"You look like a saint, Doctor Harry, and I vow that's as near as you'll ever come to it."

"She's saying something."

"I heard you, Cornelia. What's all this carrying-on?"

"Father Connolly's saying—"

Cornelia's voice staggered and bumped like a cart in a bad road. It rounded corners and turned back again and arrived nowhere. Granny stepped up in the cart very lightly and reached for the reins, but a man sat beside her and she knew him by his hands, driving the cart. She did not look in his face, for she knew without seeing, but looked instead down the road where the trees leaned over and bowed to each other and a thousand birds were singing a Mass. She felt like singing too, but she put her hand in the bosom of her dress and pulled out a rosary, and Father Connolly murmured Latin in a very solemn voice and tickled her feet.[7] Will you stop that nonsense? I'm a married woman. What if he did run away and leave me to face the priest by myself? I found another a whole world better. I wouldn't have exchanged my husband for anybody except Saint Michael[8] himself, and you may tell him that for me with a thank-you in the bargain.

Light flashed on her closed eyelids, and a deep roaring shook her. Cornelia, is that lightning? I hear thunder. There's going to be a storm. Close all the windows. Call the children in. . . . "Mother, here we are, all of us." "Is that you, Hapsy?" "Oh, no, I'm Lydia. We drove as fast as we could." Their faces drifted above her, drifted away. The rosary fell out of her hands and Lydia put it back. Jimmy tried to help, their hands fumbled together, and Granny closed two fingers around Jimmy's thumb. Beads wouldn't do, it must be something alive. She was so amazed her thoughts ran round and round. So, my dear Lord, this is my death and I wasn't even thinking about it. My children have come to see me die. But I can't, it's not time. Oh, I always hated surprises. I wanted to give Cornelia the amethyst[9] set—Cornelia, you're to have the amethyst set, but Hapsy's to wear it when she wants, and, Doctor Harry, do shut up. Nobody sent for you. Oh, my dear Lord, do wait a minute. I meant to do something about the Forty Acres, Jimmy doesn't need it and Lydia will later on, with that worthless husband of hers. I meant to finish the altar cloth and send six bottles of wine to Sister Borgia for her dyspepsia.[10] I want to send six bottles of wine to Sister Borgia, Father Connolly, now don't let me forget.

Cornelia's voice made short turns and tilted over and crashed. "Oh, Mother, oh, Mother, oh, Mother. . . ."

"I'm not going, Cornelia. I'm taken by surprise. I can't go."

You'll see Hapsy again. What about her? "I thought you'd never come." Granny made a long journey outward, looking for Hapsy. What if I don't find her? What then? Her heart sank down and down, there was no bottom to death, she couldn't come to the end of it. The blue light from Cornelia's lampshade drew into a tiny point in the center of her brain, it flickered and winked like an eye, quietly it fluttered and dwindled. Granny lay curled down within herself, amazed and watchful, staring at the point of light that was herself; her body was now only a deeper mass of shadow in an endless darkness and this darkness would curl around the light and swallow it up. God, give a sign!

For the second time there was no sign. Again no bridegroom and the priest in the house. She could not remember any other sorrow because this grief wiped them all away. Oh, no, there's nothing more cruel than this— I'll never forgive it. She stretched herself with a deep breath and blew out the light.

---

6. **nimbus:** halo.
7. **murmured . . . feet:** administered last rites, including prayers and applying holy oil to the feet.
8. **Saint Michael:** an archangel.

9. **amethyst** [am'ə thist]: purple or violet quartz, used in jewelry.
10. **dyspepsia** [dis pep'shə]: indigestion.

STUDY QUESTIONS

Recalling

1. Why does Granny Weatherall tell Doctor Harry she has taken to her bed (paragraph 5)? For what day does Granny make plans soon after Doctor Harry leaves? What does she "find" while "rummaging around" in her mind? How does it feel to her?

2. Who are Cornelia, Lydia, and Jimmy? Who was John? With whom does Granny now live?

3. Identify three thoughts that Granny has about her earlier years as a housewife and mother.

4. As she looks back on her long life, which event does Granny recall with particular anger? According to page 608, what does Granny want George to know? What does she conclude about the things she was "given back"?

5. What does Granny ask of God in the next-to-last paragraph? What happens "for the second time"? Why can Granny not remember any other sorrow, according to the last paragraph?

Interpreting

6. What happens in the last sentence of the story? With what image is life equated in this sentence and elsewhere in the story? What does Granny's attitude toward the doctor and the priest suggest about her attitude toward death?

7. What sort of life did Granny live? How is her life related to her surname? What sort of wife and mother does she seem to have been?

8. What is ironic in Granny's thought about George: "Find him and be sure to tell him I forgot him"? What might the "something not given back" on page 608 be?

9. What sort of sign might Granny want from God? What are the two "cruelties" that Granny confuses in the final paragraph?

10. Why does the jilting come back to Granny so frequently as she faces death? What is the real "jilting of Granny Weatherall"?

Extending

11. In what way is Granny's attitude toward life like that of traditional nineteenth-century pioneers? In what way is her attitude toward death different from attitudes expressed in the nineteenth century—those of Emily Dickinson, for example? How might this difference in attitude reflect modern times?

VIEWPOINT

In introducing a collection of short stories that contains "The Jilting of Granny Weatherall," Calvin Skaggs offers this analysis:

> Porter shows us a woman so scarred by her early romantic wound that she has suppressed her emotional needs. By dedicating herself to work—to raising a family and ripping a prosperous farm from the frontier—she has avoided recognizing the scar tissue that surrounds, and deadens, her life. . . . But at the moment of her death she recognizes the darkness to which her inability to forgive that first jilting has doomed her. Too late she sees that she has been jilted again, this time by the bridegroom who judges the essential nature and quality of a life.
>
> —Introduction to *The American Short Story*, Vol. 2

1. According to this analysis, what is Granny's tragic flaw, the characteristic of her personality that brings her to a tragic end? Whom does Skaggs believe is the "second bridegroom"?

2. Do you agree with this analysis of Granny's character? Why or why not?

LITERARY FOCUS

Stream of Consciousness and Flashback

In the twentieth century, with its great interest in psychology, storytellers often abandon the chronological, straight-line narrative that dominated literature for centuries. If, for example, Granny Weatherall's story were told in chronological time sequence, we would read first about her jilting, then about her marriage and the birth of her children, then about the time when she moved to Cornelia's house, and finally about the days just before her death. Clock time works that way, but the mind and the memory work differently. In our century writers began to represent the way time happens in our minds. This kind of writing is often called the **stream of consciousness,** from a phrase by the American psychologist William James.

Most of our thoughts do not come to us in complete sentences. During very few minutes in any given day do we think logically. Most of what goes on in our minds is a series of thoughts and images that switch rapidly back and forth between the present, the past, and the future, as things and ideas remind us of other things and ideas. Your own stream of consciousness is not hard for *you* to interpret because you are *in* it. For others, however, much of it would make no sense.

In some ways stream-of-consciousness writing is truer to reality than writing that suggests more orderly thinking. Yet such stream-of-consciousness fiction can also be difficult to read. In "The Jilting of Granny Weatherall" we, the readers, have to retell the story, as it were, in chronological order. We have to do some imaginative work to reorder the events, but our reward is great: We gain the illusion of being present to the private thoughts of Granny Weatherall. Porter gives us enough clues that allow us to recreate the story, and the result is an experience that we could not have had if the story had been written any other way.

One of Porter's techniques is drawn from movie making—the **flashback**, an interruption in the narrative to show an event that happened earlier. We take this technique so for granted as a narrative method in movies that we hardly notice it. A character may be reminded of something from the past, and suddenly the whole story shifts back into the past; we see something that happened earlier, and then we just as suddenly find ourselves in the present again. In this story, in the very first paragraph, we find a flashback, as Granny remembers Doctor Harry when she knew him as a little boy. Porter uses the flashback to help create the stream of consciousness.

Thinking About Stream of Consciousness and Flashback

1. Why is the stream of consciousness especially appropriate in "The Jilting of Granny Weatherall," given the story's subject matter?
2. Give another example of flashback from "The Jilting of Granny Weatherall."

COMPOSITION

Writing About Stream of Consciousness

▪ Choose three or four incidents in the life of Granny Weatherall, and write about them as if you were telling the story in the traditional way. Place the events in chronological order, and use an objective third-person point of view. When you have finished, discuss what has been gained or lost by the method that Katherine Anne Porter uses.

Writing in the Stream-of-Consciousness Manner

▪ Putting yourself in the place of one of the other characters in "The Jilting of Granny Weatherall," write a stream-of-consciousness account of what might be going on in your mind as Granny Weatherall is dying. Show how the present and past reality mix and how one thought or image suggests another.

Jerome Weidman   *born 1913*

When Jerome Weidman, who was born in New York, graduated from high school, he did not intend to be a writer. The time was the height of the Great Depression, and for Weidman "there was only one problem, and that was to eat." During the 1930s, while attending college and then law school at night, he worked as a clerk in New York City's garment district for eleven dollars a week. Reading was his pastime, and as a challenge to himself he wrote a short story based on an anecdote that he had overheard. A magazine accepted the story, and he got ten dollars for his efforts. A contest encouraged him to begin his first novel, and although it did not win the contest, the novel, *I Can Get It for You Wholesale,* was published in 1937. Weidman became a full-time writer.

Along with other novels and numerous collections of short stories, Weidman has written plays, including the musical *Fiorello!* (1960), for which he shared the Pulitzer Prize. *I Can Get It for You Wholesale,* based on the novel, was produced on Broadway in 1962. Weidman has also written several screenplays.

"My Father Sits in the Dark," from a short story collection of the same name, shows Weidman's simple and straightforward way of writing. He bases his entire story on an **anecdote,** a short account of an interesting event in someone's life. Like an old photograph, his story captures a lost time and a feeling for his father that a boy cannot forget.

Jerome Weidman

My Father Sits in the Dark

My father has a peculiar habit. He is fond of sitting in the dark, alone. Sometimes I come home very late. The house is dark. I let myself in quietly because I do not want to disturb my mother. She is a light sleeper. I tiptoe into my room and undress in the dark. I go to the kitchen for a drink of water. My bare feet make no noise. I step into the room and almost trip over my father. He is sitting in a kitchen chair, in his pajamas, smoking his pipe.

"Hello, Pop," I say.

"Hello, son."

"Why don't you go to bed, Pa?"

"I will," he says.

But he remains there. Long after I am asleep I feel sure that he is still sitting there, smoking.

Many times I am reading in my room. I hear my mother get the house ready for the night. I hear my kid brother go to bed. I hear my sister come in. I hear her do things with jars and combs until she, too, is quiet. I know she has gone to sleep. In a little while I hear my mother say good night to my father. I continue to read. Soon I become thirsty. (I drink a lot of water.) I go to the kitchen for a drink. Again I almost stumble across my father. Many times it startles me. I forget about him. And there he is—smoking, sitting, thinking.

"Why don't you go to bed, Pop?"

"I will, son."

But he doesn't. He just sits there and smokes and thinks. It worries me. I can't understand it. What can he be thinking about? Once I asked him.

"What are you thinking about, Pa?"

"Nothing," he said.

Once I left him there and went to bed. I awoke several hours later. I was thirsty. I went to the kitchen. There he was. His pipe was out. But he sat there, staring into a corner of the kitchen. After a moment I became accustomed to the darkness. I took my drink. He still sat and stared. His eyes did not blink. I thought he was not even aware of me. I was afraid.

"Why don't you go to bed, Pop?"

"I will, son," he said. "Don't wait up for me."

"But," I said, "you've been sitting here for hours. What's wrong? What are you thinking about?"

"Nothing, son," he said. "Nothing. It's just restful. That's all."

The way he said it was convincing. He did not seem worried. His voice was even and pleasant. It always is. But I could not understand it. How could it be restful to sit alone in an uncomfortable chair far into the night, in darkness?

What can it be?

I review all the possibilities. It can't be money. I know that. We haven't much, but when he is worried about money he makes no secret of it. It can't be his health. He is not reticent about that either. It can't be the health of anyone in the family. We are a bit short on money, but we are long on health. (Knock wood, my mother would say.) What can it be? I am afraid I do not know. But that does not stop me from worrying.

Maybe he is thinking of his brothers in the old country. Or of his mother and two stepmothers. Or of his father. But they are all dead. And he would not brood about them like that. I say brood, but it is not really true. He does not brood. He does not even seem to be thinking. He looks too peaceful, too, well not contented, just too peaceful, to be brooding. Perhaps it is as he says. Perhaps it is restful. But it does not seem possible. It worries me.

If I only knew what he thinks about. If I only knew that he thinks at all. I might not be able to help him. He might not even need help. It may be as he says. It may be restful.

But at least I would not worry about it.

Why does he just sit there, in the dark? Is his mind failing? No, it can't be. He is only fifty-three. And he is just as keen-witted as ever. In fact, he is the same in every respect. He still likes beet soup. He still reads the second section of the *Times* first. He still wears wing collars. He still believes that Debs[1] could have saved the country and that T.R.[2] was a tool of the moneyed interests. He is the same in every way. He does not even look older than he did five years ago. Everybody remarks about that. Well-preserved, they say. But he sits in the dark, alone, smoking, staring straight ahead of him, unblinking, into the small hours of the night.

If it is as he says, if it is restful, I will let it go at that. But suppose it is not. Suppose it is something I cannot fathom. Perhaps he needs help. Why doesn't he speak? Why doesn't he frown or laugh or cry? Why doesn't he do something? Why does he just sit there?

Finally I become angry. Maybe it is just my unsatisfied curiosity. Maybe I *am* a bit worried. Anyway, I become angry.

"Is something wrong, Pop?"

"Nothing, son. Nothing at all."

But this time I am determined not to be put off. I am angry.

"Then why do you sit here all alone, thinking, till late?"

"It's restful, son. I like it."

I am getting nowhere. Tomorrow he will be sitting there again. I will be puzzled. I will be worried. I will not stop now. I am angry.

"Well, what do you *think* about, Pa? Why do you just sit here? What's worrying you? What do you think about?"

"Nothing's worrying me, son. I'm all right. It's just restful. That's all. Go to bed, son."

My anger has left me. But the feeling of worry is still there. I must get an answer. It seems so silly. Why doesn't he tell me? I have a funny feeling that unless I get an answer I will go crazy. I am insistent.

"But what do you *think* about, Pa? What is it?"

"Nothing, son. Just things in general. Nothing special. Just things."

I can get no answer.

It is very late. The street is quiet and the house is dark. I climb the steps softly, skipping the ones that creak. I let myself in with my key and tiptoe into my room. I remove my clothes and remember that I am thirsty. In my bare feet I walk to the kitchen. Before I reach it I know he is there.

I can see the deeper darkness of his hunched shape. He is sitting in the same chair, his elbows on his knees, his cold pipe in his teeth, his unblinking eyes staring straight ahead. He does not seem to know I am there. He did not hear me come in. I stand quietly in the doorway and watch him.

Everything is quiet, but the night is full of little sounds. As I stand there motionless I begin to notice them. The ticking of the alarm clock on the icebox. The low hum of an automobile passing many blocks away. The swish of papers moved along the street by the breeze. A whispering rise and fall of sound, like low breathing. It is strangely pleasant.

The dryness in my throat reminds me. I step briskly into the kitchen.

"Hello, Pop," I say.

"Hello, son," he says. His voice is low and dreamlike. He does not change his position or shift his gaze.

I cannot find the faucet. The dim shadow of light that comes through the window from the street lamp only makes the room seem darker. I reach for the short chain in the center of the room. I snap on the light.

He straightens up with a jerk, as though he has been struck. "What's the matter, Pop?" I ask.

"Nothing," he says. "I don't like the light."

"What's the matter with the light?" I say. "What's wrong?"

---

1. **Debs:** Eugene Victor Debs (1855–1926), labor leader and Socialist candidate for President.
2. **T.R.:** Theodore Roosevelt (1858–1919), President of the United States (1901–1909).

"Nothing," he says. "I don't like the light."

I snap the light off. I drink my water slowly. I must take it easy, I say to myself. I must get to the bottom of this.

"Why don't you go to bed? Why do you sit here so late in the dark?"

"It's nice," he says. "I can't get used to lights. We didn't have lights when I was a boy in Europe."

My heart skips a beat and I catch my breath happily. I begin to think I understand. I remember the stories of his boyhood in Austria. I see the wide-beamed *kretchma*,[3] with my grandfather behind the bar. It is late, the customers are gone, and he is dozing. I see the bed of glowing coals, the last of the roaring fire. The room is already dark, and growing darker. I see a small boy, crouched on a pile of

—————
3. ***kretchma*** [krech′mə]: tavern.

twigs at one side of the huge fireplace, his starry gaze fixed on the dull remains of the dead flames. The boy is my father.

I remember the pleasure of those few moments while I stoop quietly in the doorway watching him.

"You mean there's nothing wrong? You just sit in the dark because you like it, Pop?" I find it hard to keep my voice from rising in a happy shout.

"Sure," he says. "I can't think with the light on."

I set my glass down and turn to go back to my room. "Good night, Pop," I say.

"Good night," he says.

Then I remember. I turn back. "What do you think about, Pop?" I ask.

His voice seems to come from far away. It is quiet and even again. "Nothing," he says softly. "Nothing special."

STUDY QUESTIONS

Recalling

1. What is the "peculiar habit" of the narrator's father?
2. What does the narrator wish to know in the tenth paragraph? What does his father answer when he asks?
3. What is the father's first explanation for his habit? What are four "possibilities" that the narrator reviews in trying to understand why his father sits alone in darkness?
4. What is the father's explanation of his dislike for lights? What scene does the narrator picture when he hears this explanation?
5. Once the narrator understands his father's dislike for lights, what does he feel? What question does he almost forget to ask? When he asks it, what does his father reply?

Interpreting

6. Why is the narrator puzzled, bothered, and finally angered by his father's behavior? Why is he so happy near the story's end?
7. What does the narrator's ability to picture his father's life in Austria suggest about the narrator's relationship with his father? Why is it ironic that he almost forgets to ask what his father is thinking?

8. By the story's end, do we have an idea about what the father might be thinking? If so, what might it be, and what gives us a clue?

COMPOSITION

Writing a Comparison/Contrast

▨ In this story the inner life of a character is revealed through the eyes of another character. Compare and contrast the father here with Granny Weatherall, a character who reveals her own inner life, in Katherine Anne Porter's "Jilting of Granny Weatherall" (page 604). Begin by telling what each character reveals. Then suggest what each character holds back. Conclude with your own opinion of the emotional effect of the two stories. *For help with this assignment, refer to Lesson 2 in the Writing About Literature Handbook at the back of this book.*

Writing an Anecdote

▨ In recounting an interesting event in someone's life, an anecdote often illuminates that person's character in some way. Write an anecdote about a person you know well, or if you prefer, about a character you have invented. Reveal in the anecdote something important about the subject's life or character.

John Steinbeck *1902–1968*

Often during his long career John Steinbeck enjoyed a rare combination of enormous popularity and serious critical acclaim. His great work, *The Grapes of Wrath* (1939), is among the most famous and widely read novels of this century. In its epic depiction of one dispossessed Oklahoma family's migration to California in search of a new life, it remains one of the most powerfully moving books written about the Great Depression.

John Steinbeck was born in Salinas, California, where much of his fiction is set. His varied early experiences helped shape him as a writer. When he was unable to complete his college studies at Stanford University, he worked his way to New York City on a cattle boat, hoping to get his early writing published. Failing this, he worked briefly as a newspaper reporter and then returned to California, where he continued to write while taking an assortment of jobs, including fruit picker, surveyor, caretaker on an estate, mason's assistant, and chemist's assistant. During World War II he returned to journalism, serving as a war correspondent in Italy.

Steinbeck wrote a great deal. In the two decades after 1932, he produced sixteen long works of fiction, which vary widely in length, form, and subject. *In Dubious Battle* (1936) concerns the plight of exploited migrant laborers; *Of Mice and Men* (1937) tells of the tragic friendship of two migrant workers; *Cannery Row* (1945) and *Sweet Thursday* (1954) are lighter works, full of local color and gentle humor; *The Pearl* (1947) is a retelling of a Mexican folk tale; and *Travels with Charley* (1962) is an account of the author's journey across America in a pickup truck with his poodle, Charley.

Steinbeck's novels and stories usually offer a strong sense of social justice, a heightened sensitivity to the colors and textures of the American landscape, and a compelling plot. His characters are memorable, perhaps the finest elements in his writing: people from different races and occupations, people who have lived, authentic people who seem to step right off the page. The main character of "The Leader of the People" is such a man: not in tune with his time, immersed in his memories, yet embodying an entire segment of American history.

John Steinbeck

The Leader of the People

On Saturday afternoon Billy Buck, the ranch hand, raked together the last of the old year's haystack and pitched small forkfuls over the wire fence to a few mildly interested cattle. High in the air small clouds like puffs of cannon smoke were driven eastward by the March wind. The wind could be heard whishing in the brush on the ridge crests, but no breath of it penetrated down into the ranch cup.

The little boy, Jody, emerged from the house eating a thick piece of buttered bread. He saw Billy working on the last of the haystack. Jody tramped down scuffing his shoes in a way he had been told was destructive to good shoe leather. A flock of white pigeons flew out of the black cypress tree as Jody passed, and circled the tree and landed again. A half-grown tortoise-shell cat leaped from the bunkhouse porch, galloped on stiff legs across the road, whirled and galloped back again. Jody picked up a stone to help the game along, but he was too late, for the cat was under the porch before the stone could be discharged. He threw the stone into the cypress tree and started the white pigeons on another whirling flight.

Arriving at the used-up haystack, the boy leaned against the barbed wire fence. "Will that be all of it, do you think?" he asked.

The middle-aged ranch hand stopped his careful raking and stuck his fork into the ground. He took off his black hat and smoothed down his hair. "Nothing left of it that isn't soggy from ground moisture," he said. He replaced his hat and rubbed his dry leathery hands together.

"Ought to be plenty mice," Jody suggested.

"Lousy with them," said Billy. "Just crawling with mice."

"Well, maybe, when you get all through, I could call the dogs and hunt the mice."

"Sure, I guess you could," said Billy Buck. He lifted a forkful of the damp ground-hay and threw it into the air. Instantly three mice leaped out and burrowed frantically under the hay again.

Jody sighed with satisfaction. Those plump, sleek, arrogant mice were doomed. For eight months they had lived and multiplied in the haystack. They had been immune from cats, from traps, from poison, and from Jody. They had grown smug in their security, overbearing, and fat. Now the time of disaster had come; they would not survive another day.

Billy looked up at the top of the hills that surrounded the ranch. "Maybe you better ask your father before you do it," he suggested.

"Well, where is he? I'll ask him now."

"He rode up to the ridge ranch after dinner. He'll be back pretty soon."

Jody slumped against the fence post. "I don't think he'd care."

As Billy went back to his work he said ominously, "You'd better ask him anyway. You know how he is."

Jody did know. His father, Carl Tiflin, insisted upon giving permission for anything that was done on the ranch, whether it was important or not. Jody sagged farther against the post until he was sitting on the ground. He looked up at the little puffs of wind-driven cloud. "Is it like to rain, Billy?"

"It might. The wind's good for it, but not strong enough."

"Well, I hope it don't rain until after I kill those mice."

Jody turned back and looked at the side-hill where the road from the outside world came down. The hill was washed with lean March sunshine. Silver thistles, blue lupins,[1] and a few poppies bloomed among the sage bushes. Half-

---

1. **lupins** [loo′ pinz]: plants with hand shaped leaves and variously colored flowers.

---

way up the hill Jody could see Doubletree Mutt, the black dog, digging in a squirrel hole. He paddled for a while and then paused to kick bursts of dirt out between his hind legs, and he dug with an earnestness which belied the knowledge he must have had that no dog had ever caught a squirrel by digging in a hole.

Suddenly, while Jody watched, the black dog stiffened and backed out of the hole and looked up the hill toward the cleft in the ridge where the road came through. Jody looked up too. For a moment Carl Tiflin on horseback stood out against the pale sky and then he moved down the road toward the house. He carried something white in his hand.

The boy started to his feet. "He's got a letter," Jody cried. He trotted away toward the ranch house, for the letter would probably be read aloud and he wanted to be there. He reached the house before his father did, and ran in. He heard Carl dismount from his creaking saddle and slap the horse on the side to send it to the barn where Billy would unsaddle it and turn it out.

Jody ran into the kitchen. "We got a letter!" he cried.

His mother looked up from a pan of beans. "Who has?"

"Father has. I saw it in his hand."

Carl strode into the kitchen then, and Jody's mother asked, "Who's the letter from, Carl?"

He frowned quickly. "How did you know there was a letter?"

She nodded her head in the boy's direction. "Big-Britches Jody told me."

Jody was embarrassed.

His father looked down at him contemptuously. "He *is* getting to be a Big-Britches," Carl said. "He's minding everybody's business but his own. Got his big nose into everything."

Mrs. Tiflin relented a little. "Well, he hasn't enough to keep him busy. Who's the letter from?"

Carl still frowned on Jody. "I'll keep him busy if he isn't careful." He held out a sealed letter. "I guess it's from your father."

Mrs. Tiflin took a hairpin from her head and

slit open the flap. Her lips pursed judiciously. Jody saw her eyes snap back and forth over the lines. "He says," she translated, "he says he's going to drive out Saturday to stay for a little while. Why, this is Saturday. The letter must have been delayed." She looked at the postmark. "This was mailed day before yesterday. It should have been here yesterday." She looked up questioningly at her husband, and then her face darkened angrily. "Now what have you got that look on you for? He doesn't come often."

Carl turned his eyes away from her anger. He could be stern with her most of the time, but when occasionally her temper arose, he could not combat it.

"What's the matter with you?" she demanded again.

In his explanation there was a tone of apology Jody himself might have used. "It's just that he talks," Carl said lamely. "Just talks."

"Well, what of it? You talk yourself."

"Sure I do. But your father only talks about one thing."

"Indians!" Jody broke in excitedly. "Indians and crossing the plains!"

Carl turned fiercely on him. "You get out, Mr. Big-Britches! Go on, now! Get out!"

Jody went miserably out the back door and closed the screen with elaborate quietness. Under the kitchen window his shamed, downcast eyes fell upon a curiously shaped stone, a stone of such fascination that he squatted down and picked it up and turned it over in his hands.

The voices came clearly to him through the open kitchen window. "Jody's right," he heard his father say. "Just Indians and crossing the plains. I've heard that story about how the horses got driven off about a thousand times. He just goes on and on, and he never changes a word in the things he tells."

When Mrs. Tiflin answered her tone was so changed that Jody, outside the window, looked up from his study of the stone. Her voice had become soft and explanatory. Jody knew how her face would have changed to match the tone. She said quietly, "Look at it this way,

Carl. That was the big thing in my father's life. He led a wagon train clear across the plains to the coast, and when it was finished, his life was done. It was a big thing to do, but it didn't last long enough. Look!" she continued, "it's as though he was born to do that, and after he finished it, there wasn't anything more for him to do but think about it and talk about it. If there'd been any farther west to go, he'd have gone. He's told me so himself. But at last there was the ocean. He lives right by the ocean where he had to stop."

She had caught Carl, caught him and entangled him in her soft tone.

"I've seen him," he agreed quietly. "He goes down and stares off west over the ocean." His voice sharpened a little. "And then he goes up to the Horseshoe Club in Pacific Grove,[2] and he tells people how the Indians drove off the horses."

She tried to catch him again. "Well, it's everything to him. You might be patient with him and pretend to listen."

Carl turned impatiently away. "Well, if it gets too bad, I can always go down to the bunkhouse and sit with Billy," he said irritably. He walked through the house and slammed the front door after him.

Jody ran to his chores. He dumped the grain to the chickens without chasing any of them. He gathered the eggs from the nests. He trotted into the house with the wood and interlaced it so carefully in the woodbox that two armloads seemed to fill it to overflowing.

His mother had finished the beans by now. She stirred up the fire and brushed off the stove top with a turkey wing. Jody peered cautiously at her to see whether any rancor toward him remained. "Is he coming today?" Jody asked.

"That's what his letter said."

"Maybe I better walk up the road to meet him."

Mrs. Tiflin clanged the stove lid shut. "That would be nice," she said. "He'd probably like to be met."

---

2. **Pacific Grove:** town on central California coast.

"I guess I'll just do it then."

Outside, Jody whistled shrilly to the dogs. "Come on up the hill," he commanded. The two dogs waved their tails and ran ahead. Along the roadside the sage had tender new tips. Jody tore off some pieces and rubbed them on his hands until the air was filled with the sharp wild smell. With a rush the dogs leaped from the road and yapped into the brush after a rabbit. That was the last Jody saw of them, for when they failed to catch the rabbit, they went back home.

Jody plodded on up the hill toward the ridge top. When he reached the little cleft where the road came through, the afternoon wind struck him and blew up his hair and ruffled his shirt. He looked down on the little hills and ridges below and then out at the huge green Salinas Valley.[3] He could see the white town of Salinas far out in the flat and the flash of its windows under the waning sun. Directly below him, in an oak tree, a crow congress had convened. The tree was black with crows all cawing at once.

Then Jody's eyes followed the wagon road down from the ridge where he stood, and lost it behind a hill, and picked it up again on the other side. On that distant stretch he saw a cart slowly pulled by a bay horse. It disappeared behind the hill. Jody sat down on the ground and watched the place where the cart would reappear again. The wind sang on the hilltops and the puffball clouds hurried eastward.

Then the cart came into sight and stopped. A man dressed in black dismounted from the seat and walked to the horse's head. Although it was so far away, Jody knew he had unhooked the checkrein, for the horse's head dropped forward. The horse moved on, and the man walked slowly up the hill beside it. Jody gave a glad cry and ran down the road toward them. The squirrels bumped along off the road, and a road runner flirted its tail and raced over the edge of the hill and sailed out like a glider.

Jody tried to leap into the middle of his shadow at every step. A stone rolled under his foot and he went down. Around a little bend he raced, and there, a short distance ahead, were his grandfather and the cart. The boy dropped from his unseemly running and approached at a dignified walk.

The horse plodded stumble-footed up the hill and the old man walked beside it. In the lowering sun their giant shadows flickered darkly behind them. The grandfather was dressed in a black broadcloth suit and he wore kid congress gaiters[4] and a black tie on a short, hard collar. He carried his black slouch hat[5] in his hand. His white beard was cropped close and his white eyebrows overhung his eyes like mustaches. The blue eyes were sternly merry. About the whole face and figure there was a granite dignity, so that every motion seemed an impossible thing. Once at rest, it seemed the old man would be stone, would never move again. His steps were slow and certain. Once made, no step could ever be retraced; once headed in a direction, the path would never bend nor the pace increase nor slow.

When Jody appeared around the bend, Grandfather waved his hat slowly in welcome, and he called, "Why, Jody! Come down to meet me, have you?"

Jody sidled near and turned and matched his step to the old man's step and stiffened his body and dragged his heels a little. "Yes, sir," he said. "We got your letter only today."

"Should have been here yesterday," said Grandfather. "It certainly should. How are all the folks?"

"They're fine, sir." He hesitated and then suggested shyly. "Would you like to come on a mouse hunt tomorrow, sir?"

"Mouse hunt, Jody?" Grandfather chuckled. "Have the people of this generation come down to hunting mice? They aren't very strong,

---

3. **Salinas** [sə lēn'əs] **Valley:** agricultural area in California south of San Francisco.

4. **kid congress gaiters:** old-fashioned ankle-high shoes made from the soft skin of a young goat, with an elastic insert on each side.

5. **slouch hat:** hat with a drooping brim.

the new people, but I hardly thought mice would be game for them."

"No, sir. It's just play. The haystack's gone. I'm going to drive out the mice to the dogs. And you can watch, or even beat the hay a little."

The stern, merry eyes turned down on him. "I see. You don't eat them, then. You haven't come to that yet."

Jody explained, "The dogs eat them, sir. It wouldn't be much like hunting Indians, I guess."

"No, not much—but then later, when the troops were hunting Indians and shooting children and burning teepees, it wasn't much different from your mouse hunt."

They topped the rise and started down into the ranch cup, and they lost the sun from their shoulders. "You've grown," Grandfather said. "Nearly an inch, I should say."

"More," Jody boasted. "Where they mark me on the door, I'm up more than an inch since Thanksgiving even."

Grandfather's rich throaty voice said, "Maybe you're getting too much water and turning to pith and stalk. Wait until you head out, and then we'll see."

Jody looked quickly into the old man's face to see whether his feelings should be hurt, but there was no will to injure, no punishing nor putting-in-your-place light in the keen blue eyes. "We might kill a pig," Jody suggested.

"Oh, no! I couldn't let you do that. You're just humoring me. It isn't the time and you know it."

"You know Riley, the big boar, sir?"

"Yes, I remember Riley well."

"Well, Riley ate a hole into that same haystack, and it fell down on him and smothered him."

"Pigs do that when they can," said Grandfather.

"Riley was a nice pig, for a boar, sir. I rode him sometimes, and he didn't mind."

A door slammed at the house below them, and they saw Jody's mother standing on the porch waving her apron in welcome. And they saw Carl Tiflin walking up from the barn to be at the house for the arrival.

The sun had disappeared from the hills by now. The blue smoke from the house chimney hung in flat layers in the purpling ranch cup. The puffball clouds, dropped by the falling wind, hung listlessly in the sky.

Billy Buck came out of the bunkhouse and flung a wash basin of soapy water on the ground. He had been shaving in midweek, for Billy held Grandfather in reverence, and Grandfather said that Billy was one of the few men of the new generation who had not gone soft. Although Billy was in middle age, Grandfather considered him a boy. Now Billy was hurrying toward the house too.

When Jody and Grandfather arrived, the three were waiting for them in front of the yard gate.

Carl said, "Hello, sir. We've been looking for you."

Mrs. Tiflin kissed Grandfather on the side of his beard and stood still while his big hand patted her shoulder. Billy shook hands solemnly, grinning under his straw mustache. "I'll put up your horse," said Billy, and he led the rig away.

Grandfather watched him go, and then, turning back to the group, he said as he had said a hundred times before, "There's a good boy. I knew his father, old Mule-tail Buck. I never knew why they called him Mule-tail except he packed mules."

Mrs. Tiflin turned and led the way into the house. "How long are you going to stay, Father? Your letter didn't say."

"Well, I don't know. I thought I'd stay about two weeks. But I never stay as long as I think I'm going to."

In a short while they were sitting at the white oilcloth table eating their supper. The lamp with the tin reflector hung over the table. Outside the dining-room windows the big moths battered softly against the glass.

Grandfather cut his steak into tiny pieces and chewed slowly. "I'm hungry," he said,

"Driving out here got my appetite up. It's like when we were crossing. We all got so hungry every night we could hardly wait to let the meat get done. I could eat about five pounds of buffalo meat every night."

"It's moving around does it," said Billy. "My father was a government packer. I helped him when I was a kid. Just the two of us could about clean up a deer's ham."[6]

"I knew your father, Billy," said Grandfather. "A fine man he was. They called him Mule-tail Buck. I don't know why except he packed mules."

"That was it," Billy agreed. "He packed mules."

Grandfather put down his knife and fork and looked around the table. "I remember one time we ran out of meat—" His voice dropped to a curious low singsong, dropped into a tonal groove the story had worn for itself. "There was no buffalo, no antelope, not even rabbits. The hunters couldn't even shoot a coyote. That

was the time for the leader to be on the watch. I was the leader, and I kept my eyes open. Know why? Well, just the minute the people began to get hungry they'd start slaughtering the team oxen. Do you believe that? I've heard of parties that just ate up their draft cattle. Started from the middle and worked toward the ends. Finally they'd eat the lead pair, and then the wheelers.[7] The leader of a party had to keep them from doing that."

In some manner a big moth got into the room and circled the hanging kerosene lamp. Billy got up and tried to clap it between his hands. Carl struck with a cupped palm and caught the moth and broke it. He walked to the window and dropped it out.

"As I was saying," Grandfather began again, but Carl interrupted him. "You'd better eat some more meat. All the rest of us are ready for our pudding."

Jody saw a flash of anger in his mother's eyes. Grandfather picked up his knife and fork.

---

6. **ham:** hind leg.

7. **wheelers:** cattle harnessed nearest the wheels of a vehicle.

"I'm pretty hungry, all right," he said. "I'll tell you about that later."

When supper was over, when the family and Billy Buck sat in front of the fireplace in the other room, Jody anxiously watched Grandfather. He saw the signs he knew. The bearded head leaned forward; the eyes lost their sternness and looked wonderingly into the fire; the big lean fingers laced themselves on the black knees. "I wonder," he began, "I just wonder whether I ever told you how those thieving Piutes[8] drove off thirty-five of our horses."

"I think you did," Carl interrupted. "Wasn't it just before you went up into the Tahoe[9] country?"

Grandfather turned quickly toward his son-in-law. "That's right. I guess I must have told you that story."

"Lots of times," Carl said cruelly, and he avoided his wife's eyes. But he felt the angry eyes on him, and he said, "Course I'd like to hear it again."

Grandfather looked back at the fire. His fingers unlaced and laced again. Jody knew how he felt, how his insides were collapsed and empty. Hadn't Jody been called a Big-Britches that very afternoon? He arose to heroism and opened himself to the term Big-Britches again. "Tell about Indians," he said softly.

Grandfather's eyes grew stern again. "Boys always want to hear about Indians. It was a job for men, but boys want to hear about it. Well, let's see. Did I ever tell you how I wanted each wagon to carry a long iron plate?

Everyone but Jody remained silent. Jody said, "No. You didn't."

"Well, when the Indians attacked, we always put the wagons in a circle and fought from between the wheels. I thought that if every wagon carried a long plate with rifle holes, the men could stand the plates on the outside of the wheels when the wagons were in the circle and they would be protected. It would save lives and that would make up for the extra weight of the iron. But of course the party wouldn't do it. No party had done it before and they couldn't see why they should go to the expense. They lived to regret it, too."

Jody looked at his mother and knew from her expression that she was not listening at all. Carl picked at a callus on his thumb and Billy Buck watched a spider crawling up the wall.

Grandfather's tone dropped into its narrative groove again. Jody knew in advance exactly what words would fall. The story droned on, speeded up for the attack, grew sad over the wounds, struck a dirge at the burials on the great plains. Jody sat quietly watching Grandfather. The stern blue eyes were detached. He looked as though he were not very interested in the story himself.

When it was finished, when the pause had been politely respected as the frontier of the story, Billy Buck stood up and stretched and hitched his trousers. "I guess I'll turn in," he said. Then he faced Grandfather. "I've got an old powder horn and a cap and ball pistol down to the bunkhouse. Did I ever show them to you?"

Grandfather nodded slowly. "Yes, I think you did, Billy. Reminds me of a pistol I had when I was leading the people across." Billy stood politely until the little story was done, and then he said, "Good night," and went out of the house.

Carl Tiflin tried to turn the conversation then. "How's the country between here and Monterey?[10] I've heard it's pretty dry."

"It is dry," said Grandfather. "There's not a drop of water in the Laguna Seca.[11] But it's a long pull from '87. The whole country was powder then, and in '61 I believe all the coyotes starved to death. We had fifteen inches of rain this year."

"Yes, but it all came too early. We could do with some now." Carl's eyes fell on Jody. "Hadn't you better be getting to bed?"

---

8. **Piutes** [pī´ūts]: Indians of the southwestern United States.
9. **Tahoe** [tä´hō]: mountainous area between California and Nevada.
10. **Monterey** [män´tə rā´]: city in central California.
11. **Laguna Seca:** Spanish for "dry lagoon."

Jody stood up obediently. "Can I kill the mice in the old haystack, sir?"

"Mice? Oh! Sure, kill them all off. Billy said there isn't any good hay left."

Jody exchanged a secret and satisfying look with Grandfather. "I'll kill every one tomorrow," he promised.

Jody lay in his bed and thought of the impossible world of Indians and buffaloes, a world that had ceased to be forever. He wished he could have been living in the heroic time, but he knew he was not of heroic timber. No one living now, save possibly Billy Buck, was worthy to do the things that had been done. A race of giants had lived then, fearless men, men of a staunchness unknown in this day. Jody thought of the wide plains and of the wagons moving across like centipedes. He thought of Grandfather on a huge white horse, marshaling the people. Across his mind marched the great phantoms, and they marched off the earth and they were gone.

He came back to the ranch for a moment, then. He heard the dull rushing sound that space and silence make. He heard one of the dogs, out in the doghouse, scratching a flea and bumping his elbow against the floor with every stroke. Then the wind arose again and the black cypress groaned and Jody went to sleep.

He was up half an hour before the triangle sounded for breakfast. His mother was rattling the stove to make the flames roar when Jody went through the kitchen. "You're up early," she said. "Where are you going?"

"Out to get a good stick. We're going to kill the mice today."

"Who is 'we'?"

"Why, Grandfather and I."

"So you've got him in it. You always like to have someone in with you in case there's blame to share."

"I'll be right back," said Jody. "I just want to have a good stick ready for after breakfast."

He closed the screen door after him and went out into the cool blue morning. The birds were noisy in the dawn and the ranch cats came down from the hill like blunt snakes. They had been hunting gophers in the dark, and although the four cats were full of gopher meat, they sat in a semicircle at the back door and mewed piteously for milk. Doubletree Mutt and Smasher moved sniffing along the edge of the brush, performing the duty with rigid ceremony, but when Jody whistled, their heads jerked up and their tails waved. They plunged down to him, wriggling their skins and yawning. Jody patted their heads seriously and moved on to the weathered scrap pile. He selected an old broom handle and a short piece of inch-square scrap wood. From his pocket he took a shoelace and tied the ends of the sticks loosely together to make a flail. He whistled his new weapon through the air and struck the ground experimentally, while the dogs leaped aside and whined with apprehension.

Jody turned and started down past the house toward the old haystack ground to look over the field of slaughter, but Billy Buck, sitting patiently on the back steps, called to him, "You better come back. It's only a couple of minutes till breakfast."

Jody changed his course and moved toward the house. He leaned his flail against the steps. "That's to drive the mice out," he said. "I'll bet they're fat, I'll bet they don't know what's going to happen to them today."

"No, nor you either," Billy remarked philosophically, "nor me, nor anyone."

Jody was staggered by this thought. He knew it was true. His imagination twitched away from the mouse hunt. Then his mother came out on the back porch and struck the triangle, and all thoughts fell in a heap.

Grandfather hadn't appeared at the table when they sat down. Billy nodded at his empty chair. "He's all right? He isn't sick?"

"He takes a long time to dress," said Mrs. Tiflin. "He combs his whiskers and rubs up his shoes and brushes his clothes."

Carl scattered sugar on his mush. "A man that's led a wagon train across the plains has got to be pretty careful how he dresses."

Mrs. Tiflin turned on him. "Don't do that,

Carl! Please don't!" There was more of threat than of request in her tone. And the threat irritated Carl.

"Well, how many times do I have to listen to the story of the iron plates, and the thirty-five horses? That time's done. Why can't he forget it, now it's done?" He grew angrier while he talked and his voice rose. "Why does he have to tell them over and over? He came across the plains. All right! Now it's finished. Nobody wants to hear about it over and over."

The door into the kitchen closed softly. The four at the table sat frozen. Carl laid his mush spoon on the table and touched his chin with his fingers.

Then the kitchen door opened and Grandfather walked in. His mouth smiled tightly and his eyes squinted. "Good morning," he said, and he sat down and looked at his mush dish.

Carl could not leave it there. "Did—did you hear what I said?"

Grandfather jerked a little nod.

"I don't know what got into me, sir. I didn't mean it. I was just being funny."

Jody glanced in shame at his mother, and he saw that she was looking at Carl, and that she wasn't breathing. It was an awful thing that he was doing. He was tearing himself to pieces to talk like that. It was a terrible thing to him to retract a word, but to retract it in shame was infinitely worse.

Grandfather looked sidewise. "I'm trying to get right side up," he said gently. "I'm not being mad. I don't mind what you said, but it might be true, and I would mind that."

"It isn't true," said Carl. "I'm not feeling well this morning. I'm sorry I said it."

"Don't be sorry, Carl. An old man doesn't see things sometimes. Maybe you're right. The crossing is finished. Maybe it should be forgotten, now it's done."

Carl got up from the table. "I've had enough to eat. I'm going to work. Take your time, Billy!" He walked quickly out of the dining room. Billy gulped the rest of his food and followed soon after. But Jody could not leave his chair.

"Won't you tell any more stories?" Jody asked.

"Why, sure I'll tell them, but only when—I'm sure people want to hear them."

"I like to hear them, sir."

"Oh! Of course you do, but you're a little boy. It was a job for men, but only little boys like to hear about it."

Jody got up from his place. "I'll wait outside for you, sir. I've got a good stick for those mice."

He waited by the gate until the old man came out on the porch. "Let's go down and kill the mice now," Jody called.

"I think I'll just sit in the sun, Jody. You go kill the mice."

"You can use my stick if you like."

"No, I'll just sit here a while."

Jody turned disconsolately away and walked down toward the old haystack. He tried to whip up his enthusiasm with thoughts of the fat juicy mice. He beat the ground with his flail. The dogs coaxed and whined about him, but he could not go. Back at the house he could see Grandfather sitting on the porch, looking small and thin and black.

Jody gave up and went to sit on the steps at the old man's feet.

"Back already? Did you kill the mice?"

"No, sir. I'll kill them some other day."

The morning flies buzzed close to the ground and the ants dashed about in front of the steps. The heavy smell of sage slipped down the hill. The porch boards grew warm in the sunshine.

Jody hardly knew when Grandfather started to talk. "I shouldn't stay here, feeling the way I do." He examined his strong old hands. "I feel as though the crossing wasn't worth doing." His eyes moved up the sidehill and stopped on a motionless hawk perched on a dead limb. "I tell those old stories, but they're not what I want to tell. I only know how I want people to feel when I tell them.

"It wasn't Indians that were important, nor adventures, nor even getting out here. It was a whole bunch of people made into one big crawling beast. And I was the head. It was westering[12] and westering. Every man wanted something for himself, but the big beast that was all of them wanted only westering. I was the leader, but if I hadn't been there, someone else would have been the head. The thing had to have a head.

"Under the little bushes the shadows were black at white noonday. When we saw the mountains at last, we cried—all of us. But it wasn't getting here that mattered, it was movement and westering.

"We carried life out here and set it down the way those ants carry eggs. And I was the leader. The westering was as big as God, and the slow steps that made the movement piled up and piled up until the continent was crossed.

"Then we came down to the sea, and it was done." He stopped and wiped his eyes until the rims were red. "That's what I should be telling instead of stories."

When Jody spoke, Grandfather started and looked down at him. "Maybe I could lead the people some day," Jody said.

---

12. **westering:** moving west.

The old man smiled. "There's no place to go. There's the ocean to stop you. There's a line of old men along the shore hating the ocean because it stopped them."

"In boats I might, sir."

"No place to go, Jody. Every place is taken. But that's not the worst—no, not the worst. Westering has died out of the people. Westering isn't a hunger any more. It's all done. Your father is right. It is finished." He laced his fingers on his knee and looked at them.

Jody felt very sad. "If you'd like a glass of lemonade I could make it for you."

Grandfather was about to refuse, and then he saw Jody's face. "That would be nice," he said. "Yes, it would be nice to drink lemonade."

Jody ran into the kitchen where his mother was wiping the last of the breakfast dishes. "Can I have a lemon to make a lemonade for Grandfather?"

His mother mimicked—"And another lemon to make a lemonade for you."

"No, ma'am. I don't want one."

"Jody! You're sick!" Then she stopped suddenly. "Take a lemon out of the cooler," she said softly. "Here, I'll reach the squeezer down to you."

STUDY QUESTIONS

Recalling

1. What are Jody's first three actions in the story? Now that most of the good hay is gone, what project does Jody decide to undertake?

2. What is Carl Tiflin's "lame" reason for not being pleased to learn of his father-in-law's plans to visit? According to Jody and his father, what does Jody's grandfather talk about all the time? Why does he talk about it, according to Mrs. Tiflin?

3. How are Grandfather's eyes described when Jody goes out to meet him? What is there "about his old face and figure"? What sort of steps does he take?

4. In what adventure does Jody invite his grandfather to participate? When, in his first conversation with Grandfather, Jody wonders if the old man has insulted him, what does he *not* detect in Grandfather's eyes?

5. What does Grandfather overhear his son-in-law saying about him the next morning? Why does Jody consider his father's apology "a terrible thing" for him? What does Grandfather decide he will not do anymore?

6. Does Grandfather join Jody on the mouse hunt? What does Jody decide to do after seeing Grandfather on the porch "looking small and thin and black"?

7. In his final conversation with Jody, what does Grandfather say was important about his adventures leading the wagon train? What does he say the wagon train carried out west? How does he answer when Jody says that he might "lead the people some day"?

Interpreting

8. What does the initial description of Grandfather reveal about his character and personality? What do the final paragraphs of the story suggest about his ideals and spirit? Does Carl Tiflin share his ideals?

9. What do Jody's reaction to the news of his grandfather's visit and his behavior in greeting his grandfather reveal about his feelings toward the old man? How do his feelings deepen by the story's end?

10. How do Jody's last actions in the story differ from his first? Why does he lose interest in his mouse-hunting project?

Extending

11. What, basically, is Grandfather's evaluation of "modern" life in the final paragraphs? Why would such an evaluation be particularly understandable in a story written during the Great Depression?

VIEWPOINT

Joseph Warren Beach, in noting Steinbeck's faith in human nature, writes:

He is one who feels strongly on the subject of man's essential dignity of spirit and his unexhausted possibilities for modification and improvement.

—*American Fiction 1920–1940*

■ In what sense is Grandfather's dignity maintained at the end of "The Leader of the People" despite the fact that his spirit seems broken? Which other characters modify their behavior in the story, and why are their changes improvements?

LITERARY FOCUS

Characterization

John Steinbeck is considered a master at creating believable, compelling, and memorable characters in his short stories and novels. To do so, he uses many methods of characterization (see page 540), both direct and indirect.

Consider, for example, his characterization of Grandfather. Steinbeck makes a direct statement by referring to him in the title as "the leader of the people." He presents a detailed physical description when Jody sees him, first from a distance, and then closer up. He tells what Carl Tiflin, Mrs. Tiflin, and Billy Buck all think of him. He shows him in action after his arrival. And, in the end, he lets Grandfather speak for himself and reveal his innermost thoughts. As a consequence of this subtle and varied characterization, we not only become familiar with Grandfather but in the end come to appreciate, sympathize with, and perhaps even admire him.

Steinbeck also gives us indirect information about Grandfather by creating a foil for him in the character of Carl Tiflin. A **foil** is a character who, through contrast, underscores the characteristics of another character. Carl Tiflin is almost the exact opposite of Grandfather: He is a practical man living in the present, abrupt, sometimes even un-kind. As we note the differences between Grand-father and his son-in-law, we understand Grand-father's character better and appreciate those virtues that Carl Tiflin lacks.

Thinking About Characterization

1. Look closely at another character in "The Leader of the People." What methods of char-acterization does Steinbeck use in creating and developing the character? Does the char-acter seem as well-developed as Grandfather? Why or why not?
2. What other character foils have you encoun-tered in your reading, and in what way are they foils? For example, how is Hurry Harry a foil for Cooper's Deerslayer (page 115)?

VOCABULARY

Antonyms

Antonyms are words that have opposite or nearly opposite meanings. The following words in capitals are from "The Leader of the People." Choose the word that is an antonym of each word in capitals, *as the word is used in this selection.* Write the number of each item and the letter of your choice on a separate sheet.

1. IMMUNE: (a) witty (b) serious (c) vulnerable (d) resistant
2. RETRACT: (a) annoy (b) admit (c) survive (d) lessen
3. BELIED: (a) confirmed (b) denied (c) contradicted (d) behaved
4. DISCONSOLATELY: (a) madly (b) immensely (c) eagerly (d) sorrowfully
5. OVERBEARING: (a) meek (b) fond (c) domineering (d) exhausted

COMPOSITION

Analyzing Theme Through Character

The theme of a story is often revealed through character—what a character thinks, says, does, or represents. Write an essay in which you analyze the theme of "The Leader of the People" by looking at its characters. Begin with a statement of the theme in your own words. Then support your statement with ex-amples from what characters in the story do and say. Conclude with examples from the grandfather's final long speech. *For help with this assignment, refer to Lesson 6 in the Writ-ing About Literature Handbook at the back of this book.*

Creating a Character Foil

Choose one of the characters who appear in this book—Granny Weatherall (page 604) per-haps, or Roderick Usher (page 135)—and make a list of his or her strengths and weak-nesses. Then, in a second column, list quali-ties that contrast with the strengths and weak-nesses you have listed. From your second list write a short portrait of a character who is a foil for the character you chose. In creating your foil, you may wish to examine the six methods of characterization described in the Literary Focus on page 540.

Thomas Wolfe   *1900–1938*

Almost everything about Thomas Wolfe was larger than life. He was six feet five inches tall, powerfully built, with dark, intense eyes, untidy black hair, and a wide mouth. He was enormously energetic, and he possessed the gift of total recall. He had a tremendous appetite for sensory and physical experience, which he once admitted was an "intemperate excess, an almost insane hunger." As a writer, Wolfe worked with uncontrollable, maniacal drive: He did not so much compose his stories and novels as pour them out in endless waves of images, descriptions, and remembrances. It is not surprising that his published work is uneven: Amid long stretches of unpolished writing, there appear passages of extraordinary beauty, clarity, and lyrical power.

Wolfe grew up in North Carolina. His father was a stonecutter, gifted with a vast and well-stocked memory and a love of poetry as well. Wolfe was first determined to become a playwright, but his efforts were largely ignored, and he soon turned to fiction. In 1924 he began teaching English to make a living, and in the same year started what was to become his famous first novel, *Look Homeward, Angel.* The novel was a success, and it also marked the beginning of his fruitful association with the great editor Maxwell Perkins, who had helped Wolfe shape his massive manuscripts into finished work. Both *Of Time and the River,* his second novel, and *From Death to Morning,* a collection of short stories, appeared in 1935. Three years later, Wolfe died after he had begun work on his fourth novel.

"The Far and the Near" exemplifies Wolfe's gifts as a writer: his strong sense of place, his ability to render sensory perception persuasively, and his profound awareness of the fragility of human experience.

Stone City, Iowa, Grant Wood, 1930.

Thomas Wolfe

The Far and the Near

On the outskirts of a little town upon a rise of land that swept back from the railway there was a tidy little cottage of white boards, trimmed vividly with green blinds. To one side of the house there was a garden neatly patterned with plots of growing vegetables, and an arbor[1] for the grapes which ripened late in August. Before the house there were three mighty oaks which sheltered it in their clean and massive shade in summer, and to the other side there was a border of gay flowers. The whole place had an air of tidiness, thrift, and modest comfort.

Every day, a few minutes after two o'clock in the afternoon, the limited express between the two cities passed this spot. At that moment the great train, having halted for a breathing space at the town nearby, was beginning to lengthen evenly into its stroke, but it had not yet reached the full drive of its terrific speed. It swung into view deliberately, swept past with a powerful swaying motion of the engine, a low smooth rumble of its heavy cars upon pressed steel, and then it vanished in the cut. For a moment the progress of the engine could be marked by heavy bellowing puffs of smoke that burst at spaced intervals above the edges of the meadow grass, and finally nothing could be heard but the solid clacking tempo of the wheels receding into the drowsy stillness of the afternoon.

Every day for more than twenty years, as the train approached this house, the engineer had blown on the whistle, and every day, as soon as she heard this signal, a woman had appeared on the back porch of the little house and waved to him. At first she had a small child clinging to her skirts, and now this child had grown to full womanhood, and every day she, too, came with her mother to the porch and waved.

The engineer had grown old and gray in service. He had driven his great train, loaded with its weight of lives, across the land ten thousand times. His own children had grown up and married, and four times he had seen before him on the tracks the ghastly dot of tragedy converging like a cannon ball to its eclipse of horror at the boiler head[2]—a light spring wagon filled with children, with its clustered row of small stunned faces; a cheap automobile

---

1. **arbor:** open-work lattice structure, usually shady and covered with vines.

2. **boiler head:** front section of a steam locomotive.

stalled upon the tracks, set with the wooden figures of people paralyzed with fear; a battered hobo walking by the rail, too deaf and old to hear the whistle's warning; and a form flung past his window with a scream—all this the man had seen and known. He had known all the grief, the joy, the peril, and the labor such a man could know; he had grown seamed and weathered in his loyal service, and now, schooled by the qualities of faith and courage and humbleness that attended his labor, he had grown old, and had the grandeur and the wisdom these men have.

But no matter what peril or tragedy he had known, the vision of the little house and the women waving to him with a brave free motion of the arm had become fixed in the mind of the engineer as something beautiful and enduring, something beyond all change and ruin, and something that would always be the same, no matter what mishap, grief, or error might break the iron schedule of his days.

The sight of the little house and of these two women gave him the most extraordinary happiness he had ever known. He had seen them in a thousand lights, a hundred weathers. He had seen them through the harsh bare light of wintry gray across the brown and frosted stubble of earth, and he had seen them again in the green luring sorcery of April.

He felt for them and for the little house in which they lived such tenderness as a man might feel for his own children, and at length the picture of their lives was carved so sharply in his heart that he felt that he knew their lives completely, to every hour and moment of the day, and he resolved that one day, when his years of service should be ended, he would go and find these people and speak at last with them whose lives had been so wrought[3] into his own.

That day came. At last the engineer stepped from a train onto the station platform of the town where these two women lived. His years upon the rail had ended. He was a pensioned servant of his company, with no more work to do. The engineer walked slowly through the station and out into the streets of the town. Everything was as strange to him as if he had never seen this town before. As he walked on, his sense of bewilderment and confusion grew. Could this be the town he had passed ten thousand times? Were these the same houses he had seen so often from the high windows of his cab? It was all as unfamiliar, as disquieting as a city in a dream, and the perplexity of his spirit increased as he went on.

Presently the houses thinned into the straggling outposts of the town, and the street faded into a country road—the one on which the women lived. And the man plodded on slowly in the heat and dust. At length he stood before the house he sought. He knew at once that he had found the proper place. He saw the lordly oaks before the house, the flower beds, the garden, and the arbor, and farther off, the glint of rails.

Yes, this was the house he sought, the place he had passed so many times, the destination he had longed for with such happiness. But now that he had found it, now that he was here, why did his hand falter on the gate; why had the town, the road, the earth, the very entrance to this place he loved turned unfamiliar as the landscape of some ugly dream? Why did he now feel this sense of confusion, doubt, and hopelessness?

At length he entered by the gate, walked slowly up the path and in a moment more had mounted three short steps that led up to the porch, and was knocking at the door. Presently he heard steps in the hall, the door was opened, and a woman stood facing him.

And instantly, with a sense of bitter loss and grief, he was sorry he had come. He knew at once that the woman who stood there looking at him with a mistrustful eye was the same woman who had waved to him so many thousand times. But her face was harsh and pinched and meager; the flesh sagged wearily in sallow[4]

---

3. **wrought:** formed; shaped.

---

4. **sallow:** sickly, yellowish.

folds, and the small eyes peered at him with timid suspicion and uneasy doubt. All the brave freedom, the warmth, and the affection that he had read into her gesture vanished in the moment that he saw her and heard her unfriendly tongue.

And now his own voice sounded unreal and ghastly to him as he tried to explain his presence, to tell her who he was and the reason he had come. But he faltered on, fighting stubbornly against the horror of regret, confusion, disbelief that surged up in his spirit, drowning all his former joy and making his act of hope and tenderness seem shameful to him.

At length the woman invited him almost unwillingly into the house, and called her daughter in a harsh shrill voice. Then, for a brief agony of time, the man sat in an ugly little parlor, and he tried to talk while the two women stared at him with a dull, bewildered hostility, a sullen, timorous restraint.

And finally, stammering a crude farewell, he departed. He walked away down the path and then along the road toward town, and suddenly he knew that he was an old man. His heart, which had been brave and confident when he looked along the familiar vista of the rails, was now sick with doubt and horror as it saw the strange and unsuspected visage of an earth which had always been within a stone's throw of him, and which he had never seen or known. And he knew that all the magic of that bright lost way, the vista of that shining line, the imagined corner of that small good universe of hope's desire, was gone forever, could never be got back again.

STUDY QUESTIONS

Recalling

1. What words and phrases describe the little cottage in the opening paragraph? Whom does the engineer see every day for more than twenty years when his train passes the little cottage?
2. What has the engineer known in his twenty years of service with the railroad, according to the fourth paragraph? According to the fifth paragraph, what "vision" counteracts each peril or tragedy he has known? What does he resolve in the seventh paragraph?
3. When the engineer at last visits the little cottage, what sort of woman stands looking at him? What vanishes in the moment he sees her and hears her unfriendly tongue? How does the woman invite him into the cottage, according to the next-to-last paragraph?
4. What does the engineer know about himself as he leaves the cottage in the final paragraph?

Interpreting

5. What did the engineer's mind do to the little cottage and its inhabitants for all the years he saw them?

6. Why might the engineer have placed so much importance on his vision? Why would he feel old after his vision is destroyed?
7. What is the significance of the story's title?

Extending

8. Do you think the engineer should have visited the cottage? In his place, would you have done so? Explain your answers.

COMPOSITION

Writing a Comparison/Contrast

■ Compare and contrast the engineer's vision of the little house and its inhabitants, seen every day from his passing train, with his actual closeup encounter with them after his years of service on the train are over. In what ways does the reality fall short of the vision?

Writing an Advertisement

■ Suppose the little house were for sale. Write an ad appealing to the tastes of someone like the engineer, someone who has worked hard all his life and is now seeking to purchase a retirement home with his savings. Use vivid language and persuasive adjectives.

Thomas Wolfe **633**

© Rollie McKenna

Delmore Schwartz   *1913–1966*

Delmore Schwartz was born in Brooklyn, New York. He attended the University of Wisconsin, New York University, and Harvard. He later taught at several universities, including Harvard, Princeton, and the University of Chicago, and he served as editor for the important periodicals *Partisan Review* and *The New Republic.*

Schwartz was primarily a poet and a literary critic, but he also wrote short stories and plays. In 1960 he was awarded the prestigious Bollingen Prize for poetry for his collection *Summer Knowledge,* and he has also been praised for his first collection of stories, *The World Is a Wedding* (1948).

"In Dreams Begin Responsibilities" is the title story of Schwartz's first important book, published in 1938. It makes clear that Schwartz was not afraid to take risks, to experiment with a fascinating new way to tell a story and still inject it with great emotional intensity.

Delmore Schwartz

In Dreams Begin Responsibilities

I

I think it is the year 1909. I feel as if I were in a motion picture theater, the long arm of light crossing the darkness and spinning, my eyes fixed on the screen. This is a silent picture as if an old Biograph[1] one, in which the actors are dressed in ridiculously old-fashioned clothes, and one flash succeeds another with sudden jumps. The actors too seem to jump about and walk too fast. The shots themselves are full of dots and rays, as if it were raining when the picture was photographed. The light is bad.

It is Sunday afternoon, June 12th, 1909, and my father is walking down the quiet streets of Brooklyn on his way to visit my mother. His clothes are newly pressed and his tie is too

tight in his high collar. He jingles the coins in his pockets, thinking of the witty things he will say. I feel as if I had by now relaxed entirely in the soft darkness of the theater; the organist peals out the obvious and approximate emotions on which the audience rocks unknowingly. I am anonymous, and I have forgotten myself. It is always so when one goes to the movies, it is, as they say, a drug.

My father walks from street to street of trees, lawns and houses, once in a while coming to an avenue on which a streetcar skates and gnaws, slowly progressing. The conductor, who has a handlebar mustache, helps a young lady wearing a hat like a bowl with feathers on to the car. She lifts her long skirts slightly as she mounts the steps. He leisurely makes change and rings his bell. It is obviously Sunday, for everyone is wearing Sunday clothes,

---

1. **Biograph:** company that produced films in the early 1900s.

and the streetcar's noises emphasize the quiet of the holiday. Is not Brooklyn the City of Churches? The shops are closed and their shades drawn, but for an occasional stationery store or drugstore with great green balls in the window.

My father has chosen to take this long walk because he likes to walk and think. He thinks about himself in the future and so arrives at the place he is to visit in a state of mild exaltation. He pays no attention to the houses he is passing, in which the Sunday dinner is being eaten, nor to the many trees which patrol each street, now coming to their full leafage and the time when they will room the whole street in cool shadow. An occasional carriage passes, the horse's hooves falling like stones in the quiet afternoon, and once in a while an automobile, looking like an enormous upholstered sofa, puffs and passes.

My father thinks of my mother, of how nice it will be to introduce her to his family. But he is not yet sure that he wants to marry her, and once in a while he becomes panicky about the bond already established. He reassures himself by thinking of the big men he admires who are married: William Randolph Hearst,[2] and William Howard Taft, who has just become President of the United States.

My father arrives at my mother's house. He has come too early and so is suddenly embarrassed. My aunt, my mother's sister, answers the loud bell with her napkin in her hand, for the family is still at dinner. As my father enters, my grandfather rises from the table and shakes hands with him. My mother has run upstairs to tidy herself. My grandmother asks my father if he has had dinner, and tells him that Rose will be downstairs soon. My grandfather opens the conversation by remarking on the mild June weather. My father sits uncomfortably near the table, holding his hat in his hand. My grandmother tells my aunt to take my father's hat. My uncle, twelve years old, runs into the house, his hair tousled. He shouts a greeting to my father, who has often given him a nickel, and then runs upstairs. It is evident that the respect in which my father is held in this household is tempered by a good deal of mirth. He is impressive, yet he is very awkward.

II

Finally my mother comes downstairs, all dressed up, and my father being engaged in conversation with my grandfather becomes uneasy, not knowing whether to greet my mother or continue the conversation. He gets up from the chair clumsily and says "hello" gruffly. My grandfather watches, examining their congruence,[3] such as it is, with a critical eye, and meanwhile rubbing his bearded cheek roughly, as he always does when he reflects. He is worried; he is afraid that my father will not make a good husband for his oldest daughter. At this point something happens to the film, just as my father is saying something funny to my mother; I am awakened to myself and my unhappiness just as my interest was rising. The audience begins to clap impatiently. Then the trouble is cared for but the film has been returned to a portion just shown, and once more I see my grandfather rubbing his bearded cheek and pondering my father's character. It is difficult to get back into the picture once more and forget myself, but as my mother giggles at my father's words, the darkness drowns me.

My father and mother depart from the house, my father shaking hands with my mother once more, out of some unknown uneasiness. I stir uneasily also, slouched in the hard chair of the theater. Where is the older uncle, my mother's older brother? He is studying in his bedroom upstairs, studying for his final examination at the College of the City of New York, having been dead of rapid pneumonia for the last twenty-one years. My mother and father walk down the same quiet streets once more. My mother is holding my father's

---

2. **William Randolph Hearst:** publisher of newspapers and magazines in the United States (1863–1951).

3. **congruence** [kong′groo əns]: match; appropriateness.

arm and telling him of the novel which she has been reading; and my father utters judgments of the characters as the plot is made clear to him. This is a habit which he very much enjoys, for he feels the utmost superiority and confidence when he approves and condemns the behavior of other people. At times he feels moved to utter a brief "Ugh"—whenever the story becomes what he would call sugary. This tribute is paid to his manliness. My mother feels satisfied by the interest which she has awakened; she is showing my father how intelligent she is, and how interesting.

They reach the avenue, and the streetcar leisurely arrives. They are going to Coney Island[4] this afternoon, although my mother considers that such pleasures are inferior. She has made up her mind to indulge only in a walk on the boardwalk and a pleasant dinner, avoiding the riotous amusements as being beneath the dignity of so dignified a couple.

My father tells my mother how much money he has made in the past week, exaggerating an amount which need not have been exaggerated. But my father has always felt that actualities somehow fall short. Suddenly I begin to weep. The determined old lady who sits

4. **Coney Island:** amusement park and beach in Brooklyn, N.Y.

next to me in the theater is annoyed and looks at me with an angry face, and being intimidated, I stop. I drag out my handkerchief and dry my face, licking the drop which has fallen near my lips. Meanwhile I have missed something, for here are my mother and father alighting at the last stop, Coney Island.

III

They walk toward the boardwalk, and my father commands my mother to inhale the pungent air from the sea. They both breathe in deeply, both of them laughing as they do so. They have in common a great interest in health, although my father is strong and husky, my mother frail. Their minds are full of theories of what is good to eat and not good to eat, and sometimes they engage in heated discussions of the subject, the whole matter ending in my father's announcement, made with a scornful bluster, that you have to die sooner or later anyway. On the boardwalk's flagpole, the American flag is pulsing in an intermittent wind from the sea.

My father and mother go to the rail of the boardwalk and look down on the beach where a good many bathers are casually walking about. A few are in the surf. A peanut whistle pierces the air with its pleasant and active whine, and my father goes to buy peanuts. My mother remains at the rail and stares at the ocean. The ocean seems merry to her; it pointedly sparkles and again and again the pony waves are released. She notices the children digging in the wet sand, and the bathing costumes of the girls who are her own age. My father returns with the peanuts. Overhead the sun's lightning strikes and strikes, but neither of them are at all aware of it. The boardwalk is full of people dressed in their Sunday clothes and idly strolling. The tide does not reach as far as the boardwalk, and the strollers would feel no danger if it did. My mother and father lean on the rail of the boardwalk and absently stare at the ocean. The ocean is becoming rough; the waves come in slowly, tugging strength from far back. The moment before they somersault, the moment when they arch their backs so beautifully, showing green and white veins amid the black, that moment is intolerable. They finally crack, dashing fiercely upon the sand, actually driving, full force downward, against the sand, bouncing upward and forward, and at last petering out into a small stream which races up the beach and then is recalled. My parents gaze absentmindedly at the ocean, scarcely interested in its harshness. The sun overhead does not disturb them. But I stare at the terrible sun which breaks up sight, and the fatal, merciless, passionate ocean, I forget my parents. I stare fascinated and finally, shocked by the indifference of my father and mother, I burst out weeping once more. The old lady next to me pats me on the shoulder and says "There, there, all of this is only a movie, young man, only a movie," but I look up once more at the terrifying sun and the terrifying ocean, and being unable to control my tears, I get up and go to the men's room, stumbling over the feet of the other people seated in my row.

IV

When I return, feeling as if I had awakened in the morning sick for lack of sleep, several hours have apparently passed and my parents are riding on the merry-go-round. My father is on a black horse, my mother on a white one, and they seem to be making an eternal circuit for the single purpose of snatching the nickel rings[5] which are attached to the arm of one of the posts. A hand-organ is playing; it is one with the ceaseless circling of the merry-go-round.

For a moment it seems that they will never get off the merry-go-round because it will never stop. I feel like one who looks down on the avenue from the fiftieth story of a building. But at length they do get off; even the music of the hand-organ has ceased for a moment. My father has acquired ten rings, my mother only

---

5. **nickel rings:** A nickel ring could be exchanged for a free ride.

two, although it was my mother who really wanted them.

They walk on along the boardwalk as the afternoon descends by imperceptible degrees into the incredible violet of dusk. Everything fades into a relaxed glow, even the ceaseless murmuring from the beach, and the revolutions of the merry-go-round. They look for a place to have dinner. My father suggests the best one on the boardwalk and my mother demurs,[6] in accordance with her principles.

However they do go to the best place, asking for a table near the window, so that they can look out on the boardwalk and the mobile ocean. My father feels omnipotent as he places a quarter in the waiter's hand as he asks for a table. The place is crowded and here too there is music, this time from a kind of string trio. My father orders dinner with a fine confidence.

As the dinner is eaten, my father tells of his plans for the future, and my mother shows with expressive face how interested she is, and how impressed. My father becomes exultant. He is lifted up by the waltz that is being played, and his own future begins to intoxicate him. My father tells my mother that he is going to expand his business, for there is a great deal of money to be made. He wants to settle down. After all, he is twenty-nine, he has lived by himself since he was thirteen, he is making more and more money, and he is envious of his married friends when he visits them in the cozy security of their homes, surrounded, it seems, by the calm domestic pleasures, and by delightful children, and then, as the waltz reaches the moment when all the dancers swing madly, then, then with awful daring, then he asks my mother to marry him, although awkwardly enough and puzzled, even in his excitement, at how he had arrived at the proposal, and she, to make the whole business worse, begins to cry, and my father looks nervously about, not knowing at all what to do now, and my mother says: "It's all I've wanted from the moment I saw you," sobbing, and he

6. **demurs** [di murz′]: objects.

finds all of this very difficult, scarcely to his taste, scarcely as he had thought it would be, on his long walks over Brooklyn Bridge in the revery of a fine cigar, and it was then that I stood up in the theater and shouted: "Don't do it. It's not too late to change your minds, both of you. Nothing good will come of it, only remorse, hatred, scandal, and two children whose characters are monstrous." The whole audience turned to look at me, annoyed, the usher came hurrying down the aisle flashing his searchlight, and the old lady next to me tugged me down into my seat, saying: "Be quiet. You'll be put out, and you paid thirty-five cents to come in." And so I shut my eyes because I could not bear to see what was happening. I sat there quietly.

V

But after awhile I begin to take brief glimpses, and at length I watch again with thirsty interest, like a child who wants to maintain his sulk although offered the bribe of candy. My parents are now having their picture taken in a photographer's booth along the boardwalk. The place is shadowed in the mauve light which is apparently necessary. The camera is set to the side on its tripod and looks like a Martian man. The photographer is instructing my parents in how to pose. My father has his arm over my mother's shoulder, and both of them smile emphatically. The photographer brings my mother a bouquet of flowers to hold in her hand but she holds it at the wrong angle. Then the photographer covers himself with the black cloth which drapes the camera and all that one sees of him is one protruding arm and his hand which clutches the rubber ball which he will squeeze when the picture is finally taken. But he is not satisfied with their appearance. He feels with certainty that somehow there is something wrong in their pose. Again and again he issues from his hidden place with new directions. Each suggestion merely makes matters worse. My father is becoming impatient. They try a seated pose. The photographer explains that he has pride, he is not interested in all of this for the money, he wants to make beautiful pictures. My father says: "Hurry up, will you? We haven't got all night." But the photographer only scurries about apologetically, and issues new directions. The photographer charms me. I approve of him with all my heart, for I know just how he feels, and as he criticizes each revised pose according to some unknown idea of rightness, I become quite hopeful. But then my father says angrily: "Come on, you've had enough time, we're not going to wait any longer." And the photographer, sighing unhappily, goes back under his black covering, holds out his hand, says: "One, two, three, Now!",

and the picture is taken, with my father's smile turned to a grimace and my mother's bright and false. It takes a few minutes for the picture to be developed and as my parents sit in the curious light they become quite depressed.

VI

They have passed a fortune teller's booth, and my mother wishes to go in, but my father does not. They begin to argue about it. My mother becomes stubborn, my father once more impatient, and then they begin to quarrel, and what my father would like to do is walk off and leave my mother there, but he knows that that would never do. My mother refuses to budge. She is near to tears, but she feels an uncontrollable desire to hear what the palm-reader will say. My father consents angrily, and they both go into a booth which is in a way like the photographer's, since it is draped in black cloth and its light is shadowed. The place is too warm, and my father keeps saying this is all nonsense, pointing to the crystal ball on the table. The fortune teller, a fat, short woman, garbed in what is supposed to be Oriental robes, comes into the room from the back and greets them, speaking with an accent. But suddenly my father feels that the whole thing is intolerable; he tugs at my mother's arm, but my mother refuses to budge. And then, in terrible anger, my father lets go of my mother's arm and strides out, leaving my mother stunned. She moves to go after my father, but the fortune teller holds her arm tightly and begs her not to do so, and I in my seat am shocked more than can ever be said, for I feel as if I were walking a tightrope a hundred feet over a circus audience and suddenly the rope is showing signs of breaking, and I get up from my seat and begin to shout once more the first words I can think of to communicate my terrible fear and once more the usher comes hurrying down the aisle flashing his searchlight, and the old lady pleads with me, and the shocked audience has turned to stare at me, and I keep shouting: "What are they doing? Don't they know what they are doing? Why doesn't my mother go after my father? If she does not do that, what will she do? Doesn't my father know what he is doing?" But the usher has seized my arm and is dragging me away, and as he does so, he says: "What are *you* doing? Don't you know that you can't do whatever you want to do? Why should a young man like you, with your whole life before you, get hysterical like this? Why don't you *think* of what you're doing? You can't act like this even if other people aren't around! You will be sorry if you do not do what you should do, you can't carry on like this, it is not right, you will find that out soon enough, everything you do matters too much," and he said that dragging me through the lobby of the theater into the cold light, and I woke up into the bleak winter morning of my twenty-first birthday, the windowsill shining with its lip of snow, and the morning already begun.

STUDY QUESTIONS

Recalling

1. What does the narrator imagine himself to be doing in the opening paragraphs? Where is his father going? When does this incident take place?
2. Where does the father take the mother in section II? What does the mother feel she has shown by interesting him in her conversation? What does the father do when he tells her how much money he made that week?
3. As the couple go to the rail of the boardwalk in section III, what "strikes overhead" that they scarcely notice? In what "harsh" scene are they scarcely interested? Is the narrator equally uninterested in these things?
4. What are the couple doing in the opening paragraphs of section IV? How does the mother react when the father suggests they eat at the best restaurant on the boardwalk? Where do the couple eat?
5. What plans does the father discuss as they dine? What does he ask the mother? What does the mother say as she begins sobbing? What does the narrator stand up and shout?
6. About what do the couple quarrel in section VI? What does the father do when he decides the "whole thing" is intolerable? What does the fortune teller do? What does the narrator shout?
7. What does the "usher" say to the narrator as he drags him from the "theater"? To what does the narrator awaken in the final paragraph?

Interpreting

8. In general, what characteristics do the father and mother seem to have? Do we find anything positive or touching about their day's outing? If so, what? How does the title apply to both the father and the mother?

9. What do the glaring sun, the ominous ocean, and the fortune teller's staying hand all foreshadow, or predict? Why do the couple fail to notice the sun and ocean? Why does the narrator notice?

10. Where in the story does the narrator's negative view of his parents' marriage change for the positive?

11. What do the usher's remarks and the fact that the narrator awakens to his twenty-first birthday suggest has happened to the narrator at the story's end? Why is it impossible for the narrator to be against his parents' marriage any longer? How does the title apply to the narrator?

Extending

12. What does the fact that the narrator imagines events so crucial to his life as the plot of a *movie* suggest to you about the significance of the mass media in the twentieth century? What effect do you think movies and television shows have had on Americans' perceptions, on their views of themselves and the world?

LITERARY FOCUS

Point of View: The Frame Story

The **point of view** of a work of fiction is the position from which the characters and action are seen by the author. One special means of creating point of view is to use a **frame story,** a story in which another story takes place. The author begins with one story and one character or set of characters. Then, *within that story,* the author introduces another story and another character or set of characters. Frequently a character in the frame story narrates the story it contains.

The frame story of "In Dreams Begin Responsibilities" involves a narrator who imagines that he is in a movie theater watching a film about his own parents. The story of his parents, which unfolds in the film that the narrator describes, is the story within the story.

One advantage of the frame story is that it provides a writer with a kind of double voice: Both the frame story and the inner story can express the theme. Each story can comment on the other and can thus reinforce and deepen the overall meaning. For example, at the end of Schwartz's story, the narrator awakens from a dream and realizes *from his dream* that life will not always be just as he wants it, that "everything you do matters too much."

Thinking About the Frame Story

■ Several times in the story the narrator interrupts the movie to weep or to shout at the screen. At these moments the frame story and the inner story converge. How do these moments help to clarify the theme of the story?

COMPOSITION

Analyzing the Title of a Story

■ Write an essay in which you discuss the title in terms of its significance to the whole story. Consider the kinds of "dreams" that occur in the story. What are the "responsibilities" that the author is concerned with?

Writing a Story Within a Story

■ Using the structure of "In Dreams Begin Responsibilities" as a model, write a short story within a story. Begin with a character watching a movie. Then allow the character to become "involved" in the movie in some way. Feel free to invent an ending different from the kind Schwartz uses.

Eudora Welty   *born 1909*

Eudora Welty has lived virtually all of her life in Jackson, Mississippi, where she was born. She was educated at the Mississippi State College for Women and at the University of Wisconsin. Early in her career she studied advertising copywriting and worked as a government publicity agent. During World War II she was briefly a staff member of the *New York Times Book Review,* for which she wrote reviews of battlefield reports from North Africa under the pseudonym "Michael Ravenna."

She is best known for her short stories, which have appeared in several collections, including *A Curtain of Green* (1941), *The Wide Net* (1943), and *Thirteen Stories* (1965). She has also written several novels, including *Delta Wedding* (1946), *The Ponder Heart* (1954), and *The Optimist's Daughter* (1972), for which she was awarded the Pulitzer Prize. She is the author of a children's book, *The Shoe Bird* (1964), and of a collection of photographs of Mississippi, *One Time, One Place* (1971).

With grace and gentle humor, an eye for the eccentric and for telling details, and a wonderful ear for language and dialogue, Eudora Welty has in her fiction traced and defined a broad range of southern experience. Yet by doing so, she has also touched the universal. "A Worn Path" concerns an old woman's labored journey, but, as the author herself notes, it is also about "the deep-grained habit of love."

Eudora Welty

A Worn Path

It was December—a bright frozen day in the early morning. Far out in the country there was an old Negro woman with her head tied in a red rag, coming along a path through the pinewoods. Her name was Phoenix Jackson. She was very old and small and she walked slowly in the dark pine shadows, moving a little from side to side in her steps, with the balanced heaviness and lightness of a pendulum in a grandfather clock. She carried a thin, small cane made from an umbrella, and with this she kept tapping the frozen earth in front of her. This made a grave and persistent noise in the still air, that seemed meditative like the chirping of a solitary little bird.

She wore a dark striped dress reaching down to her shoe tops, and an equally long apron of bleached sugar sacks, with a full pocket: all neat and tidy, but every time she took a step she might have fallen over her shoelaces, which dragged from her unlaced shoes. She looked straight ahead. Her eyes were blue with age. Her skin had a pattern all its own of numberless branching wrinkles and as though a whole little tree stood in the middle of her forehead, but a golden color ran underneath, and the two knobs of her cheeks were illumined by a yellow burning under the dark. Under the red rag her hair came down on her neck in the frailest of ringlets, still black, and with an odor like copper.

Now and then there was a quivering in the thicket. Old Phoenix said, "Out of my way, all you foxes, owls, beetles, jack rabbits, coons and wild animals! . . . Keep out from under these feet, little bobwhites. . . . Keep the big wild hogs out of my path. Don't let none of those come running my direction. I got a long way." Under her small black-freckled hand her cane, limber as a buggy whip, would switch at the brush as if to rouse up any hiding things.

On she went. The woods were deep and still. The sun made the pine needles almost too bright to look at, up where the wind rocked. The cones dropped as light as feathers. Down in the hollow was the mourning dove—it was not too late for him.

The path ran up a hill. "Seem like there is chains about my feet, time I get this far," she said, in the voice of argument old people keep to use with themselves. "Something always take a hold of me on this hill—pleads I should stay."

After she got to the top she turned and gave a full, severe look behind her where she had come. "Up through pines," she said at length. "Now down through oaks."

Her eyes opened their widest, and she started down gently. But before she got to the bottom of the hill a bush caught her dress.

Her fingers were busy and intent, but her skirts were full and long, so that before she could pull them free in one place they were caught in another. It was not possible to allow the dress to tear. "I in the thorny bush," she said. "Thorns, you doing your appointed work. Never want to let folks pass, no sir. Old eyes thought you was a pretty little *green* bush."

Finally, trembling all over, she stood free, and after a moment dared to stoop for her cane.

"Sun so high!" she cried, leaning back and looking, while the thick tears went over her eyes. "The time getting all gone here."

At the foot of this hill was a place where a log was laid across the creek.

"Now comes the trial," said Phoenix.

Putting her right foot out, she mounted the log and shut her eyes. Lifting her skirt, leveling her cane fiercely before her, like a festival figure in some parade, she began to march across. Then she opened her eyes and she was safe on the other side.

"I wasn't as old as I thought," she said.

But she sat down to rest. She spread her skirts on the bank around her and folded her hands over her knees. Up above her was a tree in a pearly cloud of mistletoe. She did not dare to close her eyes, and when a little boy brought her a plate with a slice of marble-cake on it she spoke to him. "That would be acceptable," she said. But when she went to take it there was just her own hand in the air.

So she left that tree, and had to go through a barbed-wire fence. There she had to creep and crawl, spreading her knees and stretching her fingers like a baby trying to climb the steps. But she talked loudly to herself: she could not let her dress be torn now, so late in the day, and she could not pay for having her arm or her leg sawed off if she got caught fast where she was.

At last she was safe through the fence and risen up out in the clearing. Big dead trees, like black men with one arm, were standing in the purple stalks of the withered cotton field. There sat a buzzard.

"Who you watching?"

In the furrow she made her way along.

"Glad this not the season for bulls," she said, looking sideways, "and the good Lord made his snakes to curl up and sleep in the winter. A pleasure I don't see no two-headed snake coming around that tree, where it come once. It took a while to get by him, back in the summer."

She passed through the old cotton and went into a field of dead corn. It whispered and shook and was taller than her head. "Through the maze now," she said, for there was no path.

Then there was something tall, black, and skinny there, moving before her.

At first she took it for a man. It could have been a man dancing in the field. But she stood still and listened, and it did not make a sound. It was silent as a ghost.

"Ghost," she said sharply, "who be you the ghost of? For I have heard of nary death close by."

But there was no answer—only the ragged dancing in the wind.

She shut her eyes, reached out her hand, and touched a sleeve. She found a coat and inside that an emptiness, cold as ice.

"You scarecrow," she said. Her face lighted. "I ought to be shut up for good," she said with laughter. "My senses is gone. I too old. I the oldest people I ever know. Dance, old scarecrow," she said, "while I dancing with you."

She kicked her foot over the furrow, and with mouth drawn down, shook her head once or twice in a little strutting way. Some husks blew down and whirled in streamers about her skirts.

Then she went on, parting her way from side to side with the cane, through the whispering field. At last she came to the end, to a wagon track where the silver grass blew between the red ruts. The quail were walking around like pullets, seeming all dainty and unseen.

"Walk pretty," she said. "This the easy place. This the easy going."

She followed the track, swaying through the quiet bare fields, through the little strings of trees silver in their dead leaves, past cabins silver from weather, with the doors and windows boarded shut, all like old women under a spell sitting there. "I walking in their sleep," she said, nodding her head vigorously.

In a ravine she went where a spring was silently flowing through a hollow log. Old Phoenix bent and drank. "Sweet-gum[1] makes the water sweet," she said, and drank more. "Nobody know who made this well, for it was here when I was born."

The track crossed a swampy part where the moss hung as white as lace from every limb. "Sleep on, alligators, and blow your bubbles." Then the track went into the road.

Deep, deep the road went down between the high green-colored banks. Overhead the live-oaks met, and it was as dark as a cave.

A black dog with a lolling tongue came up out of the weeds by the ditch. She was meditating, and not ready, and when he came at her she only hit him a little with her cane. Over she went in the ditch, like a little puff of milkweed.[2]

Down there, her senses drifted away. A dream visited her, and she reached her hand up, but nothing reached down and gave her a pull. So she lay there and presently went to talking. "Old woman," she said to herself, "that black dog come up out of the weeds to stall you off, and now there he sitting on his fine tail, smiling at you."

A white man finally came along and found her—a hunter, a young man, with his dog on a chain.

"Well, Granny!" he laughed. "What are you doing there?"

"Lying on my back like a June bug waiting to be turned over, mister," she said, reaching up her hand.

He lifted her up, gave her a swing in the air, and set her down. "Anything broken, Granny?"

"No sir, them old dead weeds is springy enough," said Phoenix, when she had got her breath. "I thank you for your trouble."

"Where do you live, Granny?" he asked, while the two dogs were growling at each other.

"Away back yonder, sir, behind the ridge. You can't even see it from here."

"On your way home?"

"No sir, I going to town."

"Why, that's too far! That's as far as I walk when I come out myself, and I get something for my trouble." He patted the stuffed bag he carried, and there hung down a little closed claw. It was one of the bobwhites, with its beak hooked bitterly to show it was dead. "Now you go on home, Granny!"

"I bound to go to town, mister," said Phoenix. "The time come around."

---

1. **Sweet-gum:** fragrant juice from sweet-gum trees.

2. **milkweed:** plant with milky juice and feathery seeds.

He gave another laugh, filling the whole landscape. "I know you old colored people! Wouldn't miss going to town to see Santa Claus!"

But something held old Phoenix very still. The deep lines in her face went into a fierce and different radiation. Without warning, she had seen with her own eyes a flashing nickel fall out of the man's pocket onto the ground.

"How old are you, Granny?" he was saying.

"There is no telling, mister," she said, "no telling."

Then she gave a little cry and clapped her hands and said, "Git on away from here, dog! Look! Look at that dog!" She laughed as if in admiration. "He ain't scared of nobody. He a big black dog." She whispered, "Sic him!"

"Watch me get rid of that cur," said the man. "Sic him, Pete! Sic him!"

Phoenix heard the dogs fighting, and heard the man running and throwing sticks. She even heard a gunshot. But she was slowly bending forward by that time, further and further forward, the lids stretched down over her eyes, as if she were doing this in her sleep. Her chin was lowered almost to her knees. The yellow palm of her hand came out from the fold of her apron. Her fingers slid down and along the ground under the piece of money with the grace and care they would have in lifting an egg from under a setting hen. Then she slowly straightened up, she stood erect, and the nickel was in her apron pocket. A bird flew by. Her lips moved. "God watching me the whole time. I come to stealing."

The man came back, and his own dog panted about them. "Well, I scared him off that time," he said, and then he laughed and lifted his gun and pointed it at Phoenix.

She stood straight and faced him.

"Doesn't the gun scare you?" he said, still pointing it.

"No, sir, I seen plenty go off closer by, in my day, and for less than what I done," she said, holding utterly still.

He smiled, and shouldered the gun. "Well, Granny," he said, "you must be a hundred years old, and scared of nothing. I'd give you a dime if I had any money with me. But you take my advice and stay home, and nothing will happen to you."

"I bound to go on my way, mister," said Phoenix. She inclined her head in the red rag. Then they went in different directions, but she could hear the gun shooting again and again over the hill.

She walked on. The shadows hung from the oak trees to the road like curtains. Then she smelled woodsmoke, and smelled the river, and she saw a steeple and the cabins on their steep steps. Dozens of little black children whirled around her. There ahead was Natchez[3] shining. Bells were ringing. She walked on.

In the paved city it was Christmas time. There were red and green electric lights strung and crisscrossed everywhere, and all turned on in the daytime. Old Phoenix would have been lost if she had not distrusted her eyesight and depended on her feet to know where to take her.

She paused quietly on the sidewalk where people were passing by. A lady came along in the crowd, carrying an armful of red-, green- and silver-wrapped presents; she gave off perfume like the red roses in hot summer, and Phoenix stopped her.

"Please, missy, will you lace up my shoe?" She held up her foot.

"What do you want, Grandma?"

"See my shoe," said Phoenix. "Do all right for out in the country, but wouldn't look right to go in a big building."

"Stand still then, Grandma," said the lady. She put her packages down on the sidewalk beside her and laced and tied both shoes tightly.

"Can't lace 'em with a cane," said Phoenix. "Thank you, missy. I doesn't mind asking a nice lady to tie up my shoe, when I gets out on the street."

Moving slowly and from side to side, she

---

3. **Natchez:** town in southern Mississippi.

went into the big building, and into a tower of steps, where she walked up and around and around until her feet knew to stop.

She entered a door, and there she saw nailed up on the wall the document that had been stamped with the gold seal and framed in the gold frame, which matched the dream that was hung up in her head.

"Here I be," she said. There was a fixed and ceremonial stiffness over her body.

"A charity case, I suppose," said an attendant who sat at the desk before her.

But Phoenix only looked above her head. There was sweat on her face, the wrinkles in her skin shone like a bright net.

"Speak up, Grandma," the woman said. "What's your name? We must have your history, you know. Have you been here before? What seems to be the trouble with you?"

Old Phoenix only gave a twitch to her face as if a fly were bothering her.

"Are you deaf?" cried the attendant.

But then the nurse came in.

"Oh, that's just old Aunt Phoenix," she said. "She doesn't come for herself—she has a little grandson. She makes these trips just as regular as clockwork. She lives away back off the Old Natchez Trace."[4] She bent down. "Well, Aunt Phoenix, why don't you just take a seat? We won't keep you standing after your long trip." She pointed.

The old woman sat down, bolt upright in the chair.

"Now, how is the boy?" asked the nurse.

Old Phoenix did not speak.

"I said, how is the boy?"

But Phoenix only waited and stared straight ahead, her face very solemn and withdrawn into rigidity.

"Is his throat any better?" asked the nurse. "Aunt Phoenix, don't you hear me? Is your grandson's throat any better since the last time you came for the medicine?"

---

4. **Old Natchez Trace:** road between Natchez and Nashville, Tennessee, used in the early 1800s.

With her hands on her knees, the old woman waited, silent, erect and motionless, just as if she were in armor.

"You mustn't take up our time this way, Aunt Phoenix," the nurse said. "Tell us quickly about your grandson, and get it over. He isn't dead, is he?"

At last there came a flicker and then a flame of comprehension across her face, and she spoke.

"My grandson. It was my memory had left me. There I sat and forgot why I made my long trip."

"Forgot?" The nurse frowned. "After you came so far?"

Then Phoenix was like an old woman begging a dignified forgiveness for waking up frightened in the night. "I never did go to school, I was too old at the Surrender,"[5] she said in a soft voice. "I'm an old woman without an education. It was my memory fail me. My little grandson, he is just the same, and I forgot it in the coming."

"Throat never heals, does it?" said the nurse, speaking in a loud, sure voice to old Phoenix. By now she had a card with something written on it, a little list. "Yes. Swallowed lye. When was it?—January—two, three years ago—"

Phoenix spoke unasked now. "No, missy, he not dead, he just the same. Every little while his throat begin to close up again, and he not able to swallow. He not get his breath. He not able to help himself. So the time come around, and I go on another trip for the soothing medicine."

"All right. The doctor said as long as you came to get it, you could have it," said the nurse. "But it's an obstinate case."

---

5. **the Surrender:** surrender of the Confederate army at the end of the Civil War on April 9, 1865.

"My little grandson, he sit up there in the house all wrapped up, waiting by himself," Phoenix went on. "We is the only two left in the world. He suffer and it don't seem to put him back at all. He got a sweet look. He going to last. He wear a little patch quilt and peep out holding his mouth open like a little bird. I remembers so plain now. I not going to forget him again, no, the whole enduring time. I could tell him from all the others in creation."

"All right." The nurse was trying to hush her now. She brought her a bottle of medicine. "Charity," she said, making a check mark in a book.

Old Phoenix held the bottle close to her eyes, and then carefully put it into her pocket.

"I thank you," she said.

"It's Christmas time, Grandma," said the attendant. "Could I give you a few pennies out of my purse?"

"Five pennies is a nickel," said Phoenix stiffly.

"Here's a nickel," said the attendant.

Phoenix rose carefully and held out her hand. She received the nickel and then fished the other nickel out of her pocket and laid it beside the new one. She stared at her palm closely, with her head on one side.

Then she gave a tap with her cane on the floor.

"This is what come to me to do," she said. "I going to the store and buy my child a little windmill they sells, made out of paper. He going to find it hard to believe there such a thing in the world. I'll march myself back where he waiting, holding it straight up in this hand."

She lifted her free hand, gave a little nod, turned around, and walked out of the doctor's office. Then her slow step began on the stairs, going down.

STUDY QUESTIONS

Recalling

1. What details in the first two paragraphs describe Phoenix Jackson?
2. Identify at least two obstacles Phoenix encounters on her journey. What does she see when she closes her eyes after sitting down to rest from her arduous crossing of the creek?
3. What does the hunter who rescues Phoenix from the ditch drop from his pocket during their conversation? What does Phoenix do to divert his attention? What does she say after she puts her acquisition in her apron pocket?
4. To what town is Phoenix going? What holiday is being celebrated?
5. What explanation does Phoenix give for her inability to answer the questions posed by the attendant and the nurse? Why does Phoenix come to Natchez regularly? What happened to her grandson two or three years ago?
6. What does the attendant give Phoenix? What does Phoenix decide to do with the money she has acquired?

Interpreting

7. What do the many difficulties of Phoenix's journey suggest about its importance? What motivates Phoenix's expedition to Natchez?
8. What sort of person is Phoenix Jackson? What do her thoughts after she picks up the hunter's nickel suggest about the importance she places on a nickel? What does her decision about how to spend the money reveal about her character?
9. What might be the significance of the story's being set at Christmas time?
10. In what sense is the title of the story literal? In what sense is Phoenix's love for her grandson itself "a worn path"?

Extending

11. Does this story satisfy the requirements of Regional literature, as defined by Hamlin Garland on page 297? Does it go beyond the regional to the universal as all great Regionalist works do? Defend your answers.

VIEWPOINT

Commenting on the ways in which a short story differs from a novel, Eudora Welty has said:

A short story is confined to one mood, to which everything in the story pertains. Characters, setting, time, events, are all subject to the mood. And you can try more ephemeral, more fleeting things in a story— you can work more by suggestion—than in a novel. Less is resolved, more is suggested, perhaps.
—*Writers at Work: The Paris Review Interviews*

▨ Would you agree that "A Worn Path" is "confined to one mood"? How would you describe that mood? What do you think the story suggests about Phoenix's brave journey?

VOCABULARY

Biblical and Mythological Allusions

The name Phoenix refers to a miraculous bird of Egyptian and Greek mythology that, after living for five hundred years, supposedly built itself a great funeral pyre, died in the flames, and arose from the ashes to live again. Welty's use of the name suggests the durability of her main character.

What would the following names suggest about a character? Use a dictionary to find the biblical or mythological allusions each makes.

1. Cassandra
2. Minerva
3. Penelope
4. Orpheus
5. Demeter
6. Thalia
7. Job
8. Cain
9. Ishmael
10. Freya

COMPOSITION

Writing a Comparison/Contrast

▨ Briefly compare and contrast the theme of this story with that of John Steinbeck's "Leader of the People" (page 618). Begin with a comparison of the journeys each describes. Then contrast the importance of the journeys to the people in the stories. Conclude with a statement about the heroism each exemplifies. *For help with this assignment, refer to Lesson 2 in the Writing About Literature Handbook at the back of this book.*

Describing a Character

▨ Welty characterizes Phoenix through physical description and description of her movements. Invent a character engaged in a particular action. Describe the action with details that characterize the performer of the action.

Walter Van Tilburg Clark *1909–1971*

A literary descendant of Bret Harte (page 301), Walter Van Tilburg Clark also wrote about the American West—its tough character, frontier towns, rugged landscapes, and rigorous climate. He used these materials, however, only as a point of departure for his short stories and novels; generally he moved on to broader philosophical issues.

The most famous example is his novel *The Ox-Bow Incident* (1940). On the one hand, it is a tale of cowboys, cattle rustling, and a lynching; on the other hand, it is an imaginative and compelling examination of the nature and meaning of justice and of humanity's responsibility in the fair dispensation of it.

Clark was born in East Orland, Maine, but grew up largely in Reno, Nevada. He returned to New England to attend graduate school at the University of Vermont. For ten years, during which he wrote and published his first two novels and several short stories, he also taught English and dramatics and coached athletics in public schools in Cazenovia, New York.

In 1945, following the publication of his second novel, *The City of Trembling Leaves,* Clark gave up teaching and with his family moved to New Mexico and later to Nevada, California, and Montana to concentrate on his writing. *The Track of the Cat* (1949), again set in the West, tells of the hunt by three brothers for a vicious black panther. *The Watchful Gods and Other Stories* appeared in 1950.

Clark's many interests included geology and Indian lore. Among his most serious concerns—as "The Portable Phonograph" makes evident—were natural conservation and the future survival of the human race.

Walter Van Tilburg Clark

The Portable Phonograph

The red sunset, with narrow, black cloud strips like threats across it, lay on the curved horizon of the prairie. The air was still and cold, and in it settled the mute darkness and greater cold of night. High in the air there was wind, for through the veil of the dusk, the clouds could be seen gliding rapidly south and changing shapes. A queer sensation of torment, of two-sided, unpredictable nature, arose from the stillness of the earth air beneath the violence of the upper air. Out of the sunset, through the dead, matted grass and isolated weed stalks of the prairie, crept the narrow and deeply rutted remains of a road. In the road, in places, there were crusts of shallow, brittle ice. There were little islands of an old oiled pavement in the road too, but most of it was mud, now frozen rigid. The frozen mud still bore the toothed impress of great tanks, and a wanderer on the neighboring undulations might have stumbled, in this light, into large, partially filled-in and weed-grown cavities, their banks channeled and beginning to spread into badlands. These pits were such as might have been made by falling meteors, but they were not. They were the scars of gigantic bombs, their rawness already made a little natural by rain, seed, and time. Along the road there were rakish remnants of fence. There was also, just visible, one portion of tangled and multiple barbed wire still erect, behind which was a shelving[1] ditch with small caves, now very quiet and empty, at intervals in its back wall. Otherwise there was no structure or remnant of a structure visible over the dome of the darkling[2] earth, but only, in sheltered hollows, the darker shadows of young trees trying again.

Under the wuthering[3] arch of the high wind, a V of wild geese fled south. The rush of their pinions[4] sounded briefly, and the faint, plaintive notes of their expeditionary talk. Then they left a still greater vacancy. There was the smell and expectation of snow, as there is likely to be when the wild geese fly south. From the remote distance, toward the red sky, came faintly the protracted howl and quick yap-yap of a prairie wolf.

North of the road, perhaps a hundred yards, lay the parallel and deeply entrenched course of a small creek, lined with leafless alders and willows. The creek was already silent under ice. Into the bank above it was dug a sort of cell, with a single opening like the mouth of a mine tunnel. Within the cell there was a little red of fire, which showed dully through the opening, like a reflection or a deception of the imagination. The light came from the chary[5] burning of four blocks of poorly aged peat, which gave off a petty warmth and much acrid smoke. But the precious remnants of wood, old fence posts and timbers from the long-deserted dugouts, had to be saved for the real cold, for the time when a man's breath blew white, the moisture in his nostrils stiffened at once when he stepped out, and the expansive blizzards paraded for days over the vast open, swirling and settling and thickening till the dawn of the cleared day when the sky was a thin blue-green and the terrible cold, in which a man could not live for three hours unwarmed, lay over the uniformly drifted swell of the plain.

Around the smoldering peat four men were seated cross-legged. Behind them, traversed by their shadows, was the earth bench, with two old and dirty army blankets, where the owner

---

1. **shelving:** sloping.
2. **darkling:** growing dark; deeply shadowed.
3. **wuthering:** blowing with a dull roar.
4. **pinions:** wings.
5. **chary** [chār′ē]: sparing; careful.

of the cell slept. In a niche in the opposite wall were a few tin utensils which caught the glint of the coals. The host was rewrapping in a piece of daubed burlap four fine, leather-bound books. He worked slowly and very carefully, and at last tied the bundle securely with a piece of grass-woven cord. The other three looked intently upon the process, as if a great significance lay in it. As the host tied the cord, he spoke. He was an old man, his long, matted beard and hair gray to nearly white. The shadows made his brows and cheekbones appear gnarled, his eyes and cheeks deeply sunken. His big hands, rough with frost and swollen by rheumatism, were awkward but gentle at their task. He was like a prehistoric priest performing a fateful ceremonial rite. Also his voice had in it a suitable quality of deep, reverent despair, yet perhaps at the moment, a sharpness of selfish satisfaction. "When I perceived what was happening," he said, "I told myself, 'It is the end. I cannot take much; I will take these.'

"Perhaps I was impractical," he continued. "But for myself, I do not regret, and what do we know of those who will come after us? We are the doddering remnant of a race of mechanical fools. I have saved what I love; the soul of what was good in us is here; perhaps the new ones will make a strong enough beginning not to fall behind when they become clever."

He rose with slow pain and placed the wrapped volumes in the niche with his utensils. The others watched him with the same ritualistic gaze.

"Shakespeare, the Bible, *Moby-Dick,* the *Divine Comedy*,"[6] one of them said softly. "You might have done worse, much worse."

"You will have a little soul left until you die," said another harshly. "That is more than is true of us. My brain becomes thick, like my hands." He held the big, battered hands, with their black nails, in the glow to be seen.

"I want paper to write on," he said. "And there is none."

---

6. *Moby-Dick,* the *Divine Comedy:* Herman Melville's great novel and Dante's poetic masterpiece.

The fourth man said nothing. He sat in the shadow farthest from the fire, and sometimes his body jerked in its rags from the cold. Although he was still young, he was sick and coughed often. Writing implied a greater future than he now felt able to consider.

The old man seated himself laboriously, and reached out, groaning at the movement, to put another block of peat on the fire. With bowed heads and averted eyes, his three guests acknowledged his magnanimity.

"We thank you, Doctor Jenkins, for the reading," said the man who had named the books.

They seemed then to be waiting for something. Doctor Jenkins understood, but was loath[7] to comply. In an ordinary moment he would have said nothing. But the words of *The Tempest*,[8] which he had been reading, and the religious attention of the three, made this an unusual occasion.

"You wish to hear the phonograph," he said grudgingly.

The two middle-aged men stared into the fire, unable to formulate and expose the enormity of their desire.

The young man, however, said anxiously, between suppressed coughs, "Oh, please," like an excited child.

The old man rose again in his difficult way, and went to the back of the cell. He returned and placed tenderly upon the packed floor, where the firelight might fall upon it, an old portable phonograph in a black case. He smoothed the top with his hand, and then opened it. The lovely green-felt-covered disc became visible.

"I have been using thorns as needles," he said. "But tonight, because we have a musician among us"—he bent his head to the young man, almost invisible in the shadow—"I will use a steel needle. There are only three left."

The two middle-aged men stared at him in speechless adoration. The one with the big

---

7. **loath** [lōth]: reluctant.
8. ***The Tempest:*** play by Shakespeare, which takes place on an isolated island.

hands, who wanted to write, moved his lips, but the whisper was not audible.

"Oh, don't!" cried the young man, as if he were hurt. "The thorns will do beautifully."

"No," the old man said. "I have become accustomed to the thorns, but they are not really good. For you, my young friend, we will have good music tonight.

"After all," he added generously, and beginning to wind the phonograph, which creaked, "they can't last forever."

"No, nor we," the man who needed to write said harshly. "The needle, by all means."

"Oh, thanks," said the young man. "Thanks," he said again in a low, excited voice, and then stifled his coughing with a bowed head.

"The records, though," said the old man when he had finished winding, "are a different matter. Already they are very worn. I do not play them more than once a week. One, once a week, that is what I allow myself.

"More than a week I cannot stand it; not to hear them," he apologized.

"No, how could you?" cried the young man. "And with them here like this."

"A man can stand anything," said the man who wanted to write, in his harsh, antagonistic voice.

"Please, the music," said the young man.

"Only the one," said the old man. "In the long run, we will remember more that way."

He had a dozen records with luxuriant gold and red seals. Even in that light the others could see that the threads of the records were becoming worn. Slowly he read out the titles, and the tremendous, dead names of the composers and the artists and the orchestras. The three worked upon the names in their minds, carefully. It was difficult to select from such a wealth what they would at once most like to remember. Finally, the man who wanted to write named Gershwin's[9] "New York."

"Oh, no!" cried the sick young man, and then could say nothing more because he had to cough. The others understood him, and the harsh man withdrew his selection and waited for the musician to choose.

The musician begged Doctor Jenkins to read the titles again, very slowly, so that he could remember the sounds. While they were read, he lay back against the wall, his eyes closed, his thin, horny hand pulling at his light beard, and listened to the voices and the orchestras and the single instruments in his mind.

---

9. **Gershwin's:** referring to George Gershwin (1898–1937), American composer.

When the reading was done, he spoke despairingly. "I have forgotten," he complained; "I cannot hear them clearly.

"There are things missing," he explained.

"I know," said Doctor Jenkins. "I thought that I knew all of Shelley[10] by heart. I should have brought Shelley."

"That's more soul than we can use," said the harsh man. "*Moby-Dick* is better.

"We can understand that," he emphasized.

The Doctor nodded.

"Still," said the man who had admired the books, "we need the absolute if we are to keep a grasp on anything.

"Anything but these sticks and peat clods and rabbit snares," he said bitterly.

"Shelley desired an ultimate absolute," said the harsh man. "It's too much," he said. "It's no good; no earthly good."

The musician selected a Debussy[11] nocturne. The others considered and approved. They rose to their knees to watch the Doctor prepare for the playing, so that they appeared to be actually in an attitude of worship. The peat glow showed the thinness of their bearded faces, and the deep lines in them, and revealed the condition of their garments. The other two continued to kneel as the old man carefully lowered the needle onto the spinning disc, but the musician suddenly drew back against the wall again, with his knees up, and buried his face in his hands.

At the first notes of the piano, the listeners were startled. They stared at each other. Even the musician lifted his head in amazement, but then quickly bowed it again, strainingly, as if he were suffering from a pain he might not be able to endure. They were all listening deeply, without movement. The wet, blue-green notes tinkled forth from the old machine, and were individual, delectable presences in the cell. The individual, delectable presences swept into a sudden tide of unbearably beautiful dissonance, and then continued fully the swelling and ebbing of that tide, the dissonant inpourings, and the resolutions, and the diminishments, and the little, quiet wavelets of interlude lapping between. Every sound was piercing and singularly sweet. In all the men except the musician, there occurred rapid sequences of tragically heightened recollection. He heard nothing but what was there. At the final, whispering disappearance, but moving quietly so that the others would not hear him and look at him, he let his head fall back in agony, as if it were drawn there by the hair, and clenched the fingers of one hand over his teeth. He sat that way while the others were silent, and until they began to breathe again normally. His drawn-up legs were trembling violently.

Quickly Doctor Jenkins lifted the needle off, to save it and not to spoil the recollection with scraping. When he had stopped the whirling of the sacred disc, he courteously left the phonograph open and by the fire, in sight.

The others, however, understood. The musician rose last, but then abruptly, and went quickly out at the door without saying anything. The others stopped at the door and gave their thanks in low voices. The Doctor nodded magnificently.

"Come again," he invited, "in a week. We will have the 'New York.'"

When the two had gone together, out toward the rimed[12] road, he stood in the entrance, peering and listening. At first, there was only the resonant boom of the wind overhead, and then far over the dome of the dead, dark plain, the wolf cry lamenting. In the rifts of clouds, the Doctor saw four stars flying. It impressed the Doctor that one of them had just been obscured by the beginning of a flying cloud at the very moment he heard what he had been listening for, a sound of suppressed coughing. It was not nearby, however. He believed that down against the pale alders he could see the moving shadow.

With nervous hands he lowered the piece of canvas which served as his door, and pegged

10. **Shelley:** Percy Bysshe Shelley (1792–1822), English poet.

11. **Debussy** [deb′yoo sē′]: Claude Debussy (1862–1918), French composer.

12. **rimed:** frosty.

it at the bottom. Then quickly and quietly, looking at the piece of canvas frequently, he slipped the records into the case, snapped the lid shut, and carried the phonograph to his couch. There, pausing to stare at the canvas and listen, he dug earth from the wall and disclosed a piece of board. Behind this there was a deep hole in the wall into which he put the phonograph. After a moment's consideration, he went over and reached down his bundle of books and inserted it also. Then, guardedly, he once more sealed up the hole with the board and the earth. He also changed his blankets, and the grass-stuffed sack which served as a pillow, so that he could lie facing the entrance. After carefully placing two more blocks of peat upon the fire, he stood for a long time watching the stretched canvas, but it seemed to billow naturally with the first gusts of a lowering wind. At last he prayed, and got in under his blankets, and closed his smoke-smarting eyes. On the inside of the bed, next the wall, he could feel with his hand the comfortable piece of lead pipe.

STUDY QUESTIONS

Recalling

1. Identify five details in the first paragraph that help capture a bleak and desolate landscape. What are the pits that "might have been made by falling meteors" but were not?
2. To whom is the host, Doctor Jenkins, compared in the fourth paragraph? What does he say in the fourth and fifth paragraphs?
3. When the characters are introduced, what activity has just concluded? What important activity follows?
4. Describe the physical reaction that the musician has as he listens to the Debussy nocturne.
5. After his visitors have left, what does Doctor Jenkins do "with nervous hands"? Where does he put the phonograph, the records, and the books? What does he face when he lies down to sleep, and what does he feel with his hand?

Interpreting

6. What cataclysmic event has occurred that left these four men "the doddering remnant of a race of mechanical fools"? In using the term "mechanical fools," what does Doctor Jenkins suggest has caused this event?
7. Briefly describe the feelings the four men have for the books, the phonograph, and the records. What is suggested by the depiction of their activities in terms of ritual or religious ceremony?

8. Why does Doctor Jenkins hide the phonograph, records, and books after his guests leave? What is suggested by his feeling for the "comfortable piece of lead pipe"?
9. What is the irony of Doctor Jenkins' final action? What does the story suggest is the true cause of violence and destruction?

Extending

10. Do you agree with the suggestions about human nature made in this story? Why or why not?

COMPOSITION

Analyzing a Symbol

The portable phonograph is clearly the central symbol in Clark's story. Write an essay in which you analyze its significance. Begin by telling what it means to the characters in the story. Then tell what it means to you. *For help with this assignment, refer to Lesson 5 in the Writing About Literature Handbook at the back of this book.*

Creating a Time Capsule

A time capsule is designed to be found and opened by future generations. Make a list of ten things you would preserve if you had to create a time capsule to protect objects against a disaster. Write a sentence for each object, telling why your think it should be preserved and defining its value for people in the future.

Walter Van Tilburg Clark **655**

James Agee   *1909–1955*

James Agee was a poet, novelist, and screen writer. This lyrical and sensitive stylist was also one of the most incisive and influential American film critics of the 1930s and 1940s.

Agee was born in Knoxville, Tennessee, and grew up in the Cumberland Mountain region. During vacations from school he worked in wheat fields in Kansas and Nebraska. From this background he developed a strong attachment to the land, which provided a source for much of his later writing.

At Harvard, where he attended college, Agee wrote poetry and was editor of the Harvard *Advocate. Permit Me Voyage* (1934), a collection of verse, contained a foreword by the poet Archibald MacLeish (page 478), who praised Agee for his "delicate and perceptive ear."

In the summer of 1936, on a joint assignment for *Fortune* magazine, Agee and the great photographer Walker Evans lived for several weeks among sharecroppers in Alabama. Deeply affected by what he saw, he wrote a passionate and poetic commentary intended to accompany Evans' evocative photographs of the sharecroppers' life. Although the article never appeared in the magazine, both text and photographs were published in book form in 1941, as *Let Us Now Praise Famous Men.*

After 1948 Agee concentrated on writing for films, and his best scripts were *The African Queen* (1951) and *The Night of the Hunter* (1955). He also wrote a novella, *The Morning Watch* (1951), and a novel, *A Death in the Family* (1957), which was awarded the Pulitzer Prize. Agee's film criticism is collected in *Agee on Film* (1958).

Like Thomas Wolfe, James Agee was often Romantic and even undisciplined in his writing, allowing his works to take on their own shapes as they grew, without forms imposed by the author. Yet, as MacLeish noted, Agee possessed a true poet's ear and a remarkable sense of rhythm. He had a sharply perceptive eye for detail. All of these qualities give his finest prose the lyrical beauty of poetry. "Knoxville: Summer, 1915" is a perfect example of Agee's achievement—a remembrance of childhood, rich in sensory impressions and nostalgic feeling. Written in 1947, it was later added as an introduction to his masterpiece, *A Death in the Family.*

James Agee

Knoxville: Summer, 1915

We are talking now of summer evenings in Knoxville, Tennessee, in the time that I lived there so successfully disguised to myself as a child. It was a little bit mixed sort of block, fairly solidly lower middle class, with one or two juts apiece on either side of that. The houses corresponded: middle-sized gracefully fretted[1] wood houses built in the late nineties and early nineteen hundreds, with small front and side and more spacious back yards, and trees in the yards, and porches. These were softwooded trees, poplars, tulip trees, cottonwoods. There were fences around one or two of the houses, but mainly the yards ran into each other with only now and then a low hedge that wasn't doing very well. There were few good friends among the grown people, and they were not poor enough for the other sort of intimate acquaintance, but everyone nodded and spoke, and even might talk short times, trivially, and at the two extremes of the general or the particular, and ordinarily nextdoor neighbors talked quite a bit when they happened to run into each other, and never paid calls. The men were mostly small businessmen, one or two very modestly executives, one or two worked with their hands, most of them clerical, and most of them between thirty and forty-five.

But it is of these evenings I speak.

Supper was at six and was over by half past. There was still daylight, shining softly and with a tarnish, like the lining of a shell; and the carbon lamps[2] lifted at the corners were on in the light, and the locusts were started, and the fire flies were out, and a few frogs were flopping in the dewy grass, by the time the fathers and the children came out. The children ran out first hell bent and yelling those names by which they were known; then the fathers sank out leisurely in crossed suspenders, their collars removed and their necks looking tall and shy. The mothers stayed back in the kitchen washing and drying, putting things away, recrossing their traceless footsteps like the lifetime journeys of bees, measuring out the dry cocoa for breakfast. When they came out they had taken off their aprons and their skirts were dampened and they sat in rockers on their porches quietly.

It is not of the games children play in the evening that I want to speak now, it is of a contemporaneous atmosphere that has little to do with them: that of the fathers of families, each in his space of lawn, his shirt fishlike pale in the unnatural light and his face nearly anonymous, hosing their lawns. The hoses were attached at spiggots that stood out of the brick foundations of the houses. The nozzles were variously set but usually so there was a long sweet stream of spray, the nozzle wet in the hand, the water trickling the right forearm and the peeled-back cuff, and the water whishing out a long loose and low-curved cone, and so gentle a sound. First an insane noise of violence in the nozzle, then the still irregular sound of adjustment, then the smoothing into steadiness and a pitch as accurately tuned to the size and style of stream as any violin. So many qualities of sound out of one hose: so many choral differences out of those several hoses that were in earshot. Out of any one hose, the almost dead silence of the release, and the short still arch of the separate big drops, silent as a held breath, and the only noise the flattering noise on leaves and the slapped grass at the fall of each big drop. That, and the intense hiss with the intense stream; that, and that same intensity not growing less but growing more quiet and delicate with the

1. **fretted:** having ornamental borders of symmetrically arranged vertical and horizontal straight lines.
2. **carbon lamps:** lamps with carbon filaments.

turn of the nozzle, up to that extreme tender whisper when the water was just a wide bell of film. Chiefly, though, the hoses were set much alike, in a compromise between distance and tenderness of spray (and quite surely a sense of art behind this compromise, and a quiet deep joy, too real to recognize itself), and the sounds therefore were pitched much alike; pointed by the snorting start of a new hose; decorated by some man playful with the nozzle; left empty, like God by the sparrow's fall, when any single one of them desists: and all, though near alike, of various pitch; and in this unison. These sweet pale streamings in the light lift out their pallors and their voices all together, mothers hushing their children, the hushing unnaturally prolonged, the men gentle and silent and each snail-like withdrawn into the quietude of what he singly is doing, and gentle happy and peaceful, tasting the mean[3] goodness of their living like the last of their suppers in their mouths; while the locusts carry on this noise of hoses on their much higher and sharper key. The noise of the locust is dry, and it seems not to be rasped or vibrated but urged from him as if through a small orifice by a breath that can never give out. Also there is never one locust but an illusion of at least a thousand. The noise of each locust is pitched in some classic locust range out of which none of them varies more than two full tones: and yet you seem to hear each locust discrete from all the rest, and there is a long, slow, pulse in their noise, like the scarcely defined arch of a long and high set bridge. They are all around in every tree, so that the noise seems to come from nowhere and everywhere at once, from the whole shell heaven, shivering in your flesh and teasing your eardrums, the boldest of all the sounds of night. And yet it is habitual to summer nights, and is of the great order of noises, like the noises of the sea and of the blood her precocious grandchild, which you realize you are hearing only when you catch yourself listening.

Meantime from low in the dark, just outside the swaying horizons of the hoses, conveying always grass in the damp of dew and its strong green-black smear of smell, the regular yet spaced noises of the crickets, each a sweet cold silver noise three-noted, like the slipping each time of three matched links of a small chain.

But the men by now, one by one, have silenced their hoses and drained and coiled them. Now only two, and now only one, is left, and you see only ghostlike shirt with the sleeve garters,[4] and sober mystery of his mild face like the lifted face of large cattle enquiring of your presence in a pitchdark pool of meadow; and now he too is gone; and it has become that time of evening when people sit on their porches, rocking gently and talking gently and watching the street and the standing up into their sphere of possession of the trees, of birds hung havens, hangars. People go by; things go by. A horse, drawing a buggy, breaking his hollow iron music on the asphalt; a loud auto; a quiet auto; people in pairs, not in a hurry, scuffling, switching their weight of aestival[5] body, talking casually, the taste hovering over them of vanilla, strawberry, pasteboard and starched milk, the image upon them of lovers and horsemen, squared with clowns in hueless amber. A streetcar raising its iron moan; stopping, belling and starting; stertorous;[6] rousing and raising again its iron increasing moan and swimming its gold windows and straw seats on past and past and past, the bleak spark crackling and cursing above it like a small malignant spirit set to dog its tracks; the iron whine rises on rising speed; still risen, faints; halts; the faint stinging bell; rises again, still fainter, fainting, lifting, lifts, faints forgone: forgotten. Now is the night one blue dew.

Now is the night one blue dew, my father has drained, he has coiled the hose.

---

4. **sleeve garters:** elastic bands worn over shirt sleeves to regulate their length.
5. **aestival** [es′tə vəl]: relating to summer.
6. **stertorous:** loud, raspy.

---

3. **mean:** humble.

A scene in Knoxville, Tennessee, c. 1915.

Low on the length of lawns, a frailing[7] of fire who breathes.

Content, silver, like peeps of light, each cricket makes his comment over and over in the drowned grass.

A cold toad thumpily flounders.

Within the edges of damp shadows of side yards are hovering children nearly sick with joy of fear, who watch the unguarding of a telephone pole.

Around white carbon corner lamps bugs of all sizes are lifted elliptic, solar systems. Big hardshells bruise themselves, assailant: he is fallen on his back, legs squiggling.

Parents on porches: rock and rock: From damp strings morning glories: hang their ancient faces.

The dry and exalted noise of the locusts from all the air at once enchants my eardrums.

On the rough wet grass of the back yard my father and mother have spread quilts. We all lie there, my mother, my father, my uncle, my aunt, and I too am lying there. First we were sitting up, then one of us lay down, and

_____
7. **frailing:** delicate light.

then we all lay down, on our stomachs, or on our sides, or on our backs, and they have kept on talking. They are not talking much, and the talk is quiet, of nothing in particular, of nothing at all in particular, of nothing at all. The stars are wide and alive, they seem each like a smile of great sweetness, and they seem very near. All my people are larger bodies than mine, quiet, with voices gentle and meaningless like the voices of sleeping birds. One is an artist, he is living at home. One is a musician, she is living at home. One is my mother who is good to me. One is my father who is good to me. By some chance, here they are, all on this earth; and who shall ever tell the sorrow of being on this earth, lying, on quilts, on the grass, in a summer evening, among the sounds of night. May God bless my people, my uncle, my aunt, my mother, my good father, oh, remember them kindly in their time of trouble; and in the hour of their taking away.

After a little I am taken in and put to bed. Sleep, soft smiling, draws me unto her: and those receive me, who quietly treat me, as one familiar and well-beloved in that home: but will not, oh, will not, not now, not ever; but will not ever tell me who I am.

STUDY QUESTIONS

Recalling

1. According to the opening paragraph, what are the narrator's subject and setting (time *and* place)?
2. Name at least three sounds of the summer evening that the narrator describes. What three "categories" of people are described in the third paragraph?
3. Who lies on the quilts in the next-to-last paragraph? Of what do they speak? What prayer does the narrator offer at the end of the paragraph?
4. What is the narrator's closing thought?

Interpreting

5. Briefly describe the style in which this story is written. Why is the poem in the middle of the story less of an interruption than it would be in many other prose narratives?
6. What particular qualities of the life pictured here emerge by the story's end? What seems to be the narrator's attitude toward his family? Give details to support your answer.
7. What does the final paragraph suggest about the narrator's reasons for remembering his childhood in such detail? What does it suggest such memories can never do to the narrator's satisfaction?

Extending

8. To what extent do you think our childhood environment determines who we are? What other factors do you think are important in determining our personalities? Discuss.

COMPOSITION

Writing a Comparison/Contrast

■ Write a short essay comparing the poetic style of "Knoxville: Summer, 1915" to the spare style of Hemingway's "In Another Country" (page 518). Begin by describing the author's purpose in each selection. Then explain how each author's style relates to his purpose, giving examples from the selection to support your descriptions of each author's style. Conclude with your own opinion of the total effect of each of the styles on the reader. *For help with this assignment, refer to Lesson 2 in the Writing About Literature Handbook at the back of this book.*

Writing an Evocative Remembrance

■ Remember an experience or a place that still gives you a special feeling when you think of it. Describe your recollection as imaginatively and as clearly as you can. Include details that evoke sensory impressions, such as particular sounds, sights, and smells.

Elizabeth Enright   *1909–1968*

Elizabeth Enright began her career as an illustrator of children's books. She wrote several stories to accompany her illustrations and later stopped illustrating in order to concentrate on writing.

Enright was born in Oak Park, Illinois, but lived most of her life in New York City. Her parents were professional artists, her mother an illustrator, her father a political cartoonist; her uncle was the famous architect Frank Lloyd Wright. As a child in this "environment of paint brushes and India ink and water colors and drawing boards," Elizabeth Enright enjoyed imitating her parents. By her own account, she drew all over telephone books, blackboards, sidewalks, her mother's best writing paper, and, when no other medium was available, on her own bare knees.

She studied art in New York and Paris, and after several years as an illustrator for magazines, she published her first book, *Kintu: A Congo Adventure* (1955), for which she supplied the text as well. *Borrowed Summer and Other Stories* (1946) contains her first writing for adults. It was followed by *The Moment Before the Rain* (1955), *The Riddle of the Fly and Other Stories* (1959), and *Doublefields: Memories and Stories* (1966).

One critic noted that Enright's best stories are "seen through the disabused [undeceived] eyes of women." The main character in "The Signature" is a good example of such a woman. In detailing her quest for identity—a common quest in post–World War II fiction—Enright also makes some strong comments about the possible future identities of us all.

Elizabeth Enright

The Signature

The street was wide and sloped gently upward ahead of me. It was paved with hard-baked dust almost white in the early-afternoon light, dry as clay and decked with bits of refuse. On either side the wooden houses stood blind to the street, all their shutters closed. The one- and two-story buildings—some of them set back a little; there was no sidewalk—had door yards with dusted grass and bushes, but many of them stood flush to the road itself with nothing but a powdered weed or two for grace. All of the houses had an old, foreign look, and all were unpainted, weather-scoured to the same pale color, except for the eaves of some which had been trimmed with wooden zigzags and painted long ago, like the crude, faded shutters, in tones of blue or red.

The sky was blanched with light, fronded with cirrus,[1] unemphatic; just such a sky as one finds near the sea, and this, in addition to the scoured, dry, enduring look of the town, persuaded me that an ocean or harbor must be somewhere near at hand. But when I came up over the rise of the road, I could find no furred line of blue at any horizon. All I could see was the great town—no, it was a city—spread far and wide, low lying, sun bleached, and unknown to me. And this was only one more thing that was unknown to me, for not only was I ignorant of the name of the city, but I was ignorant of my own name, and of my own life, and nothing that I seized on could offer me a clue. I looked at my hands: they were the hands of a middle-aged women, coarsening at the joints, faintly blotched. On the third finger of the left hand there was a golden wedding ring, but who had put it there I could not guess. My body in the dark dress, my dust-chalked shoes were also strangers to me, and I

was frightened and felt that I had been frightened for a long time, so long that the feeling had become habitual—something that I could live with, in a pinch, or, more properly, something that until this moment I had felt that I could live with. But now I was in terror of my puzzle.

I had the conviction that if I could once see my own face, I would remember who and what I was, and why I was in this place. I searched for a pane of glass to give me my reflection, but every window was shuttered fast. It was a season of drought, too, and there was not so much as a puddle to look into; in my pocket there was no mirror and my purse contained only a few bills of a currency unknown to me. I took the bills out and looked at them; they were old and used and the blue numerals and characters engraved on them were also of a sort I had never seen before, or could not remember having seen. In the center of each bill, where ordinarily one finds the pictures of a statesman or a monarch, there was instead an angular, spare symbol: a laterally elongated diamond shape with a heavy vertical line drawn through it at the center, rather like an abstraction of the human eye. As I resumed my walking I was aware of an impression that I had seen this symbol recently and often, in other places, and at the very moment I was thinking this I came upon it again, drawn in chalk on the side of a house. After that, watching for it, I saw it several times: marked in the dirt of the road, marked on the shutters, carved on the railing of a fence.

It was this figure, this eye-diamond, which reminded me, by its persistence, that the eye of another person can be a little mirror, and now with a feeling of excitement, of possible hope, I began walking faster, in search of a face.

From time to time I had passed other peo-

---

1. **fronded . . . cirrus:** having high, wispy clouds resembling fern leaves ("fronds").

ple, men and women, in the street. Their dark, anonymous clothes were like the clothes of Italian peasants, but the language they spoke was not Italian, nor did it resemble any language I had ever heard, and many of their faces had a fair Northern color. I noticed when I met these people that the answering looks they gave me, while attentive, were neither inimical[2] nor friendly. They looked at me with that certain privilege shared by kings and children, as if they possessed the right to judge, while being ignorant of, or exempt from, accepting judgment in return. There is no answer to this look and appeal is difficult, for one is already in a defensive position. Still, I had tried to appeal to them; several times I had addressed the passers-by hoping that one of them might understand me and tell me where I was, but no one could or would. They shook their heads or lifted their empty hands, and while they did not appear hostile, neither did they smile in answer to my pleading smiles. After they had passed I thought it strange that I never heard a whisper or a laugh or any added animation in their talk. It was apparently a matter of complete indifference to them that they had been approached in the street by a stranger speaking a strange language.

Knowing these things I thought that it might be difficult to accomplish my purpose, and indeed this proved to be the case. The next people I met were three women walking together; two were young and one was middle-aged. I approached the taller of the young women, for her eyes were on a level with my own, and looking steadily into them and coming close, I spoke to her.

"Can you tell me where I am?" I said to her. "Can you understand what I am saying?"

The words were a device, I expected no answer and got none of any sort. As I drew close she looked down at the ground; she would not meet my gaze. A little smile moved the corners of her lips, and she stepped aside. When I turned to her companions they also looked

away, smiling. This expression on other faces might have been called embarrassment, but not on theirs. The smile they shared seemed noncommittal, secretive, knowledgeable in a way that I could not fathom, and afterward I thought it curious that they had shown no surprise.

For a long time after that I met no one at all. I met no cat, no dog, no cabbage butterfly; not even an ant on the packed, bald dust of the road, and finally rejecting its ugliness and light I turned to the left along another street, narrower and as graceless, and walked by the same monotony of weather-beaten houses. After a few minutes I heard a sound that halted me and I stood listening. Somewhere not far away I heard children's voices. Though their words were foreign they spoke also in the common tongue of children everywhere: voices high, eruptive, excited, sparked with the universal jokes, chants, quarrels of play; and here, listening to them, my memory stirred for the first time—a memory of memory, in fact. For whatever it was that nearly illuminated consciousness was not the memory itself, but a remnant of light which glowed on the periphery of the obstacle before it: a penumbra.

Where are the children, I thought; where are they! With great urgency and longing I set out in the direction of their voices, determined to find them and in doing so to find something of myself. Their voices chattered, skipped, squabbled like the voices of sparrows, never far away, but though I turned and hunted and listened and pursued I could not find them. I never found them, and after a while I could not hear them either. The ghostly light of memory faded and was extinguished, and my despair rose up in darkness to take its place.

The next person I met was a man, young and dark-browed, and when I confronted him and asked my questions, it was without hope. I knew he would not meet my look, or let his eyes show me my longed-for, dreaded face. Yet here I was wrong; he stood before me without speaking, but the gaze with which he answered mine was so intense and undeviating that it

_____
2. **inimical:** hostile.

was I who dropped my eyes and stepped aside. I could not look, and soon I heard him going on his way.

I had been walking a long time, and the light was changing; the sun was low and full in my face. West, I said to myself; at least I know west, and I know that I am a woman, and that that is the sun. When the stars come out I will know those, too, and perhaps they will tell me something else.

After a while I sat down on a wooden step to rest. I was struck by the silence of the city around me, and I realized this was because it was a city of walkers who walked on dust instead of on pavements. I remembered that I had seen no mark of a wheel on any road, and that nothing had moved in the sky all day except for a few birds in flight.

A breath of dry wind crept along the dust at my feet, and, far away, a noise of knocking started, a sound of stakes being driven into the ground with a wooden mallet. Desolate, reiterated, it sounded as though somewhere in the city they were preparing a gallows or a barricade. Too tired and dispirited to move I sat there listening to the double knock-and-echo of each blow. A few people passed me on their way home, each of them giving me the glance of casual appraisal I had seen so often. Doors opened and doors closed, the sun went down, and soon the street was still again and the knocking stopped. Where would I sleep that night, or find a meal? I neither knew nor cared.

One by one the stars came out on the deepening sky, perfect, still, as if they were really what they seemed to be—calm ornaments for hope, promises of stillness and forever.

I looked for Venus, then Polaris,[3] then for Mars. I could not find them, and as the stars grew in number, coming imperceptibly into their light, I saw with slow-growing shock that these were not the stars I knew. The messages of this night sky were written in a language of constellations I had never seen or dreamed. I stared up at the brand-new Catherine wheels,[4] insignias, and fiery thorn crowns on the sky, and I do not think that I was really surprised when I spied at the zenith, small but bright, a constellation shaped like an elongated diamond, like the glittering abstraction of a human eye. . . .

It was just at this moment, before I could marshal or identify my thoughts in the face of such a development, that I heard a sound of trees, wind in the leaves of trees, and I realized, irrelevantly it seemed, that in all my walking in this city—how many hours, how many days?—I had not seen a single tree, and the sound of their presence was as welcome as the sound of rain is after a siege of drought. As I stood up it occurred to me that neither had I seen one child among all the strangers I had met, that though I had heard the children I had not been able to find them, and now to all the other fears was added the fear that the trees, too, would magically elude me.

The street was dark, though light was glimmering through the cracks of the closed shutters. What was left of sunset, green as water, lay on the western horizon. Yet was it really western? In a sky of new stars, was it not possible and in fact probable that what I had believed to be the sun was not really Sun at all? Then what were the compass points, what were the easts and wests of this city? And what would I find when once I found myself?

I heard the beckoning of trees again and as if they were the clue to sanity, I ran along the street in the direction of their sound. I turned a corner, and there, ah yes, there were the trees: a grove of tall, dry, paper-murmuring trees that grew in a little park or public garden where people were walking together or sitting on the dusty grass. At the center of this park or garden there was a great house of stone, the first stone building I had seen all day. It was lighted from top to bottom; the lights of its long windows twittered in gold among the

---

3. **Polaris:** North Star.

4. **Catherine wheels:** wheels with projecting spikes used in fireworks.

small leaves of the trees, and a door stood open at the head of a flight of steps.

I passed many people on the path, but now I did not look at them or ask them questions. I knew that there was nothing they could do for me. I walked straight to the steps and up them and through the door into the lighted house. It was empty, as I had expected, a great empty ringing house, but there was a splendor about it, even in its emptiness, as if those who had left it—and left it recently—had been creatures of joy, better than people and gayer than gods. But they, whoever they were, had gone. My footsteps sounded on the barren floor, and the talk of the loiterers outside, the foreign talk, came in the windows clearly on the night air.

The mirror was at the end of the hall. I walked toward it with my fists closed, and my heart walked, too, heavily in my chest. I watched the woman's figure in the dark dress and the knees moving forward. When I was close to it, I saw, low in the right-hand corner of the mirror, the scratched small outline of the eye-diamond, a signature, carved on the surface of the glass by whom, and in what cold spirit of raillery?[5] Lifting my head, I looked at my own face. I leaned forward and looked closely at my face, and I remembered everything. I remembered everything. And I knew the name of the city I would never leave, and, alas, I understood the language of its citizens.

---

5. **raillery:** taunting; teasing.

STUDY QUESTIONS

Recalling

1. How are the houses of the city described in the opening paragraph?
2. Of what things is the narrator ignorant, according to the second paragraph? What emotion does she feel? What "conviction" does she have in the third paragraph?
3. What does the narrator see on the currency in her purse? Where else does she see this sign in the third paragraph? Of what does the sign remind her?
4. How do the people on the street react when the narrator addresses them? How does the young, dark-browed man react, and why does the narrator drop her eyes and step aside?
5. What does the narrator think the knocking noises that she hears might be?
6. What does the narrator find at the end of the hall? What "signature" is on it? What happens when she looks into it? What does she know at the end of the story?

Interpreting

7. What do the shuttered windows, the passersby, the absence of children, and the knocking sounds all suggest about the world in which the narrator finds herself?

8. In what way is the eye-diamond unlike a usual signature?
9. Identify the kind of world in which the narrator finds herself. What does the final sentence suggest about her feelings?

Extending

10. How might this story be an allegory about the modern world?

COMPOSITION

Analyzing the Total Effect of a Story

Write a short essay analyzing the total effect of "The Signature." Begin with a statement about the overall impact of the story. Then explain how the author uses the following literary elements to achieve this effect: plot, character, setting, point of view, and tone. *For help with this assignment, refer to Lesson 8 in the Writing About Literature Handbook at the back of this book.*

Creating a Futuristic Setting

Write a brief description of what you think the future will be like in the place where you live. You may want to organize your description by concentrating on the sensory elements of a setting: sight, sound, smell, taste, and touch.

William Faulkner   *1897–1962*

William Faulkner created in literature a cosmos of his own, an entire world apart. Yoknapatawpha County was the name of his imagined landscape, and he proudly claimed to be its "Sole Owner and Proprietor." He populated it with a broad spectrum of remarkable characters—farmers, hunters, aristocrats, businessmen, former black slaves, dispossessed Indians, and several generations of whole families moving on different levels of southern society. He set his characters in country he knew well and against a background of history he profoundly understood. One of the greatest of American writers, Faulkner created a kind of mythical kingdom that exists simultaneously in the past and in the present.

William Faulkner spent most of his life in Oxford, Mississippi. His family was proud of its southern heritage, especially proud of a great-grandfather, Colonel William Clark Falkner, who had served with distinction in the Confederate Army, later built railroads, and had even written a popular Romantic novel, *The White Rose of Memphis*. When Faulkner was in third grade, he was asked what he wanted to do when he grew up. His prompt reply: "I want to be a writer like my great-granddaddy."

Faulkner's early experiences were varied. He loved to read, was curious about foreign literature, and even taught himself French. In 1918 he enlisted as a student flyer in the Royal Canadian Air Force but returned to Oxford a year later to attend the University of Mississippi. By then he had begun to write seriously, though his earliest efforts were in poetry.

In 1924, hoping to find work in journalism, Faulkner went to New Orleans, where he became friends with the prominent novelist and short story writer Sherwood Anderson (page 504). In that year his first book, a collection of verse entitled *The Marble Faun,* was published, but sales were poor. On Anderson's advice, Faulkner wrote his first novel, set in the South and called *Soldier's Pay*. With Anderson's recommendation, the novel was published.

After a brief stay in Europe, Faulkner returned to Oxford, where for the next few years he worked as a carpenter, house painter, deckhand, even as a golf professional—and wrote feverishly, mostly at night. He turned out poems and stories, a second novel, *Mosquitoes* (1927), and a third, *Flags in the Dust* (1927)—the first of his novels to be set in Yoknapatawpha County. Nevertheless, publishers ignored him, and, convinced that his work would never again appear in print, he decided abruptly to stop worrying about publication. "One day I seemed to shut a door," he remembered, "between me and all publishers' addresses and book lists. I said to myself, Now I can write."

At this point Faulkner embarked on what was to become his major phase, producing several books now considered to be among the greatest American novels. From 1929 to 1942, he completed two collections of stories, a second volume of poetry, and ten novels, including *The Sound and the Fury* (1929), *As I Lay Dying* (1930), *Light in August* (1932), *Absalom, Absalom!* (1936), and *The Unvanquished* (1938). Still, in spite of his great productivity, the respect of other writers, and the genuine appreciation of a handful of critics, he remained virtually unknown to the general reading public.

The complexity of Faulkner's writing style contributed to his continued obscurity. Faulkner's works are full of repetition, inconsistent punctuation, long and puzzling sentences, flashbacks, and multiple points of view. He often wrote in the stream-of-consciousness mode (see page 610). To further complicate matters, the consciousness he presented was sometimes that of a child, an idiot, or a person on the edge of madness. But as readers now understand, the difficulty of the style was in keeping with the complexity of the subject. For it was part of Faulkner's aim to represent in the consciousness of his characters the tangled interrelationships between the modern American present and the historical past.

By 1945, although his work was admired abroad—in France, especially—all seventeen of Faulkner's books had gone out of print. The great change came in 1946 with the publication of *The Portable Faulkner,* a selection of his works edited by the sympathetic critic Malcolm Cowley. A remarkable renewal of interest in Faulkner took place, as if suddenly people understood what they had not seen before. Critics began to reassess him, readers took a second look at what copies of his works they could find, and his publisher began reprinting his books. In 1950 Faulkner's *Collected Stories* won the National Book Award, and Faulkner himself was awarded the Nobel Prize.

Yoknapatawpha County stands as a grand allegory about the real American South in history. But beyond that, it is an evocation of the tremendous variety of human experience and the struggle of the human spirit everywhere. In his Nobel Prize Acceptance Speech (see page 680), Faulkner urged all writers to concern themselves above all with "the old universal truths . . . courage and honor and hope and pride and compassion and pity and sacrifice. . . ." His most famous story, "The Bear," seems at first the tale of a boy learning to hunt; by the end the boy's experience has also encompassed those "old universal truths."

William Faulkner

The Bear

He was ten. But it had already begun, long before that day when at last he wrote his age in two figures and he saw for the first time the camp where his father and Major de Spain and old General Compson and the others spent two weeks each November and two weeks again each June. He had already inherited then, without ever having seen it, the tremendous bear with one trap-ruined foot which, in an area almost a hundred miles deep, had earned for itself a name, a definite designation like a living man.

He had listened to it for years: the long legend of corncribs rifled, of shotes[1] and grown pigs and even calves carried bodily into the woods and devoured, of traps and deadfalls[2] overthrown and dogs mangled and slain, and shotgun and even rifle charges delivered at point-blank range and with no more effect than so many peas blown through a tube by a boy— a corridor of wreckage and destruction beginning back before he was born, through which sped, not fast but rather with the ruthless and irresistible deliberation of a locomotive, the shaggy tremendous shape.

It ran in his knowledge before he ever saw it. It looked and towered in his dreams before he even saw the unaxed woods where it left its crooked print, shaggy, huge, red-eyed, not malevolent but just big—too big for the dogs which tried to bay[3] it, for the horses which tried to ride it down, for the men and the bullets they fired into it, too big for the very country which was its constricting scope. He seemed to see it entire with a child's complete divination before he ever laid eyes on either— the doomed wilderness whose edges were being constantly and punily gnawed at by men with axes and plows who feared it because it

was wilderness, men myriad and nameless even to one another in the land where the old bear had earned a name, through which ran not even a mortal animal but an anachronism,[4] indomitable and invincible, out of an old dead time, a phantom, epitome and apotheosis[5] of the old wild life at which the puny humans swarmed and hacked in a fury of abhorrence and fear, like pygmies about the ankles of a drowsing elephant; the old bear solitary, indomitable and alone, widowered, childless and absolved of mortality—old Priam[6] reft of his old wife and having outlived all his sons.

Until he was ten, each November he would watch the wagon containing the dogs and the bedding and food and guns and his father and Tennie's Jim, the Negro, and Sam Fathers, the Indian, son of a slave woman and a Chickasaw[7] chief, depart on the road to town, to Jefferson, where Major de Spain and the others would join them. To the boy, at seven and eight and nine, they were not going into the Big Bottom to hunt bear and deer, but to keep yearly rendezvous with the bear which they did not even intend to kill. Two weeks later they would return, with no trophy, no head and skin. He had not expected it. He had not even been afraid it would be in the wagon. He believed that even after he was ten and his father would let him go too, for those two November weeks, he would merely make another one, along with his father and Major de Spain and General Compson and the others, the dogs which feared to bay it and the rifles and shotguns

---

1. **shotes:** young pigs.
2. **deadfalls:** traps that drop heavy weights on prey.
3. **bay:** bark at and chase in an attempt to corner.

4. **anachronism** [ə nak'rə niz'əm]: something that seems to exist out of its proper time.
5. **epitome** [i pit'ə mē] . . . **apotheosis** [ə poth'ē ō'sis]: most typical and most ideal.
6. **Priam** [prī'əm]: last king of Troy during Trojan War. His wife and sons were killed when the Greeks invaded.
7. **Chickasaw:** tribe of Indians originally from northern Mississippi and parts of Tennessee.

which failed even to bleed it, in the yearly pageant of the old bear's furious immortality.

Then he heard the dogs. It was in the second week of his first time in the camp. He stood with Sam Fathers against a big oak beside the faint crossing where they had stood each dawn for nine days now, hearing the dogs. He had heard them once before, one morning last week—a murmur, sourceless, echoing through the wet woods, swelling presently into separate voices which he could recognize and call by name. He had raised and cocked the gun as Sam told him and stood motionless again while the uproar, the invisible course, swept up and past and faded; it seemed to him that he could actually see the deer, the buck, blond, smoke-colored, elongated with speed, fleeing, vanishing, the woods, the gray solitude, still ringing even when the cries of the dogs had died away.

"Now let the hammers down," Sam said.

"You knew they were not coming here too," he said.

"Yes," Sam said, "I want you to learn how to do when you didn't shoot. It's after the chance for the bear or the deer has done already come and gone that men and dogs get killed."

"Anyway," he said, "it was just a deer."

Then on the tenth morning he heard the dogs again. And he readied the too-long, too-heavy gun as Sam had taught him, before Sam even spoke. But this time it was no deer, no ringing chorus of dogs running strong on a free scent, but a moiling[8] yapping an octave too high, with something more than indecision and even abjectness in it, not even moving very fast, taking a long time to pass completely out of hearing, leaving even then somewhere in the air that echo, thin, slightly hysterical, abject, almost grieving, with no sense of a fleeing, unseen, smoke-colored, grass-eating shape ahead of it, and Sam, who had taught him first of all to cock the gun and take position where he could see everywhere and then never move

again, had himself moved up beside him; he could hear Sam breathing at his shoulder and he could see the arched curve of the old man's inhaling nostrils.

"Hah," Sam said. "Not even running. Walking."

"Old Ben!" the boy said. "But up here!" he cried. "Way up here!"

"He do it every year," Sam said. "Once. Maybe to see who in camp this time, if he can shoot or not. Whether we got the dog yet that can bay and hold him. He'll take them to the river, then he'll send them back home. We may as well go back, too; see how they look when they come back to camp."

When they reached the camp the hounds were already there, ten of them crouching back under the kitchen, the boy and Sam squatting to peer back into the obscurity where they huddled, quiet, the eyes luminous, glowing at them and vanishing, and no sound, only that effluvium[9] of something more than dog, stronger than dog and not just animal, just beast, because still there had been nothing in front of that abject and almost painful yapping save the solitude, the wilderness, so that when the eleventh hound came in at noon and with all the others watching—even old Uncle Ash, who called himself first a cook—Sam daubed the tattered ear and the raked shoulder with turpentine and axle grease, to the boy it was still no living creature, but the wilderness which, leaning for the moment down, had patted lightly once the hound's temerity.

"Just like a man," Sam said. "Just like folks. Put off as long as she could having to be brave, knowing all the time that sooner or later she would have to be brave once to keep on living with herself, and knowing all the time beforehand what was going to happen to her when she done it."

That afternoon, himself on the one-eyed wagon mule which did not mind the smell of blood nor, as they told him, of bear, and with Sam on the other one, they rode for more than three hours through the rapid, shortening win-

---

8. **moiling:** confused.

9. **effluvium** [i floo′vē əm]: disagreeable odor.

ter day. They followed no path, no trail even that he could see; almost at once they were in a country which he had never seen before. Then he knew why Sam had made him ride the mule which would not spook. The sound one stopped short and tried to whirl and bolt even as Sam got down, blowing its breath, jerking and wrenching at the rein while Sam held it, coaxing it forward with his voice, since he could not risk tying it, drawing it forward while the boy got down from the marred one.

Then, standing beside Sam in the gloom of the dying afternoon, he looked down at the rotted overturned log, gutted and scored with claw marks and, in the wet earth beside it, the print of the enormous warped two-toed foot. He knew now what he had smelled when he peered under the kitchen where the dogs huddled. He realized for the first time that the bear which had run in his listening and loomed in his dreams since before he could remember to the contrary, and which, therefore, must have existed in the listening and dreams of his father and Major de Spain and even old General Compson, too, before they began to remember in their turn, was a mortal animal, and that if they had departed for the camp each November without any actual hope of bringing its trophy back, it was not because it could not be slain, but because so far they had had no actual hope to.

"Tomorrow," he said.

"We'll try tomorrow," Sam said. "We ain't got the dog yet."

"We've got eleven. They ran him this morning."

"It won't need but one," Sam said. "He ain't here. Maybe he ain't nowhere. The only other way will be for him to run by accident over somebody that has a gun."

"That wouldn't be me," the boy said. "It will be Walter or Major or—"

"It might," Sam said. "You watch close in the morning. Because he's smart. That's how come he has lived this long. If he gets hemmed up and has to pick out somebody to run over, he will pick out you."

"How?" the boy said. "How will he know—" He ceased. "You mean he already knows me, that I ain't never been here before, ain't had time to find out yet whether I—" He ceased again, looking at Sam, the old man whose face revealed nothing until it smiled. He said humbly, not even amazed, "It was me he was watching. I don't reckon he did need to come but once."

The next morning they left the camp three hours before daylight. They rode this time because it was too far to walk, even the dogs in the wagon; again the first gray light found him in a place which he had never seen before, where Sam had placed him and told him to stay and then departed. With the gun which was too big for him, which did not even belong to him, but to Major de Spain, and which he had fired only once—at a stump on the first day, to learn the recoil and how to reload it—he stood against a gum tree beside a little bayou[10] whose black still water crept without movement out of a canebrake[11] and crossed a small clearing and into cane again, where, invisible, a bird—the big woodpecker called Lord-to-God by Negroes— clattered at a dead limb.

It was a stand like any other, dissimilar only in incidentals to the one where he had stood each morning for ten days; a territory new to him, yet no less familiar than that other one which, after almost two weeks, he had come to believe he knew a little—the same solitude, the same loneliness through which human beings had merely passed without altering it, leaving no mark, no scar, which looked exactly as it must have looked when the first ancestor of Sam Fathers' Chickasaw predecessors crept into it and looked about, club or stone ax or bone arrow drawn and poised; different only because, squatting at the edge of the kitchen, he smelled the hounds huddled and cringing beneath it and saw the raked ear and shoulder of the one who, Sam said, had had to be brave once in order to live with herself, and saw yesterday in the earth beside the gutted log the print of the living foot.

---

10. **bayou** [bī′ oo]: marshy inlet of a lake or river.
11. **canebrake**: dense growth of cane plants.

He heard no dogs at all. He never did hear them. He only heard the drumming of the woodpecker stop short off and knew that the bear was looking at him. He never saw it. He did not know whether it was in front of him or behind him. He did not move, holding the useless gun, which he had not even had warning to cock and which even now he did not cock, tasting in his saliva that taint as of brass which he knew now because he had smelled it when he peered under the kitchen at the huddled dogs.

Then it was gone. As abruptly as it had ceased, the woodpecker's dry, monotonous clatter set up again, and after a while he even believed he could hear the dogs—a murmur, scarce a sound even, which he had probably been hearing for some time before he even remarked it, drifting into hearing and then out again, dying away. They came nowhere near him. If it was a bear they ran, it was another

bear. It was Sam himself who came out of the cane and crossed the bayou, followed by the injured bitch of yesterday. She was almost at heel, like a bird dog, making no sound. She came and crouched against his leg, trembling, staring off into the cane.

"I didn't see him," he said. "I didn't, Sam!"

"I know it," Sam said. "He done the looking. You didn't hear him neither, did you?"

"No," the boy said. "I—"

"He's smart," Sam said. "Too smart." He looked down at the hound, trembling faintly and steadily against the boy's knee. From the raked shoulder a few drops of fresh blood oozed and clung. "Too big. We ain't got the dog yet. But maybe someday. Maybe not next time. But someday."

So I must see him, he thought. *I must look at him.* Otherwise, it seemed to him that it would go on like this forever, as it had gone on with his father and Major de Spain, who was older than his father, and even with old General Compson, who had been old enough to be a brigade commander in 1865. Otherwise, it would go on so forever, next time and next time, after and after and after. It seemed to him that he could see the two of them, himself and the bear, shadowy in the limbo from which time emerged, becoming time; the old bear absolved of mortality and himself partaking, sharing a little of it, enough of it. And he knew now what he had smelled in the huddled dogs and tasted in his saliva. He recognized fear. *So I will have to see him,* he thought, without dread or even hope. *I will have to look at him.*

It was in June of the next year. He was eleven. They were in camp again, celebrating Major de Spain's and General Compson's birthdays. Although the one had been born in September and the other in the depth of winter and in another decade, they had met for two weeks to fish and shoot squirrels and turkey and run coons and wildcats with the dogs at night. That is, he and Boon Hoggenbeck and the Negroes fished and shot squirrels and ran the coons and cats, because the proved hunters, not only Major de Spain and old General Compson, who spent those two weeks sitting in a rocking chair before a tremendous iron pot of Brunswick stew, stirring and tasting, with old Ash to quarrel with about how he was making it and Tennie's Jim to pour whisky from the demijohn[12] into the tin dipper from which he drank it, but even the boy's father and Walter Ewell, who were still young enough, scorned such, other than shooting the wild gobblers with pistols for wagers on their marksmanship.

Or, that is, his father and the others believed he was hunting squirrels. Until the third day he thought that Sam Fathers believed that too. Each morning he would leave the camp

---

12. **demijohn:** large wicker-covered bottle with a narrow neck and handle.

right after breakfast. He had his own gun now, a Christmas present. He went back to the tree beside the little bayou where he had stood that morning. Using the compass which old General Compson had given him, he ranged from that point; he was teaching himself to be a better-than-fair woodsman without knowing he was doing it. On the second day he even found the gutted log where he had first seen the crooked print. It was almost completely crumbled now, healing with unbelievable speed, a passionate and almost visible relinquishment, back into the earth from which the tree had grown.

He ranged the summer woods now, green with gloom; if anything, actually dimmer than in November's gray dissolution, where, even at noon, the sun fell only in intermittent dappling upon the earth, which never completely dried out and which crawled with snakes—moccasins and water snakes and rattlers, themselves the color of the dappled gloom, so that he would not always see them until they moved, returning later and later, first day, second day, passing in the twilight of the third evening the little log pen enclosing the log stable where Sam was putting up the horses for the night.

"You ain't looked right yet," Sam said.

He stopped. For a moment he didn't answer. Then he said peacefully, in a peaceful rushing burst as when a boy's miniature dam in a little brook gives way, "All right. But how? I went to the bayou. I even found that log again. I—"

"I reckon that was all right. Likely he's been watching you. You never saw his foot?"

"I," the boy said—"I didn't—I never thought—"

"It's the gun," Sam said. He stood beside the fence, motionless—the old man, the Indian, in the battered faded overalls and the frayed five-cent straw hat which in the Negro's race had been the badge of his enslavement and was now the regalia of his freedom. The camp—the clearing, the house, the barn and its tiny lot with which Major de Spain in his turn had scratched punily and evanescently at the wilderness—faded in the dusk, back into the immemorial darkness of the woods. *The gun,* the boy thought. *The gun.*

"Be scared," Sam said. "You can't help that. But don't be afraid. Ain't nothing in the woods going to hurt you unless you corner it, or it smells that you are afraid. A bear or a deer, too, has got to be scared of a coward the same as a brave man has got to be."

The gun, the boy thought.

"You will have to choose," Sam said.

He left the camp before daylight, long before Uncle Ash would wake in his quilts on the kitchen floor and start the fire for breakfast. He had only the compass and a stick for snakes. He could go almost a mile before he would begin to need the compass. He sat on a log, the invisible compass in his invisible hand, while the secret night sounds, fallen still at his movements, scurried again and then ceased for good, and the owls ceased and gave over to the waking of day birds, and he could see the compass. Then he went fast yet still quietly; he was becoming better and better as a woodsman, still without having yet realized it.

He jumped a doe and a fawn at sunrise, walked them out of the bed, close enough to see them—the crash of undergrowth, the white scut,[13] the fawn scudding behind her faster than he had believed it could run. He was hunting right, upwind, as Sam had taught him; not that it mattered now. He had left the gun; of his own will and relinquishment he had accepted not a gambit, not a choice, but a condition in which not only the bear's heretofore inviolable anonymity but all the old rules and balances of hunter and hunted had been abrogated.[14] He would not even be afraid, not even in the moment when the fear would take him completely—blood, skin, bowels, bones, memory from the long time before it became his memory—all save that thin, clear, quenchless, immortal lucidity which alone differed him from this bear and from all the other bear and deer he would ever kill in the humility and

---

13. **scut:** short, stumpy tail.
14. **abrogated** [ab′rə gā′tid]: abolished.

pride of his skill and endurance, to which Sam had spoken when he leaned in the twilight on the lot fence yesterday.

By noon he was far beyond the little bayou, farther into the new and alien country than he had ever been. He was traveling now not only by the compass but by the old, heavy, biscuit-thick silver watch which had belonged to his grandfather. When he stopped at last, it was for the first time since he had risen from the log at dawn when he could see the compass. It was far enough. He had left the camp nine hours ago; nine hours from now, dark would have already been an hour old. But he didn't think that. He thought, *All right. Yes. But what?* and stood for a moment, alien and small in the green and topless solitude, answering his own question before it had formed and ceased. It was the watch, the compass, the stick—the three lifeless mechanicals with which for nine hours he had fended the wilderness off; he hung the watch and compass carefully on a bush and leaned the stick beside them and relinquished completely to it.

He had not been going very fast for the last two or three hours. He went no faster now, since distance would not matter even if he could have gone fast. And he was trying to keep a bearing on the tree where he had left the compass, trying to complete a circle which would bring him back to it or at least intersect itself, since direction would not matter now either. But the tree was not there, and he did as Sam had schooled him—made the next circle in the opposite direction, so that the two patterns would bisect somewhere, but crossing no print of his own feet, finding the tree at last, but in the wrong place—no bush, no compass, no watch—and the tree not even the tree, because there was a down log beside it and he did what Sam Fathers had told him was the next thing and the last.

As he sat down on the log he saw the crooked print—the warped, tremendous, two-toed indentation which, even as he watched it, filled with water. As he looked up, the wilderness coalesced, solidified—the glade, the tree he sought, the bush, the watch and the compass glinting where a ray of sunlight touched them. Then he saw the bear. It did not emerge, appear; it was just there, immobile, solid, fixed in the hot dappling of the green and windless noon, not as big as he had dreamed it, but as big as he had expected it, bigger, dimensionless against the dappled obscurity, looking at him where he sat quietly on the log and looked back at it.

Then it moved. It made no sound. It did not hurry. It crossed the glade, walking for an instant into the full glare of the sun; when it reached the other side it stopped again and looked back at him across one shoulder while his quiet breathing inhaled and exhaled three times.

Then it was gone. It didn't walk into the woods, the undergrowth. It faded, sank back into the wilderness as he had watched a fish, a huge old bass, sink and vanish back into the dark depths of its pool without even any movement of its fins.

He thought, *It will be next fall.* But it was not next fall, nor the next nor the next. He was fourteen then. He had killed his buck, and Sam Fathers had marked his face with the hot blood, and in the next year he killed a bear. But even before that accolade he had become as competent in the woods as many grown men with the same experience; by his fourteenth year he was a better woodsman than most grown men with more. There was no territory within thirty miles of the camp that he did not know—bayou, ridge, brake, landmark tree and path. He could have led anyone to any point in it without deviation, and brought them out again. He knew game trails that even Sam Fathers did not know; in his thirteenth year he found a buck's bedding place, and unbeknown to his father he borrowed Walter Ewell's rifle and lay in wait at dawn and killed the buck when it walked back to the bed, as Sam had told him how the old Chickasaw fathers did.

But not the old bear, although by now he knew its footprint better than he did his own, and not only the crooked one. He could see

any one of the three sound ones and distinguish it from any other, and not only by its size. There were other bears within those thirty miles which left tracks almost as large, but this was more than that. If Sam Fathers had been his mentor and the backyard rabbits and squirrels at home his kindergarten, then the wilderness the old bear ran was his college, the old male bear itself, so long unwifed and childless as to have become its own ungendered progenitor,[15] was his alma mater. But he never saw it.

He could find the crooked print now almost whenever he liked, fifteen or ten or five miles, or sometimes nearer the camp than that. Twice while on stand during the three years he heard the dogs strike its trail by accident; on the second time they jumped it seemingly, the voices high, abject, almost human in hysteria, as on that first morning two years ago. But not the bear itself. He would remember that noon three years ago, the glade, himself and the bear fixed during that moment in the windless and dappled blaze, and it would seem to him that it had never happened, that he had dreamed that too. But it had happened. They had looked at each other, they had emerged from the wilderness old as earth, synchronized to that instant by something more than the blood that moved the flesh and bones which bore them, and touched, pledged something, affirmed something more lasting than the frail web of bones and flesh which any accident could obliterate.

Then he saw it again. Because of the very fact that he thought of nothing else, he had forgotten to look for it. He was still-hunting with Walter Ewell's rifle. He saw it cross the end of a long blowdown, a corridor where a tornado had swept, rushing through rather than over the tangle of trunks and branches as a locomotive would have, faster than he had ever believed it could move, almost as fast as a deer even, because a deer would have spent most of

---

15. **ungendered progenitor:** its own parent; not born of any other.

that time in the air, faster than he could bring the rifle sights up to it, so that he believed the reason he never let off the shot was that he was still behind it, had never caught up with it. And now he knew what had been wrong during all the three years. He sat on a log, shaking and trembling as if he had never seen the woods before nor anything that ran them, wondering with incredulous amazement how he could have forgotten the very thing which Sam Fathers had told him and which the bear itself had proved the next day and had now returned after three years to reaffirm.

And he now knew what Sam Fathers had meant about the right dog, a dog in which size would mean less than nothing. So when he returned alone in April—school was out then, so that the sons of farmers could help with the land's planting, and at last his father had granted him permission, on his promise to be back in four days—he had the dog. It was his own, a mongrel of the sort called by Negroes a fyce, a ratter, itself not much bigger than a rat and possessing that bravery which had long since stopped being courage and had become foolhardiness.

It did not take four days. Alone again, he found the trail on the first morning. It was not a stalk; it was an ambush. He timed the meeting almost as if it were an appointment with a human being. Himself holding the fyce muffled in a feed sack and Sam Fathers with two of the hounds on a piece of plowline rope, they lay down wind of the trail at dawn of the second morning. They were so close that the bear turned without even running, as if in surprised amazement at the shrill and frantic uproar of the released fyce, turning at bay against the trunk of a tree, on its hind feet; it seemed to the boy that it would never stop rising, taller and taller, and even the two hounds seemed to take a sort of desperate and despairing courage from the fyce, following it as it went in.

Then he realized that the fyce was actually not going to stop. He flung, threw the gun away, and ran; when he overtook and grasped the frantically pinwheeling little dog, it seemed to him that he was directly under the bear.

He could smell it, strong and hot and rank. Sprawling, he looked up to where it loomed and towered over him like a cloudburst and colored like a thunderclap, quite familiar, peacefully and even lucidly familiar, until he remembered: This was the way he had used to dream about it. Then it was gone. He didn't see it go. He knelt, holding the frantic fyce with both hands, hearing the abased wailing of the hounds drawing farther and farther away, until Sam came up. He carried the gun. He laid it down quietly beside the boy and stood looking down at him.

"You've done seed him twice now with a gun in your hands," he said. "This time you couldn't have missed him."

The boy rose. He still held the fyce. Even in his arms and clear of the ground, it yapped frantically, straining and surging after the fading uproar of the two hounds like a tangle of wire springs. He was panting a little, but he was neither shaking nor trembling now.

"Neither could you!" he said. "You had the gun! Neither did you!"

"And you didn't shoot," his father said. "How close were you?"

"I don't know, sir," he said. "There was a big wood tick inside his right hind leg. I saw that. But I didn't have the gun then."

"But you didn't shoot when you had the gun," his father said. "Why?"

But he didn't answer, and his father didn't wait for him to, rising and crossing the room, across the pelt of the bear which the boy had killed two years ago and the larger one which his father had killed before he was born, to the bookcase beneath the mounted head of the boy's first buck. It was the room which his father called the office, from which all the plan-tation business was transacted; in it for the fourteen years of his life he had heard the best of all talking. Major de Spain would be there and sometimes old General Compson, and Walter Ewell and Boon Hoggenbeck and Sam Fathers and Tennie's Jim, too, because they, too, were hunters, knew the woods and what ran them.

He would hear it, not talking himself but listening—the wilderness, the big woods, bigger and older than any recorded document of white man fatuous enough to believe he had bought any fragment of it or Indian ruthless enough to pretend that any fragment of it had been his to convey. It was of the men, not white nor black nor red, but men, hunters with the will and hardihood to endure and the humility and skill to survive, and the dogs and the bear and deer juxtaposed and reliefed against it, ordered and compelled by and within the wilderness in the ancient and unremitting contest by the ancient and immitigable rules which voided all regrets and brooked no quarter, the voices quiet and weighty and deliberate for retrospection and recollection and exact remembering, while he squatted in the blazing firelight as Tennie's Jim squatted, who stirred only to put more wood on the fire and to pass the bottle from one glass to another. Because the bottle was always present, so that after a while it seemed to him that those fierce instants of heart and brain and courage and wiliness and speed were concentrated and distilled into that brown liquor which not women, not boys and children, but only hunters drank, drinking not of the blood they had spilled but some condensation of the wild immortal spirit, drinking it moderately, humbly even, not with the pagan's base hope of acquiring thereby the virtues of cunning and strength and speed, but in salute to them.

His father returned with the book and sat down again and opened it. "Listen," he said. He read the five stanzas aloud, his voice quiet and deliberate in the room where there was no fire now because it was already spring. Then he looked up. The boy watched him. "All right," his father said. "Listen." He read again, but only the second stanza this time, to the end of it, the last two lines, and closed the book and put it on the table beside him. " 'She cannot fade, though thou hast not thy bliss, for ever wilt thou love, and she be fair,' "[16] he said.

"He's talking about a girl," the boy said.

"He had to talk about something," his father said. Then he said, "He was talking about truth. Truth doesn't change. Truth is one thing. It covers all things which touch the heart—honor and pride and pity and justice and courage and love. Do you see now?"

He didn't know. Somehow it was simpler than that. There was an old bear, fierce and ruthless, not merely just to stay alive, but with the fierce pride of liberty and freedom, proud enough of that liberty and freedom to see it threatened without fear or even alarm; nay, who at times even seemed deliberately to put that freedom and liberty in jeopardy in order to savor them, to remind his old strong bones and flesh to keep supple and quick to defend and preserve them. There was an old man, son of a Negro slave and an Indian king, inheritor on the one side of the long chronicle of a people who had learned humility through suffering, and pride through the endurance which survived the suffering and injustice, and on the other side, the chronicle of a people even longer in the land than the first, yet who no longer existed in the land at all save in the solitary brotherhood of an old Negro's alien blood and the wild and invincible spirit of an old bear. There was a boy who wished to learn humility and pride in order to become skillful and worthy in the woods, who suddenly found himself becoming so skillful so rapidly that he feared he would never become worthy because he had not learned humility and pride, although he had tried to, until one day and as suddenly he discovered that an old man who could not have defined either had led him, as though by the hand, to that point where an old bear and a little mongrel dog showed him that,

by possessing one thing other, he would possess them both.

And a little dog, nameless and mongrel and many-fathered, grown, yet weighing less than six pounds, saying as if to itself, "I can't be dangerous, because there's nothing much smaller than I am; I can't be fierce, because they would call it just noise; I can't be humble, because I'm already too close to the ground to genuflect;[17] I can't be proud, because I wouldn't be near enough to it for anyone to know who was casting that shadow, and I don't even know that I'm not going to heaven, because they have already decided that I don't possess an immortal soul. So all I can be is brave. But it's all right. I can be that, even if they still call it just noise."

That was all. It was simple, much simpler than somebody talking in a book about a youth and a girl he would never need to grieve over, because he could never approach any nearer her and would never have to get any farther away. He had heard about a bear, and finally got big enough to trail it, and he trailed it four years and at last met it with a gun in his hands and he didn't shoot. Because a little dog—But he could have shot long before the little dog covered the twenty yards to where the bear waited, and Sam Fathers could have shot at any time during that interminable minute while Old Ben stood on his hind feet over them. He stopped. His father was watching him gravely across the spring-rife twilight of the room; when he spoke, his words were as quiet as the twilight, too, not loud, because they did not need to be because they would last, "Courage, and honor, and pride," his father said, "and pity, and love of justice and of liberty. They all touch the heart, and what the heart holds to becomes truth, as far as we know truth. Do you see now?"

Sam, and Old Ben, and Nip, he thought. And himself too. He had been all right too. His father had said so. "Yes, sir," he said.

---

16. " **'She . . . fair'** ": from Keats's "Ode on a Grecian Urn."

17. **genuflect** [jen′yoo flekt]: bend the knee as in worship or respect.

STUDY QUESTIONS

Recalling

1. According to the opening paragraphs, to what has the boy listened for years? For what is the bear "too big" (paragraph 3)?
2. What is Sam Father's ancestry? According to Sam, what does the bear do every year? How did the dog with the injured ear behave "just like folks"?
3. When the boy rides the one-eyed mule to a country he never saw before, what does he see in the wet earth? What does he realize for the first time? According to Sam, whom will the bear "pick out" if he must "run over" somebody?
4. During the next outing, what does the boy decide he must do so that it will not "go on like this forever"? Then, the following June, what does he leave behind and what three "lifeless mechanicals" does he abandon during his search for the bear? Does he see the bear?
5. When the boy is fourteen, in what way is he now better than most grown men? What kind of dog does he bring with him for the final hunt? What does he throw away as he runs after the dog and bear? What do both the boy and Sam fail to do?
6. How does the boy evaluate the bear on page 677? To what does he realize Sam led him? What values does the boy's father talk about in the next-to-last paragraph?

Interpreting

7. Is the boy a threat to the bear the first time he accompanies the others on the hunt? How does he change in this respect by the time of the final hunt?
8. In abandoning his "mechanical devices" on Sam's advice, of what is the boy becoming a part? On what terms is he now challenging the bear?
9. What might the bear represent? On this symbolic level, why is it significant that the bear is "mortal"?
10. Who or what is the "Nip" mentioned in the last paragraph? What do the bear, Nip, and even Sam have in common?
11. What might be the "one thing other" that the boy has learned from the dog and the bear? In failing to shoot the bear, for what things is the boy showing respect?

12. What elements of Romanticism does this story contain? Of Regionalism? With what common American themes does it deal? Why is it nevertheless a story that could not have been written in the nineteenth century?

Extending

13. Do you agree with the father's definition of truth that he provides in his last words? Why or why not?

VIEWPOINT

The critic Cleanth Brooks has commented that Faulkner's love for nature

> is certainly powerful and deep-seated, and on occasion it rises up into great rhapsodic hymns that celebrate the power and continuity of nature, finally changeless through all its apparent changes.

> —*William Faulkner: The Yoknapatawpha Country*

■ How would you apply this statement to "The Bear"? How can the story be regarded as a celebration of the permanence and power and changelessness of nature?

LITERARY FOCUS

Symbol and Theme

A **symbol** in a literary work is anything that has a meaning in itself and that also represents or suggests something larger than itself, such as an idea, a quality, a belief, or a value. The unifying symbol in this story is the great bear itself—a "shaggy tremendous shape." The bear is an actual bear, and much of the story is concerned with the process by which the boy, every year a better hunter, develops the skills needed not only to hunt the bear but merely to *see* the elusive animal. Yet, as Faulkner's descriptions suggest, the bear symbolizes, or represents, very much more. For example, it is

> an anachronism, indomitable and invincible, out of an old dead time, a phantom, epitome and apotheosis of the old wild life at which the puny humans swarmed and hacked in a fury of abhorrence and fear.

Sentences like this show how a writer can use a symbol to reveal a theme. Ageless carrier of "the old wild life," the bear, in Faulkner's vision, is one of the forces of nature from which all life springs and which humanity with the abuses of civilization, increasingly threatens.

Thinking About Symbol and Theme

■ Find two other passages in "The Bear" that illustrate the bear's symbolic function. Explain the symbolism, and then comment on its relation to the story's themes.

VOCABULARY

Sentence Completions

Each of the following sentences contains a blank with four possible words for completing the sentence. The words are from "The Bear." Choose the word that completes each sentence correctly, using the word *as it is used in this selection*. Write the number of each item and the letter of your choice on a separate sheet.

1. Two pieces of the puzzle were _____.
   (a) moiling   (c) juxtaposed
   (b) ungendered   (d) intermittent
2. The presence of an automobile was a deliberate _____ in the eighteenth-century setting of the play.
   (a) anachronism   (c) epitome
   (b) apotheosis   (d) lucidity
3. The crown and scepter are part of the queen's _____.
   (a) material   (c) effluvium
   (b) regalia   (d) canebrake
4. The new play received _____ from all the critics.
   (a) designations   (c) relinquishments
   (b) predecessors   (d) accolades
5. The various factions _____ to form a new political party.
   (a) marred   (c) reaffirmed
   (b) coalesced   (d) synchronized

COMPOSITION

Analyzing the Total Effect of a Story

■ Write an essay in which you analyze the total effect of this story. What is the impact of the story? How does the author use the following literary elements to achieve this effect: setting, character, plot, point of view, tone, symbol, and theme? *For help with this assignment, refer to Lesson 8 in the Writing About Literature Handbook at the back of this book.*

Writing Diary Entries

■ Suppose the boy in "The Bear" had been keeping a diary of his hunting experiences. Write the entries that he might have written after each outing in his pursuit of the bear. Or, if you prefer, write only the entry he might have written after his final outing and his conversation with his father. Include details about the hunt and also the boy's thoughts and feelings. You may add your own details to those already in the story.

COMPARING WRITERS

The contrasting concerns for society at large and for the individual in particular are evident in the varied themes and settings of the stories in this unit. Nevertheless, social and personal concerns are not always mutually exclusive.

1. Describe the character growth or personal learning experience that occurs in Schwartz's "In Dreams Begin Responsibilities," Steinbeck's "Leader of the People," and Faulkner's "Bear." What do these stories have to say about modern society in general or about modern America's relationship to the past?
2. What are some of the positive personal values suggested by Welty's "Worn Path," Weidman's "My Father Sits in the Dark," and Agee's "Knoxville: Summer, 1915"?
3. What do the main characters of "The Jilting of Granny Weatherall" and "The Far and the Near" have in common? Why could neither of these characters have appeared in nineteenth-century literature?
4. What social concerns are expressed in "The Portable Phonograph" and "The Signature"? Which of these stories also expresses a common personal concern of postwar literature, and what is that concern? Which has concerns similar to those expressed in Auden's poem "The Unknown Citizen" (page 575)?

NONFICTION

William Faulkner

Nobel Prize Acceptance Speech

I feel that this award was not made to me as a man but to my work—a life's work in the agony and sweat of the human spirit, not for glory and least of all for profit, but to create out of the materials of the human spirit something which did not exist before. So this award is only mine in trust. It will not be difficult to find a dedication for the money part of it commensurate with the purpose and significance of its origin. But I would like to do the same with the acclaim too, by using this moment as a pinnacle from which I might be listened to by the young men and women already dedicated to the same anguish and travail, among whom is already that one who will some day stand here where I am standing.

Our tragedy today is a general and universal physical fear so long sustained by now that we can even bear it. There are no longer problems of the spirit. There is only the question: when will I be blown up? Because of this, the young man or woman writing today has forgotten the problems of the human heart in conflict with itself which alone can make good writing because only that is worth writing about, worth the agony and the sweat.

He must learn them again. He must teach himself that the basest of all things is to be afraid; and, teaching himself that, forget it forever, leaving no room in his workshop for anything but the old verities and truths of the heart, the old universal truths lacking which any story is ephemeral and doomed—love and honor and pity and pride and compassion and sacrifice. Until he does so he labors under a curse. He writes not of love but of lust, of defeats in which nobody loses anything of value, of victories without hope and worst of all without pity or compassion. His griefs grieve on no universal bones, leaving no scars. He writes not of the heart but of the glands.

Until he relearns these things he will write as though he stood among and watched the end of man. I decline to accept the end of man. It is easy enough to say that man is immortal simply because he will endure; that when the last ding-dong of doom has clanged and faded from the last worthless rock hanging tideless in the last red and dying evening, that even then there will still be one more sound: that of his puny inexhaustible voice, still talking. I refuse to accept this. I believe that man will not merely endure: he will prevail. He is immortal, not because he alone among creatures has an inexhaustible voice, but because he has a soul, a spirit capable of compassion and sacrifice and endurance. The poet's, the writer's, duty is to write about these things. It is his privilege to help man endure by lifting his heart, by reminding him of the courage and honor and hope and pride and compassion and pity and sacrifice which have been the glory of his past. The poet's voice need not merely be the record of man, it can be one of the props, the pillars to help him endure and prevail.

Recalling

1. To whom does Faulkner address this speech, according to the first paragraph?
2. What, according to Faulkner, is the emotion that is today's tragedy? What question overrides everything else?
3. What does Faulkner say are "the old universal truths" lacking which any story is "ephemeral and doomed"?
4. What does Faulkner "decline to accept" in the fourth paragraph? Why does he believe humanity is immortal? What does he say of the poet's voice in his final sentence?

Interpreting

5. Explain in your own words the distinction Faulkner makes between valuable writing and writing that lacks value.
6. In order to determine Faulkner's purpose in this speech, discuss whether he really wants writers to *forget* the question in his second paragraph. What does his last sentence imply? In what things does he believe young writers must have faith?

Extending

7. Of which works that you have read in this unit and the two preceding units do you think Faulkner would approve, and why? Of which works do you think he would disapprove, and why? How do Faulkner's ideas differ from the ideas expressed in "The Portable Phonograph" on page 651?

COMPOSITION

Analyzing an Author's Purpose

Faulkner's speech is directed at a particular audience: all writers, present and future. He has a particular purpose as well. In an essay, analyze his purpose—what he is trying to say, what he is trying to do. Begin by stating his purpose. Then support your statement by citing the various techniques he uses to achieve his purpose—for example, imagery, use of repetition, and statements of opinion. *For help with this assignment, refer to Lesson 4 in the Writing About Literature Handbook at the back of this book.*

Expressing an Opinion Persuasively

Do you agree that humanity "will not merely endure" but will "prevail"? Express either your agreement or your disagreement with Faulkner's view. In either case, support your opinion with examples, details, facts, and well-chosen images.

Jack Kerouac   *1922–1969*

Jack Kerouac was born in Lowell, Massachusetts, where, he said, he "roamed fields and riverbanks by day and night, wrote little novels in my room, first novel written at age eleven." After serving in the Navy and as a merchant seaman, and having decided to be a "lonesome traveler," he roamed the United States and Mexico, working at an assortment of jobs, including railroad brakeman and forest ranger.

Out of his various experiences and wanderings Kerouac wrote his popular novel *On the Road* (1957), which celebrated the freedom and vigorous life of the American "traveler." The novel was a sensation, and Kerouac became the most famous of the writers and artists known as the Beat Generation. The Beats, Kerouac said, took their name from the fact that they were weary ("beat") of the ordinary, dull routine of American life. They were nonconformists who searched for the unusual, the special experience that would bring all the threads of life together in one ecstatic moment. It has also been suggested that they took their name from their search for an earthly "*beat*itude," or holiness.

On the Road was Kerouac's first attempt to write in what he called a "visual American form"—a "spontaneous prose" that would capture the vitality and impulsiveness of experience. *On the Road* does suggest that spontaneity, despite the fact that it is a highly-crafted work and was rewritten several times. Kerouac's outlook on life has been described as "an affirmative attitude in which wonder and delight take the largest place." His later books, however, never matched the success of *On the Road*.

"Alone on a Mountaintop," from Kerouac's *Lonesome Traveler*, is one of his best attempts at describing his quest. It records the wonder and delight, and the fear and serenity, of his experience as a fire lookout in northwest Washington in 1956.

Jack Kerouac

from **Lonesome Traveler**

Alone on a Mountaintop

I was a fire lookout and after two nights of trying to sleep in the boom and slap of the Forest Service floats,[1] they came for me one rainy morning—a powerful tugboat lashed to a large corral float bearing four mules and three horses, my own groceries, feed, batteries and equipment. The muleskinner's[2] name was Andy and he wore the same old floppy cowboy hat he'd worn in Wyoming twenty years ago. "Well, boy, now we're gonna put you away where we can't reach ya—you better get ready."

"It's just what I want, Andy, be alone for three solid months nobody to bother me."

"It's what you're sayin' now but you'll change your tune after a week."

I didn't believe him. I was looking forward to an experience men seldom earn in this modern world: complete and comfortable solitude in the wilderness, day and night, sixty-three days and nights to be exact. We had no idea how much snow had fallen on my mountain during the winter and Andy said: "If there didn't it means you gotta hike two miles down that hard trail every day or every other day with two buckets, boy. I ain't envyin' you—I been back there. And one day it's gonna be hot and you're about ready to broil, and bugs you can't even count 'em, and next day a li'l' ole summer blizzard come hit you around the corner of Hozomeen[3] which sits right there near Canada in your back yard and you won't be able to stick logs fast enough in that potbelly stove of yours." But I had a full rucksack loaded with turtleneck sweaters and warm shirts and pants and long wool socks bought

on the Seattle waterfront, and gloves and an earmuff cap, and lots of instant soup and coffee in my grub list.

"Shoulda brought yourself a quart of brandy, boy," says Andy shaking his head as the tug pushed our corral float up Ross Lake through the log gate and around to the left dead north underneath the immense rain shroud of Sourdough Mountain and Ruby Mountain.

"Where's Desolation Peak?" I asked, meaning my own mountain (*A mountain to be kept forever,* I'd dreamed all that spring) (O lonesome traveler!)

"You ain't gonna see it today till we're practically on top it and by that time you'll be so soakin' wet you won't care."

Assistant Ranger Marty Gohlke of Marblemount Ranger Station was with us too, also giving me tips and instructions. Nobody seemed to envy Desolation Peak except me. After two hours pushing through the storming waves of the long rainy lake with dreary misty timber rising steeply on both sides and the mules and horses chomping on their feedbags patient in the downpour, we arrived at the foot of Desolation Trail and the tugman (who'd been providing us with good hot coffee in the pilot cabin) eased her over and settled the float against a steep muddy slope full of bushes and fallen trees. The muleskinner whacked the first mule and she lurched ahead with her double-sided pack of batteries and canned goods, hit the mud with forehoofs, scrambled, slipped, almost fell back in the lake and finally gave one mighty heave and went skittering out of sight in the fog to wait on the trail for the other mules and her master. We all got off, cut the barge loose, waved to the tug man, mounted our horses and started up a sad and dripping party in heavy rain.

---

1. **floats:** raftlike platforms.
2. **muleskinner:** mule driver.
3. **Hozomeen:** Mt. Hozomeen.

At first the trail, always steeply rising, was so dense with shrubbery we kept getting shower after shower from overhead and against our out-saddled knees. The trail was deep with round rocks that kept causing the animals to slip. At one point a great fallen tree made it impossible to go on until Old Andy and Marty went ahead with axes and cleared a short cut around the tree, sweating and cursing and hacking as I watched the animals. By-and-by they were ready but the mules were afraid of the rough steepness of the short cut and had to be prodded through with sticks. Soon the trail reached alpine meadows powdered with blue lupine everywhere in the drenching mists, and with little red poppies, tiny-budded flowers as delicate as designs on a small Japanese teacup. Now the trail zigzagged widely back and forth up the high meadow. Soon we saw the vast foggy heap of a rock-cliff face above and Andy yelled "Soon's we get up high as that we're almost there but that's another two thousand feet though you think you could reach up and touch it!"

I unfolded my nylon poncho and draped it over my head, and, drying a little, or, rather, ceasing to drip, I walked alongside the horse to warm my blood and began to feel better. But the other boys just rode along with their heads bowed in the rain. As for altitude all I could tell was from some occasional frightening spots on the trail where we could look down on distant treetops.

The alpine meadow reached to timber line[4] and suddenly a great wind blew shafts of sleet on us. "Gettin' near the top now!" yelled Andy—and suddenly there was snow on the trail, the horses were chumping through a foot of slush and mud, and to the left and right everything was blinding white in the gray fog. "About five and a half thousand feet right now" said Andy rolling a cigarette as he rode in the rain.

We went down, then up another spell, down again, a slow gradual climb, and then Andy yelled "There she is!" and up ahead in the mountaintop gloom I saw a little shadowy peaked shack standing alone on the top of the world and gulped with fear:

"This my home all summer? And *this* is summer?"

The inside of the shack was even more miserable, damp and dirty, leftover groceries and magazines torn to shreds by rats and mice, the floor muddy, the windows impenetrable. But hardy Old Andy who'd been through this kind of thing all his life got a roaring fire crackling in the potbelly stove and had me lay out a pot

---

4. **timber line:** point beyond which trees cannot grow.

Photographs of the Desolation Peak lookout station and North Cascades National Park, Washington.

of water with almost half a can of coffee in it saying "Coffee ain't no good 'less it's *strong!*" and pretty soon the coffee was boiling a nice brown aromatic foam and we got our cups out and drank deep.

Meanwhile I'd gone out on the roof with Marty and removed the bucket from the chimney and put up the weather pole with the anemometer[5] and done a few other chores—when we came back in Andy was frying Spam and eggs in a huge pan and it was almost like a party. Outside, the patient animals chomped on their supper bags and were glad to rest by the old corral fence built of logs by some Desolation lookout of the Thirties.

Darkness came, incomprehensible.

In the gray morning after they'd slept in sleeping bags on the floor and I on the only bunk in my mummy bag, Andy and Marty left, laughing, saying, "Well, whatayou think now hey? We been here twelve hours and you still ain't been able to see more than twelve feet!"

"By gosh that's right, what am I going to do for watching fires?"

"Don't worry boy, these clouds'll roll away and you'll be able to see a hunnerd miles in every direction."

I didn't believe it and I felt miserable and

spent the day trying to clean up the shack or pacing twenty careful feet each way in my "yard" (the ends of which appeared to be sheer drops into silent gorges), and I went to bed early. About bedtime I saw my first star, briefly, then giant phantom clouds billowed all around me and the star was gone. But in that instant I thought I'd seen a mile-down maw[6] of grayblack lake where Andy and Marty were back in the Forest Service boat which had met them at noon.

In the middle of the night I woke up suddenly and my hair was standing on end—I saw a huge black shadow in my window. Then I saw that it had a star above it, and realized that this was Mt. Hozomeen (8080 feet) looking in my window from miles away near Canada. I got up from the forlorn bunk with the mice scattering underneath and went outside and gasped to see black mountain shapes gianting all around, and not only that but the billowing curtains of the northern lights shifting behind the clouds. It was a little too much for a city boy—the fear that the Abominable Snowman might be breathing behind me in the dark sent me back to bed where I buried my head inside my sleeping bag.

But in the morning—Sunday, July sixth—I

---

5. **anemometer:** instrument for measuring wind speed.

6. **maw:** gaping, dark opening.

was amazed and overjoyed to see a clear blue sunny sky and down below, like a radiant pure snow sea, the clouds making a marshmallow cover for all the world and all the lake while I abided in warm sunshine among hundreds of miles of snow-white peaks. I brewed coffee and sang and drank a cup on my drowsy warm doorstep.

At noon the clouds vanished and the lake appeared below, beautiful beyond belief, a perfect blue pool twenty five miles long and more, and the creeks like toy creeks and the timber green and fresh everywhere below and even the joyous little unfolding liquid tracks of vacationists' fishingboats on the lake and in the lagoons. A perfect afternoon of sun, and behind the shack I discovered a snowfield big enough to provide me with buckets of cold water till late September.

My job was to watch for fires. One night a terrific lightning storm made a dry run across the Mt. Baker National Forest without any rainfall. When I saw that ominous black cloud flashing wrathfully toward me I shut off the radio and laid the aerial on the ground and waited for the worst. Hiss! hiss! said the wind, bringing dust and lightning nearer. Tick! said the lightning rod, receiving a strand of electricity from a strike on nearby Skagit Peak. Hiss! tick! and in my bed I felt the earth move. Fifteen miles to the south, just east of Ruby Peak and somewhere near Panther Creek, a large fire raged, a huge orange spot. At ten o'clock lightning hit it again and it flared up dangerously.

I was supposed to note the general area of lightning strikes. By midnight I'd been staring so intently out the dark window I got hallucinations of fires everywhere, three of them right in Lightning Creek, phosphorescent orange verticals of ghost fire that seemed to come and go.

In the morning, there at 177° 16′ where I'd seen the big fire was a strange brown patch in the snowy rock showing where the fire had raged and sputtered out in the all-night rain that followed the lightning. But the result of this storm was disastrous fifteen miles away at McAllister Creek where a great blaze had out-lasted the rain and exploded the following afternoon in a cloud that could be seen from Seattle. I felt sorry for the fellows who had to fight these fires, the smoke-jumpers who parachuted down on them out of planes and the trail crews who hiked to them, climbing and scrambling over slippery rocks and scree slopes,[7] arriving sweaty and exhausted only to face the wall of heat when they got there. As a lookout I had it pretty easy and only had to concentrate on reporting the exact location (by instrument findings) of every blaze I detected.

Most days, though, it was the routine that occupied me. Up at seven or so every day, a pot of coffee brought to a boil over a handful of burning twigs, I'd go out in the alpine yard with a cup of coffee hooked in my thumb and leisurely make my wind speed and wind direction and temperature and moisture readings—then, after chopping wood, I'd use the two-way radio and report to the relay station on Sourdough. At 10 A.M. I usually got hungry for breakfast, and I'd make delicious pancakes, eating them at my little table that was decorated with bouquets of mountain lupine and sprigs of fir.

Early in the afternoon was the usual time for my kick of the day, instant chocolate pudding with hot coffee. Around two or three I'd lie on my back on the meadowside and watch the clouds float by, or pick blueberries and eat them right there. The radio was on loud enough to hear any calls for Desolation.

Then at sunset I'd roust up my supper out of cans of yams and Spam and peas, or sometimes just pea soup with corn muffins baked on top of the wood stove in aluminum foil. Then I'd go out to that precipitous snow slope and shovel my two pails of snow for the water tub and gather an armful of fallen firewood from the hillside like the proverbial Old Woman of Japan. For the chipmunks and conies[8] I put pans of leftovers under the shack, in the mid-

---

7. **scree slopes:** slopes covered with loose, sliding rock fragments.
8. **conies:** rabbits.

dle of the night I could hear them clanking around. The rat would scramble down from the attic and eat some too.

Sometimes I'd yell questions at the rocks and trees, and across gorges, or yodel—"What is the meaning of the void?" The answer was perfect silence, so I knew.

Before bedtime I'd read by kerosene lamp whatever books were in the shack. It's amazing how people in solitary hunger after books. After poring over every word of a medical tome, and the synopsized versions of Shakespeare's plays by Charles and Mary Lamb,[9] I climbed up in the little attic and put together torn cowboy pocket books and magazines the mice had ravaged—I also played stud poker with three imaginary players.

Around bedtime I'd bring a cup of milk almost to a boil with a tablespoon of honey in it, and drink that for my lamby[10] nightcap, then I'd curl up in my sleeping bag.

No man should go through life without once experiencing healthy, even bored solitude in the wilderness, finding himself depending solely on himself and thereby learning his true and hidden strength. Learning, for instance, to eat when he's hungry and sleep when he's sleepy.

Also around bedtime was my singing time. I'd pace up and down the well-worn path in the dust of my rock singing all the show tunes I could remember, at the top of my voice too, with nobody to hear except the deer and the bear.

In the red dusk, the mountains were symphonies in pink snow—Jack Mountain, Three Fools Peak, Freezeout Peak, Golden Horn, Mt. Terror, Mt. Fury, Mt. Despair, Crooked Thumb Peak, Mt. Challenger and the incomparable Mt. Baker bigger than the world in the distance—and my own little Jackass Ridge that completed the Ridge of Desolation. Pink snow and the clouds all distant and frilly like ancient remote cities of Buddhaland splendor, and the wind working incessantly—whish, whish—booming, at times rattling my shack.

For supper I made chop suey and baked some biscuits and put the leftovers in a pan for deer that came in the moonlit night and nibbled like big strange cows of peace—long-antlered buck and does and babies too—as I meditated in the alpine grass facing the magic moon-laned lake. And I could see firs reflected in the moonlit lake five thousand feet below, upside down, pointing to infinity.

And all the insects ceased in honor of the moon.

Sixty-three sunsets I saw revolve on that perpendicular hill—mad raging sunsets pouring in sea foams of cloud through unimaginable crags like the crags you grayly drew in pencil as a child, with every rose-tint of hope beyond, making you feel just like them, brilliant and bleak beyond words.

Cold mornings with clouds billowing out of Lightning Gorge like smoke from a giant fire but the lake cerulean[11] as ever.

August comes in with a blast that shakes your house and augurs[12] little Augusticity—then that snowy-air and woodsmoke feeling—then the snow comes sweeping your way from Canada, and the wind rises and dark low clouds rush up as out of a forge. Suddenly a green-rose rainbow appears right on your ridge with steamy clouds all around and an orange sun turmoiling . . .

> *What is a rainbow,*
> *Lord?—a hoop*
> *For the lowly*

. . . and you go out and suddenly your shadow is ringed by the rainbow as you walk on the hilltop, a lovely-haloed mystery making you want to pray.

A blade of grass jiggling in the winds of infinity, anchored to a rock, and for your own poor gentle flesh no answer.

Your oil lamp burning in infinity.

---

9. **Charles and Mary Lamb:** English Romantic authors of *Tales from Shakespeare.*
10. **lamby:** innocent.

---

11. **cerulean** [sə rōō′lē ən]: sky-blue.
12. **augurs** [ô′gərz]: foretells.

STUDY QUESTIONS

Recalling

1. For what reasons was the author "alone on a mountaintop"?
2. What were the author's first remarks when he saw the shack in which he was to live? What "huge black shadow" frightened him when he woke up on his first night and found the fog had cleared? What were his emotions upon seeing the view in the morning?
3. Summarize the author's usual daily routine described on page 686. What provided him with water? What questions did he sometimes yell at the rocks and trees? What was the answer?
4. What does the author say no one should go through life without doing (page 687)? What does he say a person learns from this experience?
5. What does the author say he felt when he watched the sunsets on the crags? How does his "poem" describe the sudden rainbow?
6. What is burning in infinity, according to the closing sentence?

Interpreting

7. What was difficult about Kerouac's summer on the mountain?
8. What did Kerouac learn to appreciate as a result of his experience? In what way did he grow? What is the significance of the oil lamp in the closing sentence?
9. What elements of Romanticism does Kerouac's narrative contain? Of Transcendentalism? What makes the narrative a distinct product of the twentieth century?

Extending

10. Why do you think both Jack Kerouac and Henry David Thoreau (page 169) were so popular with American youth of the 1950s and 1960s?

VOCABULARY

Analogies

Analogies are comparisons that point out relationships between items. Analogy items on vocabulary tests are usually written as two pairs of words. The words in the first pair are related to each other in the same way as those in the second pair: for example, SHORT : TALL : : SMALL : LARGE.

The first word in capitals in each of the following analogies is from "Alone on a Mountaintop." Complete the analogies by choosing the pair of words that is related in the same way as the pair in capital letters.

1. DESOLATION : ISOLATION : :
   (a) desperation : emptiness
   (b) loneliness : solitude
   (c) fire : slaughter
   (d) loss : misery

2. PONCHO : COAT : :
   (a) shawl : jacket
   (b) boots : galoshes
   (c) frock : dress
   (d) leather : rubber

3. ALTITUDE : HEIGHT : :
   (a) attitude : affection
   (b) volume : capacity
   (c) amplitude : amplifier
   (d) rectitude : law

4. IMPENETRABLE : PIERCE : :
   (a) unclear : unknown
   (b) spoiled : ruin
   (c) unhurt : wound
   (d) impervious : penetrate

5. PRECIPITOUS : SLOPE : :
   (a) angular : rectangle
   (b) mountainous : hilly
   (c) steep : incline
   (d) rocky : cliff

COMPOSITION

Analyzing an Author's Purpose

■ Write an essay analyzing Kerouac's purpose in "Alone on a Mountaintop." Begin by summarizing the main ideas of the work. Then tell how the author's tone suggests his attitude and the attitude he wants his reader to share. Be sure to cite any devices the author uses to achieve his purpose. *For help with this assignment, refer to Lesson 4 in the Writing About Literature Handbook at the back of this book.*

Writing a Description

■ Write a brief description of a natural scene or of some aspect of nature you have experienced. Make your description as vivid and vigorous as you can. Feel free to use some of Kerouac's descriptive techniques, such as colloquial speech, onomatopoeia, and imagery.

Carson McCullers   *1917–1967*

Individuality, selfhood, the fragile human personality—these are Carson McCullers' concerns. Her sensitive and sometimes disturbing novels and stories follow the lives of people trying desperately to gain and keep a hold on an indifferent world.

Carson McCullers was born in Columbus, Georgia. She was an accomplished musician, and her first ambitions directed her to New York City to study music. Her family sold an heirloom to provide her with the money to study at the Juilliard School of Music; unfortunately, however, all the money was lost on the subway.

She began working at various day jobs while taking writing courses at night at Columbia University. One of her teachers there spotted her talent and helped her publish her first short story. Her best known works are *The Heart Is a Lonely Hunter* (1940), *The Member of the Wedding* (1946), and *The Ballad of the Sad Cafe* (1951). *The Member of the Wedding*—the story of a sensitive teenager on the eve of her brother's wedding—was turned into a successful play by McCullers herself in 1950.

From the age of twenty-nine, McCullers was paralyzed on her left side, and this condition severely hampered her ability to work continuously. One of her books, *Clock Without Hands* (1961), took ten years to complete; she finished it by typing one page each day with one hand for a year.

An abiding concern in Carson McCullers' writing is loneliness. In this selection from *The Mortgaged Heart,* she suggests a path away from unwanted solitude and toward true belonging.

Carson McCullers

from **The Mortgaged Heart**

This city, New York—consider the people in it, the eight million of us. An English friend of mine, when asked why he lived in New York City, said that he liked it here because he could be so alone. While it was my friend's desire to be alone, the aloneness of many Americans who live in cities is an involuntary and fearful thing. It has been said that loneliness is the great American malady. What is the nature of this loneliness? It would seem essentially to be a quest for identity.

To the spectator, the amateur philosopher, no motive among the complex ricochets of our desires and rejections seems stronger or more enduring than the will of the individual to claim his identity and belong. From infancy to death, the human being is obsessed by these dual motives. During our first weeks of life, the question of identity shares urgency with the need for milk. The baby reaches for his toes, then explores the bars of his crib; again and again he compares the difference between his own body and the objects around him, and in the wavering, infant eyes there comes a pristine wonder.

Consciousness of self is the first abstract problem that the human being solves. Indeed, it is this self-consciousness that removes us from lower animals. This primitive grasp of identity develops with constantly shifting emphasis through all our years. Perhaps maturity is simply the history of those mutations that reveal to the individual the relation between himself and the world in which he finds himself.

After the first establishment of identity there comes the imperative need to lose this new-found sense of separateness and to belong to something larger and more powerful than the weak, lonely self. The sense of moral isolation is intolerable to us.

In *The Member of the Wedding*[1] the lovely twelve-year-old girl, Frankie Addams, articulates this universal need: "The trouble with me is that for a long time I have just been an *I* person. All people belong to a *We* except me. Not to belong to a *We* makes you too lonesome."

Love is the bridge that leads from the *I* sense to the *We*, and there is a paradox about personal love. Love of another individual opens a new relation between the personality and the world. The lover responds in a new way to nature and may even write poetry. Love is affirmation; it motivates the *yes* responses and the sense of wider communication. Love casts out fear, and in the security of this togetherness we find contentment, courage. We no longer fear the age-old haunting questions: "Who am I?" "Why am I?" "Where am I going?"—and having cast out fear, we can be honest and charitable.

For fear is a primary source of evil. And when the question "Who am I?" recurs and is unanswered, then fear and frustration project a negative attitude. The bewildered soul can answer only: "Since I do not understand 'Who I am,' I only know what I am *not*." The corollary of this emotional incertitude is snobbism, intolerance and racial hate. The xenophobic[2] individual can only reject and destroy, as the xenophobic nation inevitably makes war.

The loneliness of Americans does not have its source in xenophobia; as a nation we are an outgoing people, reaching always for immediate contacts, further experience. But we tend to seek out things as individuals, alone. The European, secure in his family ties and rigid class loyalties, knows little of the moral loneliness

---

1. **The Member of the Wedding:** novel and play by Carson McCullers.
2. **xenophobic** [zē'nō fō'bik]: afraid of strangers and foreigners.

The Subway, George Tooker, 1950.

that is native to us Americans. While the European artists tend to form groups or aesthetic schools, the American artist is the eternal maverick[3]—not only from society in the way of all creative minds, but within the orbit of his own art.

Thoreau took to the woods to seek the ultimate meaning of his life. His creed was simplicity and his *modus vivendi*[4] the deliberate stripping of external life to the Spartan necessities in order that his inward life could freely flourish. His objective, as he put it, was to back the world into a corner. And in that way did he discover "What a man thinks of himself, that it is which determines, or rather indicates, his fate."

On the other hand, Thomas Wolfe turned to the city, and in his wanderings around New York he continued his frenetic[5] and lifelong search for the lost brother, the magic door. He too backed the world into a corner, and as he passed among the city's millions, returning their stares, he experienced "That silent meeting [that] is the summary of all the meetings of men's lives."

Whether in the pastoral joys of country life or in the labyrinthine city, we Americans are always seeking. We wander, question. But the answer waits in each separate heart—the answer of our own identity and the way by which we can master loneliness and feel that at last we belong.

---

3. **maverick:** nonconformist; loner.
4. ***modus vivendi*** [mō′dəs vi ven′dī]: Latin for "manner of living."

5. **frenetic:** frenzied.

STUDY QUESTIONS

Recalling

1. How does McCullers define the nature of loneliness in her first paragraph? What are the "dual motives" of human beings, according to the second paragraph?
2. According to the sixth paragraph, what helps us make the bridge from "I" to "We"? What sort of fear does this emotion cast out?
3. Does McCullers feel that Americans are xenophobic? What do they nevertheless tend to do, according to the eighth paragraph? In what way are Europeans different?
4. According to McCullers' final paragraph, what are Americans always doing? What does she say can be discovered "in each separate heart"?

Interpreting

5. Explain in your own words McCullers' explanation of the cause of loneliness. What does her essay suggest is the relationship between loneliness and both love and fear?
6. What common American characteristic does McCullers suggest is the cause of American loneliness? Is McCullers suggesting that European loyalties are preferable? Consider her final paragraph in answering the second question, and explain your answer.
7. Does McCullers suggest that the city is preferable to the country—or vice versa—as the place to discover identity and solve the problem of loneliness? What does her final paragraph suggest in this regard, and why?

Extending

8. Choose one of the following ideas from McCullers' essay, and explain why you agree or disagree:

   a. Once a human being is conscious of his or her separateness, he or she has the need to lose this separateness and to belong to something larger and more powerful.
   b. Love helps cast out the fear that arises from the questions asked in the search for identity.
   c. Fear is a primary source of evil, and is caused by bewilderment at the questions asked in the search for identity.
   d. Americans are outgoing but tend to seek things as individuals, alone.

LITERARY FOCUS

The Essay

An **essay** is a moderately brief nonfiction work that deals with a particular topic. The form dates back to the French philosopher Montaigne (1533–1592), and the word *essay* comes from the French *essai,* which means "an attempt."

Essays may be classified as formal or informal. A **formal essay** is a carefully structured attempt to instruct or persuade. It has a serious tone, presents its argument logically, and generally refrains from personal references. An **informal essay** is an attempt to entertain the reader while exploring a topic. Its tone is light, its structure somewhat sprawling, and it may make personal references. In fact, informal essays are sometimes called **personal essays.**

McCullers' analysis of loneliness is an example of a formal essay. It is carefully structured, moving from point to point in logical order, reasonable, and clear. On the other hand, Jack Kerouac looks at isolation from a highly personal viewpoint. His essay is sprawling and anecdotal, creating a self-portrait and expressing a personal vision.

Thinking About the Essay

1. Outline the logic of Carson McCullers' formal essay. What are the main points she tries to persuade the reader to share?
2. Find at least two examples of informal language in Kerouac's "Alone on a Mountaintop." What other means does Kerouac employ to achieve the light tone of an informal essay?

COMPARING WRITERS

1. In his "Nobel Prize Acceptance Speech," William Faulkner discusses the fear he perceives in the modern world. How do Jack Kerouac and Carson McCullers address the problem Faulkner brings up?
2. Both Carson McCullers and Jack Kerouac seem to think that there are advantages and disadvantages to being alone. Compare the two writers' views on "aloneness."
3. McCullers' essay suggests that identity and the need to belong are common problems of modern Americans. Which selections that you have read in this unit also address these problems? What solutions do they suggest?

DRAMA

Drama consists of stories that are written to be performed for an audience. The dramatist, or playwright, writes two things: **dialogue** that the actors speak and **stage directions** that give instructions to the various people involved in putting on the play, including the actors. The actual "putting on" of the play is called **staging,** and it involves scenery, costumes, lighting, and props—movable articles like chairs or books—as well as the activities of the actors.

Drama as a form of literature dates back to the ancient Greeks and seems to have had its origins in religious ritual. The Greeks classified drama in two categories: tragedy and comedy. A **tragedy** is a play in which the main character comes to an unhappy end. A **comedy,** on the other hand, has a happy ending. Classical Greek tragedies generally involve a **protagonist,** or main character, who cuts a noble figure except for one tragic flaw that brings about his or her ruin. Usually the protagonist has one or more **antagonists—** rivals or opponents—and invariably there is a **chorus,** a group of players who narrate portions of the play and comment upon the action. Greek comedies are humorous and frequently satirical—in fact, the Greek comic playwright Aristophanes is considered the father of satire.

The Greek philosopher Aristotle defined the principles of drama as he saw them, and his ideas were adopted and adapted by classical Roman playwrights and by the great dramatists of Elizabethan England in the sixteenth and early seventeenth centuries. Classical and Elizabethan dramas were generally written in verse, and the masterpieces of the great Elizabethan playwright William Shakespeare (1564–1616) are known as much for their powerful poetry as their perceptive insights into the human heart. Shakespeare's tragedies generally follow the pattern of Greek tragedies, but most of his comedies are lighthearted romances, quite different from the biting satires of Aristophanes.

The theater audience in Elizabethan times was a motley crew: Public theaters were open to people from all ranks of English society. However, by the end of the seventeenth century, the public theaters in London had all but disappeared, and plays were performed in private theaters attended chiefly by the wealthy classes. This period saw the birth of the **comedy of manners,** a realistic and often satirical look at life in sophisticated society. This kind of play owes much of its existence to the works of the French playwright Molière (1622–1673). The comedy of manners remained a popular form throughout the eighteenth century, though English audiences of the period also enjoyed **sentimental comedies,** unrealistic tales that contain romance and tears and that usually offer a moral message.

With the Romantic movement—a movement that spurred some of the world's greatest poetry and prose—drama declined, and a rather inferior form of play, the melodrama, was born. **Melodramas** are highly emotional plays with little concern for developing convincing motivation for their characters. They were extremely popular in the nineteenth century until the influence of Realism was felt upon the stage. With Realism came the great plays of Anton Chekhov (1860–1904), a Russian, and of Henrik Ibsen (1828–1906), a Norwegian, who explore social issues and give audiences a "slice of life" as it is lived. Psychological realism came to the stage as **Expressionism,** a movement in drama that is concerned with the inner realities of characters' minds. Early Expressionist dramas are best exemplified in the plays of Sweden's Johan August Strindberg (1849–1912).

The plays of Ibsen and Strindberg have had a profound impact on all subsequent drama worldwide, for twentieth-century drama often deals with external and internal realities. Also in twentieth-century drama we see an end to the classical distinctions between tragedy and comedy. To be sure, the terms are still used, but more and more the devices of each are blended within one work, and we refer to any serious modern play as a drama.

American Drama

Up until the twentieth century American drama made little impact on American literature as a whole. The reasons for the lack of American drama are understandable: Theaters such as the elitist European ones of the eighteenth century would not flourish in America, at that time an infant democracy, and the melodrama of the nineteenth century would not attract serious American writers. There were, of course, some American plays of literary interest written before 1900: Royall Tyler's *The Contrast* (1787), America's first comedy, and the nineteenth-century verse tragedies of George Henry Boker are considered to be of literary merit. However, it was not until Realism and Expressionism began to appear on the stage that serious American writers turned to drama.

In the beginning of the twentieth century, so-called little theaters sprang up throughout the United States, theaters that encouraged serious playwrights because they were willing to produce original works by unknown talents. The first American dramatist to achieve an international reputation, Eugene O'Neill (1888–1953), began his career as a writer for the Provincetown Players, a "little theater" company begun in Provincetown, Massachusetts.

The plays of Eugene O'Neill reflect his New England background and Irish American heritage and display the Realism and interest in modern psychology characteristic of Ibsen and Strindberg. O'Neill's plays also reflect the Modernist experimentation of the early twentieth century: In *Strange Interlude* (1928) characters' thoughts are heard by the audience, and in *The Great God Brown* (1926) characters don and remove masks while they are speaking. Among O'Neill's other famous plays are *Mourning Becomes Electra* (1931), *The Ice Man Cometh* (1946), and *Long Day's Journey into Night* (1956), a semiautobiographical drama produced after the playwright's death.

Led by O'Neill, American drama flourished between the two world wars. Elmer Rice wrote a portrait of tenement life called *Street Scene* (1929); Clifford Odets explored serious social problems in *Awake and Sing!* (1935) and *Waiting for Lefty* (1935). Maxwell Anderson wrote plays in verse, and George S. Kaufman and Moss Hart entertained audiences with their witty satires.

The twenties and thirties also saw the development of a strictly American form, the **musical comedy,** which reached its peak after World War II in the works of Rodgers and Hammerstein, Lerner and Loewe, Leonard Bernstein, and Stephen Sondheim. Major American dramatists since World War II include Tennessee Williams *(The Glass Menagerie, A Streetcar Named Desire)*; William Inge *(Picnic, The Dark at the Top of the Stairs)*; Arthur Miller *(Death of a Salesman, The Crucible)*; and Edward Albee *(Who's Afraid of Virginia Woolf?)*.

Eugene O'Neill (on ladder, holding cloth) and others preparing for the first production of O'Neill's *Bound East for Cardiff*, Provincetown Playhouse, 1916.

Thornton Wilder   *1897–1975*

In 1927 Thornton Wilder was teaching French to high school students in New Jersey. That year he published a novel, his second, that he presumed would attract little more notice than had his first one. The new novel was set in Peru several centuries ago, in a time and place that would have seemed to hold little interest for Americans caught up in the exploits of Babe Ruth and Charles Lindbergh. Yet *The Bridge of San Luis Rey* proved to be an enormous success, winning the Pulitzer Prize and remaining one of the most popular American novels.

Born in Madison, Wisconsin, Wilder spent part of his youth in China, where his father was consul general. He went to Oberlin College and Yale and then studied in Rome for a year before taking up his duties as French instructor and housemaster at Lawrenceville Academy near Princeton, New Jersey. The unexpected success of his second novel brought Wilder a substantial income, and he was no longer obliged to teach for a living. Yet he continued to do so a while longer, and with great success, first at the University of Chicago and then at Harvard.

He also continued to write novels, six in the course of his lifetime, and he managed what few other novelists have been able to do: He became a successful playwright. Since his childhood Wilder had been fascinated by the theater. Accordingly, in his late thirties, this well-established novelist turned seriously to writing plays. One was a deceptively simple drama of New England village life that appeared on Broadway in 1938. That play, *Our Town,* would prove to be even more popular than his novel of colonial Peru. Wilder's other plays include *The Long Christmas Dinner* (1931) and *The Skin of Our Teeth* (1942). He was awarded the first National Medal for Literature in 1965.

Introducing **Our Town**

It has been said that not a day has passed since its original performance that *Our Town* has not been staged by some group, somewhere in America. It remains a favorite partly because of the ease with which it can be staged: no curtain, no scenery, scarcely any props beyond a few pieces of furniture and a couple of ladders. Such staging is a strong break with dramatic traditions. Yet, seeing the play, audiences soon adjust to the almost empty stage. Imagination helps us convert a wooden plank into a drugstore counter and picture above the bare floorboards the hollyhocks of Mrs. Gibbs's garden.

If Wilder's untraditional staging intrigues audiences, so does his use of one traditional device, the chorus. In classical Greek drama the chorus was a group of people who introduced the action of the play and commented on events as they progressed. By Shakespeare's day the role of chorus was acted by one person, but Realistic drama generally abandoned the chorus entirely, finding choral interruptions awkward and unrealistic. Wilder reintroduces the role of chorus with the character of the Stage Manager. In theater productions a stage manager is a person who remains behind the scenes, taking charge of the staff and seeing to changes in scenery, props, and other aspects of the play's staging. In *Our Town,* however, the Stage Manager is a character who appears on the stage as the audience is seated and immediately establishes himself as the narrator and interpreter of the events they are about to see.

Those events cannot be labeled as either comic or tragic. *Our Town* offers a rich mix of human emotions; it is simply a drama. At times it is Realistic in its depiction of everyday life as it was lived in turn-of-the-century New England. More frequently, it goes beyond Realism into the realm of Expressionism, taking us deep into the perceptions and emotions of its characters. It remains a favorite because of the warmly nostalgic view it offers of what people like to believe was a simple, appealing age. Yet most of all it retains its popularity because it speaks, with hope and love, of the burdens and blessings of being human, while reminding us of the infinite value of the ordinary and the everyday.

Thornton Wilder

Our Town

CHARACTERS *(in the order of their appearance)*

STAGE MANAGER

DR. GIBBS

JOE CROWELL

HOWIE NEWSOME

MRS. GIBBS

MRS. WEBB

GEORGE GIBBS

REBECCA GIBBS

WALLY WEBB

EMILY WEBB

PROFESSOR WILLARD

MR. WEBB

WOMAN IN THE BALCONY

MAN IN THE AUDITORIUM

LADY IN THE BOX

SIMON STIMSON

MRS. SOAMES

CONSTABLE WARREN

SI CROWELL

THREE BASEBALL PLAYERS

SAM CRAIG

JOE STODDARD

The entire play takes place in Grover's Corners, New Hampshire.

ACT 1

[*No curtain.*
No scenery.
The audience, arriving, sees an empty stage in half-light.
Presently the STAGE MANAGER, *hat on and pipe in mouth, enters and begins placing a table and three chairs downstage left, and a table and three chairs downstage right. He also places a low bench at the corner of what will be the Webb house, left.*
"Left" and "right" are from the point of view of the actor facing the audience. "Up" is toward the back wall.
As the house lights go down he has finished setting the stage and leaning against the right proscenium[1] pillar watches the late arrivals in the audience.
When the auditorium is in complete darkness he speaks.]

STAGE MANAGER. This play is called "Our Town." It was written by Thornton Wilder; produced and directed by A. . . . (or: produced by A. . . .; directed by B. . . .). In it you will see Miss C. . . .; Miss D. . . .; Miss E. . . .; and Mr. F. . . .; Mr. G. . . .; Mr. H. . . .; and many others. The name of the town is Grover's Corners, New Hampshire—just across the Massachusetts line: latitude 42 degrees 40 minutes; longitude 70 degrees 37 minutes. The First Act shows a day in our town. The day is May 7, 1901. The time is just before dawn.

[*A rooster crows.*]

The sky is beginning to show some streaks of light over in the East there, behind our mount'in. The morning star always gets wonderful bright the minute before it has to go—doesn't it?

[*He stares at it for a moment, then goes upstage.*]

Well, I'd better show you how our town lies. Up here—

[*That is: parallel with the back wall.*]

is Main Street. Way back there is the railway station; tracks go that way. Polish Town's across the tracks, and some Canuck[2] families.

[*Toward the left.*]

Over there is the Congregational Church; across the street's the Presbyterian.
Methodist and Unitarian are over there.
Baptist is down in the holla' by the river.
Catholic Church is over beyond the tracks.
Here's the Town Hall and Post Office combined; jail's in the basement.
Bryan[3] once made a speech from these very steps here.
Along here's a row of stores. Hitching posts and horse blocks in front of them. First automobile's going to come along in about five years—belonged to Banker Cartwright, our richest citizen . . . lives in the big white house up on the hill.
Here's the grocery store and here's Mr. Morgan's drugstore. Most everybody in town manages to look into those two stores once a day. Public School's over yonder. High School's still farther over. Quarter of nine mornings, noontimes, and three o'clock afternoons, the hull[4] town can hear the yelling and screaming from those schoolyards.

[*He approaches the table and chairs downstage right.*]

This is our doctor's house—Doc Gibbs'. This is the back door.

[*Two arched trellises, covered with vines and flowers, are pushed out, one by each proscenium pillar.*]

---

1. **proscenium** [prō sē′nē əm]: part of a stage in front of the curtain.

2. **Canuck** [kə nuk′]: slang for French-Canadian.
3. **Bryan:** William Jennings Bryan (1860–1925), U.S. statesman and orator.
4. **hull:** New England dialect pronunciation of "whole."

There's some scenery for those who think they have to have scenery.
This is Mrs. Gibbs' garden. Corn . . . peas . . . beans . . . hollyhocks . . . heliotrope . . . and a lot of burdock.

[*Crosses the stage.*]

In those days our newspaper come out twice a week—the Grover's Corners *Sentinel*—and this is Editor Webb's house.
And this is Mrs. Webb's garden.
Just like Mrs. Gibbs', only it's got a lot of sunflowers, too.

[*He looks upward, center stage.*]

Right here . . . 's a big butternut tree.

[*He returns to his place by the right proscenium pillar and looks at the audience for a minute.*]

Nice town, y'know what I mean?
Nobody very remarkable ever come out of it, s'far as we know.
The earliest tombstones in the cemetery up there on the mountain say 1670–1680—they're Grovers and Cartwrights and Gibbses and Herseys—same names as are around here now.
Well, as I said: it's about dawn.
The only lights on in town are in a cottage over by the tracks where a Polish mother's just had twins. And in the Joe Crowell house, where Joe Junior's getting up so as to deliver the paper. And in the depot, where Shorty Hawkins is gettin' ready to flag the 5:45 for Boston.

[*A train whistle is heard. The* STAGE MANAGER *takes out his watch and nods.*]

Naturally, out in the country—all around—there've been lights on for some time, what with milkin's and so on. But town people sleep late.
So—another day's begun.
There's Doc Gibbs comin' down Main Street now, comin' back from that baby case. And here's his wife comin' downstairs to get breakfast.

[MRS. GIBBS, *a plump, pleasant woman in the middle thirties, comes "downstairs" right. She pulls up an imaginary window shade in her kitchen and starts to make a fire in her stove.*]

Doc Gibbs died in 1930. The new hospital's named after him.
Mrs. Gibbs died first—long time ago, in fact. She went out to visit her daughter, Rebecca, who married an insurance man in Canton, Ohio, and died there—pneumonia—but her body was brought back here. She's up in the cemetery there now—in with a whole mess of Gibbses and Herseys—she was Julia Hersey 'fore she married Doc Gibbs in the Congregational Church over there.
In our town we like to know the facts about everybody.
There's Mrs. Webb, coming downstairs to get her breakfast, too.
—That's Doc Gibbs. Got that call at half past one this morning.
And there comes Joe Crowell, Jr., delivering Mr. Webb's *Sentinel.*

[DR. GIBBS *has been coming along Main Street from the left. At the point where he would turn to approach his house, he stops, sets down his—imaginary—black bag, takes off his hat, and rubs his face with fatigue, using an enormous handkerchief.*
MRS. WEBB, *a thin, serious, crisp woman, has entered her kitchen, left, tying on an apron. She goes through the motions of putting wood into a stove, lighting it, and preparing breakfast.*
Suddenly, JOE CROWELL, JR., *eleven, starts down Main Street from the right, hurling imaginary newspapers into doorways.*]

JOE CROWELL, JR. Morning, Doc Gibbs.

DR. GIBBS. Morning, Joe.

JOE CROWELL, JR. Somebody been sick, Doc?

DR. GIBBS. No. Just some twins born over in Polish Town.

JOE CROWELL, JR. Do you want your paper now?

DR. GIBBS. Yes, I'll take it. Anything serious goin' on in the world since Wednesday?

JOE CROWELL, JR. Yessir. My schoolteacher, Miss Foster, 's getting married to a fella over in Concord.

DR. GIBBS. I declare. How do you boys feel about that?

JOE CROWELL, JR. Well, of course, it's none of my business—but I think if a person starts out to be a teacher, she ought to stay one.

DR. GIBBS. How's your knee, Joe?

JOE CROWELL, JR. Fine, Doc, I never think about it at all. Only like you said, it always tells me when it's going to rain.

DR. GIBBS. What's it telling you today? Goin' to rain?

JOE CROWELL, JR. No, sir.

DR. GIBBS. Sure?

JOE CROWELL, JR. Yessir.

DR. GIBBS. Knee ever make a mistake?

JOE CROWELL, JR. No, sir.

[JOE *goes off.* DR. GIBBS *stands reading his paper.*]

STAGE MANAGER. Want to tell you something about that boy Joe Crowell there. Joe was awful bright—graduated from high school here, head of his class. So he got a scholarship to Massachusetts Tech. Graduated head of his class there, too. It was all wrote up in the Boston paper at the time. Goin' to be a great engineer, Joe was. But the war[5] broke out and he died in France. All that education for nothing.

HOWIE NEWSOME. [*Off left.*] Giddap, Bessie! What's the matter with you today?

STAGE MANAGER. Here comes Howie Newsome, deliverin' the milk.

[HOWIE NEWSOME, *about thirty, in overalls, comes along Main Street from the left, walking beside an invisible horse and wagon and carrying an imaginary rack with milk bottles. The sound of clinking milk bottles is heard. He leaves some bottles at* MRS. WEBB'S *trellis, then, crossing the stage to* MRS. GIBBS', *he stops center to talk to* DR. GIBBS.]

HOWIE NEWSOME. Morning, Doc.

DR. GIBBS. Morning, Howie.

HOWIE NEWSOME. Somebody sick?

DR. GIBBS. Pair of twins over to Mrs. Goruslawski's.

HOWIE NEWSOME. Twins, eh? This town's gettin' bigger every year.

DR. GIBBS. Goin' to rain, Howie?

HOWIE NEWSOME. No, no. Fine day—that'll burn through. Come on, Bessie.

DR. GIBBS. Hello Bessie.

[*He strokes the horse, which has remained up center.*]

How old is she, Howie?

HOWIE NEWSOME. Going on seventeen. Bessie's all mixed up about the route ever since the Lockharts stopped takin' their quart of milk every day. She wants to leave 'em a quart just the same—keeps scolding me the hull trip.

[*He reaches* MRS. GIBBS' *back door. She is waiting for him.*]

MRS. GIBBS. Good morning, Howie.

HOWIE NEWSOME. Morning, Mrs. Gibbs. Doc's just comin' down the street.

MRS. GIBBS. Is he? Seems like you're late today.

HOWIE NEWSOME. Yes. Somep'n went wrong with the separator.[6] Don't know what 'twas. [*He passes* DR. GIBBS *up center.*] Doc!

---

5. **war:** World War I (1914–1918).

6. **separator:** device for separating cream from milk.

DR. GIBBS. Howie!

MRS. GIBBS. [*Calling upstairs.*] Children! Children! Time to get up.

HOWIE NEWSOME. Come on, Bessie! [*He goes off right.*]

MRS. GIBBS. George! Rebecca!

[DR. GIBBS *arrives at his back door and passes through the trellis into his house.*]

MRS. GIBBS. Everything all right, Frank?

DR. GIBBS. Yes. I declare—easy as kittens.

MRS. GIBBS. Bacon'll be ready in a minute. Set down and drink your coffee. You can catch a couple hours' sleep this morning, can't you?

DR. GIBBS. Hm! . . . Mrs. Wentworth's coming at eleven. Guess I know what it's about, too. Her stummick ain't what it ought to be.

MRS. GIBBS. All told, you won't get more'n three hours' sleep. Frank Gibbs, I don't know what's goin' to become of you. I do wish I could get you to go away someplace and take a rest. I think it would do you good.

MRS. WEBB. Emileeee! Time to get up! Wally! Seven o'clock!

MRS. GIBBS. I declare, you got to speak to George. Seems like something's come over him lately. He's no help to me at all. I can't even get him to cut me some wood.

DR. GIBBS.

[*Washing and drying his hands at the sink.* MRS. GIBBS *is busy at the stove.*]

Is he sassy to you?

MRS. GIBBS. No. He just whines! All he thinks about is that baseball—George! Rebecca! You'll be late for school.

DR. GIBBS. M-m-m . . .

MRS. GIBBS. George!

DR. GIBBS. George, look sharp!

GEORGE'S VOICE. Yes, Pa!

DR. GIBBS. [*As he goes off the stage.*] Don't you hear your mother calling you? I guess I'll go upstairs and get forty winks.

MRS. WEBB. Walleee! Emileee! You'll be late for school! Walleee! You wash yourself good or I'll come up and do it myself.

REBECCA GIBBS' VOICE. Ma! What dress shall I wear?

MRS. GIBBS. Don't make a noise. Your father's been out all night and needs his sleep. I washed and ironed the blue gingham for you special.

REBECCA. Ma, I hate that dress.

MRS. GIBBS. Oh, hush-up-with-you.

REBECCA. Every day I go to school dressed like a sick turkey.

MRS. GIBBS. Now, Rebecca, you always look *very* nice.

REBECCA. Mama, George's throwing soap at me.

MRS. GIBBS. I'll come and slap the both of you,—that's what I'll do.

[*A factory whistle sounds.*
The CHILDREN *dash in and take their places at the tables.*
Right, GEORGE, *about sixteen, and* REBECCA, *eleven. Left,* EMILY *and* WALLY, *same ages. They carry strapped schoolbooks.*]

STAGE MANAGER. We've got a factory in our town too—hear it? Makes blankets. Cartwrights own it and it brung 'em a fortune.

MRS. WEBB. Children! Now I won't have it. Breakfast is just as good as any other meal and I won't have you gobbling like wolves. It'll stunt your growth—that's a fact. Put away your book, Wally.

WALLY. Aw, Ma! By ten o'clock I got to know all about Canada.

MRS. WEBB. You know the rule's well as I do—no books at table. As for me, I'd rather have my children healthy than bright.

EMILY. I'm both, Mama: you know I am. I'm the brightest girl in school for my age. I have a wonderful memory.

MRS. WEBB. Eat your breakfast.

WALLY. I'm bright, too, when I'm looking at my stamp collection.

MRS. GIBBS. I'll speak to your father about it when he's rested. Seems to me twenty-five cents a week's enough for a boy your age. I declare I don't know how you spend it all.

GEORGE. Aw, Ma—I gotta lotta things to buy.

MRS. GIBBS. Strawberry phosphates[7]—that's what you spend it on.

GEORGE. I don't see how Rebecca comes to have so much money. She has more'n a dollar.

REBECCA. [*Spoon in mouth, dreamily.*] I've been saving it up gradual.

MRS. GIBBS. Well, dear, I think it's a good thing to spend some every now and then.

REBECCA. Mama, do you know what I love most in the world—do you? Money.

MRS. GIBBS. Eat your breakfast.

THE CHILDREN. Mama, there's first bell. I gotta hurry. I don't want any more. I gotta hurry.

[*The* CHILDREN *rise, seize their books and dash out through the trellises. They meet, down center, and chattering, walk to Main Street, then turn left.*
The STAGE MANAGER *goes off, unobtrusively, right.*]

MRS. WEBB. Walk fast, but you don't have to run. Wally, pull up your pants at the knee. Stand up straight, Emily.

---

7. **phosphates:** soft drinks of soda water and syrup.

MRS. GIBBS. Tell Miss Foster I send her my best congratulations—can you remember that?

REBECCA. Yes, Ma.

MRS. GIBBS. You look real nice, Rebecca. Pick up your feet.

ALL. Good-bye.

[MRS. GIBBS *fills her apron with food for the chickens and comes down to the footlights.*]

MRS. GIBBS. Here, chick, chick, chick.
No, go away, you. Go away.
Here, chick, chick, chick.
What the matter with *you?* Fight, fight, fight—
that's all you do.
Hm . . . *you* don't belong to me. Where'd you come from? [*She shakes her apron.*] Oh, don't be so scared. Nobody's going to hurt you.

[MRS. WEBB *is sitting on the bench by her trellis, stringing beans.*]

Good morning, Myrtle. How's your cold?

MRS. WEBB. Well, I still get that tickling feeling in my throat. I told Charles I didn't know as I'd go to choir practice tonight. Wouldn't be any use.

MRS. GIBBS. Have you tried singing over your voice?

MRS. WEBB. Yes, but somehow I can't do that and stay on the key. While I'm resting myself I thought I'd string some of these beans.

MRS. GIBBS.

[*Rolling up her sleeves as she crosses the stage for a chat.*]

Let me help you. Beans have been good this year.

MRS. WEBB. I've decided to put up forty quarts if it kills me. The children say they hate 'em, but I notice they're able to get 'em down all winter.

[*Pause. Brief sound of chickens cackling.*]

MRS. GIBBS. Now, Myrtle. I've got to tell you something, because if I don't tell somebody I'll burst.

MRS. WEBB. Why, Julia Gibbs!

MRS. GIBBS. Here, give me some more of those beans. Myrtle, did one of those secondhand-furniture men from Boston come to see you last Friday?

MRS. WEBB. No-o.

MRS. GIBBS. Well, he called on me. First I thought he was a patient wantin' to see Dr. Gibbs. 'N he wormed his way into my parlor, and, Myrtle Webb, he offered me three hundred and fifty dollars for Grandmother Wentworth's highboy, as I'm sitting here!

MRS. WEBB. Why, Julia Gibbs!

MRS. GIBBS. He did! That old thing! Why, it was so big I didn't know where to put it and I almost give it to Cousin Hester Wilcox.

MRS. WEBB. Well, you're going to take it, aren't you?

MRS. GIBBS. I don't know.

MRS. WEBB. You don't know—three hundred and fifty dollars! What's come over you?

MRS. GIBBS. Well, if I could get the Doctor to take the money and go away someplace on a real trip, I'd sell it like that.—Y'know, Myrtle, it's been the dream of my life to see Paris, France.—Oh, I don't know. It sounds crazy, I suppose, but for years I've been promising myself that if we ever had the chance—

MRS. WEBB. How does the Doctor feel about it?

MRS. GIBBS. Well, I did beat about the bush a little and said that if I got a legacy—that's the way I put it—I'd make him take me somewhere.

MRS. WEBB. M-m-m . . . What did he say?

MRS. GIBBS. You know how he is. I haven't heard a serious word out of him since I've known him. No, he said, it might make him discontented with Grover's Corners to go traipsin' about Europe; better let well enough alone, he says. Every two years he makes a trip to the battlefields of the Civil War and that's enough treat for anybody, he says.

MRS. WEBB. Well, Mr. Webb just *admires* the way Dr. Gibbs knows everything about the Civil War. Mr. Webb's a good mind to give up Napoleon and move over to the Civil War, only Dr. Gibbs being one of the greatest experts in the country just makes him despair.

MRS. GIBBS. It's a fact! Dr. Gibbs is never so happy as when he's at Antietam or Gettysburg.[8] The times I've walked over those hills, Myrtle, stopping at every bush and pacing it all out, like we were going to buy it.

MRS. WEBB. Well, if that secondhand man's really serious about buyin' it, Julia, you sell it. And then you'll get to see Paris, all right. Just keep droppin' hints from time to time—that's how I got to see the Atlantic Ocean, y'know.

MRS. GIBBS. Oh, I'm sorry I mentioned it. Only it seems to me that once in your life before you die you ought to see a country where they don't talk in English and don't even want to.

[*The* STAGE MANAGER *enters briskly from the right. He tips his hat to the ladies, who nod their heads.*]

STAGE MANAGER. Thank you, ladies. Thank you very much.

[MRS. GIBBS *and* MRS. WEBB *gather up their things, return into their homes and disappear.*]

Now we're going to skip a few hours.
But first we want a little more information about the town, kind of a scientific account, you might say.
So I've asked Professor Willard of our State University to sketch in a few details of our past history here.

Is Professor Willard here?

[PROFESSOR WILLARD, *a rural savant, pince-nez*[9] *on a wide satin ribbon, enters from the right with some notes in his hand.*]

May I introduce Professor Willard of our State University.
A few brief notes, thank you, Professor—unfortunately our time is limited.

PROFESSOR WILLARD. Grover's Corners . . . let me see . . . Grover's Corners lies on the old Pleistocene[10] granite of the Appalachian range. I may say it's some of the oldest land in the world. We're very proud of that. A shelf of Devonian basalt crosses it with vestiges of Mesozoic[11] shale, and some sandstone outcroppings; but that's all more recent: two hundred, three hundred million years old.
Some highly interesting fossils have been found . . . I may say: unique fossils . . . two miles out of town, in Silas Peckham's cow pasture. They can be seen at the museum in our University at any time—that is, at any reasonable time. Shall I read some of Professor Gruber's notes on the meteorological situation—mean precipitation, et cetera?

STAGE MANAGER. Afraid we won't have time for that, Professor. We might have a few words on the history of man here.

PROFESSOR WILLARD. Yes . . . anthropological data: Early Amerindian[12] stock. Cotahatchee[13] tribes . . . no evidence before the tenth century of this era . . . hm . . . now entirely disappeared . . . possible traces in three families. Migration toward the end of the seventeenth century of English brachycephalic[14] blue-eyed

---

8. **Antietam** [an tē′təm] . . . **Gettysburg:** Civil war battle sites.

9. **pince-nez** [pans′nā′]: eyeglasses without temples, held on the nose by a spring.
10. **Pleistocene** [plīs′tə sēn′]: geological era in which granite was formed.
11. **Devonian** [də vō′nē ən] . . **Mesozoic** [mes′ə zō′ik]: other geological eras.
12. **Amerindian** [am′ə rin′dē ən]: American Indian.
13. **Cotahatchee** [kō′te ha′chē]: Amerindian tribe.
14. **brachycephalic** [brak′i sə fal′ik]: having a short or broad head.

stock . . . for the most part. Since then some Slav and Mediterranean—

STAGE MANAGER. And the population, Professor Willard?

PROFESSOR WILLARD. Within the town limits: 2,640.

STAGE MANAGER. Just a moment, Professor. [*He whispers into the professor's ear.*]

PROFESSOR WILLARD. Oh, yes, indeed? The population, *at the moment,* is 2,642. The Postal District brings in 507 more, making a total of 3,149. Mortality and birth rates: constant. By MacPherson's gauge: 6.032.

STAGE MANAGER. Thank you very much, Professor. We're all very much obliged to you, I'm sure.

PROFESSOR WILLARD. Not at all, sir; not at all.

STAGE MANAGER. This way, Professor, and thank you again.

[*Exit* PROFESSOR WILLARD.]

Now the political and social report: Editor Webb. Oh, Mr. Webb?

[MRS. WEBB *appears at her back door.*]

MRS. WEBB. He'll be here in a minute. . . . He just cut his hand while he was eatin' an apple.

STAGE MANAGER. Thank you, Mrs. Webb.

MRS. WEBB. Charles! Everybody's waitin'. [*Exit* MRS. WEBB.]

STAGE MANAGER. Mr. Webb is Publisher and Editor of the Grover's Corners *Sentinel.* That's our local paper, y'know.

[MR. WEBB *enters from his house, pulling on his coat. His finger is bound in a handkerchief.*]

MR. WEBB. Well . . . I don't have to tell you that we're run here by a Board of Selectmen.[15]—All males vote at the age of twenty-

one. Women vote indirect. We're lower middle class: sprinkling of professional men . . . ten per cent illiterate laborers. Politically, we're eighty-six per cent Republicans; six per cent Democrats; four per cent Socialists; rest, indifferent.

Religiously, we're eighty-five per cent Protestants; twelve per cent Catholics; rest, indifferent.

STAGE MANAGER. Have you any comments, Mr. Webb?

MR. WEBB. Very ordinary town, if you ask me. Little better behaved than most. Probably a lot duller.

But our young people here seem to like it well enough. Ninety percent of 'em graduating from high school settle down right here to live—even when they've been away to college.

STAGE MANAGER. Now, is there anyone in the audience who would like to ask Editor Webb anything about the town?

WOMAN IN THE BALCONY. Is there much drinking in Grover's Corners?

MR. WEBB. Well, ma'am, I wouldn't know what you'd call *much.* Satiddy nights the farmhands meet down in Ellery Greenough's stable and holler some. We've got one or two town drunks, but they're always having remorses every time an evangelist comes to town. No, ma'am, I'd say likker ain't a regular thing in the home here, except in the medicine chest. Right good for snake bite, y'know—always was.

BELLIGERENT MAN AT BACK OF AUDITORIUM. Is there no one in town aware of—

STAGE MANAGER. Come forward, will you, where we can all hear you. What were you saying?

BELLIGERENT MAN. Is there no one in town aware of social injustice and industrial inequality?

MR. WEBB. Oh, yes, everybody is—somethin' terrible. Seems like they spend most of their time talking about who's rich and who's poor.

BELLIGERENT MAN. Then why don't they do

---

15. **Board of Selectmen:** elected town officials.

something about it? [*He withdraws without waiting for an answer.*]

MR. WEBB. Well, I dunno. . . . I guess we're all hunting like everybody else for a way the diligent and sensible can rise to the top and the lazy and quarrelsome can sink to the bottom. But it ain't easy to find. Meanwhile, we do all we can to help those that can't help themselves and those that can we leave alone. Are there any other questions?

LADY IN A BOX. Oh, Mr. Webb? Mr. Webb, is there any culture or love of beauty in Grover's Corners?

MR. WEBB. Well, ma'am, there ain't much—not in the sense you mean. Come to think of it, there's some girls that play the piano at High School Commencement; but they ain't happy about it. No, ma'am, there isn't much culture; but maybe this is the place to tell you that we've got a lot of pleasures of a kind here: we like the sun comin' up over the mountain in the morning, and we all notice a good deal about the birds. We pay a lot of attention to them. And we watch the change of the seasons; yes, everybody knows about them. But those other things—you're right, ma'am—there ain't much. *Robinson Crusoe* and the Bible; and Handel's "Largo," we all know that; and Whistler's "Mother"[16]—those are just about as far as we go.

LADY IN A BOX. So I thought. Thank you, Mr. Webb.

STAGE MANAGER. Thank you, Mr. Webb.

[MR. WEBB *retires.*]

Now, we'll go back to the town. It's early afternoon. All 2,642 have had their dinners and all the dishes have been washed.

---

16. **Robinson Crusoe . . . "Mother":** *Robinson Crusoe* is a novel by the English writer Daniel Defoe (1660?–1731). Handel's "Largo" is a musical composition by German-born composer George Frederick Handel (1685–1759). Whistler's "Mother" refers to "Arrangement in Gray and Black: Portrait of the Artist's Mother" by American painter James McNeil Whistler (1834–1903).

[MR. WEBB, *having removed his coat, returns and starts pushing a lawn mower to and fro beside his house.*]

There's an early-afternoon calm in our town: a buzzin' and a hummin' from the school buildings; only a few buggies on Main Street—the horses dozing at the hitching posts; you all remember what it's like. Doc Gibbs is in his office, tapping people and making them say "ah." Mr. Webb's cuttin' his lawn over there; one man in ten thinks it's a privilege to push his own lawn mower.

No, sir. It's later than I thought. There are the children coming home from school already.

[*Shrill girls' voices are heard, off left.* EMILY *comes along Main Street, carrying some books. There are some signs that she is imagining herself to be a lady of startling elegance.*]

EMILY. I *can't*, Lois. I've got to go home and help my mother. I *promised.*

MR. WEBB. Emily, walk simply. Who do you think you are today?

EMILY. Papa, you're terrible. One minute you tell me to stand up straight and the next minute you call me names. I just don't listen to you. [*She gives him an abrupt kiss.*]

MR. WEBB. Golly, I never got a kiss from such a great lady before.

[*He goes out of sight.* EMILY *leans over and picks some flowers by the gate of her house.* GEORGE GIBBS *comes careening down Main Street. He is throwing a ball up to dizzying heights, and waiting to catch it again. This sometimes requires his taking six steps backward. He bumps into an* OLD LADY *invisible to us.*]

GEORGE. Excuse me, Mrs. Forrest.

STAGE MANAGER. [*As* MRS. FORREST.] Go out and play in the fields, young man. You got no business playing baseball on Main Street.

GEORGE. Awfully sorry, Mrs. Forrest. Hello, Emily.

EMILY. H'lo.

GEORGE. You made a fine speech in class.

EMILY. Well . . . I was really ready to make a speech about the Monroe Doctrine, but at the last minute Miss Corcoran made me talk about the Louisiana Purchase instead. I worked an awful long time on both of them.

GEORGE. Gee, it's funny, Emily. From my window up there I can just see your head nights when you're doing your homework over in your room.

EMILY. Why, can you?

GEORGE. You certainly do stick to it, Emily. I don't see how you can sit still that long. I guess you like school.

EMILY. Well, I always feel it's something you have to go through.

GEORGE. Yeah.

EMILY. I don't mind it really. It passes the time.

GEORGE. Yeah. Emily, what do you think? We might work out a kinda telegraph from your window to mine; and once in a while you could give me a kinda hint or two about one of those algebra problems. I don't mean the answers, Emily, of course not . . . just some little hint . . .

EMILY. Oh, I think *hints* are allowed. So—ah—if you get stuck, George, you whistle to me; and I'll give you some hints.

GEORGE. Emily, you're just naturally bright, I guess.

EMILY. I figure that it's just the way a person's born.

GEORGE. Yeah. But, you see, I want to be a farmer, and my Uncle Luke says whenever I'm ready I can come over and work on his farm and if I'm any good I can just gradually have it.

EMILY. You mean the house and everything?

[*Enter* MRS. WEBB *with a large bowl and sits on the bench by her trellis.*]

GEORGE. Yeah. Well, thanks . . . I better be getting out to the baseball field. Thanks for the talk, Emily. Good afternoon, Mrs. Webb.

MRS. WEBB. Good afternoon, George.

GEORGE. So long, Emily.

EMILY. So long, George.

MRS. WEBB. Emily, come and help me string these beans for the winter. George Gibbs let himself have a real conversation, didn't he? Why, he's growing up. How old would George be?

EMILY. I don't know.

MRS. WEBB. Let's see. He must be almost sixteen.

EMILY. Mama, I made a speech in class today and I was very good.

MRS. WEBB. You must recite it to your father at supper. What was it about?

EMILY. The Louisiana Purchase. It was like silk off a spool. I'm going to make speeches all my life.—Mama, are these big enough?

MRS. WEBB. Try and get them a little bigger if you can.

EMILY. Mama, will you answer me a question, serious?

MRS. WEBB. Seriously, dear—not serious.

EMILY. Seriously—will you?

MRS. WEBB. Of course, I will.

EMILY. Mama, am I good looking?

MRS. WEBB. Yes, of course you are. All my children have got good features; I'd be ashamed if they hadn't.

EMILY. Oh, Mama, that's not what I mean. What I mean is: am I *pretty?*

MRS. WEBB. I've already told you, yes. Now

that's enough of that. You have a nice young pretty face. I never heard of such foolishness.

EMILY. Oh, Mama, you never tell us the truth about anything.

MRS. WEBB. I *am* telling you the truth.

EMILY. Mama, were *you* pretty?

MRS. WEBB. Yes, I was, if I do say it. I was the prettiest girl in town next to Mamie Cartwright.

EMILY. But, Mama, you've got to say something about me. Am I pretty enough . . . to get anybody . . . to get people interested in me?

MRS. WEBB. Emily, you make me tired. Now stop it. You're pretty enough for all normal purposes. Come along now and bring that bowl with you.

EMILY. Oh, Mama, you're no help at all.

STAGE MANAGER. Thank you. Thank you! That'll do. We'll have to interrupt again here. Thank you, Mrs. Webb; thank you, Emily.

[MRS. WEBB *and* EMILY *withdraw.*]

There are some more things we want to explore about this town.

[*He comes to the center of the stage. During the following speech the lights gradually dim to darkness, leaving only a spot on him.*]

I think this is a good time to tell you that the Cartwright interests have just begun building a new bank in Grover's Corners—had to go to Vermont for the marble, sorry to say. And they've asked a friend of mine what they should put in the cornerstone for people to dig up . . . a thousand years from now. . . . Of course, they've put in a copy of the *New York Times* and a copy of Mr. Webb's *Sentinel.* . . . We're kind of interested in this because some scientific fellas have found a way of painting all that reading matter with a glue—a silicate glue—that'll make it keep a thousand—two thousand years.

We're putting in a Bible . . . and the Constitution of the United States—and a copy of William Shakespeare's plays. What do you say, folks? What do you think?

Y'know—Babylon[17] once had two million people in it, and all we know about 'em is the names of the kings and some copies of wheat contracts . . . and contracts for the sale of slaves. Yet every night all those families sat down to supper, and the father came home from his work, and the smoke went up the chimney—same as here. And even in Greece and Rome, all we know about the *real* life of the people is what we can piece together out of the joking poems and the comedies they wrote for the theatre back then.

So I'm going to have a copy of this play put in the cornerstone and the people a thousand years from now'll know a few simple facts about us—more than the Treaty of Versailles[18] and the Lindbergh flight.[19] See what I mean?

So—people a thousand years from now—this is the way we were in the provinces north of New York at the beginning of the twentieth century. This is the way we were: in our growing up and in our marrying and in our living and in our dying.

[*A choir partially concealed in the orchestra pit has begun singing "Blessed Be the Tie That Binds."*
SIMON STIMSON *stands directing them.*
Two ladders have been pushed onto the stage; they serve as indication of the second story in the Gibbs and Webb houses. GEORGE *and* EMILY *mount them, and apply themselves to their schoolwork.*
DR. GIBBS *has entered and is seated in his kitchen reading.*]

Well!—good deal of time's gone by. It's evening.

---

17. **Babylon** [babˈə lən]: ancient city famous for luxury and wickedness.
18. **Treaty of Versailles** [vər sīˈ]: treaty ending World War I (1919).
19. **Lindbergh flight:** first nonstop solo transatlantic flight (1927) by U.S. aviator Charles A. Lindbergh.

You can hear choir practice going on in the Congregational Church.

The children are at home doing their schoolwork.

The day's running down like a tired clock.

SIMON STIMSON. Now look here, everybody. Music come into the world to give pleasure.—Softer! Softer! Get it out of your heads that music's only good when it's loud. You leave loudness to the Methodists. You couldn't beat 'em, even if you wanted to. Now again. Tenors!

GEORGE. Hsst! Emily!

EMILY. Hello.

GEORGE. Hello!

EMILY. I can't work at all. The moonlight's so *terrible*.

GEORGE. Emily, did you get the third problem?

EMILY. Which?

GEORGE. The *third?*

EMILY. Why, yes, George—that's the easiest of them all.

GEORGE. I don't see it. Emily, can you give me a hint?

EMILY. I'll tell you one thing: the answer's in yards.

GEORGE. ! ! ! In yards? How do you mean?

EMILY. In *square* yards.

GEORGE. Oh . . . in square yards.

EMILY. Yes, George, don't you see?

GEORGE. Yeah.

EMILY. In square yards of *wallpaper*.

GEORGE. Wallpaper—oh, I see. Thanks a lot, Emily.

EMILY. You're welcome. My, isn't the moonlight *terrible?* And choir practice going on. I think if you hold your breath you can hear the train all the way to Contoocook. Hear it?

GEORGE. M-m-m—What do you know!

EMILY. Well, I guess I better go back and try to work.

GEORGE. Good night, Emily. And thanks.

EMILY. Good night, George.

SIMON STIMSON. Before I forget it: how many of you will be able to come in Tuesday afternoon and sing at Fred Hersey's wedding?—show your hands. That'll be fine; that'll be right nice. We'll do the same music we did for Jane Trowbridge's last month.

Now we'll do: "Art Thou Weary; Art Thou Languid?" It's a question, ladies and gentlemen, make it talk. Ready.

DR. GIBBS. Oh, George, can you come down a minute?

GEORGE. Yes, Pa. [*He descends the ladder.*]

DR. GIBBS. Make yourself comfortable, George; I'll only keep you a minute. George, how old are you?

GEORGE. I? I'm sixteen, almost seventeen.

DR. GIBBS. What do you want to do after school's over?

GEORGE. Why, you know, Pa. I want to be a farmer on Uncle Luke's farm.

DR. GIBBS. You'll be willing, will you, to get up early and milk and feed the stock . . . and you'll be able to hoe and hay all day?

GEORGE. Sure, I will. What are you . . . what do you mean, Pa?

DR. GIBBS. Well, George, while I was in my office today I heard a funny sound . . . and what do you think it was? It was your mother chopping wood. There you see your mother—getting up early; cooking meals all day long; washing and ironing—and still she has to go out in the back yard and chop wood. I suppose she just got tired of asking you. She just gave up and decided it was easier to do it herself. And you eat her meals, and put on the clothes she keeps nice for you, and you run off and play baseball,—like she's some hired girl we keep around the house but that we don't like very much. Well, I knew all I had to do was call your attention to it. Here's a handkerchief, son. George, I've decided to raise your spending money twenty-five cents a week. Not, of course, for chopping wood for your mother, because that's a present you give her, but because you're getting older—and I imagine there are lots of things you must find to do with it.

GEORGE. Thanks, Pa.

DR. GIBBS. Let's see—tomorrow's your payday. You can count on it—Hmm. Probably Rebecca'll feel she ought to have some more too. Wonder what could have happened to your mother. Choir practice never was as late as this before.

GEORGE. It's only half past eight, Pa.

DR. GIBBS. I don't know why she's in that old choir. She hasn't any more voice than an old crow. . . . Traipsin' around the streets at this hour of the night . . . Just about time you retired, don't you think?

GEORGE. Yes, Pa.

[GEORGE *mounts to his place on the ladder. Laughter and good nights can be heard on stage left and presently* MRS. GIBBS, MRS. SOAMES *and* MRS. WEBB *come down Main Street. When they arrive at the corner of the stage they stop.*]

MRS. SOAMES. Good night, Martha. Good night, Mr. Foster.

MRS. WEBB. I'll tell Mr. Webb; I *know* he'll want to put it in the paper.

MRS. GIBBS. My, it's late!

MRS. SOAMES. Good night, Irma.

MRS. GIBBS. Real nice choir practice, wa'n't it? Myrtle Webb! Look at the moon, will you! Tsk-tsk-tsk. Potato weather, for sure.

[*They are silent a moment, gazing up at the moon.*]

MRS. SOAMES. Naturally I didn't want to say a word about it in front of those others, but now we're alone—really, it's the worst scandal that ever was in this town!

MRS. GIBBS. What?

MRS. SOAMES. Simon Stimson!

MRS. GIBBS. Now, Louella!

MRS. SOAMES. But, Julia! To have the organist of a church *drink* and *drunk* year after year. You know he was drunk tonight.

MRS. GIBBS. Now, Louella! We all know about Mr. Stimson, and we all know about the troubles he's been through, and Dr. Ferguson knows too, and if Dr. Ferguson keeps him on there in his job the only thing the rest of us can do is just not to notice it.

MRS. SOAMES. *Not to notice it!* But it's getting worse.

MRS. WEBB. No, it isn't, Louella. It's getting better. I've been in that choir twice as long as you have. It doesn't happen anywhere near so often. . . . My, I hate to go to bed on a night like this. I better hurry. Those children'll be sitting up till all hours. Good night, Louella.

[*They all exchange good nights. She hurries downstage, enters her house and disappears.*]

MRS. GIBBS. Can you get home safe, Louella?

MRS. SOAMES. It's as bright as day. I can see Mr. Soames scowling at the window now. You'd think we'd been to a dance the way the menfolk carry on.

[*More good nights.* MRS. GIBBS *arrives at her home and passes through the trellis into the kitchen.*]

MRS. GIBBS. Well, we had a real good time.

DR. GIBBS. You're late enough.

MRS. GIBBS. Why, Frank, it ain't any later'n usual.

DR. GIBBS. And you stopping at the corner to gossip with a lot of hens.

MRS. GIBBS. Now, Frank, don't be grouchy. Come out and smell the heliotrope in the

moonlight. [*They stroll out arm in arm along the footlights.*] Isn't that wonderful? What did you do all the time I was away?

DR. GIBBS. Oh, I read—as usual. What were the girls gossiping about tonight?

MRS. GIBBS. Well, believe me, Frank—there is something to gossip about.

DR. GIBBS. Hmm! Simon Stimson far gone, was he?

MRS. GIBBS. Worst I've ever seen him. How'll that end, Frank? Dr. Ferguson can't forgive him forever.

DR. GIBBS. I guess I know more about Simon Stimson's affairs than anybody in this town. Some people ain't made for small-town life. I don't know how that'll end; but there's nothing we can do but just leave it alone. Come, get in.

MRS. GIBBS. No, not yet . . . Frank, I'm worried about you.

DR. GIBBS. What are you worried about?

MRS. GIBBS. I think it's my duty to make plans for you to get a real rest and change. And if I get a legacy, well, I'm going to insist on it.

DR. GIBBS. Now, Julia, there's no sense in going over that again.

MRS. GIBBS. Frank, you're just *unreasonable*!

DR. GIBBS. [*Starting into the house.*] Come on, Julia, it's getting late. First thing you know you'll catch cold. I gave George a piece of my mind tonight. I reckon you'll have your wood chopped for a while anyway. No, no, start getting upstairs.

MRS. GIBBS. Oh, dear. There's always so many things to pick up, seems like. You know, Frank, Mrs. Fairchild always locks her front door every night. All those people up that part of town do.

DR. GIBBS. [*Blowing out the lamp.*] They're all getting citified, that's the trouble with them. They haven't got nothing fit to burgle and everybody knows it.

[*They disappear.*
REBECCA *climbs up the ladder beside* GEORGE.]

GEORGE. Get out, Rebecca. There's only room for one at this window. You're always spoiling everything.

REBECCA. Well, let me look just a minute.

GEORGE. Use your own window.

REBECCA. I did, but there's no moon there. . . . George, do you know what I think, do you? I think maybe the moon's getting nearer and nearer and there'll be a big 'splosion.

GEORGE. Rebecca, you don't know anything. If the moon were getting nearer, the guys that sit up all night with telescopes would see it first and they'd tell about it, and it'd be in all the newspapers.

REBECCA. George, is the moon shining on South America, Canada and half the whole world?

GEORGE. Well—prob'ly is.

[*The* STAGE MANAGER *strolls on.
Pause. The sound of crickets is heard.*]

STAGE MANAGER. Nine thirty. Most of the lights are out. No, there's Constable Warren trying a few doors on Main Street. And here comes Editor Webb, after putting his newspaper to bed.

[MR. WARREN, *an elderly policeman, comes along Main Street from the right,* MR. WEBB *from the left.*]

MR. WEBB. Good evening, Bill.

CONSTABLE WARREN. Evenin', Mr. Webb.

MR. WEBB. Quite a moon!

CONSTABLE WARREN. Yepp.

MR. WEBB. All quiet tonight?

CONSTABLE WARREN. Simon Stimson is rollin' around a little. Just saw his wife movin' out to hunt for him so I looked the other way—there he is now.

[SIMON STIMSON *comes down Main Street from the left, only a trace of unsteadiness in his walk.*]

MR. WEBB. Good evening, Simon . . . Town seems to have settled down for the night pretty well. . . .

[SIMON STIMSON *comes up to him and pauses a moment and stares at him, swaying slightly.*]

Good evening . . . Yes, most of the town's settled down for the night, Simon. . . . I guess we better do the same. Can I walk along a ways with you?

[SIMON STIMSON *continues on his way without a word and disappears at the right.*]

Good night.

CONSTABLE WARREN. I don't know how that's goin' to end, Mr. Webb.

MR. WEBB. Well, he's seen a peck of trouble, one thing after another. . . . Oh, Bill . . . if you see my boy smoking cigarettes, just give him a word, will you? He thinks a lot of you, Bill.

CONSTABLE WARREN. I don't think he smokes no cigarettes, Mr. Webb. Leastways, not more'n two or three a year.

MR. WEBB. Hm . . . I hope not. Well, good night, Bill.

CONSTABLE WARREN. Good night, Mr. Webb. [*Exit.*]

MR. WEBB. Who's that up there? Is that you, Myrtle?

EMILY. No, it's me, Papa.

MR. WEBB. Why aren't you in bed?

EMILY. I don't know. I just can't sleep yet, Papa. The moonlight's so *won*-derful. And the smell of Mrs. Gibbs' heliotrope. Can you smell it?

MR. WEBB. Hm . . . Yes. Haven't any troubles on your mind, have you, Emily?

EMILY. *Troubles,* Papa? *No.*

MR. WEBB. Well, enjoy yourself, but don't let your mother catch you. Good night, Emily.

EMILY. Good night, Papa.

[MR. WEBB *crosses into the house, whistling "Blessed Be the Tie That Binds" and disappears.*]

REBECCA. I never told you about that letter Jane Crofut got from her minister when she was sick. He wrote Jane a letter and on the envelope the address was like this: It said: Jane Crofut; The Crofut Farm; Grover's Corners; Sutton County; New Hampshire; United States of America.

GEORGE. What's funny about that?

REBECCA. But listen, it's not finished: the United States of America; Continent of North America; Western Hemisphere; the Earth; the Solar System; the Universe; the Mind of God—that's what it said on the envelope.

GEORGE. What do you know!

REBECCA. And the postman brought it just the same.

GEORGE. What do you know!

STAGE MANAGER. That's the end of the First Act, friends. You can go and smoke now, those that smoke.

STUDY QUESTIONS

Recalling

1. According to the Stage Manager, when does the action of the play begin, and where does the play take place? According to the stage directions, what sort of scenery does it have?

2. In Act 1 what do we learn about the following? (a) the futures of Dr. and Mrs. Gibbs, (b) Joe Crowell's future, (c) Mrs. Gibbs's dreams, (d) the geology and anthropology of Grover's Corners, (e) Editor Webb's opinion of Grover's Corners.

3. What is Emily Webb imagining herself to be as she walks home from school, according to page 707? What is George Gibbs doing as he races down Main Street? What does Emily promise George she will do? What "serious" question does Emily ask her mother?

4. Where does the Stage Manager plan to put a copy of *Our Town* "for people to dig up a thousand years from now"? What does he say the play will tell them?

5. What is Doc Gibbs's explanation for Simon Stimson's problems, according to page 712? What is his explanation for the fact that some people in town have taken to locking their front doors at night?

6. Why does Rebecca come to her brother's room in the final scenes of Act 1? What question does she ask? What does Rebecca tell her brother about Jane Crofut's letter?

Interpreting

7. What sort of relationship does the Stage Manager set up with the audience? Is he a character living in 1901 America? Explain. What seems to be the Stage Manager's attitude toward the deaths of Doc and Mrs. Gibbs and of Joe Crowell?

8. What sort of town is Grover's Corners? What sort of people are the Gibbs and Webb families? Briefly characterize Emily and George.

9. What does the play seem to be suggesting no longer exists? What mood or attitude does this suggestion evoke in the audience?

10. What does the address described by Rebecca in the last scene do to Grover's Corners and its inhabitants? What does the "Our" in the play's title suggest?

11. Why might Wilder specifically request settings with so little scenery?

Extending

12. What aspects of life in Grover's Corners do you think are gone forever in most places in America? What aspects remain a part of life as lived in America now?

ACT 2

[*The tables and chairs of the two kitchens are still on the stage.*
The ladders and the small bench have been withdrawn.
The STAGE MANAGER *has been at his accustomed place watching the audience return to its seats.*]

STAGE MANAGER. Three years have gone by.
Yes, the sun's come up over a thousand times.
Summers and winters have cracked the mountains a little bit more and the rains have brought down some of the dirt.
Some babies that weren't even born before have begun talking regular sentences already; and a number of people who thought they were right young and spry have noticed that they can't bound up a flight of stairs like they used to, without their heart fluttering a little.
All that can happen in a thousand days.
Nature's been pushing and contriving in other ways, too: a number of young people fell in love and got married.
Yes, the mountain got bit away a few fractions of an inch; millions of gallons of water went by the mill; and here and there a new home was set up under a roof.
Almost everybody in the world gets married—you know what I mean? In our town there aren't hardly any exceptions. Most everybody in the world climbs into their graves married.
The First Act was called the Daily Life. This act is called Love and Marriage. There's another act coming after this: I reckon you can guess what that's about.

So:
It's three years later. It's 1904.
It's July 7th, just after High School Commencement. That's the time most of our young people jump up and get married.
Soon as they've passed their last examinations in solid geometry and Cicero's Orations,[1] looks

like they suddenly feel themselves fit to be married.
It's early morning. Only this time it's been raining. It's been pouring and thundering.
Mrs. Gibbs' garden, and Mrs. Webb's here: drenched.
All those bean poles and pea vines: drenched.
All yesterday over there on Main Street, the rain looked like curtains being blown along.
Hm . . . it may begin again any minute.
There! You can hear the 5:45 for Boston.

[MRS. GIBBS *and* MRS. WEBB *enter their kitchens and start the day as in the First Act.*]

And there's Mrs. Gibbs and Mrs. Webb come down to make breakfast, just as though it were an ordinary day. I don't have to point out to the women in my audience that those ladies they see before them, both of those ladies cooked three meals a day—one of 'em for twenty years, the other for forty—and no summer vacation. They brought up two children apiece, washed, cleaned the house—and *never a nervous breakdown.*
It's like what one of those Middle West poets said: You've got to love life to have life, and you've got to have life to love life[2]. . . . It's what they call a vicious circle.

HOWIE NEWSOME. [*Off stage left.*] Giddap, Bessie!

STAGE MANAGER. Here comes Howie Newsome delivering the milk. And there's Si Crowell delivering the papers like his brother before him.

[SI CROWELL *has entered hurling imaginary newspapers into doorways;* HOWIE NEWSOME *has come along Main Street with Bessie.*]

SI CROWELL. Morning, Howie.

HOWIE NEWSOME. Morning, Si. Anything in the papers I ought to know?

---

1. **Cicero's** [sis′ə rōz′] **Orations:** speeches made by the Roman orator and statesman Cicero (106–43 B.C.).

2. **You've . . . life:** Edgar Lee Masters' poem "Lucinda Matlock" (page 468) actually reads "It takes life to love life."

SI CROWELL. Nothing much, except we're losing about the best baseball pitcher Grover's Corners ever had—George Gibbs.

HOWIE NEWSOME. Reckon he is.

SI CROWELL. He could hit and run bases, too.

HOWIE NEWSOME. Yep. Mighty fine ball player. Whoa! Bessie! I guess I can stop and talk if I've a mind to!

SI CROWELL. I don't see how he could give up a thing like that just to get married. Would you, Howie?

HOWIE NEWSOME. Can't tell, Si. Never had no talent that way.

[CONSTABLE WARREN enters. They exchange good mornings.]

You're up early, Bill.

CONSTABLE WARREN. Seein' if there's anything I can do to prevent a flood. River's been risin' all night.

HOWIE NEWSOME. Si Crowell's all worked up here about George Gibbs' retiring from baseball.

CONSTABLE WARREN. Yes, sir; that's the way it goes. Back in '84 we had a player, Si—even George Gibbs couldn't touch him. Name of Hank Todd. Went down to Maine and become a parson. Wonderful ball player.—Howie, how does the weather look to you?

HOWIE NEWSOME. Oh, 'tain't bad. Think maybe it'll clear up for good.

[CONSTABLE WARREN and SI CROWELL continue on their way.

HOWIE NEWSOME brings the milk first to MRS. GIBBS' house. She meets him by the trellis.]

MRS. GIBBS. Good morning, Howie. Do you think it's going to rain again?

HOWIE NEWSOME. Morning, Mrs. Gibbs. It rained so heavy, I think maybe it'll clear up.

MRS. GIBBS. Certainly hope it will.

HOWIE NEWSOME. How much did you want today?

MRS. GIBBS. I'm going to have a houseful of relations, Howie. Looks to me like I'll need three-a-milk and two-a-cream.

HOWIE NEWSOME. My wife says to tell you we both hope they'll be very happy, Mrs. Gibbs. Know they *will*.

MRS. GIBBS. Thanks a lot, Howie. Tell your wife I hope she gits there to the wedding.

HOWIE NEWSOME. Yes, she'll be there; she'll be there if she kin. [HOWIE NEWSOME crosses to MRS. WEBB's house.] Morning, Mrs. Webb.

MRS. WEBB. Oh, good morning, Mr. Newsome. I told you four quarts of milk, but I hope you can spare me another.

HOWIE NEWSOME. Yes'm . . . and the two of cream.

MRS. WEBB. Will it start raining again, Mr. Newsome?

HOWIE NEWSOME. Well. Just sayin' to Mrs. Gibbs as how it may lighten up. Mrs. Newsome told me to tell you as how we hope they'll both be very happy, Mrs. Webb. Know they *will*.

MRS. WEBB. Thank you, and thank Mrs. Newsome and we're counting on seeing you at the wedding.

HOWIE NEWSOME. Yes, Mrs. Webb. We hope to git there. Couldn't miss that. Come on, Bessie.

[*Exit* HOWIE NEWSOME.
DR. GIBBS *descends in shirt sleeves, and sits down at his breakfast table.*]

DR. GIBBS. Well, Ma the day has come. You're losin' one of your chicks.

MRS. GIBBS. Frank Gibbs, don't you say another word. I feel like crying every minute. Sit down and drink your coffee.

DR. GIBBS. The groom's up shaving himself—only there ain't an awful lot to shave. Whistling and singing, like he's glad to leave us. Every now and then he says "I do" to the mirror, but it don't sound convincing to me.

MRS. GIBBS. I declare, Frank, I don't know how he'll get along. I've arranged his clothes and seen to it he's put warm things on—Frank! they're too *young.* Emily won't think of such things. He'll catch his death of cold within a week.

DR. GIBBS. I was remembering my wedding morning, Julia.

MRS. GIBBS. Now don't start that, Frank Gibbs.

DR. GIBBS. I was the scaredest young fella in the State of New Hampshire. I thought I'd make a mistake for sure. And when I saw you comin' down that aisle I thought you were the prettiest girl I'd ever seen, but the only trouble was that I'd never seen you before. There I was in the Congregational Church marryin' a total stranger.

MRS. GIBBS. And how do you think I felt! Frank, weddings are perfectly awful things. Farces—that's what they are! [*She puts a plate before him.*] Here, I've made something for you.

DR. GIBBS. Why, Julia Hersey—French toast!

MRS. GIBBS. 'Tain't hard to make and I had to do *something.*

[*Pause.* DR. GIBBS *pours on the syrup.*]

DR. GIBBS. How'd you sleep last night, Julia?

MRS. GIBBS. Well, I heard a lot of the hours struck off.

DR. GIBBS. Ye-e-s! I get a shock every time I think of George setting out to be a family man—that great gangling thing! I tell you Julia, there's nothing so terrifying in the world as a *son.* The relation of father and son is the darndest, awkwardest—

MRS. GIBBS. Well, mother and daughter's no picnic, let me tell you.

DR. GIBBS. They'll have a lot of troubles, I suppose, but that's none of our business. Everybody has a right to their own troubles.

MRS. GIBBS. [*At the table, drinking her coffee, meditatively.*] Yes . . . people are meant to go through life two by two. 'Tain't natural to be lonesome.

[*Pause.* DR. GIBBS *starts laughing.*]

DR. GIBBS. Julia, do you know one of the things I was scared of when I married you?

MRS. GIBBS. Oh, go along with you!

DR. GIBBS. I was afraid we wouldn't have material for conversation more'n'd last us a few weeks. [*Both laugh.*] I was afraid we'd run out and eat our meals in silence, that's a fact.—Well, you and I been conversing for twenty years now without any noticeable barren spells.

MRS. GIBBS. Well—good weather, bad weather—'tain't very choice, but I always find something to say. [*She goes to the foot of the stairs.*] Did you hear Rebecca stirring around upstairs?

DR. GIBBS. No. Only day of the year Rebecca hasn't been managing everybody's business up there. She's hiding in her room. I got the impression she's crying.

MRS. GIBBS. Lord's sakes! This has got to stop. Rebecca! Rebecca! Come and get your breakfast.

[GEORGE *comes rattling down the stairs, very brisk.*]

GEORGE. Good morning, everybody. Only five more hours to live.

[*Makes the gesture of cutting his throat, and a loud "k-k-k," and starts through the trellis.*]

MRS. GIBBS. George Gibbs, where are you going?

GEORGE. Just stepping across the grass to see my girl.

MRS. GIBBS. Now, George! You put on your overshoes. It's raining torrents. You don't go out of this house without you're prepared for it.

GEORGE. Aw, Ma. It's just a *step!*

MRS. GIBBS. George! You'll catch your death of cold and cough all through the service.

DR. GIBBS. George, do as your mother tells you! [DR. GIBBS *goes upstairs.*]

[GEORGE *returns reluctantly to the kitchen and pantomimes putting on overshoes.*]

MRS. GIBBS. From tomorrow on you can kill yourself in all weathers, but while you're in my house you'll live wisely, thank you. Maybe Mrs. Webb isn't used to callers at seven in the morning. Here, take a cup of coffee first.

GEORGE. Be back in a minute. [*He crosses the stage, leaping over the puddles.*] Good morning, Mother Webb.

MRS. WEBB. Goodness! You frightened me! Now, George, you can come in a minute out of the wet, but you know I can't ask you in.

GEORGE. Why not—?

MRS. WEBB. George, you know's well as I do: the groom can't see his bride on his wedding day, not until he sees her in church.

GEORGE. Aw!—that's just a superstition. Good morning, Mr. Webb. [*Enter* MR. WEBB.]

MR. WEBB. Good morning, George.

GEORGE. Mr. Webb, you don't believe in that superstition, do you?

MR. WEBB. There's a lot of common sense in some superstitions, George. [*He sits at the table, facing right.*]

MRS. WEBB. Millions have folla'd it, George, and you don't want to be the first to fly in the face of custom.

GEORGE. How is Emily?

MRS. WEBB. She hasn't waked up yet. I haven't heard a sound out of her.

GEORGE. Emily's *asleep!!!*

MRS. WEBB. No wonder! We were up 'till all hours, sewing and packing. Now I'll tell you what I'll do; you set down here a minute with Mr. Webb and drink this cup of coffee; and I'll go upstairs and see she doesn't come down and surprise you. There's some bacon, too; but don't be long about it.

[*Exit* MRS. WEBB.
Embarrassed silence.
MR. WEBB *dunks doughnuts in his coffee.*
More silence.]

MR. WEBB. [*Suddenly and loudly.*] Well, George, how are you?

GEORGE. [*Startled, choking over his coffee.*] Oh, fine, I'm fine. [*Pause.*] Mr. Webb, what sense could there be in a superstition like that?

MR. WEBB. Well, you see—on her wedding morning a girl's head's apt to be full of . . . clothes and one thing and another. Don't you think that's probably it?

GEORGE. Ye-e-s. I never thought of that.

MR. WEBB. A girl's apt to be a mite nervous on her wedding day. [*Pause.*]

GEORGE. I wish a fellow could get married without all that marching up and down.

MR. WEBB. Every man that's ever lived has felt that way about it, George; but it hasn't been any use. It's the womenfolk who've built up weddings, my boy. For a while now the women have it all their own. A man looks pretty small at a wedding, George. All those good women standing shoulder to shoulder making sure that the knot's tied in a mighty public way.

GEORGE. But . . . you *believe* in it, don't you, Mr. Webb?

MR. WEBB. [*With alacrity.*] Oh, yes; *oh, yes.* Don't you misunderstand me, my boy. Marriage is a wonderful thing—wonderful thing. And don't you forget that, George.

GEORGE. No, sir. Mr. Webb, how old were you when you got married?

MR. WEBB. Well, you see: I'd been to college and I'd taken a little time to get settled. But Mrs. Webb—she wasn't much older than what Emily is. Oh, age hasn't much to do with it, George—not compared with . . . uh . . . other things.

GEORGE. What were you going to say, Mr. Webb?

MR. WEBB. Oh, I don't know. Was I going to say something? [*Pause.*] George, I was thinking the other night of some advice my father gave me when I got married. Charles, he said, Charles, start out early showing who's boss, he said. Best thing to do is to give an order, even if it don't make sense; just so she'll learn to obey. And he said: if anything about your wife irritates you—her conversation, or anything—just get up and leave the house. That'll make it clear to her, he said. And, oh, yes! he said never, *never* let your wife know how much money you have, never.

GEORGE. Well, Mr. Webb . . . I don't think I could . . .

MR. WEBB. So I took the opposite of my father's advice and I've been happy ever since. And let that be a lesson to you, George, never to ask advice on personal matters. George, are you going to raise chickens on your farm?

GEORGE. What?

MR. WEBB. Are you going to raise chickens on your farm?

GEORGE. Uncle Luke's never been much interested, but I thought—

MR. WEBB. A book came into my office the other day, George, on the Philo System of raising chickens. I want you to read it. I'm thinking of beginning in a small way in the back yard, and I'm going to put an incubator in the cellar—

[*Enter* MRS. WEBB.]

MRS. WEBB. Charles, are you talking about that old incubator again? I thought you two'd be talking about things worth while.

MR. WEBB. [*Bitingly.*] Well, Myrtle, if you want to give the boy some good advice, I'll go upstairs and leave you alone with him.

MRS. WEBB. [*Pulling* GEORGE *up.*] George, Emily's got to come downstairs and eat her breakfast. She sends you her love but she doesn't want to lay eyes on you. Good-bye.

GEORGE. Good-bye.

[GEORGE *crosses the stage to his own home, bewildered and crestfallen. He slowly dodges a puddle and disappears into his house.*]

MR. WEBB. Myrtle, I guess you don't know about that older superstition.

MRS. WEBB. What do you mean, Charles?

MR. WEBB. Since the cave men: no bridegroom should see his father-in-law on the day of the wedding, or near it. Now remember that. [*Both leave the stage.*]

STAGE MANAGER. Thank you very much, Mr. and Mrs. Webb. Now I have to interrupt again here. You see, we want to know how all this began—this wedding, this plan to spend a lifetime together. I'm awfully interested in how big things like that begin.

You know how it is: you're twenty-one or twenty-two and you make some decisions; then whissssh! you're seventy: you've been a lawyer for fifty years, and that white-haired lady at your side has eaten over fifty thousand meals with you.

How do such things begin?

George and Emily are going to show you now the conversation they had when they first knew that . . . that . . . as the saying goes . . . they were meant for one another.

But before they do it I want you to try and remember what it was like to have been very young.

And particularly the days when you were first

in love; when you were like a person sleep-walking, and you didn't quite see the street you were in, and didn't quite hear everything that was said to you. You're just a little bit crazy. Will you remember that, please?

Now they'll be coming out of high school at three o'clock. George has just been elected President of the Junior Class, and as it's June, that means he'll be President of the Senior Class all next year. And Emily's just been elected Secretary and Treasurer.

I don't have to tell you how important that is.

[*He places a board across the backs of two chairs, which he takes from those at the Gibbs family's table. He brings two high stools from the wings and places them behind the board. Persons sitting on the stools will be facing the audience. This is the counter of Mr. Morgan's drugstore. The sounds of young people's voices are heard off left.*]

Yepp—there they are coming down Main Street now.

[EMILY, *carrying an armful of—imaginary—schoolbooks, comes along Main Street from the left.*]

EMILY. I can't, Louise. I've got to go home. Good-bye. Oh, Ernestine! Ernestine! Can you come over tonight and do Latin? Isn't that Cicero the worst thing—! Tell your mother you *have* to. G'bye. G'bye, Helen. G'bye, Fred.

[GEORGE, *also carrying books, catches up with her.*]

GEORGE. Can I carry your books home for you, Emily?

EMILY. [*Cooly.*] Why . . . uh . . . Thank you. It isn't far. [*She gives them to him.*]

GEORGE. Excuse me a minute, Emily. Say, Bob, if I'm a little late, start practice anyway. And give Herb some long high ones.

EMILY. Good-bye, Lizzy.

GEORGE. Good-bye, Lizzy. I'm awfully glad you were elected, too, Emily.

EMILY. Thank you.

[*They have been standing on Main Street, almost against the back wall. They take the first steps toward the audience when* GEORGE *stops and says:*]

GEORGE. Emily, why are you mad at me?

EMILY. I'm not mad at you.

GEORGE. You've been treating me so funny lately.

EMILY. Well, since you ask me, I might as well say it right out, George—[*She catches sight of a teacher passing.*] Good-bye, Miss Corcoran.

GEORGE. Good-bye, Miss Corcoran. Wha—what is it?

EMILY. [*Not scoldingly; finding it difficult to say.*] I don't like the whole change that's come over you in the last year. I'm sorry if that hurts your feelings, but I've got to—tell the truth and shame the devil.

GEORGE. A *change?* Wha—what do you mean?

EMILY. Well, up to a year ago I used to like you a lot. And I used to watch you as you did everything . . . because we'd been friends so long . . . and then you began spending all your time at *baseball* . . . and you never stopped to speak to anybody any more. Not even to your own family you didn't . . . and, George, it's a fact, you've got awful conceited and stuck-up, and all the girls say so. They may not say so to your face, but that's what they say about you behind your back, and it hurts me to hear them say it, but I've got to agree with them a little. I'm sorry if it hurts your feelings . . . but I can't be sorry I said it.

GEORGE. I . . . I'm glad you said it, Emily. I never thought that such a thing was happening to me. I guess it's hard for a fella not to have faults creep into his character.

[*They take a step or two in silence, then stand still in misery.*]

EMILY. I always expect a man to be perfect and I think he should be.

GEORGE. Oh . . . I don't think it's possible to be perfect, Emily.

EMILY. Well, my *father* is, and as far as I can see *your* father is. There's no reason on earth why you shouldn't be, too.

GEORGE. Well, I feel it's the other way round. That men aren't naturally good; but girls are.

EMILY. Well, you might as well know right now that I'm not perfect. It's not as easy for a girl to be perfect as a man, because we girls are more—more—nervous. Now I'm sorry I said all that about you. I don't know what made me say it.

GEORGE. Emily—

EMILY. Now I can see it's not the truth at all. And I suddenly feel that it isn't important, anyway.

GEORGE. Emily . . . would you like an ice-cream soda, or something, before you go home?

EMILY. Well, thank you. . . . I would.

[*They advance toward the audience and make an abrupt right turn, opening the door of Morgan's drugstore. Under strong emotion,* EMILY *keeps her face down.* GEORGE *speaks to some passers-by.*]

GEORGE. Hello, Stew—how are you? Good afternoon, Mrs. Slocum.

[*The* STAGE MANAGER, *wearing spectacles and assuming the role of* MR. MORGAN, *enters abruptly from the right and stands between the audience and the counter of his soda fountain.*]

STAGE MANAGER. Hello, George. Hello, Emily. What'll you have? Why, Emily Webb—what you been crying about?

GEORGE. [*He gropes for an explanation.*] She . . . she just got an awful scare, Mr. Morgan. She almost got run over by that hardware store wagon. Everybody says that Tom Huckins drives like a crazy man.

STAGE MANAGER. [*Drawing a drink of water.*] Well now! You take a drink of water, Emily. You look all shook up. I tell you, you've got to look both ways before you cross Main Street these days. Gets worse every year. What'll you have?

EMILY. I'll have a strawberry phosphate, thank you, Mr. Morgan.

GEORGE. No, no, Emily. Have an ice-cream soda with me. Two strawberry ice-cream sodas, Mr. Morgan.

STAGE MANAGER. [*Working the faucets.*] Two strawberry ice-cream sodas, yes sir. Yes, sir. There are a hundred and twenty-five horses in Grover's Corners this minute I'm talking to you. State Inspector was in here yesterday. And now they're bringing in these auto-mo-biles, the best thing to do is to just stay home. Why, I can remember when a dog could go to sleep all day in the middle of Main Street and nothing come along to disturb him. [*He sets the imaginary glasses before them.*] There they are. Enjoy 'em. [*He sees a customer, right.*] Yes, Mrs. Ellis. What can I do for you? [*He goes out right.*]

EMILY. They're so expensive.

GEORGE. No, no—don't you think of that. We're celebrating our election. And then do you know what else I'm celebrating?

EMILY. N-no.

GEORGE. I'm celebrating because I've got a friend who tells me all the things that ought to be told me.

EMILY. George, *please* don't think of that. I don't know why I said it. It's not true. You're—

GEORGE. No, Emily, you stick to it. I'm glad you spoke to me like you did. But you'll *see*: I'm going to change so quick—you bet I'm going to change. And, Emily, I want to ask you a favor.

EMILY. What?

GEORGE. Emily, if I go away to State Agriculture

College next year, will you write me a letter once in a while?

EMILY. I certainly will. I certainly will, George . . .

[*Pause. They start sipping the sodas through the straws.*]

It certainly seems like being away three years you'd get out of touch with things. Maybe letters from Grover's Corners wouldn't be so interesting after a while. Grover's Corners isn't a very important place when you think of all— New Hampshire; but I think it's a very nice town.

GEORGE. The day wouldn't come when I wouldn't want to know everything that's happening here. I know *that's* true, Emily.

EMILY. Well, I'll try to make my letters interesting. [*Pause.*]

GEORGE. Y'know, Emily, whenever I meet a farmer I ask him if he thinks it's important to go to Agriculture School to be a good farmer.

EMILY. Why, George—

GEORGE. Yeah, and some of them say that it's even a waste of time. You can get all those things, anyway, out of the pamphlets the government sends out. And Uncle Luke's getting old—he's about ready for me to start in taking over his farm tomorrow, if I could.

EMILY. My!

GEORGE. And, like you say, being gone all that time . . . in other places and meeting other people . . . Gosh, if anything like that can happen I don't want to go away. I guess new people aren't any better than old ones. I'll bet they almost never are. Emily . . . I feel that you're as good a friend as I've got. I don't need to go and meet the people in other towns.

EMILY. But, George, maybe it's very important for you to go and learn all that about—cattle judging and soils and those things. . . . Of course, I don't know.

GEORGE. [*After a pause, very seriously.*] Emily, I'm going to make up my mind right now. I won't go. I'll tell Pa about it tonight.

EMILY. Why, George, I don't see why you have to decide right now. It's a whole year away.

GEORGE. Emily, I'm glad you spoke to me about that . . . that fault in my character. What you said was right; but there was *one* thing wrong in it, and that was when you said that for a year I wasn't noticing people, and . . . you, for instance. Why, you say you were watching me when I did everything . . . I was doing the same about you all the time. Why, sure—I always thought about you as one of the chief people I thought about. I always made sure where you were sitting on the bleachers, and who you were with, and for three days now I've been trying to walk home with you; but something's always got in the way. Yesterday I was standing over against the wall waiting for you, and you walked home with *Miss Corcoran.*

EMILY. George! . . . Life's awful funny! How could I have known that? Why, I thought—

GEORGE. Listen, Emily, I'm going to tell you why I'm not going to Agriculture School. I think that once you've found a person that you're very fond of . . . I mean a person who's fond of you, too, and likes you enough to be interested in your character . . . Well, I think that's just as important as college is, and even more so. That's what I think.

EMILY. I think it's awfully important, too.

GEORGE. Emily.

EMILY. Y-yes, George.

GEORGE. Emily, if I *do* improve and make a big change . . . would you be . . . I mean: *could* you be . . .

EMILY. I . . . I am now; I always have been.

GEORGE. [*Pause.*] So I guess this is an important talk we've been having.

EMILY. Yes . . . yes.

GEORGE. [*Takes a deep breath and straightens his back.*] Wait just a minute and I'll walk you home.

[*With mounting alarm he digs into his pockets for the money.*
The STAGE MANAGER *enters, right.*
GEORGE, *deeply embarrassed, but direct, says to him:*]

Mr. Morgan, I'll have to go home and get the money to pay you for this. It'll only take me a minute.

STAGE MANAGER. [*Pretending to be affronted.*] What's that? George Gibbs, do you mean to tell me—!

GEORGE. Yes, but I had reasons, Mr. Morgan. Look, here's my gold watch to keep until I come back with the money.

STAGE MANAGER. That's all right. Keep your watch. I'll trust you.

GEORGE. I'll be back in five minutes.

STAGE MANAGER. I'll trust you ten years, George—not a day over. Got all over your shock, Emily?

EMILY. Yes, thank you, Mr. Morgan. It was nothing.

GEORGE. [*Taking up the books from the counter.*] I'm ready.

[*They walk in grave silence across the stage and pass through the trellis at the Webbs' back door and disappear.*
The STAGE MANAGER *watches them go out, then turns to the audience, removing his spectacles.*]

STAGE MANAGER. Well—[*He claps his hands as a signal.*] Now we're ready to get on with the wedding.

[*He stands waiting while the set is prepared for the next scene.*

STAGEHANDS remove the chairs, tables and trellises from the Gibbs and Webb houses. They arrange the pews for the church in the center of the stage. The congregation will sit facing the back wall. The aisle of the church starts at the center of the back wall and comes toward the audience.

A small platform is placed against the back wall on which the STAGE MANAGER will stand later, playing the minister. The image of a stained-glass window is cast from a lantern slide upon the back wall.

When all is ready the STAGE MANAGER strolls to the center of the stage, down front, and, musingly, addresses the audience.]

There are a lot of things to be said about a wedding; there are a lot of thoughts that go on during a wedding.

We can't get them all into one wedding, naturally, and especially not into a wedding at Grover's Corners, where they're awfully plain and short.

In this wedding I play the minister. That gives me the right to say a few more things about it. For a while now, the play gets pretty serious. Y'see, some churches say that marriage is a sacrament. I don't quite know what that means, but I can guess. Like Mrs. Gibbs said a few minutes ago: People were made to live two-by-two.

This is a good wedding, but people are so put together that even at a good wedding there's a lot of confusion way down deep in people's minds and we thought that that ought to be in our play, too.

The real hero of this scene isn't on the stage at all, and you know who that is. It's like what one of those European fellas said: every child born into the world is nature's attempt to make a perfect human being. Well, we've seen nature pushing and contriving for some time now. We all know that nature's interested in quantity; but I think she's interested in quality, too—that's why I'm in the ministry.

And don't forget all the other witnesses at this wedding—the ancestors. Millions of them. Most of them set out to live two-by-two, also. Millions of them.

Well, that's all my sermon. 'Twan't very long, anyway.

[The organ starts playing Handel's "Largo." The congregation streams into the church and sits in silence.

Church bells are heard.

MRS. GIBBS *sits in the front row, the first seat on the aisle, the right section; next to her are* REBECCA *and* DR. GIBBS. *Across the aisle* MRS. WEBB, WALLY *and* MR. WEBB. *A small choir takes its place, facing the audience under the stained-glass window.*

MRS. WEBB, *on the way to her place, turns back and speaks to the audience.*]

MRS. WEBB. I don't know why on earth I should be crying. I suppose there's nothing to cry about. It came over me at breakfast this morning; there was Emily eating her breakfast as she's done for seventeen years and now she's going off to eat it in someone else's house. I suppose that's it.

And Emily! She suddenly said: I can't eat another mouthful, and she put her head down on the table and *she* cried.

[She starts toward her seat in the church, but turns back and adds:]

Oh, I've got to say it: you know, there's something downright cruel about sending our girls out into marriage this way.

I hope some of her girl friends have told her a thing or two. It's cruel, I know, but I couldn't bring myself to say anything. I went into it blind as a bat myself.

[In half-amused exasperation.]

The whole world's wrong, that's what's the matter. There they come.

[She hurries to her place in the pew.

GEORGE *starts to come down the right aisle of the theatre, through the audience.*

Suddenly THREE MEMBERS *of his baseball team appear by the right proscenium pillar and start whistling and catcalling to him. They are dressed for the ball field.*]

THE BASEBALL PLAYERS. Eh, George, George! Hast—yaow! Look at him, fellas—he looks scared to death. Yaow! George, don't look so innocent, you old geezer. We know what you're thinking. Don't disgrace the team, big boy. Whoo-oo-oo.

STAGE MANAGER. All right! All right! That'll do. That's enough of that.

[*Smiling, he pushes them off the stage. They lean back to shout a few more catcalls.*]

There used to be an awful lot of that kind of thing at weddings in the old days—Rome, and later. We're more civilized now—so they say.

[*The choir starts singing "Love Divine, All Love Excelling—." GEORGE has reached the stage. He stares at the congregation a moment, then takes a few steps of withdrawal, toward the right proscenium pillar. His mother, from the front row, seems to have felt his confusion. She leaves her seat and comes down the aisle quickly to him.*]

MRS. GIBBS. George! George! What's the matter?

GEORGE. Ma, I don't want to grow old. Why's everybody pushing me so?

MRS. GIBBS. Why, George . . . you wanted it.

GEORGE. No, Ma, listen to me—

MRS. GIBBS. No, no, George—you're a man now.

GEORGE. Listen, Ma—for the last time I ask you . . . All I want to do is to be a fella—

MRS. GIBBS. George! If anyone should hear you! Now stop. Why, I'm ashamed of you!

GEORGE. [*He comes to himself and looks over the scene.*] What? Where's Emily?

MRS. GIBBS. [*Relieved.*] George! You gave me such a turn.

GEORGE. Cheer up, Ma. I'm getting married.

MRS. GIBBS. Let me catch my breath a minute.

GEORGE. [*Comforting her.*] Now, Ma, you save Thursday nights. Emily and I are coming over to dinner every Thursday night . . . you'll see. Ma, what are you crying for? Come on; we've got to get ready for this.

[MRS. GIBBS, *mastering her emotion, fixes his tie and whispers to him.*
In the meantime, EMILY, *in white and wearing her wedding veil, has come through the audience and mounted onto the stage. She too draws back, frightened, when she sees the congregation in the church. The choir begins: "Blessed Be the Tie That Binds."*]

EMILY. I never felt so alone in my whole life. And George over there, looking so . . .! I *hate* him. I wish I were dead. Papa! Papa!

MR. WEBB.

[*Leaves his seat in the pews and comes toward her anxiously.*]

Emily! Emily! Now don't get upset. . . .

EMILY. But Papa—I don't want to get married. . . .

MR. WEBB. Sh—sh—Emily. Everything's all right.

EMILY. Why can't I stay for a while just as I am? Let's go away—

MR. WEBB. No, no, Emily. Now stop and think a minute.

EMILY. Don't you remember that you used to say—all the time you used to say—all the time: that I was *your* girl! There must be lots of places we can go to. I'll work for you. I could keep house.

MR. WEBB. Sh . . . You mustn't think of such things. You're just nervous, Emily. [*He turns and calls.*] George! George! Will you come here a minute? [*He leads her toward* GEORGE.] Why you're marrying the best young fellow in the world. George is a fine fellow.

EMILY. But Papa—

[MRS. GIBBS *returns unobtrusively to her seat.*
MR. WEBB *has one arm around his daughter.
He places his hand on* GEORGE's *shoulder.*]

MR. WEBB. I'm giving away my daughter, George. Do you think you can take care of her?

GEORGE. Mr. Webb, I want to . . . I want to try. Emily, I'm going to do my best. I love you, Emily. I need you.

EMILY. Well, if you love me, help me. All I want is someone to love me.

GEORGE. I will, Emily. Emily, I'll try.

EMILY. And I mean for *ever.* Do you hear? For ever and ever.

[*They fall into each other's arms.
The March from* Lohengrin[3] *is heard.
The* STAGE MANAGER, *as* CLERGYMAN, *stands on the box, up center.*]

MR. WEBB. Come, they're waiting for us. Now you know it'll be all right. Come, quick.

[GEORGE *slips away and takes his place beside the* STAGE MANAGER-CLERGYMAN.
EMILY *proceeds up the aisle on her father's arm.*]

STAGE MANAGER. Do you, George, take this woman, Emily, to be your wedded wife, to have . . .

[MRS. SOAMES *has been sitting in the last row of the congregation.
She now turns to her neighbors and speaks in a shrill voice. Her chatter drowns out the rest of the clergyman's words.*]

MRS. SOAMES. Perfectly lovely wedding! Loveliest wedding I ever saw. Oh, I do love a good wedding, don't you? Doesn't she make a lovely bride?

GEORGE. I do.

STAGE MANAGER. Do you, Emily, take this man, George, to be your wedded husband—

[*Again his further words are covered by those of* MRS. SOAMES.]

MRS. SOAMES. Don't know *when* I've seen such a lovely wedding. But I always cry. Don't know why it is, but I always cry. I just like to see young people happy, don't you? Oh, I think it's lovely.

[*The ring.
The kiss.
The stage is suddenly arrested into silent tableau.
The* STAGE MANAGER, *his eyes on the distance, as though to himself.*]

---

3. ***March . . . Lohengrin*** [lō′ən grin′]: wedding march from the opera *Lohengrin* by German composer Richard Wagner (1813–1883); often called "Here Comes the Bride."

STAGE MANAGER. I've married over two hundred couples in my day.
Do I believe in it?
I don't know.
M. . . . marries N. . . . millions of them.
The cottage, the go-cart, the Sunday-afternoon drives in the Ford, the first rheumatism, the grandchildren, the second rheumatism, the deathbed, the reading of the will—

[*He now looks at the audience for the first time, with a warm smile that removes any sense of cynicism from the next line.*]

Once in a thousand times it's interesting.
—Well, let's have Mendelssohn's "Wedding March"![4]

---

4. **Mendelssohn's** [mend′əl sənz] **"Wedding March":** popular recessional march from the ballet *A Midsummer Night's Dream* by German composer Felix Mendelssohn (1809–1847).

[*The organ picks up the March.*
The BRIDE *and* GROOM *come down the aisle, radiant, but trying to be very dignified.*]

MRS. SOAMES. Aren't they a lovely couple? Oh, I've never been to such a nice wedding. I'm sure they'll be happy. I always say: *happiness,* that's the great thing! The important thing is to be happy.

[*The* BRIDE *and* GROOM *reach the steps leading into the audience. A bright light is thrown upon them. They descend into the auditorium and run up the aisle joyously.*]

STAGE MANAGER. That's all the Second Act, folks. Ten minutes' intermission.

CURTAIN

STUDY QUESTIONS

Recalling
1. How much time has passed between Acts 1 and 2? What does the Stage Manager say Act 1 is called? Act 2? What does he say about Act 3?
2. What does the Stage Manager say happens just after high school commencement?
3. What scene do Emily and George replay after George leaves the Webb house? In that scene what does Emily tell George he has become? What does he decide he is not going to do, and why?
4. Who marries the couple? What does he say about the "real hero" of the scene (page 724)? About "every child"?
5. What protest does George make to his mother just before the wedding? What does Emily protest to her father?

Interpreting
6. Why might Wilder show us the morning of the wedding before he shows us Emily and George becoming engaged?

7. In the engagement scene do Emily and George actually declare their love for each other in so many words? What does your answer suggest about their relationship?
8. Are Emily's prenuptial misgivings similar to George's? What seems to cause the misgivings of each?
9. Who is the Stage Manager suggesting is the "real hero" of the wedding? (Consider what he says about every child born.)
10. Do we know what the third act will be about, as the Stage Manager suggests? If so, what? (Consider the information the Stage Manager wanted to preserve by putting the play into a "time capsule" in Act 1.)
11. In quoting Lucinda Matlock (page 715), what is the Stage Manager suggesting about the people who live in Grover's Corners?

Extending
12. At the wedding Mrs. Soames exclaims, "The important thing is to be happy." Do you agree? Think of lives, from your reading or experience, that you admire. What besides happiness might be equally important?

ACT 3

[During the intermission the audience has seen the STAGEHANDS *arranging the stage. On the right-hand side, a little right of the center, ten or twelve ordinary chairs have been placed in three openly spaced rows facing the audience. These are graves in the cemetery.*

Toward the end of the intermission the ACTORS *enter and take their places. The front row contains: toward the center of the stage, an empty chair; then* MRS. GIBBS; SIMON STIMSON.

The second row contains, among others, MRS. SOAMES.

The third row has WALLY WEBB.

The dead do not turn their heads or their eyes to right or left, but they sit in a quiet without stiffness. When they speak their tone is matter-of-fact, without sentimentality and, above all, without lugubriousness.

The STAGE MANAGER *takes his accustomed place and waits for the house lights to go down.]*

STAGE MANAGER. This time nine years have gone by, friends—summer, 1913.

Gradual changes in Grover's Corners. Horses are getting rarer.

Farmers coming into town in Fords.

Everybody locks their house doors now at night. Ain't been any burglars in town yet, but everybody's heard about 'em.

You'd be surprised, though—on the whole, things don't change much around here. This is certainly an important part of Grover's Corners. It's on a hilltop—a windy hilltop—lots of sky, lots of clouds—often lots of sun and moon and stars. You come up here, on a fine afternoon and you can see range on range of hills—awful blue they are—up there by Lake Sunapee and Lake Winnipesaukee . . . and way up, if you've got a glass, you can see the White Mountains and Mt. Washington—where North Conway and Conway is. And, of course, our favorite mountain, Mt. Monadnock, 's right here—and all these towns that lie around it: Jaffrey, 'n East Jaffrey, 'n Peterborough, 'n Dublin; and [*Then pointing down in the audience.*]

there, quite a ways down, is Grover's Corners. Yes, beautiful spot up here. Mountain laurel and lilacs. I often wonder why people like to be buried in Woodlawn and Brooklyn when they might pass the same time up here in New Hampshire. Over there—[*Pointing to stage left.*] are the old stones—1670, 1680. Strong-minded people that come a long way to be independent. Summer people walk around there laughing at the funny words on the tombstones . . . it don't do any harm. And genealogists come up from Boston—get paid by city people for looking up their ancestors. They want to make sure they're Daughters of the American Revolution[1] and of the *Mayflower.* . . . Well, I guess that don't do any harm, either. Wherever you come near the human race, there's layers and layers of nonsense. . . .

Over there are some Civil War veterans. Iron flags on their graves . . . New Hampshire boys . . . had a notion that the Union ought to be kept together, though they'd never seen more than fifty miles of it themselves. All they knew was the name, friends—the United States of America. The United States of America. And they went and died about it.

This here is the new part of the cemetery. Here's your friend Mrs. Gibbs. 'N let me see—Here's Mr. Stimson, organist at the Congregational Church. And Mrs. Soames who enjoyed the wedding so—you remember? Oh, and a lot of others. And Editor Webb's boy, Wallace, whose appendix burst while he was on a Boy Scout trip to Crawford Notch.

Yes, an awful lot of sorrow has sort of quieted down up here. People just wild with grief have brought their relatives up to this hill. We all know how it is . . . and then time . . . and sunny days . . . and rainy days . . . 'n snow . . . We're all glad they're in a beautiful place and we're coming up here ourselves when our fit's over.

_____

1. **Daughters . . . Revolution:** society of women whose ancestors fought in the American Revolution.

Now there are some things we all know, but we don't take'm out and look at'm very often. We all know that *something* is eternal. And it ain't houses and it ain't names, and it ain't earth, and it ain't even the stars . . . everybody knows in their bones that *something* is eternal, and that something has to do with human beings. All the greatest people ever lived have been telling us that for five thousand years and yet you'd be surprised how people are always losing hold of it. There's something way down deep that's eternal about every human being. [*Pause.*]

You know as well as I do that the dead don't stay interested in us living people for very long. Gradually, gradually, they lose hold of the earth . . . and the ambitions they had . . . and the pleasures they had . . . and the things they suffered . . . and the people they loved.

They get weaned away from earth—that's the way I put it—weaned away.

And they stay here while the earth part of 'em burns away, burns out; and all that time they slowly get indifferent to what's goin' on in Grover's Corners. They're waitin'. They're waitin' for something that they feel is comin'. Something important, and great. Aren't they waitin' for the eternal part in them to come out clear?

Some of the things they're going to say maybe'll hurt your feelings—but that's the way it is: mother 'n daughter . . . husband 'n wife . . . enemy 'n enemy . . . money 'n miser . . . all those terribly important things kind of grow pale around here. And what's left when memory's gone, and your identity, Mrs. Smith?

[*He looks at the audience a minute, then turns to the stage.*]

Well! There are some *living* people. There's Joe Stoddard, our undertaker, supervising a new-made grave. And here comes a Grover's Corners boy, that left town to go out West.

[JOE STODDARD *has hovered about in the background.* SAM CRAIG *enters left, wiping his forehead from the exertion. He carries an umbrella and strolls front.*]

SAM CRAIG. Good afternoon, Joe Stoddard.

JOE STODDARD. Good afternoon, good afternoon. Let me see now: do I know you?

SAM CRAIG. I'm Sam Craig.

JOE STODDARD. Gracious sakes' alive! Of all people! I should'a knowed you'd be back for the funeral. You've been away a long time Sam.

SAM CRAIG. Yes, I've been away over twelve years. I'm in business out in Buffalo now, Joe. But I was in the East when I got news of my cousin's death, so I thought I'd combine things a little and come and see the old home. You look well.

JOE STODDARD. Yes, yes, can't complain. Very sad, our journey today, Samuel.

SAM CRAIG. Yes.

JOE STODDARD. Yes, yes. I always say I hate to supervise when a young person is taken. They'll be here in a few minutes now. I had to come here early today—my son's supervisin' at the home.

SAM CRAIG. [*Reading stones.*] Old Farmer Mc-Carty, I used to do chores for him—after school. He had the lumbago.

JOE STODDARD. Yes, we brought Farmer Mc-Carty here a number of years ago now.

SAM CRAIG. [*Staring at* MRS. GIBBS' *knees.*] Why, this is my Aunt Julia . . . I'd forgotten that she'd . . . of course, of course.

JOE STODDARD. Yes, Doc Gibbs lost his wife two-three years ago . . . about this time. And today's another pretty bad blow for him, too.

MRS. GIBBS. [*To* SIMON STIMSON: *in an even voice.*] That's my sister Carey's boy, Sam . . . Sam Craig.

SIMON STIMSON. I'm always uncomfortable when *they're* around.

MRS. GIBBS. Simon.

SAM CRAIG. Do they choose their own verses much, Joe?

JOE STODDARD. No . . . not usual. Mostly the bereaved pick a verse.

SAM CRAIG. Doesn't sound like Aunt Julia. There aren't many of those Hersey sisters left now. Let me see: where are . . . I wanted to look at my father's and mother's . . .

JOE STODDARD. Over there with the Craigs . . . Avenue F.

SAM CRAIG. [*Reading* SIMON STIMSON'S *epitaph.*] He was organist at church, wasn't he? Hm, drank a lot, we used to say.

JOE STODDARD. Nobody was supposed to know about it. He'd seen a peck of trouble. [*Behind his hand.*] Took his own life, y'know?

SAM CRAIG. Oh, did he?

JOE STODDARD. Hung himself in the attic. They tried to hush it up, but of course it got around. He chose his own epytaph. You can see it there. It ain't a verse exactly.

SAM CRAIG. Why, it's just some notes of music—what is it?

JOE STODDARD. Oh, I wouldn't know. It was wrote up in the Boston papers at the time.

SAM CRAIG. Joe, what did she die of?

JOE STODDARD. Who?

SAM CRAIG. My cousin.

JOE STODDARD. Oh, didn't you know? Had some trouble bringing a baby into the world. 'Twas her second, though. There's a little boy 'bout four years old.

SAM CRAIG. [*Opening his umbrella.*] The grave's going to be over there?

JOE STODDARD. Yes, there ain't much more room over here among the Gibbses, so they're opening up a whole new Gibbs section over by Avenue B. You'll excuse me now. I see they're comin'.

[*From left to center, at the back of the stage, comes a procession.* FOUR MEN *carry a casket, invisible to us. All the rest are under umbrellas. One can vaguely see:* DR. GIBBS, GEORGE, the WEBBS, etc. They gather about a grave in the back center of the stage, a little to the left of center.*]

MRS. SOAMES. Who is it, Julia?

MRS. GIBBS. [*Without raising her eyes.*] My daughter-in-law, Emily Webb.

MRS. SOAMES. [*A little surprised, but no emotion.*] Well, I declare! The road up here must have been awful muddy. What did she die of, Julia?

MRS. GIBBS. In childbirth.

MRS. SOAMES. Childbirth. [*Almost with a laugh.*] I'd forgotten all about that. My, wasn't life awful—[*With a sigh.*] and wonderful.

SIMON STIMSON. [*With a sideways glance.*] Wonderful, was it?

MRS. GIBBS. Simon! Now, remember!

MRS. SOAMES. I remember Emily's wedding. Wasn't it a lovely wedding! And I remember her reading the class poem at Graduation Exercises. Emily was one of the brightest girls ever graduated from High School. I've heard Principal Wilkins say so time after time. I called on them at their new farm, just before I died. Perfectly beautiful farm.

A WOMAN FROM AMONG THE DEAD. It's on the same road we lived on.

A MAN AMONG THE DEAD. Yepp, right smart farm.

[*They subside. The group by the grave starts singing "Blessed Be the Tie That Binds."*]

A WOMAN AMONG THE DEAD. I always liked that hymn. I was hopin' they'd sing a hymn.

[*Pause. Suddenly* EMILY *appears from among the umbrellas. She is wearing a white dress. Her hair is down her back and tied by a white ribbon like a little girl. She comes slowly, gazing wonderingly at the dead, a little dazed.*
She stops halfway and smiles faintly. After looking at the mourners for a moment, she

walks slowly to a vacant chair beside MRS. GIBBS *and sits down.*]

EMILY. [*To them all, quietly, smiling.*] Hello.

MRS. SOAMES. Hello, Emily.

A MAN AMONG THE DEAD. Hello, M's Gibbs.

EMILY. [*Warmly.*] Hello, Mother Gibbs.

MRS. GIBBS. Emily.

EMILY. Hello. [*With surprise.*] It's raining. [*Her eyes drift back to the funeral company.*]

MRS. GIBBS. Yes . . . They'll be gone soon, dear. Just rest yourself.

EMILY. It seems thousands and thousands of years since I . . . Papa remembered that that was my favorite hymn.
Oh, I wish I'd been here a long time. I don't like being new here. How do you do, Mr. Stimson?

SIMON STIMSON. How do you do, Emily.

[EMILY *continues to look about her with a wondering smile; as though to shut out from her mind the thought of the funeral company she starts speaking to* MRS. GIBBS *with a touch of nervousness.*]

EMILY. Mother Gibbs, George and I have made that farm into just the best place you ever saw. We thought of you all the time. We wanted to show you the new barn and a great long cement drinking fountain for the stock. We bought that out of the money you left us.

MRS. GIBBS. I did?

EMILY. Don't you remember, Mother Gibbs— the legacy you left us? Why, it was over three hundred and fifty dollars.

MRS. GIBBS. Yes, yes, Emily.

EMILY. Well, there's a patent device on the drinking fountain so that it never overflows, Mother Gibbs, and it never sinks below a certain mark they have there. It's fine.

[*Her voice trails off and her eyes return to the funeral group.*]

It won't be the same to George without me, but it's a lovely farm.

[*Suddenly she looks directly at Mrs. Gibbs.*]

Live people don't understand, do they?

MRS. GIBBS. No, dear—not very much.

EMILY. They're sort of shut up in little boxes, aren't they? I feel as though I knew them last a thousand years ago . . . My boy is spending the day at Mrs. Carter's. [*She sees* MR. CARTER *among the dead.*] Oh, Mr. Carter, my little boy is spending the day at your house.

MR. CARTER. Is he?

EMILY. Yes, he loves it there.—Mother Gibbs, we have a Ford, too. Never gives any trouble. I don't drive, though. Mother Gibbs, when does this feeling go away? Of being . . . one of *them?* How long does it . . . ?

MRS. GIBBS. Sh! dear. Just wait and be patient.

EMILY. [*With a sigh.*] I know. Look, they're finished. They're going.

MRS. GIBBS. Sh—.

[*The umbrellas leave the stage.* DR. GIBBS *has come over to his wife's grave and stands before it a moment.* EMILY *looks up at his face.* MRS. GIBBS *does not raise her eyes.*]

EMILY. Look! Father Gibbs is bringing some of my flowers to you. He looks just like George, doesn't he? Oh, Mother Gibbs, I never realized before how troubled and how . . . how in the dark live persons are. Look at him. I loved him so. From morning till night, that's all they are—troubled.

[DR. GIBBS *goes off.*]

THE DEAD. Little cooler than it was. Yes, that rain's cooled it off a little. Those northeast winds always do the same thing, don't they? If it isn't a rain, it's a three-day blow.

[*A patient calm falls on the stage. The* STAGE MANAGER *appears at his proscenium pillar, smoking.* EMILY *sits up abruptly with an idea.*]

EMILY. But, Mother Gibbs, one can go back; one can go back there again . . . into living. I feel it. I know it. Why just then for a moment I was thinking about . . . about the farm . . . and for a minute I *was* there, and my baby was on my lap as plain as day.

MRS. GIBBS. Yes, of course you can.

EMILY. I can go back there and live all those days over again . . . why not?

MRS. GIBBS. All I can say is, Emily, don't.

EMILY. [*She appeals urgently to the* STAGE MAN-AGER.] But it's true, isn't it? I can go and live . . . back there . . . again.

STAGE MANAGER. Yes, some have tried—but they soon come back here.

MRS. GIBBS. Don't do it, Emily.

MRS. SOAMES. Emily, don't. It's not what you think it'd be.

EMILY. But I won't live over a sad day. I'll choose a happy one—I'll choose the day I first knew that I loved George. Why should that be painful?

[THEY *are silent. Her question turns to the* STAGE MANAGER.]

STAGE MANAGER. You not only live it; but you watch yourself living it.

EMILY. Yes?

STAGE MANAGER. And as you watch it, you see the thing that they—down there—never know.

You see the future. You know what's going to happen afterwards.

EMILY. But is that—painful? Why?

MRS. GIBBS. That's not the only reason why you shouldn't do it, Emily. When you've been here longer you'll see that our life here is to forget all that, and think only of what's ahead, and be ready for what's ahead. When you've been here longer you'll understand.

EMILY. [Softly.] But, Mother Gibbs, how can I ever forget that life? It's all I know. It's all I had.

MRS. SOAMES. Oh, Emily. It isn't wise. Really, it isn't.

EMILY. But it's a thing I must know for myself. I'll choose a happy day, anyway.

MRS. GIBBS. No! At least, choose an unimportant day. Choose the least important day in your life. It will be important enough.

EMILY. [To herself.] Then it can't be since I was married; or since the baby was born. [To the stage manager, eagerly.] I can choose a birthday at least, can't I? I choose my twelfth birthday.

STAGE MANAGER. All right. February 11th, 1899. A Tuesday. Do you want any special time of day?

EMILY. Oh, I want the whole day.

STAGE MANAGER. We'll begin at dawn. You remember it had been snowing for several days; but it had stopped the night before, and they had begun clearing the roads. The sun's coming up.

EMILY. [With a cry; rising.] There's Main Street . . . why, that's Mr. Morgan's drugstore before he changed it! . . . And there's the livery stable.

[The stage at no time in this act has been very dark; but now the left half of the stage gradually becomes very bright—the brightness of a crisp winter morning. EMILY walks toward Main Street.]

STAGE MANAGER. Yes, it's 1899. This is fourteen years ago.

EMILY. Oh, that's the town I knew as a little girl. And, look, there's the old white fence that used to be around our house. Oh, I'd forgotten that! Oh, I love it so! Are they inside?

STAGE MANAGER. Yes, your mother'll be coming downstairs in a minute to make breakfast.

EMILY. [Softly.] Will she?

STAGE MANAGER. And you remember: your father had been away for several days; he came back on the early-morning train.

EMILY. No . . .?

STAGE MANAGER. He'd been back to his college to make a speech—in western New York, at Clinton.

EMILY. Look! There's Howie Newsome. There's our policeman. But he's dead; he died.

[The voices of HOWIE NEWSOME, CONSTABLE WARREN and JOE CROWELL, JR., are heard at the left of the stage. EMILY listens in delight.]

HOWIE NEWSOME. Whoa, Bessie!—Bessie! 'Morning, Bill.

CONSTABLE WARREN. Morning, Howie.

HOWIE NEWSOME. You're up early.

CONSTABLE WARREN. Been rescuin' a party; darn near froze to death, down by Polish Town thar. Got drunk and lay out in the snowdrifts. Thought he was in bed when I shook'm.

EMILY. Why, there's Joe Crowell . . .

JOE CROWELL. Good morning, Mr. Warren. 'Morning, Howie.

[MRS. WEBB has appeared in her kitchen, but EMILY does not see her until she calls.]

MRS. WEBB. Chil-dren! Wally! Emily! . . . Time to get up.

EMILY. Mama, I'm here! Oh! how young Mama

looks! I didn't know Mama was ever that young.

MRS. WEBB. You can come and dress by the kitchen fire, if you like; but hurry.

[HOWIE NEWSOME *has entered along Main Street and brings the milk to* MRS. WEBB'S *door.*]

Good morning, Mr. Newsome. Whhhh—it's cold.

HOWIE NEWSOME. Ten below by my barn, Mrs. Webb.

MRS. WEBB. Think of it! Keep yourself wrapped up. [*She takes her bottles in, shuddering.*]

EMILY. [*With an effort.*] Mama, I can't find my blue hair ribbon anywhere.

MRS. WEBB. Just open your eyes, dear, that's all. I laid it out for you special—on the dresser, there. If it were a snake it would bite you.

EMILY. Yes, yes . . .

[*She puts her hand on her heart.* MR. WEBB *comes along Main Street, where he meets* CONSTABLE WARREN. *Their movements and voices are increasingly lively in the sharp air.*]

MR. WEBB. Good morning, Bill.

CONSTABLE WARREN. Good morning, Mr. Webb. You're up early.

MR. WEBB. Yes, just been back to my old college in New York State. Been any trouble here?

CONSTABLE WARREN. Well, I was called up this mornin' to rescue a Polish fella—darn near froze to death he was.

MR. WEBB. We must get it in the paper.

CONSTABLE WARREN. 'Twan't much.

EMILY. [*Whispers.*] Papa.

[MR. WEBB *shakes the snow off his feet and enters his house.*
CONSTABLE WARREN *goes off, right.*]

MR. WEBB. Good morning, Mother.

MRS. WEBB. How did it go, Charles?

MR. WEBB. Oh, fine, I guess. I told'm a few things. Everything all right here?

MRS. WEBB. Yes—can't think of anything that's happened, special. Been right cold. Howie Newsome says it's ten below over to his barn.

MR. WEBB. Yes, well, it's colder than that at Hamilton College. Students' ears are falling off. It ain't Christian. Paper have any mistakes in it?

MRS. WEBB. None that I noticed. Coffee's ready when you want it.

[*He starts upstairs.*]

Charles! Don't forget; it's Emily's birthday. Did you remember to get her something?

MR. WEBB. [*Patting his pocket.*] Yes, I've got something here. [*Calling up the stairs.*] Where's my girl? Where's my birthday girl? [*He goes off left.*]

MRS. WEBB. Don't interrupt her now, Charles. You can see her at breakfast. She's slow enough as it is. Hurry up, children! It's seven o'clock. Now, I don't want to call you again.

EMILY. [*Softly, more in wonder than in grief.*] I can't bear it. They're so young and beautiful. Why did they ever have to get old? Mama, I'm here. I'm grown up. I love you all, everything. I can't look at everything hard enough.

[*She looks questioningly at the* STAGE MANAGER, *saying or suggesting: "Can I go in?" He nods briefly. She crosses to the inner door to the kitchen, left of her mother, and as though entering the room, says, suggesting the voice of a girl of twelve.*]

Good morning, Mama.

MRS. WEBB.

[*Crossing to embrace and kiss her; in her characteristic matter-of-fact manner.*]

Well, now, dear, a very happy birthday to my

girl and many happy returns. There are some surprises waiting for you on the kitchen table.

EMILY. Oh, Mama, you *shouldn't* have.

[*She throws an anguished glance at the* STAGE MANAGER.]

I can't—I can't.

MRS. WEBB. [*Facing the audience, over her stove.*] But birthday or no birthday, I want you to eat your breakfast good and slow. I want you to grow up and be a good strong girl. That in the blue paper is from your Aunt Carrie; and I reckon you can guess who brought the postcard album. I found it on the doorstep when I brought in the milk—George Gibbs . . . must have come over in the cold pretty early . . . right nice of him.

EMILY. [*To herself.*] Oh, George! I'd forgotten that. . . .

MRS. WEBB. Chew that bacon good and slow. It'll help keep you warm on a cold day.

EMILY. [*With mounting urgency.*] Oh, Mama, just look at me one minute as though you really saw me. Mama, fourteen years have gone by. I'm dead. You're a grandmother, Mama. I married George Gibbs, Mama. Wally's dead, too. Mama, his appendix burst on a camping trip to North Conway. We felt just terrible about it—don't you remember? But, just for a moment now we're all together. Mama, just for a moment we're happy. *Let's look at one another.*

MRS. WEBB. That in the yellow paper is something I found in the attic among your grandmother's things. You're old enough to wear it now, and I thought you'd like it.

EMILY. And this is from you. Why, Mama, it's just lovely and it's just what I wanted. It's beautiful!

[*She flings her arms around her mother's neck. Her mother goes on with her cooking, but is pleased.*]

MRS. WEBB. Well, I hoped you'd like it. Hunted all over. Your Aunt Norah couldn't find one in Concord, so I had to send all the way to Boston. [*Laughing.*] Wally has something for you, too. He made it at manual-training class and he's very proud of it. Be sure you make a big fuss about it. Your father has a surprise for you, too; don't know what it is myself. Sh— here he comes.

MR. WEBB. [*Off stage.*] Where's my girl? Where's my birthday girl?

EMILY. [*In a loud voice to the* STAGE MANAGER.] I can't. I can't go on. It goes so fast. We don't have time to look at one another.

[*She breaks down sobbing.*
The lights dim on the left half of the stage.
MRS. WEBB *disappears.*]

I didn't realize. So all that was going on and we never noticed. Take me back—up the hill—to my grave. But first: Wait! One more look. Good-bye, Good-bye, world. Good-bye, Grover's Corners . . . Mama and Papa. Good-bye to clocks ticking . . . and Mama's sunflowers. And food and coffee. And new-ironed dresses and hot baths . . . and sleeping and waking up. Oh, earth, you're too wonderful for anybody to realize you.

[*She looks toward the* STAGE MANAGER *and asks abruptly, through her tears:*]

Do any human beings ever realize life while they live it?—every, every minute?

STAGE MANAGER. No. [*Pause.*] The saints and poets, maybe—they do some.

EMILY. I'm ready to go back.

[*She returns to her chair beside* MRS. GIBBS. *Pause.*]

MRS. GIBBS. Were you happy?

EMILY. No . . . I should have listened to you. That's all human beings are! Just blind people.

MRS. GIBBS. Look, it's clearing up. The stars are coming out.

EMILY. Oh, Mr. Stimson, I should have listened to them.

SIMON STIMSON. [*With mounting violence; bitingly.*] Yes, now you know. Now you know! That's what it was to be alive. To move about in a cloud of ignorance; to go up and down trampling on the feelings of those . . . of those about you. To spend and waste time as though you had a million years. To be always at the mercy of one self-centered passion, or another. Now you know—that's the happy existence you wanted to go back to. Ignorance and blindness.

MRS. GIBBS. [*Spiritedly.*] Simon Stimson, that ain't the whole truth and you know it. Emily, look at that star. I forget its name.

A MAN AMONG THE DEAD. My boy Joel was a sailor—knew 'em all. He'd set on the porch evenings and tell 'em all by name. Yes, sir, wonderful!

ANOTHER MAN AMONG THE DEAD. A star's mighty good company.

A WOMAN AMONG THE DEAD. Yes. Yes, 'tis.

SIMON STIMSON. Here's one of *them* coming.

THE DEAD. That's funny. 'Tain't no time for one of them to be here. Goodness sakes.

EMILY. Mother Gibbs, it's George.

MRS. GIBBS. Sh, dear. Just rest yourself.

EMILY. It's George.

[GEORGE *enters from the left, and slowly comes toward them.*]

A MAN FROM AMONG THE DEAD. And my boy, Joel, who knew the stars—he used to say it took millions of years for that speck o' light to git to the earth. Don't seem like a body could believe it, but that's what he used to say—millions of years.

[GEORGE *sinks to his knees then falls full length at* EMILY's *feet.*]

A WOMAN AMONG THE DEAD. Goodness! That ain't no way to behave!

MRS. SOAMES. He ought to be home.

EMILY. Mother Gibbs?

MRS. GIBBS. Yes, Emily?

EMILY. They don't understand, do they?

MRS. GIBBS. No, dear. They don't understand.

[*The* STAGE MANAGER *appears at the right, one hand on a dark curtain which he slowly draws across the scene.*
In the distance a clock is heard striking the hour very faintly.]

STAGE MANAGER. Most everybody's asleep in Grover's Corners. There are a few lights on: Shorty Hawkins, down at the depot, has just watched the Albany train go by. And at the livery stable somebody's setting up late and talking. Yes, it's clearing up. There are the stars—doing their old, old crisscross journeys in the sky. Scholars haven't settled the matter yet, but they seem to think there are no living beings up there. Just chalk . . . or fire. Only this one is straining away, straining away all the time to make something of itself. The strain's so bad that every sixteen hours everybody lies down and gets a rest. [*He winds his watch.*] Hm. . . . Eleven o'clock in Grover's Corners. You get a good rest, too. Good night.

THE END

STUDY QUESTIONS

Recalling

1. How much time has elapsed between Acts 2 and 3? Which characters that we have met before are "buried" in the cemetery where Act 3 opens?

2. In his opening speech what does the Stage Manager say all the greatest people have been telling us, though some people forget? What does he ask "Mrs. Smith" near the end of this monologue?

3. How did Emily die? What warnings does Mrs. Gibbs give Emily when Emily expresses the desire to return among the living? What day does Emily choose to relive?

4. What does Emily ask her mother to do "with mounting urgency" on page 735? What does she tell the Stage Manager she did not realize? What does she ask him about human beings? What does he answer?

5. What living person comes to the cemetery near the end of the play? What is Emily's final remark to Mrs. Gibbs?

6. What does the Stage Manager say about the stars in his final speech? What does he say about "this one"?

Interpreting

7. Who is the "Mrs. Smith" that the Stage Manager addresses on page 729? What might the answer to his question be?

8. Why has revisiting a happy, seemingly innocuous day in her life been painful for Emily? What human blindness and failure does she notice?

9. To which "star" is the Stage Manager referring when he speaks of "this one" in his final speech? Is his view of this "star" negative? Explain.

10. What are some of the things this play teaches us to appreciate? Why might Wilder have chosen Grover's Corners, a regional setting, for themes that are basically universal themes?

Extending

11. When Emily asks the Stage Manager if human beings ever realize life while they live it, he replies, "The saints and poets, maybe—they do some." Based on your own reading, who are some of the poets or other writers that you think come closest to realizing life fully? Justify your answers.

VIEWPOINT

Richard Goldstone, a biographer of Thornton Wilder, acknowledges that *Our Town*

is not directly relevant to current social conditions, but neither was it relevant in 1938 [when first produced]. No one in Grover's Corners is addicted to anything stronger than coffee; no one seems to sustain any disease worse than whooping cough; crime seems unknown. . . . The village life described by Wilder, however, although it avoids the depiction of the mean, petty, ugly, and sordid, is no sentimental idyll. . . .

—*Thornton Wilder: An Intimate Portrait*

■ Which specific unpleasant and distressing aspects of life are represented in the play? Why are they included? What do they contribute to the total effect of the play?

LITERARY FOCUS

Characters in Drama

The writer of a conventional play must create his characters differently from a novelist or short story writer. A playwright cannot comment directly on the characters; all that we know of them must come through what they say and do on stage and from what other characters on stage say about them. Moreover, what is said must seem natural. The **exposition** (explaining what the situation is when the play begins, what the relationships are

among the characters, even what their names are) must arise naturally from what is said and done on stage.

Or at least it must in a conventional play. *Our Town,* however, is by no means conventional. Not only are scenery and props virtually abandoned; the stage manager, who ordinarily would be out of sight—having done his work before the audience arrives—is here allowed to remain and direct matters, much as the narrator of a novel might direct, explain, and comment on the action that he or she is describing. Thus, the Stage Manager in *Our Town* functions partly as a chorus to react to and evaluate what is happening. Even so, the various scenes from which he removes himself resemble scenes in more conventional plays, where characters reveal themselves solely through their speech and actions.

Thinking About Characters in Drama

1. Imagine Act 1 without the Stage Manager. As the play opens, two people, one middle-aged, one young, appear on stage. In what possible ways might we learn the name of the middle-aged man? Of the young man? How might we find out where the older man has been? How would we learn where the young man is going?

2. What, in your opinion, are the advantages and disadvantages of using a "chorus" or narrator in a drama, as Wilder does in *Our Town?*

Theme in Drama

Like other kinds of fiction, plays present specific *subjects* out of which general *themes* develop—themes that may relate to all of us. The specific subject of *Our Town* is life as lived by certain people in Grover's Corners, New Hampshire, in the early part of the twentieth century. But out of that specific subject grow themes that relate to lives lived at other times and places.

Some of those themes are suggested by the Stage Manager. Early in Act 2, for example, he remarks that "Nature's been pushing and contriving," moving the universe forward as though to create something better than what has preceded. "Every child born into the world," he says later, "is nature's attempt to make a perfect human being." Nature is interested, he believes, in progress toward perfection. Meanwhile, life goes on in its cyclical way, routines of birth, marriage, and death repeated over and over again.

Such general ideas, applicable to all of us but growing out of the specific events shown on stage, are what constitute the themes of the play.

Thinking About Theme in Drama

1. If an idea about change (and lack of change) is one of the themes of *Our Town,* what are some of the other themes? Consider, for example, the themes suggested by Jane Crofut's letter, by the attitudes of "the dead," by Emily's statements and pleas when she relives her twelfth birthday, and by the Stage Manager's closing remarks.
2. Do you think the play has one theme that dominates? Which one is it, and why?

Action in Drama

The conventional play moves from **exposition** (the explanation of the situation when the curtain goes up), through **rising action** (which generally involves **complication**—things going wrong or moving differently from the expected way) to a **climax** and through **falling action** to **resolution** (the unraveling or explanation of the plot). In a conventional play the protagonist, or main character, is the focal point of the action, providing a single center of attention for the play.

Our Town, however, as we have seen, is not conventional. The Stage Manager provides much of the exposition. In general, there are no complications, no climax, no effort at suspense. The purpose of the play is not to surprise or mystify or startle. Rather, it is to reveal and understand. Because an underlying theme of *Our Town* concerns the cyclical nature of life—the repeated routines by means of which our lives are led—the very structure of the play stresses repetition, as its action stresses what is ordinary and expected.

Thinking About Action in Drama

1. The action that opens Act 3 does contain some suspense, some withholding of crucial information that awakens our curiosity. What information is withheld?
2. Without using the standard devices for creating suspense, how does Wilder keep our interest focused on the action of the play?
3. Does *Our Town* have a protagonist? In what sense is the entire town the protagonist?

VOCABULARY

Antonyms

Antonyms are words that have opposite or nearly opposite meanings. The following words in capitals are from *Our Town.* Choose the word that is an antonym of each word in capitals, *as the word is used in the selection.* Write the number of each item and the letter of your choice on a separate sheet.

1. UNOBTRUSIVELY: (a) quietly (b) ominously (c) unmentionably (d) conspicuously
2. DILIGENT: (a) lazy (b) sensible (c) powerful (d) glamorous
3. SAVANT: (a) teacher (b) leader (c) ignoramus (d) philosopher
4. AFFRONTED: (a) restive (b) bereaved (c) discontented (d) mollified
5. LUGUBRIOUSNESS: (a) sorrow (b) delight (c) pride (d) monotony

COMPOSITION

Applying a Statement to a Work of Literature

Write a brief essay in defense of this statement: "*Our Town* presents a full and accurate picture of life as it is really lived, including what is truly important and leaving out only what is not important." Make sure you cite specific details from the play. *For help with this assignment, refer to Lesson 9 in the Writing About Literature Handbook at the back of this book.*

Writing a Dialogue

Try your hand at creating characters dramatically—that is, through nothing but dialogue and stage directions. Begin by writing a brief stage direction describing the setting in which your characters will find themselves. Then write a short dialogue between two or more characters. The dialogue should reveal their names, backgrounds, and something of their characteristics or attitudes. Within your dialogue include brief stage directions for actors, telling them how to move or sound when they perform your dialogue.

READING FOR APPRECIATION

Beyond the Surface

We sometimes hear people say that when they read literature they look for "hidden meanings." Yet no writer wants to *hide* his or her meanings from us. Writers want to *reveal* their meanings. Nevertheless, they seldom tell us directly what a poem or a story means.

Literature is an art of implication. It wants to surprise us, to make us participate in the experience it offers. Often it deals with the questions, the enigmas, the mysteries of our existence. No, writers do not want to hide anything from us, yet they do expect our cooperation. They expect us *to go beyond the surface.*

Look again at the poems by W. H. Auden that open this unit (page 574). In both of them, Auden expects us to go beyond the surface, to open ourselves to suggestions. In one of the poems the refrain, "If I could tell you I would let you know," may make us think: *Life is filled with mysteries and wonders, experiences we cannot fully explain.* The poet suggests that he is in love but wondering about, worrying about, what will become of this love. The poem is about uncertainty, and it asks us to share its mixture of delight and sorrow.

In "The Unknown Citizen" we look beyond the surface to see that Auden is not the speaker of the poem. He is not part of the government that seems so "concerned" for the citizen, nor does he *like* a government that judges people by statistics and reports. By the end of the poem, we know that that government would never have heard whether or not the Unknown Citizen felt free or happy. But what has happened to us as readers? We have *joined* the poet in his experience. How much less powerful these poems would be if Auden had merely *stated* his meanings!

Prose, too, asks us to look beyond the surface. In Katherine Anne Porter's "Jilting of Granny Weatherall," the point of the story is that Granny has never forgotten or forgiven the man who jilted her many years before. Her long and seemingly successful life has always been troubled by that memory. Porter's story is more moving because she allows us to watch that thought troubling Granny's mind, rising, receding, and rising to the surface again. The real action of the story is just a bit beyond Granny's consciousness. As readers beyond the surface, we gain a finer experience by not having the point spelled out for us.

Years after *Our Town* had become famous, Thornton Wilder commented that the key words in the play are "hundreds," "thousands," and "millions." He did not make this direct comment within the play itself but rather left it to his audiences to sense the meaning and emotion those words convey. As we read or watch *Our Town*, we may not say to ourselves, "Ah, there are some key words!" Yet surely we find that our experience includes the meanings Wilder intended. *Our Town* is not a realistic picture of life in a New Hampshire village. Rather, it is a meditation upon the mystery of the individual life measured against the joys and griefs of all those who have lived.

As readers we do not always see the full implications of a work of literature. That is why we study literature, discuss it, write about it: to discover what is beyond the surface. Our discussions, whether spoken or written, are attempts to share our enthusiasms and puzzlements. For literature is not only communication between writer and reader; it is communication within a community of readers, too. Each member of that community may see or feel slightly different possibilities in a story or play or poem. By sharing our thoughts, each of us comes to have a larger experience of literature and of life.

THE AMERICAN VOICE

A Usable Past

One critic has said that Americans have spent much of their time and imagination on a quest for a usable past. The years from 1930 to 1960 seem to have been spent largely in that search. The shock of the Great Depression and the cataclysm of World War II forced many Americans to think twice about what part of the American tradition was still meaningful to them. Many of the authors in this unit reveal a desire to look back at the past—whether in its personal or public aspects—and draw strength, ideas, or at least some kind of lesson from it.

Walker
My grandmothers were strong. Why am I not as they?

Wilbur
*There was perfection in the death of ferns
Which laid their fragile cheeks against the stone
A million years. . . .*

Porter
Since the day the wedding cake was not cut, but thrown out and wasted. The whole bottom dropped out of the world. . . .

Weidman
I begin to think I understand. I remember the stories of his boyhood in Austria.

Steinbeck
Jody lay in his bed and thought of the impossible world of Indians and buffaloes, a world that had ceased to be forever.

Clark
I have saved what I love; the soul of what was good in us is here; perhaps the new ones will make a strong enough beginning not to fall behind when they become clever.

Agee
We are talking now of summer evenings in Knoxville, Tennessee, in the time that I lived there so successfully disguised to myself as a child.

Faulkner
. . . not even a mortal animal but an anachronism, indomitable and invincible, out of an old dead time, a phantom, epitome and apotheosis of the old wild life.

The writers in this unit stepped back into the past to see what they could retrieve. Some found inspiring models for living. Others discovered that the past can never be exactly repeated, that in a new time new heroes and new definitions of heroism must be created.

Key to Illustrations on Pages 566–567.

1	2		8
3	4	5	9
6	7		10

1. Detail from *Room in New York,* Edward Hopper, 1932.
2. Clothes for the needy during the Depression, photographer unknown.
3. Costume designs by Patricia Zipprodt for a production of Thornton Wilder's *Our Town.*
4. Amelia Earhart, first woman to fly solo across the Atlantic Ocean (1932), postage stamp, 1963.
5. John Steinbeck, drawing by Alexis Oussenko.
6. Eudora Welty, photograph by Jill Krementz.
7. *Number 27,* Jackson Pollock, 1950.
8. Thornton Wilder, photographer unknown, 1933.
9. Guggenheim Museum in New York City, designed by Frank Lloyd Wright, 1943.
10. Celebrating the end of World War II, photographer unknown, 1945.

Key to Illustrations appears on page 837.

IN OUR TIME

1960–Present

Photograph © 1982 by Jill Krementz

The Contemporary Experience

What is it that makes the contemporary experience—the time of *our* lives—different from the past? Many historians feel that the time we ourselves live through is the most difficult to describe. Nevertheless, we produce hundreds of books each year trying to explain what it means to be a contemporary American.

The 1960s were a turbulent time in America, perhaps in reaction to the more placid 1950s. Young people in particular felt that they had to make their voices heard. They took strong, sometimes violent, stands on political matters such as American involvement in Vietnam and social matters such as the rights of black Americans and the changing role of women in American society. Many Americans searched for "peace," forming new communities in an effort to redefine the ways people might live together in the contemporary world. These efforts often involved reaching back into the past to revitalize old values and adapt them to new problems and new attitudes. Once again Americans seemed to be face to face with a New World.

As America moved into the 1970s, many of the attitudes of the sixties were absorbed into daily life while others were rejected. In the seventies Americans seemed to become more aware of their material welfare than they had been in the previous decade. The Space Age had arrived. Computers began af-

In Our Time 7

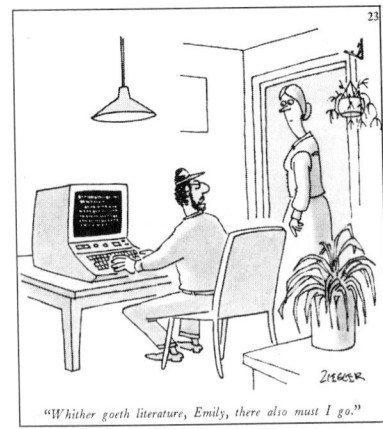

"*Whither goeth literature, Emily, there also must I go.*"

fecting everyone to a greater and greater degree each year. World and national economic problems beset almost everyone, and some of the ideals of the sixties found themselves transformed by the hard facts of making a living in the seventies.

In the 1980s we continue to balance American ideals and realities, to look closely at our goals and our impressive national achievements. Americans seem to have created a new sense of the possible without giving up the American dream.

Contemporary Literature

Surprisingly, the literature of our time is fundamentally traditional, but the traditions it follows are the traditions of Modernism. Modernism is our heritage, the extraordinary efforts and accomplishments of the writers and artists of the early decades of our century. There have been no major movements in literature since that time, only refinements, restatements, all building on the shoulders of our giants—Pound, Eliot, Frost, Stevens, Hemingway, Faulkner.

Modernism has given us forms and techniques that we have not yet exhausted. Even literature that calls itself postmodern is dependent upon the Modernist tradition. Modern free verse with its irregular rhythms, its use of association instead of direct statement, and its breakdown of standard forms still intrigues our poets. The stream-of-

consciousness technique in prose, the creation of prose poems, the imitation of storytelling techniques taken from movies, continue to be exciting when used by our contemporary novelists.

Some of our writers still seem experimental; some try to incorporate Modernist techniques into more conventional forms. However, to a certain extent, we have become so used to the "modern" style of writing and expression that we often hardly notice it. Literature is following the path taken by modern music: The "outrageous" harmonies that seemed so new in early twentieth-century music are now a part of our everyday sounds on television, in movies, and in popular songs.

Technology has greatly affected our time, of course. The paperback revolution has made more books available to more people than ever before in history. Television, computers, and word processors have changed the ways we absorb information,

the way writers write, the way all of us read and organize our thoughts. Although our time appears to many people to be an age of *images*—pictures on screens—many others realize that for the subtleties of communication we are still vitally dependent upon *words*.

The following selections can only begin to display the great variety of writing taking place in our time. Our poets are still consolidating the treasures of Modernism; many of the poems written in our time seem as if they could have been written in the 1920s. Our prose writers are trying to find ways of telling stories that will be both "new" and accessible to most people. The invention, for example, of the form called the nonfiction novel tries to do just that.

Earlier in this century, people talked about the "death of the novel," but the talk was premature. In addition to those writers represented in the following pages, there are many other American writers who have created exciting fiction in our time—among them John Cheever, Isaac Bashevis Singer, Donald Barthelme, Robert Coover, Norman Mailer, and William Gass.

Authenticity

The poet T. S. Eliot said that when it comes to the literature of one's own time, it is impossible to know who the great writers are. Eliot thought we can say

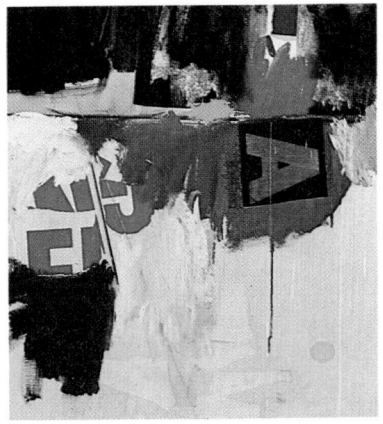

Detail from *Summer Rental, Number 2,* Robert Rauschenberg, 1960.

whether or not we feel that a work of contemporary literature is *authentic.* Yet it is the future, or time, that decides who the classic writers will be.

Only in time is there that sifting process in which some writers are forgotten and others remembered. In American literature we can see how impossible it was for men and women of the nineteenth century to know which writers we in the twentieth century would think great or interesting. In the nineteenth century almost everyone knew that Emerson was great and would become a classic, but few suspected the degree of esteem in which we would come to hold his young friend Thoreau. Emily Dickinson was unknown then, and Herman Melville was forgotten.

One thing, however, is certain. The great writers survive because they are *authentic.* A writer may be sincere but may simply not be in touch with what is truly important to his or her time. A writer may intend to write well, but only *mastery* of the art of writing will allow what is genuine, what is authentic, to be fully expressed. We are continually judging the writ-

ers of our time, and authenticity—the full expression of the genuine—is our best guide.

We find in the writers of our own time a familiar American reality. A father and son flying a kite together, a mother and son riding bikes, someone driving a car to town to mail a letter, a baseball player, a man with a flower on his fire escape—these are more familiar to us than Melville's whaling voyage, Cooper's frontiersman, or Taylor's spinning wheel. Yet what is important is the use our contemporaries make of their material, the transformation they make of the everyday into the universal, the authenticity of the experience they offer.

Whatever the greatness or

popularity of the writers of our time, they share one quality: freedom of style and content. They take as their material any and every aspect of American experience. They are the heirs of Poe and Hawthorne, of Whitman and Dickinson, of Mark Twain and Willa Cather and Ernest Hemingway and Gertrude Stein. An American writer today can *choose* his or her literary ancestors according to need or taste. An American writer writes as he or she chooses, using traditional or experimental styles or combining the best of both.

No schools or movements dominate the American writing scene today. Our artists are heirs to the entire American past. We have our contemporary Romantics, our Realists and Naturalists, our Regionalists, our Traditionalists, our Modernists. We can enjoy them all, as long as what they write is authentic, as long as it speaks to our hearts and minds, as long as it gives us pleasure and insight.

With the help of American writers like these, we try to understand our time. For that is one of the main uses of literature—to find the language that makes sense of our experience.

TIME LINE

1960–Present AMERICAN EVENTS

1960   John Updike, *Rabbit, Run*

1961   President John Kennedy establishes Peace Corps

        Joseph Heller, *Catch–22*

1962   John Steinbeck wins Nobel Prize for Literature

        Rachel Carson's *Silent Spring* sparks environmental reform movement

1963   President John Kennedy assassinated

        Martin Luther King, Jr., "I Have a Dream" speech

        Bernard Malamud, *Idiots First*

1964   Saul Bellow, *Herzog*

        Ralph Ellison, *Shadow and Act*

        Martin Luther King, Jr., wins Nobel Peace Prize

1965   *Ariel,* poems of Sylvia Plath, published posthumously

        John Berryman, 77 *Dream Songs*

1967   Stanley Kubrick directs *2001: A Space Odyssey*

        U.S. population: 200 million

1968   Martin Luther King, Jr., assassinated

        Robert F. Kennedy assassinated

WORLD EVENTS 1960–Present

1960   Africa: Many national independence movements begin

1961   U.S. and U.S.S.R. make first manned space flights

        East Germany: Communists build Berlin Wall

1962   World population: 1.6 billion

        Cuba: U.S. blockade forces removal of Soviet missiles

1963   U.S.S.R.: Valentina Tereshkova, first female cosmonaut

1965   England: Harold Pinter, *The Homecoming*

1966   India: Indira Gandhi becomes Prime Minister

1967   South Africa: Dr. Christiaan Barnard performs first heart transplant

1968   U.S.S.R. invades Czechoslovakia

        U.S.S.R.: Novelist Alexander Solzhenitsyn, *Cancer Ward*

1969   Neil Armstrong and Edwin
Aldrin, first men to walk on
moon

N. Scott Momaday, *The Way
to Rainy Mountain*

Robert Penn Warren,
Audubon: A Vision

1971   Voting age lowered from 21
to 18

1972   Engineer Robert Moog patents
synthesizer, electronic musical
instrument

1973   Vietnam War ends

1976   John Ashbery, *Self-Portrait in
a Convex Mirror*

Saul Bellow wins Nobel Prize
for Literature

1981   First flight of space shuttle

Elizabeth Spencer,
*The Stories
of Elizabeth Spencer*

Mark Helprin, *Ellis Island*

1982   World's first permanent
artificial heart transplant

1984   Personal computers and cable
television enter more and
more American homes

1969   Israel: Golda Meir becomes
Prime Minister

1971   Switzerland: Women gain right
to vote

1973   World oil and energy crisis

1976   China: Earthquake kills
655,000 people

1979   Iran: Ayatollah Khomeini
overthrows Shah; fifty
Americans taken hostage

U.S.S.R. invades Afghanistan

England: Trinidad-born
novelist V. S. Naipaul, *A Bend
in the River*

1981   Poland: Independent trade
union, Solidarity, suppressed

POETRY

Robert Penn Warren   *born 1905*

One of the most respected American men of letters, Robert Penn Warren has succeeded in almost every form of literature. He has written poetry, stories, novels, plays, criticism, and biography. In addition, he collaborated with critic Cleanth Brooks on two of the most influential textbooks for teaching literature, *Understanding Poetry* and *Understanding Fiction.*

During the first part of his life, Warren, who was born in Kentucky, lived, went to college, and taught in the South. Indeed, the South with all of its traditions is one of Warren's great subjects. During the 1920s he was a member of the group of southern poets called the Fugitives, writers who contributed to *The Fugitive* magazine and who wrote with a strong sense of their own region. These writers included John Crowe Ransom (page 476) and Allen Tate. In 1930 Warren joined several other southern writers to produce a book called *I'll Take My Stand,* celebrating agrarian, or rural, values in the face of the modern industrial world. He was also one of the founding editors of the *Southern Review* in 1935. Beyond working as a writer and editor, Warren pursued an outstanding career as a teacher. Among his novels, *All the King's Men* (1946)—a powerful story of southern politics—is considered a modern classic. He has won almost every major literary prize in America, including the Pulitzer Prize (twice, once for fiction, once for poetry) and the National Book Award.

Warren began writing poetry in his teens and has always written poetry while at the same time working in other forms of literature. His volume *Selected Poems: New and Old, 1923–1966* shows his steady dedication to the art. In his later years he has concentrated on poetry, publishing *Incarnation* (1968), *Audubon* (1969), *Or Else* (1974), and other volumes. His poetry reflects a profound love and understanding of his region; he is closely tied to the American land. Often narrative and usually deeply personal, sometimes even rather mystical, his poetry is nevertheless simple and unaffected.

Warren's *Audubon* illustrates a style of modern writing that began with Ezra Pound's *Cantos,* poetry that includes fragments of actual historical documents. Warren's poem is a tribute to John James Audubon (1785–1851), the great American naturalist and painter, who traveled through America studying and painting the birds and other animals native to this continent. Audubon's masterpiece is the huge volume of colored engravings called *Birds of America* (1827–1838). Warren's tribute moves back and forth between a re-creation of Audubon's life and vision (the subtitle of the poem is "A Vision") and quotations from Audubon's own writings.

Robert Penn Warren

from **Audubon: A Vision**

He walked in the world. Knew the lust of the eye.

Wrote: "Ever since a Boy I have had an astonishing desire
to see Much of the World and particularly
to acquire a true knowledge of the Birds of North
America."

5 He dreamed of hunting with Boone,[1] from imagination
painted his portrait.
He proved that the buzzard does not scent its repast,
but sights it.
He looked in the eye of the wounded white-headed eagle.

Wrote: ". . . the Noble Fellow looked at his Ennemies
with a Contemptible Eye."

10 At dusk he stood on a bluff, and the bellowing of buffalo
Was like distant ocean. He saw
Bones whiten the plain in the hot daylight.

He saw the Indian, and felt the splendor of God.

Wrote: ". . . for there I see the Man Naked from his
15   hand and yet free from acquired Sorrow."

Below the salt,[2] in rich houses, he sat, and knew insult.
In the lobbies and couloirs[3] of greatness he dangled,
And was not unacquainted with contumely.[4]

Wrote: "My Lovely Miss Pirrie of Oackley Passed by Me
20   this Morning, but did not remember how beautifull
I had rendered her face once by Painting it
at her Request with Pastelles."

Wrote: ". . . but thanks to My humble talents I can run
the gantlet[5] throu this World without her help."

Pileated Woodpecker. John James Audubon.

---

1. **Boone:** Daniel Boone (1734–1820), U.S. frontiersman.
2. **Below the salt:** in a less honored position. Guests were once seated at the upper or lower part of the table with a bowl of salt in the middle; honored guests were above the salt.
3. **couloirs** [kōōl wärz']: corridors.
4. **contumely** [kon'too mə lē]: rudeness.
5. **run the gantlet** [gônt'lit]: here, to carry on while being criticized or opposed from all sides.

Meadowlark. John James Audubon.

25 And ran it, and ran undistracted by promise of ease,
Nor even the kind condescension of Daniel Webster.[6]

Wrote: ". . . would give me a fat place was I willing to
have one; but I love indepenn and piece more
than humbug and money."

30 And proved same, but in the end, entered
On honor. Far, over the ocean, in the silken salons,[7]
With hair worn long like a hunter's, eyes shining,
He whistled the birdcalls of his distant forest.

Wrote: ". . . in my sleep I continually dream of birds."

35 And in the end, entered into his earned house,
And slept in a bed, and with Lucy.[8]

                                    But the fiddle
Soon lay on the shelf untouched, the mouthpiece
Of the flute was dry, and his brushes.

40   His mind
Was darkened, and his last joy
Was in the lullaby they sang him, in Spanish, at sunset.

He died, and was mourned, who had loved the world.

Who had written: ". . . a world which though wicked
45   enough in all conscience is *perhaps* as
                good as worlds unknown."

---

6. **Daniel Webster:** U.S. orator and statesman (1792–1852) who served
in the House of Representatives, in the Senate, and as Secretary of State.
7. **Far . . . salons:** referring to Audubon's art exhibitions in Great Britain.
8. **Lucy:** Lucy Bakewell, Audubon's wife.

William Stafford   *born 1914*

William Stafford is a poet with a strong sense of place, and his place is the American Midwest and West. A native of Kansas, in his youth he worked for the United States Forest Service, on farms, and in organizations promoting world peace. He has been a college teacher at several schools, mostly at Lewis and Clark College in Oregon.

The poet Louis Simpson has said that "if ever this country is to have a sense of itself, it will be through work like Stafford's." The qualities of Stafford's work that prompt such praise are its simplicity, its modern plain style, and its ability to make a song and a metaphor out of a common domestic experience. "Father and Son" avoids the complexities and difficulties of Modernism while it turns an everyday occurrence into a symbolic moment.

William Stafford

Father and Son

No sound—a spell—on, on out
where the wind went, our kite sent back
its thrill along the string that
sagged but sang and said, "I'm here!
5   I'm here!"—till broke somewhere,
gone years ago, but sailed forever clear
of earth. I hold—whatever tugs
the other end—I hold that string.

James Wright   *1927–1980*

James Wright has been called a poet of extraordinary compassion, one of the most life-affirming poets of our time. Born in Martins Ferry, Ohio, in 1927, Wright studied at Kenyon College and was influenced and encouraged by the poet John Crowe Ransom (page 476). His first volume of verse was published in the distinguished Yale Series of Younger Poets, devoted to publishing first volumes of poetry. After that volume, *The Green Wall* (1957), Wright continued to perfect his gift for lyric with *Saint Judas* (1959), *The Branch Will Not Break* (1963), *Shall We Gather at the River* (1968), and *Collected Poems* (1971). Like so many contemporary poets, Wright has supported himself as a university teacher. In fact, the predominance of the teacher-poet has become one of the most marked characteristics of the contemporary poetry scene.

Wright's poem "Depressed by a Book of Bad Poetry" displays the same directness, the almost transparent language, used by William Stafford (page 753) and Robert Bly (page 764). These poets make an effort *not* to sound "poetic" but to locate the poetry in an experience that, if simply told, will allow the reader to share it.

James Wright

Depressed by a Book of Bad Poetry, I Walk Toward an Unused Pasture and Invite the Insects to Join Me

Relieved, I let the book fall behind a stone.
I climb a slight rise of grass.
I do not want to disturb the ants
Who are walking single file up the fence post,
5 Carrying small white petals,
Casting shadows so frail that I can see through them.
I close my eyes for a moment, and listen.
The old grasshoppers
Are tired, they leap heavily now,
10 Their thighs are burdened.
I want to hear them, they have clear sounds to make.
Then lovely, far off, a dark cricket begins
In the maple trees.

STUDY QUESTIONS *(Hayden)*

Recalling

1. What did the speaker's father do on winter Sundays? In what terms are the father's hands described? With what observation does the first stanza close?
2. Why, according to the second stanza, did the speaker rise and dress slowly? How did he speak to his father, according to line 10?
3. What question does the speaker ask?

Interpreting

4. What is suggested by the "too" in the first line? What did the father do on other days?
5. What does line 9 suggest about the household described in this poem? What do line 14 and the father's activities suggest?
6. What does the speaker seem to regret?

Extending

7. What do you think Emily in *Our Town* (page 698) would have told the people in this household?

STUDY QUESTIONS *(Stafford)*

Recalling

1. What are the father and son doing in the first five lines? What does their kite send back along the string in line 3? What message does it send back in lines 5–7?
2. What happened to the kite, according to lines 5–7? What does the speaker still hold?

Interpreting

3. Is the speaker the father or the son? What might their "kite" be? What does "I'm here! I'm here!" suggest?
4. What is suggested by the kite's being broken? By the speaker's still holding onto the string? What else might tug at the other end?

STUDY QUESTIONS *(Wright)*

Recalling

1. What has depressed the speaker? Toward what does he walk? Whom or what does he invite to join him?
2. Whom or what does the speaker not want to disturb?
3. What adjectives describe the grasshoppers? What sort of sounds does the speaker say they make?
4. What adjectives describe the cricket? What does the cricket do?

Interpreting

5. In general terms, what gives the speaker solace, or comfort, after reading the bad poetry? Why is it appropriate that much of his solace comes from *sounds*?
5. What does this poem suggest about art and its relationship to nature?

COMPARING WRITERS

"Depressed by a Book of Bad Poetry" belongs to the long tradition of English and American nature poetry. In that tradition the troubled poet goes to the purity of nature to find healing or renewal. Compare the attitude toward nature in Wright's poem to the attitude toward nature in the excerpt from Robert Penn Warren's *Audubon* (page 749), in William Cullen Bryant's "Thanatopsis" (page 120), and in Walt Whitman's "When I Heard the Learn'd Astronomer" (page 254). Which of the poems seems to you the most moving? Which takes the most important questions as its subject? What generalizations can you make about the language of contemporary poetry as contrasted with the language of earlier American Romantic poetry?

John Ashbery   *born 1927*

One of the most brilliant and experimental of contemporary poets, John Ashbery seems always in search of a new definition of poetry. He blends a visionary, sometimes highly abstract style with the most ordinary of everyday objects and events. His subjects and tones shift with great speed—just as our minds move instantaneously from one thing to another.

John Ashbery was born in Rochester, New York, and after attending Harvard and Columbia universities, received a Fulbright scholarship that took him to France. He remained in France for almost ten years, and his poetry is deeply influenced by modern French poetry and important French literary criticism. In fact, Ashbery is often considered the leading American poet to reflect the most recent critical thinking about the direction poetry is taking in our time.

In Paris Ashbery became an art critic, a profession that he continued when he returned to New York in 1965. His close association with the "action painters" in New York is usually thought to be another influence on his writing. Action painting is abstract, and it is about the act of painting itself. In the same way, Ashbery's poems are often about the *act* of writing a poem, not about a completed meaning that a poem hands over to us.

Ashbery began publishing poems in 1956 with the volume *Some Trees*. His other books include *The Tennis Court Oath* (1962), *Self-Portrait in a Convex Mirror* (1975), *Houseboat Days* (1977), and *Paradoxes and Oxymorons* (1968), from which the following poem is taken. Ashbery once said that his poems "might be considered to be a snapshot of whatever is going on in my mind at the time," and indeed his poems are often impossible to understand if we try to get from them some meaning that can be expressed in prose. They are, however, a kind of elegant fun for the reader who can relax and allow them to happen, allow their brilliant images and playful shifting of voices to have their own way.

"Paradoxes and Oxymorons" is a poem that plays a trick upon "you" (the reader), but it is a trick designed to make a serious point. It makes us stop and stare at the eternal "paradoxes and oxymorons" at the center of writing and reading poetry. A **paradox** is an apparent contradiction. An **oxymoron** is a bringing together of contradictory things within a phrase such as *brilliant darkness*. In simple language that sounds *almost* as if we could follow its argument on a "plain level," this poem turns itself inside out as it makes us wonder where the meaning comes from in any poem. From the poet? From the poem? From us?

John Ashbery

Paradoxes and Oxymorons

This poem is concerned with language on a very plain level.
Look at it talking to you. You look out a window
Or pretend to fidget. You have it but you don't have it.
You miss it, it misses you. You miss each other.

5 The poem is sad because it wants to be yours, and cannot.
What's a plain level? It is that and other things,
Bringing a system of them into play. Play?
Well, actually, yes, but I consider play to be

A deeper outside thing, a dreamed role-pattern,
10 As in the division of grace these long August days
Without proof. Open-ended. And before you know
It gets lost in the steam and chatter of typewriters.

It has been played once more. I think you exist only
To tease me into doing it, on your level, and then you aren't there
15 Or have adopted a different attitude. And the poem
Has set me softly down beside you. The poem is you.

Summer Rental, Number 2,
Robert Rauschenberg, 1960.

STUDY QUESTIONS

Recalling

1. According to line 1, with what is this poem concerned? What is it doing in line 2? According to line 3, do you "have" the poem?
2. Why, according to stanza 2, is the poem "sad"? What question is asked in line 6?
3. What does the speaker say about your reasons for existing in stanza 4? According to lines 15–16, what has the poem done? What is it?

Interpreting

4. Is the speaker in this poem speaking to you as a poet? Who is "you" in this poem?
5. What paradox, or apparent contradiction, is expressed in line 3? What might this paradox suggest about poetry?
6. What do the last two lines suggest about the effects of a poem on its readers? In what way are these suggestions paradoxical?
7. Why is line 1 paradoxical? What does the paradox suggest about all good poetry?

Extending

8. Which do you think is more important to a poem—the poet's meaning or the reader's interpretation? Discuss.

VIEWPOINT

The critic Denis Donoghue has commented on Ashbery's intention as a poet:

I assume that Mr. Ashbery's concern is to give the process of the mind as it moves through . . . reflections, not merely the results of reflection. It is an extreme version of the common distinction between "a mind speaking" and "what is being said."

■ What are the advantages of a poet showing his mind at work—"a mind speaking"? What can we learn as we watch the process of a poem in the making? Tell in your own words what this kind of process poem reveals about "what is being said" in any poem at any time.

LITERARY FOCUS

Modern Style

Style in literature—especially modern literature—is one of the most difficult literary elements to discuss. We talk about "a writer's style," but when we have to describe that style precisely, we find that it is hard to do. We use words like *lyrical, dignified, ornate, journalistic, comic, satiric,* or even simpler but less helpful words like *dull, vivid, simple,* or *complex.* We can say that **style** is a writer's own characteristic way of writing, including virtually all the ways words are used: diction, syntax, sentence length, imagery, rhythm. As with all terms that have so many ways of being used, we should be careful when we use the term *style.* One useful distinction, however, can be kept in mind: the distinction between the style of a period and the style of an individual author.

In the world of contemporary poetry, there is no single "style of the period." Some writers use "plain" speech, not far from ordinary conversation or prose. Others use highly unusual, extraordinary speech, language that attempts to express what "ordinary" language cannot express. Some writers use short, clipped sentences; others use long, complicated constructions with many subordinate clauses and modifying phrases.

Some poets today are highly literal; they say exactly what they mean, neither more nor less. Some are highly metaphorical, requiring us to penetrate complex constructions of images. Some are objective, trying to eliminate as far as possible the personality of the poet behind the poem. Some are subjective, believing that there is nothing more important than the outpouring of their own feelings.

For most of us, poems in the modern "plain" style are the most attractive poems on first reading. Marianne Moore, in her famous poem, "Poetry" (page 481), admits that "we / do not admire what / we cannot understand." Yet we would be soon bored if we understood everything at once or easily. In "Paradoxes and Oxymorons" John Ashbery makes fun of the idea of reading on a "plain level." As he demonstrates in the poem itself, the question of where "meaning" comes from is never a "plain" question. There are no unusual words in Ashbery's poem. The sentences seem short and clear as we read them one by one. Yet as we attempt to follow the argument, to fit the sentences together, we see that this poem is hardly written in a "plain" style like that of Robert Hayden's "Those Winter Sundays" (page 752) or James Wright's "Depressed by a Book of Bad Poetry" (page 754).

The modern philosopher Ludwig Wittgenstein believed that "what we cannot speak about we must pass over in silence." Poets, however, resist that silence. When the style of a modern poem turns away from simple statements, it is attempting to speak about things that cannot be spoken about in "ordinary" language. It is attempting to make meaning, to find meaning, for experience. The style—perhaps we should say the *styles* of modern poetry, whether direct or indirect, plain or fantastic—tries to be adequate to whatever experience is the subject of a poem. At times, perhaps, something that looks like a "plain level" will do. Yet when it will not do, the poets of our time devise other styles, for, as an art, poetry refuses to pass over any of our wide-ranging human experience in silence.

Thinking About Modern Style

■ Choose any poem in this book written in the twentieth century. Describe in your own words the style of the poem. Be as specific as possible, referring to the poem's diction, sentence structure, imagery, and rhythm. Most important, tell whether you think the style is adequate to the poet's experience. In other words, does the poem "work"?

VOCABULARY

Words from Greek

In the Golden Age of Greece, oratory and rhetoric, or the art of using words effectively, were highly developed arts. Greek has given us many words for figures of speech and literary elements. The title of Ashbery's poem comes from two Greek words for figures of speech.

In Greek the root *para* means "beside" or "beyond"; *doxa* means "belief." A paradox, therefore, seems beyond belief—something incredible or self-contradictory but true if you think twice about it. In Greek the root *oxy* means "sharp" or "acute," and *moron* means "foolish." An oxymoron, then, is a figure of speech that combines two ideas or words in a way that seems particularly unreasonable, such as *cruel kindness* or *wise fool.*

By using your dictionary, find out the root meanings in Greek of the following literary terms.

1. metaphor
2. irony
3. drama
4. epic
5. hyperbole
6. analogy
7. protagonist

COMPOSITION

Developing a Thesis Statement

■ Write a short composition in which you develop a thesis about some aspect of modern literature. You may want to write about style or subject matter or free verse or the modern use of any literary technique. First state your thesis in clear, concise terms. Then support the thesis with several examples drawn from selections you have read in this book. *For help with this assignment, refer to Lesson 1 in the Writing About Literature Handbook at the back of this book.*

Writing About Writing

■ Write a short composition or poem about your own act of writing. Let the reader see your "mind at work." Let the process of writing itself be your subject, and do not hesitate to experiment with new ways of expressing yourself.

Adrienne Rich *born 1929*

The poems of Adrienne Rich almost always reflect her characteristic attitude toward change. She affirms that the greatest changes in society, the large-scale changes in the way we all live and think about each other, are determined and directed by changes in the minds of *individuals.*

Adrienne Rich grew up in Baltimore, Maryland, and attended Radcliffe College in Cambridge, Massachusetts. She had begun writing poetry years before her graduation, and in the same year that she graduated from college her first volume appeared in the Yale Series of Younger Poets (1951). The poet who selected her volume for this distinction was the great W. H. Auden (page 573).

Rich's early work was neat, crafted, polished, as the title of her second volume, *The Diamond Cutters* (1955), suggests. In the early 1960s, however, Rich abandoned the style that had brought her early success. Like Robert Lowell, whose "confessional" poetry so influenced his contemporaries, Rich began to write in a freer style, talking directly about her own deepest experiences. Women readers have felt especially close to Rich, who speaks in her poems about the meaning and experience of being a woman in this century. Her later works include *Snapshots of a Daughter-in-Law* (1963), *Leaflets* (1969), *The Will to Change* (1971), and *Diving into the Wreck* (1973).

In "The Observer" Rich remembers a woman scientist who lived alone in Africa among gorillas. She compares her own life with the life she imagines for the scientist who "observes" the gorillas, far from the stress of "civilization."

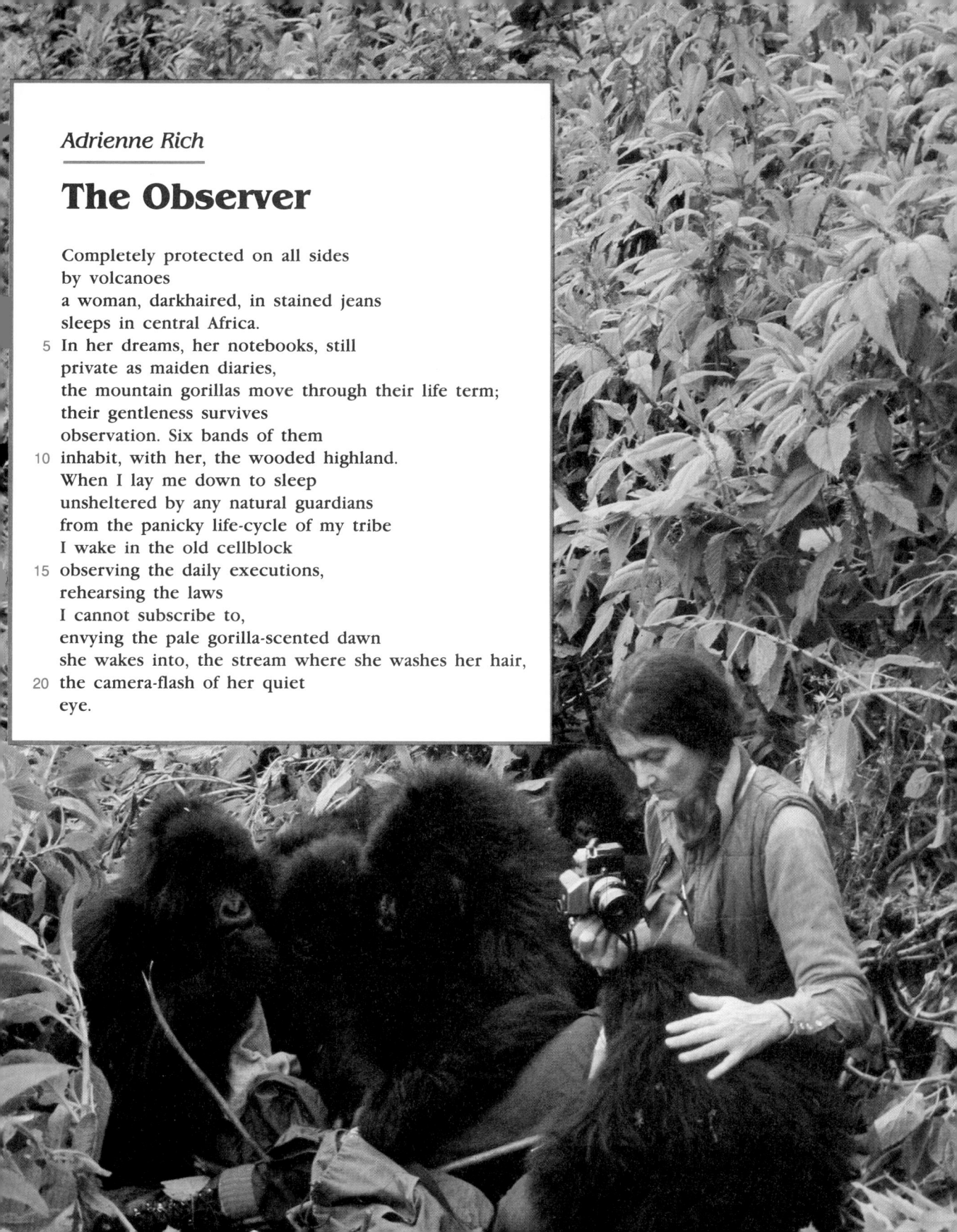

Adrienne Rich

The Observer

Completely protected on all sides
by volcanoes
a woman, darkhaired, in stained jeans
sleeps in central Africa.
5   In her dreams, her notebooks, still
private as maiden diaries,
the mountain gorillas move through their life term;
their gentleness survives
observation. Six bands of them
10   inhabit, with her, the wooded highland.
When I lay me down to sleep
unsheltered by any natural guardians
from the panicky life-cycle of my tribe
I wake in the old cellblock
15   observing the daily executions,
rehearsing the laws
I cannot subscribe to,
envying the pale gorilla-scented dawn
she wakes into, the stream where she washes her hair,
20   the camera-flash of her quiet
eye.

Alicia Ostriker   *born 1937*

Alicia Ostriker was born in New York City, and attended college and graduate school at Brandeis University in Massachusetts and the University of Wisconsin. She is an authority on the work of the English Romantic poet, William Blake. Her volumes of poetry include *Songs* (1969), *Once More Out of Darkness* (1974), and *The Mother/Child Poems* (1980). Ostriker teaches at Rutgers University in New Jersey and lives in Princeton with her husband and three children.

"His Speed and Strength," with its mythological references and its delicate similes, demonstrates how a poem may arise from our ordinary lives. The experience is not unusual—a young mother's afternoon swimming and riding with her son—but the poet makes it a special experience, a celebration.

Alicia Ostriker

His Speed and Strength

His speed and strength, which is the strength of ten
years, races me home from the pool.
First I am ahead, Niké,[1] on my bicycle,
no hands, and the *Times* crossword tucked in my rack,
5   then he is ahead, the Green Hornet,[2]
buzzing up Witherspoon,
flashing around the corner to Nassau Street.

At noon sharp he demonstrated his neat
one-and-a-half flips off the board:
10 Oh, brave. Did you see me, he wanted to know.
And I doing my backstroke laps was Juno
Oceanus,[3] then for a while I watched some black
and white boys wrestling and joking, teammates, wet
plums and peaches touching each other as if

15 it is not necessary to make hate,
as if Whitman was right and there is no death.[4]
A big wind at our backs, it is lovely, the maple boughs
ride up and down like ships. Do you mind
if I take off, he says. I'll catch you later,
20 see you. I shout and wave, as he peels
away, pedalling hard, rocket and pilot.

---

1. **Niké** [nī′kē]: in Greek mythology, goddess of victory, usually
depicted with wings.
2. **Green Hornet:** radio, television, and comic book hero.
3. **Juno Oceanus** [jo͞o′ nō ō sē′ə nəs]: here, queen of the ocean.
In Roman mythology Juno was queen of the gods.
4. **Whitman . . . death:** see "Song of Myself" (page 248).

Robert Bly   *born 1926*

Born in Minnesota, where he still lives, Robert Bly has devoted his life to poetry with an almost exclusive attention. In addition to producing several volumes of poetry—including *Silence in the Snowy Fields, Light Around the Body,* and *Sleepers Joining Hands*—he has edited poetry anthologies and published superb translations of Swedish and Spanish poets, including Pablo Neruda and Federico Garcia Lorca.

Known for his famous poetry readings, Bly does much more than *read* his poems. He *performs* them, often using masks and costumes, different voices, and gestures and dance movements. His effort is to revive poetry as an excitement, an experience that goes far beyond words on the printed page. Understandably, the songs, chants, and rituals of primitive peoples—for whom poetry was a performance—have influenced him enormously.

Bly's poems, like "Driving to Town Late to Mail a Letter," are often extremely simple, suggesting magic and mystery behind the most common American experience. Few people other than Bly, or his poetic ancestor, William Carlos Williams (page 449), would have thought to make a poem out of what most people think of as a chore or errand. Like Williams, Bly relies on the poetic eye that sees more than what the surface of things seems to offer.

Robert Bly

Driving to Town Late to Mail a Letter

It is a cold and snowy night. The main street is deserted.
The only things moving are swirls of snow.
As I lift the mailbox door, I feel its cold iron.
There is a privacy I love in this snowy night.
5 Driving around, I will waste more time.

Recalling

1. What protects the woman in Africa? In what terms are her notebooks described?
2. From what is the speaker unsheltered when she sleeps? In what does she waken?
3. Into what does the woman in Africa waken? What emotion does the speaker feel toward the woman in Africa?

Interpreting

4. Where does the speaker live? How does she feel about this world?
5. What does the speaker seem to envy about the woman in Africa?

Extending

6. Do you think it is common or unusual to want to change places with another Why?

COMPOSITION (Rich)

Writing About a Poem and Its Period

▪ "The Observer" tells of two ways of life in the modern world. Write a composition explaining what is typically modern about the speaker's experience. First identify the characteristics of modern experience reflected in Rich's poem. Then describe in your own words the advantages and disadvantages of the life of the scientist in the poem. Conclude by telling what aspects of modern life are *not* described in the poem. *For help with this assignment, refer to Lesson 10 in the Writing About Literature Handbook at the back of this book.*

Writing About a Place

▪ Write a short composition about a place in which you think a friend would like to live. Describe the place in detail, telling how the friend would live and what the friend would do there. Most important, tell, as Rich does in "The Observer," how the place would give definition and meaning to a life and a career.

STUDY QUESTIONS (Ostriker)

Recalling

1. What sort of strength does the speaker's son have, according to lines 1–2? With whom does the speaker compare her son when he races ahead on his bicycle?

2. What did the son do "at noon sharp"? What did he want to know?
3. Whom does the speaker say she felt like as she did backstroke laps in the pool? Afterward, what did she watch for a while? How does the speaker say the "wet plums and peaches" touched each other (lines 14–16)?
4. With what adjective does the speaker describe riding past the maple trees with the wind at her back? What does she do as her son "peels away" on his bicycle?

Interpreting

5. What is the speaker's attitude toward her son? Toward the day's outing? What does the title suggest is the relationship between the speaker's son and her attitude toward the day's outing?
6. What do lines 15–16 suggest the speaker has almost been able to forget during the day's outing? In what way is her son's appreciation of the outing different from hers?
7. What attitude toward youth does this poem project? Is it Romantic or Transcendentalist in any way? Explain.

Extending

8. Do you agree with the suggestions this poem makes about youth? Why or why not?

STUDY QUESTIONS (Bly)

Recalling

1. According to the title, what is the speaker doing?
2. What does the speaker love about "this snowy night"? What does he say he will do?

Interpreting

3. Is there a paradox, or discrepancy, between the activity indicated in the title and the final statement of the poem? If so, what is it?
4. Why does the speaker seem to want to continue driving around? What might he be avoiding? What sort of conflict does the poem suggest?

Extending

5. In what way is the conflict in this poem like that of the speaker in "Stopping by Woods on a Snowy Evening" (page 496)? What sort of reactions do snowy nights inspire in people?

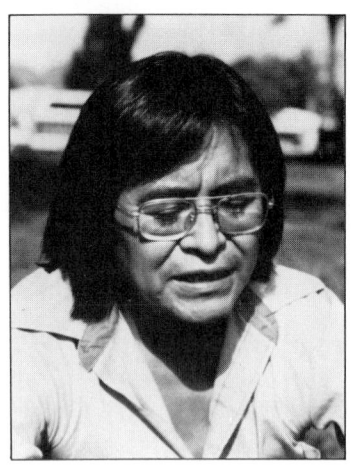

Simon J. Ortiz *born 1941*

Simon J. Ortiz was born in New Mexico, where his ancestors, people of the Acoma Pueblo tribe, lived for hundreds of years. He was educated at the University of New Mexico, where he is now a professor, and at the Writers School of the University of Iowa. Ortiz has lived most of his life in the Southwest and has dedicated himself to education, particularly to the education of Native Americans.

In his poetry Ortiz continues the long storytelling traditions of his people. When asked why he writes, Ortiz once replied: "Because Indians always tell a story. The only way to continue is to tell a story. . . . Your children will not survive unless you tell something about them—how they were born, how they came to this certain place, how they continue."

The people of Acoma Pueblo are famous for their pottery, a craft with an unbroken tradition going back to the Anasazi people who lived in New Mexico over a thousand years ago, and beyond the Anasazi into prehistory. In "My Mother and My Sisters" Ortiz reveals his respect for the craft handed down from one generation to the next, respect that can lead to a new understanding of art.

Acoma pottery,
by Marie and Joann Chino,
1982.

Simon J. Ortiz

from **My Mother and My Sisters**

My oldest sister wears thick glasses
because she can't see very well.
She makes beautifully formed pottery.
That's the thing about making dhyuuni;[1]
5 it has to do more with a sense of touching
than with seeing because fingers
have to know the texture of clay
and how the pottery is formed from lines
of shale strata and earth movements.
10 The pottery she makes is thinwalled
and has a fragile but definite balance.
In other words, her pottery has a true ring
when it is tapped with a finger knuckle.

Here, you try it;
15 you'll know what I mean.

The design that my mother is painting
onto the bowl is done with a yucca[2] stem
    brush.
My other sister says, "Our mother,
she can always tell when someone else
    has used
20 a brush that she is working with," because
she has chewed it and made it into her
    own way.
She paints with movements whose origin
has only to do with years of knowing
just the right consistency of paint,
25 the tensile vibrancy of the yucca stem,
and the design that things are supposed
    to have.

She can always tell.

---

1. **dhyuuni** [dē hyōō′nē]: "pottery" in Keresan
[ker′ə sən], language of the Acoma Pueblo Indians.
2. **yucca** [yuk′ə]: flowering desert plant, with a woody
stem and stiff sword-shaped leaves.

STUDY QUESTIONS

Recalling
1. According to lines 1–13, why does the speaker's oldest sister wear thick glasses? Why can she nevertheless make beautifully formed pottery?
2. What "test" indicates the definite balance of the pottery? What does the speaker ask us to do in lines 14–15?
3. What does the other sister say about her mother's brush in lines 16–26? What does the speaker say about the mother's movements as she paints?

Interpreting
4. What do lines 23 and 26 suggest about the nature of Pueblo pottery making? What does line 21 suggest? What attitude toward the mother's talent do the speaker and the other daughter share?
5. Briefly describe the language in which this poem is written. Is it "poetic"? Is it precise? In light of your answers, state the probable purpose of this poem, the reason the poet has written it.
6. What is the effect of lines 14–15 on the reader?

Extending
7. Why do you think so many people in modern America find it important to pass down traditional arts and customs from generation to generation? How might their practices be related to Carson McCullers' description of the loneliness of modern Americans on page 690?

Olga Cabral *born 1909*

The poetry of Olga Cabral reminds us of the continuing contributions of other cultures to the vitality of American writing. Olga Cabral was born in Port of Spain, Trinidad, West Indies. She lives in New York, where she has been an active writer for many years, as well as owner and manager of an art gallery. Cabral has written children's books but in recent years has concentrated on poetry. Her first volume, *Cities and Deserts* (1959), has been followed by four others, including *The Evaporated Man* (1968), *The Darkness in My Pockets* (1976), and *Occupied Country* (1976).

"(HELP!)" is a poem about identity. The voice in the poem cries out, afraid of becoming W. H. Auden's "unknown citizen" (page 575).

Olga Cabral

(HELP!)

i.

Help! I am trapped inside a pair of parentheses!
Will somebody read me the sentence
in which I am imprisoned?
`What is the meaning of the paragraph
5 in which I briefly appear? How did I get stuck
in the quagmire of this terrifying page
that sounds like gibberish?
`Does it make any sense at all
with/or without me?
10 `Does the Twentieth Century
make sense at all?

ii.

`Help! I'm a prisoner in an index file!
I've been stapled with steel hooks—I'm bleeding
all over the 4 x 5 cards!
15 A facsimile of myself is masquerading
in my place. I've been reduced to
some holes in a punch card, a code number
in somebody's data bank.
`No one has noticed this imposter:
20 myself who daily impersonates myself.
What was the original like
I wonder?

Diana Chang   *born 1934*

Like so many poets of modern America, Diana Chang brings to her work the experience of another language and another culture. Diana Chang was born in New York, grew up in China until the end of World War II, then returned to the United States to attend Barnard College, from which she graduated in 1955. Her poetry and novels often reflect her background. *The Frontiers of Love* (1956), for example, is set in wartime Shanghai, where Chang herself lived. Her other novels include *The Only Game in Town* and *Eye to Eye*. Chang also edited *The American Pen,* the magazine of the international writers' association, P. E. N.

"Most Satisfied by Snow" is written in the spare style of the oriental poetry that was so appealing to the early Imagists (see page 441). It suggests rather than tells, and like so many American Romantic lyrics, it suggests another way to come to terms with the natural world.

Diana Chang

Most Satisfied by Snow

Against my windows,
fog knows
what to do, too

Spaces pervade
5 us, as well

But occupied by snow,
I see

Matter
matters

10 I, too,
flowering

Lucha Corpi   *born 1945*

Lucha Corpi is part of the great renaissance in Latin American and South American literature that is now taking place and being felt in the United States. Lucha Corpi was born in Veracruz, Mexico. She came to California when she was nineteen and studied at the University of California at Berkeley and San Francisco State University. Corpi, who has held a fellowship in creative writing from the National Endowment for the Arts, now lives and teaches English in Oakland, California. Her poems have appeared in literary magazines and anthologies, and in a collection, *Fireflight* (1976).

"Emily Dickinson" is from Lucha Corpi's collection *Palabras de Mediodia (Noon Words).* Written originally in Spanish, the collection has been translated into English by Catherine Rodriguez-Nieto. In special praise of these translations, Corpi herself said, "My verses are proud of their twins." Corpi's tribute to Dickinson celebrates all poetry that escapes the limitations of time and place.

Lucha Corpi

Emily Dickinson

Like you, I belong to yesterday,
to the bays where
day is anchored to
wait for its hour.

5   Like me, you belong to today,
the progression of that hour
when what is unborn
begins to throb.

We are cultivators of
10 the unsayable, weavers
of singulars,[1] migrant
workers in search of
floating gardens[2] as yet
unsown, as yet unharvested.

---

1. **weavers of singulars:** in Spanish, *singulares* means "unique things," or "creations."
2. **floating gardens:** probably a reference to the floating gardens of Xochimilco (hō chē mēl′kō) in Mexico City.

STUDY QUESTIONS (Cabral)

Recalling

1. In the first section where does the speaker say she is trapped? What question does she ask in lines 4 – 5?
2. What does the terrifying page on which the speaker is trapped sound like, according to line 7? What questions does the speaker ask in lines 8 – 11?
3. In the second section where does the speaker say she is prisoner? What does she say is masquerading in her place? What question does she ask in the last two lines?

Interpreting

4. What do lines 10 – 11 reveal about the place in which the speaker feels trapped? What is she therefore really asking in lines 4 – 5? What is she suggesting in line 7?
5. What does being trapped in a pair of *parentheses* suggest about the speaker's self-image? What does the index-file analogy suggest are the causes of this self-image?
6. What does this poem imply are major problems of the twentieth century?

Extending

7. What advice would you give the speaker about breaking out of the "parentheses" and the "index file" in which she feels trapped?

STUDY QUESTIONS (Chang)

Recalling

1. What does the speaker state the fog against her windows "knows"? What does she observe about people in lines 4 – 5?
2. What does the speaker see because she is "occupied by snow"? What does she observe about herself in line 11?

Interpreting

3. With what aspect of the weather does the speaker associate the "spaces" human beings? What might these "spaces" be?
4. With what aspect of the weather does the speaker associate the "matter" of human beings? What does the title therefore suggest about her attitude toward this "matter"? What do lines 10 – 11 suggest the "matter" of human beings might do?
5. In what sense are the "windows" in line 1 literal? In what sense are they figurative?

6. State the meaning of this poem in your own words. What aspects of the poem seem Romantic? What aspects seem Imagist (page 441)?

Extending

7. How is the image of the snow in this poem different in its connotations from the snow imagery of Robert Frost (page 496)?

STUDY QUESTIONS (Corpi)

Recalling

1. In what way is the speaker like Emily Dickinson, according to line 1? According to line 5?
2. What sort of "cultivator" does the speaker call herself and Emily Dickinson? What sort of "migrant workers" are they?

Interpreting

3. What do the images in lines 1 – 8 suggest about Dickinson's and the speaker's poetry? That is, in what sense do they belong to "yesterday"? Why do they belong to "today"?
4. What does this poem imply about art in general? About Emily Dickinson's art in particular?

VOCABULARY (Corpi)

Words from Spanish

Many words we use in modern American English have crossed over from the Spanish language. Use a dictionary to explain the meanings and etymology, or word history, of each of the following words.

1. arroyo	5. cordovan	9. iguana
2. bonanza	6. mantilla	10. canyon
3. tornado	7. puma	11. tango
4. castanet	8. plaza	12. siesta

COMPARING WRITERS

■ Lucha Corpi says that she and Emily Dickinson are "cultivators of the unsayable." How does this phrase apply to the other poets on pages 748 – 769? Choose any four poets from those pages, and describe in your own words the central theme, the "unsayable" idea or emotion, that each is trying to express. Tell what it is that makes each theme difficult or impossible to express. Compare the writers, and demonstrate with examples which poet, in your opinion, succeeds best in saying the "unsayable."

FICTION

Bernard Malamud   *1914–1986*

In accepting the National Book Award in 1959 for *The Magic Barrel,* a collection of stories, Bernard Malamud said: "I am quite tired of the colossally deceitful devaluation of man in this day. . . . The devaluation exists because [humanity] accepts it without protest." Malamud's fiction protests that devaluation. Though he understands the pressures of history and society on the individual, Malamud always keeps his faith in the ability of the human spirit to endure and overcome.

Bernard Malamud was born in Brooklyn, New York; his parents were Russian immigrants. He graduated from City College of New York and Columbia University, and while teaching evening classes he began writing short stories, which appeared in *Harper's Bazaar, Partisan Review, Commentary,* and other magazines. Malamud has continued a career as both a teacher and a novelist, winning wide recognition for such books as *The Assistant* (1957), *Idiots First* (1963), and *Dubin's Lives* (1979). His novel of injustice in czarist Russia, *The Fixer* (1966), won both the National Book Award and the Pulitzer Prize.

Malamud's fiction portrays the struggles, defeats, and triumphs of ordinary people—shopkeepers, pawnbrokers, tenement dwellers. He uses the experience of Jewish people as an allegory for all of human experience: His characters are often pursued by a sense of injustice, burdened with grief, and strengthened by their own persistent clinging to life. They are intensely aware of the past while trying to make a life for themselves in the modern world. Malamud's protagonists seek a kind of nobility; they strive to maintain their beliefs and principles while coming to terms with the realities and compromises of living. The mixture of victory and defeat in their lives gives Malamud's work its tragicomic character.

Malamud's style is artfully simple. His language captures the essence of American Yiddish, mainly through its syntax but also in its vocabulary. His stories contain a robust humor, striking contrasts, a strong sense of compassion, and a complete understanding of his characters and their way of life. He writes of the Jewish experience, he said, "because I know it."

"The First Seven Years" is representative of Malamud's folklike style and of his ability to create believable characters. Like so many of his stories, it has the quality of a realistic fairy tale. It is both a down-to-earth story of real people and a fable with a message.

Bernard Malamud

The First Seven Years

Feld, the shoemaker, was annoyed that his helper, Sobel, was so insensitive to his reverie that he wouldn't for a minute cease his fanatic pounding at the other bench. He gave him a look, but Sobel's bald head was bent over the last[1] as he worked and he didn't notice. The shoemaker shrugged and continued to peer through the partly frosted window at the near-sighted haze of falling February snow. Neither the shifting white blur outside, nor the sudden deep remembrance of the snowy Polish village where he had wasted his youth could turn his thoughts from Max the college boy, (a constant visitor in the mind since early that morning when Feld saw him trudging through the snow-drifts on his way to school) whom he so much respected because of the sacrifices he had made throughout the years—in winter or direst heat—to further his education. An old wish returned to haunt the shoemaker: that he had had a son instead of a daughter, but this blew away in the snow for Feld, if anything, was a practical man. Yet he could not help but contrast the diligence of the boy, who was a peddler's son, with Miriam's unconcern for an education. True, she was always with a book in her hand, yet when the opportunity arose for a college education, she had said no she would rather find a job. He had begged her to go, pointing out how many fathers could not afford to send their children to college, but she said she wanted to be independent. As for education, what was it, she asked, but books, which Sobel, who diligently read the classics, would as usual advise her on. Her answer greatly grieved her father.

A figure emerged from the snow and the door opened. At the counter the man withdrew from a wet paper bag a pair of battered shoes for repair. Who he was the shoemaker for a moment had no idea, then his heart trembled as he realized, before he had thoroughly discerned the face, that Max himself was standing there, embarrassedly explaining what he wanted done to his old shoes. Though Feld listened eagerly, he couldn't hear a word, for the opportunity that had burst upon him was deafening.

He couldn't exactly recall when the thought had occurred to him, because it was clear he had more than once considered suggesting to the boy that he go out with Miriam. But he had not dared speak, for if Max said no, how would he face him again? Or suppose Miriam, who harped so often on independence, blew up in anger and shouted at him for his meddling? Still, the chance was too good to let by: all it meant was an introduction. They might long ago have become friends had they happened to meet somewhere, therefore was it not his duty—an obligation—to bring them together, nothing more, a harmless connivance to replace an accidental encounter in the subway, let's say, or a mutual friend's introduction in the street? Just let him once see and talk to her and he would for sure be interested. As for Miriam, what possible harm for a working girl in an office, who met only loud-mouthed salesmen and illiterate shipping clerks, to make the acquaintance of a fine scholarly boy? Maybe he would awaken in her a desire to go to college; if not—the shoemaker's mind at last came to grips with the truth—let her marry an educated man and live a better life.

When Max finished describing what he wanted done to his shoes, Feld marked them, both with enormous holes in the soles which he pretended not to notice, with large white-chalk x's, and the rubber heels, thinned to the nails, he marked with o's, though it troubled him he might have mixed up the letters. Max

---

1. **last:** foot-shaped block on which shoes are made or repaired.

inquired the price, and the shoemaker cleared his throat and asked the boy, above Sobel's insistent hammering, would he please step through the side door there into the hall. Though surprised, Max did as the shoemaker requested, and Feld went in after him. For a minute they were both silent, because Sobel had stopped banging, and it seemed they understood neither was to say anything until the noise began again. When it did, loudly, the shoemaker quickly told Max why he had asked to talk to him.

"Ever since you went to high school," he said, in the dimly-lit hallway, "I watched you in the morning go to the subway to school, and I said always to myself, this is a fine boy that he wants so much an education."

"Thanks," Max said, nervously alert. He was tall and grotesquely thin, with sharply cut features, particularly a beak-like nose. He was wearing a loose, long slushy overcoat that hung down to his ankles, looking like a rug draped over his bony shoulders, and a soggy, old brown hat, as battered as the shoes he had brought in.

"I am a business man," the shoemaker abruptly said to conceal his embarrassment, "so I will explain you right away why I talk to you. I have a girl, my daughter Miriam—she is nineteen—a very nice girl and also so pretty that everybody looks on her when she passes by in the street. She is smart, always with a book, and I thought to myself that a boy like you, an educated boy—I thought maybe you will be interested sometime to meet a girl like this." He laughed a bit when he had finished and was tempted to say more but had the good sense not to.

Max stared down like a hawk. For an uncomfortable second he was silent, then he asked, "Did you say nineteen?"

"Yes."

"Would it be all right to inquire if you have a picture of her?"

"Just a minute." The shoemaker went into the store and hastily returned with a snapshot that Max held up to the light.

"She's all right," he said.

Feld waited.

"And is she sensible—not the flighty kind?"

"She is very sensible."

After another short pause, Max said it was okay with him if he met her.

"Here is my telephone," said the shoemaker, hurriedly handing him a slip of paper. "Call her up. She comes home from work six o'clock."

Max folded the paper and tucked it away into his worn leather wallet.

"About the shoes," he said. "How much did you say they will cost me?"

"Don't worry about the price."

"I just like to have an idea."

"A dollar—dollar fifty. A dollar fifty," the shoemaker said.

At once he felt bad, for he usually charged two twenty-five for this kind of job. Either he should have asked the regular price or done the work for nothing.

Later, as he entered the store, he was startled by a violent clanging and looked up to see Sobel pounding with all his might upon the naked last. It broke, the iron striking the floor and jumping with a thump against the wall, but before the enraged shoemaker could cry out, the assistant had torn his hat and coat from the hook and rushed out into the snow.

So Feld, who had looked forward to anticipating how it would go with his daughter and Max, instead had a great worry on his mind. Without his temperamental helper he was a lost man, especially since it was years now that he had carried the store alone. The shoemaker had for an age suffered from a heart condition that threatened collapse if he dared exert himself. Five years ago, after an attack, it had appeared as though he would have either to sacrifice his business upon the auction block and live on a pittance thereafter, or put himself at the mercy of some unscrupulous employee who would in the end probably ruin him. But just at the moment of his darkest despair, this Polish refugee, Sobel, appeared one night from the street and begged for work. He was a stocky man, poorly dressed, with a bald head that had once been blond, a severely plain face and soft blue eyes prone to tears over the sad books he read, a young man but old—no one would have guessed thirty. Though he confessed he knew nothing of shoemaking, he said

he was apt and would work for a very little if Feld taught him the trade. Thinking that with, after all, a landsman,[2] he would have less to fear than from a complete stranger, Feld took him on and within six weeks the refugee rebuilt as good a shoe as he, and not long thereafter expertly ran the business for the thoroughly relieved shoemaker.

Feld could trust him with anything and did, frequently going home after an hour or two at the store, leaving all the money in the till, knowing Sobel would guard every cent of it. The amazing thing was that he demanded so little. His wants were few; in money he wasn't interested—in nothing but books, it seemed—which he one by one lent to Miriam, together with his profuse, queer written comments, manufactured during his lonely rooming house evenings, thick pads of commentary which the shoemaker peered at and twitched his shoulders over as his daughter, from her fourteenth year, read page by sanctified page, as if the word of God were inscribed on them. To protect Sobel, Feld himself had to see that he received more than he asked for. Yet his conscience bothered him for not insisting that the assistant accept a better wage than he was getting, though Feld had honestly told him he could earn a handsome salary if he worked elsewhere, or maybe opened a place of his own. But the assistant answered, somewhat ungraciously, that he was not interested in going elsewhere, and though Feld frequently asked himself what keeps him here? why does he stay? he finally answered it that the man, no doubt because of his terrible experiences as a refugee, was afraid of the world.

After the incident with the broken last, angered by Sobel's behavior, the shoemaker decided to let him stew for a week in the rooming house, although his own strength was taxed dangerously and the business suffered. However, after several sharp nagging warnings from both his wife and daughter, he went finally in search of Sobel, as he had once before, quite

---

2. **landsman:** fellow countryman.

recently, when over some fancied slight—Feld had merely asked him not to give Miriam so many books to read because her eyes were strained and red—the assistant had left the place in a huff, an incident which, as usual, came to nothing for he had returned after the shoemaker had talked to him, and taken his seat at the bench. But this time, after Feld had plodded through the snow to Sobel's house—he had thought of sending Miriam but the idea became repugnant to him—the burly landlady at the door informed him in a nasal voice that Sobel was not at home, and though Feld knew this was a nasty lie, for where had the refugee to go? still for some reason he was not completely sure of—it may have been the cold and his fatigue—he decided not to insist on seeing him. Instead he went home and hired a new helper.

Having settled the matter, though not entirely to his satisfaction, for he had much more to do than before, and so, for example, could no longer lie late in bed mornings because he had to get up to open the store for the new assistant, a speechless, dark man with an irritating rasp as he worked, whom he would not trust with the key as he had Sobel. Furthermore, this one, though able to do a fair repair job, knew nothing of grades of leather or prices, so Feld had to make his own purchases; and every night at closing time it was necessary to count the money in the till and lock up. However, he was not dissatisfied, for he lived much in his thoughts of Max and Miriam. The college boy had called her, and they had arranged a meeting for this coming Friday night. The shoemaker would personally have preferred Saturday, which he felt would make it a date of the first magnitude, but he learned Friday was Miriam's choice, so he said nothing. The day of the week did not matter. What mattered was the aftermath. Would they like each other and want to be friends? He sighed at all the time that would have to go by before he knew for sure. Often he was tempted to talk to Miriam about the boy, to ask whether she thought she would like his type—he had told

her only that he considered Max a nice boy and had suggested he call her—but the one time he tried she snapped at him—justly—how should she know?

At last Friday came. Feld was not feeling particularly well so he stayed in bed, and Mrs. Feld thought it better to remain in the bedroom with him when Max called. Miriam received the boy, and her parents could hear their voices, his throaty one, as they talked. Just before leaving, Miriam brought Max to the bedroom door and he stood there a minute, a tall, slightly hunched figure wearing a thick, droopy suit, and apparently at ease as he greeted the shoemaker and his wife, which was surely a good sign. And Miriam, although she had worked all day, looked fresh and pretty. She was a large-framed girl with a well-shaped body, and she had a fine open face and soft hair. They made, Feld thought, a first-class couple.

Miriam returned after 11:30. Her mother was already asleep, but the shoemaker got out of bed and after locating his bathrobe went into the kitchen, where Miriam, to his surprise, sat at the table, reading.

"So where did you go?" Feld asked pleasantly.

"For a walk," she said, not looking up.

"I advised him," Feld said, clearing his throat, "he shouldn't spend so much money."

"I didn't care."

The shoemaker boiled up some water for tea and sat down at the table with a cupful and a thick slice of lemon.

"So how," he sighed after a sip, "did you enjoy?"

"It was all right."

He was silent. She must have sensed his disappointment, for she added, "You can't really tell much the first time."

"You will see him again?"

Turning a page, she said that Max had asked for another date.

"For when?"

"Saturday."

"So what did you say?"

"What did I say?" she asked, delaying for a moment—"I said yes."

Afterwards she inquired about Sobel, and Feld, without exactly knowing why, said the assistant had got another job. Miriam said nothing more and began to read. The shoemaker's conscience did not trouble him; he was satisfied with the Saturday date.

During the week, by placing here and there a deft question, he managed to get from Miriam some information about Max. It surprised him to learn that the boy was not studying to be either a doctor or lawyer but was taking a business course leading to a degree in accountancy. Feld was a little disappointed because he thought of accountants as bookkeepers and would have preferred "a higher profession." However, it was not long before he had investigated the subject and discovered that Certified Public Accountants were highly respected people, so he was thoroughly content as Saturday approached. But because Saturday was a busy day, he was much in the store and therefore did not see Max when he came to call for Miriam. From his wife he learned there had been nothing especially revealing about their meeting. Max had rung the bell and Miriam had got her coat and left with him—nothing

more. Feld did not probe, for his wife was not particularly observant. Instead, he waited up for Miriam with a newspaper on his lap, which he scarcely looked at so lost was he in thinking of the future. He awoke to find her in the room with him, tiredly removing her hat. Greeting her, he was suddenly inexplicably afraid to ask anything about the evening. But since she volunteered nothing he was at last forced to inquire how she had enjoyed herself. Miriam began something noncommittal but apparently changed her mind, for she said after a minute, "I was bored."

When Feld had sufficiently recovered from his anguished disappointment to ask why, she answered without hesitation, "Because he's nothing more than a materialist."

"What means this word?"

"He has no soul. He's only interested in things."

He considered her statement for a long time but then asked, "Will you see him again?"

"He didn't ask."

"Suppose he will ask you?"

"I won't see him."

He did not argue; however, as the days went by he hoped increasingly she would change her mind. He wished the boy would telephone, because he was sure there was more to him than Miriam, with her inexperienced eye, could discern. But Max didn't call. As a matter of fact he took a different route to school, no longer passing the shoemaker's store, and Feld was deeply hurt.

Then one afternoon Max came in and asked for his shoes. The shoemaker took them down from the shelf where he had placed them, apart from the other pairs. He had done the work himself and the soles and heels were well built and firm. The shoes had been highly polished and somehow looked better than new. Max's Adam's apple went up once when he saw them, and his eyes had little lights in them.

"How much?" he asked, without directly looking at the shoemaker.

"Like I told you before," Feld answered sadly. "One dollar fifty cents."

Max handed him two crumpled bills and received in return a newly-minted silver half dollar.

He left. Miriam had not been mentioned. That night the shoemaker discovered that his new assistant had been all the while stealing from him, and he suffered a heart attack.

Though the attack was very mild, he lay in bed for three weeks. Miriam spoke of going for Sobel, but sick as he was Feld rose in wrath against the idea. Yet in his heart he knew there was no other way, and the first weary day back in the shop thoroughly convinced him, so that night after supper he dragged himself to Sobel's rooming house.

He toiled up the stairs, though he knew it was bad for him, and at the top knocked at the door. Sobel opened it and the shoemaker entered. The room was a small, poor one, with a single window facing the street. It contained a narrow cot, a low table and several stacks of books piled haphazardly around on the floor along the wall, which made him think how queer Sobel was, to be uneducated and read so much. He had once asked him, Sobel, why you read so much? and the assistant could not answer him. Did you ever study in a college someplace? he had asked, but Sobel shook his head. He read, he said, to know. But to know what, the shoemaker demanded, and to know, why? Sobel never explained, which proved he read much because he was queer.

Feld sat down to recover his breath. The assistant was resting on his bed with his heavy back to the wall. His shirt and trousers were clean, and his stubby fingers, away from the shoemaker's bench, were strangely pallid. His face was thin and pale, as if he had been shut in this room since the day he had bolted from the store.

"So when you will come back to work?" Feld asked him.

To his surprise, Sobel burst out, "Never."

Jumping up, he strode over to the window that looked out upon the miserable street. "Why should I come back?" he cried.

"I will raise your wages."

"Who cares for your wages!"

The shoemaker, knowing he didn't care, was at a loss what else to say.

"What do you want from me, Sobel?"

"Nothing."

"I always treated you like you was my son."

Sobel vehemently denied it. "So why you look for strange boys in the street they should go out with Miriam? Why you don't think of me?"

The shoemaker's hands and feet turned freezing cold. His voice became so hoarse he couldn't speak. At last he cleared his throat and croaked, "So what has my daughter got to do with a shoemaker thirty-five years old who works for me?"

"Why do you think I worked so long for you?" Sobel cried out. "For the stingy wages I sacrificed five years of my life so you could have to eat and drink and where to sleep?"

"Then for what?" shouted the shoemaker.

"For Miriam," he blurted—"for her."

The shoemaker, after a time, managed to say, "I pay wages in cash, Sobel," and lapsed into silence. Though he was seething with excitement, his mind was coldly clear, and he had to admit to himself he had sensed all along that Sobel felt this way. He had never so much as thought it consciously, but he had felt it and was afraid.

"Miriam knows?" he muttered hoarsely.

"She knows."

"You told her?"

"No."

"Then how does she know?"

"How does she know?" Sobel said, "because she knows. She knows who I am and what is in my heart."

Feld had a sudden insight. In some devious way, with his books and commentary, Sobel had given Miriam to understand that he loved her. The shoemaker felt a terrible anger at him for his deceit.

"Sobel, you are crazy," he said bitterly. "She will never marry a man so old and ugly like you."

Sobel turned black with rage. He cursed the shoemaker, but then, though he trembled to hold it in, his eyes filled with tears and he broke into deep sobs. With his back to Feld, he stood at the window, fists clenched, and his shoulders shook with his choked sobbing.

Watching him, the shoemaker's anger diminished. His teeth were on edge with pity for the man, and his eyes grew moist. How strange and sad that a refugee, a grown man, bald and old with his miseries, who had by the skin of his teeth escaped Hitler's incinerators,[3] should

fall in love, when he had got to America, with a girl less than half his age. Day after day, for five years he had sat at his bench, cutting and hammering away, waiting for the girl to become a woman, unable to ease his heart with speech, knowing no protest but desperation.

"Ugly I didn't mean," he said half aloud.

Then he realized that what he had called ugly was not Sobel but Miriam's life if she married him. He felt for his daughter a strange and gripping sorrow, as if she were already Sobel's bride, the wife, after all, of a shoemaker, and had in her life no more than her mother had had. And all his dreams for her—why he had slaved and destroyed his heart with anxiety and labor—all these dreams of a better life were dead.

The room was quiet. Sobel was standing by the window reading, and it was curious that when he read he looked young.

"She is only nineteen," Feld said brokenly. "This is too young yet to get married. Don't ask her for two years more, till she is twenty-one, then you can talk to her."

Sobel didn't answer. Feld rose and left. He went slowly down the stairs but once outside, though it was an icy night and the crisp falling snow whitened the street, he walked with a stronger stride.

But the next morning, when the shoemaker arrived, heavy-hearted, to open the store, he saw he needn't have come, for his assistant was already seated at the last, pounding leather for his love.

---

3. **Hitler's incinerators:** During World War II in Europe, the Nazis, under the dictatorship of Adolf Hitler (1889–1945), operated concentration camps in which millions of Jews were killed.

STUDY QUESTIONS

Recalling

1. According to the first paragraph, why does Feld, the shoemaker, respect Max? What does Miriam say about books and education? From whom does she get advice on her reading?

2. About what does Feld speak privately to Max when Max comes into the store with a pair of shoes? What startles Feld when he returns to the store after his conversation with Max?

3. For what reason did Sobel leave the shop in a huff once before? What does Feld do this time when Sobel does not return to work?

4. What does Miriam say about Max after their second date? Is she interested in seeing him again?
5. What causes Feld's heart attack? After he recovers, whom does he go to see?
6. Why has Sobel worked for so many years for a low wage? What does Feld say "bitterly" when Sobel confesses his plans and dreams? What does Feld then finally tell Sobel, and how does Feld walk when he leaves Sobel?

Interpreting
7. What does being educated seem to mean to Feld? To Miriam? To Max?
8. Compare Max and Sobel. Why is it ironic that Feld admires Max because of the sacrifice he has made to further his education and does not admire Sobel?
9. Is Feld a sympathetic character? Is he materialistic? Does he change by the story's end? Explain your answers.

Extending
10. Who do you think would make a better husband for Miriam, Sobel or Max? Do you think Miriam will marry Sobel when she is twenty-one? Explain your answers.

VIEWPOINT

In discussing Malamud's concerns, Sidney Richman writes:

Throughout his fiction, the theme of victory through defeat is constant; for it is only when his needs remain unsatisfied that Malamud's hero can recognize the form of his most human needs.

—Bernard Malamud

■ Explain how Feld the shoemaker achieves "victory through defeat." What are the "most human needs" that he recognizes at the end of the story? What needs will "remain unsatisfied"?

LITERARY FOCUS

Revelation and Epiphany
Most modern stories do not follow the old-fashioned rules for stories: They do not end with a neat resolution of the hero's problems, tying up all the loose ends in a clearly comic or tragic con-

clusion. Instead, they often focus on a moment of **revelation,** a point at which a character comes to see something with a deep understanding. The character may achieve self-knowledge or a deeper knowledge of another character; relationships between characters may become clear; the meaning and implications of an event may take shape.

The moment of revelation was an important literary technique for the influential Irish novelist James Joyce. Joyce called such a moment an **epiphany** (a "showing forth"), a sudden flash of recognition in which the essential truth about something is perceived. Many modern fiction writers have used the epiphany to give a new kind of structure to their stories.

Thinking About Revelation and Epiphany
1. Identify the moment of revelation for Feld in "The First Seven Years." Describe in your own words the insight he gains.
2. Does Sobel also have an epiphany? Support your opinion with quotations from the story.

COMPOSITION

Developing a Thesis Statement
■ Write a brief composition stating and developing a thesis statement about "The First Seven Years." First make a clear thesis statement by completing this sentence: "Both Feld and the reader of the story come to understand that. . . ." Then support your statement with quotations from the text and with your own experience as a reader. *For help with this assignment, refer to Lesson 1 in the Writing About Literature Handbook at the back of this book.*

Writing About a Concept
■ A concept is usually difficult to write about because it is not concrete. Nevertheless, writers of fiction do succeed in making concepts come alive through characters. Write a brief story or narrative poem in which you try to convey the meaning of a concept, such as *loyalty, respect, success,* or *love.* You may want to create a dramatic scene, allowing two or more characters to embody different attitudes toward the concept. Have the actions and words of the characters reveal the meaning of the concept. Do not *tell* your readers what you mean; *show* them.

Photograph © 1982 by Jill Krementz

William Saroyan *1908–1981*

William Saroyan enjoyed an emotional, even sentimental attachment to America. He set much of his fiction in uniquely American locales—the local grocery store, the telegraph office, the small-town neighborhood. Fiercely antimaterialistic, he championed the humble, imprudent, plain yet poetic people who would never be rich or famous, or ever be sorry about it.

Born of Armenian immigrant parents in Fresno, California, Saroyan lived in an orphanage for a few years just after his father's death. He sold papers when he was eight, and while in high school he worked as a telegraph messenger. Later he held jobs in a law office, a grocery, a vineyard, and a post office. From 1942 to 1945, after becoming a famous writer, he served in the United States Army.

Saroyan's literary career began with short stories, and he had more than five hundred of these published. He also wrote a few plays, one of which—*The Time of Your Life* (1939)—won the Pulitzer Prize (though Saroyan declined the award). In addition, he wrote movie screenplays, including the one for *The Human Comedy,* which he later rewrote as a novel.

When some reviewers criticized him for excessive optimism, Saroyan replied: "Out of ignorance and desperation, poverty and pain, . . . emerge intelligence and grace, humor and resignation, decency and integrity." His characters are warmly human and lovable, and he treats them with sympathy and gentle humor. His style achieves a sense of spontaneity, as if he were telling a story to a neighbor over a backyard fence. His language is simple, natural, and familiar, full of colloquial American idioms.

"There Was a Young Lady of Perth" is a fondly remembered tale of a young writer's first attempts to compose a limerick. A **limerick** is a humorous five-line poem in which the first, second, and fifth lines rhyme and have the rhythm ∪ʹ∪∪ʹ∪∪ʹ. The third and fourth lines rhyme with each other and have the rhythm ∪∪ʹ∪∪ʹ. The narrator of the story suggests that in a limerick "somebody from somewhere tried to do something and as a result something unexpected happened." As Saroyan's tale progresses, we realize that this is not only the pattern of a limerick but also the pattern of the story itself.

George M. Cohan, from a "Great Americans" advertisement.

William Saroyan

There Was a Young Lady of Perth

I sold the first issue of *Liberty* magazine. In it was the beginning of the memoirs of George M. Cohan, and a limerick contest, for which the first prize was an enormous sum of money. Was it five thousand dollars, fifty thousand, or five hundred thousand? In any case, it was enough to make me stop and think about there having been a young lady of Perth.

Now, of course, I'm not unaware that most people don't remember the first issue of *Liberty* magazine, if in fact they remember the second. How could they? The magazine saw the light of day when I was not much more than eleven or twelve, or thirteen or fourteen.

Did I sell it, or did I buy it? Did I make a profit of two and a half cents, or did I throw away a nickel? Memory fails me, and while it's not as bad as if a bank had failed me, it's bad

enough, because I *deal* in memory. And when memory fails me, I'm in trouble. I have either got to invent, or I have got to do research.

I can invent fair to middling, feeling an awful liar all the while, but I can't do research worth a bottle cap. I forget what I'm looking for and wind up with six or seven other things that I can't use. I don't mind inventing if there is a little aesthetic truth in it, as we say in the profession—"versimilitude," I once heard one writer say, but I can't vouch for either the spelling or the aptness. *Very similar* would have to be the words I would use, because I can spell those words and believe I know what they mean.

George M. Cohan happened to be a man I admired even more than I admired Benjamin Franklin, who was quite simply one of the truly great cutups in my life, as of course (later on, and in a different way) George M. Cohan was. I knew Ben had put up a kite and taken a chance on electrocution in order to invent electricity, and I knew he had written a boy's story called *The Autobiography of,* but the thing I liked about him was his easygoing way of getting to be a great man. Finally, they sent him to Paris as the ambassador, and he *enchanted* the French, in their own words.

And so, in that first issue of *Liberty* magazine I was eager to find out how George M. Cohan had begun his life, because George, the Yankee Doodle Dandy, was still alive and kicking. I thought it would be interesting to find out his secret of success, in case someday our paths were to cross. There was no such chance with Ben Franklin, of course.

Was the year 1924? If so, Ben had been dead for some time, and George M. was surely not much more than thirty. Or might it have been forty? Thirty or forty, he was certainly at the height of his fame, writing plays, singing, dancing, and being an all-round American Boy, born on Independence Day. They made a movie about him, but I presumed they had done it for money, so I never saw it.

The world was different then, whether it was 1924, or a couple of years earlier, or a couple later. It was just plain different. It wasn't necessarily better, and in all probability it was worse, but an American Boy had a chance in those days, on his own, unsponsored, so to say. All he needed was willingness, wit, and vitality, and so it was great to be an American, to be under voting age, to be unknown, to have the challenge there night and day, still unmet.

Liberty magazine had a fine editorial policy, although I have forgotten precisely what it was. In the name of something, somebody meant to be an American Boy, and to make money. I envied him, although I didn't know his name. He was back of the whole thing, though, and the arrival of his magazine into my life an event of some importance.

After work, I examined the magazine from cover to cover to find out what it came to, and then I read George M. Cohan's contribution, which I found fascinating, because he was swift, confident, and talented. He was born backstage, and as soon as he could walk he went out and wowed 'em, singing, dancing, and telling jokes.

The photographs of George and his beautiful sister and his handsome father and mother were an inspiration, but in those days the theater wasn't my line, and so if I was to get started in the business of making my fame and fortune, out of the pages of *Liberty* magazine, it would have to be by winning the limerick contest, by making something out of the fact that there *was* a young lady of Perth, if in fact that was what it was, as it probably wasn't, although it was certainly the equivalent of it.

The trouble was I didn't know anything about limericks, but *Liberty* magazine gave a brief history of them, how they had originated in a place called Limerick, and the magazine also gave three or four illustrations of perfect ones. These were incredibly clever, apt, wise, and witty. Somebody from somewhere tried to do something and as a result something unexpected happened. In a way, that was a little like the story of my life up to that time, and now it was time for a change. Instead of being the subject of a limerick, I wanted to be a writer of one, I wanted to be the writer of the greatest limerick of all time, because that would mean that I would win the contest, I would win the money, and people would say, "There goes the American Boy who wrote the limerick."

I couldn't think of a second line, though. There was a young lady of Perth; who she was or what she was up to, I couldn't guess.

I kept it in mind, though. I had the first line, supplied by the magazine, and all I needed next was a second line that was so extraordinary that the rest of the lines of the limerick would fall into place and sound like perfection itself. The words that rhymed with Perth were "worth," "mirth," "birth," "dearth," "girth," and, of course, "earth"—all good usable words. There *was* an earth, there *was* a birth, there were mirth and worth and the others, and so all I really needed to do was rattle them together and throw them out like dice, for a natural. With my conscious mind, the mind that was supposed to be equal to such a challenge, equal to thought, I had little luck. "There was a young lady of Perth who didn't know what she was worth," for instance, just wasn't right.

And so I slept on it, or, to be a little more exact, it slept on me. The young lady of Perth was here, there, and everywhere, but the limerick remained incomplete, and I woke up in the morning knowing I had been in a fight and hadn't won.

That first issue of *Liberty* magazine passed from me to my brother, who also took an interest in the limerick contest, and then to my sisters, so that before the second issue of the magazine came out everybody in my family was at work trying to win fame and fortune as a limerick writer. We weren't good at it, though. I don't know who fell out first, but I know it wasn't me. I think it was my brother, who tended to be cynical about contests in general, and about theories of how easy it is to rise in the world. He said it just wasn't an overnight proposition. A man of thirteen, he believed, was a little less likely to be invited to Washington to discuss educational reform with President Harding than a man of sixteen, for instance. But a man of sixteen was less likely than a man of nineteen, and our neighborhood was pretty well stocked with nineteen-year-old American Boys who knew a thing or two about educational reform—throw out teachers who had remained stupid after considerable schooling. That was the basic educational reform principle of the neighborhood.

I noticed with regret my brother's scorn for the limerick-writing contest, and I made up my mind to be different. I made up my mind to have stick-to-itiveness, because I had heard that everybody who had ever amounted to anything had had stick-to-itiveness. I reasoned that if *they* had had it, and had *needed* it, and had won through to success on *account* of it, I was

going to have it, too. Every evening when I got home from work I checked with the other contestants, only to discover, after two or three such checks, that everybody had given up. I also discovered that my persistence, or stick-to-itiveness, was being taken for a nuisance.

Somebody said, "To heck with the young lady of Perth. This is Fresno."

This amounted to nothing better than the waving of the white flag, surrender, armistice, failure, humiliation. I was flabbergasted and more determined than ever to win the contest.

There was time, the deadline was still ten or eleven days off, and I felt confident that long before the required midnight postmark of the final day I would have my limerick neatly written and on its way to *Liberty* magazine in—wherever it was. I don't believe it was in New York, or in Chicago, either. I just don't remember where it was, but it was somewhere, and this place could be reached by train mail in a matter of six or seven days. There was no airmail in those days.

One afternoon the chain on my bike broke while I was sprinting, and I was sent over the handle bars onto the pavement. Something was always happening to my bike. It wasn't holding up, but nobody ever said, "They don't make them the way they used to." The wire spokes of the wheel were always loosening, and while I had a spoke tightener, as every practical-minded messenger had, whenever I tightened a couple of loose spokes I noticed that the alignment of the wheel became unbalanced. You had to be an expert even in a thing like that.

The dive was on my head, which was at least a little protected by the blue cap of Postal Telegraph, or at any rate would have been had the cap not fallen off just before my head struck the pavement, when I needed it most.

It was quite a jolt, but, as always, I hoped there had been no witnesses, for I despised having accidents, and I resented help and sympathy.

The minute my head hit the pavement the whole winning limerick came to me, and I was stunned by the brilliance and rightness of it, the simplicity and inevitability of it, and by the fact that it had taken a foolish accident to bring the thing around. I was all set to begin committing it to memory before I forgot it when an elderly lady of Fresno hurried up and asked, as a mother or a grandmother might, "Are you all right?"

"Yes, ma'am, it's nothing, thank you." All quickly said, so she would be satisfied and move along, but no, she wanted to chat.

"Are you sure? Here, let me help you up."

Well, then I realized I was still flat on my back, so I leaped to my feet, picked up the fallen bike, and began to unwheel the chain, which had become entangled around the hub.

There was no getting away from her, or rather no getting her away from me. On and on she chatted, and of course my upbringing compelled me to answer every question respectfully.

At last I was able to walk away with my bike. It was time to commit the limerick to memory, but all I could remember was the first line again. The thing was lost.

I was still so mad that evening when I got home that my brother couldn't help noticing.

"What's the matter with you?"

"Lousy chain broke again."

I didn't want to tell him about the limerick because I was afraid he wouldn't believe me, and a younger brother hates not being believed. I'd *had* that whole limerick right after I had dived, and it was the winning one, too. I'd had it, and then that nice old lady of Fresno had come up and had made me forget it. My brother examined my head and told me there was a bump there. I told him I *knew* there was a bump there. He wasn't really satisfied with my reason for being mad, and little by little he won me over to a full confession. I was astonished that he *didn't* disbelieve me. On the contrary, he was sure that I *had* had the winning limerick and had lost it.

"The thing to do," he said, "is to get it back."

"How?"

"The same way."

"Sprint and break the chain and dive on my head? Nothing doing."

"That's how it came to you. That's how you'll get it back. If you want something badly enough, you've got to pay the price for it."

"It was an accident," I said. "I'm not going to have an accident on purpose. I don't think it's possible in the first place, and even if it were, even if I *had* another accident, how do I know what kind of limerick I'd get out of it? It might not be the winner at all."

"Suit yourself," my brother said.

Now, it never occurred to me that he was having fun, and I kept thinking about his suggestion. After supper we went out to the back yard, where our wheels were. I looked at mine, with the chain as good as new again, repaired by Frank the Portuguese bike man, from whom we had bought our bikes, secondhand, and after a moment I got on the bike real slow and easy and rode out across the empty lot adjoining our back yard, and then out onto the sidewalk of San Benito Avenue, and then out onto the pavement of M Street, and there I began to sprint. My brother came running after me, shouting, "For goodness sake, I was only kidding, don't do it, you'll kill yourself."

Well, the fact is I really hadn't *meant* to do it, I had only meant to sprint, racing, going as fast as I could go, as a kind of test of the fates. The chain was strong, and it just wasn't likely to break—unless the fates wanted me to take another dive, get back the winning limerick, and be on my way to fame and fortune. I heard my brother. The memory of what it was I had a lot of—stick-to-itiveness—came back to me, and I decided I *would* do my best to make that repaired chain snap and break, after all. I raced three blocks to Ventura Avenue without luck; the chain was as strong as ever. My brother rode up on his wheel and said, "Now, look, if you really think that that's the way to get the lost limerick back, I'll do everything I can to help you."

"How?"

"I'll hold you about two feet above the pavement—that's enough—and drop you. It's safer that way."

We were riding back on M Street in any case, so we rode on up to the Rainier Brewery, a kind of Bavarian red-brick castle entangled in railroad tracks and company roads, and we rode around the brewery, closed now, finished for the day, and we discussed the problem. After a while we dismounted and sat on the steps of the brewery to discuss procedure a little further and to make sure that nobody was around. The coast was clear and procedure had been agreed upon, when Eddie Imirian and Johnny Suni came up, bouncing an old tennis ball. My brother and I were challenged to a game of handball against the brewery wall. We won 21 to 18, and then it was dark, but Eddie and Johnny wanted another game, so we played in the dark and won 21 to 12.

When we reached our house, the boys sat with us on our front porch steps and talked about school. It looked as if they never wanted to go home, but finally they did, and my brother said, "Well, how about it?"

"The tar on San Benito Avenue isn't hard enough," I said.

"Want to try the sidewalk?"

"It's *harder* than the pavement I hit."

"Whatever you say."

Well, we were both pretty tired, but it seemed to me this was a matter of stick-to-itiveness if I ever saw one, so I quickly said, "Let's try her."

My brother was holding me around the knees, about two feet over the sidewalk, and was all set to drop me on my head when my mother came out on the front porch with a pitcher of tahn on a tray. "Oh-oh," my brother said.

Well, it was now or never, so I said, "Let go."

Now, I was all set to get back the winning limerick, but my brother didn't let go.

"Why are you holding your brother that way?" my mother said.

"Just exercise," my brother said. "We take turns."

He let me down, and I took him around the knees and held him precisely as he had held me. For a moment I thought of dropping *him,* without plan, but I thought better of it and didn't.

"Come and drink tahn," my mother said.

I let him down and we went up onto the porch and drank two big glasses each of the best drink in the world. Put two cups of yogurt in a pitcher, add four or five cups of cold water, stir, and drink.

Well, the drink was great, because it helped you to know how alive you were, and what a privilege it was.

One of my sisters began to play *Dardanella* on the piano, and the other began to sing. My brother and I listened and looked around at where we were, and then up at the sky, full of stars. It was kind of silly, in a way, living in a house like that, nothing to it really, a few boards and a little wallpaper, and us, in a whole neighborhood like that, but what could you do? The tahn was great. The air was full of something that made you know you were alive, and the sky seemed a lot like something almost as good as money in the bank.

Pretty soon my sisters came out on the porch. We all sat around and talked and told jokes and laughed. I liked it, but I kept feeling I was losing my stick-to-itiveness, and that was the one thing I couldn't afford to lose. After about an hour we went inside to close up for the night.

My brother dropped me headfirst onto my bed, but all I did was bounce. The winning limerick didn't come back. And then I dropped him, and all *he* did was bounce.

I did my best with my conscious mind, and sent in a limerick, and lost.

I read every installment of George M. Cohan's life, and I envied him. I read the winning limerick, too. It didn't come to very much.

About forty years later I reached Perth,

which is on the west coast of Australia. It seemed like a nice place, something like Fresno. I saw the young lady of Perth in person. I saw her six or seven *hundred* times, as a matter of fact. I *spoke* to her six or seven times. She replied in a nice Australian accent. There was nothing suitable for a limerick in her.

She was just a nice girl.

In 1939 I met George M. Cohan in the of-fices of a theater in New York. He was a gentle, kindly fellow with a touch of sorrow in his eyes.

Liberty magazine changed hands a couple of times, and then gave up the ghost.

I forgot all about limericks. Also, stick-to-itiveness.

I decided that *don't-stick-to-itiveness* is a pretty usable philosophy, too, especially for a writer.

STUDY QUESTIONS

Recalling

1. About how old was the narrator when the first issue of *Liberty* magazine came out? Why was he interested in reading about George M. Cohan, according to the sixth paragraph?

2. In about what year did the incident take place? How was the world different then?

3. For what reasons did the narrator want to be the writer of "the greatest limerick of all time"? What kept him working on the limerick contest when others in his family gave up?

4. What happened to generate the "winning limerick" in the narrator's mind? What caused him to "lose" it?

5. What did the narrator feel he was losing when he and his family "sat around and talked and joked and laughed" on the porch? What did he decide about this loss, according to the final paragraph?

6. What does the narrator report about Perth and George M. Cohan in the last section?

Interpreting

7. What does the story suggest is at the root of the narrator's "stick-to-itiveness"? What does his admiration for Franklin (page 56) and George M. Cohan have to do with it?

8. Briefly describe the narrator as an adult. Why is it significant that he has been to Perth and met George M. Cohan? In saying that "the world" was different in 1924, what does he suggest about himself?

9. What sort of scene is the scene on the porch? How might it help explain the narrator's comment in his final paragraph? What does the story suggest might be more important than "stick-to-itiveness," especially to a writer?

Extending

10. Do you agree with the narrator's view of "stick-to-itiveness," or perseverance? How would you define success?

COMPOSITION

Writing About a Narrator

■ A story that uses a first-person narrator, as "There Was a Young Lady of Perth" does, challenges the reader. After all, the narrator may be forgetting something important or deliberately not telling the whole story or slanting the interpretation of what happened. Write a composition about Saroyan's narrator. What elements in the story persuade you to believe everything the narrator says? What elements give you some doubt? Cite specific passages that show why you do or do not accept the narrator's version of the story.

Writing a Limerick

■ Complete the limerick beginning "There was a young lady of Perth," or write one with your own opening line. Remember the source of the humor in a limerick is usually situational irony: When someone tries to do something, something unexpected happens.

Elizabeth Spencer   *born 1921*

A vital sense of place is the hallmark of Elizabeth Spencer's stories. Whether writing of the South, where she grew up, or of Italy, where she lived for a few years, Spencer captures the essence of locale. She dramatizes the influence of places on people, describing scenes with photographic accuracy and describing people with insight and understanding.

Elizabeth Spencer was born into a family whose ancestors had lived in Carrol County, Mississippi, since the 1830s. She attended college in Mississippi and did graduate work in Tennessee. She taught school in both states and then worked as a reporter for the Nashville *Tennessean.* It is not surprising, then, that her first novel portrayed the intricate workings of a small southern town and the complex relationships of a family that spanned several generations. That novel, *Fire in the Morning* (1948), was called one of the finest first novels published that year.

Spencer followed her first success with two other novels deeply rooted in the southern experience, *This Crooked Way* (1952) and *The Voice at the Back Door* (1956). Her stories have gained even more praise than her novels and have appeared in magazines such as the *New Yorker, Atlantic Monthly,* and *Virginia Quarterly.* Spencer received a Guggenheim Fellowship in 1953 and traveled to Italy, where she lived for two years. A new place then entered her fiction, providing the setting for her most popular work, the novella *The Light in the Piazza.*

Spencer wrote "Port of Embarkation" during the 1970s, re-creating the sadness and tension of a family farewell during World War II. It is a deceptively simple story of what happens when war takes a man out of his accustomed place and causes great changes for those who are left behind.

Elizabeth Spencer

Port of Embarkation

It was nearly noon of the day my father went back to his unit and thence to overseas service in World War II that I saw the horses. They were coming up the hill from the field, and all I could see first was the delicately scalloped, chestnut tips of their four ears all set forward, which showed their effort, one pair lower than the other. Then their forelocks and long, down-plunging, toiling heads rose to view, the chins dipped low and lather from the bits[1] splashing down, to foam across the twinned chests. I saw the black harness, heard the shout of the driver, and had the impression of a heavily laden wagon, though who the driver was—somebody working for us? a stranger?—and what the wagon carried, I did not know.

The team of great strong chestnut horses lingered in my mind's vision even after I woke on the bed in the far corner of the sleeping porch where I had gone to cry myself to sleep, not wanting anyone to see my tears. The hill up from the field was blocked from my view by the whole of the house, which lay between. But caught in the dream, I lay still in the midday July heat, willing for a time for it to extend its power. There was indeed a moment of further increase when I knew that the nearer horse had white-stockinged hind legs, and that the hill, though steep, was nothing to the power of the team which nobly crested it.

And this was all.

In the center of the house I ran into my mother, who also showed signs of having been crying, but who at once asked where my brother was. He had said he was going somewhere, but I had forgotten where. We went into the kitchen together, trying to act as if it were any other day—we were a reserved kind of family—and found that my brother had already gotten into the lunch and had eaten most of it. We would have to scramble eggs, or drive uptown to the grocery, and we preferred not to have to go out and talk to people. An alternative was to locate my brother and get him to bring us something, but this would undoubtedly provoke a quarrel between him and my mother. My brother was stubborn and seemed to be unfeeling with us all, but I had caught the worst of his nature, for, being smaller and younger I was the object of bullying and threats.

In the hallway to which I had returned, to look past the white front porch, across the positive, relentless sun glare of the yard, toward the fall of the hill, to where I had dreamed the horses ascending, I could hear my mother's and brother's voices. Though he had missed my father's departure with us in the car to the airport, he had been somewhere around, it would seem, all the time.

"That food you got into, that was mine and Estelle's lunch. You knew that, didn't you?"

"No, I didn't know it. How would I?"

"You must have heard us say we didn't want to go out, we'd have a cold lunch, I'd make the potato salad and an aspic, then stuff some eggs. You said you wouldn't be here. There's not enough left for one, now, much less both of us."

"Can't you just fix some more?"

"I certainly don't want to, I guess I can. . . ." The down-turning of their encounter was like fire in a log smothering down to smoke; then (I knew it would come by the tension in my middle), my mother's voice flared up like flame.

"Why can't you be more considerate! That's all I ever want to know. You're the man of the house now. Your father told you that, last night at dinner. We'd like to count on you, we need

---

1. **bits:** metal mouthpieces on bridles, used for controlling horses.

to count on you, but you . . . ! What do you care?"

"The way you tell it, I don't care about nothing."

"Do you? I'd dearly love to know."

"What you want me to do? You want me to go uptown and get something for your nourishment?"

My mother started crying. He was that sarcastic. "Oh, we'll manage. We'll manage somehow."

Mother eventually found a can of crab meat and made another salad and we sat down to a good lunch. Iced tea, crisp and lemony brown, is comforting after you've been crying, especially on a hot day. It soothes out your feelings.

"We're going to be stuck here all summer," I remarked, "with the way he acts. It's all on purpose," I added, which was not a good thought to give her.

She put her hand to her head. "I think he has problems," she said. "I think something worries him deep down."

"Like what?" I asked.

"How do we know each other's problems unless we tell them? How do I know? Maybe there's some girl he likes who doesn't like him, maybe he doesn't know what to do with himself, maybe he hates it about your father and doesn't want to show it."

"Maybe he's just mean and doesn't like us and wants to show that."

"I wish you wouldn't talk like that," Mother said. She looked frail and she was upset, but she could come out with things full force. "It may interest you to know, Missy, that I love you both the same. I've always said that, and it's true. Your brother knows I love him. He'd have to know that."

That afternoon Mother and I went to the picture show in a neighboring town. Our town was too small to have anything but a flea bag for a movie house, so we generally went over to a larger town. The larger towns, having more pavement and less shade, were hotter than our own. We parked between two white slanted lines, each a paintbrush wide, and walked to the movie house. The sidewalk burned through the soles of our shoes.

"If anybody sees us and asks," Mother said, "I'm going to say we went just to get our minds off everything."

"I'll say that too," I said.

Movies in those days were not, I think, air-conditioned, but they were air-cooled, which was not a bad substitute. They had large concealed fans, almost silent, which blew over ice, so that a constant breeze was stirring, moist and pleasant. If something in this apparatus broke, as it sometimes did, you sat there in the dark, sweltering and wondering whether or not the movie was interesting enough to hold you in discomfort.

That day nothing broke and the movie, *Up in Arms,* with Danny Kaye and Dinah Shore, seemed to be making the war a great big joke. We were complete suckers for what they were doing and sat there shaking with laughter.

When we went out together we heard a voice from the lobby where a wave of hot air was coming in through the front door which the matinee crowd was pushing open.

"Hey, wasn't that swell?"

It was my brother, standing in a knot of other boys. He was laughing and talking out to us. Mother stood stock still when she saw him and I almost laughed aloud, not at the movie, but at them, because she was good and ready in her mind to bless him out[2] for going to a movie the day his father went to port of embarkation, but then, there she was herself. The only difference was that she had her excuse ready and he, undoubtedly, did not.

"Got a ride home now," Brother said to the boys he was with. He came over to us. "Lemme tag a ride," he said. Then he flung an arm around each of us. You could think he was showing off for the benefit of the boys. But, as always with him, you couldn't altogether tell why he was doing anything. He was just doing it, that was all. "I'll buy you girls a Coke," he said.

We went next door to a little hamburger shop and sat in a booth. We ordered Cokes and glasses of ice, the way we all liked them. Then we went to the car, where hot air had to be let out before we could even get in; and Brother drove us home.

All during the time we had been sitting and drinking the Cokes together he had kept laughing and talking about the movie. "It's that scat singing,"[3] he said. "I can't see how he does it, 'less they speed up the sound track. I tried it but it didn't work."

"You tried to sing!" my mother exclaimed. "I never knew you to sing a note."

"Oh, I got talents. I got lots of talents." He was laughing at both of us. We might have been people he knew slightly. He was almost sixteen and I was just twelve.

After supper that night my father telephoned to cheer us up. "I've been talking to some of the other officers," he said. "They don't see how the war can go on more than another year at the most. I may not even get there."

I was on one phone, Mother on the other, but we couldn't get my brother to hear us as he was moving the furniture in his room, making an awful racket. Wasn't it important that they spoke? No matter what my father said, we all knew the war was reaching its height. He was heading straight to its heart.

"What's going on there?"

"It's Brother," Mother said. "He's started changing his room around. Wait, I'm going to call him again."

"There're a hundred people lined up to use this phone. I've got to get off it in three minutes or my name is mud. Listen, Ginny, you and Estelle both, don't bother that boy."

"We're going to try to do everything right," Mother said. "Don't you worry, not about anything."

"You let him be his own way. Just let him be."

"I promise, Nat. Oh, I do!"

Then we were hollering good-by, this morn-

A soldier says goodbye, photograph by Alfred Eisenstadt, 1944.

ing all over again, until the phone clicked off. From my brother's room, immediately after the click, something fell and smashed.

My mother and I rubbed ourselves with 6-12[4] and went to sit out on the porch in the dark. We hadn't done much of anything, but I felt tired to death.

Neighbors' lights glowed through the trees. Down the hill, the fields slept densely under dewfall. Lightning bugs drifted against a black row of bushes at the field's distant edge. In all that lay out there, I knew the road where I had seen the horses in my dream was rising up as it always did, but I couldn't make it out.

---

2. **bless him out:** scold him.
3. **scat singing:** jazz singing; improvising with meaningless syllables, often imitating a musical instrument.

---

4. **6-12:** brand of insect repellent.

"I had this dream this morning after Daddy left," I said. I told her about the horses, the wagon, and driver.

She didn't say anything, and I wondered if I should have mentioned it. I hadn't tried to think what it meant, if anything.

Finally she said, "It's funny what you dream." I wondered whether she would ever think of it again. Maybe she would.

We heard a door slam above us and my brother's heavy steps, coming downstairs. I felt the powerful sway of her promise to my father on the phone, his demand for it all the greater by coming through from afar, as though from an unseeable beyond: *Let him be his own way. Just let him be.*

I heard her talking to herself, whispering that she would try.

STUDY QUESTIONS

Recalling

1. What day is this story about, according to the opening paragraph? What does the narrator dream in the first two paragraphs?
2. According to the second paragraph, why did the narrator go to the corner of the porch? What signs does she detect in her mother when she runs to her?
3. What does the brother do to provoke an argument? What does his mother remind him about his father's conversation on the night before? How does the mother explain the boy's behavior to his sister?
4. Where do the narrator and her mother go that afternoon? Do they enjoy themselves?
5. Where does the brother take his mother and sister after he meets them? What does he "keep doing" as they sit and drink? What does the mother exclaim when the brother reveals he has tried scat singing?
6. Who phones the house that night? What does the brother do during the phone call? What promise does the mother make to the caller?

Interpreting

7. Describe the difference between the brother's behavior on the day of the father's departure and the mother's and sister's behavior.
8. In his lunchtime behavior, is the brother being "the man of the house"? In taking his mother and sister out, what is the brother trying to do? What does the conversation about his singing suggest about his character?
9. What does the father's advice to his wife suggest about his attitude toward his son?

10. What event might the sister's dream about the horses predict in the future lives of the characters? How does this future possibility relate to the events of the story?

Extending

11. How does a family draw the line between letting adolescents "be" and applying discipline? Discuss.

COMPOSITION

Writing About a Title

▮ The title of a story often aids the reader in interpreting the events, understanding the characters, and grasping the story's theme. Write a brief composition explaining the possible meanings of the title "Port of Embarkation." Begin by defining the word *embarkation*. Explain what it means for the father of the family. Then explain what it means for the other characters, who are at a figurative or symbolic port of embarkation. Use quotations from the story to support your explanations.

Imagining a Character's Thoughts

▮ At an important moment in "Port of Embarkation," when the father telephones his family, the brother remains in his room. Spencer never tells us what is going through his mind at this time. She leaves it up to us to imagine his thoughts and emotions. Write several paragraphs presenting the thoughts and emotions of the brother during this scene. What questions is he asking himself? Why does he not come to the telephone? What causes the noises that come from his room?

Truman Capote *1924–1986*

Almost all of Truman Capote's works focus directly or indirectly on the theme of innocence. His fiction poses problems and asks questions, blurring the boundaries between innocence and ignorance, innocence and guilt, innocence and maturity.

Truman Capote was born in New Orleans, Louisiana, but attended schools in New York and Connecticut. He worked for the *New Yorker* magazine, first as a cataloguer of cartoons, later as a writer. Capote's first novel *(Other Voices, Other Rooms)* was published in 1948. He followed that with other successful novels, among them *The Grass Harp* (1951), *Breakfast at Tiffany's* (1958), and a "nonfiction novel," *In Cold Blood* (1966). A writer who has tried many different media, Capote has also produced stage plays, nonfiction, television plays, and movie scripts.

Capote's skill as a fiction writer has won him many awards. Twice he was given the O. Henry Memorial Award for a short story (in 1943 for "Miriam" and in 1946 for "Shut a Final Door"). He won the National Institute of Arts and Letters creative writing award in 1959 and the Mystery Writers of America Edgar Award (named for Edgar Allan Poe) in 1966 for *In Cold Blood.* Capote also received an Emmy Award in 1967 for the television adaption of his short story "A Christmas Memory."

In Cold Blood presents an insightful look into a violent crime, but Capote is equally adept at comedy, mystery, and delicate stories of sensitive human relationships. His style is pure, the result of much rewriting. Close attention to meaningful detail, an ear for dialogue, and a facility for creating fresh metaphors give his writing a crisp realism. An adept storyteller, Capote weaves a compassionate understanding of character into intriguing, often suspenseful plots.

"Miriam," one of Capote's most popular stories, is a combination of suspense and compassionate characterization. Its mystery is more than a matter of plot: It is the mystery of human emotions.

Truman Capote

Miriam

For several years Mrs. H. T. Miller had lived alone in a pleasant apartment (two rooms with kitchenette) in a remodeled brownstone[1] near the East River. She was a widow: Mr. H. T. Miller had left a reasonable amount of insurance. Her interests were narrow, she had no friends to speak of, and she rarely journeyed farther than the corner grocery. The other people in the house never seemed to notice her: her clothes were matter of fact, her hair iron-gray, clipped, and casually waved; she did not use cosmetics, her features were plain and inconspicuous, and on her last birthday she was sixty-one. Her activities were seldom spontaneous: she kept the two rooms immaculate, smoked an occasional cigarette, prepared her own meals, and tended a canary.

Then she met Miriam. It was snowing that night. Mrs. Miller had finished drying the supper dishes and was thumbing through an afternoon paper when she saw an advertisement of a picture playing at a neighborhood theater. The title sounded good, so she struggled into her beaver coat, laced her galoshes, and left the apartment, leaving one light burning in the foyer—she found nothing more disturbing than a sensation of darkness.

The snow was fine, falling gently, not yet making an impression on the pavement. The wind from the river cut only at street crossings. Mrs. Miller hurried, her head bowed, oblivious as a mole burrowing a blind path. She stopped at a drugstore and bought a package of peppermints.

A long line stretched in front of the box office; she took her place at the end. There would be (a tired voice groaned) a short wait for all seats. Mrs. Miller rummaged in her leather handbag till she collected exactly the correct change for admission. The line seemed to be taking its own time and, looking around for some distraction, she suddenly became conscious of a little girl standing under the edge of the marquee.

Her hair was the longest and strangest Mrs. Miller had ever seen: absolutely silver-white, like an albino's. It flowed waist-length in smooth, loose lines. She was thin and fragilely constructed. There was a simple, special elegance in the way she stood with her thumbs in the pockets of a tailored plum velvet coat.

Mrs. Miller felt oddly excited, and when the little girl glanced toward her, she smiled warmly. The little girl walked over and said, "Would you care to do me a favor?"

"I'd be glad to, if I can," said Mrs. Miller.

"Oh, it's quite easy. I merely want you to buy a ticket for me; they won't let me in otherwise. Here, I have the money." And gracefully she handed Mrs. Miller two dimes and a nickel.

They went into the theater together. An usherette directed them to a lounge; in twenty minutes the picture would be over.

"I feel just like a genuine criminal," said Mrs. Miller gaily, as she sat down. "I mean that sort of thing's against the law, isn't it? I do hope I haven't done the wrong thing. Your mother knows where you are, dear? I mean she does, doesn't she?"

The little girl said nothing. She unbuttoned her coat and folded it across her lap. Her dress underneath was prim and dark blue. A gold chain dangled about her neck and her fingers, sensitive and musical-looking, toyed with it. Examining her more attentively, Mrs. Miller decided the truly distinctive feature was not her hair, but her eyes; they were hazel, steady, lacking any childlike quality whatsoever and, because of their size, seemed to consume her small face.

Mrs. Miller offered a peppermint. "What's your name, dear?"

"Miriam," she said, as though, in some cu-

---

1. **brownstone:** house with brown stone facade.

rious way, it were information already familiar.

"Why, isn't that funny? My name's Miriam too. And it's not a terribly common name either. Now, don't tell me your last name's Miller!"

"Just Miriam."

"But isn't that funny?"

"Moderately," said Miriam, and rolled the peppermint on her tongue.

Mrs. Miller flushed and shifted uncomfortably. "You have such a large vocabulary for such a little girl."

"Do I?"

"Well, yes," said Mrs. Miller, hastily changing the topic to: "Do you like the movies?"

"I really wouldn't know," said Miriam. "I've never been before."

Women began filling the lounge; the rumble of the newsreel[2] bombs exploded in the distance. Mrs. Miller rose, tucking her purse under her arm. "I guess I'd better be running now if I want to get a seat," she said. "It was nice to have met you."

Miriam nodded ever so slightly.

It snowed all week. Wheels and footsteps moved soundlessly on the street, as if the business of living continued secretly behind a pale but impenetrable curtain. In the falling quiet there was no sky or earth, only snow lifting in the wind, frosting the window glass, chilling the rooms, deadening and hushing the city. At all hours it was necessary to keep a lamp lighted, and Mrs. Miller lost track of the days: Friday was no different from Saturday and on Sunday she went to the grocery: closed, of course.

That evening she scrambled eggs and fixed a bowl of tomato soup. Then, after putting on a flannel robe and cold-creaming her face, she

_____

2. **newsreel:** short motion picture of current events.

propped herself up in bed with a hot-water bottle under her feet. She was reading the *Times* when the doorbell rang. At first she thought it must be a mistake and whoever it was would go away. But it rang and rang and settled to a persistent buzz. She looked at the clock: a little after eleven; it did not seem possible, she was always asleep by ten.

Climbing out of bed, she trotted barefoot across the living room. "I'm coming; please be patient." The latch was caught; she turned it this way and that way and the bell never paused an instant. "Stop it!" she cried. The bolt gave way and she opened the door an inch. "What in heaven's name?"

"Hello," said Miriam.

"Oh . . . why, hello," said Mrs. Miller, stepping hesitantly into the hall. "You're that little girl."

"I thought you'd never answer, but I kept my finger on the button; I knew you were home. Aren't you glad to see me?"

Mrs. Miller did not know what to say. Miriam, she saw, wore the same plum velvet coat and now she had also a beret to match; her white hair was braided in two shining plaits and looped at the ends with enormous white ribbons.

"Since I've waited so long, you could at least let me in," she said.

"It's awfully late."

Miriam regarded her blankly. "What difference does that make? Let me in. It's cold out here and I have on a silk dress." Then, with a gentle gesture, she urged Mrs. Miller aside and passed into the apartment.

She dropped her coat and beret on a chair. She was indeed wearing a silk dress. White silk. White silk in February. The skirt was beautifully pleated and the sleeves long; it made a faint rustle as she strolled about the room. "I like your place," she said. "I like the rug; blue's my favorite color." She touched a paper rose in a vase on the coffee table. "Imitation," she commented wanly. "How sad. Aren't imitations sad?" She seated herself on the sofa, daintily spreading her skirt.

"What do you want?" asked Mrs. Miller.

"Sit down," said Miriam. "It makes me nervous to see people stand."

Mrs. Miller sank to a hassock. "What do you want?" she repeated.

"You know, I don't think you're glad I came."

For a second time Mrs. Miller was without an answer; her hand motioned vaguely. Miriam giggled and pressed back on a mound of chintz[3] pillows. Mrs. Miller observed that the girl was less pale than she remembered; her cheeks were flushed.

"How did you know where I lived?"

Miriam frowned. "That's no question at all. What's your name? What's mine?"

"But I'm not listed in the phone book."

"Oh, let's talk about something else."

Mrs. Miller said, "Your mother must be insane to let a child like you wander around at all hours of the night . . . and in such ridiculous clothes. She must be out of her mind."

Miriam got up and moved to a corner where a covered bird cage hung from a ceiling chain. She peeked beneath the cover. "It's a canary," she said. "Would you mind if I woke him? I'd like to hear him sing."

"Leave Tommy alone," said Mrs. Miller anxiously. "Don't you dare wake him."

"Certainly," said Miriam. "But I don't see why I can't hear him sing." And then, "Have you anything to eat? I'm starving! Even milk and a jam sandwich would be fine."

"Look," said Mrs. Miller, arising from the hassock, "look, if I made some nice sandwiches will you be a good child and run along home? It's past midnight, I'm sure."

"It's snowing," reproached Miriam. "And cold and dark."

"Well, you shouldn't have come here to begin with," said Mrs. Miller, struggling to control her voice. "I can't help the weather. If you want anything to eat you'll have to promise to leave."

---

3. **chintz** [chints]: colorful, patterned, cotton fabric, usually glazed.

Miriam brushed a braid against her cheek. Her eyes were thoughtful, as if weighing the proposition. She turned toward the bird cage. "Very well," she said, "I promise."

How old is she? Ten? Eleven? Mrs. Miller, in the kitchen, unsealed a jar of strawberry preserves and cut four slices of bread. She poured a glass of milk and paused to light a cigarette. *And why has she come?* Her hand shook as she held the match, fascinated, till it burned her finger. The canary was singing—singing as he did in the morning and at no other time. "Miriam," she called, "Miriam, I told you not to disturb Tommy." There was no answer. She called again; all she heard was the canary. She inhaled the cigarette and discovered she had lighted the cork-tip end and . . . oh, really, she mustn't lose her temper.

She carried the food in on a tray and set it on the coffee table. She saw first that the bird cage still wore its night cover. And Tommy was singing. It gave her a queer sensation. And no one was in the room. Mrs. Miller went through an alcove leading to her bedroom; at the door she caught her breath.

"What are you doing?" she asked.

Miriam glanced up, and in her eyes there was a look that was not ordinary. She was standing by the bureau, a jewel case opened before her. For a minute she studied Mrs. Miller, forcing their eyes to meet, and she smiled. "There's nothing good here," she said. "But I like this." Her hand held a cameo brooch. "It's charming."

"Suppose—perhaps you'd better put it back," said Mrs. Miller, feeling suddenly the need of some support. She leaned against the doorframe; her head was unbearably heavy; a pressure weighted the rhythm of her heartbeat. The light seemed to flutter defectively. "Please, child—a gift from my husband. . . ."

"But it's beautiful and I want it," said Miriam. *"Give it to me."*

As she stood, striving to shape a sentence which would somehow save the brooch, it came to Mrs. Miller there was no one to whom she might turn; she was alone; a fact that had not been among her thoughts for a long time. Its sheer emphasis was stunning. But here in her own room in the hushed snow city were evidences she could not ignore or, she knew with startling clarity, resist.

Miriam ate ravenously, and when the sandwiches and milk were gone, her fingers made cobweb movements over the plate, gathering crumbs. The cameo gleamed on her blouse, the blond profile like a trick reflection of its wearer. "That was very nice," she sighed, "though now an almond cake or a cherry would be ideal. Sweets are lovely, don't you think?"

Mrs. Miller was perched precariously on the hassock, smoking a cigarette. Her hair net had slipped lopsided and loose strands straggled down her face. Her eyes were stupidly concentrated on nothing, and her cheeks were mottled in red patches, as though a fierce slap had left permanent marks.

"Is there a candy . . . a cake?"

Mrs. Miller tapped ash on the rug. Her head swayed slightly as she tried to focus her eyes. "You promised to leave if I made the sandwiches," she said.

"Dear me, did I?"

"It was a promise and I'm tired and I don't feel well at all."

"Mustn't fret," said Miriam. "I'm only teasing."

She picked up her coat, slung it over her arm, and arranged her beret in front of a mirror. Presently she bent close to Mrs. Miller and whispered, "Kiss me good night."

"Please . . . I'd rather not," said Mrs. Miller.

Miriam lifted a shoulder, arched an eyebrow. "As you like," she said, and went directly to the coffee table, seized the vase containing the paper roses, carried it to where the hard surface of the floor lay bare, and hurled it downward. Glass sprayed in all directions and she stamped her foot on the bouquet.

Then slowly she walked to the door, but before closing it she looked back at Mrs. Miller with a slyly innocent curiosity.

Mrs. Miller spent the next day in bed, rising once to feed the canary and drink a cup of tea;

she took her temperature and had none, yet her dreams were feverishly agitated; their unbalanced mood lingered even as she lay staring wide-eyed at the ceiling. One dream threaded through the others like an elusively mysterious theme in a complicated symphony, and the scenes it depicted were sharply outlined, as though sketched by a hand of gifted intensity: a small girl, wearing a bridal gown and a wreath of leaves, led a gray procession down a mountain path, and among them there was unusual silence till a woman at the rear asked, "Where is she taking us?" "No one knows," said an old man marching in front. "But isn't she pretty?" volunteered a third voice. "Isn't she like a frost flower—so shining and white?"

Tuesday morning she woke up feeling better; harsh slats of sunlight, slanting through Venetian blinds, shed a disrupting light on her unwholesome fancies. She opened the window to discover a thawed, mild-as-spring day; a sweep of clean new clouds crumpled against a vastly blue, out-of-season sky; and across the low line of rooftops she could see the river and smoke curving from tugboat stacks in a warm wind. A great silver truck plowed the snow-banked street, its machine sound humming on the air.

After straightening the apartment, she went to the grocer's, cashed a check, and continued to Schrafft's, where she ate breakfast and chatted happily with the waitress. Oh, it was a wonderful day . . . more like a holiday . . . and it would be so foolish to go home.

She boarded a Lexington Avenue bus and rode up to Eighty-sixth Street; it was here that she had decided to do a little shopping.

She had no idea what she wanted or needed, but she idled along, intent only upon the passers-by, brisk and preoccupied, who gave her a disturbing sense of separateness.

It was while waiting at the corner of Third Avenue that she saw the man: an old man, bowlegged and stooped under an armload of bulging packages; he wore a shabby brown coat and a checkered cap. Suddenly she real-ized they were exchanging a smile; there was nothing friendly about this smile, it was merely two cold flickers of recognition. But she was certain she had never seen him before.

He was standing next to an el[4] pillar, and as she crossed the street he turned and followed. He kept quite close; from the corner of her eye she watched his reflection wavering on the shopwindows.

Then in the middle of the block she stopped and faced him. He stopped also and cocked his head, grinning. But what could she say? Do? Here, in broad daylight, on Eighty-sixth Street? It was useless and, despising her own helplessness, she quickened her steps.

Now Second Avenue is a dismal street, made from scraps and ends; part cobblestone, part asphalt, part cement; and its atmosphere of desertion is permanent. Mrs. Miller walked five blocks without meeting anyone, and all the while the steady crunch of his footfalls in the snow stayed near. And when she came to a florist's shop, the sound was still with her. She hurried inside and watched through the glass door as the old man passed; he kept his eyes straight ahead and didn't slow his pace, but he did one strange, telling thing: he tipped his cap.

"Six white ones, did you say?" asked the florist. "Yes," she told him, "white roses."

From there she went to a glassware store and selected a vase, presumably a replacement for the one Miriam had broken, though the price was intolerable and the vase itself (she thought) grotesquely vulgar. But a series of unaccountable purchases had begun, as if by prearranged plan—a plan of which she had not the least knowledge or control.

She bought a bag of glazed cherries, and at a place called the Knickerbocker Bakery she paid forty cents for six almond cakes.

Within the last hour the weather had turned cold again; like blurred lenses, winter clouds cast a shade over the sun, and the skel-

---

4. **el:** elevated railroad.

eton of an early dusk colored the sky; a damp mist mixed with the wind and the voices of a few children who romped high on mountains of gutter snow seemed lonely and cheerless. Soon the first flake fell, and when Mrs. Miller reached the brownstone house, snow was falling in a swift screen and foot tracks vanished as they were printed.

The white roses were arranged decoratively in the vase. The glazed cherries shone on a ceramic plate. The almond cakes, dusted with sugar, awaited a hand. The canary fluttered on its swing and picked at a bar of seed.

At precisely five the doorbell rang. Mrs. Miller *knew* who it was. The hem of her house coat trailed as she crossed the floor. "Is that you?" she called.

"Naturally," said Miriam, the word resounding shrilly from the hall. "Open this door."

"Go away," said Mrs. Miller.

"Please hurry—I have a heavy package."

"Go away," said Mrs. Miller. She returned to the living room, lighted a cigarette, sat down and calmly listened to the buzzer; on and on and on. "You might as well leave. I have no intention of letting you in."

Shortly the bell stopped. For possibly ten minutes Mrs. Miller did not move. Then, hearing no sound, she concluded Miriam had gone. She tiptoed to the door and opened it a sliver; Miriam was half reclining atop a cardboard box with a beautiful French doll cradled in her arms.

"Really, I thought you were never coming," she said peevishly. "Here, help me get this in, it's awfully heavy."

It was not spell-like compulsion that Mrs. Miller felt, but rather a curious passivity; she brought in the box, Miriam the doll. Miriam curled up on the sofa, not troubling to remove her coat or beret, and watched disinterestedly as Mrs. Miller dropped the box and stood trembling, trying to catch her breath.

"Thank you," she said. In the daylight she looked pinched and drawn, her hair less luminous. The French doll she was loving wore an exquisite powdered wig and its idiot glass eyes sought solace in Miriam's. "I have a surprise," she continued. "Look into my box."

Kneeling, Mrs. Miller parted the flaps and lifted out another doll; then a blue dress which she recalled as the one Miriam had worn that first night at the theater; and of the remainder she said, "It's all clothes. Why?"

"Because I've come to live with you," said Miriam, twisting a cherry stem. "Wasn't it nice of you to buy me the cherries—"

"But you can't! Go away—go away and leave me alone!"

"—and the roses and the almond cakes? How really wonderfully generous. You know, these cherries are delicious. The last place I lived was with an old man; he was terribly poor and we never had good things to eat. But I think I'll be happy here." She paused to snuggle her doll closer. "Now, if you'll just show me where to put my things . . . ."

Mrs. Miller's face dissolved into a mask of ugly red lines; she began to cry, and it was an unnatural, tearless sort of weeping, as though, not having wept for a long time, she had forgotten how. Carefully she edged backward till she touched the door.

She fumbled through the hall and down the stairs to a landing below. She pounded frantically on the door of the first apartment she came to; a short, redheaded man answered and she pushed past him. "Say, what is this?" he said. "Anything wrong, lover?" asked a young woman who appeared from the kitchen, drying her hands. And it was to her that Mrs. Miller turned.

"Listen," she cried, "I'm ashamed behaving this way, but—well, I'm Mrs. H. T. Miller and I live upstairs and"—she pressed her hands over her face—"it sounds so absurd. . . ."

The woman guided her to a chair, while the man excitedly rattled pocket change. "Yeah?"

"I live upstairs and there's a little girl visiting me, and I suppose that I'm afraid of her. She won't leave and I can't make her and—she's going to do something terrible. She's already stolen my cameo, but she's about to do something worse—something terrible!"

The man asked, "Is she a relative, huh?"

Mrs. Miller shook her head. "I don't know who she is. Her name's Miriam, but I don't know for certain who she is."

"You gotta calm down, honey," said the woman, stroking Mrs. Miller's arm. "Harry here'll tend to this kid. Go on, lover." And Mrs. Miller said, "The door's open—5A."

After the man left, the woman brought a towel and bathed Mrs. Miller's face. "You're very kind," Mrs. Miller said. "I'm sorry to act like such a fool, only this wicked child. . . ."

"Sure, honey," consoled the woman. "Now, you better take it easy."

Mrs. Miller rested her head in the crook of her arm; she was quiet enough to be asleep. The woman turned a radio dial; a piano and a husky voice filled the silence and the woman, tapping her foot, kept excellent time. "Maybe we oughta go up too," she said.

"I don't want to see her again. I don't want to be anywhere near her."

"Uh huh, but what you shoulda done, you shoulda called a cop."

Presently they heard the man on the stairs. He strode into the room frowning and scratching the back of his neck. "Nobody there," he said, honestly embarrassed. "She musta beat it."

"Harry, you're a jerk," announced the woman. "We been sitting here the whole time and we woulda seen . . ." She stopped abruptly, for the man's glance was sharp.

"I looked all over," he said, "and there just ain't nobody there. Nobody, understand?"

"Tell me," said Mrs. Miller, rising, "tell me, did you see a large box? Or a doll?"

"No, ma'am, I didn't."

And the woman, as if delivering a verdict, said, "Well, for cryinoutloud. . . ."

Mrs. Miller entered her apartment softly; she walked to the center of the room and stood quite still. No, in a sense it had not changed: the roses, the cakes, and the cherries were in place. But this was an empty room, emptier than if the furnishings and familiars were not present, lifeless and petrified as a funeral parlor. The sofa loomed before her with a new strangeness: its vacancy had a meaning that would have been less penetrating and terrible had Miriam been curled on it. She gazed fixedly at the space where she remembered setting the box and for a moment the hassock spun desperately. And she looked through the window; surely the river was real, surely snow was falling. But then one could not be certain witness to anything: Miriam, so vividly *there* . . . and yet, where was she? Where, where?

As though moving in a dream, she sank to a chair. The room was losing shape; it was dark and getting darker and there was nothing to be done about it; she could not lift her hand to light a lamp.

Suddenly, closing her eyes, she felt an upward surge, like a diver emerging from some deeper, greener depth. In times of terror or immense distress there are moments when the mind waits, as though for a revelation, while a skein of calm is woven over thought; it is like sleep, or a supernatural trance; and during this lull one is aware of a force of quiet reasoning: well, what if she had never really known a girl named Miriam? That she had been foolishly frightened on the street? In the end, like everything else, it was of no importance. For the only thing she had lost to Miriam was her identity, but now she knew she had found again the person who lived in this room, who cooked her own meals, who owned a canary, who was someone she could trust and believe in: Mrs. H. T. Miller.

Listening in contentment, she became aware of a double sound: a bureau drawer opening and closing; she seemed to hear it long after completion—opening and closing. Then gradually the harshness of it was replaced by the murmur of a silk dress and this, delicately faint, was moving nearer and swelling in intensity till the walls trembled with the vibration and the room was caving under a wave of whispers. Mrs. Miller stiffened and opened her eyes to a dull, direct stare.

"Hello," said Miriam.

STUDY QUESTIONS

Recalling

1. What does the opening paragraph tell us about Mrs. Miller's living conditions, interests, and activities? How does she meet Miriam?
2. What is unusual about Miriam's appearance and her name? What kind of dress does Miriam wear on her first visit to Mrs. Miller's apartment? What comments and requests does she make? What does she do when Mrs. Miller will not kiss her good night?
3. What dream does Mrs. Miller have?
4. Describe the man whom Mrs. Miller encounters on her shopping trip. What purchases does she make on her trip?
5. Explain how Miriam gains access to Mrs. Miller's apartment at five o'clock. What does Mrs. Miller's neighbor discover when he goes up to Mrs. Miller's apartment? According to his girlfriend, why would it have been impossible for anyone to have "beat it"?
6. According to the final paragraphs, what had Mrs. Miller "lost" to Miriam? What has she found again when Miriam departs?

Interpreting

7. What evidence suggests that Miriam is real? That she is a figment of Mrs. Miller's imagination? What do the last two paragraphs imply about Mrs. Miller's future relationship with the girl?
8. Describe the kind of life Mrs. Miller led before meeting Miriam, and explain what might prompt her initial kindness to the girl. Explain the relevance of the things Mrs. Miller purchases on her shopping trip. Why is her reluctance to open the door for Miriam ironic?
9. What might be the relationship between Miriam and the old man whom Mrs. Miller encounters on the street? Can we be sure?
10. Has Miriam's appearance had any positive effects on Mrs. Miller? Explain.
11. Interpret Mrs. Miller's dream and the general significance Miriam might have in her life. Is there one interpretation to this story? What does the story force the reader to do?

Extending

12. Despite its ambiguity and elements of fantasy, what does this story suggest to you about people and the way they behave?

LITERARY FOCUS

Suspense and Foreshadowing

Suspense is that quality in a story that makes us uncertain or tense about the outcome of events. As readers, we want to know what will happen next and if a character will be saved or lost, happy or unhappy.

There are two types of suspense. In the first and most common we do not know the outcome of events, and the suspense is a matter of plot—*what* will happen. In the second type the outcome is inevitable: We know the plot, but the suspense is a matter of the author's style and characterizations—*how* things will happen.

Many different elements help to create suspense. Characters may not possess some important information: Will they learn the truth? Characters may not possess some important object: Will they obtain it? Writers sometimes increase suspense by the use of **foreshadowing**—presenting events or characters in such a way as to hint at what is going to happen to them.

Thinking About Suspense and Foreshadowing

1. What questions draw us into "Miriam"? What information is withheld from us?
2. Find examples of foreshadowing in the story.
3. What happens to the tension in the story when Miriam leaves the apartment? Why?

COMPOSITION

Writing About Theme

■ Write a brief composition on the theme of "Miriam." Before writing, review the plot, and list the major events. Determine the significance of each major event, and look for the development of a theme. State the theme clearly. Then, using examples from the story, show how the theme is revealed through characterization, setting, plot, point of view, and tone. *For help with this assignment, refer to Lesson 6 in the Writing About Literature Handbook at the back of this book.*

Narrating a Scene

■ Narrate a scene in which unexplainable events occur to an ordinary person. First present the person, as Capote does in the first paragraph of "Miriam." Then begin the action, first with normal activity. Gradually introduce events that baffle the character and the reader.

John Updike   *born 1932*

"We must write where we stand," John Updike once said. "Wherever we do stand, there is life: And an imitation of the life we know, however narrow, is our only ground." In his writing Updike gives us "the life we know," revealing the universal through the fine details of the everyday.

John Updike was born in the small town of Shillington, Pennsylvania. When he was thirteen, his family moved to a farm. Both locations, lightly disguised, provide the setting for much of his early fiction. Updike graduated from Harvard and attended the Ruskin School of Drawing and Fine Art in England. He worked first as a cartoonist, then as a staff writer, for the *New Yorker,* the magazine in which many of his stories first appeared.

Updike is a prolific and popular writer, and his published works include novels, collections of stories, poems, essays, and reviews. His novels, however, have won him the greatest acclaim. They include *The Centaur* (1963), *Couples* (1968), *The Coup* (1978), and the trilogy *Rabbit, Run* (1960), *Rabbit Redux* (1971), and *Rabbit Is Rich* (1981).

Several character types appear repeatedly in Updike's fiction. One is the sensitive, sometimes egotistical adolescent groping with uncertainty. Another is the former high school athlete, once a star, who now seems a misfit in the workaday adult world. A third type is the middle-class man or woman who has "missed the moment," lost the opportunity for a great achievement, and who now feels trapped and frustrated. Updike's stories place people like these in ordinary situations that occur in ordinary places such as the high school classroom, the local supermarket, the family car, the small apartment. His characters often seem to be not quite happy, not quite secure, not quite satisfied with their lives.

John Updike's technical skill is sometimes overlooked because he deals with such everyday subjects, but he has a keen eye for the revealing detail and a sharp ear for colloquial dialogue. His language is alive with original metaphors and phrasing, always witty, sometimes melancholy. He is expert at stream of consciousness, ironic twists, and comic situations. In "The Slump" Updike uses one of his favorite images—the world of sports as a metaphor for life, the athlete as a metaphor for the achiever in all of us.

John Updike

The Slump

They say reflexes, the coach says reflexes, even the papers now are saying reflexes, but I don't think it's the reflexes so much—last night, as a gag to cheer me up, the wife walks into the bedroom wearing one of the kids' rubber gorilla masks and I was under the bed in six-tenths of a second, she had the stopwatch on me. It's that I can't see the ball the way I used to. It used to come floating up with all seven continents showing, and the pitcher's thumbprint, and a grass smooch or two, and the Spalding guarantee in ten-point sans-serif,[1] and *whop!* I could feel the sweet wood with the bat still cocked. Now, I don't know, there's like a cloud around it, a sort of spiral vagueness, maybe the Van Allen belt,[2] or maybe I lift my eye in the last second, planning how I'll round second base, or worrying which I do first, tip my cap or slap the third-base coach's hand. You can't see a blind spot, Kierkegaard[3] says, but in there now, between when the ball leaves the bleacher background and I can hear it plop all fat and satisfied in the catcher's mitt, there's somehow just nothing, where there used to be a lot, everything in fact, because they're not keeping me around for my fielding, and already I see the afternoon tabloid has me down as trade bait.

The flutters don't come when they used to. It used to be, I'd back the convertible out of the garage and watch the electric eye put the door down again and drive in to the stadium, and at about the bridge turnoff I'd ease off grooving with the radio rock, and then on the lot there'd be the kids waiting to get a look and that would start the big butterflies, and when the attendant would take my car I'd want

1. **ten-point sans-serif** [san ser′if]: referring to the size and style of the lettering.
2. **Van Allen belt:** belt of radiation around the earth.
3. **Kierkegaard** [kēr′kə gärd′]: Søren [sœ′rən] Kierkegaard (1813–1855), Danish philosopher.

to shout *Stop, thief,* and walking down that long cement corridor I'd fantasize like I was going to the electric chair and the locker room was some dream after death, and I'd wonder why the suit fit, and how these really immortal guys, that I recognized from the bubble-gum cards I used to collect, knew my name. *They* knew *me.* And I'd go out and the stadium mumble would scoop at me and the grass seemed too precious to walk on, like emeralds, and by the time I got into the cage I couldn't remember if I batted left or right.

Now, hell, I move over the bridge singing along with the radio, and brush through the kids at just the right speed, not so fast I knock any of them down, and the attendant knows his Labor Day tip is coming, and we wink, and in the batting cage I own the place, and take my cuts, pop five or six into the bullpen as easy as dropping dimes down a sewer. But when the scoreboard lights up, and I take those two steps up from the dugout, the biggest two steps in a ballplayer's life, and kneel in the circle, giving the crowd the old hawk profile, where once the flutters would ease off, now they dig down and begin.

They say I'm not hungry, but I still feel hungry, only now it's a kind of panic hungry, and that's not the right kind. Ever watch one of your little kids try to catch a ball? He gets so excited with the idea he's going to catch it he shuts his eyes. That's me now. I walk up to the plate, having come all this way—a lot of hotels, a lot of shagging—and my eyes feel shut. And I stand up there trying to push my eyeballs through my eyelids, and my retinas register maybe a little green, and the black patch of some nuns in far left field. That's panic hungry.

Kierkegaard called it dread.[4] It queers the works. My wife comes at me without the gorilla mask and when in the old days, *whop!,* now she slides by with a hurt expression and a flicker of gray above her temple. I go out and ride the power mower and I've already done it

so often the lawn is brown. The kids get me out of bed for a little fungo and it scares me to see them trying, busting their lungs, all that shagging ahead of them. In Florida—we used to love it in Florida, the smell of citrus and marlin, the flat pink sections where the old people drift around smiling with transistor plugs in their ears—we lie on the beach after a workout and the sun seems a high fly I'm going to lose and the waves keep coming like they've been doing for a billion years, up to the plate, up to the plate. Kierkegaard probably has the clue, somewhere in there, but I picked up *Concluding Unscientific Postscript*[5] the other day and I couldn't see the print, that is, I could see the lines, but there wasn't anything on them, like the rows of deep seats in the shade of the second deck on a Thursday afternoon, just a single ice-cream vendor sitting there, nobody around to sell to, a speck of white in all that shade, old Søren Sock himself, keeping his goods cool.

I think maybe if I got beaned. That's probably what the wife is hinting at with the gorilla mask. A change of pace, like the time DiMaggio[6] broke his slump by Topping's[7] telling him to go to a night club and get plastered. I've stopped ducking, but the trouble is, if you're not hitting, they don't brush you back. On me, they've stopped trying for even the corners; they put it right down the pike. I can see it in his evil eye as he takes the sign and rears back, I can hear the catcher snicker, and for a second of reflex there I can see it like it used to be, continents and cities and every green tree distinct as a stitch, and the hickory sweetens in my hands, and I feel the good old sure hunger. Then something happens. It blurs, skips, fades, I don't know. It's not caring enough, is what it probably is, it's knowing that none of it—the stadium, the averages—is really there, just *you* are there, and it's not enough.

---

4. **dread:** In *The Concept of Dread* Kierkegaard stated that profound fear is natural to the human condition.

5. ***Concluding Unscientific Postscript:*** one of Kierkegaard's major works.
6. **DiMaggio:** Joe DiMaggio (born 1914), New York Yankee baseball player (1936–1951).
7. **Topping's:** Dan Topping, one of a group that owned the Yankees between 1945 and 1964.

STUDY QUESTIONS

Recalling

1. According to the first paragraph, what do the coach and papers say has caused the narrator's slump? What does the narrator say has caused it?
2. How did the baseball appear when the narrator used to see it clearly (paragraph 1)? How does it appear now?
3. How did the narrator once feel when he gave his car to the stadium attendant? How does the narrator now greet the stadium attendant? When do the flutters begin now?
4. How do "they" explain the cause of the slump in paragraph 4? How does the narrator describe his present kind of hunger? What does he say Kierkegaard calls it?
5. What is the narrator's explanation of his slump in the final sentence?

Interpreting

6. What do the contrasts in paragraph 3 and 4 suggest about the changes that have occurred in the narrator's attitude toward playing baseball? What was his old "hunger" a hunger for?
7. With what is the baseball coming at the narrator compared twice in the story? What does this comparison suggest that the baseball represents? What does the narrator's "blind spot" suggest about his current attitude toward life?
8. Explain the philosophical implications of the final sentence with regard to the narrator's present condition—his "slump"—and its causes.

Extending

9. What does this story suggest to you about fame? About aging? About modern life in general? Do you agree with these suggestions? Why or why not?

VIEWPOINT

In assessing Updike's fiction Robert Detweiler has written:

Updike's accomplishment is in dramatizing the eternal human problems in terms of arresting contemporary techniques. (He may often be writing about the same failings that bothered the Victorians, but he handles them in a modern manner.)

—John Updike

What are the "eternal human problems" that are dramatized in "The Slump"? What is particularly "contemporary" in Updike's literary techniques?

COMPOSITION

Writing About Diction and Sentence Structure

Write a brief composition about the appropriateness of the language and sentence structure in "The Slump." Begin with a general statement about the character of the narrator and the subject of the story. Then show with examples how the language is natural for the narrator and appropriate for his subject. Continue by discussing how the sentence structure suits the temperament of the narrator at this point in his life. Conclude by relating the narrator's language and sentence structure to the total effect the story has on you.

Writing a Monologue

Invent a character who doubts his or her ability in an occupation, a sport, a school subject, or a social grace. Write a first-person monologue expressing that character's doubts, fears, and struggle to succeed. Keep the language consistent with the subject, the character's background, and the character's state of mind.

William Goyen   *1915–1983*

Lyric and realistic, delicate and harsh, William Goyen's stories leave unforgettable impressions. His characters are revealed with a moving combination of precision and compassion.

Goyen was born in Trinity, Texas, and graduated from Rice University. He has taught at the New School for Social Research and at Columbia University in New York City. His works of fiction include *The House of Breath* (1950), *In a Farther Country* (1955), *The Faces of Blood Kindred* (1960), and *The Fair Sister* (1963).

The characters in Goyen's fiction have often lost their purposes in life, their ideals, or their capacity to communicate with one another. They search for some way of bridging the chasm between the past and present. Their stories are carefully told, the product of close observation and hard-earned craft. While many of Goyen's stories possess a gothic quality, "The Moss Rose" is quite realistic in style. By the end of the story, however, the reader sees the deep significance of the main character's seemingly ordinary observations.

William Goyen

The Moss Rose

"Portulaca," the Third Avenue man said to him at the door of his shop when he asked the name of what he thought was a box of moss-rose plants for sale on the sidewalk.

"Aren't they moss roses?" he asked.

"Portulaca," the man said.

"Do they have orange and yellow and crimson blossoms?"

"That's right," the man said.

"And they aren't moss roses?"

"Portulaca," he said again.

He went on up Third Avenue saying the word to himself as he walked, so as not to forget it. *Portulaca.* "I guess that's what they call them up here," he said to himself.

He had grown up with them—*moss roses*—always in some flower bed, by a grave, by a

pump where the ground was moist, in a hanging kettle on a porch. They were a part of another landscape, a flower illustration of many remembered scenes in another country. Here they were, on Third Avenue in New York City. Or were they the same—could they be? Oh, he thought, I guess people up here know and have this common little flower—why shouldn't they? But such a name as they've given it! *Portulaca.*

The El[1] was quiet, the train was gone. Though the complicated and permanent-looking structure was there, soon it would be torn down. Third Avenue was quieter. People who had lived for years with the noise of the El interrupting their sleep and conversation and

_____
1. **The El:** elevated railroad.

who had learned naturally to scream above it, still spoke in Third Avenue voices; but the train, the reason, was gone.

The children yelled in resounding voices on the sidewalks, though the noise over which they yelled had vanished; and he wondered if ever their voices would soften or modulate. No, they would go on through life yelling with powerful voices developed against the monster whose tracks they had been bred alongside. It would be the El going on through them; it was not really destroyed. They seemed the children of the El, and the tracks and platform had bred children who looked a little like them, curiously, as their parents did, so that their faces, bearing, physiognomy reflected the resisted force—as people who live in constant wind or on stony landscapes reflect the natural phenomenon which opposes them in daily life.

These Third Avenue people had the same vagabond, noisy air and quality that the ramshackle train and platform symbolized. The El had created a genus of humanity, almost as the plow had shaped his own; they looked as if they had performed some laborious job with the El, as an instrument of their daily bread, although it did not feed them or reward them with anything but noise and dirt. Still it shaped a style of life for them. Over the years a race had adapted itself to an inhuman presence and had learned, almost as if by imitating or mimicking it, a mode of life that enabled them to absorb it into their daily life, and to endure. They were a kind of grimly happy, sailorlike, reckless people, carefree, poor, tough and loudmouthed, big-throated and hoarse-voiced. The old, who had lived so long with it, seemed very tired by it. They sat in their straight chairs on the sidewalks or on the steps of their buildings and conversed in loud voices—a gypsy breed with their Third Avenue dog, again his own special breed: a serene, somewhat sad, seasoned hound, resigned, fearless and friendly.

Portulaca, he said, walking along. Little moss rose. Well, he was homesick. But wasn't everyone? he consoled himself. By a certain time something, some structure, in every life is gone, and becomes a memory. But it has caused something: a change, an attitude, an aspect. It is the effect of what was, he thought, going on, that is the long-lastingness in us.

Thinking this, he looked up at the sides of the buildings and saw that the "Portulaca" grew here and there on the Third Avenue people's fire escapes. It was a rather common summer flower on Third Avenue! Well, the moss rose belongs to them, too, as it did to the old guard back home, he thought. Somehow the little moss rose was a part of any old order, any old, passing bunch, and it clung to those who represented the loss of old fixtures of everyday life, it was that faithful a friend. Now it seemed right that it grow along Third Avenue in boxes and pots on rusty and cluttered and bedraggled fire escapes, as it had in a house he knew once that was inhabited by a flock of raggle-taggle kinfolks, full of joy and knowing trouble and taggling and scrabbling along, a day at a time, toward a better day, surely, they avowed. So, in that old home far away, the moss rose used to look out on a train track, though the scarce train was an event when it chose to pass that way, as if it might be some curious animal out of the woods that had taken a daring path by the house. Still, something of the same configuration was here.

Portulaca! Little moss rose! he thought. The same patterns do exist all over the world, in cities and towns, wherever people live and arrange life around themselves, a bridge over a creek or a tunnel under a river, there is a way to manage. And a sudden sight of this human pattern in one place restores a lost recognition of it in another, far away, through an eternal image of a simple flower, in the hands and care of both; and in a moment's illumination there was in him the certain knowledge of unity forever working to stitch and tie, like a quilt, the human world into a simple shape of repetition and variation of what seems a meaningless and haphazard design whose whole was hostile to its parts and seemed set on disordering them.

He went back to the shop and told the man

he would like to try a Portulaca plant. On his fire escape, just off Third Avenue, it would grow and bloom the fragile starlike blossoms of the moss rose he had loved so deeply in another place and would love here as well, though it might be a little different from the old one—something in the leaf, slight but different. Yet, everything changes, he thought, slowly it all changes. Do we resign ourselves to that? Is youth passing when we see this—the fierce battle of youth that would not accept change and loss? But there is always the relationship of sameness, too, in all things, which identifies the old ancestor: the *relatedness;* we'll cling to that, to that continuous stem around which only the adornments change, he thought. What if the leaf is a little different? The family is the same . . . the bloom is akin—Portulaca or moss rose. Though the El was gone and the house of kinfolk vanished, two beings as different as man and woman, he would water and tend and foster the old moss-rose family that was still going on.

Sitting on his fire escape, after planting the moss rose in a discarded roasting pan, he looked out through the grillwork of the fire escape and saw the gaunt white-headed man who resembled so much his grandfather in his small room across the courtyard through the Trees of Heaven,[2] where he sat night and day, serene and waiting. Where was his home? Did he know a land where the moss rose bloomed? In his waiting, in his drab, monotonous loneliness, there was a memory living, surely. Who knew, one day it might freshen in him at the sight of something that lingered in the world out of his past, right in the neighborhood, just out of his window, and gladden him for an hour.

Squatting on the fire escape, he thought of his own dreams and hopes. As he sat with the little plant, gazing at it for a long time, a memory rose from it like a vapor, eluded him, and sank back into it. He sat patiently, to catch the memory that glimmered over the petals. What hummingbird remembrance, elusive and darting from his mind, still took its flavor, its bit of sweetness, from the moss rose? And then it came up clear and simple to him, the memory in the moss rose.

It was in the back yard of The Place, as it was called by all who lived there, long ago, under a cool shade tree in Texas. A clump of moss roses grew, without anybody asking it to, in the moist ground around the pump like ringlets of hair wreathed with red and orange and yellow blossoms. He had hung the bucket by its handle over the neck of the pump, and Jessy his small sister held one of his hands while he jacked the pump with the other. The chinaberry trees were still fresh before the sun would make them limp, the chickens were pert, the dew was still on everything, even the woodpile, and the sand in the road still cool. Their old Cherokee rose, that his grandmother had planted when she was a young woman in this house, was gay and blooming at every leaf and thorn, and frolicking all over the fence, down and up and around, locking itself and freeing itself—it would quieten down in the hot afternoon.

Over the squeaking of the pump, he heard a voice and a word . . . "star . . . star." He turned to Jessy and saw that she had picked one of the moss roses and offered it to him, a tiny red star, on the palm of her hand. The bloom was so wonderous and the gift so sudden that he had thought, at that moment, that all life might be something like this twinkling offering. When they went in, the bucket filled, and their mother asked what they had been doing, Jessy had answered, "Picking stars . . ."

Now the place was gone, the water dried up, no doubt, the moss rose finished. Jessy was dead these many years; moss roses grew around her small grave—unless they had been overcome by weeds; he had not gone back to that graveyard for a long time. Here on his fire escape (the landlady had once advertised it as a "renovated terrace") was a fragile remnant of that vanished world; he would tend it; it would no doubt bloom, in time. To find that simple joy again, what could he do to recapture it, to recapture what had been, long ago in the moss

---

2. **Trees of Heaven:** hardy shade trees, cultivated especially in cities because they resist pollution.

rose and in himself—that ready acceptance, that instantaneous belief, in that pure joy of morning, in one sweet summer, long ago at the water pump, holding his sister's tiny hand? All that had followed, as he had grown, dimmed and tarnished that small blinking star: error and disenchantment and loss.

I used to dream of a little fresh sunrise town like that one where we stood once, at the water pump, he said to himself, where I would be, as fixed upon the ground as the moss rose round the pump, rising in the early morning in vigor to my work and moving and living round it, drawing more and more life to it, through me. Instead, work and life seem to have withdrawn from me more and more, to have pushed life back from where it began, into cities and stone buildings, onto pavements, to have impoverished me even of memories that would save me despair, in a huge grassless city where no flowers bloom on the ground.

When the moss rose bloomed again for him, this time on a fire escape in a great city where he sat with gray streaks in his hair, he would be grateful for that. There might even grow another star to pick. So he would watch, day by day, for the flowers to appear, speaking patiently to himself, and again for the hundredth time, that some change was imperative round which to rebuild, out of which to call back the fullness of forgotten signs of love and visions of hope. Believe that it is right ahead, he said to himself, sitting with the plant on the fire escape. Start with one little plain, going-on thing to live around and to take up an old beginning from. Until slowly, slowly, hope and new life will grow and leaf out from it to many places and to many old forgotten promises.

William Goyen **809**

STUDY QUESTIONS

Recalling

1. What does the main character call Portulaca? Of what are these plants a part, according to the ninth paragraph? Where is the man when he sees the plants in this story?
2. What does the main character decide he is as he muses over the word *Portulaca* (paragraph 13)? What "certain knowledge" does he get in "a moment's illumination"?
3. What did the main character's sister Jessy once call moss roses? What did she do with the moss rose she picked? What has happened to Jessy?
4. According to the final paragraphs, how has the character's life differed from what it once was and what he once dreamed it would be?
5. What will the man watch for, according to the last paragraph? What does he decide is "imperative"? What will it "call back"? What does he tell himself to believe?

Interpreting

6. Basically, what does the man think the residents of Third Avenue are like at the beginning of the story? What people or life style do the residents of Third Avenue represent? What is the relationship between the moss rose and the El?
7. What is the man himself like before he has his "moment's illumination"? What is significant about his not having visited his sister's grave for a long time?
8. Explain in your own words the knowledge the man receives in his "moment's illumination." What is his new attitude at the end of the story? What does the moss rose represent for him?

Extending

9. How do you think the past can be important in helping us live in the present? Do you agree that "the same patterns . . . exist all over the world, in cities and towns"? Why or why not?

VOCABULARY

Synonyms

A **synonym** is a word that has the same or nearly the same meaning as another word. *Comfort* and *solace* are synonyms. The words in capital letters are from "The Moss Rose." Choose the word that is nearest the meaning of each word in capitals, *as it is used in the selection.*

1. RESOUNDING: (a) twice (b) loud (c) vanishing (d) quickening
2. MODULATE: (a) model (b) harden (c) adjust (d) extinguish
3. PHYSIOGNOMY: (a) features (b) back (c) skeleton (d) torso
4. RAMSHACKLE: (a) stylish (b) old (c) fixed (d) unkempt
5. AVOWED: (a) moved (b) changed (c) declared (d) retired

COMPOSITION

Writing About a Symbol

▓ "The Moss Rose" is a tightly constructed story that centers on the symbol of the moss rose. It does, however, also use the elevated train as a symbol. Write a brief composition about the Third Avenue El in this story. First tell how it is brought into the story, and what function it serves. Then discuss what it contributes to the theme and the effect on the theme if the El were not included. *For help with this assignment, refer to Lesson 5 in the Writing About Literature Handbook at the back of this book.*

Writing About Memory

▓ Write a short composition, or a poem if you wish, about how the memory of something past can influence the behavior of a person in the present. For example, the memory of a triumphant moment can spur someone to try again a difficult task. Following Goyen's example in "The Moss Rose," create a specific situation that dramatizes the effect of a memory.

Mark Helprin *born 1947*

Mark Helprin's novel, *Refiner's Fire,* and his collections of short stories—*A Dove of the East* and *Ellis Island*—have won him widespread praise. A graduate of Harvard and a student of Middle Eastern culture, Helprin has published most of his stories in magazines, particularly the *New Yorker*.

The settings for Helprin's stories range from New York and Massachusetts to Europe, North Africa, and the Middle East. His characters vary just as much. His first collection included stories about a young musician in Paris, a cattle rancher in Jamaica, a young girl working in a typewriter-ribbon factory, a priest who goes to Rome to die, and a soldier about to take part in a Civil War battle. His stories have been described as creating "strange, magical worlds." They often seem to float somewhere between reality and the country of the imagination. Indeed, Helprin has been praised for his "celebration of the transforming power of imagination."

Permeating Helprin's best stories is the quality of love—love of men and women, of landscapes, of beauty, of courage. "White Gardens" is such a story. It portrays one of those moments "when that which is truly important arises," and we realize the power of the love of life itself.

Model for Active Reading

In this selection, and in one selection in each unit, you will find notes in the right-hand margin that highlight parts of the selection. These notes point out important ideas of the period—in this case, contemporary ideas—and draw your attention to literary elements and techniques covered in the Literary Focuses. Page numbers in the notes will refer you to more extensive discussions of these important ideas and elements.

Mark Helprin

White Gardens

It was August. In the middle of his eulogy the priest said, "Now they must leave us, to repose in white gardens," and then halted in confusion, for he had certainly meant green gardens. But he was not sure. No one in the overcrowded church knew what he meant by white gardens instead of green, but they felt that the mistake was in some way appropriate, and most of them would remember for the rest of their lives the moment afterward, when he had glanced at them in alarm and puzzlement.

Contemporary idea: Literature dramatizes the difficulty of expression and communication among people (page 744).

The stone church in Brooklyn,[1] on one of the long avenues stretching to the sea, was full of firefighters, the press, uncharacteristically quiet city politicians in tropical suits, and the wives and eighteen children of the six men who, in the blink of an eye, had dropped together through the collapsing roof of a burning building, deep into an all-consuming firestorm.

Everyone noticed that the wives of the firemen who had died looked exceptionally beautiful. The young women—with the golden hair of summer, in dark print dresses—several of whom carried flowers, and the older, more matronly women who were less restrained because they understood better what was to become of them, all had a frightening, elevated quality which seemed to rule the parishioners and silence the politicians.

The priest was tumbling over his own words, perhaps because he was young and too moved to be eloquent according to convention. He looked up after a long silence and said, simply, "repose of rivers . . ." They strained to understand, but couldn't, and forgave him immediately. His voice was breaking—not because so many were in the church, for in the raw shadow of the event itself, their numbers were unimpressive. It wasn't that the Mayor was in the crowd: the Mayor had become just a man, and no one felt the power of his office. It may have been the heat. The city had been under siege for a week. Key West[2] humidity and rains had swept across Brooklyn, never-ending, trying to cover it with the sea. The sun was shining now, through a powerful white haze, and the heat inside the church was phenomenal and frightening, ninety-five degrees—like a boiler room. All the seasons have their mystery, and perhaps the mystery of summer is that it overwhelms with easy life, and makes one feel improperly immortal.

Setting (page 148): The time and place of the story suggest and support the theme.

One of the wives glanced out a high window and saw white smoke billowing from a chimney. Even in this kind of weather, she

---

1. **Brooklyn:** one of the five boroughs of New York City.
2. **Key West:** westernmost island of the Florida Keys.

thought, they have to turn on the furnaces to make hot water. The smoke rushed past the masonry as if the chimney were the stack of a ship. She had been to a fireman's funeral before, and she knew what it was going to be like when the flag-draped coffin was borne from the church and placed on the bed of a shiny new engine. Hundreds of uniformed men would snap to attention, their blue hats aligning suddenly. Then the procession would flow away like a blue river, and she, the widow (for she was now the widow), would stagger into a waiting black car to follow after it.

She was one of the younger wives, one of those who were filled with restrained motion, one of the ones in a dark print dress with flowers. She was looking to the priest for direction, but he was coming apart, and as he did she could not keep out of her mind the million things she was thinking, the things which came to her for no reason, just the way the priest had said "white gardens," and "repose of rivers." She thought of the barges moving slowly up the Hudson in a tunnel of silver and white haze, and of the wind-polished bridges standing in the summer sun. She thought of the men in the church. She knew them. They were firefighters; they were rough, and they carried with them in the church more ambition, sadness, power, courage, greed, and anger than she cared to think about on this day. But despite their battalion's worth of liveliness and strength, they were drawn to the frail priest whose voice broke every now and then in the presence of the wives and the children and the six coffins.

She thought of Brooklyn, of its vastness, and of the things that were happening in Brooklyn, right then. Even as the men were buried, traffic on the streets and parkways would be thick as blood; a hundred million emotions would pass from soul to soul, into the air, into walls in dark hot rooms, into thin groves of trees in the parks. Even as the men were buried in an emerald field dazzling with row upon row of bone-white gravestones, there would be something of resurrection and life all over Brooklyn. But now it was still, and the priest was lost in a moment during which everyone was brought together, and the suited children and lovely wives learned that there are quiet times when the world is touched, and when that which is truly important arises to claim all allegiances.

"It is bitter," said the priest, finally in control of himself, "bitter that only through windows like these do we see clearly into past and future, that in such scenes we burn through our temporal[3]

---

3. **temporal:** worldly; not spiritual.

Contemporary idea: A finely crafted modern style does not necessarily avoid emotional involvement (page 745).

Contemporary idea: Out of life's common events, not romanticized, come profound meanings (page 745).

concerns to see that everything that was, is; and that everything that is, will always be." She looked at him, bending her head slightly and pursing her lips in an expression of love and sadness, and he continued. "For we shall always have green gardens, and we shall always have white gardens, too."

Now they knew what he meant, and it shot like electricity through the six wives, the eighteen children, and the blue river of men.

> **Symbol** (page 187): The gardens, standing for two aspects of life, carry the theme of the story.

> **Revelation and epiphany** (page 780): A flash of insight is the climax of the story.

STUDY QUESTIONS

Recalling

1. Where is the story set? For what reason are the people gathered there?
2. What apparent error does the priest make in the opening paragraph? To what are the fire-fighters drawn "despite their battalion's worth of liveliness and strength" (paragraph 6)?
3. According to the seventh paragraph, where will the men be buried? What three things does the young wife realize will happen in Brooklyn "even as the men are buried"?
4. What does the priest say when he is "finally in control of himself"? How do the congregation react to his final speech, according to the last paragraph?
5. What image is used twice in the story to describe the procession of firemen?

Interpreting

6. What is the significance of the profession of the men who have died and the way they died? Why are they important to the people?
7. What does the "resurrection and life all over Brooklyn" suggest about the death of the six firemen? How is the image of the "blue stream" related to this suggestion?
8. When the priest first uses "white gardens," are his words intentional? When he uses the term a second time, are his words intentional? What might he mean by "white gardens"? Why must those mourning the dead firemen think of "white gardens" as well as "green gardens"?

Extending

9. In what sense are these six firemen traditional heroes? In what sense are they modern heroes? Who, in your opinion, are some of the other heroes of the modern world, and why?

COMPOSITION

Writing About Color Symbols

▣ Helprin uses colors in a poetic and symbolic way in "White Gardens." Write a brief composition on the use of colors in this story. First identify the story's uses of *white;* tell what you think it stands for and how it conveys the theme of the story. Then identify other colors used in the story. Tell what they symbolize and how they compare or contrast to the uses of white. *For help with this assignment, refer to Lesson 5 in the Writing About Literature Handbook at the back of this book.*

Writing a Description

▣ Write a brief prose description, or a poem if you wish, using colors to create a vivid scene for your reader. Imagine the scene as if you were a painter choosing colors from your palette. Do not hesitate to name unusual colors or describe conventional colors in new ways. If you attach symbolic meanings to the colors, be sure your reader sees your reasons for doing so.

COMPARING WRITERS

▣ The great modern philosopher George Santayana said, "The local is the only universal." Writers have always known that the great issues of life must be presented in concrete, immediate terms, but many modern writers seem to confine themselves deliberately to the domestic, the everyday, the very ordinary. Discuss how the short story writers on pages 772–809 use the ordinary to express the extraordinary. Describe the scenes and events in the stories. Then tell what insight or universal meaning the writer draws from each.

NONFICTION

Leonard Bernstein   *born 1918*

Leonard Bernstein—composer, conductor, pianist, teacher, and author—was born in Lawrence, Massachusetts. He discovered music at the age of ten, when an old upright piano belonging to a relative was brought into the Bernstein home. He studied to be a pianist at first, but later his interest shifted to conducting, and in 1943 he was invited to join the New York Philharmonic as assistant conductor. When the illustrious conductor Bruno Walter was unable to appear one day, Bernstein was summoned to stand in. His brilliant performance under difficult circumstances immediately established his reputation.

Bernstein is an articulate artist who not only conducts and composes music but also teaches it and writes books about it. His own compositions include the scores for several popular musicals— *On the Town* (1944), *Wonderful Town* (1953), *Candide* (1956), and *West Side Story* (1957). He wrote the music for the film *On the Waterfront* (1954) and has composed the scores for several ballets. Bernstein composed his *Mass* especially for the opening of the John F. Kennedy Center for the Performing Arts in Washington, D.C., in September 1971. His enlightening and entertaining books include *The Joy of Music* (1959), *The Infinite Variety of Music* (1966), and *Findings* (1982).

Bernstein has won numerous honors not only for his musical accomplishments but also for his efforts to further international good will. In his 1962 essay "What Makes Music American?" he discusses nationalistic music, music that seems to belong to a particular people and culture, and he attempts to define the characteristics inherent in truly American music.

Flag, Jasper Johns, 1958.

Leonard Bernstein

What Makes Music American?

I don't think there's anyone in the country—or in the world, for that matter—who wouldn't know right away that Gershwin's[1] music—say, "An American in Paris"—is American music. It's got "America" written all over it, not just in the title and not just because the composer was American. But it's in the music itself: It sounds American, smells American, makes you feel American when you hear it.

Now, why is that? What makes certain music seem to *belong* to us?

Almost every country or nation has some kind of music that sounds right and natural for its people. We call it "nationalistic" music. Sometimes it's just folk music, very simple songs—or not even songs: maybe just prayers for rain banged out on Congo drums, or a sort

---

1. **Gershwin's:** referring to George Gershwin (1898–1937), American composer and jazz pianist.

of primitive chanting in the Arab style, or dance music like a mazurka from Poland or a reel from Ireland. You couldn't mistake a Spanish rhythm in a million years. For instance, in the "Spanish Rhapsody," by Ravel,[2] the rhythm, with the sound of the castanets or the tambourine, makes the music definitely Spanish in character. In most countries people have been singing the same little tunes for hundreds of years. They have inherited them from their forefathers, who got them from their forefathers. So when the Russians hear a Tchaikovsky[3] symphony, they feel closer to it than, say, a Frenchman does, or than we do.

Now take the ancestors of some of America's leading composers. Howard Hanson's parents came from Sweden, Walter Piston's from Italy, and George Gershwin's from Russia, while Charles Ives came from a long line of New England whalers, who were originally British.

With all these different forefathers we have, what is it that we all have in common that we could call our folk music? That's a tough question. We haven't had very much time to develop a folk music. Don't forget, America is a very new country compared with all those others. We're not even two hundred years old yet! And so our music is also still very young.

Our really serious American music didn't even begin until about seventy-five years ago. At that time, the few American composers we had just imitated the European composers, like Brahms, Liszt, and Wagner.[4] For instance, there was a very fine composer named George W. Chadwick, who wrote expert, deeply felt music; but much of it is difficult to distinguish from Brahms or Wagner.

Around the beginning of our twentieth century, American composers started to feel self-conscious about not writing American-sounding music. And it took a foreigner to make them feel it. He was the Czechoslovakian composer Dvořák,[5] who came here on a visit and was amazed to find all our composers writing the same kind of music he wrote. So he said to the American composers, "Look, why don't you use your own folk music when you write? You've got marvelous stuff here, the music of the Indians, who are the real native Americans. Use it!" But he was forgetting the important thing, that Indian music has nothing to do with most of us. Our forefathers were not Indians, and so the Indians' music is not our music.

But Dvořák didn't worry about that, and he got so excited that he decided to write an American symphony himself and show us how it could be done. So he made up some Indian themes (and some Negro themes, because he decided also that Negro folk music was American), and he wrote a whole "New World" Symphony around those themes. The trouble was that the music doesn't sound American at all. It sounds Czech, which is what it should sound, and very pretty it is, too.

In spite of this, Dvořák made a big impression on the American composers of his time. They all got excited, too, and began to write hundreds of so-called American pieces with Indian and Negro melodies in them. . . . You can't just decide to be American; you can't be nationalistic on purpose. That was the mistake, but it was a natural mistake to make at the beginning. Those early composers were just learning to be Americans.

However, out of this period came some pretty fine music, by Edward MacDowell, for instance. Among other things, he wrote a suite that uses Indian folk material in it, but I still can't say that it sounds really American. Then there was a composer named Henry Gilbert, who was also very talented and who was more

2. **Ravel** [rə vel′]: Maurice Ravel (1875–1937), French composer.

3. **Tchaikovsky** [chĭ kôf′skē]: Peter Ilich Tchaikovsky (1840–1893), Russian composer.

4. **Brahms** [brämz], **Liszt** [list] . . . **Wagner** [väg′nər]: Johannes Brahms (1833–1897), German; Franz Liszt (1811–1866), Hungarian; Richard Wagner (1813–1883), German.

5. **Dvořák** [dvôr′zhäk]: Anton Dvořák (1841–1904), Czech composer.

interested in Negro themes. And there were many others. But there was still no real American music.

By the time the First World War was over, something new and very special had happened in American music. Jazz had been born, and it changed everything. At last there was something like an American folk music that belonged to all Americans. Everybody danced the fox-trot and knew how to sing "Alexander's Ragtime Band," whether they were from Texas, North Dakota, or South Carolina. So any serious composer growing up in America at that time couldn't keep jazz out of his ears or out of his music. It was part of him; it was in the air he breathed. Aaron Copland began to write pieces like "Music for the Theater," which is filled with jazz ideas, and they were played not by jazz bands or dance orchestras but by great and serious organizations like the Boston Symphony Orchestra.

This rage for jazz was so strong that European composers began using it in their music too—composers like Ravel, even Stravinsky.[6]

But certainly the composer who used jazz most was Gershwin. When he wrote his "Rhapsody in Blue" in 1924, he really rocked New York, and then the whole country, and finally the whole civilized world.

Here at last was a real, natural folk influence. . . . But our composers were still being American on purpose, so to speak. Only now they were using jazz to be American, instead of Indian and Creole[7] themes.

Then, during the thirties the jazz influence became a part of their living and breathing, and the composers didn't even have to think twice about it. They just wrote music, and it came out American all by itself. That was much better.

For instance, take the rhythms of jazz. The thing that makes jazz rhythms so special is something called "syncopation," which means getting an accent where you don't expect it, or getting a strong beat where a weak beat should be.

In the thirties syncopation became part of the music, so much so that the music doesn't even sound like jazz any more. In other words, it was no longer using syncopation on purpose, but just by accident, by habit. A brand-new American rhythm had come out of jazz and had become a natural part of our musical speech. For instance, a composer named Roger Sessions wrote a piece for organ, a chorale prelude. A chorale prelude is a serious piece with a religious atmosphere, the last place in the world where you'd expect to find syncopated accents. But there they were, deep in the music, making it American but without sounding like jazz.

It was like the English language spoken with an American accent. The accent, the rhythm, the speed all came out of our way of moving and living. Just think what a difference there is between the English spoken by the British poet Keats and the English of an American poet! Listen to Keats:

> Bright star, would I were steadfast as thou
>   art!
> Not in lone splendor hung aloft the night,
> And watching, with eternal lids apart,
>   Like Nature's patient, sleepless eremite,[8]
> The moving waters at their priestlike task
>   Of pure ablution[9] round earth's human
>   shores. . . .[10]

Now compare that English with this English by an American poet named Kenneth Fearing:

> And wow he died as wow he lived,
>   going whop to the office and blooie
>   home to

---

6. **Stravinsky** [strä vin′skē]: Igor Stravinsky (1882–1971), Russian-born composer who later became an American citizen.
7. **Creole** [krē′ōl]: characteristic of the descendants of the original French and Spanish settlers on the Gulf Coast, especially in Louisiana.

8. **eremite** [er′ə mīt]: religious recluse; hermit.
9. **ablution**: washing, especially as a religious ceremony.
10. **Bright star . . . shores**: from Keats's lyric "Bright Star."

sleep and
biff got married and bam had children
and
oof got fired,
zowie did he live and zowie did he die. . . .[11]

Almost like two different languages, aren't they?

Well, something like that happened to American music. The jazz influence grew to be such a deep part of our musical language that it changed the whole sound of our music.

I don't want to give you the idea that jazz is the whole story. Actually, it's only a small part of it, though an extremely important one. There are many other things about American music that make it sound American, things that have nothing to do with jazz but have to do with different sides of our American personality. One of the main personality traits in our music is the one of youth—loud, strong, and wildly optimistic. William Schuman is a composer who is a perfect example of this quality. His "American Festival Overture" is full of rip-roaring vitality and reminds you of kids having a marvelous time. In fact, this overture was based on a street call that Schuman used when he was a kid, when the fellows used to call each other to come out and play: "Wee-aw-kee!"

Then there's another kind of American vitality, not so much of the city but belonging more to the rugged West, and full of pioneer energy. The music of Roy Harris has lots of it.

Then there's a kind of loneliness to be found in a lot of American music that's different from other kinds of loneliness. You find it in the way the notes are spaced out very far apart, like the wide, open spaces our huge country is full of. You can even see it in the way the music is written. A good example is the section of Copland's ballet "Billy the Kid" that describes a quiet night on the prairie.

Then there's a kind of sweet, simple, sentimental quality that gets into our music from hymn singing, especially from Southern Baptist hymns. We find this kind of very American, naive quality in Virgil Thomson's opera *The Mother of Us All.*

Then we have another kind of sentimentality that comes out of our popular songs—a sort of crooning pleasure, like taking a long, warm bath, as in Randall Thompson's Second Symphony, which has a theme that is almost like a song Sinatra sings.

There are as many sides to American music as there are to the American people—our great, varied, many-sided democracy. And perhaps that's the main quality of all: the manysidedness. Think of all the races and personalities from all over the globe that make up our country: French, German, Scotch, Italian, African, Scandinavian, and all the rest. So what our composers are nourished on, finally, is a folk music that is probably the richest in the world. And all of it is American, whether it's jazz, or square-dance tunes, or cowboy songs, or hillbilly music, or rock 'n' roll, or Cuban mambos or Mexican huapangos, or Missouri hymn singing. It's like all the different accents we have in our speech: there's a little Mexican in some Texas accents, and a little Swedish in the Minnesota accent, and a little Slavic in the Brooklyn accent, and a little Irish in the Boston accent. But it's all American, just like Copland's "Billy the Kid," which also has a Mexican accent here and a Brooklyn accent there. As you listen to it, you hear the sweet, slow cowboy drawl in the first tune, then rip-roaring American rhythms in the gunfight that follows, not to mention the honky-tonk sound of an old-fashioned Western saloon. And hearing all these "accents," you can feel strongly what it means to be an American, a descendant of all the nations on the earth.

---

11. **And wow . . . did he die:** from Kenneth Fearing's poem "Dirge." (See page 584 for another poem by Fearing, "Cracked Record Blues.")

Leonard Bernstein **819**

STUDY QUESTIONS

Recalling

1. How does Bernstein define "nationalistic music" (paragraph 3)? What does he say American musicians have had little time to do (paragraph 6)?
2. According to Bernstein, when did really serious American music begin? What did Dvořák do after he visited America? What impact did he have on American composers?
3. According to Bernstein, what "new and special" development in American music occurred after World War I? Which American composer did it affect the most?
4. Identify at least six characteristics of American music that Bernstein mentions in his last six paragraphs. What does the last paragraph say about the "folk music" that "nourishes" American composers?

Interpreting

5. What does Bernstein basically mean by "serious music"?
6. Explain the importance of jazz to American music, as Bernstein see it.
7. What, ultimately, does American music suggest, according to Bernstein?

Extending

8. What problem do you find in Bernstein's comparison of English Romantic poet John Keats with the twentieth-century American poet Kenneth Fearing (page 584)? Which American poet do you think would have been a better choice for Bernstein's purpose, and why?

LITERARY FOCUS

Exposition

Exposition is one of the four main types of prose writing. The others are description (see page 92), narration (see page 113), and persuasion (see page 22).

Most essays use exposition to give information or to explain the nature of a particular subject. If you were to write an essay telling about some important aspects of modern dance technique or how to hit a backhand in tennis or how to make a pizza, your essay would be expository.

In "What Makes Music American?" Leonard Bernstein discusses the qualities in American music that make it American. To do so, he uses some important methods of exposition. He *defines* nationalistic music and *illustrates* his definition with several examples. He *identifies* some important American and European composers. He *analyzes* the nationalistic qualities of early American music and jazz. He *compares and contrasts* the English language and the American language. Finally, he *classifies* American music according to American characteristics.

Thinking About Exposition

■ Identify and discuss at least two other specific examples of expository methods in Bernstein's essay. Tell which method is used—definition, illustration, identification, analysis, comparison and contrast, or classification.

VOCABULARY

Words from Music

In his essay on American music, Leonard Bernstein uses many musical terms that have entered into our everyday vocabulary. Using your dictionary or a dictionary of musical terms, define each of the following words. Tell what each word means as a musical term and then tell what meaning it also has in our everyday vocabulary.

1. rhapsody	4. symphonic	7. theme
2. suite	5. prelude	8. opera
3. overture	6. tune	9. solo

COMPOSITION

Writing About Nonfiction

■ Write a brief composition about Bernstein's purpose in the essay "What Makes Music American?" Begin by stating his purpose in your own words. Then identify the techniques he uses to accomplish his purpose, such as facts, examples, and opinions. Conclude by summarizing Bernstein's conclusions and telling whether you think he has accomplished his purpose. *For help with this assignment, refer to Lesson 4 in the Writing About Literature Handbook at the back of this book.*

Writing an Expository Essay

■ Name an experience or an achievement that you consider especially American. Write an essay in which you identify and discuss the qualities that make it genuinely American. Use as many of the methods of exposition as you can.

Ralph Ellison   *born 1914*

Ralph Ellison's central theme is freedom, not only social and political freedom but the inner freedom of the individual spirit. This is the freedom Ellison himself achieved when he decided, as he said, "to run the risk of his own humanity."

Ralph Ellison grew up in Oklahoma City, Oklahoma. He loved music from an early age, played the trumpet in high school, and was especially inspired by jazz. From 1933 to 1936 he studied music and composition at Tuskegee Institute in Alabama. A new interest in sculpture drew him to New York City, where he also performed as a jazz musician.

In New York Ellison met the writers Langston Hughes and Richard Wright, who inspired and encouraged him to write. Ellison had read widely in American literature and had been particularly influenced by T. S. Eliot's poem *The Waste Land.* Now Hughes and Wright pointed him toward other great writers—Dostoevsky, Conrad, Joyce, Faulkner, and Hemingway among them. As he studied their works, Ellison learned the lessons of modernism and began to write seriously himself.

Ellison's first novel, *Invisible Man,* appeared in 1952. For its intense, deeply affecting, sometimes harrowing portrayal of a young black man growing up in the South and in Harlem, it won the National Book Award and immediate recognition as a classic of modern literature. In a poll of two hundred writers and critics, *Invisible Man* was named the most distinguished novel published in America between 1945 and 1965.

Ellison has lectured widely on black culture and folklore and has taught literature and creative writing at numerous colleges and universities. His second book, *Shadow and Act* (1964), is a collection of interviews and essays, including "Hidden Name and Complex Fate"—in which the author ponders the significance of the name his father gave him.

Ralph Ellison

from Hidden Name and Complex Fate

Our names, being the gift of others, must be made our own.

Once while listening to the play of a two-year-old girl who did not know she was under observation, I heard her saying over and over again, at first with questioning and then with sounds of growing satisfaction, "I am Mimi Livisay? . . . *I* am Mimi Livisay. I *am* Mimi Livisay . . . I am *Mimi* Li-visay! I am Mimi . . ."

And in deed and in fact she was—or became so soon thereafter, by working playfully to establish the unity between herself and her name.

For many of us this is far from easy. We must learn to wear our names within all the noise and confusion of the environment in which we find ourselves; make them the center of all of our associations with the world, with man and with nature. We must charge them with all our emotions, our hopes, hates, loves, aspirations. They must become our masks and our shields and the containers of all those values and traditions which we learn and/or imagine as being the meaning of our familial past. . . .

Perhaps, taken in aggregate, these European names which (sometimes with irony, sometimes with pride, but always with personal investment) represent a certain triumph of the spirit, speaking to us of those who rallied, reassembled and transformed themselves and who under dismembering pressures refused to die. "Brothers and sisters," I once heard a Negro preacher exhort, "let us make up our faces before the world, and our names shall sound throughout the land with honor! For we ourselves are our *true* names, not their epithets! So let us, I say, Make Up Our Faces and Our Minds!"

Perhaps my preacher had read T. S. Eliot, although I doubt it. And in actuality, it was unnecessary that he do so, for a concern with names and naming was very much a part of that special area of American culture from which I come, and it is precisely for this reason that this example should come to mind in a discussion of my own experience as a writer.

Undoubtedly, writers begin their *conditioning* as manipulators of words long before they become aware of literature—certain Freudians[1] would say at the breast.[2] Perhaps. But if so, that is far too early to be of use at this moment. Of this, though, I am certain: that despite the misconceptions of those educators who trace the reading difficulties experienced by large numbers of Negro children in Northern schools to their Southern background, these children are, in *their* familiar South, facile manipulators of words. I know, too, that the Negro community is deadly in its ability to create nicknames and to spot all that is ludicrous in an unlikely name or that which is incongruous in conduct. Names are not qualities; nor are words, in this particular sense, actions. To assume that they are could cost one his life many times a day. Language skills depend to a large extent upon a knowledge of the details, the manners, the objects, the folkways, the psychological patterns, of a given environment. Humor and wit depend upon much the same awareness, and so does the suggestive power of names.

"A small brown bowlegged Negro with the name 'Franklin D. Roosevelt Jones' might sound like a clown to someone who looks at him from the outside," said my friend Albert Murray, "but on the other hand he just might turn out to be a fireside operator. He might just lie back in all of that comic juxtaposition of

---

1. **Freudians** [froi′dē ənz]: adherents of the psychoanalytical theories and methods of Sigmund Freud (1856–1939).
2. **at the breast:** in earliest infancy.

names and manipulate you deaf, dumb and blind—and you not even suspecting it, because you're thrown out of stance by his name! There you are, so dazzled by the F. D. R. image—which you *know* you can't see—and so delighted with your own superior position that you don't realize that its *Jones* who must be confronted."

Well, as you must suspect, all of this speculation on the matter of names has a purpose, and now, because it is tied up so ironically with my own experience as a writer, I must turn to my own name.

For in the dim beginnings, before I ever thought consciously of writing, there was my own name, and there was, doubtless, a certain magic in it. From the start I was uncomfortable with it, and in my earliest years it caused me much puzzlement. Neither could I understand what a poet was, nor why, exactly, my father had chosen to name me after one. Perhaps I could have understood it perfectly well had he named me after his own father, but that name had been given to an older brother who died and thus was out of the question. But why hadn't he named me after a hero, such as Jack Johnson,[3] or a soldier like Colonel Charles Young, or a great seaman like Admiral Dewey, or an educator like Booker T. Washington, or a great orator and abolitionist like Frederick Douglass? Or again, why hadn't he named me (as so many Negro parents had done) after President Teddy Roosevelt?

Instead, he named me after someone called Ralph Waldo Emerson, and then, when I was three, he died. It was too early for me to have understood his choice, although I'm sure he must have explained it many times, and it was also too soon for me to have made the connection between my name and my father's love for reading. Much later, after I began to write and work with words, I came to suspect that he was aware of the suggestive powers of names and of the magic involved in naming.

I recall an odd conversation with my mother during my early teens in which she mentioned their interest in, of all things, prenatal culture! But for a long time I actually knew only that my father read a lot, and that he admired this remote Mr. Emerson, who was something called a "poet and philosopher" —so much so that he named his second son after him.

I knew, also, that whatever his motives, the combination of names he'd given me caused me no end of trouble from the moment when I could talk well enough to respond to the ritualized question which grownups put to very young children. Emerson's name was quite familiar to Negroes in Oklahoma during those days when World War I was brewing, and adults, eager to show off their knowledge of literary figures, and obviously amused by the

---

3. **Jack Johnson:** American boxing champion (1908–1915).

joke implicit in such a small brown nubbin[4] of a boy carrying around such a heavy moniker,[5] would invariably repeat my first two names and then to my great annoyance, they'd add "Emerson."

And I, in my confusion, would reply, "No, *no, I'm* not Emerson; he's the little boy who lives next door." Which only made them laugh all the louder. "Oh no," they'd say, "*you're* Ralph Waldo Emerson," while I had fantasies of blue murder.

For a while the presence next door of my little friend, Emerson, made it unnecessary for me to puzzle too often over this peculiar adult confusion. And since there were other Negro boys named Ralph in the city, I came to suspect that there was something about the combination of names which produced their laughter. Even today I know of only one other Ralph who had as much comedy made out of his name, a campus politician and deep-voiced orator whom I knew at Tuskegee, who was called in friendly ribbing, *Ralph Waldo Emerson Edgar Allan Poe,* spelled Powe. This must have been quite a trial for him, but I had been initiated much earlier.

During my early school years the name continued to puzzle me, for it constantly evoked in the faces of others some secret. It was as though I possessed some treasure or some defect, which was invisible to my own eyes and ears; something which I had but did not *possess,* like a piece of property in South Carolina, which was mine but which I could not have until some future time. I recall finding, about this time, while seeking adventure in back alleys—which possess for boys a superiority over playgrounds like that which kitchen utensils possess over toys designed for infants—a large photographic lens. I remember nothing of its optical qualities, of its speed or color correction, but it gleamed with crystal mystery and it was beautiful.

---

4. **nubbin:** something small or undeveloped.
5. **moniker:** slang for "name" or "nickname."

Mounted handsomely in a tube of shiny brass, it spoke to me of distant worlds of possibility. I played with it, looking through it with squinted eyes, holding it in shafts of sunlight, and tried to use it for a magic lantern. But most of this was as unrewarding as my attempts to make the music come from a phonograph record by holding the needle in my fingers.

I could burn holes through newspapers with it, or I could pretend that it was a telescope, the barrel of a cannon, or the third eye of a monster—*I* being the monster—but I could do nothing at all about its proper function of making images; nothing to make it yield its secret. But I could not discard it.

Older boys sought to get it away from me by offering knives or tops, agate marbles or whole zoos of grass snakes and horned toads in trade, but I held on to it. No one, not even the white boys I knew, had such a lens, and it was my own good luck to have found it. Thus I would hold on to it until such time as I could acquire the parts needed to make it function. Finally I put it aside and it remained buried in my box of treasures, dusty and dull, to be lost and forgotten as I grew older and became interested in music.

I had reached by now the grades where it was necessary to learn something about Mr. Emerson and what he had written, such as the "Concord Hymn" and the essay "Self-Reliance," and in following his advice, I reduced the "Waldo" to a simple and, I hoped, mysterious "W," and in my own reading I avoided his works like the plague. I could no more deal with my name—I shall never really master it— than I could find a creative use for my lens. . . .

I could suppress the name of my namesake out of respect for the achievements of its original bearer but I cannot escape the obligation of attempting to achieve some of the things which he asked of the American writer. As Henry James suggested, being an American is an arduous task, and for most of us, I suspect, the difficulty begins with the name.

STUDY QUESTIONS

Recalling

1. What idea about names does Ellison introduce in his first sentence? In paragraph 4, what does he say we must learn?
2. What does Ellison say his name "constantly evoked" during his early school years (page 824)? What does he say possessing such a name was like?
3. What "mysterious object" did Ellison, as a boy, find in a "back alley"? Of what did it "speak to him"? What does he say he could *not* do with it? How did he react when other boys wanted him to trade it away?
4. What influenced Ellison to reduce "Waldo" to "W," according to page 824? To what does he compare his boyhood failure to "master" his name? What can he now not "escape," according to his final paragraph?

Interpreting

5. Identify three people or groups to which this essay pays tribute. What effects does Ellison suggest these people or groups had on forming his identity and career?
6. Consider the first five paragraphs of the essay. What modern need or dilemma does Ellison suggest is tied to the interest in one's name?
7. Why is Ellison's comparison between his name and his lens especially appropriate?
8. To what idea of Transcendentalism (page 154) is Ellison referring when he explains why he shortens his middle name to "W"? To what theme or concern of Emerson's does he refer in his last paragraph?
9. Basically, why does Ellison still feel he has been unable to "possess" his name?

Extending

10. People sometimes change their names from the names they are given at birth. Why do you think they do this, and how do such changes relate to the ideas expressed in this essay?

COMPOSITION

Writing About Nonfiction

Ellison covers many different topics in "Hidden Name and Complex Fate." He incorporates details, anecdotes, and opinions, all of which point toward the main topic—his name. Write a composition analyzing Ellison's purpose in this essay. How does he use his examples and opinions to help achieve his purpose? *For help with this assignment, refer to Lesson 4 in the Writing About Literature Handbook at the back of this book.*

Writing About Names

Choose a name that is interesting to you—the name of a person, a place, a group, or an organization. Write a composition about the meaning you find in it. Discuss its origin, its associations, and any hidden meaning it seems to have. Include in your composition your own observations about how our names affect our everyday experiences.

N. Scott Momaday   *born 1934*

The novelist and poet N. Scott Momaday, a Kiowa Indian, acknowledges his vital interest in all aspects of American Indian history, culture, and art. Since 1963, along with writing, he has taught American Indian literature, folklore, and mythology at many universities.

Momaday was born in Lawton, Oklahoma. In addition to teaching, his father was a distinguished artist and his mother was a respected author. Momaday attended schools on Apache, Navaho, and Pueblo reservations in the Southwest before entering the University of New Mexico in 1952. He has written several highly acclaimed books, including *House Made of Dawn,* awarded the Pulitzer Prize for fiction in 1969, *Angle of Geese and Other Poems* (1974), *The Gourd Dancer* (1976), and *The Names* (1976).

Momaday is best known for *The Way to Rainy Mountain* (1969). This delicate and yet vibrant collection of imaginatively interwoven stories and legends of the Kiowa presents a picture of their history, mythology, and world view. In this section Momaday remembers his own past and the past of his people.

N. Scott Momaday

from The Way to Rainy Mountain

A single knoll rises out of the plain in Oklahoma, north and west of the Wichita Range. For my people, the Kiowas,[1] it is an old landmark, and they gave it the name Rainy Mountain. The hardest weather in the world is there. Winter brings blizzards, hot tornadic winds arise in the spring, and in summer the prairie is an anvil's edge. The grass turns brittle and brown, and it cracks beneath your feet. There are green belts along the rivers and creeks, linear groves of hickory and pecan, willow and witch hazel. At a distance in July or August the steaming foliage seems almost to writhe in fire.

Great green and yellow grasshoppers are everywhere in the tall grass, popping up like corn to sting the flesh, and tortoises crawl about on the red earth, going nowhere in the plenty of time. Loneliness is an aspect of the land. All things in the plain are isolate; there is no confusion of objects in the eye, but *one* hill or *one* tree or *one* man. To look upon that landscape in the early morning, with the sun at your back, is to lose the sense of proportion. Your imagination comes to life, and this, you think, is where Creation was begun.

I returned to Rainy Mountain in July. My grandmother had died in the spring, and I wanted to be at her grave. She had lived to be very old and at last infirm. Her only living

---

1. **Kiowas** [kī′ō wäz]: Plains Indians who migrated from Montana and other western states to Oklahoma.

daughter was with her when she died, and I was told that in death her face was that of a child.

I like to think of her as a child. When she was born, the Kiowas were living the last great moment of their history. For more than a hundred years they had controlled the open range from the Smoky Hill River to the Red, from the headwaters of the Canadian to the fork of the Arkansas and Cimarron. In alliance with the Comanches, they had ruled the whole of the southern Plains. War was their sacred business, and they were among the finest horsemen the world had ever known. But warfare for the Kiowas was preeminently a matter of disposition rather than of survival, and they never understood the grim, unrelenting advance of the U.S. Cavalry. When at last, divided and ill-provisioned, they were driven onto the Staked Plains in the cold rains of autumn, they fell into panic. In Palo Duro Canyon they abandoned their crucial stores to pillage and had nothing then but their lives. In order to save themselves, they surrendered to the soldiers at Fort Sill and were imprisoned in the old stone corral that now stands as a military museum. My grandmother was spared the humiliation of those high gray walls by eight or ten years, but she must have known from birth the affliction of defeat, the dark brooding of old warriors.

Her name was Aho, and she belonged to the last culture to evolve in North America. Her forebears came down from the high country in western Montana nearly three centuries ago. They were a mountain people, a mysterious tribe of hunters whose language has never been positively classified in any major group. In the late seventeenth century they began a long migration to the south and east. It was a journey toward the dawn, and it led to a golden age. Along the way the Kiowas were befriended by the Crows, who gave them the culture and religion of the Plains. They acquired horses, and their ancient nomadic spirit was suddenly free of the ground. They acquired Tai-me, the sacred Sun Dance doll, from that moment the object and symbol of their worship, and so shared in the divinity of the sun. Not least, they acquired the sense of destiny, therefore courage and pride. When they entered upon the southern Plains they had been transformed. No longer were they slaves to the simple necessity of survival; they were a lordly and dangerous society of fighters and thieves, hunters and priests of the sun. According to their origin myth, they entered the world through a hollow log. From one point of view, their migration was the fruit of an old prophecy, for indeed they emerged from a sunless world.

Although my grandmother lived out her long life in the shadow of Rainy Mountain, the immense landscape of the continental interior lay like memory in her blood. She could tell of the Crows, whom she had never seen, and of the Black Hills, where she had never been. I wanted to see in reality what she had seen more perfectly in the mind's eye, and traveled fifteen hundred miles to begin my pilgrimage.

Yellowstone, it seemed to me, was the top of the world, a region of deep lakes and dark timber, canyons and waterfalls. But, beautiful as it is, one might have the sense of confinement there. The skyline in all directions is close at hand, the high wall of the woods and deep cleavages of shade. There is a perfect freedom in the mountains, but it belongs to the eagle and the elk, the badger and the bear. The Kiowas reckoned their stature by the distance they could see, and they were bent and blind in the wilderness.

Descending eastward, the highland meadows are a stairway to the plain. In July the inland slope of the Rockies is luxuriant with flax and buckwheat, stonecrop[2] and larkspur. The earth unfolds and the limit of the land recedes. Clusters of trees, and animals grazing far in the distance, cause the vision to reach away and wonder to build upon the mind. The sun follows a longer course in the day, and the sky is immense beyond all comparison. The great billowing clouds that sail upon it are shadows

---

2. **stonecrop:** a flowering plant found on rocks and walls.

that move upon the grain like water, dividing light. Farther down, in the land of the Crows and Blackfeet, the plain is yellow. Sweet clover takes hold of the hills and bends upon itself to cover and seal the soil. There the Kiowas paused on their way; they had come to the place where they must change their lives. The sun is at home on the plains. Precisely there does it have the certain character of a god. When the Kiowas came to the land of the Crows, they could see the dark lees[3] of the hills at dawn across the Bighorn River, the profusion of light on the grain shelves, the oldest deity ranging after the solstices. Not yet would they veer southward to the caldron of the land that lay below; they must wean their blood[4] from the northern winter and hold the mountains a while longer in view. They bore Tai-me in procession to the east.

A dark mist lay over the Black Hills, and the land was like iron. At the top of a ridge I caught sight of Devil's Tower upthrust against the gray sky as if in the birth of time the core of the earth had broken through its crust and the motion of the world was begun. There are things in nature that engender an awful quiet in the heart of man; Devil's Tower is one of them. Two centuries ago, because they could not do otherwise, the Kiowas made a legend at the base of the rock. My grandmother said:

Eight children were there at play, seven sisters and their brother. Suddenly the boy was struck dumb; he trembled and began to run upon his hands and feet. His fingers became claws, and his body was covered with fur. Directly there was a bear where the boy had been. The sisters were terrified; they ran, and the bear after them. They came to the stump of a great tree, and the tree spoke to them. It bade them climb upon it, and as they did so it began to rise into the air. The bear came to kill them, but they were just beyond its reach. It reared against the tree and scored the bark all around with its claws. The seven sisters were borne into the sky, and they became the stars of the Big Dipper.

From that moment, and so long as the legend lives, the Kiowas have kinsmen in the night sky. Whatever they were in the mountains, they could be no more. However tenuous their well-being, however much they had suffered and would suffer again, they had found a way out of the wilderness.

My grandmother had a reverence for the sun, a holy regard that now is all but gone out of mankind. There was a wariness in her, and an ancient awe. She was a Christian in her later years, but she had come a long way about, and she never forgot her birthright. As a child she had been to the Sun Dances; she had taken part in those annual rites, and by them she had learned the restoration of her people in the presence of Tai-me. She was about seven when the last Kiowa Sun Dance was held in 1887 on the Washita River above Rainy Mountain Creek. The buffalo were gone. In order to consummate the ancient sacrifice—to impale the head of a buffalo bull upon the medicine tree—a delegation of old men journeyed into Texas, there to beg and barter for an animal from the Goodnight herd. She was ten when the Kiowas came together for the last time as a living Sun Dance culture. They could find no buffalo; they had to hang an old hide from the sacred tree. Before the dance could begin, a company of soldiers rode out from Fort Sill under orders to disperse the tribe. Forbidden without cause the essential act of their faith, having seen the wild herds slaughtered and left to rot upon the ground, the Kiowas backed away forever from the medicine tree. That was July 20, 1890, at the great bend of the Washita. My grandmother was there. Without bitterness, and for as long as she lived, she bore a vision of deicide.[5]

Now that I can have her only in memory, I see my grandmother in the several postures that were peculiar to her: standing at the wood stove on a winter morning and turning meat in

---

3. **lees:** sheltered sides, away from the wind.
4. **wean their blood:** become acclimated by removing themselves gradually.

5. **deicide** [dē′ə sīd]: killing of a god.

a great iron skillet; sitting at the south window, bent above her beadwork, and afterwards, when her vision failed, looking down for a long time into the fold of her hands; going out upon a cane, very slowly as she did when the weight of age came upon her; praying. I remember her most often at prayer. She made long, rambling prayers out of suffering and hope, having seen many things. I was never sure that I had the right to hear, so exclusive were they of all mere custom and company. The last time I saw her she prayed standing by the side of her bed at night, naked to the waist, the light of a kerosene lamp moving upon her dark skin. Her long, black hair, always drawn and braided in the day, lay upon her shoulders and against her breasts like a shawl. I do not speak Kiowa, and I never understood her prayers, but there was something inherently sad in the sound, some merest hesitation upon the syllables of sorrow. She began in a high and descending pitch, exhausting her breath to silence; then again and again—and always the same intensity of effort, of something that is, and is not, like urgency in the human voice. Transported so in the dancing light among the shadows of her room, she seemed beyond the reach of time. But that was illusion; I think I knew then that I should not see her again.

Houses are like sentinels in the plain, old keepers of the weather watch. There, in a very little while, wood takes on the appearance of great age. All colors wear soon away in the wind and rain, and then the wood is burned gray and the grain appears and the nails turn red with rust. The windowpanes are black and opaque; you imagine there is nothing within, and indeed there are many ghosts, bones given up to the land. They stand here and there against the sky, and you approach them for a longer time than you expect. They belong in the distance; it is their domain.

Once there was a lot of sound in my grandmother's house, a lot of coming and going, feasting and talk. The summers there were full of excitement and reunion. The Kiowas are a summer people; they abide the cold and keep to themselves, but when the season turns and the land becomes warm and vital they cannot hold still; an old love of going returns upon them. The aged visitors who came to my grandmother's house when I was a child were made of lean and leather, and they bore themselves upright. They wore great black hats and bright ample shirts that shook in the wind. They rubbed fat upon their hair and wound their braids with strips of colored cloth. Some of them painted their faces and carried the scars of old and cherished enmities. They were an old council of warlords, come to remind and be reminded of who they were. Their wives and daughters served them well. The women might indulge themselves; gossip was at once the mark and compensation of their servitude. They made loud and elaborate talk among themselves, full of jest and gesture, fright and false alarm. They went abroad in fringed and flowered shawls, bright beadwork and German silver.[6] They were at home in the kitchen, and they prepared meals that were banquets.

There were frequent prayer meetings, and great nocturnal feasts. When I was a child I played with my cousins outside, where the lamplight fell upon the ground and the singing of the old people rose up around us and carried away into the darkness. There were a lot of good things to eat, a lot of laughter and surprise. And afterwards, when the quiet returned, I lay down with my grandmother and could hear the frogs away by the river and feel the motion of the air.

Now there is a funeral silence in the rooms, the endless wake of some final word. The walls have closed in upon my grandmother's house. When I returned to it in mourning, I saw for the first time in my life how small it was. It was late at night, and there was a white moon, nearly full. I sat for a long time on the stone steps by the kitchen door. From there I could see out across the land; I could see the long row of trees by the creek, the low light upon the rolling plains, and the stars of the Big Dipper. Once I looked at the moon and caught

---

6. **German silver:** alloy resembling real silver.

sight of a strange thing. A cricket had perched upon the handrail, only a few inches away from me. My line of vision was such that the creature filled the moon like a fossil. It had gone there, I thought, to live and die, for there, of all places, was its small definition made whole and eternal. A warm wind rose up and purled[7] like the longing within me.

The next morning I awoke at dawn and went out on the dirt road to Rainy Mountain.

---

7. **purled:** rippled.

It was already hot, and the grasshoppers began to fill the air. Still, it was early in the morning, and the birds sang out of the shadows. The long yellow grass on the mountain shone in the bright light, and a scissortail[8] hied above the land. There, where it ought to be, at the end of a long and legendary way, was my grandmother's grave. Here and there on the dark stones were ancestral names. Looking back once, I saw the mountain and came away.

---

8. **scissortail:** small gray and pink bird with a forked tail.

STUDY QUESTIONS

Recalling

1. Why did Momaday go to Rainy Mountain in July?

2. What does Momaday say the Kiowas were living when his grandmother was born (paragraph 3)? What does he say she must have known from birth?

3. What legend was inspired by Devil's Tower? What does Momaday say the Kiowas have as long as the legend lives?

4. What happened the last time the Kiowa came together as a living Sun Dance culture?

5. How does Momaday describe his grandmother's prayers on page 829? From what did she seem beyond reach the last time he saw her praying? What word does he use to contradict this perception?

6. Identify at least two events that once took place in Momaday's grandmother's house. What does Momaday notice about the house for the first time when he returns to it in mourning? What stars does he see above the plain that night? What thought does he have about the cricket he sees against the moon?

Interpreting

7. To what two things or people does Momaday pay respect in visiting Rainy Mountain? How are the two associated in his mind?

8. What did the Kiowa lose in 1890? What do the lifelong practices of Momaday's grandmother and her neighbors suggest the Kiowa did not lose?

9. What does the appearance of the Big Dipper in the next-to-last paragraph suggest? What does the image of the cricket suggest about Momaday's grandmother and her people?

Extending

10. How can literature help preserve the past?

COMPOSITION

Applying a Statement About Literature

■ It has been said that the subject of Momaday's writing is "a time that is gone forever, a landscape that is incomparable, and a human spirit which endures." Write a brief composition applying this statement to the selection from *The Way to Rainy Mountain*. First explain the comment in your own words. Then apply each part of the statement to specific examples from the selection. Conclude with your own observations about how the statement can apply to other works of literature as well. *For help with this assignment, refer to Lesson 9 in the Writing About Literature Handbook at the back of this book.*

Writing About Traditions

■ One of Momaday's greatest concerns is the survival of traditions. Write an informal essay about the survival of a tradition in your own time. You may want to write about a tradition you see fading away and that you would like to restore. Consider also writing about a tradition you would like to begin. Include your opinions on the meaning and value of the tradition.

Saul Bellow   *born 1915*

When leading authors and critics were asked to name the twenty best books written since World War II, four of Saul Bellow's novels—*Herzog* (1964), *Henderson the Rain King* (1959), *Seize the Day* (1956), and *The Adventures of Augie March* (1953)—made the list. Bellow is often referred to as the most important American writer of his generation. He is, as the critic Leslie Fiedler said, "of all our novelists the one we need most to understand."

Saul Bellow was born in Lachine, Quebec, Canada. Both his parents had emigrated there from Russia, where his father had been an importer of Egyptian onions. Growing up, Bellow learned four languages—English, Hebrew, Yiddish, and French. When he was nine, his family moved to Chicago, where, Bellow recalls, he spent most of his time in libraries. He attended the University of Chicago and then Northwestern University, from which he graduated in 1937 with honors in sociology and anthropology.

With a scholarship to the University of Wisconsin, Bellow was on his way toward an academic career in anthropology when he discovered a more urgent calling—literature. "Every time I worked on my thesis, it turned out to be a story," he told one interviewer. "I disappeared for the Christmas holidays and I never came back."

Bellow's first two novels, *Dangling Man* (1944) and *The Victim* (1947), won him a small following. *The Adventures of Augie March* won not only greater attention but the National Book Award as well, as did *Herzog* and *Mr. Sammler's Planet* (1970). His two most recent novels are *Humboldt's Gift* (1975), which was awarded the Pulitzer Prize, and *The Dean's December* (1982). In 1976 Bellow was awarded the Nobel Prize for Literature.

Saul Bellow's novels generally concern people alienated by their urban environments but not defeated by them. In novels filled with exuberance, comic invention, and intellectual brilliance, Bellow dramatizes the lives of characters who seem misplaced, disoriented, trapped. Yet these characters come face to face with others who are tough, energetic, and street-wise. As one writer put it, Bellow's achievement lies in his "combination of cultural sophistication and the wisdom of the streets."

In his Nobel Prize Acceptance Speech, Bellow explores the power and value of literature in our time. In stirring language he calls on writers—and on readers—to return to "the center," to the human concerns that are "simple and true."

Saul Bellow receiving Nobel Prize for Literature
from Sweden's King Karl Gustaf, December 1976.

Saul Bellow

from Nobel Prize Acceptance Speech

Every year we see scores of books and articles by writers who tell Americans what a state they are in. All reflect the current crises; all tell us what we must do about them—these analysts are produced by the very disorder and confusion they prescribe for. It is as a novelist that I am considering the extreme moral sensitivity of our contemporaries, their desire for perfection, their intolerance of the defects of society, the touching, the comical boundlessness of their demands, their anxiety, their irritability, their sensitivity, their tender-mindedness, their goodness, their convulsiveness, the recklessness with which they experiment with drugs and touch-therapies[1] and bombs. . . .

And art and literature—what of them? Well, there is a violent uproar but we are not absolutely dominated by it. We are still able to think, to discriminate, and to feel. The purer, subtler, higher activities have not succumbed to fury or to nonsense. Not yet. Books continue to be written and read. It may be more difficult to cut through the whirling mind of a modern reader but it is still possible to reach

---

1. **touch-therapies:** any of various group psychotherapies in which patients touch one another as part of the treatment.

the quiet zone. In the quiet zone we novelists may find that he is devoutly waiting for us. When complications increase, the desire for essentials increases too. The unending cycle of crises that began with the First World War has formed a kind of person, one who has lived through strange and terrible things, and in whom there is an observable shrinkage of prejudices, a casting off of disappointing ideologies, an ability to live with many kinds of madness, and an immense desire for certain durable human goods—truth, for instance; freedom; wisdom. I don't think I am exaggerating; there is plenty of evidence for this. Disintegration? Well, yes. Much is disintegrating but we are experiencing also an odd kind of refining process. . . .

Hegel[2] long ago observed that art no longer engaged the central energies of man. These energies were now engaged by science—a "relentless spirit of rational inquiry." Art had moved to the margins. There it formed "a wide and splendidly varied horizon." . . .

There were European writers in the Nineteenth Century who would not give up the connection of literature with the main human enterprise. The very suggestion would have shocked Tolstoi and Dostoevski.[3] But in the West a separation between great artists and the general public took place. Artists developed a marked contempt for the average reader and the bourgeois[4] mass. The best of them saw clearly enough what sort of civilization Europe had produced, brilliant but unstable, vulnerable, fated to be overtaken by catastrophe.

Despite a show of radicalism and innovation our contemporaries are really very conservative. They follow their Nineteenth Century leaders and hold to the old standards, interpreting history and society much as they were interpreted in the last century. What would writers do today if it occurred to them that literature might once again engage those "central energies," if they were to recognize that an immense desire had arisen for a return from the periphery, for what is simple and true?

Of course we can't come back to the center simply because we wish to, though the realization that we are wanted might electrify us. The force of the crisis is so great that it might summon us back. But prescriptions are futile. One can't tell writers what to do. The imagination must find its own path. But one can fervently wish that they—that we—would come back from the periphery. We writers do not represent mankind adequately. What account do Americans give of themselves, what accounts of them are given by psychologists, sociologists, historians, journalists, and writers? In a kind of contractual daylight they see themselves in the ways with which we are desperately familiar. These images of contractual daylight, so boring to Robbe-Grillet[5] and to me, originate in the contemporary world view: We put into our books the consumer, civil servant, football fan, lover, television viewer. And in the contractual daylight version their life is a kind of death. There is another life coming from an insistent sense of what we are which denies these daylight formulations and the false life—the death-in-life—they make for us. For it is false, and we know it, and our secret and incoherent resistance to it cannot stop—that resistance arises from persistent intuitions. Perhaps humankind cannot bear too much reality, but neither can it bear too much unreality, too much abuse of the truth. . . .

What is at the center now? At the moment, neither art nor science but mankind determining, in confusion and obscurity, whether it will endure or go under. The whole species—everybody—has gotten into the act. At such a time it is essential to lighten ourselves, to dump encumbrances, including the encumbrances of education and all organized plati-

2. **Hegel** [hā′gəl]: Georg Wilhelm Friedrich [gā′ôrk vil′helm frē′driкн] Hegel (1770–1831), German philosopher.
3. **Tolstoi** [tōl′stoi] . . . **Dostoevski** [dos′tə yef′skē]: Leo Tolstoi (1828–1910) and Feodor [fyô′dôr] Dostoevski (1821–1881), Russian novelists.
4. **bourgeois** [boor zhwä′]: materialistic, conventional, middle-class.
5. **Robbe-Grillet** [rōb′grē yā′]: Alain Robbe-Grillet (born 1922), French novelist.

tudes, to make judgments of our own, to perform acts of our own. Conrad[6] was right to appeal to that part of our being which is a gift. We must look for that gift under the wreckage of many systems. The collapse of those systems may bring a blessed and necessary release from formulations, from misleading conceptions of being and consciousness. With increasing frequency I dismiss as "merely respectable" opinions I have long held—or thought I held—and try to discern what I have really lived by, and what others really live by. As for Hegel's art freed from "seriousness" and glowing on the margins, raising the soul above painful involvement in the limitations of reality through the serenity of form, that can exist nowhere now, during this struggle for survival. However, it is not as though the people who engaged in this struggle had only a rudimentary humanity, without culture, and knew nothing of art. Our very vices, our mutilations, show how rich we are in thought and culture. How much we know. How much we can feel. The struggles that convulse us make us want to simplify, to reconsider, to eliminate the tragic weakness which prevented writers—and readers—from being at once simple and true.

Writers are greatly respected. The intelligent public is wonderfully patient with them, continues to read them and endures disappointment after disappointment, waiting to hear from art what it does not hear from theology, philosophy, social theory, and what it cannot hear from pure science. Out of the struggle at the center has come an immense, painful longing for a broader, more flexible, fuller, more coherent, more comprehensive account of what we human beings are, who we are, and what this life is for. At the center humankind struggles with collective powers for its freedom, the individual struggles with dehumanization for the possession of his soul. If writers do not come again into the center it will not be because the center is pre-empted.

It is not. They are free to enter. If they so wish.

The essence of our real condition, the complexity, the confusion, the pain of it is shown to us in glimpses, in what Proust[7] and Tolstoi thought of as "true impressions." This essence reveals, and then conceals itself. When it goes away it leaves us again in doubt. But our connection remains with the depths from which these glimpses come. The sense of our real powers, powers we seem to derive from the universe itself, also comes and goes. We are reluctant to talk about this because there is nothing we can prove, because our language is inadequate, and because few people are willing to risk the embarrassment. They would have to say, "There is a spirit" and that is taboo. So almost everyone keeps quiet about it, although almost everyone is aware of it.

The value of literature lies in these intermittent "true impressions." A novel moves back and forth between the world of objects, of actions, of appearances, and that other world from which these "true impressions" come and which moves us to believe that the good we hang onto so tenaciously—in the face of evil, so obstinately—is no illusion.

No one who has spent years in the writing of novels can be unaware of this. The novel can't be compared to the epic, or to the monuments of poetic drama. But it is the best we can do just now. It is a sort of latter-day lean-to, a hovel in which the spirit takes shelter. A novel is balanced between a few true impressions and the multitude of false ones that make up most of what we call life. It tells us that for every human being there is a diversity of existences, that the single existence is itself an illusion in part, that these many existences signify something, tend to something, fulfill something; it promises us meaning, harmony and even justice. What Conrad said was true, art attempts to find in the universe, in matter as well as in the facts of life, what is fundamental, enduring, essential.

---

6. **Conrad:** Joseph Conrad (1857–1924), English novelist of Polish birth, whose books often deal with honor, morality, alienation, and guilt.

7. **Proust** [proost]: Marcel Proust (1871–1922), French novelist.

STUDY QUESTIONS

Recalling

1. What does Bellow say he is considering as a novelist (paragraph 1)? What does he say happens "when complications increase" (paragraph 2)? What sort of person does he say has been produced by the cycle of crises that began with World War I?

2. What did Hegel observe about art? What was Hegel's opinion about art "on the margin"?

3. According to page 833, what is at the center now, and what sort of people are involved in it? With what and for what does Bellow say humankind struggles "at the center"? With what and for what does he say the individual struggles?

4. What does Bellow say is shown to us "in glimpses"? What does he say literature can do in this regard? With which of Conrad's ideas about art does Bellow agree in his final sentence?

Interpreting

5. What kind of literature is Hegel's literature "on the periphery"? To what sort of audience does it appeal? Does Bellow approve of such literature?

6. Summarize Bellow's opinion of modern human beings. What does he believe that all of us understand, at least "in glimpses"?

7. For what kind of literature does Bellow argue?

Extending

8. Which twentieth-century American writers that you have read do you think are "on the periphery"? Which do you think address "the center"? Support your answers.

VIEWPOINT

Howard Harper, Jr., sees a pattern in the lives of the characters in Bellow's fiction:

> . . . the protagonist undergoes an internal crisis precipitated by external events; as he searches for a way out his existence becomes increasingly subjective and restricted; at last he recognizes and accepts the common humanity which his situation reveals to him, and in his subsequent commitment to the fullness of life he becomes free and fully human.
>
> —*Contemporary Literature*

Compare Harper's description of what happens to Bellow's characters with the struggles of modern people whom Bellow describes in his Nobel address. What is the "internal crisis" the modern world faces? In the speech what does Bellow say we need to "recognize and accept"? What "commitment" must we make to become "fully human"?

COMPOSITION

Writing About Literature and Its Period

Write a brief composition demonstrating how Bellow's Nobel address is deeply rooted in the contemporary experience. First identify the problems Bellow describes, and tell how they are like other statements of modern problems made in this unit. Then tell what solutions and sources of strength Bellow recommends and why they are particularly contemporary. Conclude with your own opinion of Bellow's assessment of the literature of our time. *For help with this assignment, refer to Lesson 10 in the Writing About Literature Handbook at the back of this book.*

Writing an Essay of Opinion

Throughout history writers have tried to describe the value of literature. Saul Bellow believes that the value of literature in our time lies in its ability to uncover a realm of "true impressions" that "moves us to believe that the good we hang onto . . . is no illusion." Write an essay telling what, in your opinion, is the value of literature. Make your essay formal or informal as you wish. Be sure, however, to give clear statements of your opinions and to back them up with examples whenever possible.

COMPARING WRITERS

Each of the nonfiction selections on pages 815–834—by Leonard Bernstein, Ralph Ellison, N. Scott Momaday, and Saul Bellow—concerns a figurative return to "the center," a search for or movement toward the essence or true identity of something important. Compare the four authors in this section. What does each one seek? What is the essence or center that each values? What "road" does each take to reach his goal? How do their methods and approaches differ?

READING FOR APPRECIATION

The Aural Imagination

Literature begins with a human voice speaking. Earlier in this book we talked about the sound of prose and the sound of poetry, to remind ourselves of the importance—and the pleasure—of *hearing* literature. The selections in this unit remind us once again how essential it is to hear not only the speakers of nonfiction and the songs of poets but also the variety of characters in fiction.

Just as we heard the emotion in Patrick Henry's speech, so we can hear the excitement in Leonard Bernstein's "What Makes Music American?" Bernstein's essay was first a lecture. Can we hear it *exactly* as he once delivered it? No, because only a tape recorder would indicate his pauses and emphases. Still we can hear in our minds a reasonable version of the sound of that lecture. We can hear the relaxed, informal, American way of talking. We can hear the starts and stops, the parenthetical explanations, the afterthoughts, of everyday speech:

"I don't think there's anyone in the country—or in the world, for that matter—who wouldn't know right away that Gershwin's music—say, 'An American in Paris'—is American Music. It's got 'American' written all over it. . . ."

This colloquial writing is easy enough to hear. It comes alive because we read it with an aural imagination, imagining an actual person talking.

In poetry too, of course, we listen for the music of the poem or the special tone of the poet. In Olga Cabral's "(HELP!)" we give a sound to the poet's outcry:

"Help! I'm a prisoner in an index file!"

The poem is serious, yet it uses a comic tone to make its point. It is an exaggerated manner of expression, and it demands an exaggerated reading. Through our aural imaginations, we become, for a few moments, the prisoner in the file.

Fiction writing makes a different kind of demand on our aural imagination. In fiction we want to hear the voice of imaginary characters, sometimes a great number of them, talking at once, having conversations, responding to each other. In Elizabeth Spencer's "Port of Embarkation," for example, the dialogue of the characters asks us to imagine rapid shifts of tone. We want to hear the tension in the voices during this dramatic exchange between a concerned mother and her confused and troubled son:

"That food you got into, that was mine and Estelle's lunch. You knew that, didn't you?"

"No, I didn't know it. How would I?"

"You must have heard us say we didn't want to go out, we'd have a cold lunch, I'd make the potato salad and an aspic, then stuff some eggs. You said you wouldn't be here. There's not enough left for one, now, much less both of us."

"Can't you just fix some more?"

"I certainly don't want to, I guess I can. . . ."

How quickly the mother's tone changes toward the end of that dialogue, softening. How much we will miss if we don't hear that change! How would you read that sentence, as the mother would speak it?

How would you sound the final word in Truman Capote's "Miriam"? Miriam's "Hello" is not simple. The sound, the tone, must convey many implications. It is cheerful, youthful, and sinister—all at once.

Each of these works of fiction—in fact, any story or novel you will ever read—calls your aural imagination into action. It is through this use of your imagination that *you*—along with the writers you read—create the characters of fiction.

THE AMERICAN VOICE

Questions

The writers of our time are questioners. In our poetry, fiction, and nonfiction they ask who we are and who we are becoming. They ask what we should be doing and why we should do it. They wonder how we can become the heroes of our own lives.

Our writers ask questions about our identity, about our relationships with one another and with the natural world, about how we are trying to express ourselves. They know that only by asking questions can we begin to answer them.

Hayden
What did I know, what did I know
Of love's austere and lonely offices?

Ashbery
What's a plain level? It is that and other things,
Bringing a system of them into play. Play?

Cabral
Does the Twentieth Century make sense at all?

Spencer
"How do we know each other's problems unless we tell them?
How do I know?"

Goyen
Yet, everything changes, he thought, slowly it all changes. Do we resign ourselves to that? Is youth passing when we see this—the fierce battle of youth that would not accept change and loss? . . .

Bellow
What is at the center now?

Throughout American literature the great artists have asked the most serious questions, and the greatest have achieved some answers. For the Puritans, the answer lay in a profound religious vision. For Emerson, the answer was a transcendental oneness with the universe. For Whitman, only a constant celebration of life was an adequate response. For Dickinson, intense personal commitment tempered with a cool sense of irony provided the greatest satisfaction. For Faulkner, a mythological world threw a light on reality. For Stevens, the power of the human imagination held the key.

There is no doubt that our writers will continue to ask questions and continue to offer answers about living. It is for this reason that we will continue to read them, need them, love them.

Key to Illustrations on Pages 742–743.

1. Computer map, photograph by Tom Tracy.

2. John Updike, photograph by Jill Krementz.

3. Liftoff of Apollo II, NASA photograph.

4. Children using computers, photograph by Mark Perlstein.

5. The St. Louis Arch, photograph by N. E. Warren.

6. William Saroyan, photograph by Jill Krementz.

7. Robert Penn Warren, photograph by Jill Krementz.

8. Dr. Sally Ride, first American woman in space, in the astronaut training module. Photograph by Katz.

9. Dr. Martin Luther King, Jr., photograph by Flip Schulke.

WRITING ABOUT LITERATURE HANDBOOK

Revising and Editing Checklist

The lessons in this handbook will help you think about literature in ways that you may be asked to when you are given essay assignments. If you think clearly about literature, you will be on your way to writing clearly about literature.

The lessons will show you how to approach writing as a process. For each essay assignment they will advise you on prewriting steps to follow, and they will suggest how you can proceed from paragraph to paragraph. Each lesson will also remind you to revise and edit your first draft into a more polished final draft. Here are specific guidelines to follow as you review your first draft.

1. Read your writing aloud. Your ear has been responding to words longer than you have been writing.
2. Use the following checklist to revise your writing. If you can answer "yes" to each question on the list, you will submit an essay that your audience will find interesting and logical.

  I. Organization
   a. Does your thesis statement in the introductory paragraph relate directly to the assignment?
   b. Are the ideas mentioned in the thesis statement then taken up in the following paragraphs with a topic sentence for each paragraph?
   c. Is there clear movement from paragraph to paragraph by means of transitions?
   d. Does the final paragraph offer a restatement of the thesis statement along with additional insights?
 II. Content
   a. Does the essay as a whole adequately answer the question posed in the assignment?
   b. Is each idea adequately developed with supporting details from the literature rather than simply stated and restated in different ways without evidence?
III. Grammar, Usage, Mechanics
   a. Is each sentence complete (no fragments, no run-ons)?
   b. Have you avoided errors in the use of verbs (especially subject-verb agreement), pronouns, and modifiers?
   c. Have you correctly capitalized and punctuated all sentences?
   d. Are all words spelled correctly?
 IV. Word Choice, Style
   a. Have you used words that are appropriate for your audience and your purpose?
   b. Have you avoided slang and clichés unless (and this should be rare) you are using them for a very special purpose or effect?
   c. Have you eliminated wordiness and vagueness?
   d. Have you varied sentence length and structure while checking for parallelism?

LESSON 1: *Developing a Thesis Statement*

The **thesis statement** of a composition, which usually occurs in the introductory paragraph, announces the topic of the composition and your reason for writing about it. It sets forth the thesis, or proposition, that you will defend. For example, after reading an excerpt from Mark Twain's *Life on the Mississippi* (page 275 in this book), you may decide to write a composition about symbolism in the work. Symbolism, then, is the *topic*. What you will say about the topic is the *thesis*, and you will state the thesis in a *thesis statement*. Note that a thesis statement may contain more than one main clause and may even, at times, be two sentences long.

> *Example:* The Mississippi River possesses rich symbolic significance in Mark Twain's *Life on the Mississippi;* the author uses the river to reflect on his emergence into adulthood and on the passing of boyhood dreams.

A thesis statement is *not* merely a fact; it is a position, or interpretation, based on the facts of the literary selection. In other words, you would not have much of a thesis statement if you were to write, "The Mississippi River is prominent in Mark Twain's *Life on the Mississippi.*" That statement is merely a fact, not a position, or interpretation, based on the facts of the work.

The purpose of the thesis statement is to alert your audience to what they will read and the nature of what to expect in the following paragraphs. Each of those paragraphs will have its own topic sentence and will provide support for the opening thesis statement.

CONCEPTS TO REMEMBER

1. A thesis statement is far more detailed and specific than a general topic. The topic is often just a single word or phrase. The thesis statement is one or more complete sentences that mention your position and indicate the plan you will be following in the composition as a whole. Here is an example of the difference between topics and thesis statements:

   Byrd's *Progress to the Mines*
   a. *General Topic:* Everyday life in the southern colonies

   b. *Thesis Statement:* Byrd's *Progress to the Mines* shows that landowners in the southern colonies enjoyed a fairly high standard of living, enabling them to achieve a degree of everyday elegance and civility beyond the reach of the Puritan farmers in the north.

   The thesis statement should narrow and focus the general topic so that you can write a coherent composition within the limits of three to five paragraphs.

2. You must believe in your thesis statement. Your composition will lack conviction and your audience will not be convinced of your thesis statement if you yourself do not believe in it. In other words, in looking for something to write about, you must find a topic and then generate a thesis in which you are genuinely interested. Although your observations and your analysis of the work of literature may not involve a radically new interpretation, you should nevertheless point out *something of interest to you.* Remember that novelty for its own sake is not your goal. You want to make a clear statement of your own observations.

TYPICAL ESSAY QUESTION

The most challenging essay question may be the kind that asks you to create a thesis statement and to go on to support the thesis statement. Such an assignment may be worded as follows:

> Develop a thesis statement about a piece of literature, and in a brief essay defend your thesis with examples from the work.

PREWRITING

Assuming you have read a work carefully, ask yourself some or all of the following questions or other, similar questions. These questions are designed to help you identify which aspect of the work you want to write about and then create a thesis statement that will focus your area of concern narrowly enough so that you can handle the topic within a brief essay.

1. What is the most intriguing literary element or aspect of the work?

a. *Plot:* What is notable about the conflicts in this selection? What prepares you for the climax? What elements of foreshadowing are present? Why does the author use a frame story?
b. *Characters:* Do any of the characters experience interesting growth or change? Would a compare/contrast approach produce significant insights?
c. *Setting:* How is the setting a reflection of the characters or of another element of the work? What impact does the setting have on events in the selection?
d. *Point of View:* Why is the point of view appropriate for the selection?
e. *Theme:* Why is the theme intriguing? How is it made clear throughout the work? How do all the literary elements contribute to presenting the theme?
f. *Symbol:* What is the purpose of any symbol that the author has used?
g. *Irony:* What type of irony (verbal, situational, dramatic) does the author use? What effect does it have on your understanding of theme, characters, and so on?
h. *Tone:* How does the author achieve his or her tone in this work?
i. *Purpose:* What is the author's purpose? What techniques does the author use to achieve that purpose?
j. *Total Effect:* What is the total impact of the work? How is it achieved?

2. Why is this element or aspect of the work interesting? Is it central to understanding the work? Do other elements or aspects support the one you have chosen to write about?
3. Can you support your idea about the element you have selected? What support can you find in the text itself? If it is part of the assignment, what evidence can you find in secondary sources, such as the author's biography or critics' writings? (See Lesson 3: Citing Evidence for more information about primary and secondary sources.)
4. What are some of the arguments against your thesis statement? How would you go about responding to these arguments?

The following example shows a thesis statement generated for the excerpt from the *Walum Olum,* which appears on page 8 of this book.

Example: In the *Walum Olum* the Delaware Indians demonstrate that they have a highly sophisticated, complex world view by presenting the great manito as a living paradox—a single force that contains all opposites.

WRITING AN ESSAY PARAGRAPH BY PARAGRAPH

1. Begin the introductory paragraph with the thesis statement. Fill out the introductory paragraph with definitions of terms or with clarification of your thesis statement.
2. In the following paragraphs give at least two specific examples from the *Walum Olum* to support your thesis statement.
3. In your concluding paragraph repeat your thesis statement in different words, and indicate that the preceding paragraphs have shown that the thesis statement is defensible.

WRITING A ONE–PARAGRAPH ANSWER

All the preceding advice on structure applies as well to written responses that are only one paragraph long. If you are limited to one paragraph, begin with a strong topic sentence. Each of your following sentences should develop one aspect of the topic sentence. You will not have as much room for supporting details as in a five-paragraph essay, but you nevertheless must give evidence to support the topic sentence. For example, using the thesis statement from Prewriting Step 4 as a topic sentence, you can devote a few sentences to the Delawares' world view and then a few to the manito as a paradox. You can conclude this one-paragraph response with a **clincher** sentence, which sums up the evidence you have presented.

REVISING AND EDITING

See page 841 for detailed reminders about improving your writing.

ASSIGNMENTS

1. Write a composition supporting the thesis statement given here for the *Walum Olum.*
2. Do one of the assignments called "Developing a Thesis Statement" that appear after the selections by John Smith (page 22), Nathaniel Hawthorne (page 188), John Ashbery (page 759), and Bernard Malamud (page 780).

Lesson 2: *Writing a Comparison/Contrast*

When you are studying two literary works, a very effective way to clarify your understanding of each is to compare and contrast their similarities and differences. Whether the works are stories, novels, or poems, you can examine their content and techniques to see how they are alike and how they differ in relation to each other.

CONCEPTS TO REMEMBER

1. *To compare* in this lesson means "to examine two or more literary works for the purpose of noting similarities." *To contrast* means "to examine two or more literary works for the purpose of noting differences."
2. In stories and novels you can compare and contrast these elements: plot, characters, settings, points of view, tones, themes, symbols, and irony.
3. In poetry you can compare and contrast these elements: speakers, sound devices, rhythm, rhyme, imagery, and figurative speech.

TYPICAL ESSAY QUESTION

When you are asked to compare and contrast two literary works, you will often have to answer an essay assignment like this one:

Select two pieces of literature that you have read. Compare and contrast the two pieces by pointing out the similarities and differences in content and literary techniques.

PREWRITING

1. Use the following questions and others like them to compare and contrast two works.

   a. What plot elements in each are similar?
   b. How are the characters similar or different? Do the characters change, or do they remain the same throughout the story?
   c. From what point of view is each story told?
   d. What is the setting of each piece? In what year does it take place?
   e. The tone of each piece may be serious, comic, straightforward, ironic, angry, etc. Are the tones of the two pieces alike or different?
   f. What theme is each author expressing?
   g. What symbols are used? How?

   h. How is irony used in each piece?
   i. What is the total impact of each piece?

2. Use the following questions and others like them to compare and contrast two poems.

   a. Does each poem focus on the actions of a character? On a place? On a thing? On an event?
   b. Does each poem focus on an idea? A feeling?
   c. What is your emotional response to each?
   d. On what does each poem cause you to reflect?
   e. Who is the speaker in each poem?
   f. What sound devices are used in each?
   g. What kind of rhyme and rhythm is used?
   h. How does each poem use imagery?
   i. What figures of speech are used in each?

3. Prepare a chart (see the opposite page) on which to record your answers to the questions in Prewriting Step 1 or Step 2 and to any other questions that you have devised.

WRITING PARAGRAPH BY PARAGRAPH

1. Begin your introductory paragraph with a thesis statement that restates the main points of the assignment. State the major similarities and differences in meaning and technique.

   Example: Although the two American Indian poems "Listen! Rain Approaches!" and "Calling One's Own" have different subjects and themes, different lengths, and different voices, they are similar in their attention to nature, their dependence upon imagery, and the repetition of lines or words.

2. Use one of the following options for organizing the body of the essay:

   Option A

   Introductory paragraph
   Next paragraph: Tell about one selection.
   Next paragraph: Tell about the second selection.
   Next paragraph: Discuss similarities and differences based on two preceding paragraphs.
   Concluding paragraph

SIMILARITIES AND DIFFERENCES IN POEMS

SELECTIONS: (1) "Listen! Rain Approaches!" and (2) "Calling One's Own"

	SPEAKER	SOUND	IMAGERY / FIGURATIVE LANGUAGE	THEME OR MEANING
SELECTION 1	Speaker calls to reader/listener directly.	*Irregular rhythm:* gives impression of gusts of wind *Parallel construction* in the two stanzas: gives feeling of cycle *Assonance:* East, bean	*Visual image:* fields of green crops literally tied with lightning and then with rainbow *Sound image:* bluebird as herald, announcing beginning and end of storm with equal joy	Poem describes an event; we reflect on nature's cycle. Rain is a life force that connects and is necessary to all living things. The storm is a process that we all must endure, and it has beauty from beginning to end.
SELECTION 2	Speaker addresses the beloved, not the reader, directly.	*Rhythm:* relatively even, with variations *Alliteration:* "*B*ehold me! *b*lood of my *b*eating heart!" "A *sh*ining river the *sh*adows of clouds darken." *Repetition of words:* "Awake" at beginning and end	*Visual image:* "A shining river the shadows of clouds darken"; "A forest streams to the sun in the moon of bright nights." *Smell image:* "fragrance of flowers in the morning" *Touch image:* "Furrows the cold wind drew" *Metaphors:* beloved called "flower of the forest"; "sky treading bird of the prairie"; "The breath of your mouth is the fragrance of flowers. . . ." *Personification:* "my heart sings"; "the water's face"; "Earth smiles"; "waters smile"	Poem describes effect of love in terms of nature: Nearness of loved one makes the world beautiful; anger of loved one is like storm darkening the world.

Option B

Introductory paragraph
Next paragraph: Discuss the similarities in meaning and elements in each selection.
Next paragraph: Discuss the differences in meaning and elements in each selection.
Concluding paragraph

3. In the concluding paragraph use different words to remind readers of your thesis. Focus on whether the two selections are more alike or more different.

REVISING AND EDITING

See page 841 for detailed reminders about improving your writing.

ASSIGNMENTS

1. Use the preceding chart to write a comparison/contrast for the two poems.
2. Do one of the "Writing a Comparison/Contrast" assignments that follow the selections by Bradford (page 29), Byrd (page 39), Robinson (page 359), Hemingway (page 524), Weidman (page 616), Welty (page 649), and Agee (page 660).

LESSON 3: *Citing Evidence*

When you write a paragraph or an essay of literary analysis, you must provide details—evidence—in support of the generalization you have made in your topic sentence or thesis statement. Compare the following two paragraphs. Sample A consists only of general statements which just repeat the idea of the topic sentence but do not bolster or advance the idea. Sample B is stronger and more substantial.

Sample A

    In his "Speech at the Virginia Convention" Patrick Henry offers several arguments for his position in favor of fighting the British. He wants his listeners to agree with his position. He feels it is necessary to take up arms against the British, and he cites arguments to persuade his listeners to agree with him.

Sample B

    In his "Speech at the Virginia Convention" Patrick Henry offers several arguments for his position in favor of fighting the British. First of all, he explains that although it is natural to have hope, the colonists must face facts and admit that the British ministry has been planning the use of force by making "warlike preparations which cover our waters and darken our land." Second, he points out that the colonists have already tried and exhausted the approach of talking with the British. He says, ". . . we have been trying that for the last ten years." Third, Henry reminds his listeners of the importance of maintaining freedom. Fourth, Henry aruges that they are "armed in the holy cause of liberty" and that "God . . . will raise up friends to fight our battles for us."

CONCEPTS TO REMEMBER

    Evidence may be in the form of a paraphrase or in the form of a direct quotation.

1. A **paraphrase** is a restatement in your own words of the sense of a piece of writing. When you paraphrase, you should indicate the source either within the context of your paraphrase (Paraphrase A) or in a footnote or endnote that you refer your reader to by placing a raised numeral at the end of your paraphrase (Paraphrase B).

Paraphrase A

    In his speech before the delegates of the 1775 Virginia Convention, Patrick Henry states unequivocally that the matter they are deciding is nothing less than whether the colonists can consider themselves free people or slaves.

Paraphrase B

    Some patriots such as Patrick Henry believed that they had to decide how to view themselves—as free people or as slaves.[1]

2. When you use a **direct quotation,** you use precisely the same words and the same word order as your source. Remember that you must use quotation marks, quote the author exactly, and indicate any omission by the use of ellipses and any addition by the use of brackets.

Direct Quotation A

    In "The Devil and Tom Walker" Washington Irving describes Tom Walker's wife and the relationship between the husband and wife by writing that she was ". . . a termagant, fierce of temper, loud of tongue, and strong of arm. . . . and his [Tom's] face sometimes showed signs that their conflicts were not confined to words."

Direct Quotation B

    In an effort to convince his listeners that all efforts have been exhausted in dealing with the king of England, Patrick Henry reminds them:

> We have petitioned; we have remonstrated; we have supplicated; we have prostrated ourselves before the throne. . . . Our petitions have been slighted . . . our supplications have been disregarded; and we have been spurned with contempt from the foot of the throne![1]

TYPICAL ESSAY QUESTION

    You should always cite evidence in support of your thesis statement. Some essay questions make a particular point of reminding you to do so. The following essay assignment is an example.

CITING EVIDENCE

SELECTION: "Speech in the Virginia Convention"

THESIS: Patrick Henry offers several arguments for his position in favor of fighting the British.

ARGUMENT	SUPPORTING QUOTATION	SUPPORTING PARAPHRASE
The British preparations	p. 67: "those warlike preparations which cover our waters and darken our land . . ."	The British are gathering the navy and the army.
Uselessness of talking	p. 67: "And what have we to oppose them? Shall we try argument? Sir, we have been trying that for the last ten years. Have we anything new to offer upon the subject? Nothing."	We have already tried to reason with the British but to no avail. There is nothing left to discuss.
The goal of the colonists	p. 67: "If we wish to be free, if we mean to preserve inviolate those inestimable privileges for which we have been so long contending, if we mean not basely to abandon the noble struggle in which we have been so long engaged, and which we have pledged ourselves never to abandon until the glorious object of our contest shall be obtained—we must fight!"	Freedom is precious and has long been our goal; we must not give up.
The strength of the colonists	p. 68: "Sir, we are not weak, if we make a proper use of those means which the God of nature hath placed in our power. Three millions of people, armed in the holy cause of liberty, and in such a country as that which we possess, are invincible by any force which our enemy can send against us. Besides, sir, we shall not fight our battles alone."	The colonists have God on their side in this battle.

Write a brief essay in which you give your opinion or make a generalization about a particular piece of literature. First clearly state your opinion. Then cite specific examples to support it.

PREWRITING

1. Gather material in support of your thesis by reading and rereading the piece of literature.
2. Prepare a chart on which you can list (on the left) the arguments you will present in support of your thesis. In the middle column add exact quotations that defend each argument you list. In the right-hand column, offer a paraphrase of each quotation. Then when you write your first draft, you will have options to pick from as you cite evidence. The chart at the top of this page was prepared during prewriting by the person who later produced Sample B, which appears near the beginning of this lesson.

USING FOOTNOTES OR ENDNOTES AND BIBLIOGRAPHY ENTRIES

A **footnote** or **endnote** gives source information for a statement in your composition. It tells who wrote the source, the title of the source, where it was published, by whom, and when. Footnotes appear at the bottom of the page that contains the idea or quotation taken from a source. Endnotes appear on a page at the end of your composition.

A **bibliography** is an alphabetical arrangement by last name of author of all the sources used in writing a composition. The bibliography appears at the end of the composition.

ASSIGNMENT

Do one of the assignments called "Citing Evidence" that appear after the selections by Jonathan Edwards (p. 45), Thomas Jefferson (p. 80), and Robert Penn Warren (p. 751)

LESSON 4: *Writing About Nonfiction*

Nonfiction comes in several different forms—for example, the biography, the autobiography, the essay, the diary, the journal. Nonfiction works may be only a few paragraphs long, or they may be book length. When you write about any kind of nonfiction, however, you can use the same kind of analysis. You can discuss the author's purpose in writing the piece and show how the author achieves that purpose.

CONCEPTS TO REMEMBER
1. The **purpose** of a piece of nonfiction is the central idea, or general statement about life, that the author wishes to make.
2. To communicate the purpose, the author uses various techniques such as sensory details, facts, statistics, examples, and opinions.

TYPICAL ESSAY QUESTION
When you are asked to write about a piece of nonfiction, you are often answering an assignment such as the following:

Select a piece of nonfiction that you have read. An author always has a purpose in writing nonfiction. To accomplish this purpose, the author may use various techniques such as sensory details, facts, statistics, examples, and opinions.

What is the purpose of the piece of nonfiction you have read? Cite with examples the particular techniques that the author uses to accomplish the purpose of the piece.

PREWRITING
1. To determine the author's purpose in writing a work of nonfiction, ask yourself the following questions:

   a. What, if anything, does the title suggest about the author's opinion of the subject of the essay, diary, or journal or about the person in the biography or autobiography?
   b. What opinion about life in general is suggested by the experiences that the author relates?

   c. What opinion about the subject or about people in general is suggested by details (including sensory details, facts, statistics, examples, and opinions)?
   d. What ideas about the world in general are suggested by details of setting?
   e. What tone, or attitude, toward the subject is revealed by the author's style?

2. Based on your answers to the preceding questions, prepare a statement of the author's purpose, and, on a chart like the one on the following page, record the techniques that the author uses to achieve that purpose. The filled-in chart represents an analysis of a section of *The Journal* of Christopher Columbus, adapted into a modern version by William Carlos Williams (page 15).

WRITING PARAGRAPH BY PARAGRAPH
1. Begin the introductory paragraph with a thesis statement. It should specify the author's purpose and state which techniques are used to accomplish this purpose.

   Example: In *The Journal* Christopher Columbus sets out to record the crew's despair, his desperate attempts to keep up the morale of his crew, and the joy of the discovery of land at last. The author uses sensory details, facts, statistics, examples, and opinions that help make the piece not just a dry captain's log but a story of suspense and drama.

2. In each of the body paragraphs, show how the author uses one technique to make the purpose clear.
3. In the concluding paragraph restate in other words the thesis statement from the introductory paragraph. Here you might include your own reaction to the author's efforts—a summary of your own opinion of the work.

REVISING AND EDITING
See page 841 for detailed reminders about improving your writing.

PURPOSE AND TECHNIQUES

SELECTION: from *The Journal*

PURPOSE: To record the facts and events of Columbus' voyage as well as Columbus' and the crew's feelings as they encountered difficulties, disappointments, and the discovery of a strange new land and people.

SENSORY DETAILS	FACTS	STATISTICS
"The sea water was found to be less salt. . . . This I caused the men to taste." "The breezes were always soft." "Bright green trees, the whole land so green . . ."	*He documents clues in the search for land:* "We observed much more weed appearing . . . a live crab." "On that morning appeared a white bird . . . not in the habit of sleeping on the sea." *Discoveries:* "their legs are straight, all in one line and no belly. They came to the ship in canoes, made out of the trunk of a tree, all in one piece. . . ." "There are also whales. I saw no beasts on land save parrots and lizards."	Keeps log including dates, course, number of leagues traveled. Reduces number of leagues to lessen the distance so as not to upset the men at thought of how far from Spain they really are

EXAMPLES	OPINIONS
Of joy: "Martin Alonzo . . . with joy called out that he had sighted land. . . ." *Of despair:* ". . . what had been said to be land was only clouds . . . despair of the crew redoubled at this disappointment." *Of his attempts to keep up morale:* "I comforted them as best I could, begging them to endure a while longer for all that would be theirs in the end." *Of delightful new discoveries:* "The fish so unlike ours that it is wonderful. Some are the shape of dories and of the finest colors, so bright that there is not a man who would not be astounded."	*Feelings of despair and determination at "endless" journey:* "I fell on my knees and gave thanks to the Lord, so heavy had been my burdens these latter days at the despair among the men and the murmurs among them that I should have to turn back. . . . The crew here became even louder in their complaints but I gave as little heed as I was able though many were now openly mutinous and would have done me harm if they dared." *Of the new land:* "Gardens of the most beautiful trees I ever saw. I saw many trees very unlike those of our country. Branches growing in different ways and all from one trunk; one twig is one form and another is a different shape and so unlike that it is the greatest wonder in the world to see the diversity. . . ." ". . . I walked among the trees which was the most beautiful thing which I had ever seen."

ASSIGNMENTS

1. Use the above chart for *The Journal* to write an essay in which you discuss the author's purpose and the techniques he used to achieve that purpose.

2. Do one of the assignments that follow the selections by Patrick Henry (page 69), Thomas Paine (page 84), Henry David Thoreau (page 177), Frederick Douglass (page 230), William Faulkner (page 681), Jack Kerouac (page 688), Leonard Bernstein (page 820), and Ralph Ellison (page 825), or select another piece of literature from this book and write an essay in which you discuss the author's purpose and the techniques used to achieve that purpose.

LESSON 5: *Writing About a Quotation or a Symbol*

Often a quotation from a piece of literature stands out. Whether the work is fiction, poetry, or non-fiction, sometimes just one line sums up its whole meaning so vividly that the line itself comes to represent the entire work. In the same way, a writer may use a symbol to create a vivid impression in a reader's mind. Just as a quotation can summarize an idea or opinion in a dramatic way, so a symbol can come to represent the message that the writer wishes to communicate. Because quotations and symbols express the writer's meaning so clearly and concisely, you should learn how to analyze them and relate them to a work as a whole.

CONCEPTS TO REMEMBER

1. A powerful quotation may have vivid adjectives and strong action verbs. It may use strong parallel structure that gives dramatic rhythm to a sentence. It may use metaphorical language. It may appeal strongly to the reader's emotions or senses. It may have a universal meaning.
2. A **symbol** is something that stands for itself but also for something larger than itself. It may be a person, an animal, an inanimate object, or an action. A writer often uses a concrete object to express an abstract idea, a quality, or a belief. A symbol may also appeal to a reader's emotions and can provide a dramatic way to express an idea, communicate a message, or clarify meaning.

TYPICAL ESSAY QUESTION

When you are asked to write about a quotation or a symbol, you may find an essay question such as this:

Identify a quotation [or symbol] from a piece of literature. Explain the specific meaning of the quotation [or symbol] in the piece of literature. Then discuss the significance of the quotation [or symbol] in the work as a whole, explaining how it relates to a theme or main idea of the work.

PREWRITING

For a quotation
1. Identify a quotation from a given work of literature. Ask yourself the following questions if

you need help in selecting a quotation that would be a good subject for an essay:

a. Is there a sentence that has gained fame?
b. Is there a sentence with strong parallel structure, emotional appeal, or notable simplicity?
c. Does the work begin or end with a particularly impressive statement?

For example, in considering Patrick Henry's speech at the Virginia Convention (page 66), you can select "give me liberty or give me death!" It is already famous, but even if it were not famous it would be a good quotation to discuss because of its strong parallelism, simplicity, and placement at the end of the speech.

2. Explain in your own words the meaning of the quotation. That is, restate any figurative language, and fill in any information your reader may need in order to understand the quotation. Make sure you explain when, where, and why the statement was made. For example, if you were working with the quotation "give me liberty or give me death!" you could explain that Henry, speaking in 1775, means he would rather die than live in America under the oppression of England.

For a symbol
1. Identify a symbol from a piece of literature. Look for a concrete object that seems to stand for something abstract above and beyond its concrete meaning. Ask yourself the following questions for help in selecting a symbol:

a. Does the title of the selection alert you to symbolism? For example, the title of Hawthorne's story "The Minister's Black Veil" (page 179) might alert you to an object with a symbolic meaning in the story.
b. Has the author given particular emphasis to one object or other detail and thereby perhaps raised it to the level of a symbol? For example, in Benjamin Franklin's *Autobiography* (page 58) the writer develops in great detail the incident of the puffy rolls.
c. Does the object seem to be representative of something *of another kind*? Remember

that you would not say a robin is symbolic of all birds; a robin is merely representative of all birds. You would, however, say that a robin is symbolic of spring; a robin is an animal, whereas spring is an aspect of time, something *of different kind.*

2. Explain the meaning of the symbol. That is, tell what abstract idea, quality, or belief is called to mind by the given person, animal, object, or action. For example, the puffy rolls and Franklin's actions with them seem to symbolize the young man's generosity.

For both a quotation and a symbol

3. Identify a main idea or theme of the piece of literature by asking yourself questions such as the following. Remember that a main idea or theme should be stated in a complete sentence as a *general* truth.

    a. What ideas about life does the selection's title suggest?
    b. What do the particular *events* and *conflicts* reveal about life in general?
    c. What might these particular *people* or *characters* with these personality traits tell us about life in general?
    d. What view of the world do the *setting* and its details offer us?

For example, answers to these questions should help you see the following main ideas:

Revolution may be the only resort people have if they want to obtain freedom from oppression.—Henry

Young men can be both absurd and sincere.—Franklin

4. Once you have identified the main idea or theme of the work, make notes on how the quotation or symbol relates to the work as a whole. Ask the following questions:

    a. Does the quotation or symbol *summarize* the theme or main idea?
    b. Does the quotation or symbol *illustrate* the theme or main idea?

WRITING PARAGRAPH BY PARAGRAPH

1. Begin your introductory paragraph with a thesis statement that tells what quotation or symbol you are going to write about and that identifies a theme or main idea of the literary work.

Examples

For a quotation: Patrick Henry's famous quotation "give me liberty or give me death!" is the dramatic statement with which he ends his impassioned speech to the Virginia Convention. The speech as a whole argues that at times people must pick up arms if they are to have the freedom they crave.

For a symbol: In his *Autobiography* Benjamin Franklin gives prominence to the story of the puffy rolls, which serve as a symbol of young Franklin's actions. The writer sees himself and young men in general as capable of acting both absurdly and sincerely.

2. In the next paragraph tell the specific meaning of the quotation or symbol. Explain, if necessary, how you arrived at your understanding of the quotation or symbol.

3. In the next paragraph explain in what way the quotation or symbol fits into the literary work as a whole.

4. In your concluding paragraph you might tell how the analysis of the quotation or symbol has helped you understand better the nature of the piece as a whole. Decide whether the quotation or symbol added anything to the piece.

REVISING AND EDITING

See page 841 for detailed reminders about improving your writing.

ASSIGNMENTS

1. Using the information in this lesson, write an essay explaining the significance of the Henry quotation or the Franklin symbol.
2. Do one of the assignments called "Writing About a Quotation" or "Writing About a Symbol" that appear after the selections by James Fenimore Cooper (page 118), Ralph Waldo Emerson (page 168), Sarah Orne Jewett (page 319), Jack London (page 352), Theodore Roethke (page 580), Walter Van Tilburg Clark (page 655), William Goyen (page 810), and Mark Helprin (page 814), or select another piece of literature from this book, and write about a symbol or a quotation within the work.

LESSON 6: *Writing About Theme*

The **theme** of a literary work is its underlying central idea or generalization about life. A theme, therefore, is more than just the specific topic or subject of a story. Whether the work is a novel, short story, or play, its theme expresses an opinion or raises a question about human nature or the meaning of human experience. For example, the subject of a short story called "Through the Tunnel" is "a young boy's trials and success at swimming through an underwater passage." The theme might be stated this way: "A young person must take risks and develop courage in order to achieve independence and adulthood." You may or may not agree with the theme, but if the selection is well written, you will gain a fresh and moving insight into the human condition, and you will be able to write about that.

CONCEPTS TO REMEMBER

1. Most pieces of literature have only one theme, although the theme can be worded in several ways. Some works, however, may contain several themes; such is the case with a long, complex novel.
2. Sometimes the theme may be clearly stated. Usually, however, the theme is implied or suggested through other elements. The author uses characterization, setting, events, point of view, and tone to develop the theme.

TYPICAL ESSAY QUESTION

When you are asked to write about the theme of a selection, you are often answering an essay assignment such as the following:

Identify the theme of a work of literature. Show how the author illuminates this theme through characterization, setting, events, point of view, and tone.

PREWRITING

1. Identify the subject of a selection that you have read. The selection may have more than one subject, but select only one. For example, the subject of "The Devil and Tom Walker" (page 105) is "Tom's bargain with the Devil."
2. Keeping the subject in mind, ask yourself the following questions so that you can move beyond the subject of the selection to its theme.

a. What do various characters (or the main character) think, say, and do about the subject?
b. What are character's key traits? Does the character change at all?
c. How do the time, place, clothing, and other details of setting serve as a suitable background for the work's subject?
d. What do the events and conflicts have to do with the subject matter?
e. What do the selection's climax and resolution have to do with the selection's subject matter?
f. From whose point of view is the story told, and how does this point of view affect you?
g. What tone does the writer use, and how does that tone affect your reaction to the subject matter?

3. Prepare a chart to record your answers to the questions in Prewriting Step 2. The chart on the opposite page is a sample prepared for "The Devil and Tom Walker."
4. Examine the completed chart, and try to develop a statement of the theme of the selection. For example, for "The Devil and Tom Walker" you might state the theme as follows: "Those who are consumed by greed are doomed to suffer the consequences of their greed—the corruption of all that is good in human nature and the inevitable destruction of the soul."

WRITING PARAGRAPH BY PARAGRAPH

1. Begin your introductory paragraph with a thesis statement that restates the main ideas of the assignment. Indicate what the theme of the selection is, being certain to state the theme in terms of a generalization about human nature or experience. Then show how the theme is illuminated through the other elements of the selection.

Example: The theme of "The Devil and Tom Walker" is that those who are consumed by greed are doomed to suffer the consequences of their greed, including the corruption of all that is good in human nature and the inevitable destruction of the

EVENTS ILLUMINATING THEME

SELECTION: "The Devil and Tom Walker"

SUBJECT OF STORY: Tom Walker's bargain with the Devil

CHARACTERIZATION	SETTING	EVENTS
Tom Walker's traits: Extremely miserly and greedy—so miserly he starves his horses and lives in what looks like bleak poverty. Although he has a moral streak (would not become a slave trader), he is pitiless toward those who owe him money. *Tom's wife's traits:* Even greedier than he; obstinate, shrewish; quite willing to sell her soul to the Devil to gain riches.	*House:* First setting evokes feeling of gloom. Tom's "forlorn-looking" house with "air of starvation" is symbol of Tom's miserly, bleak existence. *Scene of meetings with the Devil:* Swamp and dark woods ominous and foreboding, gloomy, full of quagmires, pits; quagmires are symbols of irrevocable doom.	*Conflicts:* Refuses to sell his soul—to spite his wife, who is anxious for him to do it. Then Tom's greed and pleasure at the Devil's having taken his wife overcome his reluctance. *Climax:* He becomes rich, but as he gets old, becomes afraid. Becomes fanatically religious in attempt to cheat the Devil. His own greed tricks him into calling forth the Devil. *Resolution:* The Devil appears and carries him off forever.

POINT OF VIEW	TONE	
Omniscient point of view: Narrator tells about all events and what the characters think and feel. Describes characters in detail so that we have very clear pictures of Tom, his wife, and the Devil.	Tone is simple, direct, with a slight touch of ironic humor, especially in description of characters. Tone conveys sense of inevitability: Tom cannot change the consequences of what he has done.	

soul. All the elements in the story—characterization, setting, events, point of view, and tone—contribute to the sense of doom and ultimate retribution as the Devil comes to claim Tom's soul.

2. In the next paragraph focus on how the characters, setting, and events reveal and bring to life the generalization which you feel the selection makes.

3. In the next paragraph focus on how the point of view illustrates the theme.

4. In the next paragraph focus on how the tone clarifies the theme.

5. In the concluding paragraph restate your thesis statement. Explain whether the elements of the selection led you to understand a theme new to you or whether they helped renew an awareness that you had.

REVISING AND EDITING

See page 841 for detailed reminders about improving your writing.

ASSIGNMENTS

1. Use the chart for "The Devil and Tom Walker" to write about theme. How do characterization, setting, events, point of view, and tone illustrate the theme that greedy people cannot escape the consequences of their greed?

2. Choose one of the assignments that follow the selections by William Cullen Bryant (page 124), Willa Cather (page 563), John Steinbeck (page 629), and Truman Capote (page 801), or select another piece of literature from this book, and show how all the other elements illuminate its theme.

LESSON 7: *Writing About Poetry*

Poetry is very much like music in the way it uses rhythm and sound to capture a mood, convey feelings, and communicate a message. Composers use various musical techniques to create a song; poets use various literary techniques to convey the sense, or meaning, of a poem. These techniques include choice of the speaker, sound, imagery, and figurative language. Poets emphasize different techniques in different poems depending on which they feel work best to express the meaning of the poem. You should learn to think about all these techniques so that when you write an essay about a poem, you will be able to show the connection between the techniques of the poem and its meaning.

CONCEPTS TO REMEMBER

1. The **speaker** of the poem is the voice of the poem. Sometimes the speaker is the poet himself or herself; sometimes the speaker is a character or thing created by the poet.
2. Among the sound devices that a poet may use are **onomatopoeia** (a word or phrase that actually imitates or suggests the sound of what it describes); **alliteration** (the repetition of initial consonant sounds); **consonance** (the repetition of similar consonant sounds preceded by different accented vowels); **assonance** (the repetition of vowel sounds).
3. Other aspects of sound in poetry are **rhyme** (the repetition at regular intervals of similar or identical sounds) and **rhythm** (the pattern created by arranging stressed and unstressed syllables).
4. A poem's images may appeal to one or more senses.
5. The most common kinds of figurative language available to a poet are metaphor, simile, and personification. (**Metaphor** is a figure of speech in which two unlike things are compared without the use of *like* or *as;* **simile** is a comparison using *like* or *as;* **personification** is a figure of speech in which an animal, object, or idea is described as having human form or characteristics.)

TYPICAL ESSAY QUESTION

When you are asked to write about poetry, you are often answering an assignment such as the following one:

Select a poem that you have read. What is the meaning of the poem? What techniques does the poet use to reveal this meaning? Techniques include the selection of the speaker, sound devices, imagery, and the use of figurative language.

PREWRITING

1. Use the following questions to help you determine the meaning of the poem:

   a. Does the poem focus on the actions of a character?
   b. Does the poem describe a person, place, or thing?
   c. Does the poem focus on an idea? Does it focus on a feeling?
   d. What emotional response does the poem seem to call up in you?
   e. After your immediate emotional response to the poem, on what does the poem cause you to reflect?

2. Prepare a chart on which to record your statement of the meaning of the poem and your observations about the techniques of the poem. The following chart represents an analysis of "Thanatopsis" by William Cullen Bryant (page 120). Each column deals with one of the poetic techniques.

THE MEANING AND TECHNIQUES OF A POEM
SELECTION: "Thanatopsis"
MEANING: Do not fear death, for it is a part of life and a part of nature's endless cycle of life and death.

SELECTION OF SPEAKER	SOUND	IMAGERY	FIGURATIVE LANGUAGE
Narrator addresses reader/listener with a soothing, teacherlike tone.	*Rhythm:* varies; generally iambic pentameter, but the stress pattern varies, particularly at the end of a line. *Alliteration:* "move in majesty"; "Old Ocean's"; "favorite phantom"; sound contributes to a peaceful mood.	Images paint a picture of eternal nature—timeless, majestic, all life united in earth: "Old Ocean's gray and melancholy waste"; "vales stretching in pensive quietness"; "hills rock-ribbed and ancient."	*Metaphors:* "the narrow house" (coffin); "the great tomb of man" (earth); earth as "couch," or bed; "silent halls of death" *Main metaphor:* earth as tomb for all *Personification:* "She [Nature] has a voice of gladness and a smile."

WRITING PARAGRAPH BY PARAGRAPH

1. Begin your introductory paragraph with a thesis statement, which should restate the main points of the assignment. Indicate that the various techniques used by the poet all serve to enhance and present effectively the underlying meaning of the poem.

   Example: In "Thanatopsis" by William Cullen Bryant, the speaker tells us that we should not fear death but accept it peacefully as part of nature's eternal cycle of life and death. All the poetic techniques illustrate the timeless glory of nature, the oneness of all living things with nature, and the eternal cycle of life and death.

2. In each of the following paragraphs, discuss one or two of the techniques that the poet uses to underscore the poem's meaning—choice of speaker, sound devices, imagery, and figurative language. Show how each technique enhances the meaning, which you have discussed in your introductory paragraph.

3. In the next paragraph discuss further the meaning of the poem.

4. In the concluding paragraph restate your thesis statement. You might here go into greater detail on the emotional impact of the poem—now that you have analyzed the elements used to create emotion in the poem.

ASSIGNMENTS

1. Use the chart for "Thanatopsis" to write an essay about poetry. What is the meaning of the poem? What techniques does the poet use to reveal this meaning?

2. Do the assignment called "Writing About Poetry" that appears after the selections by Edgar Allan Poe (page 134), Walt Whitman (page 259), Ezra Pound (page 441), and T. S. Eliot (page 448), or select another piece of literature from this book.

LESSON 8: *Writing About the Total Effect*

Color, light, texture and line—painters use these visual elements and others to create visions of their world. Like painters, writers have a palette. Their literary palette includes plot, characters, setting, point of view, tone, theme, symbol, and irony. A skillful writer combines these elements to create a total effect or impact on the reader. To see just how the writer achieves this impact, you can study the work and analyze each element's contribution to the whole. Often you will find that, as in a painting, one element dominates. However, all the elements are deftly woven together to support that key element. In this way the author—or painter—creates a unified effect.

CONCEPTS TO REMEMBER

Review the lessons dealing with writing about the various literary elements individually. Review the definitions and important concepts in each lesson.

TYPICAL ESSAY QUESTION

When you are asked to write about the total effect of a selection, you are often answering an essay question such as the following:

Select a piece of literature that you have read. What is the total effect of the piece—that is, what is its impact on the reader? How does the author use the following literary elements to achieve this effect: plot, character, setting, point of view, tone, theme, symbol, and irony?

PREWRITING

1. Ask yourself the following questions as you reflect on the piece of literature:

   a. What is the impact of the work? Specifically, does the work irritate you, delight you, sadden you? Does it surprise you, or does it support an opinion or impression you already had? Does the work remind you of something else or contrast greatly with something else?
   b. Which literary element dominates?
   c. How do the other literary elements support or relate to the dominant element?

2. Prepare a chart on which to record your answers to the questions in Step 1. The chart should have columns for the question, the answer, and the details that support your answer. Remember that more than one answer may be possible; however, any answer should be supported with details. For the excerpt from *The Deerslayer* on page 115, a chart might look like the one on the following page.

WRITING PARAGRAPH BY PARAGRAPH

1. Begin the introductory paragraph with a thesis statement. The thesis statement should express the total effect of the work on the reader and note that all the key literary elements work together to create this impact.

   Example: The dominant literary element of *The Deerslayer* is character, but all the elements work together to create the total effect of the piece, which causes the reader to ponder the rules for survival in the wilderness and the definition of a "man."

2. In the next paragraph focus on the dominant literary element, and show by the inclusion of details how it contributes to the total effect.
3. In the following paragraphs discuss additional literary elements, and show by the inclusion of details how each element supports or relates to the dominant element.
4. In the concluding paragraph remind your audience that all the elements work together to produce the total impact.

REVISING AND EDITING

See page 841 for detailed reminders about improving your writing.

ASSIGNMENTS

1. Use the chart for *The Deerslayer* to write about the total effect of the work. How does the author use the key elements to achieve this effect?
2. Do the assignment called "Writing About the Total Effect" that appears after the selections by Edgar Allan Poe (page 149), Elizabeth Enright (page 665), and William Faulkner (page 679), or select another piece of literature from this book, and show how all the elements combine to achieve the total effect.

ANALYSIS OF THE TOTAL EFFECT
SELECTION: from *The Deerslayer*

QUESTIONS	ANSWER	DETAILS
A. WHAT IS THE IMPACT OF THE WORK?	Reader is struck by the difference in the two frontiersmen's attitudes toward killing and what makes a "man."	*Deerslayer:* "I hold it unlawful to take the life of man, except in open and generous warfare." *Harry:* "I shall not frequent your society long, friend, unless you look higher than four-footed beasts to practice your rifle on."
B. WHAT IS THE DOMINANT LITERARY ELEMENT?	*Character:* The author describes in great detail the differences in appearance, manner, and attitudes between Deerslayer and Harry. The basic conflict between these two is introduced by these descriptions.	*Deerslayer:* slight frame, "unusual agility"; expression of "guileless truth . . . earnestness of purpose . . . sincerity of feeling"; smart, neat *Harry:* "a dashing, reckless, offhand manner . . . gigantic frame . . . good-humored and handsome"; rough but not vulgar, thanks to "so noble a physique"; carelessly dressed
C. HOW DO THE OTHER ELEMENTS SUPPORT THE STORY?	*Plot:* The device of having the two men pause to eat in a clearing after having lost their way in the forest provides the opportunity to introduce two adversary characters.	"Both set themselves about making the preparations for their usual frugal but hearty meal. We will profit by this pause . . . to give the reader some idea of the appearance of the men."
	Setting: The lonely wilderness of the frontier is suitable backdrop for the conflict between Deerslayer and Harry.	"affording forest covers to the . . . native warrior as he trode the secret and bloody warpath"
	Point of view: Omniscient narrator underscores conflict by letting us into each character's mind.	*Deerslayer's mind:* "collision between mortification and correct feeling . . . , uprightness of heart soon getting the better of false pride and frontier boastfulness." *Harry's mind:* "as if he felt a noble scorn for the trifling accessories of dress and ornaments"
	Tone: serious, foreboding of conflict and tragedy to come	"He was as zealous a friend as his companion was dangerous as an enemy."
	Theme: conflict of opinion about how to survive in nature and about what makes a hero	Descriptions of dress, physical appearance, manners, and conversation all develop the conflicts between Deerslayer and Harry.
	Symbol: Deer—Deerslayer shot the deer that the two men eat. They disagree about whether shooting deer proves manhood.	*Harry:* "Fall to, and prove your manhood on this poor devil of a doe with your teeth, as you've already done with your rifle." *Deerslayer:* "Nay, nay, Harry, there's little manhood in killing a doe, and that too out of season. . . ."
	Irony: The peaceful setting contrasts with the conversation (situational irony).	"Centuries of summer suns"; "noble oaks and pines"; "brilliant light of a cloudless day in June"

LESSON 9: *Applying a Statement About Literature*

Sometimes a statement about life or literature in general can illuminate a particular work of literature. The statement seems to penetrate to the heart of a situation or lay bare the essential meaning of a piece of literature. It is your job to explain precisely why the general statement fits the specific piece of literature so well.

TYPICAL ESSAY QUESTION

A common essay question involves giving you a statement, asking you to explain the meaning of the statement, and then requesting you to show how the statement relates to a work you select or to a work specified in the essay question.

Example: As people mature, they sometimes form bittersweet memories of the dreams and adventures of childhood. Using *Life on the Mississippi,* show how this statement applies to Mark Twain's life.

PREWRITING

1. To make sure you understand the general statement and can do the first part of the assignment, paraphrase the statement and define any key terms in the statement.

   Example: As people grow up, they can see the pain as well as the joy of certain childhood experiences, plans, and illusions. They can look back with both a realization of how naive they were and a fondness for the way they were.

2. Prepare a chart that helps you focus on the essay assignment and the piece of literature. The left column will contain questions to help you connect the essay assignment to specific literary elements in the work. In the middle column jot down quotations or other specifics from the work as answers to the questions on the left. Cite specifics from *throughout* the work; remember that giving only one specific is not sufficient evidence to prove a point. In the right column explain more fully the relationship of evidence from the middle column to the essay question and to the particular piece of literature. The chart on the following page was filled in after rereading Mark Twain's *Life on the Mississippi* (page 275).

WRITING PARAGRAPH BY PARAGRAPH

1. Begin the introductory paragraph with a thesis statement that ties the given statement to a specific work.

   Example: The events, characters, setting, and point of view in Mark Twain's *Life on the Mississippi* illustrate that as people mature, they sometimes form bittersweet memories of the dreams and adventures of childhood.

   The rest of this paragraph might offer a quick summary of the work or a generalization about its main idea or theme. In addition, you might paraphrase any part of the thesis statement to assure that your audience knows precisely what it is you are setting out to prove.

2. In each of the following paragraphs, discuss how the given statement about the work connects with a specific literary element in the work. Be sure to cite examples of each literary element.

3. In the concluding paragraph emphasize that the evidence presented from the work demonstrates the applicability of the statement to this particular piece of literature.

REVISING AND EDITING

See page 841 for detailed reminders about improving your writing.

ASSIGNMENTS

1. Use the chart on the following page to write a well-developed essay about the application of the following statement to Mark Twain's *Life on the Mississippi:* As people mature, they sometimes form bittersweet memories of the dreams and adventures of childhood.

2. Do one of the assignments called "Applying a Statement About Literature" that follow the selections by Bret Harte (page 310), Stephen Crane (page 425), Thornton Wilder (page 739), and N. Scott Momaday (page 830). Or select another piece of literature from this book, and find a statement that applies to it. Then explain what the statement means and how it relates to the piece.

APPLICATION OF GENERAL STATEMENT TO SPECIFIC WORK

SELECTION: from *Life on the Mississippi*

GENERAL STATEMENT: As people mature, they sometimes form bittersweet memories of the dreams and adventures of childhood.

LITERARY ASPECT	EVIDENCE FROM WORK	RELATIONSHIP OF EVIDENCE AND STATEMENT
WHAT *EVENTS* IN THE WORK DOES THE STATEMENT BRING TO MIND?	Twain's comrades' changing ambitions (clown, minstrel, pirate, steamboatman) Arrival of boat: "the people fasten their eyes upon the coming boat as upon a wonder they are seeing for the first time" Trying to learn the river: "I entered upon the small enterprise . . . with the easy confidence of my time of life." "It was pleasant enough information, but I could not see the bearing of it." "Here was something fresh—this thing of getting up in the middle of the night to go to work."	On the one hand, Twain sees how daily events seemed serious to young boys but implies that day-to-day life was really carefree. On the other hand, Twain implies that he did not take seriously enough certain important events.
WHAT DETAILS ABOUT *CHARACTERS* DOES THE STATEMENT BRING TO MIND?	". . . the captain stands by the big bell, calm, imposing, the envy of all." ". . . an envied deckhand stands picturesquely . . ." "I was stung, but I was obliged to admire [Mr. Bixby's] easy confidence."	Twain sees that as a boy he romanticized all the people he looked up to, painfully wishing he could be like them. He also realizes that he was generous and right in giving them credit for jobs well done.
WHAT DETAILS ABOUT *SETTING* DOES THE STATEMENT BRING TO MIND?	Major setting = river: "I could make neither head nor tail of it. . . . My heart broke again, for it was plain that I had to learn this troublesome river *both* ways." Secondary setting = boats: The young apprentice is enthralled by glamour of the big New Orleans boat ("here was a sumptuous glass temple") and degrades the *Paul Jones*.	Twain remembers how the river caused him grief but also how the whole experience elated him.
WHAT DOES THE *POINT OF VIEW* HAVE TO DO WITH THE STATEMENT?	"If I had really known what I was about to require of my faculties, I should not have had the courage to begin." "I was set aside in disgrace. . . ." "I used to have fine inspirations of prudence in those days."	First-person point of view is what makes this piece a candidate for consideration in light of the statement. It allows us to see the examples of "bittersweet memories" and of Twain's recognizing both his naiveté and his fondness for his younger self.

LESSON 10: *Writing About Literature and Its Period*

Great writers, whether of fiction or nonfiction, can enter into a dialogue with their age. Their works reflect—indeed, sometimes create—the religious, economic, social, and political developments of a period.

CONCEPTS TO REMEMBER

1. You learn about a period through literature (a primary source) or through analyses of the period such as history textbooks (secondary sources). Make sure that you look carefully at a work of literature and not "read more into it" than is really there. Some works of literature are more characteristic of their periods than other works. On the other hand, some works of literature seem almost as though they could have been created during any period.

2. When thinking about literature and its period, you must remember to pay particular attention to the writer's tone, or attitude. In order to understand how the work relates to the period, you have to determine if the author is being satiric, supportive, optimistic, or pessimistic—to mention just a few possible tones.

TYPICAL ESSAY QUESTION

When you are asked to write about literature and its period, you are often answering an essay question like this one:

Write an essay showing how an author exemplifies a given literary period. Identify the period. State each characteristic of the period, and for each give examples from the work under discussion.

PREWRITING

1. Identify the literary or historical period during which the piece of literature was created. List the major characteristics of the period.

2. Ask yourself the following questions or similar ones as you read or reread a piece of literature:

   a. *Social Customs* What manners and customs of the time does the work present? What seems to be the author's attitude toward them? What does the work say or imply about interpersonal relationships, roles, occupations, and social responsibilities?

   b. *Economy* What attitude does the author seem to have toward the economic conditions of the age (toward trade and working conditions, toward agrarian or industrial pressures)? What information about these conditions does the author supply?

   c. *Politics* What is the author's reaction to the political situation? Specifically, what does the author seem to think about the ruling powers? The laws? Other political systems?

   d. *Philosophy and Religion* Does the work present religious beliefs accepted during the period in question? Do scenes take place within traditional religious institutions? How are religious people characterized? What seems to be the author's attitude toward the human ability to do good or evil? What seems to be the author's attitude toward the interaction of human beings and the natural world?

3. Prepare a chart that will help you to focus on the most important parts of the essay question. At the top of the chart, identify and define the period. In the left column list ideas about the period that you have been able to determine based on either secondary sources or on answers to the questions in Prewriting Step 2. In the right column cite specifics, including direct quotations from the work, for each of the generalizations on the left. Such a chart for the excerpt from Thoreau's *Walden* (page 171) might look like the one on the following page.

WRITING PARAGRAPH BY PARAGRAPH

1. Begin the introductory paragraph with a thesis statement that identifies the period. In addition, the thesis statement should indicate that the work being analyzed exemplifies key characteristics of that period.

Example: The American Transcendentalism movement of the mid-1880s has several characteristics that are notably present in Thoreau's *Walden,* particularly an emphasis on idealism, individualism, optimism, and the unity of God, nature, and humanity.

LITERATURE AND ITS PERIOD

SELECTION: Excerpts from *Walden*

PERIOD: The age of Transcendentalism—a period of Romantic optimism and extraordinary creativity in American culture (approximately 1840–1860), which laid particular emphasis on idealism, individualism, and the unity of God, nature, and humanity

CHARACTERISTICS OF THE PERIOD	EXAMPLES FROM THE WORK
Romantic optimism belief in human perfectibility and in ability of mind and spirit to transcend matter	"But alert and healthy natures remember that the sun rose clear. It is never too late to give up our prejudices." "What old people say you cannot do, you try and find that you can. Old deeds for old people, and new deeds for new." ". . . if one advances confidently in the direction of his dreams, and endeavors to live the life which he has imagined, he will meet with a success unexpected in common hours."
Idealism natural world a reflection of universal truths possibility of reaching high spiritual goals	"I went to the woods because I wished to live deliberately, to front only the essential facts of life, and see if I could not learn what it had to teach." ". . . if it were sublime, to know it by experience . . ." "If you have built castles in the air, your work need not be lost. . . ."
Individualism self-reliance controlling one's own destiny energy and self-motivation	"I should not talk so much about myself if there were anybody else whom I knew as well." ". . . I desire that there may be as many different persons in the world as possible; but I would have each one be very careful to find out and pursue his own way. . . ." "If a man does not keep pace with his companions, perhaps it is because he hears a different drummer."
Unity of God, nature, and humanity inseparability of the divine and the human	"The winds which passed over my dwelling were such as sweep over the ridges of mountains, bearing the broken strains, or celestial parts only, of terrestrial music."

2. In each of the following paragraphs, discuss one or more of the major characteristics of the period, and cite examples from the work that illustrate that particular characteristic.
3. In the concluding paragraph reiterate that this author and the specific work being studied exemplify key characteristics of the period.

REVISING AND EDITING

See page 841 for detailed reminders about improving your work.

ASSIGNMENTS

1. Write a well-developed essay in which you identify characteristics of American Transcendentalism and show how Thoreau's *Walden* exemplifies key characteristics of that period.
2. Do one of the assignments called "Writing About Literature and Its Period" that follows the selections by Hamlin Garland (page 339), Adrienne Rich (page 765), and Saul Bellow (page 835), or show how another piece of literature from this book exemplifies its period.

HANDBOOK OF LITERARY TERMS

ALLEGORY *A story with a symbolic meaning used to teach a moral principle.* Many of Hawthorne's stories, such as "The Minister's Black Veil" (p. 179), are allegories dealing with pride, isolation, love, and sympathy.

See page 178.

ALLITERATION *The repetition of sounds at the beginnings of words and of sounds within words.* Notice the repetition of the *s* sound in these lines from "Success is counted sweetest" (p. 267):

Success is counted sweetest
By those who ne'er succeed

See page 131.
See also ASSONANCE,
CONSONANCE.

ALLUSION *A short reference to a person, a place, an event, or another work of literature.* The reference, which the reader is expected to know, clarifies a point or expands its meaning. For example, in Masters' "Cassius Hueffer" (p. 467) the poet uses a famous line from Shakespeare's *Julius Caesar* to shed additional light on the complex and ironic personality of Cassius Hueffer:

"His life was gentle, and the elements so mixed in him
That nature might stand up and say to all the world,
This was a man."

See page 29.

ALMANAC *An annual collection of statistics, weather forecasts, current events, and other useful or entertaining information.* Franklin's *Poor Richard's Almanack* remains interesting reading today, especially for its proverbs.

See page 57.

AMERICANISM *A word or phrase that has originated in America:* for example, *Sun Belt, slam-dunk, hot dog.*

See page 259.

ANALOGY *A comparison made between two things to show the similarities between them.* Analogies explain something unfamiliar by comparing it to something familiar. In *Of Plymouth Plantation* (p. 24), for example, Bradford draws an analogy between the Puritans' "wandering" and that of the Israelites in Egypt:

"When they had wandered in the desert wilderness out of the way, and found no city to dwell in, both hungry and thirsty, their soul was overwhelmed in them."

See page 39.
See also SIMILE, METAPHOR.

ANAPEST *A poetic foot consisting of two unstressed syllables followed by a stressed syllable.*

See page 123.
See also FOOT.

ANECDOTE *A short account of an interesting event in someone's life.* Anecdotes are used to raise or illustrate a point, to explain an idea, or to describe personality. In "My Father Sits in the Dark" (p. 613) the author explains his father's habit with an anecdote that begins: "Once I left him there and went to bed. . . . I went to the kitchen. There he was. . . ."

See page 612.
See also
CHARACTERIZATION.

ANTAGONIST *A person or force that opposes the protagonist in a story or drama.* The antagonist in "To Build a Fire" (p. 341), for example, is the bitter cold and snow of the Klondike against which the man (the protagonist) must struggle.

See page 693.
See also PLOT, CONFLICT.

APHORISM *A short, pointed statement expressing a wise or clever observation about life.* For example:

No gains without pains.

—*Poor Richard's Almanack*

APOSTROPHE *A figure of speech in which a writer directly addresses an inanimate object, idea, or absent person.* In "Oread" (p. 456), for example, the poet addresses the sea:

Whirl up, sea—
whirl your pointed pines

See page 206.
See also
PERSONIFICATION.

ASIDE *In drama a short speech spoken by a character in an undertone or directly to the audience so that other characters on stage do not hear it.*

ASSONANCE *The repetition of similar vowel sounds in a line of poetry.* For example:

And the Raven, never fl*i*tt*i*ng, st*i*ll *i*s s*i*tt*i*ng, st*i*ll *i*s s*i*tt*i*ng

—"The Raven"

See page 131.
See also ALLITERATION, CONSONANCE, REPETITION.

AUTOBIOGRAPHY *The story of a person's life told by the person who lived it.* An autobiography, such as Ben Franklin's, contains objective facts as well as subjective feelings.

See page 58.
See also BIOGRAPHY.

BIOGRAPHY *A factual account of a person's life written by someone other than the subject.* A biography that comments on the subject's work as well as life is called a **critical biography.**

See page 230.
See also AUTOBIOGRAPHY.

BLANK VERSE *Unrhymed iambic pentameter.* Blank verse attempts to suggest spoken English; every line, therefore, need not be perfectly regular. Robert Frost's "Birches" (p. 500) is written in blank verse:

When I see birches bend to left and right
Across the lines of straighter darker trees

See page 123.
See also METER, FOOT, SCANSION.

CAESURA *The pause or break in a line of poetry, usually created by punctuation.* The caesura falls generally, but not necessarily, at the middle of a line. For example:

Once upon a midnight dreary, // while I pondered, weak and weary

—"The Raven"

See page 201.
See also METER.

CHARACTER *A person in a literary work.* Some characters are **flat**—built around a single trait, quality, or idea. **Stereotypes,** or **stock characters,** such as the noble hero and fiendish villain are usually flat characters. Butler, the landowner in Hamlin Garland's "Under the Lion's Paw" (p. 327), is a flat character.

A **round character** possesses a variety of traits, often complex and contradictory, making the character more like a real human being. Henry Fleming of *The Red Badge of Courage* (p. 368), for example, is a round character who exhibits conflicting behavior and attitudes toward the war.

See page 309.
See also CHARACTERIZATION.

CHARACTERIZATION *The ways an author develops the personalities of characters.* In **direct characterization** the writer states a character's personality. For example, in "To Build a Fire" (p. 341):

The man was without imagination.

In **indirect characterization** the writer reveals personality through physical description, action, thoughts, speech, or perceptions of the character or of other characters. Most frequently the reader must infer the personality from these suggestions. For example, the sensitivity of the narrator in "My Father Sits in the Dark" (p. 613) is revealed through his thoughts about his father.

See page 309.
See also CHARACTER.

CHORUS *In drama one or more characters who comment on the action.* In classical Greek drama the chorus is made up of a number of people. In *Our Town* (p. 698) the Stage Manager functions as a chorus.

CLASSICISM *A form of art that stresses reason and order over emotion and personal concerns.* The literature and art of ancient Greece and Rome are considered classical. The movement of the eighteenth century to imitate the balanced, orderly rationality of the ancients was called **neoclassicism.** Romanticism was in part a reaction to the neoclassic movement.

See page 101.

CLIMAX *The point of highest dramatic tension or excitement in a literary work.* The climax of "To Build a Fire" (p. 341), for example, occurs when the man loses his last match while alone in the bitter cold. He and the reader realize this means he is doomed.

See page 309.
See also PLOT, CONFLICT.

COLLOQUIAL LANGUAGE *The everyday language we use in conversation.* Mark Twain mastered the art of rendering colloquial speech in print. For example:

" 'What might it be that you've got in the box?' And Smiley says, sorter indifferent-like, 'It might be a parrot, or it might be a canary, maybe, but it ain't—it's only just a frog.' "

—"The Celebrated Jumping Frog of Calaveras County"

> See page 291.
> See also LITERAL
> LANGUAGE, DIALECT.

CONCEIT   *A lengthy, unusual comparison, often extended throughout an entire poem.* In "Huswifery" (p. 33), for example, the poet speaks of himself as an instrument in God's hands, the way a spinning wheel is an instrument in a housewife's hands. The comparison runs through the entire poem.

> See page 34.
> See also METAPHOR.

CONFESSIONAL POETRY   *A type of modern poetry in which poets speak with openness and frankness about their own lives.* Robert Lowell, John Berryman, Sylvia Plath, and Anne Sexton are the most important American confessional poets.

> See page 581.

CONFLICT   *The struggle that the protagonist of a story or drama undergoes.* The conflict can be external or internal, taking place within the character's mind. Each event in a plot relates to the conflict. In "The Bear" (p. 668), for example, the boy struggles to hunt the bear and to understand what the bear means to him.

> See pages 309, 351.
> See also ANTAGONIST.

CONNOTATION   *The suggestions or associations carried with a word beyond its denotation, or literal meaning.* For example:

The *summer* soldier and the *sunshine* patriot will, in this crisis, shrink from the service of their country. . . .

—"The American Crisis"

The connotations of *summer* and *sunshine* suggest that the author is referring to people who are soldiers and patriots only during good times.

> See page 197.

CONSONANCE   *The repetition of consonant sounds in a line of poetry.* For example:

Beat! beat! drums!—blow! bugles! blow!

—"Beat! Beat! Drums!"

> See page 131.
> See also ASSONANCE,
> ALLITERATION.

COUPLET   *Two consecutive lines of poetry that rhyme.* For example, these lines from "To My Dear and Loving Husband" (p. 31):

If ever two were one, then surely we.
If ever man were loved by wife, then thee.

> See page 87.

DACTYL   *A poetic foot consisting of one stressed syllable followed by two unstressed syllables.* ($'$ ˘ ˘).

> See page 123.
> See also FOOT.

DENOTATION   *The literal meaning, or dictionary definition, of a word.*

> See page 197.
> See also LITERAL
> LANGUAGE, CONNOTATION.

DENOUEMENT   *The resolution of a story, as the conflict is resolved and the knot of the plot is untied.* After the climax of "The Far and the Near" (p. 631), when the trainman discovers that his "dream family" is quite ordinary, he comes to some conclusions about himself and his future.

> See page 309.
> See also PLOT

DESCRIPTION   *Writing that creates a picture of a person, place, or thing.* The specific details of description enhance poems, stories, and nonfiction. Columbus, for example, uses vivid and concrete details as he describes in his *Journal* (p. 15) a type of tree he had never before seen:

. . . thus one branch has leaves like those of a cane, and others like those of a mastic tree; and on a single tree there are five different kinds.

> See page 92.
> See also IMAGE,
> NARRATION,
> EXPOSITION,
> PERSUASION.

DIALECT   *The way of speaking and writing that is particular to a specific region of the country.* Mark Twain was a successful writer of dialect, capturing subtle differences of pronunciation and vocabulary. For example:

. . . he was the curiosest man about always betting on anything that turned up you ever see. . . .

—"The Celebrated Jumping Frog of Calaveras County"

> See page 118.

DIALOGUE *The conversation of characters in a drama, short story, novel, or dramatic poem.*

See page 693.

DICTION *The choice of words to fit the character, theme, setting, or subject in a poem, story, essay, or play.* Notice how Emily Dickinson chooses words that intensify the violence of the action in "Apparently with no surprise" (p. 264):

The Frost *beheads* it at its play—
In accidental *power*—
The blonde *Assassin* passes on—

See page 197.

DRAMA *A story acted out with spoken dialogue before an audience.* The dramatist, or playwright, usually provides dialogue and stage directions that give instructions about scenery, costumes, gestures, movements, and lighting.

See page 693.

DRAMATIC MONOLOGUE *A long speech by one character in a play or poem, usually revealing the character's thoughts.* "The Love Song of J. Alfred Prufrock" (p. 443), is a dramatic monologue in which the speaker reveals his fears and frustrations.

See page 447.

DRAMATIC POEM *A poem that reveals character through dialogue and monologue.* While there is some narrative in a dramatic poem, the focus is on character, not events. In "The Love Song of J. Alfred Prufrock" (p. 443), for example, Prufrock speaks to himself and to the reader; he also imagines conversations with other people.

See page 272.
See also NARRATIVE POEM, LYRIC POEM.

END–STOPPED LINE *A line of poetry that ends with a pause both in punctuation and in thought.* For example:

By the rude bridge that arched the flood,
Their flag to April's breeze unfurled
—"Concord Hymn"

See page 201.
See also RUN–ON LINE.

EPIC *A long narrative poem that traces the adventures of a hero.* Composed during ancient and medieval times, epics usually intertwine myth and history, reflecting the values of the societies in which they originate. In epics gods and goddesses often intervene in the affairs of humans, as they do in Homer's *Iliad* and *Odyssey*. Though usually referred to as a myth, the *Walum Olum* of the Delaware Indians may also be considered an epic. Other than some long works by American Indians, however, there are no genuine American literary epics, though Longfellow's *Song of Hiawatha* (1855) attempted to imitate epic form and style.

See also NARRATIVE POEM.

EPIPHANY *A term used by Irish writer James Joyce to describe the moment of revelation or recognition in which a character in a story perceives an essential truth.* In Saroyan's "There Was a Young Lady of Perth" (p. 782), for instance, during one brief moment the narrator realizes that he does not need a life of fame and fortune.

See page 780.

ESSAY *A moderately brief nonfiction work that deals with a particular topic.* Essays may be classified as formal or informal. A **formal essay** is a carefully structured attempt to instruct or persuade. It has a serious tone and presents its argument logically. Ralph Waldo Emerson's *Nature* (p. 161) is a formal essay on the subject of the relationship between the human world and the natural world.

An **informal essay** usually attempts to entertain the reader while exploring a given topic. Its tone is light, its structure somewhat sprawling. Because the informal essay often makes personal references, it is sometimes called the **personal essay.** "Hidden Name and Complex Fate" (p. 822) is an informal essay presenting the author's personal view on the subject of names.

See page 692.

EXPOSITION *The background information vital to the reader's understanding of a story.* The exposition generally comes at the beginning of a story, presenting the characters and situation. The opening paragraph of "A Worn Path" (p. 643), for example, introduces the reader to the time, place, and central character: "It was December—a bright frozen day in the early morning. Far out in the country there was an old Negro woman with her head tied in a red rag. . . ."

See page 309.
See also DESCRIPTION, NARRATION, PLOT.

FABLE *A tale, usually ending with a moral, in which animals behave as if they were human beings.* Some of the most famous fables are those of the Greek writer Aesop and those of the French writer

LaFontaine. Mark Twain openly called his fable "A Fable."

See page 289.

FIGURATIVE LANGUAGE *Language that is not meant to be taken literally.* Often figurative language uses a concrete image to express an abstract idea: for example, "Love your Neighbor; yet don't pull down your Hedge." In this proverb from *Poor Richard's Almanack* (p. 57), "Hedge" is not meant literally. It is an image representing the idea of protection of privacy.

See also LITERAL
LANGUAGE, SIMILE,
METAPHOR.

FIGURE OF SPEECH *A word or expression that is not meant to be taken literally.* **Similes** and **metaphors** are figures of speech.

See page 164.
See also FIGURATIVE
LANGUAGE.

FLASHBACK *An interruption in a narrative to show an event that happened earlier.* This technique is used in stream-of-consciousness writing, as well as in generally conventional narratives. For example, in "The Jilting of Granny Weatherall" (p. 604), Granny remembers scenes of her past life that make her final moments in the story more meaningful.

See page 611.

FOIL *A character who through contrast underscores the characteristics of another.* The dog in "To Build a Fire" (p. 341), for example, exhibits a caution and respect for the cold of the Klondike that the man obviously lacks.

See page 628.
See also
CHARACTERIZATION.

FOOT *The basic unit of meter in a line of poetry.* Usually a foot consists of one stressed syllable and one or two unstressed syllables. Common feet in American poetry are:

The **iamb**, an unstressed syllable followed by a stressed syllable. For example:

Aňd só / ma̅y yóu / whoev́ / e̅r dares̒ / dǐsgráce
—"To His Excellency, General Washington"

The **trochee,** a stressed syllable followed by an unstressed syllable. For example:

Onće uṗ / oń a̅ / midnighͭt / dreaŕy̆ / aśs I̅
—"The Raven"

The **anapest,** two unstressed syllables followed by a stressed syllable. For example:

When the heart́ / iň his̒ breast́ / like a̅ trip͐ / hǎmmer̆ beat́s
—"A Fable for Critics"
James Russell Lowell

The **dactyl,** a stressed syllable followed by two unstressed syllables. For example:

This̒ is̅ the / forest́ prim͐ / evaĺ. The̅ / muŕmurinğ / pineś and the̅ / hemlŏcks̆
—"Evangeline"
Henry Wadsworth Longfellow

The **spondee,** two stressed syllables. For example:

Iň all̒ / his̒ course̒; / nŏr yet́ / iň the̅ / cóld ground́
—"Thanatopsis"

See page 123.
See also METER.

FORESHADOWING *A method of increasing suspense by presenting events or characters in such a way as to hint at what is going to happen to them.* Foreshadowing often contains a large element of irony. For example, in Thomas Wolfe's "The Far and the Near" (page 631), the trainman's disappointment is foreshadowed when his vision of the little house is said to be fixed in his mind as "something beautiful and enduring, something beyond all change."

See page 801.

FRAME STORY *A story that serves as a framework within which another story is told.* "In Dreams Begin Responsibilities" (p. 634) uses a frame story.

See page 641.

FREE VERSE *Poetry that has an irregular rhythm and line length and that avoids a predetermined verse structure.* Free verse uses the cadences of natural speech and rarely rhymes. Walt Whitman's poetry, for example, is free verse:

This is the city and I am one of the citizens,
Whatever interests the rest interests me, politics,
wars, markets, newspapers, schools—
—"Song of Myself"

See page 251.
See also METER, RHYTHM.

HAIKU *A Japanese verse form consisting of three lines, usually describing an image of a subject in na-*

ture. The first line is limited to five syllables, the second line to seven syllables, and the third line to five syllables. Haiku influenced the Imagist poets.

See page 441.

HEROIC COUPLET _A pair of rhymed lines in iambic pentameter._ For example:

Ĭ príze / thy lóve / mŏre thán / whŏle mínes / ŏf góld
Ŏr áll / thĕ rí / chĕs thát / thĕ Eást / dŏth hóld.
—"To My Dear and Loving Husband"

See page 87.
See also RHYTHM.

IAMB _A poetic foot consisting of an unstressed syllable followed by a stressed syllable_ (˘ ´).

See also FOOT, IAMBIC
PENTAMETER.

IAMBIC PENTAMETER _A line of poetry composed of five iambic feet._

Prŏceéd / grĕat chíef / wĭth vír / tŭe ón / thy síde
—"To His Excellency, General Washington"

See page 362.
See also RHYTHM, BLANK
VERSE, HEROIC COUPLET.

IMAGE _A "picture" in the reader's mind created by words._ Images can describe the sensory experiences of seeing, hearing, tasting, smelling, feeling. In Columbus' "Journal" (p. 15), for example, the image helps the reader "see" the canoes approaching:

. . . made out of the trunk of a tree, all in one piece, and wonderfully worked, propelled with a paddle like a baker's shovel . . .

Ezra Pound said that an image "presents an intellectual and emotional complex in an instant of time."

See page 34.
See also IMAGERY.

IMAGERY _The collection of mental pictures, or images, in a literary work._ Visual imagery is most common, but a writer can also suggest images that appeal to the senses of sound, taste, smell, and touch. Consider this image of sight:

The purple petals, fallen in the pool,
Made the black water with their beauty gay.
—"The Rhodora"

See page 213.
See also DESCRIPTION

IMAGISM _An influential literary movement that took place in Europe and America from about 1910 to 1920._ The Imagist poet creates a single sharp image that evokes an emotional response in the reader. Invented by Ezra Pound and furthered by H. D., Imagism was in part a reaction to the "bad habits" of nineteenth-century poets who were too explicit in their commentary and too repetitious in their subjects, patterns, and meters. Pound's "In a Station of the Metro" (p. 438) is the most famous example of Imagism.

See page 441.

IRONY _The awareness—by author, character, or reader—of a contrast or a difference between the way things seem and the way they really are._
Verbal irony occurs when words that appear to be saying one thing mean something quite different. In W. H. Auden's "Unknown Citizen" (p. 575), for example, the poet suggests that something very definitely is wrong, making the last lines ironic:

Was he free? Was he happy? The question is absurd:
Had anything been wrong, we should certainly have heard.

Situational irony occurs when what is expected to happen is not what actually comes to pass. In "The Far and the Near" (p. 631), for example, the trainman is sadly surprised to find the dull and ordinary where he expected the romantic and beautiful.
Dramatic irony occurs when events that mean one thing to the characters mean something quite different to the reader. _Our Town_ (p. 698) is full of dramatic irony. The breakfast scenes, for example, seem ordinary to the characters, but the audience sees the universal elements and significance in the actions.

See page 359.

JOURNAL _A daily record of events kept by an individual who is a participant in or witness to these events._ Journals are often valuable historical documents. Mary Chesnut's _Journal_ gives us a view of the Civil War by one who lived through it.

See page 238.

LIMERICK _A humorous five-line poem in which the first, second, and fifth lines rhyme and have the rhythm ˘ ´/ ˘ ˘ ´/ ˘ ˘ ´, and the third and fourth lines rhyme with each other and have the rhythm ˘ ˘ ´/ ˘ ˘ ´._ Saroyan uses the limerick in "There Was a Young Lady of Perth" (p. 782). A sample limerick:

There was an old man of Peru
Who dreamt he was eating his shoe.

He awoke in the night
In a terrible fright,
And found it was perfectly true!

See page 781.

LITERAL LANGUAGE *Language that means exactly what it says.*

See page 164.
See also FIGURATIVE
LANGUAGE.

LYRIC POEM *A poem that expresses primarily the personal thoughts and feelings of the poet.* Lyric poems are short and attempt to achieve a single, unified effect. "Success is counted sweetest" (p. 267) is an example of a lyric poem.

See page 273.
See also NARRATIVE POEM,
DRAMATIC POEM.

METAPHOR *A comparison that identifies one thing with another, seemingly very different thing.* For example, in *Of Plymouth Plantation* (p. 24), to emphasize how vast the Pilgrims' troubles were, Bradford speaks of "a sea of troubles."

See page 39.
See also SIMILE, ANALOGY,
CONCEIT.

METER *A generally regular pattern of stressed and unstressed syllables in a line of poetry.* Meter is determined by the number and kind of feet in a line. For example, the meter of Longfellow's "Psalm of Life" (p. 199) is trochaic tetrameter: Each line has four (tetra) trochaic feet (one stressed syllable followed by one unstressed syllable).

See page 122.
See also SCANSION, FOOT,
BLANK VERSE.

MODERNISM *A collective term for the radically new ideas, forms, styles, and attitudes that revolutionized all the arts during the first three decades of our century.* American writers, many of whom traveled frequently to Europe, experimented with new, more objective styles and freer-flowing forms in poetry, drama, and fiction. World War I triggered a shift in values, and writers of the period were quick to reflect the change. The complacency and optimism of previous generations were replaced by a more desperate attempt to make sense of the modern world.

See page 429.

MOTIVATION *The reason or group of reasons why a character in fiction acts in a certain way.* Motivation makes characters believable. Sometimes the author will state directly why a character behaves in a certain way. Jack London, for example, explains his character's risking his life in the cold in "To Build a Fire" (p. 341): "The trouble with him was that he was without imagination."

Many times the author implies the motivation, enabling readers to draw it out of their knowledge of the character. For example, in "The First Seven Years" (p. 773) readers infer why Sobel quit his job.

See page 325.
See also CHARACTER.

NARRATION *Writing that tells a story, moving from event to event, usually in chronological order.* A narrative may be factual, like "The Alligators of East Florida" (p. 89), or fictional, like "The Fall of the House of Usher" (p. 135).

See page 113.
See also DESCRIPTION,
EXPOSITION, PERSUASION.

NARRATIVE POEM *A poem that tells a story.* The **epic** is a long poem of heroic adventure. The **ballad** is a shorter narrative poem, often set to music. "Janet Waking" (p. 477) is a narrative poem.

See page 272.
See also DRAMATIC POEM,
LYRIC POEM.

NARRATOR *One who narrates, or tells, a story.* The young sister, a character in the story, is narrator of "Point of Embarkation" (p. 789). A story may be narrated in the first person or the third person. The author may serve as narrator. Sometimes even a play may have a narrator, as in *Our Town* (p. 698).

See also POINT OF VIEW.

NATURALISM *A literary movement that portrays people caught within forces of nature or society that are beyond their understanding or control.* Naturalism was an outgrowth of Realism, responding to theories in science, psychology, human behavior, and social thought current in the late nineteenth century. The naturalist uses a quasi-scientific "facts-only" approach, heavy in detail. While the subject matter of naturalistic writing is often grim, the purpose generally is to highlight ills so that they can be corrected. Hamlin Garland's "Under the Lion's Paw" (p. 327), for example, dramatized the plight of farmers.

See page 297.

NOVEL *A book-length prose fiction.* Types of novels include the **picaresque,** a loose series of episodes recounting the adventures of wanderers and lovable rogues; **sentimental,** a highly emotional tale of romance and tears; **gothic,** a tale of mystery and fear; **philosophical,** a story that raises profound questions about life and humankind; **psychological,** a narrative that probes the complexity of its characters' thinking, behavior, and motivation; **realistic,** a story that focuses objectively on ordinary life; **naturalistic,** a story of characters trapped by overwhelming forces of nature or society; **regional,** a tale in which the peculiarities of a particular setting play a major role; **satiric,** or novel of **social witticism,** a story whose purpose is to uncover evils in society for the purpose of correction; **stream-of-consciousness,** a narrative told through the free-flowing consciousness of the narrator.

> See page 363.
> See also REALISM, REGIONALISM, NATURALISM.

OCTAVE *An eight-line poem or stanza.*

> See SONNET.

ONOMATOPOEIA *The use of words with sounds that suggest their meanings.* For example:

> So strong you *thump* O terrible drums—
> —"Beat! Beat! Drums!"

> See page 131.

ORAL TRADITION *Stories, songs, tales, and myths of a people passed down by word of mouth from one generation to another.* Much American Indian literature was originally preserved in the oral tradition.

> See page 14.

ORATORY *Formal public speaking, often characterized by a blend of argument and emotion.* Orators such as Patrick Henry (p. 65) greatly influenced the shaping of America in its early years.

> See page 68.
> See also PERSUASION.

PARALLELISM *The repetition of phrases or sentences so that the repeated parts are alike in structure or meaning.* Parallelism gives emphasis to thoughts especially in persuasive writing. For example:

> To err is human, to repent divine; to persist, devilish.
> —*Poor Richard's Almanack*

> See page 84.

PARODY *A humorous imitation.* A parody imitates another work's plot, characters, or style, usually through exaggeration. "The Fall of the House of Usher" by Reed Whittemore (p. 593) parodies the plot of Poe's story of the same title.

> See page 594.

PERSONIFICATION *A figure of speech in which human qualities are given to objects, animals, and ideas.* For example:

> Earth smiles—the waters smile—even the sky of clouds smiles—
> —"Calling One's Own"

> See page 206.
> See also METAPHOR.

PERSUASION *Writing that attempts to sway the reader to think or act in a particular way.* In "The Beauty of the World" (p. 44), for example, Jonathan Edwards tries to convince people of the superiority of spiritual beauty, so they will strive to be holy and virtuous.

> See page 22.

PLOT *In a short story, novel, or play the series of events that leads from beginning to end.* Each event is related to the **conflict,** the struggle that the main character undergoes. Usually a plot begins with **exposition,** the background of setting and situation. Some interesting element, the **narrative hook,** draws readers into the story. Events that contribute to the conflict are called the **rising action,** leading to the **climax,** or point of highest dramatic tension. The **falling action** presents the results of the climax, and the **resolution** gives the final outcome. The resolution is sometimes called **denouement,** meaning "untying," since the term refers to the untying of the "knot" of the plot.

> See page 309.

POINT OF VIEW *The relationship of the storyteller, or narrator, to the story.* A story has a **first-person point of view** if one of the characters, referred to as "I," tells the story, as in "My Father Sits in the Dark" (p. 613).

A story has a **limited third-person point of view** if the narrator reveals the thoughts of only one character but refers to that character as "he" or "she." "The Celebrated Jumping Frog of Calaveras County" (p. 284), for example, is told from a limited third-person point of view.

A narrator who tells the thoughts of all the characters and who tells things that no one character could know uses the **omniscient** (all-knowing), or **third-**

person, point of view. Bret Harte uses this point of view in "The Outcasts of Poker Flat" (p. 302).

See page 319.
See also SHORT STORY.

PROTAGONIST *The central character of a story, novel, play, or dramatic poem.* The action usually revolves around the protagonist, who generally receives the reader's sympathies. Henry Fleming is the protagonist of *The Red Badge of Courage* (p. 368) because the novel follows his every thought and action.

See page 309.
See also PLOT,
ANTAGONIST.

QUATRAIN *A stanza or poem with four lines.* For example, Emerson uses the quatrain in "Concord Hymn" (page 165):

> By the rude bridge that arched the flood,
>   Their flag to April's breeze unfurled,
> Here once the embattled farmers stood
>   And fired the shot heard round the world.

See also SONNET.

REALISM *A literary movement to produce literature that represents ordinary life as it actually is lived.* In part, Realism was a reaction against the Romantic emphasis on the strange, idealistic, and long-ago and far-away. The Realist is more objective than subjective and often writes about middle- and lower-class people and reveals democratic sympathies. *The Red Badge of Courage* (p. 368), which presents a nonidealized picture of war, is a Realist novel.

See page 296.
See also REGIONALISM.

REFRAIN *A line or group of lines repeated at regular intervals in a poem.* "Go Down, Moses" (p. 223), for example, includes a refrain, which would be recited or sung by a chorus:

> Go down, Moses,
>   Way down in Egypt land
> Tell old Pharoah,
>   Let my people go!

See page 201.
See also REPETITION.

REGIONALISM *A literary movement that focused on the special atmosphere, or "local color," of a particular area.* The regionalist re-creates accurately the activities, dialect, appearance, and customs of the characters, as well as the environment in which they live. Bret Harte, for example, conveyed the local color of the West ("The Outcasts of Poker Flat," p. 302). Sarah Orne Jewett did the same for rural New England ("A White Heron," p. 311).

See page 310.
See also REALISM.

REGIONALISMS *Words or phrases peculiar to a particular region.* Twain captures some southwestern regionalisms in "The Celebrated Jumping Frog of Calaveras County" (p. 284) with sentences like this:

> Jumping on a *dead level* was his *strong suit,* you understand; and when it come to that, Smiley would *ante up* money on him as long as he had a *red.*

See page 310.

REPETITION *A device used to emphasize the importance of words and ideas particularly in persuasive writing and poetry.* For example, in Patrick Henry's "Speech in the Virginia Convention" (p. 66), Henry repeats the words *freedom* and *slavery* many times, and uses other words (*subjugation, supplication, submission, chains*) that repeat the important ideas that he wants his audience to bear in mind.

Repetition can also add a musical quality to poetry. Poets deliberately repeat sounds, words, phrases, and lines for the musical sound and for emphasis. **Alliteration, assonance, consonance, refrain,** and **rhyme** are common means of repetition for the poet. **Parallelism** is a form of repetition used often in prose as well as in poetry.

See page 131.

RHYME *The use of similar or identical sounds in the accented syllables of two or more words.* When the rhyme occurs at the ends of lines, it is called **end rhyme:**

> We'll honor George, our Sovereign, while he sits on
>   the *throne,*
> If he grants us liberty, no other king we'll *own.*

When the rhyme occurs within the line, it is called **internal rhyme.**

> Of the *bold* Americans, who scorn to be *controlled.*

When the rhyme is not exact, it is called **approximate,** or **slant, rhyme:**

> We'll honor George, our sovereign, on any reason-
>   able *terms,*
> But if he don't grant us liberty, we'll all lay down
>   our *arms.*

—"The Bold Americans"

See pages 131, 272.
See also RHYME SCHEME.

RHYME SCHEME *The pattern of end rhymes in a poem.* The rhyme scheme is determined by assigning a different letter of the alphabet to each new rhyming sound. The rhyme scheme in the first stanza of Taylor's "Huswifery" (p. 33), for example, is determined this way:

Make me, O Lord, Thy spinning wheel complete.	*a*
Thy holy word my distaff make for me.	*b*
Make mine affections Thy swift flyers neat,	*a*
And make my soul Thy holy spool to be.	*b*
My conversation make to be Thy reel,	*c*
And reel the yarn thereon spun of Thy wheel.	*c*

See page 167.
See also STANZA.

RHYTHM *The arrangement of stressed and unstressed syllables in a poem.* When the rhythm forms a regular pattern, it is called **meter.** The rhythm in "Desert Places" (p. 497) is regular:

And lone / ly as / it is / that lone / liness

Will be / more lone / ly ere / it will / be less

The rhythm in "A Noiseless Patient Spider" (p. 254) is irregular:

A noiseless patient spider,
I marked where on a little promontory
  it stood isolated.

See page 122.

RISING ACTION *That part of a story's plot that adds complications to the problems and increases reader interest.* In Truman Capote's "Miriam" (p. 794), for example, the action rises as the mysterious child continues to impose upon the woman.

See page 309.

ROMANCE *A prose narrative that is far removed from the incidents of ordinary life.* It makes greater use of the marvelous, improbable, and unbelievable. Generally, though, the emotions of the characters are true to human nature. Hawthorne's "Minister's Black Veil" (p. 179) is a romance.

See page 156.
See also NOVEL,
ROMANTICISM.

ROMANTICISM *A literary movement of the late eighteenth and early nineteenth centuries.* Romantic literature generally exhibits some of these six characteristics: (1) a profound love of nature; (2) a focus on the self and the individual; (3) a fascination with the supernatural, the mysterious, the gothic; (4) a yearning for the picturesque and the exotic; (5) a deep-rooted idealism; (6) a passionate nationalism, or love of country.

Literature as diverse as Cooper's adventure story *The Deerslayer* and Bryant's poem on death, "Thanatopsis," are Romantic.

See page 101.
See also CLASSICISM.

RUN–ON LINE *A line of poetry that has no pause at the end but flows into the next line.* Poets can vary rhythm by using run-on lines. For example:

Bid Time and Nature gently space
The shaft we raise to them and thee.

—"Concord Hymn"

See page 201.
See also END–STOPPED
LINE.

SATIRE *Writing that holds up someone or something to ridicule or serious criticism.* Satire may be in the form of poetry or prose, of fiction or nonfiction. Consistent in all satires is the desire to correct some ill or evil in society. Some satires are gentle, poking good-natured fun; others are harsh and bitter. "(HELP!)" (p. 768) is a satire of twentieth-century depersonalization.

See page 576.

SCANSION *The analysis of a poem to determine its meter.* This is done by marking syllables in a line of poetry as being stressed (′) or unstressed (˘). For example:

"'Tis some / visi / tor," I / muttered, /

"tapping / at my / chamber / door."

—"The Raven"

See page 123.
See also FOOT, IAMBIC
PENTAMETER.

SESTET *A six-line poem or stanza.*

See SONNET.

SETTING *The time and place in which events occur in a literary work.* The setting of Mark Helprin's "White Gardens" (p. 812), for example, is a funeral in a Brooklyn, New York, church during a recent summer.

See page 309.
See also PLOT.

SHORT STORY *A brief prose narrative that usually*

can be read in one sitting. A short story generally contains the following major elements:

Plot—the series of events leading from beginning to end.

Characterization—the way an author develops the personalities of characters.

Setting—the time and place in which events occur.

Point of view—the perspective of the storyteller, or narrator.

Theme—the main idea of the story.

Style—the writer's way of writing, determined by the diction, structure, imagery, etc.

See page 309.
See also NOVEL.

SIMILE *A figure of speech that states a comparison by using* like *or* as *to indicate the comparison.* For example:

When you look upon me I am satisfied as
    flowers that drink dew.
                                        —"Calling One's Own"

See page 39.
See also METAPHOR,
ANALOGY.

SOLILOQUY *A long speech spoken by a character who is alone on stage.* This speech usually reveals the private thoughts and emotions of the character.

See also DRAMATIC
MONOLOGUE.

SONNET *A lyric poem of fourteen lines written in iambic pentameter.* **Shakespearean,** or **English, sonnets** have three quatrains (groups of four lines) followed by a rhymed couplet, with the rhyme scheme *abab cdcd efef gg.* The English sonnet presents its main thought in the three quatrains, with a conclusion presented in the couplet.

Petrarchan, or **Italian, sonnets** divide into a group of eight lines, or octave, followed by a group of six lines, or sestet. The rhyme scheme for the octave is *abba abba* and for the sestet *cdecde* or *cd cd ee.* In the Italian sonnet the octave presents a single thought, with the sestet expanding, contradicting, or developing it in some other way.

Jean Toomer's "November Cotton Flower" (p. 471) is a modified Shakespearean sonnet. Paul Laurence Dunbar's "Douglass" (p. 361) is a Petrarchan sonnet.

See page 362.

SPEAKER *The voice of a poem, sometimes that of the poet, sometimes that of a fictional person or even a thing.* The speaker's words communicate a particular tone, or attitude, toward the subject of the poem. For example, the speaker in Masters' "Lucinda Matlock" (p. 468) is a woman whose tone is vigorous and full of the love of life.

See also POINT OF VIEW.

SPIRITUAL *A folk song, generally dealing with earthly bondage or religious faith.* "Go Down, Moses" (p. 223) is a famous spiritual.

See page 222.

SPONDEE *A poetic foot consisting of two stressed syllables (' ').*

See page 123.

STAGE DIRECTIONS *Instructions written by the playwright about scenery, costumes, gestures, movements, and lighting for a play or drama.* In *Our Town* (p. 698), for example, the directions about the lack of scenery, the stage manager's hat and pipe, and the use of chairs are examples of stage directions.

STANZA *A group of lines forming a unit in a poem.* Stanzas usually contain from two to eight lines and often have a definite rhyme scheme. The stanzas in "The Raven" (p. 127) have six lines and a rhyme scheme of *abcbbb.*

Common stanzas are the **couplet,** two lines; the **tercet,** three lines; the **quatrain,** four lines; the **sestet,** six lines; the **octave,** eight lines.

See page 167.

STREAM OF CONSCIOUSNESS *A technique of writing that imitates the flow of thoughts, feelings, images, and memories through the mind of a character in a work of fiction.* The traditional chronological narrative is replaced by a seemingly jumbled collection of things running through the mind, forcing the reader to piece together the "plot" of an incident. "The Jilting of Granny Weatherall" (p. 604), for example, is the stream of Granny's thoughts.

See page 610.
See also FLASHBACK.

STYLE *A writer's characteristic way of writing determined by his diction, imagery, tone, and choice of literary devices.* Frost's style, for example, has a natural rhythm and conversational tone, with many images of nature. Wallace Stevens is more abstract in his imagery; his lines are tighter. Cummings' style is easily recognized for its lack of conventional form, punctuation, and capitalization.

See page 425.

SUSPENSE *That quality in a story that makes the reader uncertain or tense about the outcome of events.* In one type of suspense, readers do not know what will happen next, as in "The Portable Phonograph" (p. 651). In a second type of suspense, readers know the plot but wonder about *how* things will happen.

See page 801.
See also FORESHADOWING.

SYMBOL *A person, place, or thing that has meaning in itself and also stands for something other than itself.* Symbols often help convey meaning in stories and poems. For example, the flag in "Success is counted sweetest" (p. 267) is a physical object, but it symbolizes the conquest of one army over another:

Not one of all the purple Host
Who took the Flag today
Can tell the definition
So clear of Victory.

See page 187.

THEME *The main idea that the writer of a literary work communicates to the reader.* The theme is usually expressed as a statement about life. Some stories have a **stated theme,** announced explicitly, usually at the end of the story. Most stories have **implied themes** revealed indirectly through the unfolding of the events. The implied theme of Ernest Hemingway's "In Another Country" (p. 518), for example, is that pain and loss, especially during war, can numb the spirit.

See page 309.
See also PLOT.

TONE *The attitude the writer takes toward his or her subject, characters, and readers.* The Declaration of Independence, for example, has a formal tone:

When in the course of human events it becomes necessary for one people to dissolve the political bands which have connected them to another . . .

Twain's autobiography reflects a personal, affectionate tone:

The moment we were underway I began to prowl about the great steamer and fill myself with joy. She was as clean and as dainty as a drawing room. . . .
—*Life on the Mississippi*

See page 502.

TRANSCENDENTALISM *An American philosophical and artistic attitude based on the belief that the most fundamental truths about life and death can be reached only by going beyond the world of the senses.* Knowledge of this kind comes not through the mind's logic but through a deep, free intuition that transcendentalists recognized as the "highest power of the Soul." The essays of Emerson convey much of the Transcendentalist philosophy.

See page 154.

TROCHEE *A poetic foot consisting of a stressed syllable followed by an unstressed syllable (´ ˘).*

See page 123.
See also FOOT.

VILLANELLE *A poem of nineteen lines divided into five tercets (three-line stanzas) and a final quatrain, using the rhyme scheme* aba aba aba aba abaa. There are only two rhymes in a villanelle, and eight of the nineteen lines are repeated. Lines 6, 12, and 18 repeat line 1; lines 9, 15, and 18 repeat line 3. Auden's "If I Could Tell You" (p. 574) is an example of a modern villanelle.

GLOSSARY

The following glossary lists words from the selections that may be unfamiliar to you. Although many of the words have several different meanings, they are defined only as they are used in the selections. Some words may be familiar to you in other contexts but may have unusual meanings in the text.

Each glossary entry contains a pronunciation, a part of speech, and a definition. Some words are used in more than one way in the textbook and therefore have more than one definition and occasionally more than one part of speech. Related words are often combined in one entry: The main form (for example, the adjective *callow*) is defined, and another form (for example, the noun *callowness*) is run on after the main definition. Adverbs ending in *-ly* are usually run on after the definition of the adjective form.

Some unusual words or meanings of words are labeled AR-CHAIC (old-fashioned), OBSOLETE (no longer in use), RARE, or POETIC. Other special usage labels include COLLOQUIAL, SLANG, CHIEFLY BRITISH, MILITARY, and so on. Occasionally an unfamiliar idiomatic expression is used within a selection; in such cases the main word of the expression is listed, followed by a definition of the idiom.

The following abbreviations are used in this glossary:

n.	noun	*conj.*	conjunction
v.	verb	*prep.*	preposition
adj.	adjective	*interj.*	interjection
adv.	adverb	*pl.*	plural
pron.	pronoun	*n.pl.*	plural noun

A

abase [ə bās′] *v.* to humiliate; degrade.

abate [ə bāt′] *v.* to lessen; reduce.

abdicate [ab′də kāt′] *v.* to give up (a high office or throne).

abeyance [ə bā′əns] *n.* the state of being stopped temporarily.

abhorrence [ab hôr′əns, -hor′-] *n.* hatred or disgust.

abject [ab′jekt, ab jekt′] *adj.* having lost one's spirit and self-respect; wretched.

abominate [ə bom′ə nāt′] *v.* to hate.

absolve [ab zolv′, -solv′] *v.* to set free from responsibility or blame.

abut [ə but′] *v.* to be next to; border on.

accolade [ak′ə lād′, -läd′] *n.* a sign of respect or praise.

acquiesce [ak′wē es′] *v.* to agree or accept quietly.

acquire [ə kwīr′] *v.* to gain possessions. **—acquirer,** *n.*

acrid [ak′rid] *adj.* bitter; sharp.

admonish [ad mon′ish] *v.* **1.** to caution; warn. **2.** to scold mildly. **—admonition** [ad′mə nish′ən], *n.*

adversity [ad vur′sə tē] *n.* a state of misery or trouble.

affinity [ə fin′ə tē] *n.* connection; similarity.

affliction [ə flik′shən] *n.* something that causes pain, distress, or suffering.

affright [ə frīt′] *v.* ARCHAIC. to terrify. **—*n.* ARCHAIC. great fear.

affront [ə frunt′] *v.* to insult. **—*n.* an insult.

agate [ag′it] *n.* a hard stone with striped or patterned colors.

aggregate [ag′rə git, -gāt′] *n.* a group of things taken as a whole; total.

aghast [ə gast′] *adj.* horrified.

alacrity [ə lak′rə tē] *n.* readiness; promptness; eagerness.

albino [al bī′nō] *n.* a person lacking in normal coloring and therefore having whitish skin and hair and pink eyes.

align [ə līn′] *v.* to line up; straighten. **—alignment,** *n.*

allege [ə lej′] *v.* to declare or state positively but without proof.

alleviate [ə lē′vē āt′] *v.* to lesson; relieve. **—alleviation,** *n.*

allot [ə lot′] *v.* to assign.

allurement [ə loor′mənt] *n.* attraction; temptation.

allusion [ə lōō′zhən] *n.* a casual or indirect reference.

almshouse [ämz′hous′] *n.* ARCHAIC. a publicly supported home for the poor.

altercation [ôl′tər kā′shən, al′-] *n.* an angry, noisy argument.

altitude [al′tə tōōd′, tūd′] *n.* height.

anathema [ə nath′ə mə] *n.* a curse.

angling [ang′gling] *n.* fishing with a hook and line.

annex [ə neks′] *v.* to add on.

anon [ə non′] *adv.* at another time; soon.

ante [an′tē] *v.* to put up (money) for a bet.

anthropological [an′thrə pə loj′i kəl] *adj.* relating to the study of mankind.

antipathy [an tip′ə thē] *n.* a strong dislike.

apex [ā′peks] *n.* the highest point; climax.

apotheosis [ə poth′ē ō′sis, ap′ə thē′ə-] *n.* the perfect example or model.

appease [ə pēz′] *v.* **1.** to make calm or quiet. **2.** to gain favor by pleasing acts. **—appeasingly,** *adv.*

appellation [ap′ə lā′shən] *n.* a name.

apprehension [ap′ri hen′shən] *n.* fear of something that might happen. **—apprehensive,** *adj.*

arbitrary [är′bə trer′ē] *adj.* based on someone's choice or whim.

arduous [är′jōō əs] *adj.* difficult.

armistice [är′mi stis] *n.* a temporary stopping of fighting; truce.

armorial [är môr′ē əl] *adj.* relating to or bearing a coat of arms, a design representing a family.

aromatic [ar′ə mat′ik] *adj.* having a strong, pleasant smell.

array [ə rā′] *n.* fine clothing.

articulate [är tik′yə lit] *adj.* clearly separated.

artifice [är′tə fis] *n.* trickery.

askance [ə skans′] *adv.* with distrust or disapproval.

aspire [əs pīr′] *v.* to have an ambition to achieve something.

assail [ə sāl′] *v.* to attack with actions or words.

assent [ə sent′] *v.* to agree. **—*n.* agreement; consent.

assiduous [ə sij′ōō əs] *adj.* careful and persistent; hardworking.

asunder [ə sun′dər] *adv.* info pieces; apart.

atone [ə tōn′] *v.* to make up for; repay. **—atonement,** *n.*

audacious [ô dā′shəs] *adj.* bold; fearless; daring. **—audaciously,** *adv.*

auditor [ô′də tər] *n.* a listener.

auger [ô′gər] *n.* a tool for making holes; drill.

aught [ôt] *n.* anything.

austere [ôs tēr′] *adj.* strict; harsh; self-denying.

avail [ə vāl′] *v.* to be of use or help.

averse [ə vurs′] *adj.* not willing; opposed.

avow [ə vou′] *v.* to declare.

B

balk [bôk] *v.* to frustrate or block.

barbaric [bär bar′ik] *adj.* primitive; savage.

bark [bärk] *n.* a boat.

batter [bat′ər] *v.* to beat; pound.

bearing [bãr′ing] *n.* connection to the subject; relevance.

bedraggled [bi drag′əld] *adj.* falling apart; broken down.

befall [bi fôl′] *v.* to happen.

beguile [bi gīl′] *v.* to pass (time) pleasantly.

belie [bi lī′] *v.* to disguise; give a false impression of.

belligerent [bə lij′ər ənt] *adj.* wanting to fight; hostile.

beneficence [bə nef′ə səns] *n.* kindness; generosity.

bereaved [bi rēvd′] *adj.* having suffered a loss, especially through death.

blanch [blanch] *v.* to turn white or pale.

blight [blīt] *adj.* something that damages or destroys.

blithe [blīth, blīth] *adj.* lighthearted; carefree.

boatswain [bō′sən, bōt′swān′] *n.* a ship's officer who is in charge of some equipment and directs the crew.

bracken [brak′ən] *n.* a growth of large, thick ferns.

brook [brook] *v.* to put up with; tolerate. —**brook no quarter** to tolerate no mercy or consideration.

bulwarks [bool′wərks] *n.pl.* the side of a ship above the deck.

burdock [bur′dok] *n.* a plant with clusters of purple flowers with prickles.

C

cadaverous [kə dav′ər əs] *adj.* like a corpse; pale. —**cadaverousness,** *n.*

calamity [kə lam′ə tē] *n.* disaster.

callus [kal′əs] *n.* a hard, thick patch of skin.

capitulate [kə pich′ə lāt′] *v.* to surrender.

caravel [kar′ə vel′] *n.* a small sailing ship, especially one of the 15th and 16th centuries.

career [kə rēr′] *v.* to rush at top speed.

carrion [kar′ē ən] *n.* the flesh of dead animals.

casing [kā′sing] *n.* a frame.

castanets [kas′tə nets′] *n.pl.* an instrument consisting of two small, rounded pieces of wood, bone, ivory, etc., that are tied to the thumb and clicked together with the hand.

causeway [kôz′wā′] *n.* a raised road, usually across water or swampland.

cavalcade [kav′əl kād′, kav′əl kād′] *n.* a group, as a procession, moving along in sequence.

cavity [kav′ə tē] *n.* a hole.

cavort [kə vôrt′] *v.* to leap; prance.

celestial [sə les′chəl] *adj.* relating to the sky or heaven.

celibacy [sel′ə bə sē] *n.* the state of being unmarried.

censer [sen′sər] *n.* a container for burning incense.

censure [sen′shər] *n.* an official statement of disapproval.

chase [chās] *n.* animals to be hunted.

chattel [chat′əl] *n.* a possession.

chink [chingk] *n.* a crack.

chronic [kron′ik] *adj.* constant; always present.

cipher [sī′fər] *v.* to do arithmetic; calculate; figure.

civility [si vil′ə tē] *n.* politeness.

clerical [kler′i kəl] *adj.* of a clergyman.

coalesce [kō′ə les′] *v.* to come together; blend into a whole.

collocation [kol′ə kā′shən] *n.* arrangement.

comely [kum′lē] *adj.* attractive; handsome or pretty.

commendable [kə men′də bəl] *adj.* worthy of praise.

commendation [kom′ən dā′shən] *n.* recommendation; praise.

commensurate [kə men′sər it, -shər-] *adj.* equal; corresponding in degree.

commiseration [kə miz′ə rā′shən] *n.* an expression of sorrow or compassion for someone; sympathy.

commodity [kə mod′ə tē] *n.* a useful item; product.

compact [kəm pakt′] *v.* to press firmly together; make solid.

complacent [kəm plā′sənt] *adj.* satisfied.

comport [kəm pôrt′] *v.* to agree; match.

comprised [kəm prīzd′] *adj.* included.

compulsion [kəm pul′shən] *n.* the act of forcing or being forced.

concentric [kən sen′trik] *adj.* having the same center.

conciliate [kən sil′ē āt′] *v.* to win the friendliness or calm the anger of.

concision [kən sizh′ən] *n.* the act of stating in few words; briefness.

condescension [kon′di sen′shən] *n.* the act of lowering oneself to do something.

conducive [kən dōō′siv, -dū′-] *adj.* helping to bring about.

confirmed [kən furmd′] *adj.* firmly set; unchanging; habitual.

confound [kən found′, kon-] *v.* to mix up; confuse.

conjecture [kən jek′chər] *n.* the act of guessing possible reasons or conclusions.

connivance [kə nī′vəns] *n.* a secret plan; scheme.

consort [kən sôrt′] *v.* to spend time together; be a companion.

consternation [kon′stər nā′shən] *n.* shock or dismay that leads to confusion.

constituent [kən stich′ōō ənt] *n.* a person represented by another.

consummate [*v.*, kon′sə māt′; *adj.*, kən sum′it, kon′sə mit] *v.* to complete; accomplish. —*adj.* excellent; expert.

contempt [kən tempt′] *n.* scorn; disdain.

contend [kən tend′] *v.* to struggle; fight.

contractual [kən trak′chōō əl] *adj.* of or like a contract, or formal agreement.

contrivance [kən trī′vəns] *n.* a machine.

contrive [kən trīv′] *v.* to plan; scheme.

convulse [kən vuls′] *v.* to shake or disturb violently.

convulsive [kən vul′siv] *adj.* marked by violent action or emotion. —**convulsiveness,** *n.*

corollary [kôr′ə ler′ē, kor′-] *n.* something that follows or results.

countenance [coun′tə nəns] *n.* a person's face.

course [kôrs] *v.* to move rapidly; race.

covert [kuv′ərt, kō′vərt] *adj.* secret; stealthy. —**covertly,** *adv.*

crackle [krak′əl] *v.* to make a series of slight, sharp sounds.

craze [krāz] *v.* to make tiny cracks in.

credulity [kri dōō′li tē, -dū′-] *n.* willingness to believe too easily.

crescendo [kri shen′dō] *adj.* increasing in loudness.

---

at; āpe; cär; end; mē; it; īce; hot; ōld; fôrk; wood; fōōl; oil; out; up; ūse; turn; ə in ago; taken, pencil, lemon, circus; bat; chin; dear; five; game; hit; hw in white; joke; kit; lid; man; not; singer; pail; ride; sat; shoe; tag; thin; this; very; wet; yes; zoo; zh in treasure; KH in loch, German ach; N in French bon; œ in French feu, German schön

crestfallen [krest′fô′lən] *adj.* discouraged; depressed.

crypt [kript] *n.* an underground room or enclosed space.

cyclonic [sī klon′ik] *adj.* like a cyclone.

cynicism [sin′ə siz′əm] *n.* doubt of the sincerity or truth of the motives or values of others.

D

dapple [dap′əl] *v.* to mark with spots.

daub [dôb] *v.* to paint roughly or messily.

decline [di klīn′] *v.* to slope down.

deem [dēm] *v.* to think; judge; consider.

deferential [def′ə ren′shəl] *adj.* respectful.

degenerate [di jen′ər it] *adj.* fallen to a lower condition.

dehumanization [dē hū′mə niz ā′shən, dē ū′-] *n.* the taking away of qualities that make one a human being or an individual.

delectable [di lek′tə bəl] *adj.* delightful; delicious.

demeanor [di mē′nər] *n.* behavior; manner.

denominate [di nom′ə nāt′] *v.* to call; name.

denunciation [di nun′sē ā′shən] *n.* an accusation; criticism.

depository [di poz′ə tôr′ē] *n.* a place for storing things safely.

depravity [di prav′ə tē] *n.* wickedness; immorality.

depreciate [di prē′shē āt′] *v.* to make seem of little value.

deputation [dep′yə tā′shən] *n.* a group of people given authority to represent others.

derision [di rizh′ən] *n.* the act of laughing at or making fun of.

designation [dez′ig nā′shən] *n.* a distinguishing name or title.

desolate [des′ə lit] *adj.* lonely; uninhabited. —**desolation** [des′ə lā′shən], *n.*

destine [des′tin] *v.* to fix beforehand; predetermine.

destitute [des′tə tōōt′, -tūt′] *adj.* lacking.

devise [di vīz′] *v.* LAW. to leave to in a will.

diffident [dif′ə dənt] *adj.* lacking self-confidence; shy. —**diffidently,** *adv.*

diffusion [di fū′zhən] *n.* a spreading out.

digress [di gres′, dī-] *v.* to wander from the subject being discussed.

dilate [dī lāt′, di-] *v.* to enlarge or widen.

dilatory [dil′ə tôr′ē] *adj.* delaying; slow.

diligent [dil′ə jənt] *adj.* careful; persistent; hard-working.

dirge [durj] *n.* a slow, mournful piece of music.

disavow [dis′ə vou′] *v.* to deny responsibility for or connection with.

discern [di surn′, -zurn′] *v.* to perceive; detect; make out.

disconsolate [dis kon′sə lit] *adj.* unable to be comforted; hopelessly sad. —**disconsolately,** *adv.*

discourse [dis′kôrs′] *n.* **1.** conversation. **2.** a long talk or lecture. —*v.* to talk; converse.

discrete [dis krēt′] *adj.* separate.

discriminate [dis krim′ə nāt′] *v.* to show prejudice.

disintegrate [dis in′tə grāt′] *v.* to break up; come apart. —**disintegration,** *n.*

disjointed [dis join′tid] *adj.* not continuous or logical; disconnected. —**disjointedly,** *adv.*

dismast [dis mast′] *v.* to remove the mast of (a ship); take away or destroy the long pole supporting the sails.

disparage [dis par′ij] *v.* to speak of as having little value; belittle.

dispel [dis pel′] *v.* to break up and drive away; cause to disappear.

disposed [dis pōzd′] *adj.* willing; inclined.

disposition [dis′pə zish′ən] *n.* usual behavior or attitude; character.

dissolution [dis′ə lōō′shən] *n.* a breaking up; ending; dissolving.

dissonant [dis′ə nənt] *adj.* not in harmony. —**dissonance,** *n.*

dissuade [di swād′] *v.* to persuade not to do something.

distraught [dis trôt′] *adj.* very troubled or confused.

ditty [dit′ē] *n.* a little song.

diverge [di vurj′, dī-] *v.* to move in different directions.

divest [di vest′, dī-] *v.* to deprive.

divulge [di vulj′] *v.* to reveal; disclose.

dog days uncomfortably hot days of July and August.

doltish [dōl′tish] *adj.* stupid.

dominion [də min′yən] *n.* rule; power.

draggle [drag′əl] *v.* to make dirty by dragging on the ground.

E

ecclesiastical [i klē′zē as′ti kəl] *adj.* relating to the church.

eddy [ed′ē] *n.* a water or air current moving in a circular motion —*v.* to move in a circular motion.

educe [i dōōs′, i dūs′] *v.* to draw out; extract.

efface [i fās′] *v.* to wipe out; erase.

egotism [ē′gə tiz′əm, eg′ə-] *n.* conceitedness; self-centeredness.

élan [ā län′] *n.* spirit; energy; enthusiasm.

elevation [el′ə vā′shən] *n.* great joyfulness or liveliness.

elliptic [i lip′tik] *adj.* oval.

elongate [i lông′gāt] *v.* to lengthen.

elude [i lōōd′] *v.* to avoid being seen or understood by. —**elusive** [i lōō′siv], *adj.*

emaciated [i mā′shē ā′tid] *adj.* extremely thin.

embassy [em′bə sē] *n.* a group of people representing others.

encumbrance [en kum′brəns] *n.* something that holds one back; a burden.

endow [en dou′] *v.* to provide.

engender [en jen′dər] *v.* to produce; cause.

enigmatic [en′ig mat′ik, ē′nig-] *adj.* mysterious; puzzling.

enmity [en′mə tē] *n.* hatred.

entreaty [en trē′tē] *n.* a humble request.

entrenchment [en trench′mənt] *n.* a trench or ditch used for protection.

enumeration [i nōō′mə rā′shən, i nū′-] *n.* a list.

envoy [en′voi, än′-] *n.* a messenger.

ephemeral [i fem′ər əl] *adj.* lasting only a short time; fleeting.

epithet [ep′ə thet′] *n.* a descriptive word or phrase coming before or after or replacing a name.

equanimity [ēk′wə nim′ə tē, ek′-] *n.* calmness; self-control.

equity [ek′wə tē] *n.* fairness; justice.

equivocal [i kwiv′ə kəl] *adj.* having more than one meaning; ambiguous.

eradicate [i rad′ə kāt′] *v.* to pull out by the roots.

eruptive [i rup′tiv] *adj.* bursting out.

ethereal [i thēr′ē əl] *adj.* **1.** delicate; exquisite. **2.** relating to the upper regions of space; heavenly.

eulogy [u′lə jē] *n.* a statement praising someone who has died.

evanescent [ev′ə nes′ənt] *adj.* impermanent; fleeting. —**evanescently,** *adv.*

evangelist [i van′jə list] *n.* a preacher.

evince [i vins′] *v.* to give evidence of; indicate.

exhilaration [ig zil′ə rā′shən] *n.* a lively, excited feeling.

exhort [ig zôrt′] *v.* to attempt to persuade; urge strongly.

expatriate [eks pā′trē āt′] *v.* to force to leave one's country; exile.

expedient [iks pē′dē ənt] *adj.* useful for achieving a purpose; advantageous. —*n.* something useful for achieving a purpose. —**expediency,** *n.*

expeditionary [eks′pə dish′ə ner′ē] *adj.* relating to a journey.

expire [iks pīr′] *v.* to die.

expletive [eks′plə tiv] *n.* an exclamation or curse.

expostulation [iks pos′chə lā′shən] *n.* protest; objection.

extemporize [iks tem′pə rīz′] *v.* to make or do without preparation or to fill an immediate need; improvise.

extenuate [iks ten′ū āt′] *v.* to make seem less serious.

extort [iks tôrt′] *v.* to take by force or threats.

exude [ig zood′, ik sood′] *v.* to drip or ooze out.

exult [ig zult′] *v.* to be joyful; rejoice. —**exultation** [eg′zul tā′shən, ek′sul-] *n.*

F

facilitate [fə sil′ə tāt′] *v.* to make easier.

facsimile [fak sim′ə lē] *n.* a copy.

faculty [fak′əl tē] *n.* a power of the mind.

fantasize [fan′tə sīz′] *v.* to imagine; daydream.

farce [färs] *n.* a ridiculous display; pretense.

fatuous [fach′oo əs] *adj.* foolish. —**fatuousness,** *n.*

feign [fān] *v.* ARCHAIC. to imagine.

felicitous [fi lis′ə təs] *adj.* **1.** suitable; appropriate. **2.** happy; fortunate.

felonious [fə lō′nē əs] *adj.* POETIC. wicked; villainous.

fervid [fur′vid] *adj.* showing great feeling or intensity.

figurative [fig′yər ə tiv] *adj.* not actual or literal; metaphoric. —**figuratively,** *adv.*

figure [fig′yər] *n.* a series of dance steps.

firmament [fur′mə mənt] *n.* the sky.

fissure [fish′ər] *n.* a deep crack.

fitful [fit′fəl] *adj.* stopping and starting; irregular.

flail [flāl] *n.* a tool made up of a freely swinging stick at the end of a long handle, used to separate grains from their husks.

flay [flā] *v.* **1.** to skin. **2.** to scold harshly.

flush [flush] *adv.* in line; level.

folio [fō′lē ō′] *n.* a book of the largest standard size.

forbear [fôr bâr′] *v.* to keep from doing; resist.

formulate [fôr′myə lāt′] *v.* to reduce to a fixed phrase or rule.

forthwith [fôrth′with′, -with′] *adv.* immediately.

founder [foun′dər] *v.* to sink.

foundry [foun′drē] *n.* a place where metal is melted and formed into shapes.

fracas [frā′kəs] *n.* a loud disturbance.

freight [frāt] *v.* to load.

fritter [frit′ər] *v.* to waste little by little.

frugality [froo gal′ə tē] *n.* thriftiness; unwastefulness.

fungo [fun′gō] *n.* a ball tossed up by a batter and hit for practice.

G

garrulous [gar′ə ləs, gar′yə-] *adj.* talkative.

gauge-cock [gāj′kok] a valve or faucet that is used to determine the amount of liquid in a container.

genealogist [jē′nē ol′ə jist, -al′-, jen′ē-] *n.* someone who traces the descent of a person or family from ancestors.

geological [jē′ə log′i kəl] *adj.* relating to the study of the structure and development of the earth's crust.

gill [gil] *n.* the organ for breathing in fish.

girt [gurt] *v.* to surround.

goad [gōd] *v.* to push; poke; urge.

gossamer [gos′ə mər] *adj.* delicate; filmy.

grapple [grap′əl] *v.* to struggle.

grog [grog] *n.* an alcoholic drink.

guileless [gīl′lis] *adj.* not sly or crafty; candid.

H

hack [hak] *n.* a carriage that can be rented.

handselled [han′səld] *adj.* related to beginnings; original.

haply [hap′lē] *adv.* ARCHAIC. by chance or luck.

hardihood [här′dē hood′] *n.* boldness; courage.

hazard [haz′ərd] *v.* to risk.

heather [heth′ər] *n.* an evergreen plant with stalks of small pinkish flowers, common in the British Isles.

heft [heft] *n.* weight; heaviness.

heliotrope [hē′lē ə trōp′, hēl′yə-] *n.* a plant with clusters of white or purplish flowers.

hie [hī] *v.* to move quickly; hurry.

hoary [hôr′ē] *adj.* **1.** white or gray with age. **2.** old; ancient.

hobgoblin [hob′gob′lin] *n.* a cause of concern or needless anxiety.

husband [huz′bənd] *v.* to handle economically.

I

ideology [ī′dē ol′ə jē, id′ē-] *n.* the ideas or theories that make up a political or social system.

illimitable [i lim′i tə bəl] *adj.* that cannot be limited or measured.

illiterate [i lit′ər it] *adj.* unable to read or write.

imbue [im bū′] *v.* to fill; spread through.

imminent [im′ə nənt] *adj.* about to happen; threatening.

immitigable [i mit′i gə bəl] *adj.* that cannot be made less severe or painful.

immune [i mūn′] *adj.* protected against or unaffected by something harmful.

impalpable [im pal′pə bəl] *adj.* that cannot be touched.

impassive [im pas′iv] *adj.* not showing any feelings. —**impassiveness,** *n.*

impenetrable [im pen′ə trə bəl] *adj.* that cannot be passed through.

imperceptible [im′pər sep′tə bəl] *adj.* extremely small or slow; not noticeable.

impersonate [im pur′sə nāt′] *v.* to act the part of; imitate.

impetuous [im pech′oo əs] *adj.* rushing forcefully; violent.

impetus [im′pə təs] *n.* a spurring to action; incentive.

impious [im′pē əs] *adj.* not showing respect for God.

implement [im′plə mənt] *n.* **1.** a tool. **2.** something used to achieve a purpose.

implication [im′plə kā′shən] *n.* something hinted or suggested.

---

at; āpe; cär; end; mē; it; īce; hot; ōld; fôrk; wood; fool; oil; out; up; ūse; turn; ə in ago; taken, pencil, lemon, circus; bat; chin; dear; five; game; hit; hw in white; joke; kit; lid; man; not; singer; pail; ride; sat; shoe; tag; thin; this; very; wet; yes; zoo; zh in treasure; KH in loch, German ach; N in French bon; œ in French feu, German schön

importunate [im por′chə nit] *adj.* bothersomely urgent; demanding.

impotent [im′pət ənt] *adj.* weak; helpless.

imprecation [im′pri kā′shən] *n.* a curse.

impregnable [im preg′nə bəl] *adj.* that cannot be entered by force or captured; unconquerable.

impressible [im pres′ə bəl] *adj.* able to be marked by pressing or influenced.

impropriety [im′prə prī′ə tē] *n.* improper behavior.

inaccessible [in′ək ses′ə bəl] *adj.* unreachable.

inaccommodate [in′ə kom′ə dāt] *adj.* unsuitable; unfit.

inanimate [in an′ə mit] *adj.* not living.

incantation [in′kan tā′shən] *n.* the chanting of magical spells or charms.

incense [in sens′] *v.* to anger greatly.

incertitude [in sur′tə tōōd′, -tūd′] *n.* uncertainty; doubt.

incessant [in ses′ənt] *adj.* never stopping; constant. —**incessantly,** *adv.*

incongruous [in kong′grōō əs] *adj.* inconsistent; inappropriate.

incorrigible [in kôr′ə jə bəl, -kor′-] *adj.* not capable of being corrected or improved.

indecorous [in dek′ər əs, in′di kôr′əs] *adj.* not proper or well-mannered.

indolence [ind′əl əns] *n.* laziness.

indomitable [in dom′ə tə bəl] *adj.* that cannot be controlled or conquered.

ineffable [in ef′ə bəl] *adj.* that cannot be put into words; indescribable.

inexplicable [in′iks plik′ə bəl, in eks′pli kə-] *adj.* not explainable or understandable.

infelicitous [in′fə lis′ə təs] *adj.* not appropriate.

inferential [in′fə ren′shəl] *adj.* concluded or figured out from facts or assumptions. —**inferentially,** *adv.*

infest [in fest′] *v.* to spread over; overrun.

ingenuity [in′jə nōō′ə tē, -nū′-] *n.* cleverness.

ingenuous [in jen′ū əs] *adj.* open; simple; naive.

iniquity [in ik′wə tē] *n.* wickedness.

inordinate [in ôr′də nit] *adj.* excessive.

inscrutable [in skrōō′tə bəl] *adj.* difficult to understand; mysterious.

insensible [in sen′sə bəl] *adj.* 1. not capable of feeling. 2. not aware. —**insensibly,** *adv.*

insidious [in sid′ē əs] *adj.* sly; deceitful.

insipid [in sip′id] *adj.* bland; tasteless.

insistent [in sis′tənt] *adj.* standing firmly; persistent.

insolence [in′sə ləns] *n.* disrespectfulness; impertinence.

inspiration [in′spə rā′shən] *n.* a breathing in.

intercept [in′tər sept′] *v.* NOW RARE. to interfere with; hinder.

interment [in tur′mənt] *n.* burial.

intermittent [in′tər mit′ənt] *adj.* stopping at intervals; going on and off.

interpose [in′tər pōz′] *v.* to come between; interrupt.

intimate [in′tə māt′] *v.* to hint; suggest.

intractable [in trak′tə bəl] *adj.* difficult to handle or work with.

introspective [in trə spek′tiv] *adj.* looking inward; examining one's own thoughts and feelings.

invariable [in vâr′ē ə bəl] *adj.* not changing; always the same. —**invariably,** *adv.*

inviolable [in vī′ə lə bəl] *adj.* that must not be disturbed or debased; sacred.

inviolate [in vī′ə lit, -lāt′] *adj.* whole; pure; sacred.

irreproachable [ir′i prō′chə bəl] *adj.* faultless.

irruption [i rup′shən] *n.* OBSOLETE. a violent outburst: variation of **eruption**.

isolate [ī′sə lāt, is′ə-] *adj.* separated from others.

J

jaded [jā′did] *adj.* worn out; exhausted.

jag [jag] *n.* a sharp point that juts out.

jeopardy [jep′ər dē] *n.* great danger.

jocular [jok′yə lər] *adj.* 1. joking; merry. 2. like a joke; funny.

juxtapose [juks′tə pōz′] *v.* to put next to one another.

K

kindred [kin′drid] *adj.* similar; related.

L

languid [lang′gwid] *adj.* lacking liveliness.

lapse [laps] *n.* the passing of time.

latter-day [lat′ər dā′] *adj.* modern.

lattice [lat′is] *n.* a structure made of crossed strips of wood or metal, used as a screen, shutter, etc.

laurel [lôr′əl, lor′-] *n.* 1. an evergreen tree or bush with large leaves and yellowish flowers. 2. a wreath or crown made of laurel leaves and worn as a symbol of honor.

lean-to [lēn′tōō′] *n.* a small, rough building with a roof that slopes in one direction, the higher end leaning against a wall or other support.

levy [lev′ē] *v.* to conduct or wage (war).

libel [lī′bəl] *v.* to write or print damaging information about a person.

license [lī′səns] *n.* freedom.

lineage [lin′ē ij] *n.* family descent; ancestry.

literalist [lit′ər əl ist] *n.* a realist.

livid [liv′id] *adj.* grayish or whitish; pale. —**lividly,** *adv.*

loll [lol] *v.* to hang loosely; droop.

lowering [lo′ə ring] *adj.* dark; threatening.

lucid [lōō′sid] *adj.* 1. clear; understandable. 2. thinking clearly; rational. —**lucidity,** *n.*

ludicrous [lōō′də krəs] *adj.* ridiculous.

lugubrious [loo gōō′brē əs, -gū′-] *adj.* exaggeratedly sad or mournful. —**lugubriousness,** *n.*

lurid [loor′id] *adj.* glowing through smoke or haze.

lusty [lus′tē] *adj.* strong; vigorous. —**lustily,** *adv.*

M

mace [mās] *n.* a heavy club.

magnanimity [mag′nə nim′ə tē] *n.* generosity and forgivingness; nobility.

malediction [mal′ə dik′shən] *n.* a curse.

malevolence [mə lev′ə ləns] *n.* ill will; spite.

mangy [mān′jē] *adj.* low; contemptible.

manifest [man′ə fest] *v.* to show; reveal.

mansion [man′shən] *n.* a dwelling, usually large and luxurious.

mantle [mant′əl] *n.* something that covers or envelops.

mar [mär] *v.* to damage; spoil.

martial [mar′shəl] *adj.* relating to war.

materialist [mə tēr′ē ə list] *n.* a person more interested in possessions and physical comfort than in ideas and beliefs.

maudlin [môd′lin] *adj.* foolishly sentimental.

maul [môl] *n.* a heavy hammer.

maxim [mak′sim] *n.* a short statement expressing a rule or principle; saying.

mayhem [mā′hem, mā′əm] *n.* LAW. the injuring or crippling of a person.

mean [mēn] *adj.* average.

means [mēnz] *n.pl.* **1.** something used to achieve a purpose. **2.** resources.

mediate [mē′dē āt′] *v.* to settle differences; bring opposing sides together. —**mediator,** *n.*

mentor [men′tər] *n.* an adviser or teacher.

mercenary [mur′sə ner′ē] *n.* a soldier paid to fight in the army of a foreign country.

meteorological [mē′tē ər ə loj′i kəl] *adj.* referring to weather.

meticulous [mi tik′yə ləs] *adj.* extremely concerned or careful about details.

miasma [mī az′mə, mē-] *n.* fumes coming from a swamp or from decaying matter, once thought to be poisonous.

mimic [mim′ik] *v.* to copy; imitate.

minister [min′is tər] *v.* to give; provide.

ministry [min′is trē] *n.* the members of a government administration.

misanthropic [mis′ən throp′ik, miz′-] *adj.* having hatred or contempt for people.

misgiving [mis giv′ing] *n.* a feeling of doubt or worry.

mitigate [mit′ə gāt′] *v.* to make less intense or painful.

mobile [mō′bəl, -bēl] *adj.* able to move or flow; changeable.

mode [mōd] *n.* a way of doing something; method.

moderate [mod′ər it] *adj.* mild. —**moderately,** *adv.*

modulate [moj′ə lāt′] *v.* to change in pitch or intensity.

molder [mōl′dər] *v.* to crumble; decay.

morass [mə ras′] *n.* an area of soft, wet ground; marsh.

mottled [mot′əld] *adj.* spotted or streaked with color.

mutation [mū tā′shən] *n.* a change.

myriad [mir′ē əd] *adj.* very many; countless.

mystic [mis′tik] *adj.* mysterious.

mystical [mis′ti kəl] *adj.* relating to experiences beyond human reasoning; spiritual; mysterious.

N

natty [nat′ē] *adj.* neat; trim.

nectar [nek′tər] *n.* a delicious drink.

nocturne [nok′turn′] *n.* a dreamy, romantic musical composition appropriate to the evening.

O

obdurate [ob′dər it, ob′dyər-] *adj.* stubborn; unbending; hardened.

obeisance [ō bā′səns, ō bē′-] *n.* a respectful movement or gesture; bow.

obliterate [ə blit′ə rāt′] *v.* to wipe out; erase.

obscurity [əb skyoor′ə tē] *n.* darkness; unclearness; cloudiness.

obtrude [əb trood′] *v.* to call attention to or force on others without being asked.

obtuse [əb toos′, -tūs′] *adj.* slow in understanding; insensitive.

occult [ə kult′, ok′ult] *adj.* relating to things beyond normal experience; secret; mysterious.

octavo [ok tā′vō, -tä′-] *n.* a book about six by nine inches in size.

omnipotent [om nip′ət ənt] *adj.* having unlimited power.

onset [ôn′set′, on′-] *n.* beginning.

oppress [ə pres′] *v.* **1.** to rule over or keep down unfairly or cruelly. **2.** to weigh down; depress. —**oppressive,** *adj.*

orifice [ôr′ə fis, or′-] *n.* a hole; opening.

ostentation [os′tən tā′shən] *n.* a showing off; pretentiousness. —**ostentatious,** *adj.*

oust [oust] *v.* to drive out.

overbearing [ō′vər bâr′ing] *adj.* arrogant.

P

pall [pôl] *n.* a cloth used to cover a coffin.

pallid [pal′id] *adj.* pale; whitish.

palpable [pal′pə bəl] *adj.* understandable; obvious.

palsy [pôl′zē] *n.* a condition marked by a shaking or trembling of a part of the body.

parable [par′ə bəl] *n.* a short story that illustrates a basic truth or moral principle.

paradoxical [par′ə dok′sə kəl] *adj.* seemingly contradictory or nonsensical but probably true.

parley [pär′lē] *n.* a conference for settling a dispute.

parsimony [pär′sə mō′nē] *n.* thriftiness; stinginess; miserliness.

passivity [pa siv′ə tē] *n.* lack of resistance; tendency to give in; meekness.

pathos [pā′thos] *n.* a feeling of sympathy or compassion.

patriarch [pā′trē ärk′] *n.* a father, founder, or leader; respected old man.

peat [pēt] *n.* partially decayed plant matter that is dried and used as a fuel.

pedestrian [pə des′trē ən] *adj.* moving on foot; walking.

pension [pen′shən] *v.* to grant (someone who has retired) regular payments of money.

pensive [pen′siv] *adj.* dreamily or sadly thoughtful. —**pensively,** *adv.*

pent [pent] *adj.* kept in; shut up.

penumbra [pi num′brə] *n.* the partially shaded area surrounding an area of total eclipse or shadow.

perdition [pər dish′ən] *n.* hell.

peremptory [pə remp′tər ē] *adj.* not permitting argument or delay; commanding. —**peremptorily,** *adv.*

perennial [pə ren′ē əl] *adj.* present all year.

periphery [pə rif′ər ē] *n.* the edge; perimeter.

perpetual [pər pech′oo əl] *adj.* eternal.

pertinacity [purt′ən as′ə tē] *n.* firmness; stubbornness.

perturbation [pur′tər bā′shən] *n.* the state of being disturbed or upset.

perusal [pə roo′zəl] *n.* study; examination.

pervade [pər vād′] *v.* to spread throughout.

perversion [pər vur′zhən, -shən] *n.* distortion.

pestilent [pes′tə lənt] *adj.* deadly.

phenomenon [fə nom′ə non′, -nən] *n., pl.* **phenomena** a fact or event that can be observed.

phosphorescent [fos′fə res′ənt] *adj.* shining or glowing after exposure to light.

---

at; āpe; cär; end; mē; it; īce; hot; ōld; fôrk; wood; fool; oil; out; up; ūse; turn; ə in ago; taken, pencil, lemon, circus; bat; chin; dear; five; game; hit; hw in white; joke; kit; lid; man; not; singer; pail; ride; sat; shoe; tag; thin; this; very; wet; yes; zoo; zh in treasure; KH in loch, German ach; N in French bon; œ in French feu, German schön

phraseology [frā′zē ol′ə jē] *n.* wording.

physiognomy [fiz′ē og′nə mē, -on′ə mē] *n.* features; expression; appearance.

pilfer [pil′fər] *v.* to steal.

pinnacle [pin′ə kəl] *n.* a peak.

pittance [pit′əns] *n.* a small amount of money.

platitude [plat′ə tōod′, -tūd′] *n.* a dull, commonplace remark or idea.

plunge [plunj] *v.* to throw oneself; rush.

politic [pol′ə tik] *adj.* carefully polite.

pomp [pomp] *n.* showiness; splendor.

poncho [pon′chō] *n.* a garment made of a piece of waterproof material with a hole for the head, worn as a raincoat.

ponderous [pon′dər əs] *adj.* heavy and clumsy.

poop [pōōp] *n.* a raised deck at the back of a ship.

portend [pôr tend′] *v.* to give a sign or warning of (a future happening).

portent [pôr′tent] *n.* a sign or warning of something that will happen; omen.

posterity [pos ter′ə tē] *n.* descendants.

precipitous [pri sip′ə təs] *adj.* extremely steep; almost straight up and down.

precocious [pri kō′shəs] *adj.* more mature than is usual for one's age.

predecessor [pred′ə ses′ər] *n.* one who came before.

predispose [prē′dis pōz′] *v.* to make inclined (to do something) ahead of time.

pre-empt [prē empt′] *v.* to take or claim before others can.

prerogative [pri rog′ə tiv] *n.* a special right or power.

presage [pres′ij, pri sāj′] *v.* to give a sign or warning of (a future happening).

prescience [prē′shē əns, presh′ē-] *n.* knowledge of events before they happen.

presume [pri zōom′] *v.* to do without permission; be overly bold; dare.

prevail [pri vāl′] *v.* to triumph.

prevalent [prev′ə lənt] *adj.* common.

pristine [pris′tēn] *adj.* pure; unspoiled.

procure [prə kyoor′] *v.* to get; obtain.

prodigy [prod′ə jē] *n.* RARE. an amazing occurrence.

profuse [prə fūs′] *adj.* abundant.

progenitor [prō jen′ə tər] *n.* source; forerunner; ancestor.

prolixity [prō lik′sə tē] *n.* wordiness.

propitious [prə pish′əs] *adj.* favorable; gracious.

prostrate [pros′trāt] *adj.* lying flat or with the face down. —*v.* to cause to lie flat or give in; make humble.

protract [prō trakt′] *v.* to draw out; lengthen.

proverbial [prə vur′bē əl] *adj.* of a proverb or saying.

prowess [prou′is] *n.* extraordinary ability or skill.

proximity [prok sim′ə tē] *n.* nearness.

prudence [prōod′əns] *n.* carefulness; caution.

psalm [säm, sälm] *n.* a religious song or poem.

psalmist [sä′mist, säl′mist] *n.* one who writes psalms.

pullet [pool′it] *n.* a young hen.

puny [pū′nē] *adj.* small; weak; unimportant. —**punily,** adv.

Q

quaff [kwäf, kwaf] *v.* to drink thirstily.

quagmire [kwag′mīr′, kwog′-] *n.* soft, wet ground that one's feet sink into.

quartermaster [kwôr′tər mas′tər] *n.* a person on a ship who takes care of navigation and signals.

quarto [kwôr′tō] *n.* a book about nine by twelve inches in size.

querulous [kwer′ə ləs, kwer′yə-] *adj.* complaining; irritable.

R

rally [ral′ē] *v.* to recover; revive.

ramshackle [ram′shak′əl] *adj.* appearing ready to fall apart; rickety.

rapt [rapt] *adj.* showing great joy or pleasure.

ravenous [rav′ə nəs] *adj.* extremely hungry. —**ravenously,** *adv.*

reaffirm [rē′ə furm′] *v.* to declare again to be true.

recluse [rek′lōōs, ri klōōs′] *n.* a person who lives shut off from the world.

recoil [ri koil′, rē′koil′] *n.* the distance that a gun jumps back when fired.

recompense [rek′əm pens′] *v.* to repay. —*n.* repayment.

reconnoiter [rē′kə noi′tər, rek′ə-] *v.* to explore an area for information about the enemy.

recreate [rek′rē āt′] *v.* to refresh by play or relaxation.

rectitude [rek′tə tōod′, -tūd′] *n.* correctness.

recumbent [ri kum′bənt] *adj.* lying down; resting.

redolent [red′əl ənt] *adj.* filled with a certain quality; suggestive.

redoubtable [ri dou′tə bəl] *adj.* causing fear.

reft [reft] *adj.* robbed or deprived.

regalia [ri gā′lē ə, -gāl′yə] *n.pl.* badges, symbols, or clothing indicating a certain position.

regenerate [ri jen′ə rāt′] *v.* to renew; reform; improve.

reign [rān] *n.* the period of rule or dominance.

reiterate [rē it′ə rāt′] *v.* to repeat.

relent [ri lent′] *v.* to become less stern or stubborn; soften.

relief [ri lēf′] *n.* clearness of outline; contrast.

relinquish [ri ling′kwish] *v.* to give up; surrender. —**relinquishment,** *n.*

remonstrance [ri mon′strəns] *n.* protest.

remonstrate [ri mon′strāt] *v.* to protest.

render [ren′dər] *v.* to represent in a picture; portray.

renovate [ren′ə vāt′] *v.* to make like new.

repast [ri past′] *n.* a meal.

replenish [ri plen′ish] *v.* to fill or supply again, as with fuel.

replete [ri plēt′] *adj.* filled.

reprieve [ri prēv′] *n.* a postponement of punishment.

resignation [rez′ig nā′shən] *n.* unresisting or passive acceptance.

resolve [ri zolv′] *v.* to decide.

resounding [ri zoun′ding] *adj.* ringing; echoing.

respite [res′pit] *n.* a period of rest or relief.

reticent [ret′ə sənt] *adj.* reluctant to speak; reserved.

retina [ret′ən ə] *n.* the part of the eye that is sensitive to light and receives the image formed by the lens.

retract [ri trakt′] *v.* to take back.

retrospection [ret′rə spek′shən] *n.* the act of looking back on the past.

revel [rev′əl] *v.* to celebrate wildly and noisily. —**reveler,** *n.*

rhetoric [ret′ər ik] *n.* showy language.

ricochet [rik′ə shā′] *n.* a slanting rebound of an object off a surface.

rife [rīf] *adj.* abundant; filled (with).

rift [rift] *v.* to break open; split.

ritualize [rich′ōō ə līz′] *v.* to make into a formal ceremony or custom.

rote [rōt] *n.* a repetitive or routine procedure. —**by rote** by memory rather than with thought.

rout [rout] *n.* a fast, confused running away or retreat.

rude [rōōd] *adj.* roughly made or done.

S

sagacious [sə gā′shəs] *adj.* having sound judgment; wise. —**sagacity** [sə gas′ə tē], *n.*

sally [sal′ē] *v.* to go out; set out; leave.

sanctify [sangk′tə fī′] *v.* to make holy.

sanctity [sangk′tə tē] *n.* holiness.

savant [sa vänt′, sə-, sav′ənt] *n.* a person with great learning or knowledge.

scant [skant] *v.* to give less than enough.

scoff [skof, skôf] *v.* to show contempt; jeer.

scruple [skrōō′pəl] *v.* to hesitate to do something because it may be wrong.

scuttle [skut′əl] *v.* to move with short, rapid steps.

semblance [sem′bləns] *n.* appearance; likeness.

sententious [sen ten′shəs] *adj.* fond of using trite phrases or maxims. —**sententiously,** *adv.*

sepulcher [sep′əl kər] *n.* a grave or tomb.

sepulchral [si pul′krəl] *adj.* tomblike; gloomy.

servile [sur′vil, -vīl] *adj.* slavelike.

sexton [seks′tən] *n.* a church official who takes care of church property.

shag [shag] *v.* to run after balls during practice.

shoal [shōl] *adj.* shallow.

shroud [shroud] *n.* a cloth for wrapping a dead body for burial.

shy [shī] *v.* to jump back suddenly when frightened.

simper [sim′pər] *v.* to say with a silly smile.

sinew [sin′ū] *v.* to strengthen or support.

singular [sing′gyə lər] *adj.* strange; remarkable.

skein [skān] *n.* a coil of thread or yarn.

skim [skim] *v.* to glide.

skirt [skurt] *v.* to move along the edge; pass around.

skulk [skulk] *v.* to move or hide stealthily or fearfully.

slough[1] [sluf] *n.* a snake's outer skin.

slough[2] [slou] *n.* an area of deep mud.

smite [smīt] *v.* to strike hard.

solace [sol′is] *v.* to comfort; console. —*n.* comfort; relief.

solicitous [sə lis′ə təs] *adj.* full of concern or anxiety. —**solicitude,** *n.*

soliloquy [sə lil′ə kwē] *n.* the act of talking to oneself.

solstice [sol′stis] *n.* either of two times during the year (**summer solstice** and **winter solstice**) when the sun is farthest from the equator.

sooth [sōōth] *n.* ARCHAIC. truth.

sophistication [sə fis′tə kā′shən] *n.* the state of being cultured and experienced.

sough [sou, suf] *v.* to make a sighing or rustling sound. —**soughingly,** *adv.*

souvenir [sōō′və nēr′, sōō′və nēr′] *n.* something kept as a reminder of a person or event.

spasmodic [spaz mod′ik] *adj.* happening in short, violent bursts; stopping and starting.

specific [spi sif′ik] *n.* a remedy for a particular ailment.

specter [spek′tər] *n.* a ghost. —**spectral** [spek′trəl], *adj.*

speculative [spek′yə lā′tiv, -lə tiv] *adj.* relating to thinking about or considering something.

spoil [spoil] *n.* something looted or robbed.

spook [spōōk] *v.* COLLOQUIAL. to become frightened; jump suddenly because of fright.

squander [skwon′dər] *v.* to spend foolishly; waste.

stance [stans] *n.* the placement of the body or feet.

statistician [stat′is tish′ən] *n.* a person who collects and organizes numerical data about a subject.

staunch [stônch, stänch] *adj.* firm; loyal; determined. —**staunchness,** *n.*

stereotyped [ster′ē ə tīpt′, stēr′-] *adj.* typical; not individual.

strand [strand] *n.* a string or thread.

stratum [strā′təm, strat′əm, strä′təm] *n., pl.* **strata** a layer.

stricken [strik′ən] *adj.* strongly affected or distressed by something unpleasant, painful, etc.

strife [strīf] *n.* struggle; conflict.

stringency [strin′jən sē] *n.* harshness; strictness.

stubble [stub′əl] *n.* the bottoms of stalks of grain left after harvesting.

subjugation [sub′jə gā′shən] *n.* the state of being ruled over or controlled.

sublime [sə blīm′] *adj.* lofty; noble; glorious.

subsistence [səb sis′təns] *n.* means of living; livelihood.

subterranean [sub′tə rā′nē ən] *adj.* underground; hidden.

succor [suk′ər] *n.* help or relief.

suffer [suf′ər] *v.* to allow.

sufferance [suf′ər əns, suf′rəns] *n.* toleration.

suffice [sə fīs′] *v.* **1.** to be enough. **2.** to satisfy.

suit [sōōt] *v.* ARCHAIC. to agree; correspond.

sumptuous [sump′chōō əs] *adj.* luxurious; splendid.

sundry [sun′drē] *n.* some number; various ones.

supine [sōō pīn′] *adj.* not active; not resisting or caring; meek. —**supinely,** *adv.*

supple [sup′əl] *adj.* able to bend easily; limber; flexible.

supplication [sup′lə kā′shən] *n.* the act of asking humbly for something.

suppress [sə pres′] *v.* to hold back or keep in.

surcease [sur sēs′] *n.* an end; stopping.

surmise [sər mīz′] *v.* to guess; imagine.

sward [swôrd] *n.* grassy ground.

swathe [swoth, swôth] *v.* to wrap.

synchronize [sing′krə nīz′] *v.* to cause to happen together or at the same speed.

synopsize [si nop′sīz] *v.* to shorten; summarize.

T

tablet [tab′lit] *n.* a flat piece of wood, stone, etc.

tacit [tas′it] *adj.* not stated but suggested or understood.

taint [tānt] *n.* a hint of decay or contamination.

temerity [tə mer′ə tē] *n.* foolhardy boldness; recklessness.

temperance [tem′pər əns, tem′prəns] *n.* restraint; moderation.

tempered [tem′pərd] *adj.* having been brought to the correct texture or hardness.

tenacious [ti nā′shəs] *adj.* tending to hang on and not give up; stubborn. —**tenaciously,** *adv.*

---

at; āpe; cär; end; mē; it; īce; hot; ōld; fôrk; wood; fōōl; oil; out; up; ūse; turn; ə in ago; taken, pencil, lemon, circus; bat; chin; dear; five; game; hit; hw in white; joke; kit; lid; man; not; singer; pail; ride; sat; shoe; tag; thin; this; very; wet; yes; zoo; zh in treasure; KH in loch, German ach; N in French bon; œ in French feu, German schön

---

tensile [ten′sil, -sīl] *adj.* pulled tightly; taut.

tenuity [ti nōō′ə tē, -nū′-, -te-] *n.* thinness.

tenuous [ten′ū əs] *adj.* weak; flimsy.

tenure [ten′yər] *n.* the conditions under which or length of time for which an office or position is held.

terrestrial [tə res′trē əl] *adj.* earthly.

testimonial [tes′tə mō′nē əl] *n.* a showing of appreciation.

thanatopsis [than′ə top′sis] *n.* a view of death.

thither [thith′ər] *adv.* there.

thoroughfare [thur′ə fār′] *n.* a main street.

thrall [thrôl] *adj.* ARCHAIC. enslaved.

throe [thrō] *n.* a sudden, sharp pain or muscular contraction.

timorous [tim′ər əs] *adj.* fearful; timid.

toilsome [toil′səm] *adj.* involving work; difficult.

torpidity [tôr pid′ə tē] *n.* lack of energy or interest; dullness.

torpor [tôr′pər] *n.* a state of inactivity, or sluggishness.

torrential [tô ren′chəl, tə-] *adj.* streaming violently or rapidly.

transcendent [tran sen′dənt] *adj.* beyond ordinary experience or physical existence.

transfigure [trans fig′yər] *v.* to change the appearance of.

transient [tran′shənt] *adj.* staying for a short time; temporary.

transition [tran zish′ən] *n.* a moving from one condition or stage to another.

transpire [tran spīr′] *v.* to happen.

transverse [trans vurs′, tranz-] *adj.* going across.

travail [trə vāl′, trav′āl] *n.* 1. difficult work. 2. great pain.

trellis [trel′is] *n.* a structure made of crossed strips of wood, on which vines grow.

tremor [trem′ər] *n.* a trembling or shaking.

tremulous [trem′yə ləs] *adj.* trembling; shaking.

trepidation [trep′ə dā′shən] *n.* fear; anxiety.

trestle [tres′əl] *n.* a framework for supporting something.

tribute [trib′ūt] *n.* something given or done as a sign of respect or gratitude.

triviality [triv′ē al′ə tē] *n.* the state of being ordinary or unimportant.

type [tīp] *n.* a thing or person that represents another.

typify [tip′ə fī′] *v.* to represent; symbolize.

U

unaccountable [un′ə koun′tə bəl] *adj.* unexplainable; mysterious.

unction [ungk′shən] *n.* strong feeling or intensity in one's speech or behavior.

undeviating [un dē′vē ā′ting] *adj.* not turning to the side or branching off.

undistracted [un′dis trak′tid] *adj.* not having one's attention drawn to something else.

undulation [un′jə lā′shən, -dyə-] *n.* a wavelike motion.

unfurl [un furl′] *v.* to open; unroll.

ungainly [un gān′lē] *adj.* awkward or unattractive.

unitary [ū′nə ter′ē] *adj.* being one; single.

unnerve [un nurv′] *v.* to frighten or upset.

unobtrusive [un′əb trōō′siv] *adj.* not calling attention to itself.

unperverted [un′pər vur′tid] *adj.* not turned from what is good or right.

unprecedented [un pres′ə den′tid] *adj.* not having happened before; without match; new.

unremitting [un′ri mit′ing] *adj.* not letting up; constant.

unseared [un sērd′] *adj.* not scorched or withered.

unseemly [un sēm′lē] *adj.* not proper.

unsubstantiality [un′səb stan′shē al′ə tē] *n.* unreality.

unwonted [un wôn′tid, -wôn′-] *adj.* not common or usual.

urn [urn] *n.* a pot for serving hot drinks.

V

vagabond [vag′ə bond′] *adj.* like a person who moves from place to place; wandering.

vagary [və gãr′ē, vā′gər ē] *n.* a strange action or idea.

vainglory [vān′glôr′ē, vān glôr′ē] *n.* boastful conceit; vanity.

vale [vāl] *n.* CHIEFLY POETIC. a valley.

valid [val′id] *adj.* sound; convincing; correct.

vanquish [vang′kwish, van′-] *v.* to defeat; conquer.

vaulted [vôl′tid] *adj.* having an arched ceiling.

vehement [vē′ə mənt] *adj.* having great force or feeling. —**vehemently,** *adv.*

venerable [ven′ər ə bəl] *adj.* deserving respect because of age, character, or achievements.

vent [vent] *n.* a way for passage; outlet.

verisimilitude [ver′ə si mil′ə tōōd′, -tud′] *n.* the appearance of truth or reality.

verity [ver′ə tē] *n.* a belief or principle accepted as true.

vernacular [vər nak′yə lər] *adj.* the language commonly spoken by people in a particular place.

vest [vest] *v.* to give a person or group the right to or control of.

vibrancy [vī′brən sē] *n.* the quality of pulsating with life or energy.

vicarious [vī kãr′ē əs, vi-] *adj.* acting in place of another. —**vicariously,** *adv.*

vindictive [vin dik′tiv] *adj.* wanting revenge; vengeful.

virtuosity [vur′chōō os′ə tē] *n.* great skill in music, art, etc.

visage [viz′ij] *n.* a person's face.

vituperative [vī tōō′pə rā′tiv, -pər ə tiv, -tū′-, vi-] *adj.* harshly insulting or scolding.

vociferation [vō sif′ə rā′shən] *n.* a loud outcry.

volatility [vol′ə til′ə tē] *n.* the state of flying or moving around constantly; liveliness; explosiveness.

volley [vol′ē] *n.* a burst of bullets, words, etc., sent out at once.

W

waft [waft, wäft] *v.* to send or carry gently through or as if through air or water.

waggery [wag′ər ē] *n.* mischievous playfulness or joking.

wax [waks] *v.* to become; grow.

wean [wēn] *v.* to accustom (someone) gradually to stopping or losing something.

whetstone [hwet′stōn′, wet′-] *n.* a stone for sharpening blades.

whirr [hwur, wur] *v.* to move rapidly with a buzzing sound.

wily [wī′lē] *adj.* sly; crafty. —**winess,** *n.*

wistful [wist′fəl] *adj.* longing sadly; yearning. —**wistfully,** *adv.*

wont [wônt, wônt, wunt] *adj.* accustomed; used.

wrangle [rang′gəl] *v.* to quarrel or argue noisily.

wreak [rēk] *v.* to let out or express fully; inflict.

wreathe [rēth] *v.* to twist or coil.

wrought [rôt] past tense and past participle of **work.**

Z

zenith [zē′nith] *n.* the point in the sky directly above the observer.

INDEX OF TITLES BY THEME

INDEX OF TITLES BY GENRE

INDEX OF SKILLS

Page numbers in boldface italics indicate entries in the Writing About Literature Handbook.
Page numbers in italics indicate entries in the Handbook of Literary Terms.

Modern style, 758–759
Monologue, 447
Mood, 148–149
Motivation, 325, *868*

Narration, 113, *868*
Narrator, 319, 424, *868*
Native American literature, 7, 8, 12, 13
Naturalism, 297, 364, 367, 427, *868*
New Critics, 476
Novel, 114, 156, 363, *869*
  gothic, 363
  historical, 114
  picaresque, 363
  of sentiment, 363

Octave, 167, 362, *869*
Onomatopoeia, 131, 464, *869*
  and jazz rhythms, 464
Oral tradition, 7, 14, *869*
Oratory, 65, 68–69, 96, 241, *869*
Oxymoron, 756

Paradox, 756
Parallelism, 84, *869*
Paraphrase, 292
Parody, 594, *869*
Pathetic fallacy, 401
Personification, 206, *869*
Persuasion, 84, *869*
Pictograph, 8
Picture writing, 8
Playwright, 693
Plot, 309, 424, *869*
Poetry, 201, 272–273, 432, 487, 581,
    598, 600, 760, **854–855**
  ballad, 272
  confessional, 581, 598, 600, 760
  dramatic, 272–273, *865*
  epic, 272
  Imagist, 432
  lyric, 273, *868*
  mock-epic, 272
  narrative, 272, *868*
  repetition in, 201
  shape of, 487
  types of, 272–273
Point of view, 319, 424, 641,
    869–870
  first person, 319
  limited third person, 424
  omniscient, 319, 424
  third person, 319
Political writing, 50
Protagonist, 309, 424, 693, 739, *870*
Proverbs, 57
Pseudonym, 104, 274, 642
Psychological realism, 364
Puritan literature, 3, 23

Quatrain, 167, 362, 580, *870*

Realism, 296–297, 356, 363–364, 366,
    427, 694, 697, *870*
Refrain, 201, 580, *870*
Regionalism, 297, 364, *870*
Renaissance, 153
Repetition, 14, 69, 84, 131, 201, 524,
    870
  in oral tradition, 14, 69
  in persuasive writing, 84
  in poetry, 201
  as sound device, 131
Resolution, 309, 739
Revelation, 780
Rhetorical question, 69
Rhyme, 131, 167, 272, 580, *870*
  approximate, 272
  end, 167
  exact, 272
  imperfect, 272
  internal, 131
  near, 272
  off, 272
  perfect, 272
  slant, 272
Rhyme scheme, 167, *871*
Rhythm, 122–123, 201, 214, 251, 454,
    464, *871*
  irregular, 251
  jazz, 464
  syncopated, 464
Rising action, 309, 739, *871*
Romance, 156, *871*
Romanticism, 101, 119, 132, 465, 595,
    598, 656, 694, *871*
Run-on line, 201, *871*

Satire, 511, 576, *871*
Scanning, 123, *871*
Sensory language, 92
Sestet, 167, 362, *871*
Setting, 148–149, 309, 424, *871*
  atmosphere and mood in, 148–149
  in novel, 424
  in short story, 309
Short story, 309, *871–872*
Simile, 39, 164, *872*
Single effect, 130–131, 135
Sonnet, 362, *872*
  English (Shakespearean), 362
  Italian (Petrarchan), 362
Sound devices, 131
South American literature, 770
Southern colonial literature, 3, 35
Spirituals, 222, *872*
Stage directions, 693, *872*
Staging, 693
Stage manager, 697, 738
Stanza, 167–168, *872*
  ballad, 167
  heroic, 167
  hymnal, 168

Stream of consciousness, 431–432, 603,
    610–611, 667, *872*
Style, 3, 23, 425, 492, 524, 758–759,
    872
  journalistic prose, 524
  modern, 758–759
  of a novel, 425
  Ornate, 3
  Plain, 3, 23, 492, 758
Suspense, 801, *873*
Suspension of disbelief, 148,
Symbol, 187–188, 678–679, **850–851,**
    873
  and theme, 678–679

Tercet, 167, 580
Tetrameter, 167
Theme, 309, 425, 562, 678–679, 738–
    739, **852–853,** *873*
  in drama, 738–739
  in novel, 425
  in short story, 309, 562
  and symbol, 678–679
Tone, 502, 836, *873*
Total effect, 292, **856–857**
Tragedy, 693
Transcendental Club, 159
Transcendentalism, 154–155, 246, *873*
Trimeter, 123, 167
Triplet, 167

Vernacular, 274
Verse paragraph, 167
Villanelle, 580, *873*
Visual pattern, 454
Vivid language, 84
Voice, 96

Word choice, 197

COMPOSITION SKILLS

Page numbers in boldface italics
indicate entries in the Writing About
Literature Handbook.

ANALYTICAL

Author's purpose, analyzing an, 681, 688
Autobiography, writing about, 64
Character, writing about, 197, 325, 469,
    540
Coherence, analyzing, 243
Comparison/contrast, writing a, 29, 39,
    95, 359, 524, 616, 633, 649, 660,
    844–845
Contrasting tones, analyzing, 291
Descriptive writing, analyzing, 92
Diary, writing about a, 238
Diction and sentence structure, writing
    about, 805

Index of Skills **889**

Evidence, citing, 45, 80, 510, **846–847**
Imagery, writing about, 213
Literature and its period, writing about, 339, 835, **860–861**
Narrative, summarizing a, 113
Narrator, writing about a, 787
Nonfiction, writing about, 177, 230, 820, 825, **848–849**
Oratory, writing about, 69
Paraphrase, writing a, 487
Personification, writing about, 206
Persuasion, writing about, 84
Poetry, writing about, 134, 259, 273, 355, 441, 448, 454, 477, 491, 765, **854–855**
Quotation, writing about a, 118, 352, 580, **850–851**
Researching and writing, 751
Sentence, writing about a, 168
Statement about literature, applying a, 310, 425, 739, 830, **858–859**
Stream of consciousness, writing about, 611
Symbol, writing about a, 319, 655, 810, 814, **850–851**
Theme, writing about, 124, 503, 563, 801, **852–853**
and tone, 503
Theme through character, analyzing, 629
Thesis statement, developing a, 22, 188, 759, 780, **842–843**
Title, writing about a, 34, 641, 792
Total effect, writing about the, 149, 665, 679, **856–857**
Work and its author, writing about a, 583

CREATIVE

Abstract idea, writing about an, 273
Advertisement, writing an, 39, 633
Anecdote, writing an, 616
Aphorisms, writing, 64
Character, writing about, 563
Character foil, creating a, 629
Character sketch, writing a, 197, 310

Character's thoughts, imagining a, 792
Classical allusions, writing with, 134
Colors, writing about, 814
Concept, writing about a, 780
Continuation of a story, writing a, 510
Controlling image, using a, 34
Description, writing a, 45, 92, 118, 149, 188, 325, 352, 491, 503, 540, 649, 688
of a character, 649
of a character's movements, 325
of a conflict, 352
of a hero, 118
of a setting, 149
of a symbol, 188
Dialogue, writing a, 739
Diary, writing a, 29, 679
Different point of view, retelling from a, 113
Dramatic monologue, writing a, 448
Editorial, writing an, 69, 339
Epitaph, writing an, 469
Essay, writing an, 168, 177, 820, 835
expository, 820
personal, 177
persuasive, 168
Fable, writing a, 291
Free verse, writing, 259, 454
Irony, using situational or dramatic, 359
Journal entry, writing a, 238
Letter, writing a, 22, 80, 95
to the editor, 80
literary, 95
Limerick, writing a, 787
Memory, writing about, 213, 660, 810
Monologue, writing a, 805
Names, writing about, 825
Narrative, writing a, 477, 524
Nature, writing about, 124
Opinion, expressing an, 681
Oral tribute, writing an, 243
Past, writing about the, 583
Personification, writing a, 206, 355
Persuasion, writing, 84
Place, writing about a, 765
Poem, writing a, 441, 487, 751
with documents, 751

Imagist, 441
with shape, 487
villanelle, 580
Review, writing a, 230
Scene, narrating a, 801
Setting, creating a, 319, 665
Story within a story, writing a, 641
Stream-of-consciousness manner, writing in the, 611
Time capsule, creating a, 655
Topic, researching a, 425
Traditions, writing about, 830
Writing, writing about, 759

VOCABULARY SKILLS

TEST–TAKING SKILLS

Analogies, 273, 588, 688
Antonyms, 39, 124, 352, 629, 739
Sentence completions, 29, 87, 563, 679
Synonyms, 22, 64, 483, 810

WORD STUDY

Abstract words, 168
Allusions, biblical and mythological, 649
Americanisms, 259
Compound words, 592
Concrete language, 425
Denotation and connotation, 197
Derivations, 92, 759, 771
from Greek, 759
from Latin, 92
from Spanish, 771
Diction (word choice) and style, 243
Loaded words, 80
Native American words, 14
Regionalisms, 310
Shades of meaning, recognizing, 149
Slang, 540
Vivid action words, 352
Vivid adjectives, 213
Word origins and overtones, 448
Words from music, 820

INDEX OF AUTHORS AND TITLES